THE SIDE DISH BIBLE

ALSO BY AMERICA'S TEST KITCHEN

FOR A FULL LISTING OF ALL OUR BOOKS

CooksIllustrated.com

AmericasTestKitchen.com

PRAISE FOR AMERICA'S TEST KITCHEN TITLES

Selected as the Cookbook Award Winner of 2019 in the Health and Special Diet Category

INTERNATIONAL ASSOCIATION OF CULINARY PROFESSIONALS (IACP) ON *THE COMPLETE DIABETES COOKBOOK*

"Diabetics and all health-conscious home cooks will find great information on almost every page."

BOOKLIST (STARRED REVIEW) ON *THE COMPLETE DIABETES COOKBOOK*

"True to its name, this smart and endlessly enlightening cookbook is about as definitive as it's possible to get in the modern vegetarian realm."

MEN'S JOURNAL ON *THE COMPLETE VEGETARIAN COOKBOOK*

Selected as an Amazon Best Book of 2015 in the Cookbooks and Food Writing Category

AMAZON ON *THE COMPLETE VEGETARIAN COOKBOOK*

"This is a wonderful, useful guide to healthy eating."

PUBLISHERS WEEKLY ON *NUTRITIOUS DELICIOUS*

"The sum total of exhaustive experimentation . . . anyone interested in gluten-free cookery simply shouldn't be without it."

NIGELLA LAWSON ON *THE HOW CAN IT BE GLUTEN-FREE COOKBOOK*

Selected as one of the 10 Best New Cookbooks of 2017

THE LA TIMES ON *THE PERFECT COOKIE*

"Use this charming, focused title to set a showstopping table for special occasions."

LIBRARY JOURNAL ON *ALL-TIME BEST HOLIDAY ENTERTAINING*

"A one-volume kitchen seminar, addressing in one smart chapter after another the sometimes surprising whys behind a cook's best practices. . . . You get the myth, the theory, the science, and the proof, all rigorously interrogated as only America's Test Kitchen can do."

NPR ON *THE SCIENCE OF GOOD COOKING*

"If you're a home cook who loves long introductions that tell you why a dish works followed by lots of step-by-step hand holding, then you'll love *Vegetables Illustrated*."

THE WALL STREET JOURNAL ON *VEGETABLES ILLUSTRATED*

"The 21st-century *Fannie Farmer Cookbook* or *The Joy of Cooking*. If you had to have one cookbook and that's all you could have, this one would do it."

CBS SAN FRANCISCO ON *THE NEW FAMILY COOKBOOK*

"Some 2,500 photos walk readers through 600 painstakingly tested recipes, leaving little room for error."

ASSOCIATED PRESS ON *THE AMERICA'S TEST KITCHEN COOKING SCHOOL COOKBOOK*

"This encyclopedia of meat cookery would feel completely overwhelming if it weren't so meticulously organized and artfully designed. This is Cook's Illustrated at its finest."

THE KITCHN ON *THE COOK'S ILLUSTRATED MEAT BOOK*

"The go-to gift book for newlyweds, small families, or empty nesters."

ORLANDO SENTINEL ON *THE COMPLETE COOKING FOR TWO COOKBOOK*

"Some books impress by the sheer audacity of their ambition. Backed by the magazine's famed mission to test every recipe relentlessly until it is the best it can be, this nearly 900-page volume lands with an authoritative wallop."

CHICAGO TRIBUNE ON *THE COOK'S ILLUSTRATED COOKBOOK*

"This impressive installment from America's Test Kitchen equips readers with dozens of repertoire-worthy recipes. . . . This is a must-have for beginner cooks and more experienced ones who wish to sharpen their skills."

PUBLISHERS WEEKLY (STARRED REVIEW) ON *THE NEW ESSENTIALS COOKBOOK*

THE SIDE DISH BIBLE

1001 PERFECT RECIPES FOR EVERY VEGETABLE, RICE, GRAIN, AND BEAN DISH YOU'LL EVER NEED

AMERICA'S TEST KITCHEN

Library of Congress Cataloging-in-Publication Data has been applied for

ISBN 978-1-945256-99-8

AMERICA'S TEST KITCHEN
21 Drydock Avenue, Boston, MA 02210

Manufactured in the United States of America
10 9 8 7 6 5 4 3 2 1

Distributed by Penguin Random House Publisher Services
Tel: 800.733.3000

Pictured on front cover Super-Stuffed Baked Potatoes (page 79)
Pictured on back cover (clockwise from top left)
Radicchio Salad with Pear, Parsley, and Blue Cheese (page 226), Easiest-Ever Biscuits (page 498), Roasted Asparagus with Lemon-Mint Gremolata (page 41), Grilled Tomatoes (page 388), Boston Baked Beans (page 198)

Editorial Director, Books **ADAM KOWIT**

Executive Food Editor **DAN ZUCCARELLO**

Deputy Food Editor **STEPHANIE PIXLEY**

Executive Managing Editor **DEBRA HUDAK**

Senior Editors **SACHA MADADIAN, KAUMUDI MARATHÉ, AND SARA MAYER**

Associate Editor **NINA DENISON**

Assistant Editors **KELLY CORMIER AND BRENNA DONOVAN**

Editorial Assistants **TESS BERGER AND SARA ZATOPEK**

Art Director, Books **LINDSEY TIMKO CHANDLER**

Deputy Art Directors **COURTNEY LENTZ AND ALLISON BOALES**

Associate Art Director **KATIE BARRANGER**

Photography Director **JULIE BOZZO COTE**

Photography Producer **MEREDITH MULCAHY**

Senior Staff Photographers **STEVE KLISE AND DANIEL J. VAN ACKERE**

Staff Photographer **KEVIN WHITE**

Additional Photography **KELLER + KELLER AND CARL TREMBLAY**

Food Styling **TARA BUSA, ISABELLE ENGLISH, CATRINE KELTY, CHANTAL LAMBETH, KENDRA MCKNIGHT, ASHLEY MOORE, MARIE PIRAINO, MARY JANE SAWYER, MAEVE SHERIDAN, ELLE SIMONE SCOTT, KENDRA SMITH, AND SALLY STRAUB**

Photoshoot Kitchen Team

Photo Team Manager **TIMOTHY MCQUINN**

Assistant Test Cooks **SARAH EWALD, HANNAH FENTON, JACQUELINE GOCHENOUER, AND ERIC HAESSLER**

Senior Manager, Publishing Operations **TAYLOR ARGENZIO**

Imaging Manager **LAUREN ROBBINS**

Production and Imaging Specialists **DENNIS NOBLE, JESSICA VOAS, AND AMANDA YONG**

Copy Editor **CHERYL REDMOND**

Proofreaders **PAT JALBERT-LEVINE AND VICKI ROWLAND**

Indexer **ELIZABETH PARSON**

Chief Creative Officer **JACK BISHOP**

Executive Editorial Directors **JULIA COLLIN DAVISON AND BRIDGET LANCASTER**

CONTENTS

WELCOME TO AMERICA'S TEST KITCHEN

This book has been tested, written, and edited by the folks at America's Test Kitchen. Located in Boston's Seaport District in the historic Innovation and Design Building, it features 15,000 square feet of kitchen space, including multiple photography and video studios. It is the home of *Cook's Illustrated* magazine and *Cook's Country* magazine and is the workday destination for more than 60 test cooks, editors, and cookware specialists. Our mission is to test recipes over and over again until we understand how and why they work and until we arrive at the best version.

We start the process of testing a recipe with a complete lack of preconceptions, which means that we accept no claim, no technique, and no recipe at face value. We simply assemble as many variations as possible, test a half-dozen of the most promising, and taste the results blind. We then construct our own recipe and continue to test it, varying ingredients, techniques, and cooking times until we reach a consensus. As we like to say in the test kitchen, "We make the mistakes so you don't have to." The result, we hope, is the best version of a particular recipe, but we realize that only you can be the final judge of our success (or failure). We use the same rigorous approach when we test equipment and taste ingredients.

All of this would not be possible without a belief that good cooking, much like good music, is based on a foundation of objective technique. Some people like spicy foods and others don't, but there is a right way to sauté, there is a best way to cook a pot roast, and there are measurable scientific principles involved in producing perfectly beaten, stable egg whites. Our ultimate goal is to investigate the fundamental principles of cooking to give you the techniques, tools, and ingredients you need to become a better cook. It is as simple as that.

To see what goes on behind the scenes at America's Test Kitchen, check out our social media channels for kitchen snapshots, exclusive content, video tips, and much more. You can watch us work (in our actual test kitchen) by tuning in to *America's Test Kitchen* or *Cook's Country* on public television or on our websites. Download our award-winning podcast Proof, which goes beyond recipes to solve food mysteries (AmericasTestKitchen.com/proof), or listen in to test kitchen experts on public radio (SplendidTable.org) to hear insights that illuminate the truth about real home cooking. Want to hone your cooking skills or finally learn how to bake—with an America's Test Kitchen test cook? Enroll in one of our online cooking classes. And you can engage the next generation of home cooks with kid-tested recipes from America's Test Kitchen Kids.

However you choose to visit us, we welcome you into our kitchen, where you can stand by our side as we test our way to the best recipes in America.

facebook.com/AmericasTestKitchen
twitter.com/TestKitchen
youtube.com/AmericasTestKitchen
instagram.com/TestKitchen
pinterest.com/TestKitchen

AmericasTestKitchen.com
CooksIllustrated.com
CooksCountry.com
OnlineCookingSchool.com
AmericasTestKitchen.com/kids

INTRODUCTION

Who hasn't struggled over figuring out what side dishes to make, often resorting to making the same ones over and over again? We created *The Side Dish Bible* to vanquish this dilemma by putting 1,001 foolproof recipes at everyone's fingertips. Our mission is to aid home cooks in navigating the vast landscape of side dish possibilities and help you find the perfect recipe for any and every occasion.

In order to accomplish this, we organized the book into purposefully themed chapters. They help you find what you're looking for, even if you don't know what that is. "Basics You Can Count On" is a set of recipes for anyone plagued by weeknight inertia. These recipes have fewer ingredients and are simpler to prepare, with many of them ready in 30 minutes or less, like Pan-Steamed Broccolini with Shallot, Easy Parmesan Risotto, and Skillet Chickpeas. "Roast Your Vegetables" shows how hands-off roasting enhances everything prepared that way, from Roasted Artichokes with Lemon Vinaigrette to Roasted Delicata Squash.

Consult "Up Your Vegetable Game" to find more interesting ways to prepare familiar ingredients such as Pan-Roasted Cabbage and Sautéed Radishes or to explore less-familiar ingredients like Whole Romanesco with Berbere and Yogurt-Tahini Sauce and Stir-Fried Japanese Eggplant. Potato lovers will want to try all 57 recipes in "Potatoes Every Way" as well as the irresistible recipes in "Fries and Crispy Sides." Wholesome and hearty complements abound in "Perfect Rice and Great Grains" and "Best Beans and Lentils."

Lessen the pressure of having guests with "Dinner Party Winners" and "Holiday Classics"; each chapter is full of ideas and inspiration. You'll find reliable standbys like Roasted Red Potatoes with Sea Salt and Savory Noodle Kugel as well as discover new favorites like Miso Celery Root Puree and Farro with Fennel and Parmesan.

If you're looking to take the party on the road, we provide a trunkload of side dishes that can be made ahead and will travel well in "Potluck Favorites" and "Not Your Mother's Casseroles." Want to make side dishes using your grill, slow cooker, or pressure cooker? There are chapters devoted to those cooking methods too. And "The Bread Basket" offers recipes to round out your table with an appealing selection of rolls, biscuits, cornbread, and more.

The main dish may take center stage, but don't keep your side dishes on the sidelines. Experiment and have fun. *The Side Dish Bible* has every kind of side dish imaginable, from the classics to years' worth of new choices—it's the only side dish cookbook you will ever need.

BASICS YOU CAN COUNT ON

■ FAST (30 minutes or less total time)   ■ MAKE AHEAD   ■ VEGAN
Photos: Foolproof Boiled Corn; Sautéed Cherry Tomatoes

Roasted Artichokes with Lemon and Basil
SERVES 4 `VEGAN`

WHY THIS RECIPE WORKS For an easy and quick side dish, frozen artichokes are a great starting point. We found that roasting them brought out their delicate, vegetal flavor. But frozen artichokes contain a considerable amount of water, which can prevent browning and dilute flavor. To solve this problem, we preheated a baking sheet in a very hot oven; tossed the artichokes and a couple of garlic cloves with olive oil, salt, and pepper; and then spread everything out on the sizzling sheet. The excess water quickly evaporated during roasting, giving us golden-brown, deeply flavored artichokes. Lining the baking sheet with foil made cleanup a snap. After the garlic cooled slightly, we minced it and tossed it in a simple dressing of just lemon juice, more olive oil, and basil, which highlighted the artichokes' flavor without overpowering it. To thaw frozen artichokes quickly, microwave them in a covered bowl for 3 to 5 minutes; drain them and pat dry before using.

18 ounces frozen artichokes, thawed and patted dry
2 garlic cloves, peeled
3 tablespoons extra-virgin olive oil, divided
½ teaspoon table salt
⅛ teaspoon pepper
1 tablespoon lemon juice
1 tablespoon chopped fresh basil

1. Adjust oven rack to middle position, place aluminum foil–lined rimmed baking sheet on rack, and heat oven to 450 degrees. Toss artichokes and garlic with 2 tablespoons oil, salt, and pepper in bowl. Spread vegetables evenly over hot baking sheet and roast until browned around edges, 15 to 20 minutes.

2. Remove vegetables from oven and let cool slightly. Mince roasted garlic, then combine with lemon juice, basil, and remaining 1 tablespoon oil in large bowl. Add roasted artichokes and toss to coat. Season with salt and pepper to taste. Serve.

PER SERVING Cal 140; **Total Fat** 11g, **Sat Fat** 1.5g; **Chol** 0mg; **Sodium** 610mg; **Total Carb** 9g, **Dietary Fiber** 0g, **Total Sugars** 1g; **Protein** 3g

VARIATIONS
Roasted Artichokes with Fennel, Mustard, and Tarragon
Roast 1 small fennel bulb, trimmed and sliced thin, along with artichokes and garlic. Reduce lemon juice to 1 teaspoon, substitute 1 tablespoon minced fresh tarragon for basil, and add 1 tablespoon whole-grain mustard to dressing.

Roasted Artichokes with Lemon and Basil

Roasted Artichokes with Olives, Bell Pepper, and Lemon
Roast ½ cup coarsely chopped pitted kalamata olives and 1 coarsely chopped red bell pepper along with artichokes and garlic. Substitute 1 tablespoon minced fresh parsley for basil.

Broiled Asparagus
SERVES 4 `FAST` `VEGAN`

WHY THIS RECIPE WORKS Many people simply steam asparagus, but we think that broiling it is a great alternative. Broiling concentrates its flavor, helps to lightly caramelize its exterior, and, perhaps best of all, can be done in just minutes for a perfect quick side dish. And while we enjoyed the spears as is—with a little oil, salt and pepper, and lemon juice—we also came up with a simple balsamic glaze and an Asian vinaigrette to multiply our weeknight options. All we had to do was drizzle the dressings over the hot asparagus before serving. To ensure even cooking, choose asparagus that is roughly ½ inch thick. This asparagus can be served warm, at room temperature, or even chilled if desired.

- 1 pound asparagus, trimmed
- 1 tablespoon extra-virgin olive oil
- ½ teaspoon table salt
- ¼ teaspoon pepper
- 1 teaspoon lemon juice (optional)

Adjust oven rack 6 inches from broiler element and heat broiler. Toss asparagus with oil in bowl and season with salt and pepper. Lay asparagus in single layer on rimmed baking sheet. Broil, shaking pan occasionally, until asparagus is tender and lightly browned, about 10 minutes. Transfer asparagus to platter and sprinkle with lemon juice, if using. Serve.

PER SERVING Cal 50; **Total Fat** 3.5g, **Sat Fat** 0g; **Chol** 0mg; **Sodium** 290mg; **Total Carb** 4g, **Dietary Fiber** 2g, **Total Sugars** 2g; **Protein** 3g

VARIATIONS
Broiled Asparagus with Balsamic Glaze
Simmer ¾ cup balsamic vinegar in 8-inch skillet over medium heat until reduced to ¼ cup, 15 to 20 minutes. Off heat, stir in ¼ cup extra-virgin olive oil; drizzle over broiled asparagus before serving.

Broiled Asparagus with Soy-Ginger Vinaigrette
Substitute vegetable oil for olive oil. Whisk ¼ cup lime juice (2 limes), 3 tablespoons toasted sesame oil, 3 tablespoons soy sauce, 2 thinly sliced scallions, 2 minced garlic cloves, 1 tablespoon grated fresh ginger, and 1 tablespoon honey together in bowl; drizzle over broiled asparagus before serving.

TRIMMING ASPARAGUS

1. Remove 1 stalk of asparagus from bunch and bend at thicker end until it snaps.

2. With broken asparagus as guide, trim tough ends from remaining asparagus bunch using chef's knife.

Steamed Broccoli with Lime-Cumin Dressing
SERVES 4 **FAST** **VEGAN**

WHY THIS RECIPE WORKS The tricky part about steaming broccoli is keeping the delicate florets from turning to mush while simultaneously cooking the dense stalks through until they are tender. Some recipes solve this by ignoring the stalks altogether, but we like the contrasting flavors and textures of the florets and stalks. We discovered that we could steam both the stalks and the florets as long as we took the time to carefully prepare both. To guarantee even cooking, we cut the florets into large 1-inch pieces and cut the stalks into small ¼-inch pieces. This resulted in tender, evenly cooked broccoli in about 5 minutes. To dress our broccoli simply, we made a quick bright dressing flavored with lime and cumin. You will need a collapsible steamer basket for this recipe.

DRESSING
- ¼ cup finely chopped red onion
- 3 tablespoons extra-virgin olive oil
- 1 teaspoon grated lime zest plus 1 tablespoon juice
- ½ teaspoon ground cumin
- ⅛ teaspoon hot sauce, plus extra for serving

BROCCOLI
- 1½ pounds broccoli, florets cut into 1-inch pieces, stalks peeled and sliced ¼ inch thick

1. FOR THE DRESSING Whisk all ingredients together in large bowl; set aside for serving.

2. FOR THE BROCCOLI Bring 1 inch water to boil in Dutch oven. Place broccoli in collapsible steamer basket, then transfer basket to pot. Cover and cook until broccoli is tender and bright green, about 5 minutes.

3. Transfer broccoli to bowl with dressing and gently toss to combine. Season with salt and extra hot sauce to taste. Serve warm or at room temperature.

PER SERVING Cal 140; **Total Fat** 11g, **Sat Fat** 1.5g; **Chol** 0mg; **Sodium** 40mg; **Total Carb** 8g, **Dietary Fiber** 3g, **Total Sugars** 2g; **Protein** 3g

VARIATION
Steamed Broccoli with Spicy Balsamic Dressing and Black Olives
Whisk ¼ cup chopped pitted kalamata olives, ¼ cup extra-virgin olive oil, 2 teaspoons balsamic vinegar, 2 teaspoons red wine vinegar, 1 minced garlic clove, ½ teaspoon red pepper flakes, and ¼ teaspoon salt together in bowl. Substitute for lime-cumin dressing.

Skillet Broccoli with Olive Oil and Garlic

3 tablespoons extra-virgin olive oil, divided
2 garlic cloves, minced
½ teaspoon minced fresh thyme
1 pound broccoli florets, cut into 1-inch pieces
¼ teaspoon table salt
3 tablespoons water

1. Combine 1 tablespoon oil, garlic, and thyme in bowl. Heat remaining 2 tablespoons oil in 12-inch skillet over medium-high heat until just smoking. Add broccoli and salt and cook, without stirring, until beginning to brown, about 2 minutes.

2. Add water, cover, and cook until broccoli is bright green but still crisp, about 2 minutes. Uncover and continue to cook until water has evaporated and broccoli is crisp-tender, about 2 minutes.

3. Clear center of pan, add garlic mixture, and cook, mashing mixture into skillet, until fragrant, about 30 seconds. Stir garlic mixture into broccoli. Season with salt and pepper to taste. Serve.

PER SERVING Cal 130; **Total Fat** 11g, **Sat Fat** 1.5g; **Chol** 0mg; **Sodium** 180mg; **Total Carb** 6g, **Dietary Fiber** 3g, **Total Sugars** 2g; **Protein** 3g

VARIATION
Skillet Broccoli with Sesame Oil and Ginger
Omit thyme. In garlic mixture, substitute 1 tablespoon toasted sesame oil for olive oil and add 1 tablespoon grated fresh ginger. Substitute 2 tablespoons vegetable oil for oil when cooking broccoli.

Skillet Broccoli with Olive Oil and Garlic
SERVES 4 FAST VEGAN

WHY THIS RECIPE WORKS Since broccoli makes for a fast and easy side dish, we turn to it frequently. But the outcome has to be bright green, crisp-tender, and flavorful. For broccoli that was nicely browned on the outside and fully tender within, we borrowed a trick from stir-frying: We got out a skillet to first brown broccoli florets for color and then we quickly steamed them to cook them through. Finally we sautéed the florets with some aromatics for a boost in flavor. We kept it simple and flavored our broccoli with just garlic and thyme to let its natural essence shine. The best thing about this stir-fry method is that we could do all the steps in quick succession in a skillet with a tight-fitting lid. Either a traditional or a nonstick 12-inch skillet will work for this recipe. Using broccoli florets, rather than a bunch of broccoli, can save valuable prep time for this side dish. If buying broccoli in a bunch instead, you will need about 1½ pounds of broccoli in order to yield 1 pound of florets.

Pan-Steamed Broccolini with Shallot
SERVES 4 FAST

WHY THIS RECIPE WORKS Broccolini is baby broccoli and it makes an elegant alternative to broccoli; it has long asparagus-like stalks and just a few delicate florets. Its anatomy makes it tricky to cook because the florets are quicker to cook than the stems. To ensure even cooking, we split the thicker broccolini stalks down the middle so that they were the same size as the thinner ones in the bunch. Then we steamed the broccolini in a skillet, turning out evenly cooked stalks and gently wilted greens. To add some flavor and modest richness to this green and lean vegetable, we turned to butter and added shallot, lemon zest, and thyme to gently complement the broccolini's sweet flavor. For a differently flavored variation, we loved the zing of fresh ginger and the sweetness of honey. There's no need to split stalks that are ¼ inch or thinner. Broccolini is also sold as baby broccoli or asparation. You will need a 12-inch skillet with a tight-fitting lid for this recipe.

1 pound broccolini, trimmed
⅓ cup water
½ teaspoon table salt
2 tablespoons unsalted butter
2 teaspoons minced shallot
1 teaspoon grated lemon zest
1 teaspoon minced fresh thyme
¼ teaspoon pepper

1. Cut broccolini stalks measuring more than ½ inch in diameter at base in half lengthwise. Cut stalks measuring ¼ to ½ inch in diameter at base in half lengthwise, starting below where florets begin and keeping florets intact. Leave stalks measuring less than ¼ inch in diameter at base whole.

2. Bring water to boil in 12-inch skillet. Add broccolini and sprinkle with salt. Cover, reduce heat to medium-low, and cook for 3 minutes. Uncover and gently toss broccolini with tongs. Cover and continue to cook until broccolini is bright green and crisp-tender, 3 to 5 minutes. Uncover and continue to cook until any remaining liquid has evaporated, about 30 seconds.

3. Off heat, push broccolini to 1 side of skillet. Add butter, shallot, lemon zest, thyme, and pepper to cleared side of skillet and stir to combine. Using tongs, toss broccolini with butter mixture until evenly coated. Serve.

PER SERVING Cal 80; **Total Fat** 6g, **Sat Fat** 3.5g; **Chol** 15mg; **Sodium** 330mg; **Total Carb** 4g, **Dietary Fiber** 3g, **Total Sugars** 1g; **Protein** 4g

VARIATION
Pan-Steamed Broccolini with Ginger
Reduce lemon zest to ½ teaspoon. Substitute 2 teaspoons grated fresh ginger and ¼ teaspoon honey for shallot and thyme.

TRIMMING BROCCOLINI

Trim only tough, dry ends from broccolini. Slit thicker stalks measuring ¼ to ½ inch in diameter in half lengthwise starting below florets.

Broiled Broccoli Rabe

Broiled Broccoli Rabe
SERVES 4 **FAST** **VEGAN**

WHY THIS RECIPE WORKS Broccoli rabe is broccoli's spicy Italian cousin. Many recipes tend to wash out its distinctive flavor, but when we learned that most of the vegetable's bitterness comes from an enzymatic reaction triggered when the florets are cut or chewed, we kept the leafy parts of the vegetable whole. The heat from cooking deactivated the enzyme, taming much of the bitterness. We skipped stovetop methods and instead quickly broiled the rabe, which created deep caramelization without overcooking the pieces and gave them a sweetness that complemented their bitterness. Broiling the rabe took just minutes and required nothing more than a rimmed baking sheet. Because the amount of heat generated by a broiler varies from oven to oven, we recommend keeping an eye on the broccoli rabe as it cooks. If the leaves are getting too dark or not browning in the time specified in the recipe, adjust the distance of the oven rack from the broiler element.

3 tablespoons extra-virgin olive oil, divided
1 pound broccoli rabe, trimmed
1 garlic clove, minced
¾ teaspoon kosher salt
¼ teaspoon red pepper flakes
   Lemon wedges

1. Adjust oven rack 4 inches from broiler element and heat broiler. Brush rimmed baking sheet with 1 tablespoon oil.

2. Cut tops (leaves and florets) of broccoli rabe from stalks, keeping tops whole, then cut stalks into 1-inch pieces. Transfer to prepared sheet.

3. Combine remaining 2 tablespoons oil, garlic, salt, and pepper flakes in small bowl. Pour oil mixture over broccoli rabe and toss to combine.

4. Broil until exposed half of leaves are well browned, 2 to 2½ minutes. Using tongs, toss to expose unbrowned leaves. Return sheet to oven and continue to broil until most leaves are lightly charred and stalks are crisp-tender, 2 to 2½ minutes. Serve with lemon wedges.

PER SERVING Cal 120; **Total Fat** 11g, **Sat Fat** 1.5g; **Chol** 0mg; **Sodium** 250mg; **Total Carb** 4g, **Dietary Fiber** 3g, **Total Sugars** 0g; **Protein** 4g

Skillet-Roasted Brussels Sprouts with Chile, Peanuts, and Mint

Skillet-Roasted Brussels Sprouts with Lemon and Pecorino Romano
SERVES 4   FAST

WHY THIS RECIPE WORKS With this method in just 10 minutes you can make the best Brussels sprouts you have ever tasted. To create stovetop Brussels sprouts that were deeply browned on the cut sides while still bright green on the uncut sides and crisp-tender within, we started the sprouts in a cold skillet with plenty of oil and cooked them covered. This gently heated the sprouts and created a steamy environment that cooked them through without adding any extra moisture. We then removed the lid and continued to cook the sprouts cut sides down so they had time to develop a substantial, caramelized crust. Using enough oil to completely coat the skillet ensured that all the sprouts made full contact with the fat to brown evenly. Parmesan cheese can be substituted for the Pecorino, if desired. You will need a 12-inch nonstick skillet with a tight-fitting lid for this recipe.

1 pound Brussels sprouts, trimmed and halved
5 tablespoons extra-virgin olive oil
1 tablespoon lemon juice
¼ teaspoon table salt
¼ cup shredded Pecorino Romano cheese

1. Arrange Brussels sprouts in single layer cut sides down in 12-inch nonstick skillet and drizzle oil evenly over them. Cover skillet, place over medium-high heat, and cook until Brussels sprouts are bright green and cut sides have started to brown, about 5 minutes.

2. Uncover and continue to cook until cut sides of Brussels sprouts are deeply and evenly browned and paring knife meets little to no resistance, 2 to 3 minutes, adjusting heat and moving Brussels sprouts as needed to prevent overbrowning. While Brussels sprouts cook, combine lemon juice and salt in bowl.

3. Off heat, add lemon juice mixture to skillet and stir to evenly coat Brussels sprouts. Season with salt and pepper to taste. Transfer to platter, sprinkle with Pecorino, and serve.

PER SERVING Cal 230; **Total Fat** 20g, **Sat Fat** 4g; **Chol** 5mg; **Sodium** 280mg; **Total Carb** 9g, **Dietary Fiber** 4g, **Total Sugars** 2g; **Protein** 5g

Skillet-Roasted Brussels Sprouts with Chile, Peanuts, and Mint

Omit lemon juice, pepper, and Pecorino. Combine 1 stemmed, seeded, and minced Fresno chile, 2 teaspoons lime juice, 1 teaspoon fish sauce, and ¼ teaspoon table salt in small bowl. Off heat, add chile mixture to skillet and stir to evenly coat sprouts. Season with salt to taste. Transfer sprouts to large plate, sprinkle with 2 tablespoons finely chopped dry-roasted peanuts and 2 tablespoons chopped fresh mint, and serve.

Skillet-Roasted Brussels Sprouts with Gochujang and Sesame Seeds

Gochujang is a savory Korean red chili paste that can be found in Asian markets or large supermarkets.

Substitute 1 tablespoon gochujang and 1 tablespoon rice vinegar for lemon juice and 2 teaspoons toasted sesame seeds for Pecorino.

Skillet-Roasted Brussels Sprouts with Mustard and Brown Sugar

Omit Pecorino. Substitute 1 tablespoon Dijon mustard, 1 tablespoon packed brown sugar, 2 teaspoons white wine vinegar, and ⅛ teaspoon cayenne pepper for lemon juice.

Skillet-Roasted Brussels Sprouts with Pomegranate and Pistachios

Substitute 1 tablespoon pomegranate molasses and ½ teaspoon ground cumin for lemon juice. Substitute ¼ cup shelled pistachios, toasted and chopped fine, and 2 tablespoons pomegranate seeds for Pecorino.

Sautéed Sliced Brussels Sprouts
SERVES 4 TO 6 **FAST** **VEGAN**

WHY THIS RECIPE WORKS A quick-cooking method is the ideal way to produce sweet, crisp-tender Brussels sprouts. Shredding sprouts one by one with a knife is a laborious task, so we pulled out the food processor to power through a pound and a half of sprouts. A quick soak in cold water helped keep the Brussels sprouts from burning as we sautéed them. Letting them cook undisturbed for a few minutes also encouraged browning, which added some sweetness, and stirring in lemon juice and parsley at the end of cooking provided a shot of brightness and freshness. For an irresistible variation, we used the classic pairing of Brussels sprouts and smoky, salty bacon. Briefly soaking the shredded sprouts reduces bitterness while providing extra moisture, which helps the vegetable steam; do not skip this step.

1½ pounds Brussels sprouts, trimmed
1 tablespoon vegetable oil
1 teaspoon table salt
¼ teaspoon pepper
2 tablespoons chopped fresh parsley
1 tablespoon lemon juice

1. Working in batches, use food processor fitted with slicing disk to process Brussels sprouts until thinly sliced. Transfer Brussels sprouts to large bowl, cover with cold water, and let sit for 3 minutes. Drain well and set aside.

2. Heat oil in 12-inch nonstick skillet over medium heat until shimmering. Add Brussels sprouts, salt, and pepper. Cover and cook, without stirring, until Brussels sprouts are wilted and lightly browned on bottom, about 4 minutes.

3. Stir and continue to cook, uncovered, until Brussels sprouts are crisp-tender, about 3 minutes, stirring once halfway through cooking. Off heat, stir in parsley and lemon juice. Season with salt and pepper to taste. Serve.

PER SERVING Cal 70; **Total Fat** 2.5g, **Sat Fat** 0g; **Chol** 0mg; **Sodium** 410mg; **Total Carb** 9g, **Dietary Fiber** 4g, **Total Sugars** 2g; **Protein** 4g

Sautéed Sliced Brussels Sprouts with Bacon

Before cooking Brussels sprouts, cook 4 slices chopped bacon in skillet over medium heat until crisp, 5 to 7 minutes. Transfer bacon to paper towel–lined plate and pour off all but 1 tablespoon fat from skillet. Cook sprouts as directed, substituting fat left in skillet for oil. Substitute cider vinegar for lemon juice and sprinkle sprouts with bacon before serving.

Sautéed Cabbage with Parsley and Lemon
SERVES 4 TO 6 **FAST** **VEGAN**

WHY THIS RECIPE WORKS Here in the test kitchen, we tend to think that cabbage doesn't always get the credit it deserves. It can be so much more than bland and limp, and it is a perfect candidate for a simple side dish to make on a busy weeknight. We decided to pan-steam and sauté the cabbage over relatively high heat to cook it quickly and add an extra layer of flavor from browning. A precooking step of soaking the cabbage reduced any bitterness while providing extra moisture to help the cabbage steam. Cooked onion helped reinforce sweetness, and lemon juice provided a pleasant punch while fresh parsley offered a bright finish. You will need a 12-inch nonstick skillet with a tight-fitting lid for this recipe.

Sautéed Cabbage with Parsley and Lemon

1 small head green cabbage (1¼ pounds),
  cored and sliced thin
2 tablespoons vegetable oil, divided
1 onion, halved and sliced thin
¾ teaspoon table salt, divided
¼ teaspoon pepper
¼ cup chopped fresh parsley
1½ teaspoons lemon juice

1. Place cabbage in large bowl, cover with cold water, and let sit for 3 minutes. Drain well.

2. Heat 1 tablespoon oil in 12-inch nonstick skillet over medium-high heat until shimmering. Add onion and ¼ teaspoon salt and cook, stirring occasionally, until softened and lightly browned, 5 to 7 minutes; transfer to bowl.

3. Heat remaining 1 tablespoon oil in now-empty skillet over medium-high heat until shimmering. Add cabbage and sprinkle with pepper and remaining ½ teaspoon salt. Cover and cook, without stirring, until cabbage is wilted and lightly browned on bottom, about 3 minutes. Stir and continue to cook, uncovered, until cabbage is crisp-tender and lightly browned in places,

about 4 minutes, stirring once halfway through cooking. Off heat, stir in onion, parsley, and lemon juice. Season with salt and pepper to taste, and serve.

PER SERVING Cal 80; **Total Fat** 4.5g; **Sat Fat** 0g; **Chol** 0mg; **Sodium** 320mg; **Total Carb** 8g, **Dietary Fiber** 3g, **Total Sugars** 4g; **Protein** 1g

VARIATIONS

Sautéed Cabbage with Bacon and Caraway Seeds

Substitute red cabbage for green. Whisk 1 tablespoon cider vinegar and 2 teaspoons packed brown sugar together in medium bowl. Omit oil. Cook 4 slices chopped bacon in skillet over medium heat until crisp, 5 to 7 minutes. Transfer bacon to paper towel–lined plate and pour off all but 1 tablespoon fat into bowl (reserve fat). Substitute red onion for onion and cook in fat in skillet until softened, about 5 minutes. Add 1 teaspoon caraway seeds and cook for 1 minute; transfer to bowl with vinegar mixture. Cook cabbage in 1 tablespoon reserved fat. Stir bacon into cabbage with onion mixture before serving.

Sautéed Cabbage with Fennel and Garlic

Substitute savoy cabbage for green. Substitute extra-virgin olive oil for vegetable oil and 1 cored and thinly sliced fennel bulb for onion. Cook fennel bulb until softened, 8 to 10 minutes, then add 2 garlic cloves, minced to paste, and ¼ teaspoon red pepper flakes and continue to cook until fragrant, about 30 seconds. Omit pepper. Substitute fennel fronds for parsley and increase lemon juice to 2 teaspoons. Drizzle cabbage with 1 tablespoon extra-virgin olive oil and sprinkle with 2 tablespoons grated Parmesan before serving.

Simple Cream-Braised Cabbage
SERVES 4 **FAST**

WHY THIS RECIPE WORKS The French have been cooking the simple but elegant side dish of cabbage in cream for ages, and when we tried it, we loved the sophisticated blend of flavors, complemented by the slight residual crunch of the cabbage. Our easy one-pan preparation for green cabbage highlights the vegetable's natural sweetness. To cut the richness of the cream, we incorporated lemon juice for its acidity and shallot for its subtle, sweet onion flavor. The cabbage needed only minutes to braise in the skillet before it was ready to serve. You will need a 12-inch skillet with a tight-fitting lid for this recipe.

¼ cup heavy cream
1 shallot, minced
1 teaspoon lemon juice
½ head green cabbage, cored and sliced thin (4 cups)

Boiled Carrots with Cumin, Lime, and Cilantro

as helped them cook faster. After draining, we added olive oil for richness and some citrus for brightness. A bit of spice and some fresh herbs completed this simple side. For even cooking, the carrot pieces should be of similar size. Choose carrots that are between 1 and 1½ inches in diameter.

1 pound carrots, peeled
2 teaspoons table salt
1 tablespoon extra-virgin olive oil
1 tablespoon chopped fresh cilantro
½ teaspoon lime zest plus 1 teaspoon juice, plus extra juice for seasoning
½ teaspoon cumin seeds, crushed

1. Cut carrots into 1½- to 2-inch lengths. Leave thin pieces whole, halve medium pieces lengthwise, and quarter thick pieces lengthwise.

2. Bring 2 cups water to boil in medium saucepan over high heat. Add carrots and salt, cover, and cook until tender, about 6 minutes.

3. Drain carrots, then return to saucepan. Stir in oil, cilantro, lime zest and juice, and cumin seeds and stir to coat. Season with extra lime juice to taste, and serve.

PER SERVING Cal 70; **Total Fat** 4g, **Sat Fat** 0.5g; **Chol** 0mg; **Sodium** 1230mg; **Total Carb** 10g, **Dietary Fiber** 3g, **Total Sugars** 5g; **Protein** 1g

VARIATIONS

Boiled Carrots with Fennel Seeds and Citrus

Substitute ½ teaspoon orange zest for lime zest. Substitute ½ teaspoon fennel seeds, crushed, for cumin, and parsley for cilantro.

Boiled Carrots with Mint and Paprika

Omit lime zest. Substitute sherry vinegar for lime juice, ½ teaspoon paprika for cumin, and mint for cilantro.

Bring cream, shallot, and lemon juice to simmer in 12-inch skillet over medium heat. Add cabbage and toss to coat. Cover and cook, stirring occasionally, until cabbage is wilted but still bright green, 7 to 9 minutes. Season with salt and pepper to taste. Serve.

PER SERVING Cal 90; **Total Fat** 5g, **Sat Fat** 3.5g; **Chol** 15mg; **Sodium** 30mg; **Total Carb** 9g, **Dietary Fiber** 3g, **Total Sugars** 5g; **Protein** 2g

Boiled Carrots with Cumin, Lime, and Cilantro
SERVES 4 **FAST** **VEGAN**

WHY THIS RECIPE WORKS Carrots are nutritious, inexpensive, and available year-round, so it's no wonder they're a common go-to vegetable to round out a meal. Boiling is the quickest, simplest way to produce tender, well-seasoned carrots. We cut 1 pound of carrots into 1½- to 2-inch lengths and then halved or quartered them lengthwise, depending on thickness, so that they all cooked at the same rate. Well-salted water not only added seasoning but also helped the carrots retain some of their natural sugars as well

Glazed Baby Carrots
SERVES 4 **FAST**

WHY THIS RECIPE WORKS Baby carrots are super convenient and lend themselves to a range of flavorings that bring out their inherent sweetness. The problem is that the baby carrots themselves have an aged, porous texture, which we suspect is the result of their processing method. To prevent these little carrots from tasting soft and spongy, we browned them first before steaming them until tender and coating them with a simple glaze. The browning firmed up their exterior texture and prevented the interior from taking on that spongy texture. With our cooking method down, we created a few variations with herbs and other flavors. Be sure to pat the carrots dry before cooking or they will not brown in step 1.

- 1 tablespoon vegetable oil
- 1 pound baby carrots, patted dry
- 1 cup water
- 3 tablespoons brown sugar
- ⅛ teaspoon table salt
- 1 tablespoon unsalted butter

1. Heat oil in 12-inch nonstick skillet over medium-high heat until shimmering. Add carrots and cook until well browned, 5 to 7 minutes. Stir in water, brown sugar, and ⅛ teaspoon salt, cover, and simmer gently until largest carrot is just tender, about 10 minutes.

2. Uncover, increase heat to medium-high, and simmer rapidly, stirring occasionally, until sauce is slightly thickened and carrots are well coated, 3 to 5 minutes. Stir in butter, season with salt and pepper to taste, and serve.

PER SERVING Cal 140; **Total Fat** 7g, **Sat Fat** 2g; **Chol** 10mg; **Sodium** 160mg; **Total Carb** 21g, **Dietary Fiber** 3g, **Total Sugars** 15g; **Protein** 1g

VARIATIONS
Glazed Baby Carrots with Cayenne
Add pinch cayenne pepper to skillet with water and brown sugar.

Glazed Baby Carrots with Curry
Add 1 teaspoon curry powder to skillet with water and brown sugar.

Glazed Baby Carrots with Rosemary
Add 1 (3-inch) sprig fresh rosemary to skillet with water and brown sugar; discard rosemary sprig before serving.

Pan-Roasted Cauliflower with Garlic and Lemon
SERVES 4 TO 6 **FAST** **VEGAN**

WHY THIS RECIPE WORKS Roasting cauliflower caramelizes its sugars and transforms this mild-mannered vegetable into something sweet and nutty-tasting. We wanted to create a stovetop method that would deliver oven-like results in a faster time frame. Heating oil and adding the florets resulted in the craggy exteriors browning before the interiors softened. Adding water to the pan to soften the florets resulted in anemic, bland cauliflower. But starting the oil and cauliflower together in a cold pan, first covered

Pan-Roasted Cauliflower with Garlic and Lemon

and then uncovered, resulted in caramelized, tender florets. A combination of sautéed garlic and lemon zest, plus fresh chopped parsley, perked up the flavor. With a sprinkle of crunchy toasted bread crumbs, our newfangled pan-roasted cauliflower was complete. You will need a 12-inch nonstick skillet with a tight-fitting lid for this recipe.

- 1 slice hearty white sandwich bread, torn into 1-inch pieces
- 5 tablespoons extra-virgin olive oil, divided
  Pinch plus 1 teaspoon table salt, divided
- 1 head cauliflower (2 pounds), cut into 1½-inch florets
- ½ teaspoon pepper
- 1 garlic clove, minced
- 1 teaspoon grated lemon zest, plus lemon wedges for serving
- ¼ cup chopped fresh parsley

1. Pulse bread in food processor to coarse crumbs, about 10 pulses. Heat bread crumbs, 1 tablespoon oil, pinch salt, and pinch pepper in 12-inch nonstick skillet over medium heat, stirring frequently, until bread crumbs are golden brown, 3 to 5 minutes. Transfer crumbs to bowl and wipe out skillet.

2. Combine 2 tablespoons oil and cauliflower florets in now-empty skillet and sprinkle with remaining 1 teaspoon salt and ½ teaspoon pepper. Cover skillet and cook over medium-high heat until florets start to brown and edges just start to become translucent (do not lift lid during this time), about 5 minutes.

3. Uncover and continue to cook, stirring occasionally, until golden, about 12 minutes.

4. Push florets to edges of skillet. Add garlic, lemon zest, and remaining 2 tablespoons oil to center and cook, stirring with silicone spatula, until fragrant, about 30 seconds. Stir garlic mixture into florets and continue to cook, stirring occasionally, until florets are tender but still firm, about 3 minutes.

5. Remove skillet from heat and stir in parsley. Transfer florets to platter and sprinkle with bread crumbs. Serve, passing lemon wedges separately.

PER SERVING Cal 160; **Total Fat** 12g, **Sat Fat** 2g; **Chol** 0mg; **Sodium** 480mg; **Total Carb** 10g, **Dietary Fiber** 3g, **Total Sugars** 3g; **Protein** 3g

VARIATIONS
Pan-Roasted Cauliflower with Capers and Pine Nuts

Omit bread and reduce oil to ¼ cup. Reduce salt in step 2 to ¾ teaspoon. Substitute 2 tablespoons capers, rinsed and minced, for garlic. Substitute 2 tablespoons minced fresh chives for parsley and stir in ¼ cup toasted pine nuts with chives in step 5.

Pan-Roasted Cauliflower with Cumin and Pistachios

Omit bread and reduce oil to ¼ cup. Heat 1 teaspoon cumin seeds and 1 teaspoon coriander seeds in 12-inch nonstick skillet over medium heat, stirring frequently, until lightly toasted and fragrant, 2 to 3 minutes. Transfer to spice grinder or mortar and pestle and coarsely grind. Wipe out skillet. Substitute ground cumin-coriander mixture, ½ teaspoon paprika, and pinch cayenne pepper for garlic; lime zest for lemon zest; and 3 tablespoons chopped fresh mint for parsley. Sprinkle with ¼ cup pistachios, toasted and chopped, before serving with lime wedges.

Cauliflower Rice
SERVES 4 TO 6   **FAST**

WHY THIS RECIPE WORKS A shape-shifter of a vegetable, cauliflower is often used in place of rice. It's easy to process the florets into rice-size granules that cook up pleasantly fluffy. Using the food processor made quick work of breaking down the florets and created a fairly consistent texture. Next, we needed to give our neutral-tasting cauliflower a boost in flavor; a shallot and a small amount of chicken broth did the trick. To ensure that the cauliflower was tender but still maintained a pleasant, rice-like chew, we first steamed it in a covered pot, then finished cooking it uncovered to evaporate any remaining moisture. This recipe can easily be doubled; use a Dutch oven and increase the cooking time to about 25 minutes in step 2.

- 1 head cauliflower (2 pounds), cut into 1-inch florets (6 cups)
- 1 tablespoon extra-virgin olive oil
- 1 shallot, minced
- ½ cup chicken or vegetable broth
- ¾ teaspoon table salt
- 2 tablespoons minced fresh parsley

1. Working in 2 batches, pulse cauliflower florets in food processor until finely ground into ¼- to ⅛-inch pieces, 6 to 8 pulses, scraping down sides of bowl as needed; transfer to bowl.

2. Heat oil in large saucepan over medium-low heat until shimmering. Add shallot and cook until softened, about 3 minutes. Stir in cauliflower, broth, and salt. Cover and cook, stirring occasionally, until cauliflower is tender, 12 to 15 minutes.

3. Uncover and continue to cook, stirring occasionally, until cauliflower rice is almost completely dry, about 3 minutes. Off heat, stir in parsley and season with salt and pepper to taste. Serve.

PER SERVING Cal 60; **Total Fat** 3g, **Sat Fat** 0.5g; **Chol** 0mg; **Sodium** 380mg; **Total Carb** 8g, **Dietary Fiber** 3g, **Total Sugars** 3g; **Protein** 3g

CUTTING CAULIFLOWER INTO FLORETS

1. Pull off any leaves, then cut out core of cauliflower using paring knife.

2. Separate florets from inner stem using tip of knife. Cut larger florets into smaller pieces by slicing through stem end.

Curried Cauliflower Rice

Add ¼ teaspoon ground cardamom, ¼ teaspoon ground cinnamon, and ¼ teaspoon ground turmeric to saucepan with shallot. Substitute 1 tablespoon minced fresh mint for parsley and stir ¼ cup toasted sliced almonds into cauliflower rice with mint.

Tex-Mex Cauliflower Rice

Add 1 minced garlic clove, 1 teaspoon ground cumin, and 1 teaspoon ground coriander to saucepan with shallot in step 2. Substitute 2 tablespoons minced fresh cilantro for parsley and stir 1 teaspoon lime juice into cauliflower rice with cilantro.

Foolproof Boiled Corn

SERVES 4 TO 6 **FAST**

WHY THIS RECIPE WORKS You might think that you don't need a recipe for boiled corn, but who hasn't pulled out the ears too early only to reveal underdone, starchy kernels or let them sit in the cooling water too long, turning mushy and shriveled? Corn season is so fleeting that we wanted a foolproof method for perfect corn every time. There are two key variables at play: starches and pectin. As corn heats, the starches in the kernels absorb water, swell, and gelatinize, and the corn "milk" becomes smoother, silkier, and more translucent. Simultaneously, the pectin dissolves, so the corn softens. To produce perfectly done, juicy corn every time, we learned that the ideal doneness range is 150 to 170 degrees—when the starches have gelatinized but a minimum amount of the pectin has dissolved. Here's how you get there: bringing a measured amount of water to a boil, shutting off the heat, dropping in six ears of corn, and letting the corn stand for at least 10 minutes. Serve with a flavored salt, if desired.

6 ears corn, husks and silk removed
Unsalted butter, softened

1. Bring 4 quarts water to boil in large Dutch oven. Turn off heat, add corn to water, cover, and let sit for at least 10 minutes or up to 30 minutes.

2. Serve immediately, passing butter, salt, and pepper separately.

PER SERVING Cal 90; **Total Fat** 2.5g, **Sat Fat** 0g; Chol 0mg; **Sodium** 0mg; **Total Carb** 18g, **Dietary Fiber** 2g, **Total Sugars** 5g; **Protein** 4g

---

TAKE IT UP A NOTCH

A sprinkle of flavored salt enhances everything from boiled or grilled corn to roasted vegetables to plain white rice.

Chili-Lime Salt
MAKES 3 TABLESPOONS

2 tablespoons kosher salt
4 teaspoons chili powder
¾ teaspoon grated lime zest

Combine all ingredients in small bowl. (Salt can be refrigerated for up to 1 week.)

Cumin-Sesame Salt
MAKES 3 TABLESPOONS

1 tablespoon cumin seeds
1 tablespoon sesame seeds
1 tablespoon kosher salt

Toast cumin seeds and sesame seeds in 8-inch skillet over medium heat, stirring occasionally, until fragrant and sesame seeds are golden brown, 3 to 4 minutes. Transfer mixture to cutting board and let cool for 2 minutes. Mince mixture until well combined. Transfer mixture to small bowl and stir in salt. (Salt can be stored at room temperature for up to 1 month.)

Pepper-Cinnamon Salt
MAKES 2 TABLESPOONS

1 tablespoon kosher salt
1 tablespoon coarsely ground pepper
¼ teaspoon ground cinnamon

Combine all ingredients in small bowl. (Salt can be stored at room temperature for up to 1 month.)

Broiled Eggplant with Basil

1. Spread eggplant over rimmed baking sheet lined with paper towels, sprinkle both sides with salt, and let sit for 30 minutes.

2. Adjust oven rack 4 inches from broiler element and heat broiler. Thoroughly pat eggplant dry, arrange in single layer on aluminum foil–lined baking sheet, and brush both sides with oil. Broil eggplant until tops are mahogany brown, 3 to 4 minutes. Flip eggplant and broil until second side is brown, 3 to 4 minutes.

3. Transfer eggplant to platter, season with pepper to taste, and sprinkle with basil. Serve.

PER SERVING Cal 90; Total Fat 7g; Sat Fat 1g; Chol 0mg; Sodium 580mg; Total Carb 7g, Dietary Fiber 3g, Total Sugars 4g; Protein 1g

VARIATION
Broiled Eggplant with Sesame-Miso Glaze
Any type of miso will work well here. Mirin is a sweet Japanese cooking wine; sherry can be substituted for the mirin if necessary.

Substitute vegetable oil for olive oil and 1 sliced scallion for basil. Whisk 3 tablespoons mirin, 1 tablespoon miso, and 1 tablespoon tahini together in bowl. After browning second side, brush with miso mixture, sprinkle with 1 tablespoon sesame seeds, and continue to broil until miso and seeds are browned, about 2 minutes.

Broiled Eggplant with Basil
SERVES 4 TO 6 VEGAN

WHY THIS RECIPE WORKS Broiling is a great way to enjoy eggplant as a simple side dish. While you can jazz it up if you want, all you really need is a sprinkling of fresh herbs. That said, if you try to simply slice and broil eggplant, it will steam in its own juices rather than brown. So to get broiled eggplant with great color and texture, we started by salting it to draw out its moisture. After 30 minutes, we patted the slices dry, moved them to a baking sheet (lined with aluminum foil for easy cleanup), and brushed them with oil. With the excess moisture taken care of, all the eggplant required was a few minutes per side under the blazing-hot broiler to turn a beautiful mahogany color. With its concentrated roasted flavor, the only accent needed was a sprinkling of fresh basil. Make sure to slice the eggplant thin so that the slices will cook through by the time the exterior is browned.

1½ pounds eggplant, sliced into ¼-inch-thick rounds
1½ teaspoons table salt
 3 tablespoons extra-virgin olive oil
 2 tablespoons chopped fresh basil

Sautéed Green Beans with Garlic and Herbs
SERVES 4 FAST

WHY THIS RECIPE WORKS For tender and lightly browned green beans using just one pan, we looked to sautéing. We discovered that simply sautéing the raw beans in hot oil resulted in blackened exteriors and undercooked interiors. So, for the best results, we sautéed the beans until spotty brown, and then added a little water to the pan and covered it so the beans could cook through. Once the beans were bright green but still crisp, we lifted the lid to evaporate the water and promote browning. A little butter added to the pan at this stage lent richness and encouraged even more browning. A few additional ingredients—garlic, herbs, and lemon—added flavor without overcomplicating things. This recipe yields crisp-tender beans. If you prefer a slightly more tender texture, increase the water by 1 tablespoon and increase the covered cooking time by 1 minute. You will need a 12-inch nonstick skillet with a tight-fitting lid for this recipe.

- 4 teaspoons extra-virgin olive oil
- 1 pound green beans, trimmed and cut into 2-inch lengths
- ¼ teaspoon table salt
- ⅛ teaspoon pepper
- ¼ cup water
- 1 tablespoon unsalted butter, softened
- 3 garlic cloves, minced
- 1 teaspoon minced fresh thyme
- 2 teaspoons lemon juice

1. Heat oil in 12-inch nonstick skillet over medium-high heat until just smoking. Add beans, salt, and pepper and cook, stirring occasionally, until spotty brown, 4 to 6 minutes. Add water, cover, and cook until beans are bright green and still crisp, about 2 minutes.

2. Uncover, increase heat to high, and continue to cook until liquid evaporates, about 3 minutes. Add butter, garlic, and thyme and cook, stirring often, until beans are crisp-tender, lightly browned, and beginning to wrinkle, 1 to 3 minutes. Off heat, stir in lemon juice and season with salt and pepper to taste. Serve.

PER SERVING Cal 110; **Total Fat** 8g, **Sat Fat** 2.5g; **Chol** 10mg; **Sodium** 150mg; **Total Carb** 9g, **Dietary Fiber** 3g, **Total Sugars** 4g; **Protein** 2g

Sautéed Green Beans with Garlic and Herbs

VARIATIONS
Sautéed Green Beans with Ginger and Sesame
Omit lemon juice. Substitute 1 teaspoon toasted sesame oil for butter, 1 teaspoon grated fresh ginger for garlic, and 1 tablespoon Asian chili-garlic paste for thyme. Sprinkle green beans with 2 teaspoons toasted sesame seeds before serving.

Sautéed Green Beans with Roasted Red Peppers and Basil
Substitute extra-virgin olive oil for butter, 1 minced shallot for garlic, and ⅛ teaspoon red pepper flakes for thyme. Add ⅓ cup chopped jarred roasted red peppers to skillet with shallot. Substitute 1 teaspoon red wine vinegar for lemon juice. Stir in 2 tablespoons chopped fresh basil with vinegar.

Skillet Green Beans with Walnuts
SERVES 8 **FAST**

WHY THIS RECIPE WORKS When you want to serve a simple green vegetable, green beans often come to mind. To steer clear of the steamed green beans rut, we chose to sauté green beans in butter to develop toasty flavors and then quickly steam them to ensure a crisp texture. We dressed up our beans with toasted walnuts, which we spiced with brown sugar and ginger for warmth and cayenne pepper and black pepper for the perfect amount of lingering heat. You will need a 12-inch skillet with a tight-fitting lid for this recipe.

- ⅔ cup chopped walnuts
- 4 tablespoons unsalted butter, cut into 4 pieces, divided
- 1 tablespoon brown sugar
- ¾ teaspoon ground ginger
- ¼ teaspoon table salt
- ¼ teaspoon pepper
  Pinch cayenne pepper
- 2 pounds green beans, stem ends trimmed
- ¼ cup water

1. Toast walnuts in large skillet over medium-low heat until golden, about 5 minutes. Add 2 tablespoons butter and cook, stirring constantly, until butter is nutty brown, about 2 minutes. Stir in sugar, ginger, salt, pepper, and cayenne and cook until fragrant, about 30 seconds. Transfer walnut mixture to bowl and reserve. Wipe out skillet.

2. Melt remaining 2 tablespoons butter in now-empty skillet over medium-high heat. Cook beans, stirring occasionally, until spotty brown, about 8 minutes. Add water and cook, covered, over medium-low heat until beans are nearly tender, about 3 minutes. Remove lid and cook until liquid evaporates, about 1 minute. Off heat, add reserved walnut mixture. Season with salt and pepper to taste, and serve.

PER SERVING Cal 160; **Total Fat** 12g, **Sat Fat** 4g; **Chol** 15mg; **Sodium** 80mg; **Total Carb** 11g, **Dietary Fiber** 4g, **Total Sugars** 6g; **Protein** 4g

Quick Roasted Green Beans
SERVES 4 **FAST** **VEGAN**

WHY THIS RECIPE WORKS Mature supermarket green beans are often tough and dull, needing special treatment to become tender and flavorful. Braising works, but if the stovetop is getting crowded as dinnertime approaches, roasting is a great option. We wanted to find out if this technique could help transform older green beans, giving them a flavor comparable to sweet, fresh-picked beans. A remarkably simple test produced outstanding results: Beans roasted in a 450-degree oven with only olive oil, salt, and pepper transformed aged specimens into deeply caramelized, full-flavored beans. Just 20 minutes of roasting reversed the aging process (converting starch back to sugar) and encouraged flavorful browning. One tablespoon of oil was enough to lend flavor and moisture without making the beans greasy. Lining the pan with aluminum foil prevented scorching and made for easy cleanup.

    1 pound green beans, trimmed
    1 tablespoon extra-virgin olive oil
    ½ teaspoon table salt

1. Adjust oven rack to middle position and heat oven to 450 degrees. Line rimmed baking sheet with aluminum foil. Spread green beans on sheet and drizzle with oil. Using your hands, toss to coat evenly. Sprinkle with salt, toss to coat, and distribute in even layer. Roast for 10 minutes.

2. Remove sheet from oven. Using tongs, redistribute green beans. Continue roasting until green beans are dark golden brown in spots and have started to shrivel, 10 to 12 minutes.

3. Season with salt and pepper to taste, and serve.

PER SERVING Cal 70; **Total Fat** 3.5g, **Sat Fat** 0.5g; **Chol** 0mg; **Sodium** 300mg; **Total Carb** 8g, **Dietary Fiber** 3g, **Total Sugars** 4g; **Protein** 2g

VARIATIONS
Quick Roasted Green Beans with Red Onion and Walnuts
Combine 1 tablespoon balsamic vinegar, 1 teaspoon honey, 1 teaspoon minced fresh thyme, and 2 thinly sliced garlic gloves in small bowl; set aside. Roast ½ medium red onion, cut into ½-inch-thick wedges, along with green beans. Remove sheet from oven. Using tongs, coat beans and onion evenly with vinegar/honey mixture; redistribute in even layer. Continue roasting until onions and beans are dark golden brown in spots and beans have started to shrivel, 10 to 12 minutes. Season with salt and pepper to taste and toss well to combine. Transfer to serving dish, sprinkle with ⅓ cup toasted and chopped walnuts, and serve.

Quick Roasted Green Beans with Sun-Dried Tomatoes, Goat Cheese, and Olives
While green beans roast, combine ½ cup coarsely chopped oil-packed sun-dried tomatoes, ½ cup pitted kalamata olives, quartered lengthwise, 1 tablespoon lemon juice, 2 teaspoons minced fresh oregano, and 1 teaspoon extra-virgin olive oil in medium bowl. Add green beans; toss well to combine, and season with salt and pepper to taste. Transfer to serving dish, top with ½ cup crumbled goat cheese, and serve.

Quick Roasted Sesame Green Beans
While green beans roast, combine 1 tablespoon minced garlic, 1 teaspoon minced fresh ginger, 2 teaspoons honey, ½ teaspoon toasted sesame oil, and ¼ teaspoon red pepper flakes in small bowl. Remove sheet from oven. Using tongs, coat green beans evenly with garlic mixture; redistribute in even layer. Continue roasting until dark golden brown in spots and starting to shrivel, 10 to 12 minutes. Season with salt to taste and toss well to combine. Transfer to serving dish, sprinkle with 4 teaspoons toasted sesame seeds, and serve.

Simple Sautéed Kale
SERVES 6 TO 8 **MAKE AHEAD** **VEGAN**

WHY THIS RECIPE WORKS Notoriously fibrous and tough, kale is often long-cooked. For a faster way to prepare this hearty green, we sautéed it. To account for the leaves and woody stems cooking at different rates, we cut the leaves into rough 2-inch pieces and the stems into smaller ½-inch pieces so they cooked in the same amount of time. To jump-start the cooking process, we softened all the kale at once by blanching it in boiling water in a Dutch oven first. Once the kale was drained and pressed of excess water, we heated sliced garlic and a dash of red pepper flakes in extra-virgin olive oil in the now-empty Dutch oven and then added the kale. After 5 minutes of stirring, the kale was completely tender and infused with garlicky flavor. A final drizzle of olive oil gave it a glossy sheen and extra richness. You can substitute Lacinato kale (also known as dinosaur or Tuscan kale) for the curly kale in this recipe, if desired. It's important to boil the kale in the full 4 quarts of water; with less water it can become too salty.

1½ pounds curly kale
   Table salt for blanching kale
6 tablespoons extra-virgin olive oil, divided
4 garlic cloves, sliced thin
¼ teaspoon red pepper flakes

1. Bring 4 quarts water to boil in Dutch oven over medium-high heat.

2. Meanwhile, stem kale by cutting away leafy green portion from both sides of stem. Cut leaves into 2-inch pieces. Trim and discard bases of stems thicker than ½ inch. Cut remaining stems into ½-inch pieces. Transfer kale to large bowl and wash thoroughly.

3. Add 2 tablespoons salt to boiling water. Add kale to pot, 1 handful at a time, submerging with tongs as needed. Cook, stirring occasionally, until leaves are tender and stems are just al dente, about 5 minutes. Drain in colander and let sit for 5 minutes, occasionally pressing on kale with rubber spatula to release excess moisture. (Drained kale can be refrigerated for up to 3 days.)

4. Heat ¼ cup oil in now-empty pot over medium heat until shimmering. Add garlic and pepper flakes and cook until garlic is lightly browned, 30 to 60 seconds. Add kale and cook, stirring frequently, until stems are tender, about 5 minutes. Season with salt and pepper to taste. Transfer to platter and drizzle with remaining 2 tablespoons oil. Serve.

PER SERVING Cal 140; Total Fat 11g, Sat Fat 1.5g; Chol 0mg; Sodium 105mg; Total Carb 8g, Dietary Fiber 3g, Total Sugars 2g; Protein 4g

VARIATION
Simple Sautéed Kale with Crispy Pepperoni and Cherry Peppers

Add ½ cup pepperoni, cut into ¼-inch pieces, to shimmering oil in step 4 and cook until rust-colored, 3 to 5 minutes. Using slotted spoon, transfer pepperoni to plate, then add garlic and pepper flakes to remaining oil in pot. Sprinkle kale with pepperoni and 2 tablespoons chopped jarred hot cherry peppers before serving.

Garlicky Swiss Chard with Walnuts and Feta

Garlicky Swiss Chard
SERVES 4 TO 6 FAST VEGAN

WHY THIS RECIPE WORKS Swiss chard is a hearty green that lends itself to flavorful, versatile preparations. To avoid watery, overcooked chard, we started cooking the greens in a covered pot just until they wilted. Then we uncovered the pot and continued to cook the greens until all the liquid evaporated. Cutting the tough stems smaller than the tender leaves was crucial, as it meant that we could throw both stems and leaves into the pot at the same time and still get evenly cooked results. Sautéing plenty of garlic in olive oil before adding the chard gave this simple side a big hit of flavor, while a splash of mild white wine vinegar and red pepper flakes added brightness and subtle heat. You will need a large Dutch oven for this recipe.

3 tablespoons extra-virgin olive oil, divided
6 garlic cloves, minced
2 pounds Swiss chard, stems chopped fine, leaves sliced into ½-inch-wide strips
¼ teaspoon table salt
⅛ teaspoon red pepper flakes
1 teaspoon white wine vinegar

1. Cook 2 tablespoons oil and garlic in large Dutch oven over medium-low heat, stirring occasionally, until garlic is light golden and fragrant, about 3 minutes. Stir in chard, salt, and pepper flakes. Increase heat to high, cover, and cook, stirring occasionally, until chard is wilted but still bright green, 2 to 4 minutes.

2. Uncover and continue to cook, stirring often, until liquid evaporates, 4 to 6 minutes. Stir in vinegar and remaining 1 tablespoon oil. Season with salt and pepper to taste. Serve.

PER SERVING Cal 90; **Total Fat** 7g, **Sat Fat** 1g; **Chol** 0mg; **Sodium** 390mg; **Total Carb** 6g, **Dietary Fiber** 2g, **Total Sugars** 2g; **Protein** 3g

VARIATIONS

Garlicky Swiss Chard with Golden Raisins and Goat Cheese

Add ¼ cup golden raisins to pot with chard. Sprinkle chard with ⅓ cup crumbled goat cheese and ¼ cup hazelnuts, toasted and chopped, before serving.

Garlicky Swiss Chard with Walnuts and Feta

Sprinkle chard with ⅓ cup crumbled feta cheese and ¼ cup walnuts, toasted and chopped, before serving.

Asian-Style Swiss Chard

Add 1 tablespoon grated fresh ginger to pot with chard. In step 2, substitute 1 tablespoon toasted sesame oil for oil and substitute 4 teaspoons soy sauce for vinegar. Sprinkle chard with 3 tablespoons sliced scallion and ¼ cup salted dry-roasted peanuts, chopped, before serving.

PREPPING HEARTY GREENS

1. To prepare kale, Swiss chard, or collard greens, cut away leafy green portion from either side of stalk or stem using chef's knife.

2. Stack several leaves and either slice leaves crosswise or chop them into pieces (as directed in recipe). Wash and dry leaves after they are cut, using a salad spinner.

Quick Collard Greens
SERVES 4 TO 6 **FAST** **VEGAN**

WHY THIS RECIPE WORKS Collard greens are strong, assertive leaves that we think deserve more attention as a side dish contender. Our quick blanch-and-sauté recipe gave us the same tender results as long braising. Stemming the greens was a necessary first step, and blanching the leaves in salted water tenderized them quickly and neutralized their bitter qualities. To remove excess water left from blanching, we used a spatula to press on the drained greens, and then rolled them up in a dish towel to dry them further. We chopped the compressed collards into thin slices perfect for quickly sautéing with pungent, aromatic garlic and spicy red pepper flakes, which provided immediate potent seasoning. You can substitute mustard or turnip greens for the collards; reduce their boiling time to 2 minutes.

 Table salt for cooking collard greens
2½ pounds collard greens, stemmed and halved lengthwise
 3 tablespoons extra-virgin olive oil
 2 garlic cloves, minced
¼ teaspoon red pepper flakes

1. Bring 4 quarts water to boil in large pot over high heat. Stir in 1 tablespoon salt, then add collard greens, 1 handful at a time. Cook until tender, 4 to 5 minutes. Drain and rinse with cold water until greens are cool, about 1 minute. Press greens with rubber spatula to release excess liquid. Place greens on dish towel and compress into 10-inch log. Roll up towel tightly, then remove greens from towel. Cut greens crosswise into ¼-inch slices.

2. Heat oil in 12-inch nonstick skillet over medium-high heat until just smoking. Scatter greens in skillet and cook, stirring frequently, until just beginning to brown, 3 to 4 minutes. Stir in garlic and pepper flakes and cook until greens are spotty brown, 1 to 2 minutes. Season with salt and pepper to taste, and serve.

PER SERVING Cal 100; **Total Fat** 8g, **Sat Fat** 1g; **Chol** 0mg; **Sodium** 115mg; **Total Carb** 6g, **Dietary Fiber** 4g, **Total Sugars** 1g; **Protein** 3g

Sautéed Mushrooms with Shallots and Thyme

Sautéed Mushrooms with Shallots and Thyme
SERVES 4 FAST

WHY THIS RECIPE WORKS Simply sautéed white mushrooms make a delicious and versatile side dish. But mushrooms tend to shrink quite a bit when sautéed, so what looks like plenty when raw seems to shrivel away to nothing when cooked. We wanted a quick sauté method that resulted in a big enough quantity to make an ample side dish. We discovered that overloading the skillet and extending the cooking time allowed the mushrooms to give up just enough liquid to eventually fit in a single layer and cook properly without shrinking away to nothing. They browned very nicely after we added a little butter to the skillet, and from there it was easy to enhance the dish with shallot, thyme, and Marsala—a classic flavor combination for complementing mushrooms. Halve or quarter mushrooms depending on their sizes.

1 tablespoon vegetable oil
1½ pounds white mushrooms, trimmed and halved if small or quartered if medium or large
1 tablespoon unsalted butter
1 shallot, minced
1 tablespoon minced fresh thyme or 1 teaspoon dried
¼ cup dry Marsala

1. Heat oil in 12-inch nonstick skillet over medium-high heat until shimmering. Add mushrooms and cook, stirring occasionally, until they release their liquid, about 5 minutes. Increase heat to high and cook, stirring occasionally, until liquid has evaporated, about 8 minutes.

2. Stir in butter, reduce heat to medium, and cook, stirring often, until mushrooms are dark brown, about 8 minutes.

3. Stir in shallot and thyme and cook until shallot is softened, about 3 minutes. Add Marsala and cook until evaporated, about 2 minutes. Season with salt and pepper to taste, and transfer to platter. Serve.

PER SERVING Cal 120; **Total Fat** 7g, **Sat Fat** 2g; **Chol** 10mg; **Sodium** 105mg; **Total Carb** 9g, **Dietary Fiber** 0g, **Total Sugars** 7g; **Protein** 3g

VARIATION
Sautéed Mushrooms with Sesame and Ginger
Substitute 1 tablespoon vegetable oil for butter and 2 tablespoons mirin and 2 tablespoons soy sauce for Marsala. Omit shallot and thyme. After browning mushrooms in step 2, stir in 1 tablespoon toasted sesame seeds and 1 tablespoon grated fresh ginger and cook until fragrant, about 30 seconds. Stir in 1 teaspoon toasted sesame oil and sprinkle with 2 thinly sliced scallions after seasoning with salt and pepper to taste in step 3.

Sautéed Okra
SERVES 4 FAST VEGAN

WHY THIS RECIPE WORKS Okra is an inexpensive, nutritious vegetable that is often overlooked. This could be because it's often associated with having an unpleasant texture. As okra is boiled or braised, the inside can become gelatinous (or, to put it another way, slimy). That's obviously a deal breaker, whether in our test kitchen or in your kitchen at home. We wanted to develop a simple stovetop okra recipe that highlighted its nutty flavor and was as crisp-tender as any other green vegetable. We found that quickly sautéing whole pods over medium-high heat was a great way to minimize their slipperiness and maximize their fresh flavor and crisp texture. Do not substitute frozen okra here.

2 tablespoons plus 1 teaspoon extra-virgin olive oil, divided
1 pound okra, stemmed
1 garlic clove, minced
Lemon wedges

1. Heat 2 tablespoons oil in 12-inch skillet over medium-high heat until just smoking. Add okra and cook, stirring occasionally, until crisp-tender and well browned on most sides, 5 to 7 minutes.

2. Push okra to sides of skillet. Add garlic and remaining 1 teaspoon oil to center and cook, mashing mixture into pan, until fragrant, about 30 seconds. Stir mixture into okra, season with salt and pepper to taste, and serve immediately with lemon wedges.

PER SERVING Cal 110; Total Fat 8g, Sat Fat 1g; Chol 0mg; Sodium 5mg; Total Carb 8g, Dietary Fiber 3g, Total Sugars 1g; Protein 2g

TRIMMING OKRA

Trim tough, woody stems from okra pods before cooking. If using pods whole, be sure to leave top "cap" just below stem intact. This prevents whole okra from turning gooey during cooking.

Simple Pureed Parsnips
SERVES 4 **FAST** **MAKE AHEAD**

WHY THIS RECIPE WORKS For a change of pace from mashed potatoes, we looked to parsnips for a quick and simple puree. We steamed the parsnips, rather than boiling them, before processing them in the food processor. This gave us a puree with pure, sweet, and intense flavor. Because parsnips are not as high in starch as potatoes, you can puree them in a food processor without turning them into a gummy mess—unlike potatoes. If you don't want to take out your food processor, you can puree the parsnips using any of the tools you might use to mash potatoes, though you will get a more rustic consistency.

1½ pounds parsnips, peeled, cut into 2½-inch lengths, and thick ends halved lengthwise
1½ tablespoons unsalted butter, softened

1. Bring 1 inch water to boil in covered Dutch oven over medium-high heat (water should not touch bottom of steamer basket).

2. Arrange parsnips in steamer basket. Set steamer basket inside Dutch oven, cover, and cook until they can be easily pierced with paring knife, about 10 minutes. Reserve cooking liquid.

3. Puree parsnips in food processor until smooth, about 1 minute, adding reserved cooking liquid as needed to achieve desired consistency. Return puree to now-empty Dutch oven and reheat over medium-low heat, stirring in butter. Season with salt and pepper to taste. Serve immediately. (Puree can be refrigerated for up to 3 days or frozen in airtight container for up to 1 month.)

PER SERVING Cal 150; Total Fat 4.5g, Sat Fat 2.5g; Chol 10mg; Sodium 15mg; Total Carb 26g, Dietary Fiber 7g, Total Sugars 7g; Protein 2g

VARIATION
Creamy Parsnip Puree with Shallots
While parsnips are cooking, melt butter in 12-inch skillet over medium heat. Add 3 chopped shallots and cook until golden, 2 to 3 minutes. Substitute ¼ cup chicken broth and ¼ cup milk for reserved cooking liquid, adding more milk as needed to achieve desired consistency. Top puree with shallots and serve.

Quick Buttered Peas
SERVES 4 **FAST**

WHY THIS RECIPE WORKS When it comes to making a quick side dish, frozen peas are hard to beat. Because frozen peas have already been blanched, the keys to cooking with them are to avoid overcooking them and to pair the peas with other ingredients that don't require much prep. After sautéing shallot, thyme, and garlic in butter, we simply added the peas and let them cook for a few minutes for a fresh and bright-tasting side dish. Using a skillet allowed the peas to heat quickly and evenly over the large surface. Adding a bit of sugar helped highlight the peas' sweet flavor. Do not thaw the peas before adding them to the skillet. You will need a 12-inch nonstick skillet with a tight-fitting lid for this recipe.

2 tablespoons unsalted butter
1 shallot, minced
1 teaspoon minced fresh thyme
1 garlic clove, minced
1 pound frozen peas
2 teaspoons sugar

Melt butter in 12-inch nonstick skillet over medium-high heat. Add shallot, thyme, and garlic and cook until softened and fragrant, about 2 minutes. Add peas and sugar, cover, and cook, stirring occasionally, until peas are heated through, about 4 minutes. Season with salt and pepper to taste. Serve.

PER SERVING Cal 150; Total Fat 6g, Sat Fat 3.5g; Chol 15mg, Sodium 0mg; Total Carb 19g, Dietary Fiber 5g, Total Sugars 8g; Protein 7g

Sautéed Snow Peas with Lemon and Parsley
SERVES 4 FAST VEGAN

WHY THIS RECIPE WORKS Not just for stir-fries, sweet, grassy snow peas are the star of this speedy side. We wanted to caramelize them a bit to highlight and amplify their delicate flavor. First we tried stir-frying, but the constant stirring left us with greasy, overcooked pods without any browning. Adding a sprinkle of sugar and cooking the peas without stirring for a short time helped to achieve the flavorful sear we were after, and then we continued to cook them, stirring constantly, until they were just crisp-tender. To boost flavor, we quickly sautéed a mixture of minced shallot, oil, and lemon zest in the pan before stirring everything together. A squeeze of lemon juice and a sprinkling of parsley just before serving kept this dish fresh and bright. Chives, tarragon, cilantro, or basil can be substituted for the parsley.

 1 tablespoon vegetable oil, divided
 1 small shallot, minced
 1 teaspoon finely grated lemon zest plus 1 teaspoon juice
 ¼ teaspoon table salt
 ⅛ teaspoon pepper
 ⅛ teaspoon sugar
 12 ounces snow peas, strings removed
 1 tablespoon minced fresh parsley

1. Combine 1 teaspoon oil, shallot, and lemon zest in bowl. In separate bowl, combine salt, pepper, and sugar.

2. Heat remaining 2 teaspoons oil in 12-inch nonstick skillet over high heat until just smoking. Add snow peas, sprinkle with salt mixture, and cook, without stirring, for 30 seconds. Stir briefly, then cook, without stirring, for 30 seconds. Continue to cook, stirring constantly, until peas are crisp-tender, 1 to 2 minutes.

3. Push peas to sides of skillet. Add shallot mixture to center and cook, mashing mixture into skillet, until fragrant, about 30 seconds. Stir shallot mixture into peas. Stir in lemon juice and parsley and season with salt and pepper to taste. Serve.

PER SERVING Cal 70; **Total Fat** 3.5g; **Sat Fat** 0g; **Chol** 0mg; **Sodium** 150mg; **Total Carb** 7g, **Dietary Fiber** 0g, **Total Sugars** 4g; **Protein** 2g

VARIATIONS
Sautéed Snow Peas with Garlic, Cumin, and Cilantro
Add 2 minced garlic cloves and ½ teaspoon toasted and cracked cumin seeds to shallot mixture in step 1. Substitute ½ teaspoon lime zest for lemon zest, lime juice for lemon juice, and cilantro for parsley.

Sautéed Snow Peas with Shallot, Lemon Grass, and Basil
Substitute 2 teaspoons minced fresh lemon grass for lemon zest, lime juice for lemon juice, and basil for parsley.

Spinach with Garlic and Lemon
SERVES 4 FAST VEGAN

WHY THIS RECIPE WORKS The harmonization of fresh spinach, savory garlic, and bright lemon is a classic favorite for good reason. We sought tender sautéed leaves seasoned with the perfect balance of garlic and lemon. For the spinach, we found that we greatly preferred the hearty flavor and texture of curly-leaf spinach over baby spinach, which wilted down into mush. We cooked the spinach in extra-virgin olive oil and then used tongs to squeeze the cooked spinach in a colander over the sink to get rid of all the excess moisture. Lightly toasted minced garlic, cooked after the spinach, added a sweet nuttiness. As for seasoning, all the spinach needed was salt and a squeeze of lemon juice. Leave some water clinging to the spinach leaves after rinsing to help encourage steam when cooking. Two pounds of flat-leaf spinach (about three bunches) can be substituted for the curly-leaf spinach, but do not use baby spinach because it is much too delicate.

 3 tablespoons extra-virgin olive oil, divided
 20 ounces curly-leaf spinach, stemmed
 2 garlic cloves, minced
    Lemon juice

1. Heat 1 tablespoon oil in Dutch oven over high heat until shimmering. Add spinach 1 handful at a time, stirring and tossing each handful to wilt slightly before adding more. Cook spinach, stirring constantly, until uniformly wilted, about 1 minute. Transfer spinach to colander and squeeze between tongs to release excess liquid. Wipe pot dry with paper towels.

2. Add garlic and remaining 2 tablespoons oil to now-empty pot and cook over medium heat until fragrant, about 30 seconds. Add squeezed spinach and toss to coat. Off heat, season with salt and lemon juice to taste. Serve.

PER SERVING Cal 130; **Total Fat** 11g, **Sat Fat** 1.5g; **Chol** 0mg; **Sodium** 110mg; **Total Carb** 5g, **Dietary Fiber** 3g, **Total Sugars** 0g; **Protein** 3g

Sautéed Cherry Tomatoes

SERVES 4 TO 6 **FAST** **VEGAN**

WHY THIS RECIPE WORKS Sautéing cherry tomatoes turns them into a terrific year-round side dish. We look for plump tomatoes with smooth skin—signs that the tomatoes are fully ripe. Because they contain a lot of liquid, these tomatoes cook very quickly; it took only a minute for them to soften in a hot skillet. Tossing them with sugar and salt encouraged light caramelization. We seasoned them with garlic and fresh basil to complement their sweetness. Grape tomatoes can be substituted for the cherry tomatoes, but because they tend to be sweeter, you will want to reduce or even omit the sugar. Do likewise if your cherry tomatoes are very sweet. Don't toss the tomatoes with the sugar and salt ahead of time or you will draw out their juice and make them overly soft.

  1 tablespoon extra-virgin olive oil
1½ pounds cherry tomatoes, halved
  2 teaspoons sugar, or to taste
  ¼ teaspoon table salt
  1 garlic clove, minced
  2 tablespoons chopped fresh basil

Heat oil in 12-inch skillet over medium-high heat until shimmering. Toss tomatoes with sugar and salt, then add to skillet and cook, stirring often, for 1 minute. Stir in garlic and cook until fragrant, about 30 seconds. Off heat, stir in basil and season with salt and pepper to taste. Serve.

PER SERVING Cal 50; **Total Fat** 2.5g, **Sat Fat** 0g; **Chol** 0mg; **Sodium** 105mg; **Total Carb** 6g, **Dietary Fiber** 1g, **Total Sugars** 4g; **Protein** 1g

Sautéed Zucchini

Sautéed Zucchini or Yellow Summer Squash

SERVES 4 **VEGAN**

WHY THIS RECIPE WORKS Zucchini and yellow summer squash are naturally watery so they often cook up soggy and bland. We wanted to make sautéed zucchini or yellow squash with concentrated flavor and an appealing texture. The key was to remove water by salting and draining the squash for 30 minutes and then patting it dry. We sautéed an onion first for some depth and then added the squash, along with lemon zest, to the hot skillet, where the squash became tender and lightly browned with minimal stirring. A little lemon juice and parsley stirred in off the heat lent bright flavors. Do not add more salt when cooking, or the dish will be too salty. Basil, mint, or tarragon can be substituted for the parsley.

1½ pounds zucchini or yellow summer squash,
    sliced ¼ inch thick
  1 tablespoon table salt
  3 tablespoons extra-virgin olive oil
  1 small onion, chopped fine
  1 teaspoon grated lemon zest plus 1 tablespoon juice
  1 tablespoon minced fresh parsley

1. Toss zucchini with salt in colander set over bowl and let drain until roughly ⅓ cup water drains from zucchini, about 30 minutes. Pat zucchini dry with paper towels and carefully wipe away any residual salt.

2. Heat oil in 12-inch nonstick skillet over medium heat until shimmering. Add onion and cook until almost softened, about 3 minutes. Increase heat to medium-high, add zucchini and lemon zest, and cook until zucchini is golden brown, about 10 minutes.

3. Off heat, stir in lemon juice and parsley and season with pepper to taste. Transfer zucchini to serving dish. Serve.

PER SERVING Cal 130; **Total Fat** 11g, **Sat Fat** 1.5g; **Chol** 0mg; **Sodium** 1760mg; **Total Carb** 7g, **Dietary Fiber** 2g, **Total Sugars** 5g; **Protein** 2g

SIMPLE GREEN SALADS

Salads are a nice addition to any table. These easy and interesting salads combine various greens with flavorful ingredients such as nuts, olives, and cheese.

BASIC GREEN SALAD
SERVES 4 **FAST** **VEGAN**

½ garlic clove, peeled
8 ounces (8 cups) lettuce, torn into
   bite-size pieces if necessary
   Extra-virgin olive oil
   Vinegar

Rub inside of salad bowl with garlic. Add lettuce. Holding thumb over mouth of olive oil bottle to control flow, slowly drizzle lettuce with small amount of oil. Toss greens very gently. Continue to drizzle with oil and gently toss until greens are lightly coated and just glistening. Sprinkle with small amounts of vinegar, salt, and pepper to taste and gently toss to coat. Serve.

PER SERVING Cal 20; **Total Fat** 1.5g, **Sat Fat** 0g; **Chol** 0mg; **Sodium** 0mg; **Total Carb** 2g, **Dietary Fiber** 1g, **Total Sugars** 1g, **Protein** 1g

TRICOLOR SALAD WITH BALSAMIC VINAIGRETTE
SERVES 4 to 6 **FAST** **VEGAN**

1 small head radicchio (6 ounces), cored and cut into
   1-inch pieces
1 head Belgian endive (4 ounces), cut into 2-inch pieces
3 ounces (3 cups) baby arugula
1 tablespoon balsamic vinegar
1 teaspoon red wine vinegar
⅛ teaspoon table salt
   Pinch pepper
3 tablespoons extra-virgin olive oil

Gently toss radicchio, endive, and arugula together in large bowl. Whisk balsamic vinegar, red wine vinegar, salt, and pepper together in small bowl. Whisking constantly, slowly drizzle in oil. Drizzle vinaigrette over salad and gently toss to coat. Season with salt and pepper to taste. Serve.

PER SERVING Cal 80; **Total Fat** 7g, **Sat Fat** 1g; **Chol** 0mg; **Sodium** 60mg; **Total Carb** 3g, **Dietary Fiber** 1g, **Total Sugars** 1g, **Protein** 1g

Tricolor Salad with Balsamic Vinaigrette

NOTES FROM THE TEST KITCHEN

Buying Salad Greens

Not only is there a dizzying array of greens available at the supermarket now, but in a good market you can buy the same greens more than one way: full heads, prewashed in a bag, in a clamshell, and loose in bulk bins. Which is the right choice for you? A sturdy lettuce like romaine can be washed and stored for up to a week, making it a good option for many nights' worth of salads. Bags of prewashed baby spinach, arugula, and mesclun mix offer great convenience, but be sure to turn over the bags and inspect the greens as closely as you can; the sell-by date alone doesn't ensure quality, so if you see moisture in the bag or hints of blackened leaf edges, move on.

Don't buy bags of already-cut lettuce that you can otherwise buy as whole heads, like romaine, Bibb, or red leaf. Precut lettuce will be inferior in quality because the leaves begin to spoil once they are cut (bagged hearts of romaine are fine but stay away from bags of cut romaine). Endive and radicchio are always sold in heads, and because they are sturdy and will last a while, they are nice to have on hand to complement other greens and just to add more interest to a salad. And when a special salad is planned for company, for the best results you should buy the greens either the day of the party or the day before.

GREEN SALAD WITH MARCONA ALMONDS AND MANCHEGO CHEESE
SERVES 4 to 6 FAST

- 6 ounces (6 cups) mesclun greens
- 5 teaspoons sherry vinegar
- 1 shallot, minced
- 1 teaspoon Dijon mustard
- ¼ teaspoon table salt
- ¼ teaspoon pepper
- ¼ cup extra-virgin olive oil
- ⅓ cup Marcona almonds, chopped coarse
- 2 ounces Manchego cheese, shaved

Place mesclun in large bowl. Whisk vinegar, shallot, mustard, salt, and pepper together in small bowl. Whisking constantly, slowly drizzle in oil. Drizzle vinaigrette over mesclun and gently toss to coat. Season with salt and pepper to taste. Serve, topping individual portions with almonds and Manchego.

PER SERVING Cal 190; **Total Fat** 17g, **Sat Fat** 4g; **Chol** 5mg; **Sodium** 200mg; **Total Carb** 2g, **Dietary Fiber** 1g, **Total Sugars** 1g; **Protein** 4g

GREEN SALAD WITH ARTICHOKES AND OLIVES
SERVES 4 to 6 FAST

- 1 romaine lettuce heart (6 ounces), cut into 1-inch pieces
- 3 ounces (3 cups) baby arugula
- 1 cup jarred whole baby artichoke hearts packed in water, quartered, rinsed, and patted dry
- ⅓ cup fresh parsley leaves
- ⅓ cup pitted kalamata olives, halved
- 2 tablespoons white wine vinegar or white balsamic vinegar
- 1 small garlic clove, minced
- ¼ teaspoon table salt
  Pinch pepper
- 3 tablespoons extra-virgin olive oil
- 1 ounce Asiago cheese, shaved

Gently toss romaine, arugula, artichoke hearts, parsley, and olives together in large bowl. Whisk vinegar, garlic, salt, and pinch pepper together in small bowl. Whisking constantly, drizzle in oil. Drizzle vinaigrette over salad and gently toss to coat. Season with salt and pepper to taste. Serve, topping individual portions with Asiago.

PER SERVING Cal 110; **Total Fat** 9g, **Sat Fat** 2g; **Chol** 5mg; **Sodium** 270mg; **Total Carb** 5g, **Dietary Fiber** 1g, **Total Sugars** 2g; **Protein** 3g

ARUGULA SALAD WITH FENNEL AND PARMESAN
SERVES 4 to 6 FAST

- 6 ounces (6 cups) baby arugula
- 1 large fennel bulb, stalks discarded, bulb halved, cored, and sliced thin
- 1½ tablespoons lemon juice
- 1 small shallot, minced
- 1 teaspoon Dijon mustard
- 1 teaspoon minced fresh thyme
- 1 small garlic clove, minced
- ⅛ teaspoon table salt
  Pinch pepper
- ¼ cup extra-virgin olive oil
- 1 ounce Parmesan cheese, shaved

Gently toss arugula and fennel together in large bowl. Whisk lemon juice, shallot, mustard, thyme, garlic, salt, and pepper together in small bowl. Whisking constantly, slowly drizzle in oil. Drizzle dressing over salad and gently toss to coat. Season with salt and pepper to taste. Serve with Parmesan.

PER SERVING Cal 130; **Total Fat** 11g, **Sat Fat** 2g; **Chol** 5mg; **Sodium** 180mg; **Total Carb** 5g, **Dietary Fiber** 2g, **Total Sugars** 2g; **Protein** 3g

MAKING A SIMPLE GREEN SALAD

1. MEASURE OUT AND TOSS GREENS Measure out greens and gently toss with any additional vegetables.

2. MAKE DRESSING To make dressing base, whisk together vinegar or lemon juice and seasonings. To fully emulsify, slowly drizzle oil into base, whisking constantly.

3. DRIZZLE DRESSING OVER SALAD Evenly drizzle vinaigrette over salad and gently toss to coat. Add salt, pepper, and any additions like cheese and nuts and serve.

Fastest-Ever Baked Potatoes

2. Carefully transfer potatoes to oven and cook directly on hot oven rack until paring knife easily pierces flesh, about 20 minutes. Remove potatoes from oven and make dotted X on top of each potato with tines of fork. Press in at ends of each potato to release steam and push flesh up and out. Serve.

PER SERVING Cal 180; **Total Fat** 0g; **Sat Fat** 0g; **Chol** 0mg; **Sodium** 10mg; **Total Carb** 41g, **Dietary Fiber** 3g, **Total Sugars** 1g; **Protein** 5g

Pan-Roasted Potatoes

SERVES 4 **FAST** **VEGAN**

WHY THIS RECIPE WORKS We wanted an outstanding stovetop-roasted potato recipe (extra-crisp on the outside and moist and creamy on the inside) to turn to when our oven wasn't free. The key was choosing the right potato and cutting it uniformly: Red Bliss potatoes, cut in half if they're small or quartered if they're medium, offer a great crust and a moist interior. The winning cooking technique for our stovetop-roasted potatoes was to first brown the potatoes over high heat, cover, and finish the cooking over low heat, which allowed the insides to cook through while the outsides stayed crisp. For even cooking and proper browning, the potatoes must be cooked in a single layer and should not be crowded in the pan, so be sure to use a heavy-duty 12-inch skillet. A nonstick skillet simplifies cleanup but is not essential. We prefer to use small or medium potatoes (1½ to 3 inches in diameter) here because they are easier to cut into uniform pieces.

    2 pounds small or medium red potatoes,
       cut into 1-inch pieces
    3 tablespoons extra-virgin olive oil, divided
    ¼ teaspoon table salt

1. Toss potatoes with 1 tablespoon oil and salt in bowl. Microwave on high, uncovered, until potatoes soften but still hold their shape, about 10 minutes, gently stirring twice during cooking. Drain potatoes thoroughly.

2. Heat remaining 2 tablespoons oil in 12-inch nonstick skillet over medium-high heat until shimmering. Add potatoes, cut side down, in single layer and cook until golden brown on first side, 5 to 7 minutes.

3. Gently stir potatoes, rearrange in single layer, and cook until tender and deep golden brown on second side, 5 to 7 minutes longer. Season with salt and pepper to taste, and serve.

PER SERVING Cal 250; **Total Fat** 11g, **Sat Fat** 1.5g; **Chol** 0mg; **Sodium** 190mg; **Total Carb** 36g, **Dietary Fiber** 4g, **Total Sugars** 3g; **Protein** 4g

Fastest-Ever Baked Potatoes

SERVES 4 **VEGAN**

WHY THIS RECIPE WORKS Everyone loves a baked potato. Unfortunately, not everyone loves waiting an hour for their side dish to be ready to serve. When there isn't enough time to bake a potato through completely in the oven, we like to jump-start the cooking in the microwave. We discovered that cooking the potatoes in the microwave for 6 minutes or so until they began to soften, then transferring them to a very hot oven, worked well and shaved over half an hour off the traditional baked potato cooking time. For this recipe, look for evenly sized russet potatoes with firm, unblemished skin. Try topping baked potatoes with a flavored butter (page 289), if desired. When you have more time, try making our Best Baked Potatoes (page 77).

    4 russet potatoes (8 ounces each), unpeeled

1. Adjust oven rack to middle position and heat oven to 450 degrees. Poke several holes in each potato with fork. Microwave potatoes until slightly softened, 6 to 12 minutes, turning potatoes over halfway through cooking.

Pan-Roasted Potatoes with Garlic and Rosemary
Combine 1 teaspoon olive oil, 2 minced garlic cloves, and 2 teaspoons minced fresh rosemary in bowl. After browning potatoes in step 3, clear center of pan, add garlic mixture, and cook, mashing garlic into skillet, until fragrant, about 30 seconds. Stir garlic mixture into potatoes.

Pan-Roasted Potatoes with Lemon and Chives
Toss potatoes with 2 tablespoons minced fresh chives and 2 teaspoons grated lemon zest before serving.

Pan-Roasted Potatoes with Southwestern Spices
Combine ½ teaspoon chili powder, ½ teaspoon paprika, ¼ teaspoon ground cumin, and ⅛ teaspoon cayenne pepper in bowl. Toss pinch of spice mixture with potatoes before microwaving in step 1. Stir remaining spice mixture into potatoes before browning on second side in step 3.

Simple Mashed Sweet Potatoes
SERVES 4 **FAST** **MAKE AHEAD**

WHY THIS RECIPE WORKS We like our mashed sweet potatoes to taste like sweet potatoes, not the flavorings they were cooked with. To maximize their natural flavor, we steamed the potatoes in just 6 tablespoons of water (boiling them in a lot of water dilutes their flavor). We added butter, sugar, salt, and pepper to the potatoes before cooking. Then we simply mashed everything together in the same saucepan. This recipe can be doubled and prepared in a Dutch oven; increase the cooking time to 40 to 50 minutes.

2 pounds sweet potatoes, peeled and sliced ¼ inch thick
6 tablespoons water
4 tablespoons unsalted butter, cut into 4 pieces
1 teaspoon sugar
1 teaspoon table salt
½ teaspoon pepper

1. Combine potatoes, water, butter, sugar, salt, and pepper in large saucepan. Cover and cook over medium-low heat, stirring occasionally, until potatoes crumble easily when poked with paring knife, 25 to 30 minutes.

2. Using potato masher, mash potatoes thoroughly until smooth and no lumps remain. Season with salt and pepper to taste. Serve. (Mashed sweet potatoes can be refrigerated for up to 2 days.)

PER SERVING Cal 250; **Total Fat** 11g, **Sat Fat** 7g; **Chol** 30mg; **Sodium** 690mg; **Total Carb** 35g, **Dietary Fiber** 6g, **Total Sugars** 11g; **Protein** 3g

Simple Mashed Sweet Potatoes

Mashed Sweet Potatoes with Maple and Orange
Omit sugar. Stir 2 tablespoons maple syrup, 1 teaspoon minced fresh thyme, and ½ teaspoon grated orange zest into potato mixture after mashing in step 2.

Mashed Sweet Potatoes with Curry and Golden Raisins
Add 2 teaspoons curry powder to saucepan with potatoes in step 1. Stir ½ cup golden raisins and 2 tablespoons minced fresh cilantro into potato mixture after mashing in step 2.

Mashed Sweet Potatoes with Jalapeño, Garlic, and Scallions
Add 1 stemmed, seeded, and minced jalapeño chile and 2 minced garlic cloves to saucepan with potatoes in step 1. Stir 2 thinly sliced scallions into potato mixture after mashing in step 2.

Stovetop White Rice
SERVES 4 TO 6 `VEGAN`

WHY THIS RECIPE WORKS White rice seems like an easy enough side dish to make, but it can be deceptively temperamental, quickly dissolving into unpleasant, gummy grains. For really great long-grain rice with distinct separate grains that didn't clump together, we rinsed the rice of excess starch first. Then, to add a rich dimension, we sautéed the grains in butter (or vegetable oil) before covering them with water. After simmering the rice until all of the liquid was absorbed, we placed a dish towel between the lid and pot to absorb excess moisture and ensure dry, fluffy grains. A nonstick saucepan works best here, although a traditional saucepan will also work. Basmati, jasmine, or Texmati rice can be substituted for the long-grain rice. To jazz up plain rice, try tossing in some minced fresh herbs and/or citrus zest, or use a flavored butter (page 289) or flavored salt (page 14).

1 tablespoon unsalted butter or vegetable oil
2 cups long-grain white rice, rinsed
3 cups water
1 teaspoon table salt

Melt butter in large saucepan over medium heat. Add rice and cook, stirring often, until grain edges begin to turn translucent, about 2 minutes. Add water and salt and bring to simmer. Cover, reduce heat to low, and simmer gently until rice is tender and water is absorbed, about 20 minutes. Off heat, lay clean dish towel underneath lid and let rice sit for 10 minutes. Gently fluff rice with fork. Season with salt and pepper to taste. Serve.

PER SERVING Cal 240; **Total Fat** 2g, **Sat Fat** 1.5g; **Chol** 5mg; **Sodium** 390mg; **Total Carb** 49g, **Dietary Fiber** 1g, **Total Sugars** 0g; **Protein** 4g

RINSING RICE AND GRAINS

Place rice or grains in fine-mesh strainer and rinse under cool water until water runs clear, occasionally stirring lightly with your hand. Let drain briefly.

Foolproof Baked White Rice
SERVES 6 TO 8 `VEGAN`

WHY THIS RECIPE WORKS A hands-off recipe for perfect rice is a cook's ace in the hole. We've found that using the gentle heat of the oven is the most foolproof way to cook rice. When we tried to use our usual stovetop ratios of liquid to rice for this easy baked rice, we found that the grains were a bit too crunchy. Adding a little extra liquid greatly improved the texture and produced distinct, clump-proof grains. For an accurate measurement of boiling water, bring a full kettle of water to a boil and then measure out the desired amount.

4½ cups boiling water
2⅔ cups long-grain white rice, rinsed
1 tablespoon extra-virgin olive oil
¾ teaspoon table salt

Adjust oven rack to middle position and heat oven to 450 degrees. Combine boiling water, rice, oil, and salt in 13 by 9-inch baking dish. Cover dish tightly with double layer of aluminum foil. Bake until liquid is absorbed and rice is tender, 20 to 25 minutes. Remove dish from oven, uncover, and fluff rice with fork, scraping up any rice that has stuck to bottom. Re-cover dish with foil and let rice sit for 10 minutes. Season with salt and pepper to taste. Serve.

PER SERVING Cal 240; **Total Fat** 2g, **Sat Fat** 0g; **Chol** 0mg; **Sodium** 230mg; **Total Carb** 49g, **Dietary Fiber** 1g, **Total Sugars** 0g; **Protein** 4g

Simple Rice Pilaf
SERVES 4 TO 6 `VEGAN`

WHY THIS RECIPE WORKS There are several keys to making a good rice pilaf. First, rinsing the rice to remove excess starch produces a pilaf with distinct grains. It's also crucial to find the right ratio of liquid to grains to achieve the best texture. We found that 2½ cups of water to 1½ cups of rice worked perfectly. We built a base of flavor by cooking chopped onion with butter before stirring in the rice, letting the grains toast slightly. Then we added boiling water and let the rice cook until all of the liquid was absorbed. Placing a dish towel under the lid while the rice finished steaming off the heat absorbed excess moisture and guaranteed our rice was perfectly fluffy. Be sure to rinse the rice until the water runs clear. A nonstick saucepan is crucial to prevent the wet rice from sticking to the pan; for the most evenly cooked rice, use a wide-bottomed saucepan with a tight-fitting lid. Basmati, jasmine, or Texmati rice can be substituted for the long-grain rice.

Simple Rice Pilaf

VARIATION
Simple Herbed Rice Pilaf

Add 2 minced garlic cloves and 1 teaspoon minced fresh thyme to pot with rice. When fluffing cooked rice, stir in ¼ cup minced fresh parsley and 2 tablespoons minced fresh chives.

Easy Parmesan Risotto
SERVES 4 **FAST**

WHY THIS RECIPE WORKS Risotto is synonymous with long, involved cooking, but we found a way to make this side in less time. The microwave helped us cut back on some of the cooking time of most standard recipes. Microwaving Arborio rice with some broth and a little butter allowed the grains to soften quickly while we started the aromatic base of chopped onion and minced garlic on the stove. Then, we simply transferred the rice mixture to the saucepan with the aromatics and continued to cook it, stirring constantly, to achieve a creamy consistency. To add bright and fresh notes, we stirred in basil and lemon zest and juice at the end, as well as Parmesan and more butter for added richness and creaminess. If the finished risotto is too thick, stir in hot water, a few tablespoons at a time, to adjust the consistency.

- 1 cup Arborio rice
- 4 cups chicken broth, divided
- 6 tablespoons unsalted butter, divided
- 1 onion, chopped fine
- 2 garlic cloves, minced
- ½ cup chopped fresh basil
- 2 teaspoons grated lemon zest plus 2 tablespoons juice
- 2 ounces Parmesan cheese, grated (1 cup), plus extra for serving

1. Combine rice, 2 cups broth, and 2 tablespoons butter in bowl. Cover and microwave until rice is softened and most of liquid is absorbed, about 15 minutes.

2. Meanwhile, melt 2 tablespoons butter in medium saucepan over medium-high heat. Add onion and cook until softened, about 3 minutes. Stir in garlic and cook until fragrant, about 30 seconds.

3. Stir in hot rice mixture and remaining 2 cups broth. Bring to simmer and cook, stirring constantly, until rice is tender, 5 to 7 minutes. Off heat, stir in basil, lemon zest and juice, Parmesan, and remaining 2 tablespoons butter. Season with salt and pepper to taste. Serve, passing extra Parmesan separately.

PER SERVING Cal 400; **Total Fat** 20g, **Sat Fat** 13g; **Chol** 55mg; **Sodium** 710mg; **Total Carb** 43g, **Dietary Fiber** 3g, **Total Sugars** 3g; **Protein** 12g

---

- 3 tablespoons unsalted butter or vegetable oil
- 1 small onion, chopped fine
- 1 teaspoon table salt
- 1½ cups long-grain white rice, rinsed
- 2½ cups boiling water

1. Melt butter in large nonstick saucepan over medium heat. Add onion and salt and cook until softened, 5 to 7 minutes.

2. Stir in rice and cook until edges begin to turn translucent, about 3 minutes. Stir in boiling water and return to boil. Reduce heat to low, cover, and gently simmer until water is completely absorbed, 16 to 18 minutes.

3. Off heat, uncover and lay clean dish towel over saucepan; cover and let sit for 10 minutes. Fluff rice with fork, season with salt and pepper to taste, and serve.

PER SERVING Cal 220; **Total Fat** 6g, **Sat Fat** 3.5g; **Chol** 15mg; **Sodium** 390mg; **Total Carb** 37g, **Dietary Fiber** 0g, **Total Sugars** 1g; **Protein** 4g

Foolproof Baked Brown Rice
SERVES 4   `VEGAN`

WHY THIS RECIPE WORKS A lot of people like to swap out their white rice for its hearty, healthful cousin. For hands-off baked brown rice, we cooked the rice in the oven to approximate the controlled, indirect heat of a rice cooker, eliminating the risk of scorching. Experimenting with proportions, we discovered why most brown rice is sodden and overcooked: Most brown rice recipes call for a 2:1 water-to-rice ratio, but we found that 2⅓ cups water to 1½ cups rice gave us perfectly cooked rice. Medium-grain or short-grain brown rice can be substituted for the long-grain rice. For an accurate measurement of boiling water, bring a full kettle of water to a boil, then measure out the desired amount. An 8-inch ceramic baking dish with a lid may be used instead of the baking dish and foil. To double the recipe, use a 13 by 9-inch baking dish; the baking time need not be increased.

2⅓ cups boiling water
1½ cups long-grain brown rice, rinsed
 2 teaspoons extra-virgin olive oil
½ teaspoon table salt

Adjust oven rack to middle position and heat oven to 375 degrees. Combine boiling water, rice, oil, and salt in 8-inch square baking dish. Cover dish tightly with double layer of aluminum foil. Bake until rice is tender and water is absorbed, about 1 hour. Remove dish from oven, uncover, and gently fluff rice with fork, scraping up any rice that has stuck to bottom. Cover dish with clean dish towel and let rice sit for 5 minutes. Uncover and let rice sit for 5 minutes longer. Season with salt and pepper to taste. Serve.

PER SERVING Cal 280; **Total Fat** 4.5g, **Sat Fat** 0.5g; **Chol** 0mg; **Sodium** 300mg; **Total Carb** 53g, **Dietary Fiber** 2g, **Total Sugars** 0g; **Protein** 5g

Foolproof Baked Brown Rice

Easy Baked Quinoa with Lemon, Garlic, and Parsley
SERVES 4   `VEGAN`

WHY THIS RECIPE WORKS There are many ways to prepare quinoa, but this hands-off method delivers perfectly cooked quinoa every time—plus, it's simple to incorporate flavorful add-ins. For the cooking liquid we turned to chicken broth (vegetable broth worked well, too), which we microwaved with lemon zest until just boiling. We poured the hot liquid over the quinoa, which we had combined with olive oil and garlic in a baking dish. We then covered the dish with foil and placed it in the oven. Lemon juice and parsley stirred in before serving lent bright notes to this side dish. We like the convenience of prewashed quinoa. If you buy unwashed quinoa (or if you are unsure whether it's washed), rinse it before cooking to remove its bitter protective coating (called saponin).

1½ cups prewashed white quinoa
 2 tablespoons extra-virgin olive oil
 2 garlic cloves, minced
1½ cups chicken or vegetable broth
 1 teaspoon grated lemon zest plus 1 teaspoon juice
¼ teaspoon table salt
 2 tablespoons minced fresh parsley

1. Adjust oven rack to middle position and heat oven to 450 degrees. Combine quinoa, oil, and garlic in 8-inch square baking dish.

2. Microwave broth, lemon zest, and salt in covered bowl until just boiling, about 5 minutes. Pour hot broth over quinoa mixture and cover dish tightly with double layer of aluminum foil. Bake quinoa until tender and no liquid remains, about 25 minutes.

3. Remove dish from oven, uncover, and fluff quinoa with fork, scraping up any quinoa that has stuck to bottom. Re-cover dish with foil and let stand for 10 minutes. Fold in lemon juice and parsley, and season with salt and pepper to taste. Serve.

PER SERVING Cal 310; **Total Fat** 11g, **Sat Fat** 1.5g; Chol 0mg; **Sodium** 340mg; **Total Carb** 42g, **Dietary Fiber** 5g, **Total Sugars** 2g; **Protein** 11g

VARIATIONS

Easy Baked Quinoa with Scallions and Feta

Substitute 4 thinly sliced scallions for parsley. Fold ½ cup crumbled feta into quinoa before serving.

Easy Baked Quinoa with Tomatoes, Parmesan, and Basil

Omit lemon zest, lemon juice, and parsley. Fold 1 finely chopped tomato, ½ cup grated Parmesan, and 2 tablespoons chopped fresh basil into quinoa before serving.

Easy Baked Quinoa with Curry, Cauliflower, and Cilantro

Substitute 2 teaspoons curry powder for lemon zest, and fresh cilantro for parsley. Sprinkle 2 cups small cauliflower florets evenly into dish before baking.

Egg Noodles with Browned Butter and Caraway

SERVES 6 **FAST**

WHY THIS RECIPE WORKS Egg noodles are a no-brainer side dish for hearty meat stews or roasts, but they're generally pretty boring. We wanted to jazz up these noodles a bit to make a side dish worthy of joining any main course on the plate. We lightly chopped caraway seeds and toasted them with butter in a skillet to deepen their flavor. This also browned the butter, which contributed a nice nutty flavor to the dish when we stirred them in with the noodles. Adding some cold butter at the end kept the noodles creamy. Give the caraway seeds a gentle chop with a chef's knife; it brings out their flavor and helps disperse them throughout the dish. The test kitchen's favorite egg noodles are Pennsylvania Dutch Wide Egg Noodles (also sold as Mueller's). Do not use dried dill or chives in this recipe; their dusty flavor spoils the noodles.

Egg Noodles with Browned Butter and Caraway

1 (12-ounce) bag egg noodles
 Table salt for cooking egg noodles
4 tablespoons unsalted butter, cut into 4 pieces, divided
1 teaspoon caraway seeds, chopped
2 tablespoons finely chopped fresh dill or chives

1. Bring 4 quarts water to boil in Dutch oven. Add noodles and 1 tablespoon salt to boiling water and cook until al dente. Drain noodles and return to pot.

2. Meanwhile, melt 3 tablespoons butter in small saucepan over medium-low heat. Add caraway seeds and cook, swirling pan occasionally, until butter is nutty brown and fragrant, about 5 minutes. Add browned butter mixture, herbs, and remaining butter to pot with noodles and toss to combine. Season with salt to taste. Serve.

PER SERVING Cal 150; **Total Fat** 9g, **Sat Fat** 5g; Chol 35mg; **Sodium** 135mg; **Total Carb** 14g, **Dietary Fiber** 0g, **Total Sugars** 0g; **Protein** 3g

Simple Couscous
SERVES 6 `FAST` `VEGAN`

WHY THIS RECIPE WORKS Couscous is one of the fastest and easiest side dishes to prepare. It is traditionally served under stews and braises to soak up the flavorful sauce. Because it often plays sidekick, the grain is too often left bland and unexciting. We knew it had the potential to be a quick and tasty side dish, and we were determined to develop a classic version as well as a handful of flavor-packed variations that would make convenient stand-alone sides. We found that toasting the couscous grains in olive oil before adding liquid deepened their flavor and helped them cook up light and separate. And to bump up the flavor even further, we replaced half of the cooking water with broth. After just 7 minutes of steeping, the couscous was fluffy, tender, and flavorful enough to stand on its own while also ready to accompany any sauce with which it was paired. For our dressed-up variations, dried fruit, nuts, and citrus juice added textural interest and sweet, bright notes.

>   2 tablespoons extra-virgin olive oil
>   2 cups couscous
>   1 cup water
>   1 cup chicken or vegetable broth
>   1 teaspoon table salt

Heat oil in medium saucepan over medium-high heat until shimmering. Add couscous and cook, stirring frequently, until grains are just beginning to brown, 3 to 5 minutes. Stir in water, broth, and salt. Cover, remove saucepan from heat, and let sit until couscous is tender, about 7 minutes. Gently fluff couscous with fork and season with pepper to taste. Serve.

PER SERVING Cal 260; **Total Fat** 5g, **Sat Fat** 0.5g; **Chol** 0mg; **Sodium** 390mg; **Total Carb** 45g, **Dietary Fiber** 3g, **Total Sugars** 0g; **Protein** 7g

VARIATIONS
Simple Couscous with Carrots, Raisins, and Pine Nuts
Increase oil to 3 tablespoons. Before adding couscous to saucepan, add 2 peeled and grated carrots and ½ teaspoon ground cinnamon and cook until softened, about 2 minutes. Add ½ cup raisins to saucepan with couscous and increase water to 1¼ cups. Before serving, stir in ⅓ cup toasted pine nuts, 3 tablespoons minced fresh cilantro, ½ teaspoon grated orange zest, and 1 tablespoon orange juice.

Simple Couscous with Dates and Pistachios

Simple Couscous with Dates and Pistachios
Increase oil to 3 tablespoons. Add ½ cup chopped pitted dates, 1 tablespoon grated fresh ginger, and ½ teaspoon ground cardamom to saucepan with couscous. Increase water to 1¼ cups. Before serving, stir in ¾ cup coarsely chopped toasted pistachios, 3 tablespoons minced fresh cilantro, and 2 teaspoons lemon juice.

Simple Pearl Couscous
SERVES 6 `FAST` `VEGAN`

WHY THIS RECIPE WORKS Pearl couscous, also known as Jerusalem couscous or Israeli couscous, has larger grains than regular couscous and boasts a chewy texture and toasty flavor. We wanted a foolproof method for cooking pearl couscous to serve as a simple side dish or as the base for flavorful salads. To give the couscous as much flavor as possible, we toasted the spheres in oil to bring out their nuttiness. Once they turned golden brown, we added a measured amount of water that the pearls soaked up during cooking. This absorption method helped produce more evenly cooked results than simply boiling the couscous like regular pasta. Plus, once covered, the pot required little attention. When the water was completely absorbed, the warm couscous could be simply tossed with extra-virgin olive oil and salt and pepper before serving or cooled and dressed up with a bold vinaigrette plus plenty of fresh add-ins. Do not substitute regular couscous in this dish, as it requires a different cooking method and will not work in this recipe. If you're making a salad, transfer the couscous to a rimmed baking sheet and let it cool completely, about 15 minutes.

> 2 cups pearl couscous
> 1 tablespoon extra-virgin olive oil
> 2½ cups water
> ½ teaspoon table salt

Heat couscous and oil in medium saucepan over medium heat, stirring frequently, until about half of grains are golden brown, about 5 minutes. Stir in water and salt, increase heat to high, and bring to boil. Reduce heat to medium-low, cover, and simmer, stirring occasionally, until water is absorbed and couscous is tender, 9 to 12 minutes. Off heat, let couscous sit, covered, for 3 minutes. Serve.

PER SERVING Cal 250; **Total Fat** 2.5g; **Sat Fat** 0g; **Chol** 0mg; **Sodium** 200mg; **Total Carb** 48g, **Dietary Fiber** 0g, **Total Sugars** 1g; **Protein** 8g

VARIATIONS
Simple Pearl Couscous with Radishes and Watercress
SERVES 6
Do not substitute regular couscous in this dish, as it requires a different cooking method and will not work in this recipe.

> ¼ cup extra-virgin olive oil, divided
> 2 cups pearl couscous
> 2½ cups water
> ½ teaspoon plus ⅛ teaspoon table salt, divided
> 3 tablespoons sherry vinegar
> 1 teaspoon Dijon mustard
> 1 teaspoon smoked paprika
> ¼ teaspoon sugar
> 2 ounces (2 cups) watercress, torn into bite-size pieces
> 6 scallions, sliced thin
> 6 radishes, trimmed and cut into matchsticks
> 1½ cups coarsely chopped parsley
> ½ cup walnuts, toasted and chopped, divided
> 4 ounces goat cheese, crumbled (1 cup)

Simple Pearl Couscous with Radishes and Watercress

1. Heat 1 tablespoon oil and couscous in medium saucepan over medium heat, stirring frequently, until about half of grains are golden brown, about 5 minutes. Stir in water and ½ teaspoon salt, increase heat to high, and bring to boil. Reduce heat to medium-low, cover, and simmer, stirring occasionally, until water is absorbed and couscous is tender, 9 to 12 minutes. Off heat, let couscous sit, covered, for 3 minutes. Transfer couscous to rimmed baking sheet and let cool completely, about 15 minutes.

2. Whisk vinegar, mustard, paprika, sugar, remaining 3 tablespoons oil, and remaining ⅛ teaspoon salt together in large bowl. Add couscous, watercress, scallions, radishes, parsley, and 6 tablespoons walnuts and gently toss to combine. Season with salt and pepper to taste and transfer to serving bowl. Let sit for 5 minutes. Sprinkle with goat cheese and remaining 2 tablespoons walnuts and serve.

Simple Pearl Couscous with Tomatoes, Olives, and Ricotta Salata
SERVES 6
Do not substitute regular couscous in this dish, as it requires a different cooking method and will not work in this recipe. Crumbled feta cheese can be substituted for the ricotta salata.

¼ cup extra-virgin olive oil, divided
2 cups pearl couscous
2½ cups water
½ teaspoon plus ⅛ teaspoon table salt, divided
3 tablespoons red wine vinegar
1 teaspoon Dijon mustard
12 ounces grape tomatoes, quartered
2 ounces (2 cups) baby spinach, sliced ¼ inch thick
1½ cups coarsely chopped fresh basil
3 ounces ricotta salata cheese, crumbled (¾ cup), divided
⅔ cup pitted kalamata olives, sliced
½ cup pine nuts, toasted, divided
¼ cup minced fresh chives

1. Heat 1 tablespoon oil and couscous in medium saucepan over medium heat, stirring frequently, until about half of grains are golden brown, about 5 minutes. Stir in water and ½ teaspoon salt, increase heat to high, and bring to boil. Reduce heat to medium-low, cover, and simmer, stirring occasionally, until water is absorbed and couscous is tender, 9 to 12 minutes. Off heat, let couscous sit, covered, for 3 minutes. Transfer couscous to rimmed baking sheet and let cool completely, about 15 minutes.

2. Whisk vinegar, mustard, remaining 3 tablespoons oil, and remaining ⅛ teaspoon salt together in large bowl. Add couscous, tomatoes, spinach, basil, ½ cup ricotta salata, olives, 6 tablespoons pine nuts, and chives and gently toss to combine. Season with salt and pepper to taste and transfer to serving bowl. Let sit for 5 minutes. Sprinkle with remaining ¼ cup ricotta salata and remaining 2 tablespoons pine nuts and serve.

Creamy Orzo with Peas and Parmesan

SERVES 4 FAST

WHY THIS RECIPE WORKS Orzo is most commonly known as a small pasta meant for soup, yet it makes a creamy risotto-style side dish on its own. This makes sense if you consider that orzo is similar in size, shape, and starchiness to Arborio rice, yet it has the benefit of cooking through much more quickly. Frozen peas added texture and color to our easy orzo side dish, and Parmesan, stirred in at the end of cooking, added satisfying richness and creaminess. If the finished orzo is too thick, stir in hot water, a few tablespoons at a time, to adjust the consistency.

2 tablespoons unsalted butter
1 onion, chopped fine
¼ teaspoon table salt

Creamy Orzo with Peas and Parmesan

2 garlic cloves, minced
1 cup orzo
¼ cup dry white wine
3¾ cups chicken broth
2 ounces Parmesan cheese, grated (1 cup)
½ cup frozen peas, thawed

1. Melt butter in large saucepan over medium-high heat. Add onion and salt and cook until softened, about 5 minutes. Stir in garlic and cook until fragrant, about 30 seconds. Stir in orzo and cook for 1 minute.

2. Stir in wine and cook until evaporated, about 1 minute. Stir in broth, bring to boil, and cook, stirring often, until orzo is tender and creamy, about 15 minutes. Off heat, vigorously stir in Parmesan until creamy. Stir in peas and let sit off heat until peas are heated through and sauce has thickened slightly, about 2 minutes. Season with salt and pepper to taste, and serve.

PER SERVING Cal 160; **Total Fat** 4.5g, **Sat Fat** 2g; **Chol** 10mg; **Sodium** 810mg; **Total Carb** 14g, **Dietary Fiber** 1g, **Total Sugars** 2g; **Protein** 13g

Creamy Orzo with Fennel

Omit peas. Add 1 fennel bulb, cored, trimmed, and chopped, to pot with onion in step 1; cook until lightly browned, about 10 minutes. Add ¼ teaspoon fennel seeds and pinch red pepper flakes to pot with garlic.

Creamy Orzo with Bacon and Scallions

Omit butter, peas, and Parmesan. Cook 3 slices chopped bacon in pot over medium-high heat until crisp, about 5 minutes; transfer to paper towel–lined plate. Add onion to rendered bacon fat and cook as directed. Stir in 2 thinly sliced scallions and sprinkle with crisp bacon before serving.

Southwestern Black Bean Salad

SERVES 6 TO 8   **FAST**

WHY THIS RECIPE WORKS For a black bean salad with bold but balanced flavors, we wanted to avoid falling into the trap of piling on an endless array of ingredients. We found that a judicious mixture of black beans, corn, avocado, tomato, and cilantro gave us just the right combination of flavors and textures. Sautéing the corn (both fresh and frozen worked well) in a skillet until it was toasty and just starting to brown added a pleasant nuttiness to the kernels. We wanted a dressing with plenty of kick, so we used lots of lime juice plus spicy chipotle chile. A teaspoon of honey balanced the bright citrus. Raw onion was too harsh in the dressing, but thinly sliced scallions lent a mild onion flavor. You will need 3 to 4 ears of corn in order to yield 2 cups of fresh kernels. If using frozen corn, be sure to thaw and drain it before cooking.

- ¼ cup extra-virgin olive oil, divided
- 2 cups fresh or frozen corn
- 4 scallions, sliced thin
- ⅓ cup lime juice (3 limes)
- 1 tablespoon minced canned chipotle chile in adobo sauce
- 1 teaspoon honey
- ½ teaspoon table salt
- ½ teaspoon pepper
- 2 (15-ounce) cans black beans, rinsed
- 2 avocados, halved, pitted, and chopped
- 2 tomatoes, cored and chopped
- ¼ cup minced fresh cilantro

1. Heat 2 tablespoons oil in 12-inch skillet over medium-high heat until shimmering. Add corn and cook until spotty brown, about 5 minutes; let cool slightly.

Southwestern Black Bean Salad

2. Whisk scallions, lime juice, chipotle chile in adobo, honey, salt, and pepper together in large bowl. Slowly whisk in remaining 2 tablespoons oil until incorporated. Add toasted corn, beans, avocados, tomatoes, and cilantro and toss to combine. Season with salt and pepper to taste. Serve.

PER SERVING Cal 130; **Total Fat** 8g, **Sat Fat** 1g; **Chol** 0mg; **Sodium** 190mg; **Total Carb** 13g, **Dietary Fiber** 4g, **Total Sugars** 2g; **Protein** 3g

Black Beans with Chipotle

SERVES 4   **FAST**

WHY THIS RECIPE WORKS There's nothing more convenient than canned beans, which can be quickly transformed into a delicious side. For black beans with a smoky flavor profile, we turned to canned chipotle in adobo sauce—another great shortcut ingredient—and cooked it with garlic and oil. Then we added a can of black beans along with chicken broth and let the mixture simmer until slightly thickened and cohesive. Finally, we stirred in some cilantro and lime juice to round out the flavors with a bright kick.

2 tablespoons vegetable oil
1 garlic clove, minced
½ teaspoon minced canned chipotle chile in adobo sauce
1 (15-ounce) can black beans, rinsed
½ cup chicken broth
2 tablespoons minced fresh cilantro
2 teaspoons lime juice

Heat oil in 12-inch nonstick skillet over medium-high heat until shimmering. Add garlic and chipotle chile in adobo and cook until fragrant, about 30 seconds. Stir in black beans and broth, bring to simmer, and cook until heated through and sauce is slightly thickened, about 4 minutes. Stir in cilantro and lime juice and season with salt and pepper to taste. Serve.

PER SERVING Cal 120; **Total Fat** 7g, **Sat Fat** 0.5g; **Chol** 0mg; **Sodium** 310mg; **Total Carb** 12g, **Dietary Fiber** 4g, **Total Sugars** 1g; **Protein** 4g

Easy Boston Beans

Easy Boston Beans
SERVES 4 `FAST`

WHY THIS RECIPE WORKS Iconic Boston baked beans usually take hours to make but we wanted a way to enjoy them when time is tight. We doctored up canned pinto beans to replicate the long-simmered flavor of the original. Cooking onion in rendered bacon fat added rich, meaty flavor. Molasses, mustard, and vinegar contributed savory depth while the beans briefly simmered in a quick sauce. We like the flavor of spicy brown mustard here; however, Dijon or whole-grain mustard can be substituted.

2 slices bacon, chopped
1 onion, chopped fine
2 (15-ounce) cans pinto beans, rinsed
1½ cups chicken broth
½ cup molasses
1½ tablespoons spicy brown mustard
1½ teaspoons cider vinegar

1. Cook bacon in large saucepan over medium heat until fat is rendered, about 5 minutes. Stir in onion and cook until softened, about 5 minutes.

2. Stir in beans, broth, molasses, mustard, and vinegar. Simmer, stirring often, until beans are softened and sauce is thickened slightly, 15 to 20 minutes. Season with salt and pepper to taste and serve.

PER SERVING Cal 310; **Total Fat** 6g, **Sat Fat** 2g; **Chol** 10mg; **Sodium** 940mg; **Total Carb** 55g, **Dietary Fiber** 8g, **Total Sugars** 34g; **Protein** 11g

Easy White Bean Gratin
SERVES 4 `FAST`

WHY THIS RECIPE WORKS In the traditional versions of Tuscan-inspired white bean gratin, dried beans are gently cooked for hours over low heat allowing the beans to break down and bind together. To make a more practical version of this rustic side dish, we re-created it using time-saving canned beans. It took several attempts before we found a good path: Mashing some of the beans before adding them to the pan gave the finished dish a creamy, saucy texture in just 10 minutes. Simmering the beans in chicken broth allowed them to absorb rich, savory flavor. We limited supporting ingredients to the classics: onion, garlic, rosemary, and Parmesan, and finished the dish under the broiler until the cheese became golden. Make sure to rinse the beans thoroughly before cooking to get rid of excess salt. You will need a 10-inch ovensafe skillet for this recipe.

2 (15-ounce) cans white beans or cannellini beans, rinsed, divided
2 tablespoons extra-virgin olive oil
1 onion, chopped fine

3 garlic cloves, minced

1 teaspoon minced fresh rosemary or ¼ teaspoon dried

2 cups chicken broth

2 ounces Parmesan cheese, grated (1 cup)

1. Adjust oven rack 6 inches from broiler element and heat broiler. Place ⅔ cup beans in bowl and mash smooth with potato masher.

2. Heat oil in 10-inch ovensafe skillet over medium-high heat until shimmering. Add onion and cook until softened and lightly browned, 7 to 10 minutes. Stir in garlic and rosemary and cook until fragrant, about 30 seconds.

3. Stir in broth and simmer until slightly thickened, 3 to 5 minutes. Stir in mashed beans and remaining whole beans and bring to brief simmer. Off heat, sprinkle with Parmesan. Transfer skillet to broiler and broil until cheese is golden and edges are bubbling, 3 to 5 minutes. Let cool slightly before serving.

PER SERVING Cal 260; **Total Fat** 11g, **Sat Fat** 3g; **Chol** 10mg; **Sodium** 850mg; **Total Carb** 26g, **Dietary Fiber** 7g, **Total Sugars** 4g; **Protein** 14g

Skillet Chickpeas

Skillet Chickpeas

SERVES 4 **FAST** **VEGAN**

WHY THIS RECIPE WORKS With their nutty flavor and creamy texture, canned chickpeas make a terrific side dish when simply sautéed with a few flavorful ingredients. To easily transform our chickpeas, we reached for garlic and red pepper flakes. We cut garlic into thin slices and sautéed them in extra-virgin olive oil to maintain their presence and mellow their flavor. We softened an onion with this base, then added the chickpeas with vegetable broth, which imparted a savory backbone to the dish without overpowering it. As final touches, parsley and lemon juice gave our chickpeas a burst of freshness.

3 tablespoons extra-virgin olive oil

4 garlic cloves, sliced thin

⅛ teaspoon red pepper flakes

1 onion, chopped fine

2 (15-ounce) cans chickpeas, rinsed

1 cup chicken or vegetable broth

2 tablespoons minced fresh parsley

2 teaspoons lemon juice

1. Cook oil, garlic, and pepper flakes in 12-inch nonstick skillet over medium heat, stirring often, until garlic is lightly golden, about 2 minutes. Stir in onion and cook until softened and lightly browned, 5 to 7 minutes.

2. Stir in chickpeas and broth, cover, and simmer until chickpeas are heated through, about 7 minutes. Uncover, increase heat to high, and simmer until liquid has reduced to light glaze, about 3 minutes. Off heat, stir in parsley and lemon juice. Season with salt and pepper to taste, and serve.

PER SERVING Cal 180; **Fat** 12g, **Sat Fat** 1.5g; **Chol** 0mg; **Sodium** 330mg; **Total Carb** 14g, **Dietary Fiber** 4g, **Total Sugars** 2g; **Protein** 5g

THINLY SLICING GARLIC

Pick flattest side of peeled clove and hold it face down against cutting board. Then carefully slice garlic thin, holding clove securely. If middle of clove contains green stem, use tip of paring knife to pull it out.

ROAST YOUR VEGETABLES

■ FAST (30 minutes or less total time)   ■ MAKE-AHEAD   ■ VEGAN

Photos (clockwise from top left): Roasted Brussels Sprouts with Walnuts and Lemon; Roasted Winter Squash Halves; Roasted Artichokes with Lemon Vinaigrette; Roasted Butternut Squash with Goat Cheese, Pecans, and Maple

Roasted Artichokes with Lemon Vinaigrette
SERVES 4 VEGAN

WHY THIS RECIPE WORKS Artichokes are a perfect candidate for roasting, as it concentrates their delicate, nutty flavor. We prepped the artichokes for the oven by trimming the leaves, halving the artichokes, and removing the fuzzy chokes. Submerging the prepped artichokes in water and lemon juice kept them from oxidizing, and tossing them with oil and roasting cut side down encouraged browning. Because they have so much surface area, artichokes can dry out and toughen in the oven, so we covered them to let them steam and tenderize in their own juice. The fresh tang of citrus pairs well with artichokes' earthy flavor, so we roasted some halved lemons alongside the artichokes and used the deeply flavorful juice in a vinaigrette. We whisked the juice with garlic and Dijon mustard before drizzling in and emulsifying some olive oil to create a bright, intense dressing. If your artichokes are larger than 8 to 10 ounces, strip away another layer or two of the toughest outer leaves. Serve these either warm or at room temperature.

  3 lemons, divided
  4 artichokes (8 to 10 ounces each)
  ½ cup plus 1 tablespoon extra-virgin olive oil, divided
  ¾ teaspoon table salt, divided
  Pinch pepper
  2 teaspoons chopped fresh parsley
  1 small garlic clove, minced to paste
  ½ teaspoon Dijon mustard

1. Adjust oven rack to lower-middle position and heat oven to 475 degrees. Cut 1 lemon in half, squeeze halves into container filled with 2 quarts water, then add spent halves. Working with 1 artichoke at a time, trim stem to about ¾ inch and cut off top quarter of artichoke. Break off bottom 3 or 4 rows of tough outer leaves by pulling them downward. Using kitchen shears, trim off top portion of outer leaves. Using paring knife, trim outer layer of stem and base, removing any dark green parts. Cut artichoke in half lengthwise, then remove fuzzy choke and any tiny inner purple-tinged leaves using small spoon. Submerge prepped artichokes in lemon water.

2. Coat bottom of 13 by 9-inch baking dish with 1 tablespoon oil. Remove artichokes from lemon water, shaking off excess water. Toss artichokes with 2 tablespoons oil, ¼ teaspoon salt, and pepper; gently rub oil and seasonings between leaves. Arrange artichokes cut side down in prepared dish. Trim ends of remaining 2 lemons, halve crosswise, and arrange cut side up next to artichokes in dish. Cover tightly with aluminum foil and roast until cut sides of artichokes begin to brown and bases and leaves are tender when poked with tip of paring knife, 25 to 30 minutes.

3. Transfer artichokes to serving platter. Let lemons cool slightly, then squeeze into fine-mesh strainer set over bowl, extracting as much juice and pulp as possible; press firmly on solids to yield 1½ tablespoons juice. Whisk parsley, garlic, mustard, and remaining ½ teaspoon salt into juice. Whisking constantly, slowly drizzle in remaining 6 tablespoons oil until emulsified. Season with salt and pepper to taste. Serve artichokes with dressing.

PER SERVING Cal 330; **Total Fat** 32g, **Sat Fat** 4.5g; **Chol** 0mg; **Sodium** 830mg; **Total Carb** 10g, **Dietary Fiber** 5g, **Total Sugars** 1g; **Protein** 3g

PREPARING ARTICHOKES FOR ROASTING

1. Using sharp chef's knife, trim stem to about ¾ inch long and cut off top quarter of artichoke.

2. Break off bottom 3 or 4 rows of tough outer leaves by pulling them downward.

3. Using paring knife, trim outer layer of stem and base, removing any dark green parts.

4. Halve artichoke lengthwise, then remove fuzzy choke and any inner tiny purple-tinged leaves using small spoon.

Roasted Asparagus

SERVES 4 TO 6 `FAST` `VEGAN`

WHY THIS RECIPE WORKS Oven roasting can bring out the best in seasonal vegetables. But when it comes to delicate asparagus, simply tossing the spears with oil, salt, and pepper and spreading them on a baking sheet doesn't always produce reliably crisp-tender spears. After a few tests, we discovered that thicker asparagus (½ to ¾ inch in diameter) held up better to roasting. To ensure a hard sear on our spears, we preheated the baking sheet and resisted the urge to give it a shake during roasting. The result? Intense, flavorful browning on one side of the asparagus and vibrant green on the other. For complementary seasoning, we took our cue from Italian cuisine and prepared a bright garnish of minced fresh herbs called a gremolata. All of our versions reinforced the stalks' vibrant flavor and gave this simple side a more distinct presence. You can use white or green asparagus in this recipe; if using white, peel just the outermost layer of the bottom halves of the spears. Serve with one of our gremolatas, if desired.

Roasted Asparagus

2 pounds thick asparagus
2 tablespoons plus 2 teaspoons extra-virgin olive oil, divided
½ teaspoon table salt
¼ teaspoon pepper

1. Adjust oven rack to lowest position, place rimmed baking sheet on rack, and heat oven to 500 degrees.

2. Trim bottom inch of asparagus spears and discard. Peel bottom halves of spears until white flesh is exposed. Place asparagus in large baking pan and toss with 2 tablespoons oil, salt, and pepper.

3. Transfer asparagus to preheated sheet and spread into even layer. Roast, without moving asparagus, until undersides of spears are browned, tops are vibrant green, and tip of paring knife inserted at base of largest spear meets little resistance, 8 to 10 minutes. Transfer asparagus to platter, drizzle with remaining 2 teaspoons oil, and serve immediately.

PER SERVING Cal 80; **Total Fat** 6g, **Sat Fat** 1g; **Chol** 0mg; **Sodium** 190mg; **Total Carb** 6g, **Dietary Fiber** 3g, **Total Sugars** 3g; **Protein** 4g

---

TAKE IT UP A NOTCH

A gremolata is a bright garnish of minced fresh herbs, garlic, and citrus zest that can be used to dress up all kinds of vegetables and other dishes.

Lemon-Mint Gremolata
MAKES ¼ CUP

2 tablespoons minced fresh mint
2 tablespoons minced fresh parsley
1 garlic clove, minced
½ teaspoon grated lemon zest

Combine all ingredients in bowl.

Tarragon-Lemon Gremolata
Substitute tarragon for mint.

Cilantro-Lime Gremolata
Omit mint and cayenne. Substitute ¼ cup minced fresh cilantro for parsley and lime zest for orange zest.

Roasted Beets

Roasted Beets

SERVES 4 `VEGAN`

WHY THIS RECIPE WORKS Roasted fresh beets are intensely sweet and firm with deep, rich flavor. So what, exactly, is the best way to roast a beet? We tried several different methods. The first approach simply blasted untrimmed beets in a hot oven. This took hours and shrank the beets to a fraction of their size, and the skins dried to desiccated husks. Another method involved roasting the beets in a covered baking dish partially filled with water. They tasted so bland that they might as well have been boiled. A third approach roasted the beets in a covered dish with no water. This made an incredible mess, as the exuded beet juices stuck fast to the bottom of the dish. For our last and winning method, we wrapped each unpeeled beet tightly in foil and roasted them on a baking sheet. The beets cooked to perfect softness in their own moisture. The results tasted every bit as sweet as those roasted uncovered, but they cooked in half the time and peeled easily.

1 pound beets, trimmed
2 tablespoons extra-virgin olive oil

1. Adjust oven rack to middle position and heat oven to 400 degrees. Wrap beets individually in aluminum foil and place on rimmed baking sheet. Roast until beets can be easily pierced with paring knife, 45 minutes to 1 hour, removing beets individually from oven as they finish cooking.

2. Open foil packets to allow steam to escape and let cool slightly. Once beets are cool enough to handle, rub off skins with paper towels. Slice beets ¼ inch thick and place in medium bowl.

3. Add oil, season with salt and pepper to taste, and toss to combine. Serve warm or at room temperature.

PER SERVING Cal 100; **Total Fat** 7g, **Sat Fat** 1g; **Chol** 0mg; **Sodium** 60mg; **Total Carb** 7g, **Dietary Fiber** 2g, **Total Sugars** 5g; **Protein** 1g

VARIATIONS
Roasted Beets with Dill-Walnut Vinaigrette
Increase oil to 6 tablespoons. While beets cool in step 2, whisk oil, 1 minced shallot, 1½ tablespoons minced fresh dill, 1 tablespoon red wine vinegar, and 2 teaspoons lemon juice together in medium bowl. Add cooled, sliced beets and ½ cup toasted, chopped walnuts to bowl with vinaigrette and gently toss to combine.

Roasted Beets with Ginger Butter and Chives
Omit oil. While beets cool in step 2, melt 4 tablespoons unsalted butter in 8-inch skillet over medium heat. Add 1 (1-inch) piece fresh ginger, peeled and cut into matchsticks, to skillet and cook until fragrant and crispy, 3 to 4 minutes. Off heat, add 1 tablespoon minced fresh chives and stir to combine. Add butter mixture to bowl with beets in step 3.

Roasted Broccoli

SERVES 6 `FAST` `VEGAN`

WHY THIS RECIPE WORKS Broccoli can be tricky to roast given its awkward shape; dense, woody stalks; and shrubby florets. We wanted a roasted broccoli recipe that would give us evenly cooked broccoli—both stalks and florets—and add concentrated flavor and dappled browning. The way we prepared the broccoli was the key. We sliced the crown in half and then cut each half into uniform wedges. We cut the stalks into rectangular pieces slightly smaller than the more delicate wedges. This promoted even cooking and great browning by maximizing contact with the hot baking sheet. Preheating the baking sheet on the lowest rack of the oven gave us even better browning. Tossing a scant ½ teaspoon of sugar over the broccoli along with salt, pepper, and a splash of olive oil gave us crisp-tipped florets and blistered and browned stalks that were sweet and full-flavored.

1¾ pounds broccoli

3 tablespoons extra-virgin olive oil

½ teaspoon sugar

½ teaspoon table salt

   Pinch pepper

   Lemon wedges

1. Adjust oven rack to lowest position, place rimmed baking sheet on rack, and heat oven to 500 degrees. Cut broccoli horizontally at juncture of crowns and stalks. Cut crowns into 4 wedges if 3 to 4 inches in diameter or 6 wedges if 4 to 5 inches in diameter. Trim tough outer peel from stalks, then cut into ½-inch-thick planks 2 to 3 inches long.

2. Toss broccoli with oil, sugar, salt, and pepper in bowl. Working quickly, lay broccoli in single layer, flat sides down, on hot sheet. Roast until stalks are well browned and tender and florets are lightly browned, 9 to 11 minutes. Serve with lemon wedges.

PER SERVING Cal 90; Total Fat 7g, Sat Fat 1g; Chol 0mg; Sodium 220mg; Total Carb 6g, Dietary Fiber 2g, Total Sugars 2g; Protein 2g

VARIATIONS

Roasted Broccoli with Garlic

Stir 1 tablespoon minced garlic into oil before tossing it with raw broccoli.

Roasted Broccoli with Shallots and Fennel Seeds

While broccoli roasts, heat 1 tablespoon extra-virgin olive oil in 8-inch skillet over medium heat until shimmering. Add 3 thinly sliced shallots and cook until softened and lightly browned, 5 to 6 minutes. Stir in 1 teaspoon cracked fennel seeds and cook until shallots are golden brown, 1 to 2 minutes; remove from heat. Toss roasted broccoli with shallot mixture before serving.

CUTTING A BROCCOLI CROWN INTO WEDGES

1. Cut broccoli horizontally at juncture of crown and stalk, then cut crown in half through central stalk.

2. Cut crowns that measure 3 to 4 inches in diameter into 4 wedges, and crowns that measure 4 to 5 inches in diameter into 6 wedges.

Roasted Brussels Sprouts

SERVES 6 TO 8 VEGAN

WHY THIS RECIPE WORKS Oven roasting is a simple and quick way to produce Brussels sprouts that are well caramelized on the outside and tender on the inside. To ensure that we achieved this balance, we started out roasting the tiny cabbages, covered in foil, with a little bit of water. This created a steamy environment, which cooked the sprouts through. We then removed the foil and allowed the exterior to dry out and caramelize. If you can find only large sprouts (greater than 1½ inches in diameter), quarter them instead of halving them.

2¼ pounds Brussels sprouts, trimmed and halved

3 tablespoons extra-virgin olive oil

1 tablespoon water

¾ teaspoon table salt

¼ teaspoon pepper

1. Adjust oven rack to upper-middle position and heat oven to 500 degrees. Toss Brussels sprouts with oil, water, salt, and pepper in bowl. Arrange Brussels sprouts in single layer cut sides down on rimmed baking sheet.

2. Cover sheet tightly with aluminum foil and roast for 10 minutes. Remove foil and continue to roast until Brussels sprouts are well browned and tender, 10 to 12 minutes. Season with salt and pepper to taste. Serve.

PER SERVING Cal 100; Total Fat 6g, Sat Fat 1g; Chol 0mg; Sodium 250mg; Total Carb 10g, Dietary Fiber 4g, Total Sugars 3g; Protein 4g

VARIATIONS

Roasted Brussels Sprouts with Bacon and Pecans

While Brussels sprouts roast, cook 4 slices finely chopped bacon in 10-inch skillet over medium heat until crisp, 7 to 10 minutes. Using slotted spoon, transfer bacon to paper towel–lined plate and reserve 1 tablespoon fat. Toss roasted Brussels sprouts with 2 tablespoons olive oil, reserved bacon fat, chopped bacon, and ½ cup finely chopped toasted pecans. Season with salt and pepper to taste, and serve.

Roasted Brussels Sprouts with Garlic, Red Pepper Flakes, and Parmesan

While Brussels sprouts roast, cook 3 tablespoons extra-virgin olive oil, 2 minced garlic cloves, and ½ teaspoon red pepper flakes in 8-inch skillet over medium heat until garlic is golden and fragrant, about 1 minute. Remove from heat. Toss roasted Brussels sprouts with garlic oil and sprinkle with ¼ cup grated Parmesan cheese before serving.

Roasted Brussels Sprouts with Walnuts and Lemon

Toss roasted Brussels sprouts with ⅓ cup walnuts, toasted and chopped fine; 3 tablespoons melted unsalted butter; and 1 tablespoon lemon juice before serving.

Roasted Carrots

SERVES 4 TO 6

WHY THIS RECIPE WORKS Carrots will be the star side at any meal if you use this simple roasting method. We found that the key was to cut the carrots into large batons, which gave us evenly cooked results and optimized their browning. Tossing the carrots with melted butter, salt, and pepper richly seasoned the spears and lining the baking sheet with parchment prevented the butter from burning. Sealing the carrots under aluminum foil kept their moisture in while their interiors turned tender and creamy. We then uncovered the baking sheet to finish roasting the carrots with direct exposure to the oven's heat, stirring them around periodically until their surface moisture evaporated and they took on gorgeous caramelized streaks. Seasoned with salt and pepper, these carrots are simple, sweet perfection, but we also created a few variations with a host of interesting flavors.

1½ pounds carrots, peeled
2 tablespoons unsalted butter, melted
½ teaspoon table salt
¼ teaspoon pepper

1. Adjust oven rack to middle position and heat oven to 425 degrees. Cut carrots in half crosswise, then cut them lengthwise into halves or quarters as needed to create uniformly sized pieces. Toss carrots, melted butter, salt, and pepper together in bowl.

2. Transfer carrots to parchment paper–lined rimmed baking sheet and spread into single layer. Cover baking sheet tightly with aluminum foil and roast for 15 minutes. Remove foil and roast, stirring twice, until carrots are well browned and tender, 30 to 35 minutes. Transfer to serving dish, season with salt and pepper to taste, and serve.

PER SERVING Cal 80; **Total Fat** 4g, **Sat Fat** 2.5g; **Chol** 10mg; **Sodium** 270mg; **Total Carb** 11g, **Dietary Fiber** 3g, **Total Sugars** 5g; **Protein** 1g

Roasted Carrots and Shallots with Lemon and Thyme

VARIATIONS

Roasted Carrots and Fennel with Toasted Almonds and Lemon

Reduce amount of carrots to 1 pound. Add 1 small fennel bulb, cored and sliced ½ inch thick, to bowl with carrots; roast as directed. Toss vegetables with ¼ cup toasted sliced almonds, 2 teaspoons minced fresh parsley, and 1 teaspoon lemon juice before serving.

Roasted Carrots and Parsnips with Rosemary

Reduce amount of carrots to 1 pound. Add 8 ounces parsnips, peeled, halved crosswise, and cut lengthwise into halves or quarters as needed to create uniformly sized pieces, and 1 teaspoon minced fresh rosemary to bowl with carrots; roast as directed. Toss vegetables with 2 teaspoons minced fresh parsley before serving.

Roasted Carrots and Shallots with Lemon and Thyme

Reduce amount of carrots to 1 pound. Add 6 shallots, peeled and halved lengthwise, and 1 teaspoon minced fresh thyme to bowl with carrots; roast as directed. Toss vegetables with 1 teaspoon lemon juice before serving.

Roasted Carrot Noodles

SERVES 4 TO 6

WHY THIS RECIPE WORKS Knowing that roasting carrots draws out their natural sugars and intensifies their flavor, we set out to create an interesting roasted carrot side dish. Since spiralized vegetables have become popular, we used a spiralizer to cut carrots into uniform ⅛-inch noodles; this ensured that the carrots cooked evenly. Cooking the carrots covered for half the roasting time steamed them slightly and prevented them from drying out. We then uncovered the baking sheet and returned it to the oven to allow the noodles' surface moisture to evaporate, encouraging light caramelization and creating perfectly tender noodles. We kept the flavorings simple to allow the carrots' flavor to shine— just a handful of fresh thyme for earthy notes and a spoonful of honey to accent the carrots' natural sweetness. Choose carrots that are at least 1½ inches in diameter for this recipe.

- 2 **pounds carrots, peeled**
- 2 **tablespoons extra-virgin olive oil, divided**
- 2 **teaspoons minced fresh thyme or ½ teaspoon dried**
- 1 **teaspoon honey**
- ½ **teaspoon table salt**
- ½ **teaspoon pepper**

1. Adjust oven rack to middle position and heat oven to 375 degrees. Using spiralizer, cut carrots into ⅛-inch-thick noodles, then cut noodles into 12-inch lengths. Toss carrots with 1 tablespoon oil, thyme, honey, salt, and pepper on rimmed baking sheet. Cover carrots tightly with aluminum foil and roast for 15 minutes. Remove foil and continue to roast until carrots are tender, 10 to 15 minutes.

2. Transfer carrots to serving platter, drizzle with remaining 1 tablespoon oil, and season with salt and pepper to taste. Serve.

PER SERVING Cal 100; **Total Fat** 5g, **Sat Fat** 0.5g; **Chol** 0mg; **Sodium** 290mg; **Total Carb** 14g, **Dietary Fiber** 4g, **Total Sugars** 7g; **Protein** 1g

VARIATIONS

Roasted Carrot Noodles with Garlic, Red Pepper Flakes, and Basil

Substitute 2 thinly sliced garlic cloves and ½ teaspoon red pepper flakes for thyme. Toss roasted carrots with oil and 1 tablespoon chopped fresh basil before serving.

Roasted Carrot Noodles

Roasted Carrot Noodles with Shallot, Dill, and Orange

Substitute 1 thinly sliced shallot for thyme. Toss roasted carrots with oil, 1 tablespoon minced fresh dill, 1 teaspoon grated orange zest, and 1 tablespoon orange juice before serving.

SPIRALIZING CARROTS

1. Trim carrot so it will fit on prongs. Secure vegetable between prongs and blade surface.

2. Spiralize by turning crank. Pull noodles straight and cut into correct lengths as directed by recipe.

Roasted Carrots and Shallots

SERVES 4

WHY THIS RECIPE WORKS For a side dish that shows off carrots' long shape, we sliced whole carrots lengthwise before roasting them. Choosing medium carrots ensured that they would become tender in the time they took to brown. Halved shallots lent a sweet background note and a final sprinkle of fresh thyme added another layer of flavor. Choose carrots that are between 1 and 1¼ inches in diameter. If your carrots are smaller, leave them whole; if they're larger, extend the roasting time slightly.

1½ pounds carrots, peeled and halved lengthwise
  4 shallots, peeled and halved through root end
  2 tablespoons unsalted butter, melted
  ½ teaspoon table salt
  ¼ teaspoon pepper
  1 tablespoon chopped fresh thyme

1. Adjust oven rack to lowest position and heat oven to 450 degrees. Toss carrots, shallots, melted butter, salt, and pepper together in bowl.

2. Spread carrot-shallot mixture in even layer on rimmed baking sheet, cut sides down. Roast until tender and cut sides are well browned, about 25 minutes.

3. Sprinkle with thyme. Using spatula, transfer to platter. Serve.

PER SERVING Cal 140; Total Fat 6g, Sat Fat 3.5g; Chol 15mg; Sodium 400mg; Total Carb 21g, Dietary Fiber 6g, Total Sugars 10g; Protein 2g

VARIATION

Spice-Roasted Carrots and Shallots with Pumpkin Seeds and Yogurt

Add ½ teaspoon ground cumin, ½ teaspoon ground coriander, and ⅛ teaspoon cayenne pepper to carrot-shallot mixture in step 1. Substitute cilantro for thyme. Whisk ¼ cup plain whole-milk yogurt, 1 tablespoon lemon juice, ¼ teaspoon salt, and ⅛ teaspoon pepper together in bowl; drizzle yogurt sauce over vegetables on platter. Sprinkle with 2 tablespoons toasted pumpkin seeds.

Roasted Cauliflower

SERVES 4 TO 6 **VEGAN**

WHY THIS RECIPE WORKS Because of its shape, roasting cauliflower is a challenge. Our solution was twofold: First, instead of slicing florets, which don't always brown evenly, we cut a head of cauliflower into eight wedges, which gave us more surface area for browning. Next, we started the wedges covered in foil so they

Roasted Cauliflower

could steam before finishing them uncovered, so the cauliflower had enough time to caramelize on both sides but not dry out. Sweet and rich in flavor, our roasted cauliflower needs little enhancement.

  1 head cauliflower (2 pounds), cut into 8 equal wedges
  ¼ cup extra-virgin olive oil, divided

1. Adjust oven rack to lowest position and heat oven to 475 degrees. Place cauliflower wedges cut side down on parchment paper–lined rimmed baking sheet. Drizzle with 2 tablespoons oil and season with salt and pepper to taste; rub gently to distribute oil and seasonings.

2. Cover sheet tightly with aluminum foil and roast for 10 minutes. Remove foil and continue to roast until bottoms of cauliflower wedges are golden, about 15 minutes. Remove sheet from oven and, using spatula, carefully flip wedges. Return sheet to oven and continue to roast until cauliflower is golden all over, about 15 minutes. Season with salt and pepper to taste, transfer to platter, drizzle with remaining 2 tablespoons oil, and serve.

PER SERVING Cal 120; Total Fat 10g, Sat Fat 1.5g; Chol 0mg; Sodium 45mg; Total Carb 8g, Dietary Fiber 3g, Total Sugars 3g; Protein 3g

Roasted Cauliflower with Paprika and Chorizo

In step 1, combine 2 tablespoons oil and 1½ teaspoons smoked paprika in small bowl before drizzling over cauliflower. Distribute ½ red onion, cut into ½-inch-thick slices, on baking sheet around cauliflower before roasting. In step 2, after removing aluminum foil, distribute 6 ounces chorizo sausage, halved lengthwise and sliced ½ inch thick, on sheet with cauliflower. Whisk remaining 2 tablespoons oil with 2 teaspoons sherry vinegar in large bowl. Toss roasted cauliflower mixture with oil-vinegar mixture. Season with salt and pepper to taste, transfer to platter, and sprinkle with 2 tablespoons chopped fresh parsley.

Roasted Cauliflower with Bacon and Scallions

In step 1, combine 2 tablespoons oil and 4 minced garlic cloves in small bowl before drizzling over cauliflower. Distribute 6 slices bacon, cut into ½-inch pieces, and ½ onion, cut into ½-inch-thick slices, on baking sheet around cauliflower before roasting. In step 2, whisk remaining 2 tablespoons oil with 2 teaspoons cider vinegar in large bowl. Toss roasted cauliflower mixture with oil-vinegar mixture. Season with salt and pepper to taste, transfer to platter, and sprinkle with 2 thinly sliced scallions.

Roasted Cauliflower with Curry and Lime

In step 1, combine 2 tablespoons oil and 1½ teaspoons curry powder in small bowl before drizzling over cauliflower. Distribute ½ onion, cut into ½-inch-thick slices, on baking sheet around cauliflower before roasting. In step 2, whisk remaining 2 tablespoons oil with 2 teaspoons lime juice in large bowl. Toss roasted cauliflower with oil–lime juice mixture. Season with salt and pepper to taste; transfer to platter; and sprinkle with ¼ cup cashews, toasted and chopped, and 2 tablespoons chopped fresh cilantro.

Spicy Roasted Cauliflower

Stir 2 teaspoons curry powder or chili powder into oil in bowl before seasoning cauliflower in step 1.

CUTTING CAULIFLOWER FOR ROASTING

After trimming away any leaves and cutting stem flush with bottom of head, carefully slice into 8 equal wedges, keeping core and florets intact.

Roasted Celery Root with Yogurt and Sesame Seeds
SERVES 6 TO 8

WHY THIS RECIPE WORKS Celery root is often overlooked as a vegetable side. This knobby tuber has crisp white flesh that tastes like celery crossed with parsley with a hint of anise. Roasting is a great method for unlocking its herbal flavor and creamy texture. By cooking celery root slices on the bottom oven rack at a high temperature, we were able to caramelize the exteriors and concentrate the flavors. Tangy yogurt, with reinforced brightness from both lemon juice and zest, complemented the rich and savory celery root. To finish, we sprinkled an aromatic combination of toasted sesame and coriander seeds and dried thyme over the top before adding cilantro leaves to freshen the dish. To prepare celery root, use a chef's knife to cut ½ inch from both root end and opposite end; rest one cut end on a cutting board and cut down from top to bottom of the root, removing wide strips of skin.

- ¼ cup plain yogurt
- ¼ teaspoon grated lemon zest plus 1 teaspoon juice
- ½ teaspoon plus 2 pinches table salt, divided
- 1 teaspoon sesame seeds, toasted
- 1 teaspoon coriander seeds, toasted and crushed
- ¼ teaspoon dried thyme
- 2½ pounds celery root, trimmed, peeled, halved, and sliced ½ inch thick
- 3 tablespoons extra-virgin olive oil
- ¼ teaspoon pepper
- ¼ cup fresh cilantro leaves

1. Adjust oven rack to lowest position and heat oven to 425 degrees. Whisk yogurt, lemon zest and juice, and pinch salt together in bowl. In separate bowl, combine sesame seeds, coriander seeds, thyme, and pinch salt. Set both aside until ready to serve.

2. Toss celery root with oil, remaining ½ teaspoon salt, and pepper and arrange on rimmed baking sheet in single layer. Roast celery root until bottom sides toward back of oven are well browned, 25 to 30 minutes. Rotate baking sheet and continue to roast until bottom sides toward back of oven are well browned, 6 to 10 minutes.

3. Use metal spatula to flip each piece and continue to roast until celery root is very tender and other sides are browned, 10 to 15 minutes. Transfer celery root to platter, drizzle with yogurt sauce, and sprinkle with seed mixture and cilantro. Serve.

PER SERVING Cal 110; **Total Fat** 6g, **Sat Fat** 1g; **Chol** 0mg; **Sodium** 310mg; **Total Carb** 12g, **Dietary Fiber** 2g, **Total Sugars** 2g; **Protein** 2g

Roasted Celery Root Bites with Chimichurri

SERVES 6 TO 8

WHY THIS RECIPE WORKS This innovative recipe highlights the earthy, creamy qualities of celery root and allows it to be eaten, skin and all, in a rustic, satisfying side dish. We started by scrubbing and halving—but not peeling—the root. We wrapped both halves in tightly sealed foil packets along with butter, water, salt, and pepper. With heat and time, the rough, tough exterior broke down, and after a little over an hour of roasting in a 400-degree oven, the entire root was rendered creamy, tender, and aromatic. We then broke the halves apart by hand into random, jagged chunks, providing greater surface area for crisping up during the final stint on the stovetop. For the chimichurri, we anchored bright red wine vinegar and fresh herbs in a rich and fruity extra-virgin olive oil, and spooned a generous amount over the tops of the roasted pieces.

   1 large celery root (2 pounds), trimmed and halved
1¼ teaspoons table salt, divided
   ¼ teaspoon pepper, divided
   6 tablespoons hot water, divided
   2 tablespoons unsalted butter, divided
   2 teaspoons dried oregano
1⅓ cups fresh parsley leaves
   ⅔ cup fresh cilantro leaves
   6 garlic cloves, minced
   ½ teaspoon red pepper flakes
   ¼ cup red wine vinegar
   ½ cup plus 3 tablespoons extra-virgin olive oil, divided

1. Adjust oven rack to middle position and heat oven to 400 degrees. Stack two 16 by 12-inch sheets of aluminum foil. Season 1 celery root half with ⅛ teaspoon salt and ⅛ teaspoon pepper, place cut side down in center of foil, and drizzle with 1 tablespoon water and 1 tablespoon butter. Crimp foil tightly around celery root to seal; transfer to rimmed baking sheet. Repeat with 2 sheets of foil, remaining celery root half, ⅛ teaspoon salt, ⅛ teaspoon pepper, 1 tablespoon water and remaining 1 tablespoon butter.

2. Roast celery root until tender and skewer inserted into center meets little resistance (you will need to unwrap foil to test), 1 hour to 1 hour 20 minutes, rotating sheet halfway through roasting.

3. Meanwhile, combine remaining ¼ cup hot water, oregano, and remaining 1 teaspoon salt in small bowl; let sit for 5 minutes to soften oregano. Pulse parsley, cilantro, garlic, and pepper flakes in food processor until coarsely chopped, about 10 pulses. Add water mixture and vinegar and pulse until combined. Transfer to bowl and slowly whisk in ½ cup oil until incorporated. Set chimichurri aside until ready to serve.

4. Carefully open foil packets to allow steam to escape and let sit until celery root is cool enough to touch, about 15 minutes. Using your hands, break celery root into rough 1-inch chunks. Heat 1½ tablespoons oil in 12-inch nonstick skillet over high heat until shimmering. Add half of celery root chunks and cook, turning occasionally, until well browned on all sides, 6 to 8 minutes. Transfer celery root to serving platter and tent with foil to keep warm. Repeat with remaining 1½ tablespoons oil and celery root; transfer to platter. Drizzle with chimichurri. Serve.

PER SERVING Cal 250; **Total Fat** 22g, **Sat Fat** 4.5g; **Chol** 10mg; **Sodium** 470mg; **Total Carb** 11g, **Dietary Fiber** 2g, **Total Sugars** 2g; **Protein** 2g

Roasted Fennel with Rye Crumble

SERVES 4 TO 6

WHY THIS RECIPE WORKS Subtly caramelized wedges of perfectly roasted fennel make an elegant presentation. To start, we cut fennel bulbs into 1-inch-thick wedges through the core before tossing them in a mixture of butter, lemon juice, and thyme and shingling them evenly into a baking dish. Covering the dish with aluminum foil for the first half-hour of roasting ensured that the edges didn't dry out. With the fennel in the oven, we used the time to make a simple bread-crumb topping in the food processor. After testing different flavor combinations, we decided upon hearty rye bread, earthy caraway seeds, and nutty Parmesan cheese, which combined to beautifully complement the flavor of the roasted fennel. Once the fennel wedges were nearly tender, we uncovered the dish and sprinkled this mixture evenly over the top, baking until the crumble was crisped and deep golden brown and the fennel perfectly tender. Do not core the fennel bulb before cutting it into wedges; the core helps to hold the layers of fennel together during cooking.

   6 tablespoons unsalted butter, melted, divided
   1 tablespoon lemon juice
1¼ teaspoons table salt, divided
   ½ teaspoon minced fresh thyme or ¼ teaspoon dried
   ¼ teaspoon plus ⅛ teaspoon pepper, divided
   2 fennel bulbs, stalks discarded, bulbs halved and cut into 1-inch wedges
   3 ounces rye bread, cut into 1-inch pieces (3 cups)
   1 ounce Parmesan cheese, grated (½ cup)
   1 teaspoon caraway seeds

Roasted Fennel with Rye Crumble

1. Adjust oven rack to middle position and heat oven to 425 degrees. Whisk 3 tablespoons melted butter, lemon juice, 1 teaspoon salt, thyme, and ¼ teaspoon pepper together in large bowl. Add fennel and toss to coat. Arrange fennel cut side down in single layer in 13 by 9-inch baking dish. Cover dish with aluminum foil and bake until fennel is nearly tender, 25 to 30 minutes.

2. Meanwhile, pulse bread, Parmesan, caraway seeds, remaining ¼ teaspoon salt, remaining ⅛ teaspoon pepper, and remaining 3 tablespoons melted butter in food processor to coarse crumbs, about 20 pulses; set aside.

3. Remove foil from dish and sprinkle fennel with bread-crumb mixture. Continue to bake, uncovered, until fennel is tender and topping is browned and crisp, 15 to 20 minutes. Let cool for 5 minutes before serving.

PER SERVING Cal 180; **Total Fat** 13g, **Sat Fat** 8g; **Chol** 35mg; **Sodium** 700mg; **Total Carb** 13g, **Dietary Fiber** 3g, **Total Sugars** 4g; **Protein** 4g

Roasted Green Beans with Almonds and Mint

SERVES 4 TO 6   VEGAN

WHY THIS RECIPE WORKS Roasting green beans has a lot going for it: It's supersimple, it frees up your stovetop, and it gives mature, tough supermarket green beans a flavor comparable to sweet, fresh-picked beans. We knew these quick-cooking beans could only handle a short stay in the oven before they overcooked, so we ensured plenty of flavor-boosting color by tossing them with some sugar along with olive oil, salt, and pepper. Spreading them over a baking sheet and sealing them under aluminum foil allowed them to steam gently to perfect doneness in the oven. We uncovered the green beans for the final 10 minutes so the sugar could caramelize, turning the beans an appealing blistered, speckled brown. To add some lively bite to the flavorful beans, we tossed them with a warm lime vinaigrette and fresh mint, and topped them off with crunchy almonds. To trim green beans quickly, line up a handful so the stem ends are even and then cut off the stems with one swipe of the knife.

1½ pounds green beans, trimmed
6 tablespoons extra-virgin olive oil, divided
¾ teaspoon sugar
¾ teaspoon kosher salt, divided
½ teaspoon pepper, divided
2 garlic cloves, minced
1 teaspoon grated lime zest plus 4 teaspoons juice
1 teaspoon Dijon mustard
¼ cup fresh mint leaves, torn
¼ cup whole blanched almonds, toasted and chopped

1. Adjust oven rack to lowest position and heat oven to 475 degrees. Combine green beans, 2 tablespoons oil, sugar, ½ teaspoon salt, and ¼ teaspoon pepper in bowl. Evenly distribute green beans on rimmed baking sheet.

2. Cover sheet tightly with aluminum foil and roast for 10 minutes. Remove foil and continue to roast until green beans are spotty brown, about 10 minutes, stirring halfway through roasting.

3. Meanwhile, combine garlic, lime zest, and remaining ¼ cup oil in large bowl and microwave until bubbling, about 1 minute; let mixture steep for 1 minute. Whisk lime juice, mustard, remaining ¼ teaspoon salt, and remaining ¼ teaspoon pepper into garlic mixture.

4. Transfer green beans to bowl with dressing, add mint, and toss to combine. Transfer to serving dish and sprinkle with almonds. Serve.

PER SERVING Cal 190; **Total Fat** 16g, **Sat Fat** 2g; **Chol** 0mg; **Sodium** 420mg; **Total Carb** 9g, **Dietary Fiber** 4g, **Total Sugars** 4g; **Protein** 3g

Roasted Green Beans with Pecorino and Pine Nuts

Substitute lemon zest and juice for lime zest and juice, 2 tablespoons chopped fresh basil for mint, and toasted pine nuts for almonds. Sprinkle green beans with ½ cup shredded Pecorino Romano before serving.

Roasted Green Beans with Goat Cheese and Hazelnuts

Substitute orange zest for lime zest, 2 teaspoons orange juice for 2 teaspoons lime juice, 2 tablespoons minced fresh chives for mint, and skinned hazelnuts for almonds. Sprinkle green beans with ½ cup crumbled goat cheese before serving.

Roasted Kohlrabi with Crunchy Seeds
SERVES 4 `FAST` `VEGAN`

WHY THIS RECIPE WORKS Kohlrabi is a member of the turnip family with a flavor reminiscent of broccoli and celery root. A simple, quick roast with a trio of flavorful seeds is an excellent way to bring mild-tasting kohlrabi to the dinner table. A very hot oven browned the kohlrabi beautifully, and the ¾-inch pieces cooked in just 20 minutes. Usually seeds are toasted before being included in a dish, but here the high heat of the oven rendered that extra step unnecessary. Lining the baking sheet with foil prevented the kohlrabi from sticking to the pan. As the kohlrabi roasts, make sure to shake the pan once or twice to encourage even browning.

2 tablespoons extra-virgin olive oil
2 teaspoons sesame seeds
1 teaspoon poppy seeds
½ teaspoon fennel seeds, cracked
½ teaspoon table salt
¼ teaspoon pepper
2 pounds kohlrabi, trimmed, peeled, and
    cut into ¾-inch pieces

1. Adjust oven rack to middle position and heat oven to 450 degrees. Combine oil, sesame seeds, poppy seeds, fennel seeds, salt, and pepper in large bowl. Add kohlrabi and toss to coat.

2. Spread kohlrabi onto aluminum foil–lined rimmed baking sheet and roast, stirring occasionally, until browned and tender, about 20 minutes. Season with salt and pepper to taste. Serve.

PER SERVING Cal 100; **Total Fat** 8g, **Sat Fat** 1g; **Chol** 0mg; **Sodium** 310mg; **Total Carb** 7g, **Dietary Fiber** 4g, **Total Sugars** 3g; **Protein** 2g

Roasted Mushrooms with Parmesan and Pine Nuts
SERVES 4

WHY THIS RECIPE WORKS Rich, meaty mushrooms are an ideal side since they partner with almost any protein, and roasting turns them deeply flavorful. We chose a woodsy blend of cremini and shiitake mushrooms. The unusual step of brining the mushrooms first turned out to be the key to flavorful, moist roasted mushrooms. This quick process seasoned the mushrooms evenly and allowed them to absorb moisture through their gills and cut surfaces, which improved the texture of the drier shiitakes in particular. We roasted the brined mushrooms for just under an hour, until they were darkly browned. For a rich finish, we tossed them in butter, lemon juice, Parmesan, parsley, and toasted pine nuts.

5 teaspoons table salt, for brining
1½ pounds cremini mushrooms, trimmed and left whole
    if small, halved if medium, or quartered if large
1 pound shiitake mushrooms, stemmed, caps larger
    than 3 inches halved
2 tablespoons extra-virgin olive oil
1 ounce Parmesan cheese, grated (½ cup)
2 tablespoons pine nuts, toasted
2 tablespoons chopped fresh parsley
2 tablespoons unsalted butter, melted
1 teaspoon lemon juice

1. Adjust oven rack to lowest position and heat oven to 450 degrees. Whisk 5 teaspoons salt into 2 quarts water in large container until dissolved. Add cremini and shiitake mushrooms, cover with plate or bowl to submerge, and let sit for 10 minutes.

2. Drain mushrooms, then pat dry with paper towels. Transfer mushrooms to rimmed baking sheet and toss with oil to coat. Roast until liquid has completely evaporated, 35 to 45 minutes.

3. Carefully stir mushrooms and continue to roast until mushrooms are deeply browned, 5 to 10 minutes.

4. Transfer mushrooms to large serving bowl and toss with Parmesan, pine nuts, parsley, melted butter, and lemon juice. Season with salt and pepper to taste. Serve immediately.

PER SERVING Cal 230; **Total Fat** 18g, **Sat Fat** 6g; **Chol** 20mg; **Sodium** 220mg; **Total Carb** 10g, **Dietary Fiber** 0g, **Total Sugars** 7g; **Protein** 9g

Roasted Mushrooms with Sesame and Scallions

Substitute 2 teaspoons toasted sesame oil for butter and ½ teaspoon rice vinegar for lemon juice. Omit Parmesan and substitute 2 teaspoons toasted sesame seeds for nuts and 2 thinly sliced scallions for parsley.

Roasted Mushrooms with Harissa and Mint

Omit Parmesan and pine nuts and increase lemon juice to 2 teaspoons. Substitute 2 tablespoons mint for parsley. Add 1 minced garlic clove, 2 teaspoons harissa, ¼ teaspoon ground cumin, and ¼ teaspoon salt to mushroom mixture in step 4.

Roasted Mushrooms with Roasted Garlic and Smoked Paprika

Add 3 unpeeled garlic cloves to sheet with mushrooms in step 2. Remove garlic from sheet in step 3 when stirring mushrooms. When garlic is cool to touch, peel and mash. Omit Parmesan and pine nuts and substitute 2 teaspoons sherry vinegar for lemon juice. Add mashed garlic, ½ teaspoon smoked paprika, and ¼ teaspoon salt to mushroom mixture in step 4.

Roasted King Trumpet Mushrooms
SERVES 4

WHY THIS RECIPE WORKS King trumpet mushrooms (or king oyster mushrooms) are large, stumpy mushrooms that have little aroma or flavor when raw, but cooking transforms them: They become deeply savory, with the meaty texture of squid or tender octopus. We wanted to highlight this quality by preparing these mushrooms almost like a piece of meat. We halved and crosshatched each mushroom, creating attractive "fillets," and then salted them. Roasting the mushrooms cut side down in a hot oven resulted in plump and juicy well-seasoned mushrooms with a nicely browned exterior crust. These mushrooms are delicious on their own, with just a squeeze of lemon, but we also developed two potent sauces. Look for trumpet mushrooms that are 3 to 4 ounces in size.

1¾ pounds king trumpet mushrooms
½ teaspoon table salt
4 tablespoons unsalted butter, melted
Lemon wedges

1. Adjust oven rack to lowest position and heat oven to 500 degrees. Trim bottom ½ inch of mushroom stems, then halve mushrooms lengthwise. Cut ⅟₁₆-inch-deep slits on cut side of mushrooms, spaced ½ inch apart, in crosshatch pattern. Sprinkle cut side of mushrooms with salt and let sit for 15 minutes.

2. Brush mushrooms evenly with melted butter, season with pepper to taste, and arrange cut side down on rimmed baking sheet. Roast until mushrooms are browned on cut side, 20 to 24 minutes. Transfer to serving platter. Serve with lemon wedges.

PER SERVING Cal 140; **Total Fat** 11g, **Sat Fat** 7g; **Chol** 30mg; **Sodium** 300mg; **Total Carb** 7g, **Dietary Fiber** 0g, **Total Sugars** 5g; **Protein** 3g

Roasted King Trumpet Mushrooms

TAKE IT UP A NOTCH

These supersavory sauces perfectly complement roasted mushrooms.

Red Wine–Miso Sauce

Bring 1 cup dry red wine, 1 cup vegetable broth, 2 teaspoons sugar, and ½ teaspoon soy sauce to simmer in 10-inch skillet over medium heat and cook until reduced to ⅓ cup, 20 to 25 minutes. Off heat, whisk in 5 teaspoons miso and 1 tablespoon unsalted butter until smooth. Serve with mushrooms.

Browned Butter–Lemon Vinaigrette

Melt 4 tablespoons unsalted butter in 10-inch skillet over medium heat. Cook, swirling constantly, until butter is dark golden brown and has nutty aroma, 3 to 5 minutes. Off heat, whisk in 2 tablespoons lemon juice, 1 teaspoon Dijon mustard, 1 teaspoon maple syrup, ¼ teaspoon salt, and ⅛ teaspoon pepper. Serve with mushrooms.

Roasted Okra with Fennel and Oregano

Roasted Okra with Fennel and Oregano
SERVES 4 TO 6 VEGAN

WHY THIS RECIPE WORKS High-heat roasting is an easy way to bring out the best in whole okra pods. A very hot (500-degree) oven, with its dry environment, kept the okra from becoming too gelatinous, instead producing okra with pleasant texture inside and a beautifully browned outside. To speed things along, we preheated the baking sheet on the lowest rack. We took our seasoning in a Mediterranean direction, tossing the okra with cracked fennel seeds and dried oregano, along with a fair amount of oil, which gave us a good sear on the okra and helped the spices to toast and bloom. All the okra needed was a squeeze of citrus to add brightness, and we had a simple, delicious dish that had okra skeptics asking for seconds. Do not substitute frozen okra here.

1½ pounds okra, stemmed
3 tablespoons extra-virgin olive oil
2 teaspoons dried oregano
2 teaspoons fennel seeds, cracked
¼ teaspoon table salt
  Lemon wedges

1. Adjust oven rack to lowest position, place rimmed baking sheet on rack, and heat oven to 500 degrees. Toss okra with oil, oregano, fennel seeds, and salt in bowl.

2. Working quickly, carefully transfer okra to hot baking sheet and spread into single layer. Roast until okra is crisp-tender and well browned on most sides, 20 to 25 minutes, stirring occasionally to ensure even browning. Season with salt and pepper to taste. Serve with lemon wedges.

PER SERVING Cal 100; **Total Fat** 7g, **Sat Fat** 1g; **Chol** 0mg; **Sodium** 105mg; **Total Carb** 8g, **Dietary Fiber** 4g, **Total Sugars** 1g; **Protein** 2g

VARIATIONS

Roasted Okra with Sesame and Cumin
Substitute 1 tablespoon sesame seeds for oregano, 2 teaspoons cracked cumin seeds for fennel seeds, and lime wedges for lemon. Toss cooked okra with 1 teaspoon toasted sesame oil after roasting in step 2.

Roasted Okra with Smoked Paprika and Cayenne
Substitute 1 tablespoon smoked paprika for oregano and ⅛ teaspoon cayenne pepper for fennel seeds.

Roasted Caramelized Onions
MAKES 2 CUPS MAKE-AHEAD

WHY THIS RECIPE WORKS Caramelized onions are too good to be relegated to condiment status: They make a luxurious side dish all on their own. Our method turns the onions soft and sweet in the oven where the steady heat cooks them evenly. After slicing 4 pounds of onions and stirring them into melted butter in a Dutch oven, much of our work was done. The onions roasted in the covered pot, cooking down and shedding their moisture. An hour in, we gave the pot a stir, loosening any bits stuck to the sides and bottom. Leaving the lid ajar for the last hour and a half encouraged all excess moisture to evaporate, giving us deeper browning and concentrated flavor. Scraping up and stirring the fond into the golden strands made them richer. Be sure to use yellow onions here.

3 tablespoons unsalted butter
4 pounds onions, halved and sliced ¼ inch thick
1 teaspoon table salt

1. Adjust oven rack to lower-middle position and heat oven to 400 degrees. Coat inside of Dutch oven with vegetable oil spray.

2. Melt butter in prepared pot over medium-low heat. Stir in onions and salt. Cover, place pot in oven, and roast for 1 hour (onions will be moist and slightly reduced in volume).

Roasted Caramelized Onions

3. Working quickly, remove pot from oven and stir onions, scraping bottom and sides of pot. Partially cover, return pot to oven, and continue to roast until onions are deep golden brown, 1½ to 1¾ hours, stirring onions and scraping bottom and sides of pot every 30 minutes.

4. Remove pot from oven, stir to scrape up any browned bits, and season onions with salt and pepper. Serve warm or at room temperature. (Onions can be refrigerated for up to 1 week.)

PER SERVING Cal 130; **Total Fat** 4.5g, **Sat Fat** 2.5g; **Chol** 10mg; **Sodium** 300mg; **Total Carb** 21g, **Dietary Fiber** 4g, **Total Sugars** 10g; **Protein** 2g

VARIATION

Roasted Caramelized Shallots
MAKES ABOUT 1 CUP

Because shallots are somewhat expensive and time-consuming to prepare, we scaled this variation down.

Reduce amount of butter to 2 tablespoons; substitute 16 large shallots, peeled and quartered, for onions; and reduce amount of salt to ½ teaspoon. Reduce covered roasting time in step 2 to 45 minutes, and partially covered roasting time in step 3 to 1 hour.

Roasted Bell Peppers
MAKES 1½ CUPS **FAST** **VEGAN**

WHY THIS RECIPE WORKS The simple process of roasting bell peppers transforms them into soft, succulent sweetness. They are great as a simple side on their own but are also incredibly versatile. They can be used to top pizzas and sandwiches; in pasta sauces, frittatas or omelets; or in salads. For roasted bell peppers that boasted plenty of sweet flavor and were properly softened but not mushy, we turned to the broiler. Cutting the bell peppers into three pieces each so that they would lie flat helped them cook evenly. Broiling the pieces until the skin was well charred ensured maximum flavor in the flesh beneath. Steaming the roasted bell pepper pieces in a pouch fashioned from the aluminum foil on which they were cooked expedited both peeling and cleanup. Cooking times will vary depending on the broiler and the thickness of the bell pepper walls, so watch the bell peppers carefully as they cook. Use any color of peppers here, but since green bell peppers retain some bitterness even when roasted, we think they are best used as a complement to sweeter red, yellow, and orange bell peppers. We like to serve roasted bell peppers as a side dish alongside chicken or steak.

3 large bell peppers

1. Line rimmed baking sheet with aluminum foil and spray with vegetable oil spray. Slice ½ inch from top and bottom of each bell pepper. Gently remove stems from tops. Twist and pull out each core, using knife to loosen at edges if necessary. Cut slit down 1 side of each bell pepper.

2. Turn each bell pepper skin side down and gently press so it opens to create long strip. Slide knife along insides of bell peppers to remove remaining ribs and seeds.

3. Arrange bell pepper strips, tops, and bottoms skin side up on prepared sheet and flatten all pieces with your hand. Adjust oven rack 3 to 4 inches from broiler element and heat broiler. Broil until skin is puffed and most of surface is well charred, 10 to 13 minutes, rotating sheet halfway through broiling.

4. Using tongs, pile bell peppers in center of foil. Gather foil over bell peppers and crimp to form pouch. Let steam for 10 minutes. Open foil packet carefully and spread out bell peppers. When cool enough to handle, peel bell peppers and discard skins. Serve.

PER SERVING Cal 10; **Total Fat** 0g, **Sat Fat** 0g; **Chol** 0mg; **Sodium** 0mg; **Total Carb** 3g, **Dietary Fiber** 1g, **Total Sugars** 1g; **Protein** 1g

Roasted Radishes with Yogurt-Tahini Sauce

SERVES 4 TO 6 `FAST`

WHY THIS RECIPE WORKS While they're great raw or in salads, radishes are a worthy candidate for roasting. Their crisp texture holds up well to high heat, yielding a tender but meaty interior. Roasting also mellows the spiciness of radishes, concentrating their natural sugars for a nutty, slightly sweet flavor. We started by roasting halved radishes cut side down in oil. These radishes were mild and slightly sweet, but also too bland for a finished dish and lacking any golden-brown color—a bit anemic. To facilitate browning and to complement the nuttiness of the radishes, we tossed them in a mixture of melted butter and white miso and then roasted them on the bottom rack of the oven. The butter produced superior browning on the cut side, while the miso added a pleasing savory quality. To make the most of our radishes, we used the mild, peppery green tops in a simple salad, pairing them both with a tangy yogurt-tahini sauce and a sprinkling of pistachios and sesame seeds. This is a simple but elegant side dish, with bold and complementary flavors that bring out the unexpectedly sweeter side of radishes. If you can't find radishes with their greens, you can substitute baby arugula or watercress.

Roasted Radishes with Yogurt-Tahini Sauce

½ cup plain whole-milk yogurt

2 tablespoons tahini

1 teaspoon grated lemon zest plus 4 teaspoons juice, divided

1 garlic clove, minced

½ teaspoon plus ⅛ teaspoon table salt, divided

¼ teaspoon pepper

2 tablespoons chopped toasted pistachios or almonds

1½ teaspoons toasted sesame seeds

⅛ teaspoon ground cumin

3 tablespoons unsalted butter, melted

5½ teaspoons white miso (optional), divided

1½ teaspoons honey

2 pounds radishes with their greens, root ends of radishes trimmed, radishes halved lengthwise, 8 cups greens reserved

1 teaspoon extra-virgin olive oil

1. Adjust oven rack to lowest position and heat oven to 500 degrees. Whisk yogurt, tahini, lemon zest and 1 tablespoon juice, garlic, ¼ teaspoon salt, and ⅛ teaspoon pepper together in bowl; set aside for serving. Combine pistachios, sesame seeds, cumin, and ⅛ teaspoon salt in small bowl; set aside for serving.

2. Line rimmed baking sheet with aluminum foil. Whisk melted butter; 5 teaspoons miso, if using; 1 teaspoon honey; and remaining ¼ teaspoon salt in large bowl until smooth. Add radishes and toss to coat. Arrange radishes cut side down on prepared sheet and roast until tender and well browned on cut side, 10 to 15 minutes.

3. Whisk oil; remaining 1 teaspoon lemon juice; remaining ½ teaspoon miso, if using; remaining ½ teaspoon honey; ¼ teaspoon salt, and remaining ⅛ teaspoon pepper in clean large bowl until smooth. Add radish greens and toss to coat. Season with salt and pepper to taste.

4. Spread portion of yogurt-tahini sauce over bottom of individual serving plates. Top with roasted radishes and radish greens, sprinkle with pistachio mixture, and serve.

PER SERVING Cal 160; **Total Fat** 12g, **Sat Fat** 4.5g; **Chol** 20mg; **Sodium** 420mg; **Total Carb** 12g, **Dietary Fiber** 4g, **Total Sugars** 6g; **Protein** 4g

Slow-Roasted Tomatoes

MAKES ABOUT 1½ CUPS MAKE-AHEAD VEGAN

WHY THIS RECIPE WORKS If you've never roasted tomatoes, you should. It's a largely hands-off technique that yields the ultimate bright, concentrated, savory-sweet tomatoes that are soft but retain their shape. For intensely flavored tomatoes, we started by cutting large tomatoes into thick slices and arranging them on a foil-lined rimmed baking sheet. Drizzling on plenty of extra-virgin olive oil helped the tomatoes roast faster. Adding smashed garlic cloves lent flavor and fragrance to both the tomatoes and the oil. Avoid using tomatoes smaller than 3 inches in diameter; they have a smaller ratio of flavorful jelly to skin than larger tomatoes. To double the recipe, adjust the oven racks to the upper-middle and lower-middle positions, use two baking sheets, increase the roasting time in step 2 to 40 minutes, and rotate and switch the sheets halfway through baking. In step 3, increase the roasting time to 1½ to 2½ hours. These tomatoes are great as a side to roasted fish, meat, or other vegetables.

3 pounds large tomatoes, cored, bottom ⅛ inch trimmed, and sliced ¾ inch thick
2 garlic cloves, peeled and smashed
¼ teaspoon dried oregano
¼ teaspoon kosher salt
¾ cup extra-virgin olive oil

1. Adjust oven rack to middle position and heat oven to 425 degrees. Line rimmed baking sheet with aluminum foil. Arrange tomatoes in even layer on prepared sheet, with larger slices around edge and smaller slices in center. Place garlic cloves on tomatoes. Sprinkle with oregano and salt and season with pepper. Drizzle oil evenly over tomatoes.

2. Roast for 30 minutes, rotating sheet halfway through roasting. Remove sheet from oven. Reduce oven temperature to 300 degrees and prop open door with wooden spoon to cool oven. Using thin spatula, flip tomatoes.

3. Return tomatoes to oven and cook until spotty brown, skins are blistered, and tomatoes have collapsed to ¼ to ½ inch thick, 1 to 2 hours. Remove from oven and let cool completely, about 30 minutes. Discard garlic and serve. (Tomatoes and oil can be refrigerated in airtight container for up to 5 days or frozen for up to 2 months.)

PER SERVING Cal 290; **Total Fat** 28g, **Sat Fat** 4g; **Chol** 0mg; **Sodium** 60mg; **Total Carb** 9g, **Dietary Fiber** 3g, **Total Sugars** 6g; **Protein** 2g

Quicker Roasted Tomatoes

MAKES ABOUT 2 CUPS MAKE-AHEAD VEGAN

WHY THIS RECIPE WORKS For this recipe, we focused on finding a quick oven-drying technique that would transform plum tomatoes into slightly chewy, savory-sweet morsels with deep, concentrated tomato flavor. Roasting the tomatoes in smaller pieces and at a slightly higher oven temperature than is typical of other recipes did the trick. Seasoning them first with salt and herbs as well as sugar not only bumped up their savory profile but also strengthened their sweetness. Adding sliced garlic to the quartered tomatoes before roasting them provided another dimension of flavor. To double this recipe, adjust the oven racks to the upper-middle and lower-middle positions, divide the tomatoes evenly between two parchment paper–lined rimmed baking sheets, and rotate and switch the sheets halfway through baking. Plum tomatoes work best for this recipe. Other tomato varieties will work, but they may be slightly softer after roasting.

2 pounds plum tomatoes, cored
4 garlic cloves, sliced thin
1 tablespoon extra-virgin olive oil
1½ teaspoons sugar
1½ teaspoons kosher salt
½ teaspoon dried oregano
½ teaspoon dried thyme
⅛ teaspoon red pepper flakes

1. Adjust oven rack to middle position and heat oven to 350 degrees. Quarter tomatoes lengthwise. Working with 1 tomato quarter at a time, position tomatoes seed side up on cutting board. Using paring knife, cut interior pulp and seeds from tomatoes and discard. Transfer tomatoes to large bowl. Add garlic, oil, sugar, salt, oregano, thyme, and pepper flakes and toss to thoroughly combine.

2. Line rimmed baking sheet with parchment paper. Arrange tomatoes, skin side down, in even layer on prepared sheet. Place any garlic that has fallen onto sheet on top of tomatoes.

3. Bake until tomatoes are shriveled, dry, and dark around edges, 1 hour to 1 hour 10 minutes. Let cool completely on sheet, about 15 minutes. Serve. (Tomatoes can be refrigerated for up to 5 days. For longer storage, place tomatoes in jar, cover with extra-virgin olive oil, and refrigerate for up to 2 weeks.)

PER SERVING Cal 40; **Total Fat** 2g, **Sat Fat** 0g; **Chol** 0mg; **Sodium** 220mg; **Total Carb** 6g, **Dietary Fiber** 1g, **Total Sugars** 4g; **Protein** 1g

Roasted Delicata Squash

SERVES 6 TO 8

WHY THIS RECIPE WORKS Delicata is the easiest winter squash to cook because its prettily striated skin is so thin that it doesn't need to be peeled before cooking and eating. Roasting intensifies delicata squash's mildly sweet and earthy flavors, so we simply sliced the squash into half-moons and roasted the pieces on a baking sheet with a combination of olive oil and butter until tender and golden brown, covering them with foil for the first 20 minutes to ensure each bite cooked up creamy and moist, and flipping the pieces once. A bright sauce made with fresh herbs, garlic, and sherry vinegar lent a bold, contrasting flavor punch without overshadowing our star vegetable. To ensure even cooking, choose squashes that are similar in size and shape.

HERB SAUCE
- ¼ cup minced fresh parsley or chives
- ¼ cup extra-virgin olive oil
- 2 tablespoons sherry vinegar
- 2 garlic cloves, minced
- 1 teaspoon smoked paprika
- ¼ teaspoon table salt

SQUASH
- 3 delicata squashes (12 to 16 ounces each), ends trimmed, halved lengthwise, seeded, and sliced crosswise ½ inch thick
- 4 teaspoons extra-virgin olive oil
- ½ teaspoon table salt
- 2 tablespoons unsalted butter, cut into 8 pieces

1. FOR THE SAUCE Stir all ingredients together in bowl; set aside for serving.

2. FOR THE SQUASH Adjust oven rack to lowest position and heat oven to 425 degrees. Toss squash, oil, and salt in bowl to coat. Arrange squash in single layer on rimmed baking sheet. Cover tightly with aluminum foil and bake until squash is tender when pierced with tip of paring knife, 18 to 20 minutes.

3. Uncover and continue to bake until side touching baking sheet is golden brown, 8 to 11 minutes. Remove squash from oven and, using thin metal spatula, flip slices over. Scatter butter pieces over squash. Return to oven and continue to bake until side touching baking sheet is golden brown, 8 to 11 minutes. Transfer squash to serving platter and drizzle with herb sauce. Serve.

PER SERVING Cal 150; **Total Fat** 12g; **Sat Fat** 3g; **Chol** 10mg; **Sodium** 220mg; **Total Carb** 11g, **Dietary Fiber** 2g; **Total Sugars** 2g; **Protein** 1g

Roasted Delicata Squash

Roasted Butternut Squash with Browned Butter and Hazelnuts

SERVES 4 TO 6

WHY THIS RECIPE WORKS The popular London-based chef Yotam Ottolenghi introduced us to an alternative squash universe. He roasts thin skin-on half-moons of squash and then tosses them with savory ingredients, from chiles and lime to toasted nuts and spiced yogurt, which serve as a successful foil to the squash's natural sweetness. We decided to bring this approach into the test kitchen and put our own spin on it. Our first move was to lose both the skin and the white layer of flesh underneath, both of which tasters found unappealing. To achieve deeper caramelization on the squash slices, we positioned the baking sheet on the lowest oven rack. We then flipped the squash (and rotated the baking sheet) partway through roasting so that both sides could caramelize. Melted butter produced better browning than olive oil, thanks to its milk proteins that undergo the Maillard reaction, leading to more complex flavors and aromas. These slices emerged perfectly caramelized, wonderfully sweet, and tender. The crowning touch was a few toppings that provided a mix of contrasting textures and bold flavors. You can buy prepeeled squash, but the flavor of freshly peeled squash is superior.

SQUASH

1 large (2½- to 3-pound) butternut squash, peeled, seeded, and sliced crosswise ½ inch thick
3 tablespoons unsalted butter, melted
½ teaspoon table salt
½ teaspoon pepper

TOPPING

3 tablespoons unsalted butter, cut into 3 pieces
⅓ cup hazelnuts, toasted, skinned, and chopped
1 tablespoon water
1 tablespoon lemon juice
Pinch table salt
1 tablespoon minced fresh chives

1. **FOR THE SQUASH** Adjust oven rack to lowest position and heat oven to 425 degrees. Toss squash with melted butter, salt, and pepper in bowl to coat. Arrange squash in single layer on rimmed baking sheet. Roast squash until side touching sheet toward back of oven is well browned, 25 to 30 minutes. Rotate sheet and continue to bake until side touching sheet toward back of oven is well browned, 6 to 10 minutes. Remove squash from oven and use metal spatula to flip each piece. Return to oven and roast until squash is very tender and side touching sheet is browned, 10 to 15 minutes.

2. **FOR THE TOPPING** While squash roasts, melt butter with hazelnuts in 8-inch skillet over medium-low heat. Cook, stirring frequently, until butter and hazelnuts are brown and fragrant, about 2 minutes. Immediately remove skillet from heat and stir in water (butter will foam and sizzle). Let cool for 1 minute. Stir in lemon juice and salt.

3. Transfer squash to large platter. Drizzle butter mixture evenly over squash. Sprinkle with chives. Serve warm or at room temperature.

PER SERVING Cal 210; **Total Fat** 15g, **Sat Fat** 7g; **Chol** 30mg; **Sodium** 200mg; **Total Carb** 20g, **Dietary Fiber** 4g, **Total Sugars** 4g; **Protein** 3g

VARIATIONS
Roasted Butternut Squash with Goat Cheese, Pecans, and Maple

Omit topping. Stir 2 tablespoons maple syrup and pinch cayenne pepper together in small bowl. Before serving, drizzle maple mixture over squash and sprinkle with ⅓ cup crumbled goat cheese; ⅓ cup pecans, toasted and chopped coarse; and 2 teaspoons fresh thyme leaves.

Roasted Butternut Squash with Radicchio and Parmesan

Omit topping. Whisk 1 tablespoon sherry vinegar, ½ teaspoon mayonnaise, and pinch salt together in small bowl. While whisking constantly, slowly drizzle in 2 tablespoons extra-virgin olive oil until combined. Before serving, drizzle vinaigrette over squash and sprinkle with ½ cup coarsely shredded radicchio; ½ ounce Parmesan cheese, shaved into thin strips; and 3 tablespoons toasted pine nuts.

Roasted Butternut Squash with Tahini and Feta

Omit topping. Whisk 1 tablespoon tahini, 1 tablespoon extra-virgin olive oil, 1½ teaspoons lemon juice, 1 teaspoon honey, and pinch salt together in small bowl. Before serving, drizzle tahini mixture over squash and sprinkle with ¼ cup finely crumbled feta cheese; ¼ cup shelled pistachios, toasted and chopped fine; and 2 tablespoons chopped fresh mint.

Roasted Butternut Squash with Yogurt and Sesame Seeds

Omit topping. Whisk 3 tablespoons plain Greek yogurt, 4 teaspoons extra-virgin olive oil, 4 teaspoons water, and pinch salt together in small bowl. Combine 1 teaspoon toasted sesame seeds, 1 teaspoon toasted and crushed coriander seeds, ¼ teaspoon dried thyme, and pinch salt in second small bowl. Before serving, drizzle yogurt mixture over squash and sprinkle with sesame seed mixture and ¼ cup fresh cilantro leaves.

PREPPING BUTTERNUT SQUASH

1. Lop ends off squash and use chef's knife to cut it into 2 pieces where bulb meets neck .

2. Use vegetable peeler to peel away skin and fibrous yellow flesh down to bright orange flesh.

3. Halve neck end and bulb end, then scoop out seeds and pulp. Place squash flat side down on cutting board and cut into pieces as directed in recipe.

Roasted Baby Pattypan Squash
SERVES 4 TO 6 · FAST

WHY THIS RECIPE WORKS Beautiful yellow-and-green pattypans come in a variety of sizes; here we chose baby ones for their tender skin and vibrant flavor (some say the squash loses flavor as it matures). We wanted to create a recipe where the summery squash would retain its beautiful shape and color while getting good browning. Roasting was the fastest and easiest way to get a decent amount of squash done in one batch, and we knew a couple of tricks to help things along. First, we cut the squash in half horizontally, creating flower-shaped slabs. Then we cranked the oven to 500 degrees and preheated a sheet pan, for improved searing. Tossing the squash in butter and honey both complemented the squash's own sweet and creamy profile and promoted browning. We didn't even have to flip the squash—they were beautifully browned on the cut side, retained their bright color on top, and were fully cooked through. Use baby pattypan squashes between 1½ and 2 inches in diameter.

> 3 tablespoons unsalted butter, melted
> 1 teaspoon honey
> ¼ teaspoon table salt
> ⅛ teaspoon pepper
> 1½ pounds baby pattypan squash, halved horizontally

Adjust oven rack to lowest position, place rimmed baking sheet on rack, and heat oven to 500 degrees. Whisk melted butter, honey, salt, and pepper in large bowl until honey has fully dissolved. Add squash and toss to coat. Working quickly, arrange squash cut side down on hot sheet. Roast until cut side is browned and squash is tender, 15 to 18 minutes. Season with salt and pepper to taste. Serve.

PER SERVING Cal 70; **Total Fat** 6g, **Sat Fat** 3.5g; **Chol** 15mg; **Sodium** 100mg; **Total Carb** 5g, **Dietary Fiber** 1g, **Total Sugars** 3g; **Protein** 1g

VARIATIONS
Roasted Baby Pattypan Squash with Lemon and Basil
Whisk ½ teaspoon lemon zest and 1 tablespoon lemon juice into butter mixture. Sprinkle squash with 2 tablespoons chopped fresh basil before serving.

Roasted Baby Pattypan Squash with Chile and Lime
Omit pepper. Whisk 1 minced Thai chile pepper, ½ teaspoon lime zest, and 1 tablespoon lime juice into butter mixture. Sprinkle squash with 2 tablespoons chopped fresh mint before serving.

Roasted Baby Pattypan Squash

Roasted Winter Squash Halves
SERVES 4 · VEGAN

WHY THIS RECIPE WORKS Winter squashes, such as acorn and butternut, with their tough skin and dense interior, are ideal for slow cooking and are best when roasted until well done, which helps develop the sweetest flavor and smoothest texture. Though varieties of winter squash vary significantly in size and texture, we were hoping to develop a one-recipe-fits-all approach. After some experimentation, we found that roasting the unpeeled and seeded halves cut side down gave a slightly better texture than roasting them cut side up. We found it best to cook the squash on an aluminum foil–lined baking sheet that had been oiled. The oil promoted better browning and reduced the risk of sticking, and the foil made cleanup easy. This recipe can be made with butternut, acorn, buttercup, kabocha, or delicata squash. The roasting time will vary depending on the kind of squash you use.

> 2 tablespoons extra-virgin olive oil, divided
> 2 pounds winter squash, halved lengthwise and seeded

1. Adjust oven rack to middle position and heat oven to 400 degrees. Line rimmed baking sheet with aluminum foil and grease foil with 1 tablespoon oil. Brush cut sides of squash with remaining 1 tablespoon oil and place cut side down on prepared baking sheet. Roast until fork inserted into center meets little resistance, 30 to 50 minutes.

2. Remove squash from oven and flip cut side up. If necessary, cut large pieces in half to yield 4 pieces. Season with salt and pepper to taste, and serve.

PER SERVING Cal 150; **Total Fat** 7g, **Sat Fat** 1g; **Chol** 0mg; **Sodium** 5mg; **Total Carb** 24g, **Dietary Fiber** 3g, **Total Sugars** 5g; **Protein** 2g

VARIATIONS

Roasted Winter Squash Halves with Soy Sauce and Maple Syrup

Substitute vegetable oil for olive oil. While squash roasts, combine 3 tablespoons maple syrup, 2 tablespoons soy sauce, and ½ teaspoon grated fresh ginger in bowl. After flipping cooked squash cut side up in step 2, brush with maple mixture and return to oven until well caramelized, 5 to 10 minutes.

Roasted Winter Squash Halves with Browned Butter and Sage

While squash roasts, melt 6 tablespoons unsalted butter in 8-inch skillet over medium heat. Add 6 thinly sliced fresh sage leaves and cook, swirling pan often, until butter is golden and sage is crisp, 4 to 5 minutes. Drizzle sage butter over squash before serving.

Roasted Winter Squash Salad with Za'atar and Parsley

SERVES 4 TO 6

WHY THIS RECIPE WORKS The sweet, nutty flavor of roasted butternut squash pairs best with bold flavors that balance that sweetness. To fill this role in our squash salad, we chose the eastern Mediterranean spice blend za'atar (a pungent combination of toasted sesame seeds, thyme, and sumac). We found that using high heat and placing the oven rack in the lowest position produced perfectly browned squash with a firm center in about 30 minutes. Dusting the za'atar over the hot squash worked much like toasting the spice, boosting its flavor. For a foil to the tender squash, we landed on toasted pumpkin seeds; they provided the textural accent the dish needed and reinforced the squash's flavor while pomegranate seeds added a burst of tartness and color. We prefer to use our homemade Za'atar, but you can substitute store-bought.

3 pounds butternut squash, peeled, seeded, and cut into ½-inch pieces (8 cups)
¼ cup extra-virgin olive oil, divided
¾ teaspoon table salt, divided
½ teaspoon pepper
1 teaspoon za'atar
1 small shallot, minced
2 tablespoons lemon juice
2 tablespoons honey
¾ cup fresh parsley leaves
⅓ cup roasted unsalted pepitas
½ cup pomegranate seeds

1. Adjust oven rack to lowest position and heat oven to 450 degrees. Toss squash with 1 tablespoon oil and season with ½ teaspoon salt and pepper. Arrange squash in single layer in rimmed baking sheet and roast until well browned and tender, 30 to 35 minutes, stirring halfway through roasting. Sprinkle squash with za'atar and let cool for 15 minutes.

2. Whisk shallot, lemon juice, honey, and remaining ¼ teaspoon salt together in large bowl. Whisking constantly, slowly drizzle in remaining 3 tablespoons oil. Add squash, parsley, and pepitas and gently toss to coat. Arrange salad on platter and sprinkle with pomegranate seeds. Serve.

PER SERVING Cal 250; **Total Fat** 13g, **Sat Fat** 2g; **Chol** 0mg; **Sodium** 310mg; **Total Carb** 32g, **Dietary Fiber** 5g, **Total Sugars** 12g; **Protein** 5g

---

TAKE IT UP A NOTCH

Za'atar is a brightly flavored, aromatic eastern Mediterranean spice blend that is a combination of dried herbs, toasted sesame seeds, and tart, citrusy sumac. It is used as a seasoning and also as a flavorful topping for lots of side dishes.

Za'atar
MAKES ABOUT ⅓ CUP

2 tablespoons dried thyme
1 tablespoon dried oregano
1½ tablespoons sumac
1 tablespoon sesame seeds, toasted
¼ teaspoon table salt

Process thyme and oregano in spice grinder or mortar and pestle until finely ground and powdery. Transfer to bowl and stir in sumac, sesame seeds, and salt. (Za'atar can be stored at room temperature in airtight container for up to 1 year.)

Perfect Roasted Root Vegetables

1 celery root (14 ounces), peeled
4 carrots, peeled and cut into 2½-inch lengths, halved
  or quartered lengthwise if necessary to create pieces
  ½ to 1 inch in diameter
12 ounces parsnips, peeled and sliced on bias 1 inch thick
10 small shallots, peeled
1 teaspoon kosher salt
12 ounces turnips, peeled, halved horizontally, and each
  half quartered
3 tablespoons vegetable oil
2 tablespoons chopped fresh parsley

1. Adjust oven rack to middle position, place rimmed baking sheet on rack, and heat oven to 425 degrees. Cut celery root into ¾-inch-thick rounds. Cut each round into ¾-inch-thick planks about 2½ inches in length.

2. Toss celery root, carrots, parsnips, and shallots with salt in large bowl; season with pepper to taste. Microwave, covered, until small pieces of carrot are just pliable enough to bend, 8 to 10 minutes, stirring halfway through microwaving. Drain vegetables and return them to bowl. Add turnips and oil and toss to coat.

3. Working quickly, remove sheet from oven and carefully transfer vegetables to sheet; arrange in even layer. Roast for 25 minutes.

4. Using thin metal spatula, stir vegetables and arrange in even layer. Rotate sheet and continue to roast until vegetables are golden brown and celery root is tender when pierced with tip of paring knife, 15 to 25 minutes longer. Transfer to platter, sprinkle with parsley, and serve.

PER SERVING Cal 170; **Total Fat** 7g, **Sat Fat** 0.5g; **Chol** 0mg; **Sodium** 520mg; **Total Carb** 24g, **Dietary Fiber** 7g, **Total Sugars** 10g; **Protein** 3g

Perfect Roasted Root Vegetables

SERVES 6   VEGAN

WHY THIS RECIPE WORKS Roasting a mix of humble root vegetables until perfectly tender and caramelized takes them to new heights. For the perfect roasted medley, we chose a combination of celery root, carrots, parsnips, and turnips to create a nice balance of deep flavors and contrasting textures. To ensure that the vegetables would roast evenly, we cut each one into a specific shape so they would cook at the same rate. Softened shallots also added flavor to the finished dish. All that our simple roasted side dish needed for flavoring was salt, pepper, and some fresh parsley sprinkled on top before serving. Use turnips that are roughly 2 to 3 inches in diameter. Instead of sprinkling the roasted vegetables with chopped parsley, you can substitute tarragon or chives. Alternatively, we also love these vegetables garnished with either our Bacon-Shallot Topping or Orange-Parsley Salsa (page 61).

Roasted Root Vegetables with Lemon-Caper Sauce

SERVES 4 TO 6   VEGAN

WHY THIS RECIPE WORKS A vibrant sauce lightens up and elevates this hearty mix of red potatoes, carrots, shallots, and Brussels sprouts. To ensure that the vegetables would roast evenly, we cut them into comparably sized pieces. Arranging the Brussels sprouts in the center of the baking sheet, with the other vegetables around the perimeter, kept the more delicate sprouts from charring in the hot oven. Before roasting, we tossed all of the vegetables with olive oil, garlic, thyme, rosemary, and a little sugar (to promote browning). Then, once all of the vegetables were perfectly tender and caramelized, we tossed them with a simple, bright, and lively Mediterranean-inspired dressing of parsley, lemon, and capers.

1 pound Brussels sprouts, trimmed and halved

1 pound red potatoes, unpeeled, cut into 1-inch pieces

8 shallots, peeled and halved

4 carrots, peeled and cut into 2-inch lengths, thick ends halved lengthwise

6 garlic cloves, peeled

3 tablespoons extra-virgin olive oil, divided

2 teaspoons minced fresh thyme

1 teaspoon minced fresh rosemary

1 teaspoon sugar

¾ teaspoon table salt

¼ teaspoon pepper

2 tablespoons minced fresh parsley

1½ tablespoons capers, rinsed and minced

1 tablespoon lemon juice, plus extra for seasoning

1. Adjust oven rack to middle position and heat oven to 450 degrees. Toss Brussels sprouts, potatoes, shallots, carrots, garlic, 1 tablespoon oil, thyme, rosemary, sugar, salt, and pepper together in bowl.

2. Spread vegetables into single layer on rimmed baking sheet, arranging Brussels sprouts cut side down in center of sheet. Roast until vegetables are tender and golden brown, 30 to 35 minutes, rotating sheet halfway through roasting.

3. Whisk parsley, capers, lemon juice, and remaining 2 tablespoons oil together in large bowl. Add roasted vegetables and toss to combine. Season with salt, pepper, and extra lemon juice to taste. Serve.

PER SERVING Cal 200; **Total Fat** 8g, **Sat Fat** 1g; **Chol** 0mg; **Sodium** 410mg; **Total Carb** 32g, **Dietary Fiber** 7g, **Total Sugars** 9g; **Protein** 6g

ARRANGING VEGETABLES FOR EVEN ROASTING

Spread vegetables in single layer, arranging Brussels sprouts cut side down in center of baking sheet and shallots, potatoes, and carrots around perimeter.

When you want to dress up roasted root vegetables, try garnishing them with either a deeply savory crisp bacon topping or a bright salsa.

Bacon-Shallot Topping
MAKES ABOUT ⅓ CUP

4 slices bacon, cut into ¼-inch pieces

¼ cup water

2 tablespoons minced shallot

1 tablespoon sherry vinegar

2 tablespoons minced fresh chives

Bring bacon and water to boil in 8-inch skillet over high heat. Reduce heat to medium; cook until water has evaporated and bacon is crispy, about 10 minutes. Transfer bacon to paper towel–lined plate and pour off all but ½ teaspoon fat from skillet. Add shallot and cook, stirring frequently, until softened, 2 to 4 minutes. Off heat, add vinegar. Transfer shallot mixture to bowl and stir in bacon and chives. Spoon over vegetables before serving.

Orange-Parsley Salsa
MAKES ABOUT ½ CUP

¼ cup slivered almonds

¼ teaspoon ground cumin

¼ teaspoon ground coriander

1 orange

½ cup fresh parsley leaves, minced

2 garlic cloves, minced

2 teaspoons extra-virgin olive oil

1 teaspoon cider vinegar

¼ teaspoon kosher salt

1. Toast almonds in 10-inch skillet over medium-high heat until fragrant and golden brown, 5 to 6 minutes. Add cumin and coriander; continue to toast, stirring constantly, until fragrant, about 45 seconds. Immediately transfer to bowl.

2. Cut away peel and pith from orange. Use paring knife to slice between membranes to release segments. Cut segments into ¼-inch pieces. Stir orange pieces, parsley, garlic, oil, vinegar, and salt into almond mixture. Let stand for 30 minutes. Spoon over vegetables before serving.

POTATOES EVERY WAY

For more ways with Potatoes, see other chapters for fried (pages 140–145), gratins (pages 290–292), salads (pages 313–317), casseroles (pages 348–355), and grilled (pages 381–385) potatoes. For a full listing of potato recipes, see the Index.

■ FAST (30 minutes or less total time)   ■ MAKE-AHEAD   ■ VEGAN
Photos (clockwise from top left): Cumin and Chili Roasted Sweet Potato Wedges; Duck Fat–Roasted Potatoes; Roasted Smashed Potatoes; Super-Stuffed Baked Potatoes

Buttermilk Mashed Potatoes

SERVES 4 **FAST**

WHY THIS RECIPE WORKS We like our buttermilk mashed potatoes rich and tangy, like a baked potato drenched in butter and sour cream. But simply stirring buttermilk into boiled and mashed potatoes didn't yield the flavorful results we were after. Cooking the potatoes directly in the buttermilk, which we thinned with a little water, was the key to success. Buttermilk is acidic, which slows cooking, but a pinch of baking soda balanced the acid so that the potatoes cooked through in a reasonable amount of time. Because simmering the buttermilk dulled its flavor slightly, we added a little reserved buttermilk at the end to revive the tanginess.

- 2 pounds Yukon Gold potatoes, peeled, quartered, and cut into ½-inch pieces
- 1 cup buttermilk, divided
- 6 tablespoons water
- 6 tablespoons unsalted butter, cut into 6 pieces, divided
- ½ teaspoon table salt
- ⅛ teaspoon baking soda

1. Combine potatoes, ¾ cup buttermilk, water, 2 tablespoons butter, salt, and baking soda in Dutch oven. Bring to boil over medium-high heat. Cover, reduce heat to low, and simmer, stirring occasionally, until potatoes are tender and paring knife slips easily in and out of potatoes, 20 to 25 minutes.

2. Uncover and cook over medium heat until liquid has nearly evaporated, about 3 minutes. Off heat, add remaining 4 tablespoons butter and mash potatoes smooth with potato masher. Using silicone spatula, fold in remaining ¼ cup buttermilk until absorbed. Season with salt and pepper to taste, and serve.

PER SERVING Cal 340; **Total Fat** 17g, **Sat Fat** 11g; **Chol** 50mg; **Sodium** 410mg; **Total Carb** 37g, **Dietary Fiber** 0g, **Total Sugars** 3g; **Protein** 7g

VARIATIONS

Buttermilk Mashed Potatoes with Leeks and Chives

While potatoes are cooking, melt 1 tablespoon unsalted butter in 8-inch nonstick skillet over medium heat. Add 1 leek, white and light green parts only, halved lengthwise, sliced ¼ inch thick, and washed thoroughly. Cook, stirring occasionally, until lightly browned, about 8 minutes. Add leek and 3 tablespoons minced fresh chives to potatoes with buttermilk in step 2.

Buttermilk Ranch Mashed Potatoes

Add ⅓ cup sour cream, 3 very thinly sliced scallions, 2 tablespoons minced fresh parsley, and 1 minced garlic clove along with buttermilk in step 2.

Ultimate French-Style Mashed Potatoes

Ultimate French-Style Mashed Potatoes

SERVES 8

WHY THIS RECIPE WORKS *Pommes purée* are ultrasilky and buttery mashed potatoes that make a decadent and elegant side. The traditional recipe poses a number of challenges, including peeling piping-hot whole boiled potatoes, laboriously beating a full pound of cold butter into the potatoes, and passing the puree multiple times through a special sieve. Our recipe eliminates all those things. Instead of using water, we cooked peeled, diced potatoes directly in the milk and butter that would be incorporated into the mash. This approach eliminated the need to beat in the butter after the fact and also captured the potato starch released during cooking. This was essential to producing an emulsified texture in which the butter doesn't separate out. You will need a food mill or potato ricer for this recipe.

- 2 pounds Yukon Gold potatoes, peeled and cut into 1-inch pieces
- 20 tablespoons (2¼ sticks) unsalted butter
- 1⅓ cups whole milk
- 1 teaspoon table salt

1. Place potatoes in fine-mesh strainer and rinse under cold running water until water runs clear; set aside to drain.

2. Heat butter, milk, and salt in large saucepan over low heat until butter has melted. Add potatoes, increase heat to medium-low, and cook until liquid just starts to boil. Reduce heat to low, partially cover, and gently simmer until potatoes are tender and paring knife slips easily in and out of potatoes, 30 to 40 minutes, stirring every 10 minutes.

3. Drain potatoes in fine-mesh strainer set over large bowl, reserving cooking liquid. Wipe saucepan clean with paper towels. Return cooking liquid to now-empty saucepan and place over low heat.

4. Set food mill fitted with finest disk or ricer over saucepan. Working in batches, transfer potatoes to hopper and process. Using whisk, recombine potatoes and cooking liquid until smooth, 10 to 15 seconds (potatoes should almost be pourable). Season with salt and pepper to taste. Serve immediately.

PER SERVING Cal 350; **Total Fat** 29g, **Sat Fat** 18g; **Chol** 80mg; **Sodium** 310mg; **Total Carb** 19g, **Dietary Fiber** 0g, **Total Sugars** 2g; **Protein** 4g

Loaded Rustic Mashed Potatoes

Rustic Mashed Potatoes
SERVES 4 FAST

WHY THIS RECIPE WORKS For simple, uncomplicated mashed potatoes, we left the skins on and sliced the potatoes before boiling them. Choosing starchier russet potatoes, rather than Yukon Golds or Red Bliss, gave us a fluffier mash, and cooking and mashing the potatoes in the same saucepan saved on cleanup. For the dairy component, a mix of rich (but not too rich) half-and-half and melted butter gave us the comforting flavor and silky texture we were after. Don't be tempted to use another kind of potato here; your mash won't be as fluffy. Scrub the potatoes well before using.

2 pounds russet potatoes, unpeeled, sliced ½ inch thick
¾ teaspoon table salt, plus salt for cooking potatoes
1 cup half-and-half
10 tablespoons unsalted butter, cut into 10 pieces
½ teaspoon pepper

1. Place potatoes and 1 tablespoon salt in large saucepan, add water to cover by 1 inch, and bring to boil over high heat. Reduce heat to medium and simmer until potatoes are tender and paring knife slips easily in and out of potatoes, 18 to 22 minutes.

2. Meanwhile, combine half-and-half and butter in 2-cup liquid measuring cup and microwave, covered, until butter is melted and mixture is warm to touch, about 2 minutes.

3. Drain potatoes and return them to saucepan. Using potato masher, mash potatoes until smooth and no lumps remain. Stir in half-and-half mixture, pepper, and ¾ teaspoon salt until fully combined. Season with salt and pepper to taste. Serve.

PER SERVING Cal 500; **Total Fat** 34g, **Sat Fat** 22g; **Chol** 95mg; **Sodium** 480mg; **Total Carb** 44g, **Dietary Fiber** 3g, **Total Sugars** 4g; **Protein** 7g

VARIATION
Loaded Rustic Mashed Potatoes
Cook 4 slices chopped bacon in skillet over medium heat until crispy, 5 to 7 minutes; transfer to paper towel–lined plate. Decrease half-and-half to ¾ cup and butter to 8 tablespoons. Stir cooked bacon, ½ cup shredded cheddar, ¼ cup sour cream, and ¼ cup minced fresh chives into potatoes after half-and-half mixture is incorporated.

Crushed Red Potatoes with Oregano and Capers

Crushed Red Potatoes with Garlic and Herbs
SERVES 4 TO 6

WHY THIS RECIPE WORKS Boiled-and-buttered red potatoes should have flavor through and through, but when left whole the flavor remains resolutely on the outside, leaving the interiors a bit bland. To achieve something tastier, we simmered 2 pounds of red potatoes until they were completely tender, drained them, and then melted some butter in the empty pot before adding minced garlic, fresh chives and parsley, salt, and pepper. We then added the still-steaming potatoes, lightly pressed each with the back of a spoon until it broke apart, and gently stirred everything to ensure the buttery herb mixture worked its way into all the nooks and crannies (and every bite). Be sure to use small red potatoes measuring 1 to 2 inches in diameter, and use a gentle hand when crushing them.

2 pounds small red potatoes, unpeeled
½ teaspoon table salt, plus salt for cooking potatoes
6 tablespoons unsalted butter
1 garlic clove, minced
2 tablespoons minced fresh chives
2 tablespoons minced fresh parsley
¼ teaspoon pepper

1. Place potatoes and 2 tablespoons salt in Dutch oven and cover with water by 1 inch. Bring to boil over high heat. Reduce heat to medium-high and simmer until paring knife slips easily in and out of potatoes, about 20 minutes. (Potatoes should be very tender.) Drain potatoes in colander.

2. In now-empty pot, melt butter over medium heat. Add garlic and cook until fragrant, about 30 seconds. Off heat, stir in chives, parsley, salt, and pepper.

3. Add potatoes to pot. Press each potato with back of spoon or spatula to lightly crush (do not mash; potatoes should still have texture). Stir to coat potatoes with butter mixture (potatoes will break up slightly; this is OK). Serve.

PER SERVING Cal 210; **Total Fat** 11g, **Sat Fat** 7g; **Chol** 30mg; **Sodium** 220mg; **Total Carb** 24g, **Dietary Fiber** 3g, **Total Sugars** 2g; **Protein** 3g

VARIATIONS
Crushed Red Potatoes with Garlic and Smoked Paprika
Substitute extra-virgin olive oil for butter and heat until shimmering. Sprinkle 1 teaspoon smoked paprika over crushed potatoes on platter before serving.

Crushed Red Potatoes with Oregano and Capers
Substitute 1 tablespoon chopped fresh oregano, 1 tablespoon rinsed capers, and 1 tablespoon lemon juice for chives and parsley. Decrease salt in step 2 to ¼ teaspoon.

GETTING THE TEXTURE JUST RIGHT

Press on cooked potatoes with wooden spoon until they crack open and are lightly crushed. Stir gently to further break down potatoes and distribute seasoned butter.

Roasted Smashed Potatoes

1. Adjust oven racks to top and lowest positions and heat oven to 500 degrees. Arrange potatoes on rimmed baking sheet, pour water into sheet, and wrap tightly with aluminum foil. Cook on lower rack until paring knife slips easily in and out of center of potatoes (poke through foil to test), 25 to 30 minutes. Remove foil and let cool for 10 minutes. If any water remains on sheet, blot dry with paper towel.

2. Drizzle 3 tablespoons oil over potatoes and roll to coat. Space potatoes evenly on sheet and place second baking sheet on top. Press down firmly on second sheet, flattening potatoes until ⅓ to ½ inch thick. Sprinkle with thyme, season with salt and pepper, and drizzle evenly with remaining 3 tablespoons oil. Roast potatoes on upper rack for 15 minutes, then transfer potatoes to lower rack and roast until well browned, 20 to 30 minutes. Serve immediately.

PER SERVING Cal 350; **Total Fat** 21g, **Sat Fat** 3g; **Chol** 0mg; **Sodium** 330mg; **Total Carb** 36g, **Dietary Fiber** 4g, **Total Sugars** 3g; **Protein** 4g

Braised Red Potatoes with Lemon and Chives
SERVES 4 TO 6

WHY THIS RECIPE WORKS Braising is a fantastic way to deliver creamy interiors and crispy exteriors with red potatoes. We combined halved small red potatoes, butter, and salted water (plus thyme for flavoring) in a 12-inch skillet and simmered the potatoes until they were perfectly creamy and the water was fully evaporated. Then we let the potatoes continue to cook in the now-dry skillet until their cut sides browned in the butter, developing the rich flavor and crispy edges. These potatoes were so good that they needed minimal seasoning: We simply tossed them with some minced garlic (softened in the simmering water along with the potatoes), lemon juice, chives, and pepper. Use small red potatoes measuring 1 to 2 inches in diameter. You will need a 12-inch nonstick skillet with a tight-fitting lid for this recipe.

1½ pounds small red potatoes, unpeeled, halved
  2 cups water
  3 tablespoons unsalted butter
  3 garlic cloves, peeled
  3 sprigs fresh thyme
  ¾ teaspoon table salt
  1 teaspoon lemon juice
  ¼ teaspoon pepper
  2 tablespoons minced fresh chives

Roasted Smashed Potatoes
SERUS 4 `VEGAN`

WHY THIS RECIPE WORKS These smashed potatoes combine the creamy, smooth texture of mashed potatoes and the satisfying crunch of deep-fried potatoes. Success started with choosing the right potato; only small red potatoes, with their moist texture and thin skin, fit the bill. Before we smashed them, we parcooked them on a baking sheet covered with foil to soften them. Unlike boiling, which can wash out flavor, this steaming approach kept the potatoes earthy and sweet. After a short rest, we drizzled them with olive oil and smashed them all at once by placing a second baking sheet on top and pushing down evenly and firmly. After adding chopped fresh thyme, more olive oil, and another stint in the oven, we ended up with browned, crisped potatoes that were super-creamy inside. Use small red potatoes measuring 1 to 2 inches in diameter. Remove the potatoes from the baking sheet as soon as they are done browning—they will toughen if left too long.

  2 pounds small red potatoes, unpeeled
  ¾ cup water
  6 tablespoons extra-virgin olive oil, divided
  1 teaspoon chopped fresh thyme

1. Arrange potatoes in single layer, cut side down, in 12-inch nonstick skillet. Add water, butter, garlic, thyme sprigs, and salt and bring to simmer over medium-high heat. Reduce heat to medium, cover, and simmer until potatoes are just tender, about 15 minutes.

2. Remove lid and use slotted spoon to transfer garlic to cutting board; discard thyme sprigs. Increase heat to medium-high and simmer vigorously, swirling skillet occasionally, until water evaporates and butter starts to sizzle, 15 to 20 minutes. When cool enough to handle, mince garlic to paste. Transfer paste to bowl and stir in lemon juice and pepper.

3. Continue to cook potatoes, swirling skillet frequently, until butter browns and cut sides of potatoes turn spotty brown, 4 to 6 minutes. Off heat, add chives and garlic mixture and toss to coat thoroughly. Serve.

PER SERVING Cal 130; **Total Fat** 6g, **Sat Fat** 3.5g; **Chol** 15mg; **Sodium** 310mg; **Total Carb** 19g, **Dietary Fiber** 2g, **Total Sugars** 2g; **Protein** 2g

VARIATIONS

Braised Red Potatoes with Dijon and Tarragon
Substitute 2 teaspoons Dijon mustard for lemon juice and 1 tablespoon minced fresh tarragon for chives.

Braised Red Potatoes with Miso and Scallions
Reduce salt to ½ teaspoon. Substitute 1 tablespoon red miso paste for lemon juice and 3 thinly sliced scallions for chives.

Bacon-Braised Red Potatoes
SERVES 4

WHY THIS RECIPE WORKS Braising red potatoes on the stovetop produces a dead-simple side dish full of flavor. Here we added bacon and a sliced onion to the mix and simmered them with our halved red potatoes in water until the potatoes were just tender. The water performed two functions: It seasoned the potatoes while cooking them through and rendered the bacon fat. We then removed the lid and boosted the heat to first evaporate the liquid and then lightly brown the potatoes and onion and crisp the bacon. Finishing the dish with some fresh thyme gave it a bright herbal boost. For the best results, use potatoes that measure about 1½ inches in diameter. You will need a 12-inch nonstick skillet with a tight-fitting lid for this recipe.

Bacon-Braised Red Potatoes

1½ pounds small red potatoes, unpeeled, halved
2½ cups water
1 onion, halved and sliced ½ inch thick
2 slices thick-cut bacon, cut into 1-inch pieces
¼ teaspoon table salt
¼ teaspoon pepper
2 teaspoons chopped fresh thyme

1. Arrange potatoes cut side down in single layer in 12-inch nonstick skillet. Add water, onion, bacon, salt, and pepper. Bring to simmer over medium-high heat. Reduce heat to medium, cover, and simmer until potatoes are just tender, 18 to 20 minutes.

2. Uncover skillet and increase heat to medium-high. Simmer vigorously until water has nearly evaporated and potatoes begin to sizzle, about 10 minutes. Continue to cook, stirring occasionally, until potatoes and onion are spotty brown and bacon fat is completely rendered, 5 to 7 minutes. Off heat, stir in thyme and season with salt and pepper to taste. Serve.

PER SERVING Cal 190; **Total Fat** 6g, **Sat Fat** 2g; **Chol** 10mg; **Sodium** 270mg; **Total Carb** 30g, **Dietary Fiber** 3g, **Total Sugars** 4g; **Protein** 5g

O'Brien Potatoes

SERVES 4

WHY THIS RECIPE WORKS O'Brien potatoes, a side dish falling somewhere on the spud spectrum between hash browns and home fries, has two constants: bell peppers and—you guessed it—potatoes. The rest was up to us. We preferred waxy firm unpeeled red potatoes to Yukon Golds or russets. To achieve both tenderness and browning, we employed a hybrid cooking method: We started by braising the potatoes along with onion, green and red bell pepper, and oil until the spuds were almost tender. Removing the lid allowed the liquid to evaporate so the potatoes and vegetables could brown in the oil. Using chicken broth as the cooking liquid added extra flavor, and Worcestershire sauce and scallions added savory depth and freshness. Use waxy red potatoes, which hold their shape better than other varieties. You will need a 12-inch nonstick skillet with a tight-fitting lid for this recipe.

2 tablespoons vegetable oil
1½ pounds red potatoes, unpeeled, cut into ½-inch pieces
1 green bell pepper, stemmed, seeded, and cut into ½-inch pieces
1 red bell pepper, stemmed, seeded, and cut into ½-inch pieces
1 onion, chopped
½ cup chicken broth
2 teaspoons Worcestershire sauce
1½ teaspoons table salt
4 scallions, sliced thin

1. Heat oil in 12-inch nonstick skillet over medium heat until shimmering. Add potatoes, green and red bell peppers, and onion and stir to coat with oil. Stir in broth, Worcestershire, and salt. Cover and cook, stirring occasionally, until potatoes are tender, about 15 minutes.

2. Uncover and increase heat to medium-high. Cook, stirring occasionally, until liquid has evaporated and potatoes and bell peppers are spotty brown, about 12 minutes. Season with salt and pepper to taste, stir in scallions, and serve.

PER SERVING Cal 220; **Total Fat** 8g, **Sat Fat** 0.5g; **Chol** 0mg; **Sodium** 1010mg; **Total Carb** 35g, **Dietary Fiber** 5g, **Total Sugars** 6g; **Protein** 5g

Greek-Style Garlic-Lemon Potatoes

SERVES 4 TO 6   VEGAN

WHY THIS RECIPE WORKS In Greece, potato wedges are cooked in plenty of olive oil until browned and crisp and are accented by classic Greek flavors of lemon and oregano. For our version, we chose Yukon Golds, which hold their shape nicely and cook up with pleasantly fluffy interiors, and browned them in a nonstick skillet in olive oil to give them deep flavor and color. We then covered the pan to let the potatoes finish cooking through. A combination of juice and zest gave them full lemon flavor, and we added a modest amount of garlic to give them an aromatic backbone. Letting the lemon, garlic, and oregano cook briefly with the potatoes gave the dish a rounded, cohesive flavor profile. A final sprinkling of parsley added welcome freshness. You will need a 12-inch nonstick skillet with a tight-fitting lid for this recipe.

3 tablespoons extra-virgin olive oil, divided
1½ pounds Yukon Gold potatoes, peeled and cut lengthwise into ¾-inch-thick wedges
1½ tablespoons minced fresh oregano
3 garlic cloves, minced
2 teaspoons grated lemon zest plus 1½ tablespoons juice
½ teaspoon table salt
½ teaspoon pepper
1½ tablespoons minced fresh parsley

1. Heat 2 tablespoons oil in 12-inch nonstick skillet over medium-high heat until shimmering. Add potatoes cut side down in single layer and cook until golden brown on first side (skillet should sizzle but not smoke), about 6 minutes. Using tongs, flip potatoes onto second cut side and cook until golden brown, about 5 minutes. Reduce heat to medium-low, cover, and cook until potatoes are tender, 8 to 12 minutes.

2. Meanwhile, whisk remaining 1 tablespoon oil, oregano, garlic, lemon zest and juice, salt, and pepper together in small bowl. When potatoes are tender, gently stir in garlic mixture and cook, uncovered, until fragrant, about 2 minutes. Off heat, gently stir in parsley and season with salt and pepper to taste. Serve.

PER SERVING Cal 150; **Total Fat** 7g, **Sat Fat** 1g; **Chol** 0mg; **Sodium** 200mg; **Total Carb** 18g, **Dietary Fiber** 0g, **Total Sugars** 0g; **Protein** 2g

VARIATIONS
Greek-Style Garlic-Lemon Potatoes with Olives and Feta
Stir ½ cup crumbled feta cheese and 2 tablespoons chopped pitted kalamata olives into potatoes with parsley.

Greek-Style Garlic-Lemon Potatoes with Spinach and Anchovies

You can make this recipe without the anchovies if preferred. Stir 1 teaspoon minced anchovies along with garlic mixture into skillet in step 2, then add 2½ ounces baby spinach (2½ cups) and gently stir to distribute. Omit parsley.

Better Hash Browns

SERVES 4 TO 6 `MAKE-AHEAD` `VEGAN`

WHY THIS RECIPE WORKS A side of freshly made hash browns makes a nice treat for breakfast or brunch. For better hash browns, we shredded Yukon Gold potatoes and rinsed them in salted water to prevent discoloration. After squeezing excess moisture from the potatoes, we parcooked them in the microwave, which removed more moisture and jump-started the gelatinization of the potato starch so that the potatoes were cohesive even before they went into the skillet. Molding the hash browns in a cake pan was easy and also made a smoother potato cake. We prefer using the shredding disk of a food processor to shred the potatoes, but you can use the large holes of a box grater if you prefer.

    4 teaspoons table salt, for brining
2½ pounds Yukon Gold potatoes, peeled and shredded
    ¼ teaspoon pepper
    ¼ cup vegetable oil, divided

1. Spray 8-inch round cake pan with vegetable oil spray. Whisk 2 cups water and salt in large bowl until salt dissolves. Transfer potatoes to salt water and toss briefly to coat. Immediately drain in colander. Place 2½ cups potatoes in center of clean dish towel. Gather ends together and twist tightly to wring out excess moisture. Toss dried potatoes with pepper in large bowl. Microwave until very hot and slightly softened, about 5 minutes. Place remaining potatoes in towel and wring out excess moisture. Add to microwaved potatoes and toss with 2 forks until mostly combined (potatoes will not combine completely). Continue to microwave until potatoes are hot and form cohesive mass when pressed with spatula, about 6 minutes, stirring halfway through microwaving.

2. Transfer potatoes to prepared pan and let cool until no longer steaming, about 5 minutes. Using your lightly greased hands, press potatoes firmly into pan to form smooth disk. Refrigerate until cool, at least 20 minutes or up to 24 hours (if refrigerating longer than 30 minutes, wrap pan with plastic wrap once potatoes are cool).

3. Heat 2 tablespoons oil in 10-inch skillet over medium heat until shimmering. Invert potato cake onto plate and carefully slide cake into skillet. Cook, swirling skillet occasionally to distribute oil evenly and prevent cake from sticking, until bottom of cake is brown and crispy, 6 to 8 minutes. (If not browning after 3 minutes, turn heat up slightly. If browning too quickly, reduce heat.) Slide cake onto large plate. Invert onto second large plate. Heat remaining 2 tablespoons oil until shimmering. Carefully slide cake, browned side up, back into skillet. Cook, swirling skillet occasionally, until bottom of cake is brown and crispy, 5 to 6 minutes. Carefully slide cake onto plate and invert onto serving plate. Cut into wedges and serve.

PER SERVING Cal 220; **Total Fat** 9g, **Sat Fat** 0.5g; **Chol** 0mg; **Sodium** 200mg; **Total Carb** 28g, **Dietary Fiber** 0g, **Total Sugars** 0g; **Protein** 4g

Potato and Celery Root Roesti with Lemon-Parsley Crème Fraîche

SERVES 2 OR 3

WHY THIS RECIPE WORKS Roesti is a large golden-brown potato pancake of simply seasoned grated potatoes fried in butter that has its origins in Switzerland. To prepare a pan-fried cake with plenty of heartiness and bright flavor, we swapped out nearly half of the potatoes for celery root. To achieve a tender, creamy interior, we eliminated excess moisture by salting the shredded vegetables and then wringing them dry in a dish towel. A small amount of cornstarch ensured that the roesti held together to create a crunchy, crisp crust that helped to hold the pancake together when we turned it over. Preparing a rich but bright sauce to accompany it was as simple as combining tangy crème fraîche with parsley and lemon zest and juice. Use the large holes of a box grater to shred the potatoes and celery root. You will need a 10-inch nonstick skillet with a tight-fitting lid for this recipe.

    1 pound russet potatoes, peeled and shredded
  14 ounces celery root, trimmed, peeled, and shredded
    ⅛ teaspoon table salt, plus salt for salting vegetables
    ¼ cup crème fraîche
    3 tablespoons minced fresh parsley, divided
2½ teaspoons grated lemon zest, divided, plus
        ½ teaspoon juice
    2 teaspoons cornstarch
    ¼ teaspoon pepper
    4 tablespoons unsalted butter, divided

1. Toss potatoes and celery root with ¾ teaspoon salt, then let drain in colander for 30 minutes. Meanwhile, whisk crème fraîche, 1 tablespoon parsley, ½ teaspoon lemon zest, lemon juice, and ⅛ teaspoon salt together in bowl. Cover and refrigerate until ready to serve.

Potato and Celery Root Roesti with Lemon-Parsley Crème Fraîche

2. Working in 3 batches, wrap potato mixture in clean dish towel and wring tightly to squeeze out as much liquid as possible; transfer to large bowl. Add remaining 2 tablespoons parsley, remaining 2 teaspoons lemon zest, cornstarch, and pepper, and toss to combine.

3. Melt 2 tablespoons butter in 10-inch nonstick skillet over medium-low heat. Add potato mixture and spread into even layer. Cover and cook for 5 minutes. Uncover and, using greased spatula, gently press potato mixture to form compact, round cake. Cook, pressing on cake occasionally, until bottom is deep golden brown, about 10 minutes.

4. Run spatula around edge of pan and shake pan to loosen roesti; slide onto large plate. Melt remaining 2 tablespoons butter in now-empty skillet. Invert roesti onto second plate, then slide it, browned side up, back into skillet. Cook, pressing on cake occasionally, until bottom is well browned, about 15 minutes. Transfer roesti to wire rack and let cool for 5 minutes. Cut into wedges and serve with crème fraîche sauce.

PER SERVING Cal 360; **Total Fat** 22g, **Sat Fat** 14g; **Chol** 55mg; **Sodium** 135mg; **Total Carb** 36g, **Dietary Fiber** 4g, **Total Sugars** 3g; **Protein** 5g

Texas Potato Pancakes
SERVES 4 TO 6

WHY THIS RECIPE WORKS The Texas version of German potato pancakes boast moist, fluffy interiors surrounded by supremely crunchy, lacy exteriors. When developing our recipe, we found that the water content of the potatoes inhibited the crispiness of the pancakes. Wringing out the shredded potatoes in a dish towel sent a lot of this water down the drain. Choosing russet potatoes, with their high starch content, and adding extra flour guaranteed maximum crunch. Shred the potatoes and onion on the large holes of a box grater or with the shredding disk of a food processor. The potato shreds may take on a red hue if left to sit out for a few minutes before cooking. This does not affect their flavor.

2 pounds russet potatoes, peeled and shredded
½ cup all-purpose flour
2 large eggs, lightly beaten
⅓ cup shredded onion
1¼ teaspoons table salt
1¼ cups vegetable oil, plus extra as needed
Sour cream
Applesauce

1. Adjust oven rack to middle position and heat oven to 200 degrees. Set wire rack in rimmed baking sheet and place in oven. Line large plate with triple layer of paper towels.

2. Place half of potatoes in center of clean dish towel. Gather ends together and twist tightly to squeeze out as much liquid as possible. Transfer to large bowl and repeat with remaining potatoes.

3. Stir flour, eggs, onion, and salt into potatoes until combined. Heat oil in 12-inch skillet over medium heat to 325 degrees. Using ⅓-cup dry measuring cup, place 3 portions of potato mixture in skillet and press into 4-inch disks with back of spoon.

4. Cook until deep golden brown, 3 to 4 minutes per side, carefully flipping pancakes with 2 spatulas. Transfer pancakes to paper towel–lined plate to drain, about 15 seconds per side, then transfer to prepared wire rack in oven.

5. Repeat with remaining potato mixture in 3 batches, stirring mixture, if necessary, to recombine and adding extra oil to skillet as needed to maintain ¼-inch depth. Season pancakes with salt and pepper to taste. Serve immediately, passing sour cream and applesauce separately.

PER SERVING Cal 330; **Total Fat** 20g, **Sat Fat** 2g; **Chol** 60mg; **Sodium** 125mg; **Total Carb** 31g, **Dietary Fiber** 2g, **Total Sugars** 1g; **Protein** 6g

Short-Order Home Fries

1. Place potatoes and 1 tablespoon butter in large bowl and microwave, covered, until edges of potatoes begin to soften, 5 to 7 minutes, stirring halfway through cooking.

2. Meanwhile, melt 1 tablespoon butter in 12-inch nonstick skillet over medium heat. Add onion and cook until softened and golden brown, 8 to 10 minutes. Transfer to small bowl.

3. Melt remaining 2 tablespoons butter in now-empty skillet over medium heat. Add potatoes and pack down with spatula. Cook, without moving, until bottoms of potatoes are brown, 5 to 7 minutes. Turn potatoes, pack down again, and continue to cook until well browned and crisp, 5 to 7 minutes. Reduce heat to medium-low and continue to cook until potatoes are crusty, 9 to 12 minutes, stirring occasionally. Stir in onion, garlic salt, and salt and season with pepper to taste. Serve.

PER SERVING Cal 250; **Total Fat** 11g, **Sat Fat** 7g; **Chol** 30mg; **Sodium** 550mg; **Total Carb** 33g, **Dietary Fiber** 0g, **Total Sugars** 1g; **Protein** 4g

Short-Order Home Fries
SERVES 4

WHY THIS RECIPE WORKS The real secret to serving up crisp diner-style home fries is precooking the potatoes. Roasting or boiling the potatoes took too much time for a breakfast side, so we turned to the microwave to jump-start their cooking before frying them in a large skillet. We found that packing the potatoes down with a spatula and cooking them a few minutes before turning them and then repeating these steps ensured that they were evenly browned and extra-crunchy. Finally, we stirred in some sautéed onion and garlic salt to give our home fries a deep, savory flavor. Although we prefer the sweetness of Yukon Gold potatoes, other medium-starch potatoes, such as red potatoes, can be substituted. If you want to spice things up, add a pinch of cayenne pepper.

1½ pounds Yukon Gold potatoes, unpeeled, cut into ¾-inch pieces
  4 tablespoons unsalted butter, divided
  1 onion, chopped fine
  ½ teaspoon garlic salt
  ½ teaspoon table salt

Lyonnaise Potatoes
SERVES 4 **FAST**

WHY THIS RECIPE WORKS Lyonnaise potatoes are a French take on pan-fried potatoes and onions, traditionally made with leftover potatoes. To start with raw potatoes, we first cooked thickly sliced potatoes in a skillet until tender before adding a sliced onion. We then cooked the two vegetables together in a covered skillet until the onion was tender. We finished the dish with a sprinkling of minced fresh parsley, which added bright color and freshness. You will need a 12-inch nonstick skillet with a tight-fitting lid for this recipe.

  4 tablespoons unsalted butter
  2 pounds Yukon Gold potatoes, peeled and sliced ½ inch thick
1¼ teaspoons table salt, divided
  1 onion, halved and sliced thin
  ½ teaspoon pepper
  1 tablespoon minced fresh parsley

1. Melt butter in 12-inch nonstick skillet over medium heat. Add potatoes and ¾ teaspoon salt and cook, covered, until just tender and golden brown, about 15 minutes, flipping potatoes occasionally to ensure even browning.

2. Reduce heat to medium-low. Add onion, remaining ½ teaspoon salt, and pepper; cover and continue to cook until onion is tender and golden brown, about 10 minutes, stirring occasionally. Season with salt and pepper to taste. Transfer to serving platter and sprinkle with parsley. Serve.

PER SERVING Cal 270; **Total Fat** 11g, **Sat Fat** 7g; **Chol** 30mg; **Sodium** 740mg; **Total Carb** 37g, **Dietary Fiber** 1g, **Total Sugars** 1g; **Protein** 5g

Roasted Red Potatoes
SERVES 4 **VEGAN**

WHY THIS RECIPE WORKS These effortless roasted potatoes deliver perfectly crisp and tender potatoes in less than an hour. To arrive at our ideal—potatoes with deep golden, crisp crusts and creamy, soft interiors—we took advantage of the high moisture content of red potatoes. Rather than parboiling the potatoes (a common step that dims their subtle flavor), we arranged them cut side down on a foil-lined rimmed baking sheet and covered them with foil; they turned tender as they steamed in their own moisture. Finishing the potatoes uncovered crisped the outsides to a perfect golden brown. Contact with the baking sheet was important to browning, so we flipped the potatoes partway through for crispness on every side. This recipe was so easy, we had no trouble developing a few appealing variations. If using very small potatoes, cut them in half instead of into wedges and flip them cut side up during the final 10 minutes of roasting.

- 2 pounds red potatoes, unpeeled, cut into ¾-inch wedges
- 3 tablespoons extra-virgin olive oil
- ½ teaspoon table salt
- ¼ teaspoon pepper

1. Adjust oven rack to middle position and heat oven to 425 degrees. Line rimmed baking sheet with aluminum foil. Toss potatoes with oil in bowl and season with salt and pepper. Arrange potatoes in single layer on prepared sheet, with either cut side facing down. Cover with foil and roast for 20 minutes.

2. Remove foil and roast until sides of potatoes touching pan are crusty and golden, about 15 minutes. Flip potatoes over and roast until crusty and golden on second side, about 8 minutes. Season with salt and pepper to taste, and serve.

PER SERVING Cal 250; **Total Fat** 11g, **Sat Fat** 1.5g; **Chol** 0mg; **Sodium** 330mg; **Total Carb** 36g, **Dietary Fiber** 4g, **Total Sugars** 3g; **Protein** 4g

Roasted Red Potatoes with Shallot, Lemon, and Thyme

VARIATIONS
Roasted Red Potatoes with Garlic and Rosemary
During final 3 minutes of roasting, sprinkle 2 tablespoons minced fresh rosemary over potatoes. Toss roasted potatoes with 1 garlic clove, minced to paste, before serving.

Roasted Red Potatoes with Shallot, Lemon, and Thyme
During final 3 minutes of roasting, sprinkle 1 teaspoon minced fresh thyme over potatoes. Toss roasted potatoes with 1 garlic clove, minced to paste; 1 minced shallot; ½ teaspoon grated lemon zest; and 1 teaspoon lemon juice before serving.

Roasted Red Potatoes with Feta, Olives, and Oregano
During final 3 minutes of roasting, sprinkle 1 tablespoon minced fresh oregano over potatoes. Combine ½ cup crumbled feta cheese; 12 pitted and chopped kalamata olives; 1 tablespoon lemon juice; and 1 garlic clove, minced to paste, in bowl. Toss roasted potatoes with feta mixture before serving.

Duck Fat–Roasted Potatoes
SERVES 6

WHY THIS RECIPE WORKS When roasting most vegetables, olive oil is usually our fat of choice, but this roasted potato recipe calls for a richer option—duck fat—for potatoes that are crisp on the outside, moist on the inside, and exploding with meaty, savory flavor. We peeled and cut Yukon Gold potatoes into chunks to maximize their crispable surface area. We encouraged thorough seasoning and deeper browning by boiling the chunks with a touch of baking soda and plenty of salt and then, after draining them, we vigorously stirred them to rough up their exterior before working in the duck fat. This coated the potatoes with a film of starchy, fatty paste for a rich, crisp shell. A preheated baking sheet gave them a jump start on browning. Turning the potatoes partway through roasting ensured even doneness. Finally, we stirred in an extra tablespoon of duck fat, this time seasoned with rosemary, and roasted the potatoes until they were well browned. Duck fat is available in the meat department in many supermarkets. Alternatively, substitute chicken fat, lard, or a mixture of 3 tablespoons of bacon fat and 3 tablespoons of extra-virgin olive oil.

3½ pounds Yukon Gold potatoes, peeled and cut into 1½-inch pieces
⅓ cup plus 1 teaspoon kosher salt, divided
½ teaspoon baking soda
6 tablespoons duck fat, divided
1 tablespoon chopped fresh rosemary

1. Adjust oven rack to top position, place rimmed baking sheet on rack, and heat oven to 475 degrees.

2. Bring 10 cups water to boil in Dutch oven over high heat. Add potatoes, ⅓ cup salt, and baking soda. Return to boil and cook for 1 minute; drain potatoes. Return potatoes to pot and place over low heat. Cook, shaking pot occasionally, until surface moisture has evaporated, about 2 minutes. Off heat, add 5 tablespoons fat and 1 teaspoon salt; mix with silicone spatula until potatoes are coated with thick paste, about 30 seconds.

3. Remove sheet from oven, transfer potatoes to sheet, and spread into even layer. Roast for 15 minutes.

4. Remove sheet from oven. Using thin metal spatula, turn potatoes. Roast until golden brown, 12 to 15 minutes. Meanwhile, combine rosemary and remaining 1 tablespoon fat in bowl.

5. Remove sheet from oven. Spoon rosemary-fat mixture over potatoes and turn again. Continue to roast until potatoes are well browned and rosemary is fragrant, 3 to 5 minutes. Season with salt and pepper to taste. Serve immediately.

PER SERVING Cal 300; **Total Fat** 13g, **Sat Fat** 4.5g; **Chol** 15mg; **Sodium** 300mg; **Total Carb** 40g, **Dietary Fiber** 0g, **Total Sugars** 0g; **Protein** 5g

Roasted Parmesan Potatoes
SERVES 4 TO 6

WHY THIS RECIPE WORKS These irresistible cheesy potato rounds are coated with Parmesan cheese and roasted until crunchy. We sliced Yukon Gold potatoes into thick rounds and tossed them in seasoned cornstarch to dry their surface and enhance crisping. A very hot oven achieved the best color and flavor before we introduced the cheese. Parmesan processed with rosemary, pepper, and more cornstarch created an easy savory topping that we sprinkled over the slices. We made sure the topping stuck by pressing it onto the potatoes; we then flipped the slices and returned them to the same place on the baking sheet to rapidly crisp the cheese during the last minutes of roasting. Once cooled, the potatoes came off the baking sheet with ease, coated in crispy cheese. Look for potatoes that are 2½ to 3 inches long. Use a good-quality Parmesan cheese. Serve with Garlic and Chive Sour Cream (page 82), if desired.

2 pounds Yukon Gold potatoes, unpeeled, cut into ½-inch-thick slices
4 teaspoons cornstarch, divided
1 teaspoon table salt
1½ teaspoons pepper, divided
1 tablespoon extra-virgin olive oil
6 ounces Parmesan cheese, cut into 1-inch pieces
2 teaspoons minced fresh rosemary

1. Adjust oven rack to lower-middle position and heat oven to 500 degrees. Spray rimmed baking sheet liberally with vegetable oil spray. Place potatoes in large bowl.

2. Combine 2 teaspoons cornstarch, salt, and 1 teaspoon pepper in small bowl. Sprinkle cornstarch mixture over potatoes and toss until potatoes are thoroughly coated and cornstarch is no longer visible. Add oil and toss to coat.

3. Arrange potatoes in single layer on prepared sheet and roast until golden brown on top, about 20 minutes.

4. Meanwhile, process Parmesan, rosemary, remaining 2 teaspoons cornstarch, and remaining ½ teaspoon pepper in food processor until cheese is finely ground, about 1 minute.

5. Remove potatoes from oven. Sprinkle Parmesan mixture evenly over and between potatoes (cheese should cover surface of baking sheet), pressing on potatoes with back of spoon to adhere. Using 2 forks, flip slices over onto same spot on sheet.

6. Roast until cheese between potatoes turns light golden brown, 5 to 7 minutes. Transfer sheet to wire rack and let potatoes cool for 15 minutes. Transfer potatoes, cheese side up, and accompanying cheese to serving dish and serve.

PER SERVING Cal 280; **Total Fat** 10g, **Sat Fat** 4.5g; **Chol** 20mg; **Sodium** 900mg; **Total Carb** 29g, **Dietary Fiber** 0g, **Total Sugars** 0g; **Protein** 16g

Cheesy Ranch Potatoes

Cheesy Ranch Potatoes
SERVES 4

WHY THIS RECIPE WORKS If you love the flavors of garlic, onion, and dill, then these crispy potatoes are for you. Our aim with this recipe was to pack roasted potatoes with a big punch of classic ranch flavor. We began by tossing Yukon Gold potato chunks with a special ranch seasoning blend and olive oil before roasting them. To add further interest, we sprinkled the just-roasted potatoes with shredded cheddar cheese, some fresh dill, and chopped cilantro. The heat from the cooked potatoes melted the cheese and helped bloom the flavors of the herbs. We finished the dish by whisking together a creamy ranch sauce, which we drizzled over the roasted potatoes right before serving. Be sure to leave the potatoes undisturbed while they roast. If you stir them, the potatoes will cook before they acquire flavorful browning. Be sure to scrub and dry the potatoes thoroughly before cutting them.

SAUCE
¼ cup mayonnaise
¼ cup sour cream
2 tablespoons milk
2 tablespoons chopped fresh cilantro
1 tablespoon distilled white vinegar
2 teaspoons chopped fresh dill
1 teaspoon granulated garlic
1 teaspoon onion powder
¼ teaspoon table salt
¼ teaspoon pepper

POTATOES
2 pounds Yukon Gold potatoes, unpeeled, cut into 1-inch chunks
¼ cup extra-virgin olive oil
2 teaspoons granulated garlic
2 teaspoons onion powder
1 teaspoon table salt
1 teaspoon pepper
8 ounces sharp cheddar cheese, shredded (2 cups)
1 tablespoon chopped fresh cilantro
2 teaspoons chopped fresh dill

1. FOR THE SAUCE Whisk all ingredients together in bowl. Cover and set aside while potatoes cook.

2. FOR THE POTATOES Adjust oven rack to middle position and heat oven to 400 degrees. Toss potatoes, oil, granulated garlic, onion powder, salt, and pepper together in bowl.

3. Arrange potatoes in single layer on rimmed baking sheet. Roast until potatoes are tender and deep golden brown on bottoms, 35 to 40 minutes. Sprinkle potatoes with cheddar, return sheet to oven, and continue to roast until cheese is melted, about 3 minutes longer.

4. Transfer potatoes to platter. Sprinkle with cilantro and dill. Serve with sauce.

PER SERVING Cal 670; **Total Fat** 45g, **Sat Fat** 17g; **Chol** 75mg; **Sodium** 1200mg; **Total Carb** 47g, **Dietary Fiber** 1g, **Total Sugars** 1g; **Protein** 21g

Foil-Roasted Potatoes
SERVES 6

WHY THIS RECIPE WORKS To easily roast 2 pounds of small red potatoes, we deployed an aluminum foil pouch. Crimping together the edges of two sheets of foil created the cooking pouch for our hybrid steaming-and-roasting method. It also made cleanup a breeze. Chopped fresh thyme and rosemary and butter added rich, savory flavor, but the butter alone couldn't get the potatoes browned enough. For the best browning, we found that placing the baking sheet on the bottom oven rack, close to the heat source, was the solution. Use small red potatoes measuring 1 to 2 inches in diameter.

2 pounds small red potatoes, unpeeled, halved

2 teaspoons chopped fresh rosemary

1¼ teaspoons table salt

1 teaspoon chopped fresh thyme

½ teaspoon pepper

4 tablespoons unsalted butter, cut into ½-inch pieces

3 garlic cloves, sliced thin

1. Adjust oven rack to lowest position and heat oven to 400 degrees. Toss potatoes, rosemary, salt, thyme, and pepper in large bowl until potatoes are well coated.

2. Line rimmed baking sheet with 16 by 12-inch sheet of aluminum foil. Spread potato mixture evenly over foil, leaving 1½-inch border. Flip potatoes cut sides down. Scatter butter and garlic over potatoes. Place second 16 by 12-inch sheet of foil over potatoes. Beginning at 1 corner, fold foil inward in ½-inch increments 2 to 3 times to seal edge. Continue folding around perimeter of foil to create sealed packet.

3. Transfer sheet to oven and bake until potatoes are tender, about 40 minutes. Let potatoes cool for 5 minutes. Using tongs, tear away top sheet of foil, being careful of escaping steam. Serve.

PER SERVING Cal 180; **Total Fat** 8g, **Sat Fat** 4.5g; **Chol** 20mg; **Sodium** 510mg; **Total Carb** 25g, **Dietary Fiber** 3g, **Total Sugars** 2g; **Protein** 3g

Roasted Fingerling Potatoes with Parsley, Lemon, and Garlic

Roasted Fingerling Potatoes with Mixed Herbs

SERVES 4 VEGAN

WHY THIS RECIPE WORKS When roasted whole, fingerling potatoes come out creamy and tender. We tossed scrubbed potatoes with oil and transferred them to a metal baking pan. Covered with foil to start, the potatoes steamed without drying out in the hot oven. Finishing them uncovered and shaking the pan allowed for even browning. Tossing the hot potatoes with flavorings after cooking allowed the herbs to retain their fresh, vibrant appearance and flavor; they also clung nicely and became fragrant on contact with the hot potatoes. Fingerlings vary in size; to ensure that they are all cooked through, check the doneness of the largest potato. If using a glass or ceramic baking dish, increase the roasting time in step 1 by 5 minutes. This recipe can be doubled; roast the potatoes in two 13 by 9-inch baking pans on the same oven rack.

2 pounds fingerling potatoes, unpeeled

3 tablespoons vegetable oil

2 teaspoons chopped fresh thyme

2 teaspoons chopped fresh sage

½ teaspoon table salt

1. Adjust oven rack to middle position and heat oven to 450 degrees. In 13 by 9-inch baking pan, toss potatoes with oil until evenly coated. Arrange potatoes in even layer. Cover pan tightly with aluminum foil. Transfer pan to oven and roast 15 minutes.

2. Carefully remove foil (steam will escape). Shake pan and continue to roast, uncovered, until potatoes are spotty brown and tender, and largest potato can be pierced easily with tip of paring knife, about 20 minutes, shaking pan halfway through roasting.

3. While potatoes roast, chop thyme, sage, and salt until finely minced and well combined. Transfer potatoes and oil to bowl and toss with herb mixture until evenly coated. Transfer potatoes to platter. Let cool for 5 minutes before serving.

PER SERVING Cal 270; **Total Fat** 11g, **Sat Fat** 1g; **Chol** 0mg; **Sodium** 300mg; **Total Carb** 40g, **Dietary Fiber** 5g, **Total Sugars** 1g; **Protein** 4g

Roasted Fingerling Potatoes with Parsley, Lemon, and Garlic

Substitute 2 tablespoons chopped fresh parsley, 2 teaspoons grated lemon zest, and 1 minced garlic clove for thyme and sage. Finely mince ingredients with salt as directed in step 3 and toss with cooked potatoes.

Roasted Fingerling Potatoes with Pecorino and Black Pepper

Omit thyme and sage. Once cooked potatoes have been transferred to bowl in step 2, toss with salt, 2 teaspoons pepper, and 2 tablespoons grated Pecorino Romano cheese. Sprinkle potatoes with another 2 tablespoons grated Pecorino Romano before serving.

Salt-Crusted Fingerling Potatoes

SERVES 4 TO 6   VEGAN

WHY THIS RECIPE WORKS We started developing this recipe with a nontraditional ingredient: seawater. In our research, we found a number of recipes that called for it, so we wanted to try cooking our potatoes in a saline solution to see if we could develop a salty crust and an interesting minerally flavor. The potatoes we tested were creamy and tender and had a unique briny flavor profile. But this was just not practical. To mimic the effect, we boiled fingerling potatoes in a skillet with 1 teaspoon of salt and enough water to almost cover them. Covering the skillet for the first 15 minutes of cooking ensured that the potatoes cooked through and were fluffy and tender. Removing the lid for the second half of cooking allowed the water to evaporate, giving the potatoes a crackly, salty sheen.

- 4 cups water
- 1 teaspoon table salt
- 2 pounds fingerling potatoes, unpeeled
- 2 sprigs fresh rosemary

1. Whisk water and salt in 12-inch skillet until salt is dissolved, about 15 seconds. Add potatoes and rosemary sprigs (potatoes may not be fully submerged) and bring to simmer over medium-high heat. Reduce heat to medium-low, cover, and cook until potatoes are nearly tender, about 15 minutes.

2. Uncover and increase heat to medium-high. Simmer vigorously until all water has evaporated and potatoes are fully tender, 15 to 20 minutes. Discard rosemary sprigs. Serve.

PER SERVING Cal 120; **Total Fat** 0g, **Sat Fat** 0g; **Chol** 0mg; **Sodium** 400mg; **Total Carb** 27g, **Dietary Fiber** 4g, **Total Sugars** 1g; **Protein** 3g

Best Baked Potatoes with Herbed Goat Cheese Topping

Best Baked Potatoes

SERVES 4   VEGAN

WHY THIS RECIPE WORKS Baked potatoes are one of those dishes most home cooks think they don't need a recipe for, but following our precise roasting technique guarantees a perfect potato—with a fluffy interior, deliciously crispy skin, and even seasoning. Our testing pointed us to an ideal doneness temperature: 205 degrees. Baking russet potatoes elevated on a wire rack prevented a leathery ring from forming beneath the peel, and using an instant-read thermometer ensured we hit the 205-degree sweet spot every time. Coating the potatoes in salty water before baking seasoned the skin; brushing on vegetable oil once the potatoes were cooked through and then baking the potatoes for an additional 10 minutes promised the crispiest exterior possible. Open up the potatoes immediately after removal from the oven in step 3 so steam can escape. Top the potatoes as desired, with one of our variations, or with a quick creamy sauce (page 82).

- 2 tablespoons table salt, for brining
- 4 small russet potatoes (8 ounces each), unpeeled, each lightly pricked with fork in 6 places
- 1 tablespoon vegetable oil

1. Adjust oven rack to middle position and heat oven to 450 degrees. Dissolve salt in ½ cup water in large bowl. Place potatoes in bowl and toss so exteriors of potatoes are evenly moistened. Transfer potatoes to wire rack set in rimmed baking sheet and bake until center of largest potato registers 205 degrees, 45 minutes to 1 hour.

2. Remove potatoes from oven and brush tops and sides with oil. Return potatoes to oven and bake for 10 minutes.

3. Remove potatoes from oven and, using paring knife, make 2 slits, forming X, in each potato. Using clean dish towel, hold ends and squeeze slightly to push flesh up and out. Season with salt and pepper to taste. Serve immediately.

PER SERVING Cal 210; **Total Fat** 3.5g, **Sat Fat** 0g; **Chol** 0mg; **Sodium** 10mg; **Total Carb** 41g, **Dietary Fiber** 3g, **Total Sugars** 1g; **Protein** 5g

VARIATIONS
Best Baked Potatoes with Herbed Goat Cheese Topping
Mash 4 ounces softened goat cheese with fork. Stir in 2 tablespoons extra-virgin olive oil, 2 tablespoons minced fresh parsley, 1 tablespoon minced shallot, and ½ teaspoon lemon zest. Season with salt and pepper to taste, and dollop on potatoes before serving.

Best Baked Potatoes with Creamy Egg Topping
Stir 3 chopped hard-cooked eggs, ¼ cup sour cream, 1½ tablespoons minced cornichons, 1 tablespoon minced fresh parsley, 1 tablespoon Dijon mustard, 1 tablespoon minced capers, and 1 tablespoon minced shallot together in bowl. Season with salt and pepper to taste, and dollop over potatoes before serving.

Twice-Baked Potatoes with Bacon, Cheddar, and Scallions
SERVES 8

WHY THIS RECIPE WORKS Twice-baked potatoes—essentially baked potatoes whose flesh has been removed, mashed with dairy and seasonings, mounded back into the shells, and baked again— offer a variety of textures and flavors in a single bite. Done well, the skin is chewy and substantial without being tough, with just a hint of crispiness to play off the smooth, creamy filling. In the course of developing our perfect rendition, tasters preferred a filling made with combination of sharp cheddar and sour cream enriched with butter, sautéed onion, and a sprinkling of crispy bacon. A final sprinkling of scallions added contrast. Be sure to leave a layer of potato inside the potato skins; it helps them retain their shape when stuffed and baked.

4 small russet potatoes (8 ounces each), unpeeled, rubbed lightly with vegetable oil, each lightly pricked with fork in 6 places
4 slices bacon, chopped fine
1 onion, chopped fine
6 ounces sharp cheddar cheese, shredded (1½ cups), divided
1 cup sour cream
4 tablespoons unsalted butter, softened
2 scallions, sliced thin

1. Adjust oven rack to upper-middle position and heat oven to 400 degrees. Place potatoes directly on hot oven rack and bake until skins are crisp and deep brown and paring knife easily pierces flesh, about 1 hour, flipping potatoes halfway through baking. Transfer potatoes to wire rack and let cool slightly, about 10 minutes. Increase oven temperature to 500 degrees.

2. Meanwhile, cook bacon in 10-inch nonstick skillet over medium heat until crispy, 5 to 7 minutes. Using slotted spoon, transfer bacon to paper towel–lined plate. Add onion to fat left in skillet and cook over medium heat until softened and lightly browned, 5 to 7 minutes; set aside. Line rimmed baking sheet with aluminum foil and set wire rack in sheet.

3. Using oven mitt to handle hot potato, cut each potato in half lengthwise. Using soupspoon, scoop flesh from each half into medium bowl, leaving ¼- to ½-inch thickness of flesh in each shell. Transfer potato shells to prepared rack.

4. Mash potato flesh with fork until smooth. Stir in 1 cup cheddar, sour cream, butter, and sautéed onion, and season with salt and pepper to taste. Spoon mixture into potato shells, mounding at center. Sprinkle with remaining ½ cup cheddar and crisp bacon.

5. Bake until shells are crisp and filling is heated through, 10 to 15 minutes. Sprinkle with scallions and serve.

PER SERVING Cal 340; **Total Fat** 23g, **Sat Fat** 12g; **Chol** 60mg; **Sodium** 240mg; **Total Carb** 24g, **Dietary Fiber** 2g, **Total Sugars** 2g; **Protein** 10g

VARIATIONS
Twice-Baked Potatoes with Bacon, Blue Cheese, and Caramelized Onions
For more caramelized onion flavor, add an extra onion.
Substitute ½ cup crumbled blue cheese for cheddar. Add 1 tablespoon brown sugar to onion in step 2; cook until onion is very soft and deeply browned, about 20 minutes.

Southwestern Twice-Baked Potatoes
Substitute 1½ cups shredded pepper Jack cheese for cheddar. Add 3 minced garlic cloves to onion during final minute of cooking in step 2. Add 1 teaspoon minced canned chipotle chile in adobo sauce to mashed potato mixture in step 4.

Super-Stuffed Baked Potatoes

Super-Stuffed Baked Potatoes
SERVES 6

WHY THIS RECIPE WORKS These stuffed baked potatoes feature fluffy potato, garlic, herbs, and creamy cheese in crisp potato skin shells. Precooking the potatoes in the microwave cut down cooking time. And while most stuffed baked potato recipes call for cutting the potato in half, we lopped off just the top quarter of the potato. Prepared this way, the potato shells held more filling. But after we hollowed out the potatoes, there wasn't enough stuffing to fully fill each one, so we cooked an extra potato and used its flesh to top off the others. This recipe calls for seven potatoes but makes six servings; the remaining potato is used for its flesh.

- 7 large russet potatoes, unpeeled, each lightly pricked with fork in 6 places
- 3 tablespoons unsalted butter, melted, plus 3 tablespoons unsalted butter
- ¾ teaspoon table salt, divided
- 1 (5.2-ounce) package Boursin cheese, crumbled, divided
- ½ cup half-and-half
- 2 garlic cloves, minced
- ¼ cup chopped fresh chives, divided
- 1 teaspoon pepper

1. Adjust oven rack to middle position and heat oven to 475 degrees. Set wire rack in rimmed baking sheet. Place potatoes on paper towel and microwave until tender, 20 to 25 minutes, turning potatoes over after 10 minutes.

2. Slice and remove top quarter of each potato, let cool for 5 minutes, then scoop out flesh, leaving ¼-inch layer of potato on inside. Discard 1 potato shell. Brush remaining shells inside and out with 3 tablespoons melted butter and sprinkle interiors with ¼ teaspoon salt. Transfer potatoes, scooped side up, to prepared baking sheet and bake until skins begin to crisp, about 15 minutes.

3. Meanwhile, mix half of Boursin with half-and-half in bowl until blended. Cook remaining 3 tablespoons butter and garlic in saucepan over medium-low heat until garlic is straw-colored, 3 to 5 minutes. Stir in Boursin mixture until combined.

4. Set ricer or food mill over medium bowl and press or mill potatoes into bowl. Gently fold in warm Boursin mixture, 3 tablespoons chives, pepper, and remaining ½ teaspoon salt until well incorporated. Remove potato shells from oven and fill with potato-cheese mixture. Top with remaining crumbled Boursin and bake until tops of potatoes are golden brown, about 15 minutes. Sprinkle with remaining 1 tablespoon chives. Serve.

PER SERVING Cal 570; **Total Fat** 24g, **Sat Fat** 15g; **Chol** 60mg; **Sodium** 480mg; **Total Carb** 80g, **Dietary Fiber** 6g, **Total Sugars** 4g; **Protein** 12g

MAKING SUPER STUFFED POTATOES

1. Slice off top quarter of microwaved potato.

2. Use spoon to scoop out interior, leaving ¼-inch layer of potato in shell.

Crispy Baked Potato Fans

Crispy Baked Potato Fans
SERVES 4 MAKE-AHEAD

WHY THIS RECIPE WORKS Also known as Hasselback potatoes, baked potato fans are a stunning side dish consisting of whole potatoes with a fluffy interior, a crisp exterior, and a cheesy bread-crumb topping. To begin, we found that using russet potatoes were the best choice because of their starchy flesh and fluffy texture. Taking the time to rinse the potatoes of surface starch after they were sliced prevented them from sticking together, while trimming off the end of each potato gave the remaining slices room to fan out. To prevent overcooking the potatoes in a very hot oven, we precooked them in the microwave before baking. A topping of fresh bread crumbs, melted butter, two kinds of cheese, garlic powder, and paprika is the crowning touch. To ensure that the potatoes fan out evenly, look for uniformly shaped potatoes.

BREAD-CRUMB TOPPING
- 1 slice hearty white sandwich bread, torn into quarters
- 4 tablespoons unsalted butter, melted
- 2 ounces Monterey Jack cheese, shredded (½ cup)
- ¼ cup grated Parmesan cheese
- 1 teaspoon paprika
- ½ teaspoon garlic powder
- ¼ teaspoon table salt
- ¼ teaspoon pepper

POTATO FANS
- 4 russet potatoes, unpeeled
- 2 tablespoons extra-virgin olive oil

1. FOR THE BREAD-CRUMB TOPPING Adjust oven rack to middle position and heat oven to 200 degrees. Pulse bread in food processor until coarsely ground, about 5 pulses. Bake bread crumbs on rimmed baking sheet until dry, about 20 minutes. Let cool for 5 minutes, then combine crumbs, melted butter, Monterey Jack, Parmesan, paprika, garlic powder, salt, and pepper in large bowl. (Bread-crumb topping can be refrigerated in zipper-lock bag for 2 days.)

2. FOR THE POTATO FANS Heat oven to 450 degrees. Cut ¼ inch from bottom and ends of potatoes, then slice potatoes crosswise at ¼-inch intervals, leaving ¼ inch of potato intact. Gently rinse potatoes under running water, let drain, and transfer, sliced side down, to plate. Microwave until slightly soft to touch, 6 to 12 minutes, flipping potatoes halfway through microwaving.

3. Line rimmed baking sheet with aluminum foil. Arrange potatoes, sliced side up, on prepared baking sheet. Brush potatoes all over with oil and season with salt and pepper. Bake until skin is crisp and potatoes are beginning to brown, 25 to 30 minutes. Remove potatoes from oven and heat broiler.

4. Carefully top potatoes with stuffing mixture, pressing gently to adhere. Broil until bread crumbs are deep golden brown, about 3 minutes. Serve.

PER SERVING Cal 570; **Total Fat** 25g; **Sat Fat** 12g; **Chol** 50mg; **Sodium** 420mg; **Total Carb** 73g, **Dietary Fiber** 5g, **Total Sugars** 3g; **Protein** 15g

VARIATION
Blue Cheese and Bacon Baked Potato Fans
Cook 4 slices bacon in skillet over medium heat until crispy, 5 to 7 minutes; transfer to paper towel–lined plate. Let cool, then crumble. In step 1, substitute ⅓ cup crumbled blue cheese for Monterey Jack. Just before serving, sprinkle bacon over potatoes.

Lighthouse Inn Potatoes

Lighthouse Inn Potatoes

SERVES 8 TO 10 MAKE-AHEAD

WHY THIS RECIPE WORKS The recipe for Lighthouse Inn Potatoes came from an iconic inn on the Connecticut shore. Chunks of potatoes are baked in a rich cream sauce and topped with golden bread crumbs. The original recipe calls for day-old cooked potatoes, but we wanted to develop a version that didn't rely on leftovers. We cooked starchy russet potatoes in light cream and butter and added a bit of baking soda to neutralize the potatoes' acidic tannins (which can cause the sauce to curdle) and aid in creating a velvety, unbroken sauce. After topping the potato mixture with buttery, cheesy bread crumbs, we baked the dish until the potatoes were bubbling and the bread crumbs were golden brown. We prefer the texture of light cream for this recipe, but heavy cream will also work. Do not use half-and-half; it has a tendency to break. Grate the Parmesan on a rasp-style grater.

2 ounces Parmesan cheese, grated (1 cup)
1 cup panko bread crumbs
4 tablespoons unsalted butter, melted, plus
   6 tablespoons cut into 6 pieces, divided
2¼ teaspoons table salt, divided
2½ pounds russet potatoes, peeled and
   cut into 1-inch pieces
3 cups light cream, divided
⅛ teaspoon baking soda
1 teaspoon pepper

1. Adjust oven rack to middle position and heat oven to 375 degrees. Combine Parmesan, panko, melted butter, and ¼ teaspoon salt in bowl; set aside.

2. Bring potatoes, 2½ cups cream, baking soda, remaining 2 teaspoons salt, and pepper to boil in large saucepan over medium-high heat. Reduce heat to low and cook at bare simmer, stirring often, until paring knife slides easily into potatoes without them crumbling, 20 to 25 minutes.

3. Off heat, stir remaining ½ cup cream and remaining 6 tablespoons butter into potato mixture until butter has melted, about 1 minute. Transfer potato mixture to 13 by 9-inch baking dish. Sprinkle Parmesan-panko mixture over top. Bake, uncovered, until bubbling around edges and surface is golden brown, 15 to 20 minutes. Let cool for at least 15 minutes. Serve. (After potato mixture has been transferred to baking dish, let cool completely, cover with aluminum foil, and refrigerate for up to 24 hours. Before applying topping, bake, covered, until heated through, about 35 minutes. Apply topping and continue to bake, uncovered, 15 to 20 minutes.)

PER SERVING Cal 330; Total Fat 20g, Sat Fat 13g; Chol 60mg; Sodium 700mg; Total Carb 30g, Dietary Fiber 2g, Total Sugars 4g; Protein 8g

Mashed Sweet Potatoes

SERVES 4 MAKE-AHEAD

WHY THIS RECIPE WORKS Sweet potatoes have a deep, natural sweetness that doesn't require much assistance. So our mashed sweet potatoes include only a select few ingredients. Using a small amount of heavy cream, in combination with butter, stole the show. For seasonings, the baking spices often added to mashed sweet potatoes were simply distracting; we used just a little sugar, salt, and pepper. The silky puree has enough body to hold its shape while sitting on a fork, and it pushes this root vegetable's deep, earthy flavor to the forefront, where it should be.

2 pounds sweet potatoes, peeled, quartered lengthwise,
   and sliced crosswise ¼ inch thick
4 tablespoons unsalted butter, cut into 4 pieces
2 tablespoons heavy cream
1 teaspoon sugar
½ teaspoon table salt

1. Cook potatoes, butter, cream, sugar, and salt in large saucepan, covered, over low heat, stirring occasionally, until potatoes fall apart when poked with fork, 35 to 45 minutes.

2. Off heat, mash potatoes in saucepan with potato masher until smooth. Season with salt and pepper to taste, and serve. (Mashed sweet potatoes can be refrigerated for up to 2 days.)

PER SERVING Cal 280; **Total Fat** 14g, **Sat Fat** 9g; **Chol** 40mg; **Sodium** 400mg; **Total Carb** 35g, **Dietary Fiber** 6g, **Total Sugars** 12g; **Protein** 3g

VARIATIONS

Mashed Sweet Potatoes with Garlic and Coconut

Substitute ½ cup coconut milk for butter and cream, and add 1 small minced garlic clove and ¼ teaspoon red pepper flakes to pot with potatoes. Stir in 1 tablespoon minced fresh cilantro just before serving.

Indian-Spiced Mashed Sweet Potatoes with Raisins and Cashews

Substitute dark brown sugar for granulated sugar and add ¾ teaspoon garam masala to saucepan along with sweet potatoes in step 1. Stir ¼ cup golden raisins and ¼ cup roasted unsalted cashews, chopped, into mashed sweet potatoes just before serving.

TAKE IT UP A NOTCH

These quick, tangy sauces are good with roasted potatoes and go especially well with baked white and baked sweet potatoes.

Garlic and Chive Sour Cream
MAKES ABOUT ½ CUP

- ½ cup sour cream
- 1 tablespoon minced fresh chives
- 1 garlic clove, minced
- ⅛ teaspoon table salt

Combine all ingredients in small bowl. Refrigerate until ready to serve.

Garam Masala Yogurt
MAKES ABOUT ½ CUP

- ½ cup plain yogurt
- 2 teaspoons lemon juice
- ½ teaspoon garam masala
- ⅛ teaspoon table salt

Combine all ingredients in small bowl. Refrigerate until ready to serve.

Best Baked Sweet Potatoes with Garlic and Chive Sour Cream

Best Baked Sweet Potatoes
SERVES 4 VEGAN

WHY THIS RECIPE WORKS The goal when baking sweet potatoes is entirely different than when baking russets: creamy—rather than fluffy—flesh with deeply complex flavor. Sweet potatoes bake differently than russets due to their lower starch level and higher sugar content. We learned that to bake a whole sweet potato to the point where its exterior was nicely tanned and its interior was silky and sweetly caramelized, the potato needed to reach 200 degrees and stay there for an hour, long enough for the starches to gelatinize and the moisture to evaporate for concentrated flavor. To keep our recipe efficient, we microwaved the potatoes until they hit 200 degrees and then transferred them to a hot oven to linger. Putting them on a wire rack set in a foil-lined rimmed baking sheet allowed air to circulate around the potatoes and also caught any sugar that oozed from the potatoes as they roasted. A quick, flavored sour cream or yogurt topping provides a cool, creamy finishing touch.

4 small sweet potatoes (8 ounces each), unpeeled, each lightly pricked with fork in 3 places

1. Adjust oven rack to middle position and heat oven to 425 degrees. Place potatoes on large plate and microwave until potatoes yield to gentle pressure and register 200 degrees, 6 to 9 minutes, flipping potatoes every 3 minutes.

2. Set wire rack in aluminum foil–lined rimmed baking sheet and spray with vegetable oil spray. Transfer potatoes to prepared rack and bake for 1 hour (exteriors of potatoes will be lightly browned and potatoes will feel very soft when squeezed).

3. Slit each potato lengthwise. Using clean dish towel, hold ends and squeeze slightly to push flesh up and out. Season with salt and pepper to taste, and serve.

PER SERVING Cal 85; **Total Fat** 0g, **Sat Fat** 0g; **Chol** 0mg; **Sodium** 53mg; **Total Carb** 19g, **Dietary Fiber** 2g, **Total Sugars** 4g; **Protein** 1g

Roasted Sweet Potatoes

Roasted Sweet Potatoes
SERVES 6 TO 8   VEGAN

WHY THIS RECIPE WORKS Roasted sweet potatoes can turn out starchy and wan, but our method produces potatoes with a nicely caramelized exterior, a smooth, creamy interior, and an earthy sweetness. Cutting them into ¾-inch-thick rounds and laying them flat on a baking sheet ensured even cooking. A few experiments proved that a lower roasting temperature resulted in a sweeter potato, so we started the sliced potatoes in a cold (versus preheated) oven and covered them with aluminum foil; this allowed plenty of time for their starches to convert to sugars. We removed the foil after 30 minutes and continued to roast the potatoes until their bottom edges were golden brown. Choose potatoes that are as even in width as possible; trimming the small ends prevents them from burning. If you prefer not to peel the potatoes, just scrub them well before cutting.

3 pounds sweet potatoes, peeled, ends squared off, sliced into ¾-inch-thick rounds
2 tablespoons extra-virgin olive oil
1 teaspoon table salt
¼ teaspoon pepper

1. Line rimmed baking sheet with aluminum foil and spray with vegetable oil spray. Toss potatoes, oil, salt, and pepper together in bowl. Arrange potatoes in single layer on prepared sheet and cover tightly with aluminum foil.

2. Adjust oven rack to middle position and place potatoes in cold oven. Turn oven to 425 degrees and cook potatoes for 30 minutes.

3. Remove baking sheet from oven and discard foil. Return potatoes to oven and cook until bottom edges of potatoes are golden brown, 15 to 25 minutes.

4. Remove baking sheet from oven and, using thin metal spatula, flip slices over. Continue to roast until bottom edges of potatoes are golden brown, 18 to 22 minutes. Let potatoes cool for 5 to 10 minutes, then serve.

PER SERVING Cal 140; **Total Fat** 3.5g, **Sat Fat** 0g; **Chol** 0mg; **Sodium** 370mg; **Total Carb** 26g, **Dietary Fiber** 4g, **Total Sugars** 8g; **Protein** 2g

VARIATIONS
Roasted Sweet Potatoes with Maple-Thyme Glaze
Whisk ¼ cup maple syrup, 2 tablespoons melted unsalted butter, and 2 teaspoons minced fresh thyme together in bowl. Brush mixture over both sides of partially cooked potatoes when flipping in step 4, then continue to roast potatoes as directed.

Roasted Sweet Potatoes with Spiced Brown Sugar Glaze

Cook ¼ cup packed light brown sugar, 2 tablespoons apple juice, 2 tablespoons unsalted butter, ¼ teaspoon ground cinnamon, ¼ teaspoon ground ginger, and ⅛ teaspoon ground nutmeg in small saucepan over medium heat until butter has melted and sugar is dissolved, 2 to 4 minutes. Brush mixture over both sides of partially cooked potatoes when flipping in step 4, then continue to roast potatoes as directed.

ROASTING SWEET POTATOES

1. Rinse peeled sweet potatoes and cut into ¾-inch-thick rounds.

2. Cover baking sheet tightly with foil and place in cold oven. Turn oven to 425 degrees and cook potatoes for 30 minutes.

3. Remove top layer of foil and return potatoes to oven to continue roasting until bottom edges are golden brown, 15 to 25 minutes.

4. Flip slices over with spatula and continue to roast until bottom edges are golden brown, 18 to 22 minutes. Let cool before serving.

Roasted Sweet Potato Wedges

Roasted Sweet Potato Wedges
SERVES 4 TO 6   **VEGAN**

WHY THIS RECIPE WORKS Roasted sweet potato wedges are as satisfying as sweet potato fries but without all the grease. Sweet potatoes release a sweet syrup-like liquid as they cook, turning the wedges mushy. The key, we learned, was to cut the sweet potatoes into wide, obtuse wedges so they would hold their shape while roasting. Cut thinner, the wedges burned before their interiors had the chance to cook through. As for seasoning, sweet potatoes have plenty of flavor on their own, so we initially limited the seasoning to salt and pepper, tossing them with some olive oil to encourage browning. (We came up with some spicy and sweet variations later.) Arranging the wedges skin side down on a baking sheet encouraged the skins to brown while keeping the interiors pleasantly soft and tender—no turning needed. After about 30 minutes in a hot oven, the wedges were perfectly creamy and sweet, with plenty of crunch. We prefer to use small potatoes, about 8 ounces each, because it ensures that the wedges fit more uniformly on the baking sheet; they should be of similar size so they cook at the same rate. Be sure to scrub and dry the whole potatoes thoroughly before cutting them into wedges and tossing them with the oil and spices.

2 pounds small sweet potatoes (8 ounces each),
   unpeeled, cut lengthwise into 1½-inch wedges

2 tablespoons extra-virgin olive oil

½ teaspoon table salt

½ teaspoon pepper

1. Adjust oven rack to middle position and heat oven to 450 degrees. Line rimmed baking sheet with parchment paper. Toss potatoes, oil, salt, and pepper together in bowl.

2. Arrange potatoes, skin side down, in single layer on prepared sheet. Roast until lightly browned and tender, about 30 minutes, rotating sheet halfway through roasting. Serve.

PER SERVING Cal 160; **Total Fat** 4.5g, **Sat Fat** 0.5g; **Chol** 0mg; **Sodium** 280mg; **Total Carb** 27g, **Dietary Fiber** 5g, **Total Sugars** 8g; **Protein** 2g

VARIATIONS

Cumin and Chili Roasted Sweet Potato Wedges
Add 2 teaspoons ground cumin, 2 teaspoons chili powder, and 1 teaspoon garlic powder to potato mixture in step 1.

Curry Roasted Sweet Potato Wedges
Add 4 teaspoons curry powder to potato mixture in step 1.

Cinnamon-Sugar Roasted Sweet Potato Wedges
Omit pepper. Add 2 teaspoons ground cinnamon, 2 teaspoons sugar, and pinch ground nutmeg to potato mixture in step 1.

Roasted Spiralized Sweet Potatoes with Walnuts and Feta
SERVES 4 TO 6   `FAST`

WHY THIS RECIPE WORKS Spiralized sweet potatoes make a beautiful yet simple side dish. We used a spiralizer to cut the potatoes into ⅛-inch-thick noodles that would cook quickly. We found that simply roasting the potatoes in a hot oven, uncovered, for about 12 minutes gave us the result we were after: sweet potatoes that were tender but not mushy, with just a bit of caramelization. To finish the dish, we sprinkled on ¼ cup each of tangy feta and rich toasted walnuts, plus a generous sprinkle of fresh parsley. Sweet potato noodles are quite delicate; be careful when tossing them with the oil and seasonings in step 2, and again when transferring them to the serving platter before serving. If you do not have a spiralizer, you can use a mandoline or V-slicer fitted with a ⅛-inch julienne attachment. Make sure to position the vegetables on the mandoline so that the resulting noodles are as long as possible. We do not recommend cutting vegetable noodles by hand.

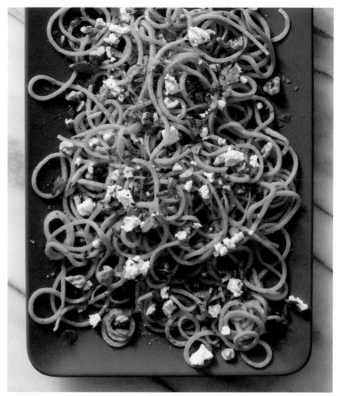

Roasted Spiralized Sweet Potatoes with Walnuts and Feta

2 pounds sweet potatoes, peeled and ends squared off

1 tablespoon extra-virgin olive oil, plus extra for serving

¼ teaspoon table salt

⅛ teaspoon pepper

¼ cup walnuts, toasted and chopped

1 ounce feta cheese, crumbled (¼ cup)

2 tablespoons chopped fresh parsley

1. Adjust oven rack to middle position and heat oven to 450 degrees. Using spiralizer, cut sweet potatoes into ⅛-inch-thick noodles, then cut noodles into 12-inch lengths.

2. Toss potato noodles, oil, salt, and pepper together in bowl, then spread on rimmed baking sheet. Roast until just tender, 12 to 14 minutes, stirring once halfway through roasting.

3. Season potatoes with salt and pepper to taste, and transfer to serving platter. Sprinkle walnuts, feta, and parsley over top, then drizzle with extra oil to taste. Serve.

PER SERVING Cal 160; **Total Fat** 6g, **Sat Fat** 1.5g; **Chol** 5mg; **Sodium** 210mg; **Total Carb** 24g, **Dietary Fiber** 4g, **Total Sugars** 7g; **Protein** 3g

UP YOUR VEGETABLE GAME

■ FAST (30 minutes or less total time)　　■ VEGAN
Photos: Garlicky Broccolini; Pan-Roasted Cabbage

Braised Artichokes with Tomatoes and Thyme
SERVES 4

WHY THIS RECIPE WORKS Gently braising fresh artichokes and creating a flavorful sauce at the same time creates an everyday side dish that keeps the focus on the flavor of these vegetable gems. A braising liquid of white wine and chicken broth imparted acidity and depth of flavor. Subtle thyme complemented the artichokes' delicate flavor, and anchovies amplified the savory qualities of the dish. Canned tomatoes are common in braises, but tasters detected an unpleasant metallic note; replacing them with halved cherry tomatoes at the end of cooking preserved the brightness of the sauce and added welcome splashes of color. If your artichokes are larger than 8 to 10 ounces, strip away another layer or two of the toughest outer leaves.

1 lemon, halved
4 artichokes (8 to 10 ounces each)
2 tablespoons extra-virgin olive oil
1 onion, chopped fine
¾ teaspoon table salt
¼ teaspoon pepper
3 garlic cloves, minced
2 anchovy fillets, rinsed, patted dry, and minced
1 teaspoon minced fresh thyme or ¼ teaspoon dried
½ cup dry white wine
1 cup chicken broth
6 ounces cherry tomatoes, halved
2 tablespoons chopped fresh parsley

1. Squeeze lemon halves into container filled with 2 quarts water, then add spent halves. Working with 1 artichoke at a time, trim stem to about ¾ inch and cut off top quarter of artichoke. Break off bottom 3 or 4 rows of tough outer leaves by pulling them downward. Using kitchen shears, trim off top portion of outer leaves. Using paring knife, trim stem and base, removing any dark green parts. Cut artichoke in half lengthwise, then remove fuzzy choke and any tiny inner purple-tinged leaves using small spoon. Cut each half into 1-inch-thick wedges and submerge wedges in lemon water.

2. Heat oil in 12-inch skillet over medium heat until shimmering. Add onion, salt, and pepper and cook until softened and lightly browned, 5 to 7 minutes. Stir in garlic, anchovies, and thyme and cook until fragrant, about 30 seconds. Stir in wine and cook until almost evaporated, about 1 minute. Stir in broth and bring to simmer.

3. Remove artichokes from lemon water, shaking off excess water, and add to skillet. Cover, reduce heat to medium-low, and simmer until artichokes are tender, 20 to 25 minutes.

Braised Artichokes with Tomatoes and Thyme

4. Stir in tomatoes, bring to simmer, and cook until tomatoes start to break down, 3 to 5 minutes. Off heat, stir in parsley and season with salt and pepper to taste. Serve.

PER SERVING Cal 150; **Total Fat** 8g, **Sat Fat** 1g; **Chol** 0mg; **Sodium** 720mg; **Total Carb** 14g, **Dietary Fiber** 5g, **Total Sugars** 4g; **Protein** 4g

Roman-Style Stuffed Braised Artichokes
SERVES 4 **VEGAN**

WHY THIS RECIPE WORKS Stuffed artichokes are a traditional Italian side dish. We achieved a bright, robust stuffing with a blend of minced fresh parsley and mint, garlic, lemon zest, and fresh bread crumbs moistened with extra-virgin olive oil. The stuffing infused the artichokes with flavor as they braised. Cooking the artichokes took little more than half an hour in a large Dutch oven filled with just enough water to cover the stems three-quarters of the way. (Any more liquid made for sodden stems and a gummy filling.) To prevent the uncooked filling from spilling out, we placed each artichoke stem end down into a thickly cut onion ring. For even cooking, we then rotated the artichokes at the midway point so that the stem ends were facing up. Serve each artichoke with a spoon so that diners can coax out the stuffing. If your artichokes are larger than 8 to 10 ounces, strip away another layer or two of the toughest outer leaves.

 1 slice hearty white sandwich bread, crust removed, cut into ½-inch pieces
 1 lemon, halved
 4 artichokes (8 to 10 ounces each)
 ½ cup extra-virgin olive oil
 ¼ cup minced fresh parsley, stems reserved
 ½ cup minced fresh mint
 4 garlic cloves, minced
 ¾ teaspoon table salt, divided
 1 onion, cut crosswise into ½-inch-thick slices and separated into rings

1. Pulse bread in food processor to fine crumbs, about 10 pulses; transfer to medium bowl. Grate 1 tablespoon zest from lemon and add to bowl; set aside. Squeeze lemon halves into container filled with 2 quarts water, then add spent halves.

2. Working with 1 artichoke at a time, trim stem to about ¾ inch and cut off top quarter of artichoke. Break off bottom 3 or 4 rows of tough outer leaves by pulling them downward. Using kitchen shears, trim off top portion of outer leaves. Using paring knife, trim stem and base, removing any dark green parts. Spread leaves to reveal fuzzy choke at center. Using spoon, remove fuzzy choke. Rinse artichokes well, then submerge prepped artichokes in lemon water.

3. Add oil, parsley leaves, mint, garlic, and ½ teaspoon salt to bowl with bread crumbs and stir until well combined; season with pepper to taste. Using small spoon, divide filling evenly among artichokes, placing it in center of artichoke, where choke was.

4. Spread onion rings evenly over bottom of Dutch oven. Sprinkle reserved parsley stems and remaining ¼ teaspoon salt over onion rings. Set artichokes stem ends down into onion rings. Fill pot with enough cold water so that stems are three-quarters submerged.

5. Cover and bring to boil over medium-high heat. Reduce heat to medium-low and simmer for 15 minutes. Using tongs, rotate artichokes so stem ends face up, using tongs to keep filling in place. Cover and cook until tip of paring knife is easily inserted into artichoke heart, about 15 minutes. Serve.

PER SERVING Cal 300; **Total Fat** 28g, **Sat Fat** 4g; **Chol** 0mg; **Sodium** 490mg; **Total Carb** 9g, **Dietary Fiber** 2g, **Total Sugars** 1g; **Protein** 2g

Parmesan-Crusted Asparagus

Parmesan-Crusted Asparagus
SERVES 4 TO 6

WHY THIS RECIPE WORKS A cheesy, crisp coating makes asparagus irresistible. To make the coating stay put we had to first salt the spears to rid them of excess moisture. Then we whipped a combination of honey and egg whites to soft peaks, tossed the asparagus spears in the mixture, and pressed them with a bread crumb–grated Parmesan combo. For the best cheese flavor, we sprinkled more cheese on the spears at the end of roasting. Look for asparagus spears between ½ and ¾ inch in diameter. Work quickly when tossing the asparagus with the egg whites, as the salt on the asparagus will rapidly begin to deflate the whites.

 2 pounds thick asparagus, trimmed
 ¾ teaspoon table salt, divided
 3 ounces Parmesan cheese, grated (1½ cups), divided
 ¾ cup panko bread crumbs
 1 tablespoon unsalted butter, melted and cooled
 ⅛ teaspoon pepper
   Pinch cayenne pepper
 2 large egg whites
 1 teaspoon honey

1. Adjust oven rack to middle position and heat oven to 450 degrees. Line rimmed baking sheet with aluminum foil and spray with vegetable oil spray. Using fork, poke holes up and down asparagus spears. Toss asparagus with ½ teaspoon salt and let sit for 30 minutes on paper towel–lined baking sheet.

2. Meanwhile, combine 1 cup Parmesan, panko, melted butter, pepper, cayenne, and remaining ¼ teaspoon salt in bowl. Transfer half of panko mixture to shallow dish; set aside remaining panko mixture. Using stand mixer fitted with whisk attachment, whip egg whites and honey on medium-low speed until foamy, about 1 minute. Increase speed to medium-high and whip until soft peaks form, 2 to 3 minutes. Scrape into 13 by 9-inch baking dish and toss asparagus in mixture. Working with 1 spear at a time, dredge half of asparagus in panko and transfer to prepared sheet. Refill shallow dish with remaining panko mixture and repeat with remaining half of asparagus.

3. Bake asparagus until just beginning to brown, 6 to 8 minutes. Sprinkle with remaining ½ cup Parmesan and continue to bake until cheese is melted, panko is golden brown, and tip of paring knife inserted at base of largest spear meets little resistance, 6 to 8 minutes. Serve.

PER SERVING Cal 140; **Total Fat** 6g, **Sat Fat** 3g; **Chol** 15mg; **Sodium** 580mg; **Total Carb** 13g, **Dietary Fiber** 2g, **Total Sugars** 3g; **Protein** 11g

Stir-Fried Asparagus with Shiitake Mushrooms

Stir-Fried Asparagus with Shiitake Mushrooms
SERVES 4 FAST VEGAN

WHY THIS RECIPE WORKS Asparagus, like many vegetables, is a natural candidate for stir-frying because it cooks in a flash. The intense heat beautifully caramelizes it, while the short cooking time ensures that it emerges crisp-tender. Starting with a hot skillet and then stirring the asparagus only occasionally during cooking allowed the asparagus to char before it overcooked and brought out a natural sweetness that paired perfectly with a potent Asian-inspired sauce. Thinly sliced shiitake mushrooms complemented the fresh-flavored asparagus and added some heft to this side dish. To ensure that the asparagus and mushrooms cooked evenly, we added a bit of water, which created a small amount of steam that cooked the vegetables through before evaporating and leaving behind a flavorful, clingy glaze. Look for asparagus spears no thicker than ½ inch.

2 tablespoons water
1 tablespoon soy sauce
1 tablespoon dry sherry
2 teaspoons packed brown sugar
2 teaspoons grated fresh ginger
1 teaspoon toasted sesame oil
1 tablespoon vegetable oil
1 pound thin asparagus, trimmed and cut on bias into 2-inch lengths
4 ounces shiitake mushrooms, stemmed and sliced thin
2 scallions, green parts only, sliced thin on bias

1. Combine water, soy sauce, sherry, sugar, ginger, and sesame oil in bowl.

2. Heat vegetable oil in 12-inch nonstick skillet over high heat until smoking. Add asparagus and mushrooms and cook, stirring occasionally, until asparagus is spotty brown, 3 to 4 minutes. Add soy sauce mixture and cook, stirring twice, until asparagus is crisp-tender, 1 to 2 minutes. Transfer to platter, sprinkle with scallion greens, and serve.

PER SERVING Cal 80; **Total Fat** 4.5g, **Sat Fat** 0g; **Chol** 0mg; **Sodium** 230mg; **Total Carb** 7g, **Dietary Fiber** 2g, **Total Sugars** 5g; **Protein** 3g

Stir-Fried Asparagus with Red Bell Pepper

Omit soy sauce, sherry, brown sugar, ginger, and sesame oil. Reduce water to 1 tablespoon. Whisk 1 tablespoon orange juice, 1 tablespoon rice vinegar, 1 tablespoon granulated sugar, 1 teaspoon ketchup, and ½ teaspoon table salt into water. Substitute 1 stemmed and seeded red bell pepper cut into 2-inch-long matchsticks for shiitakes.

Braised Asparagus, Peas, and Radishes with Tarragon
SERVES 4 TO 6 FAST VEGAN

WHY THIS RECIPE WORKS Braising asparagus is an unexpected but delightful way to capitalize on its tender springtime freshness. To turn early-season asparagus into a side dish, we started by softening minced shallot in olive oil with additional aromatics. To build a flavorful braising liquid, we poured in water and lemon and orange zest and dropped in a bay leaf. Adding the vegetables in stages ensured that each cooked at its own rate and maintained a crisp texture. Peppery radishes, which turned soft and sweet with cooking, nicely complemented the greener notes of asparagus and peas (frozen peas were reliably sweet, and adding them off the heat prevented overcooking). In no time at all, we had a simple, warm dish of radiant vegetables in an invigorating, complex broth, proof positive that braising can bring out the best in even the most delicate flavors. Chopped tarragon added a final note of freshness. Look for asparagus spears no thicker than ½ inch.

¼ cup extra-virgin olive oil
1 shallot, sliced into thin rounds
2 garlic cloves, sliced thin
3 fresh thyme sprigs
Pinch red pepper flakes
10 radishes, trimmed and quartered
1¼ cups water
2 teaspoons grated lemon zest
2 teaspoons grated orange zest
1 bay leaf
1 teaspoon table salt
1 pound thin asparagus, trimmed and cut into 2-inch lengths
2 cups frozen peas
4 teaspoons chopped fresh tarragon

1. Cook oil, shallot, garlic, thyme sprigs, and pepper flakes in Dutch oven over medium heat until shallot is just softened, about 2 minutes. Stir in radishes, water, lemon zest, orange zest, bay leaf, and salt and bring to simmer. Reduce heat to medium-low, cover, and cook until radishes can be easily pierced with tip of paring knife, 3 to 5 minutes. Stir in asparagus, cover, and cook until tender, 3 to 5 minutes.

2. Off heat, stir in peas, cover, and let sit until heated through, about 5 minutes. Discard thyme sprigs and bay leaf. Stir in tarragon and season with salt and pepper to taste. Serve.

PER SERVING Cal 140; **Total Fat** 9g, **Sat Fat** 1.5g; **Chol** 0mg; **Sodium** 400mg; **Total Carb** 11g, **Dietary Fiber** 4g, **Total Sugars** 4g; **Protein** 4g

Braised Beets with Lemon and Almonds
SERVES 4 TO 6 VEGAN

WHY THIS RECIPE WORKS Braising beets on the stovetop maximized their sweet, earthy flavor—with minimal mess. We partially submerged the beets in just 1¼ cups of water so that they partially simmered and partially steamed. Halving the beets cut down our cooking time even further. In just 45 minutes, the beets were tender and their skins slipped off easily. We reduced the braising liquid and added brown sugar and vinegar to make a glossy glaze. Shallot, toasted almonds, fresh mint and thyme, and a little lemon zest finished the dish. Look for beets that are 2 to 3 inches in diameter. You can use an 11-inch straight-sided sauté pan in place of the Dutch oven in this recipe. The beets can be served warm or at room temperature. If serving at room temperature, add the nuts (or seeds, if making the variation with lime and pepitas) and fresh herbs right before serving.

1½ pounds beets, trimmed and halved horizontally
1¼ cups water
¾ teaspoon table salt, divided
3 tablespoons distilled white vinegar
1 tablespoon packed light brown sugar
1 shallot, sliced thin
1 teaspoon grated lemon zest
¼ teaspoon pepper
½ cup whole almonds, toasted and chopped
2 tablespoons chopped fresh mint
1 teaspoon chopped fresh thyme

1. Place beets, cut side down, in single layer in Dutch oven. Add water and ¼ teaspoon salt and bring to simmer over high heat. Reduce heat to low, cover, and simmer until beets are tender and can be easily pierced with paring knife, 45 to 50 minutes.

2. Transfer beets to cutting board to cool slightly. Meanwhile, increase heat to medium-high and reduce cooking liquid, stirring occasionally, until pan is almost dry, 5 to 6 minutes. Add vinegar and sugar, return to boil, and cook, stirring constantly with heat-resistant spatula, until spatula leaves wide trail when dragged through glaze, 1 to 2 minutes. Remove pan from heat.

3. Once beets are cool enough to handle, rub off skins with paper towels and cut into ½-inch wedges. Add beets, shallot, lemon zest, remaining ½ teaspoon salt, and pepper to glaze and toss to coat. Transfer to platter; sprinkle with almonds, mint, and thyme; and serve.

PER SERVING Cal 120; **Total Fat** 6g, **Sat Fat** 0.5g; **Chol** 0mg; **Sodium** 360mg; **Total Carb** 13g, **Dietary Fiber** 4g, **Total Sugars** 8g; **Protein** 4g

VARIATIONS
Braised Beets with Lime and Pepitas
Omit thyme. Substitute lime zest for lemon zest, toasted pepitas for almonds, and cilantro for mint.

Braised Beets with Orange and Walnuts
Substitute orange zest for lemon zest, walnuts for almonds, and parsley for mint.

Braised Beets with Ginger and Cashews
Substitute 4 scallions, white parts sliced thin, for shallot and green parts sliced thin on bias for mint and thyme, 1 teaspoon grated fresh ginger for lemon zest, and cashews for almonds.

Sautéed Beet Greens with Raisins and Almonds
SERVES 2 OR 3 `FAST` `VEGAN`

WHY THIS RECIPE WORKS If you find beet greens attached to the beets at your market, bring them home with you—they are mild and delicious. Among blanching, steaming, microwaving, and wilting, we found the simplest, most straightforward recipe for these tender greens to be wilting on the stovetop. We simply tossed the leaves, still wet from washing, into a heated pot, covered it, and cooked them, stirring occasionally, until the greens wilted via the steam from their own liquid. We then found that we got even better results when combining this technique with sautéing—we heated oil in a Dutch oven, added the wet greens, covered and steamed them until wilted, and then uncovered the pan and cooked on high until all the liquid evaporated. Sweet golden raisins and crunchy almonds gave the greens Mediterranean flavors. For the variation, onion, fresh ginger and jalapeño, and curry, along with a touch of cream, moved the greens east to India.

Sautéed Beet Greens with Raisins and Almonds

2 pounds beet greens, stemmed and chopped
3 tablespoons extra-virgin olive oil
2 garlic cloves, minced
¼ teaspoon red pepper flakes
¼ cup golden raisins, chopped
½ teaspoon grated lemon zest
3 tablespoons slivered almonds, toasted

1. Wash and drain beet greens, leaving greens slightly wet. Heat oil in Dutch oven over medium-high heat until shimmering. Add garlic and pepper flakes and cook until golden, about 30 seconds. Add raisins and wet greens. Cover and cook, stirring occasionally, until greens are wilted but still bright green, about 3 minutes.

2. Stir in lemon zest. Increase heat to high and cook, uncovered, until liquid evaporates, 2 to 3 minutes. Stir in almonds and season with salt and pepper to taste. Serve.

PER SERVING Cal 250; **Total Fat** 18g, **Sat Fat** 2.5g; **Chol** 0mg; **Sodium** 390mg; **Total Carb** 20g, **Dietary Fiber** 7g, **Total Sugars** 11g; **Protein** 6g

Sautéed Beet Greens with Indian Spices

Omit oil, pepper flakes, raisins, lemon zest, and almonds. Before cooking greens in step 1, heat 2 teaspoons vegetable oil in Dutch oven over medium-high heat until shimmering. Add 1 small onion, chopped fine, and cook until softened, about 5 minutes. Add garlic; 1 teaspoon minced fresh ginger; ½ jalapeño chile, seeded and minced; 2 teaspoons curry powder; and ½ teaspoon ground cumin and cook until fragrant, about 1 minute. After evaporating liquid in pan in step 2, add ¼ cup heavy cream and 2 teaspoons packed brown sugar and cook until cream thickens, about 2 minutes. Serve.

Sautéed Baby Bok Choy with Miso Sauce

SERVES 4 **FAST** **VEGAN**

WHY THIS RECIPE WORKS Bok choy is a mild-flavored type of Chinese cabbage with crisp stalks and dark green leaves like spinach. Part of the allure of baby bok choy is showing off its small size but left whole, it's difficult to clean. Cutting the bok choy in half lengthwise gave us better access to the dirt and also helped the stalks become perfectly tender-crisp before the leaves went limp. We spun the bok choy dry after washing to avoid adding too much water to the skillet. A stint of steaming gave the stalks the head start they needed to soften before sautéing. Miso, mirin, and sugar formed the base of a salty-sweet sauce. If using heads larger than 2 ounces, quarter them instead of halving. You will need a 12-inch nonstick skillet with a tight-fitting lid for this recipe.

4 teaspoons vegetable oil, divided
1 teaspoon grated fresh ginger
1 garlic clove, minced
2 tablespoons white miso
1 tablespoon mirin
2 teaspoons sugar
½ teaspoon cornstarch
8 small heads baby bok choy (1½ to 2 ounces each), halved, washed thoroughly, and spun dry
2 tablespoons water

1. Combine 1 teaspoon oil, ginger, and garlic in small bowl. Whisk miso, mirin, sugar, and cornstarch together in second small bowl.

2. Heat remaining 1 tablespoon oil in 12-inch nonstick skillet over medium heat until shimmering. Add bok choy and water and immediately cover. Cook, covered, shaking skillet occasionally, for 2 minutes. Uncover, toss bok choy, and then push bok choy to sides of skillet. Add ginger-garlic mixture to center and

Sautéed Baby Bok Choy with Chili-Garlic Sauce

cook, stirring constantly, until fragrant, about 20 seconds. Stir ginger-garlic mixture into bok choy and continue to cook, stirring constantly, until all water has evaporated, stems are crisp-tender, and leaves are wilted, 1 to 2 minutes. Add miso mixture and cook, stirring constantly, until sauce is thickened and coats bok choy, about 15 seconds. Serve.

PER SERVING Cal 90; **Total Fat** 5g, **Sat Fat** 0g; **Chol** 0mg; **Sodium** 290mg; **Total Carb** 9g, **Dietary Fiber** 1g, **Total Sugars** 6g; **Protein** 2g

VARIATIONS

Sautéed Baby Bok Choy with Chili-Garlic Sauce

Omit ginger. Substitute 1 tablespoon soy sauce for miso and chili-garlic sauce for mirin. Increase garlic to 2 cloves and decrease sugar to 1 teaspoon.

Sautéed Baby Bok Choy with Shallot and Fish Sauce

Omit ginger. Substitute 1 tablespoon fish sauce for miso, water for mirin, and brown sugar for white sugar. Increase cornstarch to 1 teaspoon. Add 2 tablespoons minced shallot to garlic mixture and ¼ teaspoon red pepper flakes to fish sauce mixture in step 1.

Braised Bok Choy with Shiitake Mushrooms

Braised Bok Choy with Garlic

SERVES 4 TO 6   **FAST**   **VEGAN**

WHY THIS RECIPE WORKS Larger heads of bok choy take well to being braised in a covered pan with some seasoned liquid, as with kale or another sturdy green. We first stir-fried the stalks to give them some light color and then added the greens and some broth and let the bok choy simmer away. After a few minutes, the stalks were soft but not mushy, their texture creamy and delicious, the leaves completely tender. Best of all, the bok choy's flavor seemed more robust and earthy. This dish is fairly brothy, making it an excellent accompaniment to seared pork chops, sautéed chicken breasts, or a firm fish like cod. You will need a 12-inch nonstick skillet with a tight-fitting lid for this recipe.

- 2 tablespoons vegetable oil
- 1½ pounds bok choy, stalks halved lengthwise then cut crosswise into ½-inch pieces, greens sliced into ½-inch-thick pieces
- 4 garlic cloves, minced
- ½ cup chicken or vegetable broth
- 1 teaspoon rice vinegar

1. Heat oil in 12-inch nonstick skillet over high heat until just smoking. Add bok choy stalks and cook, stirring constantly, until edges begin to turn translucent, about 5 minutes. Stir in garlic and cook until fragrant, about 30 seconds. Add broth and bok choy greens. Cover, reduce heat to medium-low, and cook, stirring occasionally, until bok choy is just tender, about 4 minutes.

2. Uncover, increase heat to medium-high, and cook for 2 minutes. Stir in vinegar and season with salt and pepper to taste. Serve.

PER SERVING Cal 60; **Total Fat** 5g, **Sat Fat** 0g; **Chol** 0mg; **Sodium** 115mg; **Total Carb** 3g, **Dietary Fiber** 1g, **Total Sugars** 1g; **Protein** 2g

VARIATION
Braised Bok Choy with Shiitake Mushrooms
Microwave 1 cup water and ¼ ounce dried shiitake mushrooms, covered, until steaming, about 1 minute. Let sit until softened, about 5 minutes. Drain mushrooms in fine-mesh strainer lined with coffee filter, reserve ½ cup strained liquid, and slice mushrooms ¼ inch thick. Substitute 1 tablespoon grated fresh ginger for 2 garlic cloves and substitute mushroom liquid and mushrooms for broth.

Stir-Fried Bok Choy with Soy Sauce and Ginger
SERVES 4 TO 6   **FAST**   **VEGAN**

WHY THIS RECIPE WORKS Stir-frying nicely preserves the crisp-tender texture of bok choy stalks. We sliced the bok choy heads and started the stalks first in the skillet, then added the greens later. This way, both stalks and greens ended up perfectly cooked. Be sure to add the ginger, and then the soy sauce mixture, just as the edges of the stalks turn translucent; otherwise, the stalks won't retain their bite.

- 2 tablespoons soy sauce
- 1 teaspoon sugar
- 2 tablespoons vegetable oil
- 1½ pounds bok choy, stalks halved lengthwise then cut crosswise into ½-inch pieces, greens sliced into ½-inch-thick pieces
- 1 tablespoon grated fresh ginger

1. Whisk soy sauce and sugar in small bowl until sugar has dissolved.

2. Heat oil in 12-inch nonstick skillet over high heat until just smoking. Add bok choy stalks and cook, stirring constantly, until edges begin to turn translucent, about 5 minutes. Stir in ginger and cook until fragrant, about 30 seconds. Add bok choy greens and soy sauce mixture and cook, stirring frequently, until greens are wilted and tender, about 1 minute. Serve.

PER SERVING Cal 60; **Total Fat** 5g, **Sat Fat** 0g; **Chol** 0mg; **Sodium** 370mg; **Total Carb** 3g, **Dietary Fiber** 1g, **Total Sugars** 2g; **Protein** 2g

VARIATION
Stir-Fried Bok Choy with Oyster Sauce and Garlic
Substitute 2 tablespoons oyster sauce (or substitute hoisin sauce, if desired) and 1 tablespoon rice vinegar for soy sauce. Add 2 minced garlic cloves with ginger.

Skillet-Charred Broccoli
SERVES 4 `FAST` `VEGAN`

WHY THIS RECIPE WORKS Charring broccoli gives it a deeply roasted, lightly smoky flavor and crispy edges. Barely stirring the broccoli for the first portion of the cooking time allowed it to develop dark, frizzled edges. But stirring more frequently toward the end of cooking ensured that all the pieces were equally browned and tender. Smoked paprika played up the natural smokiness of the charred broccoli, and some fragrant basil added freshness. The skillet may look very full when you add the broccoli to it in step 1, but the pieces of broccoli will shrink as they cook.

  6 tablespoons extra-virgin olive oil
1½ pounds broccoli florets, cut into 2-inch pieces
  1 teaspoon smoked paprika
  ¾ teaspoon table salt
  ½ teaspoon ground coriander
  ¼ teaspoon pepper
  2 tablespoons chopped fresh basil
    Lemon wedges

1. Heat oil in 12-inch nonstick skillet over medium heat until shimmering. Add broccoli, paprika, salt, coriander, and pepper and stir to combine. Cook until broccoli is dark brown and crispy in spots, about 15 minutes, stirring every 5 minutes.

2. Continue to cook until broccoli is tender and well charred, 6 to 8 minutes, stirring once every 2 to 3 minutes as needed. Transfer broccoli to platter. Season with salt and pepper to taste. Sprinkle with basil and serve with lemon wedges.

PER SERVING Cal 240; **Total Fat** 22g, **Sat Fat** 3g; **Chol** 0mg; **Sodium** 480mg; **Total Carb** 9g, **Dietary Fiber** 4g, **Total Sugars** 3g; **Protein** 5g

Skillet-Charred Broccoli

VARIATION
Skillet-Charred Broccoli with Sesame Seeds and Yogurt Sauce
Substitute ground cumin for smoked paprika and 1 tablespoon toasted sesame seeds for basil. Whisk ¼ cup plain whole-milk yogurt, 2 tablespoons tahini, 1 tablespoon lemon juice, ¼ teaspoon salt, and ⅛ teaspoon pepper together in bowl; drizzle yogurt sauce over broccoli on platter.

Pan-Roasted Broccoli with Lemon Browned Butter
SERVES 6 `FAST`

WHY THIS RECIPE WORKS The first step to perfecting our pan-roasted broccoli recipe was to transform a head of broccoli into pieces that would cook evenly. First, we trimmed the florets into small pieces and the stalks into oblong coins. Then we layered the stalks evenly in a hot, lightly oiled skillet, and once they began to brown we added the florets along with seasoned water and allowed the mixture to steam until nearly tender. A lemony browned butter was the finishing touch.

BROCCOLI

3 tablespoons water
¼ teaspoon table salt
⅛ teaspoon pepper
2 tablespoons vegetable oil
1¾ pounds broccoli, florets cut into 1½-inch pieces, stalks peeled and sliced ¼ inch thick on bias

LEMON BROWNED BUTTER

4 tablespoons unsalted butter, cut into 4 pieces
1 small shallot, minced
2 garlic cloves, minced
¼ teaspoon table salt
⅛ teaspoon pepper
1½ teaspoons lemon juice
½ teaspoon minced fresh thyme

1. FOR THE BROCCOLI Stir water, salt, and pepper in small bowl until salt dissolves. Heat oil in 12-inch nonstick skillet over medium-high heat until just smoking. Add broccoli stalks in even layer and cook, without stirring, until browned on bottoms, about 2 minutes. Add florets and toss to combine. Cook, without stirring, until bottoms of florets just begin to brown, 1 to 2 minutes.

2. Add water mixture and immediately cover skillet. Cook until broccoli is bright green but still crisp, about 2 minutes. Uncover and continue to cook until water has evaporated, stalks are tender, and florets are tender-crisp, about 2 minutes; transfer to bowl.

3. FOR THE LEMON BROWNED BUTTER Melt butter in now-empty skillet over medium-high heat and continue to cook, swirling occasionally, until butter is browned and releases nutty aroma, about 1½ minutes. Off heat, add shallot, garlic, salt, and pepper, and stir constantly until garlic and shallot are fragrant, about 1 minute. Stir in lemon juice and thyme. Return broccoli to skillet and toss to coat with browned butter. Serve.

PER SERVING Cal 140; **Total Fat** 12g, **Sat Fat** 5g; **Chol** 20mg; **Sodium** 220mg; **Total Carb** 6g, **Dietary Fiber** 2g, **Total Sugars** 2g; **Protein** 2g

VARIATIONS

Pan-Roasted Broccoli with Creamy Gruyère Sauce

In step 3, melt 1 tablespoon unsalted butter in empty skillet over medium heat. Add 1 thinly sliced shallot and cook until softened, about 2 minutes. Stir in ½ cup heavy cream, ½ teaspoon Dijon mustard, ½ teaspoon dry sherry, ⅛ teaspoon salt, and pinch cayenne pepper. Increase heat to medium-high and cook until mixture bubbles and thickens, about 1 minute. Off heat, stir in 3 tablespoons finely grated Gruyère cheese and 1 teaspoon lemon juice until cheese is melted. Substitute for lemon browned butter. Sprinkle broccoli with 1 tablespoon finely grated Gruyère before serving.

Pan-Roasted Broccoli with Spicy Southeast Asian Flavors

Omit lemon browned butter. Combine 1 tablespoon creamy peanut butter, 1 tablespoon hoisin, 2 teaspoons lime juice, 2 minced garlic cloves, 1 teaspoon packed brown sugar, and ¾ teaspoon Asian chili-garlic sauce together in bowl. In step 2, do not transfer broccoli to bowl. Instead, add ¼ cup chopped basil to skillet and cook until leaves wilt, about 30 seconds. Add sauce to skillet and toss to coat. Sprinkle with 2 tablespoons chopped unsalted roasted peanuts before serving.

Garlicky Broccolini
SERVES 4 **FAST**

WHY THIS RECIPE WORKS Broccolini is a cross between broccoli and Chinese broccoli and has crisp yet tender stalks and delicate tips. To prepare it we tried sautéing broccolini then letting it steam through, but the delicate tips scorched. Instead, we brought salted water to a boil in a skillet, added the broccolini, and covered the pan to trap the steam. Minutes later, we removed the lid to reveal tender, emerald-green stalks. Another minute over the heat evaporated any remaining water. Slitting the thicker stalks in half lengthwise below the florets ensured the stalks cooked evenly. Garlic and red pepper flakes, plus a sprinkling of Parmesan before serving, was all the broccolini needed. You will need a 12-inch nonstick skillet with a tight-fitting lid for this recipe.

2 tablespoons extra-virgin olive oil
2 garlic cloves, minced
⅛ teaspoon red pepper flakes
⅓ cup water
½ teaspoon table salt
1 pound broccolini, trimmed, bottom 2 inches of stems thicker than ½ inch halved lengthwise
2 tablespoons grated Parmesan cheese

1. Combine oil, garlic, and pepper flakes in bowl. Bring water and salt to boil in 12-inch nonstick skillet. Add broccolini, cover, reduce heat to medium-low, and cook until bright green and tender, about 5 minutes.

2. Uncover and cook until liquid evaporates, about 30 seconds. Clear center of skillet, add garlic mixture, and cook, mashing mixture into skillet, until fragrant, about 30 seconds. Stir garlic mixture into broccolini. Transfer to platter, sprinkle with Parmesan, and serve.

PER SERVING Cal 110; **Total Fat** 9g, **Sat Fat** 1.5g; **Chol** 5mg; **Sodium** 390mg; **Total Carb** 4g, **Dietary Fiber** 3g, **Total Sugars** 0g; **Protein** 5g

Broccoli Rabe with Garlic and Red Pepper Flakes

1. Cut broccolini stalks measuring more than ½ inch in diameter at base in half lengthwise. Cut stalks measuring ¼ to ½ inch in diameter at base in half lengthwise, starting below where florets begin and keeping florets intact. Leave stalks measuring less than ¼ inch in diameter at base whole.

2. Cook pancetta in Dutch oven over medium heat until crisp, 6 to 8 minutes. Using slotted spoon, transfer pancetta to paper towel–lined plate; set aside.

3. Add 1 tablespoon oil, garlic, and pepper flakes to fat left in pot and cook over medium heat until fragrant, about 30 seconds. Add broccolini and cook, stirring frequently, until bright green, about 5 minutes. Add water, cover, and cook until broccolini is tender, about 5 minutes.

4. Uncover and continue to cook until liquid has evaporated, about 1 minute. Off heat, stir in pancetta, vinegar, and remaining 1½ teaspoons oil. Season with salt and pepper to taste. Transfer to platter, sprinkle with Parmesan, and serve.

PER SERVING Cal 180; **Total Fat** 14g, **Sat Fat** 4g; **Chol** 20mg; **Sodium** 580mg; **Total Carb** 5g, **Dietary Fiber** 3g, **Total Sugars** 1g; **Protein** 11g

Broccolini with Pancetta and Parmesan

SERVES 4 `FAST`

WHY THIS RECIPE WORKS Meaty pancetta, garlic, and red pepper flakes upgrade broccolini and make its flavor pop. Using a Dutch oven instead of a skillet gave us enough room to render the pancetta and sauté-steam the broccolini with water all in the same pot. Splitting the thicker stalks, which can sometimes be tough and woody, allowed them to cook evenly. (We left stalks that were ¼ inch or less as is.) A couple teaspoons of balsamic vinegar added a sweet intensity and a shower of Parmesan cheese pulled everything together. If you can't find pancetta, you can use bacon instead. You will need a large Dutch oven for this recipe.

　1　pound broccolini, trimmed
　3　ounces pancetta, cut into ½-inch pieces
1½　tablespoons extra-virgin olive oil, divided
　2　garlic cloves, minced
　¼　teaspoon red pepper flakes
　¾　cup water
　2　teaspoons balsamic vinegar
　1　ounce Parmesan cheese, grated (½ cup)

Broccoli Rabe with Garlic and Red Pepper Flakes

SERVES 4 `FAST` `VEGAN`

WHY THIS RECIPE WORKS Broccoli rabe, also known as rapini, is naturally bitter, and for some that bitterness can be overwhelming. We developed a quick and dependable method of cooking this assertive vegetable that delivered less bitterness and rounder, more balanced flavor. We found that blanching the rabe in salted water tamed its bitterness. We then sautéed the blanched rabe with garlic and red pepper flakes, which complemented the vegetable's strong flavor. A salad spinner makes easy work of drying the blanched broccoli rabe. You can reduce the amount of red pepper flakes if you prefer to make this dish less spicy.

　14　ounces broccoli rabe, trimmed and cut into 1-inch pieces
　　　Table salt for blanching broccoli rabe
　2　tablespoons extra-virgin olive oil
　3　garlic cloves, minced
　¼　teaspoon red pepper flakes

1. Bring 3 quarts water to boil in large saucepan. Fill large bowl with ice water. Add broccoli rabe and 2 teaspoons salt to boiling water and cook until wilted and tender, about 2½ minutes. Drain rabe, then transfer to bowl of ice water. Drain again and thoroughly pat dry.

2. Heat oil, garlic, and pepper flakes in 10-inch skillet over medium heat until garlic begins to sizzle, 3 to 4 minutes. Increase heat to medium high, add broccoli rabe, and cook, stirring to coat with oil, until heated through, about 1 minute. Season with salt to taste, and serve.

PER SERVING Cal 90; **Total Fat** 8g, **Sat Fat** 1g; **Chol** 0mg; **Sodium** 180mg; **Total Carb** 4g, **Dietary Fiber** 3g, **Total Sugars** 0g; **Protein** 3g

Broccoli Rabe with White Beans
SERVES 4 TO 6 `FAST`

WHY THIS RECIPE WORKS Broccoli rabe and creamy white beans are a classic pairing in Italian cooking. The pleasantly sharp greens and mellow beans complement each other incredibly well. We found that a simple sauté showcased the rabe's bold flavor. Cutting the broccoli rabe into 1-inch pieces meant that the pieces cooked evenly and quickly turned tender. Canned beans were the obvious choice to make this an easy weeknight side dish or light dinner. Adding the beans early in the cooking process gave them time to absorb the flavors of the garlic-infused olive oil. A little chicken broth tied the dish together while adding savory depth. Parmesan cheese and a squeeze of lemon brightened this simple but flavor-packed side.

¼ cup extra-virgin olive oil, divided
3 garlic cloves, sliced thin
¼ teaspoon red pepper flakes
1 pound broccoli rabe, trimmed and cut into
   1-inch pieces
1 (15-ounce) can cannellini beans, rinsed
¼ cup chicken or vegetable broth
½ teaspoon table salt
   Grated Parmesan cheese
   Lemon wedges

Cook 2 tablespoons oil, garlic, and pepper flakes in Dutch oven over medium heat until garlic is golden brown, 2 to 4 minutes. Stir in broccoli rabe, beans, broth, and salt and cook, stirring occasionally, until broccoli rabe is tender, 4 to 6 minutes. Off heat, stir in remaining 2 tablespoons oil and season with salt and pepper to taste. Serve, passing Parmesan and lemon wedges separately.

PER SERVING Cal 140; **Total Fat** 10g, **Sat Fat** 1.5g; **Chol** 0mg; **Sodium** 360mg; **Total Carb** 10g, **Dietary Fiber** 4g, **Total Sugars** 1g; **Protein** 6g

Caesar Brussels Sprouts

Braised Brussels Sprouts with Mustard-Herb Butter
SERVES 4 `FAST`

WHY THIS RECIPE WORKS Braising is one of the simplest ways to produce tender, not-too-bitter, attractively green-colored Brussels sprouts with little fuss. We flavored the sprouts simply with butter, Dijon mustard, herbs, and a squeeze of lemon. You can braise the sprouts in chicken or vegetable broth instead of water; if you try that, adjust the amount of salt you add accordingly. Halve sprouts greater than 1½ inches in diameter.

1 pound Brussels sprouts, trimmed
   Table salt for cooking Brussels sprouts
4 tablespoons unsalted butter, melted
1 tablespoon Dijon mustard
1 tablespoon minced fresh chives, parsley, or tarragon
   Lemon wedges

1. Bring Brussels sprouts, ½ cup water, and ½ teaspoon salt to simmer in 12-inch skillet over medium-high heat. Cover, reduce heat to medium-low, and cook until tender, 8 to 10 minutes, shaking skillet halfway through cooking to redistribute sprouts. Drain well.

2. Combine melted butter, mustard, and chives in large bowl. Add Brussels sprouts and gently toss to coat. Season with salt and pepper to taste. Serve with lemon wedges.

PER SERVING Cal 150; **Total Fat** 11g, **Sat Fat** 7g; **Chol** 30mg; **Sodium** 115mg; **Total Carb** 9g, **Dietary Fiber** 4g, **Total Sugars** 2g; **Protein** 3g

Caesar Brussels Sprouts
SERVES 4 TO 6

WHY THIS RECIPE WORKS We were after tender Brussels sprouts coated in a pleasantly pungent Caesar dressing. Slicing the sprouts thin meant the dressing didn't have anything to cling to, and whole or halved sprouts were too cumbersome. We landed on cutting the sprouts into quarters; they maintained their shape during cooking, and the dressing clung to each cut side. For the dressing, we combined lemon juice, Worcestershire, mustard, garlic, and anchovies along with mayonnaise for a bright yet creamy Caesar dressing. For the best results, be sure to choose Brussels sprouts with small, tight heads. The skillet may seem very full at first in step 2, but the Brussels sprouts will shrink as they cook.

DRESSING
1½ tablespoons lemon juice
1 tablespoon mayonnaise
1 tablespoon Worcestershire sauce
1 tablespoon Dijon mustard
3 garlic cloves, minced
3 anchovy fillets, rinsed and minced
½ teaspoon pepper
¼ teaspoon table salt
3 tablespoons extra-virgin olive oil

BRUSSELS SPROUTS
2 pounds Brussels sprouts, trimmed and quartered
5 tablespoons extra-virgin olive oil, divided
½ teaspoon table salt, divided
¼ cup panko bread crumbs
1 ounce Parmesan cheese, grated (½ cup)

1. FOR THE DRESSING Whisk lemon juice, mayonnaise, Worcestershire, mustard, garlic, anchovies, pepper, and salt in large bowl until combined. Slowly whisk in oil until emulsified; set aside.

2. FOR THE BRUSSELS SPROUTS Combine Brussels sprouts, ¼ cup oil, and ¼ teaspoon salt in 12-inch nonstick skillet. Cover skillet, place over medium heat, and cook, stirring occasionally, until Brussels sprouts are bright green and have started to brown, about 10 minutes.

3. Uncover and continue to cook, stirring occasionally, until Brussels sprouts are deeply and evenly browned and paring knife slides in with little to no resistance, about 5 minutes longer. Transfer Brussels sprouts to rimmed baking sheet and let cool for 15 minutes. Wipe skillet clean with paper towels.

4. Combine panko, remaining 1 tablespoon oil, and remaining ¼ teaspoon salt in now-empty skillet and cook over medium heat, stirring frequently, until golden brown, 2 to 4 minutes. Transfer to small bowl and stir in Parmesan.

5. Add Brussels sprouts to dressing and gently toss to combine. Transfer to a platter, sprinkle with panko mixture, and serve.

PER SERVING Cal 290; **Total Fat** 22g, **Sat Fat** 3.5g; **Chol** 5mg; **Sodium** 600mg; **Total Carb** 17g, **Dietary Fiber** 6g, **Total Sugars** 4g; **Protein** 8g

Pan-Roasted Cabbage
SERVES 6   FAST

WHY THIS RECIPE WORKS Oven-roasted cabbage is meltingly tender. We wanted that caramelized goodness on the stovetop. A small head of cabbage cut into six wedges fit comfortably in a 12-inch skillet. Adding some water to the skillet steamed the wedges, helping them cook through evenly. A simple mix of butter, caraway seeds, basil, and lemon juice finished this satisfying side dish. When slicing the cabbage into wedges, be sure to leave the core intact so the wedges don't fall apart when flipped in step 2. Avoid heads of cabbage that weigh more than 2 pounds; the larger wedges will not fit in the skillet. You will need a 12-inch nonstick skillet with a tight-fitting lid for this recipe.

6 tablespoons water, divided
2 tablespoons vegetable oil
1 head green cabbage (2 pounds), cut into 6 wedges through core
1 teaspoon table salt
4 tablespoons unsalted butter, cut into 4 pieces
3 tablespoons chopped fresh basil
½ teaspoon caraway seeds
½ teaspoon pepper
1 tablespoon lemon juice

1. Combine ¼ cup water and oil in 12-inch nonstick skillet. Arrange cabbage wedges cut side down in single layer in skillet. Sprinkle with salt and cook over medium heat, uncovered, until water has evaporated and wedges are well browned, 16 to 20 minutes.

2. Flip wedges to second cut side, and add remaining 2 tablespoons water to skillet. Cover and cook until wedges are tender and second side is well browned, 4 to 6 minutes.

3. Scatter butter among wedges and cook, uncovered, until butter is melted and bubbling, about 1 minute. Sprinkle with basil, caraway seeds, and pepper and continue to cook, using large spoon halfway through cooking to baste wedges with melted butter (tilting skillet so butter pools at low point and can be easily scooped into spoon), until fragrant, about 1 minute.

4. Transfer wedges to serving platter. Off heat, stir lemon juice into any remaining butter in skillet, then spoon over wedges. Season with salt and pepper to taste. Serve.

PER SERVING Cal 150; **Total Fat** 12g, **Sat Fat** 5g; **Chol** 20mg; **Sodium** 420mg; **Total Carb** 9g, **Dietary Fiber** 4g, **Total Sugars** 5g; **Protein** 2g

Smothered Cabbage
SERVES 4 TO 6

WHY THIS RECIPE WORKS Humble cabbage can be very satisfying. It is full of great flavor, and also full of water. By covering the cabbage as it cooked, we controlled the amount of liquid that stayed in the pot. Adding butter and pepper to the cooking liquid ensured a rich, seasoned sauce that coated the cabbage. One-inch pieces of potato added body to the dish, and finishing the cooking uncovered reduced the excess liquid and thickened the sauce. Buy larger Yukon Gold potatoes to ensure that you can cut 1-inch pieces; potatoes cut smaller will overcook.

> 5 tablespoons unsalted butter
> 1 onion, sliced thin
> 1 large head green cabbage (3 pounds), cored and cut into 1-inch pieces
> 1½ cups chicken broth
> 10 ounces Yukon Gold potato, peeled and cut into 1-inch pieces
> 1½ teaspoons table salt
> ½ teaspoon pepper

1. Melt butter in Dutch oven over medium heat. Add onion and cook until soft, about 4 minutes. Stir in cabbage, broth, potatoes, salt, and pepper and bring to boil. Reduce heat to medium-low, cover, and simmer until cabbage is wilted and potatoes are fork-tender, 12 to 15 minutes, stirring occasionally.

2. Increase heat to medium-high, uncover, and cook until liquid has nearly evaporated, about 12 minutes, gently stirring occasionally with silicone spatula. Serve.

PER SERVING Cal 200; **Total Fat** 9g, **Sat Fat** 6g; **Chol** 25mg; **Sodium** 770mg; **Total Carb** 24g; **Dietary Fiber** 6g; **Total Sugars** 9g; **Protein** 5g

Slow-Cooked Whole Carrots with Pine Nut Relish

Slow-Cooked Whole Carrots
SERVES 4 TO 6

WHY THIS RECIPE WORKS Why spend 1 hour and 45 minutes cooking carrots? Because slow cooking whole carrots greatly enhances their sweetness and makes them meltingly tender from one end to the other. Gently "steeping" the carrots in warm water before cooking them firmed up the vegetable's cell walls so that they could be cooked for a long time without falling apart. We also topped the carrots with a circle of parchment that sat directly on the food during cooking to ensure that the moisture in the pan cooked the carrots evenly. Finishing cooking at a simmer evaporated the liquid and concentrated the carrots' flavor so that they tasted their best whether served plain or with a flavorful relish. Choose carrots that are between ¾ to 1¼ inches in diameter. You can use rainbow carrots in this recipe, if desired. You will need a skillet with a tight-fitting lid for this recipe.

3 cups water
1 tablespoon unsalted butter
½ teaspoon table salt
12 carrots (1½ to 1¾ pounds), peeled

1. Fold 12-inch square of parchment paper into quarters to create 6-inch square. Fold bottom right corner of square to top left corner to create triangle. Fold triangle again, right side over left, to create narrow triangle. Cut off ¼ inch of tip of triangle to create small hole. Cut base of triangle straight across where it measures 5 inches from hole. Open paper round.

2. Bring water, butter, and salt to simmer in 12-inch skillet over high heat. Remove pan from heat, add carrots in single layer, and place parchment round on top of carrots. Cover skillet and let sit for 20 minutes.

3. Remove lid from skillet, leaving parchment round in place, and bring to simmer over high heat. Reduce heat to medium-low and simmer until almost all water has evaporated and carrots are very tender, about 45 minutes. Discard parchment round, increase heat to medium-high, and continue to cook carrots, shaking pan frequently, until lightly glazed and all water has evaporated, 2 to 4 minutes. Transfer carrots to platter, top with relish, if using, and serve.

PER SERVING Cal 60; **Total Fat** 2g, **Sat Fat** 1g; **Chol** 5mg; **Sodium** 260mg; **Total Carb** 9g, **Dietary Fiber** 3g, **Total Sugars** 5g; **Protein** 1g

FOLDING PARCHMENT FOR SLOW-COOKED CARROTS

1. Cut parchment into 11-inch circle, then cut 1-inch hole in center, folding paper as needed to cut out hole.

2. Lay parchment circle on top of carrots, underneath lid, to help retain and evenly distribute moisture during cooking.

These easy relishes are made with bold ingredients. Just a small amount complements earthy vegetables like carrots. Spoon any of these over the carrots before serving.

Red Pepper and Almond Relish
MAKES ABOUT ¾ CUP

½ cup finely chopped jarred roasted red peppers
¼ cup slivered almonds, toasted and chopped coarse
2 tablespoons extra-virgin olive oil
2 tablespoons minced fresh parsley
1 tablespoon white wine vinegar
1 teaspoon minced fresh oregano
¼ teaspoon table salt

Combine all ingredients in bowl.

Green Olive and Golden Raisin Relish
MAKES ABOUT 1 CUP

⅓ cup raisins
1 tablespoon water
½ cup pitted green olives, chopped
1 shallot, minced
2 tablespoons extra-virgin olive oil
1 tablespoon red wine vinegar
1 tablespoon minced fresh parsley
½ teaspoon ground fennel
¼ teaspoon table salt

Microwave raisins and water in medium bowl until hot, about 1 minute; let stand for 5 minutes. Stir in olives, shallot, oil, vinegar, parsley, ground fennel, and salt.

Pine Nut Relish
MAKES ABOUT ¾ CUP

⅓ cup pine nuts, toasted
1 shallot, minced
1 tablespoon sherry vinegar
1 tablespoon minced fresh parsley
1 teaspoon honey
½ teaspoon minced fresh rosemary
¼ teaspoon smoked paprika
¼ teaspoon table salt
Pinch cayenne pepper

Combine all ingredients in bowl.

Chopped Carrot Salad with Mint, Pistachios, and Pomegranate Seeds

SERVES 4 TO 6 **FAST** **VEGAN**

WHY THIS RECIPE WORKS It's easy to transform everyday carrots into a vibrant salad. Finely chopping carrots in the food processor, instead of shredding them slaw-style, produced a delicately crunchy and light-textured base. We first used the food processor to chop rich pistachios and two bunches of fragrant mint. We tossed the chopped carrots with a simple dressing enlivened with honey and paprika, stirred in the mint and pistachios, and added pomegranate seeds for some juicy, tart sweetness. We prefer the convenience and hint of bitterness that leaving the carrots unpeeled lends to the salad. Be sure to scrub the carrots well before using.

¾ cup shelled pistachios, toasted
¼ cup extra-virgin olive oil
3 tablespoons lemon juice
1 tablespoon honey
1 teaspoon table salt
½ teaspoon pepper
½ teaspoon smoked paprika
⅛ teaspoon cayenne pepper
1 pound carrots, unpeeled, trimmed and
   cut into 1-inch pieces
1 cup pomegranate seeds, divided
½ cup minced fresh mint

1. Pulse pistachios in food processor until coarsely chopped, 10 to 12 pulses; transfer to small bowl. Whisk oil, lemon juice, honey, salt, pepper, paprika, and cayenne together in large bowl until combined.

2. Process carrots in now-empty food processor until finely chopped, 10 to 20 seconds, scraping down sides of bowl as needed. Transfer carrots to bowl with dressing. Add ½ cup pomegranate seeds, mint, and half of pistachios and toss to combine. Season with salt to taste. Transfer to platter, sprinkle with remaining ½ cup pomegranate seeds and pistachios, and serve.

PER SERVING Cal 240; **Total Fat** 17g, **Sat Fat** 2.5g; **Chol** 0mg; **Sodium** 440mg; **Total Carb** 20g, **Dietary Fiber** 5g, **Total Sugars** 11g; **Protein** 5g

VARIATION

Chopped Carrot Salad with Radishes and Sesame Seeds

Omit pistachios. Substitute 3 tablespoons vegetable oil and 2 teaspoons toasted sesame oil for olive oil. Substitute rice vinegar for lemon juice and increase honey to 2 tablespoons and salt to 1¼ teaspoons. Substitute 1½ teaspoons Korean red pepper flakes (gochugaru) for paprika, cayenne, and pepper. Before processing carrots, pulse 8 ounces radishes, trimmed and halved, in food processor until coarsely but evenly chopped, 10 to 12 pulses; add to dressing. Substitute ¼ cup toasted sesame seeds for pomegranate seeds and cilantro for mint.

Chopped Carrot Salad with Mint, Pistachios, and Pomegranate Seeds

Braised Cauliflower with Garlic and White Wine

SERVES 4 TO 6 **FAST** **VEGAN**

WHY THIS RECIPE WORKS When properly cooked and imaginatively flavored, braised cauliflower is nutty and slightly sweet, with a pleasing texture. However, it's easy to overcook cauliflower. To avoid this, we knew we would need to quickly braise the florets. Cutting the florets into 1½-inch pieces reduced the total cooking time and sautéing them in olive oil also imparted nuttiness. Because we wanted the cauliflower to braise for only a short amount of time, we maximized its impact by creating an ultraflavorful broth that the vegetable could absorb. White wine and broth made for a complexly flavored base, and a generous amount of garlic along with a pinch of red pepper flakes added punch and deeper flavor. For the best texture and taste, make sure to brown the cauliflower well in step 1. You will need a 12-inch skillet with a tight-fitting lid for this recipe.

- 3 tablespoons plus 1 teaspoon extra-virgin olive oil, divided
- 3 garlic cloves, minced
- ⅛ teaspoon red pepper flakes
- 1 head cauliflower (2 pounds), cut into 1½-inch florets
- ¼ teaspoon table salt
- ⅓ cup chicken or vegetable broth
- ⅓ cup dry white wine
- 2 tablespoons minced fresh parsley

1. Combine 1 teaspoon oil, garlic, and pepper flakes in small bowl. Heat remaining 3 tablespoons oil in 12-inch skillet over medium-high heat until shimmering. Add cauliflower florets and salt and cook, stirring occasionally, until florets are golden, 7 to 9 minutes.

2. Push florets to sides of skillet. Add garlic mixture to center and cook, mashing mixture into skillet, until fragrant, about 30 seconds. Stir garlic mixture into florets.

3. Stir in broth and wine and bring to simmer. Reduce heat to medium-low, cover, and cook until florets are crisp-tender, 4 to 6 minutes. Off heat, stir in parsley and season with salt and pepper to taste. Serve.

PER SERVING Cal 120; Total Fat 8g, Sat Fat 1.5g; Chol 0mg; Sodium 180mg; Total Carb 8g, Dietary Fiber 3g, Total Sugars 3g; Protein 3g

VARIATIONS

Braised Cauliflower with Capers and Anchovies

Add 2 rinsed and minced anchovy fillets and 1 tablespoon rinsed and minced capers to oil mixture in step 1. Stir 1 tablespoon lemon juice into cauliflower with parsley in step 3.

Braised Cauliflower with Sumac and Mint

Omit wine. Substitute 2 teaspoons ground sumac for pepper flakes and increase broth to ½ cup. In step 3, once cauliflower is crisp-tender, uncover and continue to cook until liquid is almost evaporated, about 1 minute. Substitute 2 tablespoons chopped fresh mint for parsley and stir ¼ cup plain yogurt into cauliflower with mint.

Browned and Braised Cauliflower with Garlic, Ginger, and Soy
SERVES 4 TO 6 FAST VEGAN

WHY THIS RECIPE WORKS We wanted another method for properly cooking often-overcooked cauliflower and settled on a combination of sautéing and braising to cut down on the cook time and to avoid soggy results. Sautéing concentrated the cauliflower's flavor; we then added liquid and flavorings to the pan and cooked the florets, covered, until they were just crisp-tender. The deep flavor of the browned cauliflower held up well to bolder, more complex flavor combinations, so we used bright Asian-inspired flavors for one version and rich Indian spices for another. You will need a 12-inch nonstick skillet with a tight-fitting lid for this recipe.

- 2 tablespoons grated fresh ginger
- 2 garlic cloves, minced
- 1 teaspoon toasted sesame oil
- 1½ tablespoons vegetable oil
- 1 head cauliflower (2 pounds), cored and cut into 1-inch florets
- ¼ cup water
- 2 tablespoons soy sauce
- 2 tablespoons rice vinegar
- 1 tablespoon dry sherry
- 2 scallions, minced

1. Combine ginger, garlic, and sesame oil in bowl. Heat vegetable oil in 12-inch nonstick skillet over medium-high heat until just smoking. Add cauliflower and cook, stirring occasionally, until beginning to brown, 6 to 7 minutes.

2. Clear center of skillet, add ginger mixture, and cook, mashing mixture into skillet, until fragrant, about 30 seconds. Stir ginger mixture into cauliflower.

3. Reduce heat to low and add water, soy sauce, vinegar, and sherry. Cover and cook until florets are crisp-tender, 4 to 5 minutes. Off heat, stir in scallions and season with pepper to taste. Serve.

PER SERVING Cal 90; Total Fat 4.5g, Sat Fat 0.5g; Chol 0mg; Sodium 350mg; Total Carb 9g, Dietary Fiber 3g, Total Sugars 3g; Protein 4g

Browned and Braised Cauliflower with Indian Spices

Cooking the spices for a minute or two removes their raw edge and allows their flavors to deepen. You will need a 12-inch non-stick skillet with a tight-fitting lid for this recipe.

1½ tablespoons vegetable oil
1 head cauliflower (2 pounds), cored and cut into 1-inch florets
½ onion, sliced thin
1 teaspoon ground coriander
1 teaspoon ground cumin
1 teaspoon ground turmeric
¼ teaspoon red pepper flakes
¼ cup water
¼ cup plain yogurt
1 tablespoon lime juice
¼ cup minced fresh cilantro

1. Heat oil in 12-inch nonstick skillet over medium-high heat until just smoking. Add cauliflower and cook, stirring occasionally, until just softened, 2 to 3 minutes. Stir in onion and cook until florets begin to brown and onion softens, about 4 minutes.

2. Stir in coriander, cumin, turmeric, and pepper flakes; cook until spices are fragrant, 1 to 2 minutes. Reduce heat to low and add water, yogurt, and lime juice. Cover and cook until florets are crisp-tender, about 6 minutes. Stir in cilantro and season with salt and pepper to taste. Serve.

Cauliflower Cakes
SERVES 4

WHY THIS RECIPE WORKS Vegetable cakes are simple, filling, and a unique way to serve vegetables. For cauliflower cakes with complex flavors, a creamy interior, and a crunchy browned exterior, we started with the cauliflower. To ensure that its flavor didn't get lost and to drive off excess moisture that would otherwise make our cakes fall apart, we cut the cauliflower into florets and roasted them until they were well browned and tender. Tossing the florets with warm spices bloomed the spices' flavors and gave the cakes an aromatic backbone. Next we needed a binder to hold the shaped cakes together. Egg and flour are standard additions, but we also added some goat cheese to provide extra binding, creaminess, and tangy flavor. Though these cakes held together, they were very soft and tricky to flip in the pan. Refrigerating the cakes for 30 minutes before cooking them proved to be the best solution. In addition to lemon wedges, serve with a yogurt sauce (recipe follows), if desired.

Cauliflower Cakes

1 head cauliflower (2 pounds), cored and cut into 1-inch florets
¼ cup extra-virgin olive oil, divided
1 teaspoon ground turmeric
1 teaspoon ground coriander
1 teaspoon table salt
½ teaspoon ground ginger
¼ teaspoon pepper
4 ounces goat cheese, softened
2 scallions, sliced thin
1 large egg, lightly beaten
2 garlic cloves, minced
1 teaspoon grated lemon zest, plus lemon wedges for serving
¼ cup all-purpose flour

1. Adjust oven rack to middle position and heat oven to 450 degrees. Toss cauliflower with 1 tablespoon oil, turmeric, coriander, salt, ginger, and pepper. Transfer to aluminum foil–lined rimmed baking sheet and spread into single layer. Roast until cauliflower is well browned and tender, about 25 minutes. Let cool slightly, then transfer to large bowl.

2. Line clean rimmed baking sheet with parchment paper. Mash cauliflower coarse with potato masher. Stir in goat cheese, scallions, egg, garlic, and lemon zest until well combined. Sprinkle flour over cauliflower mixture and stir to incorporate. Using your wet hands, divide mixture into 4 equal portions, pack gently into ¾-inch-thick cakes, and place on prepared sheet. Refrigerate cakes until chilled and firm, about 30 minutes.

3. Line large plate with paper towels. Heat remaining 3 tablespoons oil in 12-inch nonstick skillet over medium heat until shimmering. Gently lay cakes in skillet and cook until deep golden brown and crisp, 5 to 7 minutes per side. Drain cakes briefly on prepared plate. Serve with lemon wedges.

PER SERVING Cal 310; **Total Fat** 22g, **Sat Fat** 7g; **Chol** 60mg; **Sodium** 800mg; **Total Carb** 19g, **Dietary Fiber** 5g, **Total Sugars** 5g; **Protein** 12g

---

TAKE IT UP A NOTCH

These light and refreshing sauces can be dolloped over anything from vegetables to rice to grain dishes.

Yogurt-Herb Sauce

MAKES ABOUT 1 CUP

  1 cup plain yogurt
  2 tablespoons minced fresh cilantro
  2 tablespoons minced fresh mint
  1 garlic clove, minced

Whisk yogurt, cilantro, mint, and garlic in bowl until combined. Season with salt and pepper to taste. Let sit until flavors meld, about 30 minutes. (Sauce can be refrigerated for up to 2 days.)

Cucumber-Yogurt Sauce

MAKES ABOUT 2½ CUPS

Cilantro, mint, parsley, or tarragon can be substituted for the dill if desired.

  1 cup plain Greek yogurt
  2 tablespoons extra-virgin olive oil
  2 tablespoons minced fresh dill
  1 garlic clove, minced
  1 cucumber, peeled, halved lengthwise, seeded, and shredded

Whisk yogurt, oil, dill, and garlic in medium bowl until combined. Stir in cucumber and season with salt and pepper to taste. (Sauce can be refrigerated for up to 1 day.)

Whole Pot-Roasted Cauliflower with Tomatoes and Olives

Whole Pot-Roasted Cauliflower with Tomatoes and Olives

SERVES 4 TO 6

WHY THIS RECIPE WORKS Whole cauliflower braised in an aromatic tomato sauce is a showstopper side (or a light main dish). The recipes we came across all started by searing the cumbersome cauliflower first in hopes of browning the exterior, but we found this task unwieldy—and when all was said and done, browning was spotty at best. Once it was coated in a piquant sauce of chunky tomatoes, golden raisins, and salty capers and olives, we couldn't taste or see the difference between browned and unbrowned cauliflower. So we skipped the hassle. To ensure all of the rich flavors penetrated the dense vegetable, we started by cooking it upside down and spooned some of the sauce into the crevices between the stalk and florets. Then we flipped it right side up, spooned more sauce over the top, and left the pot uncovered to finish cooking. The sauce thickened but remained plentiful and the flavors intensified as the cauliflower became fork-tender.

2 (28-ounce) cans whole peeled tomatoes
2 tablespoons extra-virgin olive oil, plus extra for serving
6 anchovy fillets, rinsed and minced
6 garlic cloves, minced
¼ teaspoon red pepper flakes
¼ teaspoon table salt
1 head cauliflower (2 pounds)
¼ cup golden raisins
¼ cup pitted kalamata olives, chopped coarse
3 tablespoons capers, rinsed
1 ounce Parmesan cheese, grated (½ cup)
¼ cup minced fresh parsley

1. Adjust oven rack to middle position and heat oven to 450 degrees. Pulse tomatoes and their juice in food processor until coarsely chopped, 6 to 8 pulses.

2. Cook oil, anchovies, garlic, and pepper flakes in Dutch oven over medium heat, stirring constantly, until fragrant, about 2 minutes. Stir in tomatoes and salt, bring to simmer, and cook until slightly thickened, about 10 minutes.

3. Meanwhile, trim outer leaves of cauliflower and cut stem flush with bottom florets. Stir raisins, olives, and capers into tomatoes in pot, then nestle cauliflower, stem side up, into sauce. Spoon some of sauce over top, cover, transfer pot to oven, and roast until cauliflower is just tender (paring knife slips in and out of core with some resistance), 30 to 35 minutes.

4. Uncover pot and using tongs, flip cauliflower stem side down. Spoon some of sauce over cauliflower, then scrape down sides of pot. Continue to roast, uncovered, until cauliflower is tender, 10 to 15 minutes.

5. Remove pot from oven. Sprinkle cauliflower with Parmesan and parsley and drizzle with extra oil. Cut cauliflower into wedges and serve, spooning sauce over individual portions.

PER SERVING Cal 190; **Total Fat** 7g, **Sat Fat** 1.5g; **Chol** 5mg; **Sodium** 1060mg; **Total Carb** 25g, **Dietary Fiber** 5g, **Total Sugars** 14g; **Protein** 9g

Whole Romanesco with Berbere and Yogurt-Tahini Sauce
SERVES 4

WHY THIS RECIPE WORKS Like its pale cauliflower relative, colorful romanesco is perfect for cooking whole. We started with the microwave, partially cooking the romanesco. Then we brushed melted butter over it and transferred it to the oven to finish cooking and develop some browning. We basted the broiled romanesco with more butter and the flavors of berbere, a warmly aromatic and highly flavorful Ethiopian spice blend. A bright, cooling yogurt sauce and

Whole Romanesco with Berbere and Yogurt-Tahini Sauce

crunchy pine nuts finished off this beautiful side dish. If you can't find a 2-pound head of romanesco, purchase two 1-pound heads, and reduce the microwaving time in step 2 to 5 to 7 minutes.

YOGURT-TAHINI SAUCE
½ cup whole-milk yogurt
2 tablespoons tahini
½ teaspoon grated lemon zest plus 1 tablespoon juice
1 garlic clove, minced

ROMANESCO
1 head romanesco or cauliflower (2 pounds)
6 tablespoons unsalted butter, cut into 6 pieces, divided
¼ teaspoon table salt
½ teaspoon paprika
¼ teaspoon cayenne pepper
¼ teaspoon ground coriander
⅛ teaspoon ground allspice
⅛ teaspoon ground cardamom
⅛ teaspoon ground cumin
⅛ teaspoon pepper
2 tablespoons toasted and coarsely chopped pine nuts
1 tablespoon minced fresh cilantro

1. **FOR THE SAUCE** Whisk all ingredients together in bowl until combined. Season with salt and pepper to taste and set aside until ready to serve.

2. **FOR THE ROMANESCO** Adjust oven rack 6 inches from broiler element and heat broiler. Trim outer leaves of romanesco and cut stem flush with bottom florets. Microwave romanesco and 3 tablespoons butter in large, covered bowl until paring knife slips easily in and out of core, 8 to 12 minutes.

3. Transfer romanesco, stem side down, to 12-inch ovensafe skillet. Brush romanesco evenly with melted butter from bowl and sprinkle with salt. Transfer skillet to oven and broil until top of romanesco is spotty brown, 8 to 10 minutes. Meanwhile, microwave remaining 3 tablespoons butter, paprika, cayenne, coriander, allspice, cardamom, cumin, and pepper in now-empty bowl, stirring occasionally, until fragrant and bubbling, 1 to 2 minutes.

4. Using pot holder, remove skillet from oven and transfer to wire rack. Being careful of hot skillet handle, gently tilt skillet so butter pools to one side. Using spoon, baste romanesco until butter is absorbed, about 30 seconds.

5. Cut romanesco into wedges and transfer to platter. Season with salt to taste and sprinkle pine nuts and cilantro over top. Serve with sauce.

PER SERVING Cal 330; **Total Fat** 27g, **Sat Fat** 14g; **Chol** 50mg; **Sodium** 230mg; **Total Carb** 15g, **Dietary Fiber** 5g, **Total Sugars** 6g; **Protein** 9g

Honey Butter Corn

Honey Butter Corn
SERVES 4 **FAST**

WHY THIS RECIPE WORKS Fresh corn on the cob, shucked, boiled, and buttered, is a summertime treasure. But with enough repetition, even treasures can become a little tired. We wanted to create a simple, easy recipe that added pizzazz to summer corn by enhancing its fresh, sweet flavor. We started by stripping the kernels off of six cobs of freshly husked corn. To develop deep corn flavor, we browned the kernels in a skillet in a little vegetable oil. After about 9 minutes (with a bit of stirring), the corn was tender and had loads of flavorful browning. To highlight its sweet, nutty flavor even more, we melted butter into the hot kernels to give each little nub a glistening, rich coating. Some fresh thyme lent its signature fragrance and gave the corn a savory anchor. Finally, just a little bit of a surprising ingredient—honey—brought the dish together by gently accentuating the corn's sweetness. We prefer fresh corn in this recipe, but you can substitute 4½ cups of thawed frozen corn, if desired.

2 tablespoons vegetable oil
6 ears corn, kernels cut from cobs (4½ cups)
¾ teaspoon table salt
½ teaspoon pepper
3 tablespoons unsalted butter, cut into 3 pieces
2 tablespoons honey
1 tablespoon fresh thyme leaves

1. Heat oil in 12-inch nonstick skillet over medium-high heat until shimmering. Add corn, salt, and pepper and cook, stirring occasionally, until tender and spotty brown, 8 to 10 minutes.

2. Off heat, stir in butter, honey, and thyme until butter is melted and mixture is combined, about 30 seconds. Serve.

PER SERVING Cal 310; **Total Fat** 19g, **Sat Fat** 6g; **Chol** 25mg; **Sodium** 440mg; **Total Carb** 36g, **Dietary Fiber** 3g, **Total Sugars** 15g; **Protein** 6g

VARIATION
Miso Honey Butter Corn
Reduce honey to 1 tablespoon. Substitute 2 scallions, sliced thin on bias, for thyme. Add 1 tablespoon white miso paste and 1 teaspoon soy sauce with butter in step 2.

Garden-Fresh Corn with Zucchini and Herbs
SERVES 4 **FAST** **VEGAN**

WHY THIS RECIPE WORKS We love fresh corn on the cob during its all-too-brief season, and are always on the search for new inspiration to maximize this summer favorite. In this iteration, a variety of fresh garden herbs and a light touch with the cooking are the keys to success. To capture all of the fresh corn's natural sweetness, we "milked" the cob by scraping it with the back of a knife. We then briefly sautéed the corn to bring out its summery flavors, and combined it with zucchini (another summertime must-have vegetable), a variety of soft herbs, and the corn milk for a fresh, cohesive summer side dish.

> 5 ears corn, kernels cut from cobs (about 5 cups), cobs reserved
> 1 tablespoon vegetable oil
> 2 zucchini, chopped fine
> 3 garlic cloves, minced
> 2 tablespoons minced fresh basil
> 1 tablespoon minced fresh chives
> 1 tablespoon minced fresh parsley
> 1½ teaspoons lemon juice

1. Working over bowl, run back of knife down each corn cob to scrape away milk, reserving milk. Heat oil in 12-inch skillet over medium-high heat until shimmering. Add zucchini and cook until softened and browned at edges, about 3 minutes.

2. Add corn kernels and cook until deep yellow and softened, about 2 minutes. Add garlic and cook until fragrant, about 30 seconds. Off heat, stir in corn milk, basil, chives, parsley, and lemon juice. Season with salt and pepper to taste. Serve.

PER SERVING Cal 160; **Total Fat** 7g, **Sat Fat** 0g; **Chol** 0mg; **Sodium** 10mg; **Total Carb** 27g, **Dietary Fiber** 3g, **Total Sugars** 9g; **Protein** 6g

VARIATIONS
Garden-Fresh Corn with Sausage and Sage
Omit garlic. Substitute 5 ounces crumbled breakfast sausage for zucchini. Substitute 1 teaspoon chopped fresh sage and 1 tablespoon chopped fresh thyme for basil, chives, and parsley. Add 1 finely chopped red bell pepper to skillet after cooking breakfast sausage in step 1, and cook until softened, about 1 minute. Stir in 2 tablespoons maple syrup with herbs before serving.

Garden-Fresh Southwestern Corn
Omit garlic. Substitute 1 finely chopped red onion for zucchini. Substitute 3 tablespoons minced fresh cilantro for basil, chives, and parsley. Substitute 2 teaspoons lime juice for lemon juice.

Add 1 finely chopped red bell pepper to skillet after cooking red onion in step 1, and cook until softened, about 1 minute. Stir in 1 teaspoon minced canned chipotle chile in adobo sauce with cilantro before serving.

Sautéed Corn with Cherry Tomatoes, Ricotta Salata, and Basil
SERVES 4 TO 6 **FAST**

WHY THIS RECIPE WORKS To take full advantage of the summer corn season, we wanted a quick recipe for sautéed corn bursting with fresh flavor. First we cut the kernels from the raw ears. To replicate the lightly charred, smoky flavor and satisfying texture of grilled corn, we seared the corn, without stirring it, in a little oil in a skillet. This caramelized the corn, contributing a rich sweetness and a deep toasted quality while ensuring the corn retained some crunch. Then, to balance the sweetness, we added toasted garlic chips, ricotta salata, and lemon juice. Cherry tomatoes and basil freshened the dish. We call for a range of lemon juice because fresh corn can vary in sweetness. If ricotta salata is unavailable, substitute a mild feta cheese.

> 2 tablespoons vegetable oil
> 3 garlic cloves, sliced thin
> 4 ears corn, kernels cut from cobs (4 cups)
> ½ teaspoon table salt
> 6 ounces cherry tomatoes, halved
> 1½ ounces ricotta salata cheese, crumbled (⅓ cup), divided
> ¼ cup shredded fresh basil
> 1–2 tablespoons lemon juice
> ¼ teaspoon pepper

1. Cook oil and garlic in 12-inch nonstick skillet over medium heat, stirring frequently, until garlic is light golden brown and fragrant, 2 to 3 minutes. Using slotted spoon, transfer garlic to large bowl, leaving oil in skillet.

2. Return skillet to medium-high heat and heat until shimmering. Add corn and sprinkle with salt. Cook, without stirring, until corn is browned on bottom and beginning to pop, about 3 minutes. Stir and continue to cook, stirring once or twice, until corn is spotty brown all over, 2 to 3 minutes. Transfer corn to bowl with garlic.

3. Stir in tomatoes, half of ricotta salata, basil, 1 tablespoon lemon juice, and pepper. Season with salt, pepper, and remaining lemon juice to taste. Sprinkle with remaining ricotta salata and serve.

PER SERVING Cal 130; **Total Fat** 8g, **Sat Fat** 1.5g; **Chol** 5mg; **Sodium** 120mg; **Total Carb** 14g, **Dietary Fiber** 2g, **Total Sugars** 4g; **Protein** 4g

Sautéed Corn with Black Beans and Bell Pepper

1. Heat 1 tablespoon oil in 12-inch nonstick skillet over medium heat. Add onion, bell pepper, and jalapeño and cook, stirring occasionally, until onion is softened, 4 to 6 minutes. Add garlic, cumin, and ¼ teaspoon salt and cook until fragrant, about 1 minute. Add beans and cook until warmed through, about 1 minute; transfer mixture to large bowl and wipe out skillet.

2. Heat remaining 1 tablespoon oil in now-empty skillet over medium-high heat until shimmering. Add corn and sprinkle with remaining ½ teaspoon salt. Cook, without stirring, until corn is browned on bottom and beginning to pop, about 3 minutes. Stir and continue to cook, stirring once or twice, until corn is spotty brown all over, 2 to 3 minutes. Transfer corn to bowl with black bean mixture.

3. Stir in cilantro and 2 tablespoons lime juice. Season with salt and remaining lime juice to taste. Serve.

Sautéed Corn with Miso and Scallions
SERVES 4 TO 6

Mirin is a sweet Japanese cooking wine; sherry can be substituted for the mirin if necessary. We call for a range of vinegar because fresh corn can vary in sweetness.

 2 tablespoons vegetable oil, divided
 6 scallions, white parts minced, green parts
  sliced thin on bias
 1 teaspoon grated fresh ginger
 2 tablespoons white miso
1-2 tablespoons rice vinegar
 4 ears corn, kernels cut from cobs (4 cups)
 ¼ teaspoon table salt
 1 tablespoon mirin
 1 tablespoon toasted sesame seeds

1. Heat 1 tablespoon oil in 12-inch nonstick skillet over medium heat. Add scallion whites and ginger and cook, stirring frequently, until softened, 1 to 2 minutes. Transfer mixture to large bowl and whisk in miso and 1 tablespoon vinegar. Wipe out skillet.

2. Heat remaining 1 tablespoon oil in now-empty skillet over medium-high heat until shimmering. Add corn and sprinkle with salt. Cook, without stirring, until corn is browned on bottom and beginning to pop, about 3 minutes. Stir and continue to cook, stirring once or twice, until corn is spotty brown all over, 2 to 3 minutes. Add mirin and cook until evaporated, about 1 minute. Transfer corn to bowl with scallion mixture.

3. Stir in scallion greens. Season with salt and remaining vinegar to taste. Sprinkle with sesame seeds and serve.

VARIATIONS
Sautéed Corn with Black Beans and Bell Pepper
SERVES 4 TO 6

We call for a range of lime juice because fresh corn can vary in sweetness. To make this dish spicier, add in the chile seeds.

 2 tablespoons vegetable oil, divided
 ½ red onion, chopped fine
 ½ red bell pepper, stemmed, seeded, and cut into
  ¼-inch pieces
 1 jalapeño chile, stemmed, seeded, and minced
 1 garlic clove, minced
 ½ teaspoon ground cumin
 ¾ teaspoon table salt, divided
 1 (15-ounce) can black beans, rinsed
 3 ears corn, kernels cut from cobs (3 cups)
 ½ cup minced fresh cilantro
2-3 tablespoons lime juice

Creamed Corn

SERVES 4 TO 6 **FAST**

WHY THIS RECIPE WORKS Corn and cream make a terrific combination; their sweet flavors mingle to bring out the best in each other. Those who dread creamed corn have probably had only the canned version, which contains no cream at all—only water, thickeners, sugar, and who-knows-what else. We set out to rescue this side dish and return it to its rightful place at the summertime table. To start, we stripped plump, yellow kernels from a stack of husked corn cobs and simmered the kernels gently in water, to deactivate the natural enzymes that might cause the cream to curdle. This cooking liquid turned into a flavorful, concentrated corn broth. To thicken this broth, we blended a portion of the kernels with ¼ cup of cream until smooth and then added this puree back to the rest of the corn in the saucepan, which gave it the perfect texture. Do not substitute frozen corn for fresh.

> 7 ears corn, kernels cut from cobs (about 7 cups)
> 1¼ cups water
> ¼ cup heavy cream
> 1⅛ teaspoons table salt
> ¼ teaspoon pepper

1. Combine corn and water in large saucepan and bring to boil over high heat. Cover, reduce heat to low, and cook, stirring occasionally, until corn is crisp-tender, about 20 minutes.

2. Remove saucepan from heat and transfer 1½ cups corn mixture to blender. Add cream, salt, and pepper and process until smooth, about 1 minute. Stir pureed corn mixture into corn mixture in saucepan and season with salt and pepper to taste. (If creamed corn looks thin, return to low heat and cook gently until thickened slightly, about 3 minutes.) Serve.

PER SERVING Cal 140; **Total Fat** 7g, **Sat Fat** 2.5g; **Chol** 10mg; **Sodium** 440mg; **Total Carb** 21g, **Dietary Fiber** 2g, **Total Sugars** 6g, **Protein** 5g

VARIATIONS
Creamed Corn with Bacon and Scallions
Cook 2 slices chopped bacon in 10-inch skillet over medium-high heat until crispy, 5 to 7 minutes; transfer to paper towel–lined plate. Stir crisped bacon and 2 minced scallions into saucepan with pureed corn before serving.

Creamed Corn with Chipotle and Cilantro
Add 2 teaspoons minced canned chipotle chile in adobo sauce to blender with corn. Stir 2 tablespoons minced fresh cilantro into saucepan with pureed corn before serving.

Smashed Sichuan Cucumbers

Smashed Sichuan Cucumbers

SERVES 4 **FAST** **VEGAN**

WHY THIS RECIPE WORKS Smashed cucumbers is a Sichuan dish that is typically served with rich, spicy food. We started with English cucumbers, which are nearly seedless and have thin, crisp skins. Placing them in a zipper-lock bag and smashing them into large, irregular pieces sped up a salting step that helped expel excess water. The craggy pieces also did a better job of holding on to the dressing. Using black vinegar, an aged rice-based vinegar, added a mellow complexity to the soy and sesame dressing. We prefer the complex flavor of Chinese *Chinkiang* (or *Zhenjiang*) black vinegar in this dish, but if you can't find it, you can substitute 2 teaspoons of rice vinegar and 1 teaspoon of balsamic vinegar. A rasp-style grater makes quick work of turning the garlic into a paste. We like to drizzle the cucumbers with Sichuan chili oil when serving them with milder dishes such as grilled fish or chicken.

> 2 (14-ounce) English cucumbers, ends trimmed
> 1½ teaspoons kosher salt
> 4 teaspoons Chinese black vinegar
> 1 teaspoon garlic, minced to paste

1 tablespoon soy sauce

2 teaspoons toasted sesame oil

1 teaspoon sugar

1 teaspoon sesame seeds, toasted

1. Cut each cucumber crosswise into 3 equal lengths and place in zipper-lock bag. Seal bag. Using small skillet or rolling pin, firmly but gently smash cucumbers until flattened and split lengthwise into 3 or 4 spears each. Tear spears into rough 1-inch pieces and transfer to colander set in large bowl. Toss cucumbers with salt and let sit for at least 15 minutes or up to 30 minutes.

2. Meanwhile, whisk vinegar and garlic together in medium bowl; let sit for at least 5 minutes or up to 15 minutes.

3. Whisk soy sauce, oil, and sugar into vinegar mixture to dissolve sugar. Add cucumbers, discarding any extracted liquid, and sesame seeds to bowl with dressing and toss to combine. Serve immediately.

PER SERVING Cal 40; **Total Fat** 2.5g; **Sat Fat** 0g; **Chol** 0mg; **Sodium** 650mg; **Total Carb** 3g, **Dietary Fiber** 1g, **Total Sugars** 2g; **Protein** 2g

Thai-Style Stir-Fried Eggplant with Garlic-Basil Sauce

Thai-Style Stir-Fried Eggplant with Garlic-Basil Sauce

SERVES 4 **FAST**

WHY THIS RECIPE WORKS Eggplant is the perfect base for Asian-inspired stir-fries, as it soaks up the flavor-packed sauce and softens to a melt-in-your-mouth consistency. We wanted to achieve a great Thai-style eggplant side dish without having to take the extra effort to salt or pretreat the eggplant before cooking (after all, stir-fries are supposed to come together quickly, not involve a lot of additional work). We started by cooking the eggplant for about 10 minutes. In that time we were able to drive off the excess moisture and brown the eggplant, all in one 12-inch skillet. To complement the earthy eggplant, we also added a sweet red bell pepper to the skillet. We tested adding additional vegetables, but anything more felt superfluous and hid the great flavor and texture of the sautéed eggplant. For the Thai-style sauce, we used a combination of water and fish sauce flavored with brown sugar, lime, and red pepper flakes. Stirring in a generous amount of basil and scallions to finish perfected our quick eggplant stir-fry. Do not peel the eggplant; leaving the skin on helps it hold together during cooking.

SAUCE

½ cup water

¼ cup fish sauce

2 tablespoons packed brown sugar

2 teaspoons grated lime zest plus 1 tablespoon juice

2 teaspoons cornstarch

⅛ teaspoon red pepper flakes

VEGETABLES

2 tablespoons plus 1 teaspoon vegetable oil, divided

6 garlic cloves, minced

1 tablespoon grated fresh ginger

1 pound eggplant, cut into ¾-inch pieces

1 red bell pepper, stemmed, seeded, and cut into ¼-inch pieces

½ cup fresh basil leaves, torn into rough ½-inch pieces

2 scallions, sliced thin

1. FOR THE SAUCE Whisk all ingredients together in bowl.

2. FOR THE VEGETABLES Combine 1 teaspoon oil, garlic, and ginger in bowl. Heat remaining 2 tablespoons oil in 12-inch nonstick skillet over high heat until shimmering. Add eggplant and bell pepper and cook, stirring often, until well browned and tender, 8 to 10 minutes.

3. Clear center of skillet, add garlic mixture, and cook, mashing mixture into skillet, until fragrant, about 30 seconds. Stir garlic mixture into vegetables. Whisk sauce to recombine, then add to skillet. Cook, stirring constantly, until sauce is thickened, about 30 seconds. Off heat, stir in basil and scallions and serve.

PER SERVING Cal 170; **Total Fat** 9g, **Sat Fat** 0.5g; **Chol** 0mg; **Sodium** 700mg; **Total Carb** 22g, **Dietary Fiber** 4g, **Total Sugars** 12g; **Protein** 4g

Stir-Fried Japanese Eggplant
SERVES 4 TO 6 **FAST** **VEGAN**

WHY THIS RECIPE WORKS Since eggplant is neutral in flavor, it is something of a blank canvas taking on whatever flavors are cooked with it. In this stir-fry, a deeply savory sauce clings to and flavors Japanese eggplant. Japanese eggplant is typically longer and more slender than other varieties. It is practically seedless and has a thinner skin so it can absorb lots of sauce. We cooked pieces of eggplant over high heat in a shallow skillet which allowed the eggplant's excess moisture to evaporate quickly, leaving the eggplant browned and tender. For our sauce, we opted for classic stir-fry flavors: soy sauce, Chinese rice wine, and, for umami depth, hoisin sauce. Just a teaspoon of cornstarch was enough to thicken it to the glossy consistency characteristic of restaurant-style stir-fries. Scallions and fresh cilantro lent the dish some herbaceous notes that played nicely off the savory sauce. This recipe works equally well with globe or Italian eggplants. You can substitute dry sherry for the Chinese rice wine.

SAUCE
- ½ cup chicken or vegetable broth
- ¼ cup Chinese rice wine
- 3 tablespoons hoisin sauce
- 1 tablespoon soy sauce
- 1 teaspoon cornstarch
- 1 teaspoon toasted sesame oil

EGGPLANT
- 6 garlic cloves, minced
- 2 tablespoons plus 1 teaspoon vegetable oil, divided
- 1 tablespoon grated fresh ginger
- 1½ pounds Japanese eggplant, cut into ¾-inch pieces
- 2 scallions, sliced thin on bias
- ½ cup fresh cilantro sprigs, cut into 2-inch pieces
- 1 tablespoon sesame seeds, toasted

1. FOR THE SAUCE Whisk all ingredients together in bowl; set aside.

Charred Sichuan-Style Japanese Eggplant

2. FOR THE EGGPLANT Combine garlic, 1 teaspoon oil, and ginger in small bowl. Heat 1 tablespoon oil in 12-inch nonstick skillet over high heat until just smoking. Add half of eggplant and cook, stirring frequently, until browned and tender, 4 to 5 minutes; transfer to bowl. Repeat with remaining 1 tablespoon oil and remaining eggplant.

3. Return first batch of eggplant and any accumulated juices to skillet and push to sides. Add garlic-ginger mixture to center and cook, mashing mixture into skillet, until fragrant, about 30 seconds. Stir garlic-ginger mixture into eggplant. Whisk sauce to recombine, then add to skillet and cook until eggplant is well coated and sauce is thickened, about 30 seconds. Off heat, stir in scallions and cilantro and sprinkle with sesame seeds. Serve.

PER SERVING Cal 140; **Total Fat** 7g, **Sat Fat** 0.5g; **Chol** 0mg; **Sodium** 330mg; **Total Carb** 13g, **Dietary Fiber** 3g, **Total Sugars** 6g; **Protein** 3g

VARIATIONS
Sesame-Basil Stir-Fried Japanese Eggplant
Substitute 2 tablespoons fish sauce, 2 tablespoons packed brown sugar, and 1 tablespoon rice vinegar for hoisin sauce. Substitute ½ cup torn fresh basil leaves for cilantro.

Sweet Chili-Garlic Stir-Fried Japanese Eggplant

Substitute 3 tablespoons chili-garlic sauce and 2 tablespoons packed brown sugar for hoisin sauce.

Charred Sichuan-Style Japanese Eggplant

SERVES 4 TO 6   VEGAN

WHY THIS RECIPE WORKS In this eggplant stir-fry, we took advantage of the fact that eggplant can absorb serious quantities of oil by providing the eggplant with a tasty, spicy Sichuan-style chili oil to soak up. To speed cooking and get great char on the eggplant, we used the microwave to slightly dehydrate it before putting it in a smoking-hot pan. Some green bell pepper, scallions, and cilantro sprigs provided a fresh and cooling reprieve to the rest of the dish. We like to serve this dish with plenty of white rice (page 28) to tame the heat. Fermented black beans are actually soybeans that have been packed in salt and fermented; they can be found in the Asian section of most supermarkets, in Asian specialty markets, and online. Use a spice grinder to grind the chiles. Remove the eggplant from the microwave immediately so that the steam can escape. This recipe works equally well with globe or Italian eggplants. You can substitute dry sherry for the Chinese rice wine.

⅓ cup plus 3 tablespoons vegetable oil, divided
2 garlic cloves, sliced thin
15 bird chiles, ground fine (1½ tablespoons)
1 (½-inch) piece fresh ginger, peeled and sliced thin
1 star anise pod
½ cup fermented black beans
6 tablespoons Chinese rice wine, divided
¼ cup hoisin sauce
1 tablespoon sugar
1½ pounds Japanese eggplant, halved lengthwise, then cut crosswise into 1½-inch pieces
½ teaspoon table salt
1 green bell pepper, stemmed, seeded, and cut into 1-inch pieces
¼ cup water
6 scallions, green parts cut into 1-inch pieces, white parts sliced thin
½ cup fresh cilantro sprigs, cut into 2-inch pieces

1. Heat ⅓ cup oil, garlic, bird chiles, ginger, and star anise in small saucepan over medium-high heat until sizzling. Reduce heat to low and gently simmer until garlic and ginger are soft but not browned, about 5 minutes. Let cool off heat for 5 minutes. Stir in black beans, 2 tablespoons rice wine, hoisin, and sugar until combined; set aside.

2. Toss eggplant with salt in bowl. Line entire surface of large plate with double layer of coffee filters and lightly spray with vegetable oil spray. Spread eggplant in even layer on coffee filters. Microwave until eggplant is dry and shriveled to one-third of its original size, about 10 minutes, flipping halfway through to dry sides evenly (eggplant should not brown). Transfer eggplant immediately to paper towel–lined plate.

3. Heat 2 tablespoons oil in 12-inch skillet over high heat until just smoking. Add eggplant in even layer and cook, stirring occasionally, until charred on most sides, 5 to 7 minutes. Push eggplant to sides of skillet and add remaining 1 tablespoon oil and bell pepper to center. Cook, without stirring, until bell pepper is lightly charred, about 3 minutes.

4. Reduce heat to medium, add water and remaining ¼ cup rice wine, scraping up any browned bits, and cook until liquid is reduced by half, about 15 seconds. Stir in scallion greens and cook until just wilted, about 15 seconds. Off heat, stir in garlic–black bean sauce. Transfer to platter and top with scallion whites and cilantro. Serve immediately.

PER SERVING Cal 660; **Total Fat** 46g, **Sat Fat** 3g; **Chol** 0mg; **Sodium** 740mg; **Total Carb** 42g, **Dietary Fiber** 8g, **Total Sugars** 21g; **Protein** 14g

Braised Belgian Endives

SERVES 4

WHY THIS RECIPE WORKS Belgian endives are small torpedo-shaped heads of tightly packed white leaves that have a pleasantly bitter flavor. Braising transforms them into a side dish with complex flavor—mellow, sweet, and rich. We browned Belgian endives in butter and sugar then braised them quickly in white wine and chicken broth for deep yet bright flavor. To avoid discoloration, do not cut the endives far in advance of cooking. The halved endives can fall apart easily, so move them in the pan by grasping the curved sides gingerly with tongs and supporting the cut sides with a spatula while lifting and turning. You will need a 12-inch skillet with a tight-fitting lid for this recipe.

3 tablespoons unsalted butter, divided
½ teaspoon sugar
¼ teaspoon table salt
4 heads Belgian endive (4 ounces each), halved lengthwise
¼ cup dry white wine
¼ cup chicken or vegetable broth
½ teaspoon minced fresh thyme
1 tablespoon minced fresh parsley
1 teaspoon lemon juice

1. Melt 2 tablespoons butter in 12-inch skillet over medium-high heat. Sprinkle sugar and salt evenly in skillet and set endives cut sides down in single layer. Cook, shaking skillet occasionally to prevent sticking, until golden brown, about 5 minutes (reduce heat if endives brown too quickly). Carefully flip endives and cook until curved sides are golden brown, about 3 minutes.

2. Flip endives cut sides down, then add wine, broth, and thyme to skillet. Cover, reduce heat to low, and simmer until leaves open up slightly and endives are tender when poked with tip of paring knife, 13 to 15 minutes (add 2 tablespoons water during cooking if pan appears dry). Transfer endives to serving platter and cover with aluminum foil to keep warm.

3. Increase heat to medium-high and bring liquid in skillet to boil; reduce heat and simmer until reduced to syrupy consistency, 1 to 2 minutes. Off heat, whisk in remaining 1 tablespoon butter, parsley, and lemon juice. Season with salt and pepper to taste, spoon sauce over endives, and serve.

PER SERVING Cal 100; **Total Fat** 8g, **Sat Fat** 5g; **Chol** 25mg; **Sodium** 180mg; **Total Carb** 4g, **Dietary Fiber** 2g, **Total Sugars** 1g; **Protein** 1g

VARIATION
Braised Belgian Endive with Bacon and Cream
Omit butter and lemon juice. Before cooking endives, cook 3 slices bacon, cut into ¼-inch pieces, in 12-inch skillet over medium heat until crisp, 5 to 7 minutes. Transfer bacon to paper towel–lined plate and set aside. Pour off all but 2 tablespoons fat from skillet and continue with step 1. Add 2 tablespoons heavy cream to skillet with parsley in step 3. Sprinkle crisped bacon over endives before serving.

Sesame-Hoisin Braised Escarole

Sesame-Hoisin Braised Escarole
SERVES 4 **FAST** **VEGAN**

WHY THIS RECIPE WORKS Escarole is a milder member of the endive family with pale green, crisp leaves. To enliven our quick and easy braised escarole side dish we chose a savory Asian flavor profile. Starting with a generous 2 pounds of escarole, we sautéed half of the greens before adding the rest to fit everything in the pot. We then removed the lid to allow most of the liquid to evaporate as the escarole finished cooking. A chopped onion, browned to bring out its sweetness, served as a simple flavor foundation. For seasoning, we combined hoisin sauce, soy sauce, rice vinegar, and sesame oil, along with red pepper flakes, which added some welcome heat. Adding the sauce during the last few minutes ensured it would have enough time to season the greens without over-reducing. A sprinkle of toasted sesame seeds gave this dish a little textural contrast and more sesame flavor.

2 tablespoons extra-virgin olive oil
1 onion, chopped fine
1 garlic clove, minced
¼ teaspoon red pepper flakes
2 heads escarole (2 pounds), trimmed and sliced ½ inch thick, divided
¼ teaspoon table salt
1 tablespoon hoisin sauce
1 tablespoon rice vinegar
1 tablespoon toasted sesame oil
2 teaspoons soy sauce
2 tablespoons sesame seeds, toasted

1. Heat olive oil in Dutch oven over medium heat until shimmering. Add onion and cook until softened and lightly browned, 5 to 7 minutes. Stir in garlic and pepper flakes and cook until fragrant, about 30 seconds. Stir in half of escarole and cook until beginning to wilt, about 2 minutes. Stir in remaining escarole and salt. Cover, reduce heat to medium-low, and cook, stirring occasionally, until greens are tender, about 10 minutes.

2. Uncover and increase heat to medium. Stir in hoisin, vinegar, sesame oil, and soy sauce. Cook until most of liquid has evaporated, about 3 minutes. Season with salt and pepper to taste. Transfer to platter, sprinkle with sesame seeds, and serve.

PER SERVING Cal 180; **Total Fat** 13g, **Sat Fat** 1.5g; **Chol** 0mg; **Sodium** 410mg; **Total Carb** 12g, **Dietary Fiber** 7g, **Total Sugars** 3g; **Protein** 4g

Braised Fennel with Radicchio and Parmesan
SERVES 4

WHY THIS RECIPE WORKS Fennel is a celery-like vegetable with a lively anise flavor. For a richly flavored side dish, we cut fennel bulbs into thick slabs and braised them with wine and aromatics. Leaving the fennel in the skillet even after the liquid had evaporated developed a caramelized crust. To balance the sweetness of the fennel, we stirred in a whole head of radicchio, sometimes known as Italian chicory, cooking it with water, honey, and butter to tame its edge and create a rich sauce. All this dish needed was some Parmesan cheese and toasted pine nuts for richness and crunch, and some minced fennel fronds for a bright finish. Do not core the fennel bulb before cutting it into slabs; the core will help hold the layers of fennel together during cooking. You can serve this dish over polenta (page 192) as a main course.

- 4 tablespoons unsalted butter, divided
- 3 fennel bulbs, 2 tablespoons fronds minced, stalks discarded, bulbs cut lengthwise into ½-inch-thick slabs
- ½ cup dry white wine
- ½ teaspoon grated lemon zest plus 2 teaspoons juice
- ½ teaspoon table salt
- ¼ teaspoon pepper
- 1 head radicchio (10 ounces), halved, cored, and sliced thin
- ¼ cup water
- 2 teaspoons honey
- 2 tablespoons pine nuts, toasted and chopped Shaved Parmesan cheese

1. Melt 3 tablespoons butter in 12-inch skillet over medium heat. Arrange fennel in single layer over bottom of skillet, then drizzle with wine and sprinkle with lemon zest, salt, and pepper. Cover, reduce heat to medium-low, and cook for 15 minutes. (Skillet will be crowded at first, but fennel will shrink as it cooks.)
2. Flip fennel. Continue to cook, covered, until fennel is tender and well browned, about 7 minutes per side. Transfer fennel to serving platter and tent with aluminum foil.

3. Add radicchio, water, and honey to skillet and cook over low heat, scraping up any browned bits, until wilted, 3 to 5 minutes. Off heat, stir in lemon juice and remaining 1 tablespoon butter until melted and thickened slightly. Season with salt and pepper to taste. Pour radicchio and sauce over fennel, then sprinkle with pine nuts, minced fennel fronds, and shaved Parmesan. Serve.

PER SERVING Cal 240; **Total Fat** 14g, **Sat Fat** 7g; **Chol** 0mg; **Sodium** 400mg; **Total Carb** 20g, **Dietary Fiber** 6g, **Total Sugars** 10g; **Protein** 4g

Skillet-Charred Green Beans
SERVES 4 **FAST** **VEGAN**

WHY THIS RECIPE WORKS Skillet-charring green beans produces browned beans with satisfying chew and deep flavor. After softening the beans in the microwave, we cooked them in a skillet, not stirring them so they developed deep color on one side before letting them blister all over. We seasoned the charred beans with lemony salt and pepper. Microwave thinner, tender beans for 6 to 8 minutes and thicker, tougher beans for 10 to 12 minutes. To make the green beans without a microwave, bring ¼ cup of water to a boil in a skillet over high heat. Add the green beans, cover, and cook for 5 minutes. Transfer the beans to a paper towel–lined plate and wash the skillet before proceeding with the recipe.

- ½ teaspoon grated lemon zest plus 1 teaspoon juice
- ½ teaspoon kosher salt
- ¼ teaspoon pepper
- 1 pound green beans, trimmed
- 2 tablespoons vegetable oil

1. Combine lemon zest, salt, and pepper in small bowl. Set aside.
2. Rinse green beans but do not dry. Place in medium bowl, cover, and microwave until fully tender, 6 to 12 minutes, stirring every 3 minutes. Using tongs, transfer green beans to paper towel–lined plate and let drain.
3. Heat oil in 12-inch nonstick skillet over high heat until just smoking. Add green beans in single layer. Cook, without stirring, until green beans begin to blister and char, 4 to 5 minutes. Toss green beans and continue to cook, stirring occasionally, until green beans are softened and charred, 4 to 5 minutes longer. Using tongs, transfer green beans to serving bowl, leaving any excess oil in skillet. Sprinkle with lemon-salt mixture and lemon juice and toss to coat. Serve.

PER SERVING Cal 100; **Total Fat** 7g, **Sat Fat** 0.5g; **Chol** 0mg; **Sodium** 150mg; **Total Carb** 8g, **Dietary Fiber** 3g, **Total Sugars** 4g; **Protein** 2g

Skillet-Charred Green Beans with Crispy Bread-Crumb Topping

Process 2 tablespoons panko bread crumbs in spice grinder or mortar and pestle until uniformly ground to medium-fine consistency that resembles couscous. Cook panko and 1 tablespoon vegetable oil in 12-inch nonstick skillet over medium-low heat, stirring frequently, until light golden brown, 5 to 7 minutes. Remove skillet from heat; add ¾ teaspoon kosher salt, ¼ teaspoon pepper, and ¼ teaspoon red pepper flakes; and stir to combine. Transfer panko mixture to bowl; set aside. Wash out skillet thoroughly and dry with paper towels. Proceed with recipe as directed, substituting panko mixture for lemon-salt mixture.

Skillet-Charred Green Beans with Crispy Sesame Topping

Process 3 tablespoons sesame seeds, 1 tablespoon panko bread crumbs, and 1 teaspoon Sichuan peppercorns in spice grinder or mortar and pestle until uniformly ground to medium-fine consistency that resembles couscous. Cook sesame seed mixture and 2 teaspoons vegetable oil in 12-inch nonstick skillet over medium-low heat, stirring frequently, until light golden brown, 5 to 7 minutes. Remove skillet from heat; add ¼ teaspoon kosher salt, 1 teaspoon Korean red pepper flakes, and ½ teaspoon grated orange zest and stir to combine. Transfer sesame seed mixture to bowl; set aside. Wash out skillet thoroughly and dry with paper towels. Proceed with recipe as directed, substituting sesame seed mixture for lemon-salt mixture Sprinkle with 2 scallions, green parts only sliced thin, and serve.

Sautéed Green Beans with Mushrooms and Dukkah
SERVES 4

WHY THIS RECIPE WORKS For a fresh update on traditional green bean casserole, we took inspiration from Middle Eastern flavors. We traded the casserole dish for a skillet and sautéed meaty cremini mushrooms with shallots. Next we sautéed fresh green beans until crisp-tender, which retained both their nutritional value and vibrant color. Adding a simple, bold mixture of lemon zest, garlic, and parsley during the last minutes of cooking brought plenty of flavor, as did lemon juice. To deliver creaminess without weighing down the vegetables, we drizzled on yogurt. Finally, we sprinkled the dish with dukkah, an irresistible Middle Eastern blend of roasted chickpeas, pistachios, and toasted seeds. It made all the flavors pop and was the perfect crunchy finish to our side dish. You will need a 12-inch nonstick skillet with a tight-fitting lid. We prefer to use our homemade Dukkah (page 117), but you can substitute store-bought dukkah if you wish.

Sautéed Green Beans with Mushrooms and Dukkah

5 teaspoons extra-virgin olive oil, divided
1 garlic clove, minced
2 tablespoons minced fresh parsley
1 teaspoon grated lemon zest plus 2 teaspoons lemon juice
8 ounces cremini mushrooms, trimmed and sliced thin
3 shallots, halved and sliced thin
½ teaspoon table salt
⅛ teaspoon pepper
1 pound green beans, trimmed and cut into 2-inch lengths
¼ cup water
⅓ cup organic plain low-fat yogurt
2 tablespoons dukkah

1. Combine 1 tablespoon oil, garlic, parsley, and lemon zest in bowl; set aside. Heat 1 teaspoon oil in 12-inch nonstick skillet over medium heat until shimmering. Add mushrooms, shallots, salt, and pepper, cover, and cook until mushrooms have released their liquid, about 5 minutes. Uncover, increase heat to high, and cook, stirring occasionally, until mushrooms are golden, about 8 minutes. Transfer to clean bowl.

2. Heat remaining 1 teaspoon oil in now-empty skillet over medium heat until shimmering. Add green beans and cook, stirring occasionally, until spotty brown, 4 to 6 minutes. Add water, cover, and cook until green beans are bright green and still crisp, about 2 minutes.

3. Uncover, increase heat to high, and cook until water evaporates, 30 to 60 seconds. Stir in oil-garlic mixture and mushrooms and cook until beans are crisp-tender, 1 to 3 minutes. Off heat, stir in lemon juice and season with salt and pepper to taste. Transfer to platter, drizzle with yogurt, and sprinkle with dukkah. Serve.

PER SERVING Cal 150; **Total Fat** 8g, **Sat Fat** 1g; **Chol** 0mg; **Sodium** 380mg; **Total Carb** 17g, **Dietary Fiber** 4g, **Total Sugars** 8g; **Protein** 5g

---

TAKE IT UP A NOTCH

Dukkah is a Mediterranean condiment made from a blend of nuts, seeds, and spices. It makes a flavorful crunchy garnish for vegetables and salads.

Dukkah
MAKES 2 CUPS

    1   (15-ounce) can chickpeas, rinsed and patted dry
    1   teaspoon extra-virgin olive oil
    ½   cup shelled pistachios, toasted
    ⅓   cup black sesame seeds, toasted
    2½ tablespoons coriander seeds, toasted
    1   tablespoon cumin seeds, toasted
    2   teaspoons fennel seeds, toasted
    1½ teaspoons pepper
    1¼ teaspoons table salt

1. Adjust oven rack to middle position and heat oven to 400 degrees. Toss chickpeas with oil and spread in single layer on rimmed baking sheet. Roast until browned and crisp, 40 to 45 minutes, stirring every 5 to 10 minutes; let cool completely.

2. Process chickpeas in food processor until coarsely ground, about 10 seconds; transfer to bowl. Pulse pistachios and sesame seeds in now-empty food processor until coarsely ground, about 15 pulses; transfer to bowl with chickpeas. Process coriander, cumin, and fennel seeds in again-empty food processor until finely ground, 2 to 3 minutes; transfer to bowl with chickpeas. Add pepper and salt and toss until well combined. (Dukkah can be refrigerated for up to 1 month.)

Green Beans with Tomatoes and Olives
SERVES 4 TO 6   VEGAN

WHY THIS RECIPE WORKS For a fresh take on green beans, we looked to the Mediterranean. While many recipes for green beans call for blanching and then sautéing them, we sautéed the green beans first to get browning and then added water to the pan and covered it to steam them. Once the green beans were fully tender, we uncovered the pan and stirred in a mixture of tomatoes, olives, garlic, vinegar, and olive oil to infuse them with flavor. A final sprinkling of basil brightened things up. The green beans don't need to be cut into perfect 2-inch pieces; a little variety in length is fine.

    5   ounces grape tomatoes, halved
    ½   cup pitted kalamata olives, halved
    ¼   cup extra-virgin olive oil, divided
    1   shallot, minced
    1   tablespoon red wine vinegar
    2   garlic cloves, minced
    1¼ teaspoons table salt, divided
    ½   teaspoon plus ⅛ teaspoon pepper, divided
    1½ pounds green beans, trimmed and cut into
        2-inch lengths
    ½   cup water
    3   tablespoons chopped fresh basil

1. Combine tomatoes, olives, 2 tablespoons oil, shallot, vinegar, garlic, 1 teaspoon salt, and ½ teaspoon pepper in bowl. Set aside.

2. Heat remaining 2 tablespoons oil in 12-inch skillet over medium heat until shimmering. Add green beans, remaining ¼ teaspoon salt, and remaining ⅛ teaspoon pepper and cook, stirring occasionally, until spotty brown, 5 to 7 minutes.

3. Add water, cover, and cook until green beans are nearly tender, 5 to 7 minutes. Stir in tomato mixture and cook, uncovered, until green beans are fully tender and tomatoes just begin to break down, about 2 minutes. Off heat, stir in basil and season with salt and pepper to taste. Serve.

PER SERVING Cal 140; **Total Fat** 10g, **Sat Fat** 1.5g; **Chol** 0mg; **Sodium** 430mg; **Total Carb** 10g, **Dietary Fiber** 4g, **Total Sugars** 5g; **Protein** 3g

Mediterranean Braised Green Beans

5 tablespoons extra-virgin olive oil, divided
1 onion, chopped fine
4 garlic cloves, minced
  Pinch cayenne pepper
1½ cups water
½ teaspoon baking soda
1½ pounds green beans, trimmed and cut into
  2- to 3-inch lengths
1 (14.5-ounce) can diced tomatoes, drained with
  juice reserved, chopped
1 tablespoon tomato paste
1 teaspoon table salt
¼ teaspoon pepper
¼ cup chopped fresh parsley
  Red wine vinegar

1. Adjust oven rack to lower-middle position and heat oven to 275 degrees. Heat 3 tablespoons oil in Dutch oven over medium heat until shimmering. Add onion and cook, stirring occasionally, until softened, 3 to 5 minutes. Add garlic and cayenne and cook until fragrant, about 30 seconds. Add water, baking soda, and green beans and bring to simmer. Reduce heat to medium-low and cook, stirring occasionally, for 10 minutes. Stir in tomatoes and their juice, tomato paste, salt, and pepper.

2. Cover pot, transfer to oven, and cook until sauce is slightly thickened and green beans can be easily cut with side of fork, 40 to 50 minutes. Stir in parsley and season with vinegar to taste. Drizzle with remaining 2 tablespoons oil and serve warm or at room temperature.

PER SERVING Cal 170; **Total Fat** 12g, **Sat Fat** 1.5g; **Chol** 0mg; **Sodium** 680mg; **Total Carb** 13g, **Dietary Fiber** 4g; **Total Sugars** 6g; **Protein** 3g

Mediterranean Braised Green Beans
SERVES 4 TO 6 `VEGAN`

WHY THIS RECIPE WORKS Braising green beans takes more time than sautéing or steaming them, but you can simultaneously cook and flavor the beans with this slower method, which works especially well for older, tougher supermarket beans. We first cooked the green beans in baking soda and water, which softened their fibrous skins. Then we added canned diced tomatoes and tomato paste and moved the pot to the oven for hands-off gentle simmering until the sauce thickened and the green beans became infused with the tomato and garlic and turned meltingly tender. A sprinkle of parsley and red wine vinegar added bright notes to the finished dish. These green beans taste great both warm and at room temperature.

VARIATION
Mediterranean Braised Green Beans with Mint and Feta
Add ¾ teaspoon ground allspice with garlic and cayenne. Substitute 2 tablespoons chopped fresh mint for parsley. Omit 2 tablespoons oil in step 2. Sprinkle green beans with ½ cup crumbled feta cheese before serving.

Stir-Fried Sichuan Green Beans

SERVES 4 **FAST**

WHY THIS RECIPE WORKS Sichuan green beans, usually deep-fried in oil, have a wrinkled appearance, slightly chewy texture, and intense flavor. To make them at home, we stir-fried the beans until their skins began to shrivel and char in spots. For the sauce, we used dry mustard and sherry for their subtle tang and red pepper flakes and white pepper for their aromatic warmth and muskiness. Ground pork absorbed the sauce perfectly, adding meaty richness. Sliced scallions and sesame oil were the finishing touches.

2 tablespoons soy sauce
2 tablespoons water
1 tablespoon dry sherry
1 teaspoon sugar
½ teaspoon cornstarch
¼ teaspoon white pepper
¼ teaspoon red pepper flakes
¼ teaspoon dry mustard
2 tablespoons vegetable oil
1 pound green beans, trimmed and cut into 2-inch lengths
4 ounces ground pork
3 garlic cloves, minced
1 tablespoon grated fresh ginger
3 scallions, white and light green parts only, sliced thin
1 teaspoon toasted sesame oil

1. Whisk soy sauce, water, sherry, sugar, cornstarch, pepper, pepper flakes, and mustard in small bowl until sugar dissolves.

2. Heat vegetable oil in 12-inch nonstick skillet over high heat until just smoking. Add green beans and cook, stirring frequently, until crisp-tender and skins are shriveled and blackened in spots, 5 to 8 minutes (reduce heat to medium-high if green beans begin to darken too quickly). Transfer green beans to large plate and cover loosely with aluminum foil to keep warm.

3. Reduce heat to medium-high and add pork to now-empty skillet. Cook, breaking pork into small pieces with wooden spoon, until no longer pink, about 2 minutes. Push pork to sides of skillet. Add garlic and ginger to center and cook, mashing mixture into skillet, until fragrant, 30 seconds. Stir mixture into pork; transfer to platter.

4. Whisk sauce to recombine, then add to again-empty skillet. Cook over high heat until sauce is thickened and reduced slightly, about 15 seconds. Return green beans and pork to skillet and gently toss to coat with sauce. Off heat, stir in scallions and sesame oil. Serve immediately.

PER SERVING Cal 200; **Total Fat** 15g; **Sat Fat** 3g; **Chol** 20mg; **Sodium** 610mg; **Total Carb** 12g, **Dietary Fiber** 4g, **Total Sugars** 6g; **Protein** 8g

Collard Greens with Golden Raisins and Almonds

SERVES 4 TO 6 **FAST**

WHY THIS RECIPE WORKS For a fresh take on collard greens, we decided to steam and then sauté them. Cutting the greens into 2-inch pieces helped them soften quickly but left greater texture than thinner slices, while draining and pressing the excess water from the steamed collards kept them from getting waterlogged. A generous dose of extra-virgin olive oil for sautéing the collards, along with sweet raisins, delicate shallots, toasted almonds, and umami-rich grated Parmesan, elevated humble collards into a more elegant side. You can substitute kale for the collards. Leave the collards slightly wet after washing; the moisture helps them to steam properly in step 1.

2 pounds collard greens, stemmed and cut into 2-inch pieces
1½ teaspoons table salt, divided
¾ teaspoon pepper, divided
6 tablespoons extra-virgin olive oil, divided
½ cup golden raisins
2 shallots, sliced thin
4 garlic cloves, sliced thin
⅛ teaspoon red pepper flakes
¼ cup grated Parmesan cheese, plus extra for serving
¼ cup sliced almonds, toasted
Lemon wedges

1. Add collard greens, 1 teaspoon salt, and ½ teaspoon pepper to Dutch oven. Cover and cook over medium-high heat until tender, 14 to 17 minutes, stirring occasionally. (If pot becomes dry, add ¼ cup water so collards continue to steam.) Drain greens in colander, pressing with silicone spatula to release excess liquid. Wipe pot clean with paper towels.

2. Heat ¼ cup oil in now-empty pot over medium heat until shimmering. Add raisins, shallots, garlic, and pepper flakes and cook until just beginning to brown, 2 to 4 minutes. Add greens, remaining ½ teaspoon salt, and remaining ¼ teaspoon pepper and cook until heated through, about 3 minutes. Off heat, stir in Parmesan and season with salt and pepper to taste.

3. Transfer greens to platter. Drizzle with remaining 2 tablespoons oil and sprinkle with almonds. Serve with lemon wedges and extra Parmesan.

PER SERVING Cal 250; **Total Fat** 18g; **Sat Fat** 3g; **Chol** 5mg; **Sodium** 490mg; **Total Carb** 18g, **Dietary Fiber** 5g, **Total Sugars** 11g; **Protein** 6g

Simple Dandelion Greens

SERVES 6 TO 8 `FAST` `VEGAN`

WHY THIS RECIPE WORKS Dandelion greens are easily accessible, nutritious, and unabashedly bitter. After testing various methods, we preferred to boil rather than steam them; the greens stayed brighter green in color and less muddy-tasting. We looked at possible additions: olives, feta cheese, tomatoes, and herbs but, in the end, tasters wanted their dandelion greens both perfectly cooked and free of distracting adjunct flavors. Olive oil, salt, and lemon were all that were needed to get the best flavor from the greens. This side dish can be served warm, at room temperature, or chilled. Use mature dandelion greens for this recipe; do not use baby dandelion greens.

    2 pounds dandelion greens, trimmed and
       cut into 2-inch lengths
       Table salt for blanching dandelion greens
    ¼ cup extra-virgin olive oil
       Flake sea salt
       Lemon wedges

1. Bring 4 quarts water to boil in large pot over high heat. Add dandelion greens and 1 tablespoon salt and cook until thickest stems are just tender, 4 to 7 minutes. Drain greens in colander and, using silicone spatula, gently press greens to release excess liquid.

2. Transfer greens to serving platter, drizzle with oil, and season with sea salt to taste. Serve with lemon wedges.

PER SERVING Cal 110; **Total Fat** 8g, **Sat Fat** 1g; **Chol** 0mg; **Sodium** 85mg; **Total Carb** 10g, **Dietary Fiber** 4g, **Total Sugars** 1g; **Protein** 3g

Simple Dandelion Greens

Pan-Steamed Kale with Garlic

SERVES 4 `FAST` `VEGAN`

WHY THIS RECIPE WORKS For a quick-cooking kale side dish that focused on kale's bold flavor while achieving a tender but not sodden texture, we quickly steamed the leaves in a cup of chicken broth (vegetable broth works well, too). Once the kale was tender, we cooked off any excess liquid and finished it with complementary ingredients that accented the kale's natural earthiness without overpowering it. With such an easy cooking method at hand, we decided to come up with a few variations for dressing up our simple kale. We added crunchy almonds and chewy, sweet raisins in one, smoky chorizo in another, and savory pancetta in a third.

    1   cup chicken or vegetable broth
    3   tablespoons extra-virgin olive oil, divided
    1¼   pounds curly kale, stemmed and cut into
         2-inch pieces (14 cups)
    2   garlic cloves, sliced thin
    ⅛   teaspoon red pepper flakes
    1   teaspoon lemon juice, plus extra for seasoning

1. Bring broth and 2 tablespoons oil to boil in Dutch oven over high heat. Add kale, cover, and reduce heat to medium-high. Cook until kale is tender with some resilience, about 7 minutes, stirring halfway through cooking. While kale cooks, combine garlic, pepper flakes, and remaining 1 tablespoon oil in small bowl.

2. Uncover, increase heat to high, and cook, stirring frequently, until liquid has evaporated and kale starts to sizzle, 2 to 3 minutes. Push kale to 1 side of pot, add garlic mixture to empty side, and cook until garlic is fragrant, about 1 minute. Stir garlic mixture into kale. Off heat, stir in lemon juice. Season with salt and extra lemon juice to taste. Serve.

PER SERVING Cal 170; **Total Fat** 12g, **Sat Fat** 1.5g; **Chol** 0mg; **Sodium** 200mg; **Total Carb** 13g, **Dietary Fiber** 5g, **Total Sugars** 4g; **Protein** 6g

Pan-Steamed Kale with Almonds and Raisins

Regular raisins can be substituted for the golden raisins, if desired.

Add ¼ cup golden raisins to Dutch oven with kale in step 1. Substitute ¼ teaspoon garam masala for garlic and pepper flakes. Sprinkle kale with 2 tablespoons toasted slivered almonds before serving.

Pan-Steamed Kale with Chorizo

For the best results, use a cured Spanish-style chorizo for this recipe.

Cook 3 ounces Spanish-style chorizo sausage, quartered lengthwise and sliced ¼ inch thick, and oil in Dutch oven over medium-high heat, stirring frequently, until starting to brown, about 3 minutes. Off heat, using slotted spoon, transfer chorizo to bowl. Proceed with recipe, adding broth to fat left in pot, omitting garlic and pepper flakes, and substituting red wine vinegar for lemon juice. Sprinkle kale with reserved chorizo before serving.

Pan-Steamed Kale with Pancetta

Use a mortar and pestle or a spice grinder to crush the fennel seeds.

Cook 2 ounces finely chopped pancetta and 2 tablespoons oil in Dutch oven over medium-high heat, stirring frequently, until browned, about 3 minutes. Off heat, using slotted spoon, transfer pancetta to bowl. Proceed with recipe, adding broth to fat left in pot and substituting ½ teaspoon fennel seeds, crushed, for garlic and pepper flakes and balsamic vinegar for lemon juice. Sprinkle kale with 2 tablespoons toasted pine nuts and reserved pancetta before serving.

Pan-Steamed Kale with Pancetta

Garlicky Braised Kale

SERVES 4 TO 6 **VEGAN**

WHY THIS RECIPE WORKS Our straightforward one-pot approach turns kale tender without taking hours or leaving it awash in excess liquid. Adding the greens one handful at a time to a seasoned cooking liquid and letting them wilt briefly before adding more allowed us to fit the large volume of leaves into the pot more easily. When the kale had almost the finished tender texture we wanted, we removed the pot lid to allow the liquid to cook off. Garlic, lemon, and red pepper is a classic flavor combination. This technique works equally well with other sturdy winter greens, such as collards or mustard greens.

    3 tablespoons extra-virgin olive oil, divided
    1 onion, chopped fine
    5 garlic cloves, minced
    ⅛ teaspoon red pepper flakes
    1 cup chicken or vegetable broth
    1 cup water
    ¼ teaspoon table salt
    2 pounds kale, stemmed and cut into 2-inch pieces
    2 teaspoons lemon juice, plus extra for seasoning

1. Heat 2 tablespoons oil in Dutch oven over medium heat until shimmering. Add onion and cook until softened and lightly browned, 5 to 7 minutes. Stir in garlic and pepper flakes and cook until fragrant, about 30 seconds. Stir in broth, water, and salt and bring to simmer.

2. Stir in kale, 1 handful at a time, and cook until beginning to wilt, about 5 minutes. Cover, reduce heat to medium-low, and simmer, stirring occasionally, until kale is tender, 25 to 35 minutes.

3. Uncover and increase heat to medium-high. Cook, stirring occasionally, until most of liquid has evaporated (bottom of pot will be almost dry and kale will begin to sizzle), 8 to 12 minutes. Off heat, stir in lemon juice and remaining 1 tablespoon oil. Season with salt, pepper, and extra lemon juice to taste. Serve.

PER SERVING Cal 130; **Total Fat** 8g, **Sat Fat** 1g; **Chol** 0mg; **Sodium** 160mg; **Total Carb** 13g, **Dietary Fiber** 5g, **Total Sugars** 4g; **Protein** 6g

VARIATIONS

Garlicky Braised Kale with Bacon and Onion

Cook 6 slices bacon, cut into ¼-inch pieces, over medium heat until crisp, 5 to 7 minutes. Using slotted spoon, transfer bacon to paper towel–lined plate, then pour off all but 2 tablespoons fat. Substitute rendered fat for 2 tablespoons oil; 1 red onion, halved and sliced thin, for chopped onion; and cider vinegar for lemon juice. Stir reserved bacon into kale before serving.

Garlicky Braised Kale with Coconut and Curry

Substitute 2 teaspoons grated fresh ginger and 1 teaspoon curry powder for red pepper flakes and 1 (14-ounce) can coconut milk for water. Substitute lime juice for lemon juice and sprinkle kale with ⅓ cup toasted chopped cashews before serving.

Braised Leeks
SERVES 4

Braised Leeks

WHY THIS RECIPE WORKS The unique onion-like sweetness of leeks makes them a delicious side dish, especially when braised, which gives them a tender, creamy texture and deep flavor. The key to perfectly braised leeks was cooking them to the ideal doneness, so they'd be nicely caramelized on the outside and soft but not mushy on the inside. Large leeks held together well in the pan and didn't overcook. We halved the leeks lengthwise and set them in the skillet cut side down; a sprinkling of sugar boosted caramelization. Finally, we added wine, broth, and thyme to the pan, simmered the leeks until tender, and then reduced the liquid to a flavorful glaze. Look for leeks about 1 inch in diameter and trim them to fit in the skillet. Leave enough of the root intact to hold the layers together. The leeks can fall apart easily when cooking, so handle them gently.

- 3 tablespoons unsalted butter, divided
- ½ teaspoon sugar
- ¼ teaspoon table salt
- 4 large leeks (2¾ pounds), white and light green parts only, halved lengthwise, root ends trimmed, and washed thoroughly
- ¼ cup dry white wine
- ¼ cup chicken broth
- ½ teaspoon minced fresh thyme
- 1 tablespoon minced fresh parsley (optional)
- 1 teaspoon lemon juice

1. Adjust oven rack to middle position and heat oven to 200 degrees. Place serving platter on rack. Melt 2 tablespoons butter in 12-inch nonstick skillet over medium-high heat. Sprinkle sugar and salt evenly over bottom of skillet and add leeks cut sides down in single layer. Cook, shaking skillet occasionally, until golden brown, about 5 minutes, adjusting heat as needed if browning too quickly.

2. Add wine, broth, and thyme. Reduce heat to low, cover, and simmer until leeks lose their vibrant color and turn translucent and paring knife inserted into root end meets little resistance, about 10 minutes.

3. Gently transfer leeks to warmed platter, leaving liquid in skillet; cover leeks and set aside. Return liquid to simmer over medium-high heat and cook until syrupy, 1 to 2 minutes. Off heat, whisk in remaining 1 tablespoon butter; parsley, if using; and lemon juice and season with salt and pepper to taste. Spoon sauce over leeks and serve immediately.

PER SERVING Cal 100; **Total Fat** 6g, **Sat Fat** 3.5g; **Chol** 15mg; **Sodium** 135mg; **Total Carb** 9g, **Dietary Fiber** 1g, **Total Sugars** 3g; **Protein** 1g

Stir-Fried Portobellos with Soy-Maple Glaze
SERVES 4 **VEGAN**

WHY THIS RECIPE WORKS Hefty, meaty portobello mushrooms, in combination with snow peas and carrots, make for a super-satisfying vegetable stir-fry that's great as is or served over rice (page 28). Cooking the mushrooms in two batches kept them from steaming in their own juices, guaranteeing even cooking and browning, and adding a quick glaze gave the mushrooms a strong sweet-salty flavor boost. We then stir-fried the snow peas and carrots in the same skillet until crisp-tender, added garlic and ginger and cooked until they were just fragrant, and stirred in the mushrooms and sauce to coat everything with its glossy goodness.

GLAZE
3 tablespoons maple syrup

2 tablespoons mirin

1 tablespoon soy sauce

SAUCE
½ cup chicken or vegetable broth

2 tablespoons soy sauce

1½ tablespoons mirin

2 teaspoons rice vinegar

2 teaspoons cornstarch

2 teaspoons toasted sesame oil

VEGETABLES
3 tablespoons vegetable oil, divided

2 garlic cloves, minced

2 teaspoons grated fresh ginger

¼ teaspoon red pepper flakes

2 pounds portobello mushroom caps, gills removed, cut into 2-inch wedges, divided

8 ounces snow peas, strings removed and sliced ¼ inch thick on bias

2 carrots, peeled and cut into 2-inch-long matchsticks

1. **FOR THE GLAZE** Whisk all ingredients together in bowl.

2. **FOR THE SAUCE** Whisk all ingredients together in bowl.

3. **FOR THE VEGETABLES** Combine 1 teaspoon oil, garlic, ginger, and pepper flakes in bowl. Heat 1 tablespoon oil in 12-inch nonstick skillet over high heat until shimmering. Add half of mushrooms and cook, without stirring, until browned on one side, 2 to 3 minutes. Flip mushrooms, reduce heat to medium, and cook until second side is browned and mushrooms are tender, about 5 minutes. Transfer to second bowl. Repeat with 1 tablespoon oil and remaining mushrooms.

Stir-Fried Portobellos with Soy-Maple Glaze

4. Return all mushrooms to pan, add glaze, and cook over medium-high heat, stirring frequently, until glaze is thickened and mushrooms are coated, 1 to 2 minutes. Transfer mushrooms to bowl.

5. Wipe now-empty skillet clean with paper towels. Heat remaining 2 teaspoons oil in clean skillet over high heat until shimmering. Add snow peas and carrots and cook, stirring occasionally, until vegetables are crisp-tender, about 5 minutes. Clear center of skillet, add garlic mixture, and cook, mashing mixture into skillet, until fragrant, about 30 seconds. Stir garlic mixture into vegetables.

6. Return mushrooms to skillet. Whisk sauce to recombine, then add to skillet. Cook, stirring constantly, until sauce is thickened, 1 to 2 minutes. Serve.

PER SERVING Cal 290; **Total Fat** 14g, **Sat Fat** 1.5g; **Chol** 0mg; **Sodium** 810mg; **Total Carb** 33g, **Dietary Fiber** 4g, **Total Sugars** 23g; **Protein** 9g

Greek Stewed Okra with Tomatoes

SERVES 6 TO 8 | VEGAN

WHY THIS RECIPE WORKS The bright-tasting but warmly spiced tomato sauce that envelops whole okra pods in this recipe allows the vegetal green freshness of the okra to shine through. Greek-style tomato sauce is often seasoned with cinnamon, allspice, and other warm baking spices. For our spin on the sauce, we also included onion, garlic, and lemon juice to strike the perfect sweet-savory balance. A sprinkling of minced parsley added some brightness and color to the finished dish. We found that salting the okra pods before stewing them minimized their slippery qualities. While we prefer the flavor and texture of fresh okra in this recipe, you can substitute thawed frozen whole okra.

2 pounds okra, stemmed
¾ teaspoon table salt, plus salt for salting okra
2 (28-ounce) cans whole peeled tomatoes, drained
½ cup extra-virgin olive oil
1 onion, chopped fine
5 garlic cloves, sliced thin
½ teaspoon ground allspice
¼ teaspoon ground cinnamon
¼ teaspoon pepper
2 tablespoons lemon juice
¼ cup minced fresh parsley

1. Toss okra with 2 teaspoons salt in colander and let sit for 1 hour, tossing again halfway through. Rinse well and set aside.

2. Process tomatoes in food processor until smooth, about 1 minute. Heat oil in Dutch oven over medium heat until shimmering. Add onion and cook until softened and lightly browned, 5 to 7 minutes. Stir in garlic, allspice, cinnamon, remaining ¾ teaspoon salt, and pepper and cook until fragrant, about 30 seconds. Stir in tomatoes and lemon juice and bring to simmer. Cook, stirring occasionally, until thickened slightly, about 10 minutes.

3. Stir in okra and return to simmer. Reduce heat to medium-low, cover, and cook, stirring occasionally, until okra is just tender, 20 to 25 minutes. Season with salt and pepper to taste. Sprinkle with parsley and serve.

PER SERVING Cal 200; **Total Fat** 14g, **Sat Fat** 2g; **Chol** 0mg; **Sodium** 1110mg; **Total Carb** 16g, **Dietary Fiber** 5g, **Total Sugars** 6g; **Protein** 3g

Charred Sichuan-Style Okra

Charred Sichuan-Style Okra

SERVES 4 | VEGAN

WHY THIS RECIPE WORKS Since okra stands up so well to the heat and punch of Creole cuisine, it makes sense that it would also pair well with a spicy Sichuan flavor profile. We started by making a concentrated chile oil, with the tingle-inducing flavor of Sichuan peppercorns. Broad bean chili paste gave our sauce heat and the distinct umami of fermented beans. Hoisin sauce and rice wine brought sweetness, acidity, and body to the sauce. Last but not least, scallions provided fresh balance. Charring the okra pods whole before cloaking them with the sauce lent a beautiful sear to the exterior and kept good texture on the inside. Altogether, this is a sumptuous showstopper of a side dish. If you can't find dried bird chiles (Thai red chiles), you can substitute ground red pepper flakes. Asian broad bean chili paste (or sauce) is readily available online; our favorite is from Pixian. Lee Kum Kee makes a good supermarket option. Use a spice grinder to grind the bird chiles and Sichuan peppercorns. Do not substitute frozen okra here.

⅓ cup plus 2 tablespoons vegetable oil, divided

2 garlic cloves, sliced thin

1 (½-inch) piece fresh ginger, peeled and sliced into thin rounds

5 dried bird chiles, ground fine (1½ teaspoons)

1 teaspoon Sichuan peppercorns, ground fine (½ teaspoon)

1 star anise pod

6 tablespoons Chinese rice wine or dry sherry, divided

¼ cup hoisin sauce

3 tablespoons Asian broad bean chili paste

1 pound okra, stemmed

¼ cup water

6 scallions, white parts sliced thin on bias, green parts cut into 1-inch pieces

12 sprigs fresh cilantro, chopped

1. Combine ⅓ cup oil, garlic, ginger, ground chiles, ground Sichuan peppercorns, and star anise in small saucepan and cook over medium-high heat until sizzling, 1 to 2 minutes. Reduce heat to low and gently simmer until garlic and ginger are softened but not browned, about 5 minutes. Let cool off heat for 5 minutes, then stir in 2 tablespoons rice wine, hoisin, and chili paste until combined; set aside.

2. Heat remaining 2 tablespoons oil in 12-inch skillet over medium-high heat until just smoking. Add okra and cook, stirring occasionally, until okra is crisp-tender and well browned on most sides, 5 to 7 minutes.

3. Stir remaining ¼ cup rice wine, water, and scallion greens and whites into skillet with okra, reduce heat to medium, and cook until liquid is reduced by half and scallion greens are just wilted, about 15 seconds. Off heat, stir in garlic-hoisin mixture until combined. Discard star anise and sprinkle with cilantro. Serve immediately.

PER SERVING Cal 360; **Total Fat** 28g, **Sat Fat** 2g; **Chol** 0mg; **Sodium** 770mg; **Total Carb** 18g, **Dietary Fiber** 4g, **Total Sugars** 6g; **Protein** 3g

Pan-Roasted Parsnips
SERVES 6 TO 8 `FAST` `VEGAN`

WHY THIS RECIPE WORKS Our streamlined technique replicates the sweet caramelized flavor of oven-roasted parsnips on the stovetop. After browning the parsnips in oil, we added water to the pan before covering it; this created a gentle steaming effect that guaranteed perfectly cooked parsnips every time. We cut the parsnips into ½-inch-thick pieces on the bias to assure even browning and cooking, as well as an attractive presentation.

Pan-Roasted Cilantro-Lime Parsnips

Look for parsnips no wider than 1 inch at their base, or you may need to remove their fibrous cores before cooking. You will need a 12-inch skillet with a tight-fitting lid for this recipe.

2 tablespoons vegetable oil

2 pounds parsnips, peeled and cut ½ inch thick on bias

½ cup water

¾ teaspoon table salt

1 tablespoon minced fresh parsley
Lemon wedges

1. Heat oil in 12-inch skillet over medium-high heat until shimmering. Add parsnips and cook, stirring occasionally, until golden, 8 to 10 minutes.

2. Add water and salt and bring to simmer. Cover, reduce heat to medium-low, and cook, stirring occasionally, until vegetables are tender and liquid has evaporated, 8 to 10 minutes. Stir in parsley and season with salt and pepper to taste. Serve with lemon wedges.

PER SERVING Cal 100; **Total Fat** 4g, **Sat Fat** 0g; **Chol** 0mg; **Sodium** 230mg; **Total Carb** 17g, **Dietary Fiber** 5g, **Total Sugars** 5g; **Protein** 1g

Pan-Roasted Cilantro-Lime Parsnips

Add 1 teaspoon chili powder to skillet with parsnips in step 1. Substitute 2 tablespoons cilantro for parsley. Add ¾ teaspoon lime zest plus 1 tablespoon lime juice to parsnips with cilantro in step 2. Serve with lime wedges.

Pan-Roasted Orange Parsnips

Substitute 1 teaspoon fresh minced thyme for parsley. Add ¾ teaspoon orange zest to parsnips with thyme in step 2. Serve with orange wedges.

Sautéed Parsnips with Ginger, Maple, and Fennel Seeds

SERVES 4   **FAST**   **VEGAN**

WHY THIS RECIPE WORKS Sautéing parsnips is dead-easy. Cutting them into uniform sticks, a smoking-hot pan, and minimal stirring caramelized and cooked through the parsnips in just minutes. Since parsnips have warm spice and licorice-like notes, we made a glaze that brought out those qualities and had the perfect sweet, salty, and tart balance. You can substitute anise seeds for fennel. Look for parsnips no wider than 1 inch at their base, or you may need to remove their fibrous cores before cooking.

    2 tablespoons soy sauce
    2 tablespoons balsamic vinegar
    1 tablespoon maple syrup
 1½ teaspoons fennel seeds
    2 tablespoons minced fresh ginger
    2 tablespoons plus 1 teaspoon vegetable oil, divided
 1½ pounds parsnips, peeled and cut into 2-inch-long by
        ½-inch-wide matchsticks

1. Stir soy sauce, vinegar, maple syrup, and fennel seeds together in bowl; set aside. Combine ginger and 1 teaspoon oil in separate bowl; set aside.

2. Heat remaining 2 tablespoons oil in 12-inch skillet over medium-high heat until just smoking. Add parsnips and cook, stirring occasionally, until well charred and crisp-tender, 5 to 7 minutes.

3. Push parsnips to sides of skillet. Add ginger mixture to center and cook, mashing mixture into pan, until fragrant, about 30 seconds. Stir ginger into parsnips. Add soy mixture and toss to coat parsnips; cook until liquid is reduced to syrupy glaze, about 15 seconds. Serve immediately.

PER SERVING Cal 210; **Total Fat** 9g, **Sat Fat** 0.5g; **Chol** 0mg; **Sodium** 480mg; **Total Carb** 32g, **Dietary Fiber** 7g, **Total Sugars** 11g; **Protein** 3g

Smashed Minty Peas

SERVES 4 TO 6   **FAST**

WHY THIS RECIPE WORKS Simply boiling peas doesn't add much flavor. To cook and flavor our peas at the same time, we simmered them in a sauce; this allowed the peas to quickly absorb the sauce's flavor. To intensify the sweetness of the peas, we added a small amount of sugar. Pulsing the cooked peas, lettuce, and mint in a food processor until coarsely mashed produced a delicious side dish with a pleasing texture. Do not thaw the peas before adding them to the saucepan. Be careful not to overprocess the peas; they can quickly go from smashed to pureed.

    1 pound frozen peas
    2 cups chopped Boston or Bibb lettuce
    ½ cup chicken broth
    2 tablespoons chopped fresh mint
    4 tablespoons unsalted butter
    ½ teaspoon sugar

1. Bring all ingredients to simmer in medium saucepan over medium-high heat. Cover and cook until peas are tender, 8 to 10 minutes.

2. Transfer mixture to food processor and pulse until coarsely mashed, about 10 pulses, scraping down sides of bowl as needed. Season with salt and pepper to taste. Serve.

PER SERVING Cal 130; **Total Fat** 7g, **Sat Fat** 4.5g; **Chol** 20mg; **Sodium** 50mg; **Total Carb** 11g, **Dietary Fiber** 4g, **Total Sugars** 4g; **Protein** 5g

Sugar Snap Peas with Pine Nuts, Fennel, and Lemon Zest

SERVES 4   **FAST**   **VEGAN**

WHY THIS RECIPE WORKS Sugar snap peas are a cross between English peas and snow peas. They have sweet, crisp edible pods with small juicy peas inside. To ensure that the pods and their peas cooked through at the same rate, we used a hybrid method to steam the sugar snap peas briefly before quickly sautéing them; the trapped steam transferred heat more efficiently than air, so the peas cooked through faster. Cutting the sugar snap peas in half further reduced the cooking time, so the pods retained more of their snap, and as a bonus, the pockets captured the seasonings rather than letting them slide to the bottom of the platter. Sprinkling the snap peas with a dukkah-like mix of finely chopped pine nuts, fennel seeds, and seasonings dressed up this simple preparation with distinct (but not overwhelming) flavor

Sugar Snap Peas with Pine Nuts, Fennel, and Lemon Zest

2. Heat oil in now-empty skillet over medium heat until shimmering. Add snap peas and water, immediately cover, and cook for 2 minutes. Uncover, add garlic, and continue to cook, stirring frequently, until moisture has evaporated and snap peas are crisp-tender, about 2 minutes. Off heat, stir in basil and three-quarters of pine nut mixture. Transfer snap peas to platter and sprinkle with remaining pine nut mixture. Serve.

PER SERVING Cal 100; **Total Fat** 7g, **Sat Fat** 0.5g; **Chol** 0mg; **Sodium** 140mg; **Total Carb** 8g, **Dietary Fiber** 3g, **Total Sugars** 3g; **Protein** 3g

VARIATION

Sugar Snap Peas with Almonds, Coriander, and Orange Zest

Omit pepper flakes. Substitute sliced almonds for pine nuts, coriander seeds for fennel seeds, ¼ teaspoon orange zest for lemon zest, and cilantro for basil.

Blistered Shishito Peppers
SERVES 4 TO 6 FAST VEGAN

WHY THIS RECIPE WORKS Japanese shishito peppers are bright-tasting, citrusy, mild green chiles with thin skins and a crisp texture. We found that cooking the little peppers whole in a small amount of oil worked just as well deep-frying and was far less messy and laborious. The larger granules of kosher salt sprinkled on top add a wonderful crunch, but you can use regular table salt instead, if you prefer. You can find shishito peppers at most well-stocked supermarkets or the farmers' market.

2 tablespoons vegetable oil
8 ounces shishito peppers

Heat oil in 12-inch skillet over medium-high heat until just smoking. Add shishito peppers and cook, without stirring, until skins are blistered, 3 to 5 minutes. Using tongs, flip peppers and continue to cook until blistered on second side, 3 to 5 minutes. Transfer to serving bowl, season with kosher salt to taste, and serve.

PER SERVING Cal 50; **Total Fat** 4.5g, **Sat Fat** 0g; **Chol** 0mg; **Sodium** 0mg; **Total Carb** 2g, **Dietary Fiber** 1g, **Total Sugars** 1g; **Protein** 0g

and crunch. Do not substitute ground fennel for the fennel seeds in this recipe. You will need a 12-inch skillet with a tight-fitting lid for this recipe.

3 tablespoons pine nuts
1 teaspoon fennel seeds
½ teaspoon grated lemon zest
½ teaspoon kosher salt
⅛ teaspoon red pepper flakes
2 teaspoons vegetable oil
12 ounces sugar snap peas, strings removed, halved crosswise on bias
2 tablespoons water
1 garlic clove, minced
3 tablespoons chopped fresh basil

1. Toast pine nuts in 12-inch skillet over medium heat, stirring frequently, until just starting to brown, about 3 minutes. Add fennel seeds and continue to toast, stirring constantly, until pine nuts are lightly browned and fennel is fragrant, about 1 minute. Transfer pine nut mixture to cutting board. Sprinkle lemon zest, salt, and pepper flakes over pine nut mixture. Chop mixture until finely minced and well combined. Transfer to bowl and set aside.

Smoky Shishito Peppers with Espelette and Lime

Smoky Shishito Peppers with Espelette and Lime

SERVES 4 **FAST** **VEGAN**

WHY THIS RECIPE WORKS Tame shishito peppers are the perfect base to showcase finishing spices. We created combinations from the more basic—the always appetite-whetting combo of heat and acid with dried chile and lime—to the refined and aromatic such as fennel pollen, Aleppo pepper, and lemon. If you can't find ground Espelette pepper, you can substitute 1 teaspoon Aleppo pepper or ¼ teaspoon paprika plus ¼ teaspoon red pepper flakes. The skillet will look full. You can use your preferred coarse finishing salt in this recipe. You can find shishito peppers at most well-stocked supermarkets or the farmers' market.

- 1 teaspoon ground dried Espelette pepper
- 1 teaspoon smoked paprika
- ½ teaspoon coarse finishing salt
- ¼ teaspoon grated lime zest, plus lime wedges for serving
- 2 tablespoons vegetable oil
- 8 ounces shishito peppers

Combine Espelette pepper, paprika, salt, and lime zest in small bowl; set aside. Heat oil in 12-inch skillet over medium-high heat until just smoking. Add shishitos and cook, without moving, until skins are blistered, about 3 minutes. Using tongs, flip shishitos and continue to cook until blistered on second side, about 3 minutes. Transfer to serving platter and sprinkle with spice mixture. Serve with lime wedges.

PER SERVING Cal 80; **Total Fat** 7g, **Sat Fat** 0.5g; **Chol** 0mg; **Sodium** 290mg; **Total Carb** 3g, **Dietary Fiber** 1g, **Total Sugars** 1g; **Protein** 1g

VARIATIONS

Shishito Peppers with Fennel Pollen, Aleppo, and Lemon

If you can't find fennel pollen, you can substitute an equal amount of toasted, cracked fennel seeds.

Substitute Aleppo pepper for Espelette pepper, fennel pollen for paprika, and lemon zest and wedges for lime zest and wedges.

Shishito Peppers with Mint, Poppy Seeds, and Orange

Substitute dried mint for Espelette pepper, poppy seeds for paprika, and orange zest and wedges for lime zest and wedges.

Shishito Peppers with Mustard and Bonito Flakes

Omit Espelette pepper. Substitute dry mustard for paprika. Sprinkle 2 tablespoons bonito flakes over shishitos just before serving.

Sour Cream and Onion Smashed Potatoes

SERVES 4 TO 6

WHY THIS RECIPE WORKS Sour cream and onion go hand-in-glove with potatoes. Waxy small red potatoes were the best choice in our rustic recipe, as they held their shape and texture through cooking. When we first added the sour cream the potatoes became gluey before we could fully incorporate it. Instead, we mixed the sour cream directly into melted butter and other dairy before adding the mixture to the cooked potatoes. This meant less stirring, which eliminated the glueyness caused by overworking. This technique also helped to meld the flavors. We use sliced scallions for bold onion flavor, but handled the whites and greens differently: We sautéed the whites in butter before mixing them with the warmed half-and-half and sour cream and added the scallion greens raw for a fresh layer of onion flavor. If the potatoes are too thick after folding in the sour cream in step 3, stir in additional half-and-half, 1 tablespoon at a time, until they reach the desired consistency. This recipe can be doubled.

2 pounds small red potatoes
4 tablespoons unsalted butter
4 scallions, white parts minced, green parts sliced thin
1 cup sour cream
½ cup half-and-half
1 teaspoon table salt
¼ teaspoon pepper

1. Bring potatoes and enough water to cover by 1 inch to boil in large pot over high heat. Reduce heat to medium and simmer until potatoes are tender, about 30 minutes.

2. Meanwhile, melt butter in medium saucepan over medium-low heat. Cook scallion whites until translucent, about 5 minutes. Whisk in sour cream, half-and-half, salt, and pepper until smooth. Remove from heat, cover, and keep warm.

3. Drain potatoes in colander and return to dry pot; let stand 5 minutes. Using silicone spatula, break potatoes into large chunks. Fold in sour cream mixture until incorporated and only small chunks of potato remain. Stir in scallion greens and season with salt and pepper to taste. Serve.

PER SERVING Cal 279; **Total Fat** 18g; **Sat Fat** 11g; **Chol** 48mg; **Sodium** 535mg; **Total Carb** 27g, **Dietary Fiber** 3g, **Total Sugars** 4g; **Protein** 5g

French Mashed Potatoes with Cheese and Garlic
SERVES 6

WHY THIS RECIPE WORKS *Aligot* is French cookery's rich, cheesy take on mashed potatoes. These potatoes get their elastic, satiny texture through prolonged, vigorous stirring. We wanted to create cheesy, garlicky mashed potatoes with the same smooth, elastic texture and stretch as the French original. After testing different potatoes, we found medium-starch Yukon Golds to be the clear winner, yielding a puree with a mild, buttery flavor and a light, creamy consistency. We boiled the potatoes and then used a food processor to "mash" them. Traditional aligot uses butter and crème fraîche to add flavor and creaminess but we substituted whole milk, which provided depth without going overboard. For the cheese, a combination of mild mozzarella and nutty Gruyère proved just right. As for the stirring, too much and the potatoes turned rubbery, too little and the cheese didn't marry with the potatoes for that essential elasticity. The finished potatoes should have a smooth and slightly elastic texture. White cheddar can be substituted for the Gruyère. For richer, stretchier mashed potatoes, double the mozzarella.

2 pounds Yukon Gold potatoes, peeled and cut into ½-inch-thick slices
1½ teaspoons table salt, plus salt for cooking potatoes
6 tablespoons unsalted butter
2 garlic cloves, minced
1–1½ cups whole milk, divided
4 ounces mozzarella cheese, shredded (1 cup)
4 ounces Gruyère cheese, shredded (1 cup)

1. Place potatoes and 1 tablespoon salt in large saucepan; add water to cover by 1 inch. Partially cover saucepan with lid and bring to boil over high heat. Reduce heat to medium-low and simmer until potatoes are tender and just break apart when poked with fork, 12 to 17 minutes. Drain potatoes and dry saucepan.

2. Pulse potatoes, butter, garlic, and salt in food processor until butter is melted and incorporated, about 10 pulses. Add 1 cup milk and continue to process until potatoes are smooth and creamy, about 20 seconds, scraping down sides of bowl halfway through.

3. Return potato mixture to saucepan and set over medium heat. Stir in cheeses, 1 cup at a time, until incorporated. Continue to cook potatoes, stirring vigorously, until cheese is fully melted and mixture is smooth and elastic, 3 to 5 minutes. If mixture is difficult to stir and seems thick, stir in 2 tablespoons milk at a time (up to ½ cup) until potatoes are loose and creamy. Season with salt and pepper to taste. Serve immediately.

PER SERVING Cal 400; **Total Fat** 23g; **Sat Fat** 14g; **Chol** 70mg; **Sodium** 890mg; **Total Carb** 31g, **Dietary Fiber** 0g, **Total Sugars** 4g; **Protein** 15g

Braised Radicchio with Apple and Cream
SERVES 4 **FAST**

WHY THIS RECIPE WORKS The Chioggia variety of radicchio looks like a small head of red cabbage. It has an enjoyably bitter flavor that mellows with cooking and braising is an easy and delicious way to cook radicchio. Slicing the heads into thin strips ensured a short cooking time. Cream proved to be a great braising liquid, considerably tempering the vegetable's assertiveness. After just 5 minutes in a covered pan, the radicchio was wilted and tender. We then removed the cover and allowed the excess liquid to evaporate as the radicchio continued to simmer for another minute or so. Don't be alarmed if the cream turns a lovely shade of purple. This dish is especially good with pork.

2 tablespoons unsalted butter

1 onion, chopped fine

1 Granny Smith apple, peeled, cored, and cut into ½-inch pieces

2 heads radicchio (1¼ pounds), halved, cored, and sliced ½ inch thick

½ cup heavy cream

1 tablespoon sugar

1 tablespoon cider vinegar

Melt butter in Dutch oven over medium-high heat. Add onion and apple and cook, stirring occasionally, until golden, 5 to 6 minutes. Stir in radicchio, cream, and sugar, cover, and cook until radicchio is tender, about 5 minutes. Uncover and simmer until liquid is reduced slightly, about 1 minute. Stir in vinegar and season with salt and pepper to taste. Serve.

PER SERVING Cal 260; **Total Fat** 17g, **Sat Fat** 11g; **Chol** 50mg; **Sodium** 65mg; **Total Carb** 24g, **Dietary Fiber** 3g, **Total Sugars** 11g; **Protein** 5g

Sautéed Radishes
SERVES 4 TO 6 FAST

WHY THIS RECIPE WORKS Raw radishes are peppery-hot and juicy but the heat of cooking changes them completely. Heat concentrates the natural sugars in radishes so that their characteristic pungency disappears and is replaced by a milder, almost turnip-like sweetness. We started by cooking quartered radishes in butter over moderate heat. The butter provided substantial browning and lent subtle, nutty notes to the radishes. And since radishes contain relatively little water, within 10 minutes they were golden brown all over and perfectly tender, with a slight bite. To provide some textural variety and color, we cooked the greens at the end, so that they retained a slight crispness that complemented the heartier radish pieces. We've provided two variations, but feel free to try this with any number of spice mixes. If you can't find radishes with their greens, you can substitute baby arugula or watercress, or skip step 2.

3 tablespoons unsalted butter, cut into 3 pieces, divided

1½ pounds radishes with their greens, radishes trimmed and quartered, 8 cups greens reserved

1 garlic clove, minced

⅜ teaspoon table salt, divided

¼ teaspoon pepper, divided

Lemon wedges

Sautéed Radishes

1. Melt 2 tablespoons butter in 12-inch skillet over medium-high heat. Add radishes, ¼ teaspoon salt, and ⅛ teaspoon pepper and cook, stirring occasionally, until radishes are lightly browned and crisp-tender, 10 to 12 minutes. Stir in garlic and cook until fragrant, about 30 seconds; transfer to bowl.

2. Melt remaining 1 tablespoon butter in now-empty skillet over medium heat. Add radish greens, ⅛ teaspoon salt, and ⅛ teaspoon pepper and cook, stirring frequently, until wilted, about 1 minute. Off heat, stir in radishes and season with salt and pepper to taste. Serve with lemon wedges.

PER SERVING Cal 70; **Total Fat** 6g, **Sat Fat** 3.5g; **Chol** 15mg; **Sodium** 95mg; **Total Carb** 4g, **Dietary Fiber** 2g, **Total Sugars** 2g; **Protein** 1g

VARIATIONS
Sautéed Radishes with Chili and Lime
Stir 1 teaspoon paprika and ½ teaspoon chili powder into radishes with garlic. Substitute lime wedges for lemon.

Sautéed Radishes with Vadouvan Curry and Almonds

We prefer the flavor of vadouvan curry here, but any variety will work.

Omit lemon wedges. Substitute 1½ teaspoons vadouvan curry for garlic. Sprinkle with 2 tablespoons coarsely chopped toasted almonds before serving.

Braised Radishes
SERVES 4 FAST

WHY THIS RECIPE WORKS When developing this speedy recipe for stovetop-braised radishes, we discovered that sautéing the radishes briefly in butter before adding liquid to the pan helped to bring out their natural flavor. For the braising liquid, broth proved to be the best choice: Wine made the radishes taste too harsh and acidic, while water rendered them bland. The sweet oniony flavor of chives worked well with the radishes, which themselves were surprisingly sweet when braised. This radish side dish goes well with chicken, pork, or fish.

- 1 tablespoon unsalted butter
- 1 shallot, minced
- ¼ teaspoon table salt
- 1 pound radishes, trimmed and halved if small or quartered if large
- ⅓ cup chicken or vegetable broth
- 2 teaspoons minced fresh chives

1. Melt butter in 12-inch skillet over medium-high heat. Add shallot and salt, and cook until softened, 2 to 3 minutes. Add radishes and broth, cover, and cook until radishes are tender, about 10 minutes, stirring halfway through cooking.

2. Uncover and continue to cook until liquid thickens slightly, about 1 minute. Stir in chives and season with salt and pepper to taste. Serve.

PER SERVING Cal 50; Total Fat 3g, Sat Fat 2g; Chol 10mg; Sodium 240mg; Total Carb 5g, Dietary Fiber 2g, Total Sugars 3g; Protein 1g

VARIATION
Creamy Braised Radishes with Garlic and Thyme

Omit chives. Substitute 3 minced garlic cloves for shallot and cook until fragrant, about 30 seconds. Reduce broth to ¼ cup and add 2 tablespoons heavy cream and 1 teaspoon minced fresh thyme to skillet with radishes.

Spice-Roasted Butternut Squash
SERVES 4

WHY THIS RECIPE WORKS Butternut squash is great when cut into cubes and roasted on its own—until you taste it spiced up. We turned to the spice cabinet to accent squash's earthy, sweet flavor in a new way. We found that warm spices, such as cinnamon and cumin, have a delicate sweetness of their own, which complemented that quality in the squash. For a tender texture and nice browning, we cut the squash into 1-inch pieces and roasted it in a 425-degree oven after tossing the pieces with the mix of spices. We made this spiced squash a more special side by drizzling it with an easy butter sauce, flavored with honey, lemon, and thyme. It was a rich and sweet but also a bright counterpoint to the spices. When peeling the squash, be sure also to remove the fibrous yellow flesh just beneath the skin.

- 3 tablespoons extra-virgin olive oil
- 1¼ teaspoons table salt, divided
- 1 teaspoon pepper
- 1 teaspoon ground cumin
- 1 teaspoon ground cinnamon
  Pinch cayenne pepper
- 3 pounds butternut squash, peeled, seeded, and cut into 1-inch pieces
- 2 tablespoons unsalted butter
- 1 tablespoon honey
- 1 teaspoon chopped fresh thyme or ¼ teaspoon dried
- 1 teaspoon lemon juice

1. Adjust oven rack to middle position and heat oven to 425 degrees. Line rimmed baking sheet with parchment paper. Whisk oil, 1 teaspoon salt, pepper, cumin, cinnamon, and cayenne together in large bowl. Add squash and toss until evenly coated. Arrange squash in even layer on prepared sheet and roast until tender and browned on bottom, 30 to 35 minutes.

2. Meanwhile, microwave butter, honey, and remaining ¼ teaspoon salt in small bowl until butter is melted, about 30 seconds. Stir in thyme and lemon juice. Using spatula, transfer squash to serving platter. Drizzle with butter mixture and serve.

PER SERVING Cal 317; Total Fat 16g, Sat Fat 5g; Chol 15mg; Sodium 852mg; Total Carb 46g, Dietary Fiber 8g, Total Sugars 12g; Protein 4g

VARIATIONS
Spice-Roasted Butternut Squash with Honey-Lime Butter

Substitute ground allspice for cinnamon, 1 tablespoon minced fresh chives for thyme, and lime juice for lemon juice.

Spice-Roasted Butternut Squash with Honey-Orange Butter

Substitute ground coriander for cinnamon, oregano for thyme, and orange juice for lemon juice.

Spaghetti Squash with Garlic and Parmesan

SERVES 4 TO 6

WHY THIS RECIPE WORKS Spaghetti squash has delicately flavored creamy flesh that separates into noodle-y strands. Many recipes bury the squash under a sauce, but our simple recipe lets the unique flavor and texture of the squash shine through. Brushing the squash halves with oil and roasting them cut side down brought out the sweetness of the flesh. Once the squash was cooked, shredding it was as simple as holding the halves over a bowl and scraping them with a fork. After draining the excess liquid, we dressed the squash with Parmesan, fresh basil, lemon juice, and garlic for a flavorful side dish that tasted like summer.

1 (2½-pound) spaghetti squash, halved lengthwise and seeded
2 tablespoons extra-virgin olive oil, divided
½ teaspoon table salt
¼ teaspoon pepper
¼ cup grated Parmesan cheese
1 tablespoon chopped fresh basil
1 teaspoon lemon juice
1 garlic clove, minced

1. Adjust oven rack to middle position and heat oven to 450 degrees. Brush cut sides of squash with 1 tablespoon oil and sprinkle with salt and pepper. Place squash cut side down on rimmed baking sheet. Roast until squash is tender when pierced with tip of paring knife, 25 to 30 minutes.

2. Flip squash over and let cool slightly. Holding squash with clean dish towel over large bowl, use fork to scrape squash flesh from skin while shredding it into fine pieces; discard skin.

3. Drain excess liquid from bowl, then gently stir in Parmesan, basil, lemon juice, garlic, and remaining 1 tablespoon oil. Season with salt and pepper to taste, and serve.

PER SERVING Cal 100; **Fat** 7g, **Sat Fat** 1.5g, **Chol** 5mg; **Sodium** 300mg; **Total Carb** 10g, **Dietary Fiber** 2g, **Total Sugars** 4g; **Protein** 3g

Sautéed Baby Spinach with Chickpeas and Sun-Dried Tomatoes

VARIATION
Spaghetti Squash with Asian Flavors

Omit Parmesan, basil, lemon juice, garlic, and remaining 1 tablespoon oil in step 3. Toss shredded squash with 2 thinly sliced scallions, 1 tablespoon soy sauce, 2½ teaspoons vegetable oil, 1 teaspoon rice vinegar, ½ teaspoon toasted sesame oil, and ½ teaspoon toasted sesame seeds before serving.

Sautéed Baby Spinach with Almonds and Golden Raisins

SERVES 4 **FAST** **VEGAN**

WHY THIS RECIPE WORKS Baby spinach is undeniably convenient—no tough stems to remove or sandy grit to rinse out—but cooking often turns these very tender greens into a watery, mushy mess. We were determined to find a method for cooking baby spinach that would give us a worthwhile side dish. Parcooking the spinach in the microwave turned out to be the best way to help the vegetable release plenty of liquid. We pressed the microwaved spinach against a colander to eliminate more water, coarsely chopped it, and pressed it again. Then all we had to do was quickly sauté it. We then combined the spinach with a few complementary flavors and appealing textures to finish the dish. If you don't have a bowl large enough to accommodate the entire amount of spinach, cook it in a smaller bowl in two batches. Reduce the water to 2 tablespoons per batch and cook the spinach for about 1½ minutes.

18 ounces (18 cups) baby spinach
¼ cup water
2 tablespoons plus 2 teaspoons extra-virgin olive oil, divided
½ cup golden raisins
4 garlic cloves, sliced thin crosswise
¼ teaspoon red pepper flakes
¼ teaspoon table salt
⅓ cup slivered almonds, toasted
2 teaspoons sherry vinegar

1. Microwave spinach and water in covered bowl until spinach is wilted and decreased in volume by half, 3 to 4 minutes. Remove bowl from microwave and keep covered for 1 minute. Carefully transfer spinach to colander and, using back of silicone spatula, gently press spinach against colander to release excess liquid. Transfer spinach to cutting board and chop. Return spinach to colander and press again.

2. Cook 2 tablespoons oil, raisins, garlic, and pepper flakes in 10-inch skillet over medium-high heat, stirring constantly, until garlic is light golden brown and beginning to sizzle, 3 to 6 minutes. Stir in spinach and salt and cook until uniformly wilted and glossy green, about 2 minutes. Stir in almonds and vinegar. Drizzle with remaining 2 teaspoons oil and season with salt to taste. Serve immediately.

PER SERVING Cal 240; Total Fat 14g, Sat Fat 1.5g; Chol 0mg; Sodium 250mg; Total Carb 23g, Dietary Fiber 4g, Total Sugars 15g; Protein 6g

VARIATIONS

Sautéed Baby Spinach with Pecans and Feta

Omit raisins and pepper flakes. Substitute 4 thinly sliced shallots for garlic. Cook shallots until golden brown, 3 to 5 minutes, in step 2. Substitute red wine vinegar for sherry vinegar and toasted and chopped pecans for almonds. Sprinkle spinach with ⅓ cup crumbled feta cheese before serving.

Sautéed Baby Spinach with Chickpeas and Sun-Dried Tomatoes

Omit raisins, pepper flakes, and sherry vinegar. Add ¾ cup rinsed canned chickpeas and ½ cup drained and thinly sliced oil-packed sun-dried tomatoes to skillet with spinach in step 2. Substitute 2 tablespoons grated Parmesan cheese for almonds. Sprinkle spinach with 6 tablespoons grated Parmesan cheese before serving.

Sautéed Spinach with Yogurt and Dukkah
SERVES 4 FAST

WHY THIS RECIPE WORKS Sautéing spinach is fast and easy and a good way to preserve most of its healthful benefits. And we were pleased to find that the tanginess of yogurt paired perfectly with spinach's earthy flavor. To emphasize the yogurt's tang, we added lemon zest and juice and drizzled it over our garlicky spinach. To elevate the flavor, we sprinkled on dukkah, the Middle Eastern nut and seed blend, which lent the dish a nice textural contrast. Two pounds of flat-leaf spinach (about three bunches) can be substituted for the curly-leaf spinach; do not substitute delicate baby spinach. We prefer to use our homemade Dukkah (page 117), but you can substitute store-bought dukkah if you wish.

½ cup plain low-fat yogurt
1½ teaspoons grated lemon zest plus 1 teaspoon juice
3 tablespoons extra-virgin olive oil, divided
20 ounces curly-leaf spinach, stemmed
2 garlic cloves, minced
¼ cup dukkah

1. Combine yogurt and lemon zest and juice in bowl, and season with salt and pepper to taste; set aside for serving. Heat 1 tablespoon oil in Dutch oven over high heat until shimmering. Add spinach, 1 handful at a time, and cook, stirring constantly, until wilted, about 1 minute. Transfer spinach to colander and squeeze between tongs to release excess liquid.

2. Wipe pot dry with paper towels. Add remaining 2 tablespoons oil and garlic to now-empty pot and cook over medium heat until fragrant, about 30 seconds. Add spinach and toss to coat, gently separating leaves to evenly coat with garlic oil. Off heat, season with salt and pepper to taste. Transfer spinach to platter, drizzle with yogurt sauce, and sprinkle with dukkah. Serve.

PER SERVING Cal 180; Total Fat 14g, Sat Fat 2.5g; Chol 5mg; Sodium 240mg; Total Carb 10g, Dietary Fiber 4g, Total Sugars 2g; Protein 6g

Creamed Spinach
SERVES 4 FAST

WHY THIS RECIPE WORKS Many creamed spinach recipes drown fresh spinach in a stodgy, heavy sauce. Wanting to reinvigorate this classic side dish, we reduced the amount of cream to ¼ cup and combined it with Boursin, a flavorful herbed cheese, which turned into a simple sauce. To avoid a watery sauce, we drained and pressed excess liquid from the cooked spinach before adding it to the creamy sauce. Leave some water clinging to the spinach leaves after rinsing to help encourage steam when cooking. Two pounds of flat-leaf spinach (about three bunches) can be substituted for the curly-leaf spinach; do not substitute delicate baby spinach.

1 tablespoon extra-virgin olive oil
20 ounces curly-leaf spinach, stemmed and chopped coarse
1 (5.2-ounce) package Boursin Garlic & Fine Herbs cheese
¼ cup heavy cream

1. Heat oil in Dutch oven over high heat until shimmering. Add spinach, 1 handful at a time, stirring and tossing each handful to wilt slightly before adding more. Cook spinach, stirring constantly, until uniformly wilted, about 1 minute. Transfer spinach to colander and squeeze between tongs to release excess liquid.

2. Wipe now-empty pot dry with paper towels. Whisk Boursin and cream together in pot and simmer over medium-high heat until thickened, about 2 minutes. Add squeezed spinach and toss to coat. Off heat, season with salt and pepper to taste. Serve.

PER SERVING Cal 270; **Total Fat** 25g, **Sat Fat** 14g; **Chol** 55mg; **Sodium** 340mg; **Total Carb** 7g, **Dietary Fiber** 3g, **Total Sugars** 2g; **Protein** 7g

Broiled Tomatoes with Goat Cheese and Bread Crumbs
SERVES 4 TO 6 **FAST**

WHY THIS RECIPE WORKS Broiled tomatoes make for an impressive-looking side dish and come together super-fast. We sliced ripe tomatoes into planks (instead of halves) to create more surface area and to allow for a more substantial topping. We first sprinkled goat cheese over the planks, then added a mixture of bread crumbs, Parmesan, and fresh basil. The success of this dish depends on using ripe, flavorful tomatoes. If you can't get your hands on in-season field-grown tomatoes, buy vine-ripened tomatoes; they are juicier and more flavorful than other varieties.

1 cup panko bread crumbs
2 tablespoons extra-virgin olive oil
1 ounce Parmesan cheese, grated (½ cup)
1 tablespoon chopped fresh basil
¼ teaspoon table salt
⅛ teaspoon pepper
2 pounds very ripe, in-season tomatoes, cored and sliced ¾ inch thick
1 ounce goat cheese, crumbled (¼ cup)

1. Adjust oven rack 6 inches from broiler element and heat broiler. Toss panko with oil in bowl, spread over rimmed baking sheet, and broil until golden, about 1 minute. Transfer to separate bowl and stir in Parmesan, basil, salt, and pepper.

2. Lay tomato slices on rimmed baking sheet and season with salt and pepper. Broil until heated through, about 3 minutes.

3. Remove tomatoes from broiler. Sprinkle with goat cheese and top with panko mixture. Continue to broil tomatoes until everything is heated through, about 2 minutes. Serve.

PER SERVING Cal 150; **Total Fat** 7g, **Sat Fat** 2g; **Chol** 5mg; **Sodium** 230mg; **Total Carb** 16g, **Dietary Fiber** 2g, **Total Sugars** 4g; **Protein** 6g

GRATING HARD CHEESE

When grating Parmesan and other hard cheeses, use a rasp-style grater. It produces lighter, fluffier shreds of cheese that melt seamlessly into all kinds of dishes and sauces.

Stuffed Tomatoes
SERVES 6

WHY THIS RECIPE WORKS Stuffed tomatoes are elegant and delicious. To concentrate flavor and get rid of excess moisture, we seasoned hollowed-out tomato shells with salt and sugar and let them drain. Couscous proved the best base for the filling, combined with chopped baby spinach and Gruyère cheese. We rehydrated the couscous with the reserved tomato juice, ensuring plenty of savory flavor. A topping of panko bread crumbs—pretoasted for proper browning—mixed with more cheese added crunch and richness, and a drizzle of the cooking liquid mixed with red wine vinegar provided a piquant final touch. Look for large tomatoes, about 3 inches in diameter.

6 large tomatoes (8 to 10 ounces each)
1 tablespoon plus ½ teaspoon kosher salt, divided
1 tablespoon sugar
4½ tablespoons extra-virgin olive oil, divided
¼ cup panko bread crumbs
3 ounces Gruyère cheese, shredded (¾ cup), divided
1 onion, halved and sliced thin
2 garlic cloves, minced

⅛ teaspoon red pepper flakes

8 ounces (8 cups) baby spinach, chopped

1 cup couscous

½ teaspoon grated lemon zest

1 tablespoon red wine vinegar

1. Adjust oven rack to middle position and heat oven to 375 degrees. Cut top ½ inch off stem end of tomatoes and set aside. Using melon baller, scoop out tomato pulp into fine-mesh strainer set over bowl. Press on pulp with wooden spoon to extract juice, setting aside juice and discarding pulp. (You should have about ⅔ cup tomato juice. If not, add water as needed to equal ⅔ cup.)

2. Combine 1 tablespoon salt and sugar in bowl. Sprinkle each tomato cavity with 1 teaspoon salt mixture, then turn tomatoes upside down on plate to drain for 30 minutes.

3. Combine 1½ teaspoons oil and panko in 10-inch skillet and toast over medium-high heat, stirring frequently, until golden brown, about 3 minutes. Transfer to bowl and let cool for 10 minutes. Stir in ¼ cup Gruyère.

4. Heat 2 tablespoons oil in now-empty skillet over medium heat until shimmering. Add onion and remaining ½ teaspoon salt and cook until softened, 5 to 7 minutes. Stir in garlic and pepper flakes and cook until fragrant, about 30 seconds. Add spinach, 1 handful at a time, and cook until wilted, about 3 minutes. Stir in couscous, lemon zest, and reserved tomato juice. Off heat, cover, and let sit until couscous has absorbed liquid, about 7 minutes. Transfer couscous mixture to bowl and stir in remaining ½ cup Gruyère. Season with salt and pepper to taste.

5. Coat bottom of 13 by 9-inch baking dish with remaining 2 tablespoons oil. Blot tomato cavities dry with paper towels and season with salt and pepper to taste. Pack each tomato with couscous mixture, about ½ cup per tomato, mounding excess. Top stuffed tomatoes with 1 heaping tablespoon panko mixture. Place tomatoes in prepared dish. Season reserved tops with salt and pepper to taste and place in empty spaces in dish.

6. Bake, uncovered, until tomatoes have softened but still hold their shape, about 20 minutes. Using slotted spoon, transfer to serving platter. Whisk vinegar into oil remaining in dish, then drizzle over tomatoes. Place tops on tomatoes and serve.

PER SERVING Cal 340; **Total Fat** 16g, **Sat Fat** 4.5g; **Chol** 15mg; **Sodium** 800mg; **Total Carb** 38g, **Dietary Fiber** 5g, **Total Sugars** 9g; **Protein** 11g

VARIATIONS

Stuffed Tomatoes with Currants and Pistachios

Substitute crumbled feta for Gruyère. Stir 2 tablespoons currants and 2 tablespoons chopped pistachios into cooked couscous mixture with feta.

Hasselback Tomatoes

Stuffed Tomatoes with Olives and Orange

Substitute shredded Manchego for Gruyère. Substitute ¼ teaspoon grated orange zest for lemon zest. Stir ¼ cup chopped pitted kalamata olives into cooked couscous mixture with Manchego.

Hasselback Tomatoes

SERVES 4 TO 6 **FAST**

WHY THIS RECIPE WORKS For a summery-fresh side dish, we "hasselbacked" plum tomatoes by slicing them accordion-style almost to their bottoms. Then we stuffed them with a vibrant homemade basil pesto and topped them with flavorful Gruyère cheese. We placed the stuffed tomatoes under the broiler for just about 5 minutes to slightly soften them without turning them to mush and to melt the cheese. For the best results, we recommend buying ripe tomatoes of similar weight and size. We developed this recipe with tomatoes that averaged 3 ounces in weight and 2½ inches in length.

8 ripe plum tomatoes, cored

7 ounces Gruyère cheese, shredded (1¾ cups), divided

1½ cups fresh basil leaves

6 tablespoons extra-virgin olive oil

¼ cup panko bread crumbs

1 garlic clove, minced

1¼ teaspoons table salt, divided

1¼ teaspoons pepper, divided

1. Line rimmed baking sheet with aluminum foil and set wire rack in sheet. Using serrated knife, cut ¼-inch-thick slice from 1 long side of each tomato. Turn tomatoes onto cut sides so they sit flat, then slice crosswise at ¼-inch intervals, leaving bottom ¼ inch of each tomato intact.

2. Process ¾ cup Gruyère, basil, oil, panko, garlic, ½ teaspoon salt, and ½ teaspoon pepper in food processor until smooth, scraping down sides of bowl as needed, about 10 seconds.

3. Adjust oven rack 6 inches from broiler element and heat broiler. Combine remaining ¾ teaspoon salt and remaining ¾ teaspoon pepper in bowl. Carefully open tomato slices and sprinkle with salt-pepper mixture. Using small spoon, spread basil mixture evenly between tomato slices (about 2 tablespoons per tomato).

4. Arrange tomatoes on prepared wire rack. Sprinkle remaining 1 cup Gruyère over tomatoes. Broil until cheese is golden brown, about 5 minutes. Serve.

PER SERVING Cal 290; **Total Fat** 25g, **Sat Fat** 8g; **Chol** 35mg; **Sodium** 730mg; **Total Carb** 7g, **Dietary Fiber** 1g, **Total Sugars** 2g; **Protein** 11g

PREPPING HASSELBACK TOMATOES

1. Using paring knife, remove core.

2. Using serrated knife, cut ¼-inch-thick slice from 1 long side of each tomato. Turn tomatoes onto cut sides so they sit flat, then slice crosswise at ¼-inch intervals, leaving bottom ¼ inch intact.

Zucchini with Creamy Peas and Herbs
SERVES 4

WHY THIS RECIPE WORKS We found that the secret to a zucchini recipe that would expel extra water and leave behind zucchini with concentrated flavor was to combine two recommended methods: salting and draining as well as shredding and squeezing. For this sautéed zucchini recipe, we grated the zucchini with a box grater, tossed the shreds with salt, drained them in a colander, and wrung them out in a dish towel. We tossed the now-dry shreds with a little olive oil and added them to a hot nonstick skillet, where they became tender and lightly browned with only minimal stirring. Adding frozen peas and fresh dill and turning everything creamy took our zucchini to a whole new level.

5 medium zucchini (about 8 ounces each), ends trimmed

Table salt for salting zucchini

1 tablespoon plus 1 teaspoon vegetable oil, divided

1 bunch scallions, white parts chopped fine, green parts sliced thin

1 cup frozen peas, thawed

½ cup heavy cream

2 tablespoons chopped fresh dill leaves or mint

Lemon wedges

1. Cut each zucchini crosswise into several pieces, each 2 to 3 inches long. Shred each piece on large holes of box grater, rotating as needed to avoid shredding seeds and core; you should have about 10 cups shredded zucchini. Toss zucchini with 1½ teaspoons salt and place in colander set in medium bowl; let drain 5 to 10 minutes. Wrap zucchini in dish towel, in batches if necessary, and wring out excess moisture.

2. Place zucchini in medium bowl and break up any large clumps. Drizzle 2 teaspoons oil over zucchini and toss to combine thoroughly.

3. Heat remaining 2 teaspoons oil in 12-inch nonstick skillet over medium heat until shimmering. Add white parts of scallions and cook, stirring, until softened and beginning to brown, about 3 minutes. Increase heat to high; add zucchini and spread evenly in pan with tongs; cook until bottom layer browns, about 2 minutes; stir well, breaking up any clumps with tongs, then cook until "new" bottom layer browns, about 2 minutes more. Add peas and cream and cook, stirring, until cream is mostly reduced, about 2 minutes. Off heat, stir in dill and salt and pepper to taste. Transfer to platter and serve immediately with lemon wedges.

PER SERVING Cal 214; **Total Fat** 15g, **Sat Fat** 7g; **Chol** 40mg; **Sodium** 72mg; Total Carb 16g, **Dietary Fiber** 5g, **Total Sugars** 9g; **Protein** 6g

Stewed Zucchini

SERVES 6 TO 8 `VEGAN`

WHY THIS RECIPE WORKS Looking for yet another way to take advantage of an abundance of zucchini, we developed a stewed version in which the vegetable retained its individual character while still coming together in a deeply flavored, cohesive stew. After testing a variety of recipes, we landed on the classic combination of zucchini and tomatoes. We started by browning seeded zucchini on the stovetop (in batches to ensure thorough, even browning) and set it aside while we built a savory tomato sauce. Tasters found canned diced tomatoes mealy, canned crushed tomatoes sludgy and cloying, and fresh tomatoes inconsistent in quality. Canned whole peeled tomatoes, processed until smooth, gave the dish the right balance of tomato flavor and silky texture. A smattering of olives complemented the sauce. Once our sauce had simmered and thickened, we stirred in the browned zucchini and transferred the pot to the oven to allow it to gently finish cooking and develop deep, concentrated flavor. A garnish of shredded fresh mint, stirred in at the end, added brightness. If possible, use smaller, in-season zucchini, which have thinner skins and fewer seeds.

- 1 (28-ounce) can whole peeled tomatoes
- 3 tablespoons extra-virgin olive oil, divided
- 5 zucchini (8 ounces each), trimmed, quartered lengthwise, seeded, and cut into 2-inch lengths
- 1 onion, chopped fine
- ¾ teaspoon table salt
- 3 garlic cloves, minced
- 1 teaspoon minced fresh oregano or ¼ teaspoon dried
- ¼ teaspoon red pepper flakes
- 2 tablespoons chopped pitted kalamata olives
- 2 tablespoons shredded fresh mint

1. Adjust oven rack to lower-middle position and heat oven to 325 degrees. Process tomatoes and their juice in food processor until completely smooth, about 1 minute; set aside.

2. Heat 2 teaspoons oil in Dutch oven over medium-high heat until just smoking. Brown one-third of zucchini, about 3 minutes per side; transfer to bowl. Repeat with 4 teaspoons oil and remaining zucchini in 2 batches; transfer to bowl.

3. Add remaining 1 tablespoon oil, onion, and salt to now-empty pot and cook, stirring occasionally, over medium-low heat until onion is very soft and golden brown, 9 to 11 minutes. Stir in garlic, oregano, and pepper flakes and cook until fragrant, about 30 seconds. Stir in olives and tomatoes, bring to simmer, and cook, stirring occasionally, until sauce has thickened, about 30 minutes.

Stewed Zucchini

4. Stir in zucchini and any accumulated juices, cover, and transfer pot to oven. Bake until zucchini is very tender, 30 to 40 minutes. Stir in mint and adjust sauce consistency with hot water as needed. Season with salt and pepper to taste. Serve.

PER SERVING Cal 100; **Total Fat** 6g, **Sat Fat** 1g; **Chol** 0mg; **Sodium** 420mg; **Total Carb** 10g, **Dietary Fiber** 2g, **Total Sugars** 6g; **Protein** 3g

PREPPING ZUCCHINI FOR STEWING

Trim off top and bottom of zucchini, then quarter lengthwise. Rest each quarter on trimmed side and cut through core to remove seeds. Cut cored zucchini quarters into 2-inch lengths.

FRIES AND CRISPY SIDES

■ FAST (30 minutes or less total time)　■ MAKE-AHEAD　■ VEGAN

Photos (clockwise from top left): Crispy Vegetable Fritters; Fried Zucchini Sticks; Corn Fritters; Polenta Fries

Easier French Fries

SERVES 4 TO 6 `VEGAN`

WHY THIS RECIPE WORKS Everyone loves crispy, salt-flecked French fries, but making them can be fairly involved and require precise timing. This foolproof, low-fuss method guarantees crispy fries with a tender interior and lots of potato flavor. We found that the key was to start the potatoes in room-temperature oil, bring the oil to boiling, and then cook the fries over high heat until golden. This let the potatoes' interiors soften and cook through before the exteriors started to crisp. Lower-starch Yukon Gold potatoes yielded the crispiest exteriors and creamiest interiors when cooked by this method. Letting the potatoes cook in the oil for 20 minutes before stirring gave them time to form a crust that prevented them from sticking. (Thinner fries are less likely to stick.) This recipe will not work with russets or sweet potatoes. Use a Dutch oven that holds 6 quarts or more for this recipe.

2½ pounds Yukon Gold potatoes, unpeeled
1½ quarts peanut or vegetable oil for frying

1. Line rimmed baking sheet with triple layer of paper towels. Using chef's knife, square off sides of potatoes. Cut potatoes lengthwise into ¼-inch planks, then slice each plank into ¼-inch-thick fries. Combine potatoes and oil in large Dutch oven. Cook over high heat until oil has reached rolling boil, about 5 minutes.

2. Once boiling, continue to cook, without stirring, until potatoes are limp but exteriors are beginning to firm, about 15 minutes.

3. Using tongs, stir potatoes, gently scraping up any that stick, and continue to cook, stirring occasionally, until golden and crisp, 5 to 10 minutes. Using wire skimmer or slotted spoon, transfer fries to prepared sheet. Season with salt to taste, and serve.

PER SERVING Cal 260; **Total Fat** 12g, **Sat Fat** 1g; **Chol** 0mg; **Sodium** 200mg; **Total Carb** 33g, **Dietary Fiber** 0g, **Total Sugars** 0g: **Protein** 4g

CUTTING FRENCH FRIES

1. Square off sides of scrubbed, unpeeled potatoes. Cut potatoes lengthwise into ¼-inch-thick planks.

2. Slice each plank into ¼-inch-thick fries.

Easier French Fries

Steak Fries

SERVES 4 `MAKE-AHEAD` `VEGAN`

WHY THIS RECIPE WORKS Thick wedges of skin-on steak fries are the rustic cousins of skinny French fries. We found a way to achieve a great steak fry that was crisp on the outside, tender on the inside, and full of potato flavor. Starchy russet potatoes worked best here. It was crucial to chill the potatoes in cold water before plunging them into hot oil; this allowed them to cook more slowly and evenly. After drying the potatoes, we par-fried them at a low temperature to help cook the interiors without browning them. Following a rest, we fried the potatoes again at a higher temperature to brown and crisp the exteriors. This double frying produced fries that were evenly cooked, with fluffy middles and crisp exteriors. Use a Dutch oven that holds 6 quarts or more for this recipe.

2½ pounds russet potatoes, unpeeled, cut lengthwise into
    ¾-inch-thick wedges (about 12 wedges per potato)
2 quarts peanut oil for frying

1. Place cut potatoes in large bowl, cover with cold water by at least 1 inch, and then cover with ice cubes. Refrigerate for at least 30 minutes or up to 3 days.

2. Add oil to large Dutch oven until it measures about 1½ inches deep and heat over medium-low heat to 325 degrees. Set wire rack in rimmed baking sheet and line with triple layer of paper towels.

3. Pour off ice and water, quickly wrap potatoes in clean dish towel, and thoroughly pat them dry. Increase heat to medium-high and add potatoes, 1 handful at a time, to hot oil. Fry, stirring with wire skimmer or slotted spoon, until potatoes are limp and soft and have turned from white to gold, about 10 minutes. (Oil temperature will drop 50 to 60 degrees.) Use skimmer or slotted spoon to transfer fries to prepared sheet; let rest for at least 10 minutes. (Fries can sit at room temperature for up to 2 hours.)

4. When ready to serve fries, reheat oil to 350 degrees. Using paper towels as funnel, pour potatoes into hot oil. Discard paper towels and line rack with another triple layer of paper towels. Fry potatoes, stirring fairly constantly, until medium brown and puffed, 8 to 10 minutes. Transfer to paper towel–lined rack to drain. Season with salt and pepper to taste. Serve immediately.

PER SERVING Cal 720; **Total Fat** 56g, **Sat Fat** 4g; **Chol** 0mg; **Sodium** 15mg; **Total Carb** 51g, **Dietary Fiber** 4g, Total sugars 2g: **Protein** 6g

FRYING STEAK FRIES

1. Heat oil in Dutch oven over medium-low heat to 325 degrees.

2. Increase heat and add chilled and dried potatoes, 1 handful at a time, to hot oil. Fry, stirring with wire skimmer, until potatoes turn soft and from white to gold.

3. Transfer fries to paper towels to drain and rest. When ready to serve fries, reheat oil. Add potatoes and fry, stirring constantly, until brown and puffed. Transfer to paper towels to drain. Season and serve.

Oven Fries
SERVES 3 TO 4   `VEGAN`

WHY THIS RECIPE WORKS The ease and neatness of oven fries is an engaging proposition. We were after fries with a golden, crisp crust and a richly creamy interior. We soaked peeled russet potatoes, cut into wedges, in hot water for 10 minutes to remove excess starch. To further prevent the potatoes from sticking, we poured oil, salt, and pepper on the baking sheet, instead of on the potatoes, which elevated them just enough off of the pan. We covered the potatoes with aluminum foil to steam them for the first 5 minutes of cooking and then uncovered them and continued to bake until they were golden and crisp. Take care to cut the potatoes into evenly sized wedges so that all of the pieces will cook at about the same rate. A nonstick baking sheet works particularly well for this recipe. Use a heavy-duty rimmed baking sheet; the intense heat of the oven may cause lighter pans to warp. If you prefer not to peel the potatoes, just scrub them well before cutting.

2¼ pounds russet potatoes, peeled and cut lengthwise into 10 to 12 even wedges
  5 tablespoons vegetable oil, divided
  ¾ teaspoon table salt
  ¼ teaspoon pepper

1. Adjust oven rack to lowest position and heat oven to 475 degrees. Place potatoes in large bowl, cover with hot tap water, and soak for 10 minutes. Meanwhile, coat 18 by 12-inch heavy-duty rimmed baking sheet with ¼ cup oil and sprinkle evenly with salt and pepper.

2. Drain potatoes, then spread out over paper towel–lined baking sheet and thoroughly pat dry. Rinse and wipe out now-empty bowl. Return potatoes to bowl and toss with remaining 1 tablespoon oil. Arrange potatoes in single layer on oiled and seasoned baking sheet, cover tightly with aluminum foil, and bake 5 minutes.

3. Remove foil and continue to bake until bottoms of potatoes are spotty golden brown, 15 to 20 minutes, rotating sheet halfway through roasting time.

4. Using metal spatula and tongs, scrape to loosen potatoes from pan, then flip each wedge, keeping potatoes in single layer. Continue baking until fries are golden and crisp, 5 to 15 minutes, rotating pan as needed if fries are browning unevenly. Transfer baked fries to paper towel–lined baking sheet and let drain. Season with salt and pepper to taste, and serve.

PER SERVING Cal 330; **Total Fat** 18g, **Sat Fat** 1.5g; **Chol** 0mg; **Sodium** 450mg; **Total Carb** 39g, **Dietary Fiber** 3g, **Total Sugars** 1g: **Protein** 5g

Thick-Cut Oven Fries

2. Halve potatoes lengthwise and turn halves cut sides down on cutting board. Trim thin slice from both long sides of each potato half, discarding trimmings. Slice potatoes lengthwise into ⅓- to ½-inch-thick planks.

3. Combine water and cornstarch in large bowl, making sure no lumps of cornstarch remain on bottom of bowl. Microwave, stirring every 20 seconds, until mixture begins to thicken, 1 to 3 minutes. Remove from microwave and continue to stir until mixture thickens to pudding-like consistency. (If necessary, add up to 2 tablespoons water to achieve correct consistency.)

4. Transfer potatoes to bowl with cornstarch mixture and toss until each plank is evenly coated. Arrange planks on prepared sheet, leaving small gaps between planks. (Some cornstarch mixture will remain in bowl.) Cover sheet tightly with lightly greased aluminum foil and bake for 12 minutes.

5. Remove foil and bake until bottom of each fry is golden brown, 10 to 18 minutes. Remove sheet from oven and, using thin metal spatula, carefully flip each fry. Return sheet to oven and continue to bake until second sides are golden brown, 10 to 18 minutes. Sprinkle fries with salt. Using spatula, carefully toss fries to distribute salt. Transfer fries to paper towel–lined plate. Season with salt to taste. Serve.

PER SERVING Cal 200; **Total Fat** 7g, **Sat Fat** 0.5g; **Chol** 0mg; **Sodium** 200mg; **Total Carb** 30g, **Dietary Fiber** 0g, **Total Sugars** 0g: **Protein** 4g

Thick-Cut Oven Fries
SERVES 4 TO 6 **VEGAN**

WHY THIS RECIPE WORKS Great thick-cut oven fries have the crispy crust and rich flavor of deep-fried fries. Since oven fries don't heat fast enough to drive out their water, they don't develop a crust like fried fries. A cornstarch slurry coating helped them to crisp up. Using both vegetable oil spray and oil on the baking sheet gave the fries true fried flavor and prevented sticking. Covering the sheet with foil initially ensured that the potatoes were tender by the time they were browned. Use a heavy-duty rimmed baking sheet; the intense heat of the oven may cause lighter pans to warp.

 3 tablespoons vegetable oil
 2 pounds Yukon gold potatoes, unpeeled
 ¾ cup water
 3 tablespoons cornstarch
 ½ teaspoon table salt

1. Adjust oven rack to lowest position and heat oven to 425 degrees. Generously spray rimmed baking sheet with vegetable oil spray. Pour oil into prepared sheet and tilt sheet until surface is evenly coated with oil.

VARIATION
Thick-Cut Steakhouse Oven Fries
Toss fries with 1 teaspoon Classic Steak Rub (recipe follows) before serving.

TAKE IT UP A NOTCH

This earthy, herbal rub is a popular steakhouse seasoning. Toss it with fries, sprinkle on a loaded baked potato, or toss with mushrooms before roasting.

Classic Steak Rub
MAKES ABOUT ½ CUP

 2 tablespoons peppercorns
 3 tablespoons coriander seeds
 4 teaspoons dried dill
 2 teaspoons red pepper flakes

Process peppercorns and coriander seeds in spice grinder until finely ground, about 30 seconds; transfer to small bowl. Stir in dill and pepper flakes. (Rub can be stored at room temperature for up to 1 month.)

Patatas Bravas
SERVES 4 TO 6

WHY THIS RECIPE WORKS *Patatas bravas* are a favorite Spanish tapas preparation of crispy, well-browned potato pieces served with a smoky, spicy tomato-based sauce and a garlicky mayonnaise called *alioli*. To create an ultracrispy crust without double frying, we parboiled russet potatoes with baking soda, which triggered a chain reaction that caused the pectin on the exteriors of the potatoes to release a layer of starch that, when fried, developed into a thick crust. We tossed the parcooked potatoes with kosher salt, which roughed up the surfaces of the potatoes, creating nooks and crannies through which steam could escape. The nooks and crannies also trapped oil, helping to make an even more substantial crunchy crust. For our sauce, we cooked tomato paste, cayenne, sweet smoked paprika, garlic, and water, finishing with sherry vinegar. Adding mayonnaise allowed us to create a single creamy hybrid bravas sauce. Bittersweet or hot smoked paprika can be used in place of sweet, if desired. If you make this substitution, be sure to taste the sauce before deciding how much cayenne to add, if any. A rasp-style grater makes quick work of turning the garlic into a paste.

SAUCE

- 1 tablespoon vegetable oil
- 2 teaspoons garlic, minced to paste
- 1 teaspoon sweet smoked paprika
- ½ teaspoon kosher salt
- ½–¾ teaspoon cayenne pepper
  Pinch red pepper flakes
- ¼ cup tomato paste
- ½ cup water
- 2 teaspoons sherry vinegar
- ¼ cup mayonnaise

POTATOES

- 2¼ pounds russet potatoes, peeled and cut into 1-inch pieces
- ½ teaspoon baking soda
- 1½ teaspoons kosher salt
- 3 cups vegetable oil for frying

1. FOR THE SAUCE Heat oil in small saucepan over medium-low heat until shimmering. Add garlic, paprika, salt, cayenne, and pepper flakes and cook until fragrant, about 30 seconds. Add tomato paste and cook for 30 seconds. Whisk in water and bring to boil over high heat. Reduce heat to medium-low and simmer until slightly thickened, 4 to 5 minutes. Transfer sauce to bowl, stir in vinegar, and let cool completely, about 20 minutes. Once cool, whisk in mayonnaise.

Patatas Bravas

2. FOR THE POTATOES Bring 2 quarts water to boil in large saucepan over high heat. Add potatoes and baking soda. Return to boil and cook for 1 minute. Drain potatoes.

3. Return potatoes to now-empty saucepan and place over low heat. Cook, shaking saucepan occasionally, until any surface moisture has evaporated, 30 seconds to 1 minute. Remove from heat. Add salt and stir with silicone spatula until potatoes are coated with thick, starchy paste, about 30 seconds. Transfer potatoes to rimmed baking sheet in single layer to cool.

4. Set wire rack in second rimmed baking sheet and line with triple layer of paper towels. Heat oil in large Dutch oven to 375 degrees over high heat. Add all potatoes (they should just be submerged in oil) and cook, stirring occasionally with wire skimmer or slotted spoon, until deep golden brown and crispy, 20 to 25 minutes.

5. Using skimmer or slotted spoon, transfer potatoes to prepared rack. Season with salt to taste. Spoon ½ cup sauce onto bottom of serving platter or 1½ tablespoons sauce onto individual plates. Arrange potatoes over sauce and serve immediately, passing remaining sauce separately.

PER SERVING Cal 320; **Total Fat** 22g, **Sat Fat** 2g; **Chol** 5mg; **Sodium** 630mg; **Total Carb** 29g, **Dietary Fiber** 2g, **Total Sugars** 2g: **Protein** 4g

Crisp Roasted Potatoes
SERVES 4 TO 6 `VEGAN`

WHY THIS RECIPE WORKS Roasted potatoes, with their crunchy crusts and creamy interiors, can be as good as French fries—and a lot easier to prepare. Our unique roasting method produces a crunchier exterior than the often leathery result you get from simply tossing spuds with oil and putting them in the oven. We first cut Yukon Gold potatoes (their balance of moisture and starch produced the best texture) into thick rounds to maximize contact with the baking sheet and minimize flipping. Parcooking the potatoes was the key to better crisping: This brought starch to the surface and coated the slices with it; once the moisture evaporated in the oven, the starch crisped and browned. We tossed the parcooked slices with olive oil and salt to rough them up, which released more starch for further browning. Spread on a hot baking sheet, the slices began crisping on contact. We let the first side brown deeply before flipping them to build great color on the other side.

2½ pounds Yukon Gold potatoes, unpeeled, cut into ½-inch-thick slices
1 teaspoon table salt, divided, plus salt for cooking potatoes
5 tablespoons extra-virgin olive oil, divided

1. Adjust oven rack to lowest position, place rimmed baking sheet on rack, and heat oven to 450 degrees. Place potatoes and 1 tablespoon salt in Dutch oven, then cover with 1 inch cold water. Bring to boil over high heat, then reduce heat and gently simmer until exteriors of potatoes have softened but centers offer resistance when poked with paring knife, about 5 minutes. Drain potatoes well and transfer to large bowl.

2. Drizzle potatoes with 2 tablespoons oil and sprinkle with ½ teaspoon salt; using silicone spatula, toss to combine. Repeat with 2 tablespoons oil and remaining ½ teaspoon salt and continue to toss until exteriors of potato slices are coated with starchy paste, 1 to 2 minutes.

3. Working quickly, remove sheet from oven and drizzle remaining 1 tablespoon oil over surface. Carefully transfer potatoes to preheated sheet and spread into even layer (place end pieces skin side up). Roast until bottoms of potatoes are golden brown and crisp, 15 to 25 minutes, rotating sheet after 10 minutes.

4. Remove sheet from oven and, using metal spatula and tongs, loosen potatoes from pan and carefully flip each slice. Continue to roast until second side is golden and crisp, 10 to 20 minutes, rotating sheet as needed to ensure potatoes brown evenly. Season with salt and pepper to taste, and serve immediately.

PER SERVING Cal 260; Total Fat 12g, Sat Fat 1.5g; Chol 0mg; Sodium 400mg; Total Carb 33g, Dietary Fiber 0g, Total Sugars 0g: Protein 4g

Crisp Roasted Fingerling Potatoes

Crisp Roasted Fingerling Potatoes
SERVES 4 TO 6 `VEGAN`

WHY THIS RECIPE WORKS Fingerling potatoes are prized for their good flavor, ultrathin skins, and creamy texture. But roasting them can be tricky because they have relatively little starch and starch facilitates crisp browning. We solved this by boiling halved fingerlings with ½ cup of salt and a little baking soda. The salt created a creamy interior and seasoned the potatoes, and the baking soda encouraged the release of additional starch on the surface. After boiling, we let the potatoes cool to vent steam, dried them, and arranged them cut side down on a hot baking sheet so that the now-starch-covered potatoes would develop a crisp crust in the oven. Look for fingerling potatoes measuring approximately 3 inches long and 1 inch in diameter.

2 pounds fingerling potatoes, unpeeled, halved lengthwise
½ cup table salt
½ teaspoon baking soda
2 tablespoons extra-virgin olive oil
¼ teaspoon pepper

1. Adjust oven rack to lowest position, place rimmed baking sheet on rack, and heat oven to 500 degrees. Bring 2 quarts water to boil in large saucepan. Add potatoes, salt, and baking soda, return to simmer, and cook until potatoes are tender but centers offer slight resistance when pierced with paring knife, 7 to 10 minutes. Drain potatoes in colander and shake vigorously to roughen edges. Transfer potatoes to large platter lined with dish towel and arrange cut side up. Let sit until no longer steaming and surface is tacky, about 5 minutes.

2. Transfer potatoes to large bowl and toss with 1 tablespoon oil and pepper. Working quickly, remove sheet from oven and drizzle remaining 1 tablespoon oil over surface. Arrange potatoes cut side down on sheet in even layer. Roast until cut sides are crisp and skins spotty brown, 20 to 25 minutes, rotating sheet halfway through roasting. Flip potatoes cut side up and let cool on sheet for 5 minutes. Serve.

PER SERVING Cal 160; **Total Fat** 4.5g, **Sat Fat** 0.5g; **Chol** 0mg; **Sodium** 300mg; **Total Carb** 27g, **Dietary Fiber** 4g, **Total Sugars** 1g: **Protein** 3g

Thick-Cut Sweet Potato Fries
SERVES 6 TO 8 **VEGAN**

WHY THIS RECIPE WORKS Sweet potatoes cook very differently than white potatoes—they're much lower in starch, for one thing, so getting them to crisp can be a challenge. To make up for this, we first blanched sweet potato wedges with salt and baking soda, which seasoned them and softened their exterior, before dunking them in a slurry of water and cornstarch. When tossed with this slurry, the softened outer layer of potato sloughed off, creating a substantial, pleasingly orange crust that stayed crisp. To keep the fries from sticking to the pan, we fried them in a nonstick skillet, which had the benefit of allowing us to use less oil. These fries are good served plain but for a finishing touch to complement the natural sweetness of the fries, we made a spicy Belgian-style dipping sauce. If your sweet potatoes are shorter than 4 inches in length, do not cut the wedges crosswise.

SPICY FRY SAUCE (OPTIONAL)
- 6 tablespoons mayonnaise
- 1 tablespoon Asian chili-garlic sauce
- 2 teaspoons white vinegar

FRIES
- ½ cup cornstarch
- ¼ cup kosher salt for cooking potatoes
- 1 teaspoon baking soda

Thick-Cut Sweet Potato Fries

- 3 pounds sweet potatoes, peeled, cut lengthwise into ¾-inch-thick wedges, wedges halved crosswise
- 3 cups peanut or vegetable oil for frying

1. FOR THE SPICY FRY SAUCE Combine mayonnaise, chili-garlic sauce, and vinegar in bowl and set aside for serving.

2. FOR THE FRIES Adjust oven rack to middle position and heat oven to 200 degrees. Set wire rack in rimmed baking sheet. Whisk cornstarch and ½ cup cold water together in large bowl; set aside.

3. Bring 2 quarts water, salt, and baking soda to boil in Dutch oven. Add potatoes and return to boil. Reduce heat to simmer and cook until exteriors turn slightly mushy (centers will remain firm), 3 to 5 minutes. Whisk cornstarch slurry to recombine. Using slotted spoon, transfer potatoes to bowl with slurry.

4. Using silicone spatula, fold potatoes with slurry until slurry turns light orange, thickens to paste, and clings to potatoes.

5. Heat oil in 12-inch nonstick skillet over high heat to 325 degrees. Using tongs, carefully add one-third of potatoes to oil, making sure that potatoes aren't touching one another. Fry until crispy and lightly browned, 7 to 10 minutes, using tongs to flip potatoes halfway through frying. Adjust burner, if necessary, to maintain oil temperature between 280 and 300 degrees. Using slotted spoon, transfer fries to prepared rack (fries that stick together can be separated). Season with salt to taste, and transfer to oven to keep warm. Return oil to 325 degrees and repeat with remaining potatoes in 2 batches. Serve immediately with sauce, if desired.

PER SERVING Cal 260; **Total Fat** 14g, **Sat Fat** 1g; **Chol** 0mg; **Sodium** 260mg; **Total Carb** 33g, **Dietary Fiber** 4g, **Total Sugars** 8g: **Protein** 2g

Beer-Battered Onion Rings
SERVES 4 TO 6 `VEGAN`

WHY THIS RECIPE WORKS To create onion rings with maximum crunch and tender onions, we soaked onion slices in a mixture of beer and malt vinegar to soften them and to build flavor. After testing many different batters, we settled on one that combined flour, salt, pepper, baking powder, and cornstarch with more beer. The beer gave the coating flavor, and its carbonation provided lift to the batter. The baking powder contributed to a coating that was thick and substantial yet light, while cornstarch added crunch. Tasters preferred the gentle flavor of sweet onions, but you can substitute ordinary yellow onions. Use a full-bodied beer. Use a Dutch oven that holds 6 quarts or more for this recipe.

2   Vidalia onions, sliced into ½-inch-thick rounds
3   cups beer, divided
2   teaspoons malt vinegar
1   teaspoon table salt, divided
¾   teaspoon pepper, divided
2   quarts peanut or vegetable oil for frying
¾   cup all-purpose flour
¾   cup cornstarch
1   teaspoon baking powder

1. Combine onion rounds, 2 cups beer, vinegar, ½ teaspoon salt, and ½ teaspoon pepper in large bowl, cover, and refrigerate for at least 30 minutes or up to 2 hours.

2. Line rimmed baking sheet with triple layer of paper towels. Adjust oven rack to middle position and heat oven to 200 degrees. Add oil to large Dutch oven until it measures about 1½ inches deep and heat over medium-high heat to 350 degrees. While oil heats, combine flour, cornstarch, baking powder, remaining ½ teaspoon salt, and remaining ¼ teaspoon pepper in second large bowl. Slowly whisk in ¾ cup beer until just combined (some lumps will remain). Whisk in remaining beer as needed, 1 tablespoon at a time, until batter falls from whisk in steady stream and leaves faint trail across surface of batter.

Beer-Battered Onion Rings

3. Drain onions and pat dry with paper towels. Separate into rings. Transfer one-third of rings to batter. Carefully transfer battered rings to oil. Fry until rings are golden brown and crisp, about 5 minutes, flipping halfway through frying. Drain rings on prepared baking sheet, season with salt and pepper to taste, and transfer to oven to keep warm. Return oil to 350 degrees and repeat with remaining onion rings and batter in 2 batches. Serve.

PER SERVING Cal 280; **Total Fat** 12g, **Sat Fat** 1g; **Chol** 0mg; **Sodium** 470mg; **Total Carb** 32g, **Dietary Fiber** 1g, **Total Sugars** 2g: **Protein** 2g

FRYING ONION RINGS

To prevent fused rings, fry battered onion rings in small batches. Transfer to hot oil 1 ring at a time so they don't stick together.

Oven-Fried Onion Rings

SERVES 4 TO 6 `MAKE-AHEAD`

WHY THIS RECIPE WORKS Onion rings are the perfect accompaniment to burgers, barbecue, and other casual fare. We wanted an oven method that produced tender, sweet onions with a super-crunchy coating. We made a batter with buttermilk, egg, and flour, but when we put the baking sheet in the oven the batter slid right off the onions. Coating the onion rings with flour first gave the batter something to cling to. But we wanted even more crunch. For an extra layer of coating, we turned to crushed saltines and crushed potato chips. We preheated the oil in the baking sheet before adding the coated onions so they'd start crisping right away. The result: crisp, crunchy oven-fried onion rings with deep-fried flavor.

  2 large yellow onions
  ½ cup all-purpose flour, divided
  1 large egg, room temperature
  ½ cup buttermilk, room temperature
  ½ teaspoon table salt
  ¼ teaspoon pepper
  ¼ teaspoon cayenne pepper
 30 square saltines
  4 cups kettle-cooked potato chips
  6 tablespoons vegetable oil, divided

1. Adjust oven racks to lower-middle and upper-middle positions and heat oven to 450 degrees. Slice onions into ½-inch-thick rounds, separate rings, and discard any rings smaller than 2 inches in diameter. Place ¼ cup flour in shallow dish. Beat egg and buttermilk in medium bowl. Whisk remaining ¼ cup flour, salt, pepper, and cayenne into buttermilk mixture. Pulse saltines and chips in food processor until finely ground, about 10 pulses; place in separate shallow dish.

2. Working with one at a time, dredge onion rings in flour, shaking off excess. Dip in buttermilk mixture, allowing excess to drip back into bowl, then drop into crumb coating, turning rings over to coat evenly. Transfer to large plate. (Onion rings can be refrigerated for up to 1 hour. Let sit at room temperature for 30 minutes before baking.)

3. Pour 3 tablespoons oil each onto 2 rimmed baking sheets. Transfer to oven and heat until just smoking, about 8 minutes. Carefully tilt heated sheets to coat evenly with oil, then arrange onion rings on sheets. Bake, flipping onion rings over and switching and rotating sheets halfway through baking, until golden brown on both sides, about 15 minutes. Briefly drain onion rings on paper towels. Serve immediately.

PER SERVING Cal 370; **Total Fat** 22g, **Sat Fat** 2.5g; **Chol** 30mg; **Sodium** 430mg; **Total Carb** 37g, **Dietary Fiber** 1g, **Total Sugars** 4g: **Protein** 6g

Asparagus Fries

Asparagus Fries

SERVES 4 TO 6 `FAST`

WHY THIS RECIPE WORKS Making asparagus fries is a good way to turn this common vegetable into something special. We relied on the tried-and-true three-step breading technique of dipping the spears into flour, then beaten eggs, and finally bread crumbs, but we found that the coating wasn't adhering as steadfastly as we wanted. To get around this, we rinsed the spears under cold running water before dipping them in the flour. The residual moisture was just enough to help the flour (and the bread-crumb coating) stick. We used fresh bread to amplify the sweetness of the crumbs. A bright yet creamy sauce made with sour cream, lemon juice, and mustard was the perfect accompaniment. Do not use asparagus that is thinner than ½ inch here. The bottom 1½ inches or so of asparagus is woody and needs to be trimmed. To know where to cut the spears, grip one spear about halfway down; with your other hand, hold the stem between your thumb and index finger about 1 inch from the bottom and bend the spear until it snaps. Using this spear as a guide, cut the remaining spears with your knife.

½ cup sour cream
1 tablespoon lemon juice
1 tablespoon Dijon mustard
1½ teaspoons table salt, divided
¾ teaspoon pepper, divided
¼ cup plus 3 tablespoons all-purpose flour, divided
3 large eggs
4 slices hearty white sandwich bread, torn into 1-inch pieces
1 pound (½-inch-thick) asparagus, trimmed
1 quart peanut or vegetable oil for frying

1. Combine sour cream, lemon juice, mustard, ½ teaspoon salt, and ¼ teaspoon pepper in bowl; set aside sauce.

2. Place ¼ cup flour in shallow dish. Beat eggs in second shallow dish. Process bread, remaining 1 teaspoon salt, remaining ½ teaspoon pepper, and remaining 3 tablespoons flour in food processor until finely ground, about 1 minute. Transfer bread-crumb mixture to 13 by 9-inch baking dish.

3. Place asparagus in colander and rinse under cold running water. Shake colander to lightly drain asparagus (asparagus should still be wet). Transfer one-third of asparagus to flour and toss to lightly coat; dip in egg, allowing excess to drip off; then transfer to bread-crumb mixture and press lightly to adhere. Transfer breaded asparagus to baking sheet. Repeat with remaining asparagus in 2 batches.

4. Line large plate with paper towels. Heat oil in large Dutch oven over medium-high heat to 350 degrees. Carefully add one-third of asparagus to hot oil and cook until golden brown, 1 to 2 minutes. Transfer to prepared plate. Return oil to 350 degrees and repeat with remaining asparagus in 2 batches. Serve with sauce.

PER SERVING Cal 280; **Total Fat** 16g, **Sat Fat** 3g; **Chol** 100mg; **Sodium** 780mg; **Total Carb** 24g, **Dietary Fiber** 1g, **Total Sugars** 4g; **Protein** 8g

PERFECTING FRIED ASPARAGUS

1. Moisten spears under cold running water to help breading stick evenly.

2. Toss moistened spears in flour, dip them in beaten egg, and coat them in bread crumbs before frying.

Fried Zucchini Sticks
SERVES 4 TO 6 · FAST · VEGAN

WHY THIS RECIPE WORKS Fried zucchini sticks are a delicious pub-style side that makes great use of summer's ubiquitous vegetable. Since zucchini has a high water content, working quickly when frying to prevent moisture from leaching from the zucchini was key. We cut the zucchini into spears and removed the watery inner seed pulp. Then we floured the spears, shook off the excess, and coated the zucchini in a light beer batter seasoned with garlic powder and cayenne. A little cornstarch in the batter helped the sticks to fry up nice and crisp. To keep the spears crisp, we fried them quickly in hot (375-degree) oil, drained them briefly, and served them right away with a mayonnaise-based dipping sauce. Use a Dutch oven that holds 6 quarts or more for this recipe. Dredge the zucchini just before frying for the best texture. This recipe can easily be doubled. Serve with Aioli (page 150).

2 zucchini, trimmed
¾ cup plus 1 tablespoon all-purpose flour
¼ cup cornstarch
1 teaspoon baking powder
1 teaspoon garlic powder
1 teaspoon table salt
¾ teaspoon pepper
¾ teaspoon cayenne pepper
¾ cup lager, such as Budweiser
2 quarts peanut or vegetable oil for frying

1. Quarter zucchini lengthwise. Using vegetable peeler, shave seeds from inner portion of each quarter. Halve each quarter lengthwise, then cut in half crosswise. (You should have 32 pieces total.)

2. Whisk flour, cornstarch, baking powder, garlic powder, salt, pepper, and cayenne together in large bowl. Set aside ½ cup flour mixture. Slowly whisk beer into remaining flour mixture until consistency of pancake batter (you may have leftover beer).

3. Set wire rack in rimmed baking sheet and line with triple layer of paper towels. Add oil to large Dutch oven until it measures about 1½ inches deep and heat over medium-high heat to 375 degrees.

4. Toss half of zucchini in bowl with reserved flour mixture until evenly coated. Set fine-mesh strainer over second large bowl and transfer zucchini and flour mixture to strainer. Shake to remove all excess flour mixture from zucchini (catching excess in second bowl).

5. Transfer zucchini to batter and stir to coat. Using tongs, drop each spear into hot oil and stir quickly to prevent pieces from clumping together. Cook until light golden brown, about 4 minutes. Adjust burner, if necessary, to maintain oil temperature between 350 and 375 degrees.

These easy stir-together sauces are perfect for dipping all kinds of fried vegetables.

Lemon-Chive Dipping Sauce

½ cup mayonnaise
2 tablespoons minced fresh chives
1 teaspoon grated lemon zest plus 1 tablespoon juice
1 teaspoon Worcestershire sauce
1 teaspoon Dijon mustard
¼ teaspoon garlic powder

Whisk all ingredients together in bowl. Cover and refrigerate until ready to serve. (Sauce can be refrigerated for up to 3 days.)

Sriracha Dipping Sauce

½ cup mayonnaise
1½ tablespoons sriracha
2 teaspoons lime juice
¼ teaspoon garlic powder

Whisk all ingredients together in bowl. Cover and refrigerate until ready to serve. (Sauce can be refrigerated for up to 1 week.)

Polenta Fries

6. Transfer spears to prepared rack and season with salt. Return oil to 375 degrees and repeat with remaining zucchini spears, flour mixture, and batter. Serve.

PER SERVING Cal 270; **Total Fat** 19g, **Sat Fat** 1.5g; **Chol** 0mg; **Sodium** 470mg; **Total Carb** 20g, **Dietary Fiber** 1g, **Total Sugars** 2g: **Protein** 3g

Polenta Fries
SERVES 4 `MAKE-AHEAD`

WHY THIS RECIPE WORKS For a fresh take on how to use polenta, we found that if we cooked polenta and then chilled it until firm, we could slice it into thin sticks that would become crisp when fried—and irresistible when dipped into a rich, heady sauce like saffron aioli, which complements the corn flavor without overwhelming it. We began our testing of polenta fries using instant polenta so we could minimize time on the stove. Stirring oregano and lemon zest into the fully cooked polenta lent an aromatic backbone to our fries and helped to brighten the flavor. We then poured our flavored polenta into a straight-sided 13 by

9-inch baking pan to set up in the refrigerator for easy slicing. Once our fries were cut, we looked at methods for cooking them. Deep frying resulted in fries that clumped together and stuck to the bottom of the pot, but pan frying resulted in perfectly crisp fries with a tender and fluffy interior. We seasoned the fries lightly with salt as they came out of the pan. Do not substitute coarse-ground cornmeal or traditional polenta. You can use your preferred coarse finishing salt in this recipe.

4 cups water
1 teaspoon table salt
1 cup instant polenta
½ teaspoon dried oregano
1 teaspoon grated lemon zest
½ cup vegetable oil
  Flake sea salt
1 recipe Saffron Aioli (page 150)

1. Line 13 by 9-inch baking pan with parchment paper and grease parchment. Bring water to boil in large saucepan and add salt. Slowly add polenta in steady stream while stirring constantly with wooden spoon. Reduce heat to low and cook, uncovered, stirring often, until polenta is soft and smooth, 3 to 5 minutes.

Aioli is a garlicky emulsion sauce that is quickly whipped together in a food processor. It is delicious served with cooked vegetables and fries and other potatoes.

Aioli
MAKES ABOUT ¾ CUP

If necessary, remove the green germ (or stem) in the garlic before pressing or grating it; the germ will give the aioli a bitter, hot flavor. Ground white pepper is preferred because it's not as visible in the finished aioli as black pepper, but either can be used.

- 1 garlic clove, peeled
- 2 large egg yolks
- 4 teaspoons lemon juice
- ¼ teaspoon table salt
- ⅛ teaspoon sugar
- ¾ cup extra-virgin olive oil

1. Mince garlic to paste. Measure out 1 teaspoon garlic; discard remaining garlic.

2. Process garlic, egg yolks, lemon juice, salt, sugar, and pepper to taste in food processor until combined, about 10 seconds. With food processor running, gradually add oil in slow steady stream (process should take about 30 seconds); scrape down sides of bowl with silicone spatula and process 5 seconds. Season with salt and pepper to taste, and serve. (Aioli can be refrigerated for up to 3 days.)

Rosemary-Thyme Aioli
Serve this robust aioli with grilled vegetables.
Add 1 teaspoon chopped fresh rosemary and 1 teaspoon chopped fresh thyme to food processor with garlic.

Saffron Aioli
Saffron aioli is a nice accompaniment to polenta fries.
Combine 1 teaspoon boiling water and ⅛ teaspoon saffron threads, crumbled, in small bowl; let steep for 10 minutes. Add saffron to food processor with garlic; transfer finished aioli to bowl, cover with plastic wrap, and refrigerate at least 2 hours to allow saffron flavor to bloom. Stir before serving.

Basil or Dill Aioli
This mellow herb-flavored aioli pairs nicely with all kinds of vegetables.
Stir 2 tablespoons minced fresh basil or 1 tablespoon minced fresh dill into aioli just before serving.

2. Off heat, stir in oregano and lemon zest and season with salt and pepper to taste. Pour polenta into prepared pan. Refrigerate, uncovered, until firm and sliceable, about 1 hour. (Polenta can be covered and refrigerated for up to 24 hours.)

3. Gently flip chilled polenta out onto cutting board and discard parchment. Cut polenta in half lengthwise, then slice each half crosswise into sixteen ¾-inch-wide fries. (You will have 32 fries total.)

4. Adjust oven rack to middle position and heat oven to 200 degrees. Set wire rack in rimmed baking sheet. Heat oil in 12-inch nonstick skillet over medium heat until shimmering and edge of polenta sizzles when dipped in oil. Fry half of polenta until crisp and beginning to brown, 6 to 7 minutes per side. Transfer to prepared rack, season with finishing salt to taste, and keep warm in oven. Repeat with remaining polenta. Serve warm with saffron aioli.

PER SERVING Cal 400; **Total Fat** 31g, **Sat Fat** 3.5g; **Chol** 30mg; **Sodium** 640mg; **Total Carb** 27g, **Dietary Fiber** 2g, **Total Sugars** 0g: **Protein** 3g

Jewish-Style Fried Artichokes
SERVES 4 TO 6 **FAST** **VEGAN**

WHY THIS RECIPE WORKS In this classic Roman dish, baby artichokes are pared down to their tender core and delicate inner leaves, cooked in hot extra-virgin olive oil until crispy and browned, and then sprinkled with sea salt and served with lemon. The cooking method was the key to success. Dropping the prepped artichokes into hot oil produced scorched, bitter leaves, while starting them in cold oil resulted in uneven browning. So we landed on an approach in the middle. We started the artichokes in extra-virgin olive oil heated to a moderate 300 degrees until the hearts were just cooked through; we then removed them while we increased the heat to 325 degrees. The artichokes required just 1 to 2 minutes in the hotter oil to develop golden, supercrisp leaves. Baby artichokes are a must here, as their tender hearts cook quickly and their soft leaves become shatteringly crisp. Use a Dutch oven that holds 6 quarts or more for this recipe.

- 1 lemon, halved, plus lemon wedges for serving
- 2 pounds baby artichokes (2 to 4 ounces each)
- 3 quarts extra-virgin olive oil for frying
  Flake sea salt

1. Squeeze lemon halves into 4 cups cold water in large bowl; add spent halves. Working with 1 artichoke at a time, peel and trim stem to remove dark green layer, then cut off top quarter of artichoke. Break off tough outer leaves by pulling them downward until you reach delicate yellow leaves. Cut artichokes in half lengthwise and submerge in lemon water.

2. Line rimmed baking sheet with dish towel. Remove artichokes from lemon water, shaking off excess water, and transfer to prepared sheet; discard water and spent halves. Thoroughly pat artichokes dry and transfer to clean bowl.

3. Set wire rack in now-empty baking sheet and line with triple layer of paper towels. Add oil to large Dutch oven until it measures about 2 inches deep and heat over medium-high heat to 300 degrees. Carefully add artichokes to oil and cook until tender, pale green, and edges of leaves just begin to brown, 2 to 3 minutes. Using skimmer or slotted spoon, transfer artichokes to prepared sheet.

4. Heat oil over medium-high heat to 325 degrees. Return artichokes to oil and cook until golden and crisp, 1 to 2 minutes. Using skimmer or slotted spoon, transfer artichokes to sheet. Season with flake sea salt to taste. Serve with lemon wedges.

PER SERVING Cal 140; **Total Fat** 12g, **Sat Fat** 1.5g; **Chol** 0mg; **Sodium** 55mg; **Total Carb** 6g, **Dietary Fiber** 3g, **Total Sugars** 1g: **Protein** 2g

Cauliflower Buffalo Bites

Fried Brussels Sprouts
SERVES 6 TO 8 `FAST`

WHY THIS RECIPE WORKS Fried Brussels sprouts are crunchy, nutty, and totally irresistible and our easy frying method brings out their best. Brussels sprouts splatter when they hit hot oil, so we submerged them in room-temperature oil and heated the oil and the sprouts together. As long as we cooked the Brussels sprouts until they were dark brown, this method produced beautifully crisped sprouts. Serve with a dipping sauce (page 149), if desired.

2 **pounds Brussels sprouts, trimmed and halved**
1 **quart peanut or vegetable oil for frying**

1. Line rimmed baking sheet with triple layer of paper towels. Combine Brussels sprouts and oil in Dutch oven. Cook over high heat, gently stirring occasionally, until dark brown throughout and crispy, 20 to 25 minutes.

2. Using wire skimmer or slotted spoon, transfer Brussels sprouts to prepared sheet. Roll gently so paper towels absorb excess oil. Season with salt to taste. Serve immediately.

PER SERVING Cal 260; **Total Fat** 24g, **Sat Fat** 2.5g; **Chol** 5mg; **Sodium** 140mg; **Total Carb** 10g, **Dietary Fiber** 4g, **Total Sugars** 2g: **Protein** 4g

Cauliflower Buffalo Bites
SERVES 4 TO 6

WHY THIS RECIPE WORKS These fried cauliflower bites are crunchy, tangy, and spicy. Our goal was to come up with a flavorful, crisp coating that would hold up under the Buffalo sauce. A mixture of cornstarch and cornmeal gave us an ultracrisp exterior. But because cauliflower is not naturally moist (like chicken), the mixture didn't stick, so first we dipped the florets in canned coconut milk, which had just the right viscosity. We got decent results when we baked our bites, but we absolutely flipped over the crackly crust and tender interior we achieved through frying. An herby ranch dressing was a cooling foil to the kick of the bites. We prefer Frank's RedHot Original Cayenne Pepper Sauce, but other hot sauces can be used. When you open the can of coconut milk, you may notice that it's separated—there may be a more solid mass above the watery liquid. If so, be sure to mix it together before measuring. Use a Dutch oven that holds 6 quarts or more for this recipe.

RANCH DRESSING

½ cup mayonnaise

2 tablespoons plain yogurt

1 teaspoon white wine vinegar

1½ teaspoons minced fresh chives

1½ teaspoons minced fresh dill

¼ teaspoon garlic powder

⅛ teaspoon table salt

⅛ teaspoon pepper

BUFFALO SAUCE

4 tablespoons unsalted butter, cut into 4 pieces

½ cup hot sauce

1 tablespoon packed dark brown sugar

2 teaspoons cider vinegar

CAULIFLOWER

2 quarts peanut or vegetable oil for frying

¾ cup cornstarch

¼ cup cornmeal

½ teaspoon table salt

¼ teaspoon pepper

⅔ cup canned coconut milk

1 tablespoon hot sauce

1 pound cauliflower florets, cut into 1½-inch pieces

1. FOR THE RANCH DRESSING Whisk all ingredients together in bowl until smooth. Refrigerate until serving. (Dressing can be refrigerated for up to 4 days.)

2. FOR THE BUFFALO SAUCE Melt butter in small saucepan over low heat. Whisk in hot sauce, brown sugar, and vinegar until combined. Remove from heat and cover to keep warm; set aside.

3. FOR THE CAULIFLOWER Line platter with triple layer of paper towels. Add oil to large Dutch oven until it measures about 1½ inches deep and heat over medium-high heat to 400 degrees. While oil heats, combine cornstarch, cornmeal, salt, and pepper in small bowl. Whisk coconut milk and hot sauce together in large bowl. Add cauliflower; toss to coat well. Sprinkle cornstarch mixture over cauliflower; fold with silicone spatula until thoroughly coated.

4. Fry half of cauliflower, adding 1 or 2 pieces to oil at a time, until golden and crisp, gently stirring as needed to prevent pieces from sticking together, about 3 minutes. Using slotted spoon, transfer fried cauliflower to prepared platter.

5. Return oil to 400 degrees and repeat with remaining cauliflower. Transfer ½ cup sauce to clean large bowl, add fried cauliflower, and gently toss to coat. Serve immediately with ranch dressing and remaining sauce.

PER SERVING Cal 510; **Total Fat** 45g, **Sat Fat** 13g; **Chol** 25mg; **Sodium** 950mg; **Total Carb** 25g, **Dietary Fiber** 2g, **Total Sugars** 4g: **Protein** 3g

Corn Fritters
MAKES 12 FRITTERS `FAST`

WHY THIS RECIPE WORKS A Southern favorite, fresh corn fritters are a nice side to poultry, steaks, or chops. For light fritters, we minimized the number of added fillers, processing some of the corn kernels to use as a thickener rather than more flour or cornmeal. This helped the fresh corn flavor shine through. Browning the corn puree drove off excess moisture and deepened the flavor. Cayenne, nutty Parmesan, and oniony chives balanced the natural sweetness of the corn, and some cornstarch helped to crisp the exteriors. Serve with a flavorful mayonnaise (page 153), if desired.

3 ears corn, kernels cut from cobs (about 3 cups), divided

1 teaspoon vegetable oil plus ½ cup for frying

⅛ teaspoon plus ¼ teaspoon table salt, divided

¼ cup all-purpose flour

¼ cup minced fresh chives, divided

2 tablespoons grated Parmesan cheese

1 tablespoon cornstarch

⅛ teaspoon pepper

Pinch cayenne pepper

1 large egg, lightly beaten

1. Process 1½ cups corn in food processor to uniform coarse puree, 15 to 20 seconds, scraping down sides of bowl halfway through processing; set aside.

2. Heat 1 teaspoon oil in 12-inch nonstick skillet over medium-high heat until shimmering. Add remaining 1½ cups corn and ⅛ teaspoon salt and cook, stirring frequently, until light golden, 3 to 4 minutes. Transfer to large bowl.

3. Return skillet to medium heat, add corn puree, and cook, stirring frequently, until puree is consistency of thick oatmeal (puree should cling to spatula rather than dripping off), about 5 minutes. Stir puree into corn in bowl. Rinse skillet and wipe dry with paper towels.

4. Stir flour, 3 tablespoons chives, Parmesan, cornstarch, pepper, cayenne, and remaining ¼ teaspoon salt into corn mixture until well combined. Gently stir in egg until incorporated.

5. Line rimmed baking sheet with paper towels. Heat remaining ½ cup oil in now-empty skillet over medium heat until shimmering. Drop six 2-tablespoon portions batter into skillet, then flatten with spatula into 2½-inch disks. Fry until deep golden brown on both sides, 2 to 3 minutes per side. Transfer fritters to prepared sheet. Repeat with remaining batter.

6. Transfer fritters to serving platter and sprinkle with remaining 1 tablespoon chives. Serve immediately.

PER SERVING Cal 130; **Total Fat** 11g, **Sat Fat** 1g; **Chol** 15mg; **Sodium** 100mg; **Total Carb** 7g, **Dietary Fiber** 1g, **Total Sugars** 1g: **Protein** 2g

Hushpuppies

Hushpuppies

MAKES ABOUT 25 **FAST** MAKE-AHEAD

WHY THIS RECIPE WORKS Hushpuppies are bite-size fried cornmeal dumplings served as a side dish throughout the South. We wanted ours to boast a crisp crust, tender center, and strong corn flavor without any cornmeal grit or extra effort. A combination of cornmeal and flour struck the perfect balance between being too soft and too dense, with great flavor. To kick up the hushpuppies' flavor, we stirred in cayenne and finely chopped onion. Buttermilk contributed a nice tang, and baking soda's reaction with its acidity provided a light texture and a golden-brown crust. With all of our batter's components in place, we let the whisked mixture sit to thicken before dropping heaping tablespoons into hot oil. Within minutes, our hushpuppies fried into golden mini fritters we couldn't wait to devour. Avoid coarsely ground cornmeal for this recipe, as it will make the hushpuppies gritty. If you don't have buttermilk on hand, make clabbered milk by whisking 2¼ teaspoons of lemon juice into ¾ cup of milk and letting it stand at room temperature until slightly thickened, about 10 minutes. Use a Dutch oven that holds 6 quarts or more for this recipe.

These flavored mayos nicely complement fritters, vegetable cakes, and more.

Chipotle-Maple Mayonnaise
MAKES ⅔ CUP

- ½ cup mayonnaise
- 1 tablespoon maple syrup
- 1 tablespoon minced canned chipotle chile in adobo sauce
- ½ teaspoon Dijon mustard

Whisk all ingredients together in bowl until smooth.

Red Pepper Mayonnaise
MAKES 1¼ CUPS
Letting the minced garlic sit in the lemon juice mellows the garlic's flavor.

- 1½ teaspoons lemon juice
- 1 garlic clove, minced
- ¾ cup jarred roasted red peppers, rinsed and patted dry
- ½ cup mayonnaise
- 2 teaspoons tomato paste

Combine lemon juice and garlic in small bowl and let sit for 15 minutes. Process red peppers, mayonnaise, tomato paste, and lemon juice mixture in food processor until smooth, about 15 seconds, scraping down sides of bowl as needed. Season with salt to taste. Refrigerate until thickened, about 2 hours.

Basil Mayonnaise
MAKES ¾ CUP

- ½ cup mayonnaise
- ½ cup fresh basil leaves
- 1 tablespoon water
- 1 teaspoon lemon juice

Process all ingredients in blender until smooth, about 10 seconds, scraping down sides of blender jar as needed; transfer to bowl and season with salt and pepper to taste.

¾ cup (3¾ ounces) fine-ground cornmeal

½ cup (2½ ounces) all-purpose flour

1½ teaspoons baking powder

½ teaspoon baking soda

¾ teaspoon table salt

¼ teaspoon cayenne pepper

¾ cup buttermilk

2 large eggs

¼ cup onion, chopped fine

2 quarts peanut or vegetable oil for frying

1. Combine cornmeal, flour, baking powder, baking soda, salt, and cayenne in large bowl. Whisk in buttermilk, eggs, and onion until combined. Let batter sit at room temperature for 10 minutes or up to 1 hour.

2. Set wire rack in rimmed baking sheet. Add oil to large Dutch oven until it measures about 1½ inches deep and heat over medium-high heat to 350 degrees. Working with half of batter, drop heaping tablespoons into oil and fry until deep golden brown, 2 to 3 minutes, turning hushpuppies halfway through frying. Transfer to prepared wire rack. Return oil to 350 degrees and repeat with remaining batter. Serve. (Hushpuppies can be refrigerated for up to 2 days. Reheat in 450-degree oven for about 10 minutes before serving.)

PER SERVING Cal 90; Total Fat 7g, Sat Fat 0.5g; Chol 15mg; Sodium 135mg; Total Carb 6g, Dietary Fiber 0g, Total Sugars 0g: Protein 1g

VARIATIONS

Corn and Red Pepper Hushpuppies

Add 1 cup corn kernels (fresh or frozen, thawed); ½ red bell pepper, chopped fine; and 2 thinly sliced scallions to batter in step 1.

Crab and Chive Hushpuppies

Add 8 ounces crabmeat (picked over for shells), 2 tablespoons Dijon mustard, and 2 tablespoons minced fresh chives to batter in step 1.

Ham and Cheddar Hushpuppies

Add 4 ounces finely chopped deli ham, 1 cup shredded sharp cheddar cheese, 2 tablespoons Dijon mustard, and 2 thinly sliced scallions to batter in step 1.

Rhode Island Johnnycakes

Rhode Island Johnnycakes
MAKES 12 **FAST**

WHY THIS RECIPE WORKS Johnnycakes are rich, crisp corn cakes that are delicious on their own or served as a side dish for soups and stews. For johnnycakes that would stack up in our own kitchen, we took a tip from polenta recipes, combining the dry ingredients before whisking them into a pot of boiling water. This step allowed the cornmeal to cook more thoroughly, softening its naturally gritty texture. Resting the batter for 15 minutes thickened it to the consistency of mashed potatoes. After plopping mounds of batter into the pan, we let the cakes cook for at least 6 minutes to form a crust on the bottom, preventing them from breaking apart when flipped. Gently flattening the cakes to about ¼ inch allowed them to cook through. As is, these were a perfect side dish; served with a simple maple butter, they proved a standout alternative to pancakes. Do not try to turn the johnnycakes too soon or they will fall apart. If you prefer crispier johnnycakes, press the pancakes thinner in step 5.

1 cup johnnycake meal or stone-ground cornmeal

2 teaspoons sugar

¾ teaspoon table salt

2¾ cups water, plus extra hot water for thinning batter
2 tablespoons unsalted butter
2 tablespoons vegetable oil, divided

1. Adjust oven rack to middle position and heat oven to 200 degrees. Set wire rack in rimmed baking sheet.

2. Whisk johnnycake meal, sugar, and salt together in bowl. Bring water to boil in large saucepan. Slowly whisk johnnycake meal mixture into boiling water until no lumps remain; continue to cook until thickened, about 30 seconds. Off heat, whisk in butter. Pour batter into bowl, cover with plastic wrap, and let sit until slightly firm, about 15 minutes.

3. Rewhisk batter until smooth. Batter should be consistency of ploppable mashed potatoes; if not, thin with 1 to 2 tablespoons extra hot water until mixture drops easily from spoon.

4. Heat 1 tablespoon oil in 12-inch nonstick skillet over medium heat until shimmering (or heat nonstick griddle to 400 degrees). Using greased ¼-cup dry measuring cup, drop 6 evenly spaced scoops of batter into skillet, using spoon to help release batter from cup as needed. Cook johnnycakes, without moving them, until edges appear crispy and golden brown, 6 to 8 minutes.

5. Carefully flip johnnycakes and press with spatula to flatten into 2½- to 3-inch-diameter pancakes. Continue to cook until well browned on second side, 5 to 7 minutes. Transfer johnnycakes to prepared wire rack and place in oven to keep warm. Whisk 2 to 4 tablespoons extra hot water into remaining batter to return to correct consistency. Repeat cooking with remaining 1 tablespoon oil and remaining batter. Serve.

PER SERVING Cal 80; Total Fat 4.5g, Sat Fat 1.5g; Chol 5mg; Sodium 150mg; Total Carb 10g, Dietary Fiber 0g, Total Sugars 1g: Protein 1g

---

TAKE IT UP A NOTCH

Try maple-flavored butter on roasted vegetables or cornbread as well as johnnycakes.

Maple Butter
MAKES ¼ CUP

4 tablespoons unsalted butter, softened
1 tablespoon pure maple syrup
¼ teaspoon table salt

Whisk butter, maple syrup, and salt together in bowl until combined. (Butter can be refrigerated for up to 1 week.)

Fried Fiddleheads
SERVES 6 TO 8

WHY THIS RECIPE WORKS Fiddleheads are bite-size young coiled ferns available in early spring, and in them we saw a unique frying opportunity. Our goal was deep-fried fiddleheads with a coating that was delicious and didn't obscure their signature shape. Beer batter was tasty, but the flavor was too strong and the batter completely cloaked the fiddleheads. Tasters liked the flavor and look of lacy tempura batter, but it fused the fiddleheads into large clumps. A panko crust was too tough and disguised the fiddleheads' shape. When we tried a cornmeal coating, tasters were finally satisfied. The cornmeal brought a faint sweetness and great crunch, while cornstarch kept the crust crisp and flour gave it structure—and it was light enough to still see the beautiful coils. We blanched the fiddleheads before coating and frying them, so they were cooked through by the time the crust turned golden brown. Be sure to set up the ice water bath before cooking the fiddleheads; plunging them into the cold water immediately after blanching retains their bright green color and ensures that they don't overcook. Use a Dutch oven that holds 6 quarts or more for this recipe. Serve with Lemon-Chive Dipping Sauce (page 149).

1 pound fiddleheads, trimmed and cleaned
1 teaspoon table salt, plus salt for cooking fiddleheads
⅔ cup buttermilk
1 large egg
¾ cup cornmeal
½ cup cornstarch
¼ cup all-purpose flour
½ teaspoon garlic powder
¼ teaspoon cayenne pepper
¼ teaspoon pepper
3 quarts peanut or vegetable oil for frying

1. Bring 4 quarts water to boil in large Dutch oven. Fill large bowl halfway with ice and water. Add fiddleheads and 1 tablespoon salt to boiling water and cook for 2 minutes. Using slotted spoon, transfer fiddleheads to ice water and let sit until cool, about 2 minutes. Drain, transfer fiddleheads to platter lined with triple layer of paper towels, and dry well.

2. Meanwhile, adjust oven rack to middle position and heat oven to 200 degrees. Line rimmed baking sheet with parchment paper. Set wire rack in second rimmed baking sheet and line with triple layer of paper towels. Whisk buttermilk and egg together in shallow dish. Whisk cornmeal, cornstarch, flour, garlic powder, cayenne, 1 teaspoon salt, and pepper together in second shallow dish. Working in batches, dip fiddleheads in buttermilk mixture, letting excess drip back into dish, then dredge in cornmeal mixture, pressing firmly to adhere. Transfer fiddleheads to parchment-lined sheet. Refrigerate, uncovered, for at least 30 minutes or up to 4 hours.

3. Add oil to clean, dry Dutch oven until it measures about 2 inches deep and heat over medium-high heat to 375 degrees. Carefully add half of fiddleheads to hot oil and cook, stirring as needed to prevent sticking, until fiddleheads are golden and crisp, 2 to 4 minutes. Adjust burner, if necessary, to maintain oil temperature between 350 and 375 degrees. Using wire skimmer or slotted spoon, transfer fiddleheads to prepared rack. Season with salt to taste, and transfer to oven to keep warm.

4. Return oil to 375 degrees and repeat with remaining fiddleheads. Serve immediately.

PER SERVING Cal 300; **Total Fat** 22g, **Sat Fat** 2g; **Chol** 25mg; **Sodium** 400mg; **Total Carb** 22g, **Dietary Fiber** 1g, **Total Sugars** 1g: **Protein** 5g

FRYING FIDDLEHEADS

1. Working in batches, dip fiddleheads into buttermilk mixture, letting excess drip back into bowl. Dredge fiddleheads in cornmeal mixture, pressing firmly to adhere.

2. Fry fiddleheads in hot oil for 2 to 4 minutes, then transfer to prepared rack to drain. Serve fried fiddleheads sprinkled with salt and with lemon-chive dipping sauce if desired.

Deep-Fried Okra
SERVES 4 TO 6

WHY THIS RECIPE WORKS Fried okra is, for many, simply the only way to eat okra. For a crunchy bite, we cut the pods into pieces. For a light and crispy fried exterior, we made a "glue" of buttermilk and egg in which to dip the pieces before dredging them in a mixture of cornmeal, cornstarch, and all-purpose flour. The cornmeal lent the classic Southern fried flavor profile, the cornstarch added a light crispy effect, and the flour's glutinous structure helped the coating adhere. We stirred garlic powder, cayenne, and black pepper into the cornmeal blend before dredging and frying to ramp up the flavor. You can use frozen cut okra, thawed and thoroughly patted dry, in this recipe. Use a Dutch oven that holds 6 quarts or more for this recipe.

⅔ cup buttermilk
1 large egg
¾ cup cornmeal
½ cup cornstarch
¼ cup all-purpose flour
1½ teaspoons table salt
1 teaspoon garlic powder
½ teaspoon cayenne pepper
¼ teaspoon pepper
1 pound okra, stemmed and cut into 1-inch pieces
3 quarts peanut or vegetable oil for frying
Lemon wedges
Hot sauce

1. Adjust oven rack to middle position and heat oven to 200 degrees. Line rimmed baking sheet with parchment paper. Set wire rack in second rimmed baking sheet and line with triple layer of paper towels.

2. Whisk buttermilk and egg together in shallow dish. Whisk cornmeal, cornstarch, flour, salt, garlic powder, cayenne, and pepper together in second shallow dish. Working in batches, dip okra in buttermilk mixture, letting excess drip back into dish. Dredge in cornmeal mixture, pressing firmly to adhere; transfer to parchment-lined sheet. Refrigerate, uncovered, for at least 30 minutes or up to 4 hours.

3. Add oil to large Dutch oven until it measures about 2 inches deep and heat over medium-high heat to 375 degrees. Carefully add half of okra to oil and fry, stirring as needed to prevent sticking, until okra is golden and crisp, 2 to 4 minutes. Adjust burner, if necessary, to maintain oil temperature between 350 and 375 degrees. Using wire skimmer or slotted spoon, transfer okra to prepared rack. Season with salt and transfer to oven to keep warm.

4. Return oil to 375 degrees and repeat with remaining okra. Serve immediately with lemon wedges and hot sauce.

PER SERVING Cal 480; **Total Fat** 39g, **Sat Fat** 3g; **Chol** 35mg; **Sodium** 630mg; **Total Carb** 30g, **Dietary Fiber** 3g, **Total Sugars** 2g: **Protein** 5g

Fried Sweet Plantains
SERVES 6 TO 8 **FAST** **VEGAN**

WHY THIS RECIPE WORKS Plantains, also known as "cooking bananas," are popular in Latin American cooking. Fried plantains are a savory-sweet side featuring thick slices of plantains fried in oil to create a caramel-like browned crust encasing a soft, sweet interior. We deep-fried our plantains, stirring the slices so that they would brown evenly. A sprinkling of kosher salt balanced the sweetness. Make sure to use plantains that are very ripe and black.

3 cups vegetable oil for frying

5 very ripe black plantains (8½ ounces each), peeled and sliced on bias into ½-inch pieces

Set wire rack in rimmed baking sheet. Heat oil in medium saucepan over medium-high heat until it registers 350 degrees. Carefully add one-third of plantains and cook until dark brown on both sides, 3 to 5 minutes, stirring occasionally. Using wire skimmer or slotted spoon, transfer plantains to prepared rack. (Do not place plantains on paper towels or they will stick.) Season with kosher salt. Repeat with remaining plantains in 2 batches. Serve immediately.

PER SERVING Cal 290; **Total Fat** 19g, **Sat Fat** 1.5g; **Chol** 0mg; **Sodium** 0mg; **Total Carb** 31g, **Dietary Fiber** 2g, **Total Sugars** 15g: **Protein** 1g

Fried Sunchokes
SERVES 4 TO 6 **VEGAN**

WHY THIS RECIPE WORKS Sunchokes have a vegetal taste like a cross between potatoes and artichokes. They may look like knobby potatoes, but sunchokes do not contain any starch. Instead, they are rich in inulin, a soluble fiber that provides their earthy, sweet flavor. Since sunchokes fry up really well, we first fried our sunchokes whole at a low temperature to get rid of some moisture and cook the interiors. Then we brought the oil to a hotter temperature to finish cooking them and crisp them up. These sunchokes were pretty crisp and deep golden-brown, but tasters wanted more crispy edges. So we took a page out of our potato playbook and smashed them after the initial frying. This vastly increased the number of edges, nooks, and crannies in each sunchoke, resulting in ultracrispy, crunchy fried sunchokes. Use a Dutch oven that holds 6 quarts or more for this recipe.

2 quarts peanut or vegetable oil for frying

2 pounds sunchokes, unpeeled

1. Add oil to large Dutch oven until it measures about 1½ inches deep and heat over medium-high heat to 250 degrees. Carefully add sunchokes to oil and cook, stirring occasionally, until tender and knife slips easily in and out of flesh, 30 to 35 minutes.

2. Using wire skimmer or slotted spoon, transfer sunchokes to rimmed baking sheet and let cool slightly, about 10 minutes. Space sunchokes evenly over sheet and place second baking sheet on top. Press down firmly on top sheet until sunchokes are flattened to ½-inch thickness.

3. Meanwhile, heat oil to 375 degrees. Set wire rack in top sheet and line with triple layer of paper towels. Carefully return sunchokes to oil and fry, stirring occasionally, until deep golden brown

Fried Sunchokes

and crispy, 5 to 7 minutes. Adjust burner, if necessary, to maintain oil temperature between 350 and 375 degrees. Transfer sunchokes to prepared rack and season with salt and pepper to taste. Serve.

PER SERVING Cal 220; **Total Fat** 16g, **Sat Fat** 1g; **Chol** 0mg; **Sodium** 0mg; **Total Carb** 18g, **Dietary Fiber** 2g, **Total Sugars** 10g: **Protein** 2g

VARIATIONS
Fried Sunchokes with Old Bay and Lemon
Toss fried sunchokes with 2 teaspoons Old Bay seasoning and 1 teaspoon grated lemon zest before seasoning with salt and pepper. Serve with lemon wedges.

Fried Sunchokes with Mexican Chile Oil
Microwave 2 tablespoons vegetable oil, 1 teaspoon sesame seeds, ½ teaspoon cayenne pepper, ½ teaspoon ground chipotle chile powder, ¼ teaspoon garlic powder, ⅛ teaspoon cocoa powder, ⅛ teaspoon table salt, pinch cinnamon, and pinch cumin in large bowl, stirring occasionally, until fragrant and bubbling, 1 to 3 minutes. Toss fried sunchokes with oil mixture before seasoning with salt and pepper. Serve with lime wedges.

Fried Green Tomatoes

SERVES 4 TO 6

WHY THIS RECIPE WORKS Southern cooks have long made the most of an unripe tomato crop by dipping slices of green tomatoes in milk and beaten egg, dredging them in cornmeal, and frying them to a golden crust. For a crisp, stay-put coating, we first drained slices of tomatoes on paper towels to rid them of excess moisture. We made our coating from a mixture of all-purpose flour and cornmeal, processing some of the cornmeal to a fine crumb. This minimized its natural grittiness, while keeping a portion unprocessed made for a crunchy, hearty coating. We mixed in a little bit of cayenne pepper to add a subtle kick. We then dunked the slices in egg and buttermilk and dredged them through our cornmeal blend before frying. The acid in the buttermilk helped the starchy coating absorb moisture, making it especially crisp when fried. After just a few minutes, the tomatoes developed a golden-brown crust that was so good, we found ourselves looking forward to the first frost and its bonanza of never-to-ripen green tomatoes.

1½ pounds green tomatoes, cored and sliced ¼ inch thick
⅔ cup cornmeal, divided
⅓ cup all-purpose flour
1½ teaspoons table salt
½ teaspoon pepper
⅛ teaspoon cayenne pepper
⅔ cup buttermilk
 1 large egg
 2 cups peanut or vegetable oil for frying

1. Place tomatoes on paper towel–lined rimmed baking sheet. Cover with more paper towels, let sit for 20 minutes, and pat dry. Meanwhile, process ⅓ cup cornmeal in blender until very finely ground, about 1 minute. Combine processed cornmeal, remaining ⅓ cup cornmeal, flour, salt, pepper, and cayenne in shallow dish. Whisk buttermilk and egg together in second shallow dish.

2. Working with 1 tomato slice at a time, dip in buttermilk mixture, then dredge in cornmeal mixture, pressing firmly to adhere; transfer to clean baking sheet.

3. Set wire rack in rimmed baking sheet. Heat oil in 12-inch skillet over medium-high heat to 350 degrees. Fry 4 tomato slices until golden brown on both sides, 4 to 6 minutes. Drain on prepared wire rack. Return oil to 350 degrees and repeat with remaining tomato slices in batches. Serve.

PER SERVING Cal 280; **Total Fat** 20g, **Sat Fat** 2g; **Chol** 35mg; **Sodium** 640mg; **Total Carb** 21g, **Dietary Fiber** 2g, **Total Sugars** 5g: **Protein** 5g

Fried Red Tomatoes

Fried Red Tomatoes

SERVES 4

WHY THIS RECIPE WORKS Fried green tomatoes may be more well known, but we thought red tomatoes also deserved some time in the skillet. Moisture is the enemy of a crispy crust on a fried ripe tomato. To eliminate excess moisture, we sliced plum tomatoes thin and let them drain on layers of paper towel. To help a light coating adhere to the tomatoes, we mixed buttermilk and egg in which to dip the tomatoes before dredging them in a mixture of cornmeal, flour, and Parmesan. We quickly shallow-fried the tomato slices in hot oil to sear the crust but not overcook the interior. Use two forks to turn the tomatoes quickly. This recipe can easily be doubled and cooked in two batches; change the oil and wipe out the skillet between batches.

 8 ounces plum tomatoes, ends
   trimmed, sliced ¼ inch thick
½ teaspoon granulated garlic
⅓ cup buttermilk
 1 large egg
⅔ cup cornmeal

⅓ cup all-purpose flour
1 ounce Parmesan cheese, grated (½ cup)
¾ teaspoon table salt
¼ teaspoon pepper
⅛ teaspoon cayenne pepper
½ cup vegetable oil for frying
2 tablespoons minced fresh basil
Lemon wedges

1. Line wire rack with triple layer of paper towels. Evenly space tomato slices on rack, sprinkle with granulated garlic, and let drain for 40 minutes, flipping halfway through draining.

2. Line rimmed baking sheet with parchment paper. Whisk buttermilk and egg together in shallow dish. Combine cornmeal, flour, Parmesan, salt, pepper, and cayenne in second shallow dish. Lightly pat tops of tomatoes with paper towels to remove any accumulated liquid. Working with one at a time, dip tomato slices in buttermilk mixture, then dredge in cornmeal mixture, pressing firmly to adhere; transfer to prepared sheet.

3. Heat oil in 12-inch nonstick skillet over medium-high heat until just smoking. Add all tomato slices to skillet and fry until golden brown, 2 to 4 minutes per side. Transfer to platter and sprinkle with basil. Serve with lemon wedges.

PER SERVING Cal 250; Total Fat 14g, Sat Fat 2.5g; Chol 55mg; Sodium 600mg; Total Carb 22g, Dietary Fiber 2g, Total Sugars 2g: Protein 8g

Crispy Vegetable Fritters
MAKES 12 FRITTERS; SERVES 4 TO 6 **FAST**

WHY THIS RECIPE WORKS Vegetable fritters are tender, crisp, and fun to eat. We tested a number of vegetable options and settled on a mix of shredded zucchini, shredded carrot, sliced red bell pepper, and thinly sliced onion. For the thick batter, we combined equal parts flour and cornstarch plus seltzer and baking powder to lighten the batter. We added salt to the batter just before frying so it didn't draw water out of the prepared vegetables and interfere with crispiness. We carefully monitored the temperature of the shallow oil we used to fry the fritters, turning off the burner between batches to keep the oil from overheating and to ensure that each batch came out deep golden brown, lacy, and crisp. And finally, we whipped up a creamy, bright horseradish mayonnaise to complement the crunchy fritters.

SAUCE
⅓ cup mayonnaise
1 tablespoon prepared horseradish, drained
1 tablespoon lemon juice

FRITTERS
½ cup (2½ ounces) plus 1 tablespoon all-purpose flour
½ cup (2 ounces) plus 1 tablespoon cornstarch
½ teaspoon baking powder
¾ cup seltzer
1 cup thinly sliced red bell pepper
1 cup shredded zucchini
½ cup shredded carrot
½ cup thinly sliced onion
½ cup fresh cilantro leaves
2 scallions, cut into ½-inch pieces
1 garlic clove, minced
1½ cups vegetable oil for frying
½ teaspoon table salt
½ teaspoon pepper

1. FOR THE SAUCE Whisk mayonnaise, horseradish, and lemon juice together in bowl and season with salt and pepper to taste; set aside.

2. FOR THE FRITTERS Set wire rack in rimmed baking sheet and line half of rack with triple layer of paper towels. Whisk flour, cornstarch, and baking powder together in large bowl. Add seltzer and whisk until smooth, thick batter forms. Add bell pepper, zucchini, carrot, onion, cilantro, scallions, and garlic to batter and stir until vegetables are evenly coated.

3. Add oil to 12-inch nonstick skillet until it measures about ¼ inch deep and heat over medium-high heat to 350 degrees. Stir salt and pepper into vegetable batter. Using ¼-cup dry measuring cup, place 1 portion of vegetable batter in skillet; immediately spread to 4-inch diameter with spoon so top sits slightly below surface of oil. Repeat 3 times, so you have 4 fritters in skillet. Make sure vegetables do not mound in centers of fritters. Adjust burner, if necessary, to maintain oil temperature between 300 and 325 degrees.

4. Cook on first side until deep golden brown on bottom, 2 to 4 minutes. Using 2 spatulas, flip and continue to cook until golden brown on second side, 2 to 4 minutes, moving fritters around skillet as needed for even browning. When second side of fritters is golden brown, turn off burner. Transfer fritters to paper towel–lined side of prepared rack to drain for about 15 seconds per side, then move to unlined side of rack and season with salt.

5. Return oil to 350 degrees and repeat with remaining vegetable batter in 2 batches, stirring to recombine batter as needed. Serve with sauce.

PER SERVING Cal 360; Total Fat 28g, Sat Fat 2g; Chol 0mg; Sodium 240mg; Total Carb 24g, Dietary Fiber 1g, Total Sugars 3g; Protein 2g

PERFECT RICE AND GREAT GRAINS

For rice and grain recipes in other chapters, see the Index.

■ FAST (30 minutes or less total time) ■ MAKE-AHEAD ■ VEGAN
Photos (clockwise from top left): Barley and Beet Risotto; Curried Millet Pilaf;
Spiced Baked Rice with Roasted Sweet Potatoes and Fennel; Spinach Rice

Herbed Rice and Pasta Pilaf

SERVES 4 TO 6 `VEGAN`

WHY THIS RECIPE WORKS This classic pilaf combines rice with pieces of vermicelli that have been toasted in olive oil to add richness and a nutty flavor. In order to produce perfectly tender rice and pasta in one pot, we needed both elements to cook at the same rate. Jump-starting the rice by soaking it in hot water for 15 minutes softened its outer coating and let it absorb water quickly. Toasting the thin vermicelli enhanced its nuttiness. Once the pasta and rice were cooked, we let the pilaf stand in the pot for 10 minutes with a towel under the lid to absorb steam. A handful of fresh parsley lent brightness to the finished dish. Jasmine or Texmati rice can be substituted for the basmati.

- 1½ cups basmati or long-grain white rice
- 3 tablespoons extra-virgin olive oil
- 2 ounces vermicelli pasta, broken into 1-inch lengths
- 1 onion, chopped fine
- 1 garlic clove, minced
- 2½ cups chicken or vegetable broth
- 1¼ teaspoons table salt
- 3 tablespoons minced fresh parsley

1. Place rice in medium bowl and cover with hot tap water by 2 inches; let sit for 15 minutes.

2. Using your hands, gently swish grains to release excess starch. Carefully pour off water, leaving rice in bowl. Add cold tap water to rice, swish, and pour off water. Repeat adding and pouring off cold water 4 or 5 times, until water runs almost clear. Drain rice in fine-mesh strainer.

3. Heat oil in large saucepan over medium heat until shimmering. Add pasta and cook, stirring occasionally, until browned, about 3 minutes. Add onion and garlic and cook, stirring occasionally, until onion is softened but not browned, about 4 minutes. Add rice and cook, stirring occasionally, until edges of rice begin to turn translucent, about 3 minutes. Add broth and salt and bring to boil. Reduce heat to low, cover, and simmer gently until rice and pasta are tender and broth is absorbed, about 10 minutes. Off heat, lay clean dish towel underneath lid and let pilaf sit for 10 minutes. Add parsley to pilaf and fluff gently with fork to combine. Season with salt and pepper to taste. Serve.

PER SERVING Cal 280; Total Fat 8g, Sat Fat 1g; Chol 0mg; Sodium 730mg; Total Carb 47g, Dietary Fiber 1g, Total Sugars 1g; Protein 5g

VARIATIONS

Herbed Rice and Pasta Pilaf with Yogurt

Add ¼ cup plain whole-milk yogurt, ¼ cup minced fresh dill, and ¼ cup minced fresh chives to pilaf with parsley.

Herbed Rice and Pasta Pilaf with Golden Raisins and Almonds

Stir 2 bay leaves and 1 teaspoon ground cardamom into rice mixture with broth. Discard bay leaves and sprinkle ½ cup raisins over pilaf before covering with dish towel in step 3. Add ½ cup slivered almonds, toasted and chopped coarse, to pilaf with parsley.

Herbed Rice and Pasta Pilaf with Pomegranate and Walnuts

Omit onion. Substitute 2 tablespoons grated fresh ginger and ½ teaspoon ground cumin for garlic. Substitute ½ cup walnuts, toasted and chopped, ½ cup pomegranate seeds, ½ cup chopped fresh cilantro, and 1 tablespoon lemon juice for parsley.

Spinach Rice

SERVES 4 TO 6

WHY THIS RECIPE WORKS This Greek-style pilaf is chock-full of greens. To perfect it we first tried cooking the spinach with the rice, but it floated in the cooking liquid, carrying a layer of rice up with it. That rice remained uncooked, dry, and crunchy. We found a solution by adding thawed, chopped spinach to the pilaf as it rested (after cooking), ensuring that the greens had enough heat to cook through without turning mushy or slimy. Toppings of mint, scallions, lemon juice, and feta added a layer of lively freshness and brightened the flavor of the cooked greens.

- 3 tablespoons extra-virgin olive oil, plus extra for serving
- 1 onion, chopped fine
- ½ teaspoon table salt
- ¼ teaspoon pepper
- 1½ cups long-grain white rice
- 2 garlic cloves, minced
- 1 teaspoon dried oregano
- 2½ cups chicken or vegetable broth
- 10 ounces frozen spinach, thawed, squeezed dry, and chopped
- 2 scallions, sliced thin
- 2 tablespoons chopped fresh mint
- 1 tablespoon lemon juice, plus lemon wedges for serving
- 2 ounces feta cheese, crumbled (½ cup)

1. Heat oil in large saucepan over medium-high heat until shimmering. Add onion, salt, and pepper and cook until softened, 3 to 5 minutes. Add rice and cook, stirring frequently, until edges begin to turn translucent, about 2 minutes. Add garlic and oregano and cook until fragrant, about 30 seconds.

2. Stir in broth and bring to boil. Cover, reduce heat to low, and cook until liquid is absorbed and rice is tender, about 20 minutes.

3. Off heat, sprinkle spinach on top of rice, cover, and let sit for 10 minutes. Uncover and fluff rice with fork. Stir in scallions, mint, and lemon juice, tossing gently until any clumps of spinach are broken up and thoroughly mixed into rice. Season with salt and pepper to taste. Transfer to platter and sprinkle with feta. Drizzle with extra oil and serve, passing lemon wedges separately.

PER SERVING Cal 280; **Total Fat** 9g, **Sat Fat** 2.5g; **Chol** 10mg; **Sodium** 530mg; **Total Carb** 42g, **Dietary Fiber** 2g, **Total Sugars** 2g; **Protein** 9g

Mexican Rice

Mexican Rice
SERVES 6 TO 8 `VEGAN`

WHY THIS RECIPE WORKS Cooking rice the Mexican way with tomatoes, onion, and garlic makes a flavorful, rich side dish. Our version is made of tender grains infused with fresh flavor. To keep them distinct, we rinsed the rice first to remove excess starch, then pan-fried it in oil before adding the liquid to give a satisfying texture and a mild toasted flavor. For the rice cooking liquid, we pureed fresh tomatoes with an onion and combined the mixture with vegetable broth. To add savory flavor and color, we added a little tomato paste. Baking the rice in the oven ensured even cooking. Cilantro, jalapeño, and lime juice complemented the richer tones of the cooked tomatoes, garlic, and onion. To keep the dish from being too spicy, we removed some of the jalapeño seeds. Use an ovensafe pot about 12 inches in diameter so that the rice cooks evenly and in the time indicated. We've successfully used both a straight-sided sauté pan and a Dutch oven. Whichever type of pot you use, it should have a tight-fitting, ovensafe lid.

  2 **ripe tomatoes, cored and quartered**
  1 **onion, root end trimmed, quartered**
  3 **jalapeño chiles, stemmed, divided**
  ⅓ **cup vegetable oil**
  2 **cups long-grain white rice, rinsed**
  4 **garlic cloves, minced**
  2 **cups vegetable broth**
  1 **tablespoon tomato paste**
1½ **teaspoons table salt**
  ½ **cup minced fresh cilantro**
     Lime wedges

1. Adjust oven rack to middle position and heat oven to 350 degrees. Process tomatoes and onion in food processor until smooth, about 15 seconds. Transfer mixture to liquid measuring cup and spoon off excess until mixture measures 2 cups. Remove ribs and seeds from 2 jalapeños and discard; mince flesh and set aside. Mince remaining 1 jalapeño, including ribs and seeds; set aside.

2. Heat oil in Dutch oven over medium-high heat for 1 to 2 minutes. Drop 3 or 4 grains rice in oil; if grains sizzle, oil is ready. Add rice and cook, stirring often, until rice is light golden and translucent, 6 to 8 minutes.

3. Reduce heat to medium. Stir in garlic and reserved seeded jalapeños and cook, stirring constantly, until fragrant, about 1½ minutes. Stir in pureed tomato-onion mixture, broth, tomato paste, and salt. Increase heat to medium-high and bring to boil.

4. Cover pot, transfer to oven, and cook until liquid is absorbed and rice is tender, 30 to 35 minutes, stirring well after 15 minutes. Fold in cilantro and reserved jalapeño with seeds to taste. Serve with lime wedges.

PER SERVING Cal 350; **Total Fat** 13g, **Sat Fat** 1g; **Chol** 0mg; **Sodium** 840mg; **Total Carb** 54g, **Dietary Fiber** 1g, **Total Sugars** 2g; **Protein** 6g

Mexican Brown Rice

Substitute long-grain brown rice for white rice; do not rinse rice and reduce rice frying to 3 to 3½ minutes. Increase broth to 2½ cups and increase oven cooking time to 1 to 1½ hours, stirring every 30 minutes.

Low Country Red Rice

SERVES 4 TO 6 **VEGAN**

WHY THIS RECIPE WORKS A popular side dish in the coastal regions of South Carolina and Georgia, red rice gets its signature color from tomatoes. We hoped to pare down this classic without sacrificing any flavor. We started with the test kitchen's method for rice pilaf, softening the vegetables and toasting the rice in oil before adding a combination of crushed tomatoes and chicken broth. The rice was fluffy, but the crushed tomatoes might as well have been red dye for all the flavor they added, so we sautéed some tomato paste with the vegetables to add deep tomato flavor and color. For the finishing touches, a bit of cayenne pepper gave welcome heat and a handful of chopped fresh parsley brightened up the dish. For a slightly sweeter taste, substitute a red bell pepper for the green.

- 1 tablespoon vegetable oil
- 1 onion, chopped fine
- 1 green bell pepper, stemmed, seeded, and chopped fine
- 1 celery rib, chopped fine
- 1½ cups long-grain rice
- 1 tablespoon tomato paste
- 4 garlic cloves, minced
- 1 (14.5-ounce) can diced tomatoes, drained
- 2 cups chicken or vegetable broth
- 1½ teaspoons table salt
- ¼ teaspoon cayenne pepper
- ¼ cup finely chopped fresh parsley

1. Heat oil in large saucepan over medium-high heat until shimmering. Cook onion, bell pepper, and celery until softened, about 5 minutes. Add rice and cook, stirring frequently, until edges begin to turn translucent, about 2 minutes. Stir in tomato paste and garlic and cook until fragrant, about 30 seconds.

2. Stir in tomatoes, broth, salt, and cayenne and bring to boil. Cover, reduce heat to low, and cook until liquid is absorbed and rice is tender, about 20 minutes. Remove from heat and let sit, covered, for 10 minutes. Fluff rice with fork. Stir in parsley. Serve.

PER SERVING Cal 220; **Total Fat** 2.5g, **Sat Fat** 0g; **Chol** 0mg; **Sodium** 890mg; **Total Carb** 43g, **Dietary Fiber** 2g, **Total Sugars** 3g; **Protein** 6g

Cajun Dirty Rice

Cajun Dirty Rice

SERVES 4 TO 6

WHY THIS RECIPE WORKS Frugal Cajun cooks traditionally serve up "dirty" rice as a way of using up leftover chicken giblets—the gizzard, heart, kidneys, and liver. To replicate the meaty, rich flavors of this thrifty recipe while skipping most of the innards, we kept readily available chicken livers for their distinct taste and replaced the rest with ground pork. To spice up our rice, we turned to onion, sweet red bell pepper, thyme, and a bit of cayenne pepper. Cooking the meat and vegetables separately from the rice, and combining everything once the rice was cooked through, ensured that the grains cooked evenly and didn't taste muddy. Chopped scallions gave a clean finish to our perfectly dirty rice. For a spicier dish, add more cayenne or serve with hot sauce.

- 1 tablespoon vegetable oil
- 8 ounces ground pork
- 1 onion, chopped fine
- 1 red bell pepper, stemmed, seeded, and chopped fine
- 1 celery rib, minced
- 4 ounces chicken livers, rinsed, trimmed, and chopped fine

3 garlic cloves, minced
1 teaspoon table salt
¼ teaspoon dried thyme
¼ teaspoon cayenne pepper
2¼ cups chicken broth
1½ cups long-grain white rice, rinsed
2 bay leaves
3 scallions, sliced thin

1. Heat oil in Dutch oven over medium heat until shimmering. Add pork and cook, breaking up meat with wooden spoon, until browned, about 5 minutes. Stir in onion, bell pepper, and celery and cook until softened, about 10 minutes. Add chicken livers, garlic, salt, thyme, and cayenne and cook until livers are browned, 3 to 5 minutes. Transfer meat mixture to fine-mesh strainer set over bowl and cover with aluminum foil.

2. Increase heat to high and add broth, rice, and bay leaves to now-empty pot, scraping up any browned bits. Bring to boil, reduce heat to low, cover, and cook until rice is tender, 15 to 17 minutes. Off heat, discard bay leaves and fluff rice with fork. Gently stir in drained meat mixture, discarding any accumulated juices. Sprinkle scallions over rice and serve.

PER SERVING Cal 160; Total Fat 11g, Sat Fat 3.5g; Chol 90mg; Sodium 40mg; Total Carb 3g, Dietary Fiber 1g, Total Sugars 2g; Protein 10g

Rice Salad with Oranges, Olives, and Almonds

SERVES 4 TO 6 VEGAN

WHY THIS RECIPE WORKS Our citrusy rice salad pairs tender, fluffy grains with briny olives and sweet oranges. To make sure the long-grain rice could stand up to a vinaigrette and plenty of mix-ins, we sought out a cooking method that would preserve its fresh, tender texture once cooled. Toasting the rice brought out its nutty flavor and helped to keep the grains distinct and separate. We also cooked the rice like pasta and boiled it in plenty of water, which washed away its excess starch and staved off stickiness. Spreading the cooked rice on a baking sheet allowed it to cool quickly and with less clumping. To flavor the salad, we tossed the cooled grains with a simple orange vinaigrette and fresh orange segments, chopped green olives, and crunchy toasted almonds. We let the salad sit before serving to give the flavors time to meld.

1½ cups basmati rice
2½ teaspoons table salt, divided
2 oranges, plus ¼ teaspoon grated orange zest plus 1 tablespoon juice

2 tablespoons extra-virgin olive oil
2 teaspoons sherry vinegar
1 small garlic clove, minced
½ teaspoon pepper
⅓ cup large pitted brine-cured green olives, chopped
⅓ cup slivered almonds, toasted
2 tablespoons minced fresh oregano

1. Bring 4 quarts water to boil in Dutch oven. Meanwhile, toast rice in 12-inch skillet over medium heat until faintly fragrant and some grains turn opaque, 5 to 8 minutes. Add rice and 1½ teaspoons salt to boiling water and cook, stirring occasionally, until rice is tender but not soft, about 15 minutes. Drain rice, spread onto rimmed baking sheet, and let cool completely, about 15 minutes.

2. Cut away peel and pith from oranges. Holding fruit over bowl, use paring knife to slice between membranes to release segments. Whisk oil, vinegar, garlic, orange zest and juice, remaining 1 teaspoon salt, and pepper together in large bowl. Add rice, orange segments, olives, almonds, and oregano, gently toss to combine, and let sit for 20 minutes. Serve.

PER SERVING Cal 260; Total Fat 9g, Sat Fat 1g; Chol 0mg; Sodium 1080mg; Total Carb 41g, Dietary Fiber 2g, Total Sugars 5g; Protein 5g

Curried Rice Salad

SERVES 6 FAST MAKE-AHEAD VEGAN

WHY THIS RECIPE WORKS We started our curried rice salad by again cooking the rice using the pasta method. We sautéed onion and jalapeño, then added curry powder—blooming the curry powder in oil unlocked its flavor—along with some ginger and garlic. Fresh lime juice delivered fruity, tart notes, while raisins plumped in a lime juice–sugar mixture added chewy sweetness. For a spicier salad, reserve, mince, and add the ribs and seeds from the jalapeño.

⅔ cup raisins or currants
¼ cup lime juice (2 limes)
¾ teaspoon sugar
1½ cups basmati or long-grain rice
1 tablespoon plus ¼ teaspoon table salt, divided
1 teaspoon canola oil
1 onion, chopped fine
1 jalapeño chile, stemmed, seeded, and minced
1 tablespoon grated fresh ginger
1½ teaspoons curry powder
1 garlic clove, minced
3 tablespoons chopped fresh cilantro

1. Combine raisins, lime juice, and sugar in large bowl and set aside. Bring 4 quarts water to boil in Dutch oven. Add rice and 1 tablespoon salt and cook, stirring often, until just tender, 12 to 14 minutes. Drain rice, then spread in even layer on rimmed baking sheet and let cool completely.

2. Add oil, onion, jalapeño, and remaining ¼ teaspoon salt to now-empty pot. Cook, covered, over medium-low heat, stirring occasionally, until vegetables are softened, 8 to 10 minutes. Stir in ginger, curry powder, and garlic and cook until fragrant, about 30 seconds. Off heat, stir in raisin mixture, then transfer to large bowl and let cool completely.

3. Add rice and cilantro to bowl with raisin mixture and toss to combine. Season with salt and pepper to taste, and serve. (Salad can be refrigerated for up to 1 day.)

PER SERVING Cal 230; **Total Fat** 1g, **Sat Fat** 0g; **Chol** 0mg; **Sodium** 200mg; **Total Carb** 53g, **Dietary Fiber** 1g, **Total Sugars** 15g; **Protein** 4g

Spiced Basmati Rice with Cauliflower and Pomegranate
SERVES 8 TO 10 `VEGAN`

Spiced Basmati Rice with Cauliflower and Pomegranate

WHY THIS RECIPE WORKS For a fragrant, Indian-inspired rice side dish, we started with aromatic basmati and paired it with spices like cumin for a deep smokiness and turmeric for color. To make the dish hearty, we added sweet, earthy cauliflower. Tossing the cauliflower with a generous amount of black pepper gave it heat and roasting it at a high temperature for a short time caramelized and crisped the florets. We sautéed onion and garlic, mixed in the rice and spices, and simmered it until tender. We stirred the roasted cauliflower into the cooked rice and finished the dish with a burst of sweet pomegranate seeds and a mix of fresh cilantro and mint.

1 head cauliflower (2 pounds), cored and
  cut into ¾-inch florets
¼ cup extra-virgin olive oil, divided
¾ teaspoon table salt, divided
½ teaspoon pepper
½ teaspoon ground cumin, divided
1 onion, chopped
1½ cups basmati rice, rinsed
4 garlic cloves, minced
½ teaspoon ground cinnamon
½ teaspoon ground turmeric
2¼ cups water
½ cup pomegranate seeds
2 tablespoons chopped fresh cilantro
2 tablespoons chopped fresh mint

1. Adjust oven rack to lowest position and heat oven to 475 degrees. Toss cauliflower with 2 tablespoons oil, ½ teaspoon salt, pepper, and ¼ teaspoon cumin. Arrange cauliflower in single layer in rimmed baking sheet and roast until just tender, 10 to 15 minutes; set aside.

2. Heat remaining 2 tablespoons oil in large saucepan over medium heat until shimmering. Add onion and remaining ¼ teaspoon salt and cook until softened and lightly browned, 5 to 7 minutes. Add rice, garlic, cinnamon, turmeric, and remaining ¼ teaspoon cumin and cook, stirring frequently, until grain edges begin to turn translucent, about 3 minutes.

3. Stir in water and bring to simmer. Reduce heat to low, cover, and simmer gently until rice is tender and water is absorbed, 16 to 18 minutes.

4. Off heat, lay clean dish towel underneath lid and let pilaf sit for 10 minutes. Add roasted cauliflower to pilaf and fluff gently with fork to combine. Season with salt and pepper to taste. Transfer to serving platter and sprinkle with pomegranate seeds, cilantro, and mint. Serve.

PER SERVING Cal 180; **Total Fat** 6g, **Sat Fat** 1g; **Chol** 0mg; **Sodium** 200mg; **Total Carb** 28g, **Dietary Fiber** 3g, **Total Sugars** 3g; **Protein** 4g

Spiced Baked Rice with Roasted Sweet Potatoes and Fennel

SERVES 6 TO 8 **VEGAN**

WHY THIS RECIPE WORKS This hearty rice dish combines several flavorful elements of North African cuisine—sweet potatoes, green olives, and fennel—along with the distinctive warmth of the spice blend ras el hanout. Roasting yielded sweet potatoes with firm, caramelized exteriors and soft, creamy interiors. We prepared an aromatic base of fennel and onions on the stovetop, stirring in the ras el hanout with the rice to ensure that the flavors melded and bloomed. We added enough broth so that our long-grain rice came out tender and not too crunchy, then transferred the pot to the oven. When the rice was cooked, we gently stirred in the sweet potatoes and finished with bright cilantro and lime. We prefer to make our own ras el hanout, but you can substitute store-bought ras el hanout if you wish, though note that spiciness can vary greatly by brand.

1½ pounds sweet potatoes, peeled and cut into 1-inch pieces
¼ cup extra-virgin olive oil, divided
½ teaspoon table salt
1 fennel bulb, stalks discarded, bulb halved, cored, and chopped fine
1 small onion, chopped fine
1½ cups long-grain white rice, rinsed
4 garlic cloves, minced
2 teaspoons ras el hanout
2¾ cups chicken or vegetable broth
¾ cup large pitted brine-cured green olives, halved
2 tablespoons minced fresh cilantro
Lime wedges

1. Adjust oven rack to middle position and heat oven to 400 degrees. Toss potatoes with 2 tablespoons oil and salt. Arrange potatoes in single layer in rimmed baking sheet and roast until tender and browned, 25 to 30 minutes, stirring potatoes halfway through roasting. Remove potatoes from oven and reduce oven temperature to 350 degrees.

2. Heat remaining 2 tablespoons oil in Dutch oven over medium heat until shimmering. Add fennel and onion and cook until softened, 5 to 7 minutes. Stir in rice, garlic, and ras el hanout and cook, stirring frequently, until grain edges begin to turn translucent, about 3 minutes.

3. Stir in broth and olives and bring to boil. Cover, transfer pot to oven, and bake until rice is tender and liquid is absorbed, 12 to 15 minutes.

4. Remove pot from oven and let sit for 10 minutes. Add potatoes to rice and fluff gently with fork to combine. Season with salt and pepper to taste. Sprinkle with cilantro and serve with lime wedges.

PER SERVING Cal 360; **Total Fat** 16g, **Sat Fat** 2g; **Chol** 0mg; **Sodium** 590mg; **Total Carb** 48g, **Dietary Fiber** 5g, **Total Sugars** 7g; **Protein** 5g

---

TAKE IT UP A NOTCH

Ras el hanout is a Moroccan spice blend. With its mix of warm spices like cardamom and cinnamon, it enhances the flavor of lentil dishes as well as rice.

Ras el Hanout
MAKES ABOUT ½ CUP

Ras el hanout is a complex Moroccan spice blend that traditionally features a host of warm spices. We use it to give robust flavor to rice and couscous dishes. If you can't find Aleppo pepper, you can substitute ½ teaspoon paprika and ½ teaspoon red pepper flakes.

16 cardamom pods
4 teaspoons coriander seeds
4 teaspoons cumin seeds
2 teaspoons anise seeds
½ teaspoon allspice berries
¼ teaspoon black peppercorns
4 teaspoons ground ginger
2 teaspoons ground nutmeg
2 teaspoons ground dried Aleppo pepper
2 teaspoons ground cinnamon

1. Toast cardamom, coriander, cumin, anise, allspice, and peppercorns in small skillet over medium heat until fragrant, shaking skillet occasionally to prevent scorching, about 2 minutes. Let cool to room temperature.

2. Transfer toasted spices, ginger, nutmeg, Aleppo, and cinnamon to spice grinder and process to fine powder. (Ras el hanout can be stored at room temperature in airtight container for up to 1 year.)

Persian-Style Rice with Golden Crust

Persian-Style Rice with Golden Crust
SERVES 6

WHY THIS RECIPE WORKS *Chelow* is a showpiece side, a classic Iranian dish that marries an unusually light and fluffy rice pilaf with a crispy golden-brown crust. Rinsing and soaking the rice yielded well-separated grains; many recipes soak for 24 hours, but 15 minutes in hot water provided similar hydration. Parboiling the rice and then steaming it to finish cooking was essential for evenly cooked rice and the perfect crust. We also wrapped the lid with a dish towel to absorb extra moisture and ensure fluffiness. Combining a portion of the rice with Greek yogurt and oil created a browned, flavorful crust, while chunks of butter enriched the pilaf portion. The yogurt also made the crust easier to remove from the pot, as did brushing the bottom of the pot with oil and letting the pot rest on a damp towel after cooking (rapidly cooling the pot caused the rice to contract and release). Adding cumin seeds and parsley made for a more interesting, well-rounded flavor profile. Texmati or other long-grain rice will work here. For the best results, use a Dutch oven with a bottom diameter between 8½ and 10 inches. It is important not to overcook the rice during parboiling, as it will continue to cook during steaming. Begin checking the rice at the lower end of the time range.

2 cups basmati rice
1 tablespoon table salt for brining
¼ teaspoon table salt, plus 2 tablespoons for cooking rice
5 tablespoons vegetable oil, divided
¼ cup plain Greek yogurt
1½ teaspoons cumin seeds, divided
2 tablespoons unsalted butter, cut into 8 pieces
¼ cup minced fresh parsley, divided

1. Place rice in fine-mesh strainer and rinse under cold running water until water runs clear. Place rinsed rice and 1 tablespoon salt in medium bowl and cover with 4 cups hot tap water. Stir gently to dissolve salt; let sit for 15 minutes. Drain rice in fine-mesh strainer.

2. Meanwhile, bring 8 cups water to boil in Dutch oven over high heat. Add rice and 2 tablespoons salt. Boil briskly, stirring frequently, until rice is mostly tender with slight bite in center and grains are floating toward top of pot, 3 to 5 minutes (begin timing from when rice is added to pot).

3. Drain rice in large fine-mesh strainer and rinse with cold water to stop cooking, about 30 seconds. Rinse and dry pot well to remove any residual starch. Brush bottom and 1 inch up sides of pot with 1 tablespoon oil.

4. Whisk remaining ¼ cup oil, yogurt, 1 teaspoon cumin seeds, and remaining ¼ teaspoon salt together in medium bowl. Add 2 cups parcooked rice and stir until combined. Spread yogurt-rice mixture evenly over bottom of prepared pot, packing it down well.

5. Stir remaining ½ teaspoon cumin seeds into remaining rice. Mound rice in center of pot on top of yogurt-rice base (it should look like small hill). Poke 8 equally spaced holes through rice mound but not into yogurt-rice base. Place 1 butter cube in each hole. Drizzle ⅓ cup water over rice mound.

6. Wrap pot lid with clean dish towel and cover pot tightly, making sure towel is secure on top of lid and away from heat. Cook over medium-high heat until rice on bottom is crackling and steam is coming from sides of pot, about 10 minutes, rotating pot halfway through for even cooking.

7. Reduce heat to medium-low and continue to cook until rice is tender and fluffy and crust is golden brown around edges, 30 to 35 minutes. Remove covered pot from heat and place on damp dish towel set in rimmed baking sheet; let sit for 5 minutes.

8. Stir 2 tablespoons parsley into rice, making sure not to disturb crust on bottom of pot, and season with salt to taste. Gently spoon rice onto serving platter.

9. Using thin metal spatula, loosen edges of crust from pot, then break crust into large pieces. Transfer pieces to serving platter, arranging evenly around rice. Sprinkle with remaining 2 table-spoons parsley and serve.

PER SERVING Cal 350; **Total Fat** 16g, **Sat Fat** 3g; **Chol** 10mg; **Sodium** 105mg; **Total Carb** 45g, **Dietary Fiber** 0g, **Total Sugars** 1g; **Protein** 6g

Jeweled Rice

SERVES 4 TO 6　**VEGAN**

WHY THIS RECIPE WORKS Jeweled rice is a staple in Persian cuisine and features basmati rice and candied carrots, perfumed with saffron and cardamom; its name comes from the colorful dried fruit and nuts that traditionally stud its appealingly golden surface. We love the dish's subtle balance of sweet and savory, and we were inspired to re-create it while also making it simpler and easier. With ingredients that are soaked, bloomed, parcooked, layered, and steamed, this dish typically uses almost every pot in the kitchen. We streamlined our version by cooking the rice using an easy pilaf method, adding spices and some sautéed onion to the water to infuse the rice with deep flavor. While it simmered, we candied the orange zest and carrots. Once the rice was done, we sprinkled our candied mixture and some dried fruit on top and let them plump up while the rice rested off the heat. Finally, we stirred in the nuts just before serving so they'd retain their crunch. Texmati or other long-grain white rice will work here.

1 cup sugar
6 (2-inch) strips orange zest, sliced thin lengthwise
2 carrots, peeled and cut into ¼-inch pieces
2 tablespoons extra-virgin olive oil
1 onion, chopped fine
1½ teaspoons table salt
¾ teaspoon saffron threads, crumbled
½ teaspoon ground cardamom
1½ cups basmati rice, rinsed
½ cup currants
½ cup dried cranberries
¼ cup sliced almonds, toasted
¼ cup shelled pistachios, toasted and chopped

Jeweled Rice

SLICING ORANGE ZEST THIN

1. Using vegetable peeler, remove 2-inch-long strips of orange zest from orange, avoiding bitter white pith just beneath.

2. Using chef's knife, cut zest strips lengthwise into long, thin pieces.

1. Bring 2 cups water and sugar to boil in small saucepan over medium-high heat. Stir in orange zest and carrots, reduce heat to medium-low, and simmer until carrots are tender, 10 to 15 minutes. Drain well, transfer to plate, and let cool.

2. Meanwhile, heat oil in large saucepan over medium heat until shimmering. Add onion and salt and cook until onion is softened, about 5 minutes. Stir in saffron and cardamom and cook until fragrant, about 30 seconds. Stir in rice and cook, stirring often, until grain edges begin to turn translucent, about 3 minutes. Stir in 2¼ cups water and bring to simmer. Reduce heat to low, cover, and simmer gently until liquid is absorbed and rice is tender, 16 to 18 minutes.

3. Remove pot from heat and sprinkle candied carrots and orange zest, currants, and cranberries over rice. Cover, laying clean folded dish towel underneath lid, and let sit for 10 minutes. Add almonds and pistachios and fluff gently with fork to combine. Season with salt and pepper to taste, and serve.

PER SERVING Cal 260; **Total Fat** 10g, **Sat Fat** 1g; **Chol** 0mg; **Sodium** 580mg; **Total Carb** 38g, **Dietary Fiber** 2g, **Total Sugars** 2g; **Protein** 5g

Sushi Rice

2. Bring rice and 3 cups water to boil in saucepan over medium-high heat. Cook, uncovered, until water level drops below surface of rice and small holes form, about 5 minutes.

3. Reduce heat to low, cover, and cook until rice is tender and water is fully absorbed, about 15 minutes. Serve.

PER SERVING Cal 210; **Total Fat** 0g, **Sat Fat** 0g; **Chol** 0mg; **Sodium** 0mg; **Total Carb** 48g, **Dietary Fiber** 0g, **Total Sugars** 0g; **Protein** 5g

Sushi Rice
SERVES 4 TO 6 `FAST` `VEGAN`

WHY THIS RECIPE WORKS Sushi rice, sometimes called sticky rice, is ideal for sushi because it holds together and can be rolled and shaped. Short-grain sushi rice has a higher starch content than regular rice, which gives it a characteristic sticky texture. Its slightly sweet flavor comes from the addition of seasoned rice vinegar. We love this rice not just for making sushi but also as a side dish for Asian-inspired meals. You can substitute short-grain white rice for the sushi rice. Regular rice vinegar can be substituted for the seasoned rice vinegar. Do not rinse the rice before cooking; the rice's exterior starch gives the finished dish the proper sticky texture.

- 2 cups sushi or short-grain white rice
- 2 cups water
- 2 teaspoons seasoned rice vinegar
- 1 teaspoon table salt

Bring rice, water, vinegar, and salt to boil in medium saucepan over high heat. Cover, reduce heat to low, and cook until liquid is absorbed, 7 to 9 minutes. Remove rice from heat and let sit, covered, until tender, about 15 minutes. Fluff rice with fork and serve.

PER SERVING Cal 240; **Total Fat** 0g, **Sat Fat** 0g; **Chol** 0mg; **Sodium** 390mg; **Total Carb** 53g, **Dietary Fiber** 2g, **Total Sugars** 0g; **Protein** 4g

Chinese Restaurant–Style Rice
SERVES 4 TO 6 `FAST` `VEGAN`

WHY THIS RECIPE WORKS The rice served in Chinese restaurants is soft enough to soak up savory sauces and sticky enough to be picked up with chopsticks. Chinese cooks never salt their rice, making it an ideal simple accompaniment to highly flavorful and/or soy-heavy dishes. We found that rinsing the grains removed some of their surface starch and that boiling the rice for the first 5 minutes of cooking provided enough agitation to release the remaining starch, resulting in just the right amount of stickiness. Do not stir the rice as it cooks. The finished rice can stand off the heat, covered, for up to 15 minutes. Medium-grain or jasmine rice can also be used.

- 2 cups long-grain white rice
- 3 cups water

1. Place rice in fine-mesh strainer set over bowl. Rinse under running water, swishing with your hands, until water runs clear. Drain thoroughly.

Thai-Style Sticky Rice
SERVES 4 `VEGAN`

WHY THIS RECIPE WORKS The traditional vessel for steaming Thai sticky rice (*khao niaw*, which is made from glutinous rice) is a bamboo basket set over an hourglass-shaped aluminum pot, which allows the rice to steam on all sides. We mimicked that setup by cooking rice in a cheesecloth-lined fine-mesh strainer set over a saucepan of barely simmering water. This sticky rice ably soaks up the assertive flavors of any sauce and delivers satisfying chew. This recipe requires letting the rice soak in water for at least 4 hours before cooking. When shopping, look for rice labeled "Thai glutinous rice" or "Thai sweet rice"; do not substitute other varieties. Thai glutinous rice can be found in Asian markets and online.

2 cups Thai glutinous rice

1. Place rice in medium bowl and pour enough water over rice to cover by 2 inches. Let sit at room temperature for at least 4 hours or up to 8 hours.

2. Cut 18-inch square of double-thickness cheesecloth. Line large fine-mesh strainer with cheesecloth, letting excess hang over sides. Drain rice in prepared strainer, then rinse under running water until water runs clear. Fold edges of cheesecloth over rice and pat surface of rice smooth.

3. Bring 1½ inches water to boil in large saucepan. Set strainer in saucepan (water should not touch bottom of strainer), cover with lid (it will not form tight seal), reduce heat to medium-high, and steam rice for 15 minutes. Uncover and, using tongs, flip cheesecloth bundle (rice should form a sticky mass) so side that was closer to bottom of saucepan is now on top. Cover and continue to steam until rice is just translucent and texture is tender but with a little chew, 15 to 20 minutes, checking water level occasionally and adding more if necessary.

4. Remove saucepan from heat, drain excess water from saucepan and return strainer to saucepan. Cover and let rice sit for 10 to 15 minutes before serving.

PER SERVING Cal 340; **Total Fat** 0.5g; **Sat Fat** 0g; **Chol** 0mg; **Sodium** 5mg; **Total Carb** 76g, **Dietary Fiber** 3g, **Total Sugars** 0g; **Protein** 6g

Coconut Rice with Bok Choy and Lime
SERVES 4 TO 6 `FAST` `VEGAN`

WHY THIS RECIPE WORKS Rich, creamy coconut rice is served around the globe as a cooling accompaniment to spicy curries, stir-fries, and more. Our dressed-up side dish features baby bok choy along with aromatic lemon grass, lime, and cilantro. Following the traditional method, we cooked basmati rice in coconut milk along with lemon grass, which steeped in the liquid and lent its flavor as the rice simmered. To ensure that the bok choy stalks turned tender by the time the rice was cooked, we sautéed them in the pan along with some minced shallot before adding the rice. When the rice was done, we stirred in fragrant lime zest and juice and cilantro along with the delicate bok choy greens. We prefer the flavor of basmati rice in this recipe, but long-grain white, jasmine, or Texmati rice can be substituted.

2 teaspoons vegetable oil
2 heads baby bok choy (4 ounces each), stalks sliced ½ inch thick and greens chopped
1 shallot, minced
1½ cups basmati rice, rinsed
1½ cups water
¾ cup canned coconut milk
1 lemon grass stalk, trimmed to bottom 6 inches and smashed
2 teaspoons table salt
2 tablespoons minced fresh cilantro
1 teaspoon grated lime zest plus 2 teaspoons juice

1. Heat oil in large saucepan over medium-high heat until shimmering. Add bok choy stalks and shallot and cook, stirring occasionally, until softened, about 2 minutes.

2. Stir in rice, water, coconut milk, lemon grass, and salt and bring to boil. Reduce heat to low, cover, and simmer gently until liquid is absorbed, 18 to 20 minutes.

3. Fold in cilantro, lime zest and juice, and bok choy greens; cover and cook until rice is tender, about 3 minutes. Discard lemon grass. Season with salt and pepper to taste, and serve.

PER SERVING Cal 240; **Total Fat** 8g, **Sat Fat** 5g; **Chol** 0mg; **Sodium** 800mg; **Total Carb** 38g, **Dietary Fiber** 1g, **Total Sugars** 1g; **Protein** 5g

SMASHING LEMON GRASS

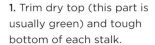

1. Trim dry top (this part is usually green) and tough bottom of each stalk.

2. Peel and discard dry outer layer until moist, tender inner stalk is exposed. Smash peeled stalk with back of chef's knife or meat pounder to release maximum flavor.

Almost Hands-Free Risotto with Parmesan
SERVES 6

WHY THIS RECIPE WORKS Classic risotto can demand half an hour of stovetop tedium for the best creamy results. Our goal was 5 minutes of stirring, tops. First, we swapped out the saucepan for a Dutch oven, which has a thick, heavy bottom, deep sides, and a tight-fitting lid—perfect for trapping and distributing heat evenly. Typical recipes dictate adding the broth in small increments after the wine has been absorbed and stirring constantly after each addition, but we added most of the broth at once and covered the pan, allowing the rice to simmer until almost all the broth had been absorbed, stirring just twice. After adding the second and final addition of broth, we stirred the pot and then turned off the heat. Without sitting over a direct flame, the sauce turned out perfectly creamy and the rice was thickened, velvety, and just barely chewy. To finish, we simply stirred in butter and a squeeze of lemon juice. This more hands-off method requires precise timing, so we strongly recommend using a timer. To make this dish vegetarian, substitute vegetable broth for the chicken broth.

- 5 cups chicken broth
- 1½ cups water
- 4 tablespoons unsalted butter, divided
- 1 large onion, chopped fine
- ¾ teaspoon table salt
- 1 garlic clove, minced
- 2 cups Arborio rice
- 1 cup dry white wine
- 2 ounces Parmesan cheese, grated (1 cup)
- 1 teaspoon lemon juice

1. Bring broth and water to boil in large saucepan over high heat. Cover and reduce heat to medium-low to maintain bare simmer.

2. Melt 2 tablespoons butter in Dutch oven over medium heat. Add onion and salt and cook until onion is softened, 4 to 5 minutes. Stir in garlic and cook until fragrant, about 30 seconds. Stir in rice and cook, stirring often, until grain edges begin to turn translucent, about 3 minutes.

3. Stir in wine and cook, stirring constantly, until fully absorbed, 2 to 3 minutes. Stir in 5 cups hot broth mixture. Reduce heat to medium-low, cover, and simmer until almost all liquid has been absorbed and rice is just al dente, 18 to 19 minutes, stirring twice during cooking.

4. Add ¾ cup hot broth mixture and stir gently and constantly until risotto becomes creamy, about 3 minutes. Stir in Parmesan. Remove pot from heat, cover, and let sit for 5 minutes. Stir in remaining 2 tablespoons butter and lemon juice. Season with salt and pepper to taste. Before serving, stir in remaining broth mixture as needed to loosen texture of risotto.

PER SERVING Cal 400; **Total Fat** 12g, **Sat Fat** 6g; **Chol** 25mg; **Sodium** 940mg; **Total Carb** 56g, **Dietary Fiber** 3g, **Total Sugars** 4g; **Protein** 12g

VARIATIONS
Almost Hands-Free Risotto with Herbs
Stir in 2 tablespoons minced fresh parsley and 2 tablespoons minced fresh chives before serving.

Almost Hands-Free Risotto with Fennel and Saffron
Add 1 fennel bulb, cored and chopped fine, to pot with onion and cook until softened, about 12 minutes. Add ¼ teaspoon ground coriander and large pinch saffron threads to pot with garlic.

Almost Hands-Free Risotto with Porcini
Add ¼ ounce rinsed and minced dried porcini mushrooms to pot with garlic. Substitute soy sauce for lemon juice.

MAKING ALMOST HANDS-FREE RISOTTO

1. Bring broth and water to boil. Cover and reduce heat to maintain simmer. In Dutch oven, add onion to butter and cook until softened. Stir in garlic.

2. Add rice, stirring often until grains are translucent on edges. Stir in wine and cook until absorbed. Stir in 5 cups hot broth. Reduce heat, cover, and simmer until rice is al dente, stirring twice.

3. Add ¾ cup broth and stir until risotto becomes creamy. Stir in Parmesan. Remove from heat, cover, and let sit. Stir in remaining butter and lemon juice.

Hearty Baked Brown Rice with Peas, Feta, and Mint

Hearty Baked Brown Rice

SERVES 4 TO 6

WHY THIS RECIPE WORKS To bulk up our Foolproof Baked Brown Rice (page 30), with aromatics and vegetables that complemented the hearty flavor and texture of the rice, we sautéed two onions until well browned before adding the rice and water to the pot. Once the rice was tender, we stirred in chopped roasted red peppers and let them warm through as the rice rested off the heat. Then we stirred in some fresh parsley and black pepper, and we served the dish with grated Parmesan cheese and bright lemon wedges. Finally, we made some simple variations—a meaty version with Andouille sausage; a Greek-inspired version with peas, feta, and mint; and a Southwestern take with black beans, bell pepper, and cilantro.

- 4 teaspoons vegetable oil
- 2 onions, chopped fine
- 2¼ cups water
- 1 cup vegetable broth
- 1½ cups long-grain brown rice, rinsed
- 1 teaspoon table salt
- ¾ cup chopped jarred roasted red peppers, drained
- ½ cup minced fresh parsley
- ¼ teaspoon pepper
- 1 ounce Parmesan cheese, grated (½ cup)
  Lemon wedges

1. Adjust oven rack to middle position and heat oven to 375 degrees. Heat oil in Dutch oven over medium heat until shimmering. Add onions and cook, stirring occasionally, until well browned, 12 to 14 minutes.

2. Add water and broth, cover, and bring to boil. Off heat, stir in rice and salt. Cover, transfer pot to oven, and bake until liquid is absorbed and rice is tender, 1 hour 5 minutes to 1 hour 10 minutes.

3. Remove pot from oven and uncover. Fluff rice with fork and stir in red peppers. Replace lid and let rice sit for 5 minutes. Stir in parsley and pepper. Serve with Parmesan and lemon wedges.

PER SERVING Cal 230; **Total Fat** 5g, **Sat Fat** 1.5g; **Chol** 5mg; **Sodium** 690mg; **Total Carb** 41g, **Dietary Fiber** 2g, **Total Sugars** 3g; **Protein** 6g

VARIATIONS
Hearty Baked Brown Rice with Andouille, Corn, and Red Pepper
Substitute 1 tablespoon extra-virgin olive oil for vegetable oil and heat in Dutch oven over medium heat until shimmering. Add 6 ounces andouille sausage, cut into ½-inch pieces, and cook until lightly browned, 4 to 6 minutes. Using slotted spoon, transfer sausage to paper towel–lined plate. Substitute 1 finely chopped red bell pepper for 1 onion. Cook bell pepper and onion in remaining fat, stirring occasionally, until well browned, 12 to 14 minutes; add 3 minced garlic cloves and cook until fragrant, about 30 seconds, before adding water and broth. Substitute ½ cup thawed frozen corn for roasted red peppers; add reserved sausage with corn. Substitute ¼ cup chopped fresh basil for parsley and omit Parmesan.

Hearty Baked Brown Rice with Black Beans and Cilantro
Substitute 1 finely chopped green bell pepper for 1 onion. Once vegetables are well browned in step 1, stir in 3 minced garlic cloves and cook until fragrant, about 30 seconds. Substitute 1 (15-ounce) can rinsed black beans for roasted red peppers and ¼ cup minced fresh cilantro for parsley. Omit Parmesan and substitute lime wedges for lemon wedges.

Hearty Baked Brown Rice with Peas, Feta, and Mint
Reduce amount of oil to 1 tablespoon and omit 1 onion. Substitute 1 cup thawed frozen peas for roasted red peppers, ¼ cup minced fresh mint for parsley, ½ teaspoon grated lemon zest for pepper, and ½ cup crumbled feta for Parmesan.

Brown Rice Pilaf with Dates and Pistachios

1½ cups long-grain brown rice, rinsed
1 bay leaf
1½ ounces pitted dates, chopped (¼ cup)
⅓ cup shelled pistachios, toasted and chopped coarse
¼ cup minced fresh mint

1. Adjust oven rack to middle position and heat oven to 375 degrees. Heat oil in Dutch oven over medium heat until shimmering. Add onion and salt and cook until softened and lightly browned, 5 to 7 minutes.

2. Stir in broth, cover, and bring to boil. Off heat, stir in rice and bay leaf. Cover, transfer pot to oven, and bake until liquid is absorbed and rice is tender, 55 to 65 minutes.

3. Remove pot from oven. Sprinkle dates over rice and let sit, covered, for 10 minutes. Discard bay leaf. Fluff rice with fork, stir in pistachios and mint, and season with salt and pepper to taste. Serve.

PER SERVING Cal 270; **Total Fat** 7g, **Sat Fat** 1g; **Chol** 0mg; **Sodium** 510mg; **Total Carb** 45g, **Dietary Fiber** 3g, **Total Sugars** 7g; **Protein** 6g

Skillet Brown Rice and Beans with Corn and Fresh Tomatoes
SERVES 6   VEGAN

WHY THIS RECIPE WORKS The sustaining combination of rice and beans is a staple in many cuisines. We wanted to make a simple weeknight version with bold Latin American flavor. White rice is traditional, but we preferred the texture, chew, and robust flavor of brown rice. After sautéing an onion, we added fresh corn and the uncooked rice to the skillet with garlic, cumin, and cayenne and sautéed them until fragrant. Then we stirred in broth and simmered the rice until tender. Canned black beans made the dish quicker; to keep them from getting mushy, we stirred them in partway through cooking. A flavorful salsa of grape tomatoes, scallions, cilantro, and lime juice added a fresh counterpoint to the rich, spicy rice and beans. We prefer the flavor of fresh corn; however, 1½ cups frozen corn, thawed and patted dry, can be substituted.

2 tablespoons extra-virgin olive oil, divided
1 onion, minced
2 ears corn, kernels cut from cobs
1 cup long-grain brown rice, rinsed
4 garlic cloves, minced
1 teaspoon cumin
  Pinch cayenne pepper
3¼ cups vegetable broth
2 (15-ounce) cans black beans, rinsed

Brown Rice Pilaf with Dates and Pistachios
SERVES 6   VEGAN

WHY THIS RECIPE WORKS We set out to enrich simple brown rice pilaf with some Middle Eastern–inspired add-ins. A combination of aromatic onions, sweet dates, earthy pistachios, and fresh mint created the flavorful yet mild profile we were after. We knew from previous testing that oven baking brown rice guaranteed an even and appealing texture. In a Dutch oven, we sautéed a base of onions, stirred in broth, rice, and a bay leaf, and baked it, covered, for about an hour. When the rice was tender, we removed it from the oven, sprinkled chopped dates over the top, covered the pot again, and let it sit for 10 minutes, just enough time for the dates to become plump and tender. After a quick fluff with a fork to incorporate a sprinkling of pistachios and mint, our pilaf was good to go. Medium-grain or short-grain brown rice can be substituted for the long-grain rice.

1 tablespoon extra-virgin olive oil
1 onion, chopped fine
½ teaspoon table salt
3¼ cups chicken or vegetable broth

Skillet Brown Rice and Beans with Corn and Fresh Tomatoes

12 ounces grape tomatoes, quartered

5 scallions, sliced thin

¼ cup minced fresh cilantro

1 tablespoon lime juice

1. Heat 1 tablespoon oil in 12-inch nonstick skillet over medium-high heat until shimmering. Add onion and cook until softened and lightly browned, 5 to 7 minutes. Stir in corn and cook until lightly browned, about 4 minutes. Stir in rice, garlic, cumin, and cayenne and cook until fragrant, about 30 seconds.

2. Stir in broth and bring to simmer. Cover, reduce heat to medium-low, and simmer gently, stirring occasionally, for 25 minutes.

3. Stir in beans, cover, and continue to simmer until liquid has been absorbed and rice is tender, 20 to 25 minutes. Season with salt and pepper to taste.

4. Combine remaining 1 tablespoon oil, tomatoes, scallions, cilantro, and lime juice in bowl and season with salt and pepper to taste. Sprinkle tomato mixture over rice and beans and serve.

PER SERVING Cal 290; **Total Fat** 7g, **Sat Fat** 1g;
Chol 0mg; **Sodium** 750mg; **Total Carb** 51g, **Dietary Fiber** 8g, **Total Sugars** 5g; **Protein** 10g

VARIATIONS

Skillet Brown Rice and Chickpeas with Coconut Milk

Substitute 2 finely chopped yellow bell peppers for corn, 1½ teaspoons garam masala for cumin, and canned chickpeas for black beans. Reduce amount of vegetable broth to 1¾ cups and add 1 (13.5-ounce) can light coconut milk to skillet with broth.

Spanish-Style Skillet Brown Rice and Chickpeas

Substitute 2 finely chopped red bell peppers for corn, pinch of crumbled saffron for cumin, and canned chickpeas for black beans.

Miso Brown Rice Cakes
SERVES 4

WHY THIS RECIPE WORKS Easy and substantial, rice cakes are a different and appealing way to serve brown rice. Here we used hearty long-grain brown rice and gave the dish a flavorful Asian twist. We paired rice with red miso and shiitake mushrooms for meatiness, and ginger and garlic for depth of flavor. We cooked the rice on the stovetop to aid in releasing starches that helped hold the cakes together when pan-fried. Once the rice was cool, we pulsed it in a food processor to break down the starches for even better binding and combined it with egg, sesame oil, miso, and scallions. Then we formed our patties and chilled them until firm. A few minutes in a hot skillet gave us crisp, browned rice cakes. We prefer the flavor of red miso here but you can use white miso. Do not substitute "light" miso; its flavor is too mild.

3 tablespoons vegetable oil, divided

8 ounces shiitake mushrooms, stemmed and chopped

2 teaspoons grated fresh ginger

2 garlic cloves, minced

3¾ cups water

1½ cups long-grain brown rice

1 teaspoon table salt, divided

4 scallions, chopped fine

1 large egg plus 1 yolk, lightly beaten

3 tablespoons red miso

1½ teaspoons sesame oil

¼ teaspoon pepper

1 recipe Sriracha Mayo (page 176)

1. Heat 1 tablespoon vegetable oil in large saucepan over medium heat until shimmering. Add mushrooms and cook until lightly browned, about 5 minutes. Stir in ginger and garlic and cook until fragrant, about 30 seconds. Add water, rice, and ½ teaspoon salt and bring to simmer. Reduce heat to low, cover, and cook until rice is tender, about 50 minutes, stirring occasionally. Spread rice mixture onto rimmed baking sheet and let cool for 15 minutes.

2. Pulse rice mixture in food processor until coarsely ground, about 10 pulses; transfer to large bowl. Stir in scallions, egg and yolk, miso, sesame oil, pepper, and remaining ½ teaspoon salt until well combined.

3. Line rimmed baking sheet with parchment paper and spray with vegetable oil spray. Using your wet hands, divide rice mixture into 8 equal portions and pack firmly into ½-inch-thick patties; lay on prepared sheet. Refrigerate rice cakes, uncovered, until chilled and firm, about 30 minutes.

4. Heat 1 tablespoon vegetable oil in 12-inch nonstick skillet over medium-high heat until shimmering. Gently lay 4 rice cakes in skillet and cook until crisp and browned on both sides, about 4 minutes per side, turning gently halfway through cooking; transfer to plate and cover to keep warm. Repeat with remaining 1 tablespoon vegetable oil and remaining rice cakes. Serve with Sriracha Mayo.

PER SERVING Cal 620; **Total Fat** 38g, **Sat Fat** 5g; **Chol** 105mg; **Sodium** 1500mg; **Total Carb** 61g, **Dietary Fiber** 3g, **Total Sugars** 5g; **Protein** 10g

---

TAKE IT UP A NOTCH

Prepared sriracha adds some heat to mayonnaise. This easy-to-make condiment is delicious with rice cakes and fried foods like vegetable fritters and onion rings.

Sriracha Mayo
MAKES ABOUT ¾ CUP

½ cup mayonnaise
1 scallion, chopped fine
2 tablespoons sriracha
1 tablespoon lime juice

Combine all ingredients in bowl. (Mayo can be refrigerated for up to 1 week.)

Baked Wild Rice
SERVES 4 TO 6 `VEGAN`

WHY THIS RECIPE WORKS Wild rice is not actually rice but a grass. We love its nuttiness in a savory side dish, but its chewy outer husk means it can take nearly an hour to become tender on the stovetop. We turned to the oven to make wild rice a hands-off affair. We started with our recipe for baked brown rice, spreading the wild rice in a baking dish, pouring boiling water over, and baking it until tender. To get the hardier grains to cook through, we had to increase both the amount of water and the cooking time. After a little more than an hour, we had evenly cooked, tender grains with great chew. The recipe can be doubled easily using a 13 by 9-inch baking dish. Be sure to cover the pot when bringing the water to a boil in step 2; any water loss due to evaporation will affect how the rice cooks. Do not use quick-cooking or presteamed wild rice in this recipe; you may need to read the ingredient list on the package carefully to determine if the wild rice is presteamed.

1½ cups wild rice, rinsed
3 cups water
2 teaspoons unsalted butter or extra-virgin olive oil
¾ teaspoon table salt

1. Adjust oven rack to middle position and heat oven to 375 degrees. Spread rice into 8-inch square glass baking dish.

2. Bring water, butter, and salt to boil in covered medium saucepan over high heat. Once boiling, stir to combine, then pour immediately over rice. Cover baking dish tightly with aluminum foil and bake until liquid is absorbed and rice is tender, 70 to 80 minutes.

3. Remove baking dish from oven, uncover, and fluff rice with fork. Re-cover dish with foil and let rice sit for 10 minutes before serving.

PER SERVING Cal 150; **Total Fat** 1.5g, **Sat Fat** 1g; **Chol** 5mg; **Sodium** 290mg; **Total Carb** 28g, **Dietary Fiber** 3g, **Total Sugars** 0g; **Protein** 5g

VARIATION
Baked Wild Rice with Almonds and Cranberries
Finely chopping the cranberries helps them soften in the steaming rice. Dried cherries can be substituted for the cranberries.

In step 2, melt butter in medium saucepan over medium heat. Add 1 finely chopped onion and salt and cook until onion is softened, 5 to 7 minutes. Stir in water. Cover pot, increase heat to high, and bring to boil before pouring over rice. Before re-covering dish with foil in step 3, stir in ¼ cup finely chopped cranberries. Sprinkle with ¼ cup toasted sliced almonds before serving.

Barley with Lemon and Herbs

SERVES 6 TO 8 **VEGAN**

WHY THIS RECIPE WORKS Barley is a hearty grain with a nutty flavor similar to brown rice. We like to cook barley like pasta—boiled in salted water and then drained—to rid the grains of their sticky starch, which is what causes them to clump. We let the cooked barley cool on a rimmed baking sheet to help it dry and then tossed it with an acid-heavy dressing (a 1:1 ratio of oil to acid instead of the typical 3:1), and aromatics and herbs to create a flavorful side. The cooking time will vary from product to product, so start checking for doneness after 25 minutes.

- 1½ cups pearl barley
- ½ teaspoon table salt plus salt for cooking barley
- 3 tablespoons extra-virgin olive oil
- 2 tablespoons minced shallot
- 1 teaspoon grated lemon zest plus 3 tablespoons juice
- 1 teaspoon Dijon mustard
- ¼ teaspoon pepper
- 6 scallions, sliced thin on bias
- ¼ cup minced fresh mint
- ¼ cup minced fresh cilantro

1. Line rimmed baking sheet with parchment paper and set aside. Bring 4 quarts water to boil in Dutch oven. Add barley and 1 tablespoon salt. Stir and cook uncovered, adjusting heat to maintain gentle boil, until barley is tender with slight chew, 25 to 45 minutes.

2. While barley cooks, whisk oil, shallot, lemon zest and juice, mustard, pepper, and ½ teaspoon salt together in large bowl.

3. Drain barley. Transfer to prepared sheet and spread into even layer. Let stand until no longer steaming, 5 to 7 minutes. Add barley to bowl with dressing and toss to coat. Add scallions, mint, and cilantro and stir to combine. Season with salt and pepper to taste. Serve.

PER SERVING Cal 190; **Total Fat** 6g, **Sat Fat** 1g; **Chol** 0mg; **Sodium** 180mg; **Total Carb** 31g, **Dietary Fiber** 6g, **Total Sugars** 1g; **Protein** 4g

VARIATIONS

Barley with Celery and Miso Dressing

Substitute 3 tablespoons seasoned rice vinegar, 1 tablespoon white miso paste, 1 tablespoon soy sauce, 1 tablespoon toasted sesame oil, 1 tablespoon vegetable oil, 2 teaspoons grated fresh ginger, 1 minced garlic clove, 1 teaspoon packed brown sugar, and ¼ to ½ teaspoon red pepper flakes for oil, shallot, lemon zest and juice, mustard, salt, and pepper in step 2. Substitute 2 celery ribs, sliced thin on bias, and 2 peeled and grated carrots for scallions. Omit mint and increase cilantro to ½ cup.

Barley with Lemon and Herbs

Barley with Fennel, Dried Apricots, and Orange

Substitute 3 tablespoons red wine vinegar and ½ teaspoon grated orange zest plus 2 tablespoons juice for lemon zest and juice. Omit mustard. Reduce oil to 2 tablespoons and add 1 minced garlic clove to dressing in step 2. Substitute 20 chopped dried California apricots and 1 small fennel bulb, 2 tablespoons fronds minced, stalks discarded, bulb halved, cored, and chopped fine, for scallions. Omit mint and substitute parsley for cilantro.

Barley with Lentils and Mushrooms

SERVES 4

WHY THIS RECIPE WORKS This barley-based dish makes a substantial side (or satisfying vegetarian main). To balance the grains, we used hearty lentils and earthy mushrooms. Tasters favored black lentils for their nutty, robust flavor and their ability to hold their shape once cooked. We were happy to find that we could cook the barley and lentils together in one pot. To keep our recipe streamlined, we set the cooked barley and lentils aside and attempted to brown the mushrooms in the same pan. Unfortunately, the mushrooms were too crowded in the pot, which caused them to steam and overcook. Using a nonstick skillet to cook the mushrooms resulted in more browning and faster cooking; the increased surface area allowed the mushrooms to make more contact with the pan. We tested many varieties of mushrooms and liked the combination of meaty portobellos with savory, flavor-rich porcini. Our tangy Tahini-Yogurt Sauce worked perfectly to balance these rich flavors, and fresh dill and strips of lemon peel brightened the earthy notes of the barley and lentils. Do not substitute hulled, hull-less, quick-cooking, or presteamed barley (read the ingredient list on the package to determine this) in this recipe. While we prefer black lentils here, lentilles du Puy, brown lentils, or green lentils can be substituted.

½ ounce dried porcini mushrooms, rinsed
1 cup pearl barley
½ cup dried black lentils, picked over and rinsed
2 tablespoons extra-virgin olive oil
1 onion, chopped fine
2 large portobello mushroom caps, cut into 1-inch pieces
3 (2-inch) strips lemon zest, sliced thin lengthwise
¾ teaspoon ground coriander
½ teaspoon table salt plus salt for cooking lentils and barley
¼ teaspoon pepper
2 tablespoons chopped fresh dill
½ cup Tahini-Yogurt Sauce

1. Microwave 1½ cups water and porcini mushrooms in covered bowl until steaming, about 1 minute. Let sit until softened, about 5 minutes. Drain mushrooms in fine-mesh strainer lined with coffee filter, reserving soaking liquid, and chop mushrooms.

2. Bring 4 quarts water to boil in Dutch oven. Add barley, lentils, and 1 tablespoon salt, return to boil, and cook until tender, 20 to 40 minutes. Drain barley and lentils, return to now-empty pot, and cover to keep warm.

3. Meanwhile, heat oil in 12-inch nonstick skillet over medium heat until shimmering. Add onion and cook until softened, about 5 minutes. Stir in portobello mushrooms, cover, and cook until portobellos have released their liquid and begin to brown, about 4 minutes.

4. Uncover, stir in lemon zest, coriander, ½ teaspoon salt, and pepper, and cook until fragrant, about 30 seconds. Stir in porcini and porcini soaking liquid, bring to boil, and cook, stirring occasionally, until liquid is thickened slightly and reduced to ½ cup, about 5 minutes. Stir mushroom mixture and dill into barley-lentil mixture and season with salt and pepper to taste. Serve, drizzling individual portions with Tahini-Yogurt Sauce.

PER SERVING Cal 440; **Total Fat** 15g, **Sat Fat** 2.5g; **Chol** 0mg; **Sodium** 670mg; **Total Carb** 63g, **Dietary Fiber** 15g, **Total Sugars** 3g; **Protein** 16g

---

Inspired by Middle Eastern ingredients, this light and refreshing sauce adds life to rice, grain, and lentil dishes.

Tahini-Yogurt Sauce
MAKES ABOUT 1 CUP

⅓ cup tahini
⅓ cup plain Greek yogurt
¼ cup water
3 tablespoons lemon juice
1 garlic clove, minced
¾ teaspoon table salt

Whisk all ingredients in bowl until combined. Season with salt and pepper to taste. Let sit until flavors meld, about 30 minutes. (Sauce can be refrigerated for up to 4 days.)

Oven-Baked Barley
SERVES 4 TO 6 VEGAN

WHY THIS RECIPE WORKS Simple cooked barley offers a great alternative to rice, and it can be similarly flavored, with herbs, toasted nuts, or vegetables. For a hands-off approach, we followed our method for baked rice, pouring boiling water over the barley to shorten the cooking time and baking the barley in the oven. Settling on the right ratio of water to barley required some testing. Barley can absorb two to three times its volume in cooking liquid, and when we tried our standard ratio the water disappeared before the barley was fully cooked. We increased the water, finally landing on 3½ cups to 1½ cups of barley. After covering the dish with a double layer of foil and giving it 70 minutes in the oven followed by a 10-minute rest, we peeled back the foil to reveal perfectly cooked barley, with grains that were separate and done without being soggy. Do not substitute hulled, hull-less, quick-cooking, or presteamed barley for the pearl barley. Be sure to cover the pot when bringing the water to a boil in step 1; any water loss due to evaporation will affect how the barley cooks.

1½ cups pearl barley, rinsed
3½ cups water
1 tablespoon unsalted butter or extra-virgin olive oil
½ teaspoon table salt

1. Adjust oven rack to middle position and heat oven to 375 degrees. Spread barley in 8-inch square baking dish. Bring water, butter, and salt to boil in covered medium saucepan over high heat.

2. Pour hot water mixture immediately over barley. Cover baking dish tightly with double layer of aluminum foil. Bake barley until tender and no liquid remains, 1 hour 10 minutes to 1 hour 20 minutes.

3. Remove baking dish from oven, uncover, and fluff barley with fork. Re-cover dish with foil and let barley sit for 10 minutes. Season with salt and pepper to taste, and serve.

PER SERVING Cal 200; **Total Fat** 3g, **Sat Fat** 1g; **Chol** 5mg; **Sodium** 200mg; **Total Carb** 39g, **Dietary Fiber** 8g, **Total Sugars** 0g; **Protein** 5g

VARIATION
Oven-Baked Barley with Porcini Mushrooms

Before adding water and salt to pot, melt 2 tablespoons unsalted butter in saucepan over medium heat. Add 1 finely chopped onion and cook until softened, 5 to 7 minutes. Stir in 1 teaspoon minced fresh thyme and ¼ ounce dried porcini mushrooms, rinsed and minced; cook until fragrant, about 30 seconds. Add water and salt to pan and bring to boil; pour hot water mixture over barley and bake as directed.

Barley Risotto with Roasted Butternut Squash

Barley Risotto
SERVES 4 TO 6 `MAKE-AHEAD`

WHY THIS RECIPE WORKS Pearl barley takes well to being cooked risotto-style; its starchy interior creates a velvety sauce when simmered—much the same as Arborio rice does—while maintaining a pleasant chewiness. We used the classic risotto cooking method, with one change: We added more broth-water because barley takes longer to cook and absorbs more liquid. To complement the hearty grain, we sautéed onion and carrot before adding the barley and liquid to the pot. We finished the dish with fresh thyme, Parmesan, and a little butter for richness. You may not need all of the broth when cooking the risotto. Do not substitute hulled, hull-less, quick-cooking, or presteamed barley (read the ingredient list on the package to determine this) in this recipe. Serve with lemon wedges and extra grated Parmesan cheese.

- 4 **cups vegetable broth**
- 4 **cups water**
- 1 **tablespoon vegetable oil**
- 1 **onion, chopped fine**
- 1 **carrot, peeled and chopped fine**
- 1½ **cups pearl barley**
- 1 **cup dry white wine**
- 1 **teaspoon minced fresh thyme**
- 2 **ounces Parmesan cheese, grated (1 cup)**
- 1 **tablespoon unsalted butter**

1. Bring broth and water to simmer in medium saucepan. Reduce heat to lowest setting and cover to keep warm.

2. Heat oil in large saucepan over medium heat until shimmering. Add onion and carrot and cook until vegetables are softened, 5 to 7 minutes. Stir in barley and cook, stirring often, until lightly toasted and aromatic, about 4 minutes. Stir in wine and cook until fully absorbed, about 2 minutes.

3. Stir in thyme and 3 cups warm broth. Simmer, stirring occasionally, until liquid is absorbed and bottom of pan is dry, 22 to 25 minutes. Stir in 2 cups warm broth and simmer, stirring occasionally, until liquid is absorbed and bottom of pan is dry, 15 to 18 minutes.

4. Continue to cook risotto, stirring often and adding remaining broth as needed to prevent pan bottom from becoming dry, until barley is cooked through but still somewhat firm in center, 15 to 20 minutes. (Barley risotto can be refrigerated for up to 3 days.) Off heat, stir in Parmesan and butter. Season with salt and pepper to taste, and serve.

PER SERVING Cal 310; **Total Fat** 8g, **Sat Fat** 2.5g; **Chol** 10mg; **Sodium** 680mg; **Total Carb** 45g, **Dietary Fiber** 9g, **Total Sugars** 2g; **Protein** 9g

Barley Risotto with Mushrooms and Red Wine

A medium-bodied dry red wine blend such as a Côtes du Rhône works nicely here.

Omit carrot. Substitute red wine for white wine and fresh rosemary for thyme. Before adding barley to pan, add 8 ounces cremini mushrooms, trimmed and cut into ½-inch pieces, and ½ ounce dried porcini mushrooms, rinsed and minced, and cook until just beginning to brown, about 4 minutes.

Barley Risotto with Roasted Butternut Squash

Omit carrot and thyme. Before adding barley to pan, add 2 cloves minced garlic and cook until fragrant, about 30 seconds. While barley cooks, toss 6 cups butternut squash, cut into ½-inch pieces, with 1 tablespoon vegetable oil and season with salt and pepper; spread onto parchment paper–lined rimmed baking sheet and roast in 450-degree oven until tender and golden brown, about 30 minutes. Stir roasted squash, 1 teaspoon minced fresh sage, and ⅛ teaspoon ground nutmeg into barley before serving.

Barley and Beet Risotto
SERVES 6

WHY THIS RECIPE WORKS Barley holds its own against the sweet earthiness of beets, which give this risotto a vibrant hue. We stirred grated raw beets into the barley—half at the start for a base of flavor, and half at the end for freshness and color. We added the beet greens for an even more vegetable-packed risotto. Use the large holes of a box grater or a food processor fitted with a shredding disk to shred the beets. Do not substitute hulled, hull-less, quick-cooking, or presteamed barley (read the ingredient list on the package to determine this). If you can't find beets with greens attached, use 10 ounces of beets and 2 cups stemmed and chopped Swiss chard.

    3 cups vegetable broth
    3 cups water
    2 tablespoons extra-virgin olive oil
    1 pound beets with greens attached, beets trimmed,
      peeled, and shredded, greens stemmed and cut into
      1-inch pieces (2 cups), divided
    1 onion, chopped
    ¾ teaspoon table salt
 1½ cups pearl barley, rinsed
    4 garlic cloves, minced
    1 teaspoon minced fresh thyme or ¼ teaspoon dried
    1 cup dry white wine
    1 ounce Parmesan cheese, grated (½ cup)
    2 tablespoons chopped fresh parsley

1. Bring broth and water to simmer in medium saucepan. Reduce heat to lowest setting and cover to keep warm.

2. Heat oil in large saucepan over medium heat until shimmering. Add half of grated beets, onion, and salt and cook until vegetables are softened, 5 to 7 minutes. Stir in barley and cook, stirring often, until fragrant, about 4 minutes. Stir in garlic and thyme and cook until fragrant, about 30 seconds. Stir in wine and cook until fully absorbed, about 2 minutes.

3. Stir in 3 cups warm broth mixture. Simmer, stirring occasionally, until liquid is absorbed and bottom of pan is dry, 22 to 25 minutes. Stir in 2 cups warm broth and simmer, stirring occasionally, until liquid is absorbed and bottom of pan is dry, 15 to 18 minutes.

4. Add beet greens and continue to cook, stirring often and adding remaining broth as needed to prevent pan bottom from becoming dry, until greens are softened and barley is cooked through but still somewhat firm in center, 5 to 10 minutes. Off heat, stir in remaining grated beets and Parmesan. Season with salt and pepper to taste and sprinkle with parsley. Serve.

PER SERVING Cal 320; **Total Fat** 7g, **Sat Fat** 1.5g; **Chol** 5mg; **Sodium** 800mg; **Total Carb** 49g, **Dietary Fiber** 10g, **Total Sugars** 5g; **Protein** 8g

Bulgur Pilaf with Cremini Mushrooms
SERVES 4 　VEGAN

WHY THIS RECIPE WORKS Some pilafs are light and fluffy; this whole-grain version is robust and hearty. Earthy mushrooms pair well with chewy, nutty-tasting bulgur. For big mushroom flavor, we chose widely available cremini mushrooms plus ¼ ounce of dried porcini, which added nice depth. Just a dash of soy sauce boosted the mushroom's umami flavor even further and gave the dish a rich mahogany color. We sautéed the mushrooms with an onion, then we added the bulgur and the cooking liquid and simmered it until tender. After removing the pot from the heat, we placed a dish towel underneath the lid (which helped absorb moisture) and let the bulgur steam gently for 10 minutes, which resulted in perfectly tender, chewy grains. When shopping, don't confuse bulgur with cracked wheat, which has a much longer cooking time and will not work in this recipe.

    2 tablespoons extra-virgin olive oil
    1 onion, chopped fine
    ¼ ounce dried porcini mushrooms, rinsed and minced
    ¼ teaspoon table salt
    8 ounces cremini mushrooms, stemmed and quartered
      if small or cut into 6 pieces if large
    2 garlic cloves, minced

Bulgur Pilaf with Cremini Mushrooms

1 cup medium-grind bulgur, rinsed
¾ cup chicken or vegetable broth
¾ cup water
1 teaspoon soy sauce
¼ cup minced fresh parsley

1. Heat oil in large saucepan over medium heat until shimmering. Add onion, porcini mushrooms, and salt and cook until onion is softened, about 5 minutes. Stir in cremini mushrooms, increase heat to medium-high, cover, and cook until cremini mushrooms have released their liquid and begin to brown, about 4 minutes.

2. Stir in garlic and cook until fragrant, about 30 seconds. Stir in bulgur, broth, water, and soy sauce and bring to simmer. Cover, reduce heat to low, and simmer until bulgur is tender, 16 to 18 minutes.

3. Off heat, lay clean dish towel underneath lid, and let bulgur sit for 10 minutes. Fluff bulgur with fork, stir in parsley, and season with salt and pepper to taste. Serve.

PER SERVING Cal 220; **Total Fat** 8g, **Sat Fat** 1g; **Chol** 0mg; **Sodium** 310mg; **Total Carb** 33g, **Dietary Fiber** 5g, **Total Sugars** 3g; **Protein** 7g

Bulgur with Chickpeas, Spinach, and Za'atar
SERVES 4 TO 6   VEGAN

WHY THIS RECIPE WORKS This simple but substantial side dish combines bulgur with creamy, nutty chickpeas and the vegetal punch of fresh spinach. To boost the flavor without calling for a laundry list of ingredients we added za'atar, an aromatic eastern Mediterranean blend of thyme, toasted sesame seeds, and tangy sumac. We found that incorporating za'atar at two points in the cooking process brought out its most complex flavor. First, to release its deep, earthy flavors, we bloomed half of the za'atar in a base of onion and garlic before adding the bulgur, chickpeas, and cooking liquid. We added the remainder of the za'atar along with the fresh spinach, off the heat; the residual heat in the bulgur was enough to perfectly soften the spinach and to highlight the za'atar's more delicate aromas. We prefer the flavor of our homemade Za'atar (page 59) but you can use store-bought. When shopping, don't confuse bulgur with cracked wheat, which has a much longer cooking time and will not work in this recipe.

3 tablespoons extra-virgin olive oil, divided
1 onion, chopped fine
½ teaspoon table salt
3 garlic cloves, minced
2 tablespoons za'atar, divided
1 cup medium-grind bulgur, rinsed
1 (15-ounce) can chickpeas, rinsed
¾ cup chicken or vegetable broth
¾ cup water
3 ounces (3 cups) baby spinach, chopped
1 tablespoon lemon juice

1. Heat 2 tablespoons oil in large saucepan over medium heat until shimmering. Add onion and salt and cook until softened, about 5 minutes. Stir in garlic and 1 tablespoon za'atar and cook until fragrant, about 30 seconds.

2. Stir in bulgur, chickpeas, broth, and water and bring to simmer. Reduce heat to low, cover, and simmer gently until bulgur is tender, 16 to 18 minutes.

3. Off heat, lay clean dish towel underneath lid and let bulgur sit for 10 minutes. Add spinach, lemon juice, remaining 1 tablespoon za'atar, and remaining 1 tablespoon oil and fluff gently with fork to combine. Season with salt and pepper to taste. Serve.

PER SERVING Cal 200; **Total Fat** 8g, **Sat Fat** 1g; **Chol** 0mg; **Sodium** 410mg; **Total Carb** 28g, **Dietary Fiber** 6g, **Total Sugars** 1g; **Protein** 6g

Tabbouleh

Sevres 4 to 6 · **VEGAN**

WHY THIS RECIPE WORKS Tabbouleh is a signature Levantine salad made of bulgur, parsley, tomato, and onion steeped in a penetrating mint and lemon dressing. We started by salting the tomatoes to rid them of excess moisture that otherwise made our salad soggy. Soaking the bulgur in lemon juice and some of the drained tomato liquid, rather than in water, allowed it to absorb lots of flavor as it softened. Chopped onion overwhelmed the salad; two mild scallions added just the right amount of punch. Parsley, mint, and a bit of cayenne pepper rounded out the dish. Adding the herbs and vegetables while the bulgur was still soaking gave the components time to mingle, resulting in a cohesive dish. When shopping, don't confuse bulgur with cracked wheat, which has a much longer cooking time and will not work in this recipe.

    3 tomatoes, cored and cut into ½-inch pieces
    ½ teaspoon table salt, divided
    ½ cup medium-grind bulgur, rinsed
    ¼ cup lemon juice (2 lemons)
    6 tablespoons extra-virgin olive oil
    ⅛ teaspoon cayenne pepper
 1½ cups minced fresh parsley
    ½ cup minced fresh mint
    2 scallions, sliced thin

1. Toss tomatoes with ¼ teaspoon salt in fine-mesh strainer set over bowl and let drain, tossing occasionally, for 30 minutes; reserve 2 tablespoons drained tomato juice. Toss bulgur with 2 tablespoons lemon juice and reserved tomato juice in bowl and let sit until grains begin to soften, 30 to 40 minutes.

2. Whisk remaining 2 tablespoons lemon juice, oil, cayenne, and remaining ¼ teaspoon salt together in large bowl. Add tomatoes, bulgur, parsley, mint, and scallions and gently toss to combine. Cover and let sit at room temperature until flavors meld and bulgur is tender, about 1 hour. Before serving, toss salad to recombine and season with salt and pepper to taste.

PER SERVING Cal 190; **Total Fat** 14g, **Sat Fat** 2g; **Chol** 0mg; **Sodium** 210mg; **Total Carb** 14g, **Dietary Fiber** 3g, **Total Sugars** 2g; **Protein** 3g

VARIATION
Spiced Tabbouleh
Add ¼ teaspoon ground cinnamon and ¼ teaspoon ground allspice to dressing with cayenne.

Tabbouleh

Bulgur Salad with Carrots and Almonds

SERVES 4 TO 6 · **VEGAN**

WHY THIS RECIPE WORKS This flavorful bulgur salad uses the same simple technique for making tabbouleh but incorporates some warm Middle Eastern spices, shredded carrot, and crunchy almonds, as well as lots of chopped fresh herbs. We softened the bulgur in a mixture of water, lemon juice, and salt for 1½ hours until it had the perfect chew. Fresh mint, cilantro, and scallions made our salad fresh and bright, and cumin and cayenne added depth of flavor. The sweet shredded carrots nicely accented the rich, nutty taste of the bulgur. When shopping, don't confuse bulgur with cracked wheat, which has a much longer cooking time and will not work in this recipe.

 1½ cups medium-grind bulgur, rinsed
    1 cup water
    6 tablespoons lemon juice (2 lemons), divided
    ¾ teaspoon table salt, divided
    ⅓ cup extra-virgin olive oil
    ½ teaspoon ground cumin

⅛ teaspoon cayenne pepper

4 carrots, peeled and shredded

3 scallions, sliced thin

½ cup sliced almonds, toasted

⅓ cup chopped fresh mint

⅓ cup chopped fresh cilantro

1. Combine bulgur, water, ¼ cup lemon juice, and ¼ teaspoon salt in bowl. Cover and let sit at room temperature until grains are softened, about 1½ hours.

2. Whisk oil, cumin, cayenne, remaining 2 tablespoons lemon juice, and remaining ½ teaspoon salt together in large bowl. Add soaked bulgur, carrots, scallions, almonds, mint, and cilantro and toss to combine. Season with salt and pepper to taste, and serve.

PER SERVING Cal 300; **Total Fat** 17g, **Sat Fat** 2g; **Chol** 0mg; **Sodium** 330mg; **Total Carb** 34g, **Dietary Fiber** 7g, **Total Sugars** 3g; **Protein** 7g

Bulgur Salad with Grapes and Feta

Bulgur Salad with Grapes and Feta
SERVES 4

WHY THIS RECIPE WORKS For a light and flavorful bulgur salad, we combined sweet, juicy grapes and tangy feta cheese. We softened the bulgur in a mixture of water, lemon juice, and salt for an hour and a half. Once the bulgur was tender and flavorful, we tossed it with more fresh lemon juice, cumin, and cayenne for depth of flavor, along with the grapes and feta. Quartering the grapes ensured that we got some sweetness in every bite. Scallions and mint gave the salad plenty of bright, fresh flavor. Finally, for textural contrast, we added crunchy toasted slivered almonds. When shopping, don't confuse bulgur with cracked wheat, which has a much longer cooking time and will not work in this recipe.

1½ cups medium-grind bulgur, rinsed

1 cup water

5 tablespoons lemon juice (2 lemons), divided

½ teaspoon table salt, divided

¼ cup extra-virgin olive oil

¼ teaspoon ground cumin

Pinch cayenne pepper

6 ounces seedless red grapes, quartered (1 cup)

½ cup slivered almonds, toasted, divided

2 ounces feta cheese, crumbled (½ cup), divided

2 scallions, sliced thin

¼ cup chopped fresh mint

1. Combine bulgur, water, ¼ cup lemon juice, and ¼ teaspoon salt in bowl. Cover and let sit at room temperature until grains are softened, about 1½ hours.

2. Whisk oil, cumin, cayenne, remaining 1 tablespoon lemon juice, and remaining ¼ teaspoon salt together in large bowl. Add soaked bulgur, grapes, ⅓ cup almonds, ⅓ cup feta, scallions, and mint and toss to combine. Season with salt and pepper to taste. Sprinkle with remaining almonds and feta before serving.

PER SERVING Cal 310; **Total Fat** 16g, **Sat Fat** 3g; **Chol** 10mg; **Sodium** 290mg; **Total Carb** 35g, **Dietary Fiber** 6g, **Total Sugars** 6g; **Protein** 8g

Warm Farro with Lemon and Herbs

Warm Farro with Lemon and Herbs
SERVES 4 TO 6 `MAKE-AHEAD` `VEGAN`

WHY THIS RECIPE WORKS Nutty, chewy farro is a popular grain in Italian cuisine and has become a favorite in the test kitchen, too. We typically use the pasta method to cook farro; the abundance of water cooks the grains evenly. For a simple way to dress up the farro, we sautéed onion and garlic to create a savory backbone. Bright lemon and herbs lent it freshness. We prefer the flavor and texture of whole farro; pearled farro can be used, but the texture may be softer. Do not use quick-cooking or presteamed farro (read the ingredient list on the package to determine this) in this recipe. The cooking time for farro can vary greatly among different brands, so we recommend beginning to check for doneness after 10 minutes.

1½ cups whole farro
¼ teaspoon table salt, plus salt for cooking farro
3 tablespoons extra-virgin olive oil, divided
1 onion, chopped fine
1 garlic clove, minced

¼ cup chopped fresh parsley
¼ cup chopped fresh mint
1 tablespoon lemon juice

1. Bring 4 quarts water to boil in Dutch oven. Add farro and 1 tablespoon salt, return to boil, and cook until grains are tender with slight chew, 15 to 30 minutes. Drain farro, return to now-empty pot, and cover to keep warm.

2. Heat 2 tablespoons oil in 12-inch skillet over medium heat until shimmering. Add onion and ¼ teaspoon salt and cook until softened, about 5 minutes. Stir in garlic and cook until fragrant, about 30 seconds.

3. Add remaining 1 tablespoon oil and farro and cook, stirring frequently, until heated through, about 2 minutes. (Farro can be refrigerated for up to 3 days.) Off heat, stir in parsley, mint, and lemon juice. Season with salt and pepper to taste. Serve.

PER SERVING Cal 240; **Total Fat** 9g, **Sat Fat** 1g; **Chol** 0mg; **Sodium** 200mg; **Total Carb** 39g, **Dietary Fiber** 1g, **Total Sugars** 3g; **Protein** 6ig

Farro with Mushrooms and Thyme
SERVES 4 `VEGAN`

WHY THIS RECIPE WORKS Mushrooms sautéed with shallot and thyme lend farro plenty of meatiness, and using sherry to deglaze the pan after the mushrooms browned added complexity to the dish. Finishing with sherry vinegar and a couple of tablespoons of fresh parsley gave a brightness and freshness that balanced the hearty, savory flavors. White mushrooms can be substituted for the cremini. Do not substitute pearled (perlato) farro for the whole farro in this recipe. If using quick-cooking or presteamed farro (read the ingredient list on the package to determine this), you will need to alter the farro cooking time in step 1.

1 cup whole farro
¼ teaspoon table salt, plus salt for cooking farro
2 tablespoons extra-virgin olive oil
8 ounces cremini mushrooms, trimmed and chopped
1 shallot, minced
1 teaspoon minced fresh thyme
2 tablespoons dry sherry
2 tablespoons minced fresh parsley
1 teaspoon sherry vinegar

1. Bring 4 quarts water to boil in Dutch oven. Stir in farro and 1 tablespoon salt and boil until tender, 15 to 20 minutes. Drain farro, transfer to large bowl, and cover to keep warm.

Farro with Mushrooms and Thyme

2. Meanwhile, heat oil in 12-inch skillet over medium-high heat until shimmering. Add mushrooms, shallot, thyme, and ¼ teaspoon salt and cook, stirring frequently, until moisture has evaporated and vegetables start to brown, 5 to 8 minutes. Stir in sherry and cook, scraping up any browned bits, until pan is almost dry, 1 to 2 minutes.

3. Add farro and cook, stirring constantly, until heated through, about 1 minute. Off heat, stir in parsley and vinegar. Season with salt and pepper to taste, and serve.

PER SERVING Cal 250; **Total Fat** 9g, **Sat Fat** 1g; **Chol** 0mg; **Sodium** 300mg; **Total Carb** 39g, **Dietary Fiber** 0g, **Total Sugars** 4g; **Protein** 7g

Parmesan Farrotto
SERVES 6

WHY THIS RECIPE WORKS Italian *farrotto* is essentially a risotto-style dish made with farro in place of the usual Arborio rice. Although it is prepared with a similar method, farro's more robust, nutty flavor gives the dish new dimension. Because much of farro's starch is trapped inside the outer bran, achieving a creamy, velvety consistency can be a challenge. We tested making farrotto with pearled farro, which has had the outer bran removed, but the flavor was lacking and the sauce turned out thin. Instead, we turned back to whole farro and, to make the starch more accessible without losing farro's hallmark chew, we ran the grains through a blender. After a few pulses, about half of the farro had cracked, freeing up enough starch to create a creamy, risotto-like consistency. Adding most of the liquid up front and cooking the farrotto in a lidded Dutch oven helped the grains cook evenly and meant we didn't have to stir constantly—just twice before mixing in the flavorings. We created a variation with pancetta, asparagus, and peas, which made this side dish even heartier. The consistency of farrotto is a matter of personal taste; if you prefer a looser texture, add more of the hot broth mixture in step 5.

1½ cups whole farro
3 cups chicken or vegetable broth
3 cups water
3 tablespoons extra-virgin olive oil, divided
½ onion, chopped fine
1 garlic clove, minced
2 teaspoons minced fresh thyme
1 teaspoon table salt
¾ teaspoon pepper
2 ounces Parmesan cheese, grated (1 cup)
2 tablespoons minced fresh parsley
2 teaspoons lemon juice

1. Pulse farro in blender until about half of grains are broken into smaller pieces, about 6 pulses.

2. Bring broth and water to boil in medium saucepan over high heat. Reduce heat to low, cover, and keep warm.

3. Heat 2 tablespoons oil in Dutch oven over medium-low heat. Add onion and cook until softened, about 5 minutes. Stir in garlic and cook until fragrant, about 30 seconds. Add farro and cook, stirring frequently, until grains are lightly toasted, about 3 minutes.

4. Stir 5 cups warm broth mixture into farro mixture, reduce heat to low, cover, and cook until almost all liquid has been absorbed and farro is just al dente, about 25 minutes, stirring twice during cooking.

5. Add thyme, salt, and pepper and cook, stirring constantly, until farro becomes creamy, about 5 minutes. Off heat, stir in Parmesan, parsley, lemon juice, and remaining 1 tablespoon oil. Adjust consistency with remaining warm broth mixture as needed (you may have broth left over). Season with salt and pepper to taste. Serve.

PER SERVING Cal 260; **Total Fat** 10g, **Sat Fat** 2.5g; **Chol** 5mg; **Sodium** 870mg; **Total Carb** 32g, **Dietary Fiber** 3g, **Total Sugars** 1g; **Protein** 11g

Farrotto with Pancetta, Asparagus, and Peas

SERVES 6

Do not use quick-cooking, presteamed, or pearled farro (read the ingredient list on the package to determine this) in this recipe. The consistency of farrotto is a matter of personal taste; if you prefer a looser texture, add more of the hot broth mixture in step 5.

1½ cups whole farro
 3 cups chicken broth
 3 cups water
 4 ounces asparagus, trimmed and cut on bias into 1-inch lengths
 4 ounces pancetta, cut into ¼-inch pieces
 2 tablespoons extra-virgin olive oil, divided
 ½ onion, chopped fine
 1 garlic clove, minced
 1 cup frozen peas, thawed
 2 teaspoons minced fresh tarragon
 ¾ teaspoon table salt
 ½ teaspoon pepper
1½ ounces Parmesan cheese, grated (¾ cup)
 1 tablespoon minced fresh chives
 1 teaspoon grated lemon zest plus 1 teaspoon juice

1. Pulse farro in blender until about half of grains are broken into smaller pieces, about 6 pulses.

2. Bring broth and water to boil in medium saucepan over high heat. Add asparagus and cook until crisp-tender, 2 to 3 minutes. Using slotted spoon, transfer asparagus to bowl and set aside. Reduce heat to low, cover broth mixture, and keep warm.

3. Cook pancetta in Dutch oven over medium heat until lightly browned and fat has rendered, about 5 minutes. Add 1 tablespoon oil and onion and cook until softened, about 5 minutes. Stir in garlic and cook until fragrant, about 30 seconds. Add farro and cook, stirring frequently, until grains are lightly toasted, about 3 minutes.

4. Stir 5 cups warm broth mixture into farro mixture, reduce heat to low, cover, and cook until almost all liquid is absorbed and farro is just al dente, about 25 minutes, stirring twice during cooking.

5. Add peas, tarragon, salt, and pepper and cook, stirring constantly, until farro becomes creamy, about 5 minutes. Off heat, stir in Parmesan, chives, lemon zest and juice, remaining 1 tablespoon oil, and reserved asparagus. Adjust consistency with remaining warm broth mixture as needed (you may have broth left over). Season with salt and pepper to taste. Serve.

PER SERVING Cal 310; **Total Fat** 12g, **Sat Fat** 3.5g; **Chol** 20mg; **Sodium** 1100mg; **Total Carb** 36g, **Dietary Fiber** 5g, **Total Sugars** 2g; **Protein** 15g

Freekeh Pilaf with Dates and Cauliflower

Freekeh Pilaf with Dates and Cauliflower

SERVES 4 TO 6   VEGAN

WHY THIS RECIPE WORKS Freekeh is a grain common across the Eastern Mediterranean and North Africa. It has a grassy, slightly smoky flavor. For a pilaf that accentuated freekeh's flavor and chew, we paired it with pan-roasted cauliflower, warm spices and aromatics, and refreshing mint. We found that simply boiling the grain like pasta was the most foolproof cooking method to achieve a chewy, firm texture. Allowing the cauliflower to soften and brown slightly before adding the remaining ingredients to the pan was essential to creating the best flavor and texture. Studded with sweet dates and toasted pistachios, our pilaf was a hearty, healthful option for a satisfying side dish. We prefer the texture of whole, uncracked freekeh; cracked freekeh can be substituted, but you will need to decrease the freekeh cooking time in step 1.

1½ cups whole freekeh
 ½ teaspoon table salt, plus salt for cooking freekeh
 ¼ cup extra-virgin olive oil, divided, plus extra for serving
 1 head cauliflower (2 pounds), cored and cut into ½-inch florets

¼ teaspoon pepper

3 ounces pitted dates, chopped (½ cup)

1 shallot, minced

1½ teaspoons grated fresh ginger

¼ teaspoon ground coriander

¼ teaspoon ground cumin

¼ cup shelled pistachios, toasted and chopped coarse

¼ cup chopped fresh mint

1½ tablespoons lemon juice

1. Bring 4 quarts water to boil in Dutch oven. Add freekeh and 1 tablespoon salt, return to boil, and cook until grains are tender, 30 to 45 minutes. Drain freekeh, return to now-empty pot, and cover to keep warm.

2. Heat 2 tablespoons oil in 12-inch nonstick skillet over medium-high heat until shimmering. Add cauliflower, ½ teaspoon salt, and pepper, cover, and cook until florets are softened and start to brown, about 5 minutes.

3. Remove lid and continue to cook, stirring occasionally, until florets turn spotty brown, about 10 minutes. Add remaining 2 tablespoons oil, dates, shallot, ginger, coriander, and cumin and cook, stirring frequently, until dates and shallot are softened and fragrant, about 3 minutes.

4. Reduce heat to low, add freekeh, and cook, stirring frequently, until heated through, about 1 minute. Off heat, stir in pistachios, mint, and lemon juice. Season with salt and pepper to taste and drizzle with extra oil. Serve.

PER SERVING Cal 360; **Total Fat** 13g, **Sat Fat** 2g; **Chol** 0mg; **Sodium** 240mg; **Total Carb** 53g, **Dietary Fiber** 12g, **Total Sugars** 13g; **Protein** 10g

Freekeh Salad with Butternut Squash, Walnuts, and Raisins

SERVES 4 TO 6 `VEGAN`

WHY THIS RECIPE WORKS We thought the unique flavor of freekeh would work perfectly with sweet roasted winter squash as a hearty side dish (or light meal). We chose widely available butternut squash. Roasting the squash resulted in lightly charred, beautifully caramelized edges; to give the squash more dimension, we paired it with fenugreek, a slightly sweet and nutty seed with a unique maple-like flavor. To bring all the elements together, we stirred in a rich yet bright tahini-lemon dressing. Chopped walnuts offered complementary crunch. We prefer the texture of whole, uncracked freekeh; cracked freekeh can be substituted, but you will need to decrease the freekeh cooking time in step 2.

Freekeh Salad with Butternut Squash, Walnuts, and Raisins

1½ pounds butternut squash, peeled, seeded, and cut into ½-inch pieces (4 cups)

1 tablespoon extra-virgin olive oil

½ teaspoon ground fenugreek

Table salt for cooking freekeh

1½ cups whole freekeh

⅓ cup golden raisins

½ cup Tahini-Lemon Dressing (page 188)

1 cup coarsely chopped cilantro

⅓ cup walnuts, toasted and chopped

1. Adjust oven rack to lowest position and heat oven to 450 degrees. Toss squash with oil and fenugreek and season with salt and pepper. Arrange squash in single layer in rimmed baking sheet and roast until well browned and tender, 30 to 35 minutes, stirring halfway through roasting; let cool to room temperature.

2. Meanwhile, bring 4 quarts water to boil in Dutch oven. Add freekeh and 1 tablespoon salt, return to boil, and cook until grains are tender, 30 to 45 minutes. Drain freekeh, transfer to large bowl, and let cool completely, about 15 minutes.

3. Combine raisins and ¼ cup hot tap water in small bowl and let sit until softened, about 5 minutes; drain raisins. Add squash, raisins, dressing, cilantro, and walnuts to bowl with freekeh and gently toss to combine. Season with salt and pepper to taste. Serve.

PER SERVING Cal 410; **Total Fat** 19g, **Sat Fat** 2.5g; **Chol** 0mg; **Sodium** 300mg; **Total Carb** 55g, **Dietary Fiber** 10g, **Total Sugars** 9g; **Protein** 9g

---

TAKE IT UP A NOTCH

This bright dressing balances the richness of sesame tahini and olive oil with the tartness of lemon juice. You can drizzle it on grain dishes as well as use it to dress salads.

Tahini-Lemon Dressing
MAKES ABOUT ½ CUP

2½ tablespoons lemon juice
2 tablespoons tahini
1 tablespoon water
1 garlic clove, minced
½ teaspoon table salt
⅛ teaspoon pepper
¼ cup extra-virgin olive oil

Whisk lemon juice, tahini, water, garlic, salt, and pepper in bowl until smooth. Whisking constantly, slowly drizzle in oil until emulsified. (Dressing can be refrigerated for up to 1 week.)

Curried Millet Pilaf
SERVES 4 TO 6

WHY THIS RECIPE WORKS Millet is a tiny cereal grass seed that has a mellow corn flavor. It's a staple in Middle Eastern and Indian cuisines, so we looked there for the flavor inspiration for this easy pilaf. Toasting the millet before simmering gave the seeds nutty depth; we first rinsed and dried the soggy seeds so they would toast properly. After some testing, we landed on a 2:1 ratio of liquid to millet, which ensured evenly cooked, fluffy seeds. We served the pilaf with a dollop of yogurt for richness and an appealing cooling counterpoint to the heat of the curry. We prefer whole-milk yogurt in this recipe, but low-fat yogurt can be substituted if desired. We have found that, unlike other grains, millet can become gluey if allowed to steam off the heat. Once all the liquid has been absorbed, use a gentle hand to stir in the basil, raisins, almonds, and scallion greens, and serve immediately.

1 tablespoon extra-virgin olive oil
3 scallions, white and green parts separated and sliced thin
1 teaspoon curry powder
1½ cups millet, rinsed and dried on dish towel
3 cups water
¾ teaspoon table salt
½ cup chopped fresh basil and/or mint
¼ cup raisins
¼ cup sliced almonds, toasted
½ cup plain yogurt

1. Heat oil in large saucepan over medium heat until shimmering. Add scallion whites and curry powder and cook until fragrant, about 1 minute. Stir in millet and cook, stirring often, until lightly browned, about 2 minutes.

2. Stir in water and salt and bring to boil. Reduce heat to low, cover, and simmer until liquid is absorbed, 15 to 20 minutes.

3. Off heat, fluff millet with fork and gently stir in basil, raisins, almonds, and scallion greens. Season with salt and pepper to taste. Serve, dolloping individual portions with yogurt.

PER SERVING Cal 280; **Total Fat** 7g, **Sat Fat** 1g; **Chol** 5mg; **Sodium** 310mg; **Total Carb** 48g, **Dietary Fiber** 10g, **Total Sugars** 6g; **Protein** 9g

---

Creamy, Cheesy Millet
SERVES 4 TO 6

WHY THIS RECIPE WORKS We wanted to take advantage of millet's starchiness to turn it into a creamy, savory side dish similar to polenta. However, it took some testing to find a method that gave us the silky consistency we were after. When we cooked the millet in the amount of liquid we'd normally use for polenta, it didn't break down enough, giving us a texture that was slightly set up, like oatmeal, not the loose consistency we wanted. Instead, we started the millet in 5 cups of liquid (4 cups of water plus 1 cup of milk to lend some richness). This made all the difference. We also slightly overcooked the millet so that the seeds burst and released their starch, creating the right creamy consistency. Since millet is very mild, we toasted it briefly before cooking to bring out its taste. We also stirred in a good amount of Parmesan and basil before serving to ensure that this dish had plenty of flavor.

1 tablespoon extra-virgin olive oil
1 shallot, minced
2 garlic cloves, minced
1 cup millet, rinsed and dried on dish towel
4 cups water

1 cup whole milk

1 teaspoon table salt

2 ounces Parmesan cheese, grated (1 cup)

2 tablespoons shredded fresh basil

1. Heat oil in large saucepan over medium heat until shimmering. Stir in shallot and cook until softened, about 2 minutes. Add garlic and cook until fragrant, about 30 seconds. Stir in millet and cook, stirring often, until fragrant and lightly browned, about 2 minutes.

2. Stir in water, milk, and salt and bring to boil. Reduce heat to low, cover, and simmer, stirring occasionally, until thick and porridgy, about 20 minutes. Uncover and continue to cook, stirring frequently, until millet is mostly broken down, 8 to 10 minutes.

3. Off heat, stir in Parmesan until melted. Sprinkle with basil and season with salt and pepper to taste. Serve.

PER SERVING Cal 220; **Total Fat** 8g, **Sat Fat** 2.5g; **Chol** 10mg; **Sodium** 580mg; **Total Carb** 30g, **Dietary Fiber** 6g, **Total Sugars** 2g; **Protein** 10g

Millet Salad with Corn and Queso Fresco

DRYING GRAINS

1. After rinsing grains, spread over rimmed baking sheet lined with clean dish towel and let dry for 15 minutes.

2. When grains are dry, pick up towel by corners and gently shake grains into bowl.

Millet Salad with Corn and Queso Fresco

SERVES 4 TO 6

WHY THIS RECIPE WORKS The mellow corn flavor and fine texture of tiny millet seeds make them versatile in savory applications. We set out to feature the small seeds in a grain-style salad that would enhance the sweet flavor of the millet. The seeds release starch as they cook, which can create large clumps. We found that boiling the millet like pasta resulted in distinct, individual cooked seeds perfect for tossing with dressing. Spreading out the millet on a baking sheet allowed it to cool and prevented clumping. With

our cooking method nailed down, we proceeded to build the flavors of our salad. We stirred in corn to complement the millet's natural flavor and to add texture, while cherry tomatoes, queso fresco, and a minced jalapeño gave the salad a Southwestern flavor profile. We whipped up a quick vinaigrette using lime zest and juice to dress our salad and add brightness. A small amount of mayonnaise helped to emulsify the dressing and more evenly coat the millet. Chopped cilantro added freshness and color to the salad. For more spice, reserve, mince, and add the ribs and seeds from the jalapeño.

1 cup millet

¼ teaspoon table salt, plus salt for cooking millet

1 teaspoon grated lime zest plus 2½ tablespoons juice (2 limes), divided

2 teaspoons honey

½ teaspoon mayonnaise

3 tablespoons extra-virgin olive oil

8 ounces cherry tomatoes, quartered

½ cup frozen corn, thawed

1½ ounces queso fresco, crumbled (⅓ cup)

¼ cup chopped fresh cilantro

1 jalapeño chile, stemmed, seeded, and minced

1. Bring 3 quarts water to boil in large pot. Add millet and 1 teaspoon salt and cook until grains are tender, about 20 minutes. Drain millet, spread onto rimmed baking sheet, drizzle with ½ tablespoon lime juice, and let cool for 15 minutes.

2. Whisk lime zest and remaining 2 tablespoons juice, honey, mayonnaise, and ¼ teaspoon salt together in large bowl. Whisking constantly, drizzle in oil. Add cooled millet and toss to combine. Fold in cherry tomatoes, corn, queso fresco, cilantro, and jalapeño. Season with salt and pepper to taste, and serve.

PER SERVING Cal 230; **Total Fat** 9g, **Sat Fat** 1.5g; Chol 0mg; **Sodium** 230mg; **Total Carb** 31g, **Dietary Fiber** 3g, **Total Sugars** 4g; **Protein** 5g

VARIATIONS
Millet Salad with Oranges, Olives, and Almonds
For this vegan option, omit tomatoes, corn, queso fresco, cilantro, and jalapeño. Substitute orange zest for lime zest, and sherry vinegar for lime juice. Fold in 2 oranges, peeled and cut into ½-inch pieces; ⅓ cup chopped pitted green olives; ⅓ cup toasted sliced almonds; and 2 tablespoons chopped fresh oregano before serving.

Millet Salad with Endive, Blueberries, and Goat Cheese
Omit tomatoes, corn, queso fresco, cilantro, and jalapeño. Omit lime zest and substitute champagne vinegar for lime juice. Fold in 2 heads thinly sliced Belgian endive, 1½ cups blueberries, ¾ cup chopped toasted pecans, and 1 cup crumbled goat cheese before serving.

Oat Berry Pilaf with Walnuts and Gorgonzola
SERVES 4 TO 6

WHY THIS RECIPE WORKS Oat berries, or oat groats, are whole oats that have been hulled and cleaned; they have great flavor and a satisfying chew. We wanted to make a flavorful oat berry pilaf with tasty add-ins. To start, we sautéed some shallot for aromatic backbone, then added the water and oat berries to the pan. Because oat berries naturally have a nutty flavor, we skipped the step of toasting them. After testing various ratios of water to oat berries, we settled on 2 cups water to 1½ cups oat berries. Creamy, pungent Gorgonzola cheese provided a nice balance to their earthy flavor. We tried stirring the cheese into the pilaf once the berries were cooked, but the result was a thick, gluey mixture. It was better to wait and simply sprinkle the cheese over the oat berries just before serving. Toasted, chopped walnuts added more

Oat Berry Pilaf with Walnuts and Gorgonzola

richness and a nice crunch. Tart cherries and a drizzle of tangy balsamic vinegar cut through the richness, while parsley gave our pilaf the freshness it needed.

  1 tablespoon extra-virgin olive oil
  1 shallot, minced
  2 cups water
1½ cups oat berries (groats), rinsed
  ¼ teaspoon table salt
  ¾ cup walnuts, toasted and chopped
  ½ cup dried cherries
  2 tablespoons minced fresh parsley
  1 tablespoon balsamic vinegar
  2 ounces Gorgonzola cheese, crumbled (½ cup)

1. Heat oil in large saucepan over medium heat until shimmering. Add shallot and cook until softened, about 2 minutes. Stir in water, oat berries, and salt and bring to simmer. Reduce heat to low, cover, and continue to simmer until oat berries are tender but still slightly chewy, 30 to 40 minutes.

2. Remove pot from heat and lay clean folded dish towel underneath lid. Let sit for 10 minutes. Fluff oat berries with fork and fold in walnuts, cherries, and parsley. Season with salt and pepper to taste and drizzle with vinegar. Serve, sprinkling individual portions with Gorgonzola.

PER SERVING Cal 380; **Total Fat** 18g, **Sat Fat** 3.5g; **Chol** 10mg; **Sodium** 230mg; **Total Carb** 42g, **Dietary Fiber** 6g, **Total Sugars** 8g; **Protein** 12g

Oat Berry, Chickpea, and Arugula Salad

Oat Berry, Chickpea, and Arugula Salad
SERVES 4 TO 6

WHY THIS RECIPE WORKS Chewy, nutty oat berries make a wonderful base for a substantial grain salad. To ensure that the oat berries retained the perfect chewy, tender texture when served cold, we cooked them in a large amount of water, pasta style, and then drained and rinsed them under cold water to stop the cooking so the grains wouldn't end up mushy. For the leafy component of our salad, assertive, peppery arugula paired well with the oat berries, and we added chickpeas for a little more heft and complementary buttery flavor and creamy texture. Roasted red peppers added sweetness and creamy feta lent the right creaminess and salty bite. A simple lemon and cilantro dressing spiked with cumin, paprika, and cayenne provided the perfect amount of spice and brightness.

1 cup oat berries (groats), rinsed
¾ teaspoon table salt, divided
3 tablespoons extra-virgin olive oil
2 tablespoons lemon juice
2 tablespoons minced fresh cilantro
1 teaspoon honey
1 garlic clove, minced
¼ teaspoon ground cumin
⅛ teaspoon paprika
   Pinch cayenne pepper
1 (15-ounce) can chickpeas, rinsed
6 ounces (6 cups) baby arugula
½ cup jarred roasted red peppers, drained, patted dry, and chopped
2 ounces feta cheese, crumbled (½ cup)

1. Bring 2 quarts water to boil in large saucepan. Add oat berries and ½ teaspoon salt, partially cover, and cook, stirring often, until tender but still chewy, 45 to 50 minutes. Drain oat berries, rinse under cold running water until cool, then transfer to large bowl.

2. Whisk oil, lemon juice, cilantro, honey, garlic, cumin, paprika, cayenne, and remaining ¼ teaspoon salt together in small bowl, then drizzle over oat berries. Stir in chickpeas, arugula, roasted red peppers, and feta. Season with salt and pepper to taste, and serve.

PER SERVING Cal 260; **Total Fat** 12g, **Sat Fat** 3g; **Chol** 10mg; **Sodium** 550mg; **Total Carb** 30g, **Dietary Fiber** 5g, **Total Sugars** 4g; **Protein** 9g

CRUMBLING FETA

To crumble feta cheese neatly, place in bowl and use fork to break off small pieces from block. Continue to break up pieces with fork until crumbles are desired size.

Creamy Parmesan Polenta with Sautéed Cherry Tomato and Fresh Mozzarella Topping

Creamy Parmesan Polenta
SERVES 4

WHY THIS RECIPE WORKS With deep corn flavor and a porridge-like texture, polenta is a classic pairing for stews and ragus but also tastes great with a variety of vegetable toppings. Why don't people cook it more often? It could be polenta's reputation for requiring almost constant stirring to avoid forming intractable lumps. We wanted smooth polenta without the fussy process. Coarse-ground degerminated cornmeal gave us a soft but hearty texture and nutty flavor. Adding a pinch of baking soda to the pot helped soften the cornmeal's endosperm, which cut down on the cooking time. The baking soda also encouraged the granules to break down and release their starch, creating a silky consistency with minimal stirring. Parmesan cheese and butter, stirred in at the last minute, ensured a satisfying, rich flavor. If the polenta bubbles or sputters even slightly after the first 10 minutes, the heat is too high and you may need a flame tamer. Serve with any of our toppings (recipes follow).

7½ cups water
1½ teaspoons table salt
    Pinch baking soda

1½ cups coarse-ground cornmeal
 4 ounces Parmesan cheese, grated (2 cups), plus extra for serving
 2 tablespoons unsalted butter

1. Bring water to boil in large saucepan over medium-high heat. Stir in salt and baking soda. Slowly pour cornmeal into water in steady stream while stirring back and forth with wooden spoon or silicone spatula. Bring mixture to boil, stirring constantly, about 1 minute. Reduce heat to lowest setting and cover.

2. After 5 minutes, whisk polenta to smooth out any lumps that may have formed, about 15 seconds. (Make sure to scrape down sides and bottom of pan.) Cover and continue to cook, without stirring, until polenta grains are tender but slightly al dente, about 25 minutes. (Polenta should be loose and barely hold its shape; it will continue to thicken as it cools.)

3. Remove from heat, stir in Parmesan and butter, and season with pepper to taste. Let sit, covered, for 5 minutes. Serve, passing extra Parmesan separately.

PER SERVING Cal 310; **Total Fat** 15g; **Sat Fat** 8g; **Chol** 35mg; **Sodium** 1410mg; **Total Carb** 31g, **Dietary Fiber** 3g, **Total Sugars** 0g; **Protein** 16g

MAKING CREAMY PARMESAN POLENTA

1. Bring water to boil over medium-high heat. Stir in salt and pinch baking soda. Slowly pour in cornmeal, stirring constantly.

2. Bring to boil, continuing to stir. Reduce heat to lowest setting and cover. After 5 minutes, whisk until smooth. Cover and continue to cook until grains are tender.

3. Remove pot from heat. Stir in cheese, olive oil, and pepper to taste. Cover and let sit for 5 minutes.

Polenta makes a great side dish on its own but is especially hearty with one of these easy vegetable toppings.

Sautéed Cherry Tomato and Fresh Mozzarella Topping
MAKES ENOUGH FOR 4 SERVINGS

- 3 tablespoons extra-virgin olive oil
- 2 garlic cloves, sliced thin
  Pinch red pepper flakes
  Pinch sugar
- 1½ pounds cherry tomatoes, halved
- 6 ounces fresh mozzarella cheese, cut into ½-inch cubes
- 2 tablespoons shredded fresh basil

Cook oil, garlic, pepper flakes, and sugar in 12-inch non-stick skillet over medium-high heat until fragrant and sizzling, about 1 minute. Stir in tomatoes and cook until just beginning to soften, about 1 minute. Off heat, season with salt and pepper to taste. Spoon mixture over individual portions of polenta, top with mozzarella and basil, and serve.

Mushroom and Rosemary Topping
MAKES ENOUGH FOR 4 SERVINGS

- 2 tablespoons unsalted butter
- 2 tablespoons extra-virgin olive oil
- 1 small onion, chopped fine
- 2 garlic cloves, minced
- 2 teaspoons minced fresh rosemary
- 1 pound mushrooms (such as white, cremini, shiitake, or oyster), stemmed and sliced thin
- ⅓ cup vegetable broth
- ¼ cup grated Parmesan cheese

Heat butter and oil in 12-inch nonstick skillet over medium-high heat until butter is melted and hot. Add onion and cook until softened and beginning to brown, 5 to 7 minutes. Stir in garlic and rosemary and cook until fragrant, about 30 seconds. Stir in mushrooms and cook, stirring occasionally, until they release their moisture, about 6 minutes. Add broth and simmer briskly until sauce thickens, about 8 minutes. Season with salt and pepper to taste. Spoon mushroom mixture over individual portions of polenta, sprinkle with Parmesan, and serve.

Quinoa Pilaf with Herbs and Lemon
SERVES 4 TO 6 `MAKE-AHEAD` `VEGAN`

WHY THIS RECIPE WORKS In theory quinoa has an appealingly nutty flavor and a crunchy texture; in practice it often turns into a mushy mess with washed-out flavor and an underlying bitterness. We wanted a simple quinoa pilaf with light, distinct grains and great flavor. We found that most recipes for quinoa pilaf turned out woefully overcooked because they call for far too much liquid. We cut the water back to ensure tender grains with a satisfying bite. We also toasted the quinoa in a dry skillet to develop its natural nutty flavor before simmering. We flavored our pilaf with some onion sautéed in butter and finished it with herbs and a squeeze of lemon juice. We like the convenience of prewashed quinoa; rinsing removes the quinoa's bitter protective coating (called saponin). If you buy unwashed quinoa (or if you are unsure whether it's washed), rinse it and then spread it out over a clean dish towel to dry for 15 minutes before cooking.

- 1½ cups prewashed white quinoa
- 2 tablespoons unsalted butter or extra-virgin olive oil
- 1 small onion, chopped fine
- ¾ teaspoon table salt
- 1¾ cups water
- 3 tablespoons chopped fresh cilantro, parsley, chives, mint, or tarragon
- 1 tablespoon lemon juice

1. Toast quinoa in medium saucepan over medium-high heat, stirring frequently, until quinoa is very fragrant and makes continuous popping sound, 5 to 7 minutes; transfer to bowl.

2. Add butter to now-empty pan and melt over medium-low heat. Add onion and salt and cook until onion is softened and light golden, 5 to 7 minutes. Stir in water and toasted quinoa, increase heat to medium-high, and bring to simmer. Cover, reduce heat to low, and simmer until grains are just tender and liquid is absorbed, 18 to 20 minutes, stirring once halfway through cooking.

3. Remove pan from heat and let sit, covered, for 10 minutes. (Quinoa can be refrigerated for up to 3 days.) Fluff quinoa with fork, stir in herbs and lemon juice, and serve.

PER SERVING Cal 200; **Total Fat** 6g, **Sat Fat** 2.5g; **Chol** 10mg; **Sodium** 300mg; **Total Carb** 29g, **Dietary Fiber** 3g, **Total Sugars** 2g; **Protein** 6g

Quinoa Pilaf with Apricots, Aged Gouda, and Pistachios

Add ½ teaspoon grated lemon zest, ½ teaspoon ground coriander, ¼ teaspoon ground cumin, and ⅛ teaspoon pepper to pot with onion and salt. Stir in ½ cup coarsely chopped dried apricots before letting quinoa sit for 10 minutes in step 3. Substitute ½ cup shredded aged gouda; ½ cup shelled pistachios, toasted and chopped; and 2 tablespoons chopped fresh mint for herbs.

Quinoa Pilaf with Chipotle, Queso Fresco, and Peanuts

Add 1 teaspoon chipotle chile powder and ¼ teaspoon ground cumin to pot with onion and salt. Substitute ½ cup crumbled queso fresco, ½ cup coarsely chopped dry-roasted unsalted peanuts, and 2 thinly sliced scallions for herbs. Substitute 4 teaspoons lime juice for lemon juice.

Quinoa Pilaf with Olives, Raisins, and Cilantro

In order for this variation to be vegan, you must use olive oil.

Add ¼ teaspoon ground cumin, ¼ teaspoon dried oregano, and ⅛ teaspoon ground cinnamon to pot with onion and salt. Stir in ¼ cup golden raisins halfway through cooking quinoa. Substitute ⅓ cup coarsely chopped pimento-stuffed green olives and 3 tablespoons chopped fresh cilantro for chopped fresh herbs. Substitute 4 teaspoons red wine vinegar for lemon juice.

Quinoa Salad with Red Bell Pepper and Cilantro

SERVES 4 VEGAN

WHY THIS RECIPE WORKS Bell peppers work especially well in room-temperature grain salads, lending a burst of crunchy, juicy sweetness. Here we chose red bell pepper, along with jalapeño and red onion for a spicy counterpoint, and fresh cilantro for a bright herbal note. All these ingredients both tasted and looked great paired with the hearty, chewy quinoa. Before serving, we tossed the salad mixture with a bright dressing flavored with lime juice, mustard, garlic, and cumin. Rinse the quinoa in a fine-mesh strainer, drain it, and then spread it on a rimmed baking sheet lined with a dish towel and let dry for 15 minutes before proceeding with the recipe. To make this dish spicier, add the chile seeds.

1 cup prewashed white quinoa, rinsed and dried
1½ cups water
¼ teaspoon table salt
½ red bell pepper, chopped fine
½ jalapeño chile, minced
2 tablespoons finely chopped red onion

Quinoa Salad with Red Bell Pepper and Cilantro

1 tablespoon minced fresh cilantro
2 tablespoons fresh lime juice
1 tablespoon extra-virgin olive oil
2 teaspoons Dijon mustard
1 garlic clove, minced
½ teaspoon ground cumin

1. Toast quinoa in large saucepan over medium heat, stirring frequently, until quinoa is lightly toasted and aromatic, about 5 minutes. Stir in water and salt and bring to simmer. Cover, reduce heat to low, and cook until water is mostly absorbed and quinoa is nearly tender, about 12 minutes. Spread quinoa out over rimmed baking sheet and set aside until tender and cool, about 20 minutes.

2. Transfer cooled quinoa to large bowl. Stir in bell pepper, jalapeño, onion, and cilantro. In separate bowl, whisk lime juice, oil, mustard, garlic, and cumin together, then pour over quinoa mixture and toss to coat. Season with salt and pepper to taste, and serve.

PER SERVING Cal 200; **Total Fat** 6g, **Sat Fat** 1g; **Chol** 0mg; **Sodium** 230mg; **Total Carb** 30g, **Dietary Fiber** 3g, **Total Sugars** 2g; **Protein** 6g

Warm Wheat Berries with Zucchini, Red Pepper, and Oregano

SERVES 4 TO 6 `VEGAN`

WHY THIS RECIPE WORKS Earthy and almost sweet, with a pleasingly firm chew, wheat berries benefit from pairing with lighter, brighter flavors such as summer vegetables and herbs. We cooked our wheat berries using the pasta method, but found that our standard ratio of salt to water (1 tablespoon to 4 quarts) prevented the grains from properly absorbing the water; they stayed hard and crunchy no matter how long we cooked them. Reducing the amount of salt was a simple fix and the grains still turned out nicely seasoned. Sautéing zucchini, red pepper, and red onion gave them great flavor; browning the vegetables in batches was essential to achieving deeper flavor. We allowed the warm wheat berries to soak in our bold-flavored vinaigrette while the vegetables were cooking. Do not add more than 1½ teaspoons of salt when cooking the wheat berries; adding more will prevent the grains from softening. If using quick-cooking or presteamed wheat berries (read the ingredient list on the package to determine this), you will need to decrease the wheat berry cooking time in step 1.

Warm Wheat Berries with Zucchini, Red Pepper, and Oregano

1½ cups wheat berries
½ teaspoon table salt, divided, plus salt for cooking wheat berries
2 tablespoons extra-virgin olive oil, divided
3 tablespoons red wine vinegar
1 garlic clove, minced
1 tablespoon grated lemon zest
1 tablespoon minced fresh oregano or 1½ teaspoons dried
1 zucchini, cut into ½-inch pieces
1 red onion, chopped
1 red bell pepper, stemmed, seeded, and cut into ½-inch pieces

1. Bring 4 quarts water to boil in Dutch oven. Add wheat berries and 1½ teaspoons salt, return to boil, and cook until tender but still chewy, 1 hour to 1 hour 10 minutes.

2. Meanwhile, whisk 1 tablespoon oil, vinegar, garlic, lemon zest, and oregano together in large bowl. Drain wheat berries, add to bowl with dressing, and gently toss to coat.

3. Heat 2 teaspoons oil in 12-inch nonstick skillet over medium-high heat until just smoking. Add zucchini and ¼ teaspoon salt and cook, stirring occasionally, until deep golden brown and beginning to char in spots, 6 to 8 minutes; transfer to bowl with wheat berries.

4. Return now-empty skillet to medium-high heat and add remaining 1 teaspoon oil, onion, bell pepper, and remaining ¼ teaspoon salt. Cook, stirring occasionally, until onion is charred at edges and pepper skin is charred and blistered, 8 to 10 minutes. Add wheat berry–zucchini mixture and cook, stirring frequently, until heated through, about 2 minutes. Season with salt and pepper to taste. Serve.

PER SERVING Cal 230; **Total Fat** 5g, **Sat Fat** 0.5g; **Chol** 0mg; **Sodium** 300mg; **Total Carb** 39g, **Dietary Fiber** 7g, **Total Sugars** 3g; **Protein** 7g

BEST BEANS AND LENTILS

For more ways with Beans and Lentils, see other chapters for basics (pages 35–37), potluck salads (332–337), slow cooker (pages 420–424), and pressure cooker (pages 431–433) beans and lentils. For a full listing of bean and lentil recipes, see the Index.

■ FAST (30 minutes or less total time)　■ MAKE-AHEAD　■ VEGAN
Photo(s): Cranberry Beans with Tequila, Green Chiles, and Pepitas; Curried Chickpeas with Garlic and Yogurt; Black-Eyed Peas with Walnuts and Pomegranate; French Lentils

Basic Black Beans

SERVES 6 `MAKE-AHEAD`

WHY THIS RECIPE WORKS We were in pursuit of black beans with the perfect texture: tender without being mushy, with enough bite to make a satisfying chew. We discovered that it was important to cook the beans in enough water; too little water and the beans on top cooked more slowly than the beans underneath. We determined that meat gave the beans a rich, deep flavor, so we tested cooking the beans with a ham hock, bacon, ham, and pork loin; the ham hock provided the smoothest background taste. In many Caribbean recipes, a *sofrito* is added to the cooked beans for flavor. We sautéed chopped vegetables—onion, garlic, and green bell pepper—in olive oil, along with some herbs and spices, until soft and then stirred the mixture into the beans. Mashing a cup of the beans with the sofrito helped to intensify all of the flavors.

BEANS

- 12 cups water
- 1 pound (2½ cups) dried black beans, picked over and rinsed
- 1 smoked ham hock (⅔ pound), rinsed
- 1 green bell pepper, stemmed, seeded, and quartered
- 1 onion
- 6 garlic cloves, minced
- 2 bay leaves
- 1½ teaspoons table salt

SOFRITO

- 2 tablespoons extra-virgin olive oil
- 1 onion, chopped fine
- 1 green bell pepper, stemmed, seeded, and chopped fine
- 8 garlic cloves, minced
- 2 teaspoons dried oregano
- ¾ teaspoon table salt
- 1½ teaspoons ground cumin
- 1 tablespoon lime juice
- ½ cup chopped fresh cilantro

1. **FOR THE BEANS** Bring all bean ingredients to boil over medium-high heat in Dutch oven, skimming surface as scum rises. Reduce heat to low and simmer, partially covered, adding more water if cooking liquid reduces to level of beans, until beans are tender but not splitting, about 2 hours. Remove ham hock. When cool enough to handle, remove ham from bone, discard bone and skin, and cut meat into bite-size pieces; set aside. Discard bay leaves.

2. **FOR THE SOFRITO** Meanwhile, heat oil in 12-inch skillet over medium heat; add onion, bell pepper, garlic, oregano, and salt; cook until vegetables soften, 8 to 10 minutes. Add cumin; cook until fragrant, about 1 minute.

3. Scoop 1 cup beans and 2 cups cooking liquid into pan with sofrito; mash beans with potato masher or fork until smooth. Simmer over medium heat until liquid is reduced and thickened, about 6 minutes. Return sofrito mixture with meat from ham hock to bean pot; simmer until beans are creamy and liquid thickens to sauce consistency, 15 to 20 minutes. Add lime juice; simmer 1 minute. Stir in cilantro and season with salt and pepper to taste. Serve. (Cooled beans can be refrigerated for up to 3 days.)

PER SERVING Cal 450; **Total Fat** 12g, **Sat Fat** 3g; **Chol** 45mg; **Sodium** 1100mg; **Total Carb** 54g, **Dietary Fiber** 2g, **Total Sugars** 9g; **Protein** 28g

VARIATIONS

Black Beans with Dry Sherry

Add 1 teaspoon ground coriander to sofrito along with cumin, substitute dry sherry for lime juice, and omit cilantro.

Black Beans with Bacon, Balsamic Vinegar, and Sweet Pepper

Cook 8 slices bacon, cut into ½-inch strips, in skillet over medium heat until crisp and browned, about 5 minutes. Transfer to paper towel–lined plate. Omit ham hock and substitute bacon fat for oil and 1 red bell pepper for green bell pepper in sofrito. Add cooked bacon to beans with sofrito and substitute 2 teaspoons balsamic vinegar for lime juice.

Boston Baked Beans

SERVES 4 TO 6 `MAKE-AHEAD`

WHY THIS RECIPE WORKS Boston baked beans are both sweet and savory and make a robust side dish in the middle of summer and winter alike. Made from the simplest ingredients, these beans are unified and refined during a long simmer. We wanted tender beans in a thick, smoky, slightly sweet sauce. For depth of flavor, we started by browning salt pork and bacon. Small white beans were preferred for their creamy texture and ability to remain intact during the long simmer. Mild molasses provided just the right amount of sweetness, while brown mustard and cider vinegar added welcome notes of spice and tanginess. We removed the lid for the last hour of cooking to reduce the sauce to a syrupy, intensified consistency that perfectly napped the beans.

- 4 ounces salt pork, rind removed, cut into ½-inch cubes
- 2 slices bacon, cut into ¼-inch pieces
- 1 onion, chopped fine
- 9 cups water
- 1 pound (2½ cups) dried small white beans, picked over and rinsed
- ½ cup plus 1 tablespoon mild molasses, divided

Boston Baked Beans

1½ tablespoons spicy brown mustard
1¼ teaspoons table salt
1 teaspoon cider vinegar

1. Adjust oven rack to lower-middle position and heat oven to 300 degrees. Place salt pork and bacon in Dutch oven; cook over medium heat, stirring occasionally, until lightly browned and most of fat is rendered, about 7 minutes. Add onion and continue to cook, stirring occasionally, until the onion is softened, 5 to 7 minutes. Add water, beans, ½ cup molasses, mustard, and salt; increase heat to medium-high and bring to a boil. Cover pot and transfer to oven.

2. Bake until beans are tender, about 4 hours, stirring once after 2 hours. Uncover and continue to bake until liquid has thickened to syrupy consistency, 1 to 1½ hours. Remove beans from oven; stir in vinegar, remaining 1 tablespoon molasses, and salt and pepper to taste. Serve. (Cooled beans can be refrigerated for up to 3 days.)

PER SERVING Cal 530; **Total Fat** 20g, **Sat Fat** 7g; **Chol** 20mg; **Sodium** 1120mg; **Total Carb** 70g, **Dietary Fiber** 12g, **Total Sugars** 26g; **Protein** 19g

Quicker Boston Baked Beans
SERVES 6 TO 8   MAKE-AHEAD

WHY THIS RECIPE WORKS The sweet, smoky flavor of Boston baked beans is hard to top, but we don't always have the luxury of devoting half a day in the kitchen to make a humble side dish. Shooting for authentic Boston beans that could be made in under 3 hours, we turned to baking soda to speed up the beans' cooking time. This addition triggered rapid softening, and after only 20 minutes on the stove, our beans were ready to bake. To create a slow-cooked, salty-sweet taste, we bolstered molasses with dark brown sugar and then upped the flavor with cider vinegar, Worcestershire, and Dijon mustard. Chopping and browning the salt pork rendered some of its fat and made it an edible flavor booster. We moved our covered pot to the oven to bake for 1½ hours followed by 30 minutes uncovered, concentrating the liquid. Our beans emerged perfectly tender, and a final stir of extra molasses and mustard served to thicken and enrich the sauce.

1 pound (2½ cups) dried navy beans, picked over and rinsed
1 tablespoon baking soda
6 ounces salt pork, rind removed, cut into ¼-inch pieces
1 onion, chopped fine
5 tablespoons packed dark brown sugar
5 tablespoons molasses, divided
2 tablespoons Worcestershire sauce
4 teaspoons Dijon mustard, divided
2 teaspoons cider vinegar
¼ teaspoon pepper

1. Adjust oven rack to middle position and heat oven to 350 degrees. Bring 3 quarts water, beans, and baking soda to boil in Dutch oven over high heat. Reduce heat to medium-high and simmer briskly for 20 minutes. Drain beans in colander. Rinse beans and pot.

2. Cook salt pork in now-empty pot over medium heat, stirring occasionally, until browned, about 10 minutes. Add onion and cook until softened, about 5 minutes. Stir in 3 cups water, sugar, ¼ cup molasses, Worcestershire, 1 tablespoon mustard, vinegar, pepper, and beans and bring to boil. Cover, transfer pot to oven, and cook until beans are nearly tender, about 1½ hours.

3. Uncover and continue to bake until beans are completely tender, about 30 minutes. Stir in remaining 1 tablespoon molasses and remaining 1 teaspoon mustard. Season with salt and pepper to taste. Serve. (Cooled beans can be refrigerated for up to 3 days.)

PER SERVING Cal 430; **Total Fat** 18g, **Sat Fat** 6g; **Chol** 20mg; **Sodium** 1130mg; **Total Carb** 54g, **Dietary Fiber** 9g, **Total Sugars** 21g; **Protein** 14g

Cowboy Beans

SERVES 4 TO 6 `MAKE-AHEAD`

WHY THIS RECIPE WORKS Cowboy beans are a top secret recipe among many pit masters, who serve them by the ladleful alongside the slabs of ribs and mounds of pulled pork. We wanted to make these creamy-textured, smoky, saucy beans at home to accompany our own barbecue. To get there, we used dried pinto or navy beans. We found that bacon was a convenient substitute for the smoky barbecued meat traditionally used. We blended mustard, barbecue sauce, and brown sugar for a sweet but spicy, deep flavor—a fair amount of garlic and onion helped, too. The secret ingredient in our recipe is coffee; its roasted, slightly bitter flavor tied all the ingredients together. This recipe uses the "quick-brine" method for soaking beans. Alternatively, you can skip step 1 and soak the beans overnight in 6 cups of water.

- 1 pound (2½ cups) dried pinto or navy beans, picked over and rinsed
- 4 slices bacon, chopped fine
- 1 onion, chopped fine
- 4 garlic cloves, minced
- 1 cup brewed coffee
- ½ cup plus 2 tablespoons barbecue sauce, divided
- ⅓ cup packed dark brown sugar
- 2 tablespoons spicy brown mustard
- 2 teaspoons table salt
- ½ teaspoon hot sauce

1. Place beans and 6 cups water in Dutch oven. Bring to boil over high heat and cook for 5 minutes. Remove pot from heat, cover, and let beans sit for 1 hour. Drain beans.

2. Adjust oven rack to lower-middle position and heat oven to 300 degrees. Cook bacon in clean, dry pot over medium heat until crispy, 5 to 7 minutes. Stir in onion and cook until beginning to brown, 6 to 8 minutes. Add garlic and cook until fragrant, about 30 seconds. Add 4½ cups water, coffee, and drained beans and bring to simmer; cook for 10 minutes. Add ½ cup barbecue sauce, sugar, mustard, salt, and hot sauce; return to simmer. Cover pot and transfer to oven.

3. Cook until beans are just tender, 2 to 2½ hours. Uncover and continue to cook, stirring occasionally, until liquid has thickened to syrupy consistency, 1 to 1½ hours. Remove from oven and stir in remaining 2 tablespoons barbecue sauce. Season with salt and pepper to taste, and serve. (Cooled beans can be refrigerated for up to 3 days.)

PER SERVING Cal 450; **Total Fat** 8g, **Sat Fat** 2.5g; **Chol** 10mg; **Sodium** 1260mg; **Total Carb** 74g, **Dietary Fiber** 18g, **Total Sugars** 26g; **Protein** 19g

Backyard Barbecue Beans

Backyard Barbecue Beans

SERVES 12 TO 16 `MAKE-AHEAD`

WHY THIS RECIPE WORKS For a standout barbecue side, we turned canned beans into a savory showstopper. Baked beans gave us an easy starting point, and mixing in pinto and cannellini beans built a multifaceted bean base. We skipped the usual step of rinsing the beans before draining them so that they would retain a viscous layer, ensuring a pleasantly thick consistency. We boosted the beans' flavor with an easy pantry sauce made with cider vinegar, granulated garlic, cayenne, and liquid smoke for that off-the-grill flavor. Browned bratwurst gave the sauce some meaty heft. We stirred the beans into this rich mixture, arranged bite-size pieces of bacon over the surface, and baked, allowing the bacon to render, crisp, and infuse the dish with its smoky flavor. Be sure to use a 13 by 9-inch metal baking pan; the volume of the beans is too great for a 13 by 9-inch ceramic baking dish, and it will overflow. We found that Bush's Original Recipe Baked Beans are the most consistent product for this recipe.

½ cup barbecue sauce

½ cup ketchup

½ cup water

2 tablespoons spicy brown mustard

2 tablespoons cider vinegar

1 teaspoon liquid smoke

1 teaspoon granulated garlic

¼ teaspoon cayenne pepper

1¼ pounds bratwurst, casings removed

2 onions, chopped

2 (28-ounce) cans baked beans

2 (15-ounce) cans pinto beans, drained

2 (15-ounce) cans cannellini beans, drained

1 (10-ounce) can Ro-Tel Original Diced Tomatoes and Green Chilies, drained

6 slices thick-cut bacon, cut into 1-inch pieces

1. Adjust oven rack to middle position and heat oven to 350 degrees. Whisk barbecue sauce, ketchup, water, mustard, vinegar, liquid smoke, granulated garlic, and cayenne together in large bowl; set aside.

2. Cook bratwurst in 12-inch nonstick skillet over medium-high heat, breaking up into small pieces with spoon, until fat begins to render, about 5 minutes. Stir in onions and cook until sausage and onions are well browned, about 15 minutes.

3. Transfer bratwurst mixture to bowl with sauce. Stir in baked beans, pinto beans, cannellini beans, and tomatoes. Transfer bean mixture to 13 by 9-inch baking pan and place pan on rimmed baking sheet. Arrange bacon pieces in single layer over top of beans.

4. Bake until beans are bubbling and bacon is rendered, about 1½ hours. Let cool for 15 minutes. Serve. (At end of step 3, beans can be wrapped in plastic and refrigerated for up to 24 hours. Proceed with recipe from step 4, increasing baking time to 1¾ hours.)

PER SERVING Cal 350; **Total Fat** 17g; **Sat Fat** 5g; **Chol** 35mg; **Sodium** 1000mg; **Total Carb** 36g, **Dietary Fiber** 2g, **Total Sugars** 16g; **Protein** 13g

Refried Beans

SERVES 4 TO 6

WHY THIS RECIPE WORKS Refried beans are a classic side dish in Mexican cuisine, perfect for serving alongside tacos, enchiladas, and beyond. We wanted a foolproof method for deeply flavored refried beans that boasted a rich, creamy texture. In traditional *frijoles refritos*, dried pinto beans are cooked in lard and mashed. In our version, we found that dried beans aren't essential—rinsed canned pinto beans worked just fine and are much

Refried Beans

more convenient. For authentic flavor, we reached for salt pork, which we sautéed to render its fat. Using the fat to cook the onion and chiles deepened the flavor of the beans. Processing a portion of the beans with broth created the creamy texture we were after, while pulsing the remaining beans ensured some chunky bites. Onion, garlic, two types of chiles, and cumin gave the dish complexity, and cilantro and lime juice added at the end gave our refried beans brightness. Make sure you rinse the beans thoroughly before cooking to get rid of excess salt.

2 (15-ounce) cans pinto beans, rinsed, divided

½ cup chicken broth, plus extra as needed

1 tablespoon vegetable oil

3 ounces salt pork, rind removed, chopped fine

1 onion, chopped fine

1 poblano chile, stemmed, seeded, and chopped fine

1 jalapeño chile, stemmed, seeded, and minced

¼ teaspoon table salt

3 garlic cloves, minced

½ teaspoon ground cumin

1 tablespoon minced fresh cilantro

2 teaspoons lime juice

1. Process all but 1 cup beans with broth in food processor until smooth, about 30 seconds, scraping down sides of bowl as needed. Add remaining beans and pulse until coarsely ground, about 5 pulses.

2. Heat oil in 12-inch nonstick skillet over medium heat until shimmering. Add salt pork and cook, stirring occasionally, until rendered and well browned, 10 to 15 minutes; discard pork, leaving fat behind in skillet.

3. Add onion, poblano, jalapeño, and salt to fat left in skillet and cook over medium heat until vegetables are softened and beginning to brown, about 8 minutes. Stir in garlic and cumin and cook until fragrant, about 30 seconds. Stir in processed beans and cook, stirring often, until well combined and thickened slightly, about 5 minutes. Off heat, stir in cilantro and lime juice and season with salt and pepper to taste. Adjust consistency with extra hot broth as needed. Serve.

PER SERVING Cal 250; **Total Fat** 15g, **Sat Fat** 4.5g; **Chol** 10mg; **Sodium** 750mg; **Total Carb** 23g, **Dietary Fiber** 6g, **Total Sugars** 2g; **Protein** 8g

VARIATION
Vegetarian Refried Beans
Substitute 1 cup water for ½ cup broth; add all of water to food processor in step 1. Omit salt pork and add vegetables to pan when oil is shimmering. Add 2 tablespoons tomato paste, ½ teaspoon dried oregano, and ½ teaspoon chipotle chile powder to skillet with garlic and cumin. Adjust consistency with extra hot water as needed before serving.

MAKING REFRIED BEANS

1. Process broth and most of beans, then add remaining beans and pulse until ground.

2. After cooking aromatics, add bean puree and cook until slightly thickened.

Cannellini Beans with Roasted Red Peppers and Kale
SERVES 4

WHY THIS RECIPE WORKS For a full-flavored one-pot take on the classic Italian combination of beans and greens, we paired cannellini beans and kale with jarred roasted red peppers. We sautéed garlic and onion with some hot red pepper flakes; the subtle spiciness balanced the sweetness of the beans and roasted peppers. We sliced the kale into thin ribbons and added it to the skillet a handful at a time to allow it to wilt. Choosing canned beans and jarred red peppers meant this dish could come together quickly and easily. For the liquid, we used a combination of water and white wine to brighten the dish. We served the dish with savory Parmesan, bright lemon wedges, and a drizzle of olive oil. Swiss chard can be substituted for the kale.

¼ cup extra-virgin olive oil, plus extra for serving
4 garlic cloves, minced
¼ teaspoon red pepper flakes
1 small red onion, halved and sliced thin
¼ teaspoon table salt
1 cup jarred roasted red peppers, sliced thin lengthwise
1 pound kale, stemmed and sliced thin crosswise
2 (15-ounce) cans cannellini beans, rinsed
½ cup dry white wine
½ cup water
1 ounce Parmesan cheese, grated (½ cup)
Lemon wedges

1. Cook oil, garlic, and pepper flakes in 12-inch skillet over medium-high heat until garlic turns golden brown, about 2 minutes. Stir in onion and salt, reduce heat to medium, and cook until onion is softened, about 5 minutes. Stir in red peppers and cook until softened and glossy, about 3 minutes.

2. Stir in kale, 1 handful at a time, and cook until wilted, about 3 minutes. Stir in beans, wine, and water and bring to simmer. Reduce heat to medium-low, cover, and cook until flavors have melded and kale is tender, 15 to 20 minutes. Season with salt and pepper to taste. Serve with Parmesan, lemon wedges, and extra oil.

PER SERVING Cal 350; **Total Fat** 17g, **Sat Fat** 3g; **Chol** 5mg; **Sodium** 840mg; **Total Carb** 33g, **Dietary Fiber** 9g, **Total Sugars** 7g; **Protein** 15g

Sicilian White Beans and Escarole

SERVES 4 **FAST** **VEGAN**

WHY THIS RECIPE WORKS White beans and escarole are a classic pairing in Sicilian cooking. Combining the buttery texture of cannellini beans with tender, slightly bitter escarole resulted in a well-balanced and simple side dish. Canned beans made this dish convenient, and their texture was a perfect counterpoint to the greens. Sautéed onions added a rich, deep flavor base without requiring too much time at the stove. Red pepper flakes lent a slight heat without overwhelming the other ingredients, and a combination of broth and water provided a flavorful backbone. We added the escarole and beans along with the liquid, and then we cooked the greens just until the leaves were wilted before cranking up the heat so the liquid would quickly evaporate. This short stint on the heat prevented the beans from breaking down and becoming mushy. Once we took the pot off the heat, we stirred in lemon juice for a bright finish and drizzled on some extra olive oil for richness. Chicory can be substituted for the escarole; however, its flavor is stronger.

1 tablespoon extra-virgin olive oil, plus extra for serving
2 onions, chopped fine
½ teaspoon table salt
4 garlic cloves, minced
⅛ teaspoon red pepper flakes
1 head escarole (1 pound), trimmed and sliced 1 inch thick
1 (15-ounce) can cannellini beans, rinsed
1 cup chicken or vegetable broth
1 cup water
2 teaspoons lemon juice

1. Heat oil in Dutch oven over medium heat until shimmering. Add onions and salt and cook until softened and lightly browned, 5 to 7 minutes. Stir in garlic and pepper flakes and cook until fragrant, about 30 seconds.

2. Stir in escarole, beans, broth, and water and bring to simmer. Cook, stirring occasionally, until escarole is wilted, about 5 minutes. Increase heat to high and cook until liquid is nearly evaporated, 10 to 15 minutes. Stir in lemon juice and season with salt and pepper to taste. Drizzle with extra oil and serve.

PER SERVING Cal 140; **Total Fat** 4g, **Sat Fat** 0.5g; **Chol** 0mg; **Sodium** 650mg; **Total Carb** 21g, **Dietary Fiber** 8g, **Total Sugars** 4g; **Protein** 7g

Chickpeas with Garlic and Parsley

Chickpeas with Garlic and Parsley

SERVES 4 TO 6 **FAST** **VEGAN**

WHY THIS RECIPE WORKS There's nothing more versatile and convenient than canned chickpeas. With their buttery, nutty flavor and creamy texture, chickpeas can make a terrific side dish when simply sautéed with a few ingredients. In search of fresh flavors that would transform our canned chickpeas, we reached for garlic and red pepper flakes. We sautéed thin garlic slices in extra-virgin olive oil to mellow their flavor. Then we softened an onion with the garlic and added the chickpeas with broth, which imparted a rich, savory backbone to the dish without overpowering it. Parsley and lemon juice added a burst of freshness.

¼ cup extra-virgin olive oil, divided
4 garlic cloves, sliced thin
⅛ teaspoon red pepper flakes
1 onion, chopped fine
¼ teaspoon table salt
2 (15-ounce) cans chickpeas, rinsed
1 cup chicken or vegetable broth
2 tablespoons minced fresh parsley
2 teaspoons lemon juice

1. Cook 3 tablespoons oil, garlic, and pepper flakes in 12-inch skillet over medium heat, stirring frequently, until garlic turns golden but not brown, about 3 minutes. Stir in onion and salt and cook until softened and lightly browned, 5 to 7 minutes. Stir in chickpeas and broth and bring to simmer. Reduce heat to medium-low, cover, and cook until chickpeas are heated through and flavors meld, about 7 minutes.

2. Uncover, increase heat to high, and continue to cook until nearly all liquid has evaporated, about 3 minutes. Off heat, stir in parsley and lemon juice. Season with salt and pepper to taste and drizzle with remaining 1 tablespoon oil. Serve.

PER SERVING Cal 170; **Total Fat** 11g, **Sat Fat** 1.5g; **Chol** 0mg; **Sodium** 430mg; **Total Carb** 16g, **Dietary Fiber** 3g, **Total Sugars** 2g; **Protein** 4g

VARIATIONS
Chickpeas with Smoked Paprika and Cilantro
Omit red pepper flakes. Add ½ teaspoon smoked paprika to skillet before chickpeas and cook until fragrant, about 30 seconds. Substitute 2 tablespoons minced fresh cilantro for parsley and 2 teaspoons sherry vinegar for lemon juice.

Chickpeas with Bell Pepper, Scallions, and Basil
Add 1 chopped red bell pepper to skillet with onion. Substitute 2 tablespoons chopped fresh basil for parsley and stir in 2 thinly sliced scallions before serving.

Chickpeas with Saffron, Mint, and Yogurt
Omit red pepper flakes. Add ⅛ teaspoon crumbled saffron threads to skillet before chickpeas and cook until fragrant, about 30 seconds. Add ⅓ cup raisins to skillet with chickpeas. Substitute 2 tablespoons minced fresh mint for parsley and stir in ¼ cup plain yogurt before serving.

RINSING CANNED BEANS

Place beans in fine-mesh strainer and rinse under cool water to remove excess starchy canning liquid. Let drain briefly.

Curried Chickpeas with Garlic and Yogurt FAST
SERVES 6

WHY THIS RECIPE WORKS For a chickpea side dish packed with flavor and flair, we started with a base of sautéed garlic and onion. We then elevated this humble legume by infusing our oil and aromatics with fragrant curry powder. In search of other easy kitchen staples to flavor our chickpeas, we reached for chicken or vegetable broth and raisins, which complemented the warm spice of the curry. Keeping the chickpeas whole provided excellent texture. We added some parsley and lime juice at the end of cooking for freshness, along with yogurt, which added a creamy tang to mellow the curry. A final drizzle of extra-virgin olive oil lent a bit of richness.

¼ cup extra-virgin olive oil, divided
4 garlic cloves, sliced thin
1 onion, chopped fine
¼ teaspoon table salt
1 teaspoon curry powder
2 (15-ounce) cans chickpeas, rinsed
1 cup chicken or vegetable broth
⅓ cup raisins
2 tablespoons minced fresh parsley
2 teaspoons lime juice
¼ cup plain low-fat yogurt

1. Combine 3 tablespoons oil and garlic in 12-inch skillet and cook over medium heat, stirring occasionally, until garlic is light golden, 3 to 5 minutes. Stir in onion and salt and cook until onion is softened and lightly browned, 5 to 7 minutes.

2. Stir in curry powder and cook until fragrant, about 30 seconds. Stir in chickpeas, broth, and raisins and bring to simmer. Cover and cook until chickpeas are warmed through and flavors meld, about 7 minutes. 3. Uncover, increase heat to high, and simmer until nearly all liquid has evaporated, about 3 minutes. Off heat, stir in parsley and lime juice. Stir in yogurt, season with salt and pepper to taste, and drizzle with remaining 1 tablespoon oil. Serve.

PER SERVING Cal 210; **Total Fat** 11g, **Sat Fat** 1.5g; **Chol** 0mg; **Sodium** 380mg; **Total Carb** 23g, **Dietary Fiber** 4g, **Total Sugars** 9g; **Protein** 5g

Greek Spinach and Chickpeas

2 tablespoons extra-virgin olive oil, plus extra for drizzling
3 garlic cloves, sliced thin
¼ teaspoon red pepper flakes
2 (15-ounce) cans chickpeas (1 can drained and rinsed, 1 can left undrained), divided
10 ounces (10 cups) baby spinach
½ cup chicken broth or vegetable broth
¼ teaspoon table salt
¼ cup chopped fresh dill
1 tablespoon lemon juice

1. Combine oil, garlic, and pepper flakes in Dutch oven and cook over medium heat until garlic is golden brown, 3 to 5 minutes.

2. Stir in 1 can drained chickpeas, 1 can chickpeas and their liquid, spinach, broth, and salt. Increase heat to medium-high and cook, stirring occasionally, until spinach is wilted and liquid is slightly thickened, about 5 minutes. Off heat, stir in dill and lemon juice. Season with salt and pepper to taste. Transfer to shallow platter and drizzle with extra oil. Serve.

PER SERVING Cal 150; **Total Fat** 6g, **Sat Fat** 0.5g; **Chol** 0mg; **Sodium** 440mg; **Total Carb** 18g, **Dietary Fiber** 5g, **Total Sugars** 2g; **Protein** 6g

Greek Spinach and Chickpeas
SERVES 4 TO 6 FAST VEGAN

WHY THIS RECIPE WORKS Chickpeas and spinach are a quintessential pairing in Greek cuisine. We wanted a side dish of chickpeas tossed with a tangle of wilted spinach in a vibrant lemon-and-dill-flavored broth inspired by some of Greece's favored ingredients. We started by heating sliced garlic and red pepper flakes in olive oil to infuse the oil with savory, spicy flavor. Canned chickpeas were the obvious choice to keep the dish weeknight-friendly. Baby spinach proved easier to work with than curly-leaf spinach, as it didn't require any stemming or chopping. We also found that cooking everything in a Dutch oven provided enough room so that we could add all the spinach at once, which was much more efficient than adding it in bunches. A little chicken broth provided a savory backbone that tied the dish together. The last trick was not draining one of the cans of chickpeas; the starchy chickpea liquid added body to the broth, giving it a subtle creaminess that was perfect for sopping up with a torn piece of crusty bread. Before serving, we stirred in some lemon juice and a hefty quarter cup of fresh dill.

Spicy Chickpeas with Turnips
SERVES 4 TO 6 MAKE-AHEAD VEGAN

WHY THIS RECIPE WORKS To turn up the heat on dinner, we combined chickpeas with hearty, satisfying turnips and dressed them up with vibrantly spiced ingredients. To start, we created a spicy and savory base of sautéed aromatics. For the main source of heat, we opted for a jalapeño. We also added extra punch with a bit of cayenne pepper. With the aromatic foundation for this dish in place, it was time to add the hearty vegetables. To keep our recipe streamlined, we chose canned chickpeas, which softened slightly with cooking. Including the starchy, seasoned liquid from the cans gave our sauce good flavor and body. To add bulk and earthy flavor to this dish, we tested a variety of root vegetables and landed on turnips, a hearty and versatile ingredient that would pick up the flavorful heat of the dish. A final touch of lemon juice was all this zesty bean dish needed before serving.

2 tablespoons extra-virgin olive oil

2 onions, chopped

2 red bell peppers, stemmed, seeded, and chopped

½ teaspoon table salt

¼ teaspoon pepper

¼ cup tomato paste

1 jalapeño chile, stemmed, seeded, and minced

5 garlic cloves, minced

¾ teaspoon ground cumin

¼ teaspoon cayenne pepper

2 (15-ounce) cans chickpeas

12 ounces turnips, peeled and cut into ½-inch pieces

¾ cup water, plus extra as needed

¼ cup chopped fresh parsley

2 tablespoons lemon juice, plus extra for seasoning

1. Heat oil in Dutch oven over medium heat until shimmering. Add onions, bell peppers, salt, and pepper and cook until softened and lightly browned, 5 to 7 minutes. Stir in tomato paste, jalapeño, garlic, cumin, and cayenne and cook until fragrant, about 30 seconds.

2. Stir in chickpeas and their liquid, turnips, and water. Bring to simmer and cook until turnips are tender and sauce has thickened, 25 to 35 minutes. (Cooled beans can be refrigerated for up to 2 days.)

3. Stir in parsley and lemon juice. Season with salt, pepper, and extra lemon juice to taste. Adjust consistency with extra hot water as needed. Serve.

PER SERVING Cal 210; **Total Fat** 7g, **Sat Fat** 0.5g; **Chol** 0mg; **Sodium** 650mg; **Total Carb** 31g, **Dietary Fiber** 7g, **Total Sugars** 9g; **Protein** 8g

Cranberry Beans with Warm Spices
SERVES 6 TO 8 MAKE-AHEAD VEGAN

WHY THIS RECIPE WORKS Cranberry beans have a delicate flavor and a creamy texture similar to that of pinto or cannellini beans. We wanted to highlight these beans in a gently spiced side dish. Since cranberry beans are rarely canned, we knew we'd have to start with dried beans. To help the beans cook up creamy and tender, we soaked them overnight in salt water before thoroughly rinsing them to remove any excess salt. We sautéed aromatic vegetables along with tomato paste for depth of flavor; just a touch of cinnamon imparted a subtle yet distinctly Turkish flavor. White wine offered acidity, and broth gave the dish a hearty backbone. Letting the beans cook through in the gentle heat of the oven ensured that they were perfectly cooked without constant monitoring. We completed our comforting dish with lemon juice and mint, which nicely balanced the warm, rich flavors of the beans. If cranberry beans are not available, you can substitute pinto beans.

Cranberry Beans with Warm Spices

3 tablespoons table salt for brining

1 pound (2½ cups) dried cranberry beans, picked over and rinsed

¼ cup extra-virgin olive oil

1 onion, chopped fine

2 carrots, peeled and chopped fine

4 garlic cloves, sliced thin

1 tablespoon tomato paste

½ teaspoon ground cinnamon

¼ teaspoon pepper

½ cup dry white wine

4 cups chicken or vegetable broth

2 tablespoons lemon juice, plus extra for seasoning

2 tablespoons minced fresh mint

1. Dissolve salt in 4 quarts cold water in large container. Add beans and soak at room temperature for at least 8 hours or up to 24 hours. Drain and rinse well.

2. Adjust oven rack to lower-middle position and heat oven to 350 degrees. Heat oil in Dutch oven over medium heat until shimmering. Add onion and carrots and cook until softened, about 5 minutes. Stir in garlic, tomato paste, cinnamon, and pepper and cook until fragrant, about 1 minute. Stir in wine, scraping up any browned bits. Stir in broth, ½ cup water, and beans and bring to boil. Cover, transfer pot to oven, and cook until beans are tender, about 1½ hours, stirring every 30 minutes. (Cooled beans can be refrigerated for up to 2 days.)

3. Stir in lemon juice and mint. Season with salt, pepper, and extra lemon juice to taste. Adjust consistency with extra hot water as needed. Serve.

PER SERVING Cal 290; **Total Fat** 8g, **Sat Fat** 1g; **Chol** 0mg; **Sodium** 400mg; **Total Carb** 40g, **Dietary Fiber** 15g, **Total Sugars** 2g; **Protein** 14g

Cranberry Beans with Tequila, Green Chiles, and Pepitas
SERVES 4 TO 6

WHY THIS RECIPE WORKS Cranberry beans have a delicate flavor and a creamy texture similar to that of pinto or cannellini beans. While originally from South America, these beans have become popular in Mexico as well, so we decided to pair them with bold Mexican flavors. To help the dried beans cook up creamy and tender, we started our recipe with an overnight soak in salt water. Then to begin building a flavorful background for the dish, we sautéed some onion and garlic with lots of paprika, some cumin seeds, and dried oregano. Once the mixture was fragrant, we added a little tequila to the pot to give the beans some kick. Cooking the mixture until the tequila evaporated prevented the dish from tasting too boozy. Next we stirred in the brined beans and water and transferred the entire pot to the oven, where the beans could cook gently without requiring constant monitoring. Once the beans were tender, we stirred in some convenient canned chiles to give the dish great spice and some brightness, then we cooked the beans uncovered for 15 minutes more to allow the sauce to thicken. A garnish of rich sour cream, crunchy pepitas, and quick pickled shallot and radishes nicely balanced the rich, warm flavors of the cranberry beans. If cranberry beans are not available, you can substitute pinto beans.

3 tablespoons table salt for brining
1 pound (2½ cups) dried cranberry beans, picked over and rinsed
¼ cup extra-virgin olive oil
1 onion, chopped fine
1 teaspoon table salt
6 garlic cloves, minced
1 tablespoon paprika
½ teaspoon cumin seeds

½ teaspoon dried oregano
¼ cup tequila
5 cups water
1 tablespoon packed brown sugar
1 bay leaf
½ cup canned chopped green chiles
½ cup roasted pepitas
½ cup sour cream or queso fresco
1 recipe Quick Pickled Shallot and Radishes

1. Dissolve 3 tablespoons salt in 4 quarts cold water in large container. Add beans and soak at room temperature for at least 8 hours or up to 24 hours. Drain and rinse well.

2. Adjust oven rack to middle position and heat oven to 325 degrees. Heat oil in Dutch oven over medium heat until shimmering. Add onion and 1 teaspoon salt and cook until onion is softened, about 5 minutes. Stir in garlic, paprika, cumin, and oregano and cook until fragrant, about 1 minute. Stir in tequila and cook until evaporated, about 30 seconds. Stir in water, sugar, bay leaf, and cranberry beans; bring to simmer. Cover, transfer pot to oven, and cook until beans are tender, stirring once halfway through cooking, about 1¼ hours.

3. Add green chiles, stirring vigorously. Return pot to oven uncovered, and cook until sauce is thickened slightly, about 15 minutes. Season with salt and pepper to taste and serve with pepitas, sour cream, and pickled vegetables.

PER SERVING Cal 340; **Total Fat** 18g, **Sat Fat** 4g; **Chol** 10mg; **Sodium** 600mg; **Total Carb** 29g, **Dietary Fiber** 8g, **Total Sugars** 5g; **Protein** 12g

---

TAKE IT UP A NOTCH

These quick pickled vegetables add a briny, peppery bite to bean dishes, salads, and more.

Quick Pickled Shallot and Radishes
MAKES ABOUT 1 CUP

5 radishes, trimmed and sliced thin
1 shallot, sliced thin
¼ cup lime juice (2 limes)
1 teaspoon sugar
⅛ teaspoon table salt

Combine all ingredients in bowl. (Pickled vegetables can be refrigerated for up to 2 days.)

Cranberry Bean Salad with Fennel, Grapes, and Pine Nuts

SERVES 6 TO 8 VEGAN

WHY THIS RECIPE WORKS *Agrodolce* is an Italian sweet-and-sour sauce made by reducing vinegar and sugar. We used it in a flavorful cranberry bean salad. We brined dried beans overnight, to ensure fewer blowouts, before rinsing and gently simmering them until tender. Next, we built a foundation for our salad. We sautéed chopped fennel until it had softened and added fennel seeds to reinforce the fresh flavor. We reduced red wine vinegar and sugar to a syrupy glaze that beautifully coated the salad. Grapes and pine nuts provided sweetness and extra crunch. A sprinkling of fennel fronds added color and underscored the fennel flavor. If cranberry beans are not available, you can substitute pinto beans.

3 tablespoons table salt for brining
1 pound (2½ cups) dried cranberry beans, picked over and rinsed
1¼ teaspoons table salt, divided
3 tablespoons extra-virgin olive oil
½ fennel bulb, cored and chopped, plus 2 tablespoons chopped fennel fronds
¼ teaspoon pepper
1 cup plus 2 tablespoons red wine vinegar, divided
½ cup sugar
1 teaspoon fennel seeds
6 ounces seedless red grapes, halved (1 cup)
½ cup pine nuts, toasted

1. Dissolve 3 tablespoons salt in 4 quarts cold water in large container. Add beans and soak at room temperature for at least 8 hours or up to 24 hours. Drain and rinse well.

2. Bring beans, 4 quarts water, and 1 teaspoon salt to boil in Dutch oven. Reduce to simmer and cook, stirring occasionally, until beans are tender, 1 to 1½ hours. Drain beans and set aside.

3. Wipe Dutch oven clean with paper towels. Heat oil in now-empty pot over medium heat until shimmering. Add fennel, remaining ¼ teaspoon salt, and pepper and cook until softened, about 5 minutes. Stir in 1 cup vinegar, sugar, and fennel seeds until sugar is dissolved. Bring to simmer and cook until liquid is thickened to syrupy glaze and edges of fennel are beginning to brown, about 10 minutes.

4. Add beans to vinegar-fennel mixture and toss to coat. Transfer to large bowl and let cool to room temperature. Add grapes, pine nuts, fennel fronds, and remaining 2 tablespoons vinegar and toss to combine. Season with salt and pepper to taste, and serve.

PER SERVING Cal 240; Total Fat 11g, Sat Fat 1g; Chol 0mg; Sodium 160mg; Total Carb 33g, Dietary Fiber 6g, Total Sugars 17g; Protein 7g

Gingery Stir-Fried Edamame

SERVES 4 FAST VEGAN

WHY THIS RECIPE WORKS: Edamame are young green soy beans and have always been a test kitchen favorite. We love snacking on them in their shells, but for a warm stir-fried side dish, we turned to shelled edamame. The toasted sesame oil amplified the nuttiness of the edamame, and a generous amount of fresh ginger gave the fresh legumes an aromatic, spicy punch. Soy sauce stirred in at the end tied all the flavors together. Superfast and superflavorful, this quick side dish makes for a great weeknight accompaniment to practically any protein. You will need a 12-inch nonstick skillet with a tight-fitting lid for this recipe.

12 ounces shelled edamame beans
½ cup water
1 tablespoon toasted sesame oil
1 scallion, minced
1 tablespoon grated fresh ginger
1 tablespoon soy sauce

1. Cook edamame and water in 12-inch nonstick skillet, covered, until edamame are nearly tender, about 7 minutes. Uncover and cook until water evaporates and edamame are tender, about 2 minutes.

2. Push edamame to sides of skillet. Add sesame oil, scallion, and ginger to center and cook, mashing mixture into pan, until fragrant, about 30 seconds. Stir mixture into edamame, then stir in soy sauce. Serve.

PER SERVING Cal 130; Total Fat 7g, Sat Fat 0.5g; Chol 0mg; Sodium 240mg; Total Carb 8g, Dietary Fiber 0g, Total Sugars 3g; Protein 11g

Edamame Salad

SERVES 4 FAST

WHY THIS RECIPE WORKS Edamame are great in salads because their fresh flavor and satisfying texture pair well with leafy greens and vegetables. Baby arugula served as the perfect base thanks to its subtle peppery flavor and tender leaves. Lots of mint and basil brought a light, summery flavor to our salad. Shallot added mild onion flavor, and just a couple of radishes added crunch and color. For the vinaigrette, we chose to use rice vinegar for its mild acidity and added a little honey for sweetness and to emulsify the dressing. One small clove of garlic added flavor without taking over the dish. The final touch was a sprinkle of sunflower seeds. You can substitute frozen edamame beans that have been thawed and patted dry for fresh edamame here.

Edamame Salad

2 tablespoons rice vinegar
1 tablespoon honey
1 small garlic clove, minced
1 teaspoon table salt
3 tablespoons extra-virgin olive oil
20 ounces shelled edamame beans
2 ounces (2 cups) baby arugula
½ cup shredded fresh basil
½ cup chopped fresh mint
2 radishes, trimmed, halved, and sliced thin
1 shallot, halved and thinly sliced
¼ cup roasted sunflower seeds

Whisk vinegar, honey, garlic, and salt together in large bowl. Slowly whisk in oil until incorporated. Add edamame, arugula, basil, mint, radishes, and shallot and toss to combine. Sprinkle with sunflower seeds and season with salt and pepper to taste. Serve.

PER SERVING Cal 340; Total Fat 21g, Sat Fat 2g; Chol 0mg; Sodium 600mg; Total Carb 21g, Dietary Fiber 2g, Total Sugars 10g; Protein 19g

Mashed Fava Beans with Cumin and Garlic
SERVES 4 TO 6 **FAST** **VEGAN**

WHY THIS RECIPE WORKS Fava beans are hugely popular in Egypt, so it's no surprise that *ful medames*, a simple dish composed of mashed fava beans flavored with cumin and garlic and topped with a host of fresh ingredients, is one of the nation's most beloved dishes. We set out to create a simplified fava bean side dish that was loyal to the dish's ancient roots. The traditional dish is made by cooking dried fava beans in a pear-shaped pot for hours until the beans are soft. We took a hint from modern recipes and opted to use canned beans, eliminating both the long cooking time and the need for a piece of specialty cookware. We cooked the unrinsed beans in their own seasoned liquid until they were tender and then mashed them gently with a potato masher. As for toppings, recipes we found varied widely, so we opted for the customary additions of chopped tomato, raw onion, and chopped hard-cooked eggs, along with some parsley and a drizzle of extra-virgin olive oil for richness. Traditionally, this dish is served as a hearty breakfast dish, as a dip, or as a side for lunch or dinner; tasters liked it best as a side dish with meat or vegetables or as a snack served with pita. It also tastes great with hard-cooked eggs.

4 garlic cloves, minced
1 tablespoon extra-virgin olive oil, plus extra for serving
1 teaspoon ground cumin
2 (15-ounce) cans fava beans
3 tablespoons tahini
2 tablespoons lemon juice, plus lemon wedges for serving
1 teaspoon pepper
1 tomato, cored and cut into ½-inch pieces
1 small onion, chopped fine
2 tablespoons minced fresh parsley
2 Easy-Peel Hard-Cooked Eggs (page 453), chopped (optional)

1. Cook garlic, oil, and cumin in medium saucepan over medium heat until fragrant, about 2 minutes. Stir in beans and their liquid and tahini. Bring to simmer and cook until liquid thickens slightly, 8 to 10 minutes.

2. Off heat, mash beans to coarse consistency using potato masher. Stir in lemon juice and pepper. Season with salt and pepper to taste. Transfer to serving dish, top with tomato, onion, parsley, and eggs, if using, and drizzle with extra oil. Serve with lemon wedges.

PER SERVING Cal 150; Total Fat 7g, Sat Fat 1g; Chol 0mg; Sodium 430mg; Total Carb 16g, Dietary Fiber 4g, Total Sugars 1g; Protein 7g

Mashed Fava Beans with Cucumbers, Olives, and Feta

Omit onion and egg. Sprinkle ½ cucumber, peeled, halved lengthwise, seeded, and cut into ½-inch pieces; ¼ cup pitted kalamata olives, halved; and ¼ cup crumbled feta cheese over beans along with tomatoes and parsley.

Spicy Mashed Fava Beans with Yogurt

Omit parsley and egg. Add 1 thinly sliced jalapeño chile and ¼ teaspoon cayenne pepper to saucepan with garlic. Substitute 3 chopped scallions for onion. Mix ⅓ cup plain yogurt with additional 1 tablespoon lemon juice and drizzle over beans before serving.

Fava Bean and Radish Salad
SERVES 4 TO 6 **VEGAN**

WHY THIS RECIPE WORKS A highlight of farmers' markets every spring, fresh fava beans are a wonderful, fuzzy green pod bean not to be passed by. Since it takes some time to prepare fresh favas, we wanted to use them in a vibrant, interesting salad that would be worth the effort. We added thin half-moons of peppery radishes to provide a nice crunchy bite as well as flecks of color to our salad. Fresh pea shoots supplied another layer of texture and a bit of natural sweetness. Basil and a lemony vinaigrette were the final additions to this light and flavorful salad that celebrates springtime in every bite. The beans inside their tough outer pod are covered with a waxy, translucent sheath that should be removed after shelling. You can substitute 1 pound (3 cups) of frozen fava beans.

    3 pounds fava beans, shelled (3 cups)
    3 tablespoons lemon juice
    2 garlic cloves, minced
    ½ teaspoon table salt
    ¼ teaspoon pepper
    ¼ teaspoon ground coriander
    ¼ cup extra-virgin olive oil
    10 radishes, trimmed, halved, and sliced thin
    1½ ounces (1½ cups) pea shoots
    ¼ cup chopped fresh basil

1. Bring 4 quarts water to boil in large pot over high heat. Meanwhile, fill large bowl halfway with ice and water. Add fava beans to boiling water and cook for 1 minute. Drain fava beans, transfer to ice water, and let sit until chilled, about 2 minutes. Transfer fava beans to triple layer of paper towels and dry well.

Using paring knife, make small cut along edge of each bean through waxy sheath, then gently squeeze sheath to release bean; discard sheath.

2. Whisk lemon juice, garlic, salt, pepper, and coriander together in large bowl. Whisking constantly, slowly drizzle in oil. Add fava beans, radishes, pea shoots, and basil and gently toss to coat. Serve immediately.

PER SERVING Cal 140; **Total Fat** 10g, **Sat Fat** 1.5g; **Chol** 0mg; **Sodium** 230mg; **Total Carb** 10g, **Dietary Fiber** 3g, **Total Sugars** 5g; **Protein** 4g

PREPPING FRESH FAVA BEANS

1. To shell favas, use paring knife and your thumb to snip off tip of pod and pull apart sides to release beans. Blanch beans and dry well.

2. Use paring knife to make small cut along edge of bean through waxy sheath, then gently squeeze sheath to release bean.

Gigante Beans with Spinach and Feta
SERVES 6 TO 8

WHY THIS RECIPE WORKS Popular throughout Greece, gigante beans are similar in size and texture to large lima beans. They have a velvety, creamy texture and earthy flavor. Greens are ubiquitous in Greek cuisine as well, so we set our sights on combining the two ingredients for a hearty, satisfying side dish. We cooked fresh spinach in a large Dutch oven using a combination steam-sauté method, which boosted the spinach's flavor as it wilted. We then stirred in our soaked and cooked beans (soaking was essential to preventing blowouts) along with tomatoes and dill. To make the dish even more impressive, we baked the greens and beans with fresh bread crumbs on top for some crunch and feta cheese for salty, tangy contrast. You can substitute flat-leaf spinach; do not substitute baby spinach. Dried gigante beans can be found at Greek and Middle Eastern markets as well as in the international food aisle of many supermarkets; if you cannot find them, substitute dried large lima beans.

Gigante Beans with Spinach and Feta

garlic and cook until fragrant, about 30 seconds. Stir in half of spinach, cover, and cook until beginning to wilt, about 2 minutes. Stir in remaining spinach, cover, and cook until wilted, about 2 minutes. Off heat, gently stir in beans, tomatoes, dill and 2 tablespoons oil. Season with salt and pepper to taste.

4. Meanwhile, adjust oven rack to middle position and heat oven to 400 degrees. Pulse bread and remaining 2 tablespoons oil in food processor to coarse crumbs, about 5 pulses. Transfer bean mixture to 13 by 9-inch baking dish and sprinkle with feta, then bread crumbs. Bake until bread crumbs are golden brown and edges are bubbling, about 20 minutes. Serve with lemon wedges.

PER SERVING Cal 310; **Total Fat** 16g, **Sat Fat** 4.5g; Chol 20mg; **Sodium** 670mg; **Total Carb** 32g, **Dietary Fiber** 7g, **Total Sugars** 7g; **Protein** 12g

Classic Succotash
SERVES 4 TO 6 FAST

WHY THIS RECIPE WORKS Succotash, which takes its name from an age-old Narragansett Indian dish, has been an American staple for generations. To our way of thinking, succotash should include little but fresh, tender sweet corn, creamy lima beans, a few flecks of bell pepper, and just enough seasoning and butter to marry the vegetables. Because fresh limas can be nearly impossible to find in most of the country, we opted for frozen lima beans. Frozen corn, unfortunately, did not work as well. Luckily, it's easy enough to find fresh corn most anywhere come midsummer. For maximum corn flavor, we scraped the cobs with the back of a knife to release any remaining bits of pulp or liquid. Chopped onion and a little minced garlic added depth and complexity. Many authentic recipes call for green bell pepper, but we found that we liked the sweet, ripe flavor of red bell pepper, which also added a bit of bright color. Seasoned with salt, pepper, and a hint of cayenne, our succotash needed only a little parsley to help bring these fresh flavors home. This quick, summery vegetable sauté is the perfect side dish for an outdoor barbecue or picnic. Only fresh corn has the proper flavor and texture for the dish.

- 3 tablespoons table salt for brining
- 8 ounces (1½ cups) dried gigante beans, picked over and rinsed
- 6 tablespoons extra-virgin olive oil, divided
- 2 onions, chopped fine
- ½ teaspoon table salt
- 3 garlic cloves, minced
- 20 ounces curly-leaf spinach, stemmed, divided
- 2 (14.5-ounce) cans diced tomatoes, drained
- ¼ cup minced fresh dill
- 2 slices hearty white sandwich bread, torn into quarters
- 6 ounces feta cheese, crumbled (1½ cups)
  Lemon wedges

1. Dissolve 3 tablespoons salt in 4 quarts cold water in large container. Add beans and soak at room temperature for at least 8 hours or up to 24 hours. Drain and rinse well.

2. Bring beans and 2 quarts water to boil in Dutch oven. Reduce to simmer and cook, stirring occasionally, until beans are tender, 1 to 1½ hours. Drain beans and set aside.

3. Wipe Dutch oven clean with paper towels. Heat 2 tablespoons oil in now-empty pot over medium heat until shimmering. Add onions and salt and cook until softened, about 5 minutes. Stir in

- 3 ears corn, kernels cut from cobs, cobs reserved
- 4 tablespoons unsalted butter
- 1 small onion, chopped fine
- ½ red bell pepper, cut into ½-inch pieces
- 2 garlic cloves, minced
- 2 cups frozen lima beans
- ¾ teaspoon table salt
- ⅛ teaspoon pepper
  Pinch cayenne pepper
- 1 tablespoon minced fresh parsley

1. Place corn kernels in medium bowl. Working with 1 cob at a time, hold cob over bowl with corn and use back of butter knife to scrape any pulp and liquid into bowl.

2. Melt butter in 12-inch nonstick skillet over medium-high heat. Add onion and bell pepper and cook, stirring frequently, until softened and beginning to brown around edges, about 5 minutes. Add garlic and cook until fragrant, about 30 seconds. Stir in lima beans, salt, pepper, cayenne, and corn and pulp and reduce heat to medium. Cook, stirring occasionally, until lima beans and corn have cooked through, about 5 minutes. Stir in parsley and serve immediately.

PER SERVING Cal 200; **Total Fat** 9g, **Sat Fat** 4.5g; **Chol** 20mg; **Sodium** 450mg; **Total Carb** 25g, **Dietary Fiber** 5g, **Total Sugars** 5g; **Protein** 6g

VARIATION

Succotash with Chile and Cilantro
Add 1 seeded and minced small jalapeño chile to skillet along with onion and bell pepper. Substitute cilantro for parsley.

Black-Eyed Peas and Collard Greens
SERVES 6 TO 8

WHY THIS RECIPE WORKS Southern tradition holds that if, on New Year's Day, you eat a plate of collards and black-eyed peas all stewed up with tomatoes, spices, and a hambone, you will experience greater wealth and prosperity in the coming year. To get a jump on acquiring said prosperity, we decided to speed up this one-pot dish a little bit. We swapped more time-consuming dried legumes for a couple of convenient cans of black-eyed peas, and gave the collards a 15-minute head start on the stove before adding the peas. We also relied on smoky bacon and savory chicken broth to quickly build a meaty backbone of flavor. For maximum good luck, be careful not to crush those black-eyed peas—stir them gently.

  6 slices bacon, cut into ½-inch pieces
  1 onion, halved and sliced thin
1¼ teaspoons table salt
  4 garlic cloves, minced
  ½ teaspoon ground cumin
  ½ teaspoon pepper
  ¼ teaspoon red pepper flakes
1½ cups chicken broth
  1 (14.5-ounce) can diced tomatoes
  1 pound collard greens, stemmed and cut into 2-inch pieces
  2 (15-ounce) cans black-eyed peas, rinsed
  1 tablespoon cider vinegar
  1 teaspoon sugar

1. Cook bacon in Dutch oven over medium heat until crispy, 5 to 7 minutes. Using slotted spoon, transfer bacon to paper towel–lined plate; set aside.

2. Pour off all but 2 tablespoons fat from pot. Add onion and salt and cook over medium heat, stirring frequently, until golden brown, about 10 minutes. Stir in garlic, cumin, pepper, and pepper flakes and cook until fragrant, about 30 seconds.

3. Stir in broth and tomatoes and their juice and bring to boil. Add collard greens, cover, and reduce heat to medium-low. Simmer until greens are tender, about 15 minutes.

4. Add black-eyed peas and cook, covered, stirring occasionally, until greens are silky and completely tender, about 15 minutes. Uncover, increase heat to medium-high, and cook until liquid is reduced by one-quarter, about 5 minutes. Stir in vinegar, sugar, and reserved bacon. Serve.

PER SERVING Cal 180; **Total Fat** 9g, **Sat Fat** 3g; **Chol** 15mg; **Sodium** 940mg; **Total Carb** 17g, **Dietary Fiber** 5g, **Total Sugars** 3g; **Protein** 8g

Black-Eyed Peas with Walnuts and Pomegranate
SERVES 4 TO 6 **FAST** **VEGAN**

WHY THIS RECIPE WORKS For a black-eyed pea salad that would boast big flavor and be ultrasimple to prepare, we decided to combine the creamy beans with the crunch of walnuts and the tart burst of flavor of pomegranate seeds. We turned to some other salad additions like scallions and parsley for fresh notes. We created a punchy dressing with lemon juice and pomegranate molasses, which offered balanced acidity and tang. Finally, we incorporated dukkah, a nut and seed blend used as a seasoning across North Africa. The dukkah added a bit more textural contrast as well as a final hit of bold and earthy flavor. We prefer to use our homemade Dukkah (page 117), but you can substitute store-bought dukkah if you wish.

  3 tablespoons extra-virgin olive oil
  3 tablespoons dukkah, divided
  2 tablespoons lemon juice
  2 tablespoons pomegranate molasses
  ¼ teaspoon table salt
  ⅛ teaspoon pepper
  2 (15-ounce) cans black-eyed peas, rinsed
  ½ cup walnuts, toasted and chopped
  ½ cup pomegranate seeds
  ½ cup minced fresh parsley
  4 scallions, sliced thin

Whisk oil, 2 tablespoons dukkah, lemon juice, pomegranate molasses, salt, and pepper in large bowl until smooth. Add peas, walnuts, pomegranate seeds, parsley, and scallions and toss to combine. Season with salt and pepper to taste. Sprinkle with remaining 1 tablespoon dukkah and serve.

PER SERVING Cal 240; Total Fat 14g, Sat Fat 2g; Chol 0mg; Sodium 440mg; Total Carb 22g, Dietary Fiber 5g, Total Sugars 5g; Protein 7g

Texas Caviar
SERVES 6 MAKE-AHEAD VEGAN

WHY THIS RECIPE WORKS You won't find any roe in Texas caviar, but that doesn't make it any less delectable. This black-eyed pea salad was created in 1940 by Helen Corbitt, the "mother of modern Texas cooking," during her stint as director of food services at the Zodiac Room in Dallas. Then, her "pickled" black-eyed peas were marinated in a simple vinaigrette and tossed with onion and garlic. We wanted to brighten the flavors while keeping things fuss-free. A highly acidic dressing was key, so we used a heavy hand with red wine vinegar and balanced it with oil, adding some sugar to soften the burn and garlic for flavor. Canned black-eyed peas saved us hours of soaking and cooking dried beans without sacrificing texture. Bypassing onions altogether, we created a crunchy, savory, earthy mélange by tossing the black-eyed peas with sliced scallions, red and green bell pepper, chopped celery, and two jalapeños. Mixed together, the salad tasted good, but it was even better after sitting for an hour (and great the next day). Though it was not real caviar, we felt pretty privileged to serve up this tasty Texas picnic dish. If you prefer a spicier salad, reserve and stir in some of the jalapeño seeds. Note that the salad needs to sit for at least an hour prior to serving.

⅓ cup red wine vinegar
3 tablespoons vegetable oil
1 tablespoon sugar
2 garlic cloves, minced
1 teaspoon table salt
½ teaspoon pepper
2 (15.5-ounce) cans black-eyed peas, rinsed
6 scallions, sliced thin

Texas Caviar

1 red bell pepper, stemmed, seeded, and chopped
1 green bell pepper, stemmed, seeded, and chopped
2 jalapeño chiles, stemmed, seeded, and minced
1 celery rib, chopped fine
¼ cup chopped fresh cilantro
¼ cup chopped fresh parsley

1. Whisk vinegar, oil, sugar, garlic, salt, and pepper together in large bowl.

2. Add peas, scallions, red bell pepper, green bell pepper, jalapeños, celery, cilantro, and parsley and toss to combine. Season with salt and pepper to taste. Let sit for at least 1 hour before serving. (Caviar can be refrigerated for up to 5 days.)

PER SERVING Cal 170; Total Fat 8g, Sat Fat 0.5g; Chol 0mg; Sodium 680mg; Total Carb 19g, Dietary Fiber 5g, Total Sugars 4g; Protein 5g

French Lentils

SERVES 6 TO 8 `VEGAN`

WHY THIS RECIPE WORKS Smaller and firmer than the more common brown and green varieties, French lentils, or *lentilles du Puy*, are a favorite in the test kitchen thanks to their rich, complex flavor and tender texture. For a simple side dish that highlighted their sweet, earthy flavors, we began by slowly cooking them with carrots, onion, and celery (a classic combination called a mirepoix). Garlic and thyme added aromatic flavors that complemented the lentils. Vegetable broth lent the dish an overwhelming sweetness, but water let the flavors of the vegetables and lentils come through. We cooked the lentils until they became completely tender, and then finished the dish with a splash of olive oil along with some parsley and lemon juice. We prefer lentilles du Puy for this recipe, but it will work with any type of lentil except red or yellow (note that cooking times will vary depending on the type used).

- 2 carrots, peeled and chopped fine
- 1 onion, chopped fine
- 1 celery rib, chopped fine
- 2 tablespoons extra-virgin olive oil, divided
- ½ teaspoon table salt
- 2 garlic cloves, minced
- 1 teaspoon minced fresh thyme or ¼ teaspoon dried
- 2½ cups water
- 1 cup lentilles du Puy, picked over and rinsed
- 2 tablespoons minced fresh parsley
- 2 teaspoons lemon juice

1. Combine carrots, onion, celery, 1 tablespoon oil, and salt in large saucepan. Cover and cook over medium-low heat, stirring occasionally, until vegetables are softened, 8 to 10 minutes. Stir in garlic and thyme and cook until fragrant, about 30 seconds.

2. Stir in water and lentils and bring to simmer. Reduce heat to low, cover, and continue to simmer, stirring occasionally, until lentils are mostly tender but still slightly crunchy, 40 to 50 minutes.

3. Uncover and continue to cook, stirring occasionally, until lentils are completely tender, about 8 minutes. Stir in remaining 1 tablespoon oil, parsley, and lemon juice. Season with salt and pepper to taste, and serve.

PER SERVING Cal 230; **Total Fat** 5g, **Sat Fat** 0.5g; **Chol** 0mg; **Sodium** 200mg; **Total Carb** 35g, **Dietary Fiber** 9g, **Total Sugars** 4g; **Protein** 12g

VARIATIONS

French Lentils with Swiss Chard

Omit carrots, celery, and parsley. Separate stems and leaves from 12 ounces Swiss chard; chop stems fine and chop leaves into ½-inch pieces. Add chard stems to pot with onion and stir chard leaves into pot after uncovering in step 3.

Curried French Lentils with Golden Raisins

Add 1 teaspoon curry powder to pot with onion. Stir ½ cup golden raisins into pot after uncovering in step 3. Substitute minced fresh cilantro for parsley.

Lentils with Spinach and Garlic Chips

SERVES 6 `VEGAN`

WHY THIS RECIPE WORKS Lentils are super economical, easy to prepare, and an excellent source of protein and other good things. Their relatively neutral flavor makes them adaptable to a range of flavors. To give our lentils an equally healthy partner, we paired them with fresh spinach. We started by sautéing sliced garlic in oil until crisp; the crunchy golden garlic chips added a nice textural contrast and infused the cooking oil with garlic flavor. We then bloomed coriander and cumin in the oil until fragrant before adding our lentils, which absorbed the warm spices as they cooked. Allowing sturdy curly-leaf spinach to wilt in the pot with the lentils was simple and avoided dirtying extra dishes. For a finishing touch, we stirred in some red wine vinegar for brightness. If you can't find curly-leaf spinach, you can substitute 12 ounces of flat-leaf spinach; do not substitute baby spinach. We prefer green or brown lentils for this recipe, but it will work with any type of lentil except red or yellow (note that cooking times will vary depending on the type used).

- 2 tablespoons extra-virgin olive oil
- 4 garlic cloves, sliced thin
- 1 onion, chopped fine
- ½ teaspoon table salt
- 1 teaspoon ground coriander
- 1 teaspoon ground cumin
- 2½ cups water
- 1 cup green or brown lentils, picked over and rinsed
- 8 ounces curly-leaf spinach, stemmed and chopped
- 1 tablespoon red wine vinegar

1. Cook oil and garlic in large saucepan over medium-low heat, stirring often, until garlic turns crispy and golden but not brown, about 5 minutes. Using slotted spoon, transfer garlic to paper towel–lined plate and season lightly with salt to taste; set aside.

2. Add onion and salt to oil left in saucepan and cook over medium heat until softened and lightly browned, 5 to 7 minutes. Stir in coriander and cumin and cook until fragrant, about 30 seconds.

3. Stir in water and lentils and bring to simmer. Cover, reduce heat to low, and simmer gently, stirring occasionally, until lentils are mostly tender but still intact, 45 to 50 minutes.

4. Stir in spinach, 1 handful at a time. Cook, uncovered, stirring occasionally, until spinach is wilted and lentils are completely tender, about 8 minutes. Stir in vinegar and season with salt and pepper to taste. Sprinkle with toasted garlic and serve.

PER SERVING Cal 160; **Total Fat** 5g, **Sat Fat** 0.5g; **Chol** 0mg; **Sodium** 220mg; **Total Carb** 21g, **Dietary Fiber** 6g, **Total Sugars** 1g; **Protein** 8g

Spiced Red Lentils
SERVES 4

WHY THIS RECIPE WORKS Heavily spiced stewed lentils are common throughout India. Split red lentils give the dish a mild, slightly nutty taste, and as the lentils slowly simmer, they break down to a smooth consistency. We wanted our lentil dish to be simple yet still embody the complex flavors of Indian cuisine, so we started with the spices. We created a balanced blend of warm spices with just a subtle layer of heat. Blooming the spices in oil until they were fragrant boosted and deepened their flavors. Onion, garlic, and ginger rounded out the aromatic flavor. Getting a porridge-like consistency required cooking the lentils with just the right amount of water: We finally settled on 4 cups water to 1¼ cups lentils for a puree that was smooth but not thin. Before serving, we added cilantro for color and freshness, diced raw tomato for sweetness and acidity, and a pat of butter for richness. You cannot substitute other types of lentils for the red lentils here; they have a very different texture. Serve over rice (page 28).

 1 tablespoon vegetable oil
½ teaspoon ground coriander
½ teaspoon ground cumin
½ teaspoon ground cinnamon
½ teaspoon ground turmeric
⅛ teaspoon ground cardamom
⅛ teaspoon red pepper flakes
 1 onion, chopped fine
 4 garlic cloves, minced
1½ teaspoons grated fresh ginger
 4 cups water

Spiced Red Lentils

8½ ounces (1¼ cups) red lentils, picked over and rinsed
 1 pound plum tomatoes, cored, seeded, and chopped
½ cup minced fresh cilantro
 2 tablespoons unsalted butter
 Lemon wedges

1. Heat oil in large saucepan over medium-high heat until shimmering. Add coriander, cumin, cinnamon, turmeric, cardamom, and pepper flakes and cook until fragrant, about 10 seconds. Stir in onion and cook until softened, about 5 minutes. Stir in garlic and ginger and cook until fragrant, about 30 seconds.

2. Stir in water and lentils and bring to boil. Reduce heat to low and simmer, uncovered, until lentils are tender and resemble coarse puree, 20 to 25 minutes.

3. Stir in tomatoes, cilantro, and butter and season with salt and pepper to taste. Serve with lemon wedges.

PER SERVING Cal 340; **Total Fat** 11g, **Sat Fat** 4g; **Chol** 15mg; **Sodium** 20mg; **Total Carb** 45g, **Dietary Fiber** 11g, **Total Sugars** 7g; **Protein** 18g

SLICE UP A SALAD OR SLAW

■ FAST (30 minutes or less total time)   ■ MAKE-AHEAD   ■ VEGAN
Photos: Wedge Salad; Beet Salad with Goat Cheese and Arugula

Arugula Salad with Pear, Almonds, Goat Cheese, and Apricots

Arugula Salad with Pear, Almonds, Goat Cheese, and Apricots

SERVES 6   **FAST**

WHY THIS RECIPE WORKS We love arugula for its peppery bite and delicate texture. For a refreshing salad, we found ingredients to temper the assertiveness of the arugula while accommodating its lively flavor. Tasters liked salads with fruit and cheese, whose sweet and salty notes balanced the sharp arugula, as well as some crunchy elements. As for the dressing, a vinaigrette made with mustard was too spicy to pair with the arugula; our surprise solution was to add a spoonful of jam, which added fruity sweetness, pulling the flavors of the salad right in line. Honey can be substituted for the apricot jam.

  3 tablespoons white wine vinegar
  1 tablespoon apricot jam
  1 small shallot, minced
 ¼ teaspoon table salt
 ⅛ teaspoon pepper
 ½ cup dried apricots, chopped
  3 tablespoons extra-virgin olive oil
 ¼ small red onion, sliced thin

  8 ounces (8 cups) baby arugula
  1 ripe but firm pear, halved, cored, and sliced
     ¼ inch thick
 ⅓ cup sliced almonds, toasted
  3 ounces goat cheese, crumbled (¾ cup)

  1. Whisk vinegar, jam, shallot, salt, and pepper together in large bowl. Add apricots, cover, and microwave until steaming, about 1 minute. Whisking constantly, slowly drizzle in oil. Stir in onion and let sit until apricots are softened and vinaigrette has cooled to room temperature, about 15 minutes.

  2. Just before serving, whisk vinaigrette to re-emulsify. Add arugula and pear and gently toss to coat. Season with salt and pepper to taste. Serve, topping individual portions with almonds and goat cheese.

PER SERVING Cal 250; **Total Fat** 13g, **Sat Fat** 3.5g; **Chol** 5mg; **Sodium** 180mg; **Total Carb** 30g, **Dietary Fiber** 5g, **Total Sugars** 23g; **Protein** 6g

Bitter Greens, Carrot, and Chickpea Salad
SERVES 4

WHY THIS RECIPE WORKS Spinach is the typical choice for tossing with a warm vinaigrette, but we wanted a lightly wilted salad featuring lettuces that don't get as much attention: curly frisée, ruffled escarole, and frilly chicory. Alone or in combination, these bitter greens make a robust canvas for bold, flavorful ingredients. But drizzling a hot vinaigrette over the greens wasn't enough to wilt them. Instead, we warmed up a Dutch oven by sautéing the salad mix-ins (carrots, raisins, and almonds), let it cool, and added the greens and lemon vinaigrette off the heat. A few turns of the tongs and the greens had just the right slightly softened texture. Nutty chickpeas and salty feta added savory heft to the salad. The volume measurement of the greens may vary depending on the variety or combination used.

VINAIGRETTE

  2 tablespoons extra-virgin olive oil
  1 tablespoon grated lemon zest plus
     6 tablespoons juice (2 lemons)
  1 tablespoon Dijon mustard
  1 tablespoon minced shallot
 ½ teaspoon ground cumin
 ½ teaspoon ground coriander
 ¼ teaspoon smoked paprika
 ¼ teaspoon cayenne pepper
 ¼ teaspoon table salt
 ¼ teaspoon pepper

SALAD

1 (15-ounce) can chickpeas, rinsed

  Pinch table salt

1 tablespoon extra-virgin olive oil

3 carrots, peeled and shredded

¾ cup raisins, chopped

½ cup slivered almonds

12 ounces (10–12 cups) bitter greens, such as escarole, chicory, and/or frisée, torn into bite-size pieces

⅓ cup mint leaves, chopped

1½ ounces feta cheese, crumbled (⅓ cup)

1. FOR THE VINAIGRETTE Whisk all ingredients together in bowl until emulsified.

2. FOR THE SALAD Toss chickpeas with 1 tablespoon vinaigrette and salt in bowl; set aside. Heat oil in Dutch oven over medium heat until shimmering. Add carrots, raisins, and almonds and cook, stirring frequently, until carrots are wilted, 4 to 5 minutes. Remove pot from heat and let cool for 5 minutes.

3. Add half of remaining vinaigrette to pot, then add half of greens and toss for 1 minute to warm and wilt. Add remaining greens and mint followed by remaining vinaigrette and continue to toss until greens are evenly coated and warmed through, about 2 minutes. Season with salt and pepper to taste. Transfer greens to serving platter, top with chickpeas and feta, and serve.

PER SERVING Cal 400; **Total Fat** 21g, **Sat Fat** 4g; **Chol** 10mg; **Sodium** 630mg; **Total Carb** 45g, **Dietary Fiber** 9g, **Total Sugars** 25g; **Protein** 10g

Kale Salad with Sweet Potatoes and Pomegranate Vinaigrette
SERVES 6 TO 8

WHY THIS RECIPE WORKS We love the earthy flavor of uncooked kale for a salad, but the texture of raw kale can be a little tough. Many recipes call for tossing it with dressing and letting it tenderize in the fridge overnight. This method didn't deliver the tender leaves we were after, and the long sitting time wasn't very convenient. Luckily, we found another technique that worked better and faster: soaking. Letting the kale soak in warm water for about 10 minutes softened the leaves and washed off any grit. We simply spun the softened kale dry in a salad spinner and patted the leaves down with paper towels until they were fully dry. Caramelized roasted sweet potatoes, shredded radicchio, crunchy pecans, a sprinkling of Parmesan cheese, and a sweet pomegranate vinaigrette turned our salad into a hearty meal-completing side. Tuscan kale (also known as dinosaur or Lacinato kale) is more tender than curly-leaf and red kale. Do not use baby kale.

Kale Salad with Sweet Potatoes and Pomegranate Vinaigrette

SALAD

1½ pounds sweet potatoes, peeled, cut into ½-inch pieces

2 teaspoons extra-virgin olive oil

½ teaspoon table salt

¼ teaspoon pepper

12 ounces Tuscan kale, stemmed and sliced crosswise into ½-inch-wide strips (7 cups)

½ head radicchio (5 ounces), cored and sliced thin

⅓ cup pecans, toasted and chopped

  Shaved Parmesan cheese

VINAIGRETTE

2 tablespoons water

1½ tablespoons pomegranate molasses

1 small shallot, minced

1 tablespoon honey

1 tablespoon cider vinegar

¼ teaspoon table salt

¼ teaspoon pepper

¼ cup extra-virgin olive oil

1. FOR THE SALAD Adjust oven rack to middle position and heat oven to 400 degrees. Toss sweet potatoes with oil and season with salt and pepper. Arrange potatoes in single layer on rimmed baking sheet and roast until browned, 25 to 30 minutes, flipping potatoes halfway through roasting. Transfer to plate and let cool for 20 minutes. Meanwhile, place kale in large bowl, cover with warm water, and swish to remove grit. Let kale sit in warm water bath for 10 minutes. Remove kale from water and spin dry in salad spinner in multiple batches. Pat kale dry with paper towels if still wet.

2. FOR THE VINAIGRETTE Whisk water, pomegranate molasses, shallot, honey, vinegar, salt, and pepper together in large bowl. Whisking constantly, slowly drizzle in oil.

3. Add potatoes, kale, and radicchio to vinaigrette and gently toss to coat. Season with salt and pepper to taste. Transfer to serving platter and sprinkle with pecans and shaved Parmesan to taste. Serve.

PER SERVING Cal 190; **Total Fat** 12g, **Sat Fat** 1.5g; **Chol** 0mg; **Sodium** 270mg; **Total Carb** 20g, **Dietary Fiber** 4g, **Total Sugars** 8g; **Protein** 3g

Crisp and Creamy Kale Salad

Crisp and Creamy Kale Salad
SERVES 2 TO 4

WHY THIS RECIPE WORKS We love kale for its versatility: It's just as good as a hearty base for a salad as it is when crisped up into crunchy, salty kale chips. To get the most out of kale, we decided to combine these two treatments for a leafy salad with pleasantly crispy elements: kale on top of kale. We used our go-to soaking method to soften the kale that would make up the base of the salad. We also used almonds in two ways; we blended some into a bright herb-and-lemon dressing to provide creamy richness, and we used more sliced almonds for crunch in the salad. The result was a simple but texturally interesting salad—one that might win over any would-be kale haters out there. We prefer Tuscan kale (also known as dinosaur or Lacinato kale) to curly-leaf kale in this recipe, but both will work. Do not use baby kale.

CRISPY KALE TOPPING
3½ ounces kale, stemmed and cut into 2-inch pieces
2 tablespoons vegetable oil
4 teaspoons sesame seeds, toasted
½ teaspoon kosher salt
¼ teaspoon sugar
¼ teaspoon cayenne pepper

SALAD
5 ounces kale, stemmed and cut into 2-inch pieces
1 cup sliced almonds, toasted, divided
1½ cups fresh parsley leaves
6 tablespoons water
¼ cup vegetable oil
¼ cup grated Pecorino Romano cheese
3 tablespoons lemon juice
2 teaspoons fresh thyme leaves
½ teaspoon kosher salt
¼ teaspoon sugar

1. FOR THE CRISPY KALE TOPPING Adjust oven rack to middle position and heat oven to 275 degrees. Line rimmed baking sheet with parchment paper. Place kale in large bowl, cover with warm water, and swish to remove grit. Let kale sit in warm water bath for 10 minutes. Remove kale from water and spin dry in salad spinner in multiple batches. Pat kale dry with paper towels if still wet. Toss kale and oil in medium bowl until kale is well coated, about 30 seconds. Spread kale evenly on prepared sheet. Wipe bowl clean with paper towels. Bake kale until dry, crispy, and translucent, 30 to 40 minutes, turning leaves halfway through baking. Carefully remove kale and return it to bowl, leaving excess oil on sheet.

2. Thoroughly combine sesame seeds, salt, sugar, and cayenne in small bowl. Gently toss crispy kale and sesame seed mixture until evenly coated and kale is broken into ½- to 1-inch pieces.

3. **FOR THE SALAD** Place kale in large bowl, cover with warm water, and swish to remove grit. Let kale sit in warm water bath for 10 minutes. Remove kale from water and spin dry in salad spinner in multiple batches. Pat kale dry with paper towels if still wet. Combine kale and ¾ cup almonds in large bowl.

4. Process parsley, water, oil, Pecorino, remaining ¼ cup almonds, lemon juice, thyme, salt, and sugar in blender on high speed until smooth and creamy, about 2 minutes, scraping down sides of blender jar halfway through processing. Transfer ¾ cup dressing to bowl with kale mixture; toss until kale is well coated. Season with salt and pepper to taste. Divide salad among shallow bowls or plates, sprinkle with crispy kale topping, and drizzle with remaining dressing. Serve.

PER SERVING Cal 420; **Total Fat** 38g, **Sat Fat** 5g; **Chol** 15mg; **Sodium** 480mg; **Total Carb** 11g, **Dietary Fiber** 5g, **Total Sugars** 3g; **Protein** 12g

Mâche Salad with Cucumber and Mint

Mâche Salad with Cucumber and Mint
SERVES 6 TO 8 `FAST` `VEGAN`

WHY THIS RECIPE WORKS Mâche, also called lamb's lettuce, is a soft, tender green that grows in delicate rosettes and is beloved in French kitchens for its sweet, nutty flavor. To turn this baby lettuce into an elegant side salad, we paired the mâche with the crisp, fresh flavor of thinly sliced cucumber. Chopped mint added brightness, and crunchy pine nuts reinforced the mâche's buttery notes. We kept the dressing simple with just lemon juice, fresh parsley, fresh thyme, and minced garlic, plus capers for some briny contrast to the rest of the salad. Mâche is a very delicate green, so be sure to handle it gently and make sure it is thoroughly dry before tossing it with the vinaigrette. If you can't find mâche, you can substitute either baby spinach or mesclun.

12 ounces (12 cups) mâche
1 cucumber, sliced thin
½ cup chopped fresh mint
⅓ cup pine nuts, toasted
1 tablespoon lemon juice
1 tablespoon minced fresh parsley
1 tablespoon capers, rinsed and minced
1 teaspoon minced fresh thyme
1 garlic clove, minced
¼ teaspoon table salt
¼ teaspoon pepper
¼ cup extra-virgin olive oil

Gently toss mâche, cucumber, mint, and pine nuts together in large bowl. Whisk lemon juice, parsley, capers, thyme, garlic, salt, and pepper together in small bowl. Whisking constantly, slowly drizzle in oil. Drizzle dressing over salad and gently toss to coat. Season with salt and pepper to taste. Serve.

PER SERVING Cal 120; **Total Fat** 11g, **Sat Fat** 1.5g; **Chol** 0mg; **Sodium** 100mg; **Total Carb** 5g, **Dietary Fiber** 2g, **Total Sugars** 1g; **Protein** 2g

Bibb Lettuce, Orange, and Jícama Salad with Honey-Mustard Vinaigrette

SERVES 4 TO 6 **FAST**

WHY THIS RECIPE WORKS Oranges and lettuce greens are a classic salad combination that makes for a refreshing side dish all year long. Soft-textured, mild-tasting Bibb lettuce is a perfect canvas for citrusy flavors, so we decided to create a version with more orange flavor than usual. We discovered two tricks to get us there: First, adding orange zest intensified the orange flavor of the vinaigrette, which also included honey and mustard. Second, cutting the oranges into sections, rather than the more usual route of slicing them into rounds, ensured that we got rid of the bitter membranes and that the sweet citrus pieces were more evenly and abundantly distributed throughout the salad. To complement the soft Bibb, jícama added its juicy crunch.

2 oranges, plus 2 teaspoons zest

3 shallots, minced

2 tablespoons red wine vinegar

1 tablespoon Dijon mustard

2 teaspoons honey

½ teaspoon table salt

¼ teaspoon pepper

¼ cup extra-virgin olive oil

2 heads Bibb lettuce (1 pound), leaves separated and torn into bite-size pieces (9 cups)

8 ounces jícama, peeled and sliced into ¼-inch matchsticks

1. Cut away peel and pith from oranges. Holding fruit over bowl, use paring knife to slice between membranes to release segments; set aside.

2. Whisk shallots, vinegar, mustard, honey, salt, pepper, and orange zest together in medium bowl. Whisking constantly, slowly drizzle in oil until combined.

3. Pour all but 2 tablespoons dressing over greens in large bowl and toss to coat. Add jícama to medium bowl with remaining dressing and toss to coat. Season with salt and pepper to taste. Divide dressed greens among individual plates, then top with jícama and orange segments. Serve immediately.

PER SERVING Cal 150; **Total Fat** 10g, **Sat Fat** 1.5g; **Chol** 0mg; **Sodium** 260mg; **Total Carb** 14g, **Dietary Fiber** 4g, **Total Sugars** 8g; **Protein** 2g

Pea Green Salad with Warm Apricot-Pistachio Vinaigrette

Pea Green Salad with Warm Apricot-Pistachio Vinaigrette

SERVES 4 TO 6 **VEGAN**

WHY THIS RECIPE WORKS Pea greens (also known as pea shoots or pea tendrils) are the leafy tips of the pea plant. Both the stems and the leaves are edible, making these delicate greens a nice choice for a light salad. We complemented the grassy pea greens by adding fresh peas, endive, and a warm, fruity vinaigrette that both offset the faintly bitter quality of the pea greens and lightly wilted them. To boost our salad with sweet springtime flavor, we steamed the peas in a skillet until just tender. In the same skillet, we toasted pistachios in oil and then added the rest of the dressing, shallots, apricots, mustard, and white wine vinegar. We made sure to add the shallot mixture to the oil off the heat, as the hot oil would sizzle. The last step was simply tossing the warmed vinaigrette with the pea greens, cooked peas, and a bit of Belgian endive for crunch. You can substitute thawed frozen peas for the fresh peas; if using frozen peas, skip step 1.

- 1 pound fresh peas, shelled (1¼ cups)
- 3 tablespoons white wine vinegar
- 2 teaspoons whole-grain mustard
- ½ teaspoon sugar
- ¼ teaspoon table salt
- ½ cup dried apricots, chopped
- 1 small shallot, halved and sliced thin
- 3 tablespoons vegetable oil
- ⅓ cup shelled pistachios, chopped
- 8 ounces (8 cups) pea greens
- 2 heads Belgian endive (8 ounces), trimmed, halved lengthwise, and sliced ¼ inch thick

1. Bring peas and ¼ cup water to simmer in 10-inch skillet over medium-high heat. Cover, reduce heat to medium-low, and cook, stirring occasionally, until peas are tender, 5 to 7 minutes. Drain peas and set aside. Wipe skillet clean with paper towels.

2. Whisk vinegar, mustard, sugar, and salt together in medium bowl. Add apricots and shallot, cover, and microwave until steaming, 30 seconds to 1 minute. Stir to submerge shallot, then let cool to room temperature, about 15 minutes.

3. Heat oil in now-empty skillet over medium heat until shimmering. Add pistachios and cook, stirring frequently, until toasted and fragrant, 1 to 2 minutes. Off heat, stir in shallot mixture and let sit until heated through, about 30 seconds.

4. Gently toss pea greens, endive, and peas with warm vinaigrette in large bowl until evenly coated and wilted slightly. Season with salt and pepper to taste. Serve.

PER SERVING Cal 180; **Total Fat** 10g, **Sat Fat** 1g; **Chol** 0mg; **Sodium** 150mg; **Total Carb** 18g, **Dietary Fiber** 6g, **Total Sugars** 10g; **Protein** 5g

Chopped Salad

Chopped Salad
SERVES 4 TO 6 **FAST**

WHY THIS RECIPE WORKS We started our chopped salad with an important step: marinating the tomatoes and cucumber in a flavorful combination of extra-virgin olive oil and red wine vinegar. This drew out excess moisture from the vegetables to help prevent a soggy salad. Then we tossed the lettuce and other stir-ins with that mixture for a fresh, assertive chopped salad. You can substitute cherry tomatoes for the grape tomatoes, if desired. To cut the romaine lettuce hearts into ½-inch pieces, cut each heart in half lengthwise and then cut each half lengthwise into quarters. Finally, cut each quarter crosswise into ½-inch pieces.

- ¼ cup extra-virgin olive oil
- 3 tablespoons red wine vinegar
- 1 shallot, minced
- ¾ teaspoon table salt, divided
- ¾ teaspoon pepper, divided
- 8 ounces grape tomatoes, halved
- ½ English cucumber, cut into ½-inch pieces
- 2 romaine lettuce hearts (12 ounces), cut into ½-inch pieces
- 4 ounces feta cheese, crumbled (1 cup)
- ¼ cup fresh basil leaves, torn into 1-inch pieces

1. Whisk oil, vinegar, shallot, ½ teaspoon salt, and ½ teaspoon pepper together in large bowl. Add tomatoes and cucumber to bowl and gently toss to coat with dressing; let tomato mixture sit for 10 minutes.

2. Add lettuce, feta, basil, remaining ¼ teaspoon salt, and remaining ¼ teaspoon pepper to tomato mixture and gently toss to combine. Season with salt and pepper to taste. Serve.

PER SERVING Cal 160; **Total Fat** 14g, **Sat Fat** 4g; **Chol** 15mg; **Sodium** 470mg; **Total Carb** 6g, **Dietary Fiber** 2g, **Total Sugars** 3g; **Protein** 4g

Salad with Crispy Spiced Chickpeas

Salad with Crispy Spiced Chickpeas
SERVES 4 TO 6

WHY THIS RECIPE WORKS The contrasting flavors (sweet, smoky, sharp) and textures (soft, crunchy, creamy) in this salad really satisfy, and the star of the show is spiced chickpeas. We cooked the chickpeas in hot oil, frying them until they were toasty and crisp, and then tossed them with smoked paprika, cumin, sugar, salt, and cayenne pepper for some heat. Crushing some of the chickpeas ensured that they clung to the lettuce and didn't roll around the salad bowl. A scant teaspoon of mayonnaise whisked with a combination of sharp but fruity cider vinegar, sweet honey, and seedy whole-grain mustard gave us a vinaigrette that was creamy yet not so heavy that it weighed down delicate mesclun leaves. Charring sliced red onion under the broiler brought out its sweetness and added an extra layer of smoke to the salad. Mesclun is typically a mixture of such specialty greens as arugula, Belgian endive, and radicchio.

SALAD
- 1 teaspoon smoked paprika
- 1 teaspoon sugar
- ½ teaspoon ground cumin
- ¾ teaspoon table salt, divided
- ¼ teaspoon cayenne pepper
- ¾ cup plus 1 tablespoon vegetable oil, divided
- 1 (15-ounce) can chickpeas, rinsed and thoroughly dried
- 1 red onion, halved and sliced through root end
- 6 ounces (6 cups) mesclun

DRESSING
- 1½ tablespoons cider vinegar
- 1 tablespoon whole-grain mustard
- 2 teaspoons honey
- 1½ teaspoons grated lemon zest
- ¾ teaspoon mayonnaise
- ¼ teaspoon table salt
- ¼ cup extra-virgin olive oil

1. FOR THE SALAD Combine paprika, sugar, cumin, ½ teaspoon salt, and cayenne in large bowl; set aside. Heat ¾ cup oil in large Dutch oven over high heat until just smoking. Add chickpeas, partially cover (to prevent splattering), and cook, stirring occasionally, until deep golden brown and crispy, 10 to 12 minutes.

2. Using slotted spoon, transfer chickpeas to paper towel–lined plate and let drain briefly. Toss chickpeas in large bowl with reserved spice mixture. Let cool slightly, then crush about half of chickpeas into coarse crumbs using fork.

3. Adjust oven rack 6 inches from broiler element and heat broiler. Toss onion with remaining 1 tablespoon oil and remaining ¼ teaspoon salt and spread over aluminum foil–lined rimmed baking sheet. Broil onion, checking often, until edges are charred, 6 to 8 minutes, stirring halfway through cooking. Let onion cool slightly, then add to spiced chickpeas along with mesclun and toss to combine.

4. FOR THE DRESSING Whisk vinegar, mustard, honey, lemon zest, mayonnaise, and salt together in bowl. Whisking constantly, drizzle in oil. Drizzle dressing over salad and toss to combine. Serve.

PER SERVING Cal 260; **Total Fat** 22g, **Sat Fat** 2g; **Chol** 0mg; **Sodium** 550mg; **Total Carb** 11g, **Dietary Fiber** 2g, **Total Sugars** 4g; **Protein** 2g

Wedge Salad

SERVES 6

WHY THIS RECIPE WORKS A crisp, chilled wedge salad is a classic accompaniment to a steakhouse-style dinner: cool, crunchy iceberg lettuce, rings of red onion, a slice or two of beefsteak tomato, and creamy blue cheese dressing. A sprinkling of diced bacon is the pièce de résistance. We wanted to replicate this salad at home to pair with dinner any night of the week. For a dressing that was neither too thick nor too runny, we used lots of crumbled Stilton—there's a reason the British call it the "king of cheeses." For balanced creaminess and tang, we included both mayonnaise and sour cream. A little milk thinned it to just the right consistency to nap the iceberg wedge. To assemble the salad, we decided on shallots rather than red onions, soaked briefly in vinegar to tame their flavor (and we used that vinegar in the dressing). Cherry tomatoes were a more flavorful year-round choice than beefsteak tomatoes. And, oh yes—the bacon. This wedge salad is so good that you barely need that T-bone.

    1 large shallot, sliced thin
    ¼ cup red wine vinegar
    4 slices bacon
    4 ounces Stilton blue cheese, crumbled (1 cup), divided
    ⅓ cup mayonnaise
    ¼ cup sour cream
    3 tablespoons milk
    1 garlic clove, minced
    ¼ teaspoon table salt
    ¼ teaspoon pepper
    1 head iceberg lettuce (2 pounds), cored and cut into
       6 wedges
   12 ounces cherry tomatoes, halved

1. Combine shallot and vinegar in bowl and let sit for 20 minutes. Meanwhile, cook bacon in 10-inch nonstick skillet over medium heat until crispy, 5 to 7 minutes. Using slotted spoon, transfer bacon to paper towel–lined plate; set aside.

2. Using fork, remove shallot from vinegar and set aside. Whisk 2 tablespoons vinegar, 3 ounces Stilton, mayonnaise, sour cream, milk, garlic, salt, and pepper in bowl until combined.

3. Arrange lettuce wedges on platter, drizzle with dressing, and top with reserved shallot and tomatoes. Crumble bacon over top and sprinkle with remaining 1 ounce Stilton. Serve.

PER SERVING Cal 290; **Total Fat** 25g, **Sat Fat** 9g; **Chol** 40mg; **Sodium** 470mg; **Total Carb** 9g, **Dietary Fiber** 3g, **Total Sugars** 6g; **Protein** 9g

Radicchio Salad with Apple, Arugula, and Parmesan

Radicchio Salad with Apple, Arugula, and Parmesan

SERVES 4 **FAST**

WHY THIS RECIPE WORKS We often cook radicchio to mellow out the sharp, pleasantly bitter flavor of this vibrant red-and-white vegetable, but it's also a welcome raw addition to many dishes, including this simple textured salad. For a sweet vinaigrette that would play off the radicchio's bitterness, we whisked together honey, white wine vinegar, olive oil, and potent Dijon mustard. For added interest and a pop of green, we tossed in a few handfuls of peppery baby arugula. Parmesan cheese, thinly shaved with a vegetable peeler (a fancy-looking touch that couldn't be easier to produce) added salty depth. Finally, a generous handful of toasted and chopped almonds and some crisp sliced apple added even more crunch. Simply coring the radicchio, chopping it into 1-inch pieces, and letting it sit in the vinaigrette for about 15 minutes before adding the other ingredients softened its fibrous texture and made for more pleasant eating. The easiest way make thin Parmesan shavings is with a sharp vegetable peeler.

3 tablespoons honey
2 tablespoons white wine vinegar
1 teaspoon Dijon mustard
1 teaspoon table salt
½ teaspoon pepper
5 tablespoons extra-virgin olive oil
1 head radicchio (10 ounces), halved, cored, and cut into 1-inch pieces
1 apple, cored, halved, and sliced thin
2 ounces (2 cups) baby arugula
2 ounces Parmesan cheese, shaved
¼ cup almonds, toasted and chopped

1. Whisk honey, vinegar, mustard, salt, and pepper together in large bowl. Whisking constantly, slowly whisk in oil until combined. Fold in radicchio and let sit until slightly softened, about 15 minutes.

2. Add apple, arugula, and Parmesan to radicchio mixture and toss to combine. Season with salt and pepper to taste. Transfer to serving platter, sprinkle with almonds, and serve.

PER SERVING Cal 360; **Total Fat** 26g, **Sat Fat** 5g; **Chol** 10mg; **Sodium** 880mg; **Total Carb** 25g, **Dietary Fiber** 3g, **Total Sugars** 18g; **Protein** 9g

VARIATION
Radicchio Salad with Pear, Parsley, and Blue Cheese
Substitute balsamic vinegar for white wine vinegar, 1 ripe pear for apple, 1 cup fresh parsley leaves for baby arugula, ½ cup crumbled blue cheese for Parmesan, and chopped toasted pistachios for almonds.

Warm Spinach Salad with Feta and Pistachios FAST
SERVES 6

WHY THIS RECIPE WORKS Served wilted in a salad, spinach takes on a milder flavor, perfect for pairing with bold mix-ins. Hardy curly-leaf spinach withstands the heat best. We began by heating extra-virgin olive oil in a Dutch oven with minced shallot; we then added a strip of lemon zest and lemon juice before tossing in the spinach off the heat. The residual heat in the pot steamed the spinach until it was warm and just wilted. Peppery radishes, feta (which we'd frozen briefly to prevent it from melting), and toasted pistachios rounded out our salad. Make sure you cook the spinach just until it begins to wilt; any longer and the leaves will overcook and clump. Be sure to use curly-leaf spinach here; do not substitute flat-leaf or baby spinach.

Warm Spinach Salad with Feta and Pistachios

1½ ounces feta cheese, crumbled (⅓ cup)
3 tablespoons extra-virgin olive oil
1 (2-inch) strip lemon zest plus 1½ tablespoons juice
1 shallot, minced
2 teaspoons sugar
10 ounces curly-leaf spinach, stemmed and torn into bite-size pieces
6 radishes, trimmed and sliced thin
3 tablespoons chopped toasted pistachios

1. Place feta on plate and freeze until slightly firm, about 15 minutes.

2. Cook oil, lemon zest, shallot, and sugar in Dutch oven over medium-low heat until shallot is softened, about 5 minutes. Off heat, discard zest and stir in lemon juice. Add spinach, cover, and let steam off heat until it just begins to wilt, about 30 seconds.

3. Transfer spinach mixture and liquid left in pot to large bowl. Add radishes, pistachios, and chilled feta and toss to combine. Season with salt and pepper to taste. Serve.

PER SERVING Cal 130; **Total Fat** 10g, **Sat Fat** 2.5g; **Chol** 5mg; **Sodium** 105mg; **Total Carb** 6g, **Dietary Fiber** 2g, **Total Sugars** 3g; **Protein** 3g

Wilted Spinach Salad with Warm Bacon-Pecan Vinaigrette FAST

SERVES 4 TO 6

WHY THIS RECIPE WORKS A warm bacon vinaigrette is a classic complement to a spinach salad. Achieving perfection with this salad was a careful balancing act; we wanted the spinach leaves (here, tender baby spinach) to be just gently wilted by the warm vinaigrette dressing. Too much or too-hot dressing and the spinach ends up overwilted and lifeless. Too little or too-cool dressing and the spinach remains chewy, raw, and less pleasant to eat. We found that the trick for ensuring a properly wilted salad was to have everything at the ready—tongs and all—before we began and then toss the spinach and serve the salad the moment the vinaigrette is at the right temperature. We chose particularly sweet, fragrant, and crisp apple varieties to emphasize and offset the bacon-pecan dressing's smoky, salty, nutty richness.

- 5 tablespoons white wine vinegar
- 1 tablespoon whole-grain mustard
- 1 teaspoon sugar
- ¼ teaspoon table salt
- 1 shallot, halved through root end and sliced thin crosswise
- 6 slices bacon, cut into ½-inch pieces
- ⅓ cup pecans, chopped
- 12 ounces (12 cups) baby spinach
- 1 Fuji or Honeycrisp apple, cored, halved, and sliced thin

1. Whisk vinegar, mustard, sugar, and salt together in small bowl. Add shallot, cover tightly with plastic wrap, and microwave until steaming, 30 to 60 seconds. Stir briefly to submerge shallot. Let cool to room temperature, about 15 minutes.

2. Cook bacon and pecans in 12-inch skillet over medium heat, stirring frequently, until bacon is crispy and pecans are toasted and fragrant, 8 to 10 minutes. Off heat, stir in shallot mixture and let sit until heated through, about 30 seconds.

3. Gently toss spinach with warm vinaigrette in large bowl until evenly coated and wilted slightly. Add apple and toss to combine. Season with salt and pepper to taste. Serve.

PER SERVING Cal 200; **Total Fat** 15g; **Sat Fat** 4g; **Chol** 20mg; **Sodium** 390mg; **Total Carb** 9g, **Dietary Fiber** 3g, **Total Sugars** 5g; **Protein** 6g

Asparagus and Arugula Salad with Cannellini Beans

Asparagus and Arugula Salad with Cannellini Beans

SERVES 4 TO 6   FAST   VEGAN

WHY THIS RECIPE WORKS To incorporate asparagus into a bright, fresh salad, choosing the right cooking method was key. Steaming produced bland, mushy spears, but sautéing the asparagus over high heat delivered deep flavor and tender texture. We sliced the spears on the bias to expose as much of the inner fibers to the cooking surface as possible. With olive oil in a hot pan, we browned some red onion before adding the asparagus pieces. Just 4 minutes of cooking was enough to produce uniformly tender pieces. Creamy cannellini beans provided a subtly nutty and smooth contrast to the asparagus. While the asparagus mixture cooled we made a simple vinaigrette of balsamic vinegar, olive oil, salt, and pepper. For the greens, we knew peppery arugula would hold up well against the other bold flavors, so we dressed and plated it before tossing the asparagus in the dressing as well. Look for asparagus spears no thicker than ½ inch.

5 tablespoons extra-virgin olive oil, divided
½ red onion, sliced thin
1 pound asparagus, trimmed and cut on bias into 1-inch lengths
½ teaspoon table salt, divided
¼ teaspoon plus ⅛ teaspoon pepper, divided
1 (15-ounce) can cannellini beans, rinsed
2 tablespoons plus 2 teaspoons balsamic vinegar
6 ounces (6 cups) baby arugula

1. Heat 2 tablespoons oil in 12-inch nonstick skillet over high heat until just smoking. Add onion and cook until lightly browned, about 1 minute. Add asparagus, ¼ teaspoon salt, and ¼ teaspoon pepper and cook, stirring occasionally, until asparagus is browned and crisp-tender, about 4 minutes. Transfer to bowl, stir in beans, and let cool slightly.

2. Whisk vinegar, remaining ¼ teaspoon salt, and remaining ⅛ teaspoon pepper together in small bowl. Whisking constantly, slowly drizzle in remaining 3 tablespoons oil. Gently toss arugula with 2 tablespoons dressing until coated. Season with salt and pepper to taste. Divide arugula among plates. Toss asparagus mixture with remaining dressing, arrange over arugula, and serve.

PER SERVING Cal 170; **Total Fat** 12g, **Sat Fat** 1.5g; **Chol** 0mg; **Sodium** 330mg; **Total Carb** 13g, **Dietary Fiber** 4g, **Total Sugars** 4g; **Protein** 5g

VARIATION
Asparagus, Red Pepper, and Spinach Salad with Goat Cheese

5 tablespoons extra-virgin olive oil, divided
1 red bell pepper, stemmed, seeded, and cut into 2-inch-long matchsticks
1 pound asparagus, trimmed and cut on bias into 1-inch lengths
½ teaspoon table salt, divided
¼ teaspoon plus ⅛ teaspoon pepper, divided
1 shallot, halved and sliced thin
1 tablespoon plus 1 teaspoon sherry vinegar
1 garlic clove, minced
6 ounces (6 cups) baby spinach
2 ounces goat cheese, crumbled (½ cup)

1. Heat 1 tablespoon oil in 12-inch nonstick skillet over high heat until just smoking. Add bell pepper and cook until lightly browned, about 2 minutes. Add asparagus, ¼ teaspoon salt, and ⅛ teaspoon pepper and cook, stirring occasionally, until asparagus

is browned and almost tender, about 2 minutes. Stir in shallot and cook until softened and asparagus is crisp-tender, about 1 minute. Transfer to bowl and let cool slightly.

2. Whisk vinegar, garlic, remaining ¼ teaspoon salt, and remaining ⅛ teaspoon pepper together in small bowl. Whisking constantly, slowly drizzle in remaining ¼ cup oil. Gently toss spinach with 2 tablespoons dressing until coated. Season with salt and pepper to taste. Divide spinach among plates. Toss asparagus mixture with remaining dressing and arrange over spinach. Sprinkle with goat cheese and serve.

Asparagus Salad with Oranges, Feta, and Hazelnuts
SERVES 4 TO 6 **FAST**

WHY THIS RECIPE WORKS Instead of cooking our asparagus, we took a much different approach and made a fresh, vibrant salad with raw asparagus. Slicing the spears thin was the key to keeping them crunchy, not woody. An herby pesto dressing complemented the freshness of the asparagus. Sweet orange segments, briny feta, and toasted hazelnuts were the finishing touches. For easier slicing, look for large asparagus spears, about ½ inch thick.

PESTO DRESSING
2 cups fresh mint leaves
¼ cup fresh basil leaves
¼ cup grated Pecorino Romano cheese
1 teaspoon grated lemon zest plus 2 teaspoons juice
1 garlic clove, minced
¾ teaspoon table salt
½ cup extra-virgin olive oil

SALAD
2 pounds asparagus, trimmed
2 oranges
4 ounces feta cheese, crumbled (1 cup)
¾ cup hazelnuts, toasted, skinned, and chopped

1. **FOR THE PESTO DRESSING** Process mint, basil, Pecorino, lemon zest and juice, garlic, and salt in food processor until finely chopped, about 20 seconds, scraping down sides of bowl as needed. Transfer to large bowl. Stir in oil and season with salt and pepper to taste.

2. **FOR THE SALAD** Cut asparagus tips from stalks into ¾-inch-long pieces. Slice asparagus stalks ⅛ inch thick on extreme bias into approximate 2-inch lengths. Cut away peel and pith from

Asparagus Salad with Oranges, Feta, and Hazelnuts

oranges. Holding fruit over bowl, use paring knife to slice between membranes to release segments. Add asparagus tips and stalks, orange segments, feta, and hazelnuts to dressing and toss to combine. Season with salt and pepper to taste. Serve.

PER SERVING Cal 32; **Total Fat** 32g; **Sat Fat** 7g; **Chol** 20mg; **Sodium** 490mg; **Total Carb** 16g, **Dietary Fiber** 7g, **Total Sugars** 8g; **Protein** 10g

CUTTING CITRUS INTO SEGMENTS

1. Slice off top and bottom of citrus, then cut away peel and pith using paring knife.

2. Holding fruit over bowl, slice between membranes to release individual segments.

Avocado Salad with Tomatoes and Radishes
SERVES 6

WHY THIS RECIPE WORKS In salad, buttery avocados demand an acidic dressing to cut their richness. Using a little mayonnaise as an emulsifier allowed us to make a creamy dressing with equal parts vinegar and olive oil. To add flavor and textural contrast, we steered clear of leafy greens and relied on crunchier vegetables like fennel and radishes and sweet, juicy fruits like cherry tomatoes and mango. A garnish of salty cheese was the perfect finishing touch to complement the creamy avocado. Arranging the dressed avocado chunks underneath the other ingredients maximized visual appeal by preventing the avocado from turning the salad a murky army green. Crumbled feta cheese can be substituted for the ricotta salata. Don't skip the step of soaking the shallot—the ice water helps tame its oniony bite.

1 large shallot, sliced thin
3 tablespoons red wine vinegar
1 garlic clove, minced
½ teaspoon mayonnaise
¾ teaspoon table salt, divided
¼ teaspoon pepper
3 tablespoons extra-virgin olive oil
3 avocados, halved, pitted, and cut into ¾-inch pieces
12 ounces cherry tomatoes, quartered
3 radishes, trimmed and sliced thin
½ cup chopped fresh basil
3 ounces ricotta salata, shaved thin

1. Place shallot in 2 cups ice water and let stand for 30 minutes; drain and pat dry.

2. Whisk vinegar, garlic, mayonnaise, ¼ teaspoon salt, and pepper together in medium bowl. Whisking constantly, drizzle in oil. Gently toss avocados with 2 tablespoons dressing and remaining ½ teaspoon salt in separate bowl, then transfer to serving platter. Toss shallot, tomatoes, radishes, and basil in bowl with remaining dressing and spoon over avocados. Sprinkle with ricotta salata and serve.

PER SERVING Cal 280; **Total Fat** 25g; **Sat Fat** 5g; **Chol** 15mg; **Sodium** 550mg; **Total Carb** 13g, **Dietary Fiber** 8g, **Total Sugars** 3g; **Protein** 5g

VARIATIONS
Avocado Salad with Oranges and Fennel
Omit pepper. Substitute sherry vinegar for red wine vinegar and ½ teaspoon hot paprika for garlic in dressing. Substitute 1 fennel bulb, cored and sliced thin, for tomatoes; ⅓ cup toasted slivered almonds for radishes; ¼ cup chopped fresh parsley for basil, and

¼ cup sliced green olives for ricotta salata. Add 1 teaspoon grated orange zest to dressing in step 2. Cut away peel and pith from 3 oranges, quarter each orange, then slice crosswise into ¼-inch-thick pieces and add to shallot mixture in step 2.

Avocado Salad with Mangos and Jícama
Reduce shallot to 1 tablespoon, minced, and skip step 1. Substitute pinch cayenne for garlic and ½ teaspoon lemon zest plus 3 tablespoons lemon juice for red wine vinegar in dressing. Substitute 2 mangos, peeled, pitted, and cut into ½-inch pieces, for tomatoes; 2 cups peeled jícama, cut into 2-inch-long matchsticks, for radishes; and feta cheese for ricotta salata. Reduce basil to ¼ cup and add ¼ cup chopped fresh mint to shallot mixture in step 2.

Tarragon-Mustard Bean Salad
SERVES 4 TO 6 `MAKE-AHEAD`

WHY THIS RECIPE WORKS String bean salad is a terrific side dish for a summertime—or anytime—gathering, especially if it can be made ahead of time. We combined green beans and yellow wax beans with a potent vinaigrette while they were still warm and then refrigerated the salad until chilled. The classic pair of honey and Dijon mustard thickened the vinaigrette enough for it to coat the beans, with the bite of the mustard and touch of cayenne pepper intensifying the overall flavor and pairing nicely with the fresh tarragon. Skipping the typical step of plunging the beans into ice water after cooking worked to this salad's advantage, causing the warm beans to soak up some of the flavorful vinaigrette and resulting in a tender, not-too-crunchy texture. The salad tasted even better after a short chilling time in the refrigerator let the flavors mingle.

    3 tablespoons extra-virgin olive oil
 1½ tablespoons white wine vinegar
 1½ tablespoons Dijon mustard
    1 tablespoon lemon juice
    2 teaspoons honey
    2 teaspoons minced fresh tarragon, dill, or parsley
    ¼ teaspoon pepper
    ⅛ teaspoon cayenne pepper
    12 ounces green beans, trimmed
    12 ounces yellow wax beans, trimmed
       Table salt, for cooking beans

1. Whisk oil, vinegar, mustard, lemon juice, honey, tarragon, pepper, and cayenne together in large bowl; set aside.

2. Bring 4 quarts water to a boil in large pot. Add beans and 2 teaspoons salt and cook until beans are crisp-tender, about 5 minutes. Drain beans, add to bowl with dressing, and toss to combine. Refrigerate for at least 30 minutes or up to 3 days. Season with salt and pepper to taste. Serve cold or at room temperature.

PER SERVING Cal 110; Total Fat 7g; Sat Fat 1g; Chol 0mg; Sodium 190mg; Total Carb 10g, Dietary Fiber 3g, Total Sugars 6g; Protein 2g

Roasted Beet Salad with Blood Oranges and Almonds
SERVES 4 TO 6

WHY THIS RECIPE WORKS To make sweet, earthy beets the star of a simple yet elegant salad, we had to find the easiest way to prepare them. When wrapped in foil and roasted, the beets were juicy and tender with a concentrated sweetness. Peeling was easier when the beets were still warm. We also tossed the sliced beets with the dressing while still warm, allowing them to absorb maximum flavor. Assertive blood oranges were a welcome counterpoint to the milder beets, and salty ricotta salata, peppery arugula, and toasted almonds rounded out the dish. You can use either golden or red beets (or a mix of both) in this recipe. To ensure even cooking, use beets that are of similar size—roughly 2 to 3 inches in diameter. If your beets are larger, the cooking time will be longer. Navel oranges, tangelos, or Cara Caras can be substituted for the blood oranges, but because they are larger you'll need just one of them.

    2 pounds beets, trimmed
    4 teaspoons sherry vinegar
    ¼ teaspoon table salt
    ¼ teaspoon pepper
    2 tablespoons extra-virgin olive oil
    2 blood oranges
    2 ounces (2 cups) baby arugula
    2 ounces ricotta salata cheese, shaved
    2 tablespoons sliced almonds, toasted

1. Adjust oven rack to middle position and heat oven to 400 degrees. Wrap beets individually in aluminum foil and place in rimmed baking sheet. Roast beets until skewer inserted into center meets little resistance (you will need to unwrap beets to test them), 45 minutes to 1 hour.

2. Carefully open foil packets and let beets sit until cool enough to handle. Carefully rub off beet skins using paper towels. Slice beets into ½-inch-thick wedges, and, if large, cut in half crosswise.

3. Whisk vinegar, salt, and pepper together in large bowl. Whisking constantly, slowly drizzle in oil. Add beets, toss to coat, and let cool to room temperature, about 20 minutes.

Roasted Beet Salad with Blood Oranges and Almonds

Beet Salad with Goat Cheese and Arugula
SERVES 6

WHY THIS RECIPE WORKS Beets work particularly well in a salad with cheese, greens, and nuts. For our take on this classic combination, we changed up the presentation and how we prepared the beets and the cheese. To cut down on the cooking time, we cubed the beets and cooked them in the microwave. Instead of serving the cheese crumbled as a topping, we thinned goat cheese with lemon juice and water and spread it on a platter, creating a creamy anchor for the beets, arugula, and toasted almonds.

2 pounds beets, trimmed, peeled, and cut into ¾-inch pieces
½ teaspoon plus ⅛ teaspoon plus 2 pinches table salt, divided
4 ounces goat cheese, crumbled (1 cup)
2 tablespoons minced fresh chives, divided
½ teaspoon grated lemon zest plus 5 teaspoons juice, divided, plus extra juice for seasoning
½ teaspoon caraway seeds
¼ teaspoon pepper
5 ounces (5 cups) baby arugula
¼ cup sliced almonds, toasted, divided
1 tablespoon extra-virgin olive oil, divided

1. In largest bowl your microwave will accommodate, stir together beets, ⅓ cup water, and ½ teaspoon salt. Cover with plate and microwave until beets can be easily pierced with paring knife, 25 to 30 minutes, stirring halfway through microwaving. Drain beets in colander and let cool.

2. In medium bowl, use silicone spatula to mash together goat cheese, 1 tablespoon chives, lemon zest and 2 teaspoons juice, caraway seeds, pepper, and ⅛ teaspoon salt. Slowly stir in up to ⅓ cup water until mixture has consistency of regular yogurt. Season with salt, pepper, and extra lemon juice to taste. Spread goat cheese mixture over serving platter.

3. In large bowl, combine arugula, 2 tablespoons almonds, 2 teaspoons oil, 1 teaspoon lemon juice, and pinch salt and toss to coat. Arrange arugula mixture on top of goat cheese mixture, leaving 1-inch border of goat cheese mixture. Add beets to now-empty bowl and toss with remaining 2 teaspoons lemon juice, remaining 1 teaspoon oil, and remaining pinch salt. Place beet mixture on top of arugula mixture. Sprinkle salad with remaining 2 tablespoons almonds and remaining 1 tablespoon chives and serve.

PER SERVING Cal 180; **Total Fat** 10g, **Sat Fat** 3.5g; **Chol** 10mg; **Sodium** 500mg; **Total Carb** 17g, **Dietary Fiber** 6g, **Total Sugars** 11g; **Protein** 8g

4. Cut away peel and pith from oranges. Quarter oranges, then slice crosswise into ½-inch-thick pieces. Add oranges and arugula to bowl with beets and gently toss to coat. Season with salt and pepper to taste. Transfer to serving platter and sprinkle with ricotta salata and almonds. Serve.

PER SERVING Cal 260; **Total Fat** 12g, **Sat Fat** 3g; **Chol** 15mg; **Sodium** 570mg; **Total Carb** 31g, **Dietary Fiber** 8g, **Total Sugars** 22g; **Protein** 7g

REMOVING SKIN FROM ROASTED BEETS

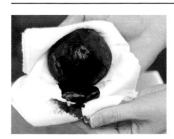

When beets are cool enough to handle, carefully rub off skins using paper towels.

Charred Beet Salad

SERVES 4 TO 6

WHY THIS RECIPE WORKS For another fresh take on the pairing of creamy, salty goat cheese and earthy, sweet beets, we charred beets to temper their sweetness and add some complementary bitterness. After roasting foil-wrapped beets, we sliced and quickly charred them on the stovetop. This step burned off some sugar without negating all of their sweetness and added the slightly bitter notes we sought. Crisp radicchio tossed with a dressing made from the beet cooking liquid complemented the beets' sweet-bitter flavor. A spread of feta and Greek yogurt replaced the traditional goat cheese component. A final flourish of pomegranate seeds provided pops of bright acidity (and fit the ruby color scheme). Be sure to scrub the beets clean before roasting, as the roasting liquid forms the basis of the dressing.

  4 ounces feta cheese, crumbled (1 cup)
  ½ cup plain Greek yogurt, divided
  1½ pounds beets, trimmed
  3 tablespoons extra-virgin olive oil
  2 tablespoons water
  2 tablespoons sherry vinegar
  1½ teaspoons table salt
  1 teaspoon pepper
  1 tablespoon vegetable oil
  4 ounces radicchio, cut into 2-inch pieces
  ½ cup pomegranate seeds
  1 tablespoon coarsely chopped fresh dill
  1 tablespoon coarsely chopped fresh tarragon

1. Adjust oven rack to middle position and heat oven to 375 degrees. Set wire rack in rimmed baking sheet. Combine feta and ¼ cup yogurt in small bowl and mash to form coarse spread; refrigerate until ready to serve.

2. Toss beets, olive oil, water, vinegar, salt, and pepper in bowl to combine. Stack two 16 by 12-inch pieces of aluminum foil on prepared rack. Arrange beets in center of foil and lift sides of foil to form bowl. Pour liquid over top and crimp foil tightly to seal.

3. Bake until beets can be easily pierced with paring knife, 1 to 1½ hours for small beets and 1½ to 2½ hours for medium to large beets. Open foil packet and set beets aside, then pour cooking liquid into large bowl (you should have about ½ cup). Whisk remaining ¼ cup yogurt into beet cooking liquid until smooth; set aside. Once beets are cool enough to handle, rub off skins with paper towels and cut into ½-inch-thick rounds.

4. Heat vegetable oil in 12-inch skillet over medium-high heat until just smoking. Arrange beets in skillet in single layer and cook until both sides are well charred, about 3 minutes per side. Transfer to cutting board and cut into 1½-inch pieces, then add to bowl with yogurt-beet dressing.

5. Add radicchio to bowl with beets and toss to combine. Season with salt and pepper to taste. Spread yogurt-feta mixture in even layer on platter. Arrange beets and radicchio over top, then sprinkle with pomegranate seeds, dill, and tarragon. Serve.

PER SERVING Cal 210; **Total Fat** 16g, **Sat Fat** 6g; **Chol** 20mg; **Sodium** 830mg; **Total Carb** 13g, **Dietary Fiber** 3g, **Total Sugars** 9g; **Protein** 6g

Beet and Carrot Noodle Salad

SERVES 6 **FAST**

WHY THIS RECIPE WORKS With their dense texture, beets make excellent vegetable "noodles." Spiralizing renders them delicate enough to eat raw. Pairing them with carrot noodles made for a visually stunning salad. The noodles' crisp-tender texture was a perfect foil for the creamy sweet-and-savory dressing. For the best noodles, use beets at least 1½ inches in diameter and carrots at least ¾ inch across at the thinnest end and 1½ inches across at the thickest end. We prefer to spiralize our own vegetables, but you can substitute store-bought spiralized raw beets and carrots. You can use smooth or chunky almond or peanut butter in this recipe.

DRESSING
  ¼ cup almond or peanut butter
  3 tablespoons tahini
  3 tablespoons lime juice (2 limes)
  1 tablespoon soy sauce
  1 tablespoon honey
  1 tablespoon grated fresh ginger
  2 garlic cloves, minced
  ½ teaspoon toasted sesame oil
  ½ cup hot water

NOODLES
  1 pound beets, trimmed and peeled
  1 pound carrots, peeled
  5 scallions, sliced thin on bias
  ¼ cup fresh cilantro leaves
  1 tablespoon sesame seeds, toasted
     Lime wedges

1. FOR THE DRESSING Whisk almond butter, tahini, lime juice, soy sauce, honey, ginger garlic, and oil in large bowl until well combined. Whisking constantly, add water, 1 tablespoon at a time, until dressing has consistency of heavy cream (you may not need all of water). Set aside.

2. FOR THE NOODLES Using spiralizer, cut beets and carrots into ⅛-inch-thick noodles; then cut beet and carrot noodles into 6-inch lengths.

3. Add beet and carrot noodles and scallions to dressing and toss well to combine. Sprinkle with cilantro and sesame seeds. Serve with lime wedges.

PER SERVING Cal 190; **Total Fat** 11g, **Sat Fat** 1.5g; **Chol** 0mg; **Sodium** 290mg; **Total Carb** 22g, **Dietary Fiber** 5g, **Total Sugars** 11g; **Protein** 6g

Broccoli Salad with Creamy Avocado Dressing
SERVES 4 TO 6   `FAST` `VEGAN`

WHY THIS RECIPE WORKS A combination of crisp broccoli, dried fruit, nuts, and creamy dressing makes for a classic picnic salad. For a fresh, modern version of this old-school favorite, we ditched the mayo-based dressing in favor of an avocado dressing. We got the best texture and flavor by quickly steaming the broccoli and then shocking it in ice water. Steaming also allowed us to cook the tougher broccoli stalks, leaving nothing to waste. By placing the chopped stalks in the boiling water and perching the florets on top to steam, we ensured that both became tender at the same time. Toasted almonds added crunch and dried cranberries provided brightness. Fresh tarragon brought everything together.

CREAMY AVOCADO DRESSING
- 1 avocado, halved, pitted, and cut into ½-inch pieces
- 2 tablespoons extra-virgin olive oil
- 1 teaspoon grated lemon zest plus 3 tablespoons juice
- 1 garlic clove, minced
- ¾ teaspoon table salt
- ¼ teaspoon pepper

BROCCOLI SALAD
- Table salt for cooking broccoli
- 1½ pounds broccoli, florets cut into 1-inch pieces, stalks peeled, halved lengthwise, and sliced ¼ inch thick
- ½ cup dried cranberries
- ½ cup sliced almonds, toasted
- 1 shallot, sliced thin
- 1 tablespoon minced fresh tarragon

Broccoli Salad with Creamy Avocado Dressing

1. FOR THE DRESSING Process avocado, oil, lemon zest and juice, garlic, salt, and pepper in food processor until smooth, about 30 seconds, scraping down sides of bowl as needed. Season with salt and pepper to taste.

2. FOR THE BROCCOLI SALAD Bring 1 cup water and ½ teaspoon salt to boil in large saucepan over high heat. Add broccoli stalks, then place florets on top of stalks so that they sit just above water. Cover and cook until broccoli is bright green and crisp-tender, about 3 minutes. Meanwhile, fill large bowl halfway with ice and water. Drain broccoli well, transfer to ice water, and let sit until just cool, about 2 minutes. Transfer broccoli to triple layer of paper towels and dry well.

2. Gently toss broccoli with dressing, cranberries, almonds, shallot, and tarragon in separate large bowl until evenly coated. Season with salt and pepper to taste. Serve.

PER SERVING Cal 210; **Total Fat** 14g, **Sat Fat** 1.5g; **Chol** 0mg; **Sodium** 320mg; **Total Carb** 22g, **Dietary Fiber** 6g, **Total Sugars** 12g; **Protein** 4g

Brussels Sprouts Salad with Pecorino and Pine Nuts

SERVES 4 TO 6

WHY THIS RECIPE WORKS To make Brussels sprouts shine in a salad, we needed to get rid of some of their vegetal rawness. Rather than cooking the sprouts, we sliced them very thin and then marinated them in a bright vinaigrette made with lemon juice and Dijon mustard. The 30-minute soak in the acidic dressing softened and seasoned the sprouts, bringing out and balancing their flavor. Toasted pine nuts and shredded Pecorino Romano added just before serving lent crunch and nutty richness.

- 2 tablespoons lemon juice
- 1 tablespoon Dijon mustard
- 1 small shallot, minced
- 1 garlic clove, minced
- ½ teaspoon table salt
- ¼ cup extra-virgin olive oil
- 1 pound Brussels sprouts, trimmed, halved, and sliced very thin
- 2 ounces Pecorino Romano cheese, shredded (⅔ cup)
- ¼ cup pine nuts, toasted

Whisk lemon juice, mustard, shallot, garlic, and salt together in large bowl. Whisking constantly, slowly drizzle in oil. Add Brussels sprouts, toss to coat, and let sit for at least 30 minutes or up to 2 hours. Stir in Pecorino and pine nuts. Season with salt and pepper to taste. Serve.

PER SERVING Cal 190; **Total Fat** 16g, **Sat Fat** 3g; **Chol** 5mg; **Sodium** 400mg; **Total Carb** 8g, **Dietary Fiber** 3g, **Total Sugars** 2g; **Protein** 6g

Moroccan-Style Carrot Salad

Moroccan-Style Carrot Salad

SERVES 4 TO 6 **FAST**

WHY THIS RECIPE WORKS This classic Moroccan salad combines grated carrots with olive oil, citrus, and warm spices like cumin and cinnamon. We first grated the carrots with a coarse grater. To complement their earthy tones, we added juicy orange segments, reserving some of the orange juice to add to the salad dressing. We balanced the sweet orange juice with a squeeze of lemon juice and small amounts of cumin, cayenne, and cinnamon. The musty aroma and slight nuttiness of the cumin nicely complemented the sweetness of the carrots. A touch of honey provided a pleasing floral note. To add color and freshness, we stirred in some minced cilantro before serving. Use the large holes of a box grater to shred the carrots.

- 2 oranges
- 1 tablespoon lemon juice
- 1 teaspoon honey
- ¾ teaspoon ground cumin
- ½ teaspoon table salt
- ⅛ teaspoon cayenne pepper
- ⅛ teaspoon ground cinnamon
- 1 pound carrots, peeled and shredded
- 3 tablespoons minced fresh cilantro
- 3 tablespoons extra-virgin olive oil

1. Cut away peel and pith from oranges. Holding fruit over bowl, use paring knife to slice between membranes to release segments. Cut segments in half crosswise and let drain in fine-mesh strainer set over large bowl, reserving juice.

2. Whisk lemon juice, honey, cumin, salt, cayenne, and cinnamon into reserved orange juice. Add drained oranges and carrots and gently toss to coat. Let sit until liquid starts to pool in bottom of bowl, 3 to 5 minutes.

3. Drain salad in fine-mesh strainer and return to now-empty bowl. Stir in cilantro and oil and season with salt and pepper to taste. Serve.

PER SERVING Cal 120; **Total Fat** 7g; **Sat Fat** 1g; **Chol** 0mg; **Sodium** 240mg; **Total Carb** 13g, **Dietary Fiber** 3g, **Total Sugars** 8g; **Protein** 1g

VARIATION

Moroccan-Style Carrot Salad with Harissa and Feta

The spiciness of store-bought harissa can vary greatly by brand.

Substitute 2 tablespoons harissa for cumin, cayenne pepper, and cinnamon. Substitute 2 tablespoons chopped fresh mint for cilantro. Stir ½ cup crumbled feta cheese into salad with mint.

Roasted Cauliflower Salad with Golden Raisins and Almonds

SERVES 4 `VEGAN`

WHY THIS RECIPE WORKS Cauliflower's delicate flavor makes it an ideal canvas for a vibrant, fresh salad. We roasted florets from one head of cauliflower until caramelized and blitzed the core in the food processor to add for a contrasting grain-like texture. A lemon vinaigrette, parsley, and mint added brightness. We stirred in a sweet and savory mix of minced shallot and golden raisins. Coriander added herbal, citrusy flavor, and toasted almonds provided crunch. Toast the sliced almonds in a dry skillet over medium heat, stirring often, until browned and fragrant, 3 to 5 minutes.

Roasted Cauliflower Salad with Golden Raisins and Almonds

1	head cauliflower (2 pounds)
5	tablespoons extra-virgin olive oil, divided
1¼	teaspoons table salt, divided
1	teaspoon pepper, divided
⅓	cup golden raisins
1	shallot, minced
1	teaspoon grated lemon zest plus 1 tablespoon juice
1	teaspoon ground coriander
1	cup fresh parsley leaves
½	cup fresh mint leaves
¼	cup sliced almonds, toasted

1. Adjust oven rack to lowest position and heat oven to 475 degrees. Trim outer leaves from cauliflower and cut stem flush with bottom of head. Flip cauliflower stem side up. Using kitchen shears, cut around stem and core to remove large florets. Chop core and set aside. Cut florets through stems into 1-inch pieces (you should have about 6 cups florets).

2. Toss florets, 1 tablespoon oil, 1 teaspoon salt, and ½ teaspoon pepper together in bowl. Transfer to rimmed baking sheet and roast until florets are tender and browned on bottoms, 12 to 15 minutes. Let cool for 15 minutes.

3. While florets are roasting, combine raisins, shallot, lemon zest and juice, coriander, remaining ¼ cup oil, remaining ¼ teaspoon salt, and remaining ½ teaspoon pepper in large bowl; set aside.

4. Transfer core to food processor and process until finely chopped, 10 to 20 seconds, scraping down sides of bowl as needed; transfer to bowl with dressing. Add parsley and mint to now-empty processor and pulse until coarsely chopped, 5 to 7 pulses, scraping down sides of bowl as needed; transfer to bowl with dressing.

5. Add florets and almonds to bowl with dressing mixture and toss to combine. Season with salt and pepper to taste. Serve.

PER SERVING Cal 310; **Total Fat** 21g, **Sat Fat** 3g; **Chol** 0mg; **Sodium** 810mg; **Total Carb** 26g, **Dietary Fiber** 7g, **Total Sugars** 15g; **Protein** 7g

VARIATIONS

Roasted Cauliflower Salad with Apricots and Hazelnuts

Substitute chopped dried apricots for golden raisins, ½ teaspoon smoked paprika for coriander, and hazelnuts, toasted, skinned, and chopped, for almonds.

Roasted Cauliflower Salad with Cranberries and Pistachios

Substitute dried cranberries for golden raisins, ground fennel for coriander, and shelled pistachios, toasted and chopped, for almonds.

Roasted Cipollini and Escarole Salad

SERVES 4 TO 6

WHY THIS RECIPE WORKS Cipollini onions, whose name means "little onions" in Italian, have more residual sugar than regular yellow or white onions; in this way, they're more similar to Vidalias. When roasted, they caramelize beautifully and develop a melt-in-your-mouth texture. We wanted a foolproof roasting method to ensure perfectly caramelized cipollini onions every time—plus a great salad to serve alongside dinner. Halving the cipollinis and roasting on the middle oven rack ensured that they cooked through until buttery and tender at the same rate as they browned and caramelized. With the goal of keeping this sweet, buttery flavor front and center, we kept this salad complementary to its northern Italian roots. Crisp and slightly bitter escarole and frisée paired well with the onions' roasted sweetness, while crunchy prosciutto and creamy blue cheese added savory richness. A tangy cracked caraway seed dressing added the final flavor balance. You can use prepeeled cipollini onions in this recipe; simply halve them through the root end and proceed with step 2.

Roasted Cipollini and Escarole Salad

1½ pounds cipollini onions
6 tablespoons extra-virgin olive oil, divided
½ teaspoon table salt, divided
⅛ teaspoon pepper
4 ounces thinly sliced prosciutto
2 tablespoons apple cider vinegar
2 teaspoons Dijon mustard
1½ teaspoons caraway seeds, toasted and cracked
1 teaspoon honey
1 head escarole (1 pound), trimmed and cut into 1-inch pieces
½ head frisée (3 ounces), trimmed and cut into 1-inch pieces
2 ounces blue cheese, crumbled (½ cup)

1. Adjust oven rack to middle position and heat oven to 400 degrees. Bring 2 quarts water to boil in large saucepan. Add onions and cook for 30 seconds. Drain in colander and run under cold water until onions are cool enough to handle, about 1 minute. Transfer onions to paper towel–lined plate and pat dry. Trim root and stem ends, then peel and discard onion skins. Halve onions through root end and transfer to bowl.

2. Add 3 tablespoons oil, ¼ teaspoon salt, and pepper to bowl with onions and toss to coat. Arrange onions cut side down on parchment paper–lined rimmed baking sheet and roast until well browned and softened, 35 to 40 minutes, rotating sheet halfway through roasting. Let cool slightly, about 10 minutes.

3. Line plate with double layer of paper towels. Lay prosciutto slices in single layer on prepared plate and microwave until rendered and beginning to crisp, 2 to 4 minutes. Set aside until cool enough to handle, then crumble into ½-inch pieces.

4. Whisk vinegar, mustard, caraway seeds, honey, and remaining ¼ teaspoon salt together in large bowl. Whisking constantly, slowly drizzle in remaining 3 tablespoons oil until combined. Add escarole, frisée, onions, and prosciutto and gently toss to combine. Season with salt and pepper to taste. Transfer to serving platter and sprinkle with blue cheese. Serve.

PER SERVING Cal 290; **Total Fat** 19g, **Sat Fat** 4.5g; **Chol** 20mg; **Sodium** 880mg; **Total Carb** 21g, **Dietary Fiber** 3g, **Total Sugars** 5g; **Protein** 10g

Shaved Celery Salad with Pomegranate-Honey Vinaigrette

SERVES 4 TO 6 **FAST**

WHY THIS RECIPE WORKS This fresh, light salad employs both celery ribs and celery root. We especially love how the combination of sweet-tart pomegranate seeds and rich, salty Pecorino Romano cheese boost the flavors and textures of the celery. Shaving the celery root thin using a vegetable peeler eliminated any need to cook the root. Chopped frisée gave the salad more substance, and toasted walnuts added another nice crunch. For the dressing, we echoed the use of pomegranate seeds by starting with pomegranate molasses, along with red wine vinegar, honey, and a shallot. Pomegranate molasses can be found in the international aisle of well-stocked grocery stores. You can substitute 1 to 2 tablespoons chopped fresh parsley for the celery leaves. Use the large holes of a box grater to shred the Pecorino Romano. A mandoline or V-slicer can also be used to shave the celery root in step 2.

- 2 tablespoons pomegranate molasses
- 1 small shallot, minced
- 1 tablespoon red wine vinegar
- 2 teaspoons honey
- ¼ teaspoon table salt
  Pinch pepper
- 2 tablespoons extra-virgin olive oil
- 14 ounces celery root, trimmed, peeled, and quartered
- 4 celery ribs, sliced thin on bias, plus ½ cup celery leaves
- 1 head frisée (6 ounces), trimmed and cut into 1-inch pieces
- 1½ ounces Pecorino Romano cheese, shredded (½ cup)
- ¼ cup pomegranate seeds, divided
- ½ cup walnuts, toasted and chopped coarse

1. Whisk pomegranate molasses, shallot, vinegar, honey, salt, and pepper together in large bowl. Whisking constantly, slowly drizzle in oil until combined.

2. Using sharp vegetable peeler, shave celery root into thin ribbons. Add celery root, celery ribs and leaves, frisée, Pecorino, and 2 tablespoons pomegranate seeds to bowl with dressing and gently toss to coat. Season with salt and pepper to taste. Transfer to platter and sprinkle with walnuts and remaining 2 tablespoons pomegranate seeds. Serve.

PER SERVING Cal 200; **Total Fat** 13g, **Sat Fat** 2.5g; **Chol** 5mg; **Sodium** 280mg; **Total Carb** 17g, **Dietary Fiber** 3g, **Total Sugars** 9g; **Protein** 5g

Fresh Corn Salad

Fresh Corn Salad

SERVES 4 TO 6 **VEGAN**

WHY THIS RECIPE WORKS A fresh corn salad is irresistible in the summer when corn is at the peak of its season. Most recipes for corn salad follow a standard method: stripping kernels off the cob, adding vegetables (usually tomatoes, onions, and/or peppers), and tossing with dressing. Instead, we found that browning the kernels lightly in a skillet for a few minutes gave even inferior, out-of-season corn a complex, nutty dimension. As for the dressing, it took equal parts oil and vinegar to create a dressing that balanced the sugary corn. Don't add the tomatoes to the toasted corn until it is cool, as otherwise the heat from the corn will partially cook them.

- 2 tomatoes, cored and cut into ½-inch pieces
- 1¼ teaspoons table salt, divided
- 2½ tablespoons extra-virgin olive oil, divided
- 5 ears corn, kernels cut from cobs (5 cups)
- 2 scallions, sliced thin
- 1½ tablespoons white wine vinegar
- ½ teaspoon pepper
- ¼ cup minced fresh parsley

1. Toss tomatoes with ½ teaspoon salt in bowl, then transfer to colander. Set colander over bowl and let drain for 30 minutes.

2. Meanwhile, heat 1 tablespoon oil in 12-inch nonstick skillet over medium-high heat until shimmering. Add corn and cook, stirring occasionally, until spotty brown, 5 to 7 minutes. Transfer to large bowl and stir in scallions, vinegar, remaining 1½ tablespoons oil, remaining ¾ teaspoon salt, and pepper; let cool to room temperature, about 20 minutes.

3. Stir in drained tomatoes and parsley. Let sit until flavors meld, about 30 minutes. Season with salt and pepper to taste. Serve.

PER SERVING Cal 140; **Total Fat** 8g, **Sat Fat** 1g; **Chol** 0mg; **Sodium** 490mg; **Total Carb** 17g, **Dietary Fiber** 2g, **Total Sugars** 5g; **Protein** 4g

VARIATIONS

Watermelon-Feta Fresh Corn Salad

Replace tomatoes with 2 cups watermelon, cut into ½-inch pieces, and 2 cucumbers, peeled, quartered lengthwise, seeded, and cut into ½-inch pieces. Stir 1 cup crumbled feta cheese into cooked and cooled corn. Replace parsley with ¼ cup minced fresh mint.

Arugula–Goat Cheese Fresh Corn Salad

Omit parsley. Replace white wine vinegar with 1½ tablespoons lemon juice. Stir in 2 cups chopped baby arugula and 1 cup crumbled goat cheese with tomatoes.

Tuscan Fresh Corn Salad

Replace white wine vinegar with 1½ tablespoons red wine vinegar. Toss 1 (15-ounce) can rinsed cannellini beans with vinaigrette and hot corn. Replace parsley with 2 tablespoons chopped fresh basil.

Mexican Corn Salad

SERVES 6 TO 8

WHY THIS RECIPE WORKS Our Mexican Corn Salad features charred kernels whose nutty, slightly bitter flavor complements corn's natural sweetness. We achieved that charring on the stove-top by cooking kernels in a small amount of oil in a covered skillet. The kernels in contact with the skillet's surface browned and charred, and the lid prevented the kernels from popping out of the hot skillet and trapped steam, which helped cook the corn. We cooked the corn in two batches to allow more kernels to make contact with the skillet and brown. After cooking the corn, we used the hot skillet to bloom chili powder and lightly cook minced garlic to temper its bite. We dressed the salad with a creamy and tangy mixture of sour cream, mayonnaise, and lime juice. Letting the corn cool before adding chopped cilantro and spicy serrano

Mexican Corn Salad

chiles preserved their bright colors and fresh flavors. If desired, substitute plain Greek yogurt for the sour cream. We like serrano chiles here, but you can substitute a jalapeño chile that has been halved lengthwise and sliced into ⅛-inch-thick half-moons. Adjust the amount of chiles to suit your taste. If cotija cheese is unavailable, substitute feta cheese.

    3 tablespoons lime juice, plus extra for seasoning
       (2 limes)
    3 tablespoons sour cream
    1 tablespoon mayonnaise
  1–2 serrano chiles, stemmed and cut into ⅛-inch-thick rings
    ¾ teaspoon table salt, divided
    2 tablespoons plus 1 teaspoon vegetable oil, divided
    6 ears corn, kernels cut from cobs (6 cups)
    2 garlic cloves, minced
    ½ teaspoon chili powder
    4 ounces cotija cheese, crumbled (1 cup)
    ¾ cup coarsely chopped fresh cilantro
    3 scallions, sliced thin

1. Combine lime juice, sour cream, mayonnaise, serrano(s), and ¼ teaspoon salt in large bowl. Set aside.

2. Heat 1 tablespoon oil in 12-inch nonstick skillet over high heat until shimmering. Add half of corn and spread into even layer. Sprinkle with ¼ teaspoon salt. Cover and cook, without stirring, until corn touching skillet is charred, about 3 minutes. Remove skillet from heat and let stand, covered, for 15 seconds, until any popping subsides. Transfer corn to bowl with sour cream mixture. Repeat with 1 tablespoon oil, remaining ¼ teaspoon salt, and remaining corn.

3. Return now-empty skillet to medium heat and add remaining 1 teaspoon oil, garlic, and chili powder. Cook, stirring constantly, until fragrant, about 30 seconds. Transfer garlic mixture to bowl with corn mixture and toss to combine. Let cool for at least 15 minutes.

4. Add cotija, cilantro, and scallions and toss to combine. Season salad with salt and up to 1 tablespoon extra lime juice to taste. Serve.

PER SERVING Cal 180; **Total Fat** 12g, **Sat Fat** 3.5g; **Chol** 15mg; **Sodium** 440mg; **Total Carb** 16g, **Dietary Fiber** 2g, **Total Sugars** 4g; **Protein** 6g

Creamy Cucumber Salad with Radishes, Lemon, and Mint

Creamy Cucumber Salad with Radishes, Lemon, and Mint

SERVES 4 TO 6

WHY THIS RECIPE WORKS Cucumbers and red onions are a great salad combo: The cucumber gives the salad some heft and juicy crunch, while the bite of red onion serves as a great foil to the cucumber's subtle flavor. In this side-dish salad recipe, we added peppery sliced radishes and brought everything together with a creamy, lemony dressing. Creamy cucumber salads can suffer from limp, flimsy slices of cucumber swimming in a diluted dressing. Here we found that laying the sliced cucumbers on a paper towel–lined baking sheet, instead of the more typical step of salting them, dried them out sufficiently while keeping them crisp. Marinating the onions in vinegar before we added them to the salad tamed their raw strength, and the thick, sour cream–based dressing resulted in a creamy—never watery—cucumber salad.

    3 cucumbers, peeled, halved lengthwise,
       seeded, and sliced thin crosswise
    ½ cup red onion, sliced thin
    3 tablespoons cider vinegar
    ½ cup sour cream
    3 tablespoons chopped fresh mint
    1 teaspoon grated lemon zest
    ½ teaspoon sugar
    ½ teaspoon table salt
    6 radishes, trimmed and sliced thin

1. Spread cucumber slices in single layer on paper towel–lined baking sheet and refrigerate for 20 minutes. Meanwhile, combine onion and vinegar in bowl and let sit for 20 minutes.

2. Whisk sour cream, mint, lemon zest, sugar, and salt together in large bowl. Add cucumbers, radishes, and onion-vinegar mixture and toss to combine. Season with salt and pepper to taste. Serve.

PER SERVING Cal 50; **Total Fat** 3.5g, **Sat Fat** 1.5g; **Chol** 10mg; **Sodium** 200mg; **Total Carb** 5g, **Dietary Fiber** 1g, **Total Sugars** 3g; **Protein** 1g

SEEDING CUCUMBERS

Peel and halve cucumber lengthwise. Run small spoon inside each cucumber half to scoop out seeds and any surrounding excess liquid.

Cucumber Salad with Olives, Oregano, and Almonds

SERVES 4 TO 6 **VEGAN**

WHY THIS RECIPE WORKS For this cucumber salad, we selected American cucumbers (our usual go-to and the kind you generally buy from the grocery store), which are crunchier than their English cousins. Draining the thinly sliced cucumbers on paper towels helped to wick away some of their moisture, and using some of the remaining liquid in the dressing gave it more fresh cucumber flavor. For the dressing, we used a base of vinegar, which we simmered to preserve its character and mellow its sharp bite. This salad is best served within 1 hour of being dressed. Slicing the cucumbers very thin allows the dressing to cling to them; aim for slices between ⅛ and ³⁄₁₆ inch thick.

> 4 cucumbers, peeled, halved lengthwise, seeded, and sliced very thin
> ⅓ cup white wine vinegar
> 1 tablespoon lemon juice
> 2 teaspoons extra-virgin olive oil
> 1½ teaspoons sugar
> 1 teaspoon table salt
> ⅛ teaspoon pepper
> ½ cup pitted kalamata olives, chopped
> ½ cup chopped fresh parsley
> 1 shallot, sliced very thin
> 1 teaspoon minced fresh oregano
> 3 tablespoons sliced almonds, toasted and chopped

1. Line baking sheet with triple layer of paper towels. Spread cucumber slices in single layer on prepared sheet; refrigerate while preparing dressing.

2. Bring vinegar to simmer in small saucepan over medium-low heat; cook until reduced to 2 tablespoons, 4 to 6 minutes. Transfer vinegar to bowl and let cool completely, about 10 minutes. Whisk in lemon juice, oil, sugar, salt, and pepper.

3. Add olives, parsley, shallot, oregano, and cucumber slices to dressing and toss to combine. Let sit for 5 minutes, then toss again, sprinkle with almonds, and serve.

PER SERVING Cal 60; **Total Fat** 4g, **Sat Fat** 0g; **Chol** 0mg; **Sodium** 430mg; **Total Carb** 5g, **Dietary Fiber** 1g, **Total Sugars** 3g; **Protein** 2g

Parsley-Cucumber Salad with Feta, Walnuts, and Pomegranate

Parsley-Cucumber Salad with Feta, Walnuts, and Pomegranate

SERVES 4 TO 6 **FAST**

WHY THIS RECIPE WORKS Sweet, crisp, nearly seedless English cucumber is just a bit less crunchy than American cucumber. Its fresh flavor and distinct texture worked perfectly with fresh parsley. A generous quantity of fresh parsley leaves served as the salad greens in this dish, which made a crisp, refreshing accompaniment to rich grilled meats or fish. The bracing vinaigrette, made from olive oil, sweet-tart pomegranate molasses, and red wine vinegar, brought layers of flavor, and a pinch of cayenne pepper lent a bit of heat. For a finishing touch and some richness, we topped the salad with thinly sliced feta cheese, chopped toasted walnuts, and juicy, jewel-like pomegranate seeds. Use flat-leaf parsley (also called Italian parsley) rather than curly parsley for this salad.

> 3 tablespoons extra-virgin olive oil
> 1 tablespoon pomegranate molasses
> 1 tablespoon red wine vinegar
> ¼ teaspoon table salt
> ⅛ teaspoon pepper
> Pinch cayenne pepper

3 cups fresh parsley leaves
1 English cucumber, halved lengthwise and sliced thin
1 cup walnuts, toasted and chopped coarse, divided
½ cup pomegranate seeds, divided
4 ounces feta cheese, sliced thin

Whisk oil, molasses, vinegar, salt, pepper, and cayenne in large bowl until fully incorporated. Add parsley and cucumber and toss to coat. Add half of walnuts and half of pomegranate seeds and toss to combine. Season with salt and pepper to taste. Transfer to platter and top with feta, remaining walnuts, and remaining pomegranate seeds. Serve.

PER SERVING Cal 280; **Total Fat** 24g, **Sat Fat** 5g; **Chol** 15mg; **Sodium** 290mg; **Total Carb** 11g, **Dietary Fiber** 3g, **Total Sugars** 6g; **Protein** 7g

Fennel Salad
SERVES 4 TO 6

WHY THIS RECIPE WORKS This salad—a mix of bright colors, lively flavors, and contrasting textures—is an edible advertisement for fennel. Since fennel is a classic Mediterranean ingredient, we aimed for an assertively flavored Mediterranean-style salad, with sweet, salty, slightly sour, and bitter flavors. For sweetness, we tossed a handful of raisins into a salad bowl, and for the salty component, we chose capers. Thinly sliced red onion contributed pungency, while Italian flat-leaf parsley added an herbal note—especially when treated more like a vegetable by tossing in whole leaves rather than mincing it. For the vinaigrette, olive oil was a given, and we liked bright, fresh lemon juice balanced with a little honey. Dijon mustard helped emulsify the vinaigrette and added bite. Letting the fennel and onion macerate with some vinaigrette seasoned the fennel nicely and softened the onion's raw bite. Just before serving, we stirred in the parsley and some toasted almonds.

3 tablespoons lemon juice
2 teaspoons Dijon mustard
2 teaspoons honey
1 teaspoon table salt
1 teaspoon pepper
¼ cup extra-virgin olive oil
2 fennel bulbs, stalks discarded, bulbs halved, cored, and sliced thin
½ red onion, halved through root end and sliced thin
½ cup golden raisins, chopped
3 tablespoons capers, rinsed and minced
½ cup fresh parsley leaves
½ cup sliced almonds, toasted

1. Whisk lemon juice, mustard, honey, salt, and pepper in large serving bowl until combined. Whisking constantly, slowly drizzle in oil until combined. Add fennel, onion, raisins, and capers and toss to coat. Cover and refrigerate for 30 minutes.

2. Stir in parsley and almonds and season with salt and pepper to taste. Serve.

PER SERVING Cal 210; **Total Fat** 13g, **Sat Fat** 1.5g; **Chol** 0mg; **Sodium** 580mg; **Total Carb** 22g, **Dietary Fiber** 5g, **Total Sugars** 15g; **Protein** 3g

Algerian-Style Fennel Salad with Oranges and Olives
SERVES 4 TO 6 FAST VEGAN

WHY THIS RECIPE WORKS: In Algeria and Tunisia, raw fennel is often used to make distinctive crisp, light salads. We liked the fennel best in this side-dish salad when it was sliced very thin for the most tender texture. Sweet, juicy oranges were an excellent flavor match for the crisp fennel. To ensure that they were evenly distributed in the salad, we cut the oranges into bite-size pieces and tossed the salad gently to keep the segments from falling apart. We added some oil-cured black olives, which are ubiquitous in the region's dishes, plus some fresh mint, lemon juice, extra-virgin olive oil, salt, and pepper. Because this dish is so simple, using high-quality ingredients is essential. Blood oranges are traditional in this dish; navel oranges, tangelos, or Cara Caras can be substituted, but since they are larger, you'll need just three of them.

¼ cup extra-virgin olive oil
2 tablespoons lemon juice
¼ teaspoon table salt
⅛ teaspoon pepper
4 blood oranges
2 fennel bulbs, stalks discarded, bulbs halved, cored, and sliced thin
½ cup pitted oil-cured black olives, sliced thin
¼ cup chopped fresh mint

1. Whisk oil, lemon juice, salt, and pepper in large serving bowl until combined; set aside.

2. Cut away peel and pith from oranges. Quarter oranges, then slice crosswise into ¼-inch-thick pieces. Add oranges, fennel, olives, and mint to bowl with dressing and gently toss to coat. Season with salt and pepper to taste. Serve.

PER SERVING Cal 160; **Total Fat** 10g, **Sat Fat** 1.5g; **Chol** 0mg; **Sodium** 180mg; **Total Carb** 17g, **Dietary Fiber** 5g, **Total Sugars** 12g; **Protein** 2g

Rhubarb, Celery, and Radish Salad with Feta and Cilantro

Rhubarb, Celery, and Radish Salad with Feta and Cilantro

SERVES 4 TO 6

WHY THIS RECIPE WORKS For a refreshing side salad with plenty of crunch that bursts with mouthwatering tart-spicy flavor, rhubarb was the perfect summer pick. Its sharp acidity, celery's herbal spiciness, and radishes' peppery element all played off each other to create a colorful salad with a uniquely bright flavor profile. Allowing the vinaigrette to sit for a while let the salt work its magic on drawing out liquid from the chopped rhubarb. The vinaigrette got even more of a flavor boost from jalapeño and lime. You can substitute ½ cup fresh parsley leaves for the celery leaves.

VINAIGRETTE

    1 rhubarb stalk, cut into ½-inch pieces
    1 jalapeño chile, stemmed, seeded, and cut into
       ½-inch pieces
    1 tablespoon grated lime zest plus 2 tablespoons juice
    1 small shallot, sliced thin
    ¼ teaspoon table salt
    ½ teaspoon pepper
    ¼ cup extra-virgin olive oil

SALAD

    2 rhubarb stalks, sliced ¼ inch thick on bias
    1 celery rib, sliced thin on bias, plus ½ cup celery leaves
    5 radishes, trimmed and cut into ¼-inch wedges
    1 teaspoon extra-virgin olive oil
    ⅛ teaspoon table salt
    ⅛ teaspoon chipotle chile powder
    2 ounces feta cheese, crumbled (½ cup)
    ½ cup fresh cilantro leaves

1. FOR THE VINAIGRETTE Pulse rhubarb, jalapeño, lime zest and juice, shallot, salt, and pepper in food processor until finely chopped, about 10 pulses. Transfer to bowl and let sit until rhubarb releases its juice, 20 to 25 minutes. Stir in oil and set aside.

2. FOR THE SALAD Toss rhubarb, celery rib, radishes, oil, salt, and chile powder together in bowl. Transfer to serving bowl and sprinkle with feta. Spoon ½ cup vinaigrette over salad and sprinkle with celery leaves and cilantro leaves. Serve, passing remaining vinaigrette separately.

PER SERVING Cal 130; **Total Fat** 12g, **Sat Fat** 3g; **Chol** 10mg; **Sodium** 220mg; **Total Carb** 4g, **Dietary Fiber** 1g, **Total Sugars** 1g; **Protein** 2g

Spaghetti Squash Salad with Tomatoes and Pecorino

SERVES 4 TO 6

WHY THIS RECIPE WORKS Spaghetti squash is a popular stand-in for real spaghetti, but we wanted to see it shine as the flavorful vegetable it is, aiming for an unexpected, fresh-tasting, salad that would highlight its grassy, nutty sweetness. We zeroed in on roasting as the best cooking method. We cut the squash in half lengthwise, removed the seeds, positioned it cut side down on a baking sheet (to maximize browning), and roasted it in a 375-degree oven. This resulted in soft, non-soggy strings of squash with a hint of caramelization. The strands were tender but firm enough to hold their shape, and the delicate but distinct nutty, squashy flavor stood out, all of which made for a fine base with which to build a salad. We tossed our cooked squash with a bright lemony vinaigrette, halved grape tomatoes, fresh basil, and Pecorino Romano cheese. We liked the results so much that we came up with two variations on this squash-centric salad.

Spaghetti Squash Salad with Chickpeas and Feta

3. Add tomatoes to bowl with squash and gently toss to coat. Transfer to serving platter and sprinkle with Pecorino, basil, shallot, and pine nuts. Drizzle with extra oil before serving.

PER SERVING Cal 210; **Total Fat** 18g, **Sat Fat** 3g; **Chol** 5mg; **Sodium** 280mg; **Total Carb** 12g, **Dietary Fiber** 3g, **Total Sugars** 5g; **Protein** 3g

VARIATIONS

Spaghetti Squash Salad with Chickpeas and Feta

Substitute 1 (15-ounce) can rinsed chickpeas for tomatoes. Substitute ½ cup crumbled feta for Pecorino. Substitute ½ cup coarsely chopped parsley for basil. Substitute 4 thinly sliced scallions for shallot. Substitute 2 tablespoons toasted and chopped pistachios for pine nuts.

Spaghetti Squash Salad with Radishes and Queso Fresco

Substitute 4 halved and thinly sliced radishes for tomatoes. Substitute ½ cup crumbled queso fresco for Pecorino. Substitute ½ cup fresh cilantro leaves for basil. Substitute ¼ cup thinly sliced red onion for shallot. Substitute 2 tablespoons pepitas for pine nuts.

---

1 (2½-pound) spaghetti squash, halved lengthwise and seeded
6 tablespoons extra-virgin olive oil, divided, plus extra for drizzling
2 teaspoons grated lemon zest plus 7 teaspoons juice
½ teaspoon table salt
½ teaspoon pepper
3 ounces grape tomatoes, halved
1 ounce Pecorino Romano cheese, grated (½ cup)
¼ cup torn fresh basil leaves
1 shallot, sliced thin
2 tablespoons pine nuts, toasted

1. Adjust oven rack to middle position and heat oven to 375 degrees. Brush cut sides of squash with 2 tablespoons oil and season with salt and pepper. Place squash cut side down on rimmed baking sheet. Roast until squash is tender when pierced with tip of paring knife, 40 to 45 minutes. Transfer squash to wire rack cut side up and let cool completely, about 1 hour.

2. Combine lemon zest and juice, remaining ¼ cup oil, salt, and pepper in large bowl. Holding squash over bowl, use fork to scrape flesh from skin into strands, discarding skin.

Simple Tomato Salad
SERVES 4 TO 6 `FAST` `VEGAN`

WHY THIS RECIPE WORKS A simple tomato salad is one of the elemental joys of summer when the tomatoes are plump and juicy. We started with the ripest tomatoes we could find, whether from the farmers' market or the grocery store. Because tomatoes are already fairly acidic, we found that a dressing made with the typical 3:1 ratio of oil to acid was too sharp here. Adjusting the amount of lemon juice to minimize the acidity perfectly balanced the salad. A minced shallot added a bit of sweetness, while toasted pine nuts added a buttery nuttiness. Torn basil leaves completed the salad with a fresh herbal note. The success of this recipe depends on using ripe, in-season tomatoes. Serve with crusty bread to sop up the dressing.

1½ pounds mixed ripe tomatoes, cored and sliced ¼ inch thick
3 tablespoons extra-virgin olive oil
1 tablespoon minced shallot
1 teaspoon lemon juice
½ teaspoon table salt
¼ teaspoon pepper
2 tablespoons pine nuts, toasted
1 tablespoon torn fresh basil leaves

Simple Tomato Salad

Marinated Tomato Salad with Arugula and Goat Cheese
SERVES 4

WHY THIS RECIPE WORKS The key to success with this salad is ridding the tomatoes of excess moisture. We salted tomato wedges, placed them on paper towels, and let them sit. The salt drew out the moisture and the towels helped wick away the liquid. The tomatoes soaked up a flavorful marinade of olive oil and red wine vinegar, flavored with arugula, basil, garlic, and pepper. Soft goat cheese was a creamy counterpoint. Let the cheese firm up in the freezer for 15 minutes before crumbling to minimize the mess.

1½ pounds tomatoes, cored and cut into
  ½-inch-thick wedges
½ teaspoon table salt
2 ounces (2 cups) baby arugula
¼ cup chopped fresh basil
2 tablespoons extra-virgin olive oil
1 tablespoon red wine vinegar
1 garlic clove, minced
½ teaspoon pepper
1 ounce goat cheese, crumbled (¼ cup)

1. Line baking sheet with triple layer of paper towels. Toss tomatoes and salt together in large bowl, then transfer to prepared sheet and let drain for 15 minutes.

2. Return tomatoes to bowl. Add arugula, basil, oil, vinegar, garlic, and pepper to bowl and toss to combine; let mixture sit for 15 minutes. Sprinkle with goat cheese and serve.

PER SERVING Cal 120; **Total Fat** 9g, **Sat Fat** 2g; **Chol** 5mg; **Sodium** 340mg; **Total Carb** 8g, **Dietary Fiber** 2g, **Total Sugars** 5g; **Protein** 3g

Arrange tomatoes on large, shallow platter. Whisk oil, shallot, lemon juice, salt, and pepper together in bowl. Spoon dressing over tomatoes. Sprinkle with pine nuts and basil. Serve immediately.

PER SERVING Cal 100; **Total Fat** 9g, **Sat Fat** 1g; **Chol** 0mg; **Sodium** 200mg; **Total Carb** 5g, **Dietary Fiber** 1g, **Total Sugars** 3g; **Protein** 1g

VARIATIONS
Simple Tomato Salad with Capers and Parsley
Omit pine nuts. Add 1 tablespoon rinsed capers, 1 rinsed and minced anchovy fillet, and ⅛ teaspoon red pepper flakes to dressing. Substitute chopped fresh parsley for basil.

Simple Tomato Salad with Pecorino Romano and Oregano
Add ½ teaspoon grated lemon zest and ⅛ teaspoon red pepper flakes to dressing. Substitute 1 ounce shaved Pecorino Romano cheese for pine nuts and 2 teaspoons chopped fresh oregano for basil.

Country-Style Greek Salad
SERVES 6 TO 8 **FAST**

WHY THIS RECIPE WORKS Most versions of Greek salad consist of iceberg lettuce, green pepper, tomato wedges, some style" salad of fresh vegetables and herbs that is popular throughout Greece. We included tomatoes, onion, and cucumbers along with fresh mint and parsley, roasted peppers, and a generous sprinkling of feta and olives. For a bright-tasting dressing, we used a combination of lemon juice and red wine vinegar and added fresh oregano, olive oil, and a small amount of garlic. Briefly marinating the cucumbers and onion in the vinaigrette both flavored the cucumbers and toned down the onion's harshness.

Country-Style Greek Salad

2. Add tomatoes, red peppers, olives, parsley, and mint to bowl with cucumber-onion mixture and toss to combine. Season with salt and pepper to taste. Transfer to serving dish and sprinkle with feta. Serve.

PER SERVING Cal 190; **Total Fat** 15g; **Sat Fat** 4g; **Chol** 15mg; **Sodium** 430mg; **Total Carb** 9g, **Dietary Fiber** 2g, **Total Sugars** 6g; **Protein** 4g

Tomato and Burrata Salad with Pangrattato and Basil
SERVES 4 TO 6

WHY THIS RECIPE WORKS Burrata is a deluxe version of fresh mozzarella in which supple cheese is bound around a filling of cream and bits of cheese. For a Caprese-inspired salad starring this decadent cheese, we combined standard and cherry tomatoes and salted them for 30 minutes. We made a bold shallot vinaigrette and topped the salad with Italian *pangrattato* (rustic garlicky bread crumbs). The success of this dish depends on using ripe, in-season tomatoes and very fresh, high-quality burrata.

1½ pounds ripe tomatoes, cored and cut into 1-inch pieces
  8 ounces ripe cherry tomatoes, halved
  ½ teaspoon plus pinch table salt, divided
  3 ounces rustic Italian bread, cut into 1-inch pieces (1 cup)
  6 tablespoons extra-virgin olive oil, divided
    Pinch pepper
  1 garlic clove, minced
  1 shallot, halved and sliced thin
1½ tablespoons white balsamic vinegar
  ½ cup chopped fresh basil
  8 ounces burrata cheese, room temperature

1. Toss tomatoes with ¼ teaspoon salt and let drain in colander for 30 minutes.

2. Pulse bread in food processor into large crumbs measuring between ⅛ and ¼ inch, about 10 pulses. Combine crumbs, 2 tablespoons oil, pinch salt, and pepper in 12-inch nonstick skillet. Cook over medium heat, stirring often, until crumbs are crisp and golden, about 10 minutes. Clear center of skillet, add garlic, and cook, mashing it into skillet, until fragrant, about 30 seconds. Stir garlic into crumbs. Transfer to plate and let cool slightly.

3. Whisk shallot, vinegar, and remaining ¼ teaspoon salt together in large bowl. Whisking constantly, slowly drizzle in remaining ¼ cup oil. Add tomatoes and basil and gently toss to combine.

---

  6 tablespoons extra-virgin olive oil
1½ tablespoons red wine vinegar
  2 teaspoons minced fresh oregano
  1 teaspoon lemon juice
  1 garlic clove, minced
  ½ teaspoon table salt
  ⅛ teaspoon pepper
  2 English cucumbers, halved lengthwise and sliced thin
  ½ red onion, sliced thin
  6 large ripe tomatoes, cored, seeded, and cut into ½-inch-thick wedges
  1 cup jarred roasted red peppers, rinsed, patted dry, and cut into ½-inch strips
  ½ cup pitted kalamata olives, quartered
  ¼ cup chopped fresh parsley
  ¼ cup chopped fresh mint
  5 ounces feta cheese, crumbled (1¼ cups)

1. Whisk oil, vinegar, oregano, lemon juice, garlic, salt, and pepper together in large bowl. Add cucumbers and onion, toss to coat, and let sit for 20 minutes.

Season with salt and pepper to taste and arrange on platter. Cut burrata into 1-inch pieces, collecting creamy liquid. Sprinkle burrata over tomatoes and drizzle with creamy liquid. Sprinkle with bread crumbs and serve immediately.

PER SERVING Cal 300; Total Fat 24g, Sat Fat 7g; Chol 25mg; Sodium 400mg; Total Carb 15g, Dietary Fiber 2g, Total Sugars 6g; Protein 10g

Cherry Tomato Salad with Basil and Fresh Mozzarella
SERVES 4 TO 6

WHY THIS RECIPE WORKS Cherry tomatoes make a delicious all-season salad. After salting them, we used a salad spinner to separate the tomato liquid from the flesh; we then reduced the liquid to a concentrate (adding shallot, olive oil, and vinegar) and reunited it with the tomatoes. Some fresh mozzarella and chopped basil filled out this great salad. If you don't have a salad spinner, wrap the bowl tightly with plastic wrap after the salted tomatoes have sat for 30 minutes and gently shake to remove seeds and excess liquid. Strain the liquid and proceed with the recipe as directed. If you have less than ½ cup of juice after spinning, proceed with the recipe using the entire amount of juice you do have and reduce it to 3 tablespoons as directed (the cooking time will be shorter).

1½ pounds cherry tomatoes, quartered
½ teaspoon sugar
¼ teaspoon table salt
8 ounces fresh mozzarella, cut into ½-inch pieces and patted dry with paper towels
1½ cups fresh basil leaves, coarsely torn
1 shallot, minced
1 tablespoon balsamic vinegar
2 tablespoons extra-virgin olive oil

1. Toss tomatoes with sugar and salt in bowl and let sit for 30 minutes. Transfer tomatoes to salad spinner and spin until seeds and excess liquid have been removed, 45 to 60 seconds, stopping to redistribute tomatoes several times during spinning. Add tomatoes, mozzarella, and basil leaves to large bowl; set aside.

2. Strain ½ cup tomato liquid through fine-mesh strainer into liquid measuring cup; discard remaining liquid. Bring tomato liquid, shallot, and vinegar to simmer in small saucepan over medium heat and cook until reduced to 3 tablespoons, 6 to 8 minutes. Transfer to small bowl and let cool to room temperature, about 5 minutes. Whisking constantly, slowly drizzle in oil. Drizzle dressing over salad and gently toss to coat. Season with salt and pepper to taste. Serve.

Cherry Tomato Salad with Basil and Fresh Mozzarella

PER SERVING Cal 180; Total Fat 13g, Sat Fat 6g; Chol 25mg; Sodium 210mg; Total Carb 7g, Dietary Fiber 2g, Total Sugars 5g; Protein 8g

VARIATIONS
Cherry Tomato Salad with Tarragon and Blue Cheese
Substitute ½ cup crumbled blue cheese for mozzarella and 1½ tablespoons chopped fresh tarragon for basil. Add ½ cup toasted and chopped pecans to bowl with drained tomatoes. Substitute cider vinegar for balsamic vinegar and add 4 teaspoons honey and 2 teaspoons Dijon mustard to saucepan with tomato liquid before cooking.

Cherry Tomato Salad with Mango and Lime-Curry Vinaigrette
Substitute 1 mango, cut into ½-inch pieces, for mozzarella and 3 tablespoons chopped fresh cilantro for basil. Add ½ cup toasted slivered almonds to bowl with drained tomatoes. Substitute 4 teaspoons lime juice for balsamic vinegar and add ¼ teaspoon curry powder to saucepan with tomato liquid before cooking.

Salad with Pickled Tomatillos, Sun-Dried Tomatoes, and Goat Cheese

SERVES 4 TO 6

WHY THIS RECIPE WORKS Most often used in Mexican dishes, tomatillos don't get enough play, in our view. To show them off in a new light, we created a salad with a different and unexpected flavor profile. To punch up the flavor of our tomatillos, we started by quick-pickling them for 30 minutes. Their crunchy skin holds up well to the pickling process and their tart flavor is enhanced by a sweet and vinegary brine. We boiled the tomatillo wedges in a simple brine of cider vinegar, sugar, water, and salt for 1 minute before transferring the mixture to a bowl. While the tomatillo pickles cooled, we built our salad. Oil-packed sun-dried tomatoes were an unexpected flavor complement, their assertively bright flavor pairing perfectly with the pickled tomatillos. Leaf lettuce made a sturdy salad base. For a zippy, punchy dressing, we used the sun-dried tomato packing oil and the tomatillo pickle brine. Creamy goat cheese balanced the acidity of the tomatillos and dressing, and toasted walnuts added a crunchy final touch.

½ cup cider vinegar

¼ cup sugar

2 tablespoons table salt, for brining tomatillos

12 ounces tomatillos, husks and stems removed, rinsed well and dried, and cut into eighths

⅓ cup oil-packed sun-dried tomatoes, patted dry and sliced thin, plus 2 tablespoons packing oil

¼ cup chopped fresh basil

1 garlic clove, minced

¼ teaspoon red pepper flakes

¼ teaspoon table salt

1 head red or green leaf lettuce (8 ounces), torn into bite-size pieces

2 ounces goat cheese, crumbled (½ cup)

¼ cup walnuts, toasted and chopped

1. Bring vinegar, sugar, 2 tablespoons water, and 2 teaspoons salt to boil in medium saucepan over medium-high heat. Add tomatillos and boil for 1 minute. Transfer mixture to bowl and let cool to room temperature, about 30 minutes. Drain tomatillos, reserving 2 tablespoons brine.

2. Whisk reserved brine, sun-dried tomato oil, basil, garlic, pepper flakes, and salt together in large serving bowl. Add pickled tomatillos, red leaf lettuce, and sun-dried tomatoes and toss to combine. Season with salt and pepper to taste. Sprinkle with goat cheese and walnuts. Serve.

PER SERVING Cal 100; **Total Fat** 7g, **Sat Fat** 2g; **Chol** 5mg; **Sodium** 260mg; **Total Carb** 7g, **Dietary Fiber** 2g, **Total Sugars** 3g; **Protein** 4g

Salad with Pickled Tomatillos, Sun-Dried Tomatoes, and Goat Cheese

Cape Gooseberry Salad with Ginger-Lime Dressing

SERVES 4 FAST

WHY THIS RECIPE WORKS Cape gooseberries, also known as goldenberries, are a close relative to tomatillos. They are small, smooth fruits with a mildly tart flavor, and they look a bit like yellow cherry tomatoes when they're out of their husks. For a salad featuring these summer gems, we balanced the gooseberries with a bold dressing and creamy, tangy goat cheese. The simple vinaigrette, made with lime juice, fresh ginger, Dijon mustard, and cayenne pepper, added bright freshness without overpowering the mild flavor of the gooseberries. Simply whisking the dressing together in the salad bowl before tossing in the remaining ingredients made the salad easy to prepare. Bibb lettuce added bulk and a delicate buttery bite to accompany the gooseberries. Mint offered a refreshing twist to the vinaigrette and complemented the lime juice and ginger. The addition of goat cheese made for a nice, creamy counterpoint to the zesty dressing and sweet gooseberries, and a final sprinkle of pistachios added a crunchy bite. Adjust the amount of lime juice depending on the sweetness level of your Cape gooseberries.

2–3 teaspoons lime juice
1 teaspoon grated fresh ginger
½ teaspoon Dijon mustard
¼ teaspoon table salt
Pinch cayenne pepper
¼ cup extra-virgin olive oil
1 head Bibb lettuce (8 ounces), leaves separated and torn into 2-inch pieces
8 ounces Cape gooseberries, husks and stems removed, rinsed well and dried, halved
¼ cup chopped fresh mint
1½ ounces goat cheese, crumbled (⅓ cup)
2 tablespoons chopped toasted pistachios

Whisk lime juice, ginger, mustard, salt, and cayenne together in large bowl. Whisking constantly, slowly drizzle in oil until well combined. Add lettuce, gooseberries, and mint and gently toss to coat. Season with salt and pepper to taste. Transfer to platter and sprinkle with goat cheese and pistachios. Serve.

PER SERVING Cal 220; **Total Fat** 19g, **Sat Fat** 4g; **Chol** 5mg; **Sodium** 210mg; **Total Carb** 9g, **Dietary Fiber** 1g, **Total Sugars** 1g; **Protein** 5g

Zucchini Noodle Salad with Tahini-Ginger Dressing

Zucchini Noodle Salad with Tahini-Ginger Dressing
SERVES 4

WHY THIS RECIPE WORKS Zucchini noodles are now really popular. The squash is easy to work with and produces long, satisfying noodles with a pleasant, neutral flavor. We wanted to create an Asian-inspired noodle salad. Leaving the noodles raw gave us a texture closer to that of real noodles. We added red bell pepper, shredded carrot, and sautéed broccoli and based our dressing on tahini, a nutty, buttery paste made from sesame seeds. Soy sauce, ginger, rice vinegar, and garlic rounded out the dressing. If possible, use smaller, in-season zucchini, which have thinner skins and fewer seeds. We prefer to spiralize our own zucchini, but you can use store-bought zucchini noodles. You'll need 2½ pounds of noodles.

½ cup tahini
5 tablespoons soy sauce
2 tablespoons rice vinegar
4 teaspoons grated fresh ginger
1 tablespoon honey
2 teaspoons hot sauce
1 garlic clove, minced
½ teaspoon table salt
2 tablespoons toasted sesame oil

12 ounces broccoli florets, cut into ½-inch pieces
3 pounds zucchini, trimmed
1 red bell pepper, stemmed, seeded, and cut into ¼-inch-wide strips
1 carrot, peeled and shredded
4 scallions, sliced thin on bias
1 tablespoon sesame seeds, toasted

1. Process tahini, soy sauce, vinegar, ginger, honey, hot sauce, garlic, and salt in blender until smooth, about 30 seconds. Transfer to large serving bowl.

2. Heat oil in 12-inch nonstick skillet over medium-high heat until shimmering. Add broccoli and cook until softened and spotty brown, about 5 minutes. Transfer to plate and let cool slightly.

3. Using spiralizer, cut zucchini into ⅛-inch-thick noodles, cutting noodles into 12-inch lengths with kitchen shears as you spiralize (every 4 or 5 revolutions). Add zucchini, bell pepper, carrot, scallions, and broccoli to bowl with dressing and toss to combine. Sprinkle with sesame seeds. Serve.

PER SERVING Cal 380; **Total Fat** 26g, **Sat Fat** 3.5g; **Chol** 0mg; **Sodium** 1610mg; **Total Carb** 31g, **Dietary Fiber** 8g, **Total Sugars** 15g; **Protein** 15g

Avocado-Grapefruit Salad

SERVES 4 TO 6 **FAST** **VEGAN**

WHY THIS RECIPE WORKS Avocado's creaminess combined with grapefruit's bright acidity makes for a complex, fresh-flavored salad. Layering the components instead of tossing them together elevated this salad by highlighting the ingredients' natural beauty and unique flavors. The sweet and tangy punch of grapefruit complemented the buttery, rich avocado. We dressed the salad with a simple vinaigrette and sprinkled it with a healthy handful of fresh herbs. A ripe avocado will yield slightly to a gentle squeeze when held in the palm of your hand. To ripen your avocados evenly, if you have plenty of time, place them in the refrigerator. Though it will take longer, the chilling slows down the production of ethylene gas (the gas that triggers ripening in many fruits and vegetables) and, therefore, the ripening process, giving the gas time to distribute evenly throughout the fruit. Be sure to store avocados near the front of the refrigerator, on the middle to bottom shelves, where the temperature is more moderate.

Avocado-Grapefruit Salad

- 3 red grapefruits
- 2 ripe avocados, halved, pitted, and sliced ¼ inch thick
- ¼ cup fresh mint leaves, torn
- ¼ cup fresh cilantro leaves
- ¼ cup blanched hazelnuts, toasted and chopped
- 3 tablespoons extra-virgin olive oil
- 1 tablespoon minced shallot
- 1 teaspoon white wine vinegar
- 1 teaspoon Dijon mustard
- 1 teaspoon sugar
- ½ teaspoon table salt

1. Cut away peel and pith from grapefruits. Holding fruit over bowl, use paring knife to slice between membranes to release segments. Reserve 2 tablespoons grapefruit juice.

2. Arrange avocado slices in single layer on large platter. Distribute grapefruit evenly over top. Sprinkle mint, cilantro, and hazelnuts over top.

3. Whisk oil, shallot, vinegar, mustard, sugar, salt, and reserved grapefruit juice together in bowl. Drizzle dressing over salad. Serve immediately.

PER SERVING Cal 270; **Total Fat** 20g, **Sat Fat** 2.5g; **Chol** 0mg; **Sodium** 220mg; **Total Carb** 24g, **Dietary Fiber** 11g, **Total Sugars** 11g; **Protein** 3g

Escarole and Orange Salad with Green Olive Vinaigrette

SERVES 4 TO 6 **FAST** **VEGAN**

WHY THIS RECIPE WORKS This escarole salad especially brightens up a winter table, but it's delicious anytime. Citrus fruits have a natural affinity for olive oil, salt, and pepper, and we combined oranges treated this way with chicory for harmonious flavor. Green olives added a briny, meaty element. To underscore the citrusy flavor, we used orange zest to boost the vinaigrette, and we cut the oranges into sections instead of larger rounds, so they were more evenly and abundantly distributed throughout the salad. That said, when arranging the orange segments on the escarole, leave behind any juice that is released; it will dilute the dressing.

- ½ cup chopped brine-cured green olives
- ⅓ cup extra-virgin olive oil
- 3 shallots, minced
- 2 tablespoons sherry vinegar
- 1 garlic clove, minced
- 2 oranges plus 1 teaspoon zest
- 1 head escarole (1 pound), trimmed and chopped
- ½ cup slivered almonds, toasted

1. Whisk olives, oil, shallots, vinegar, garlic, and orange zest in large bowl until combined. Add escarole and toss to coat. Season with salt and pepper to taste.

2. Cut away peel and pith from oranges. Holding knife over separate bowl, use paring knife to slice between membranes to release segments. Divide dressed greens among individual serving plates, top with orange segments, and sprinkle with almonds. Serve.

PER SERVING Cal 220; **Total Fat** 19g, **Sat Fat** 2g; **Chol** 0mg; **Sodium** 180mg; **Total Carb** 13g, **Dietary Fiber** 5g, **Total Sugars** 6g; **Protein** 4g

Orange-Jícama Salad with Sweet and Spicy Peppers
SERVES 8 `VEGAN`

WHY THIS RECIPE WORKS For a bold orange-based salad, we began by setting orange wedges in a strainer over a bowl to drain them of excess moisture. For flavorful dressing assertive enough to stand up to the sweet oranges, we used lime juice and olive oil and flavored the mixture with cumin and a scant amount of Dijon mustard. Jícama and red bell pepper added crunch and volume, while jalapeños added a welcome hit of heat. Cilantro and scallion greens added freshness and color. Fresh parsley can be substituted for the cilantro, if desired. Toast the cumin in a dry skillet over medium heat until fragrant (about 30 seconds) and then remove the pan from the heat so the cumin won't scorch.

- 6 oranges
- 6 tablespoons lime juice (3 limes)
- 1 teaspoon ground cumin, toasted
- ½ teaspoon Dijon mustard
- ¾ teaspoon table salt, divided
- ½ cup vegetable oil
- 2 pounds jícama, peeled and cut into 2-inch-long matchsticks
- 2 red bell peppers, stemmed, seeded, and cut into ⅛-inch-wide strips
- 4 jalapeño chiles, stemmed, seeded, quartered lengthwise, and quarters cut crosswise into ⅛-inch-thick slices
- 1 cup chopped fresh cilantro
- 6 scallions, green parts only, sliced thin on bias

1. Cut away peel and pith from oranges. Halve oranges from end to end. Cut each half lengthwise into 3 wedges, then cut crosswise into ¼-inch pieces. Place orange pieces in fine-mesh strainer set over bowl; let drain to remove excess juice.

2. Whisk lime juice, cumin, mustard, and ½ teaspoon salt together in large bowl. Whisking constantly, gradually add oil.

3. Toss jícama and bell peppers with remaining ¼ teaspoon salt in large bowl until combined. Add jícama mixture, jalapeños, cilantro, scallions, and oranges to bowl with dressing and toss well to combine. Divide salad among individual plates, drizzle with any remaining dressing in bowl, and serve immediately.

PER SERVING Cal 260; **Total Fat** 14g, **Sat Fat** 2g; **Chol** 0mg; **Sodium** 250mg; **Total Carb** 32g, **Dietary Fiber** 16g, **Total Sugars** 8g; **Protein** 3g

VARIATION
Orange, Avocado, and Watercress Salad with Ginger-Lime Vinaigrette
Be sure to use a ripe but firm avocado here. An overly ripe avocado will disintegrate in the salad.

- 6 oranges
- 2 tablespoons lime juice
- 2 tablespoons minced fresh mint
- 2 teaspoons grated fresh ginger
- ½ teaspoon Dijon mustard
- ¼ teaspoon table salt
- ⅛ teaspoon cayenne pepper
- 6 tablespoons vegetable oil
- ½ small red onion, sliced very thin
- 2 avocados
- 5 ounces (5 cups) watercress, torn into 2-inch pieces

1. Cut away peel and pith from oranges. Halve oranges from end to end. Cut each half lengthwise into 3 wedges, then cut crosswise into ¼-inch pieces. Place orange pieces in fine-mesh strainer set over bowl; let drain to remove excess juice.

2. Whisk lime juice, mint, ginger, mustard, salt, and cayenne together in large bowl. Whisking constantly, gradually add oil. Add onion and toss to coat; set aside.

3. Halve and pit avocados; cut each half lengthwise to form quarters. Using paring knife, slice flesh of each quarter (do not cut through skin) lengthwise into fifths. Using soupspoon, carefully scoop out flesh and fan slices from each quarter onto individual plates; season avocado lightly with salt.

4. Add oranges to bowl with dressing and toss to coat. Add watercress and gently toss to coat. Divide watercress mixture among individual plates, mounding it in center and arranging orange and onion pieces on top. Drizzle any remaining dressing in bowl over salads and serve immediately.

Peach and Tomato Salad

1. Whisk oil, lemon juice, salt, and pepper together in large bowl. Add peaches and gently toss to coat.

2. Shingle peaches and mozzarella on serving platter. Drizzle any remaining dressing from bowl over top. Sprinkle with basil. Season with salt and pepper to taste. Serve.

PER SERVING Cal 260; **Total Fat** 20g, **Sat Fat** 9g; **Chol** 40mg; **Sodium** 500mg; **Total Carb** 10g, **Dietary Fiber** 2g, **Total Sugars** 8g; **Protein** 14g

Peach and Tomato Salad

SERVES 4 TO 6 VEGAN

WHY THIS RECIPE WORKS At the height of summer, we like to take advantage of beautiful in-season fruits and vegetables. We combined peaches and tomatoes, being sure to choose ripe, sweet, in-season produce. Salting and draining the tomatoes helped concentrate the flavors by removing excess liquid that waters down the salad. We balanced the naturally sweet fruit with acidic cider vinegar, lemon juice, and lemon zest in the dressing. Thinly sliced shallot kept the salad on the savory side, and torn mint leaves added a fresh herbal note. Perfectly ripe peaches and tomatoes are essential to this recipe.

  1 pound ripe tomatoes, cored, cut into ½-inch-thick wedges, and wedges halved crosswise
  1 teaspoon table salt, divided
  3 tablespoons extra-virgin olive oil, plus extra for drizzling
  2 tablespoons cider vinegar
  ½ teaspoon grated lemon zest plus 1 tablespoon juice
  ½ teaspoon pepper
  1 pound ripe peaches, halved, pitted, cut into ½-inch-thick wedges, and wedges halved crosswise
  1 shallot, sliced thin
  ⅓ cup fresh mint leaves, torn

1. Combine tomatoes and ½ teaspoon salt in bowl and toss to coat; transfer to colander and let drain in sink for 30 minutes.

2. Whisk oil, vinegar, lemon zest and juice, pepper, and remaining ½ teaspoon salt together in large bowl. Add peaches, shallot, and drained tomatoes to dressing and gently toss to coat. Season with salt and pepper to taste. Transfer to platter and sprinkle with mint. Drizzle with extra oil. Serve.

PER SERVING Cal 110; **Total Fat** 7g, **Sat Fat** 1g; **Chol** 0mg; **Sodium** 390mg; **Total Carb** 11g, **Dietary Fiber** 2g, **Total Sugars** 9g; **Protein** 2g

Peach Caprese Salad

SERVES 6 FAST

WHY THIS RECIPE WORKS Caprese salad is traditionally made with slices of tomatoes and mozzarella adorned with a simple dressing of extra-virgin olive oil and balsamic vinegar. We wanted to preserve the simplicity of this summer side-dish salad while swapping in another juicy gem: ripe, fresh peaches. Fresh lemon juice in the dressing enhanced and complemented the sweetness of the peaches. Tossing the peach slices with the lemon-and-oil vinaigrette before assembling the salad ensured that it was throughly seasoned and dressed. Be sure to use ripe peaches. We like using 4-ounce balls of fresh mozzarella in this recipe.

  3 tablespoons extra-virgin olive oil
1½ tablespoons lemon juice
  ¼ teaspoon table salt
  ⅛ teaspoon pepper
  1 pound ripe peaches, quartered and pitted, each quarter cut into 4 slices
 12 ounces fresh mozzarella cheese, halved and sliced ¼ inch thick
  6 large fresh basil leaves, torn into small pieces

Purslane and Watermelon Salad

4 cups 1-inch watermelon pieces

2 teaspoons sugar

2 tablespoons extra-virgin olive oil, plus extra for drizzling

1 tablespoon cider vinegar

½ teaspoon grated lemon zest plus 1 tablespoon juice

½ teaspoon table salt

¼ teaspoon pepper

6 ounces purslane, trimmed and torn into 1½-inch pieces (6 cups)

¼ cup fresh basil leaves, torn

1 shallot, sliced thin

6 ounces fresh mozzarella cheese, torn into 1-inch pieces

1. Toss watermelon with sugar in colander set over bowl; set aside for 30 minutes.

2. Whisk oil, vinegar, lemon zest and juice, salt, and pepper together in large bowl. Add purslane, basil, shallot, and drained watermelon and gently toss to combine. Transfer to serving platter and scatter mozzarella over top. Drizzle with extra oil and season with salt and pepper to taste. Serve.

PER SERVING Cal 170; **Total Fat** 12g, **Sat Fat** 4.5g; **Chol** 20mg; **Sodium** 220mg; **Total Carb** 11g, **Dietary Fiber** 1g, **Total Sugars** 8g; **Protein** 6g

Purslane and Watermelon Salad
SERVES 4 TO 6

WHY THIS RECIPE WORKS You have probably seen purslane growing all around—in open fields, in sidewalk cracks, maybe even in your backyard—without realizing that this common foraged green is not only edible but also delicious. Its crisp, juicy stems and leaves and slightly tart, tangy flavor make it a special ingredient perfect for highlighting in a fresh salad. Since purslane is available only in the summer, we created a salad that celebrates a pairing of two fresh, summery ingredients. To start, we cubed watermelon into 1-inch hunks, tossed them with sugar, and let them drain of any excess liquid. This ensured that we wouldn't have a soupy mess on our hands. To gently balance the melon's sweetness and the purslane's tangy bite, we added thinly sliced shallot for delicate onion flavor. Tearing the purslane into 1½-inch pieces ensured that every bite would have purslane flavor. Fresh basil lent brightness, torn bits of fresh mozzarella added creamy substance, and a simple vinaigrette of olive oil, cider vinegar, and lemon brought everything together. This salad benefits from a liberal sprinkling of salt and pepper, so don't be shy when seasoning the mozzarella.

Watermelon-Tomato Salad
SERVES 4

WHY THIS RECIPE WORKS This salad screams summer, but to ensure that the fruity flavors didn't get drowned out, we had to devise a way to tame the juiciness of both fruits before combining them in a dressed salad. To do this, we tossed the cubes of watermelon with sugar and let them drain. We tossed the cherry tomatoes with a little salt and set them aside while the watermelon drained before tossing both together. Shallot added a subtle sharpness and basil introduced fresh, bright notes. Finally, we rounded out the salad with creamy fresh mozzarella and dressed it with a simple vinaigrette.

4 cups 1-inch seedless watermelon cubes

2 teaspoons sugar

12 ounces yellow cherry tomatoes, halved

¾ teaspoon table salt, divided

½ teaspoon pepper, divided

2 tablespoons extra-virgin olive oil, plus extra for drizzling

Watermelon-Tomato Salad

Cantaloupe, Plum, and Cherry Fruit Salad with Mint and Vanilla
SERVES 4 TO 6 **VEGAN**

WHY THIS RECIPE WORKS To create a fruit salad recipe with great fruit flavor, we had to rewrite a few old-school rules. We found it hard to judge the proper amount of sugar when it was added directly to the salad, so we macerated each fruit in just the amount needed to release its natural juices; we balanced the sweetness with fresh lime juice. But first, we mashed the sugar with herbs and zests (in bartending circles, this process is called muddling) to ensure even flavor distribution in our ideal fruit salad recipe. Blueberries can be substituted for cherries. Because riper fruits require more acid to balance their sweetness, the lime juice should be added to taste. Start with 1 tablespoon, then add 1 teaspoon at a time as necessary.

    4 teaspoons sugar
1–2 tablespoons minced fresh mint
    ¼ teaspoon vanilla extract
    3 cups ½-inch cantaloupe pieces
    2 plums, halved, pitted, and cut into ½-inch pieces
    8 ounces fresh sweet cherries, pitted and halved
1–2 tablespoons lime juice

Combine sugar and mint to taste in large bowl. Using silicone spatula, press mixture into side of bowl until sugar becomes damp, about 30 seconds; add vanilla. Gently toss cantaloupe, plums, and cherries with sugar mixture until combined. Let sit at room temperature, stirring occasionally, until fruit releases its juices, 15 to 30 minutes. Stir in lime juice to taste, and serve.

PER SERVING Cal 70; **Total Fat** 0g; **Sat Fat** 0g; **Chol** 0mg; **Sodium** 15mg; **Total Carb** 18g, **Dietary Fiber** 2g, **Total Sugars** 16g; **Protein** 1g

VARIATIONS
Honeydew, Mango, and Raspberry Fruit Salad with Lime and Ginger
SERVES 4

    4 teaspoons sugar
    2 teaspoons grated lime zest plus 1–2 tablespoons juice
       Pinch cayenne pepper (optional)
    3 cups ½-inch honeydew melon pieces
    1 mango, peeled, pitted, and cut into ½-inch pieces
1–2 teaspoons grated fresh ginger
    5 ounces (1 cup) raspberries

    1 tablespoon cider vinegar
    ½ teaspoon grated lemon zest plus 1 tablespoon juice
    1 shallot, sliced thin
    ¼ cup fresh basil leaves, torn
    6 ounces fresh mozzarella cheese, torn into 1-inch pieces

1. Gently combine watermelon and sugar in large bowl. Transfer watermelon to colander and set colander in now-empty bowl. Cover colander with plastic wrap and refrigerate for 30 minutes.

2. Toss tomatoes, ¼ teaspoon salt, and ¼ teaspoon pepper together in small bowl; set aside.

3. Whisk oil, vinegar, lemon zest and juice, remaining ½ teaspoon salt, and remaining ¼ teaspoon pepper together in large bowl. Add shallot, basil, drained watermelon, and tomatoes and gently toss to combine. Transfer to platter and evenly scatter mozzarella over top. Drizzle with extra oil and season with salt and pepper to taste. Serve.

PER SERVING Cal 280; **Total Fat** 18g; **Sat Fat** 8g; **Chol** 30mg; **Sodium** 740mg; **Total Carb** 20g, **Dietary Fiber** 2g, **Total Sugars** 14g; **Protein** 11g

Peach, Blackberry, and Strawberry Fruit Salad with Basil and Black Pepper

Combine sugar, zest, and cardamom in large bowl. Using silicone spatula, press mixture into side of bowl until sugar becomes damp, about 30 seconds. Gently toss nectarines, grapes, and blueberries with sugar mixture until combined. Let stand at room temperature, stirring occasionally, until fruit releases its juices, 15 to 30 minutes. Stir in lime juice to taste, and serve.

Peach, Blackberry, and Strawberry Fruit Salad with Basil and Pepper
SERVES 4 TO 6

- 4 teaspoons sugar
- 2 tablespoons chopped fresh basil
- ½ teaspoon pepper
- 1½ pounds peaches, halved, pitted, and cut into ½-inch pieces
- 10 ounces (2 cups) blackberries
- 10 ounces strawberries, hulled and quartered lengthwise (2 cups)
- 1–2 tablespoons lime juice

Combine sugar, basil, and pepper in large bowl. Using silicone spatula, press mixture into side of bowl until sugar becomes damp, about 30 seconds. Gently toss peaches, blackberries, and strawberries with sugar mixture until combined. Let sit at room temperature, stirring occasionally, until fruit releases its juices, 15 to 30 minutes. Stir in lime juice to taste, and serve.

Combine sugar, lime zest, and cayenne, if using, in large bowl. Using silicone spatula, press mixture into side of bowl until sugar becomes damp, about 30 seconds. Gently toss honeydew, mango, and ginger to taste with sugar mixture until combined. Let sit at room temperature, stirring occasionally, until fruit releases its juices, 15 to 30 minutes. Gently stir in raspberries. Stir in lime juice to taste, and serve.

Nectarine, Grape, and Blueberry Fruit Salad with Orange and Cardamom
SERVES 4 TO 6

- 4 teaspoons sugar
- 1 teaspoon grated orange zest
- ⅛ teaspoon ground cardamom
- 3 medium nectarines (about 6 ounces each), pitted and cut into ½-inch pieces
- 9 ounces large green grapes, halved lengthwise (about 2 cups)
- 10 ounces (2 cups) blueberries
- 1–2 tablespoons lime juice

Mango, Orange, and Jícama Salad
SERVES 4 TO 6 VEGAN

WHY THIS RECIPE WORKS Come winter, putting together a fresh fruit salad requires a bit more creativity than in the summertime when the summer fruit crops are at our fingertips. Working with the abundant citrus and tropical fruits available in colder months, we set our sights on a nuanced salad. A pairing of 1 part citrus fruit to 4 parts tropical fruit produced a juicy—not waterlogged—salad. We started with oranges and mangos and then we created a simple, bright dressing by heating sugar, lime juice, lime zest, red pepper flakes, and a pinch of salt to form a tangy-sweet syrup infused with just a touch of spicy heat. The mild sweetness and supercrisp texture of jícama, softened slightly in the hot syrup, contributed just enough crunch to finish off the salad. The syrup must cool before it is poured over the fruit.

3 tablespoons sugar

¼ teaspoon grated lime zest plus
3 tablespoons juice (2 limes)

¼ teaspoon red pepper flakes
Pinch salt

12 ounces jícama, peeled and cut into
¼-inch dice (1½ cups)

2 oranges

2 mangos, peeled, pitted, and cut into
½-inch dice (4 cups)

1. Bring sugar, lime zest and juice, pepper flakes, and salt to simmer in small saucepan over medium heat, stirring constantly, until sugar is dissolved, 1 to 2 minutes. Off heat, stir in jícama and let syrup cool for 20 minutes.

2. Meanwhile, cut away peel and pith from oranges. Slice into ½-inch-thick rounds, then cut rounds into ½-inch pieces. Place oranges and mangos in large bowl.

3. When syrup is cool, pour over oranges and mangos and toss to combine. Refrigerate for 15 minutes before serving.

PER SERVING Cal 120; **Total Fat** 0.5g, **Sat Fat** 0g; **Chol** 0mg; **Sodium** 30mg; **Total Carb** 30g, **Dietary Fiber** 6g, **Total Sugars** 22g; **Protein** 2g

VARIATION
Papaya, Clementine, and Chayote Salad
Chayote, also called mirliton, is often sold with other tropical fruits and vegetables. If you can't find chayote, substitute an equal amount of jícama.

Substitute 2 teaspoons grated fresh ginger for red pepper flakes; 1 chayote, peeled, halved, pitted, and cut into ¼-inch dice, for jícama; 3 clementines, peeled and each segment cut into 3 pieces, for oranges; and 2 large papayas, peeled, seeded, and cut into ½-inch dice, for mangos.

Pineapple, Grapefruit, and Cucumber Salad
Substitute ground cardamom for red pepper flakes; 1 cucumber, peeled, halved lengthwise, seeded, and cut into ¼-inch dice, for jícama; 1 grapefruit for oranges; and 1 pineapple, peeled, cored, and cut into ½-inch dice, for mangos.

Brussels Sprout and Kale Slaw with Herbs and Peanuts

Brussels Sprout and Kale Slaw with Herbs and Peanuts
SERVES 4 TO 6   `MAKE-AHEAD`   `VEGAN`

WHY THIS RECIPE WORKS Brussels sprouts and kale leaves may sound like an odd combination for a slaw, but these two vegetables are perfect together; since the uncooked leaves hold up well for hours, they're ideal for picnics and making ahead. To keep our slaw crisp and light, we left the Brussels sprouts raw and marinated them in the dressing to soften them just slightly. A warm-water soak softened the kale and rid the leaves of dirt, and a whirl in a salad spinner dried it. A simple cider and coriander vinaigrette, fresh cilantro and mint, chopped peanuts, plus a squeeze of lime juice gave this slaw a refreshing Southeast Asian profile. Tuscan kale (also known as dinosaur or Lacinato kale) is more tender than curly-leaf and red kale. Do not use baby kale. Slice the sprouts as thin as possible; if you have a food processor with a slicing disk, you can use that for the job.

⅓ cup cider vinegar

3 tablespoons sugar

½ teaspoon ground coriander

½ teaspoon table salt

¼ teaspoon pepper

2 tablespoons extra-virgin olive oil

1 pound Brussels sprouts, trimmed, halved, and sliced thin

8 ounces Tuscan kale, stemmed and sliced ¼ inch thick (4½ cups)

¼ cup salted dry-roasted peanuts, chopped coarse

1 tablespoon chopped fresh cilantro

1 tablespoon chopped fresh mint
  Lime juice

1. Whisk vinegar, sugar, coriander, salt, and pepper together in large bowl. Whisking constantly, drizzle in oil until combined. Add Brussels sprouts and toss to combine. Cover and let sit at room temperature for at least 30 minutes or up to 2 hours.

2. Place kale in large bowl, cover with warm water, and swish to remove grit. Let kale sit in warm water bath for 10 minutes. Remove kale from water and spin dry in salad spinner in multiple batches. Pat kale dry with paper towels if still wet. Add kale, peanuts, cilantro, and mint to bowl with Brussels sprouts and toss to combine. Season with salt and lime juice to taste. Serve.

PER SERVING Cal 150; **Total Fat** 8g, **Sat Fat** 1g; **Chol** 0mg; **Sodium** 220mg; **Total Carb** 16g, **Dietary Fiber** 4g, **Total Sugars** 9g; **Protein** 5g

Brussels Sprout, Red Cabbage, and Pomegranate Slaw

Brussels Sprout, Red Cabbage, and Pomegranate Slaw

SERVES 8 FAST VEGAN

WHY THIS RECIPE WORKS Shredded Brussels sprouts make a good starting point for a supercharged slaw bursting with colors, texture, and flavors. We started with a base of delicate shredded Brussels sprouts and vibrant red cabbage, liking the visual contrast of the two brassicas. To add a bright pop of sweetness, we incorporated a generous amount of pomegranate seeds. Toasted sliced almonds provided a nutty foil to the fruit. Instead of a creamy dressing, we made a sweet-tart vinaigrette of apple cider vinegar, pomegranate molasses, and olive oil. A sprinkle of fresh mint added a lively finish. Pomegranate molasses can be found in the international aisle of well-stocked supermarkets; if you can't find it, substitute 2 teaspoons of lemon juice plus 2 teaspoons of mild molasses for the tablespoon of pomegranate molasses. The Brussels sprouts and cabbage can be sliced with a knife or the slicing disk of a food processor. Either way, slice them as thin as possible.

¼ cup cider vinegar

1 tablespoon pomegranate molasses

¾ teaspoon table salt

¼ teaspoon pepper

3 tablespoons extra-virgin olive oil

1 pound Brussels sprouts, trimmed, halved, and sliced very thin

3 cups thinly sliced red cabbage

1½ cups pomegranate seeds

½ cup sliced almonds, toasted

2 tablespoons minced fresh mint

1. Whisk vinegar, pomegranate molasses, salt, and pepper in large bowl until well combined. Whisking constantly, slowly drizzle in oil until combined.

2. Add Brussels sprouts, cabbage, pomegranate seeds, almonds, and mint, and toss well to coat. Season with salt and pepper to taste. Serve.

PER SERVING Cal 140; **Total Fat** 9g, **Sat Fat** 1g; **Chol** 0mg; **Sodium** 240mg; **Total Carb** 15g, **Dietary Fiber** 5g, **Total Sugars** 8g; **Protein** 4g

Creamy Buttermilk Coleslaw

SERVES 4 `MAKE-AHEAD`

WHY THIS RECIPE WORKS No picnic, cookout, or clambake is complete without a classic creamy coleslaw. Cabbage has a high water content, and water leaching out of the vegetable can lead to a watery coleslaw. We salted and drained the cabbage first to draw out excess moisture. This allowed our coleslaw recipe to produce crisp, evenly cut pieces of cabbage lightly coated with a flavorful buttermilk dressing that clung to the cabbage instead of collecting in the bottom of the bowl. For a creamy, hefty dressing, the combination of buttermilk, mayonnaise, and sour cream proved ideal. This recipe can be easily doubled.

- ½ head red or green cabbage, cored and shredded (6 cups)
- ¼ teaspoon table salt, plus salt for salting cabbage
- 1 carrot, peeled and shredded
- ½ cup buttermilk
- 2 tablespoons mayonnaise
- 2 tablespoons sour cream
- 2 tablespoons minced fresh parsley
- 1 small shallot, minced
- ½ teaspoon cider vinegar
- ½ teaspoon sugar
- ¼ teaspoon Dijon mustard
- ⅛ teaspoon pepper

1. Toss shredded cabbage with 1 teaspoon salt in colander set over large bowl and let sit until wilted, at least 1 hour or up to 4 hours. Rinse cabbage under cold running water. Press, but do not squeeze, to drain, and blot dry with paper towels.

2. Discard liquid and wipe bowl clean with paper towels. Combine cabbage and carrot in now-empty bowl. In separate bowl, whisk together buttermilk, mayonnaise, sour cream, parsley, shallot, vinegar, sugar, mustard, remaining ¼ teaspoon salt, and pepper. Pour dressing over cabbage and toss to combine. Cover and refrigerate until chilled, at least 30 minutes or up to 1 day. Season with salt and pepper to taste. Toss to recombine before serving.

PER SERVING Cal 120; **Total Fat** 7g, **Sat Fat** 1.5g; **Chol** 10mg; **Sodium** 560mg; **Total Carb** 11g, **Dietary Fiber** 3g; **Total Sugars** 7g; **Protein** 3g

VARIATIONS
Creamy Buttermilk Coleslaw with Scallions and Cilantro

Omit Dijon mustard. Substitute 2 thinly sliced scallions and 1 tablespoon minced fresh cilantro for parsley and 1 teaspoon lime juice for cider vinegar.

Honey-Mustard Coleslaw

Lemony Buttermilk Coleslaw

Substitute 1 teaspoon lemon juice for cider vinegar. Add 1 teaspoon minced fresh thyme and 1 tablespoon minced fresh chives to dressing.

Honey-Mustard Coleslaw

SERVES 6 TO 8 `MAKE-AHEAD`

WHY THIS RECIPE WORKS Honey-mustard dressing isn't traditional in standard coleslaw, but we found that this sweet and pungent dressing was a welcome addition to an otherwise classic slaw. We first tossed the cabbage in a colander with a mixture of salt and sugar to soften it and pull out a bit of its liquid. Adding sugar enhanced the cabbage's flavor and kept the saltiness from dominating. This step also allowed us to simply stir in the sauce ingredients without having to rinse and dry the cabbage. For sharp, bold mustard flavor tamed with just the right amount of sweetness, we used twice as much mustard as honey here; tasters preferred spicy brown mustard to yellow mustard for its complexity. For a bit of welcome creaminess, we added a small amount of mayonnaise.

1 head green or red cabbage (2 pounds), cored and sliced thin (12 cups)

1½ teaspoons plus ⅛ teaspoon table salt, divided

1½ teaspoons sugar

½ cup spicy brown mustard

¼ cup honey

3 tablespoons minced fresh chives

2 tablespoons mayonnaise

½ teaspoon pepper

1. Toss cabbage with 1½ teaspoons salt and sugar in colander set over large bowl. Let sit until cabbage has wilted and released about 2 tablespoons water, at least 1 hour or up to 4 hours, stirring and pressing on cabbage occasionally with silicone spatula.

2. Discard liquid and wipe bowl clean with paper towels. Whisk mustard, honey, chives, mayonnaise, pepper, and remaining ⅛ teaspoon salt in now-empty bowl until combined. Add cabbage and toss to combine. Cover and refrigerate until chilled, at least 30 minutes or up to 2 days. Season with salt and pepper to taste. Toss to recombine before serving.

PER SERVING Cal 110; Total Fat 2.5g, Sat Fat 0g; Chol 0mg; Sodium 460mg; Total Carb 16g, Dietary Fiber 3g, Total Sugars 12g; Protein 1g

Kentucky Red Slaw

Kentucky Red Slaw

SERVES 4 TO 6 MAKE-AHEAD

WHY THIS RECIPE WORKS In the Bluegrass State, some home cooks swap out the mayonnaise in coleslaw for an unexpected ingredient: ketchup. This results in a sweeter-yet-lighter slaw with a distinctive flavor. For our version, we started with finely chopped cabbage, which is both traditional and practical, as it makes the slaw easier to pile on a barbecue sandwich. Adding just a tablespoon of oil made the cabbage more tender. Cider vinegar provided tanginess, while hot sauce and black pepper added a spicy kick. We prefer the evenly sized pieces you get from cutting the cabbage by hand, but you can also do it in a food processor. Cut the cabbage into 1-inch pieces and pulse it in two batches until it's finely chopped.

½ cup ketchup

¼ cup cider vinegar

¼ cup sugar

1 tablespoon vegetable oil

1 teaspoon hot sauce

1 teaspoon table salt

¾ teaspoon pepper

1 small head green cabbage (1¼ pounds), chopped fine (6 cups)

Whisk ketchup, vinegar, sugar, oil, hot sauce, salt, and pepper together in large bowl. Stir in cabbage until well combined. Cover and refrigerate until chilled, at least 30 minutes or up to 2 days. Season with salt and pepper to taste. Serve.

PER SERVING Cal 110; Total Fat 2.5g, Sat Fat 0g; Chol 0mg; Sodium 650mg; Total Carb 21g, Dietary Fiber 2g, Total Sugars 17g; Protein 1g

Memphis Chopped Coleslaw

SERVES 6 TO 8 MAKE-AHEAD

WHY THIS RECIPE WORKS Memphis chopped coleslaw is traditionally studded with celery seeds and crunchy green peppers and tossed with an unapologetically sugary mustard dressing that's balanced by a bracing hit of vinegar. To ensure that our slaw boasted brash—but balanced—flavor, we quickly cooked the dressing to meld the flavors and then tossed the hot dressing with the cabbage. We found that our usual trick of salting and then draining the cabbage removed excess water and wilted it to a perfect pickle-crisp texture. The salted cabbage absorbed the dressing, becoming thoroughly and evenly seasoned.

1 head green cabbage (2 pounds), cored and chopped fine (12 cups)
1 jalapeño chile, stemmed, seeded, and minced
1 carrot, peeled and shredded
1 small onion, peeled and shredded
Table salt for salting cabbage
⅔ cup packed light brown sugar
¼ cup yellow mustard
¼ cup chili sauce
¼ cup mayonnaise
¼ cup sour cream
¼ cup cider vinegar
1 teaspoon celery seeds

1. Toss cabbage with jalapeño, carrot, onion, and 2 teaspoons salt in colander set over large bowl. Let sit until cabbage has wilted and released about 2 tablespoons water, at least 1 hour or up to 4 hours. Rinse cabbage under cold running water. Press, but do not squeeze, to drain, and blot dry with paper towels.

2. Discard liquid and wipe bowl clean with paper towels. Bring sugar, mustard, chili sauce, mayonnaise, sour cream, vinegar, and celery seeds to boil in saucepan over medium heat; stir to blend. Combine cabbage and hot dressing in now-empty bowl. Cover and refrigerate until chilled, at least 30 minutes or up to 24 hours. Season with salt and pepper to taste. Toss to recombine before serving.

PER SERVING Cal 150; **Total Fat** 7g, **Sat Fat** 1.5g; **Chol** 5mg; **Sodium** 440mg; **Total Carb** 21g, **Dietary Fiber** 3g, **Total Sugars** 16g, **Protein** 2g

CHOPPING CABBAGE FOR COLESLAW

1. Cut cabbage into quarters, then trim and discard core. Separate cabbage into small stacks of leaves that flatten when pressed.

2. Cut each stack of cabbage leaves into ¼-inch-wide strips. Cut strips into ¼-inch pieces.

Spicy Barbecue Coleslaw

Spicy Barbecue Coleslaw
SERVES 8 TO 10   MAKE-AHEAD

WHY THIS RECIPE WORKS There's nothing like spice to cut through smoky, sweet, fatty barbecued meat. For our take on this beloved barbecue side dish, we used a three-pronged approach to turn up the heat. But before we could concentrate on the dressing, we needed to work on the cabbage, which contains a good amount of water. Tossing the chopped cabbage with a little salt and sugar before dressing it drew out the vegetable's excess water and kept the dressing from becoming diluted. Microwaving the cabbage for a few minutes accelerated the draining process. For the dressing, we combined horseradish, dry mustard, and cayenne to create a dynamic, spicy kick. To save time, we shredded the cabbage in a food processor fitted with a slicing disk. If you don't have a food processor, slice the cabbage wedges crosswise ⅛ inch thick. Shred the carrots on the large holes of a box grater. For an extra spicy kick, up the horseradish to 2 tablespoons. The flavors will intensify as the coleslaw chills.

1 head green cabbage (2½ pounds), quartered, cored, and shredded (12 cups)
2 tablespoons sugar
1¾ teaspoons table salt, divided
1 cup mayonnaise
⅓ cup distilled white vinegar
1 tablespoon prepared horseradish
1 teaspoon Worcestershire sauce
1 garlic clove, minced
1 teaspoon pepper
½ teaspoon dry mustard
¼ teaspoon cayenne pepper
2 carrots, peeled and shredded

1. Toss cabbage, sugar, and ½ teaspoon salt together in bowl. Microwave, covered, until just beginning to wilt, about 3 minutes. Let cool slightly, about 5 minutes. Transfer half of cabbage to center of clean dish towel. Gather ends of towel to form bundle and twist to squeeze out excess water. Transfer to clean bowl and repeat with remaining cabbage.

2. Whisk mayonnaise, vinegar, horseradish, Worcestershire, garlic, pepper, mustard, cayenne, and remaining 1¼ teaspoons salt in large bowl until smooth. Stir in cabbage and carrots, cover, and refrigerate until chilled, at least 1 hour or up to 2 days. Serve.

PER SERVING Cal 180; **Total Fat** 16g, **Sat Fat** 2.5g; **Chol** 10mg; **Sodium** 300mg; **Total Carb** 9g, **Dietary Fiber** 3g, **Total Sugars** 5g; **Protein** 2g

Tangy Apple-Cabbage Slaw

Tangy Apple-Cabbage Slaw
SERVES 6 TO 8 MAKE-AHEAD   VEGAN

WHY THIS RECIPE WORKS We wanted to discover the secrets to tender cabbage, crunchy apples, and the sweet and spicy dressing that brings them together in this Southern barbecue side dish. We liked Granny Smith apples in this recipe for their sturdy crunch and tart bite. We cut the apples into matchsticks so they could be easily mixed with the cabbage (salted and drained) while retaining their crispness. Cider vinegar gave the dressing a fruity flavor, while red pepper flakes, chopped scallions, and mustard added some punch. To help the dressing cling, we heated it—the cabbage slaw readily absorbs a hot dressing, especially if it's allowed to sit for an hour before serving. In step 1, the salted, rinsed, and dried cabbage can be refrigerated in a zipper-lock bag for up to 24 hours. To prep the apples, cut the cored apples into ¼-inch-thick planks, then stack the planks and cut them into thin matchsticks. Don't substitute other varieties of apple here; they will result in a mushy, less tangy slaw.

1 head green cabbage (2 pounds), cored and shredded
  Table salt for salting cabbage
2 Granny Smith apples, cored and cut into ¼-inch-thick matchsticks
2 scallions, sliced thin
½ cup cider vinegar
½ cup sugar
6 tablespoons vegetable oil
1 tablespoon Dijon mustard
¼ teaspoon red pepper flakes

1. Toss cabbage and salt together in colander set over medium bowl. Let sit until wilted, about 1 hour. Rinse cabbage under cold running water. Drain, dry well with paper towels, and transfer to large bowl. (At this point, cabbage can be refrigerated in zipper-lock bag for up to 24 hours.) Add apples and scallions to cabbage and toss to combine.

2. Bring vinegar, sugar, oil, mustard, and pepper flakes to boil in small saucepan over medium heat. Pour dressing over cabbage mixture and toss to coat. Cover and refrigerate until chilled, at least 1 hour or up to 24 hours. Serve.

PER SERVING Cal 200; **Total Fat** 11g, **Sat Fat** 1g; **Chol** 0mg; **Sodium** 210mg; **Total Carb** 26g, **Dietary Fiber** 4g, **Total Sugars** 21g; **Protein** 2g

Celery Root, Celery, and Apple Slaw
SERVES 4 TO 6 `FAST` `VEGAN`

WHY THIS RECIPE WORKS With so much texture and flavor, this is a slaw you'll want to have on your dinner table all year long. Many root vegetables, including celery root, stay just as crisp as cabbage once shredded and dressed in a slaw. Here we complemented celery root's distinctive flavor with the addition of its aboveground cousin celery ribs, along with sweet apples. A vinaigrette made with cider vinegar (to echo the apples) and plenty of Dijon mustard was a fresher, more flavorful alternative to the common mayonnaise-based slaw dressing. To save time, we recommend shredding and treating the celery root with the sugar and salt before prepping the remaining ingredients. You can use the large holes of a box grater or the shredding disk of a food processor to shred the celery root.

Celery Root, Celery, and Apple Slaw

1½ pounds celery root, trimmed, peeled, and shredded
¼ cup sugar, plus extra for seasoning
1½ teaspoons table salt, divided
3 tablespoons cider vinegar, plus extra for seasoning
2 tablespoons Dijon mustard
½ teaspoon pepper
½ cup extra-virgin olive oil
5 celery ribs, sliced thin on bias
2 Honeycrisp or Fuji apples, peeled, cored, and cut into 2-inch-long matchsticks
½ cup chopped fresh parsley

1. Toss celery root, sugar, and 1 teaspoon salt together in large bowl and let sit until partially wilted and reduced in volume by one-third, about 15 minutes.

2. Meanwhile, whisk vinegar, mustard, pepper, and remaining ½ teaspoon salt together in large bowl. Whisking constantly, slowly drizzle in oil until combined.

3. Transfer celery root to salad spinner and spin until excess water is removed, 10 to 20 seconds. Transfer celery root to bowl with dressing. Add celery, apples, and parsley to bowl with celery root and toss to combine. Season with salt, pepper, extra sugar, and extra vinegar to taste. Serve immediately.

PER SERVING Cal 270; **Total Fat** 19g, **Sat Fat** 2.5g; **Chol** 0mg; **Sodium** 640mg; **Total Carb** 22g, **Dietary Fiber** 4g, **Total Sugars** 12g; **Protein** 2g

CUTTING APPLES INTO MATCHSTICKS

Cut sides of apple squarely away from core. Cut each piece of apple into ¼-inch-thick slices. Stack planks and cut into matchsticks.

Endive, Beet, and Pear Slaw

1½ pounds beets, trimmed, peeled, and shredded
¼ cup sugar, plus extra for seasoning
1½ teaspoons table salt, divided
3 tablespoons sherry vinegar, plus extra for seasoning
2 tablespoons Dijon mustard
½ teaspoon pepper
½ cup extra-virgin olive oil
2 heads Belgian endive (4 ounces each), halved, cored, and sliced thin on bias
2 pears, peeled, halved, cored, and cut into ⅛-inch matchsticks
1 cup fresh cilantro leaves

1. Toss beets with sugar and 1 teaspoon salt in large bowl and let sit until partially wilted and reduced in volume by one-third, about 15 minutes.

2. Meanwhile, whisk vinegar, mustard, pepper, and remaining ½ teaspoon salt together in large serving bowl. Whisking constantly, slowly drizzle in oil until combined.

3. Transfer beets to salad spinner and spin until excess water is removed, 10 to 20 seconds. Transfer beets to bowl with dressing. Add endive, pears, and cilantro to bowl with beets and toss to combine. Season with salt, pepper, extra sugar, and extra vinegar to taste. Serve immediately.

PER SERVING Cal 260; Total Fat 19g, Sat Fat 2.5g; Chol 0mg; Sodium 570mg; Total Carb 22g, Dietary Fiber 5g, Total Sugars 15g; Protein 2g

Endive, Beet, and Pear Slaw
SERVES 4 TO 6 FAST VEGAN

WHY THIS RECIPE WORKS We always love a traditional cabbage-based slaw, but when we wanted to change things up a bit, we created this delicious, unique coleslaw using some unusual ingredients. We combined the natural mild bitterness and light texture of endive with the dense, earthy sweetness of beets and the floral fruitiness of pears. Tossing the beets with a combination of sugar and salt and then spinning them in a salad spinner extracted some of their water, which otherwise would make for a watery slaw. We let them sit in the sugar and salt while we got to work prepping the remaining ingredients and mixing up a bold, complex sherry-Dijon vinaigrette. Loaded with so much texture, flavor, and alluring color, this salad will be welcome on your table throughout the year. To save time, we recommend shredding and treating the beets before prepping the remaining ingredients. Shred the beets on the large holes of a box grater or with the shredding disk of a food processor.

Kohlrabi, Radicchio, and Apple Slaw
SERVES 4 TO 6 FAST VEGAN

WHY THIS RECIPE WORKS For a fresh and fruity take on coleslaw, we traded out cabbage for crisp, juicy kohlrabi, supplementing it with sliced Granny Smith apples and radicchio to lend contrasting sweet, tart, assertive flavor and texture and bright color to this year-round side dish. We used a box grater (you could use the shredding disk of a food processor) to quickly turn the hard kohlrabi into tender shreds. To avoid a waterlogged slaw, we tossed the shredded kohlrabi with salt and sugar to soften it slightly and draw out moisture, and then spun it in a salad spinner to dry before combining it with the other ingredients. A generous amount of fresh mint and a bright Dijon mustard–based vinaigrette tied everything together.

1½ pounds kohlrabi, trimmed, peeled, and shredded

¼ cup sugar, plus extra for seasoning

1½ teaspoons table salt, divided

½ cup extra-virgin olive oil

3 tablespoons white wine vinegar, plus extra for seasoning

2 tablespoons Dijon mustard

½ teaspoon pepper

2 Granny Smith apples, peeled, cored, and cut into matchsticks

1 small head radicchio (6 ounces), halved, cored, and sliced ½ inch thick

½ cup chopped fresh mint

1. Toss kohlrabi with sugar and 1 teaspoon salt in large bowl and let sit until partially wilted and reduced in volume by one-third, about 15 minutes. Transfer kohlrabi to salad spinner and spin until excess water is removed, 10 to 20 seconds.

2. Whisk oil, vinegar, mustard, pepper, and remaining ½ teaspoon salt in large bowl until combined. Add kohlrabi, apples, radicchio, and mint and toss to combine. Season with salt, pepper, extra sugar, and extra vinegar to taste. Serve immediately.

PER SERVING Cal 240; **Total Fat** 19g, **Sat Fat** 2.5g; **Chol** 0mg; **Sodium** 520mg; **Total Carb** 16g, **Dietary Fiber** 2g, **Total Sugars** 12g; **Protein** 2g

Southwestern Radish and Apple Slaw

Southwestern Radish and Apple Slaw
SERVES 4 **FAST**

WHY THIS RECIPE WORKS Peppery radishes, sweet-tart Granny Smith apples, and sharp red onion form the base of this satisfying but light salad-type of slaw with plenty of crunch. It's a lovely side dish for barbecued chicken but is also substantial enough to pair with a grain salad or grilled vegetables for a refreshing summertime meal. We added avocado and cotija cheese for creamy richness, and a generous amount of cilantro contributed a bright, grassy note. A dressing spiked with cumin and lime continued the Southwestern theme, and a sprinkling of toasted pepitas before serving added a final crunchy burst of flavor. If you can't find cotija cheese, use farmer's cheese or a mild feta instead.

¼ cup extra-virgin olive oil

2 tablespoons lime juice

1 tablespoon rice vinegar

1 tablespoon honey

1 teaspoon ground cumin

1 garlic clove, minced

¾ teaspoon table salt

¼ teaspoon pepper

12 ounces radishes, trimmed, each cut into 6 wedges

1 Granny Smith apple, cored and cut into 2-inch-long matchsticks

½ cup thinly sliced red onion

2 avocados, halved, pitted, and cut into ¾-inch pieces

1 cup fresh cilantro leaves

4 ounces cotija cheese, crumbled (1 cup)

⅓ cup pepitas, toasted

Whisk oil, lime juice, vinegar, honey, cumin, garlic, salt, and pepper in large bowl until combined. Add radishes, apple, and onion and toss to coat. Gently fold in avocados, cilantro, and cotija. Season with salt and pepper to taste. Sprinkle with pepitas and serve.

PER SERVING Cal 510; **Total Fat** 43g, **Sat Fat** 10g; **Chol** 30mg; **Sodium** 880mg; **Total Carb** 27g, **Dietary Fiber** 9g, **Total Sugars** 12g; **Protein** 12g

DINNER PARTY WINNERS

■ FAST (30 minutes or less total time)   ■ MAKE-AHEAD   ■ VEGAN

Photos (clockwise from top left): Pan-Steamed Asparagus with Lemon and Parmesan; Pasta with Roasted Cherry Tomatoes; Cauliflower Puree; Braised Zucchini

Arugula Salad with Figs, Prosciutto, Walnuts, and Parmesan

Apple and Celery Salad with Roquefort
SERVES 8 **FAST**

WHY THIS RECIPE WORKS Nothing says "dinner party" quite like Roquefort cheese. Stellar in composed salads, the assertive cheese benefits from using a free hand when introducing other flavors and textures, especially anything sweet, tart, or crunchy. For a sophisticated start to a company-worthy menu, we paired it with apples and crisp celery. A shot of cider vinegar gave the necessary tartness to the dressing, and a spoonful of honey tempered the vinegar's acidity and highlighted the saltiness of the cheese. For the greens, we liked a combination of mild red leaf lettuce with bold and aromatic parsley. Toasted hazelnuts provided crunch. We like the rich, creamy flavor of Roquefort in this salad, but other blue cheeses can be substituted. You can slice the apples or celery by hand or use a mandoline or V-slicer. Blanched slivered almonds can be substituted for the hazelnuts.

3 tablespoons cider vinegar
1 tablespoon honey
¼ teaspoon table salt
⅛ teaspoon pepper
3 tablespoons extra-virgin olive oil
2 celery ribs, sliced thin on bias
1 Braeburn or Fuji apple, cored, halved, and sliced thin
1 head red leaf lettuce (12 ounces), cut into 1-inch pieces
¼ cup fresh parsley leaves
6 ounces Roquefort cheese, crumbled (1½ cups)
½ cup hazelnuts, toasted, skinned, and chopped

Whisk vinegar, honey, salt, and pepper together in large bowl. Whisking constantly, drizzle in oil. Just before serving, whisk dressing to re-emulsify. Stir in celery and apple and let them absorb dressing, about 5 minutes. Add lettuce and parsley and gently toss to coat. Garnish individual portions with Roquefort and hazelnuts.

PER SERVING Cal 200; **Total Fat** 16g, **Sat Fat** 5g; **Chol** 20mg; **Sodium** 480mg; **Total Carb** 8g, **Dietary Fiber** 2g, **Total Sugars** 5g; **Protein** 6g

Arugula Salad with Figs, Prosciutto, Walnuts, and Parmesan
SERVES 6 **FAST**

WHY THIS RECIPE WORKS Every dinner party host needs a salad that's simple to make but impressive and this one delivers in spades. Figs and prosciutto, a classic duo, combine perfectly with peppery arugula for a salad that explodes with flavor in each bite: sweet, salty, and spicy. Frying the prosciutto slices heightened their flavor and gave them some crunch. We chopped dried figs to provide bites of fig throughout the salad. For the dressing, a basic mustard and balsamic vinaigrette was too spicy with the already punchy arugula. A surprise substitution—a spoonful of jam in place of the mustard—added fruity sweetness that helped to balance the salty flavors. Microwaving the vinegar, jam, shallot, and figs allowed the fruit to plump and the flavors to meld before we whisked in the olive oil. Toasted walnuts, sprinkled over the dressed arugula, gave the salad an earthy crunch, and Parmesan cheese complemented the walnuts while also reinforcing the prosciutto's salty flavor.

¼ cup extra-virgin olive oil, divided
2 ounces thinly sliced prosciutto, cut into ¼-inch-wide ribbons
3 tablespoons balsamic vinegar
1 tablespoon raspberry jam
1 small shallot, minced
¼ teaspoon table salt
⅛ teaspoon pepper
½ cup dried figs, stemmed and chopped
8 ounces (8 cups) baby arugula
½ cup walnuts, toasted and chopped
2 ounces Parmesan cheese, shaved

1. Heat 1 tablespoon oil in 10-inch nonstick skillet over medium heat. Add prosciutto and cook, stirring often, until crispy, about 7 minutes. Using slotted spoon, transfer prosciutto to paper towel–lined plate; set aside.

2. Whisk vinegar, jam, shallot, salt, and pepper together in large bowl. Stir in figs, cover, and microwave until steaming, about 1 minute. Whisking constantly, slowly drizzle in remaining 3 tablespoons oil. Let sit until figs are softened and vinaigrette has cooled to room temperature, about 15 minutes.

3. Just before serving, whisk vinaigrette to re-emulsify. Add arugula and gently toss to coat. Season with salt and pepper to taste. Serve, topping individual portions with prosciutto, walnuts, and Parmesan.

PER SERVING Cal 260; **Total Fat** 19g, **Sat Fat** 3.5g; **Chol** 15mg; **Sodium** 530mg; **Total Carb** 16g, **Dietary Fiber** 2g, **Total Sugars** 12g; **Protein** 9g

Arugula Salad with Grapes, Fennel, Gorgonzola, and Pecans
SERVES 6

WHY THIS RECIPE WORKS Arugula has a lively, peppery bite, so it's important to choose accompaniments that can stand up to it. As with the previous salad, we found that the sweet and salty notes of fruits and cheeses worked well as supporting players to arugula; tasters loved the combination of red grapes and bold Gorgonzola cheese. Thinly sliced fennel gave the salad more substance, and chopped pecans added a crunch that provided a nice counterpoint. As for the dressing, we started with oil, white wine vinegar, and shallot and added a spoonful of apricot jam for some fruity sweetness, pulling the flavors of the salad right in line.

  3 **tablespoons white wine vinegar**
  1 **small shallot, minced**
  4 **teaspoons apricot jam**
  ¼ **teaspoon table salt**
  ¼ **teaspoon pepper**
  3 **tablespoons extra-virgin olive oil**
  ½ **small fennel bulb, cored and sliced thin, plus minced fennel fronds**
  5 **ounces (5 cups) baby arugula**
  6 **ounces red seedless grapes, halved lengthwise (1 cup)**
  3 **ounces Gorgonzola cheese, crumbled (¾ cup)**
  ½ **cup pecans, toasted and chopped**

1. Whisk vinegar, shallot, jam, salt, and pepper together in large bowl. Whisking constantly, drizzle in oil. Stir in sliced fennel and let sit for 15 minutes.

Arugula Salad with Grapes, Fennel, Gorgonzola, and Pecans

2. Add arugula, grapes, and fennel fronds and gently toss to coat. Season with salt and pepper to taste. Serve, topping individual portions with Gorgonzola and pecans.

PER SERVING Cal 220; **Total Fat** 18g, **Sat Fat** 4.5g; **Chol** 10mg; **Sodium** 310mg; **Total Carb** 12g, **Dietary Fiber** 2g, **Total Sugars** 8g; **Protein** 5g

Herbed Baked Goat Cheese Salad
SERVES 8 MAKE-AHEAD

WHY THIS RECIPE WORKS Warm goat cheese atop a salad makes for an elegant dish to serve dinner guests. We coated cheese rounds with nuts instead of bread crumbs for added flavor. Giving the cheese a whirl in the food processor let us incorporate flavor-packed herbs throughout. Baking the rounds for a few minutes ensured a crunchy coating and a smooth, but not melted, interior. To avoid runny cheese rounds, we froze the rounds until completely firm before baking. Prepare the salad components and the vinaigrette while the goat cheese rounds are in the freezer. Assertive salad greens, such as a mix of arugula and frisée, work best here.

Herbed Baked Goat Cheese Salad

SALAD
- 1½ cups pecans
- 12 ounces goat cheese, softened
- 2 tablespoons minced fresh chives
- 1 teaspoon minced fresh thyme
- 2 large eggs
- 12 cups (12 ounces) hearty salad greens
  Vegetable oil spray

VINAIGRETTE
- 1 tablespoon cider vinegar
- 1 teaspoon minced shallot
- 3 tablespoons extra-virgin olive oil
- 1 teaspoon honey
- ½ teaspoon mayonnaise
- ½ teaspoon Dijon mustard
- ¼ teaspoon table salt
- ¼ teaspoon pepper

1. FOR THE SALAD Pulse pecans in food processor until finely chopped; transfer to medium bowl. Add cheese, chives, and thyme to food processor; process until smooth. Refrigerate cheese mixture in covered bowl until firm, at least 1 hour or up to 2 days.

2. Using your hands, roll 2 tablespoons chilled cheese mixture into twelve 1½-inch balls. Beat eggs in medium bowl. One at a time, dip balls in egg, then roll in nuts, pressing gently to adhere. Place balls 2 inches apart on rimmed baking sheet. Press balls into 2-inch disks with greased measuring cup. Cover with plastic wrap and freeze until completely firm, at least 2 hours or up to 1 week.

3. FOR THE VINAIGRETTE Combine vinegar and shallot in small jar; let sit for 5 minutes. Add oil, honey, mayonnaise, mustard, salt, and pepper to jar, affix lid, and shake vigorously until emulsified, about 30 seconds.

4. Adjust oven rack to upper position and heat oven to 475 degrees. Remove plastic and spray cheese lightly with oil spray. Bake until nuts are golden brown and cheese is warmed through, 7 to 10 minutes. Let cool for 3 minutes. Toss greens with vinaigrette and divide among individual plates. Serve warm cheese rounds over dressed salad.

PER SERVING Cal 320; **Total Fat** 29g, **Sat Fat** 9g; **Chol** 65mg; **Sodium** 300mg; **Total Carb** 5g, **Dietary Fiber** 3g, **Total Sugars** 2g; **Protein** 12g

Asparagus and Spinach Salad
SERVES 6 **FAST**

WHY THIS RECIPE WORKS For a bright, fresh-flavored asparagus salad, cooking the asparagus properly was paramount. Blanching and steaming both produced bland and sometimes mushy spears, while sautéing the asparagus over high heat delivered deep flavor and tender texture (and was quicker than bringing a pot of water to a boil). Strips of red pepper sautéed with the asparagus gave the salad a sweet, roasted flavor and bright color. Tossing the tender vegetables with baby spinach rounded out the fresh, crisp composition. A zesty sherry vinegar dressing gave the salad bold flavor, and the addition of creamy, delicate goat cheese made our salad rich and substantial.

- 6 tablespoons extra-virgin olive oil, divided
- 1 red bell pepper, stemmed, seeded, and cut into 1 by ¼-inch strips
- 1 pound asparagus, trimmed and cut on bias into 1-inch lengths
- ½ teaspoon table salt, divided
- ¼ teaspoon pepper, divided
- 1 shallot, sliced thin
- 4 teaspoons sherry vinegar
- 1 garlic clove, minced
- 6 ounces (6 cups) baby spinach
- 4 ounces goat cheese, cut into small chunks

Asparagus and Spinach Salad

1. Heat 2 tablespoons oil in 12-inch nonstick skillet over high heat until just smoking. Add bell pepper and cook until lightly browned, about 2 minutes. Stir in asparagus, ¼ teaspoon salt, and ⅛ teaspoon pepper and cook until asparagus is browned and almost tender, about 2 minutes. Stir in shallot and cook until softened and asparagus is crisp-tender, about 1 minute. Transfer to large plate and let cool for 5 minutes.

2. Meanwhile, whisk vinegar, garlic, remaining ¼ teaspoon salt, and remaining ⅛ teaspoon pepper together in bowl. Whisking constantly, drizzle in remaining 4 tablespoons oil.

3. Toss spinach with 2 tablespoons dressing in bowl, and divide among salad plates. Toss asparagus mixture with remaining dressing in now-empty bowl and arrange over spinach. Sprinkle with goat cheese and serve.

PER SERVING Cal 210; **Total Fat** 18g; **Sat Fat** 5g; **Chol** 10mg; **Sodium** 310mg; **Total Carb** 6g, **Dietary Fiber** 3g, **Total Sugars** 3g; **Protein** 6g

Bibb and Radicchio Salad with Orange Vinaigrette
SERVES 12 FAST

WHY THIS RECIPE WORKS For an impressive but simple salad to serve a large group, we combined crunchy, slightly bitter radicchio with mild, soft Bibb lettuce, and dressed them with a lively vinaigrette made with orange juice. To achieve a cohesive, clingy dressing, we needed to compensate for the significant amount of orange juice, so we recruited a few ingredients to help emulsify: mayonnaise, Dijon mustard, and honey. Any kind of orange juice will work in this recipe; however, freshly squeezed juice will make the flavor of the vinaigrette really sparkle.

- ½ cup orange juice
- ¼ cup white wine vinegar
- 1 shallot, minced
- 2 tablespoons minced fresh mint
- 2 teaspoons mayonnaise
- 1 teaspoon Dijon mustard
- 1 teaspoon honey
- ½ teaspoon table salt
- 1 teaspoon pepper
- ½ cup extra-virgin olive oil
- 3 heads Bibb lettuce (1½ pounds), cut into 1-inch pieces
- 1 head radicchio (10 ounces), cut into 1-inch pieces
- ½ cup sliced almonds, toasted
- 6 ounces feta, crumbled (1½ cups)

Whisk orange juice, vinegar, shallot, mint, mayonnaise, mustard, honey, salt, and pepper together in small bowl. Whisking constantly, drizzle in oil. In large bowl, gently toss lettuce, radicchio, almonds, and feta. Just before serving, whisk dressing to re-emulsify, then drizzle over salad and gently toss to coat.

PER SERVING Cal 170; **Total Fat** 15g, **Sat Fat** 3.5g; **Chol** 15mg; **Sodium** 250mg; **Total Carb** 6g, **Dietary Fiber** 1g, **Total Sugars** 3g; **Protein** 4g

TOASTING NUTS

Spread nuts in dry skillet over medium heat. Shake skillet occasionally to prevent scorching and toast until lightly browned and fragrant, 3 to 8 minutes. Watch closely since nuts can go from golden to burnt very quickly.

Chopped Carrot Salad with Fennel, Orange, and Hazelnuts

Chopped Carrot Salad with Fennel, Orange, and Hazelnuts

SERVES 4 TO 6 · FAST · VEGAN

WHY THIS RECIPE WORKS We love the combination of flavorful fennel, bright citrus, and earthy nuts for a special-occasion salad. For a little something different to serve to guests, we paired this trifecta with a chopped-carrot base. Chopping carrots in the food processor, rather than shredding them, gave us delicate yet crunchy pieces, akin to a vivid orange tabbouleh. We also pulsed the fennel to a coarse chop to harmonize with the carrots. Toasting the skinned hazelnuts enhanced their nuttiness for maximum flavor, and a citrus dressing with plenty of orange zest brought everything together. We prefer the convenience and the hint of bitterness that leaving the carrots unpeeled lends to this salad; just be sure to scrub the carrots well before using them.

- ¾ cup hazelnuts, toasted and skinned, divided
- ¼ cup extra-virgin olive oil
- 2 tablespoons white wine vinegar
- 1 teaspoon table salt
- ½ teaspoon pepper
- ¼ teaspoon grated orange zest plus ⅓ cup juice
- 1 fennel bulb, stalks discarded, bulb halved, cored, and cut into 1-inch pieces
- 1 pound carrots, trimmed and cut into 1-inch pieces
- ½ cup minced fresh chives, divided

Pulse hazelnuts in food processor until coarsely chopped, 10 to 12 pulses; transfer to small bowl. Whisk oil, vinegar, salt, pepper, and orange zest and juice in large bowl until combined. Pulse fennel in now-empty processor until coarsely chopped, 10 to 12 pulses; transfer to bowl with dressing. Process carrots in again-empty processor until finely chopped, 10 to 20 seconds, scraping down sides of bowl as needed. Transfer carrots to bowl with fennel mixture. Add ¼ cup chives and half of hazelnuts and toss to combine. Season with salt to taste. Transfer to serving platter, sprinkle with remaining ¼ cup chives and remaining hazelnuts, and serve.

PER SERVING Cal 230; **Total Fat** 18g, **Sat Fat** 2g; **Chol** 0mg; **Sodium** 460mg; **Total Carb** 14g, **Dietary Fiber** 5g, **Total Sugars** 7g; **Protein** 4g

Citrus and Radicchio Salad with Dates and Smoked Almonds

SERVES 4 TO 6 · FAST · VEGAN

WHY THIS RECIPE WORKS Brighten up your winter dinner party table with this colorful salad. In a reversal of what you might expect, we used sliced grapefruits and oranges as the base, topping them with sliced radicchio (given that citrus pieces inevitably sink to the bottom of the salad bowl, this made for a more attractive presentation). To tame the bitterness of the grapefruit and prevent its ample juice from overwhelming the other components, we treated the grapefruit (and the oranges) with sugar and salt and let them sit for 15 minutes. Draining the seasoned fruit enabled us to preemptively remove the excess juice, and reserving some to use in the simple mustard and shallot vinaigrette for the greens helped to make the salad more cohesive. Salty smoked almonds added mellow richness, and chopped dates contributed sweetness. We prefer to use navel oranges, tangelos, or Cara Caras here.

- 2 red grapefruits
- 3 oranges
- 1 teaspoon sugar
- ½ teaspoon table salt
- 3 tablespoons extra-virgin olive oil
- 1 small shallot, minced
- 1 teaspoon Dijon mustard

Citrus and Radicchio Salad with Dates and Smoked Almonds

1 small head radicchio (6 ounces), halved, cored, and sliced thin

⅔ cup chopped pitted dates, divided

½ cup smoked almonds, chopped, divided

1. Cut away peel and pith from grapefruits and oranges. Cut each fruit in half from pole to pole, then slice crosswise ¼ inch thick. Transfer to bowl, toss with sugar and salt, and let sit for 15 minutes.

2. Drain fruit in fine-mesh strainer set over bowl, reserving 2 tablespoons juice. Arrange fruit in even layer on serving platter and drizzle with oil. Whisk reserved citrus juice, shallot, and mustard together in medium bowl. Add radicchio, ⅓ cup dates, and ¼ cup almonds and gently toss to coat. Season with salt and pepper to taste. Arrange radicchio mixture over fruit, leaving 1-inch border of fruit around edges. Sprinkle with remaining ⅓ cup dates and remaining ¼ cup almonds. Serve.

PER SERVING Cal 260; **Total Fat** 13g, **Sat Fat** 1.5g; **Chol** 0mg; **Sodium** 270mg; **Total Carb** 36g, **Dietary Fiber** 7g, **Total Sugars** 27g; **Protein** 4g

Cucumber, Radish, and Watercress Salad
SERVES 8 `FAST`

WHY THIS RECIPE WORKS For an alternative to a greens-based salad that was impressive enough to serve to guests, we paired mild cucumber with spicy radishes and watercress. We seeded and salted the cucumbers and then drained them for 15 minutes to draw out excess moisture and give them good crunch (this also prevented the salad from becoming watery). This salad couldn't be simpler to prepare, and its bold and refreshing flavors will cut the richness of any main dish and complement any salty-sweet flavor profile on your dinner party table.

3 cucumbers, peeled, halved lengthwise, seeded, and cut on bias into ¼-inch pieces

½ teaspoon table salt

¼ cup rice vinegar

1 tablespoon honey

1 teaspoon grated ginger

½ teaspoon grated orange zest plus 1 tablespoon juice

½ teaspoon grated lime zest plus 1 tablespoon juice

¼ cup vegetable oil

1 pound watercress (16 cups)

8 ounces radishes, trimmed and sliced thin

1. Toss cucumbers with salt and let drain in colander for 15 minutes. In small bowl, whisk vinegar, honey, ginger, orange zest and juice, and lime zest and juice together. Whisking constantly, drizzle in oil.

2. Combine drained cucumbers, watercress, and radishes in large bowl. Just before serving, whisk dressing to re-emulsify, then drizzle over salad and gently toss to coat.

PER SERVING Cal 100; **Total Fat** 7g, **Sat Fat** 0.5g; **Chol** 0mg; **Sodium** 180mg; **Total Carb** 8g, **Dietary Fiber** 1g, **Total Sugars** 5g; **Protein** 2g

Endive Salad with Blue Cheese and Walnut Vinaigrette
SERVES 12 `FAST`

WHY THIS RECIPE WORKS A salad featuring a bitter green such as endive is the perfect foil to a rich roast or braise. We used mesclun greens as a fluffy, mild foil for the endive. Chopped walnuts brought in some crunch and echoed the walnut flavor of the walnut vinaigrette in which we dressed our salad. A garnish of soft crumbled blue cheese added flavor, texture, and just enough richness so as not to overpower a main course. If walnut oil is unavailable, simply substitute additional olive oil.

- ¼ cup lemon juice (2 lemons)
- 1 shallot, minced
- 1 teaspoon Dijon mustard
- 1 teaspoon honey
- ¼ teaspoon table salt
- ¼ teaspoon pepper
- ½ cup extra-virgin olive oil
- ⅓ cup walnut oil
- 6 heads Belgian endive (1½ pounds), leaves separated and halved crosswise
- 12 ounces mesclun greens (12 cups)
- ¾ cup walnuts, toasted and chopped
- 6 ounces blue cheese, crumbled (1½ cups)

Whisk lemon juice, shallot, mustard, honey, salt, and pepper together in small bowl. Whisking constantly, drizzle in olive oil and walnut oil. In large bowl, gently toss endive, mesclun, and walnuts together. Just before serving, whisk dressing to re-emulsify, then drizzle over salad and toss to coat. Garnish individual portions with blue cheese.

PER SERVING Cal 250; **Total Fat** 24g, **Sat Fat** 5g; **Chol** 10mg; **Sodium** 220mg; **Total Carb** 5g, **Dietary Fiber** 2g, **Total Sugars** 1g; **Protein** 5g

Frisée, Spinach, and Cucumber Salad

Frisée, Spinach, and Cucumber Salad
SERVES 12 FAST VEGAN

WHY THIS RECIPE WORKS For a refreshing salad that calls to mind a summer evening dinner party, we punctuated crunchy cucumbers and soft spinach with bites of slightly peppery, bitter frisée. The natural flavors of all three components needed nothing more than a simple lemon-shallot vinaigrette to join together as the perfect light salad. Salting the cucumbers helped to rid them of excess moisture and prevented the salad from tasting watery.

- 3 cucumbers, peeled, halved lengthwise, seeded, and sliced thin
- ¾ teaspoon table salt, divided
- 3 tablespoons lemon juice
- 1 shallot, minced
- 2 tablespoons minced fresh mint
- 1 tablespoon white wine vinegar
- 2 teaspoons Dijon mustard
- 1 garlic clove, minced
- ¼ teaspoon pepper
- ½ cup extra-virgin olive oil
- 4 small heads frisée (1 pound), cut into 2-inch pieces
- 10 ounces baby spinach (10 cups)

1. Toss cucumbers with ½ teaspoon salt and let drain in colander for 15 minutes. Whisk lemon juice, shallot, mint, vinegar, mustard, garlic, pepper, and remaining ¼ teaspoon salt together in small bowl. Whisking constantly, drizzle in oil.

2. Combine drained cucumbers, frisée, and spinach in large bowl. Just before serving, whisk dressing to re-emulsify, then drizzle over salad and gently toss to coat.

PER SERVING Cal 110; **Total Fat** 9g, **Sat Fat** 1.5g; **Chol** 0mg; **Sodium** 190mg; **Total Carb** 6g, **Dietary Fiber** 2g, **Total Sugars** 2g; **Protein** 1g

Green Bean and Potato Salad with Cilantro Dressing
SERVES 8 MAKE-AHEAD VEGAN

WHY THIS RECIPE WORKS To dress up the classic combo of vibrant, crisp green beans and creamy potatoes we added a cilantro dressing that balanced herbal flavor with richness from olive oil and walnuts. Since we were using 4 pounds of vegetables we knew we'd need a generous amount of dressing, so we started with four bunches of cilantro (stems and leaves, both), adding toasted walnuts for richness and garlic, lemon juice, and scallions for freshness and a little bite. We sliced and boiled the potatoes, then brushed them with some of the sauce while still hot so they could absorb maximum flavor. We blanched the green beans until crisp-tender, and then shocked them in ice water to halt the cooking. Don't worry about patting the beans dry before tossing them with the sauce; any water that clings to the beans helps thin out the dressing.

½ cup walnuts
4 garlic cloves, unpeeled
5 cups fresh cilantro leaves and stems, trimmed (4 bunches)
¾ cup extra-virgin olive oil
¼ cup water
2 tablespoons lemon juice
2 scallions, sliced thin
½ teaspoon table salt plus salt for cooking potatoes and green beans
⅛ teaspoon pepper
2 pounds red potatoes, sliced ½ inch thick
2 pounds green beans, trimmed and cut into 2-inch lengths

1. Toast walnuts in small heavy skillet over medium heat, stirring frequently, until just golden and fragrant, about 5 minutes; transfer to bowl. Add garlic to now-empty skillet and toast over medium heat, shaking pan occasionally, until fragrant and color deepens slightly, about 7 minutes. Let garlic cool slightly, then peel and chop.

2. Process toasted walnuts, garlic, cilantro, oil, water, lemon juice, scallions, ½ teaspoon salt, and pepper in food processor until smooth, stopping to scrape down sides of bowl as needed, about 1 minute. Transfer to bowl and season with salt and pepper to taste. (Sauce can be refrigerated for up to 2 days.)

3. Place potatoes and 1 tablespoon salt in large saucepan and add cold water to cover by 1 inch. Bring to boil. Reduce to gentle simmer and cook until potatoes are tender but not falling apart, about 10 minutes. Drain potatoes and spread evenly over rimmed baking sheet. Drizzle ½ cilantro sauce over potatoes and let cool to room temperature, about 30 minutes.

4. Meanwhile, bring 4 quarts water to boil in large Dutch oven over high heat. Fill large bowl halfway with ice and water. Add 1 tablespoon salt and green beans to boiling water and cook until crisp-tender, about 5 minutes. Transfer beans to ice water using large slotted spoon, and let sit until chilled, about 2 minutes.

5. Drain green beans well, discarding any ice. Toss beans with remaining cilantro sauce in large bowl. Gently fold in potatoes, season with salt and pepper to taste, and serve. (Salad can be refrigerated for up to 1 day; bring to room temperature before serving.)

Fingerling Potato and Arugula Salad

PER SERVING Cal 350; **Total Fat** 26g, **Sat Fat** 3.5g; Chol 0mg; **Sodium** 320mg; **Total Carb** 28g, **Dietary Fiber** 6g, **Total Sugars** 6g; **Protein** 6g

Fingerling Potato and Arugula Salad
SERVES 8 MAKE-AHEAD VEGAN

WHY THIS RECIPE WORKS A combination of tender potatoes, baby greens, and a lively vinaigrette makes for a simple but hearty, fresh-tasting salad perfect for pairing with a dinner of chicken or fish. For our potatoes, tasters unanimously sang the praises of fingerlings and felt that the distinctly elongated, narrow shape of this small potato, which sliced into petite circles, elevated the presentation of this dish to company-worthy status. We found it best to slice the fingerling potatoes and boil them in salted water, as roasting muddied the clean flavor we were after. Dressing the potatoes while still warm helped them to absorb flavor. To avoid wilting the arugula, make sure to cool the potatoes completely and toss the salad with the dressing just before serving.

5 tablespoons white wine vinegar

1 shallot, minced

1 tablespoon minced fresh thyme

1 teaspoon Dijon mustard

¾ teaspoon table salt, divided, plus salt for cooking potatoes

⅛ teaspoon pepper

⅔ cup extra-virgin olive oil

3 pounds fingerling potatoes, sliced ¼ inch thick

12 ounces cherry tomatoes, quartered

6 ounces baby arugula (6 cups)

1. Whisk vinegar, shallot, thyme, mustard, ¼ teaspoon salt, and pepper together in small bowl. Whisking constantly, drizzle in oil.

2. Place potatoes and 2 tablespoons salt in Dutch oven and add cold water to cover by 1 inch. Bring to a boil. Reduce to gentle simmer and cook until potatoes are tender but not falling apart, about 8 minutes. Drain potatoes and spread evenly over 2 rimmed baking sheets.

3. Whisk dressing to re-emulsify, then drizzle ¾ cup dressing over warm potatoes. Let potatoes cool completely, about 30 minutes. (Cooled potatoes can be refrigerated for up to 1 day; bring to room temperature before continuing with step 4.)

4. Toss tomatoes with remaining ½ teaspoon salt and let drain in colander for 30 minutes. Combine potatoes and drained tomatoes in large bowl. Just before serving, add arugula to bowl. Whisk remaining dressing to re-emulsify, then drizzle over salad and gently toss to coat.

PER SERVING Cal 320; **Total Fat** 19g, **Sat Fat** 2.5g; **Chol** 0mg; **Sodium** 320mg; **Total Carb** 33g, **Dietary Fiber** 5g, **Total Sugars** 3g; **Protein** 4g

Kale Caesar Salad

SERVES 4 **FAST** **MAKE-AHEAD**

WHY THIS RECIPE WORKS Kale is closing on romaine as the most popular green for Caesar salad. In fact, many prefer how its sturdy leaves stand up to the creamy dressing, but those leaves, which can be tough, first need to be tenderized. In order to break down the leaves and make them more palatable, we soaked them in a warm water bath. Marinating them in the Caesar dressing in the refrigerator gave the salad time to cool back down and the flavors time to meld. To balance the strong flavor of kale, we made the dressing extra-potent, with a stronger dose of lemon juice and anchovies than is typical. The kale leaves must be dressed at least 20 minutes (or up to 6 hours) before serving.

Kale Caesar Salad

SALAD

12 ounces curly kale, stemmed and cut into 1-inch pieces (16 cups)

1 ounce Parmesan cheese, grated (½ cup)

CROUTONS

3 ounces baguette, cut into ¾-inch cubes (3 cups)

2 tablespoons extra-virgin olive oil

¼ teaspoon pepper

⅛ teaspoon table salt

DRESSING

½ cup mayonnaise

¼ cup grated Parmesan cheese

2 tablespoons lemon juice

1 tablespoon white wine vinegar

1 tablespoon Worcestershire sauce

1 tablespoon Dijon mustard

3 anchovy fillets, rinsed

1 garlic clove, minced

½ teaspoon table salt

½ teaspoon pepper

¼ cup extra-virgin olive oil

1. **FOR THE SALAD** Place kale in large bowl and cover with warm tap water (110 to 115 degrees). Swish kale around to remove grit. Let kale sit in warm water bath for 10 minutes. Remove kale from water and spin dry in salad spinner in multiple batches. Pat leaves dry with paper towels if still wet.

2. **FOR THE CROUTONS** Adjust oven rack to middle position and heat oven to 350 degrees. Toss all ingredients together in bowl. Bake on rimmed baking sheet until golden and crisp, about 15 minutes. Let croutons cool completely on sheet. (Cooled croutons can be stored in airtight container at room temperature for up to 24 hours.)

3. **FOR THE DRESSING** Process mayonnaise, Parmesan, lemon juice, vinegar, Worcestershire, mustard, anchovies, garlic, salt, and pepper in blender until pureed, about 30 seconds. With blender running, slowly add oil until emulsified.

4. Toss kale with ¾ cup dressing in large bowl. Refrigerate dressed kale for at least 20 minutes or up to 6 hours. Toss Parmesan and croutons with dressed kale. Serve, passing remaining ¼ cup dressing at table.

PER SERVING Cal 550; **Total Fat** 47g; **Sat Fat** 8g; **Chol** 25mg; **Sodium** 1240mg; **Total Carb** 19g, **Dietary Fiber** 3g, **Total Sugars** 4g; **Protein** 14g

Spinach Salad with Blood Oranges and Radishes
SERVES 8 `FAST` `VEGAN`

WHY THIS RECIPE WORKS To turn sweet, tender baby spinach into a company-worthy salad, we paired it with spicy radishes and juicy blood oranges. Orange zest and a pinch of sugar enhanced the natural sweetness of the blood oranges without challenging the peppery bite of the radishes. Shredding the radishes on a box grater ensured that crunchy bites were incorporated throughout the salad. The visual appeal of this salad made it a perfect contender for a dinner-party side dish. Regular oranges can be substituted for the blood oranges.

- 2 tablespoons lemon juice
- 1 shallot, minced
- ½ teaspoon table salt
- ¼ teaspoon grated orange zest
- ¼ teaspoon sugar
- ¼ teaspoon pepper
- ⅓ cup extra-virgin olive oil
- 6 radishes, grated
- 2 blood oranges
- 12 ounces baby spinach (12 cups)

Whisk lemon juice, shallot, salt, orange zest, sugar, and pepper together in small bowl. Whisking constantly, drizzle in oil. Cut away peel and pith from oranges. Quarter oranges, then slice crosswise into ½-inch-thick pieces. Combine orange pieces and radishes in large bowl and place spinach on top. Just before serving, whisk dressing to re-emulsify, then drizzle over salad and gently toss to coat.

PER SERVING Cal 120; **Total Fat** 10g, **Sat Fat** 1.5g; **Chol** 0mg; **Sodium** 180mg; **Total Carb** 6g, **Dietary Fiber** 2g, **Total Sugars** 4g; **Protein** 1g

CUTTING ORANGES

1. Using paring knife, cut away peel and pith from orange.

2. Quarter orange, then slice crosswise into pieces as directed.

Cherry Tomato Salad with Feta and Olives
SERVES 6 `FAST` `MAKE-AHEAD` `VEGAN`

WHY THIS RECIPE WORKS Cherry tomatoes are reliably sweet and juicy year-round and make a great base for a salad, but they exude lots of liquid when cut. To get rid of some of the juice without sacrificing any tomato flavor, we quartered and salted the tomatoes before whirling them in a salad spinner to separate the seeds and juice from the flesh. After we strained out and discarded the seeds, we reduced the tomato juice to a flavorful concentrate (adding garlic, oregano, shallot, olive oil, and vinegar) and reunited it with the tomatoes. Feta cheese added richness and another layer of flavor to this great all-season salad. If cherry tomatoes are unavailable, substitute grape tomatoes cut in half along the equator. Strain the liquid and proceed with the recipe as directed. If you have less than ½ cup of juice after spinning, proceed with the recipe using the entire amount of juice and reduce it to 3 tablespoons as directed (the cooking time will be shorter).

1½ pounds cherry tomatoes, quartered
½ teaspoon sugar
¼ teaspoon table salt
1 small cucumber, peeled, halved lengthwise, seeded, and cut into ½-inch pieces
½ cup pitted kalamata olives, chopped
4 ounces feta cheese, crumbled (1 cup)
3 tablespoons chopped fresh parsley
1 shallot, minced
1 tablespoon red wine vinegar
2 garlic cloves, minced
2 teaspoons minced fresh oregano
2 tablespoons extra-virgin olive oil

1. Toss tomatoes with sugar and salt in bowl and let sit for 30 minutes. Transfer tomatoes to salad spinner and spin until seeds and excess liquid have been removed, 45 to 60 seconds, stopping to redistribute tomatoes several times during spinning. Add tomatoes, cucumber, olives, feta, and parsley to large bowl; set aside.

2. Strain ½ cup tomato liquid through fine-mesh strainer into liquid measuring cup; discard remaining liquid. Bring tomato liquid, shallot, vinegar, garlic, and oregano to simmer in small saucepan over medium heat and cook until reduced to 3 tablespoons, 6 to 8 minutes. Transfer to small bowl and let cool to room temperature, about 5 minutes. Whisking constantly, slowly drizzle in oil. Drizzle dressing over salad and gently toss to coat. Season with salt and pepper to taste. Serve.

PER SERVING Cal 130; **Total Fat** 10g, **Sat Fat** 3.5g; **Chol** 15mg; **Sodium** 320mg; **Total Carb** 8g, **Dietary Fiber** 2g, **Total Sugars** 5g; **Protein** 4g

Pan-Steamed Asparagus with Garlic
SERVES 6 FAST

WHY THIS RECIPE WORKS We wanted to preserve the fresh, sweet, grassy flavor of asparagus and ensure a crisp-tender texture by steaming it, while avoiding the pitfalls of washed-out flavor. To do that, we steamed the asparagus in just 2 tablespoons of water in a skillet along with butter, salt, and garlic. As the water evaporated, we were left with perfectly crisp-tender asparagus glossed with garlicky butter. This recipe works best with asparagus spears that are about ½ inch thick. If using thinner spears, reduce the uncovered cooking time to 1½ to 2 minutes.

2 pounds asparagus
1 tablespoon unsalted butter
2 tablespoons water
1 garlic clove, minced
½ teaspoon table salt

1. Trim bottom inch of asparagus spears; discard trimmings. Peel bottom halves of spears until white flesh is exposed. Cut spears on bias into 2-inch lengths. Melt butter in 12-inch nonstick skillet over medium-high heat. Add 2 tablespoons water, garlic, and salt and stir to combine. Add asparagus, shaking skillet to evenly distribute. Cover and cook, without stirring, for 2 minutes.

2. Uncover and continue to cook, stirring occasionally, until skillet is almost dry and asparagus is crisp-tender, 2½ to 3 minutes. Serve.

PER SERVING Cal 45; **Total Fat** 2g, **Sat Fat** 1g; **Chol** 5mg; **Sodium** 190mg; **Total Carb** 6g, **Dietary Fiber** 3g, **Total Sugars** 3g; **Protein** 4g

MAKING CHERRY TOMATO SALAD

1. Toss tomatoes, sugar, and salt together in bowl and let sit for 30 minutes.

2. Transfer tomatoes to salad spinner and spin until seeds and excess liquid have been removed, 45 to 60 seconds. Combine seeded tomatoes with cucumber, olives, feta, and parsley.

3. Strain ½ cup tomato liquid into measuring cup. Bring liquid, shallot, vinegar, garlic, and oregano to simmer over medium heat and cook until reduced to 3 tablespoons, 6 to 8 minutes. Once cool, slowly whisk in oil.

4. Drizzle dressing over salad and gently toss to coat.

Pan-Steamed Asparagus with Garlic

VARIATIONS

Pan-Steamed Asparagus with Anchovies and Red Pepper Flakes

Substitute extra-virgin olive oil for butter and heat until shimmering. Add 2 rinsed and minced anchovy fillets and ¼ teaspoon red pepper flakes to skillet with garlic. Decrease salt to ¼ teaspoon.

Pan-Steamed Asparagus with Lemon and Parmesan

Combine 1 teaspoon grated lemon zest plus 1 tablespoon juice and ¼ teaspoon pepper in small bowl. Stir lemon zest mixture into asparagus and sprinkle with ¼ cup shredded Parmesan before serving.

Pan-Steamed Asparagus with Mint and Almonds

Combine ¼ cup chopped fresh mint, 2 teaspoons sherry vinegar, and ¼ teaspoon smoked paprika in small bowl. Stir mint mixture into asparagus and sprinkle with ¼ cup sliced almonds, toasted, cooled, and lightly crushed, just before serving.

Pan-Steamed Asparagus with Shallots and Herbs

Substitute ¼ cup minced shallots for garlic. Stir ¼ cup chopped fresh chives and 2 teaspoons chopped fresh dill into asparagus before serving.

Sautéed Broccoli Rabe with Roasted Red Peppers

SERVES 6 TO 8 **FAST** **VEGAN**

WHY THIS RECIPE WORKS Broccoli rabe generally gets mixed reviews. While it's naturally bitter, it can also taste pleasantly peppery when prepared right. We found that this green vegetable was extremely appealing when combined with roasted sweet red bell peppers in an Italian-inspired side dish. Store-bought jarred roasted peppers offered convenience without sacrificing flavor. Chopping the broccoli rabe into small pieces and quickly blanching it in a large amount of salted water tamed its bitterness while retaining its round, deep flavor. Quick, dependable, and versatile, this side makes a great accompaniment to pasta and roast meat.

- 2 pounds broccoli rabe, trimmed and cut into 1-inch pieces
- ½ teaspoon table salt, plus salt for blanching broccoli rabe
- 3 tablespoons extra-virgin olive oil, divided
- 2 garlic cloves, minced
- ½ cup jarred roasted red peppers, patted dry and chopped fine

1. Bring 3 quarts water to boil in Dutch oven. Fill large bowl halfway with ice and water. Add broccoli rabe and 2 teaspoons salt to boiling water and cook until wilted and tender, about 2 minutes. Drain broccoli rabe, then transfer to ice water and let sit until chilled. Drain again and thoroughly pat dry.

2. Cook 2 tablespoons oil and garlic in now-empty Dutch oven over medium heat, stirring often, until garlic begins to sizzle, about 2 minutes. Increase heat to medium-high, add broccoli rabe, red peppers, and ½ teaspoon salt and cook, stirring to coat with oil, until heated through, about 1 minute. Season with salt and pepper to taste. Transfer to serving platter and drizzle with remaining 1 tablespoon oil. Serve.

PER SERVING Cal 80; **Total Fat** 6g, **Sat Fat** 1g; **Chol** 0mg; **Sodium** 230mg; **Total Carb** 4g, **Dietary Fiber** 3g, **Total Sugars** 1g; **Protein** 4g

VARIATION

Sautéed Broccoli Rabe with Sun-Dried Tomatoes and Pine Nuts

Omit red peppers. Add ¼ cup oil-packed sun-dried tomatoes, cut into thin strips, and ¼ teaspoon red pepper flakes to pot with garlic. Sprinkle broccoli rabe with 3 tablespoons toasted pine nuts before serving.

Broccolini with Garlic and Browned Butter

SERVES 8 **FAST**

WHY THIS RECIPE WORKS Broccolini, a cross between regular and Chinese broccoli, adds a fresh accent to any hearty main dish. The vegetable comes in small bunches but we wanted enough to serve eight, so we started with 3 pounds' worth and used a Dutch oven to lightly sauté the broccolini in oil, and then added water and covered the pot to braise it until bright green and almost fully cooked. A quick sauce of nutty browned butter enhanced the vegetable's natural sweetness. Garlic and thyme added aromatic depth to the sauce, while red pepper flakes provided a touch of heat. You will need at least a 6-quart Dutch oven for this recipe. Make sure to watch the butter closely as it browns in step 3; it can go from nutty brown to black and burnt in a matter of seconds.

- 2 tablespoons extra-virgin olive oil
- 3 pounds broccolini, trimmed
- 1 teaspoon table salt, divided
- ¾ cup water
- 6 tablespoons unsalted butter
- 4 garlic cloves, minced
- 1 teaspoon minced fresh thyme
- ¼ teaspoon red pepper flakes
- ¼ teaspoon pepper

1. Heat oil in Dutch oven over medium-high heat until just smoking. Add broccolini and ½ teaspoon salt and cook, stirring occasionally, until they begin to brown, about 5 minutes.

2. Reduce heat to medium, add water, and cover. Cook broccolini, tossing often, until bright green but still crisp, 6 to 8 minutes. Uncover and continue to cook, tossing often, until water has evaporated, and broccolini is tender, 5 to 7 minutes. Transfer to large bowl.

3. Add butter to now-empty pot and melt over medium-high heat, swirling occasionally, until butter is browned and has nutty aroma, 2 to 3 minutes. Off heat, stir in garlic, thyme, pepper flakes, remaining ½ teaspoon salt, and pepper until fragrant, about 30 seconds. Add broccolini, toss to coat evenly with browned butter, and serve.

PER SERVING Cal 140; **Total Fat** 13g, **Sat Fat** 6g; **Chol** 25mg; **Sodium** 350mg; **Total Carb** 5g, **Dietary Fiber** 4g, **Total Sugars** 1g; **Protein** 5g

Roasted Baby Carrots with Browned Butter

SERVES 12

WHY THIS RECIPE WORKS Prepared baby-cut carrots can be a lifesaver when you need a big-batch side dish that requires little effort, as they require no peeling or cutting. Roasting the carrots releases their sweetness, yielding a caramelized exterior and tender interior. Tossing the carrots with olive oil and salt and roasting them in a hot oven for 20 minutes gave us perfectly roasted carrots. To dress them up a bit, we browned some butter in a skillet while the carrots roasted and then tossed the carrots and butter together, transforming an everyday veggie snack into something sweet, nutty, and complex.

- 2 pounds baby carrots
- 2 tablespoons extra-virgin olive oil
- ½ teaspoon table salt
- 3 tablespoons unsalted butter

Adjust oven rack to middle position and heat oven to 475 degrees. Toss baby carrots with oil and salt and spread into single layer on rimmed baking sheet. Roast for 12 minutes. Shake pan and continue to roast, shaking pan occasionally, until carrots are lightly browned and tender, about 8 minutes. Meanwhile, cook butter in 8-inch skillet over medium heat, swirling occasionally, until browned, 1 to 2 minutes. Toss roasted carrots with browned butter and serve.

PER SERVING Cal 70; **Total Fat** 5g, **Sat Fat** 2g; **Chol** 10mg; **Sodium** 160mg; **Total Carb** 6g, **Dietary Fiber** 2g, **Total Sugars** 4g; **Protein** 0g

MAKING BROWNED BUTTER

1. Place butter in heavy-bottomed skillet or pot with light-colored interior. Cook, swirling pan occasionally, until butter melts and begins to foam.

2. Continue to cook, swirling pan constantly, until butter is dark golden brown and has nutty aroma, 1 to 3 minutes.

Cauliflower Puree

SERVES 6 **FAST** **VEGAN**

WHY THIS RECIPE WORKS Most experienced cooks will admit that the key to silky mashed potatoes involves loads of butter and cream. To create a similarly creamy, equally versatile puree without all the fat, we turned to cauliflower. This mild-tasting crucifer has such a low starch content that it purees like a dream, needing little help to achieve a smooth texture. In fact, its leanness makes it a great pairing for proteins that might be overwhelmed by potatoes, such as scallops. While a food processor would turn high-starch potatoes gummy, it proved perfect for pureeing steamed cauliflower, giving it a smooth, velvety texture. To make our puree reminiscent of mashed potatoes, we added thyme and a little garlic sautéed in olive oil. A dash of white wine vinegar balanced all the flavors.

- ¼ cup extra-virgin olive oil
- 2 garlic cloves, minced
- 2 teaspoons minced fresh thyme or ¾ teaspoon dried
- ½ teaspoon table salt, plus salt for cooking cauliflower
- ¼ teaspoon white wine vinegar
- 1 large head cauliflower (3 pounds), florets cut into 1-inch pieces, core peeled and sliced ¼ inch thick

1. Combine oil and garlic in 8-inch nonstick skillet. Cook over low heat, stirring occasionally, until garlic is pale golden, 9 to 12 minutes. Off heat, stir in thyme, ½ teaspoon salt, and vinegar; transfer to 1-cup liquid measuring cup and set aside to cool.

2. Meanwhile, bring 2½ cups water and ½ teaspoon salt to boil in Dutch oven over high heat. Add cauliflower, cover, and cook until cauliflower is tender, stirring once halfway through cooking, 14 to 16 minutes.

3. Drain cauliflower and transfer to food processor. Add 2 tablespoons water and process cauliflower until mostly smooth, 3 to 4 minutes, scraping down sides of bowl as needed. With processor running, drizzle in oil-garlic mixture and process until completely smooth, about 30 seconds. (If puree is too thick, add hot water, 1 tablespoon at a time, until desired consistency is reached). Season with salt and pepper to taste. Serve.

PER SERVING Cal 140; **Total Fat** 10g, **Sat Fat** 1.5g; **Chol** 0mg; **Sodium** 460mg; **Total Carb** 12g, **Dietary Fiber** 5g, **Total Sugars** 4g; **Protein** 4g

Sage–Brown Butter Celery Root Puree

Sage–Brown Butter Celery Root Puree

SERVES 6 TO 8

WHY THIS RECIPE WORKS The velvety texture and pleasantly mild flavor of celery root pureed in the food processor make it a more refined alternative to classic mashed potatoes. To develop creaminess and character in this puree, we lightly sautéed the celery root in butter, which concentrated its flavor and added richness. To bring out even deeper flavor, we simmered it in garlic-infused chicken broth. Next, it went into the food processor along with all of that rich, aromatic broth. Although starchy potatoes can turn gluey when whipped in a food processor, the celery root broke down beautifully into a smooth, luscious puree. We bloomed fresh sage in browned butter to give the celery root a nutty, savory profile. For a different take on this puree, we blended in white miso; its subtly sweet, floral flavor complements the celery root's earthiness. Another variation punches things up with prepared horseradish and scallions.

8 tablespoons unsalted butter, divided

4 pounds celery root, trimmed, peeled, and cut into 1-inch pieces

4 garlic cloves, peeled and smashed

½ cup chicken or vegetable broth, plus extra as needed

1 teaspoon table salt

¼ teaspoon pepper

1 tablespoon minced fresh sage

1½ teaspoons lemon juice

1. Melt 4 tablespoons butter in large saucepan over medium heat. Add celery root and garlic and cook, stirring occasionally, until celery root is softened and lightly browned, 10 to 12 minutes. (If after 4 minutes celery root has not started to brown, increase heat to medium-high.)

2. Stir in broth, salt, and pepper and bring to simmer over medium heat. Cover, reduce heat to low, and cook, stirring occasionally, until celery root is very tender and breaks apart when poked with fork, about 40 minutes; let cool slightly.

3. Melt remaining 4 tablespoons butter in 12-inch skillet over medium-high heat, swirling occasionally, until butter is browned and releases nutty aroma, about 1½ minutes. Off heat, stir in sage and cook, using residual heat of skillet, until fragrant, about 1 minute. Stir in lemon juice

4. Working in batches, process celery root in food processor until smooth, about 2 minutes, scraping down sides of bowl as needed. Return puree to now-empty pot and adjust consistency with extra hot broth as needed. Stir in browned butter mixture and season with salt and pepper to taste. Serve.

PER SERVING Cal 190; **Total Fat** 12g, **Sat Fat** 7g; **Chol** 30mg; **Sodium** 520mg; **Total Carb** 19g, **Dietary Fiber** 4g, **Total Sugars** 3g; **Protein** 3g

PEELING CELERY ROOT

1. Using chef's knife, cut ½ inch from both root end and opposite end of celery root.

2. Turn celery root so 1 cut side rests on board. To peel, cut from top to bottom, rotating celery root while removing wide strips of skin.

VARIATIONS

Miso Celery Root Puree

Omit sage and lemon juice. Increase garlic to 8 cloves. Decrease butter to 4 tablespoons and omit step 3. Stir ¼ cup white miso into celery root puree in saucepan in step 4.

Horseradish Celery Root Puree with Scallions

Omit sage and lemon juice. Increase garlic to 6 cloves. Decrease butter to 4 tablespoons and omit step 3. Stir 2 tablespoons prepared horseradish and 4 thinly sliced scallions into celery root puree in saucepan in step 4.

Eggplant Pecorino

SERVES 6 `MAKE-AHEAD`

WHY THIS RECIPE WORKS Based on a dish served at La Campagna in Westlake Ohio, this spin on "eggplant parm" upends the concept of the traditional casserole by showcasing (rather than masking) the eggplant as savory, faintly bitter, buttery, and satisfying. We skipped the breading and instead lightly fried superthin slices of eggplant in a thin flour-and-egg coating. A quick aromatic tomato sauce, rich fontina, and some nutty Pecorino added just enough context to amplify the eggplant—not obscure it. Do not use eggplants any bigger than 1 pound each or they won't fit into the baking dish. Depending on the size of your eggplants, you may not need to use all three to get the 20 slices needed to assemble the casserole.

SAUCE

2 tablespoons unsalted butter

¼ cup finely chopped onion

3 garlic cloves, minced

2 anchovy fillets, rinsed and minced

¾ teaspoon table salt

¼ teaspoon red pepper flakes

¼ teaspoon dried oregano

1 (28-ounce) can crushed tomatoes

1 (15 ounce) can diced tomatoes

½ teaspoon sugar

¼ cup chopped fresh basil

1 tablespoon extra-virgin olive oil

EGGPLANT

3 (10- to 16-ounce) eggplants

½ cup all-purpose flour

4 large eggs

1 cup extra-virgin olive oil

4 ounces Pecorino Romano cheese, grated (2 cups)

4 ounces fontina cheese, shredded (1 cup)

Eggplant Pecorino

4. Adjust oven rack 6 inches from broiler element and heat oven to 375 degrees. Spread 1 cup sauce in bottom of broiler-safe 13 by 9-inch baking dish. Starting with largest slices of eggplant first, place 4 slices of eggplant side by side in bottom of dish. Spread ½ cup sauce over eggplant, then sprinkle ½ cup Pecorino over top. Repeat layering 3 more times, building individual stacks of eggplant. Cover top layer of eggplant with remaining sauce, then sprinkle with fontina. (To make ahead, do not sprinkle with fontina. Cover with foil and refrigerate for up to 24 hours. Remove foil and sprinkle with fontina. Bake 20 minutes, then continue with recipe.)

5. Bake until bubbling around edges and center of casserole is hot, about 30 minutes. Broil until fontina is lightly browned, 1 to 3 minutes. Let cool for 20 minutes. Serve.

PER SERVING Cal 530; **Total Fat** 39g, **Sat Fat** 13g; Chol 110mg; **Sodium** 1150mg; **Total Carb** 34g, **Dietary Fiber** 10g, **Total Sugars** 17g; **Protein** 19g

Fennel Confit
SERVES 6 TO 8   **VEGAN**

WHY THIS RECIPE WORKS The confit technique is most often used with duck, but it's also a versatile way of transforming vegetables. Fennel is a perfect candidate, since long, slow cooking in olive oil coaxes out its hidden flavors and turns it luxuriously creamy. We found that arranging two layers of fennel slabs in the bottom of a large Dutch oven allowed us to use just 3 cups of oil rather than the 2 quarts called for in most recipes. The oil didn't fully cover the fennel, but the fennel shrank and released liquid during cooking, causing it to sink. We flavored the oil with lemon zest, garlic, and complementary fennel seeds and caraway seeds. The oven was perfect for our purpose: It provided even heat for the 2-hour cooking time and was completely hands-off. The fennel emerged buttery and aromatic, and pieces that remained above the oil became golden and caramelized. We finished with a scattering of fronds for an unforgettable dish. Don't core the fennel before cutting it; the core helps hold the slabs together during cooking.

 3 fennel bulbs, 2 tablespoons fronds minced, stalks discarded, bulbs cut lengthwise into ½-inch-thick slabs, divided
 ¼ teaspoon table salt, divided
 3 garlic cloves, lightly crushed and peeled
 3 (2-inch) strips lemon zest, plus lemon wedges for serving
 1 teaspoon caraway seeds
 1 teaspoon fennel seeds
 3 cups extra-virgin olive oil
   Flake sea salt

1. **FOR THE SAUCE** Melt butter in medium saucepan over medium-low heat. Add onion, garlic, anchovies, salt, pepper flakes, and oregano and cook until onions are softened, about 3 minutes. Stir in crushed tomatoes, diced tomatoes and their juice, and sugar and bring to simmer. Reduce heat to medium-low and simmer until slightly thickened, about 10 minutes. Off heat, stir in basil and oil. Season with salt and pepper to taste. Set aside. (Sauce can be prepared and refrigerated up to 48 hours in advance.)

2. **FOR THE EGGPLANT** Cut stem end off eggplants and discard. Cut off ¼-inch-thick slice from 1 long side of each eggplant and discard. Using mandoline or slicing knife, and starting on cut side, slice eggplants lengthwise into ¼-inch-thick slices until you have 20 slices total (you may not need all 3 eggplants).

3. Place flour in shallow dish. Beat eggs together in second shallow dish. Line baking sheet with triple layer of paper towels. Heat oil in 12-inch skillet over medium heat to 350 degrees (tilt skillet to pool oil to one side to take temperature). Working with 3 to 4 slices of eggplant per batch (depending on size of eggplant), dredge eggplant in flour, shaking off excess; dunk in egg, allowing excess to drip off; then place in hot oil. Fry until lightly browned on both sides, about 1½ minutes per side. Transfer to prepared sheet and repeat with remaining eggplant. (As eggplant cools, you can stack it to make room.)

1. Adjust oven rack to middle position and heat oven to 300 degrees. Arrange half of fennel cut side down in single layer in Dutch oven. Sprinkle with ⅛ teaspoon salt. Repeat with remaining fennel and remaining ⅛ teaspoon salt. Scatter garlic, lemon zest, caraway seeds, and fennel seeds over top, then add oil (fennel may not be completely submerged).

2. Cover pot, transfer to oven, and cook until fennel is very tender and is easily pierced with tip of paring knife, about 2 hours.

3. Remove pot from oven. Using slotted spoon, transfer fennel to serving platter, brushing off any garlic, lemon zest, caraway seeds, or fennel seeds that stick to fennel. Drizzle ¼ cup cooking oil over fennel, sprinkle with fennel fronds, and season with sea salt to taste. Serve with lemon wedges.

PER SERVING Cal 280; **Total Fat** 28g, **Sat Fat** 4g; **Chol** 0mg; **Sodium** 120mg; **Total Carb** 7g, **Dietary Fiber** 3g, **Total Sugars** 3g; **Protein** 1g

Blanched Green Beans with Bistro Mustard Vinaigrette

Blanched Green Beans with Bistro Mustard Vinaigrette
SERVES 12   MAKE-AHEAD   VEGAN

WHY THIS RECIPE WORKS Green beans are excellent candidates for the classic, simple cooking technique of blanching. Cooked quickly in rapidly boiling salted water and then rapidly cooled in ice water, green beans hold their fresh flavor, bright color, and crisp-tender texture beautifully. A rustic, slightly sharp mustard vinaigrette brought out the best in the beans without overshadowing their mild flavor. Be sure to set up the ice water bath before cooking the green beans, as plunging them in the cold water immediately after blanching both retains their bright green color and ensures that they don't overcook. These green beans are delicious at room temperature, slightly chilled, or briefly rewarmed in the microwave.

BEANS
  3 pounds green beans, trimmed
    Table salt for cooking beans

VINAIGRETTE
  6 tablespoons extra-virgin olive oil
  4 teaspoons red wine or sherry vinegar
  3 tablespoons whole-grain mustard
  1 shallot, minced
  1 garlic clove, minced
  1½ teaspoons minced fresh thyme
  ½ teaspoon table salt
  ¼ teaspoon pepper

1. **FOR THE BEANS** Bring 8 quarts of water to boil in large pot over high heat. Fill large bowl halfway with ice and water; set aside. Add beans and 2 tablespoons salt to boiling water and cook until mostly tender but still underdone, with little crunch in center, 2 to 4 minutes.

2. Drain green beans, then transfer immediately to ice water. Let green beans cool completely, about 5 minutes, then drain and pat dry with paper towels. (Green beans can be wrapped loosely in paper towels and stored in zipper-lock bag in refrigerator for up to 2 days.)

3. **FOR THE VINAIGRETTE** Shake all ingredients together in jar with tight-fitting lid. (Vinaigrette can be refrigerated for up to 2 days; bring to room temperature before using.)

4. Transfer green beans to large bowl, cover, and microwave until hot and steaming, 6 to 8 minutes. Drain away any accumulated water. Shake vinaigrette to recombine, then toss with green beans to coat. Serve immediately.

PER SERVING Cal 110; **Total Fat** 7g, **Sat Fat** 1g; **Chol** 0mg; **Sodium** 190mg; **Total Carb** 8g, **Dietary Fiber** 3g, **Total Sugars** 4g; **Protein** 2g

Haricots Verts with Garlic and Herbs
SERVES 8 **FAST** **MAKE-AHEAD**

WHY THIS RECIPE WORKS The freshness of slender haricots verts offsets the richness of substantial main dishes like prime rib and heavier sides as well. For impressive-looking beans, we boiled the beans to set their color and deepen their flavor. Mixing a garlic and thyme compound butter helped us to evenly distribute the flavors without needing to sauté the beans. To preserve the bright green color of the beans, add the lemon juice just before serving, as the acidity will cause the beans to discolor.

- 2 tablespoons unsalted butter, softened
- 4 garlic cloves, minced
- 1½ teaspoons minced fresh thyme
- ½ teaspoon table salt, plus salt for blanching haricot verts
- ¼ teaspoon pepper
- 2 pounds haricots verts, trimmed
- 1 tablespoon minced fresh parsley
- 2 teaspoons lemon juice

1. Mash butter, garlic, thyme, ½ teaspoon salt, and pepper together in bowl. (Butter can be refrigerated for up to 1 week.)

2. Bring 6 quarts water to boil in large pot over high heat. Stir in haricots verts and 1½ tablespoons salt and cook until crisp-tender, 4 to 8 minutes. Drain beans and return to pot. Add butter, cover, and let sit off heat until butter has melted, about 2 minutes. Add parsley and lemon juice, gently toss to coat, and serve.

PER SERVING Cal 70; **Total Fat** 3g; **Sat Fat** 2g; **Chol** 10mg; **Sodium** 220mg; **Total Carb** 9g, **Dietary Fiber** 2g, **Total Sugars** 2g; **Protein** 3g

Green Beans Amandine

Green Beans Amandine
SERVES 8 **FAST**

WHY THIS RECIPE WORKS The French classic of green beans and almonds is an ever-popular side dish for entertaining, perhaps because it promises something refined yet simple. Sadly, the beans often turn out limp and awash in pools of acidic sauce and the pale almonds are an afterthought. A few adjustments made all the difference: We sautéed rather than blanched the beans, adding a splash of water to cook them through. We toasted the almonds (an obvious step often skipped). And we browned the butter, lightly so as not to overpower the beans, before stirring in lemon juice. The butter's heat took the edge off the citrus, leaving behind a subtle, balanced flavor. Use a light-colored traditional skillet so that you can monitor the butter's browning.

- ⅓ cup sliced almonds
- 3 tablespoons unsalted butter, cut into 3 pieces
- 2 teaspoons lemon juice
- 2 pounds green beans, trimmed
- ½ cup water
- ½ teaspoon table salt

1. Toast almonds in 12-inch skillet over medium-low heat, stirring often, until just golden, about 6 minutes. Add butter and cook, stirring constantly, until butter is golden brown and has nutty aroma, about 3 minutes. Transfer almond-butter mixture to bowl and stir in lemon juice.

2. Add green beans, water, and salt to now-empty skillet. Cover and cook, stirring occasionally, until green beans are nearly tender, 8 to 10 minutes. Uncover, increase heat to medium-high, and cook until water evaporates, 3 to 5 minutes. Off heat, add almond-butter mixture to skillet and toss to combine. Season with salt to taste, and serve.

PER SERVING Cal 110; **Total Fat** 7g; **Sat Fat** 3g; **Chol** 10mg; **Sodium** 5mg; **Total Carb** 9g, **Dietary Fiber** 3g, **Total Sugars** 4g; **Protein** 3g

Baked Stuffed Onions with Sausage and Swiss Chard
SERVES 8

WHY THIS RECIPE WORKS For our baked stuffed onions recipe, we avoided thinking of the onions as "bowls" and instead saw them as hollowed-out, bottomless onion shells (made of a layer of three onion rings). We were able to prepare these shells in advance of cooking, which was a lot easier than trying to prepare slippery cooked onions. We tested various ways of parcooking the onions before settling on a combination method: first browning them in a skillet, and then briefly braising them. The softened and browned the onions made a perfect vehicle for the sausage and Swiss chard stuffing. Try to buy white-stemmed Swiss chard; red-stemmed chard can turn the filling an unappealing pink color. Balsamic or red wine vinegar can be substituted for the sherry vinegar. The stuffed onions pair well with roasted or grilled meats.

Baked Stuffed Onions with Sausage and Swiss Chard

  4 large (3- to 4-inch) yellow onions
  2 tablespoons extra-virgin olive oil, divided
  ½ cup chicken broth
  6 ounces sweet Italian sausage, casings removed
  ½ teaspoon table salt
  3 garlic cloves, minced
  1 pound Swiss chard, stems discarded and
      leaves chopped (8 cups)
  2 teaspoons sherry vinegar

1. Adjust oven rack to middle position and heat oven to 350 degrees. Trim off both root and stem end of onions, then slice onions in half through middle. Remove and discard brown papery onion skins along with tough, outermost layer of onion. Remove core from each onion half by pushing it out from underside, leaving just 3 of outermost layers to form bottomless shell. Chop onion cores fine and reserve for use in filling.

2. Line 13 by 9-inch baking dish with foil and set aside. Heat 1 tablespoon oil in 12-inch nonstick skillet over medium heat until shimmering. Lay 4 onion rings in skillet wide ends down and cook until edges are browned, 2 to 3 minutes. Transfer onion rings to plate without separating layers and repeat with remaining oil and onion rings.

3. Once second batch is browned, return first batch to skillet (they will overlap). Add broth, cover, and continue to cook onions over medium heat until softened, about 5 minutes. Transfer onions to prepared baking dish, browned edges facing up. Pour broth into small bowl and set aside.

4. Pinch sausage into small pieces and add to skillet. Add chopped onion cores and salt, cover, and cook over medium heat, stirring occasionally, until onions are softened, about 10 minutes. Uncover and continue to cook until onions are golden and dry, 5 to 10 minutes.

5. Stir in garlic and cook until fragrant, about 30 seconds. Stir in chard and reserved broth. Cook, tossing chard until wilted, about 2 minutes. Off heat, stir in vinegar and season with salt and pepper to taste. Spoon filling into center of onion rings

6. Bake onions until the filling is hot and bubbling, about 45 minutes. Serve.

PER SERVING Cal 100; **Total Fat** 5g, **Sat Fat** 1g; **Chol** 5mg; **Sodium** 430mg; **Total Carb** 8g, **Dietary Fiber** 2g, **Total Sugars** 3g; **Protein** 5g

Buttery Peas with Shallots and Thyme
SERVES 12 **FAST** MAKE-AHEAD

WHY THIS RECIPE WORKS Since most recipes that make up an elaborate dinner-party menu require both time and space in the oven, it's nice to have a vegetable dish that can be made on the stovetop in just minutes. In the test kitchen, we have come to depend on frozen peas for their convenience and bright flavor. To make this last-minute side dish a real breeze, prep and measure all the ingredients an hour or two in advance (keep the peas frozen).

    4 tablespoons unsalted butter
    2 shallots, minced
    2 teaspoons minced fresh thyme
    2 garlic cloves, minced
    1 tablespoon sugar
    ½ teaspoon table salt
    2 pounds frozen peas

Melt butter in 12-inch nonstick skillet over medium-high heat. Add shallots, thyme, garlic, sugar, and salt and cook until softened, about 2 minutes. Stir in peas and cook, stirring often, until thawed and heated through, 5 to 10 minutes. Season with salt and pepper to taste, and serve.

PER SERVING Cal 100; **Total Fat** 3.5g, **Sat Fat** 2.5g; **Chol** 10mg; **Sodium** 100mg; **Total Carb** 12g, **Dietary Fiber** 4g, **Total Sugars** 5g; **Protein** 4g

Stuffed Plum Tomatoes
SERVES 8 MAKE-AHEAD

WHY THIS RECIPE WORKS Stuffed tomatoes are a showpiece side dish for entertaining guests. We wanted stuffed tomatoes that tasted as good as they looked and could easily be made ahead of time. Plum tomatoes were a good starting point; their meaty, sweet flavor and small size were ideal for a side dish. Salting the tomatoes rid them of excess liquid and ensured that our stuffing wouldn't get soggy. Fresh, tangy goat cheese, lightly flavored with olive oil and basil, gave the tomatoes a creamy center and made a perfect base for our topping of fresh toasted bread crumbs. Do not overprocess the bread into fine, even crumbs; the texture of coarse, slightly uneven crumbs is preferable here. To scoop out the seeds and ribs from the tomatoes, we found it easiest to use a sharp-edged spoon, such as a grapefruit spoon or melon baller. We prefer kosher salt here because residual grains can easily be wiped away; if using table salt, reduce the amount of salt by half.

    2 slices hearty white sandwich bread, torn into quarters
    3 tablespoons extra-virgin olive oil, divided
    3 garlic cloves, minced
    ¼ cup grated Parmesan cheese
    ¼ cup chopped fresh basil, divided
    8 firm, ripe plum tomatoes
    1½ teaspoons kosher salt
    6 ounces goat cheese, softened

1. Adjust oven rack to middle position and heat oven to 325 degrees. Pulse bread in food processor to coarse crumbs, about 6 pulses. Toss crumbs, 2 tablespoons oil, and garlic together. Spread crumbs on rimmed baking sheet and bake, stirring occasionally, until lightly browned and dry, 15 to 20 minutes; set aside to cool. When cool, toss crumbs with Parmesan and 2 tablespoons basil and season with salt and pepper to taste.

2. Meanwhile, slice tomatoes in half lengthwise and scoop out inner ribs and seeds. Sprinkle insides of tomatoes with salt, then lay cut sides down on several layers of paper towels. Let tomatoes sit at room temperature for 30 minutes to 1 hour to drain.

3. Mix goat cheese with remaining 1 tablespoon oil and remaining 2 tablespoons basil. Season with salt and pepper to taste, then transfer to small zipper-lock bag and cut off tip of bag.

4. Pat insides of tomatoes dry with paper towels. Pipe 1 teaspoon goat cheese mixture into bottom of each tomato, then spoon bread crumbs evenly into tomatoes, pressing gently to adhere. Arrange tomatoes in 13 by 9-inch baking dish.

5. Bake tomatoes until cheese is heated through and crumbs are crisp, 15 to 20 minutes. Serve.

PER SERVING Cal 160; **Total Fat** 11g, **Sat Fat** 4.5g; **Chol** 10mg; **Sodium** 410mg; **Total Carb** 8g, **Dietary Fiber** 1g, **Total Sugars** 2g; **Protein** 7g

SEEDING AND STUFFING PLUM TOMATOES

1. Slice tomatoes in half lengthwise and scoop out inner ribs and seeds. Salt and lay cut side down on paper towels to drain.

2. Pat drained tomatoes dry, then pipe 1 teaspoon goat cheese mixture into bottom of each tomato and top with bread crumbs.

Braised Zucchini

SERVES 6 TO 8 `FAST` `VEGAN`

WHY THIS RECIPE WORKS Vibrant, supersummery and flavorful, this is a zucchini side dish that even squash haters could love. Braising is a speedy and convenient stovetop way to prepare zucchini, but since the vegetable contains a lot of water, it can easily end up waterlogged and flavorless. To avoid this, we first cut the zucchini into fairly large pieces, which helped to ensure that they would retain their delicate flavor and become tender without cooking down into mush. We brought the zucchini pieces to a boil in a skillet in a mixture of oil, water, basil, garlic, and pepper flakes—mild seasonings that would allow the zucchini's flavor to shine. We then covered the skillet and let it simmer for 8 minutes, just until the pieces were fork-tender. Stirring it every 2 minutes ensured even cooking. We then added cherry tomatoes and finished cooking the veggies uncovered to drive off excess moisture. Once reduced, the flavorful liquid ably coated the vegetables. If possible, use smaller, in-season zucchini, which have thinner skins and fewer seeds. Stir with a silicone spatula because it's gentle on the zucchini, which has a tendency to break apart. You will need a 12-inch skillet with a tight-fitting lid for this recipe.

- 4 zucchini, trimmed, quartered lengthwise, and cut into 2-inch lengths
- ¼ cup extra-virgin olive oil
- ¼ cup water
- 2 sprigs fresh basil
- 2 garlic cloves, sliced thin
- 1 teaspoon table salt
- ¼ teaspoon pepper
- ¼ teaspoon red pepper flakes
- 3 ounces cherry tomatoes, halved
  Lemon wedges

1. Bring zucchini, oil, water, basil sprigs, garlic, salt, pepper, and pepper flakes to boil in 12-inch nonstick skillet over medium-high heat. Cover, reduce heat to medium, and simmer until zucchini is fork-tender, about 8 minutes, stirring with silicone spatula every 2 minutes.

2. Gently stir in tomatoes and cook, uncovered, until tomatoes are just softened, about 2 minutes. Discard basil sprigs. Serve.

PER SERVING Cal 80; **Total Fat** 7g, **Sat Fat** 1g; **Chol** 0mg; **Sodium** 300mg; **Total Carb** 4g, **Dietary Fiber** 1g, **Total Sugars** 3g; **Protein** 1g

Zucchini Ribbons with Shaved Parmesan

Zucchini Ribbons with Shaved Parmesan

SERVES 6 TO 8 `FAST`

WHY THIS RECIPE WORKS This elegant alternative to salad is also a unique way to serve zucchini without softening its crunchy texture or altering its fresh flavor by cooking. We sliced the zucchini lengthwise into thin ribbons, which was not only more visually appealing than cutting it into rounds but also maximized its surface area for dressing to cling to. A vegetable peeler or mandoline made quick work of this step. We then dressed the zucchini simply with olive oil, lemon juice, mint, and shaved Parmesan cheese. Using in-season zucchini, good olive oil, and high-quality Parmesan is crucial in this simple side dish.

- 1½ pounds zucchini
- ½ cup extra-virgin olive oil
- ¼ cup lemon juice (2 lemons)
- 2 tablespoons minced fresh mint
- 6 ounces Parmesan cheese, shaved

Using vegetable peeler, slice zucchini lengthwise into very thin ribbons. Gently toss zucchini ribbons in bowl with salt and pepper to taste, then arrange attractively on platter. Drizzle with olive oil and lemon juice, sprinkle with mint and Parmesan, and serve.

PER SERVING Cal 230; **Total Fat** 20g, **Sat Fat** 5g; **Chol** 15mg; **Sodium** 390mg; **Total Carb** 3g, **Dietary Fiber** 1g, **Total Sugars** 2g; **Protein** 10g

MAKING ZUCCHINI RIBBONS

Using vegetable peeler or mandoline, slice zucchini lengthwise into very thin ribbons.

Buttery Spring Vegetables
SERVES 6 **FAST**

WHY THIS RECIPE WORKS To prevent our medley of spring vegetables from becoming waterlogged, we staggered their additions to a steamer basket so that each one ended up perfectly crisp-tender. Spreading the vegetables on a platter immediately after cooking allowed excess heat to dissipate so the vegetables didn't overcook while we made the sauce. Instead of plain melted butter, which can slip off the vegetables and pool below, we made a version of the tangy French butter sauce beurre blanc by emulsifying chilled butter into a mixture of shallot, vinegar, salt, sugar, and water. The sauce clung to each vegetable. Peel the turnips thoroughly to remove not only the tough outer skin but also the fibrous layer of flesh just beneath.

  1 **pound turnips, peeled and cut into ½-inch by ½-inch by 2-inch batons**
  1 **pound asparagus, trimmed and cut on bias into 2-inch lengths**
  8 **ounces sugar snap peas, strings removed, trimmed**
  4 **large radishes, halved and sliced thin**
  1 **tablespoon minced shallot**
1½ **teaspoons white wine vinegar**
  ¾ **teaspoon table salt**
  ¼ **teaspoon sugar**
  6 **tablespoons unsalted butter, cut into 6 pieces and chilled**
  1 **tablespoon minced fresh chives**

Buttery Spring Vegetables

1. Bring 1 cup water to boil in large saucepan over high heat. Place steamer basket over boiling water. Add turnips and asparagus to basket, cover saucepan, and reduce heat to medium. Cook until vegetables are slightly softened, about 2 minutes. Add snap peas, cover, and cook until snap peas are crisp-tender, about 2 minutes. Add radishes, cover, and cook for 1 minute. Lift basket out of saucepan and transfer vegetables to platter. Spread into even layer to allow steam to dissipate. Discard all but 3 tablespoons liquid from saucepan.

2. Return saucepan to medium heat. Add shallot, vinegar, salt, and sugar and cook until mixture is reduced to 1½ tablespoons (it will barely cover bottom of saucepan), about 2 minutes. Reduce heat to low. Add butter, 1 piece at a time, whisking vigorously after each addition, until butter is incorporated and sauce has consistency of heavy cream, 4 to 5 minutes. Remove saucepan from heat. Add vegetables and stir to coat. Dry platter and return vegetables to platter. Sprinkle with chives and serve.

PER SERVING Cal 150; **Total Fat** 11g, **Sat Fat** 7g; **Chol** 30mg; **Sodium** 350mg; **Total Carb** 10g, **Dietary Fiber** 3g, **Total Sugars** 5g; **Protein** 3g

Walkaway Ratatouille

⅓ cup plus 1 tablespoon extra-virgin olive oil, divided
2 large onions, cut into 1-inch pieces
8 large garlic cloves, peeled and smashed
1¾ teaspoons table salt, divided
¾ teaspoon pepper, divided
1½ teaspoons herbes de Provence
¼ teaspoon red pepper flakes
1 bay leaf
2 pounds plum tomatoes, peeled, cored, and chopped coarse
1½ pounds eggplant, peeled and cut into 1-inch pieces
2 small zucchini, halved lengthwise and cut into 1-inch pieces
1 red bell pepper, stemmed, seeded, and cut into 1-inch pieces
1 yellow bell pepper, stemmed, seeded, and cut into 1-inch pieces
2 tablespoons chopped fresh basil, divided
1 tablespoon minced fresh parsley
1 tablespoon sherry vinegar

Walkaway Ratatouille

SERVES 6 TO 8 **VEGAN**

WHY THIS RECIPE WORKS This nearly hands-off recipe achieves the ratatouille ideal of simply but intensely flavored (not waterlogged) vegetables while avoiding the time-intensive treatments (like salting and pressing) often used to remove excess moisture. We started by sautéing aromatics and then added chunks of eggplant and tomatoes before transferring the pot to the oven, where the dry, ambient heat would thoroughly evaporate moisture, concentrate flavors, and caramelize some of the vegetables. After 45 minutes, the tomatoes and eggplant became meltingly soft and could be mashed into a thick, silky sauce. Zucchini and bell peppers went into the pot last so that they retained some texture. Finishing the dish with fresh herbs, sherry vinegar, and olive oil tied everything together. This dish is best prepared using ripe, in-season tomatoes. If good tomatoes are not available, substitute one 28-ounce can of whole peeled tomatoes that have been drained and chopped. Ratatouille can be served warm, at room temperature, or chilled, alongside meat or fish, topped with an egg, over pasta, or on its own with crusty bread.

1. Adjust oven rack to middle position and heat oven to 400 degrees. Heat ⅓ cup oil in Dutch oven over medium-high heat until shimmering. Add onions, garlic, 1 teaspoon salt, and ¼ teaspoon pepper and cook, stirring occasionally, until onions are translucent and starting to soften, about 10 minutes. Stir in herbes de Provence, pepper flakes, and bay leaf and cook until fragrant, about 1 minute. Stir in tomatoes, eggplant, ½ teaspoon salt, and ¼ teaspoon pepper.

2. Transfer pot to oven and cook, uncovered, until vegetables are very tender and spotty brown, 40 to 45 minutes.

3. Remove pot from oven and, using potato masher, mash eggplant mixture to coarse puree. Stir in zucchini, bell peppers, remaining ¼ teaspoon salt, and remaining ¼ teaspoon pepper and return to oven. Cook, uncovered, until zucchini and bell peppers are just tender, 20 to 25 minutes.

4. Remove pot from oven, cover, and let stand until zucchini is translucent and easily pierced with tip of paring knife, 10 to 15 minutes. Using wooden spoon, scrape any browned bits from sides of pot and stir back into ratatouille. Discard bay leaf.

5. Stir in 1 tablespoon basil, parsley, and vinegar. Season with salt and pepper to taste. Transfer to large platter, drizzle with remaining 1 tablespoon oil, sprinkle with remaining 1 tablespoon basil, and serve.

PER SERVING Cal 210; **Total Fat** 12g, **Sat Fat** 1.5g; **Chol** 0mg; **Sodium** 530mg; **Total Carb** 24g, **Dietary Fiber** 7g, **Total Sugars** 12g; **Protein** 4g

Boiled Red Potatoes with Butter and Herbs

SERVES 12

WHY THIS RECIPE WORKS When cooking for a crowd, there are few things easier than simply boiling and dressing red potatoes. To serve a large group, 4 pounds of potatoes was the perfect amount. We simply boiled them in a Dutch oven for about 20 minutes before draining them and tossing them with butter and herbs. We prefer to use small red potatoes, measuring 1 to 2 inches in diameter, in this recipe. If using large potatoes, halve or quarter the potatoes and adjust the cooking time as needed. Serve with one of our compound butters instead of plain butter, if desired.

- 4 pounds small red potatoes, unpeeled
- 4 tablespoons unsalted butter, cut into 4 pieces
- 2 tablespoons minced fresh chives, tarragon, or parsley

Cover potatoes by 1 inch water in Dutch oven and bring to boil over high heat. Reduce to simmer and cook until potatoes are tender, 20 to 25 minutes. Drain potatoes, transfer to large bowl, and toss with butter until butter melts. Season with salt and pepper to taste, sprinkle with chives, and serve.

PER SERVING Cal 140; **Total Fat** 4g, **Sat Fat** 2.5g; **Chol** 10mg; **Sodium** 25mg; **Total Carb** 24g, **Dietary Fiber** 3g, **Total Sugars** 2g; **Protein** 3g

Roasted Red Potatoes with Sea Salt

SERVES 12 `VEGAN`

WHY THIS RECIPE WORKS To roast enough potatoes for a large group, we opted for extra-small red potatoes, which could simply be halved (minimizing prep) before roasting until deeply browned, with moist, creamy flesh. To ensure they would cook through without turning leathery, we gave the potatoes a head start by microwaving them with some water. Make sure to thoroughly drain the potatoes (there should be no water in the bottom of the colander). We prefer to use potatoes measuring 1 inch or less in diameter; if yours are slightly larger, you should quarter them.

- 6 pounds extra-small red potatoes, unpeeled, halved
- ⅓ cup extra-virgin olive oil
- 1 tablespoon coarse sea salt or kosher salt
- 1½ teaspoons pepper

1. Adjust oven racks to upper-middle and lower-middle positions and heat oven to 450 degrees. Combine potatoes with ½ cup water in large bowl. Cover and microwave, stirring occasionally, until potatoes begin to soften but still hold their shape, about 15 minutes.

2. Drain potatoes well, then toss with oil and sprinkle with salt and pepper. Arrange potatoes cut side down in single layer on 2 large rimmed baking sheets. Roast until cut sides are golden brown and potatoes are fully tender, about 30 minutes, switching and rotating baking sheets halfway through roasting. Transfer potatoes to serving bowl, season with salt to taste, and serve.

PER SERVING Cal 220; **Total Fat** 7g, **Sat Fat** 1g; **Chol** 0mg; **Sodium** 320mg; **Total Carb** 36g, **Dietary Fiber** 4g, **Total Sugars** 3g; **Protein** 4g

---

TAKE IT UP A NOTCH

Use these butters to flavor boiled or roasted potatoes and countless other simply cooked vegetables. We like to make a double or triple batch, roll it into a log, and freeze it so that flavored butter is always just a slice away.

Compound Butters

Whip 8 tablespoons softened unsalted butter with fork until light and fluffy. Mix in any of the ingredient combinations listed below and season with salt and pepper to taste. Wrap in plastic wrap and let rest to meld flavors, about 10 minutes, or roll into log and refrigerate. (Butter can be refrigerated in airtight container for up to 4 days or frozen, wrapped tightly in plastic wrap, for up to 2 months.)

Parsley-Caper Compound Butter

- ¼ cup minced fresh parsley
- 4 teaspoons capers, rinsed and minced

Parsley-Lemon Compound Butter

- ¼ cup minced fresh parsley
- 4 teaspoons grated lemon zest

Tarragon-Lime Compound Butter

- ¼ cup minced scallions
- 2 tablespoons minced fresh tarragon
- 4 teaspoons lime juice

Tapenade Compound Butter

- 10 oil-cured black olives, pitted and chopped fine
- 1 anchovy fillet, rinsed and minced
- 1 tablespoon brandy
- 2 teaspoons minced fresh thyme
- 2 garlic cloves, minced
- ¼ teaspoon grated orange zest

Duchess Potatoes

1¼ teaspoons table salt
½ teaspoon pepper
½ teaspoon baking powder
   Pinch nutmeg
   Vegetable oil spray

1. Adjust oven rack to upper-middle position and heat oven to 475 degrees. Meanwhile, prick potatoes all over with fork, place on plate, and microwave until tender, 18 to 25 minutes, turning potatoes over after 10 minutes.

2. Cut potatoes in half. When cool enough to handle, scoop flesh into large bowl and mash until no lumps remain. Add cream, 3 tablespoons butter, egg and yolk, salt, pepper, baking powder, and nutmeg and continue to mash until potatoes are smooth. Let cool to room temperature, about 10 minutes. Gently fold in remaining butter until pieces are evenly distributed.

3. Transfer potato mixture to piping bag fitted with ½-inch star tip. Pipe eight 4-inch-wide mounds of potato onto rimmed baking sheet. Spray lightly with vegetable oil spray and bake until golden brown, 15 to 20 minutes. Serve.

PER SERVING Cal 330; Total Fat 20g, Sat Fat 13g; Chol 105mg; Sodium 420mg; Total Carb 32g, Dietary Fiber 2g, Total Sugars 2g; Protein 6g

Duchess Potatoes
SERVES 8

WHY THIS RECIPE WORKS Duchess potatoes take mashed potatoes to the next level, enriched with egg and piped into decorative rosettes before being baked. To cook our spuds, we tried boiling, but this made them waterlogged; baking dried them out. Parcooking them in the microwave and finishing the rosettes in a hot oven proved best. For a potato mixture that was the right texture for piping, we stirred in butter, eggs, and cream while the potatoes were still hot and added more butter once the potatoes had cooled. Baking powder ensured that our picture-perfect Duchess Potatoes had the perfect airy, light texture to match. For the smoothest, most uniform texture, use a food mill or ricer to mash the potatoes. Choose potatoes of the same size so that they cook evenly.

3 pounds russet potatoes
1 cup heavy cream
6 tablespoons unsalted butter, cut into
   ¼-inch pieces and softened, divided
1 large egg plus 1 large yolk, lightly beaten

Pommes Anna
SERVES 6 TO 8

WHY THIS RECIPE WORKS Pommes Anna is a timelessly elegant potato cake with a crisp, deep brown crust covering soft, creamy potato layers—an ideal side dish for a special occasion that is certain to impress. We reached for our nonstick skillet to ensure easy release of the potatoes. Most recipes for pommes Anna call for clarified butter, but to cut down on cooking time and waste (a lot of the butter is lost with clarifying), we tossed the sliced potatoes with melted unsalted butter. We arranged the slices in pretty layered circles in the skillet as it was heating on the stovetop; we then pressed on the layered slices with the bottom of a cake pan to form a cohesive cake. Finally, we simply inverted the potato cake onto a baking sheet and then slid it onto a serving dish. Use a food processor fitted with a fine slicing disk or a mandoline to slice the potatoes; do not slice them until you are ready to assemble.

3 pounds russet or Yukon Gold potatoes,
   peeled and sliced ⅛ inch thick
5 tablespoons unsalted butter, melted
¼ cup vegetable oil
¾ teaspoon table salt, divided

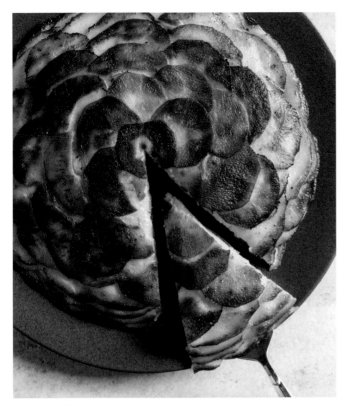

Pommes Anna

1. Adjust oven rack to lower-middle position and heat oven to 450 degrees. Toss potatoes with butter to coat.

2. Heat oil in 10-inch ovenproof nonstick skillet over medium-low heat. Begin timing, and arrange potato slices in skillet, using most attractive slices to form bottom layer, by placing 1 slice in center of skillet and overlapping more slices in circle around center slice; form another circle of overlapping slices to cover pan bottom. Season with ¼ teaspoon salt and pepper to taste. Arrange second layer of potatoes, working in opposite direction of first layer; season with ¼ teaspoon salt and pepper to taste. Repeat, layering potatoes in opposite directions and seasoning with remaining ¼ teaspoon salt and pepper to taste, until no slices remain (broken or uneven slices can be pieced together to form single slice; potatoes will mound in center of skillet). Continue to cook until 30 minutes elapse from when you began arranging potatoes in skillet.

3. Using bottom of 9-inch cake pan, press on potatoes firmly to compact. Cover skillet and place in oven; bake until potatoes begin to soften, about 15 minutes. Uncover and continue to bake until potatoes are tender when pierced with tip of paring knife and edge of potatoes near skillet is browned, about 10 minutes. Meanwhile, line rimless baking sheet or inverted rimmed baking sheet with aluminum foil and spray lightly with vegetable oil spray. Carefully drain off excess fat from potatoes by pressing bottom of cake pan against potatoes while tilting skillet. (Be sure to use heavy potholders.)

4. Set sheet foil side down on top of skillet. Using potholders, hold sheet in place with your hand and carefully invert skillet and sheet together. Lift skillet off potatoes; slide potatoes from sheet onto platter. Cut into wedges and serve immediately.

PER SERVING Cal 240; **Total Fat** 12g, **Sat Fat** 5g; **Chol** 20mg; **Sodium** 230mg; **Total Carb** 31g, **Dietary Fiber** 2g, **Total Sugars** 1g; **Protein** 4g

Potato-Artichoke Gratin
SERVES 8 TO 10

WHY THIS RECIPE WORKS This gratin combines creamy hot artichoke dip with rich, irresistible scalloped potatoes. The best part? It couldn't be easier to prepare; the convenience and quality of frozen artichokes make this satisfying side dish a fuss-free, delicious accompaniment to a roast beef or ham centerpiece at any special-occasion meal. While we prefer frozen artichokes in this recipe, 3 cups of drained jarred whole baby artichokes can also be used here, although the texture of the artichokes may be mushy. If you don't own a mandoline and don't want to slice the potatoes with a knife, you can use a cheese plane.

- 2 tablespoons unsalted butter
- 1 onion, halved and sliced thin
- 3 pounds russet potatoes, peeled and sliced ⅛ inch thick
- 2 cups heavy cream
- 1½ teaspoons table salt
- ½ teaspoon pepper
- 2 (9-ounce) boxes frozen artichokes, thawed and chopped
- 2 cups shredded Gruyère cheese, divided

1. Adjust oven rack to middle position and heat oven to 425 degrees. Melt butter in Dutch oven over medium-high heat. Cook onion until softened, about 5 minutes. Stir in potatoes, cream, salt, and pepper and bring to boil. Reduce heat to medium-low, cover, and simmer until potatoes are almost tender, about 15 minutes. Stir in artichokes and 1 cup cheese and transfer to 13 by 9-inch baking dish.

2. Sprinkle with remaining cheese and bake until golden brown and potatoes are completely tender, about 20 minutes. Let cool for 10 minutes. Serve.

PER SERVING Cal 400; **Total Fat** 27g, **Sat Fat** 17g; **Chol** 85mg; **Sodium** 540mg; **Total Carb** 29g, **Dietary Fiber** 4g, **Total Sugars** 3g; **Protein** 11g

Potato Gratin with Leeks and Fennel

SERVES 12 **MAKE-AHEAD**

WHY THIS RECIPE WORKS Tender leeks, aromatic fennel, and creamy potatoes are the perfect trifecta for a welcoming gratin. For some textural and flavor variety, we combined russet potatoes with a lesser amount of sweet potatoes. Slicing the potatoes very thin—⅛ inch thick—ensured that they would cook through and be tender. We jump-started the leeks and fennel in a skillet along with butter, aromatics, and white wine, then tossed them with the sliced potatoes, along with heavy cream and whole milk, dividing the vegetable medley evenly to make two gratins. To bake them, we pressed the vegetables into flat layers in two shallow gratin dishes which allowed maximum surface area and browned crust. (We portioned the gratin into two smaller dishes rather than a single large dish so that it can be reheated more quickly. We like to use shallow 2-quart gratin dishes, but 8 by 8-inch baking dishes will also work.) To finish, we sprinkled rich grated Gruyère cheese over the top. Use a food processor fitted with a fine slicing disk or a mandoline to slice the potatoes; do not slice them until you are ready to assemble.

- 4 pounds russet potatoes, peeled and sliced ⅛ inch thick
- 1½ pounds sweet potatoes, peeled and sliced ⅛ inch thick
- 2 cups heavy cream
- 1 cup whole milk
- 4 tablespoons unsalted butter
- 12 ounces leeks, white and light green parts only, sliced ⅛ inch thick
- 2 fennel bulbs, stalks discarded, bulbs halved, cored, and sliced ⅛ inch thick
- 5 teaspoons table salt
- 1 teaspoon fennel seeds
- 4 garlic cloves, minced
- 1½ teaspoons minced fresh thyme, or ½ teaspoon dried
- ½ cup dry white wine
- ½ teaspoon pepper
- 6 ounces Gruyère cheese, grated (1½ cups)

1. Adjust oven rack to middle position and heat oven to 375 degrees. Divide potatoes and sweet potatoes evenly between 2 large bowls. Divide cream and milk evenly between 2 bowls and toss to coat potatoes; set aside.

2. Melt butter in 12-inch nonstick skillet over medium-high heat. Add leeks, fennel, salt, and fennel seeds; cover and cook, stirring occasionally, until vegetables are wilted and have given off some liquid, 5 to 7 minutes. Uncover and continue to cook until most of liquid has evaporated, 3 to 5 minutes. Stir in garlic and thyme and cook until fragrant, about 30 seconds. Stir in wine

and pepper and cook until mostly evaporated, about 1 minute. Divide leek mixture evenly between 2 bowls of potatoes and toss to combine.

3. Turn bowls of potatoes into 2 shallow 2-quart gratin dishes, pressing potatoes into flat, even layer. Cover dishes tightly with foil, arrange each on rimmed baking sheet lined with foil, and bake until potatoes are completely tender, 1¾ to 2 hours, rotating sheets halfway through baking. (Gratins can be cooled until warm about 45 minutes, wrapped in plastic, and refrigerated for up to 2 days. To serve, bring to room temperature and continue with step 4.)

4. Increase oven temperature to 450 degrees. Unwrap gratins and sprinkle Gruyère evenly over top. Bake gratins on oven rack until cheese is golden brown and edges are bubbling, about 30 minutes. Serve warm.

PER SERVING Cal 450; **Total Fat** 24g, **Sat Fat** 15g; **Chol** 75mg; **Sodium** 960mg; **Total Carb** 48g, **Dietary Fiber** 6g, **Total Sugars** 8g; **Protein** 11g

Mashed Sweet Potatoes with Chipotle and Lime

SERVES 4

WHY THIS RECIPE WORKS We wanted to highlight the natural flavor of sweet potatoes against a slightly spicy flavor backdrop. We steamed the potatoes in water and then added some butter, chipotle chile, sugar, salt, and pepper. When the potatoes were cooked through, we mashed everything together and then stirred in chives and lime zest for a lively Southwestern flavor profile. This recipe can be easily doubled and prepared in a Dutch oven; increase the cooking time to 40 to 50 minutes.

- 2 pounds sweet potatoes, peeled and sliced ¼ inch thick
- 6 tablespoons water
- 4 tablespoons unsalted butter, cut into 4 pieces
- 2 teaspoons minced canned chipotle chile in adobo sauce
- 1 teaspoon sugar
- 1 teaspoon table salt
- ½ teaspoon pepper
- 2 tablespoons minced fresh chives
- 1 teaspoon grated lime zest

1. Combine potatoes, water, butter, chipotle, sugar, salt, and pepper in large saucepan. Cover and cook over medium-low heat, stirring occasionally, until potatoes crumble easily when poked with paring knife, 25 to 30 minutes.

2. Remove from heat. Using potato masher, mash potatoes thoroughly until smooth and no lumps remain. Stir in chives and lime zest. Season with salt and pepper to taste. Serve.

PER SERVING Cal 400; **Total Fat** 22g, **Sat Fat** 14g; **Chol** 60mg; **Sodium** 720mg; **Total Carb** 47g, **Dietary Fiber** 7g, **Total Sugars** 11g; **Protein** 4g

Rice Pilaf for a Crowd
SERVES 10 TO 12   `MAKE-AHEAD`

WHY THIS RECIPE WORKS Rice pilaf is a crowd pleaser and can pair with any number of main dishes. We turned to our Dutch oven in order to make enough rice for a crowd, cooking an onion in 4 tablespoons of butter and then lightly toasting 3 cups of basmati rice. Then we added the water and a bay leaf and let the rice cook until the liquid was absorbed. Our recipe is great as is, but it also makes an ideal canvas for our flavorful variations We noted the best flavor and texture with basmati rice, but you can substitute long-grain rice, if desired. If you choose to reheat the rice in small servings, adjust the microwaving time accordingly.

  4 tablespoons unsalted butter
  1 onion, chopped fine
    Pinch table salt
  3 cups basmati rice
4½ cups water
  1 bay leaf

1. Melt butter in Dutch oven over medium heat. Add onion and salt and cook until softened, 5 to 7 minutes. Stir in rice and cook, stirring occasionally, until rice is fragrant and edges begin to turn translucent, about 3 minutes.

2. Add water and bay leaf, increase heat to medium-high, and bring to boil. Cover, reduce heat to low, and cook until water is absorbed, about 15 minutes.

3. Off heat, remove lid and place dish towel over pot; replace lid. Let sit for 10 minutes. Discard bay leaf.

4. Fluff rice with fork, season with salt and pepper to taste, and serve. (Rice can be transferred to a microwave-safe bowl, covered, and refrigerated for up to 2 days. To reheat, microwave covered bowl on high power until rice is hot, 12 to 14 minutes. Fluff rice with fork and season with salt and pepper to taste.)

PER SERVING Cal 220; **Total Fat** 3.5g, **Sat Fat** 2.5g; **Chol** 10mg; **Sodium** 15mg; **Total Carb** 40g, **Dietary Fiber** 0g, **Total Sugars** 0g; **Protein** 4g

Rice Pilaf for a Crowd

VARIATIONS
Rice Pilaf with Currants and Cinnamon
Add 2 minced garlic cloves, 1 teaspoon ground turmeric, and ½ teaspoon ground cinnamon to pot after sautéing onion in step 1. Cook until fragrant, about 30 seconds. Sprinkle ½ cup dried currants over cooked rice before letting rice stand in step 3.

Indian-Spiced Rice Pilaf with Dates and Parsley
Add 2 minced garlic cloves, 1 tablespoon grated fresh ginger, ¼ teaspoon ground cinnamon, and ¼ teaspoon ground cardamom to pot after sautéing onion in step 1. Cook until fragrant, about 30 seconds. Before serving, stir in ½ cup chopped dates and 3 tablespoons minced fresh parsley.

Saffron Rice Pilaf with Apricots and Almonds
Add ½ teaspoon saffron with onion in step 1. Sprinkle ½ cup finely chopped dried apricots over cooked rice before letting rice stand in step 3. Before serving, stir in ½ cup toasted slivered almonds.

Easy Baked White Rice for a Crowd

SERVES 12 `VEGAN`

WHY THIS RECIPE WORKS Baking white rice is a convenient alternative to other stovetop methods. This large-scale recipe is especially handy for serving a crowd larger than that on your average weeknight. We rinsed the rice before cooking to wash away the exterior starch and minimize clumping. Moving the rice from the stovetop to the oven meant hands-free cooking and also eliminated issues like burnt rice and scorched pans. Be sure to cover the water when bringing it to a boil in step 1.

3½ cups long-grain white rice, rinsed
5¼ cups water
 1 teaspoon table salt

1. Adjust oven rack to middle position and heat oven to 375 degrees. Spread rice into 13 by 9-inch baking dish. Combine water and salt in large saucepan, cover, and bring to brief boil over high heat.

2. Immediately pour boiling water over rice and cover baking dish tightly with double layer of aluminum foil. Bake rice until tender and no water remains, 40 to 50 minutes.

3. Remove dish from oven, uncover, and fluff rice with fork, scraping up any rice that has stuck to bottom. Re-cover dish with foil and let rice sit for 10 minutes. Season with salt and pepper to taste, and serve.

PER SERVING Cal 190; **Total Fat** 0g, **Sat Fat** 0g; **Chol** 0mg; **Sodium** 200mg; **Total Carb** 42g, **Dietary Fiber** 0g, **Total Sugars** 0g; **Protein** 5g

Spring Vegetable Risotto

Spring Vegetable Risotto

SERVES 4

WHY THIS RECIPE WORKS We love the combination of fresh spring vegetables and creamy risotto, but bland flavor and a mushy texture can ruin this Italian classic. For a risotto primavera with perfectly al dente rice and flavorful vegetables, we started with a combination of asparagus and leeks. The leeks melted down beautifully, infusing the rice with their delicate flavor. Sautéing the asparagus spears and stirring them into the rice right before serving kept them from turning into mush. For a good backbone of flavor, we simmered the leek greens and the tough asparagus stems in the broth we used for cooking the rice. Then we topped the dish with a gremolata (page 41). To substitute onions for the leeks, use one coarsely chopped onion in the broth and two finely chopped onions in the risotto. This more hands-off method requires precise timing, so we strongly recommend using a timer.

 1 pound asparagus, trimmed, tough ends reserved and chopped, spears cut on bias into ½-inch lengths
 2 leeks, white and light green parts halved lengthwise, sliced thin, and washed thoroughly; dark green parts chopped
 4 cups vegetable broth
 3 cups water
 5 tablespoons unsalted butter, divided
    Pinch plus ½ teaspoon table salt, divided
    Pinch plus ½ teaspoon pepper, divided
½ cup frozen peas
 2 garlic cloves, minced
1½ cups Arborio rice
 1 cup dry white wine
1½ ounces Parmesan cheese, grated (¾ cup)
 2 teaspoons lemon juice
 1 recipe Lemon-Mint Gremolata (page 41)

1. Bring chopped asparagus ends, chopped dark green leek parts, broth, and water to boil in large saucepan over high heat. Reduce heat to medium-low, partially cover, and simmer for 20 minutes.

Strain broth through fine-mesh strainer into medium bowl, pressing on solids to extract as much liquid as possible. Return strained broth to saucepan, cover, and set over low heat to keep warm.

2. Melt 1 tablespoon butter in Dutch oven over medium heat. Add asparagus spears, pinch salt, and pinch pepper. Cook, stirring occasionally, until asparagus is crisp-tender, 4 to 6 minutes. Add peas and continue to cook for 1 minute. Transfer vegetables to plate.

3. Melt 3 tablespoons butter in now-empty Dutch oven over medium heat. Add garlic, white and light green leek parts, remaining ½ teaspoon salt, and remaining ½ teaspoon pepper. Cook, stirring occasionally, until leeks are softened, 5 to 7 minutes. Stir in rice and cook, stirring often, until grain edges begin to turn translucent, about 3 minutes.

4. Stir in wine and cook, stirring constantly, until fully absorbed, 2 to 3 minutes. Stir in 4 cups hot broth mixture. Reduce heat to medium-low, cover, and simmer until almost all liquid has been absorbed and rice is just al dente, 18 to 19 minutes, stirring twice during cooking.

5. Add ½ cup hot broth mixture and gently and constantly stir until risotto becomes creamy, about 3 minutes. Stir in Parmesan. Remove pot from heat, cover, and let sit for 5 minutes. Stir in lemon juice and remaining 1 tablespoon butter. Season with salt and pepper to taste and gently fold in asparagus and peas. Before serving, stir in remaining broth mixture as needed to loosen consistency of risotto and sprinkle individual servings with gremolata.

PER SERVING Cal 540; **Total Fat** 19g, **Sat Fat** 10g; **Chol** 45mg; **Sodium** 1290mg; **Total Carb** 71g, **Dietary Fiber** 5g, **Total Sugars** 5g; **Protein** 16g

Herbed Barley Pilaf
SERVES 8 MAKE-AHEAD

WHY THIS RECIPE WORKS This lesser-known grain is making a name for itself in restaurants and fast-casual joints as a hearty, healthy base for a side dish or meal. Firmer in texture and less likely to overcook than rice, barley makes for a substantial and easy-to-prepare alternative to other grains in classic and innovative side dishes alike. For an easy barley pilaf, we started by cooking a chopped onion in melted butter until softened. Then we stirred in the barley along with more aromatics—garlic and thyme—until the grains were lightly toasted. After letting the barley cook at a low simmer until it absorbed almost 4 cups of water, we gave it a 10-minute rest. Parsley, chives, and lemon juice added fresh, bright notes to finish off the dish. Don't substitute hulled barley for the pearl barley; hulled barley requires soaking and a longer cooking time.

4 tablespoons unsalted butter
1 onion, chopped fine
¼ teaspoon table salt
2½ cups pearl barley, rinsed and drained
3 garlic cloves, minced
2 teaspoons minced fresh thyme
3¾ cups water
⅓ cup minced fresh parsley
3 tablespoons minced fresh chives
2 teaspoons lemon juice

1. Melt butter in large saucepan over medium heat. Add onion and salt and cook, stirring occasionally, until onion is softened, 5 to 7 minutes.

2. Stir in barley, garlic, and thyme and cook, stirring often, until barley is lightly toasted and fragrant, about 3 minutes. Stir in water and bring to simmer. Reduce heat to low, cover, and continue to simmer until barley is tender and water is absorbed, 20 to 30 minutes.

3. Off heat, lay clean folded dish towel underneath lid and let sit for 10 minutes. Fluff barley with fork. Fold in parsley, chives, and lemon juice and season with salt and pepper to taste. Serve. (Pilaf can be refrigerated for up to 1 day; reheat in microwave until hot, 2 to 4 minutes, before serving.)

PER SERVING Cal 280; **Total Fat** 6g, **Sat Fat** 3.5g; **Chol** 15mg; **Sodium** 85mg; **Total Carb** 51g, **Dietary Fiber** 10g, **Total Sugars** 1g; **Protein** 7g

Farro with Fennel and Parmesan
SERVES 8 MAKE-AHEAD

WHY THIS RECIPE WORKS This wonderfully nutty, slightly sweet grain is traditionally cooked by Italians in the same manner as Arborio rice to create a creamy dish called farrotto. We found it best to modify the traditional risotto technique and employed a more hands-off hybrid approach. We sautéed the farro with aromatics to enhance its flavor and then simmered it covered with plenty of liquid until nearly tender. We then removed the lid and stirred it frequently during the last minutes of cooking, releasing starches in the farro to create a rich and creamy consistency. For a creamy texture, be sure to stir the farro often in step 3. Farro can be found at the market alongside the other grains (such as barley) or next to the dried pasta.

¼ cup extra-virgin olive oil

1 onion, chopped fine

1 fennel bulb, stalks discarded, bulb halved, cored, and chopped fine

½ teaspoon table salt

6 garlic cloves, minced

2 teaspoons minced fresh thyme

3½ cups farro

4 cups chicken broth

3 cups water, plus extra as needed

2 ounces Parmesan cheese, grated (1 cup)

½ cup minced fresh parsley

4 teaspoons balsamic vinegar

1. Heat oil in Dutch oven over medium heat until shimmering. Add onion, fennel, and ½ teaspoon salt and cook until softened, about 10 minutes. Stir in garlic and thyme and cook until fragrant, about 30 seconds. Stir in farro and cook until lightly toasted, about 3 minutes.

2. Stir in broth and water and bring to boil. Cover, reduce heat to low, and simmer until farro is nearly tender yet still firm in center, 45 to 50 minutes.

3. Uncover, increase heat to medium, and simmer, stirring often, until farro is tender and most of liquid has evaporated, about 10 minutes. If pot looks dry before farro is tender, add additional water as needed. (Farro can be covered and held at room temperature for up to 4 hours; reheat gently over medium-low heat, adding extra water as needed, before continuing.)

4. Off heat, stir in Parmesan, parsley, and vinegar. Season with salt and pepper to taste, and serve.

PER SERVING Cal 370; **Total Fat** 9g, **Sat Fat** 2g; **Chol** 5mg; **Sodium** 620mg; **Total Carb** 58g, **Dietary Fiber** 7g, **Total Sugars** 3g; **Protein** 15g

Creamy Parmesan Polenta for a Crowd
SERVES 8

WHY THIS RECIPE WORKS We love polenta for a hearty, rustic-yet-elegant side dish. And since it is so simple on its own, it's the perfect canvas for a number of added flavorings or toppings, making it an ideal choice to include on any dinner party menu. Coarse-ground degerminated cornmeal was the best choice for the texture and nutty flavor we were wanted. To serve eight people, we used 2 cups of cornmeal and cooked it in water with a pinch of baking soda, which cut down on cooking time and

eliminated the need for stirring. We stirred in Parmesan cheese and butter at the end of cooking for rich flavor and creamy texture. Do not use instant or quick-cooking polenta here. Coarse-ground degerminated cornmeal such as yellow grits (with uniform grains the size of couscous) will work, but do not use whole grain, stone-ground, or regular cornmeal. Do not omit the baking soda—it reduces the cooking time and makes for a creamier polenta. Using a high-quality Parmesan is crucial in this simple side dish. Serve with one of our flavorful polenta toppings (page 193).

9½ cups water

2 teaspoons table salt

Pinch baking soda

2 cups polenta

5 ounces Parmesan cheese, grated (2½ cups), plus extra for serving

3 tablespoons unsalted butter

1. Bring water to boil in large saucepan over medium-high heat. Stir in salt and baking soda. Slowly add polenta while whisking constantly in circular motion to prevent clumping. Bring to simmer, stirring constantly, about 1 minute. Reduce heat to lowest possible setting and cover.

2. Cook for 5 minutes, then whisk polenta to smooth out lumps, about 15 seconds. Cover and continue to cook, without stirring, until grains of polenta are tender but slightly al dente, about 30 minutes longer. (Polenta should be loose and barely hold its shape but will continue to thicken as it cools.)

3. Off heat, stir in Parmesan and butter and season with salt and pepper to taste. Let polenta sit, covered, for 5 minutes. Serve, passing additional Parmesan separately.

PER SERVING Cal 250; **Total Fat** 9g, **Sat Fat** 5g; **Chol** 25mg; **Sodium** 920mg; **Total Carb** 32g, **Dietary Fiber** 0g, **Total Sugars** 0g; **Protein** 11g

Butternut Squash Polenta
SERVES 8

WHY THIS RECIPE WORKS Butternut squash puree transforms plain polenta into a nutritious side dish while enhancing its rustic appeal. How much squash could we add without overpowering polenta's texture and sweet corn flavor? Turns out, for 1 cup of cornmeal, a whole small squash was perfect. Roasting squash halves and scooping out the creamy flesh kept the process unfussy. For fluffy, creamy polenta, we added a pinch of baking soda, which

Butternut Squash Polenta

1. Adjust oven rack to middle position and heat oven to 400 degrees. Line rimmed baking sheet with aluminum foil. Brush cut sides of squash with 1½ teaspoons oil, sprinkle with ¼ teaspoon salt and ⅛ teaspoon pepper, and place squash cut sides down on prepared baking sheet. Roast until fork inserted into center meets little resistance and sides touching sheet are deep golden brown, 40 to 50 minutes.

2. Remove squash from oven and let cool for 10 minutes. Scoop flesh of squash into medium bowl and set aside; discard skin.

3. Heat remaining 1½ teaspoons oil in large saucepan over medium heat until shimmering. Add onion and remaining ¾ teaspoon salt and cook until softened and lightly browned, 5 to 7 minutes. Add sage and nutmeg and cook until fragrant, about 30 seconds. Stir in water, bay leaf, baking soda, and remaining ¼ teaspoon pepper and bring to boil. Slowly pour cornmeal into water in steady stream while stirring back and forth with wooden spoon or silicone spatula. Bring mixture to boil, stirring constantly, about 1 minute. Reduce heat to lowest setting and cover.

4. After 5 minutes, whisk polenta to smooth out any lumps that may have formed, about 15 seconds. (Make sure to scrape down sides and bottom of saucepan.) Cover and continue to cook, whisking occasionally, until polenta grains are tender but slightly al dente, about 25 minutes longer.

5. Stir in cooked squash, increase heat to medium-low, and cook, stirring occasionally, until squash is well incorporated, about 5 minutes.

6. Off heat, stir in Parmesan and season with salt and pepper to taste. Cover and let sit for 5 minutes. Serve, topping individual portions with extra Parmesan, pepitas, and a drizzle of balsamic vinegar.

PER SERVING Cal 140; **Total Fat** 4.5g, **Sat Fat** 1g; **Chol** 5mg; **Sodium** 380mg; **Total Carb** 24g, **Dietary Fiber** 5g, **Total Sugars** 3g; **Protein** 4g

encouraged the grains to release their starches for a silky consistency with minimal stirring. To round out the flavor, we cooked the polenta with fresh sage and a pinch of nutmeg, then finished with a bit of Parmesan.

- 1 small (1½- to 2-pound) butternut squash, halved lengthwise, seeds removed
- 1 tablespoon extra-virgin olive oil, divided, plus extra for serving
- 1 teaspoon table salt, divided
- ⅛ teaspoon plus ¼ teaspoon pepper, divided
- 1 small onion, chopped fine
- 1½ teaspoons minced fresh sage
- ⅛ teaspoon ground nutmeg
- 5 cups water
- 1 bay leaf
  Pinch baking soda
- 1 cup whole-grain coarse-ground cornmeal
- 1 ounce Parmesan cheese, grated (½ cup), plus extra for serving
- 2 tablespoons pepitas, toasted
  Balsamic vinegar

Couscous with Pistachio and Cilantro

SERVES 12 · MAKE-AHEAD · VEGAN

WHY THIS RECIPE WORKS Couscous is an incredibly easy side dish, and great for a crowd because it can be served either warm or at room temperature. Though it may look like a grain, couscous is actually tiny pasta made from semolina. During our testing, we found that toasting the couscous for a few minutes before adding the liquid gave it a deeper, richer flavor. The toasted couscous can then simply be soaked in boiling water to hydrate and turn tender. For an accurate measurement of boiling water, bring a full kettle of water to a boil, then measure out the desired amount. This dish can be served warm or at room temperature.

3½ cups couscous
½ cup extra-virgin olive oil, divided, plus extra
   for drizzling
1 large onion, chopped fine
6 garlic cloves, minced
4¼ cups boiling water
1 teaspoon table salt
¾ cup pistachios, toasted (see page 269) and chopped
¼ cup lemon juice (2 lemons)
½ cup minced fresh cilantro

1. Toast couscous with 3 tablespoons oil in 12-inch skillet over medium heat, stirring occasionally, until lightly browned, 3 to 5 minutes; transfer to large bowl.

2. Heat 2 tablespoons oil in now-empty skillet over medium-high heat until shimmering. Add onion and cook until softened, about 5 minutes. Stir in garlic and cook until fragrant, about 30 seconds. Transfer to bowl with couscous.

3. Stir boiling water and salt into couscous. Cover tightly with plastic wrap and let sit until couscous is tender, about 12 minutes.

4. Fluff couscous with fork, breaking up any clumps. Add remaining 3 tablespoons oil, pistachios, and lemon juice and gently toss to incorporate. Drizzle with oil and season with salt and pepper to taste. (Couscous can be refrigerated for up to 1 day; microwave, covered, until hot, 3 to 5 minutes.) Fold in cilantro and serve warm or at room temperature.

PER SERVING Cal 340; **Total Fat** 13g, **Sat Fat** 2g; **Chol** 0mg; **Sodium** 200mg; **Total Carb** 46g, **Dietary Fiber** 4g, **Total Sugars** 3g; **Protein** 9g

Pearl Couscous with Caramelized Fennel and Spinach

Pearl Couscous with Caramelized Fennel and Spinach

SERVES 4 TO 6 `VEGAN`

WHY THIS RECIPE WORKS Larger-grained pearl couscous, as opposed to the more traditional small-grain Moroccan couscous, gives dishes a heartier texture and great visual appeal. Pearl couscous also has a unique nutty taste that we paired with baby spinach and thinly sliced anise-flavored fennel. Some lemon zest and fresh lemon juice brightened it up, and chives added freshness. Traditional couscous can simply be soaked in boiling water to rehydrate and turn tender, but the larger grains of pearl couscous require boiling or simmering. Once the couscous was tender, we sautéed the fennel along with some sliced onion; the baby spinach just needed to be stirred in off the heat until it was lightly wilted.

1½ cups pearl couscous
¼ teaspoon table salt, plus salt for cooking couscous
2 tablespoons extra-virgin olive oil, divided
3 fennel bulbs, stalks discarded, bulbs halved, cored,
   and sliced thin
½ onion, halved and sliced ¼ inch thick
2 garlic cloves, minced
½ teaspoon grated lemon zest plus 1 tablespoon juice,
   divided
4 ounces (4 cups) baby spinach
3 tablespoons minced fresh chives

1. Bring 4 quarts water to boil in Dutch oven. Stir in couscous and 1 tablespoon salt and cook until tender, about 5 minutes. Drain couscous, transfer to large bowl, and cover to keep warm.

2. Wipe now-empty pot dry, add 1½ tablespoons oil, and place over medium-low heat until shimmering. Add fennel, onion, and ¼ teaspoon salt, cover, and cook, stirring occasionally, until vegetables have softened and released their liquid, about

15 minutes. Uncover, increase heat to medium-high, and cook, stirring often, until lightly browned and liquid has evaporated, 15 to 20 minutes.

3. Stir in garlic and lemon zest and cook until fragrant, about 1 minute. Off heat, stir in spinach, cover, and let sit until spinach is wilted, about 2 minutes. Stir in couscous, lemon juice, chives, and remaining 1½ teaspoons oil. Season with salt and pepper to taste, and serve warm or at room temperature.

PER SERVING Cal 260; **Total Fat** 5g, **Sat Fat** 0.5g; **Chol** 0mg; **Sodium** 270mg; **Total Carb** 47g, **Dietary Fiber** 4g, **Total Sugars** 6g; **Protein** 8g

Orzo with Lemon, Basil, and Feta for a Crowd
SERVES 8 **FAST** MAKE-AHEAD

WHY THIS RECIPE WORKS To produce separate, distinct pieces of orzo, we cooked the orzo in abundant boiling water and rinsed it in cold water to prevent sticking. So that it would play well with a wide range of dishes, we kept the flavor bright but uncomplicated with lemon, garlic, feta cheese, and plenty of chopped basil. Rinsing the pasta under cold water halted the cooking process and kept the orzo from sticking together.

- 1 pound orzo
  Table salt for cooking orzo
- 3 tablespoons extra-virgin olive oil
- 2 teaspoons grated lemon zest plus 2 tablespoons juice
- 2 garlic cloves, minced
- 8 ounces feta cheese, crumbled (2 cups)
- ½ cup chopped fresh basil

Bring 4 quarts water to boil in large pot. Add orzo and 1 tablespoon salt and cook, stirring often, until tender. Drain orzo and rinse under cold water. Transfer orzo to large bowl and toss with oil, lemon zest and juice, and garlic. Fold in feta and season with salt and pepper to taste. (Orzo can be refrigerated for up to 2 days; bring to room temperature before serving.) Fold in basil and serve.

PER SERVING Cal 330; **Total Fat** 12g, **Sat Fat** 5g; **Chol** 25mg; **Sodium** 340mg; **Total Carb** 44g, **Dietary Fiber** 0g, **Total Sugars** 4g; **Protein** 12g

Pasta with Roasted Cherry Tomatoes
SERVES 6 TO 8

WHY THIS RECIPE WORKS Slow-roasted tomatoes offer a sweet depth of flavor to pasta, but we didn't want to spend 2 hours waiting for the oven to work its magic for our pasta with roasted cherry tomatoes. By choosing cherry tomatoes instead of bigger varieties and turning up the oven to 500 degrees, we were able to achieve the same richness of flavor in just 20 minutes. Nestling sliced garlic cloves into the tomatoes softened their edge without burning them. Tossed with pasta, basil, and Parmesan, the dish delivered deep flavor. You will need 3 pints of cherry tomatoes for this recipe; you can use an equal amount of grape tomatoes. Linguine or capellini can be substituted for the spaghetti.

- 3 tablespoons extra-virgin olive oil, divided
- 5 garlic cloves, sliced thin
- 2 teaspoons tomato paste
- 1½ teaspoons table salt, plus salt for cooking pasta
- 1 teaspoon sugar
- ¼ teaspoon pepper
- ⅛ teaspoon red pepper flakes
- 1¾ pounds cherry tomatoes
- 1 pound spaghetti
- ½ cup coarsely chopped fresh basil
- 1 ounce Parmesan cheese, grated (½ cup), plus extra for serving

1. Adjust oven rack to middle position and heat oven to 500 degrees. Line rimmed baking sheet with parchment paper. Whisk 2 tablespoons oil, garlic, tomato paste, 1½ teaspoons salt, sugar, pepper, and pepper flakes together in large bowl. Add tomatoes and toss to combine.

2. Transfer tomato mixture to prepared sheet and push tomatoes toward center of sheet. Scrape any remaining garlic and tomato paste from bowl into center of tomatoes. Bake until tomatoes are blistered and browned, about 20 minutes.

3. Bring 4 quarts water to boil in large pot. Add pasta and 1 tablespoon salt and cook, stirring often, until al dente. Reserve 1 cup cooking water, then drain pasta and return it to pot.

4. Add basil, roasted tomato mixture, ½ cup reserved cooking water, and remaining 1 tablespoon oil to pasta and toss to combine. Adjust consistency with remaining reserved cooking water as needed and season with salt and pepper to taste. Transfer to serving dish and sprinkle with Parmesan. Serve, passing extra Parmesan separately.

PER SERVING Cal 290; **Total Fat** 8g, **Sat Fat** 1.5g; **Chol** 5mg; **Sodium** 590mg; **Total Carb** 46g, **Dietary Fiber** 1g, **Total Sugars** 4g; **Protein** 10g

POTLUCK FAVORITES

■ FAST (30 minutes or less total time)   ■ MAKE-AHEAD   ■ VEGAN

Photos (clockwise from top left): All-American Potato Salad; Sweet and Tangy Coleslaw; Spinach and Strawberry Salad with Poppy Seed Dressing; Cold Soba Noodle Salad

Asparagus Salad with Radishes, Pecorino Romano, and Croutons

SERVES 4 TO 6   **FAST**

WHY THIS RECIPE WORKS Raw asparagus is just as delicious as cooked and makes an ideal base for a quick potluck-worthy salad. The raw asparagus is mildly sweet and nutty, with a delicate crunch and none of the sulfurous flavors that cooked asparagus sometimes has. Peeling the spears left them too fibrous, but as long as we chose the right ones (bright green, firm, and crisp, with tightly closed tips) and sliced them very thin on the bias, we could leave the spears unpeeled and avoid woodiness while still keeping things crunchy. This technique worked best with thicker spears. To complement the asparagus, we wanted an herby dressing, and turned to mint and basil. A high ratio of herbs to oil created a pesto-style dressing potent enough to enhance but not mask the flavor of the asparagus. We processed the herbs with Pecorino Romano cheese, garlic, lemon, and salt before adding extra-virgin olive oil. A few radishes, more Pecorino, and homemade croutons rounded out the salad.

CROUTONS

- 2 tablespoons unsalted butter
- 1 tablespoon extra-virgin olive oil
- 2 slices hearty white sandwich bread, crusts discarded, cut into ½-inch pieces
- ⅛ teaspoon table salt

PESTO DRESSING

- 2 cups fresh mint leaves
- ¼ cup fresh basil leaves
- ¼ cup grated Pecorino Romano cheese
- 1 teaspoon grated lemon zest plus 2 teaspoons juice
- 1 garlic clove, minced
- ¾ teaspoon table salt
- ½ cup extra-virgin olive oil

SALAD

- 2 pounds thick asparagus, trimmed
- 5 radishes, trimmed and sliced thin
- 2 ounces Pecorino Romano cheese, shaved (¾ cup)

1. FOR THE CROUTONS Heat butter and oil in 12-inch nonstick skillet over medium heat until butter is melted. Add bread pieces and salt and cook, stirring frequently, until golden brown, 7 to 10 minutes. Season with salt and pepper to taste and set aside.

2. FOR THE PESTO DRESSING Process mint, basil, Pecorino, lemon zest and juice, garlic, and salt in food processor until smooth, about 20 seconds, scraping down sides of bowl as needed. With processor running, slowly add oil until incorporated; transfer to large bowl and season with salt and pepper to taste.

Asparagus Salad with Radishes, Pecorino Romano, and Croutons

3. FOR THE SALAD Cut asparagus tips from spears into ¾-inch-long pieces. Slice asparagus spears ⅛ inch thick on bias. Add asparagus tips and spears, radishes, and Pecorino to dressing and toss to combine. Season with salt and pepper to taste. Transfer salad to serving platter and top with croutons. Serve.

PER SERVING Cal 330; **Total Fat** 29g; **Sat Fat** 8g; Chol 20mg; **Sodium** 580mg; **Total Carb** 11g, **Dietary Fiber** 2g, **Total Sugars** 2g, **Protein** 7g

VARIATION

Asparagus Salad with Grapes, Goat Cheese, and Almonds

Omit croutons. Substitute 6 ounces thinly sliced grapes for radishes and 4 ounces crumbled goat cheese for Pecorino in the salad. Add ¾ cup toasted and chopped almonds to salad in step 3.

Broccoli Salad with Raisins and Walnuts

SERVES 4 TO 6 `FAST` `MAKE-AHEAD`

WHY THIS RECIPE WORKS Most recipes for broccoli salad leave the broccoli raw, but we found that cooking it briefly in boiling water improved both its flavor and its appearance. Adding the hardier stems to the cooking water before the florets leveled the playing field, so both became tender at the same time. Drying the broccoli in a salad spinner rid it of excess moisture, so the dressing—a tangy mayo-and-vinegar mixture—wouldn't get watered down. As an added benefit, when treated this way, the broccoli retained its color, flavor, and crunch in the fridge. Toasted walnuts and golden raisins brought more crunch and salty-sweet balance to this side dish. When prepping the broccoli, keep the stems and florets separate. If you don't own a salad spinner, lay the broccoli on a clean dish towel to dry in step 2.

- ½ cup golden raisins
- 1½ pounds broccoli, florets cut into 1-inch pieces, stalks peeled and sliced ¼ inch thick
- ½ cup mayonnaise
- 1 tablespoon balsamic vinegar
- ½ teaspoon table salt
- ¼ teaspoon pepper
- ½ cup walnuts, toasted and chopped
- 1 large shallot, minced

1. Bring 3 quarts water to boil in Dutch oven. Fill large bowl halfway with ice and water. Combine ½ cup of boiling water and raisins in small bowl, cover, and let sit for 5 minutes; drain.

2. Meanwhile, add broccoli stalks to pot of boiling water and cook for 1 minute. Add florets and cook until slightly tender, about 1 minute. Drain broccoli, then transfer to bowl of ice water and let sit until chilled, about 5 minutes. Drain again, transfer broccoli to salad spinner, and spin dry.

3. Whisk mayonnaise, vinegar, salt, and pepper together in large bowl. Add broccoli, raisins, walnuts, and shallot to bowl with dressing and toss to combine. Season with salt and pepper to taste, and serve. (Salad can be refrigerated for up to 6 hours.)

PER SERVING Cal 250; **Total Fat** 19g, **Sat Fat** 2.5g; **Chol** 5mg; **Sodium** 340mg; **Total Carb** 18g, **Dietary Fiber** 3g, **Total Sugars** 12g; **Protein** 4g

Cauliflower Salad with Chermoula and Carrots

Cauliflower Salad with Chermoula and Carrots

SERVES 4 TO 6 `VEGAN`

WHY THIS RECIPE WORKS Chermoula is a traditional Moroccan marinade made with hefty amounts of cilantro, lemon, and garlic that pack a big flavor punch. While this dressing is usually used as a marinade for meat and fish, we decided to make it the flavor base for a zippy cauliflower salad in an effort to spice up a vegetable that can be bland. We focused first on the cooking method of the starring vegetable. Roasting was the best choice to add deep flavor to the cauliflower and balance the bright chermoula. To keep the cauliflower from overbrowning before the interior was cooked, we started it covered and let it steam until barely tender. Then we removed the foil, added sliced onion, and returned the pan to the oven to let both the onion and the cauliflower caramelize. Adding the onion to the pan once the cauliflower was uncovered ensured that they would finish cooking at the same time. Finally, to highlight the natural sweetness of the cooked vegetables, we added shredded carrot and raisins, two common North African ingredients. Use the large holes of a box grater to shred the carrot.

SALAD

- 1 head cauliflower (2 pounds), cored and cut into 2-inch florets
- 2 tablespoons extra-virgin olive oil
- ½ teaspoon table salt
- ¼ teaspoon pepper
- ½ red onion, sliced ¼ inch thick
- 1 cup shredded carrot
- ½ cup raisins
- 2 tablespoons chopped fresh cilantro
- 2 tablespoons sliced toasted almonds

CHERMOULA

- ¾ cup fresh cilantro leaves
- ¼ cup extra-virgin olive oil
- 2 tablespoons lemon juice
- 4 garlic cloves, minced
- ½ teaspoon ground cumin
- ½ teaspoon paprika
- ¼ teaspoon table salt
- ⅛ teaspoon cayenne pepper

1. **FOR THE SALAD** Adjust oven rack to lowest position and heat oven to 475 degrees. Toss cauliflower with oil and sprinkle with salt and pepper. Spread on parchment paper–lined rimmed baking sheet, cover tightly with aluminum foil, and roast until softened, 5 to 7 minutes.

2. Remove foil and scatter onion on sheet. Roast until vegetables are tender, cauliflower is deep golden, and onion slices are charred at edges, 10 to 15 minutes, stirring halfway through roasting. Let cool slightly, about 5 minutes.

3. **FOR THE CHERMOULA** Process all ingredients in food processor until smooth, about 1 minute, scraping down sides of bowl as needed; transfer to large bowl. Add cauliflower-onion mixture, carrot, and raisins and toss to combine. Season with salt and pepper to taste, sprinkle with cilantro and almonds. Serve warm or at room temperature.

PER SERVING Cal 240; **Total Fat** 16g, **Sat Fat** 2g; **Chol** 0mg; **Sodium** 350mg; **Total Carb** 22g, **Dietary Fiber** 4g, **Total Sugars** 14g; **Protein** 4g

Marinated Eggplant with Capers and Mint

Marinated Eggplant with Capers and Mint
SERVES 4 TO 6   `MAKE-AHEAD`   `VEGAN`

WHY THIS RECIPE WORKS Marinated eggplant is a classic Greek dish popular for sharing. It has a surprisingly creamy texture and a deep yet tangy flavor. We wanted an easy recipe that would keep the eggplant in the spotlight, with a complementary, brightly flavored marinade. To start, we experimented with cooking techniques: We tried frying but found that the eggplant absorbed too much oil; pan frying in batches required too much time for a simple side dish; and roasting yielded either leathery eggplant skin or undercooked and tough flesh. We found that broiling was perfect; we could achieve flavorful browning on the eggplant and it cooked through nicely. To encourage even more browning, we first salted the eggplant, which drew out excess moisture. As for the marinade, a Greek-inspired combination of extra-virgin olive oil (using only a few tablespoons kept the eggplant from turning greasy), red wine vinegar, capers, lemon zest, oregano, garlic, and mint worked perfectly. When making this dish ahead, we found that the flavor was better if we brought the eggplant to room temperature before serving. If using table salt, reduce all of the salt amounts in the recipe by half.

1½ pounds Italian eggplant, sliced into 1-inch thick rounds
1 teaspoon kosher salt
¼ cup extra-virgin olive oil, divided
4 teaspoons red wine vinegar
1 tablespoon capers, rinsed and minced
1 garlic clove, minced
½ teaspoon grated lemon zest
½ teaspoon minced fresh oregano
¼ teaspoon pepper
3 tablespoons minced fresh mint

1. Spread eggplant on paper towel–lined baking sheet, sprinkle each side with ½ teaspoon salt, and let sit for 30 minutes.

2. Adjust oven rack 4 inches from broiler element and heat broiler. Pat eggplant thoroughly dry with paper towels, arrange on aluminum foil–lined rimmed baking sheet in single layer, and lightly brush both sides with 1 tablespoon oil. Broil eggplant until mahogany brown and lightly charred, 6 to 8 minutes per side.

3. Whisk remaining 3 tablespoons oil, vinegar, capers, garlic, lemon zest, oregano, and pepper together in large bowl. Add eggplant and mint and gently toss to combine.

4. Let eggplant cool to room temperature, about 1 hour. Season with pepper to taste, and serve. (Marinated eggplant can be refrigerated for up to 3 days.)

PER SERVING Cal 120; **Total Fat** 10g; **Sat Fat** 1.5g; **Chol** 0mg; **Sodium** 130mg; **Total Carb** 7g, **Dietary Fiber** 3g, **Total Sugars** 4g; **Protein** 1g

Green Bean Salad with Cilantro Sauce

Green Bean Salad with Cilantro Sauce
SERVES 6 TO 8 **FAST** **MAKE-AHEAD** **VEGAN**

WHY THIS RECIPE WORKS In this vibrant green bean salad, sweet green beans and grassy cilantro really shine. For a variation on pesto, we swapped out basil for bright, herbal cilantro and traded pine nuts for walnuts. Some lemon juice rounded out the flavors and loosened the sauce. We blanched and shocked the beans to set their green color and ensure that they were evenly cooked. Be sure to set up the ice water bath before cooking the green beans, as plunging them in the cold water immediately after blanching retains their bright green color and keeps them from overcooking.

2 pounds green beans, trimmed
½ teaspoon table salt, plus salt for cooking green beans
¼ cup walnuts
2 garlic cloves, unpeeled
2½ cups fresh cilantro leaves and stems, tough stem ends trimmed (about 2 bunches)
½ cup extra-virgin olive oil
4 teaspoons lemon juice
1 scallion, sliced thin
⅛ teaspoon pepper

1. Bring 4 quarts water to boil in large pot over high heat. Fill large bowl halfway with ice and water. Add green beans and 1 tablespoon salt to boiling water and cook until crisp-tender, 2 to 4 minutes. Drain beans, then transfer immediately to ice water. Let beans cool completely, about 5 minutes, then drain again and return to now-empty bowl.

2. Meanwhile, cook walnuts and garlic in dry 8-inch skillet over medium heat, stirring often, until toasted and fragrant, 5 to 7 minutes; transfer to bowl. Let garlic cool slightly, then peel and chop.

3. Process walnuts, garlic, cilantro, oil, lemon juice, scallion, ½ teaspoon salt, and pepper in food processor until smooth, about 1 minute, scraping down sides of bowl as needed. Season with salt and pepper to taste. Add cilantro sauce to green beans and toss to coat, and serve. (Salad can be refrigerated for up to 4 hours.)

PER SERVING Cal 190; **Total Fat** 16g; **Sat Fat** 2g; **Chol** 0mg; **Sodium** 230mg; **Total Carb** 9g, **Dietary Fiber** 3g; **Total Sugars** 4g; **Protein** 3g

Caesar Green Bean Salad

SERVES 4 TO 6 **FAST** **MAKE-AHEAD**

WHY THIS RECIPE WORKS It's hard to beat a classic Caesar salad. We decided to take that savory dressing and elevate the flavor of green beans with it for a no-fuss potluck-worthy side. To keep things easy, we blanched green beans in boiling salted water, and rather than shocking them in ice water, transferred the beans to a baking sheet to cool. To make a Caesar dressing that would cling well to the beans, we emulsified its usual potent ingredients, minus raw egg, with a tablespoon of Dijon mustard. To add texture and crunch to the salad (and keep it traditional), we tossed in shards of Parmesan and crisp homemade croutons.

DRESSING AND GREEN BEANS

1½ tablespoons lemon juice
1 tablespoon Worcestershire sauce
1 tablespoon Dijon mustard
3 garlic cloves, minced
3 anchovy fillets, rinsed and minced to paste
½ teaspoon pepper
¼ teaspoon table salt plus salt for cooking green beans
3 tablespoons extra-virgin olive oil
1½ pounds green beans, trimmed
2 ounces Parmesan cheese, shaved with vegetable peeler, divided

CROUTONS

3 ounces baguette, cut into ½-inch pieces
2 tablespoons extra-virgin olive oil
¼ teaspoon pepper

1. FOR THE DRESSING AND GREEN BEANS Whisk lemon juice, Worcestershire, mustard, garlic, anchovies, pepper, and ¼ teaspoon salt in bowl until combined. Slowly whisk in oil until emulsified; set aside. (Dressing can be made up to 1 day in advance.)

COOLING GREEN BEANS

An alternative method to shocking green beans in ice water to stop them from cooking is to simply spread them onto a dish towel–lined baking sheet to cool.

Caesar Green Bean Salad

2. Line baking sheet with clean dish towel. Bring 4 quarts water to boil in Dutch oven. Add green beans and 1½ teaspoons salt, return to boil, and cook until tender, 5 to 7 minutes. Drain green beans in colander and spread in even layer on prepared sheet. Let green beans cool completely.

3. FOR THE CROUTONS Meanwhile, toss cut baguette, oil, and pepper in large bowl until pieces are coated with oil. Transfer to 12-inch nonstick skillet (reserve bowl). Cook over medium-high heat, stirring occasionally, until golden brown and crispy, 5 to 7 minutes. Return croutons to reserved bowl.

4. Transfer dressing, green beans, and half of Parmesan to bowl with croutons and toss to combine. Season with salt and pepper to taste. Transfer to serving dish. Sprinkle with remaining Parmesan. Serve.

PER SERVING Cal 230; **Total Fat** 15g, **Sat Fat** 3g; **Chol** 10mg; **Sodium** 580mg; **Total Carb** 17g, **Dietary Fiber** 3g, **Total Sugars** 4g; **Protein** 8g

Radicchio Chopped Salad

SERVES 4 TO 6 | FAST

WHY THIS RECIPE WORKS For an easy and elegant chopped salad, we started with radicchio and sturdy romaine as the base for a wealth of tasty add-ins. While the cucumber marinated in the dressing to soak up flavor, we readied radicchio, apple, goat cheese for tangy richness, toasted pecans, dried cranberries, and basil for freshness. To cut the romaine lettuce hearts and radicchio into ½-inch pieces, cut each in half lengthwise, then cut each half lengthwise into two. Finally, cut the quarters crosswise into ½-inch pieces.

- ¼ cup extra-virgin olive oil
- 3 tablespoons balsamic vinegar
- 1 shallot, minced
- ¾ teaspoon table salt, divided
- ¾ teaspoon pepper, divided
- ½ English cucumber, cut into ½-inch pieces
- 1 romaine lettuce heart (6 ounces), cut into ½-inch pieces
- 1 small head radicchio (6 ounces), halved, cored, and cut into ½-inch pieces
- 1 apple, cored and cut into ½-inch pieces
- 4 ounces goat cheese, crumbled (1 cup)
- ½ cup chopped toasted pecans
- ½ cup dried cranberries
- ¼ cup fresh basil leaves, torn into 1-inch pieces

1. Whisk oil, vinegar, shallot, ½ teaspoon salt, and ½ teaspoon pepper together in large bowl. Add cucumber to bowl and gently toss to coat with dressing; let rest for 10 minutes.

2. Add romaine, radicchio, apple, goat cheese, pecans, cranberries, basil, remaining ¼ teaspoon salt, and remaining ¼ teaspoon pepper to cucumber mixture and gently toss to combine. Season with salt and pepper to taste. Transfer to platter and serve.

PER SERVING Cal 290; Total Fat 20g, Sat Fat 4.5g; Chol 10mg; Sodium 390mg; Total Carb 23g, Dietary Fiber 4g, Total Sugars 17g; Protein 6g

Radicchio Chopped Salad

Cape Cod Picnic Salad

SERVES 8 TO 10 | FAST | MAKE-AHEAD

WHY THIS RECIPE WORKS Inspired by the cranberries of Cape Cod, we created a hearty picnic-perfect salad with other New England foods: maple turkey, cheddar cheese, apple, and walnuts. Tossing the apple slices with acidic lime juice prevented them from turning brown. Combining two types of greens—crisp romaine and mustardy watercress—lent flavor and textural depth to our salad. Cranberry chutney was the secret ingredient that lent mystery to the vinaigrette and tied all its other tangy ingredients together, including Dijon mustard and lime juice. With the tartness of the crisp apples, sweetness from the cranberries, satisfying crunch of walnuts, and substance of the turkey and cheese, this salad tasted just as delicious as it looked. Make sure to ask for a single piece of unsliced turkey breast at the deli counter.

- 1 red apple, cored, quartered, and cut crosswise into ¼-inch-thick slices
- 3 tablespoons lime juice, divided
- ¼ cup cranberry chutney or apricot preserves
- 2 teaspoons Dijon mustard
- ½ cup extra-virgin olive oil
- 2 heads romaine lettuce (24 ounces)
- 4 ounces (4 cups) watercress
- ½ pound piece unsliced deli maple-glazed turkey breast, diced
- ½ cup diced sharp cheddar cheese
- ¼ cup chopped walnuts, toasted
- ¼ cup dried cranberries

1. Toss apple slices with 1 tablespoon lime juice in small bowl. Whisk remaining 2 tablespoons lime juice, chutney, and mustard together in large bowl. Gradually whisk in oil until incorporated. Season with salt and pepper to taste, and reserve ¼ cup dressing in measuring cup.

2. Toss lettuce and watercress with remaining dressing in large bowl and arrange on large platter. Arrange apples, turkey, cheddar, walnuts, and cranberries on top of lettuce. Drizzle salad with remaining dressing. Serve or refrigerate for up to 1 hour.

PER SERVING Cal 220; **Total Fat** 15g, **Sat Fat** 3g; **Chol** 15mg; **Sodium** 250mg; **Total Carb** 15g, **Dietary Fiber** 2g, **Total Sugars** 10g; **Protein** 8g

Chopped Caprese Salad
SERVES 4 TO 6 **FAST** **MAKE-AHEAD**

WHY THIS RECIPE WORKS To transform a classic Italian appetizer into a tossed salad perfect for taking on the road, we had to keep a few things from getting lost in translation. To add heft, we added chopped romaine to the traditional tomato, mozzarella, and basil. Chopped globe tomatoes turned the salad watery, but halved grape tomatoes provided a pop of color and sweet, year-round tomato flavor. To further guard against watery salad, we tossed the tomatoes with salt ahead of time, seasoning them and drawing out their excess liquid. A potent oil infused with garlic, basil, and shallot seasoned the cheese, and later we used the same oil and added red wine vinegar to it to make the salad dressing. You can use cherry tomatoes in place of the grape tomatoes.

  8 ounces fresh mozzarella, cut into ½-inch pieces (1 cup)
  3 tablespoons extra-virgin olive oil
  2 tablespoons minced shallot
  1 garlic clove, minced
1¼ teaspoons table salt, divided
  ¼ teaspoon pepper
  ½ cup fresh basil leaves, divided
1½ pounds grape tomatoes, cut in half lengthwise
  2 romaine hearts (12 ounces), quartered lengthwise and cut into ½-inch pieces
  ¼ cup pitted kalamata olives, chopped
  3 tablespoons red wine vinegar

1. Combine mozzarella, oil, shallot, garlic, ¼ teaspoon salt, and pepper in bowl. Coarsely chop half of basil leaves and add to mozzarella mixture; set aside while preparing tomatoes. Combine tomatoes and remaining 1 teaspoon salt in separate bowl; transfer to colander set in sink; and let drain for 15 minutes, stirring occasionally. (Tomatoes can be prepared up to 1 hour in advance.)

2. Tear remaining basil leaves into ½-inch pieces. Gently toss tomatoes, romaine, olives, vinegar, mozzarella mixture, and basil together in large bowl. Season with salt and pepper to taste, and serve.

PER SERVING Cal 210; **Total Fat** 16g, **Sat Fat** 6g; **Chol** 25mg; **Sodium** 780mg; **Total Carb** 9g, **Dietary Fiber** 3g, **Total Sugars** 5g; **Protein** 10g

Spinach and Strawberry Salad with Poppy Seed Dressing
SERVES 4 TO 6 **VEGAN**

WHY THIS RECIPE WORKS Spinach and strawberries are a popular salad pairing, but they need to be combined in the right way. We cut back on the spinach and swapped in crisp chopped romaine for color and crunch and also bumped up the amount of strawberries to a full pound so there would be berries in every bite. For a dressing that was neither too thick nor over-the-top sweet but had plenty of poppy seed flavor, we toasted the seeds to enhance their flavor and then made a simple vinaigrette of red wine vinegar, a minimal amount of sugar, and mild vegetable oil. Red onion and toasted almonds rounded out the salad's ingredients. Poppy seeds are dark so it's hard to see when they're fully toasted. Instead, use your nose: They should smell nutty.

  ½ cup red wine vinegar
  ⅓ cup sugar
  ¾ teaspoon table salt
  ½ red onion, sliced thin
  1 tablespoon poppy seeds
  ½ cup sliced almonds, divided
  ¼ cup vegetable oil
  1 teaspoon dry mustard
  ½ teaspoon pepper
  1 pound strawberries, hulled and quartered (2½ cups)
  1 romaine lettuce heart (6 ounces), torn into bite-size pieces
  5 ounces (5 cups) baby spinach

1. Whisk vinegar, sugar, and salt together in bowl. Transfer ¼ cup vinegar mixture to small bowl and microwave until hot, about 1 minute. Add onion, stir to combine, and let sit for at least 30 minutes. (Pickled onion can be refrigerated, covered, for up to 2 days.)

2. Meanwhile, toast poppy seeds in 8-inch nonstick skillet over medium heat until fragrant and slightly darkened, 1 to 2 minutes; transfer to bowl and set aside. Add almonds to now-empty skillet, return to medium heat, and toast until fragrant and golden, 3 to 5 minutes.

3. Whisk oil, mustard, pepper, and poppy seeds into remaining vinegar mixture.

4. Combine strawberries, lettuce, spinach, and ¼ cup almonds in large bowl. Using fork, remove onions from vinegar mixture and add to salad. Add poppy seed dressing to salad and toss to combine. Season with salt and pepper to taste. Transfer salad to serving platter and top with remaining ¼ cup almonds. Serve.

PER SERVING Cal 210; **Total Fat** 14g; **Sat Fat** 1g; **Chol** 0mg; **Sodium** 310mg; **Total Carb** 22g, **Dietary Fiber** 4g, **Total Sugars** 16g; **Protein** 3g

Sugar Snap Pea Salad
SERVES 4 TO 6 `FAST` `MAKE-AHEAD`

WHY THIS RECIPE WORKS Sugar snap peas are crisp and durable, making them a good choice for a portable salad. To show off a variety of supporting ingredients to complement the sugar snap peas, we added a few handfuls of peppery arugula, some thinly sliced red radishes for a light touch of heat and color, and slices of seedless English cucumber for freshness. We tried the sugar snap peas both blanched and raw and found that the raw pods were the tastiest and crispest. For the prettiest presentation, we cut the pods in half diagonally. We dressed the components in an easy, creamy white wine vinaigrette bolstered with fresh dill and a bit of mustard for personality.

- ¼ cup mayonnaise
- 2 tablespoons extra-virgin olive oil
- 2 tablespoons white wine vinegar
- 2 tablespoons chopped fresh dill
- 1 tablespoon Dijon mustard
- 1 small garlic clove, minced
- ½ teaspoon table salt
- ¼ teaspoon pepper
- 1 pound sugar snap peas, strings removed, cut in half diagonally
- 2 ounces (2 cups) baby arugula
- ½ English cucumber, halved lengthwise and sliced thin
- 6 radishes, trimmed, halved, and sliced thin (1 cup)

1. Whisk mayonnaise, oil, vinegar, dill, mustard, garlic, salt, and pepper together in large bowl.

Sugar Snap Pea Salad

2. Add snap peas, arugula, cucumber, and radishes and toss to combine. Season with salt and pepper to taste. Serve. (The salad can be refrigerated for up to 1 hour before serving.)

PER SERVING Cal 140; **Total Fat** 12g; **Sat Fat** 1.5g; **Chol** 5mg; **Sodium** 320mg; **Total Carb** 7g, **Dietary Fiber** 2g, **Total Sugars** 4g; **Protein** 3g

PREPPING SNAP PEAS FOR SALAD

1. Strip and discard fibrous stings that run down insides of pea pods.

2. Slice each pod in half diagonally.

Roasted Zucchini and Eggplant Medley
SERVES 8 | VEGAN

WHY THIS RECIPE WORKS We were looking for a flavorful roasted vegetable side dish that could be both homey and elegant, and served either warm or at room temperature. We quickly learned that paper-thin leafy vegetables such as leeks, radicchio, and Swiss chard don't work because they became slimy when cooled, while root vegetables such as potatoes and parsnips turn starchy and mealy. We had better luck with vegetables like zucchini, eggplant, and tomatoes. After testing a range of cooking methods, broiling turned out to be the best way to achieve plenty of browning on the zucchini and eggplant without overcooking them. Broiling each vegetable separately ensured that they were perfectly done and the pan wasn't too crowded. We quickly sautéed the aromatics to caramelize them and tossed in cherry tomatoes off the heat, which just warmed them through and melded the flavors. A final sprinkle of lemon juice and basil brought welcome brightness. Undercooking the vegetables is crucial; they will continue to cook after they are removed from the oven. Leaving the skins on the eggplant and zucchini helps keep the vegetables from being mushy after they have cooled. Toasted pine nuts make a nice garnish, if desired.

Roasted Zucchini and Eggplant Medley

- 3 zucchini (about 1½ pounds), quartered lengthwise and sliced crosswise into ¾-inch-wide pieces
- ¼ cup extra-virgin olive oil, divided, plus extra for serving
- ¾ teaspoon table salt, divided
- 2 pinches pepper, divided
- 1½ pounds eggplant, cut into 1-inch cubes
- 1 onion, chopped fine
- 1 tablespoon minced fresh thyme or 1 teaspoon dried
- 3 garlic cloves, minced
- 12 ounces cherry tomatoes, quartered
- ¼ cup coarsely chopped fresh basil
- 1 tablespoon lemon juice

1. Adjust oven rack 6 inches from broiler element and heat broiler. Line rimmed baking sheet with aluminum foil and spray with vegetable oil spray.

2. Toss zucchini with 1 tablespoon oil, ¼ teaspoon salt, and pinch pepper. Spread zucchini in even layer on prepared sheet. Broil zucchini, stirring occasionally, until lightly charred around edges but slightly underdone, 7 to 10 minutes; transfer zucchini to shallow serving dish (or casserole dish). Repeat with eggplant, 1 tablespoon oil, ¼ teaspoon salt and remaining pinch pepper; transfer to serving dish.

3. Heat remaining 2 tablespoons oil in 12-inch nonstick skillet over medium heat until shimmering. Add onion, thyme, and remaining ¼ teaspoon salt and cook until lightly browned, about 10 minutes. Stir in garlic and cook until fragrant, about 30 seconds. Off heat, stir in tomatoes. Scatter onion-tomato mixture over broiled vegetables. Cover vegetables and let sit for 10 minutes.

4. Sprinkle with basil, lemon juice, and additional oil before serving. Serve warm or at room temperature.

PER SERVING Cal 130; **Total Fat** 8g, **Sat Fat** 1g; **Chol** 0mg; **Sodium** 240mg; **Total Carb** 14g, **Dietary Fiber** 5g, **Total Sugars** 8g; **Protein** 4g

VARIATION
Roasted Asparagus and Fennel Medley
Thick spears of asparagus work best here.

Substitute 2 fennel bulbs (about 1½ pounds), stalks discarded, bulbs halved, cored, and sliced into ¼-inch-thick strips, and 2 pounds thick asparagus, ends trimmed, sliced on bias into 2- to 3-inch lengths, for zucchini and eggplant. Season and broil fennel and asparagus, 1 vegetable at a time, as directed in step 2 (broiling times are the same).

Napa Cabbage Slaw with Carrots and Sesame

SERVES 6 TO 8 FAST VEGAN

WHY THIS RECIPE WORKS Napa cabbage has a more tender, delicate texture and sweeter flavor than traditional green cabbage. It also leaches even more water than regular cabbage, so we made a potent dressing with a high ratio of vinegar to oil and cooked down the dressing's vinegar to offset the diluting power of the cabbage's water. After we tossed the cabbage with the dressing and let it sit for about 5 minutes, the slaw achieved the perfect level of bright acidity. Adding colorful, crunchy carrots and scallions and a handful of sesame seeds gave the salad added layers of Asian-inspired flavor and texture.

⅓ cup white wine vinegar
2 teaspoons toasted sesame oil
2 teaspoons vegetable oil
1 tablespoon rice vinegar
1 tablespoon soy sauce
1 tablespoon sugar
1 teaspoon grated fresh ginger
¼ teaspoon table salt
1 small head napa cabbage (1½ pounds),
  cored and sliced thin (8¼ cups)
2 carrots, peeled and shredded
4 scallions, sliced thin on bias
¼ cup sesame seeds, toasted

1. Bring white wine vinegar to simmer in small saucepan over medium heat and cook until reduced to 2 tablespoons, 4 to 6 minutes. Transfer vinegar reduction to large bowl and let cool completely, about 10 minutes. Whisk in sesame oil, vegetable oil, rice vinegar, soy sauce, sugar, ginger, and salt.

2. Add cabbage and carrots to dressing and toss to coat. Let sit for 5 minutes. Add scallions and sesame seeds and toss to combine. Serve.

PER SERVING Cal 110; **Total Fat** 9g, **Sat Fat** 1.5g; **Chol** 0mg; **Sodium** 210mg; **Total Carb** 6g, **Dietary Fiber** 2g, **Total Sugars** 4g; **Protein** 2g

VARIATIONS

Napa Cabbage Slaw with Apple and Walnuts
Omit sesame oil and increase vegetable oil to 4 teaspoons. Omit soy sauce and ginger. Substitute cider vinegar for rice vinegar. Decrease sugar to 2 teaspoons and increase salt to ¾ teaspoon. Substitute 2 celery ribs, sliced thin on bias, and 1 grated Fuji apple for carrots. Substitute 3 tablespoons minced fresh chives for scallions and ½ cup walnuts, toasted and chopped fine, for sesame seeds.

Napa Cabbage Slaw with Carrots and Sesame

Napa Cabbage Slaw with Jícama and Pepitas
Omit sesame oil and increase vegetable oil to 4 teaspoons. Omit soy sauce. Substitute lime juice for rice vinegar, honey for sugar, and ½ teaspoon ground coriander for ginger. Increase salt to ¾ teaspoon. Add 1 seeded and minced jalapeño. Substitute 6 ounces jícama, peeled and grated, for carrots. Substitute ¼ cup coarsely chopped fresh cilantro for scallions and ½ cup roasted and salted pepitas, chopped fine, for sesame seeds.

Radish and Carrot Slaw with Sesame and Scallions

SERVES 6 TO 8 FAST VEGAN

WHY THIS RECIPE WORKS Raw radishes have a peppery, mustard-like flavor and crisp texture that makes them ideal for slaw-type salads. We wanted to highlight radishes by tempering their pepperiness in a nontraditional slaw. We started with a mix of globe radishes, daikon radishes, and carrot. Pretreating the carrots with salt and sugar softened them and drew out excess moisture, and the added sweetness balanced the pungent radishes. The daikons' mild flavor and crisp texture gave the salad lift with a slight sweetness. A Dijon-based sesame vinaigrette brought bold flavor, and sliced scallions contributed savory hits.

1 pound carrots, peeled and grated

¼ cup sugar

1½ teaspoons table salt, divided

½ cup vegetable oil

3 tablespoons rice vinegar, plus extra for seasoning

2 tablespoons Dijon mustard

1 tablespoon toasted sesame oil

½ teaspoon pepper

1 pound radishes, trimmed, halved, and sliced thin

4 ounces daikon radish, peeled and cut into matchsticks

10 scallions, green parts only, sliced thin on bias

1. Toss carrots with sugar and 1 teaspoon salt in colander set over large bowl and let sit until partially wilted and reduced in volume by one-third, about 15 minutes. Press, but do not squeeze, to drain, then blot dry with paper towels.

2. Whisk oil, vinegar, mustard, sesame oil, remaining ½ teaspoon salt, and pepper in separate large bowl until combined. When ready to serve, add carrots, radishes, daikon radish, and scallions and toss to combine. Season with salt, pepper, and extra vinegar to taste. Serve.

PER SERVING Cal 200; **Total Fat** 16g, **Sat Fat** 1.5g; **Chol** 0mg; **Sodium** 590mg; **Total Carb** 14g, **Dietary Fiber** 3g, **Total Sugars** 10g; **Protein** 1g

Sweet and Tangy Coleslaw

Sweet and Tangy Coleslaw

SERVES 4 [MAKE-AHEAD] [VEGAN]

WHY THIS RECIPE WORKS This crisp, noncreamy slaw starts out with a stint in the microwave. We wanted to find a speedier way to make the cabbage shed its excess water; our usual technique involves salting the cabbage for a few hours. We discovered that sugar, which we were already including in our recipe, had the same effect on cabbage that salt did. Microwaving a batch of shredded slaw that we'd tossed with salt and sugar made it shed the same amount of liquid that it had taken three hours to release at room temperature. Cooling down our cabbage was easy: We simply chilled the dressing and then refrigerated the finished coleslaw. If you don't own a salad spinner, you can drain the microwaved cabbage in a colander placed in a bowl in step 3. Use a silicone spatula to press out the excess moisture.

¼ cup cider vinegar

1 tablespoon canola oil

¼ teaspoon celery seeds

¼ teaspoon pepper

½ head green cabbage, cored and sliced thin (6 cups)

¼ cup sugar

1 teaspoon table salt

1 large carrot, peeled and shredded

2 tablespoons minced fresh parsley

1. Whisk vinegar, oil, celery seeds, and pepper together in medium bowl. Place bowl in freezer and chill until dressing is cold, 15 to 30 minutes.

2. While dressing chills, toss cabbage with sugar and salt in large bowl. Microwave cabbage, covered, until just beginning to wilt, about 1 minute. Stir briefly, then continue to microwave, covered, until cabbage is partially wilted and has reduced in volume by one-third, 30 to 60 seconds.

3. Transfer cabbage to salad spinner and spin until excess water is removed, 10 to 20 seconds.

4. Remove bowl from freezer; add carrot, parsley, and cabbage; and toss to coat. Season with salt and pepper to taste. Refrigerate until chilled, at least 15 minutes. Toss coleslaw before serving.

PER SERVING Cal 130; **Total Fat** 3.5g; **Sat Fat** 0.5g; **Chol** 0mg; **Sodium** 630mg; **Total Carb** 23g, **Dietary Fiber** 4g, **Total Sugars** 18g; **Protein** 2g

VARIATION
Sweet and Tangy Coleslaw with Red Bell Pepper and Jalapeño

Substitute 2 tablespoons lime juice for celery seeds, ½ thinly sliced red bell pepper and 1 or 2 seeded and minced jalapeños for carrot, and 1 thinly sliced scallion for parsley.

All-American Potato Salad
SERVES 4 TO 6 `MAKE-AHEAD`

WHY THIS RECIPE WORKS For classic, potluck-perfect potato salad, we like to use firm-textured Yukon Gold potatoes because they hold their shape after cooking. Our recipe benefited from the sweetness of an unexpected ingredient: pickle juice. We drizzled the warm potatoes with a mixture of pickle juice and mustard. The potatoes easily absorbed the acidic seasoning liquid right through to the middle. Mayonnaise and sour cream formed the base of our creamy dressing, seasoned with celery seeds, celery, and red onion. Chopped hard-cooked eggs stirred in at the end completed our all-American potato salad; you can omit them if you prefer. Make sure not to overcook the potatoes or the salad will be mushy. Keep the water at a gentle simmer and use the tip of a paring knife to judge their doneness; if the knife inserts easily, they are done.

- 2 **pounds Yukon Gold potatoes, peeled and cut into ¾-inch pieces**
- ½ **teaspoon table salt, plus salt for cooking potatoes**
- 3 **tablespoons dill pickle juice, divided, plus ¼ cup finely chopped dill pickles**
- 1 **tablespoon dry yellow mustard**
- ½ **teaspoon celery seeds**
- ¼ **teaspoon pepper**
- ½ **cup mayonnaise**
- ¼ **cup sour cream**
- 1 **celery rib, chopped fine**
- ½ **small red onion, chopped fine**
- 2 **Easy-Peel Hard-Cooked Eggs (page 453) (optional)**

1. Place potatoes and 1 teaspoon salt in large saucepan and add water to cover by 1 inch. Bring to boil over high heat, reduce heat to medium-low, and simmer until potatoes are just tender and paring knife can be slipped in and out of potatoes with little resistance, 10 to 15 minutes.

2. Drain potatoes thoroughly, then spread out on rimmed baking sheet. Mix 2 tablespoons pickle juice and mustard together in small bowl, then drizzle mixture over hot potatoes, and toss until evenly coated. Refrigerate until cooled, about 30 minutes.

3. Mix remaining 1 tablespoon pickle juice, chopped pickles, celery seeds, ½ teaspoon salt, pepper, mayonnaise, sour cream, celery, and onion in large bowl. Add cooled potatoes and gently toss to coat. Cover and refrigerate until chilled, about 30 minutes. (Salad can be refrigerated for up to 2 days.) Gently stir in eggs just before serving.

PER SERVING Cal 270; **Total Fat** 17g, **Sat Fat** 3.5g; **Chol** 75mg; **Sodium** 670mg; **Total Carb** 25g, **Dietary Fiber** 0g, **Total Sugars** 1g; **Protein** 6g

BLT Potato Salad
SERVES 6 TO 8 `MAKE-AHEAD`

WHY THIS RECIPE WORKS This supercharged salad combines two American classics—BLTs and potato salad. To ensure that the potatoes stayed intact and were deeply seasoned, we turned to two test kitchen tricks: We added vinegar to the cooking water, which helped the potatoes keep their shape, and then tossed the hot, drained potatoes with extra vinegar. In a BLT, the B comes first for a reason, so we opted for a generous eight slices of bacon. For the L part, we relied on a romaine lettuce heart for its flavor, color, and crunch. That left the T, and we liked cherry tomatoes for their resilience. To up the flavor of the mayo-based dressing, we added scallions, fresh chives, and dill pickle relish. To make the salad ahead of time, toss together everything but the bacon, lettuce, tomatoes, and chives; refrigerate it; and gently fold in the remaining ingredients right before serving.

- 2½ **pounds Yukon Gold potatoes, peeled and cut into ½-inch pieces**
- ¼ **cup white wine vinegar, divided**
- ½ **teaspoon table salt plus salt for cooking potatoes**
- 8 **slices bacon, cut into 1-inch pieces**
- ¾ **cup mayonnaise**
- 7 **scallions, sliced thin**
- 2 **tablespoons dill pickle relish**
- ⅛ **teaspoon pepper**
- 1 **romaine lettuce heart (6 ounces), cut into 1-inch pieces**
- 12 **ounces cherry tomatoes, halved**
- ¼ **cup chopped fresh chives**

1. Place potatoes in large saucepan and cover with cold water by 1 inch. Add 2 tablespoons vinegar and 2 tablespoons salt to pan and bring to boil over medium-high heat. Reduce heat to medium-low and simmer until potatoes are tender, 12 to 16 minutes. Drain, transfer potatoes to bowl, and toss with 1 tablespoon vinegar. Let potatoes cool for 10 minutes.

2. Meanwhile, cook bacon in 12-inch nonstick skillet over medium heat until crispy, 5 to 7 minutes. Using slotted spoon, transfer bacon to paper towel–lined plate; set aside.

3. Whisk mayonnaise, scallions, relish, ½ teaspoon salt, pepper, and remaining 1 tablespoon vinegar together in large bowl. Fold in potatoes, lettuce, tomatoes, chives, and reserved bacon. Serve.

PER SERVING Cal 230; **Total Fat** 11g, **Sat Fat** 3.5g; **Chol** 20mg; **Sodium** 470mg; **Total Carb** 24g, **Dietary Fiber** 1g, **Total Sugars** 2g; **Protein** 7g

French Potato Salad with Dijon and Fines Herbes

SERVES 4 TO 6 ⬛VEGAN

WHY THIS RECIPE WORKS Fresh green herbs and a mustard vinaigrette are the hallmarks of French-style potato salad, making it pleasing to the eye and to the palate. Small red potatoes are the traditional choice, and they should be tender but not mushy, with the flavor of the vinaigrette fully permeating the relatively bland potatoes. To eliminate torn skins and broken slices, a common pitfall of boiling skin-on red potatoes, we sliced the potatoes before boiling them. To evenly infuse the potatoes with the garlicky vinaigrette, we spread the warm potatoes on a baking sheet and poured the vinaigrette over the top. Gently folding in the fresh herbs just before serving helped keep the potatoes intact. If fresh chervil isn't available, substitute an additional ½ tablespoon of minced parsley and an additional ½ teaspoon of tarragon. Use small red potatoes measuring 1 to 2 inches in diameter.

2 pounds small red potatoes, unpeeled, sliced
  ¼ inch thick
  Table salt for cooking potatoes
1 garlic clove, peeled and threaded on skewer
¼ cup extra-virgin olive oil
1½ tablespoons champagne vinegar or white wine vinegar
2 teaspoons Dijon mustard
½ teaspoon pepper
1 small shallot, minced
1 tablespoon minced fresh chervil
1 tablespoon minced fresh parsley
1 tablespoon minced fresh chives
1 teaspoon minced fresh tarragon

French Potato Salad with Dijon and Fines Herbes

1. Place potatoes and 2 tablespoons salt in large saucepan and add water to cover by 1 inch. Bring to boil over high heat, reduce heat to medium low, and simmer until potatoes are just tender and paring knife can be slipped in and out of potatoes with little resistance, 5 to 6 minutes.

2. While potatoes are cooking, lower skewered garlic into simmering water and blanch for 45 seconds. Hold garlic under cold running water, then remove from skewer and mince.

3. Drain potatoes, reserving ¼ cup cooking water. Arrange hot potatoes close together in single layer on rimmed baking sheet. Whisk oil, minced garlic, vinegar, mustard, pepper, and reserved potato cooking water together in bowl, then drizzle evenly over potatoes. Let potatoes sit at room temperature until flavors meld, about 10 minutes.

4. Transfer potatoes to large bowl. Combine shallot and herbs in small bowl, then sprinkle over potatoes and gently combine. Serve.

PER SERVING Cal 190; **Total Fat** 10g, **Sat Fat** 1.5g; **Chol** 0mg; **Sodium** 260mg; **Total Carb** 25g, **Dietary Fiber** 3g, **Total Sugars** 2g; **Protein** 3g

French Potato Salad with Fennel, Tomato, and Olives

Omit chervil, chives, and tarragon. Increase parsley to 3 tablespoons. Add ½ bulb thinly sliced fennel, 1 cored and chopped tomato, and ¼ cup pitted oil-cured black olives, quartered, to salad with shallots and parsley. If desired, chop 1 tablespoon of the fennel fronds and add it to the salad with the parsley.

Lemon and Herb Red Potato Salad
SERVES 8 VEGAN

WHY THIS RECIPE WORKS Our lemon and herb potato salad is a lighter alternative to traditional mayonnaise-based potato salad. We boiled chunks of red potatoes and to help them keep their shape we added vinegar to the cooking water. A mixture of briny capers and tart lemon juice complemented the earthiness of the potatoes, while tarragon, parsley, and chives gave the salad a fresh character. Adding some of the vinaigrette while the potatoes were still hot let them absorb all of its flavor. To remove some of the onion's harshness after chopping, place it in a fine-mesh strainer and run it under cold water. Drain, but do not rinse, the capers here.

- 3 pounds red potatoes, unpeeled, cut into 1-inch pieces
- 2 tablespoons distilled white vinegar
- 1 teaspoon table salt, plus salt for cooking potatoes
- 2 teaspoons grated lemon zest plus 3 tablespoons juice
- ½ teaspoon pepper
- ⅓ cup extra-virgin olive oil
- ½ cup finely chopped onion, rinsed
- 3 tablespoons minced fresh tarragon
- 3 tablespoons minced fresh parsley
- 3 tablespoons minced fresh chives
- 2 tablespoons capers, minced

1. Combine potatoes, 8 cups water, vinegar, and 2 tablespoons salt in Dutch oven and bring to boil over high heat. Reduce heat to medium and cook at strong simmer until potatoes are just tender, 10 to 15 minutes.

2. Meanwhile, whisk lemon zest and juice, 1 teaspoon salt, and pepper together in large bowl. Slowly whisk in oil until emulsified; set aside.

3. Drain potatoes thoroughly, then transfer to rimmed baking sheet. Drizzle 2 tablespoons dressing over hot potatoes and gently toss until evenly coated. Let potatoes cool, about 30 minutes, stirring once halfway through cooling.

Lemon and Herb Red Potato Salad

4. Whisk dressing to recombine and stir in onion, tarragon, parsley, chives, and capers. Add cooled potatoes to dressing and gently stir to combine. Season with salt and pepper to taste. Serve warm or at room temperature.

PER SERVING Cal 210; **Total Fat** 10g, **Sat Fat** 1.5g; **Chol** 0mg; **Sodium** 450mg; **Total Carb** 29g, **Dietary Fiber** 3g, **Total Sugars** 3g; **Protein** 4g

Ranch Potato Salad
SERVES 6 TO 8 MAKE-AHEAD

WHY THIS RECIPE WORKS To dress up red potato salad, we developed a flavorful homemade ranch dressing. We doubled the amount of cilantro used in most ranch recipes and added fresh garlic and scallions for some bite. Dijon mustard and vinegar provided acidity, while roasted red peppers made a sweet counterpoint. To better season them, we first tossed hot potatoes, peeled to absorb the maximum amount of dressing, with just the Dijon and vinegar; a dash of dried dill lent more herb flavor. We prefer white wine vinegar here, but white and cider vinegars will work.

Ranch Potato Salad

3. Transfer cooled potatoes to bowl with mayonnaise mixture and toss to combine. Cover and refrigerate until well chilled, about 30 minutes. Serve. (Salad can be refrigerated for up to 2 days.)

PER SERVING Cal 250; **Total Fat** 15g, **Sat Fat** 2.5g; **Chol** 10mg; **Sodium** 650mg; **Total Carb** 25g, **Dietary Fiber** 3g, **Total Sugars** 3g; **Protein** 4g

Smashed Potato Salad

SERVES 8 TO 10   MAKE-AHEAD

WHY THIS RECIPE WORKS Southern potato salad has the perfect balance between smooth and chunky potatoes, like crossing creamy mashed potatoes with potato salad. To achieve the perfect texture, we cooked soft-skinned Yukon Gold potato chunks until just tender; then we coarsely mashed a portion of the potatoes before combining them with the remaining pieces. Adding a splash of vinegar to the potatoes while they were still hot added deep flavor. The mayo-based dressing got its tangy punch from yellow mustard and cayenne pepper. To round out the salad, we added hard-cooked eggs, celery, and onion. Chopped sweet pickles added unexpected sweetness and crunch. Use the tip of a paring knife to judge the doneness of the potatoes. If the tip inserts easily into the potato pieces, they are done. Note that the salad needs to be refrigerated for about 2 hours before serving.

3 pounds red potatoes, peeled and cut into ¾-inch pieces
1 teaspoon table salt, plus salt for cooking potatoes
¾ cup mayonnaise
½ cup buttermilk
¼ cup white wine vinegar, divided
¼ cup drained jarred roasted red peppers, chopped fine
3 tablespoons finely chopped fresh cilantro
3 scallions, chopped fine
1 garlic clove, minced
⅛ teaspoon dried dill
2 teaspoons pepper
2 tablespoons Dijon mustard

1. Bring potatoes, 1 tablespoon salt, and enough water to cover potatoes by 1 inch to boil in large pot over high heat. Reduce heat to medium and simmer until potatoes are just tender, about 10 minutes. While potatoes simmer, whisk mayonnaise, buttermilk, 2 tablespoons vinegar, red peppers, cilantro, scallions, garlic, dill, 1 teaspoon salt, and pepper together in large bowl.

2. Drain potatoes thoroughly, then spread out on rimmed baking sheet. Whisk mustard and remaining 2 tablespoons vinegar in small bowl. Drizzle mustard mixture over hot potatoes and toss until evenly coated. Refrigerate until cooled, about 30 minutes.

3 pounds Yukon Gold potatoes, unpeeled, cut into 1-inch pieces
1 teaspoon table salt, plus salt for cooking potatoes
2 tablespoons distilled white vinegar, divided
1 cup mayonnaise
3 tablespoons yellow mustard
1 teaspoon pepper
¼ teaspoon cayenne pepper
3 Easy-Peel Hard-Cooked Eggs (page 453), chopped
3 scallions, sliced thin
½ cup chopped sweet pickles
½ cup finely chopped celery
¼ cup finely chopped onion

1. Combine potatoes, 8 cups water, and 1 tablespoon salt in Dutch oven and bring to boil over high heat. Reduce heat to medium and cook at vigorous simmer until potatoes are tender, 14 to 17 minutes.

2. Drain potatoes in colander. Transfer 3 cups potatoes to large bowl, add 1 tablespoon vinegar, and coarsely mash with potato masher. Transfer remaining potatoes to rimmed baking sheet, drizzle with remaining 1 tablespoon vinegar, and gently toss to combine. Let cool completely, about 15 minutes.

3. Whisk mayonnaise, ½ cup water, mustard, pepper, cayenne, and 1 teaspoon salt together in bowl. Stir mayonnaise mixture into mashed potatoes. Fold in eggs, scallions, pickles, celery, onion, and remaining potatoes until combined. (Mixture will be lumpy.)

4. Cover and refrigerate until fully chilled, about 2 hours. Season with salt and pepper to taste. Serve.

PER SERVING Cal 290; **Total Fat** 17g, **Sat Fat** 3g; **Chol** 65mg; **Sodium** 520mg; **Total Carb** 27g, **Dietary Fiber** 0g, **Total Sugars** 2g; **Protein** 5g

Texas Potato Salad
SERVES 8 MAKE-AHEAD

WHY THIS RECIPE WORKS Texans take their potato salad seriously, cranking up the flavor with plenty of yellow mustard and spicy jalapeños. For our distinctive version, we started with classic boiled Yukon Gold potatoes. For maximum zip we made some quick homemade pickled jalapeños and seasoned the hot potatoes with their pickling solution. We mixed a whopping 6 tablespoons of yellow mustard into mayonnaise for the dressing and added a pinch of cayenne for extra kick. Chopped hard-cooked eggs and celery, along with the pickled jalapeños and red onion, completed our bold and bright potato salad.

½ cup red wine vinegar
1½ tablespoons sugar
1½ teaspoons table salt, plus salt for cooking potatoes
1 teaspoon yellow mustard seeds
½ small red onion, sliced thin
2 jalapeño chiles (1 sliced into thin rings; 1 stemmed, seeded, and minced)
3 pounds Yukon Gold potatoes, peeled and cut into ¾-inch pieces
6 tablespoons mayonnaise
6 tablespoons yellow mustard
½ teaspoon pepper
¼ teaspoon cayenne pepper
2 Easy-Peel Hard-Cooked Eggs (page 453), cut into ¼-inch pieces
1 celery rib, minced

1. Combine vinegar, sugar, 1½ teaspoons salt, and mustard seeds in bowl and microwave until steaming, about 2 minutes. Whisk until sugar and salt are dissolved. Add onion and jalapeños and set aside until cool, 15 to 20 minutes. Strain onion and jalapeños through fine-mesh strainer set over bowl. Reserve pickled vegetables and vinegar mixture separately.

Texas Potato Salad

2. Meanwhile, combine potatoes, 8 cups water, and 1 tablespoon salt in Dutch oven and bring to boil over high heat. Reduce heat to medium and simmer until potatoes are just tender, 10 to 15 minutes.

3. Drain potatoes thoroughly, then transfer to large bowl. Drizzle 2 tablespoons reserved vinegar mixture over hot potatoes and gently toss until evenly coated. (Reserve remaining vinegar mixture for another use.) Refrigerate until cool, about 30 minutes, stirring once halfway through chilling.

4. Whisk mayonnaise, mustard, pepper, and cayenne together in bowl until combined. Add mayonnaise mixture, reserved pickled vegetables, eggs, and celery to potatoes and gently stir to combine. Season with salt and pepper to taste. Cover and refrigerate to let flavors meld, about 30 minutes. Serve. (Salad can be refrigerated for up to 2 days.)

PER SERVING Cal 220; **Total Fat** 9g, **Sat Fat** 1.5g; **Chol** 50mg; **Sodium** 650mg; **Total Carb** 29g, **Dietary Fiber** 0g, **Total Sugars** 3g; **Protein** 5g

Brown Rice Salad with Asparagus, Goat Cheese, and Lemon
SERVES 4 TO 6

WHY THIS RECIPE WORKS Nutty, pleasantly chewy brown rice works perfectly in a hearty yet elegant salad. Baking the brown rice didn't work here. In an early test, we discovered that once it was cooled and drizzled with dressing, the baked rice turned gummy. Instead, we cooked the rice by boiling it in a large pot of water, which washed away its excess starches. Then we spread it out on a baking sheet to cool rapidly, preventing it from overcooking as it sat. To give the rice some bright flavor, we drizzled it with lemon juice while it was still warm. Meanwhile, we cooked pieces of asparagus in olive oil until they were browned and tender. Wanting the dressing to be zesty but simple, we whisked together olive oil, minced shallot, and fresh lemon juice and zest. We added the rice, asparagus, some crumbled goat cheese, almonds, and parsley, and let the dressing's flavors seep into the salad before serving. With a sprinkling of toasted almonds and more goat cheese and parsley, our brown rice salad was loaded with fresh, vibrant flavors. Look for asparagus spears no thicker than ½ inch.

1½ cups long-grain brown rice
¾ teaspoon table salt, plus salt for cooking rice
1 teaspoon grated lemon zest plus 3 tablespoons juice
3½ tablespoons extra-virgin olive oil, divided
1 pound asparagus, trimmed and cut into 1-inch lengths
¾ teaspoon pepper, divided
1 shallot, minced
2 ounces goat cheese, crumbled (½ cup), divided
¼ cup slivered almonds, toasted, divided
¼ cup minced fresh parsley, divided

1. Bring 4 quarts water to boil in Dutch oven. Add rice and 1½ teaspoons salt and cook, stirring occasionally, until rice is tender, 25 to 30 minutes. Drain rice, spread onto rimmed baking sheet, and drizzle with 1 tablespoon lemon juice. Let cool completely, about 15 minutes.

COOLING BROWN RICE FOR SALAD

After cooking and draining rice, spread onto rimmed baking sheet and drizzle with 1 tablespoon lemon juice. Let rice cool completely, about 15 minutes; transfer to large bowl.

2. Heat 1 tablespoon oil in 12-inch skillet over high heat until just smoking. Add asparagus, ¼ teaspoon salt, and ¼ teaspoon pepper and cook, stirring occasionally, until asparagus is browned and crisp-tender, about 4 minutes; transfer to plate and let cool slightly.

3. Whisk remaining 2½ tablespoons oil, lemon zest and remaining 2 tablespoons juice, shallot, remaining ½ teaspoon salt, and remaining ½ teaspoon pepper together in large bowl. Add rice, asparagus, 6 tablespoons goat cheese, 3 tablespoons almonds, and 3 tablespoons parsley. Gently toss to combine and let sit for 10 minutes. Season with salt and pepper to taste. Transfer to serving platter and sprinkle with remaining 2 tablespoons goat cheese, remaining 1 tablespoon almonds, and remaining 1 tablespoon parsley. Serve.

PER SERVING Cal 310; **Total Fat** 14g; **Sat Fat** 3g; **Chol** 5mg; **Sodium** 920mg; **Total Carb** 40g, **Dietary Fiber** 4g, **Total Sugars** 2g; **Protein** 8g

Egyptian Barley Salad
SERVES 4 TO 6 **MAKE-AHEAD**

WHY THIS RECIPE WORKS We set out to create a vibrantly spiced pearl barley salad with the right balance of sweetness, tang, and nuttiness. For separate, distinct grains of cooked barley, we simply boiled the grains until tender. Inspired by the flavors of Egypt, we incorporated toasty pistachios, tangy pomegranate molasses, and bright cilantro, all balanced by warm, earthy spices and sweet golden raisins. Salty feta cheese, pungent scallions, and pomegranate seeds adorned the dish for a colorful composed salad with dynamic flavors and textures. When making this salad's dressing ahead, we found that the pomegranate molasses's brightness was muted a bit. So, we made a little more dressing than we would typically need for this salad; the extra dressing gave us leeway to dress more heavily when reviving the salad from refrigerator storage. If you can't find pomegranate molasses, substitute 2 tablespoons of lemon juice, 2 teaspoons of mild molasses, and 1 teaspoon of honey. Do not substitute hulled barley or hull-less barley in this recipe. If using quick-cooking or presteamed barley (read the ingredient list on the package to determine this), you will need to decrease the barley cooking time in step 1.

1½ cups pearl barley
½ teaspoon table salt, plus salt for cooking barley
3 tablespoons extra-virgin olive oil, plus extra for serving
2 tablespoons pomegranate molasses
1 teaspoon lemon juice
½ teaspoon ground cinnamon
¼ teaspoon ground cumin
½ cup coarsely chopped fresh cilantro
⅓ cup golden raisins

Egyptian Barley Salad

¼ cup shelled pistachios, toasted and chopped

3 ounces feta cheese, cut into ½-inch cubes (¾ cup)

6 scallions, green parts only, sliced thin

½ cup pomegranate seeds

1. Bring 4 quarts water to boil in Dutch oven. Add barley and 1 tablespoon salt, return to boil, and cook until tender, 20 to 40 minutes. Drain barley, spread in rimmed baking sheet, and let cool for 15 minutes.

2. Whisk oil, pomegranate molasses, lemon juice, cinnamon, cumin, and ½ teaspoon salt together in large bowl. (Cooked barley and dressing can be refrigerated separately for up to 3 days.)

3. Add barley, cilantro, raisins, and pistachios and gently toss to combine. Season with salt and pepper to taste. Spread barley salad evenly on serving platter and arrange feta, scallions, and pomegranate seeds in separate diagonal rows on top. Drizzle with extra oil and serve. (Dressed salad can be held for up to 2 hours before serving.)

PER SERVING Cal 370; **Total Fat** 14g, **Sat Fat** 3.5g; **Chol** 15mg; **Sodium** 520mg; **Total Carb** 55g, **Dietary Fiber** 10g, **Total Sugars** 12g; **Protein** 9g

Farro Salad with Asparagus, Snap Peas, and Tomatoes
SERVES 4 TO 6

WHY THIS RECIPE WORKS After just 20 minutes of cooking, farro is ready to be turned into a hearty, fresh salad. During testing, we learned that boiling the grains in plenty of salted water and then draining them yielded nicely firm but tender farro. First, we boiled bite-size pieces of asparagus and snap peas to bring out their vibrant color and crisp-tender bite then cooked the farro in the same pot of water. A lemon-dill dressing complemented the earthy farro, and cherry tomatoes and feta cheese offered a fresh, full-flavored finish. We prefer the flavor and texture of whole farro; pearled farro can be used, but the texture may be softer. Do not use quick-cooking or presteamed farro (read the ingredient list on the package to determine this) in this recipe. The cooking time for farro can vary greatly among different brands, so we recommend beginning to check for doneness after 10 minutes.

6 ounces asparagus, trimmed and cut into 1-inch lengths

6 ounces sugar snap peas, strings removed, cut into 1-inch lengths

¼ teaspoon table salt, plus salt for cooking vegetables and farro

1½ cups whole farro

3 tablespoons extra-virgin olive oil

2 tablespoons lemon juice

2 tablespoons minced shallot

1 teaspoon Dijon mustard

¼ teaspoon pepper

6 ounces cherry tomatoes, halved

3 tablespoons chopped fresh dill

2 ounces feta cheese, crumbled (½ cup), divided

1. Bring 4 quarts water to boil in Dutch oven. Add asparagus, snap peas, and 1 tablespoon salt and cook until crisp-tender, about 3 minutes. Using slotted spoon, transfer vegetables to large plate and let cool completely, about 15 minutes.

2. Add farro to water, return to boil, and cook until grains are tender with slight chew, 15 to 30 minutes. Drain farro, spread in rimmed baking sheet, and let cool completely, about 15 minutes.

3. Whisk oil, lemon juice, shallot, mustard, ¼ teaspoon salt, and pepper together in large bowl. Add vegetables, farro, tomatoes, dill, and ¼ cup feta and gently toss to combine. Season with salt and pepper to taste. Transfer to serving platter and sprinkle with remaining ¼ cup feta. Serve.

PER SERVING Cal 280; **Total Fat** 11g, **Sat Fat** 2.5g; **Chol** 10mg; **Sodium** 400mg; **Total Carb** 41g, **Dietary Fiber** 2g, **Total Sugars** 5g; **Protein** 9g

Farro Salad with Asparagus, Snap Peas, and Tomatoes

1. Bring 4 quarts water to boil in Dutch oven. Add farro and 1 tablespoon salt, return to boil, and cook until grains are tender with slight chew, 15 to 30 minutes. Drain farro, spread in rimmed baking sheet, and let cool completely, about 15 minutes.

2. Whisk oil, lemon juice, shallot, yogurt, ¼ teaspoon salt, and pepper together in large bowl. Add farro, cucumber, tomatoes, arugula, and mint and gently toss to combine. Season with salt and pepper to taste. Serve.

Quinoa, Black Bean, and Mango Salad

SERVES 4 TO 6 **FAST** **MAKE-AHEAD** **VEGAN**

WHY THIS RECIPE WORKS We love quinoa for its intriguing and delicate texture and nutty flavor. To showcase these qualities, we toasted quinoa to bring out its flavor before adding liquid to the pan and simmering the seeds until nearly tender. We then spread the quinoa on a rimmed baking sheet so that the residual heat would finish cooking it gently as it cooled. Black beans, mango, and bell pepper lent bright flavor, color, and satisfying heft. A simple but intense dressing of olive oil, lime juice, jalapeño, cumin, and cilantro added the right amount of acidity and warmth. Finally, sliced scallions contributed bite, and avocado slices lent creamy richness. If you buy unwashed quinoa (or if you are unsure whether it's washed), be sure to rinse it before cooking to remove its bitter protective coating (called saponin).

1½ cups prewashed white quinoa
2¼ cups water
1½ teaspoons table salt, divided
 5 tablespoons lime juice (3 limes)
½ jalapeño chile, stemmed, seeded, and chopped
¾ teaspoon ground cumin
½ cup extra-virgin olive oil
⅓ cup fresh cilantro leaves
 1 red bell pepper, stemmed, seeded, and chopped
 1 mango, peeled, pitted, and cut into ¼-inch pieces
 1 (15-ounce) can black beans, rinsed
 2 scallions, sliced thin
 1 avocado, halved, pitted, and sliced thin

1. Toast quinoa in large saucepan over medium-high heat, stirring often, until quinoa is very fragrant and makes continuous popping sounds, 5 to 7 minutes. Stir in water and ½ teaspoon salt and bring to simmer. Cover, reduce heat to low, and simmer gently until most of water has been absorbed and quinoa is nearly tender, about 15 minutes.

VARIATION
Farro Salad with Cucumber, Yogurt, and Mint
SERVES 4 TO 6
We prefer the flavor and texture of whole farro; pearled farro can be used, but the texture may be softer. Do not use quick-cooking or presteamed farro (read the ingredient list on the package to determine this) in this recipe. The cooking time for farro can vary greatly among different brands, so we recommend beginning to check for doneness after 10 minutes.

1½ cups whole farro
 ¼ teaspoon table salt plus salt for cooking farro
 3 tablespoons extra-virgin olive oil
 2 tablespoons lemon juice
 2 tablespoons minced shallot
 2 tablespoons plain Greek yogurt
 ¼ teaspoon pepper
 1 English cucumber, halved lengthwise, seeded, and cut into ¼-inch pieces
 6 ounces cherry tomatoes, halved
 1 cup baby arugula
 3 tablespoons chopped fresh mint

2. Spread quinoa on rimmed baking sheet and let cool completely, about 15 minutes; transfer to large bowl. (Cooled quinoa can be refrigerated for up to 3 days.)

3. Process lime juice, jalapeño, cumin, and remaining 1 teaspoon salt in blender until jalapeño is finely chopped, about 15 seconds. With blender running, add oil and cilantro; continue to process until smooth and emulsified, about 20 seconds.

4. Add bell pepper, mango, beans, scallions, and lime-jalapeño dressing to cooled quinoa and toss to combine. Season with salt and pepper to taste. Serve, topping individual servings with avocado.

PER SERVING Cal 450; **Total Fat** 27g, **Sat Fat** 3.5g; **Chol** 0mg; **Sodium** 740mg; **Total Carb** 45g, **Dietary Fiber** 8g, **Total Sugars** 3g; **Protein** 9g

Quinoa Pilaf with Shiitakes, Edamame, and Ginger
SERVES 6 VEGAN

WHY THIS RECIPE WORKS Quinoa cooks quickly, is hands-off, and toasts up nicely, making it the perfect starting point for a vegetable-full pilaf. We started by toasting the quinoa in a dry skillet to bring out its natural nuttiness. Then we sautéed fragrant scallions, shiitakes, and ginger, letting them soften and become even more aromatic before adding our liquid. Most recipes for quinoa pilaf turn out woefully overcooked because they call for far too much liquid. We cut the water back to ensure tender grains with a satisfying bite. The fresh ginger provided a brightness to the quinoa that paired well with pungent scallions and earthy mushrooms. And because they cooked with the quinoa and weren't just mixed in toward the end, their flavors melded thoroughly. If you buy unwashed quinoa (or if you are unsure whether it's washed), be sure to rinse it before cooking to remove its bitter protective coating (called saponin).

- 1½ cups prewashed white quinoa
- 2 tablespoons vegetable oil
- 4 scallions, white parts minced, green parts sliced thin on bias
- 4 ounces shiitake mushrooms, stemmed and sliced thin
- 2 teaspoons grated fresh ginger
- ¾ teaspoon table salt
- 1¾ cups water
- ½ cup frozen shelled edamame beans, thawed and patted dry
- 4 teaspoons rice vinegar
- 1 tablespoon mirin

1. Toast quinoa in medium saucepan over medium-high heat, stirring frequently, until quinoa is very fragrant and makes continuous popping sound, 5 to 7 minutes. Transfer quinoa to bowl.

2. Return now-empty saucepan to medium-low heat, add oil, and heat until shimmering. Add scallion whites, mushrooms, ginger, and salt and cook, stirring frequently, until softened, 5 to 7 minutes.

3. Increase heat to medium-high, stir in water and toasted quinoa, and bring to simmer. Cover, reduce heat to low, and simmer until grains are just tender and liquid is absorbed, 18 to 20 minutes, stirring once halfway through cooking.

4. Remove pot from heat and stir in edamame. Lay clean folded dish towel underneath lid and let sit, covered, for 10 minutes. Fluff quinoa with fork, stir in scallion greens, vinegar, and mirin, and season with salt and pepper to taste. Serve.

PER SERVING Cal 230; **Total Fat** 8g, **Sat Fat** 1g; **Chol** 0mg; **Sodium** 300mg; **Total Carb** 31g, **Dietary Fiber** 4g, **Total Sugars** 3g; **Protein** 8g

PREPARING MANGO FOR SALAD

1. Cut thin slice from one end of mango so that it sits flat on counter. Rest mango on trimmed bottom, then cut off skin in thin strips, top to bottom.

2. Cut down along each side of flat pit to remove flesh.

3. Trim around pit to remove any remaining flesh. Cut flesh into ¼-inch pieces.

Red Rice and Quinoa Salad

SERVES 4 TO 6 **VEGAN**

WHY THIS RECIPE WORKS Red rice sports a red husk and has a nutty flavor. For a rice and grain salad that was colorful, hearty, and a little out of the ordinary, we mixed this healthful rice with nutty quinoa, cooking both in the same pot. We gave the rice a 15-minute head start and then added the quinoa to ensure that both grains were done at the same time. Then we drained them, drizzled them with lime juice, and let them cool. To make this salad fresh and a little sweet, we added dates and orange segments (and used some of the orange juice in our dressing). Cilantro and red pepper flakes added a fresh bite and a bit of spiciness to round things out. If you buy unwashed quinoa (or if you are unsure whether it's washed), be sure to rinse it before cooking to remove its bitter protective coating (called saponin).

¾ cup red rice
 Table salt for cooking grains
¾ cup prewashed white quinoa
3 tablespoons lime juice (2 limes), divided
2 oranges
1 small shallot, minced
1 tablespoon minced fresh cilantro plus 1 cup leaves
¼ teaspoon red pepper flakes
¼ cup extra-virgin olive oil
6 ounces pitted dates, chopped (1 cup)

1. Bring 4 quarts water to boil in large pot over high heat. Add rice and 1 tablespoon salt and cook, stirring occasionally, for 15 minutes. Add quinoa to pot and continue to cook until grains are tender, 12 to 14 minutes. Drain rice-quinoa mixture, spread over rimmed baking sheet, drizzle with 2 tablespoons lime juice, and let cool completely, about 15 minutes.

2. Meanwhile, cut away peel and pith from oranges. Holding fruit over bowl, use paring knife to slice between membranes to release segments. Cut segments in half crosswise. If needed, squeeze orange membranes to equal 2 tablespoons juice in bowl.

3. Whisk 2 tablespoons orange juice, remaining 1 tablespoon lime juice, shallot, minced cilantro, and pepper flakes together in large bowl. Whisking constantly, slowly drizzle in oil. Add rice-quinoa mixture, dates, orange segments, and remaining 1 cup cilantro leaves, and toss to combine. Season with salt and pepper to taste, and serve.

PER SERVING Cal 350; **Total Fat** 11g, **Sat Fat** 1.5g; **Chol** 0mg; **Sodium** 100mg; **Total Carb** 59g, **Dietary Fiber** 5g, **Total Sugars** 24g; **Protein** 6g

Red Rice and Quinoa Salad

Wheat Berry Salad with Orange and Carrots

SERVES 4 TO 6

WHY THIS RECIPE WORKS The French-inspired flavors of orange and tarragon enhance this crowd-pleasing wheat berry salad. Sweet-tart orange boosts and brightens tarragon's grassy licorice notes, creating a remarkably vibrant flavor. This combination shone against a backdrop of mildly nutty wheat berries, especially after we added shredded carrots for crunch and orange zest for a deeper citrus flavor. A simple red wine vinaigrette finished off this fresh salad with a sophisticated mix of flavors. Do not add more than 1½ teaspoons of salt when cooking the wheat berries; adding more will prevent the grains from softening. If using quick-cooking or presteamed wheat berries (read the ingredient list on the package to determine this), you will need to decrease the wheat berry cooking time in step 1.

1½ cups wheat berries
¼ teaspoon table salt, plus salt for cooking wheat berries
3 tablespoons red wine vinegar, plus extra for seasoning
1½ tablespoons Dijon mustard

1 small shallot, minced
1 garlic clove, minced
1 orange, plus ⅛ teaspoon grated orange zest
1½ teaspoons honey
2 tablespoons extra-virgin olive oil
3 carrots, peeled and shredded
1 tablespoon minced fresh tarragon

1. Bring 4 quarts water to boil in Dutch oven. Add wheat berries and 1½ teaspoons salt, return to boil, and cook until tender but still chewy, 1 hour to 1 hour 10 minutes. Drain wheat berries, spread in rimmed baking sheet, and let cool completely, about 15 minutes.

2. Whisk vinegar, mustard, shallot, garlic, orange zest, honey, and ¼ teaspoon salt in large bowl until combined. Whisking constantly, slowly drizzle in oil.

3. Cut away peel and pith from orange. Quarter orange, then slice crosswise into ¼-inch-thick pieces and add to dressing. Add wheat berries, carrots, and tarragon and gently toss to coat. Season with salt, pepper, and extra vinegar to taste. Serve.

PER SERVING Cal 240; **Total Fat** 5g, **Sat Fat** 0.5g; **Chol** 0mg; **Sodium** 310mg; **Total Carb** 41g, **Dietary Fiber** 7g, **Total Sugars** 5g; **Protein** 7g

Wheat Berry Salad with Figs, Pine Nuts, and Goat Cheese

Wheat Berry Salad with Figs, Pine Nuts, and Goat Cheese
SERVES 4 TO 6

WHY THIS RECIPE WORKS We wanted to feature the sweet flavor and juicy texture of figs in a hearty, summery grain salad. Wheat berries provided a nutty base for the fresh figs, and creamy goat cheese was a pleasantly rich, tangy element. For the dressing, we chose a zippy vinaigrette made with balsamic vinegar, shallot, mustard, and honey to highlight the figs' natural sweetness. Toasted pine nuts and parsley leaves lent crunch and fragrance. Do not add more than 1½ teaspoons of salt when cooking the wheat berries, as it will prevent the grains from softening. If using quick-cooking or presteamed wheat berries (read the ingredient list on the package to determine this), you will need to decrease the wheat berry cooking time in step 1.

1½ cups wheat berries
¼ teaspoon table salt, plus salt for cooking wheat berries
2 tablespoons balsamic vinegar
1 small shallot, minced
1 teaspoon Dijon mustard
1 teaspoon honey
¼ teaspoon pepper
3 tablespoons extra-virgin olive oil
8 ounces figs, cut into ½-inch pieces
½ cup fresh parsley leaves
¼ cup pine nuts, toasted
2 ounces goat cheese, crumbled (½ cup)

1. Bring 4 quarts water to boil in Dutch oven. Add wheat berries and 1½ teaspoons salt, return to boil, and cook until tender but still chewy, 60 to 70 minutes. Drain wheat berries, spread onto rimmed baking sheet, and let cool completely, about 15 minutes.

2. Whisk vinegar, shallot, mustard, honey, ¼ teaspoon salt, and pepper together in large bowl. Whisking constantly, slowly drizzle in oil. Add wheat berries, figs, parsley, and pine nuts and gently toss to combine. Season with salt and pepper to taste. Transfer to serving platter and sprinkle with goat cheese. Serve.

PER SERVING Cal 330; **Total Fat** 14g, **Sat Fat** 2.5g; **Chol** 5mg; **Sodium** 260mg; **Total Carb** 45g, **Dietary Fiber** 8g, **Total Sugars** 8g; **Protein** 9g

Moroccan-Style Couscous with Chickpeas
SERVES 6 FAST VEGAN

WHY THIS RECIPE WORKS Couscous can be dressed up with any number of flavors. We decided to combine couscous and chickpeas in a Moroccan-inspired dish by following a basic game plan: Toast the couscous to maximize its nutty flavor, sauté the vegetables, toast the spices, add chickpeas, simmer, and finally add the couscous, which we needed only to hydrate with boiling water. We tasted our way through a long list of vegetables and landed on carrots, onion, and peas, each of which brought a distinctive flavor, texture, and color to the dish. When it came to spices, we liked coriander, ground ginger, and a dash of ground anise, each of which supported the vegetables' flavor well. Garlic, broth, and a hefty amount of herbs stirred in at the end rounded out the dish's flavors.

¼ cup extra-virgin olive oil, divided, plus extra for serving
1½ cups couscous
2 carrots, peeled and chopped fine
1 onion, chopped fine
1 teaspoon table salt
3 garlic cloves, minced
1 teaspoon ground coriander
1 teaspoon ground ginger
¼ teaspoon ground anise seed
1¾ cups chicken or vegetable broth
    1 (15-ounce) can chickpeas, rinsed
1½ cups frozen peas
½ cup chopped fresh parsley, cilantro, and/or mint
    Lemon wedges

1. Heat 2 tablespoons oil in 12-inch skillet over medium-high heat until shimmering. Add couscous and cook, stirring frequently, until grains are just beginning to brown, 3 to 5 minutes. Transfer to bowl and wipe skillet clean with paper towels.

2. Heat remaining 2 tablespoons oil in now-empty skillet over medium heat until shimmering. Add carrots, onion, and salt and cook until softened and lightly browned, 5 to 7 minutes. Stir in garlic, coriander, ginger, and anise and cook until fragrant, about 30 seconds. Stir in broth and chickpeas and bring to simmer.

3. Stir in peas and couscous. Cover, remove skillet from heat, and let sit until couscous is tender, about 7 minutes. Add parsley to couscous and gently fluff with fork to combine. Season with salt and pepper to taste and drizzle with extra oil. Serve with lemon wedges.

PER SERVING Cal 340; **Total Fat** 10g, **Sat Fat** 1.5g; **Chol** 0mg; **Sodium** 730mg; **Total Carb** 50g, **Dietary Fiber** 6g, **Total Sugars** 4g; **Protein** 10g

Lemon and Parsley Couscous Salad
SERVES 4 TO 6 FAST

WHY THIS RECIPE WORKS This easy couscous salad is not only fast and flavorful but it actually tastes better when it has time to sit. To keep the pearls of couscous fluffy, we toasted the uncooked couscous in butter and garlic, which helped to set the starch in the pasta and prevent it from absorbing too much water; the toasting also added nutty flavor. Using a combination of chicken broth and water as our liquid added savory but not overwhelming flavor. Dressing the salad with an olive oil, citrus, and herb vinaigrette added a final layer of flavor along with crunchy almonds and scallions. You can eat the salad immediately, but it will improve if you let the flavors meld for 30 minutes or so.

2 tablespoons unsalted butter
2 garlic cloves, minced
2 cups couscous
1 cup water
1 cup chicken broth
1 teaspoon table salt
1 cup sliced almonds, toasted
6 tablespoons extra-virgin olive oil
¼ cup chopped fresh parsley
4 scallions, sliced thin
3 tablespoons lemon juice

1. Melt butter in medium saucepan over medium-high heat. Stir in garlic and cook until fragrant, about 30 seconds. Add couscous and cook, stirring frequently, until grains begin to brown, about 5 minutes. Add water, broth, and salt; stir briefly to combine, cover, and remove pan from heat. Let sit until liquid is absorbed and couscous is tender, about 7 minutes. Uncover and fluff couscous with fork.

2. Combine almonds, oil, parsley, scallions, and lemon juice in large bowl. Stir in couscous until well combined. Season with salt and pepper to taste. Serve.

PER SERVING Cal 480; **Total Fat** 26g, **Sat Fat** 5g; **Chol** 10mg; **Sodium** 480mg; **Total Carb** 50g, **Dietary Fiber** 5g, **Total Sugars** 1g; **Protein** 12g

Orzo Salad with Broccoli and Radicchio
SERVES 4 FAST MAKE-AHEAD

WHY THIS RECIPE WORKS For an orzo dish that would stand out on a potluck spread, we aimed to hit all the taste buds: salty, sweet, bitter, and sour. To give the dish a variety of balanced flavors, we included broccoli, bitter radicchio, salty sun-dried tomatoes, pine nuts, and a hefty dose of basil. Cooking the orzo in the same

Orzo Salad with Broccoli and Radicchio

1. Bring 4 quarts water to boil in large pot. Fill large bowl halfway with ice and water. Add broccoli and 1 tablespoon salt to boiling water and cook until crisp-tender, about 2 minutes. Using slotted spoon, transfer broccoli to ice water and let cool, about 2 minutes; drain and pat dry.

2. Return pot of water to boil, add orzo, and cook, stirring often, until tender. Drain orzo, rinse with cold water, and drain again, leaving pasta slightly wet. Toss orzo, broccoli, radicchio, tomatoes, Parmesan, and pine nuts together in large bowl.

3. In small bowl, whisk vinegar, garlic, honey, and 1 teaspoon salt together. Whisking constantly, drizzle in tomato oil and olive oil. Stir vinaigrette into orzo mixture. (Salad can be refrigerated for up to 1 day; refresh with warm water and additional oil as needed.) Stir in basil and season with salt and pepper to taste before serving.

PER SERVING Cal 650; **Total Fat** 40g, **Sat Fat** 6g; **Chol** 10mg; **Sodium** 1040mg; **Total Carb** 58g, **Dietary Fiber** 3g, **Total Sugars** 11g; **Protein** 19g

Pasta Salad with Broccoli and Olives
SERVES 6 TO 8   **FAST**   MAKE-AHEAD   **VEGAN**

WHY THIS RECIPE WORKS No potluck or picnic is complete without a pasta salad and, for us, store-bought pasta salad is not an option. Developing the best pasta salad recipe was an exercise in precision: While some acidity was clearly needed to brighten the flavor of the salad, too much caused the pasta to soften and dulled the vegetables, both in flavor and appearance. We liked lemon juice for contributing a nice, bright flavor that was neither puckery nor sour. When we turned our attention to the vegetables, we discovered that, as we suspected, roasting and grilling added more flavor to most vegetables (broccoli and cauliflower being the exceptions) than blanching. For a spicier salad, add more red pepper flakes to taste.

water that we used to quickly blanch the broccoli imparted a delicate vegetal flavor throughout the dish. To round out the salad, we made a sour and sweet dressing with balsamic vinegar and honey. Toasting the pine nuts intensified their nutty flavor and brought further dimension to the orzo. Sharp Parmesan added the perfect salty accent, and chopped basil gave us a fresh finish to lighten this hearty dish. Cooking the pasta until it is completely tender and leaving it slightly wet after rinsing are important for the texture of the finished salad.

¾ pound broccoli florets, cut into 1-inch pieces
 1 teaspoon table salt, plus salt for cooking broccoli
1⅓ cups orzo
 1 head radicchio, cored and chopped fine
 ½ cup oil-packed sun-dried tomatoes, rinsed, patted dry, and minced, plus 3 tablespoons packing oil
 2 ounces Parmesan cheese, grated (1 cup)
 ½ cup pine nuts, toasted
 ¼ cup balsamic vinegar
 1 garlic clove, minced
 1 teaspoon honey
 3 tablespoons extra-virgin olive oil
 ½ cup chopped fresh basil

 3 pounds broccoli, florets cut into bite-size pieces
 ¾ teaspoon table salt, plus salt for cooking broccoli and pasta
 1 garlic clove, minced
 ½ teaspoon grated lemon zest plus ¼ cup juice (2 lemons)
 ½ teaspoon red pepper flakes
 ½ cup extra-virgin olive oil
 1 pound fusilli, farfalle, orecchiette, or other bite-size pasta
 ½ cup pitted kalamata olives or other brine-cured olives, chopped
 ½ cup chopped fresh basil

1. Bring 4 quarts water to boil in large pot. Add broccoli and 1 tablespoon salt and cook until broccoli is crisp-tender, about 2 minutes. Using slotted spoon, transfer broccoli to paper towel–lined plate and let cool completely.

2. Meanwhile, whisk garlic, lemon zest and juice, pepper flakes, and ¾ teaspoon salt together in large bowl. Whisk in oil in slow, steady stream until smooth.

3. Add pasta to boiling water and cook, stirring often, until al dente. Drain pasta. Whisk dressing again to blend; add olives, basil, broccoli, and pasta to bowl; toss to mix thoroughly; and let salad cool completely. Season with salt to taste, and serve. (Pasta salad can be refrigerated for up to 24 hours; return to room temperature before serving.)

PER SERVING Cal 380; **Total Fat** 16g, **Sat Fat** 2g; **Chol** 0mg; **Sodium** 370mg; **Total Carb** 51g, **Dietary Fiber** 4g, **Total Sugars** 4g; **Protein** 12g

VARIATIONS

Pasta Salad with Grilled Eggplant, Tomatoes, and Basil

SERVES 6 TO 8

The eggplants can be broiled until golden brown if you prefer not to grill them.

  1 pound eggplant, cut into ½-inch-thick rounds
  ½ cup extra-virgin olive oil, plus extra for brushing eggplant
 1¼ teaspoons table salt, divided, plus salt for cooking pasta
  ¼ teaspoon pepper
  1 garlic clove, minced
  ½ teaspoon grated lemon zest plus ¼ cup juice (2 lemons)
  ½ teaspoon red pepper flakes
  1 pound fusilli, farfalle, orecchiette, or other bite-size pasta
  2 large tomatoes, cored, seeded, and cut into ½-inch pieces
  ½ cup chopped fresh basil

1A. FOR A CHARCOAL GRILL Open bottom vent completely. Light large chimney starter filled with charcoal briquettes (6 quarts). When top coals are partially covered with ash, pour evenly over grill. Set cooking grate in place, cover, and open lid vent completely. Heat grill until hot, about 5 minutes.

1B. FOR A GAS GRILL Turn all burners to high, cover, and heat grill until hot, about 15 minutes. Leave all burners on high. (Adjust burners as needed to maintain grill temperature of 350 degrees.)

2. Clean and oil cooking grate. Lightly brush eggplant with extra oil and sprinkle with ½ teaspoon salt and pepper. Cook until dark grill marks appear, about 10 minutes, flipping eggplant once

Pasta Salad with Roasted Fennel, Red Onions, and Sun-Dried Tomatoes

halfway through cooking. Let cool completely, then cut into bite-size pieces.

3. Meanwhile, bring 4 quarts water to boil in large pot. Whisk garlic, lemon zest and juice, pepper flakes, and ¾ teaspoon salt together in large bowl. Whisk in oil in slow, steady stream until smooth.

4. Add pasta and 1 tablespoon salt to boiling water and cook, stirring often, until al dente. Drain pasta. Whisk dressing again to blend; add tomatoes, basil, eggplant, and pasta to bowl; toss to mix thoroughly; and let salad cool completely. Season with salt to taste, and serve. (Pasta salad can be refrigerated for up to 24 hours; return to room temperature before serving.)

Pasta Salad with Roasted Fennel, Red Onions, and Sun-Dried Tomatoes

SERVES 6 TO 8

  2 fennel bulbs, stalks discarded, bulbs halved, cored, and cut into ½-inch wedges
  2 red onions, sliced into ½-inch-thick rounds
  ½ cup plus 2 tablespoons extra-virgin olive oil, divided
  1 teaspoon table salt, divided, plus salt for cooking pasta

¼ teaspoon pepper

1 garlic clove, minced

½ teaspoon grated lemon zest plus ¼ cup juice (2 lemons)

1 pound fusilli, farfalle, orecchiette, or other bite-size pasta

½ cup oil-packed sun-dried tomatoes, patted dry and sliced thin

½ cup chopped fresh basil

1. Adjust oven rack to middle position and heat oven to 425 degrees. Add fennel, onions, and 2 tablespoons oil to bowl; season with ¼ teaspoon salt and pepper; and toss to combine. Transfer vegetables to baking sheet and roast until tender and lightly browned, 15 to 17 minutes. Let cool completely.

2. Meanwhile, bring 4 quarts water to boil in large pot. Whisk garlic, lemon zest and juice, and remaining ¾ teaspoon salt together in large bowl. Season with pepper to taste, then whisk in remaining ½ cup oil in slow, steady stream until smooth.

3. Add pasta and 1 tablespoon salt to boiling water and cook, stirring often, until al dente. Drain pasta. Whisk dressing again to blend; add sun-dried tomatoes, basil, fennel and onions, and pasta to bowl; toss to mix thoroughly; and let salad cool completely. Season with salt and pepper to taste, and serve. (Pasta salad can be refrigerated for up to 24 hours; return to room temperature before serving.)

Pasta Salad with Pesto

Pasta Salad with Pesto

SERVES 6 TO 8 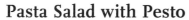 MAKE-AHEAD

WHY THIS RECIPE WORKS Pesto is too good to be restricted to warm pasta dishes. It also makes a terrific dressing for pasta salad. Pesto couldn't be simpler to make; just process fresh basil, garlic, pine nuts, Parmesan cheese, and extra-virgin olive oil together in a food processor. When we tossed the pesto directly with hot pasta the sauce became separated and greasy as the pasta cooled. We found that spreading the pasta on a baking sheet for about half an hour before adding the pesto was enough to adequately combat the problem. We also added some unusual ingredients to the pesto: To help prevent the pesto from turning dark over time, we added a handful of baby spinach, which set the bright green color, but was mild enough in flavor to let the basil shine. Mayonnaise gave our pesto a clingy, thick texture. We finished off our salad by reserving some of the toasted pine nuts to add a nice crunch and tossed in cherry tomatoes for a burst of freshness. This sturdy pasta salad, with its combination of basil and spinach, stays fresh and brightly colored for days.

2 garlic cloves, unpeeled

1 pound farfalle

1 teaspoon table salt, plus salt for cooking pasta

5 tablespoons extra-virgin olive oil, divided

3 cups fresh basil leaves, lightly bruised

1 cup baby spinach

¾ cup pine nuts, toasted, divided

2 tablespoons lemon juice

1½ ounces Parmesan cheese, grated (¾ cup), plus extra for serving

6 tablespoons mayonnaise

12 ounces cherry tomatoes, quartered

1. Bring 4 quarts water to boil in large pot. Add garlic and cook for 1 minute. Remove garlic with slotted spoon and rinse under cold water to stop cooking. Let garlic cool slightly, then peel and chop fine; set aside.

2. Add pasta and 1 tablespoon salt to boiling water and cook, stirring often, until tender. Reserve ¼ cup cooking water. Drain pasta, toss with 1 tablespoon oil, and spread in single layer on rimmed baking sheet. Let pasta and cooking water cool to room temperature, about 30 minutes.

3. Process basil, spinach, ¼ cup pine nuts, lemon juice, garlic, and 1 teaspoon salt in food processor until smooth, about 30 seconds, scraping down sides of bowl as needed. Add Parmesan, mayonnaise, and remaining ¼ cup oil and process until thoroughly combined; transfer to large bowl.

4. Toss cooled pasta with pesto, adding reserved cooking water, 1 tablespoon at a time, until pesto evenly coats pasta.

5. Fold in remaining ½ cup pine nuts and tomatoes. Season with salt and pepper to taste. Serve. (Cooled pasta can be tossed with half of pesto and refrigerated for up to 3 days; refrigerate remaining pesto separately, covered with 1 tablespoon extra-virgin olive oil. To serve, toss pasta with reserved pesto, adding hot water 1 tablespoon at a time as needed until pasta is evenly coated. Continue with step 5.)

PER SERVING Cal 470; **Total Fat** 28g, **Sat Fat** 4g; **Chol** 10mg; **Sodium** 550mg; **Total Carb** 46g, **Dietary Fiber** 2g, **Total Sugars** 3g; **Protein** 13g

Fusilli Salad with Sun-Dried Tomato Dressing

Fusilli Salad with Sun-Dried Tomato Dressing
SERVES 4 TO 6 `MAKE-AHEAD`

WHY THIS RECIPE WORKS To create a bold and satisfying pasta salad, we were inspired by the flavors of traditional antipasto. We made a bright sun-dried tomato dressing, which was a natural fit with the flavor profile of the salad. To maximize the dressing's impact, we dressed the pasta while it was still warm so it would absorb more flavor. Thickly cut salami and provolone added a salty, savory bite and richness, and sliced kalamata olives and capers added a brininess that punched up the flavor. Chopped baby spinach lent extra color and freshness. Other pasta shapes can be substituted for the fusilli.

DRESSING
6 tablespoons water
¼ cup oil-packed sun-dried tomatoes, chopped
4 teaspoons red wine vinegar
1 garlic clove, minced
¼ teaspoon pepper
½ cup extra-virgin olive oil

SALAD
8 ounces (2½ cups) fusilli
Table salt for cooking pasta
2 (¼-inch-thick) slices deli salami (4 ounces), cut into 1-inch-long matchsticks
2 (¼-inch-thick) slices deli provolone cheese (4 ounces), cut into 1-inch-long matchsticks
¼ cup pitted kalamata olives, sliced
1 tablespoon capers, rinsed and minced
1 tablespoon minced fresh parsley
2 ounces (2 cups) baby spinach, chopped

1. FOR THE DRESSING Process water, tomatoes, vinegar, garlic, and pepper in blender until smooth, 1 to 2 minutes, scraping down blender jar as needed. With blender running, slowly add oil and process until dressing is emulsified, about 15 seconds. Season with salt and pepper to taste. (Dressing can be refrigerated for up to 1 week; whisk to recombine before using.)

2. FOR THE SALAD Bring 4 quarts water to boil in large pot. Add pasta and 1 tablespoon salt and cook, stirring often, until tender. Drain pasta, then toss while still hot in bowl with dressing. Refrigerate until chilled, about 30 minutes.

3. Stir in salami, provolone, olives, capers, parsley, and spinach. Season with salt and pepper to taste. Serve.

PER SERVING Cal 460; **Total Fat** 31g, **Sat Fat** 8g; **Chol** 35mg; **Sodium** 670mg; **Total Carb** 30g, **Dietary Fiber** 1g, **Total Sugars** 1g; **Protein** 14g

Cool and Creamy Macaroni Salad

SERVES 8 TO 10 **FAST** MAKE-AHEAD

WHY THIS RECIPE WORKS Our creamy macaroni salad wraps pasta elbows and chopped celery and onion in a creamy dressing. We cooked the pasta until it was completely tender—not just al dente—and left a little moisture on it. The pasta absorbed the water rather than our creamy dressing. A fair amount of lemon juice balanced the richness of the mayonnaise. This was one of the rare occasions in which we preferred garlic powder to fresh garlic because the flavor wasn't as sharp and the powder dissolved into the smooth dressing.

- 1 pound elbow macaroni
  Table salt for cooking pasta
- ½ cup finely chopped red onion
- 1 celery rib, minced
- ¼ cup minced fresh parsley
- 2 tablespoons lemon juice
- 1 tablespoon Dijon mustard
- ⅛ teaspoon garlic powder
  Pinch cayenne pepper
- 1½ cups mayonnaise

1. Bring 4 quarts water to boil in large pot. Add macaroni and 1 tablespoon salt and cook, stirring often, until tender. Drain macaroni, rinse with cold water, and drain again, leaving macaroni slightly wet.

2. Toss macaroni, onion, celery, parsley, lemon juice, mustard, garlic powder, and cayenne together in large bowl and let sit until flavors are absorbed, about 2 minutes. Stir in mayonnaise and let sit until salad is no longer watery, 5 to 10 minutes. Season with salt and pepper to taste. Serve. (Salad can be refrigerated for up to 2 days. To serve, toss salad with 1 tablespoon hot water as needed until creamy.)

PER SERVING Cal 380; **Total Fat** 25g, **Sat Fat** 4g; **Chol** 10mg; **Sodium** 320mg; **Total Carb** 34g, **Dietary Fiber** 0g, **Total Sugars** 2g; **Protein** 6g

RINSING MACARONI

After draining cooked macaroni, rinse under cold water for 1 minute to stop cooking and rinse away excess starch. Let pasta drain briefly.

Cool and Creamy Macaroni Salad

VARIATIONS

Cool and Creamy Macaroni Salad with Curry, Apple, and Golden Raisins

Increase cayenne to ¼ teaspoon and add 1 Granny Smith apple, cored and chopped, 1 cup golden raisins, ½ cup mango chutney, and 2 teaspoons curry powder to macaroni with onion and other flavorings.

Cool and Creamy Macaroni Salad with Roasted Red Peppers and Capers

Add 1 cup jarred roasted red peppers, drained and chopped, and 6 tablespoons drained capers, chopped, to macaroni with onion and other flavorings.

Cool and Creamy Macaroni Salad with Sharp Cheddar and Chipotle

Add 1½ cups shredded extra-sharp cheddar cheese and 2 tablespoons minced canned chipotle chile in adobo sauce to macaroni with onion and other flavorings.

BBQ Macaroni Salad

SERVES 8 TO 10 **FAST** MAKE-AHEAD

WHY THIS RECIPE WORKS Pasta salad takes a road trip to the barbecue belt in this smoky, spicy side dish. Many recipes drown the pasta in ketchupy barbecue sauce, making it much too sweet and sticky. We found that a combination of mayonnaise and barbecue sauce made the best dressing, as the tang of the barbecue sauce was nicely balanced by the neutral creaminess of the mayo. To punch up the barbecue flavor, we added chili powder, garlic powder, cider vinegar, and hot sauce. For freshness and texture, bell pepper, celery, and scallions introduced just the right vegetal bite. We like the sweet, smoky flavor of Bull's-Eye Original barbecue sauce here, but feel free to substitute your favorite. Don't drain the macaroni too well before adding the other ingredients—a little extra moisture will keep the salad from drying out. The salad can also become dry as it sits; just before serving, stir in a few tablespoons of warm water to bring back its creamy texture.

    1   pound elbow macaroni
        Table salt for cooking pasta
    1   red bell pepper, stemmed, seeded, and chopped fine
    1   celery rib, minced
    4   scallions, sliced thin
    2   tablespoons cider vinegar
    1   teaspoon hot sauce
    1   teaspoon chili powder
    ⅛   teaspoon garlic powder
        Pinch cayenne pepper
    1   cup mayonnaise
    ½   cup barbecue sauce

1. Bring 4 quarts water to boil in large pot. Add pasta and 1 tablespoon salt and cook, stirring often, until al dente. Drain in colander and rinse with cold water until cool, then drain briefly so that macaroni remains moist. Transfer to large bowl.

2. Stir in bell pepper, celery, scallions, vinegar, hot sauce, chili powder, garlic powder, and cayenne and let sit until flavors meld, about 2 minutes. Stir in mayonnaise and barbecue sauce and let sit until salad texture is no longer watery, 5 to 10 minutes. Season with salt and pepper to taste. Serve. (Salad can be refrigerated for up to 2 days.)

PER SERVING Cal 340; **Total Fat** 17g, **Sat Fat** 2.5g; **Chol** 10mg; **Sodium** 370mg; **Total Carb** 40g, **Dietary Fiber** 0g, **Total Sugars** 7g; **Protein** 6g

Hawaiian Macaroni Salad

Hawaiian Macaroni Salad

SERVES 8 TO 10 **FAST** MAKE-AHEAD

WHY THIS RECIPE WORKS Hawaiians cook the macaroni for their macaroni salad until it's "fat," or very soft. Turns out they know what they're doing. While overcooking the pasta seems like a bad idea, it actually enables the macaroni to absorb more dressing. For our version, we found that the dressing had to be thin enough to soak into the pasta, so we used an equal amount of mayonnaise and milk, and a lot of each. To prevent the cider vinegar from curdling the milk, we poured the vinegar directly over the hot macaroni. After the vinegar soaked in, we poured on about half the dressing, gave the mixture a stir, and let it cool. We then stirred in the remaining dressing and added grated carrot, chopped celery for crunch, scallions, a bit of brown sugar, and some vigorous shakes of salt and black pepper.

    1⅓ cups whole milk, divided
    1⅓ cups mayonnaise, divided
    2   teaspoons packed brown sugar
    1   teaspoon pepper
    ¼   teaspoon table salt, plus salt for cooking pasta
    10 ounces elbow macaroni

5 tablespoons plus 1 teaspoon cider vinegar
3 scallions, sliced thin
1½ carrots, peeled and shredded
1½ celery ribs, chopped fine

1. Whisk 1 cup milk, ⅔ cup mayonnaise, sugar, pepper, and ¼ teaspoon salt together in bowl.

2. Meanwhile, bring 2 quarts water to boil in large pot. Add macaroni and 1½ teaspoons salt and cook until very soft, about 15 minutes. Drain macaroni and return it to pot. Add vinegar and toss until absorbed. Transfer to bowl. Let macaroni cool for 10 minutes, then stir in dressing until macaroni is well coated. Let macaroni cool completely.

3. Add scallions, carrots, celery, remaining ⅓ cup milk, and remaining ⅔ cup mayonnaise to bowl with macaroni mixture and stir to combine. Season with salt and pepper to taste. Refrigerate, covered, for at least 1 hour or up to 2 days before serving.

PER SERVING Cal 330; **Total Fat** 23g; **Sat Fat** 4g; **Chol** 15mg; **Sodium** 340mg; **Total Carb** 25g, **Dietary Fiber** 1g, **Total Sugars** 4g; **Protein** 5g

Tortellini Salad with Asparagus

Tortellini Salad with Asparagus
SERVES 4 TO 6 **FAST** MAKE-AHEAD

WHY THIS RECIPE WORKS This easy pasta salad looks fresh and colorful and will impress any gathering. We paired dried cheese tortellini with crisp asparagus and a dressing based on the flavors of classic pesto. First, we blanched the asparagus in the same water we later used to cook the tortellini, which instilled in the pasta its flavor. Once the tortellini were cooked, we tossed them in a bold dressing of olive oil, lemon juice, shallot, and garlic. To finish the salad, we added bright, juicy cherry tomatoes, fresh basil, grated Parmesan, and toasted pine nuts along with the blanched asparagus just before serving. Cooking the tortellini until it is completely tender and leaving it slightly wet after rinsing are important for the texture of the finished salad.

1 pound thin asparagus, trimmed and cut into 1-inch lengths
1 teaspoon table salt, plus salt for cooking asparagus and pasta
1 pound dried cheese tortellini
3 tablespoons lemon juice, plus extra for seasoning
1 shallot, minced
2 garlic cloves, minced
¾ teaspoon pepper
½ cup extra-virgin olive oil
12 ounces cherry tomatoes, halved
1 ounce Parmesan cheese, grated (½ cup)
¾ cup chopped fresh basil, mint, or parsley
¼ cup pine nuts, toasted

1. Bring 4 quarts water to boil in large pot. Fill large bowl halfway with ice and water. Add asparagus and 1 tablespoon salt to boiling water and cook until crisp-tender, about 2 minutes. Using slotted spoon, transfer asparagus to ice water and let cool, about 2 minutes; drain and pat dry.

2. Return pot of water to boil. Add tortellini and cook, stirring often, until tender. Drain tortellini, rinse with cold water, and drain again, leaving tortellini slightly wet.

3. Whisk lemon juice, shallot, garlic, 1 teaspoon salt, and pepper together in large bowl. Whisking constantly, drizzle in oil. Add tortellini and toss to combine.

4. Add asparagus, tomatoes, Parmesan, basil, and pine nuts and gently toss to combine. Season with salt, pepper, and extra lemon juice to taste. Serve. (Cooled tortellini, cooked asparagus, and vinaigrette can be refrigerated separately for up to 2 days.)

PER SERVING Cal 570; **Total Fat** 35g, **Sat Fat** 7g; **Chol** 50mg; **Sodium** 1240mg; **Total Carb** 51g, **Dietary Fiber** 3g, **Total Sugars** 6g; **Protein** 16g

Cold Soba Noodle Salad

SERVES 4 **FAST** **MAKE-AHEAD** **VEGAN**

WHY THIS RECIPE WORKS Soba noodles, made from buckwheat flour or a buckwheat-wheat flour blend, have a chewy texture and nutty flavor and are often enjoyed chilled. They are usually served with a dipping sauce, but we turned soy sauce, mirin, sugar, fresh ginger, and wasabi into a superflavorful dressing. The ginger added some heat, balanced by the sweetness of the sugar, and thin slices of nori (dried seaweed) sprinkled over the top added texture and a subtle briny taste. Peppery radishes and thinly sliced scallions added color and crunch. To prevent the cooked soba noodles from sticking together while we prepped the dressing, we tossed them with vegetable oil. To give this salad more heat, add additional wasabi paste to taste. Sheets of nori can be found in packets at Asian markets or in the international aisle at the supermarket. Do not substitute other types of noodles for the soba noodles here.

14 ounces dried soba noodles
    Table salt for cooking noodles
 1 tablespoon vegetable oil
¼ cup soy sauce
 3 tablespoons mirin
½ teaspoon sugar
½ teaspoon grated fresh ginger
¼ teaspoon wasabi paste or powder
 4 radishes, trimmed and shredded
 2 scallions, sliced thin on bias
 1 (8 by 2½-inch) piece nori, cut into
    matchsticks with scissors

1. Bring 4 quarts water to boil in large pot. Add noodles and 1 tablespoon salt and cook, stirring often, until tender. Drain noodles, rinse with cold water, and drain again, leaving noodles slightly wet. Transfer to large bowl and toss with oil.

2. Whisk soy sauce, mirin, sugar, ginger, and wasabi together in bowl, then pour over noodles. Add radishes and scallions and toss until well combined. (Salad and noodles can be refrigerated separately for up to 1 day; refresh with warm water and additional oil as needed.) Sprinkle individual portions with nori before serving.

PER SERVING Cal 400; **Total Fat** 4g, **Sat Fat** 0g; **Chol** 0mg; **Sodium** 1970mg; **Total Carb** 81g, **Dietary Fiber** 0g, **Total Sugars** 4g; **Protein** 17g

Chickpea Salad with Carrots, Arugula, and Olives

Chickpea Salad with Carrots, Arugula, and Olives

SERVES 4 **FAST** **VEGAN**

WHY THIS RECIPE WORKS Canned chickpeas are ideal for a salad because they absorb flavors easily and provide texture and substance. We heated the chickpeas in the microwave until they became soft and tender, which helped them quickly soak up a tangy vinaigrette. A combination of sweet carrots, peppery arugula, and briny olives transformed the chickpeas into a bright and savory salad. Shred the carrots on the large holes of a box grater or use a food processor fitted with the shredding disk.

 2 (15-ounce) cans chickpeas, rinsed
¼ cup extra-virgin olive oil
 2 tablespoons lemon juice
¾ teaspoon table salt
½ teaspoon pepper
    Pinch cayenne pepper
 3 carrots, peeled and shredded
 1 ounce (1 cup) baby arugula, chopped
½ cup pitted kalamata olives, chopped

1. Microwave chickpeas in medium bowl until hot, about 1 minute 30 seconds. Stir in oil, lemon juice, salt, pepper, and cayenne and let sit for 30 minutes.

2. Add carrots, arugula, and olives and toss to combine. Season with salt and pepper to taste. Serve.

PER SERVING Cal 270; **Total Fat** 17g, **Sat Fat** 2g; **Chol** 0mg; **Sodium** 850mg; **Total Carb** 26g, **Dietary Fiber** 6g, **Total Sugars** 5g; **Protein** 6g

VARIATIONS

Chickpea Salad with Fennel and Arugula

Substitute 1 fennel bulb, stalks discarded, bulb halved, cored, and cut into ¼-inch pieces, for carrots and olives.

Chickpea Salad with Roasted Red Peppers and Feta

Substitute ½ cup drained and chopped jarred roasted red peppers, ½ cup crumbled feta cheese, and ¼ cup chopped fresh parsley for carrots, arugula, and olives.

Marinated Chickpea and Cauliflower Salad

SERVES 6 TO 8　MAKE-AHEAD　VEGAN

WHY THIS RECIPE WORKS For an outstanding chickpea salad, we marinated earthy cauliflower and creamy chickpeas, which are robust enough to absorb the marinade without turning mushy. First we blanched the cauliflower, softening its exterior to help it absorb the dressing. Heating the marinade before tossing it with the salad also helped it to absorb. For the marinade, we bloomed saffron in hot water to coax out its distinct, complex flavors. Then we heated smashed garlic cloves in olive oil, infusing the oil with flavor and taming the garlic's harsh edge. Smoked paprika and a sprig of rosemary gave the marinade a vibrant brick-red hue and earthy, aromatic flavor. Thin slices of lemon lent bright citrus flavor. Letting the chickpeas and cauliflower rest in the marinade for at least 4 hours allowed the flavors to meld and deepen.

1 head cauliflower (2 pounds), cored and cut into 1-inch florets
2 teaspoons table salt, plus salt for cooking cauliflower
¼ teaspoon saffron threads, crumbled
¾ cup extra-virgin olive oil
10 garlic cloves, peeled and smashed
3 tablespoons sugar
1 tablespoon smoked paprika
1 small sprig fresh rosemary
¼ cup sherry vinegar
¼ teaspoon pepper

Marinated Chickpea and Cauliflower Salad

1 (15-ounce) can chickpeas, rinsed
1 lemon, sliced thin
2 tablespoons minced fresh parsley

1. Bring 2 quarts water to boil in large saucepan. Add cauliflower and 1 tablespoon salt and cook until florets begin to soften, about 3 minutes. Drain florets and transfer to paper towel–lined baking sheet.

2. Combine ½ cup hot water and saffron in bowl; set aside. Heat oil and garlic in small saucepan over medium-low heat until fragrant and beginning to sizzle but not brown, 4 to 6 minutes. Stir in sugar, paprika, and rosemary and cook until fragrant, about 30 seconds. Off heat, stir in saffron mixture, vinegar, 2 teaspoons salt, and pepper.

3. In large bowl, combine florets, saffron mixture, chickpeas, and lemon. Transfer mixture to gallon-size zipper-lock bag and refrigerate for at least 4 hours or up to 3 days, flipping bag occasionally. To serve, transfer cauliflower and chickpeas to serving bowl with slotted spoon and sprinkle with parsley.

PER SERVING Cal 280; **Total Fat** 22g, **Sat Fat** 3g; **Chol** 0mg; **Sodium** 790mg; **Total Carb** 18g, **Dietary Fiber** 4g, **Total Sugars** 7g; **Protein** 4g

Edamame Succotash

SERVES 4

WHY THIS RECIPE WORKS Traditional succotash is a delicate mixture of fresh corn and lima beans. For a modern take on old-school succotash, we decided to forgo the lima beans and turned instead to shelled edamame. We found that frozen edamame were fine in this dish, but frozen corn was less successful. Kernels scraped from fresh ears tasted much sweeter than bland frozen corn and also gave the succotash a pleasant crunch. Cooking the corn in butter with chopped onion provided an aromatic base. Finally, we punched up the flavors of our succotash with garlic, spicy jalapeño, and a pinch of cayenne. Fresh corn is key in this dish; do not substitute frozen corn. To make this dish spicier, add the jalapeño seeds to the skillet with the minced jalapeño.

  4 ears corn, husks and silk removed
  4 tablespoons unsalted butter
  ½ cup finely chopped onion
  1 red bell pepper, stemmed, seeded, and cut into
     ½-inch pieces
  ½ pound shelled frozen edamame, thawed (4 cups)
  1 teaspoon table salt
  ¼ teaspoon pepper
  2 garlic cloves, minced
  1 jalapeño chile, stemmed, seeded, and minced
     Pinch cayenne pepper
  3 tablespoons minced fresh cilantro

1. Using paring knife, cut kernels off cobs into large bowl, then use back of knife to scrape pulp from cob into bowl.

2. Melt 3 tablespoons butter in 12-inch nonstick skillet over medium-high heat. Add onion, bell pepper, edamame, salt, and pepper and cook until vegetables are tender, 10 to 12 minutes. Stir in garlic, jalapeño, and cayenne and cook until fragrant, about 1 minute. Transfer vegetables to second large bowl and cover.

3. Melt remaining 1 tablespoon butter in now-empty skillet over medium-high heat. Add corn mixture and cook until tender, 6 to 8 minutes. Transfer corn to bowl with vegetables and stir in cilantro. Season with salt and pepper to taste, and serve.

PER SERVING Cal 270; **Total Fat** 16g, **Sat Fat** 7g; **Chol** 30mg; **Sodium** 590mg; **Total Carb** 26g, **Dietary Fiber** 6g, **Total Sugars** 8g; **Protein** 11g

Lentil Salad with Olives, Mint, and Feta

Lentil Salad with Olives, Mint, and Feta

SERVES 4 TO 6 `MAKE-AHEAD`

WHY THIS RECIPE WORKS With their versatile flavor and firm-tender bite, lentils make a great base for a hearty salad. We salt-soaked the legumes, which softened their skins, leading to fewer blowouts, and then cooked them in the oven to heat them gently. Then we paired the earthy beans with a tart vinaigrette and bold mix-ins. We mixed bright white wine vinegar with extra-virgin olive oil, and added fresh mint, minced shallot, and kalamata olives. A sprinkle of rich feta finished the dish. French green lentils, or *lentilles du Puy*, are our preferred choice for this recipe; do not use red or yellow lentils. Salt-soaking helps keep the lentils intact, but if you don't have time, they'll still taste good. You will need an ovensafe medium saucepan for this recipe. The salad can be served warm or at room temperature.

  ½ teaspoon table salt, plus salt for brining
  1 cup lentilles du Puy, picked over and rinsed
  5 garlic cloves, lightly crushed and peeled
  1 bay leaf
  5 tablespoons extra-virgin olive oil
  3 tablespoons white wine vinegar

½ cup pitted kalamata olives, chopped coarse

1 large shallot, minced

½ cup chopped fresh mint

1 ounce feta cheese, crumbled (¼ cup)

1. Dissolve 1 teaspoon salt in 4 cups warm water (about 110 degrees) in bowl. Add lentils and soak at room temperature for 1 hour. Drain well.

2. Adjust oven rack to middle position and heat oven to 325 degrees. Combine lentils, 4 cups water, garlic, bay leaf, and ½ teaspoon salt in medium ovensafe saucepan. Cover, transfer saucepan to oven, and cook until lentils are tender but remain intact, 40 minutes to 1 hour.

3. Drain lentils well, discarding garlic and bay leaf. In large bowl, whisk oil and vinegar together. Add lentils, olives, and shallot and toss to combine. Season with salt and pepper to taste.

4. Transfer to serving dish, gently stir in mint, and sprinkle with feta. Serve warm or at room temperature.

PER SERVING Cal 240; **Total Fat** 14g, **Sat Fat** 2.5g; **Chol** 5mg; **Sodium** 280mg; **Total Carb** 21g, **Dietary Fiber** 5g, **Total Sugars** 1g; **Protein** 8g

VARIATIONS

Lentil Salad with Carrots and Cilantro

Omit shallot and feta. Toss 2 carrots, peeled and cut into 2-inch-long matchsticks, with 1 teaspoon ground cumin, ½ teaspoon ground cinnamon, and ⅛ teaspoon cayenne pepper in bowl; cover and microwave until carrots are tender but still crisp, 2 to 4 minutes. Substitute 3 tablespoons lemon juice for white wine vinegar, carrots for olives, and ¼ cup chopped fresh cilantro for mint.

Lentil Salad with Hazelnuts and Goat Cheese

Substitute 3 tablespoons red wine vinegar for white wine vinegar and add 2 teaspoons Dijon mustard to dressing. Omit olives and substitute ¼ cup chopped fresh parsley for mint. Substitute ¼ cup crumbled goat cheese for feta and sprinkle salad with ¼ cup coarsely chopped toasted hazelnuts before serving.

Lentil Salad with Spinach, Walnuts, and Parmesan

Substitute 3 tablespoons sherry vinegar for white wine vinegar. Place 4 cups baby spinach and 2 tablespoons water in bowl. Cover and microwave until spinach is wilted and volume is halved, about 4 minutes. Remove bowl from microwave and keep covered for 1 minute. Transfer spinach to colander and gently press to release liquid. Transfer spinach to cutting board and chop coarse. Return to colander and press again. Substitute chopped spinach for olives and mint and ¼ cup coarsely grated Parmesan cheese for feta. Sprinkle salad with ¼ cup coarsely chopped toasted walnuts before serving.

Spiced Lentil Salad with Winter Squash
SERVES 4 TO 6 **VEGAN**

WHY THIS RECIPE WORKS For a sophisticated lentil salad to add to our repertoire, we paired bold-tasting black lentils with butternut squash; the squash's sweetness was a nice foil to the earthy legume. To accentuate the delicate squash flavor, we tossed small pieces with balsamic vinegar and extra-virgin olive oil and roasted them in a hot oven. Putting the rack in the lowest position encouraged deep, even browning. Satisfied with the squash, we turned to the lentils. We soaked them in a saltwater solution to season them throughout and ensure fewer blowouts. To infuse them with more flavor as they cooked, we chose a mixture of warm, floral spices. We cooked the pot of lentils in the oven rather than on the stove for even cooking. For the dressing, we paired balsamic vinegar with a small amount of Dijon mustard for depth. Parsley and chopped red onion gave the dish some color and freshness, and toasted pepitas provided just the right amount of textural contrast. You can use *lentilles du Puy* (also called French green lentils), brown, or regular green lentils in this recipe, though cooking times will vary. Salt-soaking helps keep the lentils intact, but if you don't have time, they'll still taste good.

¼ teaspoon table salt, plus salt for brining

1 cup black lentils, picked over and rinsed

1 pound butternut squash, peeled, seeded, and cut into ½-inch pieces (3 cups)

5 tablespoons extra-virgin olive oil, divided

2 tablespoons balsamic vinegar, divided

¼ teaspoon pepper

1 garlic clove, minced

½ teaspoon ground coriander

¼ teaspoon ground cumin

¼ teaspoon ground ginger

⅛ teaspoon ground cinnamon

1 teaspoon Dijon mustard

½ cup fresh parsley leaves

¼ cup finely chopped red onion

1 tablespoon raw pepitas, toasted

1. Dissolve 1 teaspoon salt in 4 cups warm water (about 110 degrees) in bowl. Add lentils and soak at room temperature for 1 hour. Drain well.

2. Meanwhile, adjust oven racks to middle and lowest positions and heat oven to 450 degrees. Toss squash with 1 tablespoon oil, 1½ teaspoons vinegar, ¼ teaspoon salt, and pepper. Spread squash on rimmed baking sheet and roast on lower rack until well browned and tender, 20 to 25 minutes, stirring halfway through roasting. Let cool slightly, about 5 minutes. Reduce oven temperature to 325 degrees.

3. Heat 1 tablespoon oil, garlic, coriander, cumin, ginger, and cinnamon in medium saucepan over medium heat until fragrant, about 1 minute. Stir in 4 cups water and lentils. Cover, transfer saucepan to upper oven rack, and cook until lentils are tender but remain intact, 40 minutes to 1 hour.

4. Drain lentils well. Whisk remaining 3 tablespoons oil, remaining 1½ tablespoons vinegar, and mustard together in large bowl. Add squash, lentils, parsley, and onion and toss to combine. Season with salt and pepper to taste, sprinkle with pepitas, and serve warm or at room temperature.

PER SERVING Cal 260; **Total Fat** 13g, **Sat Fat** 2g; **Chol** 0mg; **Sodium** 220mg; **Total Carb** 29g, **Dietary Fiber** 7g, **Total Sugars** 3g; **Protein** 8g

White Bean Salad
SERVES 4 TO 6 `MAKE-AHEAD` `VEGAN`

WHY THIS RECIPE WORKS One of our favorite white bean recipes is this simple salad preparation that allows the creamy-sweet beans to shine. This well-balanced salad is superflavorful; we used classic Spanish flavors and ingredients to give the salad an identity. Cannellini beans worked perfectly, since they are savory and buttery. We steeped the beans in a garlicky broth, which infused them with flavor. While the beans sat, we had enough time to rid the shallot of any harshness by briefly marinating it in sherry vinegar. Red bell pepper offered sweetness and crunch, parsley provided herbal flavor, and chives gave the salad some subtle onion notes, rounding out the dish nicely.

- ¼ cup extra-virgin olive oil, divided
- 3 garlic cloves, peeled and smashed
- 2 (15-ounce) cans cannellini beans, rinsed
- 1 teaspoon table salt
- 1 tablespoon sherry vinegar
- 1 small shallot, minced
- 1 red bell pepper, stemmed, seeded, and cut into ¼-inch pieces
- ¼ cup chopped fresh parsley
- 2 teaspoons chopped fresh chives

1. Cook 1 tablespoon oil and garlic in medium saucepan over medium heat, stirring often, until garlic turns golden but not brown, about 3 minutes. Add beans, 2 cups water, and salt and bring to simmer. Remove from heat, cover, and let sit for 20 minutes.

2. Meanwhile, combine vinegar and shallot in large bowl and let sit for 20 minutes. Drain beans and discard garlic. Add beans, bell pepper, and remaining 3 tablespoons oil to shallot mixture and gently toss to combine. Let sit for 20 minutes.

3. Stir in parsley and chives and season with salt and pepper to taste. Serve.

PER SERVING Cal 180; **Total Fat** 9g, **Sat Fat** 1.5g; **Chol** 0mg; **Sodium** 350mg; **Total Carb** 17g, **Dietary Fiber** 5g, **Total Sugars** 2g; **Protein** 6g

VARIATION
White Bean Salad with Tomatoes and Olives
Substitute 1 cup quartered cherry tomatoes for bell pepper and ½ cup chopped fresh basil for parsley and chives. Add ⅓ cup chopped kalamata olives to salad before tossing to combine.

Three-Bean Salad
SERVES 4 TO 6 `FAST` `MAKE-AHEAD`

WHY THIS RECIPE WORKS Fresh beans breathe new life into our simple take on classic three-bean bean salad. First we steamed fresh romano beans and yellow wax beans to crisp-tender perfection. To avoid the need to soak and simmer dried beans for hours, canned kidney beans rounded out our trio. Letting the garlic and onion sit in the vinaigrette while preparing the beans tamed the garlic and quick-pickled the onions. A touch of honey in the bright dressing added the appropriate hint of sweetness to recall the classic formula, and a generous amount of parsley folded in just before serving contributed a lively finish. Be sure to set up the ice water bath before cooking the green beans, as plunging them in the cold water immediately after blanching retains their bright green color and ensures that they don't overcook. This salad improves if refrigerated for a few hours to let the flavors meld.

- ¼ cup cider vinegar
- 3 tablespoons extra-virgin olive oil
- 1 tablespoon honey
- 1 garlic clove, minced
- ¼ teaspoon table salt, plus salt for cooking beans
- ⅛ teaspoon and pepper
- ½ small red onion, sliced thin
- 8 ounces yellow wax beans, trimmed and halved on bias
- 8 ounces romano beans, trimmed and halved on bias
- 1 (15-ounce) can red kidney beans, rinsed
- ¼ cup minced fresh parsley

1. Whisk vinegar, oil, honey, garlic, ¼ teaspoon salt, and pepper together in large bowl. Stir in onion and set aside.

2. Bring 4 quarts water to boil in large pot over high heat. Fill large bowl halfway with ice and water. Add wax beans, romano beans, and 1 tablespoon salt to boiling water and cook until crisp-tender, 3 to 5 minutes. Drain beans, then transfer immediately to ice water. Let beans cool completely, about 5 minutes, then drain again and pat dry with paper towels.

3. Add drained wax and romano beans, kidney beans, and parsley to vinaigrette and toss to coat. Season with salt and pepper to taste. Serve. (Salad can be refrigerated for up to 2 days.)

PER SERVING Cal 140; **Total Fat** 7g, **Sat Fat** 1g; **Chol** 0mg; **Sodium** 380mg; **Total Carb** 17g, **Dietary Fiber** 5g, **Total Sugars** 6g; **Protein** 5g

Three-Bean Salad with Arugula
SERVES 6 `FAST` `MAKE-AHEAD`

WHY THIS RECIPE WORKS For another fresh take on three-bean salad that would feel at home on any picnic spread, we kept things simple. We steamed fresh green beans to crisp-tender perfection. Then we tested various combinations of beans, settling on chickpeas and kidney beans to round out the trio for an appealing mix of color, texture, and flavor. Most recipes rely on a syrupy dressing made from sugar and vinegar; we opted for a bright vinaigrette, with just a hint of honey sweetness. To keep the sharpness of the red onion in check, we marinated it briefly in the vinaigrette. One last change: Just before serving, we folded in a generous bundle of baby arugula. Be sure to set up the ice water bath before cooking the green beans, as plunging them in the cold water immediately after steaming retains their bright green color and ensures that they don't overcook. To make the salad ahead of time, toss together everything but the arugula and refrigerate it; gently fold in the arugula and season right before serving.

- 3 tablespoons cider vinegar
- 2 teaspoons honey
- 1 garlic clove, minced
- ½ teaspoon table salt
- ⅛ teaspoon pepper
- 2 tablespoons extra-virgin olive oil
- ½ small red onion, sliced thin
- 8 ounces green beans, trimmed and cut into 1-inch lengths
- 1 (15-ounce) can chickpeas, rinsed
- 1 (15-ounce) can red kidney beans, rinsed
- ¼ cup minced fresh parsley
- 3 ounces (3 cups) baby arugula

Three-Bean Salad with Arugula

1. Whisk vinegar, honey, garlic, salt, and pepper together in large bowl until well combined. Whisking constantly, slowly drizzle in oil. Stir in onion and set aside. Fill separate large bowl halfway with ice and water.

2. Bring ½ inch water to rolling boil in medium saucepan over high heat. Place green beans in steamer basket then transfer basket to saucepan. Cover, reduce heat to medium-low, and cook beans until crisp-tender, about 4 minutes. Transfer to bowl of ice water and let sit until chilled, about 5 minutes. Drain beans well and pat dry with paper towels.

3. Add green beans, chickpeas, kidney beans, and parsley to vinaigrette mixture and toss well to coat. Gently fold in arugula, and season with salt and pepper to taste. Serve.

PER SERVING Cal 150; **Total Fat** 5g, **Sat Fat** 0.5g; **Chol** 0mg; **Sodium** 430mg; **Total Carb** 20g, **Dietary Fiber** 5g, **Total Sugars** 5g; **Protein** 6g

NOT YOUR MOTHER'S CASSEROLES

■ MAKE-AHEAD   ■ VEGAN
Photos (clockwise from top left): Brussels Sprout Gratin; Loaded Sweet Potato Casserole;
Modern Cauliflower Gratin; Zucchini and Orzo Tian

Brussels Sprout Gratin

SERVES 6 TO 8

WHY THIS RECIPE WORKS Brussels sprouts can be divisive but this gratin is sure to win over even the most ardent anti-sprouter, not by covering up the vegetable but by casting its flavor in a new light. Preroasting the sprouts makes them rich and nutty, not cabbagey. We made a quick Mornay sauce, a classic cheese sauce, using a combination of Gruyère and Parmesan, to bind the casserole. To add crunch, we topped the gratin with toasted panko bread crumbs and more Gruyère. Look for smaller Brussels sprouts, no bigger than a golf ball, as they're likely to be sweeter and more tender than large ones. If you can find only large sprouts, quarter them. A broiler-safe dish is important because the sprouts cook at such a high temperature.

2½ pounds Brussels sprouts, trimmed and halved
1 tablespoon vegetable oil
¾ teaspoon plus ⅛ teaspoon table salt, divided
¾ teaspoon pepper, divided
3 tablespoons unsalted butter, divided
¼ cup panko bread crumbs
1 shallot, minced
1 garlic clove, minced
1 tablespoon all-purpose flour
1¼ cups heavy cream
¾ cup chicken broth
2 ounces Gruyère cheese, shredded (½ cup), divided
1 ounce Parmesan cheese, grated (½ cup)
  Pinch ground nutmeg
  Pinch cayenne pepper

1. Adjust oven rack to middle position and heat oven to 450 degrees. Grease 13 by 9-inch broiler-safe baking dish. Toss Brussels sprouts, oil, ½ teaspoon salt, and ¼ teaspoon pepper together in prepared dish. Bake until sprouts are well browned and tender, 30 to 35 minutes. Transfer dish to wire rack and let cool for at least 5 minutes or up to 30 minutes.

2. Meanwhile, melt 1 tablespoon butter in medium saucepan over medium heat. Add panko and cook, stirring frequently, until golden brown, about 3 minutes. Transfer to bowl and stir in ¼ teaspoon salt and ¼ teaspoon pepper; set aside. Wipe saucepan clean with paper towels.

3. Melt remaining 2 tablespoons butter in now-empty saucepan over medium heat. Add shallot and garlic and cook until just softened, about 1 minute. Stir in flour and cook for 1 minute. Whisk in cream and broth and bring to boil over medium-high heat. Once boiling, remove from heat and whisk in ¼ cup Gruyère, Parmesan, nutmeg, cayenne, remaining ¼ teaspoon pepper, and remaining ⅛ teaspoon salt until smooth.

4. Pour cream mixture over Brussels sprouts in dish and stir to combine. Sprinkle evenly with panko mixture and remaining ¼ cup Gruyère. Bake until bubbling around edges and golden brown on top, 5 to 7 minutes. Transfer dish to wire rack and let cool for 10 minutes. Serve.

PER SERVING Cal 300; **Total Fat** 23g; **Sat Fat** 13g; **Chol** 65mg; **Sodium** 460mg; **Total Carb** 16g, **Dietary Fiber** 5g, **Total Sugars** 4g; **Protein** 10g

Butternut Squash Gratin

SERVES 8 **VEGAN**

WHY THIS RECIPE WORKS Our butternut squash gratin skips the milk and cheese in order to allow the sweet, nutty flavor and brilliant color of the squash to shine through. We cut the squash into bite-size pieces to eliminate the need for precooking and then tossed them with fruity extra-virgin olive oil, salt, pepper, and fresh sage. Caramelizing the onions before layering them with the squash not only deepened their flavor but also got rid of excess moisture so the squash didn't taste steamed or waterlogged. To add crunch, we topped the casserole with toasted panko near the end of the baking time; we then finished the dish with fresh minced parsley. Do not use packaged prepeeled or chunked butternut squash for this dish.

6 tablespoons extra-virgin olive oil, divided
¼ cup panko bread crumbs
2 teaspoons table salt, divided
1¼ teaspoons pepper, divided
2 pounds onions, halved and sliced thin
¼ cup water, divided
4 teaspoons chopped fresh sage, divided
2 garlic cloves, minced
4 pounds butternut squash
¼ cup minced fresh parsley
1 teaspoon grated lemon zest

1. Adjust oven rack to middle position and heat oven to 425 degrees. Grease 13 by 9-inch baking dish. Combine 1 tablespoon oil and panko in 12-inch skillet and toast over medium-high heat, stirring frequently, until golden brown, about 3 minutes. Transfer to bowl and stir in ½ teaspoon salt and ¼ teaspoon pepper; set aside.

2. Heat 3 tablespoons oil in now-empty skillet over medium heat until shimmering. Add onions, ½ teaspoon salt, and ¼ teaspoon pepper and cook, stirring frequently, until soft and golden brown, about 30 minutes. Add 2 tablespoons water and cook, scraping up any browned bits, until water is evaporated, about 5 minutes.

Butternut Squash Gratin

Add remaining 2 tablespoons water and cook until onions are caramelized and water is evaporated, about 5 minutes. Add 2 teaspoons sage and garlic and cook until fragrant, about 30 seconds; set aside.

3. Trim ends from squash and peel. Cut in half lengthwise, then halve each piece lengthwise again and remove seeds. Cut each piece into ¼-inch-thick slices (you should have 11 cups). Toss squash, remaining 1 teaspoon salt, remaining ¾ teaspoon pepper, remaining 2 tablespoons oil, and remaining 2 teaspoons sage together in large bowl. Arrange half of squash evenly in prepared dish. Spread half of onion mixture evenly over squash. Arrange remaining squash evenly over onion mixture. Spread remaining onion mixture evenly over squash.

4. Cover dish with aluminum foil and bake until squash is nearly tender, about 40 minutes. Sprinkle panko mixture over top and continue to bake, uncovered, until squash is tender, about 15 minutes. Transfer dish to wire rack. Combine parsley and lemon zest in bowl and sprinkle over gratin. Serve.

PER SERVING Cal 250; **Total Fat** 11g, **Sat Fat** 1.5g; **Chol** 0mg; **Sodium** 600mg; **Total Carb** 40g, **Dietary Fiber** 7g, **Total Sugars** 10g; **Protein** 4g

Modern Cauliflower Gratin
SERVES 8 TO 10 `MAKE-AHEAD`

WHY THIS RECIPE WORKS To create a cauliflower gratin that was rich and flavorful without the typical heft, we relied on cauliflower's natural ability to become an ultracreamy puree (thanks to its low fiber content). To ensure that we had enough cauliflower, we used two heads. We cut them into slabs, which we then divided into florets; this ensured even cooking. We pureed the cores, stems, and some of the florets into a sauce to bind the remaining florets together. For a streamlined cooking setup, we simmered the cauliflower pieces destined to become sauce in water at the bottom of a Dutch oven and set our steamer basket filled with florets right on top. Butter and Parmesan (plus a little cornstarch) gave the sauce a richer flavor and texture without making it too heavy, and a few pantry spices lent some complexity. Tossing the florets in the sauce before placing them in the baking dish ensured that they were completely coated. Topping the gratin with Parmesan and toasted panko gave it savory crunch, and a final garnish of minced chives added color. When buying cauliflower, look for heads without many leaves. Alternatively, if your cauliflower does have a lot of leaves, buy slightly larger heads—about 2¼ pounds each. This recipe can be halved to serve 4 to 6; cook the cauliflower in a large saucepan and bake the gratin in an 8-inch square baking dish.

2 heads cauliflower (2 pounds each)
8 tablespoons unsalted butter, divided
½ cup panko bread crumbs
2 ounces Parmesan cheese, grated (1 cup)
2 teaspoons table salt
½ teaspoon pepper
½ teaspoon dry mustard
⅛ teaspoon ground nutmeg
  Pinch cayenne pepper
1 teaspoon cornstarch dissolved in 1 teaspoon water
1 tablespoon minced fresh chives

1. Adjust oven rack to middle position and heat oven to 400 degrees.

2. Pull off outer leaves of 1 head of cauliflower and trim stem. Using paring knife, cut around core to remove; halve core lengthwise and slice thin crosswise. Slice head into ½-inch-thick slabs. Cut stems from slabs to create florets that are about 1½ inches tall; slice stems thin and reserve along with sliced core. Transfer cauliflower florets to bowl, including any small pieces that may have been created during trimming, and set aside. Repeat with remaining head of cauliflower. (After trimming you should have about 3 cups of sliced stems and cores and 12 cups of florets.)

3. Combine sliced stems and cores, 2 cups florets, 3 cups water, and 6 tablespoons butter in Dutch oven and bring to boil over high heat. Place remaining florets in steamer basket (do not rinse bowl). Once mixture is boiling, place steamer basket in pot, cover, and reduce heat to medium. Steam florets in basket until translucent and stem ends can be easily pierced with paring knife, 10 to 12 minutes. Remove steamer basket and drain florets. Re-cover pot, reduce heat to low, and continue to cook stem mixture until very soft, about 10 minutes. Transfer drained florets to now-empty bowl.

4. While cauliflower is cooking, melt remaining 2 tablespoons butter in 10-inch skillet over medium heat. Add panko and cook, stirring frequently, until golden brown, 3 to 5 minutes. Transfer to bowl and let cool. Once cool, add ½ cup Parmesan and toss to combine.

5. Transfer stem mixture and cooking liquid to blender and add salt, pepper, mustard, nutmeg, cayenne, and remaining ½ cup Parmesan. Process until smooth and velvety, about 1 minute (puree should be pourable; adjust consistency with additional water as needed). With blender running, add cornstarch slurry. Season with salt and pepper to taste. Pour puree over cauliflower florets and gently toss to evenly coat. Transfer mixture to 13 by 9-inch baking dish (it will be quite loose) and smooth top with spatula. (Gratin and bread-crumb mixture can be refrigerated separately for up to 24 hours. To serve, assemble and bake gratin as directed in step 6, increasing baking time by 13 to 15 minutes.)

6. Scatter bread-crumb mixture evenly over top. Transfer dish to oven and bake until sauce bubbles around edges, 13 to 15 minutes. Let stand for 20 to 25 minutes. Sprinkle with chives and serve.

PER SERVING Cal 170; **Total Fat** 11g, **Sat Fat** 7g; **Chol** 30mg; **Sodium** 630mg; **Total Carb** 12g, **Dietary Fiber** 4g, **Total Sugars** 4g; **Protein** 6g

Cauliflower and Cheese Casserole

SERVES 8 TO 10   `MAKE-AHEAD`

WHY THIS RECIPE WORKS Sometimes nothing else will do but a bubbling pan of creamy, cheesy cauliflower. For a casserole packed with flavor, instead of steaming the cauliflower florets separately, we simmered them right in the cream that we'd use for our sauce—which we cut with chicken broth for a more well-rounded flavor. Stirring in a mixture of extra-sharp cheddar and Monterey Jack cheeses, enhanced with garlic, thyme, and dry mustard, created a decadent cheese sauce. Buttered bread crumbs added a pleasant crunch to the top of our casserole, but we thought it needed just a little something more; grinding the crumbs with a bit of reserved cheese and garlic ensured that the topping added interest as well as crunch. Roughly 6 pounds of cauliflower yields 12 cups of trimmed florets.

Cauliflower and Cheese Casserole

3 slices hearty white sandwich bread, torn into quarters
4 ounces extra-sharp cheddar cheese, shredded (1 cup), divided
4 ounces Monterey Jack cheese, shredded (1 cup), divided
4 tablespoons unsalted butter, melted, divided
3 garlic cloves, minced, divided
¾ teaspoon table salt, divided
¾ teaspoon pepper, divided
2 tablespoons all-purpose flour
1¼ cups heavy cream
¾ cup chicken broth
2 large heads cauliflower (3 pounds each), cored and cut into ¾-inch florets
2 teaspoons dry mustard
1 teaspoon dried thyme

1. Adjust oven rack to middle position and heat oven to 450 degrees. Pulse bread, 2 tablespoons cheddar, 2 tablespoons Monterey Jack, 2 tablespoons melted butter, one-third of garlic, ¼ teaspoon salt, and ¼ teaspoon pepper in food processor until coarsely ground.

2. Heat remaining 2 tablespoons melted butter, remaining garlic, and flour in Dutch oven over medium heat, stirring constantly, until golden and fragrant, about 1 minute. Slowly whisk in cream and broth. Stir in cauliflower, mustard, thyme, remaining ½ teaspoon salt, and remaining ½ teaspoon pepper and bring to boil. Reduce heat to medium-low, cover, and simmer, stirring occasionally, until cauliflower is nearly tender, 6 to 8 minutes. Off heat, stir in remaining cheddar and remaining Monterey Jack until incorporated.

3. Pour mixture into 13 by 9-inch baking dish and top with bread crumbs. (Cauliflower and bread crumbs can be refrigerated separately for up to 24 hours. Let come to room temperature, top with bread crumbs, and bake as directed.) Bake until crumbs are golden brown and crisp, 10 to 15 minutes. Let cool for 10 minutes. Serve.

PER SERVING Cal 340; **Total Fat** 24g; **Sat Fat** 15g; **Chol** 70mg; **Sodium** 500mg; **Total Carb** 23g, **Dietary Fiber** 6g, **Total Sugars** 7g; **Protein** 13g

Cheesy Corn Casserole

Cheesy Corn Casserole
SERVES 8 TO 10

WHY THIS RECIPE WORKS With a texture falling somewhere between cornbread and creamed corn, this Midwestern and Southern favorite is usually made with boxed corn muffin mix and canned creamed corn. To control the casserole's sweetness, we ditched the store-bought muffin mix and stirred together flour, cornmeal, and baking powder. Substituting frozen corn kernels for canned creamed corn resulted in a fresher-tasting casserole, and pulsing half the corn in a food processor released more corn flavor and mimicked the texture of creamed corn. Scallions, cayenne pepper, and a mix of two cheeses—Monterey Jack and Parmesan—amped up the flavor. Two pounds of fresh corn kernels (from about eight cobs) can be substituted for the frozen corn.

  8 ounces Monterey Jack cheese
  ½ cup all-purpose flour
  ⅓ cup cornmeal
  2 teaspoons baking powder
  1 teaspoon table salt
  ¼ teaspoon pepper
  ¼ teaspoon cayenne pepper
  4 scallions, white and green parts separated and
    sliced thin, divided
  2 pounds frozen corn, thawed, divided
  1 cup sour cream
  1 ounce Parmesan cheese, grated (½ cup), divided
  2 large eggs, lightly beaten
  4 tablespoons unsalted butter, melted

1. Adjust oven rack to middle position and heat oven to 350 degrees. Grease 13 by 9-inch baking dish. Cut half of Monterey Jack into ½-inch cubes. Shred remaining half of Monterey Jack on large holes of box grater; set aside. Whisk flour, cornmeal, baking powder, salt, pepper, and cayenne together in large bowl.

2. Pulse scallion whites and half of corn in food processor to coarse puree, about 10 pulses. Stir pureed corn mixture into flour mixture. Add sour cream, ¼ cup Parmesan, eggs, melted butter, cubed Monterey Jack, and remaining corn and stir until combined. Transfer mixture to prepared dish. Sprinkle with shredded Monterey Jack and remaining ¼ cup Parmesan.

3. Bake until casserole is slightly puffy and cheese is golden brown, 45 to 50 minutes. Transfer casserole to wire rack and let cool for 10 minutes. Sprinkle with scallion greens and serve.

PER SERVING Cal 290; **Total Fat** 18g, **Sat Fat** 10g; **Chol** 85mg; **Sodium** 550mg; **Total Carb** 26g, **Dietary Fiber** 3g; **Total Sugars** 4g; **Protein** 11g

VARIATION
Cheesy Corn Casserole with Jalapeños and Cilantro
Add ¼ cup minced jarred jalapeños to batter in step 2. Sprinkle with 2 tablespoons chopped fresh cilantro before serving.

Scalloped Corn
SERVES 4 TO 6 `MAKE-AHEAD`

WHY THIS RECIPE WORKS Scalloped corn is a cracker-crusted, creamy casserole traditionally made from convenience products. We swapped out canned corn for fresh and our casserole sang with pure corn flavor. To cut back on the cooking time, we started the operation on the stovetop. We simmered the corn until tender, using half-and-half rather than heavy cream, which made for a lighter and fresher-tasting casserole. To thicken, we pureed some of the corn and mixed it back in. For a topping with a balance of saltiness and sweetness, we sprinkled on a mixture of Ritz Crackers and fresh bread crumbs for the last 10 minutes of baking.

14 Ritz Crackers
1 slice hearty white sandwich bread, torn into 1-inch pieces
3 tablespoons unsalted butter, melted
12 ears corn, husks and silk removed
1¼ cups half-and-half
1½ teaspoons table salt
¼ teaspoon pepper

1. Adjust oven rack to middle position and heat oven to 450 degrees. Spray 8-inch square baking dish with vegetable oil spray. Pulse crackers, bread, and melted butter in food processor until coarsely ground, about 10 pulses; set aside.

2. Using chef's knife, cut kernels from cobs. Bring kernels, half-and-half, salt, and pepper to boil in large saucepan. Reduce heat to medium-low and simmer, covered, until corn is tender, 20 to 30 minutes.

3. Transfer 2 cups corn mixture to blender and process until thick and smooth, about 30 seconds. Return puree to saucepan and stir to combine. Transfer corn mixture to prepared dish. (Corn mixture and crumb topping can be refrigerated separately for up to 3 days. Bring corn to room temperature, cover with foil, and bake at 400 degrees for 20 minutes. Remove foil, top with crumb mixture, and bake as directed.)

4. Top corn mixture with cracker mixture and bake until golden brown, 7 to 10 minutes. Serve.

PER SERVING Cal 350; **Total Fat** 18g, **Sat Fat** 7g; **Chol** 30mg; **Sodium** 700mg; **Total Carb** 47g, **Dietary Fiber** 4g, **Total Sugars** 13g; **Protein** 11g

Spinach Gratin

Spinach Gratin
SERVES 8 TO 10 `MAKE-AHEAD`

WHY THIS RECIPE WORKS Spinach gratin promises a vibrant alternative to starchier options like potatoes, but those made with just frozen spinach can be stringy and listless while using fresh involves a mountain of spinach—and tedious prep. So we split the difference. Adapting our creamed spinach recipe, we wilted fresh spinach in a creamy, cheesy white sauce as it cooked, then added frozen whole-leaf spinach that we'd squeezed dry and chopped fine (this produced a better texture than prechopped frozen spinach). A topping of bread crumbs and Gruyère got crispy and brown in the oven, and a sprinkling of parsley and lemon zest kept the dish fresh and bright. Thaw the frozen spinach in the refrigerator overnight.

2 slices hearty white sandwich bread, torn into 1-inch pieces
8 tablespoons unsalted butter, divided
8 ounces Gruyère cheese, shredded (2 cups), divided
2 teaspoons table salt, divided
1½ teaspoons pepper, divided
1 onion, chopped fine
4 garlic cloves, minced
⅛ teaspoon cayenne pepper

2 tablespoons all-purpose flour
4 cups half-and-half
8 ounces curly-leaf spinach, stemmed and chopped
1 tablespoon Dijon mustard
⅛ teaspoon ground nutmeg
2½ pounds frozen whole-leaf spinach, thawed, squeezed dry, and chopped fine
½ cup minced fresh parsley
1 teaspoon grated lemon zest, plus lemon wedges for serving

1. Adjust oven rack to upper-middle position and heat oven to 425 degrees. Pulse bread in food processor to fine crumbs, about 10 pulses; transfer to bowl. Melt 3 tablespoons butter in microwave, about 30 seconds. Stir melted butter, ½ cup Gruyère, ½ teaspoon salt, and ½ teaspoon pepper into bread crumbs; set aside. (Crumb mixture can be refrigerated for up to 1 day.)

2. Melt remaining 5 tablespoons butter in Dutch oven over medium heat. Add onion and cook until lightly browned, 7 to 9 minutes. Stir in garlic and cayenne and cook until fragrant, about 30 seconds. Stir in flour and cook for 1 minute. Slowly whisk in half-and-half and bring to simmer. Cook, whisking occasionally, until slightly thickened and reduced to about 3½ cups, about 10 minutes.

3. Stir in curly-leaf spinach; cook until just wilted, about 30 seconds. Off heat, stir in mustard, nutmeg, remaining 1½ cups Gruyère, remaining 1½ teaspoons salt, and remaining 1 teaspoon pepper until cheese is melted. Stir in thawed frozen spinach until combined. Season with salt and pepper to taste. Transfer mixture to 13 by 9-inch baking dish. (Spinach mixture can be refrigerated for up to 24 hours. Bake at 425 degrees for 15 to 20 minutes then proceed with step 4.)

4. Sprinkle bread-crumb mixture evenly over spinach mixture. Bake until bubbling around edges and crumbs are golden brown, 15 to 17 minutes. Transfer to wire rack. Combine parsley and lemon zest in bowl; sprinkle over gratin. Let cool for 10 minutes. Serve with lemon wedges.

PER SERVING Cal 370; Total Fat 27g, Sat Fat 16g; Chol 85mg; Sodium 850mg; Total Carb 17g, Dietary Fiber 4g, Total Sugars 6g; Protein 15g

STEMMING SPINACH

Holding leaf with your hand, use your other hand to pull down and remove stem.

Swiss Chard and Kale Gratin
SERVES 8 TO 10 MAKE-AHEAD

WHY THIS RECIPE WORKS For a creamy, rich greens gratin with a crisp, flavorful bread-crumb topping, we started with a mixture of kale and Swiss chard. Sturdy kale kept the gratin fluffy and tall; Swiss chard collapsed but its plentiful tender stems added bulk. Steaming the greens in a Dutch oven cooked them quickly without the need for blanching or sautéing in batches. To keep the gratin from turning the crumb topping soggy, we limited the amount of cream to 1 cup, just enough to give the dish a silky richness. For a craggy, crisp, and flavorful topping, we used rustic bread, pulsed to a coarse texture, along with Parmesan and garlic.

2 pounds Swiss chard
1 pound curly kale, stemmed and cut into 1-inch wide strips
2 garlic cloves
4 ounces rustic white bread, cut into ¾-inch cubes (3 cups)
5 tablespoons extra-virgin olive oil, divided
1 cup Parmesan cheese, grated (2 ounces)
¾ teaspoon table salt, divided
½ teaspoon pepper, divided
1 onion, chopped coarse
1½ teaspoons minced fresh thyme
1 cup heavy cream
⅛ teaspoon ground nutmeg

1. Adjust oven rack to upper-middle position and heat oven to 375 degrees. Stem chard, reserving stems. Cut stems into 2-inch lengths and set aside. Slice leaves into 1-inch-wide ribbons. Bring 2 cups water to boil in Dutch oven over high heat. Add kale, cover, and reduce heat to medium-high. Cook until kale is wilted, about 5 minutes, stirring once halfway through cooking. Add chard leaves, cover, and continue to cook until chard is wilted, about 4 minutes, stirring once halfway through cooking. Transfer to colander set in sink and allow to drain.

2. Pulse garlic in food processor until chopped coarse, 5 to 7 pulses. Add bread cubes and 3 tablespoons oil and pulse until largest crumbs are smaller than a pea (most will be much smaller), 8 to 10 pulses. Add Parmesan, ¼ teaspoon salt, and ¼ teaspoon pepper, and pulse to combine. Transfer to bowl.

3. Add onion and chard stems to now-empty food processor and process until finely chopped, scraping down sides of bowl as needed, 20 to 30 seconds. Transfer to now-empty Dutch oven. Add thyme, remaining 2 tablespoons olive oil, remaining ½ teaspoon salt, and remaining ¼ teaspoon pepper. Cook over medium-high heat, stirring occasionally, until moisture has evaporated and mixture is just beginning to brown, 8 to 10 minutes. Remove from heat.

4. Press gently on greens in colander with spatula to remove excess moisture. Transfer greens to Dutch oven with onion mixture. Add cream and nutmeg and stir to combine. Transfer mixture to 13 by 9-inch baking dish. Sprinkle bread-crumb mixture evenly over surface. Bake until topping is golden brown and filling bubbles around edges, 20 to 25 minutes. Let cool for 10 minutes, and serve. (Greens mixture and bread-crumb mixture can be refrigerated separately for up to 24 hours. Increase baking time by 5 to 10 minutes.)

PER SERVING Cal 260; **Total Fat** 20g; **Sat Fat** 8g; **Chol** 35mg; **Sodium** 620mg; **Total Carb** 13g, **Dietary Fiber** 3g; **Total Sugars** 3g; **Protein** 9g

Summer Squash Casserole

Summer Squash Casserole
SERVES 6 TO 8

WHY THIS RECIPE WORKS Summer squash is mostly composed of water, so how could we turn this vegetable into a crisp, flavorful gratin? To drive off moisture, we microwaved the squash with salt, drained it well, and patted it dry. The salt drew out excess moisture, and microwaving broke down the vegetables' cell walls, speeding up the process. A mixture of browned onions, garlic, thyme, and salty olives boosted flavor, and a layer of panko bread crumbs mixed with Parmesan cheese soaked up excess moisture while the gratin baked. We added a final sprinkling of panko on top during the last stint in the oven to create a crunchy, well-browned crust.

- 2 tablespoons unsalted butter, softened, divided, plus 4 tablespoons melted
- 2 onions, halved and sliced thin
- ½ teaspoon table salt, plus salt for salting vegetables
- 1¼ teaspoons pepper, divided
- 3 garlic cloves, minced
- 1 tablespoon minced fresh thyme
- ½ cup dry white wine
- ½ cup pitted kalamata olives, chopped fine
- ¼ cup chopped fresh basil, divided
- 1½ pounds zucchini, sliced ¼ inch thick
- 1½ pounds yellow summer squash, sliced ¼ inch thick
- 1 cup panko bread crumbs
- 2 ounces Parmesan cheese, grated (1 cup)

1. Melt 1 tablespoon softened butter in 12-inch nonstick skillet over medium heat. Add onions, ½ teaspoon salt, and ¼ teaspoon pepper and cook, stirring occasionally, until onions are soft and golden brown, 15 to 20 minutes. Stir in garlic and thyme and cook until fragrant, about 30 seconds. Stir in wine and cook until evaporated, about 3 minutes. Off heat, stir in olives and 2 tablespoons basil; set aside.

2. Meanwhile, toss zucchini and summer squash with 2 teaspoons salt in large bowl. Microwave, covered, until slightly softened and some liquid is released, about 8 minutes, stirring halfway through microwaving. Drain in colander and let cool slightly. Arrange zucchini and summer squash on triple layer of paper towels, then cover with another triple layer of paper towels. Firmly press on slices to remove as much liquid as possible.

3. Adjust oven rack to middle position and heat oven to 450 degrees. Grease bottom and sides of 13 by 9-inch baking dish with remaining 1 tablespoon softened butter. Combine panko, Parmesan, and remaining 1 teaspoon pepper in bowl. Evenly coat baking dish with 6 tablespoons panko mixture. Stir melted butter into remaining panko mixture until well combined; set aside.

4. Arrange half of zucchini and summer squash in prepared dish and season with pepper to taste. Sprinkle ¼ cup panko mixture evenly over squash. Spread onion mixture in even layer over panko

mixture. Arrange remaining zucchini and summer squash over onion mixture and season with pepper to taste. Cover with aluminum foil and bake until just tender, about 15 minutes.

5. Remove dish from oven; discard foil. Sprinkle remaining panko mixture evenly over top. Bake, uncovered, until bubbling around edges and panko is golden brown, 10 to 15 minutes. Transfer to wire rack and let cool for 15 minutes. Sprinkle with remaining 2 tablespoons basil. Serve.

PER SERVING Cal 200; **Total Fat** 11g, **Sat Fat** 6g; **Chol** 30mg; **Sodium** 910mg; **Total Carb** 17g, **Dietary Fiber** 2g, **Total Sugars** 5g; **Protein** 7g

Summer Vegetable Gratin
SERVES 6 TO 8 **MAKE-AHEAD**

WHY THIS RECIPE WORKS This simple-to-prepare gratin transforms summer produce into something spectacular. We started with zucchini, yellow summer squash, and ripe tomatoes. To prevent the watery vegetables from turning our gratin into a soupy mess, we salted and then drained them before assembling the casserole. Baking the dish uncovered ensured that additional moisture would evaporate in the oven. Layering the especially wet tomatoes on top maximized their heat exposure and helped them caramelize. To flavor the vegetables, we tossed them with an aromatic garlic-thyme oil and then drizzled more oil over the top. Fresh bread crumbs tossed with Parmesan and shallots made a simple but elegant topping. Use only fresh, in-season vegetables for this recipe. Look for zucchini and yellow summer squash of roughly the same diameter. We like a mix of the two vegetables here but you can use just one or the other.

    1 pound zucchini, sliced ¼ inch thick
    1 pound yellow summer squash, sliced ¼ inch thick
    ½ teaspoon table salt, plus salt for salting vegetables
 1½ pounds tomatoes, cored and sliced ¼ inch thick
    6 tablespoons extra-virgin olive oil, divided
    2 onions, halved and sliced thin
    1 tablespoon minced fresh thyme
    2 garlic cloves, minced
    ½ teaspoon pepper
    1 slice hearty white sandwich bread, torn into quarters
    2 ounces Parmesan cheese, grated (1 cup)
    2 shallots, minced
    ¼ cup chopped fresh basil

Summer Vegetable Gratin

1. Toss zucchini and summer squash with 1 teaspoon salt and let drain in colander set over bowl until vegetables release at least 3 tablespoons liquid, about 45 minutes. Thoroughly pat zucchini and summer squash dry with paper towels.

2. Meanwhile, spread tomatoes on paper towel–lined baking sheet, sprinkle with ½ teaspoon salt, and let sit for 30 minutes. Thoroughly pat tomatoes dry with paper towels.

3. Heat 1 tablespoon oil in 12-inch nonstick skillet over medium heat until shimmering. Add onions and ½ teaspoon salt and cook, stirring occasionally, until softened and dark golden brown, 20 to 25 minutes; set aside.

4. Adjust oven rack to upper-middle position and heat oven to 400 degrees. Coat bottom of 13 by 9-inch baking dish (or 3-quart gratin dish) with 1 tablespoon oil. Combine 3 tablespoons oil, thyme, garlic, and pepper in bowl. Process bread in food processor until finely ground, about 10 seconds; transfer to second bowl and add Parmesan, shallots, and remaining 1 tablespoon oil.

5. Toss zucchini and summer squash with half of oil-thyme mixture and arrange in prepared dish. Sprinkle evenly with onions, then arrange tomatoes on top, overlapping them slightly. Spoon remaining oil-thyme mixture evenly over tomatoes. (Gratin and bread-crumb mixture, prepared through step 5, can be refrigerated separately for up to 24 hours.)

6. Bake until vegetables are tender and tomatoes begin to brown on edges, 40 to 45 minutes. Remove dish from oven and increase oven temperature to 450 degrees. Sprinkle bread-crumb mixture evenly over top and bake until gratin is bubbling and cheese is lightly browned, 5 to 10 minutes. Let cool for 10 minutes, then sprinkle with basil. Serve.

PER SERVING Cal 190; **Total Fat** 13g, **Sat Fat** 2.5g; **Chol** 5mg; **Sodium** 520mg; **Total Carb** 13g, **Dietary Fiber** 3g, **Total Sugars** 7g; **Protein** 6g

Tomato Gratin
SERVES 6

WHY THIS RECIPE WORKS A gratin may not be an obvious summertime side, but baking intensifies the tomatoes' natural sweetness; the crispy topping soaks up the juices released as the tomatoes cook. To avoid a watery dish, we salted tomato slices and let them sit for 30 minutes to release excess moisture. We then gave the tomato slices a whirl in the salad spinner to remove even more moisture, as well as some of their seeds and their jelly-like interiors. Then we added softened onions and thyme; layered the tomatoes in a dish; and popped it into the oven for 15 minutes. Sprinkling the makings of our crispy, cheesy crust over the tomatoes midway through baking and moving the dish to the upper-middle oven rack to brown kept the topping from getting soggy.

- 3 pounds plum tomatoes, cored and cut into ¼-inch-thick slices
- ½ teaspoon table salt, plus salt for salting tomatoes
- ½ teaspoon sugar
- ½ teaspoon pepper, divided
- 1 cup panko bread crumbs
- 2 ounces Parmesan cheese, grated (1 cup)
- ¼ cup extra-virgin olive oil, divided
- 2 onions, halved and sliced thin
- 1 tablespoon chopped fresh thyme
- 2 garlic cloves, minced

1. Adjust oven racks to upper-middle and lower-middle positions and heat oven to 450 degrees. Toss tomatoes, 1½ teaspoons salt, and sugar in bowl until combined; let sit for 30 minutes. Combine panko, Parmesan, 2 tablespoons oil, ½ teaspoon salt, and ¼ teaspoon pepper in second bowl.

2. Heat remaining 2 tablespoons oil in 12-inch skillet over medium-high heat until shimmering. Add onions and cook until softened and translucent, about 7 minutes. Stir in thyme and garlic and cook until fragrant, about 30 seconds. Season with salt and pepper to taste. Spread onion mixture in bottom of 13 by 9-inch baking dish.

3. Transfer tomatoes to salad spinner and spin to remove excess moisture. Arrange tomatoes in even layer over onion mixture and sprinkle with remaining ¼ teaspoon pepper. Transfer dish to lower rack and bake until tomatoes are tender and starting to bubble, about 15 minutes. Remove dish from oven, sprinkle evenly with panko mixture, transfer to upper rack, and bake until topping is golden brown, about 10 minutes. Transfer to wire rack and let cool for 10 minutes before serving. The gratin can be served hot, warm, or at room temperature.

PER SERVING Cal 230; **Total Fat** 13g, **Sat Fat** 2.5g; **Chol** 5mg; **Sodium** 880mg; **Total Carb** 23g, **Dietary Fiber** 3g, **Total Sugars** 8g; **Protein** 8g

Classic Potato Gratin
SERVES 4 TO 6

WHY THIS RECIPE WORKS A bubbling, creamy potato gratin is the ultimate in comfort food and is welcome anytime. For our classic recipe, we found that the potato variety mattered less than having them evenly sliced. Uniformly thin slices (easily obtained using a mandoline) yielded a gratin with distinct slices of potato bathed in a velvety sauce. The other trick was to first cook the sliced potatoes on the stovetop to get them started. As for the choice of dairy, we tried making gratins with milk, half-and-half, and heavy cream, and our favorite turned out to be half-and-half. Baked at 350 degrees for about an hour, gratins made this way had just the right balance of saturated potato and saucy liquid, without the sauce overwhelming the taste of the potato. For a more pronounced crust, sprinkle 3 tablespoons of heavy cream or grated Gruyère cheese on top of the potatoes after 45 minutes of baking.

- 1 garlic clove, peeled and smashed, divided
- 1 tablespoon unsalted butter, softened, divided
- 2 pounds potatoes, peeled and sliced ⅛ inch thick
- 2¼ cups half-and-half
- 1¼ teaspoons table salt
- ⅛ teaspoon pepper
  Pinch ground nutmeg
  Pinch cayenne pepper (optional)

1. Adjust oven rack to middle position and heat oven to 350 degrees. Rub bottom and sides of 1½-quart gratin dish or shallow baking dish with half garlic clove. Mince remaining garlic and set aside. Once garlic in dish has dried, about 2 minutes, spread dish with ½ tablespoon butter.

2. Bring potatoes; half-and-half; salt; pepper; nutmeg; cayenne, if using; and reserved minced garlic to boil in medium saucepan over medium-high heat, stirring occasionally (liquid will just barely cover potatoes). Reduce to simmer and cook until liquid thickens, about 2 minutes.

3. Pour potato mixture into prepared dish. Shake dish or use fork to distribute potatoes evenly. Gently press down potatoes until submerged in liquid. Cut remaining ½ tablespoon butter into small pieces and scatter over potatoes.

4. Bake until top is golden brown, about 1¼ hours, basting once or twice during first 45 minutes. Let rest for 5 minutes, and serve.

PER SERVING Cal 230; **Total Fat** 11g, **Sat Fat** 7g; **Chol** 35mg; **Sodium** 550mg; **Total Carb** 28g, **Dietary Fiber** 2g, **Total Sugars** 5g; **Protein** 6g

Olive Oil Potato Gratin

Olive Oil Potato Gratin
SERVES 6 TO 8

WHY THIS RECIPE WORKS Potato gratin is an inarguably delicious but also inarguably rich, luxurious side dish. For a lighter version that shifted the focus to the flavor of the potatoes, we tossed the spuds with fruity extra-virgin olive oil. We chose Yukon Gold potatoes for their rich flavor and moderate starch content, which helped them hold their shape when cooked. For a crisp, cheesy topping, we mixed more olive oil with panko bread crumbs and sprinkled the dish with salty Pecorino Romano. For added depth, we added sautéed onions, fresh thyme, and garlic.

 2 ounces Pecorino Romano cheese, grated (1 cup)
 ½ cup extra-virgin olive oil, divided
 ¼ cup panko bread crumbs
 1¼ teaspoons pepper, divided
 2 onions, halved and sliced thin
 1½ teaspoons table salt, divided
 2 garlic cloves, minced
 1 teaspoon minced fresh thyme, divided
 1 cup chicken broth, divided
 3 pounds Yukon Gold potatoes, peeled and
    sliced ⅛ inch thick

1. Adjust oven rack to upper-middle position and heat oven to 400 degrees. Grease 13 by 9-inch baking dish. Combine Pecorino, 3 tablespoons oil, panko, and ½ teaspoon pepper in bowl; set aside.

2. Heat 2 tablespoons oil in 12-inch skillet over medium heat until shimmering. Add onions, ½ teaspoon salt, and ¼ teaspoon pepper and cook, stirring frequently, until browned, about 15 minutes. Add garlic and ½ teaspoon thyme and cook until fragrant, about 30 seconds. Add ¼ cup broth and cook until nearly evaporated, scraping up any browned bits, about 2 minutes. Remove from heat; set aside.

3. Toss potatoes, remaining 3 tablespoons oil, remaining ½ teaspoon pepper, remaining 1 teaspoon salt, and remaining ½ teaspoon thyme together in bowl. Arrange half of potatoes in prepared dish, spread onion mixture in even layer over potatoes, and distribute remaining potatoes over onions. Pour remaining ¾ cup broth over potatoes. Cover dish tightly with aluminum foil and bake for 1 hour.

4. Remove foil, top gratin with reserved Pecorino mixture, and continue to bake until top is golden brown and potatoes are completely tender, 15 to 20 minutes. Let cool for 15 minutes. Serve.

PER SERVING Cal 300; **Total Fat** 16g, **Sat Fat** 3g; **Chol** 5mg; **Sodium** 610mg; **Total Carb** 31g, **Dietary Fiber** 1g, **Total Sugars** 1g; **Protein** 6g

Mashed Potato Casserole

SERVES 8 | MAKE-AHEAD

WHY THIS RECIPE WORKS Most recipes for mashed potato casserole call for simply dumping mashed potatoes in a baking dish and popping it in the oven, but these dishes always end up bland, gluey, and dense. We wanted a casserole that delivered fluffy, buttery, creamy potatoes nestled under a savory golden crust. Using half-and-half instead of the traditional heavy cream lightened the recipe, and cutting it with chicken broth kept the potatoes moist. Beating eggs into the potato mixture helped it achieve a fluffy, airy texture. For bold flavor, we added Dijon mustard and fresh chives. The casserole may also be baked in a 13 by 9-inch pan.

   4 pounds russet potatoes, peeled and cut into
      1-inch pieces
  12 tablespoons unsalted butter, cut into 12 pieces
  ½ cup half-and-half
  ½ cup chicken broth
   2 teaspoons Dijon mustard
   2 teaspoons table salt
   1 garlic clove, minced
   4 large eggs
  ¼ cup finely chopped fresh chives

1. Adjust oven rack to upper-middle position and heat oven to 375 degrees. Cover potatoes with water by 1 inch and bring to boil in large pot over high heat. Reduce heat to medium and simmer until potatoes are tender, about 20 minutes.

2. Heat butter, half-and-half, broth, mustard, salt, and garlic in saucepan over medium-low heat until smooth, about 5 minutes. Keep warm.

3. Drain potatoes and transfer to large bowl. Using stand mixer fitted with paddle, beat potatoes on medium-low speed, slowly adding half-and-half mixture, until smooth and creamy, about 1 minute. Scrape down bowl; beat in eggs, 1 at a time, until incorporated, about 1 minute. Fold in chives. (Casserole prepared through step 3, can be refrigerated for up to 24 hours. To bake, let sit at room temperature for 1 hour and continue with step 4.)

4. Transfer potato mixture to greased 3-quart baking dish. Smooth surface of potatoes, then use fork to make peaked design on top of casserole. Bake until potatoes rise and begin to brown, about 35 minutes. Let cool for 10 minutes. Serve.

PER SERVING Cal 330; **Total Fat** 21g; **Sat Fat** 12g; **Chol** 145mg; **Sodium** 700mg; **Total Carb** 29g, **Dietary Fiber** 2g, **Total Sugars** 2g; **Protein** 7g

Duchess Potato Casserole

Duchess Potato Casserole

SERVES 8 TO 10 | MAKE-AHEAD

WHY THIS RECIPE WORKS *Pommes duchesse* is a classic French preparation of piped mounds of egg-enriched mashed potatoes (for the classic, see page 290). To make an easier casserole version, we skipped the piping and baked the mashed potatoes in a baking dish. Starting with Yukon Golds gave the casserole a rich potato flavor, which we enhanced with butter, egg yolks, half-and-half, and nutmeg. To give the casserole an attractive crisp, golden-brown finish, we coated the top with a mixture of butter and egg white (the proteins in the egg white browned faster than butter; the butterfat prevented a tough skin) and then scored the surface with a paring knife before baking.

  3½ pounds Yukon Gold potatoes, peeled and
       sliced ½ inch thick
   ⅔ cup half-and-half
    1 large egg, separated, plus 2 large yolks, divided
 1¾ teaspoons plus pinch table salt, divided
   ½ teaspoon pepper
       Pinch ground nutmeg
   10 tablespoons unsalted butter, melted, divided

1. Adjust oven rack to middle position and heat oven to 450 degrees. Grease 13 by 9-inch baking dish. Place potatoes in large saucepan and add cold water to cover by 1 inch. Bring to simmer over medium-high heat. Adjust heat to maintain gentle simmer and cook until paring knife can easily slip in and out of centers of potatoes, 18 to 22 minutes. Drain potatoes.

2. While potatoes cook, combine half-and-half, 3 egg yolks, 1¾ teaspoons salt, pepper, and nutmeg in bowl. Set aside.

3. Place now-empty saucepan over low heat; set ricer or food mill over saucepan. Working in batches, transfer potatoes to hopper and process. Using silicone spatula, stir in 8 tablespoons melted butter until incorporated. Stir in reserved half-and-half mixture until combined. Transfer potatoes to prepared dish and smooth into even layer. (Potato mixture can be refrigerated for up to 24 hours.)

4. Combine egg white, remaining pinch salt, and remaining 2 tablespoons melted butter in bowl and beat with fork until combined. Pour egg white mixture over potatoes, tilting dish so mixture evenly covers surface. Using flat side of paring knife, make series of ½-inch-deep, ¼-inch-wide parallel grooves across surface of casserole. Make second series of parallel grooves across surface, at angle to first series, to create crosshatch pattern. Bake casserole until golden brown, 25 to 30 minutes, rotating dish halfway through baking. Let cool for 20 minutes. Serve.

PER SERVING Cal 260; **Total Fat** 15g, **Sat Fat** 9g; **Chol** 110mg; **Sodium** 470mg; **Total Carb** 25g, **Dietary Fiber** 0g, **Total Sugars** 1g; **Protein** 6g

Funeral Potatoes

Funeral Potatoes
SERVES 8 TO 10   MAKE-AHEAD

WHY THIS RECIPE WORKS This cheesy potato casserole is attributed to the Mormons. For ours, we softened onions in butter and added flour to create a golden roux. Chicken broth and half-and-half gave our base body. Using frozen hash browns cut hours of prep time without sacrificing flavor or texture. We stirred in shredded cheddar and let the potatoes cook in the sauce before stirring in sour cream. Crushed sour-cream-and-onion potato chips boosted the casserole's flavors and added irresistible crunch.

 3 tablespoons unsalted butter
 2 onions, chopped fine
 ¼ cup all-purpose flour
1½ cups chicken broth
 1 cup half-and-half
1¾ teaspoons table salt
 ½ teaspoon dried thyme
 ¼ teaspoon pepper
 8 ounces sharp cheddar cheese, shredded (2 cups)
 8 cups frozen shredded hash brown potatoes
 ½ cup sour cream
 4 ounces sour-cream-and-onion potato chips, crushed

1. Adjust oven rack to middle position and heat oven to 350 degrees. Melt butter in Dutch oven over medium-high heat. Add onions and cook until softened, about 5 minutes. Add flour and cook, stirring constantly, until golden, about 1 minute. Slowly whisk in broth, half-and-half, salt, thyme, and pepper and bring to boil. Reduce heat to medium-low and simmer, stirring occasionally, until slightly thickened, 3 to 5 minutes. Off heat, whisk in cheddar until smooth.

2. Stir potatoes into sauce, cover, and cook, stirring occasionally, over low heat until thawed, 10 minutes. Off heat, stir in sour cream.

3. Transfer mixture to 13 by 9-inch baking dish and top with potato chips. Bake until golden brown, 45 to 50 minutes. Let cool for 10 minutes before serving. (Potato mixture covered with foil can be refrigerated for up to 2 days. To finish, bake potatoes at 350 degrees for 20 minutes. Uncover, top with potato chips, and bake as directed.)

PER SERVING Cal 390; **Total Fat** 25g, **Sat Fat** 14g; **Chol** 65mg; **Sodium** 940mg; **Total Carb** 33g, **Dietary Fiber** 1g, **Total Sugars** 4g; **Protein** 11g

Potatoes Romanoff

SERVES 6 TO 8 `MAKE-AHEAD`

WHY THIS RECIPE WORKS Marked by a crisp top and creamy interior, potatoes romanoff is distinguished from its potato casserole cousins by the inclusion of sour cream, which turns it downright decadent. To maintain a smooth sauce (not broken and curdled) we added cream cheese and cornstarch in addition to the sour cream, and chose russet potatoes, as their starchiness helped bind this sauce and their fluffy quality kept our casserole from becoming heavy. Microwaving the potatoes sped up their cooking process so that the casserole needed only 20 minutes in the oven. We introduced the hot potatoes in two additions to keep the sour cream mixture from curdling. Chicken broth and white pepper added seasoning and savory flavor, and sharp cheddar cheese, along with scallion greens, finished the job.

3 pounds russet potatoes, peeled and cut into ½-inch pieces
2 teaspoons table salt
1¼ cups sour cream
4 ounces cream cheese, softened
1 tablespoon cornstarch
½ teaspoon white pepper
1¾ cups chicken broth
4 scallions, white parts minced, green parts sliced thin on bias
6 ounces sharp cheddar cheese, shredded (1½ cups)

1. Adjust oven rack to upper-middle position and heat oven to 425 degrees. Toss potatoes with salt in large bowl, cover, and microwave until tender, about 15 minutes, stirring once halfway through cooking.

2. Whisk sour cream, cream cheese, cornstarch, and pepper together in large bowl until combined. Whisk in chicken broth and scallion whites until incorporated. Fold in hot potatoes in 2 additions. Pour potato mixture into 8-inch square baking dish and sprinkle top with cheddar.

3. Place dish on rimmed baking sheet and bake until casserole is bubbling and cheese is browned, 15 to 20 minutes. Let cool for 20 minutes. Top with scallion greens. Serve. (Casserole can be made ahead and stored in the refrigerator for up to 24 hours. To serve, bake in a 425-degree oven for 30 to 35 minutes.)

PER SERVING Cal 320; **Total Fat** 17g, **Sat Fat** 11g; **Chol** 60mg; **Sodium** 910mg; **Total Carb** 31g, **Dietary Fiber** 2g, **Total Sugars** 3g; **Protein** 11g

Cheddar Scalloped Potatoes

SERVES 6 `MAKE-AHEAD`

WHY THIS RECIPE WORKS We love scalloped potatoes, but most recipes call for an hour or more of oven time. For a streamlined side dish, we parboiled sliced russets in heavy cream and chicken broth on the stovetop. Then we stirred in sharp cheddar and transferred the potato mixture to the oven to finish cooking. We prefer sharp cheddar here, but mild or extra-sharp cheddar can be used. A mandoline makes quick work of slicing the potatoes. Do not prepare them ahead of time or store them in water. This recipe can easily be doubled; use a large Dutch oven in step 1 and let the casserole cool for 30 minutes before serving in step 3.

2 pounds russet potatoes, peeled and sliced ¼ inch thick
1¼ cups heavy cream
1 cup chicken broth
1 teaspoon table salt
½ teaspoon pepper
8 ounces sharp cheddar cheese, shredded (2 cups), divided

1. Adjust oven rack to upper-middle position and heat oven to 425 degrees. Bring potatoes, cream, broth, salt, and pepper to simmer in large saucepan over medium-high heat.

2. Reduce heat to medium, cover, and cook, stirring occasionally, until paring knife slips in and out of potatoes easily, about 8 minutes, adjusting heat as necessary to maintain gentle simmer. Off heat, gently stir in 1 cup cheddar. (Potatoes can be cooled in baking dish, covered with foil, and refrigerated for up to 24 hours. To serve, bake covered for 20 minutes. Uncover and continue with step 3.)

3. Transfer potato mixture to 13 by 9-inch baking dish, spread into even layer, and sprinkle with remaining 1 cup cheddar. Bake until bubbling around edges and top is golden brown, about 20 minutes. Let cool for 15 minutes. Serve.

PER SERVING Cal 420; **Total Fat** 30g, **Sat Fat** 20g; **Chol** 95mg; **Sodium** 750mg; **Total Carb** 26g, **Dietary Fiber** 2g, **Total Sugars** 2g; **Protein** 14g

USING A MANDOLINE OR V-SLICER

Being sure to use safety guard, press potato against base of mandoline. Slide potato back and forth, passing over blade to thinly and evenly slice potato.

Cheddar Scalloped Potatoes

Lighter Scalloped Potatoes
SERVES 6

WHY THIS RECIPE WORKS Ultrarich, cheesy scalloped potatoes tend to be reserved for special occasions, but we think that's a shame. In an effort to make a version of this comforting side dish that we might feel better about enjoying more often, we did some careful ingredient swapping. The first thing to go was the butter, which we traded for just 1 tablespoon of canola oil. Our next target was the heavy cream. We eliminated it by using 2 percent low-fat milk, thickened and stabilized with cornstarch, which gave our potatoes the requisite creaminess. Adding some reduced-fat cream cheese and replacing the full-fat cheddar with a little Parmesan—its sharp, bold flavor meant we could use less of it—were the final adjustments needed to lighten this dish without sacrificing its characteristic creamy richness.

  1 tablespoon canola oil
  1 onion, chopped fine
  ½ teaspoon table salt
  1 garlic clove, minced
  1 teaspoon minced fresh thyme

2½ pounds russet potatoes, peeled and sliced ⅛ inch thick
  2 cups 2 percent low-fat milk
  2 bay leaves
  2 teaspoons cornstarch
  1 tablespoon water
  3 tablespoons ⅓ less fat cream cheese (neufchatel)
  2 ounces Parmesan cheese, grated (1 cup), divided
  ¼ teaspoon pepper

1. Adjust oven rack to middle position and heat oven to 450 degrees. Heat oil in Dutch oven over medium heat until shimmering. Add onion and salt and cook until softened, 5 to 7 minutes. Stir in garlic and thyme and cook until fragrant, about 30 seconds.

2. Add potatoes, milk, and bay leaves and bring to simmer. Cover, reduce heat to low, and simmer until potatoes are partially tender (tip of paring knife can be slipped into center of potato with some resistance), about 10 minutes.

3. Remove bay leaves. Whisk cornstarch and water together in bowl, then add to pot and bring to simmer. Off heat, stir in cream cheese, 2 tablespoons Parmesan, and pepper, being careful not to break up potatoes. Transfer mixture to 8-inch square baking dish.

4. Sprinkle with remaining Parmesan. Cover dish with aluminum foil and bake until bubbling around edges, about 20 minutes. Remove foil and continue to bake until potatoes are completely tender and top is golden brown, 10 to 15 minutes. Let cool for 10 minutes before serving.

PER SERVING Cal 260; **Total Fat** 8g, **Sat Fat** 3.5g; **Chol** 20mg; **Sodium** 440mg; **Total Carb** 36g, **Dietary Fiber** 2g, **Total Sugars** 6g; **Protein** 11g

Caramelized Onion and Potato Gratin
SERVES 6 TO 8

WHY THIS RECIPE WORKS This casserole dresses up creamy potato gratin with soft, sweet caramelized onions. While it usually takes at least 45 minutes to caramelize onions, we did it in a third of the time by adding brown sugar and cooking the onions over medium-high heat instead of low heat. Dark strings of caramelized onions were unappealing in the gratin, so instead of slicing the onions, we chopped them and tucked them away in the middle to form a layer of caramelized onion. Repurposing the skillet in which we'd caramelized our onions to make the sauce harvested all the browned bits that remained in the skillet for a sauce infused with onion flavor. A thick layer of melty, nutty Gruyère was the finishing touch to this sophisticated side. Thinly sliced potatoes are the key to even cooking—use a mandoline or the slicing disk of a food processor. You'll need 3 cups of chopped onions.

Caramelized Onion and Potato Gratin

2. Bring wine, cream, remaining 1 teaspoon salt, and remaining ⅔ cup broth to boil in now-empty skillet, scraping up any browned bits. Off heat, stir in vinegar; cover and keep warm.

3. Shingle half of potatoes in 13 by 9-inch baking dish; sprinkle with 1 teaspoon thyme and ½ teaspoon pepper. Spread onions over them, then top with remaining potatoes. Sprinkle with remaining ½ teaspoon pepper and remaining 1 teaspoon thyme. Pour wine mixture over the layers.

4. Bake until bubbling around edges, about 30 minutes. Top with Gruyère and bake until gratin is golden brown and fork inserted in center meets little resistance, 30 to 40 minutes. Let cool for 15 minutes. Serve.

PER SERVING Cal 340; **Total Fat** 17g, **Sat Fat** 10g; **Chol** 55mg; **Sodium** 1980mg; **Total Carb** 33g, **Dietary Fiber** 3g, **Total Sugars** 5g; **Protein** 11g

Candied Sweet Potato Casserole

SERVES 10 TO 12   MAKE-AHEAD

WHY THIS RECIPE WORKS Sweet potato casserole is a must-have side on many Thanksgiving tables, but it is often overly saccharine. For a casserole with restrained sweetness, we incorporated a more savory accent—and no marshmallows. For optimum soft texture and nuanced flavor, we steamed the sweet potatoes on the stovetop with butter and brown sugar. We kept the other flavors simple—just salt and pepper. For the candied topping, we used whole pecans; this gave the casserole a better texture and striking appearance. Tossing the nuts with egg white, brown sugar, and a little cayenne and cumin ensured a balanced topping with an inviting sheen and some welcome heat. For more intense molasses flavor, use dark brown sugar in place of light.

SWEET POTATOES
- 8 tablespoons unsalted butter, cut into 1-inch pieces
- 5 pounds sweet potatoes, peeled and cut into 1-inch cubes
- 1 cup packed light brown sugar
- ½ cup water
- 1½ teaspoons table salt
- ½ teaspoon pepper

PECAN TOPPING
- 2 cups pecans
- ½ cup packed light brown sugar
- 1 egg white, lightly beaten
- ⅛ teaspoon table salt
  - Pinch cayenne pepper
  - Pinch ground cumin

---

2 tablespoons unsalted butter
3 onions, chopped
2 teaspoons table salt, divided
1 tablespoon packed brown sugar
1 cup chicken broth, divided
⅔ cup dry white wine
⅔ cup heavy cream
1 teaspoon balsamic vinegar
3 pounds russet potatoes, peeled and sliced ⅛ inch thick
2 teaspoons minced fresh thyme, divided
1 teaspoon pepper, divided
6 ounces Gruyère cheese, shredded (1½ cups)

1. Adjust oven rack to middle position and heat oven to 350 degrees. Melt butter in 12-inch nonstick skillet over medium-high heat. Add onions and 1 teaspoon salt and cook until onions are just beginning to brown, about 5 minutes. Stir in sugar and cook, stirring frequently, until onions are golden brown, about 5 minutes. Add ⅓ cup broth and cook until onions are softened and deep golden brown and sticky, about 5 minutes. Transfer onions to medium bowl.

1. FOR THE SWEET POTATOES Melt butter in Dutch oven over medium-high heat. Add sweet potatoes, sugar, water, salt, and pepper; bring to simmer. Reduce heat to medium-low, cover, and cook, stirring often, until sweet potatoes are tender and paring knife inserted in center meets very little resistance, 45 minutes to 1 hour.

2. When sweet potatoes are tender, remove lid and bring sauce to rapid simmer over medium-high heat. Continue to simmer until sauce has reduced to glaze, 7 to 10 minutes. (Sweet potato mixture can be stored in microwave-safe bowl for up to 24 hours. To continue, microwave mixture covered until hot, 3 to 5 minutes. Continue to assemble and bake as directed.)

3. FOR THE TOPPING Meanwhile, mix all ingredients in medium bowl; set aside.

4. Adjust oven rack to middle position and heat oven to 450 degrees. Transfer sweet potato mixture to 13 by 9-inch baking dish. Spread topping over potatoes. Bake until pecans are toasted and crisp, 10 to 15 minutes. Serve immediately.

PER SERVING Cal 410; **Total Fat** 19g, **Sat Fat** 6g; **Chol** 20mg; **Sodium** 410mg; **Total Carb** 58g, **Dietary Fiber** 7g, **Total Sugars** 36g; **Protein** 4g

Loaded Sweet Potato Casserole

Loaded Sweet Potato Casserole
SERVES 6 TO 8

WHY THIS RECIPE WORKS For a savory alternative to a marshmallowy sweet potato side dish, we swapped the sweet topping for one that was cheesy and complex flavored. To make sure our sweet potatoes were tender but not mushy, we precooked them in the microwave. We also tossed the sliced potatoes with smoked paprika and garlic powder for a flavor boost before microwaving. And rather than rely on the traditional ingredients for this dish (they didn't jibe with the potatoes' sweetness), we loaded our casserole with more compatible ingredients: extra-sharp cheddar cheese, crispy bacon, sour cream, and scallions. Any shallow baking dish of similar size will work for this recipe. A mandoline makes quick work of evenly slicing the sweet potatoes.

- 3 pounds sweet potatoes, peeled and sliced ¼ inch thick
- 2 tablespoons extra-virgin olive oil
- 1 tablespoon smoked paprika
- 1 tablespoon garlic powder
- 1¼ teaspoons table salt
- ½ teaspoon pepper
- 8 ounces extra-sharp cheddar cheese, shredded (2 cups), divided
- 4 slices bacon, cut into ½-inch pieces
- 3 scallions, sliced thin on bias
  Sour cream

1. Adjust oven rack to middle position and heat oven to 400 degrees. Grease 13 by 9-inch baking dish.

2. Toss potatoes, oil, paprika, garlic powder, salt, and pepper together in large bowl. Microwave, covered, until potatoes are just tender, 10 to 12 minutes, stirring halfway through microwaving. Uncover and let sit until cool enough to handle, about 15 minutes.

3. Shingle one-third of potatoes in prepared dish, then sprinkle with ½ cup cheddar. Repeat with half of remaining potatoes and ½ cup cheddar. Shingle remaining potatoes in dish and pour any remaining liquid from bowl over top. Sprinkle with remaining 1 cup cheddar. Bake until tip of paring knife inserted into potatoes meets no resistance and cheese is spotty brown, about 30 minutes.

4. Meanwhile, cook bacon in 10-inch nonstick skillet over medium heat until crispy, 5 to 7 minutes. Using slotted spoon, transfer bacon to paper towel–lined plate.

5. Transfer dish to wire rack and let cool for 15 minutes. Sprinkle bacon and scallions over top and serve, passing sour cream separately.

PER SERVING Cal 320; **Total Fat** 18g, **Sat Fat** 8g; **Chol** 40mg; **Sodium** 720mg; **Total Carb** 29g, **Dietary Fiber** 5g, **Total Sugars** 8g; **Protein** 12g

Root Vegetable Gratin

SERVES 6 TO 8

WHY THIS RECIPE WORKS Our root vegetable gratin pairs the earthy flavor of potatoes with thinly sliced sweet rutabaga and savory celery root. We allowed these flavors to come to the forefront by using just a few aromatics (onion, garlic, and thyme), along with a little bit of Dijon mustard. We added white wine because the wine's acidity strengthened the pectin in the potatoes so that they remained intact while the denser, less-starchy rutabaga and celery root cooked through; the wine also brightened the flavors of the vegetables. To help the layers of the gratin cook through at the same rate, we covered the dish for the first portion of the cooking time. After removing the foil, we sprinkled on a layer of Parmesan enhanced panko bread crumbs that toasted while the gratin finished cooking, adding a crispy, golden crust with a nutty, cheesy flavor. Uniformly thin slices are necessary for a cohesive gratin. We recommend a mandoline for quick and even slicing, but a sharp chef's knife will also work. Because the vegetables in the gratin are tightly packed into the baking dish, it will still be plenty hot after a 25-minute rest.

Root Vegetable Gratin

1 tablespoon plus 1½ cups water, divided
2 teaspoons all-purpose flour
1½ teaspoons Dijon mustard
1½ teaspoons table salt
⅔ cup dry white wine
½ cup heavy cream
½ onion, chopped fine
1¼ teaspoons minced fresh thyme
1 garlic clove, minced
¼ teaspoon pepper
2 pounds large Yukon Gold potatoes, peeled and sliced lengthwise ⅛ inch thick
1 large celery root (1 pound), peeled, quartered, and sliced ⅛ inch thick
1 pound rutabaga, peeled, quartered, and sliced ⅛ inch thick
¾ cup panko bread crumbs
1½ ounces Parmesan cheese, grated (¾ cup)
4 tablespoons unsalted butter, melted and cooled

1. Adjust oven rack to middle position and heat oven to 375 degrees. Grease 13 by 9-inch baking dish. Whisk 1 tablespoon water, flour, mustard, and salt in medium bowl until smooth. Add wine, cream, and remaining 1½ cups water; whisk to combine. Combine onion, thyme, garlic, and pepper in second bowl.

2. Layer half of potatoes in prepared dish, arranging so they form even layer. Sprinkle half of onion mixture evenly over potatoes. Arrange celery root and rutabaga in even layer over onion mixture. Sprinkle remaining onion mixture over celery root and rutabaga. Layer remaining potatoes over onion mixture. Slowly pour wine mixture over vegetables. Using silicone spatula, gently press on vegetables to create even, compact layer. Cover dish tightly with aluminum foil and bake for 50 minutes. Remove foil and continue to bake until knife inserted in center of gratin meets no resistance, 20 to 25 minutes.

3. While gratin bakes, combine panko, Parmesan, and melted butter in bowl and season with salt and pepper to taste. Remove gratin from oven and sprinkle evenly with panko mixture. Continue to bake until panko is golden brown, 15 to 20 minutes longer. Remove gratin from oven and let stand for 25 minutes. Serve.

PER SERVING Cal 290; **Total Fat** 13g, **Sat Fat** 8g; **Chol** 35mg; **Sodium** 630mg; **Total Carb** 34g, **Dietary Fiber** 2g, **Total Sugars** 4g; **Protein** 7g

Cannellini Bean Gratin

SERVES 6 TO 8

WHY THIS RECIPE WORKS This elegant yet homey side-dish casserole features Tuscan-flavored saucy beans under a golden crust of cheese. We opted for convenient canned beans here. First we caramelized onions and deglazed the pot with white wine. Spread in the bottom of a casserole dish, the onions formed a flavorful base for our gratin. Briefly simmering the beans in vegetable broth, along with rosemary, infused the beans with subtle flavor. After stirring in some nutty Parmesan, we poured the bean mixture on top of the onions. For a cheesy crust with big impact, we sprinkled Gruyère over the top; its complex, earthy flavor perfectly complemented the creamy beans below. Make sure to cook the onions until they are well caramelized and darkly colored in step 1.

3 tablespoons extra-virgin olive oil, divided

3 onions, halved through root end and sliced thin

½ teaspoon brown sugar

6 garlic cloves, minced

⅛ teaspoon red pepper flakes

½ cup dry white wine

4 (15-ounce) cans cannellini beans, rinsed

1 cup vegetable broth

1 teaspoon minced fresh rosemary or ¼ teaspoon dried

2 ounces Parmesan cheese, grated (1 cup)

4 ounces Gruyère cheese, shredded (1 cup)

2 tablespoons minced fresh parsley

1. Adjust oven rack to middle position and heat oven to 375 degrees. Heat 2 tablespoons oil in Dutch oven over medium-high heat until shimmering. Add onions and sugar and cook, stirring frequently, until softened, about 5 minutes. Reduce heat to medium-low and continue to cook, stirring often, until onions are dark golden and caramelized, 20 to 25 minutes.

2. Stir in garlic and pepper flakes and cook until fragrant, about 30 seconds. Stir in wine and cook until nearly evaporated, about 1 minute. Transfer onions to 13 by 9-inch baking dish and spread into even layer.

3. Add beans, broth, and rosemary to now-empty pot and bring to brief simmer, about 1 minute. Off heat, gently stir in remaining 1 tablespoon oil and Parmesan. Season with salt and pepper to taste, spread evenly over onions, then sprinkle with Gruyère.

4. Bake, uncovered, until cheese is lightly golden and bubbling around edges, 15 to 20 minutes. Sprinkle with parsley and serve.

PER SERVING Cal 290; **Total Fat** 12g, **Sat Fat** 4.5g; **Chol** 20mg; **Sodium** 700mg; **Total Carb** 28g, **Dietary Fiber** 7g, **Total Sugars** 4g; **Protein** 17g

Rustic Polenta Casserole with Mushrooms and Swiss Chard

Rustic Polenta Casserole with Mushrooms and Swiss Chard

SERVES 6 TO 8 `MAKE-AHEAD`

WHY THIS RECIPE WORKS For a polenta casserole light enough to serve alongside dinner, we turned to meaty-tasting mushrooms, which we sautéed until all their liquid evaporated and they were well browned. Garlic and thyme added depth of flavor, and simmering the tomatoes with the mushrooms ensured we didn't lose any of the flavorful fond developed while cooking the mushrooms. To bulk up this dish and add a bright vegetal flavor, we used Swiss chard, which we cooked briefly in the skillet to take away its raw bite. Since the chard continues to cook in the oven, we found that it was important to reduce all the liquid from our sauce first, so the extra moisture from the chard didn't turn the sauce watery. Sprinkled with flavorful fontina cheese to finish, this combination of creamy polenta, meaty mushrooms, tomatoes, and Swiss chard made a satisfying side dish.

3 cups water

1 cup whole milk

1½ teaspoons table salt, divided

1 cup coarse-ground polenta

2 ounces Parmesan cheese, grated (1 cup)

3 tablespoons unsalted butter

3 tablespoons extra-virgin olive oil

1 onion, chopped fine

1½ pounds white mushrooms, trimmed and sliced thin

3 garlic cloves, minced

1 tablespoon minced fresh thyme or 1 teaspoon dried

1 (28-ounce) can diced tomatoes

8 ounces Swiss chard, stemmed and cut into 1-inch pieces

4 ounces fontina cheese, shredded (1 cup)

1. Adjust oven rack to middle position and heat oven to 400 degrees. Bring water and milk to boil in large saucepan over medium-high heat. Stir in 1 teaspoon salt. Slowly pour polenta into liquid in steady stream while stirring back and forth with wooden spoon. Reduce to gentle simmer, cover, and cook, stirring often, until mixture has uniformly smooth, thick consistency, 15 to 20 minutes. Off heat, stir in Parmesan and butter and season with salt and pepper to taste. Pour polenta into 13 by 9-inch baking dish and smooth into even layer.

2. Meanwhile, heat oil in 12-inch skillet over medium heat until shimmering. Add onion and remaining ½ teaspoon salt and cook until onion is softened, about 5 minutes. Add mushrooms and cook until they have released their liquid and are well browned, about 25 minutes.

3. Stir in garlic and thyme and cook until fragrant, about 30 seconds. Stir in tomatoes and their juice, bring to simmer, and cook, stirring occasionally, until sauce has thickened, about 10 minutes. Stir in chard, 1 handful at a time, and cook until wilted, 2 to 4 minutes. Season with salt and pepper to taste. Spread mushroom mixture evenly over polenta. (Casserole can be refrigerated for up to 24 hours. To serve, cover with aluminum foil and bake until bubbling at edges, about 30 minutes, then remove foil and continue with step 4.)

4. Sprinkle fontina evenly over top. Bake casserole until warmed through and cheese is melted, 10 to 15 minutes. Let cool for 5 minutes before serving.

PER SERVING Cal 300; Total Fat 17g, Sat Fat 8g; Chol 35mg; Sodium 890mg; Total Carb 26g, Dietary Fiber 2g, Total Sugars 6g; Protein 12g

Baked Cheese Grits
SERVES 6 TO 8

WHY THIS RECIPE WORKS Grits can be prepared in a variety of ways, but this lush baked version brings out the best of their sweet corn flavor. We opted for old-fashioned grits because, unlike their quick counterparts, they turn creamy but still retain some appealing coarseness once cooked. Simmering them in cream and salted water gave them full, deep flavor, while some softened chopped onion and a hit of hot sauce provided savoriness. Eggs added richness and structure, promising a texture somewhere between polenta and custardy spoonbread, and a cup of shredded extra-sharp cheddar delivered welcome tang. Spread into a baking dish, topped off with more cheese, and baked, these simple grits emerged just the creamy, rich accompaniment we craved with all our favorite brunch dishes. Do not substitute quick grits, which are finely ground and presteamed, for the old-fashioned grits called for here. Quick grits do not offer enough texture or body and will make for a gluey casserole.

3 tablespoons unsalted butter, divided

1 onion, chopped fine

4½ cups water

1½ cups heavy cream

1 teaspoon table salt

¾ teaspoon hot sauce

1½ cups old-fashioned grits

8 ounces extra-sharp cheddar cheese, shredded (2 cups), divided

4 large eggs, lightly beaten

¼ teaspoon pepper

1. Adjust oven rack to middle position and heat oven to 350 degrees. Grease 13 by 9-inch baking dish with 1 tablespoon butter.

2. Melt remaining 2 tablespoons butter in Dutch oven over medium heat. Add onion and cook, stirring often, until softened, 5 to 7 minutes. Add water, cream, salt, and hot sauce. Cover and bring mixture to boil.

3. Uncover and slowly whisk in grits. Reduce heat to low and cook, uncovered, stirring often, until grits are thick and creamy, about 15 minutes. Off heat, whisk in 1 cup cheddar, eggs, and pepper.

4. Pour mixture into prepared dish and smooth top with rubber spatula. Sprinkle remaining 1 cup cheddar over top. Bake until top is browned and grits are hot, 35 to 45 minutes. Remove grits from oven and let cool for 10 minutes before serving.

PER SERVING Cal 440; Total Fat 32g, Sat Fat 20g; Chol 185mg; Sodium 540mg; Total Carb 24g, Dietary Fiber 2g, Total Sugars 2g; Protein 14g

Baked Cheese Grits with Red Bell Pepper and Pepper Jack

Add 1 finely chopped red bell pepper to pot with onion in step 2 and increase cooking time to 8 to 10 minutes. Substitute pepper Jack for cheddar.

Farro and Broccoli Rabe Gratin

SERVES 6 **MAKE-AHEAD**

WHY THIS RECIPE WORKS This healthy, hearty casserole pairs whole-grain farro with other Italian ingredients—creamy white beans, slightly bitter broccoli rabe, and salty Parmesan—accenting the grain's nutty flavor. Toasting the farro in aromatics and oil boosted its nuttiness. We liked how small white beans blended in with the farro while giving it some creaminess and added protein. Blanching the broccoli rabe in salted water tamed its bitterness. We then sautéed it with garlic and pepper flakes for extra depth. Sun-dried tomatoes gave us the extra pop of flavor we were after in this dish. All that was left was to combine all the ingredients in a casserole dish and stick it under the broiler to brown the Parmesan dusted over the top. Do not substitute pearled (perlato), quick-cooking, or presteamed farro for the whole farro in this recipe; you may need to read the ingredient list on the package carefully to determine if the farro is presteamed.

Farro and Broccoli Rabe Gratin

2 tablespoons extra-virgin olive oil, divided
1 onion, chopped fine
1½ cups whole farro, rinsed
2 cups vegetable broth
4 ounces Parmesan cheese, grated (2 cups), divided
1 pound broccoli rabe, trimmed and cut into 2-inch lengths
   Table salt for cooking broccoli rabe
6 garlic cloves, minced
⅛ teaspoon red pepper flakes
1 (15-ounce) can small white beans or navy beans, rinsed
½ cup oil-packed sun-dried tomatoes, chopped

1. Heat 1 tablespoon oil in large saucepan over medium heat until shimmering. Add onion and cook until softened and lightly browned, 5 to 7 minutes. Stir in farro and cook until lightly toasted, about 2 minutes. Stir in broth and 1½ cups water and bring to simmer. Reduce heat to low and continue to simmer, stirring often, until farro is just tender and remaining liquid has thickened into creamy sauce, 20 to 25 minutes. Off heat, stir in 1 cup Parmesan and season with salt and pepper to taste.

2. Meanwhile, bring 4 quarts water to boil in Dutch oven. Add broccoli rabe and 1 tablespoon salt and cook until just tender, about 2 minutes. Drain broccoli rabe and transfer to bowl.

3. Wipe now-empty Dutch oven dry, add remaining 1 tablespoon oil, garlic, and pepper flakes, and cook over medium heat until fragrant and sizzling, 1 to 2 minutes. Stir in drained broccoli rabe and cook until hot and well coated, about 2 minutes. Off heat, stir in beans, farro mixture, and sun-dried tomatoes. Season with salt and pepper to taste, and transfer to 3-quart broiler-safe casserole dish. (Gratin filling can be refrigerated for up to 24 hours. To serve, stir ½ cup water into filling, cover with aluminum foil, and bake in 400-degree oven on upper-middle rack until hot throughout, about 30 minutes, before continuing with step 4.)

4. Position oven rack 6 inches from broiler element and heat broiler. Sprinkle gratin filling with remaining 1 cup Parmesan and broil until lightly browned and hot, 3 to 5 minutes. Let cool for 5 minutes before serving.

PER SERVING Cal 370; **Total Fat** 12g, **Sat Fat** 3.5g; **Chol** 15mg; **Sodium** 920mg; **Total Carb** 48g, **Dietary Fiber** 8g, **Total Sugars** 1g; **Protein** 21g

Cheesy Broccoli and Rice Casserole

Cheesy Broccoli and Rice Casserole

SERVES 8 TO 10 ⬛ MAKE-AHEAD

WHY THIS RECIPE WORKS Broccoli casserole recipes that call for condensed soup and frozen broccoli are a cinch to throw together, but we thought we could make an even better version without the convenience products. Instead of canned soup, we used a mixture of half-and-half and chicken broth. We also added extra-sharp cheddar and Parmesan cheese. To maximize the broccoli flavor, we used both the stalks and the florets. Since the stalks took longer to cook, we sautéed the chopped stalks in butter with onion and then added the rice and liquids. At first our sauce was too thick, but we realized we could eliminate the flour because the rice's natural starch gave the sauce the right consistency. Wanting a fresher topping than just cheese or canned fried onions, we made garlicky, Parmesan-enriched bread crumbs. This topping baked up crisp and added a final layer of flavor. You will need about two bunches of broccoli for this recipe.

2 slices hearty white sandwich bread, torn into quarters
1½ ounces Parmesan cheese, grated (¾ cup), divided
4 tablespoons unsalted butter, melted, plus 2 tablespoons unsalted butter

1 garlic clove, minced
2 pounds broccoli, florets cut into 1-inch pieces, stalks peeled and chopped
1 onion, chopped fine
1¼ cups long-grain white rice
4 cups chicken broth
1¼ cups half-and-half
1 teaspoon table salt
8 ounces extra-sharp cheddar cheese, shredded (2 cups)
⅛ teaspoon cayenne pepper

1. Adjust oven rack to middle position and heat oven to 400 degrees. Grease 13 by 9-inch baking dish. Pulse bread, ¼ cup Parmesan, and melted butter in food processor until coarsely ground. Add garlic and pulse to combine.

2. Microwave broccoli florets, covered, in large bowl until bright green and tender, 2 to 4 minutes; set aside. Melt remaining 2 tablespoons butter in Dutch oven over medium heat. Add onion and broccoli stalks and cook until softened, 8 to 10 minutes. Add rice and cook, stirring constantly, until rice is translucent, about 1 minute. Stir in broth, half-and-half, and salt and bring to boil. Reduce heat to medium-low and cook, stirring often, until rice is tender, 20 to 25 minutes. Off heat, mix in cheddar, cayenne, broccoli florets, and remaining ½ cup Parmesan.

3. Transfer mixture to prepared dish and top with bread-crumb mixture. (Filling and topping can be refrigerated separately for up to 24 hours. Let come to room temperature, add topping, and bake as directed.) Bake until sauce is bubbling around edges and top is golden brown, about 15 minutes. Let cool for 5 minutes. Serve.

PER SERVING Cal 260; **Total Fat** 19g, **Sat Fat** 12g; **Chol** 55mg; **Sodium** 760mg; **Total Carb** 13g, **Dietary Fiber** 2g, **Total Sugars** 4g; **Protein** 12g

Green Rice Casserole

SERVES 8 TO 10

WHY THIS RECIPE WORKS To rescue this potluck standby from canned soup–induced mediocrity, we started by infusing chicken broth with flavorful onion, garlic, and fresh thyme. We chopped thawed frozen spinach in the food processor, smoothed it out with cream cheese, and then layered it in the casserole dish with rice (raw, to prevent mushy grains) and sharp cheddar cheese before pouring our infused broth over the top. Baking the casserole covered to start allowed the rice to steam gently, and stirring it halfway through baking ensured even cooking. A crispy, Parmesan-rich layer of bread crumbs finished off the dish.

Green Rice Casserole

ground, 8 to 10 pulses; transfer to bowl and set aside. Combine spinach, cream cheese, remaining ½ teaspoon salt, and remaining ¼ teaspoon pepper in now-empty processor and process until smooth, about 10 seconds.

3. Spread spinach mixture in even layer in 13 by 9-inch baking dish. Sprinkle rice evenly over spinach mixture. Sprinkle cheddar over rice. Pour broth mixture into dish, cover tightly with double layer of aluminum foil, and bake for 25 minutes.

4. Remove dish from oven, remove foil, and stir to redistribute ingredients. Return dish to oven, increase oven temperature to 450 degrees, and continue to bake, uncovered, until all liquid is absorbed, about 15 minutes longer. Sprinkle bread-crumb mixture over top and bake until golden brown, 8 to 10 minutes. Let casserole cool for 20 minutes. Serve.

PER SERVING Cal 400; **Total Fat** 21g, **Sat Fat** 13g; **Chol** 65mg; **Sodium** 930mg; **Total Carb** 40g, **Dietary Fiber** 2g, **Total Sugars** 3g; **Protein** 15g

Zucchini and Orzo Tian
SERVES 6

WHY THIS RECIPE WORKS In this Provençal-type vegetable casserole, which would be right at home on a summertime table or potluck spread, attractively layered slices of zucchini, summer squash, and tomatoes top a filling of orzo. To ensure that the pasta and vegetables finished cooking simultaneously, we tightly shingled the vegetables on the orzo's surface, trapping the moisture within the casserole dish. Swapping out water for vegetable broth reinforced the vegetables' flavor, and shallots and garlic provided aromatic depth and sweetness. Stirring in some Parmesan gave the orzo a creamy texture, and oregano and red pepper flakes contributed floral, spicy notes to this otherwise mild dish. More cheese sprinkled on top before a few minutes under the broiler made for an appealing presentation, and chopped basil lent a fresh finish.

  3 ounces Parmesan cheese, grated (1½ cups), divided
  1 cup orzo
  2 shallots, minced
  3 tablespoons minced fresh oregano or 1 teaspoon dried
  3 garlic cloves, minced
  ⅛ teaspoon red pepper flakes
  ¼ teaspoon table salt
  1 zucchini, sliced ¼ inch thick
  1 yellow summer squash, sliced ¼ inch thick
  1 pound plum tomatoes, cored and sliced ¼ inch thick
1¾ cups vegetable broth
  1 tablespoon extra-virgin olive oil
  2 tablespoons chopped fresh basil

---

  4 tablespoons unsalted butter, divided
  1 onion, chopped fine
1½ teaspoons table salt, divided
  4 garlic cloves, minced
  ½ teaspoon minced fresh thyme
  4 cups chicken broth
  2 slices hearty white sandwich bread, torn into quarters
  1 ounce Parmesan cheese, grated (½ cup)
  ¾ teaspoon pepper, divided
1¼ pounds frozen chopped spinach,
     thawed and squeezed dry
  8 ounces cream cheese
  2 cups long-grain white rice
  8 ounces sharp cheddar cheese, shredded (2 cups)

1. Adjust oven rack to upper-middle position and heat oven to 350 degrees. Melt 2 tablespoons butter in medium saucepan over medium-low heat. Add onion and ½ teaspoon salt and cook until translucent, about 5 minutes. Add garlic and thyme and cook until fragrant, about 30 seconds. Add broth, increase heat to medium-high, and bring to boil. Cover and remove from heat.

2. Pulse bread, Parmesan, ½ teaspoon salt, ½ teaspoon pepper, and remaining 2 tablespoons butter in food processor until coarsely

1. Adjust oven rack to middle position and heat oven to 425 degrees. Combine ½ cup Parmesan, orzo, shallots, oregano, garlic, pepper flakes, and salt in bowl. Spread mixture evenly into broiler-safe 13 by 9-inch baking dish. Alternately shingle zucchini, squash, and tomatoes in tidy rows on top of orzo.

2. Carefully pour broth over top of vegetables. Bake until orzo is just tender and most of broth is absorbed, about 20 minutes.

3. Remove dish from oven, adjust oven rack 9 inches from broiler element, and heat broiler. Drizzle vegetables with oil, season with salt and pepper, and sprinkle with remaining 1 cup Parmesan. Broil until nicely browned and bubbling around edges, about 5 minutes.

4. Remove dish from oven and let rest for 10 minutes. Sprinkle with basil before serving.

PER SERVING Cal 350; **Total Fat** 11g, **Sat Fat** 4g; Chol 15mg; **Sodium** 790mg; **Total Carb** 45g, **Dietary Fiber** 3g, **Total Sugars** 10g; **Protein** 19g

Macaroni and Cheese Casserole

Macaroni and Cheese Casserole
SERVES 4 TO 6

WHY THIS RECIPE WORKS Unlike the standard saucy, béchamel-based macaroni and cheese, Southern-style macaroni and cheese is made with a cold custard and bakes into a nearly sliceable casserole. Starting with cold custard required long baking to get the center to set, which led to overcooked edges. Trading some of the whole eggs for a yolk made the custard more resilient, and starting with a hot custard reduced the baking time, which prevented the edges from overcooking. For the best cheese flavor and texture, we used easy-melting mild cheddar in the custard, reserving the sharp stuff for the top. The macaroni should still be firm after step 1.

8 ounces (2 cups) elbow macaroni
½ teaspoon table salt, plus salt for cooking pasta
8 ounces mild cheddar cheese, shredded (2 cups)
2 teaspoons cornstarch
4 tablespoons unsalted butter, divided
½ cup panko bread crumbs
½ cup finely chopped onion
3 tablespoons all-purpose flour
2 teaspoons dry mustard
¾ teaspoon pepper
⅛ teaspoon cayenne pepper
1 cup heavy cream
2 large eggs plus 1 large yolk, lightly beaten
2 teaspoons Worcestershire sauce
4 ounces sharp cheddar cheese, shredded (1 cup)

1. Adjust oven rack to upper-middle position and heat oven to 375 degrees. Bring 4 quarts water to boil in large saucepan. Add macaroni and 1 tablespoon salt and cook for 5 minutes. Drain macaroni; set aside. Toss mild cheddar with cornstarch; set aside.

2. In now-empty saucepan, melt 1 tablespoon butter over medium-low heat. Add panko and cook, stirring constantly, until golden, about 4 minutes. Transfer to bowl and set aside.

3. Melt remaining 3 tablespoons butter in now-empty saucepan over medium heat. Add onion and cook until beginning to soften, about 3 minutes. Add flour, mustard, pepper, cayenne, and ½ teaspoon salt and cook, stirring constantly, until well combined and floury smell has dissipated, about 1 minute. Whisk in cream and 2 cups water and bring to boil. Reduce heat to medium-low. Simmer until thickened, about 5 minutes.

4. Off heat, whisk in mild cheddar–cornstarch mixture until melted. Whisk in eggs and yolk and Worcestershire. Stir in macaroni. Transfer mixture to 8-inch square baking dish. Sprinkle with sharp cheddar, then panko mixture. Bake until well browned and set, 20 to 25 minutes. Let casserole cool for 20 minutes before serving.

PER SERVING Cal 590; **Total Fat** 38g, **Sat Fat** 23g; Chol 200mg; **Sodium** 710mg; **Total Carb** 41g, **Dietary Fiber** 0g, **Total Sugars** 3g; **Protein** 26g

Creamy Corn and Tomato Pasta Bake
SERVES 8 `MAKE-AHEAD`

WHY THIS RECIPE WORKS Baked pasta casseroles make for side dishes that are as convenient as they are irresistible. Wanting to avoid mushy noodles and flavorless vegetables in a thick, overly rich sauce, we began by parcooking the pasta until it was just beginning to soften so that it wouldn't overcook when baked or reheated. A combination of cream, vegetable broth, and white wine formed the basis of a simple flour-thickened sauce. Leaving the sauce a bit loose ensured that there was enough liquid to finish cooking the pasta during baking or reheating. For the vegetables, we chose a fresh combination of corn and tomatoes. Sprinkling additional cheese over the top before baking protected the pasta and ensured it cooked through evenly.

Creamy Corn and Tomato Pasta Bake

    1 pound penne
    1 teaspoon table salt, plus salt for cooking pasta
    2 tablespoons extra-virgin olive oil, divided
    1 onion, chopped
    ½ teaspoon pepper
    3 garlic cloves, minced
    1 tablespoon minced fresh thyme or 1 teaspoon dried
    ⅛ teaspoon red pepper flakes
    ¼ cup all-purpose flour
    2 cups vegetable broth
    2 cups heavy cream
    ½ cup dry white wine
    4 ears of corn, kernels cut from cobs
    8 ounces fontina cheese, shredded (2 cups), divided
    2 ounces Parmesan cheese, grated (1 cup), divided
    1 pound cherry tomatoes, halved
    1 tablespoon chopped fresh basil, parsley, or tarragon

1. Bring 4 quarts water to boil in large pot. Add pasta and 1 tablespoon salt. Cook, stirring often, until just beginning to soften, about 5 minutes. Drain pasta in colander and toss with 1 tablespoon oil; set aside.

2. Adjust oven rack to middle position and heat oven to 400 degrees. Dry now-empty pot and heat remaining 1 tablespoon oil over medium heat until shimmering. Add onion, salt, and pepper and cook until softened, about 5 minutes. Stir in garlic, thyme, and pepper flakes and cook until fragrant, about 30 seconds. Add flour and cook, stirring constantly, until golden, about 1 minute. Slowly whisk in broth, cream, and wine, smoothing out any lumps. Stir in corn and bring to simmer.

3. Off heat, gradually whisk in 1 cup fontina and ½ cup Parmesan into sauce until cheese is melted and sauce is smooth. Stir in tomatoes and pasta, breaking up any clumps. Transfer pasta mixture to 13 by 9-inch baking dish and sprinkle with remaining 1 cup fontina and ½ cup Parmesan. (Casserole can be refrigerated for up to 24 hours.)

4. Place baking dish on aluminum foil-lined rimmed baking sheet and bake until golden and bubbling around edges, 25 to 35 minutes. Let casserole cool for 20 minutes. Sprinkle with basil and serve.

PER SERVING Cal 660; **Total Fat** 38g, **Sat Fat** 21g; **Chol** 105mg; **Sodium** 920mg; **Total Carb** 60g, **Dietary Fiber** 2g, **Total Sugars** 8g; **Protein** 22g

GET FIRED UP

■ MAKE-AHEAD   ■ VEGAN
Photos (clockwise from top left): Husk-Grilled Corn; Grilled Butternut Squash;
Grilled Zucchini with Red Pepper Sauce; Grilled Vegetable and Halloumi Salad

GRILLING VEGETABLES

Grilling vegetables turns them into something special and frequently you can make some magic while your protein is resting. Each recipe in this chapter contains instructions for making a single-level or modified two-level fire using either a charcoal or a gas grill. For more information about grilling specific vegetables, see the chart on page 517.

SINGLE-LEVEL CHARCOAL FIRE
This simple arrangement is suited to foods that you want to brown but that can also overcook quickly, like vegetables. To set up the fire, distribute ash-covered coals in an even layer across the bottom of the grill. A single-level fire delivers a uniform level of heat across the entire cooking surface.

MODIFIED TWO-LEVEL (HALF-GRILL) CHARCOAL FIRE
This fire has two cooking zones: One side is intensely hot, and the other is comparatively cool. For foods that require longer cooking times, you can brown the food on the hotter side and then set it on the cooler side to finish with indirect heat. To set up the fire, distribute ash-covered coals over half of the grill, piling them in an even layer. Leave the other half of the grill free of coals.

SINGLE-LEVEL OR MODIFIED TWO-LEVEL GAS FIRE
To create a single-level fire on a gas grill, turn all the burners to the heat setting specified in the recipe after preheating the grill. To create a modified two-level fire, adjust the primary burner as directed in the recipe and turn off the other burner(s).

CLEAN AND OIL THE COOKING GRATE
Properly heating and cleaning the grill before cooking are important to successful grilling. To ensure vegetables release with ease, heat your grill before scraping it clean with a grill brush. For further insurance against sticking, grab a wad of paper towels with a pair of long-handled tongs, dip the wad into vegetable oil, and run it over the cleaned grill grate.

Grilled Artichokes with Lemon Butter

Grilled Artichokes with Lemon Butter
SERVES 4

WHY THIS RECIPE WORKS Grilling artichokes is a nice alternative to steaming them. It adds a bit of smoky char and enhances their nutty flavor. We parboiled them in a broth with lemon juice, red pepper flakes, and salt to ensure that they were completely tender and thoroughly seasoned. Brushing the artichokes with extra-virgin olive oil helped them develop flavorful char marks on the grill. A simple blend of lemon zest and juice, garlic, and butter came together easily in the microwave and was perfect for dipping or drizzling. If your artichokes are larger than 10 ounces, strip away another layer or two of the toughest outer leaves. For more on trimming artichokes, see page 40.

½ teaspoon table salt, plus salt for cooking artichokes
½ teaspoon red pepper flakes
2 lemons
4 artichokes (8 to 10 ounces each)
6 tablespoons unsalted butter
1 garlic clove, minced to paste
¼ teaspoon pepper
2 tablespoons extra-virgin olive oil

1. Combine 3 quarts water, 3 tablespoons salt, and pepper flakes in Dutch oven. Cut 1 lemon in half; squeeze juice into pot, then add spent halves. Bring to boil over high heat.

2. Meanwhile, working with 1 artichoke at a time, trim end of stem and cut off top quarter of artichoke. Break off bottom 3 or 4 rows of tough outer leaves by pulling them downward. Using kitchen shears, trim off top portion of outer leaves. Using paring knife, trim stem and base, removing any dark green parts.

3. Add artichokes to pot with boiling water mixture, cover, and reduce heat to medium-low. Simmer until tip of paring knife inserted into base of artichoke meets no resistance, 25 to 28 minutes, stirring occasionally.

4. While artichokes simmer, grate 2 teaspoons zest from remaining lemon; combine with butter, garlic, ½ teaspoon salt, and pepper in bowl. Microwave at 50 percent power until butter is melted and bubbling and garlic is fragrant, about 2 minutes, stirring occasionally. Squeeze 1½ tablespoons juice from zested lemon and stir into butter. Season with salt and pepper to taste.

5. Set wire rack in rimmed baking sheet. Place artichokes stem side up on prepared rack and let drain for 10 minutes. Cut artichokes in half lengthwise. Remove fuzzy choke and any tiny inner purple-tinged leaves using small spoon, leaving small cavity in center of each half.

6A. FOR A CHARCOAL GRILL Open bottom vent completely. Light large chimney starter filled with charcoal briquettes (6 quarts). When top coals are partially covered with ash, pour evenly over grill. Set cooking grate in place, cover, and open lid vent completely. Heat grill until hot, about 5 minutes.

6B. FOR A GAS GRILL Turn all burners to high, cover, and heat grill until hot, about 15 minutes. Leave all burners on high.

7. Clean and oil cooking grate. Brush artichokes with oil. Place artichokes on grill and cook (covered if using gas) until lightly charred, 2 to 4 minutes per side. Transfer artichokes to serving platter and tent with aluminum foil. Briefly rewarm lemon butter in microwave, if necessary, and serve with artichokes.

PER SERVING Cal 260; **Total Fat** 24g, **Sat Fat** 12g; **Chol** 45mg; **Sodium** 520mg; **Total Carb** 11g, **Dietary Fiber** 5g, **Total Sugars** 1g; **Protein** 3g

Grilled Asparagus

Grilled Asparagus
SERVES 4

WHY THIS RECIPE WORKS The main challenge with grilling delicate asparagus is protecting it from overcooking while still developing a good char. For great grilled asparagus, we opted for thicker spears, which combined maximum browning potential with a meaty, crisp-tender texture. A medium-hot fire worked best—the spears were on and off the grill in less than 10 minutes. Brushing the spears with butter rather than oil before grilling gave us crispy, nutty asparagus. The asparagus is nice served with a flavored butter (page 375), vinaigrette (page 368), or aioli (page 150). Look for asparagus spears between ½ and ¾ inch in diameter. You can use white or green asparagus in this recipe; if using white, peel just the outermost layer of the bottom halves of the spears.

1½ pounds thick asparagus
3 tablespoons unsalted butter, melted
½ teaspoon table salt
¼ teaspoon pepper

1. Trim bottom inch of asparagus spears and discard. Peel bottom halves of spears until white flesh is exposed. Brush asparagus with melted butter and season with salt and pepper.

2A. FOR A CHARCOAL GRILL Open bottom vent completely. Light large chimney starter three-quarters filled with charcoal briquettes (4½ quarts). When top coals are partially covered with ash, pour evenly over grill. Set cooking grate in place, cover, and open lid vent completely. Heat grill until hot, about 5 minutes.

2B. FOR A GAS GRILL Turn all burners to high, cover, and heat grill until hot, about 15 minutes. Turn all burners to medium-high.

3. Clean and oil cooking grate. Place asparagus in even layer on grill and cook until browned and tip of paring knife inserted at base of largest spear meets little resistance, 4 to 10 minutes, turning halfway through cooking. Serve.

PER SERVING Cal 100; **Total Fat** 8g, **Sat Fat** 5g; **Chol** 25mg; **Sodium** 290mg; **Total Carb** 5g, **Dietary Fiber** 2g, **Total Sugars** 2g; **Protein** 3g

---

TAKE IT UP A NOTCH

These quick vinaigrettes are easy to prepare and can elevate any simple vegetable or green salad to something a little more special.

Tomato-Basil Vinaigrette

    1 tomato, cored, seeded, and minced (about ½ cup)
    1 shallot, minced (about 1½ tablespoons)
 1½ tablespoons lemon juice
    1 tablespoon minced fresh basil
    3 tablespoons extra-virgin olive oil

Whisk tomato, shallot, lemon juice, basil, and oil in small bowl; season with salt and pepper to taste.

Lemon-Shallot Vinaigrette

    1 large shallot, minced (about 2 tablespoons)
    1 tablespoon minced fresh thyme
    1 teaspoon grated lemon zest plus 1 tablespoon juice
  ¼ teaspoon Dijon mustard
  ⅓ cup extra-virgin olive oil

Whisk shallot, thyme, lemon zest and juice, mustard, and oil in small bowl; season with salt and pepper to taste.

Grilled Prosciutto-Wrapped Asparagus
SERVES 4

WHY THIS RECIPE WORKS For a sophisticated twist on grilled asparagus, we dressed up the spears with savory prosciutto. Wrapping the asparagus in prosciutto before grilling resulted in crispy prosciutto—an appealing contrast to the mellow vegetable. Since grilling prosciutto concentrates and intensifies its flavor, wrapping two spears in one piece of prosciutto was the perfect ratio. Wrapping the prosciutto around the spears' middles exposed the asparagus on either end so it still picked up flavorful browning and char from the grill. Brushing the bundles with extra-virgin olive oil before grilling ensured that the prosciutto crisped without drying out, and a little pepper enhanced the dish's flavors. Off the grill, a spritz of lemon juice was all the spears needed to be ready for serving. For the best results, look for spears that are bright green in color and firm to the touch, with tightly closed tips. If you are using asparagus spears that are thicker than ½ inch in diameter, you may have to increase the grilling time. Do not use asparagus that is thinner than ½ inch in diameter.

 16 (½-inch-thick) asparagus spears, trimmed
  8 thin slices prosciutto (4 ounces)
  2 tablespoons extra-virgin olive oil
    Lemon wedges

1. Working with 2 asparagus spears at a time, tightly wrap 1 slice prosciutto around middle of spears to create bundle. (If prosciutto rips, slightly overlap ripped pieces and press with your fingers to stick it back together.) Brush bundles on both sides with oil and season with pepper to taste.

2A. FOR A CHARCOAL GRILL Open bottom vent completely. Light large chimney starter filled with charcoal briquettes (6 quarts). When top coals are partially covered with ash, pour evenly over grill. Set cooking grate in place, cover, and open lid vent completely. Heat grill until hot, about 5 minutes.

2B. FOR A GAS GRILL Turn all burners to high, cover, and heat grill until hot, about 15 minutes. Turn all burners to medium.

3. Clean and oil cooking grate. Grill asparagus bundles (covered if using gas) until prosciutto is spotty brown and paring knife slips easily in and out of asparagus, 6 to 8 minutes, flipping bundles halfway through cooking. Serve warm or at room temperature with lemon wedges.

PER SERVING Cal 130; **Total Fat** 10g, **Sat Fat** 2g; **Chol** 20mg; **Sodium** 760mg; **Total Carb** 3g, **Dietary Fiber** 1g, **Total Sugars** 1g; **Protein** 9g

Grilled Broccoli with Lemon and Parmesan
SERVES 6 TO 8

WHY THIS RECIPE WORKS Grilling broccoli produces vivid green spears with flavorful char. To avoid toughness, we peeled the stalks with a vegetable peeler and cut the head into spears small enough to cook quickly but large enough to grill easily. Since grilling alone would yield dry broccoli, we tossed the spears in olive oil and water and steamed them in sealed foil packets on the grill. As soon as the stalks and florets were evenly cooked, we placed them directly on the grill to give them perfect grill marks and plenty of flavor. A squeeze of grilled lemon and a sprinkling of Parmesan sealed the deal. To keep the packs from tearing, use heavy-duty aluminum foil. Use the large holes of a box grater to shred the Parmesan.

Grilled Broccoli with Lemon and Parmesan

¼ cup extra-virgin olive oil, plus extra for drizzling
1 tablespoon water
¾ teaspoon table salt
½ teaspoon pepper
2 pounds broccoli
1 lemon, halved
¼ cup shredded Parmesan cheese

1. Cut two 26 by 12-inch sheets of heavy-duty aluminum foil. Whisk oil, water, salt, and pepper together in large bowl.

2. Trim stalks so each entire head of broccoli measures 6 to 7 inches long. Trim tough outer peel from stalks, then cut heads in half lengthwise into spears (stems should be ½ to ¾ inch thick and florets 3 to 4 inches wide). Add broccoli to oil mixture and toss to coat well.

3. Divide broccoli between sheets of foil, cut side down and alternating direction of florets and stalks. Bring short sides of foil together and crimp tightly. Crimp long ends to seal packs tightly.

4A. FOR A CHARCOAL GRILL Open bottom vent completely. Light large chimney starter filled with charcoal briquettes (6 quarts). When top coals are partially covered with ash, pour evenly over half of grill. Set cooking grate in place, cover, and open lid vent completely. Heat grill until hot, about 5 minutes.

4B. FOR A GAS GRILL Turn all burners to high, cover, and heat grill until hot, about 15 minutes. Turn all burners to medium-high. (Adjust burners as needed to maintain grill temperature around 400 degrees.)

5. Clean and oil cooking grate. Arrange packets evenly on grill (over coals if using charcoal), cover, and cook for 8 minutes, flipping packets halfway through cooking.

6. Transfer packets to rimmed baking sheet and, using scissors, carefully cut open, allowing steam to escape away from you. (Broccoli should be bright green and fork inserted into stalks should meet some resistance.)

7. Discard foil and place broccoli and lemon halves cut side down on grill (over coals if using charcoal). Grill (covered if using gas), turning broccoli about every 2 minutes, until stalks are fork-tender and well charred on all sides, 6 to 8 minutes. Transfer broccoli to now-empty sheet as it finishes cooking. Grill lemon halves until well charred on cut side, 6 to 8 minutes.

8. Transfer broccoli to cutting board and cut into 2-inch pieces. Transfer to serving platter and season with salt and pepper to taste. Squeeze lemon over broccoli to taste, sprinkle with Parmesan, and drizzle with extra oil. Serve.

PER SERVING Cal 90; Total Fat 8g, Sat Fat 1g; Chol 0mg; Sodium 260mg; Total Carb 5g, Dietary Fiber 2g, Total Sugars 1g; Protein 2g

VARIATIONS
Grilled Broccoli with Anchovy-Garlic Butter
Omit lemon and Parmesan cheese. Whisk 4 tablespoons melted unsalted butter, 3 rinsed and minced anchovy fillets, 1 minced garlic clove, 1 teaspoon lemon juice, ½ teaspoon salt, ¼ teaspoon red pepper flakes, and ⅛ teaspoon pepper together in bowl. Drizzle butter mixture over broccoli before serving.

Grilled Broccoli with Sweet Chili Sauce

Omit lemon and Parmesan cheese. Whisk 4 teaspoons toasted sesame oil, 2½ teaspoons sugar, 2 teaspoons Asian chili-garlic sauce, 1 teaspoon distilled white vinegar, and ¼ teaspoon salt together in bowl. Drizzle oil mixture over broccoli before serving.

Grilled Butternut Squash

SERVES 4 TO 6　VEGAN

WHY THIS RECIPE WORKS Grilling brings out the best in butternut squash, leaving the flesh tender and sweet with a caramelized, smoky exterior. We peeled the squash to remove not only the tough outer skin but also the rugged fibrous layer of white flesh just beneath, which gave us supremely tender squash. However, our first few attempts at grilling the peeled, sliced squash resulted in slices that were raw on the inside and burnt on the outside. We realized that the squash was just too dense to cook through evenly on the grill, so we parboiled it before grilling. This extra step helped jump-start the cooking process so the squash could finish cooking relatively quickly over a medium-hot fire that had enough heat to caramelize its surface. This recipe calls for a lot of squash slices. Depending on the spacing of the bars on your cooking grate, you might want to cook them on a grill topper to prevent any slices from dropping down into the fire.

- 1 small butternut squash (2 pounds), peeled, seeded, and sliced ½ inch thick
  Table salt for cooking squash
- 3 tablespoons extra-virgin olive oil

1. Place squash in large pot. Cover with 2 quarts cold water. Add 1 teaspoon salt and bring to boil over high heat. Reduce heat to medium and simmer until squash is barely tender, about 3 minutes.

2. Drain squash in colander, being careful not to break up slices. Transfer squash to large bowl; drizzle oil over top. Season with salt and pepper and gently turn squash to coat both sides of each slice with oil.

3A. FOR A CHARCOAL GRILL Open bottom vent completely. Light large chimney starter three-quarters filled with charcoal briquettes (4½ quarts). When top coals are partially covered with ash, pour evenly over grill. Set cooking grate in place, cover, and open lid vent completely. Heat grill until hot, about 5 minutes.

3B. FOR A GAS GRILL Turn all burners to high, cover, and heat grill until hot, about 15 minutes. Turn all burners to medium-high.

4. Clean and oil cooking grate. Place squash on grill and cook, flipping once, until dark brown and caramelized and flesh is very tender, 8 to 10 minutes. Serve squash hot, warm, or at room temperature.

PER SERVING Cal 120; **Total Fat** 7g, **Sat Fat** 1g; **Chol** 0mg; **Sodium** 100mg; **Total Carb** 15g, **Dietary Fiber** 3g, **Total Sugars** 3g; **Protein** 1g

VARIATION
Spicy Grilled Butternut Squash with Garlic and Rosemary

Add 1 tablespoon extra-virgin olive oil to squash in step 2. After oiling, sprinkle squash with 2 tablespoons packed brown sugar, 1 teaspoon chopped fresh rosemary, 1 minced garlic clove, and ½ teaspoon red pepper flakes in place of salt and pepper. Turn squash to coat. Grill as directed.

Grilled Cabbage

SERVES 6 TO 8

WHY THIS RECIPE WORKS The fire of a hot grill tames cabbage's crunch, turning the cabbage tender, sweet, and deliciously smoky. Slicing the head into thick wedges kept it intact on the grill. To make sure the interior softened before the exterior overcooked, we salted the wedges to draw out moisture so the moisture would then turn to steam on the grill. Brushing a simple lemon vinaigrette on the cabbage both before and after grilling added bright flavor.

- 1 teaspoon table salt
- 1 head green cabbage (2 pounds), cut into 8 wedges through core
- 6 tablespoons extra-virgin olive oil
- 1 tablespoon minced fresh thyme
- 2 teaspoons minced shallot
- 2 teaspoons honey
- 1 teaspoon Dijon mustard
- ½ teaspoon grated lemon zest plus 2 tablespoons juice
- ¼ teaspoon pepper

1. Sprinkle salt evenly over cabbage wedges and let sit for 45 minutes. Whisk oil, thyme, shallot, honey, mustard, lemon zest and juice, and pepper together in bowl. Measure out and reserve ¼ cup vinaigrette for serving.

2A. FOR A CHARCOAL GRILL Open bottom vent completely. Light large chimney starter half-filled with charcoal briquettes (3 quarts). When top coals are partially covered with ash, pour evenly over grill. Set cooking grate in place, cover, and open lid vent completely. Heat grill until hot, about 5 minutes.

Grilled Cabbage

2B. FOR A GAS GRILL Turn all burners to high, cover, and heat grill until hot, about 15 minutes. Turn all burners to medium.

3. Clean and oil cooking grate. Pat cabbage wedges dry, then brush 1 cut side of wedges with half of remaining vinaigrette. Place cabbage on grill, vinaigrette side down, and cook (covered if using gas) until well browned, 7 to 10 minutes. Brush top cut side of wedges with remaining vinaigrette. Flip and cook (covered if using gas) until second side is well browned and fork-tender, 7 to 10 minutes. Transfer cabbage to serving platter and drizzle with reserved vinaigrette. Season with salt and pepper to taste. Serve.

CUTTING CABBAGE INTO WEDGES

Cut the cabbage head into wedges, being careful to keep the core intact. This will keep the wedges from breaking apart on the grill.

Easy Grilled Coleslaw
SERVES 4

WHY THIS RECIPE WORKS We love the fresh crunch of cold and creamy coleslaw, but sometimes a change of course is in order. For an updated take on a classic side dish, we used the grill to mellow the raw bite of cabbage. Leaving the core in the cabbage helped keep the leaves together while grilling, and after about 10 minutes our wedges were beautifully grill-marked and ready to be cored and cut up for the slaw. A simple tangy dressing of mayo seasoned with cider vinegar coated the charred cabbage and brought the slaw together. Carrot added earthy sweetness and fresh cilantro made this picnic staple a bit more spirited. Do not remove the core from the cabbage before grilling; it will keep the leaves intact on the grill.

½ head green cabbage (1 pound), cut into 2 wedges
2 tablespoons extra-virgin olive oil
½ teaspoon table salt
¼ teaspoon pepper
¼ cup mayonnaise
1 shallot, minced
4 teaspoons cider vinegar
1 carrot, peeled and shredded
2 tablespoons minced fresh cilantro

1A. FOR A CHARCOAL GRILL Open bottom vent completely. Light large chimney starter filled with charcoal briquettes (6 quarts). When top coals are partially covered with ash, pour evenly over grill. Set cooking grate in place, cover, and open lid vent completely. Heat grill until hot, about 5 minutes.

1B. FOR A GAS GRILL Turn all burners on high, cover, and heat grill until hot, about 15 minutes. Leave all burners on high.

2. Brush cabbage wedges with oil and sprinkle with salt and pepper.

3. Clean and oil cooking grate. Place cabbage on grill. Cook (covered if using gas), turning as needed, until cabbage is lightly charred on all sides, 8 to 12 minutes. Transfer cabbage to platter; tent with aluminum foil and let rest.

4. Whisk mayonnaise, shallot, and vinegar together in large bowl. Slice cabbage into thin strips, discarding core. Stir cabbage, carrot, and cilantro into mayonnaise mixture. Season with salt and pepper to taste. Serve.

PER SERVING Cal 200; **Total Fat** 17g, **Sat Fat** 2.5g; **Chol** 5mg; **Sodium** 420mg; **Total Carb** 10g, **Dietary Fiber** 3g, **Total Sugars** 5g; **Protein** 2g

Grilled Brined Carrots with Cilantro-Yogurt Sauce

1½ pounds young carrots with greens attached, carrots unpeeled, greens chopped (1¼ cups), divided
    Table salt for brining carrots
1¼ cups coarsely chopped fresh cilantro leaves and stems, divided
½ cup plain Greek yogurt
¼ cup dry-roasted peanuts, chopped, divided
1 jalapeño chile, stemmed, seeds reserved, and minced
1 ice cube
1 teaspoon grated fresh ginger
1 garlic clove, minced
¼ teaspoon ground coriander

Grilled Brined Carrots with Cilantro-Yogurt Sauce
SERVES 4

WHY THIS RECIPE WORKS We love grilling whole carrots, but they are tricky to season evenly. Dusting whole raw carrots with salt did nothing—the salt just bounced right off. But 45 minutes in a salty bath changed the game, thoroughly infusing the carrots with flavor. Whereas we brine meat to increase tenderness and season, our goal here was primarily seasoning (though the carrots did soften slightly in the brine). We grilled them quickly over a hot fire to develop char and smoky flavor without sacrificing crunch. Drizzled with a piquant cilantro-yogurt sauce and sprinkled with peanuts and fresh herbs, these carrots might just become your new favorite side dish during grilling season. Young carrots are immature carrots, harvested early in their growing cycle. Look for carrots that are 3 to 5 inches long and ½ to 1 inch in diameter. Peeled carrots will absorb salt more rapidly, so we don't recommend peeling them for this recipe. If you can't find carrots with their tops attached or the greens aren't in good shape, use thin carrots and 2 cups cilantro.

1. Rinse and scrub carrots to remove any dirt. Whisk 1 quart water and ¼ cup salt in large bowl until salt is dissolved. Submerge carrots in brine and let sit at room temperature for at least 45 minutes or up to 1 hour. (Carrots brined with this salt concentration will start to taste too salty if brined longer than 1 hour. Brined carrots can be removed from brine, patted dry, and refrigerated for up to 3 hours before cooking.) Transfer carrots to paper towel–lined plate and pat dry. Discard brine.

2. Meanwhile, process 1 cup cilantro, 1 cup carrot greens, yogurt, 3 tablespoons peanuts, jalapeño, ice cube, ginger, garlic, and coriander in blender on high speed until smooth and creamy, about 2 minutes, scraping down sides of blender jar halfway through processing. Taste for spiciness; if desired, add more spice by blending in reserved jalapeño seeds. Season with salt to taste. Transfer yogurt sauce to small bowl, cover, and refrigerate until ready to serve.

3A. FOR A CHARCOAL GRILL Open bottom vent completely. Light large chimney starter filled with charcoal briquettes (6 quarts). When top coals are partially covered with ash, pour evenly over half of grill. Set cooking grate in place, cover, and open lid vent completely. Heat grill until hot, about 5 minutes.

3B. FOR A GAS GRILL Turn all burners to high, cover, and heat grill until hot, about 15 minutes. Leave all burners on high.

4. Clean and oil cooking grate. Place carrots on grill (directly over coals if using charcoal) and cook, turning occasionally, until carrots are well charred on all sides and exteriors are just beginning to soften, 3 to 5 minutes for very small carrots or 5 to 7 minutes for larger ones. Transfer to serving platter.

5. Drizzle yogurt sauce over carrots, then sprinkle with remaining ¼ cup cilantro, remaining ¼ cup carrot greens, and remaining 1 tablespoon peanuts. Serve.

PER SERVING Cal 160; Total Fat 8g, Sat Fat 3.5g; Chol 5mg; Sodium 300mg; Total Carb 18g, Dietary Fiber 5g, Total Sugars 9g; Protein 6g

Grilled Brined Asparagus with Cilantro-Yogurt Sauce

Look for asparagus that is at least ½ inch thick at base.

Substitute 2 pounds thick asparagus, trimmed, for carrots and additional 1¼ cups chopped cilantro for carrot tops. Cook asparagus, turning occasionally, until spears are charred on all sides and just beginning to soften on exteriors, 2 to 4 minutes.

Grilled Brined Zucchini with Cilantro-Yogurt Sauce

Substitute 3 large zucchini, halved lengthwise, for carrots and additional 1¼ cups chopped cilantro for carrot tops. Increase salt in brine to 5 tablespoons. Place zucchini cut side down on grill and cook until well charred on bottom and flesh just begins to soften, 3 to 4 minutes. Flip zucchini and continue to cook until skin side is charred, about 2 minutes.

Charred Carrot Salad

SERVES 4 **VEGAN**

WHY THIS RECIPE WORKS Grilling carrots draws out their natural sugars and intensifies their flavor, and in this delicious salad the sweet, charred flavor of the carrots shines. To cook our carrots all the way through without overcooking them, we jump-started them in the microwave. Then we grilled them over a medium-hot fire for just a few minutes on each side. Halving the carrots lengthwise made them easier to maneuver on the grill; we then cut them into smaller pieces after grilling before we assembled the salad. To complement their smoky-sweet flavor, we made a vinaigrette with warm spices and a bit of heat from smoked paprika as well as sweetness from brown sugar and raisins, and freshness from parsley.

1½ pounds carrots, peeled and halved lengthwise
¼ cup vegetable oil, divided
¾ teaspoon table salt, divided
½ teaspoon pepper, divided
2 tablespoons white balsamic vinegar
1 teaspoon packed brown sugar
¾ teaspoon smoked paprika
   Pinch ground cinnamon
   Pinch ground allspice
⅓ cup raisins
2 tablespoons minced fresh parsley

1. Toss carrots with 1 tablespoon oil in bowl and sprinkle with ½ teaspoon salt and ¼ teaspoon pepper. Cover and microwave until softened, 6 to 8 minutes, stirring halfway through microwaving; drain well.

Charred Carrot Salad

2. Meanwhile, whisk vinegar, sugar, paprika, cinnamon, allspice, remaining ¼ teaspoon salt, and remaining ¼ teaspoon pepper together in large bowl. Whisking constantly, drizzle in remaining 3 tablespoons oil.

3A. FOR A CHARCOAL GRILL Open bottom vent completely. Light large chimney starter three-quarters filled with charcoal briquettes (4½ quarts). When top coals are partially covered with ash, pour evenly over grill. Set cooking grate in place, cover, and open lid vent completely. Heat grill until hot, about 5 minutes.

3B. FOR A GAS GRILL Turn all burners to high, cover, and heat grill until hot, about 15 minutes. Turn all burners to medium-high.

4. Clean and oil cooking grate. Place carrots on grill and cook until tender and browned on both sides, 2 to 4 minutes per side; transfer to cutting board.

5. Cut carrots into 2-inch pieces. Add carrots, raisins, and parsley to dressing and toss to coat; season with salt and pepper to taste. Serve.

PER SERVING Cal 250; **Total Fat** 14g, **Sat Fat** 1g; **Chol** 0mg; **Sodium** 540mg; **Total Carb** 28g, **Dietary Fiber** 4g, **Total Sugars** 20g; **Protein** 2g

Grilled Cauliflower

1. Whisk 2 cups water, salt, and sugar in medium bowl until salt and sugar dissolve. Holding wedges by core, gently dunk in salt-sugar mixture until evenly moistened (do not dry—residual water will help cauliflower steam). Transfer wedges, rounded side down, to large plate and cover with inverted large bowl. Microwave until cauliflower is translucent and tender and paring knife slips easily in and out of thickest stem of florets (not core), 14 to 16 minutes.

2. Carefully (bowl and cauliflower will be very hot) transfer cauliflower to paper towel–lined plate and pat dry with paper towels. Brush cut sides of wedges with 1 tablespoon oil.

3A. FOR A CHARCOAL GRILL Open bottom vent completely. Light large chimney starter three-quarters filled with charcoal briquettes (4½ quarts). When top coals are partially covered with ash, pour evenly over grill. Set cooking grate in place, cover, and open lid vent completely. Heat grill until hot, about 5 minutes.

3B. FOR A GAS GRILL Turn all burners to high, cover, and heat grill until hot, about 15 minutes. Turn all burners to medium-high.

4. Clean and oil cooking grate. Place cauliflower, cut side down, on grill and cook, covered, until well browned with spots of charring, 3 to 4 minutes. Using tongs or thin metal spatula, flip cauliflower and cook second cut side until well browned with spots of charring, 3 to 4 minutes. Flip again so cauliflower is sitting on rounded edge and cook until browned, 1 to 2 minutes.

5. Transfer cauliflower to serving platter. Drizzle with remaining 1 tablespoon oil, sprinkle with chives, and serve with lemon wedges.

PER SERVING Cal 80; **Total Fat** 5g; **Sat Fat** 1g; **Chol** 0mg; **Sodium** 95mg; **Total Carb** 8g, **Dietary Fiber** 3g, **Total Sugars** 3g; **Protein** 3g

Grilled Cauliflower
SERVES 4 TO 6   **VEGAN**

WHY THIS RECIPE WORKS Raw cauliflower has subtle flavor, but when grilled it transforms, gaining a crisp, browned exterior, a tender interior, and sweet, nutty flavor. To ensure that the cauliflower held up on the grill without falling through the grate and to provide sufficient surface area for browning, we cut the head into wedges. Cauliflower is so dense that the exteriors can brown and dry out before the interiors become tender. For an even cook, we first microwaved the cauliflower until it was cooked through and then briefly grilled it to pick up color and flavor. Dunking the cauliflower in a salt and sugar solution before microwaving seasoned it all over, even in the nooks and crannies. This dish stands well on its own, but to dress it up, serve it sprinkled with 1 tablespoon of Dukkah (page 117) or a savory relish (page 101).

¼ cup table salt, for brining
2 tablespoons sugar, for brining
1 head cauliflower (2 pounds), cut into 6 equal wedges
2 tablespoons extra-virgin olive oil, divided
1 tablespoon minced fresh chives
  Lemon wedges

Husk-Grilled Corn
SERVES 6

WHY THIS RECIPE WORKS Grilled corn on the cob is a classic. We started the corn with the husk on to prevent the kernels from drying out. But we found that if we left the husk on the whole time, the corn kernels didn't pick up the grill's signature smoky flavor. By shucking the corn, and rolling the ears in butter, and then returning the ears to the grill, we were able to perfectly caramelize the kernels and maximize the grill flavor. One last roll in the butter and our corn was ready. Substitute a flavored butter (recipes follow) for plain, if desired. Set up a cutting board and knife next to your grill to avoid traveling back and forth between kitchen and grill.

Husk-Grilled Corn

6 ears corn (unshucked)
6 tablespoons unsalted butter, softened
½ teaspoon table salt
½ teaspoon pepper

1. Cut and remove silk protruding from top of each ear of corn. Combine butter, salt, and pepper in bowl. Fold one 14 by 12-inch piece heavy-duty aluminum foil in half to create 7 by 12-inch rectangle, then crimp into boat shape long and wide enough to accommodate 1 ear of corn. Transfer butter mixture to prepared foil boat.

2A. FOR A CHARCOAL GRILL Open bottom vent completely. Light large chimney starter mounded with charcoal briquettes (7 quarts). When top coals are partially covered with ash, pour evenly over half of grill. Set cooking grate in place, cover, and open lid vent completely. Heat grill until hot, about 5 minutes.

2B. FOR A GAS GRILL Turn all burners to high, cover, and heat grill until hot, about 15 minutes. Leave all burners on high.

3. Clean and oil cooking grate. Place corn on grill (over coals, with stem ends facing cooler side of grill, for charcoal). Cover and cook, turning corn every 3 minutes, until husks have blackened all over, 12 to 15 minutes. (To check for doneness, carefully peel down small portion of husk. If corn is steaming and bright yellow,

it is ready.) Transfer corn to cutting board. Using chef's knife, cut base from corn. Using dish towel to hold corn, peel away and discard husk and silk with tongs.

4. Roll each ear of corn in butter mixture to coat lightly and return to grill (over coals for charcoal). Cook, turning as needed to char corn lightly on each side, about 5 minutes total. Remove corn from grill and roll each ear again in butter mixture. Transfer corn to platter. Serve, passing any remaining butter mixture.

PER SERVING Cal 190; **Total Fat** 14g; **Sat Fat** 7g; **Chol** 30mg; **Sodium** 190mg; **Total Carb** 18g, **Dietary Fiber** 2g, **Total Sugars** 5g; **Protein** 4g

TAKE IT UP A NOTCH

These flavorful seasoned butters complement corn on the cob as well as other simple grilled, roasted, or steamed vegetables.

Savory Butters

Whip 6 tablespoons softened unsalted butter with a fork until light and fluffy. Mix in any of the ingredient combinations listed below. The butter can be refrigerated for up to three days; bring to room temperature before using.

Rosemary-Pepper Butter

1 tablespoon minced fresh rosemary
1 small garlic clove, minced
1 teaspoon pepper
½ teaspoon table salt

Mustard-Paprika Butter

2 tablespoons spicy brown mustard
1 teaspoon smoked paprika
½ teaspoon table salt
½ teaspoon pepper

Cilantro-Lime Butter

¼ cup minced fresh cilantro,
2 teaspoons grated lime zest plus 1 tablespoon juice
1 small garlic clove, minced
½ teaspoon table salt
½ teaspoon butter

Brown Sugar–Cayenne Butter

2 tablespoons packed brown sugar
½ teaspoon table salt
½ teaspoon pepper
¼ teaspoon cayenne pepper

Mexican-Style Grilled Corn

SERVES 6

WHY THIS RECIPE WORKS In Mexico, street vendors add kick to grilled corn by slathering it with a creamy, spicy, cheesy sauce. The corn takes on an irresistibly sweet, smoky, charred flavor, which is heightened by the lime juice and chili powder in the sauce. For our own rendition of this south-of-the-border street fare, we ditched the husks, coated the ears with oil to prevent sticking, and grilled them directly on the grate over a hot fire so the corn could develop plenty of char. The traditional base for the sauce is crema, a thick, soured Mexican cream. But given its limited availability in supermarkets, we replaced the crema with a combination of mayonnaise (for richness) and sour cream (for tanginess). If you can find *queso fresco* or cotija, use either in place of the Pecorino Romano.

1½ ounces Pecorino Romano cheese, grated (¾ cup)
¼ cup mayonnaise
3 tablespoons sour cream
3 tablespoons minced fresh cilantro
4 teaspoons lime juice
1 garlic clove, minced
¾ teaspoon chili powder, divided
¼ teaspoon pepper
¼ teaspoon cayenne pepper
4 teaspoons vegetable oil
¼ teaspoon table salt
6 ears corn, husks and silk removed

1. Combine Pecorino, mayonnaise, sour cream, cilantro, lime juice, garlic, ¼ teaspoon chili powder, pepper, and cayenne in large bowl; set aside. In second large bowl, combine oil, salt, and remaining ½ teaspoon chili powder. Add corn to oil mixture and toss to coat.

2A. FOR A CHARCOAL GRILL Open bottom vent completely. Light large chimney starter filled with charcoal briquettes (6 quarts). When top coals are partially covered with ash, pour evenly over half of grill. Set cooking grate in place, cover, and open lid vent completely. Heat grill until hot, about 5 minutes.

2B. FOR A GAS GRILL Turn all burners to high, cover, and heat grill until hot, about 15 minutes. Leave all burners on high.

3. Clean and oil cooking grate. Place corn on grill (on hotter side if using charcoal) and cook (covered if using gas), turning as needed, until lightly charred on all sides, 7 to 12 minutes. Transfer corn to bowl with cheese mixture and toss to coat. Serve.

PER SERVING Cal 220; **Total Fat** 16g, **Sat Fat** 3g; **Chol** 10mg; **Sodium** 270mg; **Total Carb** 19g, **Dietary Fiber** 2g, **Total Sugars** 5g; **Protein** 6g

Mexican-Style Grilled Corn

Grilled Eggplant with Cherry Tomatoes and Cilantro Vinaigrette

SERVES 4 TO 6 `VEGAN`

WHY THIS RECIPE WORKS When grilled, eggplant skin turns beautifully brown and becomes crisp in spots. And the great advantage of grilling is that there is no need to salt the eggplant in advance because the moisture vaporizes or drips harmlessly through the cooking grate into the hot fire. We found that thinner slices can fall apart on the cooking grate; thicker pieces can better withstand the rigors of grilling. To impart flavor to the eggplant while we grilled it, we whisked together a mixture of olive oil and minced garlic and brushed it on liberally. Our vinaigrette included shallot, lime juice, and a little cayenne pepper, and we added quartered cherry tomatoes for their bright flavor. We spooned this over the grilled eggplant slices for a simple but superflavorful side dish.

½ cup plus 1 tablespoon extra-virgin olive oil, divided
1 shallot, minced
2 tablespoons minced fresh cilantro
2 tablespoons lime juice
¼ teaspoon table salt
   Pinch cayenne pepper

6 ounces cherry tomatoes, quartered

2 garlic cloves, minced

1½ pounds eggplant, sliced into ¾-inch-thick rounds

1. Whisk 6 tablespoons oil, shallot, cilantro, lime juice, salt, and cayenne together in medium bowl. Add tomatoes and toss to coat; set aside.

2. Whisk garlic and remaining 3 tablespoons oil together in small bowl and season with salt and pepper. Brush eggplant with oil mixture.

3A. FOR A CHARCOAL GRILL Open bottom vent completely. Light large chimney starter filled with charcoal briquettes (6 quarts). When top coals are partially covered with ash, pour evenly over grill. Set cooking grate in place, cover, and open lid vent completely. Heat grill until hot, about 5 minutes.

3B. FOR A GAS GRILL Turn all burners to high, cover, and heat grill until hot, about 15 minutes. Leave all burners on high.

4. Clean and oil cooking grate. Grill eggplant (covered if using gas) until browned and tender, 4 to 5 minutes per side. Transfer to serving platter. Spoon vinaigrette over eggplant. Serve immediately.

PER SERVING Cal 230; **Total Fat** 21g, **Sat Fat** 3g; **Chol** 0mg; **Sodium** 100mg; **Total Carb** 9g, **Dietary Fiber** 4g, **Total Sugars** 5g; **Protein** 2g

Grilled Eggplant and Bell Peppers with Mint-Cumin Dressing

Grilled Eggplant and Bell Peppers with Mint-Cumin Dressing

SERVES 4 TO 6

WHY THIS RECIPE WORKS For a side dish of perfectly charred-on-the-outside, tender-on-the-inside grilled vegetables, we paired eggplant with sweet bell peppers and topped them with a lively yogurt dressing. A medium-hot fire allowed us to cook the vegetables quickly without any chance of burning them; in less than 20 minutes they were perfectly tender and full of smoky flavor. We whisked up a quick mint-cumin dressing that complemented our grilled vegetables. Drizzled with dressing while still warm, the vegetables had enough flavor to be the star attraction of a meal. Serve hot, warm, or at room temperature.

1 pound eggplant, sliced into ¾-inch-thick rounds

2 red bell peppers, stemmed, seeded, and cut into 2-inch planks

5 tablespoons extra-virgin olive oil, divided

1¼ teaspoons table salt, divided

2 tablespoons plain yogurt

1 tablespoon chopped fresh mint

1 tablespoon lemon juice

1 small garlic clove, minced

½ teaspoon ground coriander

½ teaspoon ground cumin

1. Brush eggplant and bell peppers with ¼ cup oil, sprinkle with 1 teaspoon salt, and season with pepper. Whisk yogurt, mint, lemon juice, garlic, coriander, cumin, remaining 1 tablespoon oil, and remaining ¼ teaspoon salt together in bowl.

2A. FOR A CHARCOAL GRILL Open bottom vent completely. Light large chimney starter half filled with charcoal briquettes (3 quarts). When top coals are partially covered with ash, pour evenly over grill. Set cooking grate in place, cover, and open lid vent completely. Heat grill until hot, about 5 minutes.

2B. FOR A GAS GRILL Turn all burners to high, cover, and heat grill until hot, about 15 minutes. Turn all burners to medium.

3. Clean and oil cooking grate. Place eggplant and bell peppers cut sides down on grill. Cook (covered if using gas), turning as needed, until tender and caramelized, 16 to 18 minutes; transfer to platter as they finish cooking. Whisk dressing to recombine, drizzle over vegetables, and serve.

PER SERVING Cal 140; **Total Fat** 12g, **Sat Fat** 2g; **Chol** 0mg; **Sodium** 490mg; **Total Carb** 8g, **Dietary Fiber** 3g, **Total Sugars** 4g; **Protein** 1g

Grilled Fennel
SERVES 4 VEGAN

WHY THIS RECIPE WORKS There's something special about grilled fennel. The caramelization of its sugars brings out the vegetable's anise flavor and the high heat softens the tough, fibrous texture to just shy of creamy. But the bulb's awkward, uneven shape and dense, succulent texture made it difficult for us to find the right way to cut the fennel to prevent it from falling through the cooking grate. We found that plank-like cross sections with the core left intact made the most sense, and roughly ¼-inch-thick slices cooked through in just about the time the slices browned. You can also serve the fennel dressed with a vinaigrette (page 368), if desired.

2 fennel bulbs, stalks discarded, base trimmed, tough or blemished outer layers removed, bulb sliced vertically through core into ¼-inch-thick slices
3 tablespoons extra-virgin olive oil

1A. FOR A CHARCOAL GRILL: Open bottom vent completely. Light large chimney starter filled with charcoal briquettes (6 quarts). When top coals are partially covered with ash, pour evenly over half of grill. Set cooking grate in place, cover, and open lid vent completely. Heat grill until hot, about 5 minutes.

1B. FOR A GAS GRILL: Turn all burners to high, cover, and heat grill until hot, about 15 minutes. Leave all burners on high.

2. Clean and oil cooking grate. Toss fennel slices and oil together in large bowl; season with salt and pepper to taste. Grill fennel slices (on hotter side if using charcoal), turning once, until tender and streaked with dark grill marks, 7 to 9 minutes. Serve hot, warm, or at room temperature.

PER SERVING Cal 130; **Total Fat** 11g, **Sat Fat** 1.5g; **Chol** 0mg; **Sodium** 60mg; **Total Carb** 9g, **Dietary Fiber** 4g, **Total Sugars** 5g; **Protein** 1g

Grilled Onions with Balsamic Vinaigrette
SERVES 4 VEGAN

WHY THIS RECIPE WORKS Grilled onions can stand on their own as a side dish. Grilling halved onions cut side down directly over the flame until very dark ensured that they developed sufficient char-grilled flavor; we then transferred them to a covered disposable pan to finish cut side up so they would cook through evenly, turning buttery soft. Leaving the skins on kept the bottoms of the onions from burning but still allowed for plenty of caramelization. A simple balsamic vinaigrette complemented their sweetness and

Grilled Onions with Balsamic Vinaigrette

lent a burst of acidity. In step 3, be sure to err on the side of achieving darker charring, as the steaming step will soften the char's appearance and flavor.

½ cup extra-virgin olive oil, divided
3 tablespoons balsamic vinegar
1½ teaspoons table salt, divided
¼ teaspoon pepper
4 onions (8 ounces each)
1 (13 by 9-inch) disposable aluminum pan
1 tablespoon minced fresh chives

1. Whisk 6 tablespoons oil, vinegar, ½ teaspoon salt, and pepper together in bowl; set aside. Trim stem end of onions and halve onions from root end to stem end, leaving skin intact. (Root end can be trimmed, but don't remove it or the onions will fall apart.) Brush cut sides of onions with remaining 2 tablespoons oil and sprinkle each half with ⅛ of remaining teaspoon salt.

2A. FOR A CHARCOAL GRILL Open bottom vent completely. Light large chimney starter three-quarters filled with charcoal briquettes (4½ quarts). When top coals are partially covered with ash, pour evenly over grill. Set cooking grate in place, cover, and open lid vent completely. Heat grill until hot, about 5 minutes.

2B. FOR A GAS GRILL Turn all burners to high, cover, and heat grill until hot, about 15 minutes. Turn all burners to medium.

3. Clean and oil cooking grate. Place onions cut side down on grill and cook (covered if using gas) until well charred, 10 to 15 minutes, moving onions as needed to ensure even cooking. Flip onions and cook cut side up until lightly charred on skin side, about 5 minutes.

4. Transfer onions cut side up to disposable pan and cover tightly with aluminum foil. Return disposable pan to grill and cook over medium heat (covered if using gas) until onions are tender and easily pierced with paring knife, 10 to 15 minutes. Set aside to cool slightly, about 10 minutes.

5. When onions are cool enough to handle, remove and discard charred outer skin; arrange onions cut side up on serving platter. Whisk vinaigrette to recombine and drizzle evenly over onions. Sprinkle with chives, season with salt and pepper to taste, and serve.

PER SERVING Cal 360; **Total Fat** 28g, **Sat Fat** 4g; **Chol** 0mg; **Sodium** 880mg; **Total Carb** 25g, **Dietary Fiber** 4g, **Total Sugars** 13g; **Protein** 3g

Grill-Roasted Peppers with Sherry Vinaigrette
SERVES 4 VEGAN

WHY THIS RECIPE WORKS Grill roasting is a great, simple way to add deep, smoky flavor to sweet red bell peppers, making for an unexpectedly luscious side dish. To infuse the peppers with even more flavor and ensure that they were perfectly tender, we started by steaming them in a disposable pan with a mixture of olive oil, garlic, salt, and pepper. We then transferred the softened peppers to the grate to char and blacken. After the peppers were done grilling, we used the remaining oil mixture from the pan—now boosted with pepper juices and a hit of sherry vinegar—as a tangy vinaigrette for the tender peeled peppers. Take care not to overroast the peppers—when the skin puffs up and turns black, it has reached the point at which the flavor is maximized and the flesh is soft but not mushy.

¼ cup extra-virgin olive oil
3 garlic cloves, peeled and smashed
½ teaspoon table salt
¼ teaspoon pepper
1 (13 by 9-inch) disposable aluminum pan
6 red bell peppers
1 tablespoon sherry vinegar

Grill-Roasted Peppers with Sherry Vinaigrette

1. Combine oil, garlic, salt, and pepper in disposable pan. Using paring knife, cut around stems of peppers and remove cores and seeds. Place peppers in pan and turn to coat with oil. Cover pan tightly with aluminum foil.

2A. FOR A CHARCOAL GRILL Open bottom vent completely. Light large chimney starter filled with charcoal briquettes (6 quarts). When top coals are partially covered with ash, pour evenly over half of grill. Set cooking grate in place, cover, and open lid vent completely. Heat grill until hot, about 5 minutes.

2B. FOR A GAS GRILL Turn all burners to high, cover, and heat grill until hot, about 15 minutes. Turn all burners to medium-high.

3. Clean and oil cooking grate. Place pan on grill (hotter side if using charcoal) and cook, covered, until peppers are just tender and skins begin to blister, 10 to 15 minutes, rotating and shaking pan halfway through cooking.

4. Remove pan from heat and carefully remove foil (reserve foil to use later). Using tongs, remove peppers from pan, allowing juices to drip back into pan, and place on grill (hotter side if using charcoal). Grill peppers, covered, turning every few minutes until skins are blackened, 10 to 15 minutes.

5. Transfer juices and garlic in pan to medium bowl and whisk in vinegar. Remove peppers from grill, return to now-empty pan, and cover tightly with foil. Let peppers steam for 5 minutes. Using spoon, scrape blackened skin off each pepper. Quarter peppers lengthwise, add to vinaigrette in bowl, and toss to combine. Season with salt and pepper to taste, and serve.

PER SERVING Cal 190; **Total Fat** 15g, **Sat Fat** 2g; **Chol** 0mg; **Sodium** 300mg; **Total Carb** 12g, **Dietary Fiber** 4g, **Total Sugars** 7g; **Protein** 2g

VARIATION
Grill-Roasted Peppers with Rosemary

Add 1 rosemary sprig to oil mixture in step 1 (discard after grilling). Substitute red wine vinegar for sherry vinegar.

SCRAPING THE SKIN OFF A GRILLED PEPPER

Using spoon, scrape blackened skin off pepper.

Grilled Plantains

Grilled Plantains
SERVES 4 `VEGAN`

WHY THIS RECIPE WORKS Although plantains closely resemble bananas, these Latin American staples have a starchier texture and subtler flavor than bananas, making them a great option for a delicious grilled side dish. Green plantains are most often fried, but for grilling we prefer ripe, black-skinned plantains, which are softer, sweeter, and easier to peel than green ones. To prevent the peeled plantains from sticking to the cooking grate, we coated them with oil before grilling. By the time the plantains were streaked with grill marks, they were cooked through, tender, and ready to serve. Try these plantains with grilled chicken, fish, beef, or pork. For this recipe, the plantains are quartered, peeled, and then cut in half lengthwise. Make sure to use plantains that are very ripe and black.

2 large ripe plantains
2 tablespoons vegetable oil

1. Trim ends from plantains, then cut crosswise into 4 pieces. With paring knife, make slit in peel of each piece, from 1 end to other end, and then peel away skin with your fingers. Cut each piece of plantain in half lengthwise. Place plantains in large bowl, add oil, season with salt, and gently toss to coat.

2A. FOR A CHARCOAL GRILL Open bottom vent completely. Light large chimney starter three-quarters filled with charcoal briquettes (4½ quarts). When top coals are partially covered with ash, pour evenly over grill. Set cooking grate in place, cover, and open lid vent completely. Heat grill until hot, about 5 minutes.

2B. FOR A GAS GRILL Turn all burners to high, cover, and heat grill until hot, about 15 minutes. Turn all burners to medium-high.

3. Clean and oil cooking grate. Place plantains on grill and cook, turning once, until grill marks appear, 7 to 8 minutes. Serve.

PER SERVING Cal 170; **Total Fat** 7g, **Sat Fat** 1g; **Chol** 0mg; **Sodium** 0mg; **Total Carb** 29g, **Dietary Fiber** 2g, **Total Sugars** 13g; **Protein** 1g

Grilled Marinated Portobello Mushrooms

SERVES 4 TO 6 `VEGAN`

WHY THIS RECIPE WORKS When portobello mushrooms meet the grill, their texture softens and their earthy, rich flavor deepens. By wrapping each mushroom in a packet of foil, we were able to ensure that the interior fully cooked through in about 10 minutes without turning the mushrooms limp. Then we unwrapped each mushroom and let it grill uncovered for 30 to 60 seconds to sear in the grilled flavor. Cooking them gill side up trapped the juices and flavor in the meaty mushrooms. The end result was plump, juicy, and slightly charred mushrooms, with all the smoky flavor of the grill. We prefer large 5- to 6-inch portobellos for grilling because they are not prepackaged and are typically fresher. However, you can also use six 4- to 5-inch portobellos, which are usually sold three to a package; decrease their grilling time wrapped in foil to about 8 minutes.

- ½ cup extra-virgin olive oil
- 3 tablespoons lemon juice
- 6 garlic cloves, minced
- ¼ teaspoon table salt
- 4 portobello mushrooms (5 to 6 inches in diameter), stemmed

1. Combine oil, lemon juice, garlic, and salt in 1-gallon zipper-lock bag. Add mushrooms and toss to coat; press out as much air as possible and seal bag. Let sit at room temperature for 1 hour.

2. Meanwhile, cut four 12-inch square pieces of aluminum foil (or six 9-inch square pieces if using smaller mushrooms).

3A. FOR A CHARCOAL GRILL Open bottom vent completely. Light large chimney starter three-quarters filled with charcoal briquettes (4½ quarts). When top coals are partially covered with ash, pour evenly over grill. Set cooking grate in place, cover, and open lid vent completely. Heat grill until hot, about 5 minutes.

3B. FOR A GAS GRILL Turn all burners to high, cover, and heat grill until hot, about 15 minutes. Turn all burners to medium-high.

4. Clean and oil cooking grate. Remove mushrooms from marinade and place each on foil square, gill side up. Fold foil around each mushroom and seal edges. Place foil packets on grill, sealed side up, and cook (covered if using gas) until juicy and tender, 9 to 12 minutes.

5. Using tongs, unwrap mushrooms, place gill side up on grill, and cook until grill-marked, 30 to 60 seconds. Transfer to platter and serve.

PER SERVING Cal 190; **Total Fat** 19g, **Sat Fat** 2.5g; **Chol** 0mg; **Sodium** 105mg; **Total Carb** 4g, **Dietary Fiber** 1g, **Total Sugars** 2g; **Protein** 1g

Grilled Marinated Portobello Mushrooms

VARIATION
Grilled Marinated Portobello Mushrooms with Tarragon

Substitute 2 teaspoons rice vinegar for lemon juice, reduce garlic to 1 clove, and add 1 tablespoon chopped fresh tarragon to marinade.

Grilled Potatoes

SERVES 4 TO 6 `VEGAN`

WHY THIS RECIPE WORKS Grilled potatoes are perfect on their own but they are also the perfect starting point for a variety of potato salad options. We set out to find the best cooking method for how to grill new potatoes. We first skewered unpeeled potato slices and then blanched them before grilling them for just 5 minutes over high heat. The result was perfectly tender and smoky potatoes. When buying potatoes for this recipe, the color is less important than the size; make sure they are no longer than 3 inches. You will need about fifteen 10-inch metal or bamboo skewers for this recipe. If using wooden skewers, trim to lengths that can be submerged in the Dutch oven you will be using.

Because the potatoes are precooked, they need only brown on the grill; you can grill them alongside your main dish over a charcoal- or gas-grill fire of any intensity. If making a potato salad, be sure to prepare the other ingredients while the water heats so that the salad can be made immediately with potatoes that are still hot from the grill.

½ teaspoon table salt, plus salt for cooking potatoes
1½ pounds new potatoes, unpeeled, cut into eighths
2 tablespoons extra-virgin olive oil
¼ teaspoon pepper

1. In Dutch oven or stockpot, bring 4 quarts water to boil over high heat; add 1 teaspoon salt.

2. Pass skewer through center of each potato with skin facing out. Drop skewers into boiling water and boil until paring knife slips in and out of potato easily, about 10 minutes.

3. While potatoes boil, line rimmed baking sheet with paper towels. Using tongs, transfer skewers to prepared sheet; pat potatoes dry with additional paper towels. Discard paper towels (potatoes can be cooled completely, covered with plastic wrap, and kept at room temperature for up to 2 hours); brush all sides of potatoes with oil and sprinkle with ½ teaspoon salt and pepper.

4A. FOR A CHARCOAL GRILL Open bottom vent completely. Light large chimney starter filled with charcoal briquettes (6 quarts). When top coals are partially covered with ash, pour evenly over half of grill. Set cooking grate in place, cover, and open lid vent completely. Heat grill until hot, about 5 minutes.

4B. FOR A GAS GRILL Turn all burners to high, cover, and heat grill until hot, about 15 minutes. Leave all burners on high.

5. Clean and oil cooking grate. Grill skewers (on hotter side of grill if using charcoal), turning twice with tongs, until all sides are browned, 2 to 3 minutes per side. Slide hot potatoes off skewers into bowl and serve, or use immediately in one of the following recipes.

PER SERVING Cal 130; **Total Fat** 5g, **Sat Fat** 0.5g; **Chol** 0mg; **Sodium** 200mg; **Total Carb** 21g, **Dietary Fiber** 1g, **Total Sugars** 1g; **Protein** 2g

VARIATIONS

Grilled Potato and Arugula Salad with Dijon Mustard Vinaigrette
SERVES 4 TO 6
If you prefer, watercress can be substituted for the arugula.

1 recipe Grilled Potatoes (page 381)
1½ teaspoons rice vinegar, divided
½ teaspoon pepper
¼ teaspoon table salt
3 ounces (3 cups) baby arugula
1 yellow bell pepper, stemmed, seeded, and cut into ½-inch squares
3 tablespoons chives, chopped fine
2 tablespoons extra-virgin olive oil
1 small shallot, minced
1 teaspoon Dijon mustard

1. Toss hot grilled potatoes with 1 teaspoon vinegar, pepper, and salt. Add arugula, bell pepper, and chives; toss to combine.

2. Combine oil, shallot, mustard, remaining ½ teaspoon vinegar, and salt to taste in bowl. Pour over potatoes, toss to combine, and serve.

German-Style Grilled Potato Salad
SERVES 4 TO 6

1 recipe Grilled Potatoes (page 381)
1 tablespoon yellow mustard seeds
3 tablespoons red wine vinegar
¼ teaspoon table salt
⅛ teaspoon pepper
4 slices bacon, cut into ¼-inch strips
2 small shallots, minced
⅓ cup chicken broth
1 rib celery, chopped fine
2 tablespoons minced fresh parsley

1. Toast mustard seeds in 8-inch covered skillet over medium heat until popping and lightly browned, about 30 seconds. Add hot mustard seeds to vinegar.

2. Toss hot grilled potatoes with 2 tablespoons vinegar with mustard seeds, salt, and pepper.

3. Fry bacon in medium skillet over medium-high heat until brown and crispy, about 6 minutes; with slotted spoon, transfer bacon to bowl with potatoes. Reduce heat to medium, add shallots to fat in skillet and cook, stirring occasionally, until softened, about 3 minutes. Add broth and bring to boil; stir in remaining 1 tablespoon vinegar. Pour mixture over potatoes, add celery, parsley, and salt to taste; toss to combine. Serve. (Salad can be covered with plastic wrap and kept at room temperature up to 30 minutes; toss before serving.)

Spicy Grilled Potato Salad with Corn and Poblano Chiles

SERVES 4 TO 6

We prefer to use corn kernels cut from grilled corn on the cob, but boiled corn works, too. Poblano chiles are relatively mild; to alter spiciness according to your preference, decrease or increase the quantity of jalapeños in this recipe.

- 1 recipe Grilled Potatoes (page 381)
- 1 teaspoon white wine vinegar
- ¼ teaspoon table salt
- ¼ teaspoon pepper
- 2 ears grilled or boiled corn, kernels cut from cobs
- 2 poblano chiles, roasted, peeled, stemmed, seeded, and cut into ½-inch pieces
- 2 jalapeño chiles, stemmed, seeded, and minced
- 3 tablespoons lime juice (2 limes)
- ½ teaspoon sugar
- ¼ cup extra-virgin olive oil
- 3 scallions, white parts only, sliced thin
- 3 tablespoons minced fresh cilantro

1. Toss hot grilled potatoes with vinegar, salt, and pepper. Add corn, poblanos, and jalapeños; toss to combine.

2. Whisk lime juice and sugar in small bowl until sugar dissolves; whisk in oil and season with salt to taste. Pour mixture over potatoes and add scallions and cilantro, toss to combine, and serve. (Salad can be covered and kept at room temperature for up to 30 minutes; toss before serving.)

Charred Fingerling Potato Salad

SERVES 4 **VEGAN**

WHY THIS RECIPE WORKS Grilled fingerling potatoes, with their crisp skins and creamy interiors, made the perfect basis for a warm, salty-sweet salad, but cooking these small potatoes through presented a challenge. To ensure that the potatoes achieved a good grilled flavor while also cooking all the way through, we jump-started the cooking process in the microwave. We then threaded the softened potatoes onto skewers and grilled them for a few minutes. For a new take on the flavors of potato salad, we added a sweet and smoky vinaigrette with warm spices and a few extra ingredients that paired well with the charred potatoes: We got sweetness from roasted red peppers, savory crunch from toasted pecans, and a fresh bite from sliced scallions. Fingerling potatoes with a 1-inch diameter work best in this recipe; if your potatoes are thinner, you may not be able to skewer them with the cut sides facing down. You can substitute small halved red potatoes, if necessary. You will need four 12-inch metal skewers for this recipe.

Charred Fingerling Potato Salad

- 1½ pounds fingerling potatoes, unpeeled, halved lengthwise
- ¼ cup vegetable oil, divided
- ¾ teaspoon table salt, divided
- ½ teaspoon pepper, divided
- 2 tablespoons white balsamic vinegar
- 1 teaspoon packed brown sugar
- ¾ teaspoon smoked paprika
  Pinch ground cinnamon
  Pinch ground allspice
- ¾ cup jarred roasted red peppers, drained and sliced thin
- ½ cup pecans, toasted and chopped
- 2 scallions, sliced thin

1. Toss potatoes with 1 tablespoon oil in bowl and season with ½ teaspoon salt and ¼ teaspoon pepper. Cover and microwave until softened, 6 to 8 minutes, stirring halfway through microwaving. Drain potatoes well, then thread cut side down onto four 12-inch metal skewers.

2. Meanwhile, whisk vinegar, sugar, paprika, cinnamon, allspice, remaining ¼ teaspoon salt, and remaining ¼ teaspoon pepper together in large bowl. Whisking constantly, drizzle in remaining 3 tablespoons oil.

3A. FOR A CHARCOAL GRILL Open bottom vent completely. Light large chimney starter three-quarters filled with charcoal briquettes (4½ quarts). When top coals are partially covered with ash, pour evenly over grill. Set cooking grate in place, cover, and open lid vent completely. Heat grill until hot, about 5 minutes.

3B. FOR A GAS GRILL Turn all burners to high, cover, and heat grill until hot, about 15 minutes. Turn all burners to medium-high.

4. Clean and oil cooking grate. Place potatoes on grill and cook until tender and browned on both sides, 2 to 4 minutes per side; transfer to plate.

5. Carefully slide potatoes off skewers into bowl of dressing; add red peppers, pecans, and scallions; and toss to coat. Season with salt and pepper to taste, and serve.

PER SERVING Cal 360; **Total Fat** 24g, **Sat Fat** 2g; **Chol** 0mg; **Sodium** 570mg; **Total Carb** 35g, **Dietary Fiber** 6g, **Total Sugars** 8g; **Protein** 4g

Grilled Potato Packs
SERVES 4 `VEGAN`

WHY THIS RECIPE WORKS The appeal of this campfire classic is partly convenience: All you need is fire, food, and tin foil, no pots or pans required. Because the food is cooked in a contained environment over the fire, the technique combines freshness and clear flavors with the deep, caramelized taste of grilling. For a foolproof recipe that would avoid both burnt and undercooked potatoes, we found that Yukon Golds were preferable to starchy, mealy russets and small, waxy-skinned red potatoes. To ensure even grilling, we cut them into equally sized wedges and microwaved them for a few minutes before grilling them to jump-start the cooking process. Tossing the potatoes with a little oil prevented them from sticking to the foil, and a quick flip of the whole pack halfway through grilling ensured perfectly cooked, spotty brown potatoes. The sealed cooking environment of the foil pack created the perfect opportunity to add all kinds of flavors in our variations, from simple herbs to more creative ingredients like chorizo sausage or wine vinegar. To keep the packs from tearing, use heavy-duty aluminum foil or two layers of regular foil.

- 2 **pounds Yukon Gold potatoes, unpeeled**
- 1 **tablespoon extra-virgin olive oil**
- 2 **garlic cloves, chopped**
- 1 **teaspoon minced fresh thyme**
- 1 **teaspoon table salt**
- ½ **teaspoon pepper**

1. Cut each potato in half crosswise, then cut each half into 8 wedges. Place potatoes in large bowl, cover, and microwave until edges of potatoes are translucent, 4 to 7 minutes, shaking bowl to redistribute potatoes halfway through microwaving. Drain well. Gently toss potatoes with oil, garlic, thyme, salt, and pepper.

2. Cut four 14 by 10-inch sheets of heavy-duty aluminum foil. Working with one at a time, spread one-quarter of potato mixture over half of foil, fold foil over potatoes, and crimp edges tightly to seal.

3A. FOR A CHARCOAL GRILL Open bottom vent completely. Light large chimney starter filled with charcoal briquettes (6 quarts). When top coals are partially covered with ash, pour evenly over grill. Set cooking grate in place, cover, and open lid vent completely. Heat grill until hot, about 5 minutes.

3B. FOR A GAS GRILL Turn all burners to high, cover, and heat grill until hot, about 15 minutes. Turn all burners to medium-high.

4. Place hobo packs on grill and cook, covered, until potatoes are completely tender, about 10 minutes, flipping packs halfway through cooking. Cut open foil and serve.

PER SERVING Cal 220; **Total Fat** 3.5g, **Sat Fat** 0g; **Chol** 0mg; **Sodium** 590mg; **Total Carb** 41g, **Dietary Fiber** 0g, **Total Sugars** 0g; **Protein** 5g

VARIATIONS
Grilled Spanish-Style Potato Packs
Add 6 ounces thinly sliced cured chorizo sausage, 1 seeded and chopped red bell pepper, and 1 teaspoon paprika to cooked potatoes as they are tossed in step 1.

Grilled Vinegar and Onion Potato Packs
Microwave 1 halved and thinly sliced small onion with potatoes in step 1. Add 2 tablespoons white or red wine vinegar to cooked potatoes as they are tossed in step 1.

MAKING FOIL POTATO PACKS

1. Arrange microwaved potatoes on foil, fold over, and crimp.

2. Flip packs halfway through grilling for evenly charred potatoes.

Grill-Roasted Sweet Potatoes

SERVES 4

WHY THIS RECIPE WORKS Sweet potatoes cooked whole on the grill are simple and phenomenally delicious. The skin crisps up and the flesh steams to fluffy perfection, ready to be eaten with butter and salt. We found it best to lightly oil the potatoes' skin for maximum crispness. For the best results, stick with medium-size sweet potatoes and choose potatoes of similar size to ensure they cook at the same rate. We like to grill these potatoes alongside something else, such as chicken or ribs, as they will absorb a fair amount of smoke flavor. Substitute a flavored butter (page 375), if desired.

    4 sweet potatoes, unpeeled
    1 teaspoon vegetable oil
       Unsalted butter

1A. FOR A CHARCOAL GRILL Open bottom vent completely. Light large chimney starter filled with charcoal briquettes (6 quarts). When top coals are partially covered with ash, pour evenly over half of grill. Set cooking grate in place, cover, and open lid vent completely. Heat grill until hot, about 5 minutes.

1B. FOR A GAS GRILL Turn all burners to high, cover, and heat grill until hot, about 15 minutes. Leave primary burner on high and turn other burner(s) to medium.

2. Clean and oil cooking grate. Rub sweet potatoes with vegetable oil. Grill sweet potatoes, covered, over cooler side of grill, turning every 10 to 12 minutes, until tender, 45 minutes to 1 hour. (To check for doneness, insert tip of paring knife into potato. It should meet no resistance, and potato skin should be dark brown and crisp.) Remove sweet potatoes from grill.

3. Cut slit along top of each sweet potato and squeeze to push up flesh. Season with salt to taste, and serve with butter.

PER SERVING Cal 110; **Total Fat** 1g, **Sat Fat** 0g; **Chol** 0mg; **Sodium** 70mg; **Total Carb** 23g, **Dietary Fiber** 4g, **Total Sugars** 7g; **Protein** 2g

Grilled Sweet Potato Salad

SERVES 4 TO 6

WHY THIS RECIPE WORKS For a sweet and spicy spin on classic potato salad, we paired the natural sweetness of sweet potatoes, enhanced by the grill, with a boldly spiced dressing. We first tossed the potatoes with our vinaigrette in a disposable aluminum pan; the vinaigrette generated steam and helped cook the potatoes through while also seasoning them. Once the potatoes

Grilled Sweet Potato Salad

were steamed, we transferred them from the pan to the hot cooking grate to give them some flavorful char. Threading toothpicks through the onion rounds kept them intact and prevented them from falling through the grate during cooking. We sprinkled feta, scallions, and cilantro over the grilled salad to finish it off.

    1   small red onion, sliced into ½-inch-thick rounds
    3   tablespoons lime juice (2 limes), plus lime
         wedges for serving
    2   tablespoons honey
    1   teaspoon minced canned chipotle chile in
         adobo sauce
    ½   teaspoon ground cumin
    1   teaspoon table salt, divided
    ¾   teaspoon pepper, divided
    ⅓   cup vegetable oil
    2½   pounds sweet potatoes, peeled and cut into
         ½-inch-thick rounds
    1   (13 by 9-inch) disposable aluminum pan
    2   ounces feta cheese, crumbled (½ cup)
    3   scallions, sliced thin on bias
    ¼   cup chopped fresh cilantro

1. Thread 1 toothpick horizontally through each onion round. Whisk lime juice, honey, chipotle, cumin, ½ teaspoon salt, and ¼ teaspoon pepper together in large bowl. While whisking constantly, slowly drizzle in oil until combined; set aside.

2. Toss potatoes, onion rounds, ¼ cup vinaigrette, remaining ½ teaspoon salt, and remaining ½ teaspoon pepper together in separate bowl. Place onion rounds in bottom of disposable pan, layer potatoes over top, then pour in any remaining liquid from bowl. Cover disposable pan tightly with aluminum foil.

3A. FOR A CHARCOAL GRILL Open bottom vent completely. Light large chimney starter filled with charcoal briquettes (6 quarts). When top coals are partially covered with ash, pour evenly over grill. Set cooking grate in place, cover, and open lid vent completely. Heat grill until hot, about 5 minutes.

3B. FOR A GAS GRILL Turn all burners to high, cover, and heat grill until hot, about 15 minutes. Turn all burners to medium. Adjust burners as needed to maintain grill temperature around 400 degrees.

4. Clean and oil cooking grate. Place disposable pan on grill. Cover grill and cook until vegetables are tender, 20 to 25 minutes, shaking disposable pan halfway through cooking to redistribute potatoes. Remove disposable pan from grill.

5. Place vegetables on cooking grate. Cook (covered if using gas) until lightly charred and tender, 2 to 4 minutes per side. Transfer vegetables to platter. Remove toothpicks from onion rounds and separate rings. Pour remaining vinaigrette over vegetables and toss to coat. Sprinkle feta, scallions, and cilantro over top. Serve with lime wedges.

PER SERVING Cal 290; **Total Fat** 15g, **Sat Fat** 2.5g; **Chol** 10mg; **Sodium** 560mg; **Total Carb** 37g, **Dietary Fiber** 6g, **Total Sugars** 15g; **Protein** 4g

Grilled Radicchio with Garlic- and Rosemary-Infused Oil

SERVES 4 TO 6   `VEGAN`

WHY THIS RECIPE WORKS When grilled, the beautiful red-purple leaves of radicchio become lightly crisp and smoky-tasting. To keep the fragile radicchio from falling apart, we cut it through the core end into thick wedges. And for leaves that were smoky not singed, we coated the leaves liberally with olive oil and infused that oil with extra flavor by microwaving it with garlic and rosemary before brushing it on. For optimal browning, we flipped each wedge of radicchio so that the two cut sides of the wedges could rest directly against the grill grate. This simple side is great with grilled steaks.

6 tablespoons extra-virgin olive oil
1 garlic clove, minced

Grilled Radicchio with Garlic- and Rosemary-Infused Oil

1 teaspoon minced fresh rosemary or ¼ teaspoon dried
3 heads radicchio (10 ounces each), quartered
1 teaspoon table salt
½ teaspoon pepper

1. Microwave oil, garlic, and rosemary in bowl until bubbling, about 1 minute; let mixture steep for 1 minute. Brush radicchio with ¼ cup oil mixture and sprinkle with salt and pepper.

2A. FOR A CHARCOAL GRILL Open bottom vent completely. Light large chimney starter half filled with charcoal briquettes (3 quarts). When top coals are partially covered with ash, pour evenly over grill. Set cooking grate in place, cover, and open lid vent completely. Heat grill until hot, about 5 minutes.

2B. FOR A GAS GRILL Turn all burners to high, cover, and heat grill until hot, about 15 minutes. Turn all burners to medium.

3. Clean and oil cooking grate. Place radicchio on grill. Cook (covered if using gas), flipping as needed, until radicchio is softened and lightly charred, 3 to 5 minutes. Transfer to serving platter and drizzle with remaining oil mixture. Serve.

PER SERVING Cal 160; **Total Fat** 14g, **Sat Fat** 2g; **Chol** 0mg; **Sodium** 420mg; **Total Carb** 6g, **Dietary Fiber** 1g, **Total Sugars** 1g; **Protein** 2g

Grilled Caesar Salad

SERVES 6

WHY THIS RECIPE WORKS The smoky char of the grill brings a whole new dimension to the crunchy, tangy, and savory flavors of Caesar salad. To develop good char and maintain crisp lettuce without ending up with scorched, wilted, even slimy leaves, we used sturdy, compact romaine hearts, which withstood the heat of the grill better than whole heads. Halving them lengthwise and grilling on just one side gave them plenty of surface area for charring without turning limp. A hot fire meant that the heat didn't have time to penetrate and wilt the crunchy inner leaves before the exterior developed grill marks. Our boldly seasoned Caesar dressing replaced the raw egg with mayonnaise, and brushing the dressing on the cut side of the uncooked lettuce allowed it to pick up a mildly smoky flavor on the grill along with the lettuce. For the croutons, we brushed baguette slices with olive oil, toasted them over the coals, and then rubbed them with a garlic clove. We combined the lettuce and croutons, drizzled on extra dressing, and dusted everything with Parmesan.

Grilled Caesar Salad

DRESSING

- 1 tablespoon lemon juice
- 1 garlic clove, minced
- ½ cup mayonnaise
- ¼ cup grated Parmesan cheese
- 1 tablespoon white wine vinegar
- 1 tablespoon Worcestershire sauce
- 1 tablespoon Dijon mustard
- 2 anchovy fillets, rinsed
- ½ teaspoon table salt
- ½ teaspoon pepper
- ¼ cup extra-virgin olive oil

SALAD

- 1 (12-inch) baguette, sliced ½ inch thick on bias
- 3 tablespoons extra-virgin olive oil
- 1 garlic clove, peeled
- 3 romaine lettuce hearts (18 ounces), halved lengthwise through cores
- ¼ cup grated Parmesan cheese

1. FOR THE DRESSING Combine lemon juice and garlic in bowl and let stand for 10 minutes. Process lemon-garlic mixture, mayonnaise, Parmesan, vinegar, Worcestershire, mustard, anchovies, salt, and pepper in blender until smooth, about 30 seconds. With blender running, slowly add oil until incorporated. Measure out and reserve 6 tablespoons dressing for brushing romaine.

2A. FOR A CHARCOAL GRILL Open bottom vent completely. Light large chimney starter filled with charcoal briquettes (6 quarts). When top coals are partially covered with ash, pour evenly over half of grill. Set cooking grate in place, cover, and open lid vent completely. Heat grill until hot, about 5 minutes.

2B. FOR A GAS GRILL Turn all burners to high, cover, and heat grill until hot, about 15 minutes. Leave all burners on high.

3. FOR THE SALAD Clean and oil cooking grate. Brush bread with oil and grill (over coals if using charcoal), uncovered, until browned, about 1 minute per side. Transfer to serving platter and rub with garlic clove. Brush cut sides of lettuce with half of reserved dressing. Place half of lettuce cut side down on grill (over coals if using charcoal). Grill, uncovered, until lightly charred, 1 to 2 minutes. Transfer to platter with bread. Repeat with remaining reserved dressing and lettuce. Drizzle lettuce with remaining dressing. Sprinkle with Parmesan. Serve.

PER SERVING Cal 380; **Total Fat** 33g; **Sat Fat** 6g; **Chol** 15mg; **Sodium** 680mg; **Total Carb** 13g, **Dietary Fiber** 2g, **Total Sugars** 2g; **Protein** 7g

Grilled Ramps

Grilled Ramps

SERVES 4 `VEGAN`

WHY THIS RECIPE WORKS A foolproof and easy way to celebrate the distinctive fresh onion flavor and short window of availability of ramps is by simply grilling them. To ensure that the thicker white bulbous ends of the ramps cooked through without the more delicate green ends of the ramps burning, we made sure to cook the white ramp bulbs over the high heat of the grill, arranging the green ends of the ramps over the cooler side of the grill. A simple toss of oil, salt, and pepper was all the flavor boost our ramps needed. Grilled lemon quarters made for a beautiful presentation and a welcomed tart finish of flavor for this beautiful side dish. The ramp greens will blister and char quickly, so make sure to watch them carefully. Serve with grilled steak, chicken, or fish, or chop them up and add to vegetable or grain salads.

5 ounces ramps, trimmed
1 tablespoon extra-virgin olive oil
1 lemon, quartered

1A. FOR A CHARCOAL GRILL Open bottom vent completely. Light large chimney starter filled with charcoal briquettes (6 quarts). When top coals are partially covered with ash, pour evenly over half of grill. Set cooking grate in place, cover, and open lid vent completely. Heat grill until hot, about 5 minutes.

1B. FOR A GAS GRILL Turn all burners to high, cover, and heat grill until hot, about 15 minutes. Leave primary burner on high and turn off other burner(s).

2. Clean and oil cooking grate. Toss ramps with oil. Arrange ramps on grill, perpendicular to grate bars, with whites over hotter side of grill and greens over cooler side. Place lemon quarters over hotter side of grill. Grill ramps until whites are softened and lightly charred and lemons are well charred, turning ramps as needed, about 5 minutes.

3. Flip ramps so that greens are over hotter side of grill and cook, turning as needed, until greens are blistered and charred, about 15 seconds. Transfer ramps and lemon quarters to platter and season with salt and pepper to taste. Serve.

PER SERVING Cal 45; **Total Fat** 3.5g, **Sat Fat** 0.5g; **Chol** 0mg; **Sodium** 5mg; **Total Carb** 3g, **Dietary Fiber** 1g, **Total Sugars** 1g; **Protein** 1g

Grilled Tomatoes

MAKES ABOUT 2 CUPS `MAKE-AHEAD` `VEGAN`

WHY THIS RECIPE WORKS Grilling enhances tomatoes with smoky char while preserving their summery taste. A stint over a hot fire softens the tomato's flesh and concentrates its sweetness, while the smoke of the grill adds another dimension of flavor. Tomatoes cook quickly so you can grill them while your steak or other protein is resting and the coals are still hot. Cutting ripe, but still firm, tomatoes in half gave us lots of surface area to quickly caramelize and char before the flesh started to break down too much. Tossing the tomatoes with salt before grilling allowed them to release some of their liquid; the drier the tomatoes were, the more easily they caramelized. To serve the tomatoes as a simple side dish, top them with the reserved juice, 2 tablespoons of torn fresh basil leaves, 1 tablespoon of extra-virgin olive oil, and flake sea salt to taste. This recipe can easily be doubled. For the best results, use in-season, round tomatoes that are ripe yet a bit firm so they will hold their shape on the grill. Plum tomatoes may be used, but they will be drier in texture. If using plum tomatoes, halve them lengthwise. Supermarket vine-ripened tomatoes will work but won't be as flavorful.

2 pounds ripe tomatoes, cored and halved along equator
1 tablespoon extra-virgin olive oil
½ teaspoon table salt
¼ teaspoon pepper

Grilled Tomatoes

VARIATION

Marinated Grilled Tomatoes with Fresh Mozzarella
MAKES ABOUT 3 CUPS
Serve this dish at room temperature by itself, alongside crusty bread, as a topping for bruschetta or grilled pizza, or as part of an antipasto platter.

- 1 recipe Grilled Tomatoes
- 8 ounces fresh mozzarella cheese, torn into bite-size pieces and patted dry
- ¼ cup extra-virgin olive oil
- ¼ cup chopped fresh basil
- 2 tablespoons red wine vinegar
- ¼ teaspoon table salt
- ¼ teaspoon pepper
  Pinch red pepper flakes

Remove and reserve tomato skins; cut tomato flesh into ½-inch pieces and chop skins fine. Combine tomatoes, skins, mozzarella, oil, basil, vinegar, salt, pepper, and pepper flakes in bowl, submerging tomatoes and mozzarella in oil-vinegar mixture. Let sit at room temperature until flavors meld, up to 1 hour, stirring occasionally to ensure that tomatoes are evenly coated. Serve. (Mixture can be refrigerated for up to 2 days; let come to room temperature before serving.)

1. Toss tomatoes with oil, salt, and pepper in large bowl. Let sit for at least 15 minutes or up to 1 hour.

2A. FOR A CHARCOAL GRILL Open bottom vent completely. Light large chimney starter filled with charcoal briquettes (6 quarts). When top coals are partially covered with ash, pour evenly over grill. Set cooking grate in place, cover, and open lid vent completely. Heat grill until hot, about 5 minutes.

2B. FOR A GAS GRILL Turn all burners to high, cover, and heat grill until hot, about 15 minutes. Leave all burners on high.

3. Clean and oil cooking grate. Place tomatoes cut sides down on grill (reserve any juice left behind in bowl) and cook (covered if using gas) until tomatoes are charred and beginning to soften, 4 to 6 minutes.

4. Using tongs or thin metal spatula, carefully flip tomatoes and continue to cook (covered if using gas) until skin sides are charred and juice bubbles, 4 to 6 minutes. Serve. (Tomatoes can be refrigerated for up to 2 days.)

PER SERVING Cal 70; **Total Fat** 4g, **Sat Fat** 0.5g; **Chol** 0mg; **Sodium** 300mg; **Total Carb** 9g, **Dietary Fiber** 3g, **Total Sugars** 6g; **Protein** 2g

Grilled Zucchini with Red Pepper Sauce
SERVES 4 TO 6   **VEGAN**

WHY THIS RECIPE WORKS Pairing beautifully charred zucchini with a summery sauce is a great way to prepare and serve this bountiful vegetable. To encourage the zucchini to give up their moisture on the grill, we cut medium-size zukes in half lengthwise and then cut a shallow crosshatch pattern into the flesh sides of each half. We brushed the flesh sides with extra-virgin olive oil and seasoned them with salt and pepper before charring them on the grill alongside a red bell pepper. We then steamed the bell pepper and blended it with red wine vinegar, garlic, and toasted almonds to create a Spanish-inspired romesco sauce. Adding fresh basil provided an herbal punch. Look for zucchini that are no more than 2 inches in diameter and weigh about 8 ounces each to ensure correct grilling times. Clean and oil the cooking grate thoroughly to prevent the zucchini from sticking. Note that we leave the bell pepper whole (minus the stem and core) and grill only two sides of it.

4 zucchini (8 ounces each), trimmed

1 red bell pepper

1½ tablespoons plus ⅓ cup extra-virgin olive oil, divided

1¼ teaspoons table salt, divided

½ teaspoon pepper, divided

2 tablespoons sliced almonds, toasted

1½ tablespoons red wine vinegar

2 small garlic cloves, peeled

2 teaspoons chopped fresh basil

1. Cut zucchini in half lengthwise. Using paring knife, cut ½-inch crosshatch pattern, about ¼ inch deep, in flesh of each zucchini half, being careful not to cut through skin. Cut around stem of bell pepper and remove core and seeds. Brush flesh sides of zucchini with 1 tablespoon oil and sprinkle with 1 teaspoon salt and ¼ teaspoon pepper. Brush bell pepper with 1½ teaspoons oil.

2A. FOR A CHARCOAL GRILL Open bottom vent completely. Light large chimney starter filled with charcoal briquettes (6 quarts). When top coals are partially covered with ash, pour evenly over grill. Set cooking grate in place, cover, and open lid vent completely. Heat grill until hot, about 5 minutes.

2B. FOR A GAS GRILL Turn all burners to high, cover, and heat grill until hot, about 15 minutes. Turn all burners to medium-high.

3. Clean and oil cooking grate. Place zucchini, flesh side down, and bell pepper, skin side down, on cooking grate. Cook (covered if using gas) until vegetables are well charred on first side, 7 to 9 minutes, rearranging zucchini as needed to ensure even browning.

4. Flip vegetables and continue to cook (covered if using gas) until fork inserted into zucchini meets little resistance and bell pepper is charred on second side, 8 to 10 minutes longer. Transfer zucchini to plate, flesh side up, as they finish cooking. Transfer bell pepper to small bowl, cover with plastic wrap, and let sit for 5 minutes.

5. Using spoon, remove skin from bell pepper (it's OK if some small pieces of skin remain; do not rinse bell pepper to remove skin); cut into 1-inch pieces. Process bell pepper, almonds, vinegar, garlic, remaining ⅓ cup oil, remaining ¼ teaspoon salt, and remaining ¼ teaspoon pepper in blender until smooth, 30 to 60 seconds, scraping down sides of blender jar as needed. Transfer sauce to bowl and stir in basil. Season sauce with salt and pepper to taste.

6. Spread half of sauce on platter. Arrange zucchini over sauce, flesh side up. Spoon remaining sauce over zucchini, as desired. Serve.

PER SERVING Cal 190; **Total Fat** 17g, **Sat Fat** 2.5g; **Chol** 0mg; **Sodium** 500mg; **Total Carb** 7g, **Dictary Fiber** 2g, **Total Sugars** 4g; **Protein** 3g

Grilled Zucchini and Corn Salad
SERVES 4

WHY THIS RECIPE WORKS Corn and zucchini are both at their peak in midsummer and the grill provides a boost to their flavors. The direct heat of the fire enhanced the corn's natural sweetness by caramelizing the sugars in it and drew moisture out of zucchini as well as added flavorful char. Brushing the corn with flavored oil helped the kernels stay moist. For the zucchini, we cut it into planks ½ inch thick, which ensured that the flesh didn't turn to mush before the surfaces were fully charred. A few assertive ingredients—garlic, red pepper flakes, salt, and pepper—added to the oil made a quick marinade and dressing. We tossed the zucchini in the flavored oil before grilling and then dressed the warm grilled vegetables with the remaining oil, lemon juice, and fresh basil. A final sprinkle of crumbled feta added salty, creamy complexity to the flavorful corn and zucchini. Serve warm or at room temperature.

⅓ cup extra-virgin olive oil

2 garlic cloves, minced

½ teaspoon table salt

½ teaspoon pepper

¼ teaspoon red pepper flakes

2 ears corn, husks and silk removed

3 zucchini (8 ounces each), sliced lengthwise into ½-inch-thick planks

2 tablespoons chopped fresh basil

4 teaspoons lemon juice

2 ounces feta cheese, crumbled (½ cup)

1. Whisk oil, garlic, salt, pepper, and pepper flakes together in large bowl. Brush corn with 1 tablespoon oil mixture. Add zucchini to remaining oil mixture in bowl and toss to coat.

2A. FOR A CHARCOAL GRILL Open bottom vent completely. Light large chimney starter filled with charcoal briquettes (6 quarts). When top coals are partially covered with ash, pour evenly over grill. Set cooking grate in place, cover, and open lid vent completely. Heat grill until hot, about 5 minutes.

2B. FOR A GAS GRILL Turn all burners to high, cover, and heat grill until hot, about 15 minutes. Turn all burners to medium-high.

3. Clean and oil cooking grate. Place corn and zucchini on grill; reserve any oil mixture remaining in zucchini bowl. Grill, uncovered, turning corn every 2 to 3 minutes until kernels are lightly charred all over, 10 to 15 minutes total, and zucchini is well-browned and tender (not mushy), 4 to 8 minutes per side.

4. Transfer grilled vegetables to cutting board. Cut kernels from cobs. Cut zucchini on bias into ½-inch-thick slices. Add vegetables to bowl with reserved oil mixture. Add basil and lemon juice and toss to combine. Season with salt and pepper to taste. Transfer salad to platter and sprinkle with feta. Serve.

PER SERVING Cal 280; **Total Fat** 24g; **Sat Fat** 5g; **Chol** 15mg; **Sodium** 430mg; **Total Carb** 16g, **Dietary Fiber** 3g, **Total Sugars** 7g; **Protein** 6g

Grilled Zucchini and Red Onion with Lemon Vinaigrette

SERVES 4 TO 6   `VEGAN`

WHY THIS RECIPE WORKS For this summery side dish, we paired thick slices of zucchini with thick slices of sweet red onion, cutting the vegetables into similar-size pieces so that we could grill them in sync over a medium-hot fire. After about 5 minutes, faint grill marks began to appear on the undersides of the vegetables; we adjusted their position on the grill or the heat level as needed to brown both sides. Our zucchini and onions were perfectly tender and full of smoky flavor in about 20 minutes. To bump up their flavor, we whisked up a quick lemony vinaigrette with a touch of Dijon mustard to drizzle over the vegetables after they came off the grill. Lastly, we sprinkled everything with chopped fresh basil. The vegetables can be served hot, warm, or at room temperature.

- 1 red onion, sliced into ½-inch-thick rounds
- 1 pound zucchini, trimmed and sliced lengthwise into ¾-inch-thick planks
- 6 tablespoons extra-virgin olive oil, divided
- 1¼ teaspoons table salt, divided
- ½ teaspoon pepper
- 1 teaspoon grated lemon zest plus 1 tablespoon juice
- 1 garlic clove, minced
- ¼ teaspoon Dijon mustard
- 1 tablespoon chopped fresh basil

1. Thread onion rounds, from side to side, onto 2 metal skewers. Brush onion and zucchini with ¼ cup oil, sprinkle with 1 teaspoon salt, and season with pepper. Whisk lemon zest and juice, garlic, mustard, remaining 2 tablespoons oil, and remaining ¼ teaspoon salt together in bowl.

Grilled Zucchini and Red Onion with Lemon Vinaigrette

2A. FOR A CHARCOAL GRILL Open bottom vent completely. Light large chimney starter half filled with charcoal briquettes (3 quarts). When top coals are partially covered with ash, pour evenly over grill. Set cooking grate in place, cover, and open lid vent completely. Heat grill until hot, about 5 minutes.

2B. FOR A GAS GRILL Turn all burners to high, cover, and heat grill until hot, about 15 minutes. Turn all burners to medium.

3. Clean and oil cooking grate. Place onion and zucchini on grill. Cook (covered if using gas), turning as needed, until tender and caramelized, 18 to 22 minutes. Transfer vegetables to serving platter as they finish cooking. Remove onion from skewers and discard any charred outer rings. Whisk dressing to recombine and drizzle over vegetables. Sprinkle with basil and serve.

PER SERVING Cal 150; **Total Fat** 14g, **Sat Fat** 2g; **Chol** 0mg; **Sodium** 500mg; **Total Carb** 4g, **Dietary Fiber** 1g, **Total Sugars** 2g; **Protein** 1g

Grilled Ratatouille

Grilled Vegetable Kebabs with Grilled Lemon Dressing

SERVES 4   MAKE-AHEAD   VEGAN

WHY THIS RECIPE WORKS Vegetables are a great option for grilled kebabs; they cook quickly and offer a charred exterior and tender interior. To flavor our vegetables, we first tossed them with some of the dressing base before skewering and grilling them. We also grilled lemon quarters to tone down their acidity and give the juice a deeper, more complex flavor. The bell peppers sweetened over the flame, the zucchini held their shape and texture, and the portobello caps picked up both great char flavor and a meaty taste. You will need eight 12-inch metal skewers for this recipe.

- ¼ cup extra-virgin olive oil
- 1 teaspoon Dijon mustard
- 1 teaspoon minced fresh rosemary
- 1 garlic clove, minced
- ½ teaspoon table salt
- ¼ teaspoon pepper
- 6 portobello mushroom caps (5 inches in diameter), quartered

- 2 zucchini, halved lengthwise and sliced ¾ inch thick
- 2 red bell peppers, stemmed, seeded, and cut into 1½-inch pieces
- 2 lemons, quartered, divided

1. Whisk oil, mustard, rosemary, garlic, salt, and pepper together in large bowl. Measure half of mixture into separate bowl and set aside for serving. Toss mushrooms, zucchini, and bell peppers with remaining oil mixture, then thread in alternating order onto eight 12-inch metal skewers. (Vegetables and reserved dressing can be refrigerated separately for up to 24 hours. To serve, let dressing come to room temperature and continue with step 2, increasing cooking time to 20 to 24 minutes.)

2A. FOR A CHARCOAL GRILL Open bottom vent completely. Light large chimney starter half filled with charcoal briquettes (3 quarts). When top coals are partially covered with ash, pour evenly over grill. Set cooking grate in place, cover, and open lid vent completely. Heat grill until hot, about 5 minutes.

2B. FOR A GAS GRILL Turn all burners to high, cover, and heat grill until hot, about 15 minutes. Turn all burners to medium.

3. Clean and oil cooking grate. Place kebabs and lemons on grill. Cook (covered if using gas), turning as needed, until vegetables are tender and well browned and lemons are juicy and slightly charred, 16 to 18 minutes. Transfer kebabs and lemons to platter, removing skewers.

4. Juice 2 lemon quarters and whisk into reserved oil mixture. Drizzle vegetables with dressing and serve.

PER SERVING Cal 200; **Total Fat** 15g, **Sat Fat** 2g; **Chol** 0mg; **Sodium** 340mg; **Total Carb** 13g, **Dietary Fiber** 4g, **Total Sugars** 8g; **Protein** 5g

Grilled Ratatouille

SERVES 6 TO 8   VEGAN

WHY THIS RECIPE WORKS Smoky char makes the classic French vegetable dish ratatouille even better. Its vegetables, including eggplant, zucchini, onion, bell peppers, and tomatoes, take well to the grill and don't require any precooking. They are also easy to prep: Simply brush them with olive oil, season with salt and pepper, and they're good to go on the grill. The heat of the fire helps all the moisture evaporate from the vegetables. To avoid mushy, overcooked vegetables or hard, undercooked vegetables, carefully monitor the grill time for each separate vegetable. You may have to cook the vegetables in batches if they don't all fit on your grill; be prepared to take each off the grill as it is done cooking.

1 red onion, cut into ½-inch-thick slices and skewered

2 pounds eggplant, sliced into ¾-inch-thick rounds

1½ pounds zucchini or summer squash, sliced lengthwise into ½-inch-thick planks

2 bell peppers, stemmed, seeded, and halved, each half cut into thirds

1 pound tomatoes, cored and halved

¼ cup extra-virgin olive oil, plus extra for brushing

1½ teaspoons table salt

¾ teaspoons pepper

3 tablespoons sherry vinegar

¼ cup chopped fresh basil

1 tablespoon minced fresh thyme

1 garlic clove, minced to paste

1. Place onion, eggplant, zucchini, bell peppers and tomatoes on baking sheet, brush with oil, and season with salt and pepper. Whisk ¼ cup oil, vinegar, basil, thyme, and garlic together in large bowl.

2A. FOR A CHARCOAL GRILL Open bottom vent completely. Light large chimney starter three-quarters filled with charcoal briquettes (4½ quarts). When top coals are partially covered with ash, pour evenly over grill. Set cooking grate in place, cover, and open lid vent completely. Heat grill until hot, about 5 minutes.

2B. FOR A GAS GRILL Turn all burners to high, cover, and heat grill until hot, about 15 minutes. Turn all burners to medium-high.

3. Clean and oil cooking grate. Place vegetables on grill and cook, turning once, until tender and streaked with grill marks, 10 to 12 minutes for onion, 8 to 10 minutes for eggplant and squash, 7 to 9 minutes for peppers, and 4 to 5 minutes for tomatoes. Remove vegetables from grill as they are done and let cool slightly.

4. When cool enough to handle, chop vegetables into ½-inch pieces and add to oil mixture; toss to coat. Season with salt and pepper to taste, and serve warm or at room temperature.

PER SERVING Cal 130; **Total Fat** 8g, **Sat Fat** 1g; **Chol** 0mg; **Sodium** 450mg; **Total Carb** 15g, **Dietary Fiber** 5g, **Total Sugars** 9g; **Protein** 3g

Tunisian-Style Grilled Vegetables
SERVES 4 TO 6 `VEGAN`

WHY THIS RECIPE WORKS For our take on the robustly flavored Tunisian grilled vegetable salad *mechouia*, we started with the vegetable prep. Halving the eggplant, zucchini, and plum tomatoes lengthwise, and flattening the bell peppers provided the maximum surface area for charring. We also scored the eggplant and zucchini to release excess moisture as they cooked. A combination of Tunisian spices infused our vegetables with flavor, and those spices plus garlic, lemon, and a trio of herbs made a bright-tasting dressing. Equal amounts of ground coriander and cumin can be substituted for the whole spices. Serve with grilled pita bread or with Easy-Peel Hard-Cooked Eggs (page 453) and olives.

DRESSING

2 teaspoons coriander seeds

1½ teaspoons caraway seeds

1 teaspoon cumin seeds

5 tablespoons extra-virgin olive oil

½ teaspoon paprika

⅛ teaspoon cayenne pepper

3 garlic cloves, minced

¼ cup chopped fresh parsley

¼ cup chopped fresh cilantro

2 tablespoons chopped fresh mint

1 teaspoon grated lemon zest plus 2 tablespoons juice

VEGETABLES

2 red or green bell peppers, tops and bottoms trimmed, stemmed and seeded, and peppers flattened

1 small eggplant, halved lengthwise and scored on cut side

1 zucchini (8 to 10 ounces), halved lengthwise and scored on cut side

4 plum tomatoes, cored and halved lengthwise

½ teaspoon table salt

2 shallots, unpeeled

1. FOR THE DRESSING Grind coriander seeds, caraway seeds, and cumin seeds in spice grinder until finely ground. Whisk ground spices, oil, paprika, and cayenne together in bowl. Reserve 3 tablespoons oil mixture for brushing vegetables before grilling. Heat remaining oil mixture and garlic in 8-inch skillet over low heat, stirring occasionally, until fragrant and small bubbles appear, 8 to 10 minutes. Transfer to large bowl, let cool for 10 minutes, then whisk in parsley, cilantro, mint, and lemon zest and juice and season with salt to taste; set aside for serving.

2. FOR THE VEGETABLES Brush interior of bell peppers and cut sides of eggplant, zucchini, and tomatoes with reserved oil mixture and sprinkle with salt.

3A. FOR A CHARCOAL GRILL Open bottom vent completely. Light large chimney starter three-quarters filled with charcoal briquettes (4½ quarts). When top coals are partially covered with ash, pour evenly over grill. Set cooking grate in place, cover, and open lid vent completely. Heat grill until hot, about 5 minutes.

3B. FOR A GAS GRILL Turn all burners to high, cover, and heat grill until hot, about 15 minutes. Turn all burners to medium-high.

4. Clean and oil cooking grate. Place bell peppers, eggplant, zucchini, tomatoes, and shallots cut side down on grill. Cook (covered if using gas), turning as needed, until tender and slightly charred, 8 to 16 minutes. Transfer eggplant, zucchini, tomatoes, and shallots to baking sheet as they finish cooking; place bell peppers in bowl, cover with plastic wrap, and let steam to loosen skins.

5. Let vegetables cool slightly. Peel bell peppers, tomatoes, and shallots. Chop all vegetables into ½-inch pieces, then toss gently with dressing in bowl. Season with salt and pepper to taste. Serve warm or at room temperature.

PER SERVING Cal 170; **Total Fat** 12g, **Sat Fat** 1.5g; **Chol** 0mg; **Sodium** 210mg; **Total Carb** 14g, **Dietary Fiber** 5g, **Total Sugars** 7g; **Protein** 3g

Grilled Vegetable and Halloumi Salad
SERVES 4 TO 6

WHY THIS RECIPE WORKS This warm and smoky salad matches nicely charred vegetables with chunks of briny Greek halloumi cheese. Halloumi has a solid consistency and high melting point, making it perfect for grilling; it becomes beautifully charred and crisp in contrast to its chewy, warm interior. After grilling radicchio, eggplant, zucchini, and the cheese for 10 minutes, the vegetables and cheese were perfectly browned, tender, and redolent with smoky flavor. We chopped all the vegetables before tossing everything with a honey and thyme vinaigrette.

- 3 tablespoons honey
- 1 tablespoon minced fresh thyme
- ½ teaspoon grated lemon zest plus 3 tablespoons juice
- 1 garlic clove, minced
- ¾ teaspoon table salt, divided
- ⅛ teaspoon plus ½ teaspoon pepper, divided
- 1 pound eggplant, sliced into ½-inch-thick rounds
- 1 head radicchio (10 ounces), quartered
- 1 zucchini, halved lengthwise
- 1 (8-ounce) block halloumi cheese, sliced into ½-inch-thick slabs
- ¼ cup extra-virgin olive oil, divided

1. Whisk honey, thyme, lemon zest and juice, garlic, ¼ teaspoon salt, and ⅛ teaspoon pepper together in large bowl; set aside. Brush eggplant, radicchio, zucchini, and halloumi with 2 tablespoons oil and sprinkle with remaining ½ teaspoon salt and remaining ½ teaspoon pepper.

Grilled Vegetable and Halloumi Salad

2A. FOR A CHARCOAL GRILL Open bottom vent completely. Light large chimney starter half filled with charcoal briquettes (3 quarts). When top coals are partially covered with ash, pour evenly over grill. Set cooking grate in place, cover, and open lid vent completely. Heat grill until hot, about 5 minutes.

2B. FOR A GAS GRILL Turn all burners to high, cover, and heat grill until hot, about 15 minutes. Turn all burners to medium.

3. Clean and oil cooking grate. Place vegetables and halloumi on grill. Cook (covered if using gas), flipping as needed, until radicchio is softened and lightly charred, 3 to 5 minutes, and remaining vegetables and cheese are softened and lightly charred, about 10 minutes. Transfer vegetables and cheese to cutting board as they finish cooking, let cool slightly, then cut into 1-inch pieces.

4. Whisking constantly, slowly drizzle remaining 2 tablespoons oil into honey mixture. Add vegetables and halloumi and gently toss to coat. Season with salt and pepper to taste. Serve.

PER SERVING Cal 280; **Total Fat** 20g, **Sat Fat** 8g; **Chol** 30mg; **Sodium** 710mg; **Total Carb** 17g, **Dietary Fiber** 3g, **Total Sugars** 12g; **Protein** 10g

Grilled Panzanella Salad

SERVES 4 TO 6 `MAKE-AHEAD`

WHY THIS RECIPE WORKS *Panzanella* is a classic Italian salad traditionally made of stale bread and ripe vegetables, tossed together with vinaigrette. We translated the salad to the grill and filled it with smoky flavor. Grilling slices of fresh baguette brushed with olive oil and garlic gave us bread that could stand up to dressing and had a bonus layer of summery, grill-marked flavor. For the vegetables, we grilled red onion, zucchini, and red bell pepper after prepping them into uniform shapes that wouldn't fall through the grill grate. Capers with some of their brine, garlic, and Dijon mustard created a robust vinaigrette that brought everything together. The dressing can be made up to a day in advance, but the salad is best eaten the day it is made.

DRESSING

- 1 cup extra-virgin olive oil
- 3 garlic cloves, minced
- ⅓ cup white wine vinegar
- 2 tablespoons capers, minced, plus 1 tablespoon brine
- 1 teaspoon Dijon mustard
- ½ teaspoon table salt
- ½ teaspoon pepper

SALAD

- 1 red onion, halved and cut into ½-inch-thick wedges through root end
- 1 red bell pepper, stemmed, seeded, and cut into 2-inch planks
- 1 zucchini, trimmed and quartered lengthwise
- 1 (12-inch) baguette, cut on bias into 4-inch-long, 1-inch-thick slices
- ½ seedless English cucumber, cut into ½-inch pieces
- 1 cup cherry tomatoes, halved
- ½ cup chopped fresh basil
- 1½ ounces Parmesan cheese, shredded (½ cup)

1. FOR THE DRESSING Whisk oil and garlic together in bowl. Set aside ⅓ cup garlic oil for brushing vegetables and bread. Whisk vinegar, capers and brine, mustard, salt, and pepper into remaining ⅔ cup garlic oil until combined. (Dressing can be refrigerated for up to 24 hours.)

2. FOR THE SALAD Place onion, bell pepper, zucchini, and bread on rimmed baking sheet and brush all over with reserved garlic oil.

3A. FOR A CHARCOAL GRILL Open bottom vent completely. Light large chimney starter mounded with charcoal briquettes (7 quarts). When top coals are partially covered with ash, pour evenly over grill. Set cooking grate in place, cover, and open lid vent completely. Heat grill until hot, about 5 minutes.

Grilled Panzanella Salad

3B. FOR A GAS GRILL Turn all burners to high, cover, and heat grill until hot, about 15 minutes. Turn all burners to medium.

4. Clean and oil cooking grate. Transfer onion, bell pepper, and zucchini to grill and cook (covered if using gas) until well browned and tender, 6 to 12 minutes, flipping and turning as needed for even cooking. Return vegetables to sheet as they finish grilling and season with salt and pepper. Arrange bread slices on grill and cook, uncovered, until golden brown and lightly charred, 1 to 2 minutes per side. Return to sheet and season with salt and pepper.

5. Cut grilled vegetables and bread slices into ¾-inch pieces and transfer to large bowl. Add cucumber, tomatoes, basil, and ¾ cup dressing and toss to combine. Let sit for 10 minutes for flavors to blend, then season with salt and pepper to taste. Transfer salad to serving platter and sprinkle with Parmesan. Serve, passing remaining ¼ cup dressing separately.

PER SERVING Cal 450; **Total Fat** 40g, **Sat Fat** 6g; **Chol** 5mg; **Sodium** 500mg; **Total Carb** 16g, **Dietary Fiber** 2g, **Total Sugars** 4g; **Protein** 6g

USE YOUR SLOW COOKER OR PRESSURE COOKER

▪ VEGAN
Photos (clockwise from top left): Pressure-Cooker Garlicky Braised Swiss Chard with Chorizo; Slow-Cooker Butternut Squash Puree; Slow-Cooker Creamy Orzo with Parmesan and Peas; Pressure-Cooker Drunken Beans

Slow-Cooker Braised Artichokes with Garlic Butter

1. Working with 1 artichoke at a time, cut off stem at base so artichoke sits upright, then cut off top quarter of artichoke. Using kitchen shears, trim off top portion of outer leaves. Toss artichokes with 2 tablespoons lemon juice and oil in bowl, then place right side up in slow cooker. Add ½ cup water, cover, and cook until outer leaves of artichokes pull away easily and tip of paring knife inserted into base meets no resistance, 8 to 9 hours on low or 5 to 6 hours on high.

2. Microwave remaining 2 tablespoons lemon juice, butter, garlic, and salt in bowl until butter is melted. Whisk butter mixture to combine, then divide evenly among 4 serving bowls. Remove artichokes from slow cooker, letting any excess cooking liquid drain back into insert, and place artichokes in bowls with butter. Serve.

PER SERVING Cal 230; **Total Fat** 20g, **Sat Fat** 11g; **Chol** 45mg; **Sodium** 230mg; **Total Carb** 11g, **Dietary Fiber** 5g, **Total Sugars** 1g; **Protein** 3g

Slow-Cooker Braised Artichokes with Garlic Butter
SERVES 4
COOKING TIME 8 to 9 hours on low or 5 to 6 hours on high

WHY THIS RECIPE WORKS A slow cooker makes impressive whole braised artichokes accessible. We simply trimmed the artichokes and placed them upright in the slow cooker with a little water. Tossing them with a bit of lemon juice and olive oil beforehand helped to preserve their color. For a simple yet boldly flavored dipping sauce, we melted butter with more lemon juice and some minced garlic. If your artichokes are larger than 10 ounces, strip away another layer or two of the toughest outer leaves. These artichokes are delicious warm or at room temperature. You will need a 5- to 7-quart slow cooker for this recipe. This recipe will only work in a traditional slow cooker.

- 4 artichokes (8 to 10 ounces each)
- ¼ cup lemon juice (2 lemons), divided
- 1 tablespoon extra-virgin olive oil
- 6 tablespoons unsalted butter
- 3 garlic cloves, minced
- ¼ teaspoon table salt

Slow-Cooker Beets with Oranges and Walnuts
SERVES 4 TO 6
COOKING TIME 6 to 7 hours on low or 4 to 5 hours on high

WHY THIS RECIPE WORKS Moving beets to the slow cooker frees up the oven and gives them an undiluted, earthy taste. We wrapped our beets in aluminum foil and included ½ cup of water in the slow cooker to ensure that the beets cooked evenly. Rather than skin them when they were raw—a messy endeavor—we waited until the beets cooled and simply rubbed off the skins with paper towels. Cutting the beets into wedges made them easy to eat; a simple white wine vinaigrette added brightness. Orange pieces, toasted walnuts, and chives turned our slow-cooked beets into an impressive bistro-style side dish. For even cooking, we recommend using beets that are similar in size—roughly 3 inches in diameter. You will need a 4- to 7-quart oval slow cooker for this recipe. This recipe will only work in a traditional slow cooker.

- 1½ pounds beets, trimmed
- 2 oranges
- ¼ cup white wine vinegar
- 2 tablespoons extra-virgin olive oil
- 1 tablespoon honey
- ¼ cup walnuts, toasted and chopped
- 2 tablespoons minced fresh chives

1. Wrap beets individually in aluminum foil and place in slow cooker. Add ½ cup water, cover, and cook until beets are tender, 6 to 7 hours on low or 4 to 5 hours on high.

2. Transfer beets to cutting board and carefully remove foil (watch for steam). When beets are cool enough to handle, rub off skins with paper towels and cut into ½-inch-thick wedges.

3. Cut away peel and pith from oranges. Quarter oranges, then slice crosswise into ½-inch-thick pieces. Whisk vinegar, oil, and honey together in large bowl. Add beets and orange pieces, along with any accumulated juices, and toss to coat. Season with salt and pepper to taste. Sprinkle with walnuts and chives. Serve.

PER SERVING Cal 140; **Total Fat** 8g, **Sat Fat** 1g; **Chol** 0mg; **Sodium** 75mg; **Total Carb** 18g, **Dietary Fiber** 4g, **Total Sugars** 13g; **Protein** 3g

Slow-Cooker Brussels Sprouts with Lemon, Thyme, and Bacon
SERVES 4 TO 6
COOKING TIME 2 to 3 hours on high

WHY THIS RECIPE WORKS Dressed-up Brussels sprouts are perfect for any table—and for the slow cooker. Using chicken broth and thyme added savory depth, and a bit of lemon zest and juice contributed brightness. For added richness, we quickly crisped some bacon in the microwave and sprinkled it on top. When trimming the Brussels sprouts, be careful not to cut off too much of the stem end or the leaves will fall away from the core. You will need a 5- to 7-quart slow cooker for this recipe. This recipe will only work in a traditional slow cooker.

- 2 pounds Brussels sprouts, trimmed and halved through root end
- 2 cups chicken broth
  Table salt for cooking Brussels sprouts
- 4 slices bacon, chopped
- 2 tablespoons unsalted butter, melted
- 2 teaspoons grated lemon zest plus 1 tablespoon juice
- 1 teaspoon minced fresh thyme

1. Combine Brussels sprouts, broth, and ½ teaspoon salt in slow cooker. Cover and cook until Brussels sprouts are tender, 2 to 3 hours on high.

2. Line plate with double layer of coffee filters. Spread bacon in even layer on filters and microwave until crispy, about 5 minutes. Drain Brussels sprouts and return to now-empty slow cooker. Stir in melted butter, lemon zest and juice, and thyme. Season with salt and pepper to taste. Sprinkle with bacon and serve.

PER SERVING Cal 170; **Total Fat** 12g, **Sat Fat** 5g; **Chol** 20mg; **Sodium** 540mg; **Total Carb** 12g, **Dietary Fiber** 5g, **Total Sugars** 3g; **Protein** 7g

Slow-Cooker Brussels Sprouts with Lemon, Thyme, and Bacon

Slow-Cooker Sweet-and-Sour Braised Red Cabbage
SERVES 4 TO 6
COOKING TIME 5 to 6 hours on low or 3 to 4 hours on high

WHY THIS RECIPE WORKS The slow cooker, with its moist heat environment, is perfect for braising cabbage. However, adding the cabbage directly to it left the vegetable too crunchy for our liking. To get the texture just right, we had to precook it in the microwave to soften it slightly. This step had the added benefit of getting rid of excess moisture that detracted from the flavors of the dish. For the braising medium we selected sweet and fruity apple cider, enhancing it with traditional spices such as cinnamon, caraway seeds, and allspice. A bit of brown sugar rounded out the sweetness, while vinegar perked up the flavors and added balance. Since tasters found the cabbage a little lean, we added bacon, which imparted a smoky depth and richness. You will need a 5- to 7-quart slow cooker for this recipe. This recipe will only work in a traditional slow cooker.

1 head red cabbage (2 pounds), cored and sliced thin
1 tablespoon vegetable oil
½ teaspoon table salt
4 slices bacon, chopped fine
1 onion, chopped fine
1 teaspoon minced fresh thyme or ¼ teaspoon dried
½ teaspoon caraway seeds, toasted
¼ teaspoon ground cinnamon
¼ teaspoon ground allspice
1½ cups apple cider, divided
2 tablespoons packed brown sugar, plus extra for seasoning
3 bay leaves
2 tablespoons cider vinegar, plus extra for seasoning

1. Microwave cabbage, oil, and salt in covered bowl, stirring occasionally, until cabbage is softened, 15 to 20 minutes. Drain cabbage and transfer to slow cooker.

2. Cook bacon in 12-inch skillet over medium-high heat until crispy, about 5 minutes. Add onion and cook until softened and lightly browned, 5 to 7 minutes. Stir in thyme, caraway seeds, cinnamon, and allspice and cook until fragrant, about 30 seconds. Stir in ½ cup cider, scraping up any browned bits; transfer to slow cooker.

3. Stir remaining 1 cup cider, sugar, and bay leaves into slow cooker. Cover and cook until cabbage is tender, 5 to 6 hours on low or 3 to 4 hours on high.

4. Discard bay leaves. Stir in vinegar and season with salt, pepper, extra sugar, and extra vinegar to taste. Serve. (Cabbage can be held on warm or low setting for up to 2 hours.)

PER SERVING Cal 170; Total Fat 6g, Sat Fat 1.5g; Chol 10mg; Sodium 380mg; Total Carb 25g, Dietary Fiber 4g, Total Sugars 18g; Protein 6g

Slow-Cooker Glazed Carrots

SERVES 6 TO 8
COOKING TIME 5 to 6 hours on low or 3 to 4 hours on high

WHY THIS RECIPE WORKS Glazed carrots are a reliable side dish we often turn to for a holiday meal, and using the slow cooker eliminated any last-minute fuss (and freed up the stovetop). Initially we tried cooking the carrots in broth, but it detracted from their delicate, sweet flavor. In the end, water seasoned with a little sugar and salt was best for gently simmering the carrots. Once they were tender, we simply drained them and tossed them with tart orange marmalade and butter. The marmalade and butter melted to form a mock "glaze" that conveniently did not need to be reduced on the stovetop. Simple, sweet, and delicious—nothing could be easier. You will need a 4- to 7-quart slow cooker for this recipe. This recipe will only work in a traditional slow cooker.

3 pounds carrots, peeled and sliced ¼ inch thick on bias
1 tablespoon sugar
Table salt for cooking carrots
½ cup orange marmalade
2 tablespoons unsalted butter, softened

1. Combine carrots, ¾ cup water, sugar, and ¼ teaspoon salt in slow cooker. Cover and cook until carrots are tender, 5 to 6 hours on low or 3 to 4 hours on high.

2. Drain carrots and return to now-empty slow cooker. Stir in marmalade and butter. Season with salt and pepper to taste. Serve. (Carrots can be held on warm or low setting for up to 2 hours.)

PER SERVING Cal 140; Total Fat 3g, Sat Fat 2g; Chol 10mg; Sodium 180mg; Total Carb 29g, Dietary Fiber 4g, Total Sugars 20g; Protein 1g

Slow-Cooker Braised Cauliflower with Lemon-Caper Dressing

SERVES 4 TO 6 **VEGAN**
COOKING TIME 2 to 3 hours on high

WHY THIS RECIPE WORKS Braising cauliflower in a slow cooker allows it time to really absorb the flavors surrounding it. Since cauliflower can quickly go from perfectly tender to broken down, we avoided florets and instead sliced a head of cauliflower into thick wedges. A small amount of water seasoned with a little salt proved best for gently braising it. We also included a few smashed garlic cloves, thyme sprigs, and pepper flakes for added flavor. A bright dressing put a Mediterranean spin on this simple side. You will need a 5- to 7-quart oval slow cooker for this recipe. This recipe will only work in a traditional slow cooker.

4 garlic cloves, peeled and smashed
2 sprigs fresh thyme
½ teaspoon table salt
⅛ teaspoon red pepper flakes
1 head cauliflower (2 pounds)
2 tablespoons extra-virgin olive oil
1 tablespoon minced fresh parsley
2 teaspoons grated lemon zest plus 1 tablespoon juice
2 teaspoons capers, rinsed and minced

1. Combine 1 cup water, garlic, thyme sprigs, salt, and pepper flakes in slow cooker. Trim outer leaves of cauliflower and cut stem flush with bottom of head. Cut head into 8 equal wedges, keeping core and florets intact. Place wedges cut side down in slow cooker (wedges may overlap). Cover and cook until cauliflower is tender, 2 to 3 hours on high.

Slow-Cooker Braised Cauliflower with Lemon-Caper Dressing

2. Whisk oil, parsley, lemon zest and juice, and capers together in bowl. Season with salt and pepper to taste. Using slotted spoon, transfer cauliflower to serving dish, brushing away any garlic cloves or thyme sprigs that stick to it. Drizzle cauliflower with dressing. Serve.

PER SERVING Cal 80; **Total Fat** 5g, **Sat Fat** 1g; **Chol** 0mg; **Sodium** 260mg; **Total Carb** 9g, **Dietary Fiber** 3g, **Total Sugars** 3g; **Protein** 3g

Slow-Cooker Mashed Cauliflower
SERVES 8 TO 10
COOKING TIME 7 to 8 hours on low or 4 to 5 hours on high

WHY THIS RECIPE WORKS For a simple alternative to mashed potatoes, we decided to use cauliflower. Since cauliflower is low in fiber, it easily breaks down when cooked for an extended period of time, making it perfect for the slow cooker. This meant a creamy textured side dish could easily be achieved using only a potato masher. With just three key ingredients—cauliflower, water

instead of broth, and salt—we aimed to keep the flavor of the cauliflower at the fore. Because the cooking liquid isn't drained, a mere ½ cup of water proved to be just enough to allow the cauliflower to cook perfectly without causing the sweet, nutty flavor developed during the long cooking time to become washed out. Covering the cauliflower with a parchment shield ensured even cooking by trapping the steam. Our cauliflower mash tasted too lean to be considered a mashed potato alternative. We solved this with a splash of heavy cream, which provided richness, while a sprinkle of chives added a bright, fresh finish. If you prefer to buy bagged cauliflower florets, rather than a head, you will need 3 pounds. For more information on creating a parchment shield, see below. For an accurate measurement of boiling water, bring a full kettle of water to a boil and then measure out the desired amount. You will need a 5- to 7-quart slow cooker for this recipe. This recipe will only work in a traditional slow cooker.

2 heads cauliflower (4 pounds), cored and
   cut into 2-inch florets
½ cup boiling water, plus extra as needed
1½ teaspoons table salt
¼ cup heavy cream
3 tablespoons minced fresh chives

1. Combine cauliflower, boiling water, and salt in slow cooker. Press 16 by 12-inch sheet of parchment paper firmly onto cauliflower, folding down edges as needed. Cover and cook until cauliflower is very tender, 7 to 8 hours on low or 4 to 5 hours on high.

2. Discard parchment. Mash cauliflower with potato masher until almost completely broken down. Stir in cream and chives and season with salt and pepper to taste. Serve. (Cauliflower can be held on warm or low setting for up to 2 hours; adjust consistency with extra hot water as needed before serving.)

PER SERVING Cal 40; **Total Fat** 2.5g, **Sat Fat** 1.5g; **Chol** 5mg; **Sodium** 370mg; **Total Carb** 4g, **Dietary Fiber** 1g, **Total Sugars** 2g; **Protein** 2g

MAKING A PARCHMENT SHIELD

Press 16 by 12-inch sheet of parchment paper firmly onto vegetables or rice, folding down edges as needed. Parchment traps steam so it drips back into slow cooker.

Slow-Cooker Braised Kale with Garlic and Chorizo

SERVES 4 TO 6

COOKING TIME 7 to 8 hours on low or 4 to 5 hours on high

WHY THIS RECIPE WORKS A long cooking time in the slow cooker turns kale and other hearty greens meltingly soft, and gentles their strong flavors. Spanish-style chorizo (the cured, smoked type) and garlic brought a meaty, spicy kick to our greens and ensured things didn't get toned down. This kale makes a delicious bed for over-easy eggs, or could also be served over rice for a heartier side. You will need a 5- to 7-quart slow cooker for this recipe. This recipe will only work in a traditional slow cooker.

 8 ounces Spanish-style chorizo sausage, halved lengthwise and sliced ½ inch thick
 1 tablespoon extra-virgin olive oil
 2 garlic cloves, minced
1½ cups chicken broth
 ¼ teaspoon table salt
 2 pounds kale, stemmed and cut into 2-inch pieces

1. Lightly coat slow cooker with vegetable oil spray. Microwave chorizo, oil, and garlic in bowl, stirring occasionally, until fragrant, about 1 minute. Transfer to prepared slow cooker. Stir in broth and salt.

2. Microwave half of kale in covered bowl until slightly wilted, about 5 minutes, and transfer to slow cooker. Stir in remaining kale, cover, and cook until kale is tender, 7 to 8 hours on low or 4 to 5 hours on high. Season with salt and pepper to taste. Serve.

PER SERVING Cal 250; **Total Fat** 18g; **Sat Fat** 6g; **Chol** 35mg; **Sodium** 750mg; **Total Carb** 11g, **Dietary Fiber** 4g, **Total Sugars** 3g; **Protein** 14g

Slow-Cooker Braised Swiss Chard with Shiitakes and Peanuts

SERVES 4 TO 6

COOKING TIME 1 to 2 hours on high

WHY THIS RECIPE WORKS For an Asian take on braised Swiss chard, we turned to toasted sesame oil, fresh ginger, and garlic as our aromatic base. We added shiitake mushrooms, which we softened with the chard stems in the microwave before braising them along with the chard leaves. Once the chard was perfectly tender, we stirred in rice vinegar and more ginger, keeping the flavors vibrant. Butter added richness and peanuts and scallions provided crunch. You will need a 5- to 7-quart slow cooker for this recipe. This recipe will only work in a traditional slow cooker.

 2 pounds Swiss chard, stems chopped fine, leaves cut into 1-inch pieces
 4 ounces shiitake mushrooms, stemmed and sliced ¼ inch thick
 3 garlic cloves, minced
 2 teaspoons grated fresh ginger, divided
 2 teaspoons toasted sesame oil, divided
 ¼ teaspoon table salt
 ⅛ teaspoon red pepper flakes
 1 tablespoon rice vinegar
 1 tablespoon unsalted butter
 1 teaspoon sugar
 2 tablespoons chopped dry-roasted peanuts
 2 scallions, sliced thin

1. Lightly coat slow cooker with vegetable oil spray. Microwave chard stems, mushrooms, garlic, 1 teaspoon ginger, 1 teaspoon oil, salt, and pepper flakes in bowl, stirring occasionally, until vegetables are softened, about 5 minutes; transfer to prepared slow cooker. Stir in chard leaves, cover, and cook until chard is tender, 1 to 2 hours on high.

2. Stir in vinegar, butter, sugar, remaining 1 teaspoon ginger, and remaining 1 teaspoon oil. Season with salt and pepper to taste. (Swiss chard can be held on warm or low setting for up to 2 hours.) Sprinkle with peanuts and scallions and serve.

PER SERVING Cal 90; **Total Fat** 5g; **Sat Fat** 1.5g; **Chol** 5mg; **Sodium** 420mg; **Total Carb** 9g, **Dietary Fiber** 3g, **Total Sugars** 3g; **Protein** 4g

Slow-Cooker Southern Braised Collard Greens

SERVES 4 TO 6

COOKING TIME 9 to 10 hours on low or 6 to 7 hours on high

WHY THIS RECIPE WORKS Any Southerner will tell you that "lip-smacking" collard greens require long cooking and the smokiness of cured pork, and we tend to agree. Slow-cooking this hearty green in liquid tempers its assertive bitterness, making it perfectly suited to the slow cooker. After testing varying amounts of liquid, we found 4 cups to be ideal for 2 pounds of greens. This may not sound like a lot of liquid, but given the lack of significant evaporation and the slow cooker's moist environment, this amount went a long way to ensure properly cooked collards without the need for them to be fully submerged. A combination of chicken broth (rather than water) and aromatics (onion and garlic) helped the greens develop great flavor, while a ham hock imparted characteristic smokiness. To round things out, we added pepper flakes for some subtle heat. We brightened up the liquid

Slow-Cooker Southern Braised Collard Greens

at the end of cooking with cider vinegar. The leftover cooking liquid, traditionally called pot "liquor" (or "likker"), can be sopped up with cornbread or biscuits, or used to cook a second batch of collard greens, as is traditionally done in the South. You will need a 5- to 7-quart slow cooker for this recipe. This recipe will only work in a traditional slow cooker.

1 onion, chopped fine
6 garlic cloves, minced
1 tablespoon vegetable oil
1 teaspoon table salt
½ teaspoon red pepper flakes
2 pounds collard greens, stemmed and cut into
    1-inch pieces
4 cups chicken broth
1 (12-ounce) smoked ham hock, rinsed
2 tablespoons cider vinegar, plus extra for seasoning
    Hot sauce

1. Lightly coat slow cooker with vegetable oil spray. Microwave onion, garlic, oil, salt, and pepper flakes in bowl, stirring occasionally, until onion is softened, about 5 minutes; transfer to prepared

slow cooker. Stir in collard greens and broth. Nestle ham hock into slow cooker. Cover and cook until collard greens are tender, 9 to 10 hours on low or 6 to 7 hours on high.

2. Transfer ham hock to cutting board, let cool slightly, then shred into bite-size pieces using 2 forks, discarding fat, skin, and bones. Stir ham and vinegar into collard greens. Season with salt, pepper, and extra vinegar to taste. Serve with hot sauce. (Collard greens can be held on warm or low setting for up to 2 hours.)

PER SERVING Cal 200; Total Fat 11g, Sat Fat 3g;
Chol 50mg; Sodium 1020mg; Total Carb 8g, Dietary
Fiber 4g, Total Sugars 2g; Protein 18g

Slow-Cooker Stuffed Eggplant
SERVES 4
COOKING TIME 5 to 6 hours on low or 3 to 4 hours on high

WHY THIS RECIPE WORKS When slow-cooked, eggplants turn rich and creamy, losing the bitterness they have when raw. We like Italian eggplants for stuffing and two of them fit easily in a slow cooker. We adapted the simple Turkish-inspired stuffing of canned diced tomatoes, Pecorino Romano, pine nuts, and aromatics that we had developed for our oven-baked stuffed eggplant. We nestled halved eggplants cut side down in this fragrant stuffing and let them cook until tender. After removing the eggplants from the slow cooker, we gently pushed the soft flesh to the sides to create a cavity, which we filled with the aromatic tomato mixture left behind in the slow cooker. Topped with extra cheese and fresh minced parsley, these eggplants looked beautiful and were far easier to make than many traditional versions. Be sure to buy eggplants that are no more than 10 ounces; larger eggplants will not fit properly in your slow cooker. You may need to trim off the eggplant stems to help them fit. You will need a 5- to 7- quart oval slow cooker for this recipe. This recipe will only work in a traditional slow cooker.

1 onion, chopped fine
2 tablespoons extra-virgin olive oil, divided
3 garlic cloves, minced
2 teaspoons minced fresh oregano or ½ teaspoon dried
¼ teaspoon ground cinnamon
¼ teaspoon table salt
⅛ teaspoon cayenne pepper
1 (14.5-ounce) can diced tomatoes, drained
2 ounces Pecorino Romano cheese, grated (1 cup), divided
¼ cup pine nuts, toasted
1 tablespoon red wine vinegar
2 (10-ounce) Italian eggplants, halved lengthwise
2 tablespoons minced fresh parsley

Slow-Cooker Stuffed Eggplant

1. Microwave onion, 1 tablespoon oil, garlic, oregano, cinnamon, salt, and cayenne in bowl, stirring occasionally, until onion is softened, about 5 minutes; transfer to slow cooker. Stir in tomatoes, ¾ cup Pecorino, pine nuts, and vinegar. Season eggplant halves with salt and pepper and nestle cut side down into slow cooker (eggplants may overlap slightly). Cover and cook until eggplants are tender, 5 to 6 hours on low or 3 to 4 hours on high.

2. Transfer eggplant halves cut side up to serving dish. Using 2 forks, gently push eggplant flesh to sides of each half to make room for filling. Stir remaining 1 tablespoon oil into tomato mixture and season with salt and pepper to taste. Mound tomato mixture evenly into eggplants and sprinkle with parsley and remaining ¼ cup Pecorino. Serve.

PER SERVING Cal 240; **Total Fat** 17g, **Sat Fat** 3.5g; **Chol** 10mg; **Sodium** 530mg; **Total Carb** 17g, **Dietary Fiber** 5g, **Total Sugars** 8g; **Protein** 8g

Slow-Cooker Turkish Eggplant Casserole

SERVES 4 TO 6
COOKING TIME 3 to 4 hours on low or 2 to 3 hours on high

WHY THIS RECIPE WORKS Earthy and versatile, eggplant goes well with traditional Turkish spices, namely, paprika, cumin, cayenne, and cinnamon. We rubbed eggplant with a spice mixture and broiled before adding it to the slow cooker, cooking off extra moisture and keeping the slices firm. We paired it with bulgur, a grain that cooks perfectly in the steamy environment of the slow cooker. An herb-yogurt sauce added richness and tang to this spiced dish. When shopping, don't confuse bulgur with cracked wheat, which has a much longer cooking time and will not work in this recipe. You will need a 5- to 7-quart oval slow cooker for this recipe. This recipe will only work in a traditional slow cooker.

SAUCE

- 1 cup plain yogurt
- ¼ cup chopped fresh parsley
- 2 tablespoons chopped fresh mint
- 1 garlic clove, minced

BULGUR

- 2 teaspoons paprika
- 1½ teaspoons ground cumin
- 1½ teaspoons table salt, divided
- ⅛ teaspoon cayenne pepper
- ⅛ teaspoon ground cinnamon
- 1½ pounds eggplant, sliced into ½-inch-thick rounds
- ¼ cup extra-virgin olive oil, divided
- 1 onion, chopped fine
- 4 garlic cloves, minced
- 1 tablespoon tomato paste
- 1 cup medium-grind bulgur, rinsed
- 1 cup vegetable broth
- 4 tomatoes, cored and sliced ½ inch thick

1. **FOR THE SAUCE** Combine all ingredients in bowl and season with salt and pepper to taste. Refrigerate until ready to serve.

ASSEMBLING EGGPLANT CASSEROLE

After combining bulgur mixture in slow cooker, shingle alternating slices of eggplant and tomato into 3 tightly fitting rows on top. Vegetable rows may overlap slightly.

2. FOR THE BULGUR Adjust oven rack 6 inches from broiler element and heat broiler. Combine paprika, cumin, ¾ teaspoon salt, cayenne, and cinnamon in bowl. Arrange eggplant in single layer on aluminum foil–lined rimmed baking sheet, brush both sides with 3 tablespoons oil, and sprinkle with spice mixture. Broil eggplant until softened and beginning to brown, 10 to 12 minutes, flipping eggplant halfway through broiling.

3. Lightly coat slow cooker with vegetable oil spray. Microwave onion, garlic, tomato paste, remaining ¾ teaspoon salt, and remaining 1 tablespoon oil in bowl, stirring occasionally, until onion is softened, about 5 minutes; transfer to prepared slow cooker. Stir in bulgur and broth. Shingle alternating slices of eggplant and tomato into 3 tightly fitting rows on top of bulgur mixture. Cover and cook until eggplant and bulgur are tender and all broth is absorbed, 3 to 4 hours on low or 2 to 3 hours on high. Serve, passing sauce separately.

PER SERVING Cal 260; **Total Fat** 13g, **Sat Fat** 2.5g; **Chol** 5mg; **Sodium** 760mg; **Total Carb** 34g, **Dietary Fiber** 8g, **Total Sugars** 10g; **Protein** 7g

Slow-Cooker Ratatouille

Slow-Cooker Ratatouille

SERVES 8 TO 10

COOKING TIME 3 to 4 hours on low or 2 to 3 hours on high

WHY THIS RECIPE WORKS This Provençal dish is chock-full of watery vegetables. Since the slow cooker doesn't allow for evaporation, that can lead to runny ratatouille. Draining the tomatoes was a good start, and adding some instant tapioca at the outset helped, too. In the end, tossing the vegetables with olive oil and a little sugar and broiling them before they went into the slow cooker added flavorful browning and also drove off moisture. Garlic and herbes de Provence seasoned the ratatouille, and Parmesan cheese and basil finished it off. If you can't find herbes de Provence, you can use 1 teaspoon each of dried rosemary and dried thyme. You will need a 5- to 7-quart slow cooker for this recipe. This recipe will only work in a traditional slow cooker.

2 pounds eggplant, cut into ½-inch pieces
1½ pounds zucchini, cut into 1-inch pieces
2 red bell peppers, stemmed, seeded, and cut into ½-inch pieces
2 onions, chopped
½ cup extra-virgin olive oil, divided
1 tablespoon sugar
2 garlic cloves, minced
2 teaspoons herbes de Provence
1 (28-ounce) can diced tomatoes, drained
2½ teaspoons table salt
1 teaspoon instant tapioca
1 teaspoon pepper
¼ cup grated Parmesan cheese
¼ cup chopped fresh basil

1. Adjust oven rack 4 inches from broiler element and heat broiler. Line 2 rimmed baking sheets with aluminum foil and spray with vegetable oil spray. Toss eggplant, zucchini, bell peppers, and onions with 6 tablespoons oil, sugar, garlic, and herbes de Provence in large bowl. Divide vegetables evenly between prepared sheets and spread in single layer. Broil, 1 sheet at a time, until vegetables begin to brown, 10 to 12 minutes, rotating sheet halfway through broiling. Transfer vegetables and tomatoes to slow cooker.

2. Stir salt, tapioca, and pepper into vegetables. Cover and cook until vegetables are tender, 3 to 4 hours on low or 2 to 3 hours on high. Stir in Parmesan, basil, and remaining 2 tablespoons oil. Season with salt and pepper to taste. Serve. (Ratatouille can be held on warm or low setting for up to 2 hours; adjust consistency with hot water as needed before serving.)

PER SERVING Cal 180; **Total Fat** 12g, **Sat Fat** 2g; **Chol** 0mg; **Sodium** 790mg; **Total Carb** 16g, **Dietary Fiber** 4g, **Total Sugars** 9g; **Protein** 4g

Slow-Cooker Braised Fennel with Orange-Tarragon Dressing

2 garlic cloves, peeled and smashed
2 sprigs fresh thyme
1 teaspoon juniper berries
½ teaspoon table salt
2 fennel bulbs, stalks discarded, bulbs halved and cut into 1-inch wedges
2 tablespoons extra-virgin olive oil
2 teaspoons grated orange zest plus 1 tablespoon juice
1 teaspoon minced fresh tarragon

1. Combine 1 cup water, garlic, thyme sprigs, juniper berries, and salt in slow cooker. Place fennel wedges cut side down in slow cooker (wedges may overlap). Cover and cook until fennel is tender, 8 to 9 hours on low or 5 to 6 hours on high.

2. Whisk oil, orange zest and juice, and tarragon together in bowl. Season with salt and pepper to taste. Using slotted spoon, transfer fennel to platter, discarding any garlic cloves, thyme sprigs, and juniper berries that stick to it. Drizzle fennel with dressing. Serve.

PER SERVING Cal 70; Total Fat 5g, Sat Fat 0.5g; Chol 0mg; Sodium 230mg; Total Carb 6g, Dietary Fiber 2g, Total Sugars 3g; Protein 1g

Slow-Cooker Braised Fennel with Orange-Tarragon Dressing
SERVES 4 TO 6 VEGAN
COOKING TIME 8 to 9 hours on low or 5 to 6 hours on high

WHY THIS RECIPE WORKS Braising fennel in the slow cooker is a great way to infuse it with deep, savory flavor and give it a melting texture. Cutting the fennel into wedges turned out to be the key to even slow-cooking, and we made sure to braise it long enough to deliver uniformly tender but not mushy results. A combination of water, garlic, thyme, and juniper berries provided the seasoning base for this appealing side dish, and we finished it off with a simple orange-tarragon dressing. Don't core the fennel bulb before cutting it into wedges; the core will help hold the layers of fennel together during cooking. You will need a 5- to 7-quart oval slow cooker for this recipe. This recipe will only work in a traditional slow cooker.

Slow-Cooker Mediterranean Braised Green Beans
SERVES 4 TO 6 VEGAN
COOKING TIME 7 to 8 hours on low or 4 to 5 hours on high

WHY THIS RECIPE WORKS Using the slow cooker to gently braise green beans with the bold flavors of the Mediterranean turned them meltingly tender but not mushy and infused them with big taste. Canned tomatoes made this dish too watery, so we used tomato paste to provide deep flavor and minimize liquid. Onion and garlic, along with oregano, provided an aromatic backbone. For subtle heat, we included a small amount of red pepper flakes. Briny capers, added at the end of cooking, made them stand out among the beans and provided a salty kick. For extra richness, we simply stirred in a second tablespoon of olive oil just before serving. You will need a 5- to 7-quart oval slow cooker for this recipe. This recipe will only work in a traditional slow cooker.

1 onion, halved and sliced thin
2 tablespoons extra-virgin olive oil, divided
3 garlic cloves, sliced thin
2 teaspoons minced fresh oregano or ½ teaspoon dried

Slow-Cooker Mediterranean Braised Green Beans

¾ teaspoon table salt
⅛ teaspoon red pepper flakes
½ cup water
⅓ cup tomato paste
2 pounds green beans, trimmed
2 tablespoons capers, rinsed and minced
1 tablespoon chopped fresh parsley

1. Microwave onion, 1 tablespoon oil, garlic, oregano, salt, and pepper flakes in bowl, stirring occasionally, until onion is softened, about 5 minutes; transfer to slow cooker. Stir in water and tomato paste, then stir in green beans. Cover and cook until green beans are tender, 7 to 8 hours on low or 4 to 5 hours on high.

2. Stir in remaining 1 tablespoon oil, capers, and parsley. Season with salt and pepper to taste. Serve. (Green beans can be held on warm or low setting for up to 2 hours.)

PER SERVING Cal 110; **Total Fat** 5g, **Sat Fat** 1g; **Chol** 0mg; **Sodium** 480mg; **Total Carb** 14g, **Dietary Fiber** 4g, **Total Sugars** 7g; **Protein** 3g

Slow-Cooker Creamy Braised Leeks
SERVES 4 TO 6
COOKING TIME 3 to 4 hours on low or 2 to 3 hours on high

WHY THIS RECIPE WORKS Braising leeks in the slow cooker is a hands-off way to make a tender and creamy side dish to serve with chicken or fish. The slow cooker's relatively low heat and slow cooking time helped to coax out the leeks' delicate flavor. We jump-started them in the microwave, along with garlic and thyme, to build even more complex flavor. A generous amount of cream ensured a rich, velvety texture, while a splash of wine added acidity. Pecorino stirred in at the end of cooking enriched the dish further and provided an even creamier texture. Heavy cream, unlike milk or half-and-half, can be simmered without curdling, so it is essential here. You will need a 5- to 7-quart slow cooker for this recipe. This recipe will only work in a traditional slow cooker.

3 pounds leeks, white and light green parts only, halved lengthwise, sliced thin, washed thoroughly, and drained
1 tablespoon vegetable oil
2 garlic cloves, minced
2 teaspoons minced fresh thyme or ½ teaspoon dried
1 teaspoon table salt
¼ teaspoon pepper
1 cup heavy cream
½ cup dry white wine
¼ cup grated Pecorino Romano cheese

1. Microwave leeks, oil, garlic, thyme, salt, and pepper in bowl, stirring occasionally, until leeks are softened, 8 to 10 minutes; transfer to slow cooker. Stir in cream and wine, cover, and cook until leeks are tender but not mushy, 3 to 4 hours on low or 2 to 3 hours on high.

2. Stir Pecorino into leek mixture and season with salt and pepper to taste. Let sit for 5 minutes, until slightly thickened. Serve. (Leeks can be held on warm or low setting for up to 2 hours; adjust consistency with hot water as needed before serving.)

PER SERVING Cal 240; **Total Fat** 18g, **Sat Fat** 10g; **Chol** 45mg; **Sodium** 450mg; **Total Carb** 16g, **Dietary Fiber** 2g, **Total Sugars** 5g; **Protein** 3g

Slow-Cooker Classic Mashed Potatoes

Slow-Cooker Classic Mashed Potatoes

SERVES 10 TO 12

COOKING TIME 5 to 6 hours on low or 3 to 4 hours on high

WHY THIS RECIPE WORKS For perfectly moist, fluffy, and smooth mashed potatoes in the slow cooker, we used a small amount of water and a parchment shield to create a moist, steamy environment. Thinly sliced potatoes cooked more evenly than chunks, and boiling the water first jump-started the cooking process. We brushed the top layer of potatoes with melted butter to help prevent discoloration, and mashed in the rest of the butter about 4 hours later, when the potatoes were tender. (The top layer of potatoes may discolor slightly, but this won't be noticeable upon mashing.) We mashed the potatoes right in the cooking liquid, rather than draining them. Along with the added butter and some sour cream, the cooking liquid easily created a nice smooth texture when incorporated. For an accurate measurement of boiling water, bring a full kettle of water to a boil and then measure out the desired amount. For more information on creating a parchment shield, see page 401. You will need a 5- to 7-quart slow cooker for this recipe. This recipe will only work in a traditional slow cooker.

5 pounds russet potatoes, peeled and sliced ¼ inch thick
2¾ cups boiling water, plus extra as needed
2 teaspoons table salt
12 tablespoons unsalted butter, melted, divided
½ cup sour cream
3 tablespoons minced fresh chives

1. Combine potatoes, boiling water, and salt in slow cooker. Brush top layer with 3 tablespoons melted butter. Press 16 by 12-inch sheet of parchment paper firmly onto potatoes, folding down edges as needed. Cover and cook until potatoes are tender and paring knife can be slipped in and out of them with no resistance, 5 to 6 hours on low or 3 to 4 hours on high.

2. Discard parchment. Mash potatoes with potato masher until smooth. Stir in sour cream, chives, and remaining 9 tablespoons melted butter until combined. Season with salt and pepper to taste. Serve.

PER SERVING Cal 240; **Total Fat** 13g, **Sat Fat** 8g; **Chol** 35mg; **Sodium** 400mg; **Total Carb** 29g, **Dietary Fiber** 2g, **Total Sugars** 1g; **Protein** 4g

VARIATIONS

Slow-Cooker Garlic and Parmesan Mashed Potatoes
Omit sour cream and chives. Add 8 peeled and smashed garlic cloves to slow cooker along with potatoes. After mashing potatoes, stir in 1½ cups grated Parmesan along with remaining butter.

Slow-Cooker Loaded Mashed Potatoes
Omit chives. Add 3 peeled and smashed garlic cloves to slow cooker along with potatoes. While potatoes are cooking, line plate with double layer of coffee filters, spread 6 chopped slices bacon in even layer, and microwave until crispy, about 5 minutes. After mashing potatoes, stir in bacon, 2 cups shredded cheddar, and 3 thinly sliced scallions along with sour cream and remaining butter.

Slow-Cooker Olive Oil–Rosemary Mashed Potatoes
Omit sour cream and chives. Substitute 10 tablespoons extra-virgin olive oil for butter, brushing top layer of potatoes with 2 tablespoons oil. After mashing potatoes, stir in 1 teaspoon minced fresh rosemary, ½ teaspoon grated lemon zest, 1 tablespoon lemon juice, and remaining ½ cup oil.

Slow-Cooker Mashed Potatoes and Root Vegetables
Reduce russet potatoes to 3 pounds. Add 1 pound peeled parsnips, sliced ¼ inch thick, and 14 ounces peeled celery root, quartered and sliced ¼ inch thick, to slow cooker along with potatoes.

Slow-Cooker Buttermilk Smashed Red Potatoes

Slow-Cooker Buttermilk Smashed Red Potatoes

SERVES 4 TO 6
COOKING TIME 5 to 6 hours on low or 3 to 4 hours on high

WHY THIS RECIPE WORKS Rustic smashed potatoes make a satisfying side dish. We found that low-starch red potatoes were the best choice, as their compact structure held up well under mashing, and their red skins provided nice color. For the best texture, we halved the potatoes; cooked them with olive oil, garlic, and thyme; and smashed them. A combination of buttermilk and sour cream gave our potatoes a creamy consistency. Look for small red potatoes measuring 1 to 2 inches in diameter. You will need a 4- to 7-quart slow cooker for this recipe. This recipe can easily be doubled in a 7-quart slow cooker; you will need to increase the cooking time range by 1 hour. This recipe will only work in a traditional slow cooker.

- 2 pounds small red potatoes, unpeeled, halved
- 3 tablespoons extra-virgin olive oil
- 3 garlic cloves, peeled and smashed
- 2 teaspoons minced fresh thyme or ½ teaspoon dried
- 1 teaspoon table salt
- ¼ teaspoon pepper
- ⅔ cup buttermilk
- ¼ cup sour cream
- 2 tablespoons minced fresh chives

1. Combine potatoes, oil, garlic, thyme, salt, and pepper in slow cooker. Cover and cook until potatoes are tender, 5 to 6 hours on low or 3 to 4 hours on high.

2. Add buttermilk and sour cream to potatoes and, using potato masher, mash until combined and chunks of potatoes remain. Fold in chives and season with salt and pepper to taste. Serve. (Potatoes can be held on warm or low setting for up to 2 hours; adjust consistency with hot water as needed before serving.)

PER SERVING Cal 200; **Total Fat** 8g; **Sat Fat** 1g; **Chol** 5mg; **Sodium** 450mg; **Total Carb** 26g, **Dietary Fiber** 3g, **Total Sugars** 3g; **Protein** 4g

Slow-Cooker Red Potatoes with Rosemary and Garlic

SERVES 4 TO 6 **VEGAN**
COOKING TIME 5 to 6 hours on low or 3 to 4 hours on high

WHY THIS RECIPE WORKS Creamy red potatoes are a simple side that goes well with any entrée. Since they were small, the potatoes cooked through evenly. We simply tossed them with olive oil and minced garlic for richness and flavor and rosemary added woodsy notes. Look for small red potatoes measuring 1 to 2 inches in diameter. You will need a 4- to 7-quart slow cooker for this recipe. This recipe can easily be doubled in a 7-quart slow cooker; you will need to increase the cooking time range by 1 hour. This recipe will only work in a traditional slow cooker.

- 2 pounds small red potatoes, unpeeled
- 2 tablespoons extra-virgin olive oil, divided
- 3 garlic cloves, minced
- ½ teaspoon table salt
- ¼ teaspoon pepper
- 1 teaspoon minced fresh rosemary

1. Combine potatoes, 1 tablespoon oil, garlic, salt, and pepper in slow cooker. Cover and cook until potatoes are tender, 5 to 6 hours on low or 3 to 4 hours on high.

2. Stir in rosemary and remaining 1 tablespoon oil. Season with salt and pepper to taste. Serve. (Potatoes can be held on warm or low setting for up to 2 hours.)

PER SERVING Cal 150; **Total Fat** 5g; **Sat Fat** 0.5g; **Chol** 0mg; **Sodium** 220mg; **Total Carb** 25g, **Dietary Fiber** 3g, **Total Sugars** 2g; **Protein** 3g

Slow-Cooker Lemon-Herb Fingerling Potatoes

2 pounds fingerling potatoes, unpeeled
2 tablespoons extra-virgin olive oil, divided
2 scallions, white parts minced, green parts sliced thin
3 garlic cloves, minced
1 teaspoon table salt
¼ teaspoon pepper
1 tablespoon chopped fresh parsley
1 teaspoon grated lemon zest plus 1 tablespoon juice

1. Combine potatoes, 1 tablespoon oil, scallion whites, garlic, salt, and pepper in slow cooker. Cover and cook until potatoes are tender, 5 to 6 hours on low or 3 to 4 hours on high.

2. Stir in parsley, lemon zest and juice, scallion greens, and remaining 1 tablespoon oil. Season with salt and pepper to taste. Serve.

PER SERVING Cal 160; Total Fat 4.5g, Sat Fat 0.5g; Chol 0mg; Sodium 400mg; Total Carb 28g, Dietary Fiber 4g, Total Sugars 1g; Protein 3g

Slow-Cooker Mashed Sweet Potatoes
SERVES 6 TO 8
COOKING TIME 5 to 6 hours on low or 3 to 4 hours on high

WHY THIS RECIPE WORKS The deep natural sweetness of the humble sweet potato tastes far better when prepared with a minimum of ingredients. This slow-cooker mashed version is smooth and velvety, with a buttery finish. Pressing a piece of parchment on top of the potatoes resulted in even cooking, without any dry edges. For more information on creating a parchment shield, see page 401. For an accurate measurement of boiling water, bring a full kettle of water to a boil and then measure out the desired amount. You will need a 5- to 7-quart slow cooker for this recipe. This recipe can easily be doubled in a 7-quart slow cooker; you will need to increase the cooking time range by 1 hour. This recipe will only work in a traditional slow cooker.

3 pounds sweet potatoes, peeled and sliced ¼ inch thick
½ cup boiling water, plus extra as needed
1 teaspoon sugar
¾ teaspoon table salt
6 tablespoons half-and-half, warmed
3 tablespoons unsalted butter, melted

Slow-Cooker Lemon-Herb Fingerling Potatoes
SERVES 4 TO 6 VEGAN
COOKING TIME 5 to 6 hours on low or 3 to 4 hours on high

WHY THIS RECIPE WORKS Cooking small whole potatoes in the slow cooker requires no prep work, frees up your stove, and turns out perfectly tender little spuds. For this supereasy and attractive side dish, we turned to fingerlings. We could put them into the slow cooker without any liquid whatsoever, and they retained their delicate sweetness without a hint of mushiness. To enhance their flavor, we added some olive oil, garlic, and scallions. Unlike with some other slow-cooker potato dishes, they cooked through properly without our having to cover them first with a sheet of parchment paper. Look for fingerling potatoes about 3 inches long and 1 inch in diameter. You will need a 5- to 7-quart slow cooker for this recipe. This recipe can easily be doubled in a 7-quart slow cooker, but you will need to increase the cooking time range by 1 hour. This recipe will only work in a traditional slow cooker.

1. Combine potatoes, boiling water, sugar, and salt in slow cooker. Press 16 by 12-inch sheet of parchment paper firmly onto potatoes, folding down edges as needed. Cover and cook until potatoes are tender, 5 to 6 hours on low or 3 to 4 hours on high.

2. Discard parchment. Mash potatoes with potato masher until smooth. Stir in warm half-and-half and melted butter and season with salt and pepper to taste. Serve. (Sweet potatoes can be held on warm or low setting for up to 2 hours; adjust consistency with extra hot water as needed before serving.)

PER SERVING Cal 160; **Total Fat** 5g, **Sat Fat** 3.5g; **Chol** 15mg; **Sodium** 300mg; **Total Carb** 27g, **Dietary Fiber** 4g, **Total Sugars** 9g; **Protein** 3g

Slow-Cooker Maple-Orange Glazed Acorn Squash

SERVES 4 TO 6 `VEGAN`

COOKING TIME 3 to 4 hours on low or 2 to 3 hours on high

WHY THIS RECIPE WORKS A quintessential fall vegetable, acorn squash takes forever to roast and often emerges dry and a bit grainy. In the slow cooker, however, it turns tender easily without overcooking or drying out. And as an added bonus, you can perfume it with warm spices as it cooks. Here we created a cooking base made up of water, orange juice, cloves, and cinnamon and placed the squash cut side down in this flavorful mixture. And since we think a glaze greatly enhances acorn squash, we made a quick one in the microwave by combining maple syrup with coriander, cayenne pepper, and orange zest; toasted hazelnuts provided great crunch and flavor. You will need a 5-to 7-quart oval slow cooker for this recipe. This recipe will only work in a traditional slow cooker.

- 2 teaspoons grated orange zest plus ½ cup juice
- 5 whole cloves
- 1 cinnamon stick
- 2 small acorn squashes (1 pound each), quartered pole to pole and seeded
- 1 teaspoon table salt
- ½ teaspoon pepper
- ¼ cup maple syrup
- ⅛ teaspoon ground coriander
  Pinch cayenne pepper
- ¼ cup hazelnuts, toasted, skinned, and chopped
- 1 tablespoon chopped fresh parsley

Slow-Cooker Maple-Orange Glazed Acorn Squash

1. Combine 1 cup water, orange juice, cloves, and cinnamon stick in slow cooker. Season squashes with salt and pepper and shingle cut side down in slow cooker. Cover and cook until squashes are tender, 3 to 4 hours on low or 2 to 3 hours on high.

2. Using tongs, transfer squashes to serving dish, brushing away any cloves that stick to them. Microwave maple syrup, coriander, cayenne, and orange zest in bowl until heated through, about 1 minute. Season glaze with salt and pepper to taste. Drizzle glaze over squashes and sprinkle with hazelnuts and parsley. Serve.

PER SERVING Cal 200; **Total Fat** 4.5g, **Sat Fat** 0g; **Chol** 0mg; **Sodium** 590mg; **Total Carb** 42g, **Dietary Fiber** 4g, **Total Sugars** 20g; **Protein** 3g

Slow-Cooker Butternut Squash Puree

SERVES 6 TO 8

COOKING TIME 5 to 6 hours on low or 3 to 4 hours on high

WHY THIS RECIPE WORKS Having a foolproof slow-cooker method for squash can be a lifesaver, especially at holiday time. Since the flavor of butternut squash is delicate, our goal was to bump it up so it would taste great even after hours in the slow cooker. First we tried cooking the squash in water to cover, but this left us with a bland, watery puree. Since the squash exuded a lot of moisture during cooking, we thought we could reduce the amount of water dramatically. In the end, it took only a bare minimum—½ cup—to properly braise the squash, but even this small amount of water seemed to be diluting the squash flavor significantly. We considered alternative braising liquids and settled on apple cider, which accented the squash's inherent sweetness and added a brightness that tasters loved. A small amount of heavy cream and some butter lent richness to round out the flavors. For more information on creating a parchment shield, see page 401. This recipe can easily be doubled in a 7-quart slow cooker; you will need to increase the cooking time range by 1 hour. This recipe will only work in a traditional slow cooker.

- 3 pounds butternut squash, peeled, seeded, and cut into 1-inch pieces (8 cups)
- ½ cup apple cider, plus extra as needed
- ½ teaspoon table salt
- 4 tablespoons unsalted butter, melted
- 2 tablespoons heavy cream, warmed
- 2 tablespoons packed brown sugar, plus extra for seasoning

1. Combine squash, cider, and salt in slow cooker. Press 16 by 12-inch sheet of parchment paper firmly onto squash, folding down edges as needed. Cover and cook until squash is tender, 5 to 6 hours on low or 3 to 4 hours on high.

2. Discard parchment. Using potato masher, mash squash until smooth. Stir in melted butter, cream, and sugar. Season with salt, pepper, and extra sugar to taste. Serve. (Squash can be held on warm or low setting for up to 2 hours. Adjust consistency with extra hot cider as needed before serving.)

PER SERVING Cal 150; **Total Fat** 7g, **Sat Fat** 4.5g; **Chol** 20mg; **Sodium** 150mg; **Total Carb** 22g, **Dietary Fiber** 3g, **Total Sugars** 8g; **Protein** 2g

Slow-Cooker Braised Butternut Squash with Pecans and Cranberries

Slow-Cooker Braised Butternut Squash with Pecans and Cranberries

SERVES 4 TO 6 VEGAN

COOKING TIME 4 to 5 hours on low or 3 to 4 hours on high

WHY THIS RECIPE WORKS Cooking this popular winter squash in a slow cooker makes for a wonderful everyday vegetable, but slow-cooked butternut squash is also a great contribution to the holiday dinner table. We found that a small amount of liquid in the bottom of the slow cooker, plus a couple of aromatics, was all it took to deeply flavor and perfectly steam butternut squash. Pecans and dried cranberries dressed up the squash, and a quick vinaigrette tied the elements of this vegetable side together. You will need a 5-to 7-quart oval slow cooker for this recipe. This recipe will only work in a traditional slow cooker.

- 1 cup vegetable or chicken broth
- 2 garlic cloves, peeled and smashed
- 2 sprigs fresh thyme
- ¼ teaspoon table salt
- 2 pounds butternut squash, peeled, halved lengthwise, seeded, and sliced 1 inch thick
- 2 tablespoons extra-virgin olive oil

1 teaspoon grated lemon zest plus 2 teaspoons juice

¼ cup pecans, toasted and chopped

¼ cup dried cranberries

1 tablespoon minced fresh parsley

1. Combine broth, garlic, thyme sprigs, and salt in slow cooker and nestle squash in. Cover and cook until squash is tender, 4 to 5 hours on low or 3 to 4 hours on high.

2. Using slotted spoon, transfer squash to serving dish, brushing away any garlic cloves or thyme sprigs that stick to squash. Whisk oil, lemon zest, and lemon juice together in bowl. Season with salt and pepper to taste. Drizzle squash with dressing and sprinkle with pecans, cranberries, and parsley. Serve.

PER SERVING Cal 150; **Total Fat** 8g, **Sat Fat** 1g; **Chol** 0mg; **Sodium** 230mg; **Total Carb** 22g, **Dietary Fiber** 3g, **Total Sugars** 8g; **Protein** 2g

Slow-Cooker Butternut Squash Risotto

SERVES 6 TO 8

COOKING TIME 2 to 3 hours on high

WHY THIS RECIPE WORKS Risotto usually demands a cook's attention, which is why our no-fuss slow-cooker version is so appealing. We microwaved garlic and onion, then stirred in white wine, allowing the grains to absorb the liquid. Since adding all the broth at once led to blown-out grains, we stirred in 2 cups of hot broth at the outset and gently stirred in more at the end for an ultracreamy texture. Butternut squash offered sweetness and color, and butter, Parmesan, and sage ramped up the rich taste of our risotto. Arborio rice, which is high in starch, gives risotto its characteristic creaminess; do not substitute other types of rice here. For more information on creating a parchment shield, see page 401. You will need a 4- to 7-quart oval slow cooker for this recipe. This recipe will only work in a traditional slow cooker.

1 onion, chopped fine

4 tablespoons unsalted butter, divided

3 garlic cloves, minced

½ teaspoon table salt

5 cups vegetable or chicken broth, divided, plus extra as needed

½ cup dry white wine

1 pound butternut squash, peeled, seeded, and cut into ½-inch pieces (3 cups)

2 cups Arborio rice

2 ounces Parmesan cheese, grated (1 cup)

1 tablespoon minced fresh sage

1 teaspoon lemon juice

Slow-Cooker Butternut Squash Risotto

1. Lightly coat slow cooker with vegetable oil spray. Microwave onion, 2 tablespoons butter, garlic, and salt in bowl, stirring occasionally, until onion is softened, about 5 minutes; transfer to prepared slow cooker.

2. Microwave 2 cups broth and wine in 4-cup liquid measuring cup until steaming, about 5 minutes. Stir broth mixture, squash, and rice into slow cooker. Gently press 16 by 12-inch sheet of parchment paper onto surface of broth mixture, folding down edges as needed. Cover and cook until rice is almost fully tender and all liquid is absorbed, 2 to 3 hours on high.

3. Microwave remaining 3 cups broth in now-empty measuring cup until steaming, about 5 minutes. Discard parchment. Slowly stream broth into rice, stirring gently, until liquid is absorbed and risotto is creamy, about 1 minute. Gently stir in remaining 2 tablespoons butter, Parmesan, sage, and lemon juice until combined. Adjust consistency with extra hot broth as needed. Season with salt and pepper to taste. Serve.

PER SERVING Cal 290; **Total Fat** 9g, **Sat Fat** 4.5g; **Chol** 20mg; **Sodium** 740mg; **Total Carb** 45g, **Dietary Fiber** 2g, **Total Sugars** 2g; **Protein** 9g

Slow-Cooker Brown Rice with Parmesan and Herbs

SERVES 6

COOKING TIME 2 to 3 hours on high

WHY THIS RECIPE WORKS It's true that brown rice takes longer than white rice to cook, and that it can be trickier to cook evenly. We wondered if the steady, gentle heat of the slow cooker would take the challenge out of cooking brown rice. After experiments that resulted in some burnt rice and some undercooked grains, we learned that while brown rice needs a head start with boiling water in the slow cooker, it can indeed emerge with light and fluffy grains every time. Cooking on high was best, and we laid a piece of parchment paper over the rice to protect the grains on top from drying out as the water was absorbed. For more information on creating a parchment shield, see page 401. For an accurate measurement of boiling water, bring a full kettle of water to a boil and then measure out the desired amount. You will need a 5- to 7-quart oval slow cooker for this recipe. This recipe will only work in a traditional slow cooker.

- 3 cups boiling water
- 2 cups long-grain brown rice, rinsed
- 1 tablespoon unsalted butter
- ½ teaspoon table salt
- ½ teaspoon pepper
- 2 ounces Parmesan cheese, grated (1 cup)
- ½ cup chopped fresh basil, dill, or parsley
- 2 teaspoons lemon juice

1. Lightly coat slow cooker with vegetable oil spray. Combine boiling water, rice, butter, salt, and pepper in prepared slow cooker. Gently press 16 by 12-inch sheet of parchment paper onto surface of water, folding down edges as needed. Cover and cook until rice is tender and all water is absorbed, 2 to 3 hours on high.

2. Discard parchment. Fluff rice with fork, then gently fold in Parmesan, basil, and lemon juice. Season with salt and pepper to taste. Serve.

PER SERVING Cal 290; **Total Fat** 7g, **Sat Fat** 3g; **Chol** 10mg; **Sodium** 370mg; **Total Carb** 47g, **Dietary Fiber** 2g, **Total Sugars** 0g; **Protein** 9g

Slow-Cooker Mexican Rice

SERVES 6   VEGAN

COOKING TIME 2 to 3 hours on high

WHY THIS RECIPE WORKS This easy variation on plain white rice is the perfect accompaniment to enchiladas and tacos, as well as to many simply prepared meat and fish dishes. Cumin, tomato paste, and minced garlic infused the rice with flavor as it cooked, while a few ingredients stirred in before serving—cilantro, scallions, and lime juice—provided bright, zesty flavor. As with our other rice dishes, we found that long-grain white rice cooked best on high, and we laid a piece of parchment paper over the mixture to prevent the grains on top from drying out as the water was absorbed. Basmati rice can be substituted for the long-grain white rice. For more information on creating a parchment shield, see page 401. You will need a 5- to 7-quart oval slow cooker for this recipe. This recipe will only work in a traditional slow cooker.

- 1 onion, chopped fine
- 2 jalapeño chiles, stemmed, seeded, and minced
- 3 tablespoons tomato paste
- 2 tablespoons extra-virgin olive oil
- 4 garlic cloves, minced
- ½ teaspoon ground cumin
- ½ teaspoon table salt
- 3 cups vegetable or chicken broth
- 2 cups long-grain white rice, rinsed
- ¼ cup chopped fresh cilantro
- 2 scallions, sliced thin
- 1 tablespoon lime juice

1. Lightly coat slow cooker with vegetable oil spray. Microwave onion, jalapeños, tomato paste, oil, garlic, cumin, and salt in bowl, stirring occasionally, until vegetables are softened, about 5 minutes; transfer to prepared slow cooker.

2. Microwave broth in bowl until steaming, about 5 minutes. Stir broth and rice into slow cooker. Gently press 16 by 12-inch sheet of parchment paper onto surface of broth, folding down edges as needed. Cover and cook until rice is tender and all broth is absorbed, 2 to 3 hours on high.

3. Discard parchment. Fluff rice with fork, then gently fold in cilantro, scallions, and lime juice. Season with salt and pepper to taste. Serve.

PER SERVING Cal 280; **Total Fat** 5g, **Sat Fat** 0.5g; **Chol** 0mg; **Sodium** 600mg; **Total Carb** 53g, **Dietary Fiber** 1g, **Total Sugars** 2g; **Protein** 5g

Slow-Cooker Mushroom Biryani

Slow-Cooker Mushroom Biryani

SERVES 4 TO 6

COOKING TIME 2 to 3 hours on high

WHY THIS RECIPE WORKS Biryani uses fragrant long-grain basmati rice, enriching it with fresh herbs and pungent spices. Most recipes steep whole spices and cook each part of the dish separately before marrying them. Our streamlined, hands-free slow cooker version delivers on big, bold flavors without the fuss. We chose basmati rice for its nutty flavor and perfume-like aroma. Indian-inspired aromatics were first bloomed with oil in the microwave to jump-start flavor development. We then combined the bloomed spice blend, rice, and hot vegetable broth in our slow cooker before topping the rice with earthy mushrooms. Layering the mushrooms on top of the rice mixture ensured even cooking of the rice. We found that basmati rice cooked best on high. Placing a piece of parchment paper over the mixture prevented the grains on top from drying out as the water was absorbed and promoted even steaming in the rice. We added fresh spinach, herbs, and raisins before serving. Biryani is traditionally served with a cooling yogurt sauce; make it before starting the biryani to allow the flavors to meld. We prefer the flavor of basmati rice in this recipe, but long-grain white rice can be substituted. For more information on creating a parchment shield, see page 401. You will need a 5- to 7-quart oval slow cooker for this recipe. This recipe will only work in a traditional slow cooker.

SAUCE

- ¾ cup plain yogurt
- 2 tablespoons chopped fresh cilantro
- 2 tablespoons chopped fresh mint
- 1 garlic clove, minced

BIRYANI

- 1 onion, chopped fine
- 3 tablespoons extra-virgin olive oil
- 4 garlic cloves, minced
- 2 teaspoons garam masala
- 1 teaspoon table salt
- ½ teaspoon turmeric
- ⅛ teaspoon cayenne pepper
- 1½ cups vegetable broth
- 1½ cups basmati rice, rinsed
- 1 pound cremini mushrooms, trimmed and sliced thin
- 6 ounces (6 cups) baby spinach, chopped coarse
- ¼ cup raisins
- 2 tablespoons chopped fresh cilantro
- 2 tablespoons chopped fresh mint
- ⅓ cup sliced almonds, toasted

1. FOR THE SAUCE Combine all ingredients in bowl and season with salt and pepper to taste. Refrigerate until ready to serve.

2. FOR THE BIRYANI Lightly coat slow cooker with vegetable oil spray. Microwave onion, oil, garlic, garam masala, salt, turmeric, and cayenne in bowl, stirring occasionally, until onion is softened, about 5 minutes; transfer to prepared slow cooker.

3. Microwave broth in bowl until steaming, about 5 minutes. Stir broth and rice into slow cooker. Spread mushrooms evenly on top of rice mixture. Gently press 16 by 12-inch sheet of parchment paper onto surface of mushrooms, folding down edges as needed. Cover and cook until rice is tender and all broth is absorbed, 2 to 3 hours on high.

4. Discard parchment. Sprinkle spinach and raisins on top of rice, cover, and let sit until spinach is wilted, about 5 minutes. Add cilantro and mint and fluff rice with fork until combined. Season with salt and pepper to taste. Sprinkle with almonds and serve, passing sauce separately.

PER SERVING Cal 320; **Total Fat** 11g, **Sat Fat** 2g; **Chol** 5mg; **Sodium** 620mg; **Total Carb** 48g, **Dietary Fiber** 2g, **Total Sugars** 10g; **Protein** 8g

Slow-Cooker Herbed Barley Pilaf

Slow-Cooker Herbed Barley Pilaf

SERVES 6 VEGAN

COOKING TIME 3 to 4 hours on low or 2 to 3 hours on high

WHY THIS RECIPE WORKS For an everyday barley pilaf, we needed to find the right liquid-to-barley ratio for the slow cooker. After a few tests, we found that 3½ cups broth to 1½ cups barley produced grain that was cooked through once all the broth had been absorbed, though the texture was on the soft side. Reducing the amount of liquid wasn't an option because it resulted in unevenly cooked barley. To maintain a bit of the grain's firm structure and ensure even cooking, we briefly toasted the barley in the microwave before adding it to the slow cooker. All this pilaf needed were some fresh herbs before serving. Do not substitute hulled, hull-less, quick-cooking, or presteamed barley (read the ingredient list on the package to determine this) in this recipe. You will need a 4- to 7-quart slow cooker for this recipe. This recipe will only work in a traditional slow cooker.

  1 onion, chopped fine
1½ cups pearl barley, rinsed
  2 tablespoons extra-virgin olive oil, divided
  2 garlic cloves, minced
  1 teaspoon minced fresh thyme or ¼ teaspoon dried
  ½ teaspoon table salt
3½ cups vegetable or chicken broth
  ¼ cup chopped fresh basil, dill, or parsley

1. Lightly coat slow cooker with vegetable oil spray. Microwave onion, barley, 1 tablespoon oil, garlic, thyme, and salt in bowl, stirring occasionally, until onion is softened and barley is lightly toasted, about 5 minutes; transfer to prepared slow cooker. Stir in broth, cover, and cook until barley is tender and all broth is absorbed, 3 to 4 hours on low or 2 to 3 hours on high.

2. Fluff barley with fork, then gently fold in basil and remaining 1 tablespoon oil. Season with salt and pepper to taste. Serve.

PER SERVING Cal 240; **Total Fat** 6g, **Sat Fat** 0.5g; **Chol** 0mg; **Sodium** 630mg; **Total Carb** 43g, **Dietary Fiber** 9g, **Total Sugars** 2g; **Protein** 5g

Slow-Cooker Creamy Farro with Mushrooms and Thyme

SERVES 4 TO 6

COOKING TIME 3 to 4 hours on low or 2 to 3 hours on high

WHY THIS RECIPE WORKS The nutty, mild flavor of farro lends itself to almost any culinary direction. We decided on a simple Italian profile. We started by softening aromatics—shallots, porcini, garlic, and thyme—in the microwave. Cremini mushrooms lent the dish meatiness, and sherry was a natural complement and added complexity. Once our farro was tender, we stirred in just enough Parmesan to create a luxurious, creamy texture without overwhelming our well-balanced dish. Finishing with fresh parsley added brightness and freshness that balanced the hearty, savory flavors. Do not use quick-cooking or presteamed farro (the ingredient list on the package will specify the type) in this recipe. You will need a 4- to 7-quart slow cooker for this recipe. This recipe will only work in a traditional slow cooker.

  2 shallots, minced
  ½ ounce dried porcini mushrooms, rinsed and minced
  2 tablespoons extra-virgin olive oil, divided
  3 garlic cloves, minced
  2 teaspoons minced fresh thyme or ½ teaspoon dried
  ½ teaspoon table salt
  ½ teaspoon pepper
2½ cups vegetable or chicken broth, divided, plus extra as needed
  ¼ cup dry sherry

Slow-Cooker Creamy Farro with Mushrooms and Thyme

Slow-Cooker Creamy Orzo with Parmesan and Peas

SERVES 4 TO 6
COOKING TIME 1 to 2 hours on high

WHY THIS RECIPE WORKS For a side dish of tender—not mushy—orzo, we toasted our pasta in butter in the microwave before moving it to the slow cooker, and then added hot broth to jump-start its cooking. Adding grated Parmesan and a couple more pats of butter after cooking gave us a rich-tasting dish with a creamy texture. Stirring frozen peas in at the end of cooking ensured that they stayed bright and fresh-tasting. You will need a 4-to 7-quart oval slow cooker for this recipe. This recipe will only work in a traditional slow cooker.

- 1 cup orzo
- 1 onion, chopped fine
- 6 garlic cloves, minced
- 3 tablespoons unsalted butter, divided
- ½ teaspoon table salt
- 2½ cups vegetable or chicken broth, divided, plus extra as needed
- ¼ cup dry white wine
- 1 cup frozen peas, thawed
- 2 ounces Parmesan cheese, grated (1 cup)
- 1½ teaspoons grated lemon zest

1. Microwave orzo, onion, garlic, 1 tablespoon butter, and salt in bowl, stirring occasionally, until orzo is lightly toasted and onion is softened, 5 to 7 minutes; transfer to slow cooker.

2. Microwave 2 cups broth and wine in bowl until steaming, about 5 minutes. Stir broth mixture into slow cooker, cover, and cook until orzo is al dente, 1 to 2 hours on high.

3. Sprinkle peas over orzo, cover, and let sit until heated through, about 5 minutes. Microwave remaining ½ cup broth in bowl until steaming, about 2 minutes. Stir broth, Parmesan, lemon zest, and remaining 2 tablespoons butter into orzo until mixture is creamy. Adjust consistency with extra hot broth as needed. Season with salt and pepper to taste. Serve.

PER SERVING Cal 240; **Total Fat** 9g, **Sat Fat** 5g; **Chol** 20mg; **Sodium** 680mg; **Total Carb** 28g, **Dietary Fiber** 1g, **Total Sugars** 3g; **Protein** 10g

- 8 ounces cremini mushrooms, trimmed and sliced thin
- 1 cup whole farro
- 1 ounce Parmesan cheese, grated (½ cup)
- 2 tablespoons chopped fresh parsley

1. Lightly coat slow cooker with vegetable oil spray. Microwave shallots, porcini mushrooms, 1 tablespoon oil, garlic, thyme, salt, and pepper in bowl, stirring occasionally, until shallots are softened, about 5 minutes; transfer to prepared slow cooker.

2. Microwave 2 cups broth and sherry in bowl until steaming, about 5 minutes. Stir broth mixture, cremini mushrooms, and farro into slow cooker. Cover and cook until farro is tender, 3 to 4 hours on low or 2 to 3 hours on high.

3. Microwave remaining ½ cup broth in bowl until steaming, about 2 minutes. Stir broth and Parmesan into farro until mixture is creamy. Adjust consistency with extra hot broth as needed. Stir in parsley and remaining 1 tablespoon oil. Season with salt and pepper to taste. Serve.

PER SERVING Cal 220; **Total Fat** 8g, **Sat Fat** 1.5g; **Chol** 5mg; **Sodium** 600mg; **Total Carb** 30g, **Dietary Fiber** 1g, **Total Sugars** 3g; **Protein** 8g

Slow-Cooker Creamy Parmesan Polenta

SERVES 6

COOKING TIME 3 to 4 hours on low or 2 to 3 hours on high

WHY THIS RECIPE WORKS Many polenta recipes deliver rich creaminess by piling on hefty amounts of cheese and butter. Not wanting to sacrifice creaminess or texture, we focused on getting the polenta perfectly tender. Remarkably, thanks to the gentle heat of the slow cooker, our typical ratio of liquid to polenta worked just fine. Instead of using only water and stirring in lots of butter at the end, we added 1 cup of whole milk up front. This helped to deliver the same rich, creamy texture but with substantially less fat and calories. We finished the dish by steeping a sprig of rosemary in the polenta to infuse herbal flavor without adding bits of herbs that would disturb its smooth texture. Just a cup of nutty Parmesan and 2 tablespoons of butter stirred in at the end gave the polenta richness and flavor while keeping the dish light. Coarse-ground degerminated cornmeal such as yellow grits (with uniform grains the size of couscous) works best in this recipe. Avoid instant or quick-cooking products, as well as whole-grain, stone-ground, and regular cornmeal. You will need a 4- to 7-quart slow cooker for this recipe. This recipe will only work in a traditional slow cooker.

- 3 cups water, plus extra as needed
- 1 cup whole milk
- 1 cup coarse-ground cornmeal
- 2 garlic cloves, minced
- 1 teaspoon table salt
- 1 sprig fresh rosemary (optional)
- 2 ounces Parmesan cheese, grated (1 cup)
- 2 tablespoons unsalted butter

1. Lightly coat slow cooker with vegetable oil spray. Whisk water, milk, cornmeal, garlic, and salt together in prepared slow cooker. Cover and cook until polenta is tender, 3 to 4 hours on low or 2 to 3 hours on high.

2. Nestle rosemary sprig into polenta, if using, cover, and let steep for 10 minutes; discard rosemary sprig. Whisk Parmesan and butter into polenta until combined. Season with salt and pepper to taste. Serve. (Polenta can be held on warm or low setting for up to 2 hours; adjust consistency with extra hot water as needed before serving.)

PER SERVING Cal 160; **Total Fat** 8g, **Sat Fat** 4.5g; **Chol** 20mg; **Sodium** 580mg; **Total Carb** 16g, **Dietary Fiber** 2g, **Total Sugars** 2g; **Protein** 7g

Slow-Cooker No-Fuss Quinoa with Lemon

Slow-Cooker No-Fuss Quinoa with Lemon

SERVES 6   **VEGAN**

COOKING TIME 3 to 4 hours on low or 2 to 3 hours on high

WHY THIS RECIPE WORKS We love quinoa for its nutty taste and ease of preparation. To keep the grains separate and fluffy during cooking, we toasted them in the microwave before adding them to the slow cooker. We dressed the quinoa simply, with lemon and parsley, to make a universally appealing side dish. If you buy unwashed quinoa (or if you are unsure whether it's washed), be sure to rinse it before cooking to remove its bitter protective coating (called saponin). You will need a 4- to 7-quart oval slow cooker for this recipe. This recipe will only work in a traditional slow cooker.

- 1½ cups prewashed white quinoa, rinsed
- 1 onion, chopped fine
- 2 tablespoons extra-virgin olive oil, divided
- 1 teaspoon table salt
- 1¾ cups water
- 2 (2-inch) strips lemon zest plus 1 tablespoon juice
- 2 tablespoons minced fresh parsley

1. Lightly coat slow cooker with vegetable oil spray. Microwave quinoa, onion, 1 tablespoon oil, and salt in bowl, stirring occasionally, until quinoa is lightly toasted and onion is softened, about 5 minutes; transfer to prepared slow cooker. Stir in water and lemon zest. Cover and cook until quinoa is tender and all water is absorbed, 3 to 4 hours on low or 2 to 3 hours on high.

2. Discard lemon zest. Fluff quinoa with fork, then gently fold in lemon juice, parsley, and remaining 1 tablespoon oil. Season with salt and pepper to taste. Serve.

PER SERVING Cal 210; **Total Fat** 8g, **Sat Fat** 1g; **Chol** 0mg; **Sodium** 390mg; **Total Carb** 30g, **Dietary Fiber** 4g, **Total Sugars** 3g; **Protein** 6g

Slow-Cooker Beet and Wheat Berry Salad with Arugula and Apples
SERVES 4 TO 6
COOKING TIME 6 to 8 hours on low or 4 to 5 hours on high

WHY THIS RECIPE WORKS This hearty salad features wheat berries, earthy beets, crisp apple slices, and fresh arugula, all tied together with a lively vinaigrette and fresh goat cheese. The flavor of wheat berries works especially well in salads and pairs nicely with the sweet and rich beets. Even better, the wheat berries can be slowly simmered alongside the beets, which we wrapped in foil to keep the cooking even and the deep color from bleeding into the grain. Minced garlic and thyme, added right to the slow cooker, provided an aromatic backbone. Once the wheat berries were tender, we drained them and dressed them with a simple red wine vinaigrette. Baby arugula and a Granny Smith apple rounded out our salad with their bitter and sweet-tart notes respectively, and crumbled goat cheese provided a creamy, tangy counterpoint to the wheat berries and beets. To ensure even cooking, we recommend using beets that are similar in size—roughly 3 inches in diameter. If using quick-cooking or presteamed wheat berries (the ingredient list on the package specifies the type), you will need to decrease the cooking time. The wheat berries will retain a chewy texture once fully cooked. You will need a 4- to 7-quart slow cooker for this recipe. This recipe will only work in a traditional slow cooker.

1 **cup wheat berries**
2 **garlic cloves, minced**
2 **teaspoons minced fresh thyme or ½ teaspoon dried**
½ **teaspoon table salt, plus salt for cooking wheat berries**
1 **pound beets, trimmed**
1 **Granny Smith apple, peeled, cored, halved, and sliced ¼ inch thick**
4 **ounces (4 cups) baby arugula**

Slow-Cooker Beet and Wheat Berry Salad with Arugula and Apples

3 **tablespoons extra-virgin olive oil**
3 **tablespoons red wine vinegar**
  Pinch pepper
  Pinch sugar
4 **ounces goat cheese, crumbled (1 cup)**

1. Combine 5 cups water, wheat berries, garlic, thyme, and ½ teaspoon salt in slow cooker. Wrap beets individually in aluminum foil and place in slow cooker. Cover and cook until wheat berries and beets are tender, 6 to 8 hours on low or 4 to 5 hours on high.

2. Transfer beets to cutting board, open foil, and let sit until cool enough to handle. Rub off beet skins with paper towels and cut beets into ½-inch-thick wedges.

3. Drain wheat berries, transfer to large serving bowl, and let cool slightly. Add beets, apple, arugula, oil, vinegar, pepper, sugar, and ½ teaspoon salt and toss to combine. Season with salt and pepper to taste. Sprinkle with goat cheese and serve.

PER SERVING Cal 260; **Total Fat** 12g, **Sat Fat** 4g; **Chol** 10mg; **Sodium** 520mg; **Total Carb** 33g, **Dietary Fiber** 7g, **Total Sugars** 7g; **Protein** 9g

Slow-Cooker Barbecued Baked Beans

SERVES 6

COOKING TIME 8 to 9 hours on high

WHY THIS RECIPE WORKS Traditional baked beans rely on a long, slow cooking time in a low oven and careful adjustment of the cooking liquid in order to get perfectly cooked beans with just the right amount of syrupy sauce. While the gentle, steady heat of the slow cooker seemed like the perfect fit for beans, we were in for a surprise. While we were able to get silky, tender beans after 8 to 9 hours of cooking on the high setting, we weren't able to replicate those results on low, even after 16 hours of cooking. So we settled on cooking the beans exclusively on high. Our slow-cooking method perfected, we first microwaved our aromatics with chopped bacon for rich, smoky flavor. Next we added the classic flavors of barbecue sauce and coffee along with vinegar and mustard for tang. You will need a 4- to 7-quart slow cooker for this recipe. This recipe will only work in a traditional slow cooker.

- 1 onion, chopped fine
- 6 slices bacon, chopped
- 4 garlic cloves, minced
- 1 tablespoon vegetable oil
- ½ teaspoon table salt
- 5½ cups water, plus extra as needed
- 1 pound dried navy beans (2½ cups), picked over and rinsed
- ½ cup barbecue sauce, divided
- ½ cup brewed coffee
- 2 bay leaves
- 1 tablespoon cider vinegar
- 2 teaspoons dry mustard
  Hot sauce

1. Microwave onion, bacon, garlic, oil, and salt in bowl, stirring occasionally, until onion is softened, about 5 minutes; transfer to slow cooker. Stir in water, beans, ¼ cup barbecue sauce, coffee, and bay leaves. Cover and cook until beans are tender, 8 to 9 hours on high.

2. Discard bay leaves. Drain beans, reserving ¾ cup cooking liquid. Return beans to now-empty slow cooker. Stir in reserved cooking liquid, vinegar, mustard, and remaining ¼ cup barbecue sauce. Cover and cook on high until beans are thickened slightly, about 10 minutes. Season with salt, pepper, and hot sauce to taste. Serve. (Beans can be held on warm or low setting for up to 2 hours; adjust consistency with extra hot water as needed before serving.)

PER SERVING Cal 450; **Total Fat** 15g, **Sat Fat** 4g; **Chol** 20mg; **Sodium** 620mg; **Total Carb** 58g, **Dietary Fiber** 12g, **Total Sugars** 12g; **Protein** 21g

VARIATION

Slow-Cooker Peach-Bourbon Baked Beans

Omit vegetable oil, barbecue sauce, coffee, and hot sauce. Add 2 teaspoons minced fresh thyme to bowl with onion before microwaving. Increase water to 6 cups. Stir 2 cups thawed frozen peaches, cut into ½ inch pieces, and 2 tablespoons packed dark brown sugar into beans before cooking. Stir 2 tablespoons peach preserves, 2 tablespoons bourbon, 2 tablespoons packed dark brown sugar, and ½ teaspoon table salt into beans with cooking liquid. Increase cider vinegar to 4 teaspoons.

Slow-Cooker Cuban-Style Black Beans

SERVES 6

COOKING TIME 8 to 9 hours on high

WHY THIS RECIPE WORKS Served at almost every meal, black beans are at the heart of Cuban cuisine. Prior testing left us confident in our method for cooking them, so we turned our attention to building layers of flavor. Pork is commonly added to the beans for much-needed depth, so we began there. After trying bacon, ham, and a ham hock, we liked the smoky depth the ham hock lent. Instead of adding aromatics at the start of cooking, we favored the custom of stirring a *sofrito* (typically sautéed onion, garlic, and green bell pepper) into the cooked beans. Microwaving the sofrito until the vegetables were tender saved time without compromising flavor. This addition, along with minced cilantro and lime juice, provided a fresh layer of flavor without overwhelming the beans. Some recipes suggested pureeing the sofrito with some of the beans to thicken the sauce, but we preferred simply mashing them and the sofrito along with a little cooking liquid. The texture is typically looser than that achieved in other bean recipes. You will need a 4- to 7-quart slow cooker for this recipe. This recipe will only work in a traditional slow cooker.

- 6 cups water, plus extra as needed
- 1 pound dried black beans (2½ cups), picked over and rinsed
- 1 (12-ounce) smoked ham hock, rinsed
- 2 bay leaves
- 1 onion, chopped fine
- 1 green bell pepper, stemmed, seeded, and minced
- 6 garlic cloves, minced
- 2 tablespoons extra-virgin olive oil
- 2 tablespoons minced fresh oregano or 2 teaspoons dried
- 1½ teaspoons ground cumin
- ½ cup minced fresh cilantro
- 1 tablespoon lime juice, plus extra for seasoning

Slow-Cooker Cuban-Style Black Beans

1. Combine water, beans, ham hock, and bay leaves in slow cooker. Cover and cook until beans are tender, 8 to 9 hours on high.

2. Transfer ham hock to cutting board, let cool slightly, then shred into bite-size pieces using 2 forks; discarding fat, skin, and bones. Discard bay leaves.

3. Microwave onion, bell pepper, garlic, oil, oregano, and cumin in bowl, stirring occasionally, until vegetables are tender, 8 to 10 minutes.

4. Drain beans, reserving 1½ cups cooking liquid. Add vegetable mixture, one-third of beans, and reserved cooking liquid to now-empty slow cooker and mash with potato masher until mostly smooth. Stir in remaining beans, ham, cilantro, and lime juice. Season with salt, pepper, and extra lime juice to taste. Serve. (Beans can be held on warm or low setting for up to 2 hours; adjust consistency with extra hot water as needed before serving.)

PER SERVING Cal 450; **Total Fat** 13g, **Sat Fat** 3.5g; **Chol** 50mg; **Sodium** 250mg; **Total Carb** 50g, **Dietary Fiber** 1g, **Total Sugars** 8g; **Protein** 29g

Slow-Cooker Mexican-Style Beans
SERVES 6 VEGAN
COOKING TIME 8 to 9 hours on high

WHY THIS RECIPE WORKS To deliver flavorful, robust Mexican-style beans from the slow cooker we needed to amp up the aromatics and spices. Since the beans required a full 6 cups of liquid to cook evenly in the slow cooker, we knew that we would need to drain away some of that liquid after. To ensure that our beans remained full of flavor, we boosted the amount of garlic, oregano, and chili powder. For an extra taste dimension, we also added smoky chipotle chiles in adobo sauce and exchanged 1 cup of water for beer. When we stirred 1 cup of reserved cooking liquid back into the tender beans, we created a sauce that was rich and bold. A little bit of brown sugar rounded things out, and a hit of fresh lime juice and cilantro added brightness at the end. You will need a 4- to 7-quart slow cooker for this recipe. This recipe will only work in a traditional slow cooker.

1 onion, chopped fine
2 tablespoons extra-virgin olive oil, divided
4 garlic cloves, minced
1 tablespoon minced fresh oregano or 1 teaspoon dried
1 tablespoon chili powder
2 teaspoons minced canned chipotle chile in adobo sauce
1 teaspoon table salt
5 cups water, plus extra as needed
1 pound (2½ cups) dried pinto beans, picked over and rinsed
1 cup mild lager, such as Budweiser
2 tablespoons minced fresh cilantro
1 tablespoon packed brown sugar
1 tablespoon lime juice, plus extra for seasoning

1. Microwave onion, 1 tablespoon oil, garlic, oregano, chili powder, chipotle, and salt in bowl, stirring occasionally, until onion is softened, about 5 minutes; transfer to slow cooker. Stir in water, beans, and beer. Cover and cook until beans are tender, 8 to 9 hours on high.

2. Drain beans, reserving 1 cup cooking liquid. Return beans and reserved cooking liquid to now-empty slow cooker. Stir in cilantro, sugar, lime juice, and remaining 1 tablespoon oil. Season with salt, pepper, and extra lime juice to taste. Serve. (Beans can be held on warm or low setting for up to 2 hours; adjust consistency with extra hot water as needed before serving.)

PER SERVING Cal 350; **Total Fat** 5g, **Sat Fat** 0.5g; **Chol** 0mg; **Sodium** 440mg; **Total Carb** 55g, **Dietary Fiber** 19g, **Total Sugars** 7g; **Protein** 17g

Slow-Cooker Refried Beans

1 onion, chopped fine
1 poblano chile, stemmed, seeded, and minced
2 slices bacon
3 garlic cloves, minced
1 tablespoon ground cumin
1 pound (2½ cups) dried pinto beans, picked over and rinsed
6 cups chicken broth, plus extra as needed
3 tablespoons minced fresh cilantro
1 tablespoon lime juice, plus extra as needed
½ teaspoon table salt

1. Microwave onion, poblano, bacon, garlic, and cumin in bowl, stirring occasionally, until vegetables are softened, about 5 minutes; transfer to slow cooker. Stir in beans and broth, cover, and cook until beans are tender, 8 to 9 hours on high.

2. Discard bacon. Drain beans, reserving 1 cup cooking liquid. Return beans and reserved cooking liquid to now-empty slow cooker and mash with potato masher until smooth. Stir in cilantro, lime juice, and salt. Season with salt, pepper, and extra lime juice to taste. Serve. (Beans can be held on warm or low setting for up to 2 hours; adjust consistency with extra hot broth as needed before serving.)

PER SERVING Cal 340; **Total Fat** 4.5g, **Sat Fat** 1.5g; **Chol** 5mg; **Sodium** 830mg; **Total Carb** 53g, **Dietary Fiber** 19g; **Total Sugars** 5g; **Protein** 19g

Slow-Cooker Refried Beans
SERVES 6
COOKING TIME 8 TO 9 HOURS ON HIGH

WHY THIS RECIPE WORKS Homemade refried beans, infused with rich pork taste, a subtle heat, and warm spice notes, are worlds apart from the canned stuff, but making them takes time. For great refried beans for tacos, tostadas, and nachos, we put our slow cooker to work and developed a recipe that was flavor-packed but hands-off. We started with dried pintos (the usual pick for refried beans) and added them right to the slow cooker—no advance soaking or simmering needed. Chicken broth provided a flavorful cooking liquid, and garlic, onion, and cumin offered the requisite aromatic and warm spice notes. A poblano chile upped the heat level, and two slices of bacon infused the beans with smoky, savory depth. To jump-start the cooking of the aromatics and spices and deepen their flavor, we microwaved them briefly with the bacon, which rendered some fat and took the place of any vegetable oil. Once the beans were tender, we discarded the spent bacon strips and mashed the beans. Cilantro and lime juice added brightness and gave our dish authentic south-of-the-border flavor. You will need a 4- to 7-quart slow cooker for this recipe. This recipe will only work in a traditional slow cooker.

Slow-Cooker Braised White Beans with Olive Oil and Sage VEGAN
SERVES 6
COOKING TIME 8 to 9 hours on high

WHY THIS RECIPE WORKS These slow-cooked beans deliver rich flavor and a creamy, tender texture, and are perfect alongside pork, chicken, or fish. The beans themselves—we found that small white beans worked well—required no prep, other than being picked over and rinsed. So that they would take on robust flavor during their long stint in the slow cooker, we cooked them with onion, a hefty amount of garlic, and a little sage. Once the beans were perfectly done, we drained them and reserved a cup of the flavorful cooking liquid to stir back in. We mashed a portion of the beans to thicken the sauce and enhance the creamy consistency of the dish. More olive oil and fresh sage stirred in at the end heightened the earthy, herbaceous flavors. You will need a 4- to 7-quart slow cooker for this recipe. This recipe will only work in a traditional slow cooker.

1 onion, chopped fine

5 garlic cloves, minced

3 tablespoons extra-virgin olive oil, divided

2 teaspoons minced fresh sage, divided

Table salt for cooking beans

3 cups vegetable or chicken broth, plus extra as needed

3 cups water

1 pound (2½ cups) dried small white beans, picked over and rinsed

1. Microwave onion, garlic, 1 tablespoon oil, 1 teaspoon sage, and 1 teaspoon salt in bowl, stirring occasionally, until onion is softened, about 5 minutes; transfer to slow cooker. Stir in broth, water, and beans. Cover and cook until beans are tender, 8 to 9 hours on high.

2. Drain beans, reserving 1 cup cooking liquid. Return one-third of beans and reserved cooking liquid to now-empty slow cooker and mash with potato masher until smooth. Stir in remaining beans, remaining 2 tablespoons oil, and remaining 1 teaspoon sage. Season with salt and pepper to taste. Serve. (Beans can be held on warm or low setting for up to 2 hours; adjust consistency with extra hot broth as needed before serving.)

PER SERVING Cal 340; **Total Fat** 8g, **Sat Fat** 1g; **Chol** 0mg; **Sodium** 780mg; **Total Carb** 51g, **Dietary Fiber** 19g, **Total Sugars** 2g; **Protein** 16g

Slow-Cooker Braised Chickpeas

Slow-Cooker Braised Chickpeas

SERVES 6 VEGAN

COOKING TIME 8 to 9 hours on high

WHY THIS RECIPE WORKS Chickpeas have a great buttery texture and they easily soak up the flavors of other ingredients they're paired with, making them ideal for cooking in a flavor-packed broth over a long, slow stint in the slow cooker. We infused broth with distinctive sweet smoked paprika and a sliced red onion for flavor and texture. Once our chickpeas were perfectly tender and creamy, we drained them, reserving a cup of the cooking liquid to create a simple, smoky sauce. Mashing a portion of the beans enhanced the creamy consistency of the dish, and citrusy cilantro added brightness and a simple colorful finish. You will need a 4- to 7-quart slow cooker for this recipe. This recipe will only work in a traditional slow cooker.

1 red onion, halved and sliced thin

1 tablespoon extra-virgin olive oil

1 tablespoon smoked paprika

Table salt for cooking beans

3 cups vegetable or chicken broth, plus extra as needed

3 cups water

1 pound (2½ cups) dried chickpeas, picked over and rinsed

¼ cup minced fresh cilantro

1. Microwave onion, oil, paprika, and 1 teaspoon salt in bowl, stirring occasionally, until onion is softened, about 5 minutes; transfer to slow cooker. Stir in broth, water, and chickpeas. Cover and cook until chickpeas are tender, 8 to 9 hours on high.

2. Drain chickpeas, reserving 1 cup cooking liquid. Return one-third of chickpeas and reserved cooking liquid to now-empty slow cooker and mash with potato masher until smooth. Stir in remaining chickpeas and cilantro. Season with salt and pepper to taste. Serve. (Chickpeas can be held on warm or low setting for up to 2 hours; adjust consistency with extra hot broth as needed before serving.)

PER SERVING Cal 310; **Total Fat** 7g, **Sat Fat** 0g; **Chol** 0mg; **Sodium** 780mg; **Total Carb** 49g, **Dietary Fiber** 14g, **Total Sugars** 9g; **Protein** 15g

Slow-Cooker Braised Lentils with Escarole

SERVES 6 TO 8

COOKING TIME 3 to 4 hours on low or 2 to 3 hours on high

WHY THIS RECIPE WORKS Lentils are amazingly versatile: Their mild earthiness makes it easy to pair them with a wide range of flavors and, depending on the variety of lentil and the cooking method, their consistency can range from a silky, smooth dal to the slightly firm bite of a French lentil salad. For this side we envisioned something in between—distinct, tender lentils in a brothy sauce thickened by the lentils themselves. We started by deliberately veering away from our slow-cooker technique for perfect salad lentils. Usually, to ensure that they cook evenly without blowing out, we use abundant liquid, often with a touch of acid (which helps keep them firm while cooking), and then drain them. In this case, since we actually wanted to release some starches, we didn't mind a few burst lentils. So we skipped the acid and used just enough broth, fortified with some simple aromatics, to submerge our lentils. The result was just what we had hoped for—tender lentils in a ready-made sauce. We wanted to keep the dish simple, just wilting in escarole for some heft, and found its bitterness the perfect foil to the lentils' earthy base. A final stir-in of olive oil and lemon juice, and a sprinkling of Parmesan, brought our dish into perfect balance. We prefer French green lentils, or *lentilles du Puy,* for this recipe, but it will work with any type of lentil except red or yellow. You will need a 5- to 7-quart slow cooker for this recipe. This recipe will only work in a traditional slow cooker.

1 onion, chopped fine

3 tablespoons extra-virgin olive oil, divided

3 garlic cloves, minced

½ teaspoon red pepper flakes

2½ cups vegetable or chicken broth

1 cup French green lentils, picked over and rinsed

1 head escarole (1 pound), trimmed and sliced 1 inch thick

1 ounce Parmesan cheese, grated (½ cup)

1 tablespoon lemon juice, plus extra for seasoning

1. Microwave onion, 1 tablespoon oil, garlic, and pepper flakes in bowl, stirring occasionally, until onion is softened, about 5 minutes; transfer to slow cooker. Stir in broth and lentils, cover, and cook until lentils are tender, 3 to 4 hours on low or 2 to 3 hours on high.

2. Stir in escarole, 1 handful at a time, until slightly wilted. Cover and cook on high until escarole is completely wilted, about 10 minutes. Stir in Parmesan, lemon juice, and remaining 2 tablespoons oil. Season with salt, pepper, and extra lemon juice to taste. Serve.

PER SERVING Cal 140; **Total Fat** 7g, **Sat Fat** 1.5g; **Chol** 5mg; **Sodium** 250mg; **Total Carb** 13g, **Dietary Fiber** 4g, **Total Sugars** 2g; **Protein** 7g

Slow-Cooker Lentil Salad with Dill, Orange, and Spinach

SERVES 4 `VEGAN`

COOKING TIME 3 to 4 hours on low or 2 to 3 hours on high

WHY THIS RECIPE WORKS A lentil salad can be hearty, impressive, and easy to cook. But sometimes lentils overcook and break down; we found that the slow and even heat of the slow cooker was the perfect solution to great lentils every time. We discovered that cooking the lentils with plenty of liquid was necessary to ensure even doneness. Also adding a little salt and vinegar to the cooking liquid (we preferred water for a pure lentil flavor) gave us lentils that were firm yet creamy. We added aromatics to the cooking water for a flavorful backbone. Once the lentils were cooked to the ideal texture and drained, we added fresh and bright ingredients to create hearty flavor. We prefer French green lentils, or *lentilles du Puy,* for this recipe, but it will work with any type of lentil except red or yellow. You will need a 4- to 7-quart slow cooker for this recipe. This recipe will only work in a traditional slow cooker.

1 cup French green lentils, picked over and rinsed

2½ tablespoons red wine vinegar, divided

3 garlic cloves, minced

3 (2-inch) strips orange zest, plus 2 oranges

1 bay leaf

¼ teaspoon table salt, plus salt for cooking lentils

4 ounces (4 cups) baby spinach, chopped

¼ cup extra-virgin olive oil

1 shallot, minced

2 tablespoons chopped fresh dill

2 tablespoons chopped toasted pecans

1. Combine 4 cups water, lentils, 1 tablespoon vinegar, garlic, orange zest, bay leaf, and ¾ teaspoon salt in slow cooker. Cover and cook until lentils are tender, 3 to 4 hours on low or 2 to 3 hours on high.

2. Cut away peel and pith from oranges. Cut oranges into 8 wedges, then slice wedges crosswise into ¼-inch-thick pieces.

3. Drain lentils, discarding orange zest and bay leaf, and transfer to large serving bowl; let cool slightly. Add oranges, along with any accumulated juices, spinach, oil, shallot, dill, remaining 1½ tablespoons vinegar, and ¼ teaspoon salt; gently toss to combine. Season with salt and pepper to taste, sprinkle with pecans, and serve.

PER SERVING Cal 500; **Total Fat** 17g, **Sat Fat** 2g; **Chol** 0mg; **Sodium** 610mg; **Total Carb** 59g, **Dietary Fiber** 13g, **Total Sugars** 12g; **Protein** 25g

Pressure-Cooker Braised Carrots with Lemon and Chives

2 pounds carrots, peeled
½ cup water
½ teaspoon table salt
⅛ teaspoon pepper
1 tablespoon unsalted butter
1 tablespoon chopped fresh chives
1 teaspoon lemon juice, plus extra for seasoning

1. Cut carrots into 2-inch lengths. Leave thin pieces whole, halve medium pieces lengthwise, and quarter thick pieces lengthwise. Combine carrots, water, salt, and pepper in pressure cooker.

2. Lock lid in place and close pressure release valve. Select high pressure cook function and cook for 3 minutes. (If using Instant Pot, decrease cooking time to 1 minute.) Turn off pressure cooker and quick-release pressure. Carefully remove lid, allowing steam to escape away from you.

3. Stir in butter, chives, and lemon juice. Season with salt, pepper, and extra lemon juice to taste. Serve.

PER SERVING Cal 70; Total Fat 2g, Sat Fat 1g; Chol 5mg; Sodium 280mg; Total Carb 12g, Dietary Fiber 4g, Total Sugars 6g; Protein 1g

VARIATION

Pressure-Cooker Braised Carrots with Scallions and Ginger

Substitute 1 teaspoon toasted sesame oil for butter, 2 teaspoons rice vinegar for lemon juice, and 2 minced scallions for chives. Stir ½ teaspoon grated fresh ginger into carrots with oil. Season with extra rice vinegar to taste.

Pressure-Cooker Braised Carrots with Lemon and Chives
SERVES 4 TO 6

WHY THIS RECIPE WORKS Buttery braised carrots are a classic, well-loved, wonderfully all-purpose side dish, and using the pressure cooker ensures that they come out tender, not mushy, while you focus on the rest of dinner. To make sure the carrots cooked evenly, we cut them into 2-inch lengths and then halved or quartered them lengthwise, depending on their thickness, so that all the pieces were of similar size. We cooked them in a small amount of water with some salt and pepper, which seasoned the carrots throughout and accented their natural sweetness. A pat of butter, a spritz of lemon juice, and some fresh chives, added after cooking, gave the carrots richness and brightness. This recipe was developed using carrots with a diameter between 1 and 1½ inches at the thick end. If you are using larger carrots, you may have to cut them into more pieces. This recipe will only work in an electric pressure cooker.

Pressure-Cooker Garlicky Braised Swiss Chard
SERVES 4 TO 6   VEGAN

WHY THIS RECIPE WORKS Using the pressure cooker to prepare Swiss chard was a no-brainer—after all, this sturdy green takes well to braising, which turns it meltingly tender and tempers its assertive flavor. We decided on simple flavorings to keep the chard in the spotlight: A healthy dose of garlic and a pinch of red pepper flakes made for a punchy base. We used the chard stems as well to add textural contrast to our side dish; we cut them and added them to the pot along with the chard leaves. Using broth to braise the greens infused them with extra savory taste, and the chard turned out with just the right amount of chew. A splash of lemon juice at the end lightened the finished dish. This recipe will only work in an electric pressure cooker.

¼ cup extra-virgin olive oil, divided
5 garlic cloves, sliced thin
⅛ teaspoon red pepper flakes
½ cup chicken or vegetable broth
¼ teaspoon table salt
2 pounds Swiss chard, stems cut into 2-inch lengths, leaves sliced into 2-inch-wide strips
1 tablespoon lemon juice, plus extra for seasoning

1. Using highest sauté or browning function, cook 2 tablespoons oil, garlic, and pepper flakes in pressure cooker until fragrant, about 1 minute. Stir in broth and salt, then stir in chard stems and leaves, 1 handful at a time.

2. Lock lid in place and close pressure release valve. Select high pressure cook function and cook for 5 minutes. Turn off pressure cooker and quick-release pressure. Carefully remove lid, allowing steam to escape away from you.

3. Stir in lemon juice and remaining 2 tablespoons oil. Season with salt, pepper, and extra lemon juice to taste. Serve.

PER SERVING Cal 120; **Total Fat** 10g, **Sat Fat** 1.5g; **Chol** 0mg; **Sodium** 440mg; **Total Carb** 6g, **Dietary Fiber** 2g, **Total Sugars** 2g; **Protein** 3g

VARIATION
Pressure-Cooker Garlicky Braised Swiss Chard with Chorizo
Using highest sauté or browning function, heat oil in step 1 until shimmering. Add 4 ounces Spanish-style chorizo sausage, quartered lengthwise and sliced thin, and cook until just beginning to brown, about 3 minutes. Stir in garlic, pepper flakes, and ¼ teaspoon smoked paprika and proceed with recipe as directed.

Pressure-Cooker Braised Spring Vegetables
SERVES 4 TO 6 **VEGAN**

WHY THIS RECIPE WORKS This vibrant dish of fresh artichokes, asparagus, and peas captures the flavor of springtime with varying textures and verdant colors. Lovely as they are when combined, however, these vegetables don't cook at anywhere near the same rate. The pressure cooker helped us to cook each to perfection, and in just one pot. First, we cooked halved baby artichokes (in broth to infuse them with flavor); they came out tender and evenly cooked from leaf to stem. We then added asparagus and shelled fresh peas, and simmered them until just crisp-tender. Shredded basil and mint and lemon zest gave the dish an extra bright, springy taste. If you can't find fresh peas, you can substitute 1 cup frozen. This recipe will only work in an electric pressure cooker.

Pressure-Cooker Braised Spring Vegetables

1 lemon, grated to yield 2 teaspoons zest and halved
8 baby artichokes (4 ounces each)
1 tablespoon extra-virgin olive oil, plus extra for serving
3 garlic cloves, minced
¾ cup chicken or vegetable broth
½ teaspoon table salt
1 pound asparagus, trimmed and cut on bias into 2-inch lengths
1 pound fresh peas, shelled (1¼ cups)
2 tablespoons shredded fresh basil
1 tablespoon shredded fresh mint

1. Squeeze zested lemon halves into container filled with 4 cups water, then add spent halves. Working with 1 artichoke at a time, trim stem to about ¾ inch and cut off top quarter of artichoke. Break off bottom 3 or 4 rows of tough outer leaves by pulling them downward. Using paring knife, trim outer layer of stem and base, removing any dark green parts. Cut artichoke in half and submerge in lemon water.

2. Using highest sauté or browning function, cook oil and garlic in pressure cooker until fragrant, about 1 minute. Remove artichokes from lemon water, shaking off excess liquid, and add to multicooker along with broth and salt.

3. Lock lid in place and close pressure release valve. Select high pressure cook function and cook for 4 minutes. Turn off pressure cooker and quick-release pressure. Carefully remove lid, allowing steam to escape away from you. (If using Instant Pot, quick-release pressure immediately after pressure cooker reaches pressure.)

4. Add asparagus and peas and cook using highest sauté or browning function, stirring occasionally, until crisp-tender, 4 to 6 minutes. Turn off pressure cooker. Stir in basil, mint, and lemon zest, and season with salt and pepper to taste. Transfer vegetables to serving dish and drizzle with extra oil. Serve.

PER SERVING Cal 120; **Total Fat** 2.5g, **Sat Fat** 0g; **Chol** 0mg; **Sodium** 370mg; **Total Carb** 20g, **Dietary Fiber** 8g, **Total Sugars** 5g; **Protein** 7g

Pressure-Cooker Greek-Style Stewed Zucchini
SERVES 6   VEGAN

WHY THIS RECIPE WORKS This ultrasimple recipe combines a few everyday ingredients—zucchini, canned tomatoes, aromatics, and herbs—and transforms them into a savory, satisfying dish. Thanks to the pressure cooker's moist, concentrated heat, the zucchini became meltingly tender and soft but still held their shape, while the tomato sauce gained deep, bold flavor. Since zucchini naturally contain a lot of water, we started by using the sauté function to brown them in batches, ridding them of some of their excess liquid and giving them a flavor boost. To build our tomato sauce, we started with an aromatic base of onions, garlic, pepper flakes, and oregano. Canned diced tomatoes were the best option for this sauce; tasters liked that the pieces of tomato stayed fairly distinct through high-heat pressure cooking. A smattering of olives (added at the end of cooking so their flavor wouldn't dominate the dish) offered pleasant, briny bites. A traditional garnish of shredded fresh mint gave a clean, bright finish. This recipe will only work in an electric pressure cooker.

3 tablespoons extra-virgin olive oil, divided, plus extra for drizzling
5 zucchini (8 ounces each), quartered lengthwise, seeded, and cut into 2-inch lengths
1 onion, chopped fine
¾ teaspoon table salt
3 garlic cloves, minced
1 teaspoon minced fresh oregano or ¼ teaspoon dried
¼ teaspoon red pepper flakes

1 (28-ounce) can diced tomatoes
2 tablespoons chopped pitted kalamata olives
2 tablespoons shredded fresh mint

1. Using highest sauté or browning function, heat 1 tablespoon oil in pressure cooker for 5 minutes (or until just smoking). Brown half of zucchini on all sides, 3 to 5 minutes; transfer to bowl. Repeat with 1 tablespoon oil and remaining zucchini; transfer to bowl.

2. Add remaining 1 tablespoon oil, onion, and salt to now-empty pressure cooker and cook until onion is softened and lightly browned, 5 to 7 minutes. Stir in garlic, oregano, and pepper flakes and cook until fragrant, about 30 seconds. Stir in tomatoes and their juice and zucchini.

3. Lock lid in place and close pressure release valve. Select high pressure cook function and cook for 2 minutes. Turn off pressure cooker and quick-release pressure. Carefully remove lid, allowing steam to escape away from you.

4. If necessary, continue to cook zucchini mixture using highest sauté or browning function until sauce is slightly thickened. Stir in olives and season with salt and pepper to taste. Transfer to serving dish, sprinkle with mint, and drizzle with extra oil. Serve.

PER SERVING Cal 130; **Total Fat** 8g, **Sat Fat** 1g; **Chol** 0mg; **Sodium** 560mg; **Total Carb** 14g, **Dietary Fiber** 2g, **Total Sugars** 8g; **Protein** 4g

Pressure-Cooker Smashed Potatoes
SERVES 4 TO 6

WHY THIS RECIPE WORKS The chunky texture of smashed potatoes makes them a pleasant alternative to mashed. We preferred low-starch, high-moisture potatoes such as Red Bliss, as they held up best to cooking and mashing; plus, their red skins provided a nice color contrast. While the potatoes are typically boiled in a pot of water, the pressure cooker enabled us to cook them in a much smaller amount of liquid, which we turned to our advantage by using a potent mix of broth flavored with butter, garlic, and rosemary. This amped up the richness of the dish and added a subtle, alluring aroma. After cooking, we mashed in a half-cup of cream cheese to give the potatoes some additional creaminess along with a bit of tang to balance out the richness. This recipe was developed using small potatoes with a diameter between 1 and 2 inches. If you are using larger potatoes, you may have to cut them into more pieces. This recipe can be doubled in an 8-quart pressure cooker. This recipe will only work in an electric pressure cooker.

4 tablespoons unsalted butter
3 garlic cloves, minced
½ teaspoon chopped fresh rosemary
1 bay leaf
2 pounds small red potatoes, unpeeled, halved
½ cup chicken or vegetable broth
1 teaspoon table salt
4 ounces cream cheese, softened

1. Using highest sauté or browning function, melt butter in pressure cooker. Stir in garlic, rosemary, and bay leaf and cook until fragrant, about 30 seconds. Stir in potatoes, broth, and salt.

2. Lock lid in place and close pressure release valve. Select high pressure cook function and cook for 8 minutes. Turn off pressure cooker and quick-release pressure. Carefully remove lid, allowing steam to escape away from you.

3. Discard bay leaf. Add cream cheese and, using potato masher, mash until combined and chunks of potato remain. Season with salt and pepper to taste. Serve.

PER SERVING Cal 240; **Total Fat** 14g, **Sat Fat** 9g; **Chol** 45mg; **Sodium** 530mg; **Total Carb** 26g, **Dietary Fiber** 3g, **Total Sugars** 3g; **Protein** 4g

VARIATION
Pressure-Cooker Smashed Potatoes with Horseradish and Chives
Omit rosemary. Mash 2 tablespoons prepared horseradish and 1 tablespoon minced fresh chives into potatoes with cream cheese.

Pressure-Cooker Parmesan Risotto
SERVES 4 TO 6

WHY THIS RECIPE WORKS With the help of the pressure cooker's concentrated, moist heat and closed cooking environment, perfect risotto is achievable even on a weeknight. We started by blooming our aromatics, toasting the rice, and stirring in some wine. A few cups of warm broth gave the rice the proper texture. To pressure-cook the risotto, all we had to do was lock on the lid and allow the intense heat to do its work. The rice turned out perfectly tender. For the traditional creamy consistency, we encouraged the rice to release additional starch by vigorously stirring in the Parmesan at the end of cooking. Arborio rice, which is high in starch, gives risotto its characteristic creaminess; do not substitute other types of rice here. This recipe will only work in an electric pressure cooker.

Pressure-Cooker Parmesan Risotto

4 tablespoons unsalted butter, divided
½ onion, chopped fine
1 teaspoon table salt
1½ cups Arborio rice
3 garlic cloves, minced
½ cup dry white wine
3 cups chicken broth, warmed, plus extra as needed
2 ounces Parmesan cheese, grated (1 cup)
2 tablespoons minced fresh chives
1 tablespoon lemon juice

1. Using highest sauté or browning function, melt 2 tablespoons butter in pressure cooker. Add onion and salt and cook until onion is softened, 3 to 5 minutes. Stir in rice and garlic and cook until grains are translucent around edges, about 3 minutes. Stir in wine and cook until nearly evaporated, about 1 minute. Stir in warm broth, scraping up any rice that sticks to bottom of pot.

2. Lock lid in place and close pressure release valve. Select high pressure cook function and cook for 7 minutes. Turn off pressure cooker and quick-release pressure. Carefully remove lid, allowing steam to escape away from you.

3. If necessary, adjust consistency with extra hot broth or continue to cook risotto using highest sauté or browning function, stirring frequently, until proper consistency is achieved. (Risotto should be slightly thickened, and spoon dragged along bottom of pressure cooker should leave trail that quickly fills in.) Add Parmesan and remaining 2 tablespoons butter and stir vigorously until risotto becomes creamy. Stir in chives and lemon juice and season with salt to taste. Serve.

PER SERVING Cal 300; **Total Fat** 11g, **Sat Fat** 6g; **Chol** 25mg; **Sodium** 840mg; **Total Carb** 38g, **Dietary Fiber** 1g, **Total Sugars** 1g; **Protein** 10g

Pressure-Cooker Brown Rice with Shiitakes and Edamame
SERVES 6 `VEGAN`

WHY THIS RECIPE WORKS Nutty brown rice is a great base for a hearty side dish, and using the pressure cooker made it foolproof. We ignored the preset "rice" buttons found on many pressure cookers, discovering that we got more consistent results by manually setting the cook time. While rice is usually cooked using the absorption method (in which the rice soaks up all the liquid it's cooked in), we cooked ours in plenty of liquid and then drained away the extra after cooking. This resulted in more evenly cooked rice, since all of the grains were completely submerged in liquid for the whole cooking time. To add to our perfect brown rice, we used the sauté function to cook meaty shiitake mushrooms, fragrant scallions, and some grated fresh ginger, then stirred in edamame for heft and rice vinegar and mirin for brightness. This recipe will only work in an electric pressure cooker.

1½ cups short-grain brown rice, rinsed
¼ teaspoon table salt, plus salt for cooking rice
1 tablespoon vegetable oil
4 ounces shiitake mushrooms, stemmed and sliced thin
4 scallions, white parts minced, green parts sliced thin on bias
2 teaspoons grated fresh ginger
1 cup frozen edamame, thawed
4 teaspoons rice vinegar, plus extra for seasoning
1 tablespoon mirin, plus extra for seasoning
1 teaspoon toasted sesame oil

Pressure-Cooker Brown Rice with Shiitakes and Edamame

1. Combine 12 cups water, rice, and 2 teaspoons salt in pressure cooker.

2. Lock lid in place and close pressure release valve. Select high pressure cook function and cook for 8 minutes. Turn off pressure cooker and let pressure release naturally for 15 minutes. Quick-release any remaining pressure, then carefully remove lid, allowing steam to escape away from you.

3. Drain rice and transfer to large bowl. Wipe out pressure cooker with paper towels. Using highest sauté or browning function, heat vegetable oil in now-empty pressure cooker until shimmering. Add mushrooms, scallion whites, ginger, and ¼ teaspoon salt and cook until mushrooms are softened, 5 to 7 minutes. Transfer to bowl with rice, then add edamame, vinegar, mirin, sesame oil, and scallion greens and gently toss to combine. Season with extra vinegar and mirin to taste. Serve.

PER SERVING Cal 240; **Total Fat** 5g, **Sat Fat** 0g; **Chol** 0mg; **Sodium** 880mg; **Total Carb** 42g, **Dietary Fiber** 2g, **Total Sugars** 2g; **Protein** 7g

Pressure-Cooker Warm Wild Rice Salad with Pecans and Cranberries

2 cups wild rice, picked over and rinsed

8 sprigs fresh thyme

2 bay leaves

½ teaspoon table salt, plus salt for cooking rice

1 cup fresh parsley leaves

¾ cup dried cranberries

¾ cup pecans, toasted and chopped coarse

3 tablespoons unsalted butter, melted

1 shallot, minced

2 teaspoons apple cider vinegar

1. Combine 12 cups water, rice, thyme sprigs, bay leaves, and 1 tablespoon salt in pressure cooker.

2. Lock lid in place and close pressure release valve. Select high pressure cook function and cook for 18 minutes. Turn off pressure cooker and quick-release pressure. Carefully remove lid, allowing steam to escape away from you.

3. Discard thyme sprigs and bay leaves. Drain rice and transfer to large bowl. Add parsley, cranberries, pecans, melted butter, shallot, vinegar, and ½ teaspoon salt and gently toss to combine. Season with salt and pepper to taste. Serve.

PER SERVING Cal 470; **Total Fat** 17g; **Sat Fat** 4.5g; **Chol** 15mg; **Sodium** 230mg; **Total Carb** 74g, **Dietary Fiber** 7g, **Total Sugars** 18g; **Protein** 12g

Pressure-Cooker Warm Wild Rice Salad with Pecans and Cranberries

SERVES 6

WHY THIS RECIPE WORKS We found that the electric pressure cooker could produce perfect wild rice as long as we made it in enough water to keep it submerged. When prepared well, wild rice is pleasantly chewy and has a nutty, savory flavor. The pressure cooker's ability to moderate the temperature of the cooking liquid meant that every grain turned out tender and intact. Thyme sprigs and bay leaves added to the water infused the rice with flavor. To transform wild rice into a side dish with contrasting flavors and textures, we added sweet-tart dried cranberries, crunchy pecans, fresh parsley, and bright apple cider vinegar. Do not use quick-cooking or presteamed wild rice in this recipe (read the ingredient list on the package to determine this). This recipe will only work in an electric pressure cooker.

Pressure-Cooker Egyptian Barley Salad

SERVES 6

WHY THIS RECIPE WORKS This impressive and unique salad, inspired by the flavors of Egypt, relies on a bed of tender-yet-firm pearl barley as its base. Pearl barley is a great candidate for the pressure cooker; cooking the grains in plenty of water, similar to our method for brown rice, gave us perfectly even results. To further ensure separate, intact grains when pressure-cooking, we found that a natural release was essential (quick-release caused some of the grains to blow out). After cooking and then draining the barley, we spread it on a baking sheet to cool it quickly. With our perfected barley ready, we incorporated toasty pistachios, tangy pomegranate molasses, and bright, vegetal cilantro, all balanced by warm, earthy spices and sweet golden raisins. Salty feta cheese, pungent scallions, and sweet-tart pomegranate seeds adorned the top of the dish for a colorful and tasty finish. You can find pomegranate molasses in the international aisle of most well-stocked supermarkets. Do not substitute hulled, hull-less, quick-cooking, or presteamed barley (read the ingredient list on the package to determine this). This recipe will only work in an electric pressure cooker.

1½ cups pearl barley

½ teaspoon table salt, plus salt for cooking barley

3 tablespoons extra-virgin olive oil, plus extra for drizzling

2 tablespoons pomegranate molasses

½ teaspoon ground cinnamon

¼ teaspoon ground cumin

⅓ cup golden raisins

½ cup coarsely chopped fresh cilantro

¼ cup shelled pistachios, toasted and chopped

3 ounces feta cheese, cut into ½-inch cubes (¾ cup)

6 scallions, green parts only, sliced thin

½ cup pomegranate seeds

1. Combine 12 cups water, barley, and 1 tablespoon salt in pressure cooker.

2. Lock lid in place and close pressure release valve. Select high pressure cook function and cook for 8 minutes. Turn off pressure cooker and let pressure release naturally for 15 minutes. Quick-release any remaining pressure, then carefully remove lid, allowing steam to escape away from you.

3. Drain barley, spread onto rimmed baking sheet, and let cool completely, about 15 minutes. Meanwhile, whisk oil, molasses, cinnamon, cumin, and ½ teaspoon salt together in large bowl. Add cooled barley, raisins, cilantro, and pistachios and gently toss to combine. Season with salt and pepper to taste. Spread barley salad evenly into serving dish and arrange feta, scallions, and pomegranate seeds in separate diagonal rows on top. Drizzle with extra oil and serve.

PER SERVING Cal 370; **Total Fat** 14g, **Sat Fat** 3.5g; **Chol** 15mg; **Sodium** 350mg; **Total Carb** 54g, **Dietary Fiber** 9g, **Total Sugars** 12g; **Protein** 9g

Pressure-Cooker Boston Baked Beans
SERVES 6

WHY THIS RECIPE WORKS Traditional Boston baked beans consist of tender navy beans napped in a pork- and molasses-enhanced, sweet-savory sauce. Moving the cooking from a low oven (which requires careful adjustment of the cooking liquid in order to get perfectly cooked beans with just the right amount of sauce) to the pressure cooker made our baked beans bulletproof: The even, steady heat and closed environment (meaning limited evaporation) made this crowd-pleasing dish hands-off. We found that brining the beans made for a much better final product;

the cooked beans were well seasoned and held their shape through cooking. Although brining required a bit of advance planning, it couldn't have been simpler, and the next day we merely needed to combine the beans with the rest of the ingredients in the pressure cooker, and then lock on the lid. You'll get fewer blowouts if you soak the beans overnight, but if you're pressed for time you can quick-salt-soak your beans: In step 1, combine the salt, water, and beans in the pressure cooker and bring everything to a boil using the highest sauté or browning function. Turn off the pressure cooker, cover, and let the beans sit for 1 hour. Drain and rinse the beans and proceed with the recipe as directed. This recipe will only work in an electric pressure cooker.

1½ tablespoons table salt for brining

1 pound (2½ cups) dried navy beans, picked over and rinsed

6 ounces salt pork, rind removed, rinsed, and cut into 3 pieces

1 onion, halved

½ cup molasses

2 tablespoons packed dark brown sugar

2 tablespoons vegetable oil

1 tablespoon soy sauce

2 teaspoons dry mustard

1 teaspoon table salt

½ teaspoon pepper

½ teaspoon baking soda

1 bay leaf

1. Dissolve 1½ tablespoons salt in 8 cups cold water in large container. Add beans and let soak at room temperature for at least 8 hours or up to 24 hours. Drain and rinse well.

2. Combine soaked beans, 2½ cups water, salt pork, onion, molasses, sugar, oil, soy sauce, mustard, 1 teaspoon salt, ½ teaspoon pepper, baking soda, and bay leaf in pressure cooker.

3. Lock lid in place and close pressure release valve. Select high pressure cook function and cook for 50 minutes. Turn off pressure cooker and let pressure release naturally for 15 minutes. Quick-release any remaining pressure, then carefully remove lid, allowing steam to escape away from you.

4. Discard bay leaf and onion. If necessary, continue to cook beans using highest sauté or browning function until sauce has thickened and clings to beans. Serve.

PER SERVING Cal 620; **Total Fat** 29g, **Sat Fat** 9g; **Chol** 25mg; **Sodium** 1440mg; **Total Carb** 72g, **Dietary Fiber** 12g, **Total Sugars** 28g; **Protein** 19g

Pressure-Cooker Drunken Beans

SERVES 6

WHY THIS RECIPE WORKS Drunken beans is a satisfying, brothy Mexican dish that is humble yet utterly comforting: Dried pinto beans are cooked with a bit of pork or lard, a few herbs and aromatics, and beer or tequila. Since the pressure cooker had already proven to be a great ally in cooking beans, we set out to create a recipe for creamy, intact beans in a lightly thickened broth with multidimensional (not boozy) flavor. An overnight soak in salt water helped to soften the beans' skins and ensured fewer blowouts, even when cooked under pressure. Bacon gave the dish smoky, savory depth and doubled as a crisp garnish. We sautéed our aromatics—traditional onion, poblano chiles, and garlic—in the rendered bacon fat for deep flavor. A combination of tequila (added before pressure cooking) and light beer (added afterward) created good depth of flavor with subtle malty notes. This recipe will only work in an electric pressure cooker.

1½ tablespoons table salt for brining
1 pound (2½ cups) dried pinto beans, picked over and rinsed
30 sprigs fresh cilantro (1 bunch)
4 slices bacon, cut into ¼-inch pieces
1 onion, chopped fine
2 poblano chiles, stemmed, seeded, and chopped fine
¼ cup tomato paste
3 garlic cloves, minced
½ cup tequila
1 teaspoon table salt
2 bay leaves
1 cup Mexican lager
2 ounces Cotija cheese, crumbled (½ cup)
Lime wedges

1. Dissolve 1½ tablespoons salt in 8 cups cold water in large container. Add beans and let soak at room temperature for at least 8 hours or up to 24 hours. Drain and rinse well.

2. Pick leaves from 20 cilantro sprigs (reserve stems), chop fine, and refrigerate until needed. Using kitchen twine, tie remaining 10 cilantro sprigs and reserved stems into bundle. Using highest sauté or browning function, cook bacon until rendered and crisp, 10 to 12 minutes. Using slotted spoon, transfer bacon to paper towel–lined bowl; refrigerate until needed.

3. Add onion and poblanos to fat left in pressure cooker and cook until softened, 5 to 7 minutes. Stir in tomato paste and garlic and cook until fragrant, about 1 minute. Stir in tequila and cook until evaporated, about 2 minutes. Stir in 2 cups water, beans, 1 teaspoon salt, cilantro bundle, and bay leaves.

4. Lock lid in place and close pressure release valve. Select high pressure cook function and cook for 40 minutes. Turn off pressure cooker and let pressure release naturally for 15 minutes. Quick-release any remaining pressure, then carefully remove lid, allowing steam to escape away from you.

5. Discard bay leaves and cilantro bundle. Stir in beer and bacon and season with salt and pepper to taste. Serve, passing cotija, lime wedges, and chopped cilantro separately.

PER SERVING Cal 470; **Total Fat** 11g, **Sat Fat** 4g; **Chol** 20mg; **Sodium** 760mg; **Total Carb** 56g, **Dietary Fiber** 19g, **Total Sugars** 6g; **Protein** 22g

Pressure-Cooker Braised Chickpeas with Saffron and Mint

SERVES 6

WHY THIS RECIPE WORKS The pressure cooker makes cooking dried chickpeas nearly as easy as opening a can. To make sure the chickpeas were well seasoned and held their shape, we brined them first. We infused the cooking liquid with garlic, onion, and saffron to add flavor. After cooking, we simply stirred in raisins and fresh mint, along with bright lemon juice; yogurt offered a creamy finish. If you're pressed for time you can quick-salt-soak your chickpeas: In step 1, combine the salt, water, and chickpeas in the pressure cooker and bring everything to a boil using the highest sauté or browning function. Turn off the pressure cooker, cover, and let the chickpeas sit for 1 hour. Drain and rinse the chickpeas and proceed with the recipe as directed. This recipe will only work in an electric pressure cooker.

1½ tablespoons table salt for brining
1 pound (2½ cups) dried chickpeas, picked over and rinsed
3 tablespoons extra-virgin olive oil
1 onion, chopped fine
¼ teaspoon table salt
2 garlic cloves, minced
Pinch saffron threads, crumbled
2 cups chicken or vegetable broth
⅓ cup golden raisins
2 tablespoons chopped fresh mint
2 teaspoons lemon juice
Plain whole-milk yogurt

1. Dissolve 1½ tablespoons salt in 8 cups cold water in large container. Add chickpeas and let soak at room temperature for at least 8 hours or up to 24 hours. Drain and rinse well.

2. Using highest sauté or browning function, heat oil until shimmering. Add onion and ¼ teaspoon salt and cook until onion is softened and lightly browned, 5 to 7 minutes. Stir in garlic and saffron and cook until fragrant, about 30 seconds. Stir in broth and chickpeas.

3. Lock lid in place and close pressure release valve. Select high pressure cook function and cook for 20 minutes. Turn off pressure cooker and let pressure release naturally for 15 minutes. Quick-release any remaining pressure, then carefully remove lid, allowing steam to escape away from you.

4. Stir in raisins, mint, and lemon juice. Season with salt and pepper to taste. Serve with yogurt.

PER SERVING Cal 380; **Total Fat** 11g, **Sat Fat** 1g; **Chol** 0mg; **Sodium** 330mg; **Total Carb** 55g, **Dietary Fiber** 14g, **Total Sugars** 16g; **Protein** 16g

Pressure-Cooker French Lentils with Carrots and Parsley
SERVES 6 **VEGAN**

WHY THIS RECIPE WORKS This simple side has surprisingly complex flavor, thanks to French lentils, or *lentilles du Puy*. These lentils, which are firmer than regular brown or green lentils, are perfect for pressure cooking since their sturdy texture enables them to stand up well to the intense heat. To give the lentils classic French flavors, we used the sauté function to cook a traditional mirepoix (a mix of carrots, onions, and celery) along with garlic and thyme for aromatic backbone. Using water rather than broth as our cooking liquid let the other flavors come through. We were happy to find that once we locked on the lid, our work was pretty much done. A bit of lemon juice and parsley, added before serving, brightened up the dish. We prefer French green lentils for this recipe, but it will work with any type of lentils except red or yellow. This recipe will only work in an electric pressure cooker.

    2 tablespoons extra-virgin olive oil, divided
    2 carrots, peeled and chopped fine
    1 onion, chopped fine
    1 celery rib, chopped fine
    ½ teaspoon table salt
    2 garlic cloves, minced
    1 teaspoon minced fresh thyme or ¼ teaspoon dried
 2½ cups water
    1 cup French green lentils, picked over and rinsed
    2 tablespoons minced fresh parsley
    2 teaspoons lemon juice

Pressure-Cooker French Lentils with Carrots and Parsley

1. Using highest sauté or browning function, heat 1 tablespoon oil until shimmering. Add carrots, onion, celery, and salt and cook until vegetables are softened, 5 to 7 minutes. Stir in garlic and thyme and cook until fragrant, about 30 seconds. Stir in water and lentils.

2. Lock lid in place and close pressure release valve. Select high pressure cook function and cook for 24 minutes. Turn off pressure cooker and let pressure release naturally for 15 minutes. Quick-release any remaining pressure, then carefully remove lid, allowing steam to escape away from you.

3. Stir in parsley, lemon juice, and remaining 1 tablespoon oil. Season with salt and pepper to taste. Serve.

PER SERVING Cal 160; **Total Fat** 5g, **Sat Fat** 0.5g; **Chol** 0mg; **Sodium** 220mg; **Total Carb** 23g, **Dietary Fiber** 6g, **Total Sugars** 3g; **Protein** 7g

ALMOST A MEAL

■ FAST (30 minutes or less total time) ■ MAKE-AHEAD ■ VEGAN
Photos (clockwise from top left): Stovetop Macaroni and Cheese; Cauliflower Steaks with Salsa Verde; Southwestern Chopped Salad; Cuban-Style Black Beans and Rice

Cobb Chopped Salad

SERVES 4 TO 6 **FAST**

WHY THIS RECIPE WORKS This simplified Cobb salad offers the same appealing mix of flavors—buttery avocado, smoky bacon, tangy blue cheese, bright tomato, and rich hard-cooked eggs—minus the fussy assembly. Omitting the chicken made for a side salad that was nevertheless quite hearty. We started by marinating grape tomatoes and cucumber in olive oil and red wine vinegar. Then we tossed this with chopped romaine hearts and our many stir-ins for a fresh, assertive salad to eat for lunch or alongside a main course. You can substitute cherry tomatoes for the grape tomatoes. To cut the romaine lettuce hearts into ½-inch pieces, cut each heart in half lengthwise and then cut each half lengthwise into quarters. Finally, cut each quarter crosswise into ½-inch pieces.

- ¼ cup extra-virgin olive oil
- 3 tablespoons red wine vinegar
- 1 shallot, minced
- ¾ teaspoon table salt, divided
- ¾ teaspoon pepper, divided
- 8 ounces grape tomatoes, halved
- ½ English cucumber, cut into ½-inch pieces
- 2 romaine lettuce hearts (12 ounces), cut into ½-inch pieces
- 4 Easy-Peel Hard-Cooked Eggs (page 453), chopped
- 6 slices cooked bacon, crumbled
- 4 ounces blue cheese, crumbled (1 cup)
- 1 ripe avocado, cut into ½-inch pieces

1. Whisk oil, vinegar, shallot, ½ teaspoon salt, and ½ teaspoon pepper together in large bowl. Add tomatoes and cucumber to bowl and gently toss to coat with dressing; let tomato mixture sit for 10 minutes.

2. Add lettuce, eggs, bacon, blue cheese, avocado, remaining ¼ teaspoon salt, and remaining ¼ teaspoon pepper to tomato mixture and gently toss to combine. Season with salt and pepper to taste. Serve.

PER SERVING Cal 400; **Total Fat** 34g, **Sat Fat** 10g; **Chol** 155mg; **Sodium** 750mg; **Total Carb** 9g, **Dietary Fiber** 3g, **Total Sugars** 4g; **Protein** 14g

VARIATIONS

Antipasti Chopped Salad

Whisk ½ teaspoon dried oregano into oil mixture in step 1 and add ½ cup chopped pepperoncini to dressing with tomatoes. Add 6 ounces salami, cut into ½-inch pieces, to bowl with lettuce. Substitute provolone cheese, cut into ½-inch pieces, for feta and fresh parsley leaves for basil.

Southwestern Chopped Salad

Substitute lime juice for vinegar; 1 (15-ounce) can black beans, rinsed, for cucumber; shredded pepper Jack cheese for feta; and ½ cup fresh cilantro leaves for basil. Whisk 1½ teaspoons chili powder into oil mixture in step 1 and add 1 cup thawed frozen corn to dressing with tomatoes. Add 1 avocado, cut into ½-inch pieces, to bowl with lettuce.

Mediterranean Chopped Salad

SERVES 6 **FAST**

WHY THIS RECIPE WORKS The appeal of any chopped salad is that all the ingredients are cut to a uniform size, permitting a taste of everything in each bite. They are the ultimate blank canvas salad, yet many are an uninspired or haphazard mix of ingredients drowning in dressing. For a lighter, fresher take, we looked to the Mediterranean for inspiration. In place of lettuce as a base, we chose escarole: A member of the chicory family, this underutilized leafy green has a mild bitterness that pairs well with bold flavors. Next, we added chopped cucumbers and grape tomatoes (salted to remove excess moisture) and red onion. To make our salad hearty without the addition of meat, we incorporated nutty chickpeas. Kalamata olives and walnuts added richness and crunch. We tossed everything with a simple red wine vinaigrette to let the salad's flavors shine. Finally, wanting some cheese in our salad, we sprinkled on ½ cup of briny feta to round out the flavors. Cherry tomatoes can be substituted for the grape tomatoes.

- 1 cucumber, halved lengthwise, seeded, and cut into ½-inch pieces
- 10 ounces grape tomatoes, quartered
- 1 teaspoon table salt
- 3 tablespoons red wine vinegar
- 1 garlic clove, minced
- 3 tablespoons extra-virgin olive oil
- 1 (15-ounce) can chickpeas, rinsed
- ½ cup pitted kalamata olives, chopped
- ½ small red onion, chopped fine
- ½ cup chopped fresh parsley
- 1 head escarole (1 pound), trimmed and cut into ½-inch pieces
- 2 ounces feta cheese, crumbled (½ cup)
- ½ cup walnuts, toasted and chopped

1. Toss cucumber and tomatoes with salt and let drain in colander for 15 minutes.

2. Whisk vinegar and garlic together in large bowl. Whisking constantly, drizzle in oil. Add drained cucumber-tomato mixture, chickpeas, olives, onion, and parsley and toss to coat. Let sit for at least 5 minutes or up to 20 minutes.

3. Add escarole, feta, and walnuts and gently toss to combine. Season with salt and pepper to taste. Serve.

PER SERVING Cal 240; **Total Fat** 16g, **Sat Fat** 3.5g; **Chol** 15mg; **Sodium** 810mg; **Total Carb** 19g, **Dietary Fiber** 7g, **Total Sugars** 5g; **Protein** 7g

Spanish Tapas Salad
SERVES 4

WHY THIS RECIPE WORKS Loosely inspired by the flavors and components you might find on a Spanish tapas spread, this easily assembled salad is hearty enough to be dinner and a great partner for simply cooked meat or seafood. We dressed chickpeas, sautéed chorizo, and cracked green olives with a garlicky olive-oil dressing, tossed baby greens in the same dressing, and topped everything with Manchego cheese. We served our salad with a tapas favorite, *pan de tomate*. This simple but wonderful dish involves rubbing toasted bread with a garlic clove and half a tomato for sweetness and color, but we found it easier to grate the tomato separately and spread it on. Adding the bread to the skillet after sautéing the chorizo makes quick work of toasting it. You can substitute stuffed pimento olives for the cracked green olives.

½ cup extra-virgin olive oil, divided
8 ounces chorizo sausage, halved lengthwise and
   sliced into ¼-inch-thick pieces
4 (¾-inch-thick) slices crusty Italian bread
2 garlic cloves, peeled (1 minced and 1 whole)
½ cup cracked green olives, sliced thin, plus
   2 tablespoons olive brine
1 (16-ounce) can chickpeas, rinsed
5 ounces (5 cups) baby greens
   Manchego cheese, shaved
1 small tomato, halved and grated over large holes
   of box grater

1. Heat 1 tablespoon oil in 12-inch nonstick skillet over medium-high heat until just smoking. Cook chorizo until lightly browned and crisp on both sides, about 6 minutes; transfer to paper towel–lined plate.

Spanish Tapas Salad

2. Add 1 tablespoon oil to now-empty skillet and heat over medium-high heat until shimmering. Lay bread in skillet and cook until crisp and golden on first side, about 1 minute. Flip bread over, add 1 tablespoon oil, and cook until second side is crisp and golden, about 1 minute. Let bread cool slightly, then rub 1 side with whole garlic clove.

3. Meanwhile, whisk remaining 5 tablespoons oil, minced garlic, and olive brine together in large bowl. Measure 2 tablespoons vinaigrette into separate bowl and toss with cooked chorizo, olives, and chickpeas; season with salt and pepper to taste.

4. Add greens to remaining dressing and toss to coat; season with salt and pepper to taste.

5. Divide salad among individual plates or transfer to serving platter. Top with olive-chickpea mixture and Manchego. Spread grated tomato over bread, season with salt and pepper, and serve.

PER SERVING Cal 640; **Total Fat** 54g, **Sat Fat** 12g; **Chol** 50mg; **Sodium** 1280mg; **Total Carb** 20g, **Dietary Fiber** 4g, **Total Sugars** 1g; **Protein** 19g

Fattoush

SERVES 4 | VEGAN

WHY THIS RECIPE WORKS The eastern Mediterranean salad *fattoush* puts cucumbers and tomatoes at center stage along with herbs, toasted pita bread, and lemony sumac. We used an ample amount of ground sumac in the dressing to intensify the flavor and as a garnish for the salad. Many recipes call for eliminating moisture from the salad by taking the time-consuming step of seeding and salting the cucumbers and tomatoes. We skipped this to preserve the crisp texture of the cucumber and the flavorful seeds and juice of the tomatoes. Instead, we made the pita pieces more resilient by brushing them with olive oil before baking, which prevented them from becoming soggy in the dressing. The success of this recipe depends on ripe, in-season tomatoes. Sumac can be found in the spice aisle of larger supermarkets.

- 2 (8-inch) pita breads
- 7 tablespoons extra-virgin olive oil, divided
- 3 tablespoons lemon juice
- 4 teaspoons ground sumac, plus extra for sprinkling (optional)
- ¼ teaspoon minced garlic
- ¼ teaspoon table salt
- 1 pound ripe tomatoes, cored and cut into ¾-inch pieces
- 1 English cucumber, sliced ⅛ inch thick
- 1 cup arugula, chopped
- ½ cup chopped fresh cilantro
- ½ cup chopped fresh mint
- 4 scallions, sliced thin

1. Adjust oven rack to middle position and heat oven to 375 degrees. Using kitchen shears, cut around perimeter of each pita and separate into 2 thin rounds. Cut each round in half. Place pitas smooth side down on wire rack set in rimmed baking sheet. Brush 3 tablespoons oil over surface of pitas. (Pitas do not need to be uniformly coated. Oil will spread during baking.) Season with salt and pepper to taste. Bake until pitas are crisp and pale golden brown, 10 to 14 minutes. Let cool to room temperature.

2. Whisk lemon juice; sumac, if using; garlic; and salt together in small bowl and let sit for 10 minutes. While whisking constantly, slowly drizzle in remaining ¼ cup oil.

3. Break pitas into ½-inch pieces and place in large bowl. Add tomatoes, cucumber, arugula, cilantro, mint, and scallions. Drizzle dressing over top and gently toss to coat. Season with salt and pepper to taste. Serve, sprinkling individual portions with extra sumac if desired.

PER SERVING Cal 340; **Total Fat** 25g, **Sat Fat** 3.5g; **Chol** 0mg; **Sodium** 320mg; **Total Carb** 25g, **Dietary Fiber** 3g, **Total Sugars** 5g; **Protein** 5g

Crispy Thai Eggplant Salad

Crispy Thai Eggplant Salad

SERVES 3

WHY THIS RECIPE WORKS For this recipe, we took elements from Sicilian caponata—eggplant, tomatoes, herbs, and vinegary notes—and married them with intense Thai flavors. We used the microwave dehydrating method from our Charred Sichuan-Style Japanese Eggplant (page 113) and then shallow-fried the eggplant before marinating it in *nam prik*—a bright Thai condiment made with lime juice, fish sauce, rice vinegar, ginger, garlic, and chiles. We tossed in juicy cherry tomatoes, a healthy amount of fresh herbs, and crispy fried shallots for a dish that delivered all of the five tastes and as many different textures. Japanese eggplant was our unanimous favorite when we tested this recipe, but globe or Italian eggplant can be substituted if necessary. Traditional Genovese basil is a fine substitute for the Thai basil. Depending on the size of your microwave, you may need to microwave the eggplant in two batches. Be sure to remove the eggplant from the microwave immediately so that the steam can escape. We like to serve this salad with Thai-Style Sticky Rice (page 170). Use a Dutch oven that holds 6 quarts or more for this recipe.

¼ cup fish sauce

¼ cup unseasoned rice vinegar

¼ cup plus 1 teaspoon lime juice (3 limes), divided

¼ cup packed light brown sugar

1 (2-inch piece) ginger, peeled and chopped

4 garlic cloves, chopped

1 red Thai chile, seeded and sliced thin

6 ounces cherry tomatoes, halved

2 large Japanese eggplants, halved lengthwise,
then sliced crosswise 1½ inches thick

½ teaspoon table salt

2 cups vegetable oil

½ cup fresh cilantro leaves

½ cup fresh mint leaves

½ cup fresh Thai basil leaves

½ cup dry-roasted peanuts, chopped

1. Process fish sauce, vinegar, ¼ cup lime juice, sugar, ginger, garlic, and chile in blender until dressing is mostly smooth, about 1 minute. Transfer to large serving bowl and stir in tomatoes; set aside.

2. Toss eggplant with salt in medium bowl. Line entire surface of large plate with double layer of coffee filters and lightly spray with vegetable oil spray. Spread eggplant in even layer on coffee filters. Microwave until eggplant is dry and shriveled to one-third of its original size, about 10 minutes, flipping halfway through to dry sides evenly (eggplant should not brown). Transfer eggplant immediately to paper towel–lined plate.

3. Heat oil in large Dutch oven over medium-high heat to 375 degrees. Add eggplant to oil and cook until flesh is deep golden brown and edges are crispy, 5 to 7 minutes. Using skimmer or slotted spoon, transfer to paper towel–lined plate and blot to remove excess oil. Transfer to bowl with dressing.

4. Toss cilantro, mint, basil, and remaining 1 teaspoon lime juice together in small bowl. Add half of herb mixture to bowl with eggplant, tossing to combine, then sprinkle remaining herb mixture and peanuts over top. Serve.

PER SERVING Cal 560; Total Fat 38g, Sat Fat 4g; Chol 0mg; Sodium 1330mg; Total Carb 52g, Dietary Fiber 12g, Total Sugars 31g; Protein 13g

Utica Greens
SERVES 6

WHY THIS RECIPE WORKS Bitter greens can be a tough sell, but the tender, meaty escarole in this Italian American side dish from upstate New York is irresistible. The winning flavor in this dish comes from capicola (also called coppa), a dry-cured cold cut made from pork shoulder and neck meat; we found that both hot and sweet varieties put this dish on the right track. Browning the meat first established a savory base of flavor. After braising the escarole with the browned meat, onions, hot cherry peppers, and garlic, we stirred in homemade bread crumbs to absorb excess moisture. Grated Pecorino Romano along with another helping of bread crumbs contributed great crunchy texture to complement the greens' bold, hearty flavors. You can use either hot or sweet capicola here. Whichever you choose, buy a ½-inch-thick slice (or use prosciutto) at the deli counter; avoid the prepackaged thin slices, as hearty cubes of meat are traditional for this dish. Do not use store-bought bread crumbs here.

1 slice hearty white sandwich bread,
torn into 1-inch pieces

3 tablespoons extra-virgin olive oil, divided

4 ounces ½-inch-thick capicola, cut into ½-inch pieces

1 onion, chopped

¼ cup jarred sliced hot cherry peppers, chopped fine

4 garlic cloves, minced

2 large heads (2½ pounds) escarole, trimmed and
chopped

½ cup chicken broth

¾ teaspoon table salt

½ teaspoon pepper

1 ounce Pecorino Romano cheese, grated (½ cup)

1. Pulse bread and 1 tablespoon oil in food processor to coarse crumbs, about 5 pulses. Toast bread crumbs in Dutch oven over medium heat, stirring occasionally, until golden brown, about 5 minutes. Transfer crumbs to bowl; set aside. Wipe out pot with paper towels. Add remaining 2 tablespoons oil and capicola to now-empty pot and cook, stirring occasionally, until capicola begins to brown, 3 to 5 minutes. Stir in onion and cook until onion is softened and capicola is browned and crispy, about 5 minutes. Add cherry peppers and garlic and cook until fragrant, about 30 seconds.

2. Stir in half of escarole, broth, salt, and pepper. Cover and cook until greens are beginning to wilt, about 1 minute. Add remaining escarole, cover, and cook over medium-low heat, stirring occasionally, until stems are tender, about 10 minutes. Off heat, stir in Pecorino and ⅓ cup reserved bread crumbs. Top with remaining bread crumbs before serving.

PER SERVING Cal 200; Total Fat 14g, Sat Fat 3.5g; Chol 20mg; Sodium 920mg; Total Carb 12g, Dietary Fiber 6g, Total Sugars 2g; Protein 9g

Braised Greens and Squash with Coconut Curry

SERVES 4 TO 6 `VEGAN`

WHY THIS RECIPE WORKS These comforting curried vegetables could accompany all kinds of meats, roast chicken, or fish, or be served with rice for a vegetarian meal. Plenty of aromatics built flavor and rich coconut milk balanced the bitter kale while sweet butternut squash added heartiness. It was important to bloom the curry powder in oil to deepen its flavor before adding the liquid: a combination of coconut milk and vegetable broth, which brought more complexity than just coconut milk. Reserving some of the coconut milk to stir in at the end reinforced the dish's creaminess. We finished with a squeeze of lime juice for brightness and a sprinkle of crunchy roasted pepitas.

- 3 tablespoons extra-virgin olive oil, divided
- 1 onion, chopped fine
- 2 pounds butternut squash, peeled, seeded, and cut into ½-inch pieces (6 cups)
- 5 garlic cloves, minced
- 2 teaspoons grated fresh ginger
- 1 teaspoon curry powder
- 2 pounds kale, stemmed and chopped
- 1 cup vegetable broth
- 1 (13.5-ounce) can coconut milk, divided
- ½ teaspoon table salt
- 1 tablespoon lime juice
- ⅓ cup roasted pepitas

1. Heat 2 tablespoons oil in Dutch oven over medium heat until shimmering. Add onion and cook, stirring frequently, until softened, about 5 minutes. Add squash and cook, stirring occasionally, until just beginning to brown, about 5 minutes; transfer to bowl.

2. Add garlic, ginger, and curry powder to oil left in pot and cook over medium-high heat until fragrant, about 30 seconds. Add half of greens and stir until beginning to wilt, about 1 minute. Stir in remaining greens, broth, all but ½ cup coconut milk, and salt. Cover pot, reduce heat to medium-low, and cook, stirring occasionally, until kale is wilted, about 15 minutes.

3. Stir in squash and any accumulated juices, cover, and continue to cook until kale and squash are tender, 10 to 20 minutes.

4. Uncover, increase heat to medium-high, and cook, stirring occasionally, until most of liquid has evaporated and sauce has thickened, 2 to 5 minutes. Off heat, stir in remaining ½ cup coconut milk, lime juice, and remaining 1 tablespoon oil. Season with salt and pepper to taste, sprinkle with pepitas, and serve.

PER SERVING Cal 500; **Total Fat** 38g, **Sat Fat** 21g; **Chol** 0mg; **Sodium** 540mg; **Total Carb** 40g, **Dietary Fiber** 9g, **Total Sugars** 8g; **Protein** 12g

Mediterranean Braised Green Beans with Potatoes and Basil

Mediterranean Braised Green Beans with Potatoes and Basil

SERVES 4 TO 6 `VEGAN`

WHY THIS RECIPE WORKS When you slow braise green beans something magic happens: They turn soft and velvety without becoming mushy. We first simmered the beans with a pinch of baking soda to dissolve the pectin in their cell walls. Once the beans were partially softened, we stirred in acidic diced tomatoes to add sweet flavor and neutralize the baking soda so the beans wouldn't soften too much. The beans turned meltingly tender after less than an hour of simmering in a low oven. To infuse the beans with bright flavors, we added sautéed garlic and onion plus some bright lemon juice, basil, and a drizzle of olive oil. Finally, to make the dish heartier, we added in chunks of potatoes; 1-inch pieces turned tender in the same amount of time as the beans. Serve with a dollop of plain yogurt and rice or crusty bread.

- 5 tablespoons extra-virgin olive oil, divided
- 1 onion, chopped fine
- 4 garlic cloves, minced
- 2 teaspoons dried oregano
- 1½ cups water

1½ pounds green beans, trimmed and cut into
  2- to 3-inch lengths
1 pound Yukon Gold potatoes, peeled and
  cut into 1-inch pieces
½ teaspoon baking soda
1 (14.5-ounce) can diced tomatoes, drained with
  juice reserved, chopped coarse
1 tablespoon tomato paste
2 teaspoons table salt
¼ teaspoon pepper
3 tablespoons chopped fresh basil
  Lemon juice

1. Adjust oven rack to lower-middle position and heat oven to
275 degrees. Heat 3 tablespoons oil in Dutch oven over medium
heat until shimmering. Add onion and cook until softened, 5 to
7 minutes. Stir in garlic and oregano and cook until fragrant, about
30 seconds. Stir in water, green beans, potatoes, and baking soda
and bring to simmer. Reduce heat to medium-low and cook, stirring
occasionally, for 10 minutes.

2. Stir in tomatoes and their juice, tomato paste, salt, and pepper.
Cover pot, transfer to oven, and cook until sauce is slightly thickened and green beans can be cut easily with side of fork, 40 to
50 minutes.

3. Stir in basil and season with lemon juice to taste. Transfer to
bowl, drizzle with remaining 2 tablespoons oil, and serve.

PER SERVING Cal 220; **Total Fat** 12g, **Sat Fat** 1.5g;
Chol 0mg; **Sodium** 1080mg; **Total Carb** 25g, **Dietary
Fiber** 3g, **Total Sugars** 6g; **Protein** 4g

Stuffed Acorn Squash

Stuffed Acorn Squash
SERVES 4

WHY THIS RECIPE WORKS Stuffing and roasting an acorn
squash the traditional way can take hours, but our impressive
version is ready in a fraction of the time without compromising on
either flavor or texture. Our solution was to microwave the squash,
which takes about 15 minutes, and make our filling in the mean-
time. While couscous steeped off heat in boiling water, we sautéed
onion and garlic, and then added baby spinach and cooked until
it wilted before folding this mixture into the couscous along with
pine nuts and Pecorino Romano cheese. Golden raisins brought
a touch of sweetness that complemented the squash. To finish,
we just needed a sprinkle of additional cheese and a few minutes
under the broiler. Be sure to look for similar-size squash (1½ pounds
each) to ensure even cooking. For an accurate measurement of
boiling water, bring a full kettle of water to a boil, then measure
out the desired amount.

2 acorn squashes (1½ pounds each),
  halved lengthwise and seeded
3 tablespoons vegetable oil, divided
1 cup couscous
½ cup golden raisins
1 teaspoon table salt
1 cup boiling water
1 onion, chopped fine
4 garlic cloves, minced
6 ounces (6 cups) baby spinach
½ cup pine nuts, toasted
1½ ounces Pecorino Romano cheese,
  grated (¾ cup), divided

1. Brush cut side of squash with 1 tablespoon oil and place cut
side down on large plate. Microwave, covered, until tender and soft,
12 to 16 minutes.

2. Meanwhile, combine couscous, raisins, salt, and 1 tablespoon
oil in medium bowl. Stir in boiling water, cover tightly, and let sit
until liquid is absorbed and couscous is tender, about 5 minutes.
Fluff couscous with fork.

3. Heat remaining 1 tablespoon oil in 12-inch skillet over medium heat until shimmering. Add onion and cook until softened, about 5 minutes. Stir in garlic and cook until fragrant, about 30 seconds. Stir in spinach and cook until wilted and most of liquid has evaporated, about 2 minutes. Off heat, stir in couscous mixture, pine nuts, and ½ cup Pecorino. Season with salt and pepper to taste.

4. Adjust oven rack 8 inches from broiler element and heat broiler. Transfer squash cut side up to rimmed baking sheet and season with salt and pepper. Mound couscous mixture into squash, pack lightly with back of spoon, and sprinkle with remaining ¼ cup Pecorino.

5. Broil until lightly browned, 4 to 5 minutes. Serve.

PER SERVING Cal 600; **Total Fat** 26g, **Sat Fat** 3.5g; **Chol** 5mg; **Sodium** 780mg; **Total Carb** 84g, **Dietary Fiber** 8g, **Total Sugars** 22g; **Protein** 15g

Stuffed Eggplant
SERVES 8

WHY THIS RECIPE WORKS Italian eggplants are the ideal size for stuffing—and one half makes an ample side dish (serve two halves for a main dish). We wanted a version that allowed the flavor of the eggplant to shine. Drawn to the flavors of Turkey, we mixed a simple stuffing of sautéed onion, tomatoes, Pecorino Romano cheese, and pine nuts seasoned with oregano, and cinnamon, plus red wine vinegar. After roasting eggplant halves until tender, we gently pushed the soft flesh to the sides to create a cavity for our stuffing, which we sprinkled with extra cheese before returning the eggplants to the oven just until the cheese melted. If you can't find Italian eggplants, substitute small globe eggplants.

  4 Italian eggplants (10 ounces each), halved lengthwise
  ¼ cup extra-virgin olive oil, divided
1¼ teaspoons table salt, divided
  ½ teaspoon pepper
  1 onion, chopped fine
  3 garlic cloves, minced
  2 teaspoons minced fresh oregano or ½ teaspoon dried
  ¼ teaspoon ground cinnamon
  ⅛ teaspoon cayenne pepper
  1 pound plum tomatoes, cored, seeded, and chopped
  2 ounces Pecorino Romano cheese, grated (1 cup), divided
  ¼ cup pine nuts, toasted
  1 tablespoon red wine vinegar
  2 tablespoons minced fresh parsley

1. Adjust oven racks to upper-middle and lowest positions, place parchment paper–lined rimmed baking sheet on lower rack, and heat oven to 400 degrees.

Stuffed Eggplant

2. Brush cut sides of eggplant with 2 tablespoons oil and sprinkle with ¾ teaspoon salt and pepper. Place eggplant cut side down on preheated sheet and carefully cover with aluminum foil. Roast until eggplant is golden brown and tender, 50 to 55 minutes. Transfer eggplant cut side down to paper towel–lined baking sheet and let drain.

3. Meanwhile, heat remaining 2 tablespoons oil in 12-inch skillet over medium heat until shimmering. Add onion and remaining ½ teaspoon salt and cook until softened and browned, about 10 minutes. Stir in garlic, oregano, cinnamon, and cayenne and cook until fragrant, about 30 seconds. Stir in tomatoes, ¾ cup Pecorino, pine nuts, and vinegar and cook until warmed through, about 1 minute. Season with salt and pepper to taste.

4. Return eggplant cut side up to sheet. Using 2 forks, gently push eggplant flesh to sides to make room in center for filling. Mound ¼ cup filling into eggplant halves and sprinkle with remaining ¼ cup Pecorino. Roast on upper rack until cheese is melted, 5 to 10 minutes. Sprinkle with parsley. Serve.

PER SERVING Cal 170; **Total Fat** 12g, **Sat Fat** 2.5g; **Chol** 5mg; **Sodium** 400mg; **Total Carb** 13g, **Dietary Fiber** 5g, **Total Sugars** 7g; **Protein** 5g

Hasselback Eggplant with Garlic-Yogurt Sauce
SERVES 4

WHY THIS RECIPE WORKS This roasted eggplant dish offers the smoky goodness that we love in baba ghanoush—but with more textural variety and structural integrity. For a creamy interior and crispy edges, we borrowed the technique used for Hasselback potatoes. Making crosswise slices every ¼ inch down the length of the eggplant, stopping just short of slicing through, allowed steam to escape during cooking so the eggplant became tender without bursting and turning to mush. More importantly, we could pack the spaces between the slices with a sweet and spicy paste made from jarred piquillo peppers, walnuts, bread crumbs, and pomegranate molasses. Finally, we balanced the eggplant's rich spiciness and mild bitterness with a garlic-yogurt sauce. To ensure you don't cut through the eggplant in step 2, you can create a guard by placing a chopstick on either side of the eggplant. If you can't find Aleppo pepper, you can substitute 1½ teaspoons paprika and 1½ teaspoons finely chopped red pepper flakes.

Hasselback Eggplant with Garlic-Yogurt Sauce

EGGPLANT
- 1 large eggplant (1½ pounds)
- 2 teaspoons table salt, divided
- 1 cup jarred piquillo peppers, patted dry and chopped
- 1 cup walnuts, toasted
- 1 cup panko bread crumbs, divided
- 7 scallions, cut into 1-inch pieces
- 3 tablespoons pomegranate molasses
- 2 tablespoons ground dried Aleppo pepper
- 1 tablespoon lemon juice
- 1 teaspoon ground cumin
- 6 tablespoons extra-virgin olive oil, divided
- 2 tablespoons chopped fresh mint

GARLIC-YOGURT SAUCE
- 1 cup plain Greek yogurt
- 1 tablespoon lemon juice
- 1 tablespoon chopped fresh mint
- 1 garlic clove, minced
- ½ teaspoon table salt

1. FOR THE EGGPLANT Adjust oven rack to upper-middle position and heat oven to 400 degrees. Line rimmed baking sheet with aluminum foil and place wire rack in sheet.

2. Trim stem and bottom ¼ inch of eggplant, then halve lengthwise. Working with 1 half at a time, place eggplant cut side down on cutting board and slice crosswise at ¼-inch intervals, leaving bottom ¼ inch intact. Sprinkle eggplant fans evenly with 1 teaspoon salt, making sure to get salt in between slices, and let sit for 15 minutes.

3. Process piquillos, walnuts, 6 tablespoons panko, scallions, pomegranate molasses, Aleppo pepper, lemon juice, cumin, and remaining 1 teaspoon salt in food processor to coarse paste, about 30 seconds, scraping down sides of bowl as needed. With processor running, slowly add ¼ cup oil until incorporated.

4. Pat eggplant dry with paper towels. Spread 1½ cups pepper paste over eggplant, being sure to spread paste between cut sides of eggplant. Transfer eggplant fanned side up to prepared rack and roast until eggplant can be easily pierced with tip of paring knife and edges are crispy and golden brown, 40 minutes to 1 hour.

5. Remove eggplant from oven and heat broiler. Combine remaining 10 tablespoons panko, remaining 2 tablespoons oil, and 2 tablespoons pepper paste in bowl. (Set aside remaining pepper paste for another use.) Spread panko mixture evenly over top of eggplant and broil until topping is crispy and golden brown, 1 to 3 minutes. Transfer eggplant to serving platter and sprinkle with mint. Serve with yogurt sauce.

6. FOR GARLIC-YOGURT SAUCE Whisk all ingredients in bowl until combined.

PER SERVING Cal 640; **Total Fat** 45g, **Sat Fat** 10g; **Chol** 10mg; **Sodium** 1310mg; **Total Carb** 49g, **Dietary Fiber** 8g, **Total Sugars** 22g; **Protein** 13g

Stuffed Portobello Mushrooms with Spinach and Gorgonzola
SERVES 8

WHY THIS RECIPE WORKS With their naturally concave shape and wide surface area, portobello mushroom caps are perfect for roasting and stuffing. We first roasted the empty caps in a super-hot 500-degree oven. Roasting them gill side down allowed any moisture released during cooking to drain away; plus, it protected the delicate underside of the mushrooms from burning. While the mushrooms roasted, we made an easy stuffing with baby spinach, flavorful Gorgonzola cheese, and toasted walnuts that we topped with panko bread crumbs. A quick run under the broiler heated everything through and crisped up the crown of bread crumbs. You can substitute cream sherry with a squeeze of lemon juice for the dry sherry here, but do not substitute cooking sherry. Feta or goat cheese can be substituted for the Gorgonzola if desired.

  5 tablespoons extra-virgin olive oil, divided
 10 large portobello mushroom caps (8 whole,
       2 chopped fine)
 1¼ teaspoons table salt, divided
  ½ teaspoon pepper
 12 ounces (12 cups) baby spinach
  2 tablespoons water
  1 onion, chopped fine
  4 garlic cloves, minced
  ½ cup dry sherry
  4 ounces Gorgonzola cheese, crumbled (1 cup)
  1 cup walnuts, toasted and chopped
  ¾ cup panko bread crumbs

1. Adjust oven rack to upper-middle position and heat oven to 500 degrees. Brush rimmed baking sheet with 1 tablespoon oil. Lay 8 whole mushroom caps gill side down on baking sheet and brush tops with 2 tablespoons oil. Roast until tender, 10 to 12 minutes. Remove baking sheet from oven, flip mushrooms gill side up, and season with 1 teaspoon salt and pepper.

2. Meanwhile, microwave spinach, water, and remaining ¼ teaspoon salt in covered bowl until spinach is wilted, about 2 minutes. Drain spinach in colander, let cool slightly, then place in clean dish towel and squeeze out excess liquid. Transfer spinach to cutting board and chop coarse.

3. Cook onion and remaining 2 tablespoons oil in 12-inch skillet over medium-high heat until softened, about 3 minutes. Stir in chopped mushrooms and cook until they begin to release their liquid, about 4 minutes. Stir in garlic and cook until fragrant, about 30 seconds. Stir in sherry and cook until evaporated, about 2 minutes. Stir in chopped spinach, Gorgonzola, and walnuts and cook until heated through, about 1 minute. Season with salt and pepper to taste.

4. Spoon filling into roasted mushroom caps, press filling flat with back of spoon, then sprinkle with panko. Bake until panko is golden and filling is hot, 5 to 10 minutes. Serve.

PER SERVING Cal 300; **Total Fat** 23g, **Sat Fat** 5g; **Chol** 10mg; **Sodium** 580mg; **Total Carb** 16g, **Dietary Fiber** 4g, **Total Sugars** 4g; **Protein** 9g

Stuffed Zucchini with Corn, Black Beans, and Chipotle Chiles
SERVES 8

WHY THIS RECIPE WORKS Zucchini are a perfect shape for hollowing out and stuffing, and the possibilities for fillings are endless. We started by scooping the seeds out of the zucchini to reduce moisture. Then we roasted the zucchini cut side down for a flavorful sear and a head start on the cooking process. A stuffing of potato, black beans, smoky chipotle, and vegetables gave this dish satisfying heft and flavor. Finally, we returned everything to the oven for a quick final roast to cook through. For a vegetarian main, serve two halves per person. It's important to use smaller, in-season zucchini, which have thinner skins and fewer seeds.

  4 zucchini (8 ounces each)
  ¾ teaspoon table salt, divided
  ¼ teaspoon plus ⅛ teaspoon pepper, divided
  ¼ cup extra-virgin olive oil, divided
  1 red potato, unpeeled, cut into ½-inch cubes
  1 onion, chopped fine
  2 ears corn, kernels cut from cobs
  5 garlic cloves, minced
  3 canned chipotle chiles in adobo sauce, minced
  2 tomatoes, seeded and chopped
  1 (15-ounce) can black beans, rinsed
  ⅓ cup minced fresh cilantro
  6 ounces Monterey Jack cheese,
       shredded (1½ cups), divided

1. Adjust oven racks to upper-middle and lowest positions, place rimmed baking sheet on each rack, and heat oven to 400 degrees.

2. Meanwhile, halve each zucchini lengthwise. With small spoon, scoop out seeds and most of flesh so that walls of zucchini are ¼ inch thick. Sprinkle cut sides of zucchini with ½ teaspoon salt and ¼ teaspoon pepper, and brush with 2 tablespoons oil; set zucchini halves cut side down on hot baking sheet on lower rack. Toss potato cubes with 1 tablespoon oil, remaining ¼ teaspoon salt, and remaining ⅛ teaspoon pepper in small bowl and spread in single layer on hot baking sheet on upper rack. Roast zucchini

until slightly softened and skins are wrinkled, about 10 minutes; roast potatoes until tender and lightly browned, 10 to 12 minutes. Using tongs, flip zucchini halves over on baking sheet and set aside.

3. Heat remaining tablespoon oil in 12-inch skillet over medium heat until shimmering but not smoking, about 2 minutes. Add onion and cook, stirring occasionally, until softened and beginning to brown, about 10 minutes. Increase heat to medium-high; stir in corn and cook until almost tender, about 3 minutes. Add garlic and chipotle chiles; cook until fragrant, about 30 seconds. Stir in tomatoes, black beans, and cooked potato; cook, stirring occasionally, until heated through, about 3 minutes. Off heat, stir in cilantro and ½ cup Monterey Jack and season with salt and pepper to taste.

4. Divide filling evenly among squash halves on baking sheet, spooning about ½ cup into each, and pack lightly; sprinkle with remaining Monterey Jack. Return sheet to upper rack in oven, and bake zucchini until heated through and cheese is spotty brown, about 6 minutes. Serve immediately.

PER SERVING Cal 240; **Total Fat** 15g, **Sat Fat** 5g; **Chol** 20mg; **Sodium** 500mg; **Total Carb** 21g, **Dietary Fiber** 5g, **Total Sugars** 6g; **Protein** 10g

Mediterranean Stuffed Zucchini

Mediterranean Stuffed Zucchini
SERVES 8

WHY THIS RECIPE WORKS These perfectly baked zucchini boats are filled with a rich, gently spiced lamb stuffing. To avoid overcooked and flavorless zucchini, we scooped out the seeds and roasted the unstuffed zucchini cut side down. Then we returned the stuffed zucchini to the hot oven for a final burst of heat. To balance the flavor of the lamb, we settled on a trio of elements popular in Moroccan cuisine: sweet dried apricots, buttery pine nuts, and *ras el hanout*, the spice blend that includes coriander, cardamom, and cinnamon. After browning the lamb, we poured off all but a small amount of the fat to keep our filling from tasting too greasy; to offset the filling's meaty texture and add a wheaty chew, we incorporated a small amount of bulgur. It's important to use smaller, in-season zucchini, which have thinner skins and fewer seeds. We prefer to use our own ras el hanout, but you can find it in the spice aisle of most well-stocked supermarkets.

4 zucchini (8 ounces each), trimmed, halved lengthwise, and seeded
2 tablespoons plus 1 teaspoon extra-virgin olive oil, divided
1 teaspoon table salt, divided
½ teaspoon pepper, divided
8 ounces ground lamb
1 onion, chopped fine
4 garlic cloves, minced
2 teaspoons Ras el Hanout (page 167)
⅔ cup chicken broth
½ cup medium-grind bulgur, rinsed
¼ cup dried apricots, chopped fine
2 tablespoons pine nuts, toasted
2 tablespoons minced fresh parsley

1. Adjust oven racks to upper-middle and lowest positions, place rimmed baking sheet on lower rack, and heat oven to 400 degrees. Brush cut sides of zucchini with 2 tablespoons oil and sprinkle with ½ teaspoon salt and ¼ teaspoon pepper. Lay zucchini cut side down in hot sheet and roast until slightly softened and skins are wrinkled, 8 to 10 minutes. Remove zucchini from oven and flip cut side up on sheet; set aside.

2. Meanwhile, heat remaining 1 teaspoon oil in large saucepan over medium-high heat until just smoking. Add lamb, remaining ½ teaspoon salt, and remaining ¼ teaspoon pepper and cook, breaking up meat with wooden spoon, until browned, 3 to 5 minutes. Using slotted spoon, transfer lamb to paper towel–lined plate.

3. Pour off all but 1 tablespoon fat from saucepan. Add onion to fat left in saucepan and cook over medium heat until softened, about 5 minutes. Stir in garlic and ras el hanout and cook until fragrant, about 30 seconds. Stir in broth, bulgur, and apricots and bring to simmer. Reduce heat to low, cover, and simmer gently until bulgur is tender, 16 to 18 minutes.

4. Off heat, lay clean dish towel underneath lid and let pilaf sit for 10 minutes. Add pine nuts and parsley to pilaf and gently fluff with fork to combine. Season with salt and pepper to taste.

5. Pack each zucchini half with bulgur mixture, about ½ cup per zucchini half, mounding excess. Place baking sheet on upper rack and bake zucchini until heated through, about 6 minutes. Serve.

PER SERVING Cal 390; **Total Fat** 24g, **Sat Fat** 7g; **Chol** 40mg; **Sodium** 740mg; **Total Carb** 30g, **Dietary Fiber** 6g, **Total Sugars** 11g; **Protein** 16g

Zucchini and Feta Fritters
SERVES 4 TO 6

WHY THIS RECIPE WORKS These zucchini fritters, packed with feta cheese and dill and served with a yogurt sauce, make an appealing side dish or light main course. Shredding and salting the zucchini, letting it drain, and then squeezing it in a clean dish towel eliminated excess moisture, which can make the fritters soggy. To allow the zucchini's delicate flavor to shine, we bound the zucchini with just a couple of eggs and a little flour. A simple yogurt-based sauce offered the perfect finish. Use a coarse grater or the shredding disk of a food processor to shred the zucchini. Make sure to squeeze the zucchini until it is completely dry, or the fritters will fall apart in the skillet. Do not let the zucchini sit on its own for too long after it has been squeezed dry or it will turn brown. In addition to the lemon wedges, serve with Cucumber-Yogurt Sauce or Yogurt-Herb Sauce (page 105). The fritters can be served warm or at room temperature.

1 pound zucchini, shredded
    Table salt for salting zucchini
4 ounces feta cheese, crumbled (1 cup)
2 scallions, minced
2 large eggs, lightly beaten
2 tablespoons minced fresh dill
1 garlic clove, minced
¼ teaspoon pepper
¼ cup all-purpose flour
6 tablespoons extra-virgin olive oil, divided
    Lemon wedges

Zucchini and Feta Fritters

1. Adjust oven rack to middle position and heat oven to 200 degrees. Toss zucchini with 1 teaspoon salt and let drain in fine-mesh strainer for 10 minutes.

2. Wrap zucchini in clean dish towel, squeeze out excess liquid, and transfer to large bowl. Stir in feta, scallions, eggs, dill, garlic, and pepper. Sprinkle flour over mixture and stir to incorporate.

3. Heat 3 tablespoons oil in 12-inch nonstick skillet over medium heat until shimmering. Drop 2-tablespoon-size portions of batter into skillet and use back of spoon to press batter into 2-inch-wide fritter (you should fit about 6 fritters in skillet at a time). Fry until golden brown, about 3 minutes per side.

4. Transfer fritters to paper towel–lined baking sheet and keep warm in oven. Wipe skillet clean with paper towels and repeat with remaining 3 tablespoons oil and remaining batter. Serve with lemon wedges.

PER SERVING Cal 230; **Total Fat** 20g, **Sat Fat** 5g; **Chol** 80mg; **Sodium** 400mg; **Total Carb** 7g, **Dietary Fiber** 1g, **Total Sugars** 3g; **Protein** 6g

Cauliflower Steaks with Salsa Verde

SERVES 4 `MAKE-AHEAD` `VEGAN`

WHY THIS RECIPE WORKS Popularized as a plant-based reimagining of a steak, roasted thick planks of cauliflower make for not only a great vegan main but also a substantial side for any meal. In a superhot oven they develop a meaty texture and became nutty, sweet, and caramelized. Steaming the cauliflower briefly by covering the baking sheet with foil, followed by high-heat uncovered roasting, produced dramatic seared steaks with tender interiors. To elevate the dish, we paired it with a vibrant salsa verde—a blend of parsley, mint, capers, olive oil, and white wine vinegar brushing the steaks while hot so they'd soak up the sauce's robust flavor. Look for fresh, firm, white heads of cauliflower that feel heavy for their size and are free of blemishes or soft spots; florets are more likely to separate from older heads of cauliflower.

- 1½ cups fresh parsley leaves
- ½ cup fresh mint leaves
- ½ cup extra-virgin olive oil, divided
- 2 tablespoons water
- 1½ tablespoons white wine vinegar
- 1 tablespoon capers, rinsed
- 1 garlic clove, minced
- ⅛ teaspoon plus ½ teaspoon table salt, divided
- 2 heads cauliflower (2 pounds each)
- ¼ teaspoon pepper
  Lemon wedges

1. Pulse parsley, mint, ¼ cup oil, water, vinegar, capers, garlic, and ⅛ teaspoon salt in food processor until mixture is finely chopped but not smooth, about 10 pulses, scraping down sides of bowl as needed. Transfer sauce to small bowl and set aside. (Sauce can be refrigerated for up to 2 days.)

2. Adjust oven rack to lowest position and heat oven to 500 degrees. Working with 1 head cauliflower at a time, discard outer leaves of cauliflower and trim stem flush with bottom florets. Halve cauliflower lengthwise through core. Cut one 1½-inch-thick slab lengthwise from each half, trimming any florets not connected to core. (You should have 4 steaks; reserve remaining cauliflower for another use.)

3. Place steaks on rimmed baking sheet and drizzle with 2 tablespoons oil. Sprinkle with ¼ teaspoon salt and ⅛ teaspoon pepper and rub to distribute. Flip steaks and repeat with remaining ¼ teaspoon salt and ⅛ teaspoon pepper.

4. Cover baking sheet tightly with foil and roast for 5 minutes. Remove foil and roast until bottoms of steaks are well browned, 8 to 10 minutes. Gently flip and continue to roast until tender and second sides are well browned, 6 to 8 more minutes.

5. Transfer steaks to platter and brush evenly with ¼ cup salsa verde. Serve with lemon wedges and remaining salsa verde.

PER SERVING Cal 320; **Total Fat** 29g, **Sat Fat** 4.5g; **Chol** 0mg; **Sodium** 500mg; **Total Carb** 14g, **Dietary Fiber** 6g, **Total Sugars** 5g; **Protein** 5g

CUTTING CAULIFLOWER STEAKS

1. Halve cauliflower lengthwise through core.

2. Cut one 1½-inch-thick slab from each cauliflower half.

Twice-Baked Sweet Potatoes with Hazelnuts

SERVES 6

WHY THIS RECIPE WORKS Part baked potato, part casserole, twice-baked potatoes spruce up any meal—or make it. We wanted to remake this classic into an elegant but not overly heavy dish for dinner, so we swapped out starchy russets for sweet potatoes, choosing smaller potatoes for portions small enough to serve with another side. Mashing the flesh with an egg, Greek yogurt, and Parmesan produced a filling that was fluffy and just rich enough. To accentuate the earthy potatoes, we topped them with toasted hazelnuts, parsley, and chives and traded sour cream for seasoned Greek yogurt for a creamy finish.

- 4 small sweet potatoes (8 ounces each), unpeeled, each lightly pricked with fork in 3 places
- 2 tablespoons extra-virgin olive oil
- 2 shallots, sliced thin
- 2 garlic cloves, minced, divided
- ¼ cup hazelnuts, toasted, skinned, and chopped
- 2 tablespoons chopped fresh parsley
- 2 tablespoons minced fresh chives
- 2 tablespoons grated Parmesan cheese, divided
- ⅛ teaspoon pepper
- 1 large egg, lightly beaten
- ¼ cup plain 2 percent Greek yogurt, divided
- ¼ teaspoon table salt

1. Adjust oven rack to middle position and heat oven to 425 degrees. Place potatoes in shallow baking dish. Microwave until skewer glides easily through flesh, 9 to 12 minutes, flipping potatoes every 3 minutes. Let potatoes cool for 10 minutes.

2. Halve each potato lengthwise. Using spoon, scoop flesh from each half into medium bowl, leaving about ⅛- to ¼-inch thickness of flesh. Place 6 shells cut side up on wire rack set in rimmed baking sheet (discard remaining 2 shells). Bake shells until dry and slightly crispy, about 10 minutes. Remove shells from oven and reduce temperature to 325 degrees.

3. Heat oil in 10-inch skillet over medium heat until shimmering. Add shallots and cook, stirring occasionally, until softened and lightly browned, about 3 minutes. Stir in half of the garlic and cook until fragrant, about 30 seconds. Transfer mixture to second bowl. Add hazelnuts, parsley, chives, 1 tablespoon Parmesan, and pepper to shallot mixture and toss to combine.

4. Mash potato flesh with ricer, food mill, or potato masher until smooth. Whisk in egg, 1 tablespoon yogurt, remaining garlic, remaining 1 tablespoon Parmesan, and salt until well combined and fluffy.

5. Divide mashed potato mixture evenly among shells. Top each filled shell with shallot-hazelnut mixture and return filled potatoes to wire rack. When oven has reached 325 degrees, bake until topping is spotty golden brown and filling is hot, about 20 minutes.

6. Season remaining 3 tablespoons yogurt with salt and pepper and dollop onto potatoes. Serve.

PER SERVING Cal 230; **Total Fat** 9g; **Sat Fat** 1.5g; **Chol** 35mg; **Sodium** 240mg; **Total Carb** 30g, **Dietary Fiber** 6g, **Total Sugars** 10g; **Protein** 6g

Sweet Potato and Swiss Chard Gratin

Sweet Potato and Swiss Chard Gratin
SERVES 4 TO 6 `MAKE-AHEAD`

WHY THIS RECIPE WORKS For a new twist on a classic potato gratin, we created a decidedly savory and elegant sweet potato version to serve with a light dinner or as a main course with a salad or simple vegetable. We balanced the potatoes' natural sweetness with earthy, slightly bitter Swiss chard sautéed in butter with shallot, garlic, and thyme. We shingled half the sliced potatoes along the bottom of the dish, topped them with the chard, and layered on the remaining potatoes. Pouring water, wine, and cream over the vegetables encouraged the potatoes to cook evenly and imparted a welcome richness. Covering the gratin dish for the first half of baking ensured that the potatoes cooked through. We then uncovered the dish so that the excess liquid could evaporate and the cheesy topping could brown. Slicing the potatoes ⅛ inch thick is crucial for the success of this dish; use a mandoline, a V-slicer, or a food processor fitted with a ⅛-inch-thick slicing blade.

2 tablespoons unsalted butter
2 shallots, minced
2 teaspoons table salt, divided
2 pounds Swiss chard, stemmed and cut into ½-inch-wide strips
3 garlic cloves, minced
2 teaspoons minced fresh thyme
¾ teaspoon pepper
⅓ cup heavy cream
⅓ cup water
⅓ cup dry white wine
3 pounds sweet potatoes, peeled and sliced ⅛ inch thick
2 ounces Parmesan cheese, grated (1 cup)

1. Adjust oven rack to middle position and heat oven to 350 degrees. Melt butter in Dutch oven over medium-high heat. Add shallots and 1 teaspoon salt and cook until shallots are softened, about 2 minutes. Stir in chard and cook until wilted, about 2 minutes. Stir in garlic, thyme, and pepper and cook until fragrant, about 30 seconds; transfer to bowl.

2. Add cream, water, wine, and remaining 1 teaspoon salt to now-empty pot and bring to simmer over medium-high heat. Remove pot from heat and cover to keep warm.

3. Shingle half of potatoes evenly into 3-quart gratin dish (or 13 by 9-inch baking dish). Spread wilted chard mixture evenly over potatoes, then shingle remaining potatoes over top. Pour cream mixture evenly over top and sprinkle with Parmesan. (Gratin can be refrigerated for up to 24 hours.)

4. Cover dish with aluminum foil and bake for 20 minutes. Uncover and continue to bake until gratin is golden and feels tender when poked with paring knife, 40 to 50 minutes. Let cool for 10 minutes before serving.

PER SERVING Cal 320; **Total Fat** 11g, **Sat Fat** 7g; **Chol** 30mg; **Sodium** 1350mg; **Total Carb** 42g, **Dietary Fiber** 9g, **Total Sugars** 13g; **Protein** 10g

Indian-Style Spinach with Fresh Cheese (Saag Paneer)
SERVES 4 TO 6 `MAKE-AHEAD`

WHY THIS RECIPE WORKS *Saag paneer*, soft cubes of creamy cheese in a spicy pureed spinach sauce, is an Indian restaurant classic. It pairs well with any curry (meat or vegetable) and basmati rice, and re-creating it isn't as difficult as you might think. We made our own cheese by heating whole milk and buttermilk, squeezing the curds of excess moisture, then weighting the cheese down until firm enough to slice. Adding mustard greens to the spinach lent complexity that worked well with the warm spices; microwaving the greens kept the process easy. Canned diced tomatoes brightened the dish and cashews—both pureed and chopped—gave our saag paneer nutty richness. Wring the cheese tightly in step 2 and use two plates that nestle together snugly. Use commercially produced cultured buttermilk in this recipe. You can substitute 14 ounces of firm tofu cut into ½-inch pieces and drained for the cheese.

CHEESE
- 3 quarts whole milk
- 3 cups buttermilk
- 1 tablespoon table salt

SPINACH SAUCE
- 1 (10-ounce) bag curly-leaf spinach, rinsed
- ¾ pound mustard greens, stemmed and rinsed
- 3 tablespoons unsalted butter
- 1 teaspoon cumin seeds
- 1 teaspoon ground coriander
- 1 teaspoon paprika
- ½ teaspoon ground cardamom
- ¼ teaspoon ground cinnamon
- 1 onion, chopped fine
- ¾ teaspoon table salt
- 3 garlic cloves, minced
- 1 tablespoon grated fresh ginger
- 1 jalapeño chile, stemmed, seeded, and minced
- 1 (14.5-ounce) can diced tomatoes, drained and chopped
- ½ cup roasted cashews, chopped, divided
- 1 cup water
- 1 cup buttermilk
- 3 tablespoons minced fresh cilantro

1. FOR THE CHEESE Line colander with triple layer of cheesecloth and set in sink. Bring milk to boil in Dutch oven over medium-high heat. Whisk in buttermilk and salt, turn off heat, and let stand for 1 minute. Pour milk mixture through cheesecloth and let curds drain for 15 minutes.

2. Pull edges of cheesecloth together to form pouch. Twist edges of cheesecloth together, firmly squeezing out as much liquid as possible from cheese curds. Place taut, twisted cheese pouch between 2 large plates and weigh down top plate with heavy Dutch oven. Set aside at room temperature until cheese is firm and set, about 45 minutes, then remove cheesecloth. (Cheese can be wrapped in plastic wrap and refrigerated for up to 3 days.) Cut cheese into ½-inch pieces.

3. FOR THE SPINACH SAUCE Microwave spinach in covered bowl until wilted, about 3 minutes. Let cool slightly, then chop enough spinach to measure ⅓ cup. Transfer remaining spinach to blender. Microwave mustard greens in covered bowl until wilted, about 4 minutes. Let cool slightly, then chop enough mustard greens to measure ⅓ cup; combine with chopped spinach. Transfer remaining mustard greens to blender with remaining spinach.

4. Meanwhile, melt butter in 12-inch skillet over medium-high heat. Add cumin seeds, coriander, paprika, cardamom, and cinnamon and cook until fragrant, about 30 seconds. Add onion and salt and cook, stirring frequently, until softened, about 3 minutes. Stir in garlic, ginger, and jalapeño and cook, stirring frequently, until lightly browned and just beginning to stick to pan, 2 to 3 minutes. Stir in tomatoes and cook mixture until pan is dry and tomatoes are beginning to brown, 3 to 4 minutes. Remove skillet from heat.

5. Transfer half of onion mixture, ¼ cup cashews, and water to blender with greens and process until smooth, about 1 minute. Stir puree, chopped greens, and buttermilk into skillet with remaining onion mixture and bring to simmer over medium-high heat. Reduce heat to low, cover, and cook until flavors have blended, 5 minutes. Season with salt and pepper to taste. Gently fold in cheese cubes and cook until just heated through, 1 to 2 minutes. Transfer to serving dish, sprinkle with remaining ¼ cup cashews and cilantro, and serve.

PER SERVING Cal 540; **Total Fat** 29g, **Sat Fat** 15g; **Chol** 75mg; **Sodium** 1640mg; **Total Carb** 46g, **Dietary Fiber** 5g, **Total Sugars** 35g; **Protein** 27g

Garlicky Tofu Tabbouleh

SERVES 4 TO 6 `VEGAN`

WHY THIS RECIPE WORKS Tabbouleh made from bulgur, tomatoes, lemon, and heaps of fresh herbs is often served as a meze. But with just a little help, tabbouleh becomes more substantial. Enter tofu: Garlicky, savory sautéed tofu transformed this classic into a light summer meal or hearty addition to a picnic spread. Rather than using cubes of tofu, we pulsed it in the food processor to mimic the texture of the bulgur. Salting our tomatoes rid them of excess liquid, and we used their juice (rather than water) to soak the bulgur. Meanwhile, we sautéed our tofu with a hefty dose of toasted garlic. As the tofu cooled, we made a lemony dressing and then tossed everything with liberal amounts of parsley, mint, and scallions and let the whole thing sit for about an hour to let the flavors mingle. When shopping, don't confuse bulgur with cracked wheat, which has a much longer cooking time and will not work in this recipe. You can substitute firm tofu for the extra-firm in this recipe.

- 3 tomatoes, cored and cut into ½-inch pieces
- ¾ teaspoon table salt, divided
- ½ cup medium-grind bulgur, rinsed
- ¼ cup lemon juice (2 lemons), divided
- 14 ounces extra-firm tofu, cut into 2-inch pieces
- ¼ cup extra-virgin olive oil, divided
- 3 garlic cloves, minced
- ⅛ teaspoon cayenne pepper
- 1½ cups minced fresh parsley
- ½ cup minced fresh mint
- 2 scallions, sliced thin

1. Toss tomatoes with ¼ teaspoon salt in fine-mesh strainer set over bowl and let drain, tossing occasionally, for 30 minutes; reserve 2 tablespoons drained tomato juice. Toss bulgur with 2 tablespoons lemon juice and reserved tomato juice in bowl and let sit until grains begin to soften, 30 to 40 minutes.

2. Meanwhile, spread tofu on paper towel–lined baking sheet and let drain for 20 minutes. Gently press dry with paper towels and season with salt and pepper. Pulse tofu in food processor until coarsely chopped, 3 or 4 pulses. Line baking sheet with clean paper towels. Spread processed tofu over prepared sheet and press gently with paper towels to dry.

3. Heat 2 teaspoons oil in 12-inch nonstick skillet over medium-high heat until shimmering. Add tofu and cook, stirring occasionally, until tofu is lightly browned, 10 to 12 minutes. (Tofu should start to sizzle after about 1½ minutes; adjust heat as needed.) Push tofu to sides of skillet. Add 1 teaspoon oil and garlic to center and cook, mashing garlic into skillet, until fragrant, about 1 minute. Stir mixture into tofu. Transfer to bowl and let cool for 10 minutes.

Garlicky Tofu Tabbouleh

4. Whisk remaining ½ teaspoon salt, remaining 2 tablespoons lemon juice, remaining 3 tablespoons oil, and cayenne together in large bowl. Add drained tomatoes, soaked bulgur, cooled tofu, parsley, mint, and scallions and toss to combine. Cover and let sit until bulgur is tender, about 1 hour. Toss to recombine and season with salt and pepper to taste before serving.

PER SERVING Cal 210; **Total Fat** 13g; **Sat Fat** 2g; **Chol** 0mg; **Sodium** 310mg; **Total Carb** 16g, **Dietary Fiber** 3g, **Total Sugars** 2g; **Protein** 9g

Chickpeas with Spinach, Chorizo, and Smoked Paprika

SERVES 4 TO 6

WHY THIS RECIPE WORKS *Espinacas* is a traditional tapas dish found in the southern Spanish region of Andalucia consisting of tender stewed chickpeas, delicate wilted spinach, and bold North African spices. We set out to develop an adaptation of this dish that could work as part of a larger meal or stand on its own as a satisfying main dish. For the flavor backbone, we stuck with the classic southern Spanish flavors of saffron, garlic, smoked paprika, and cumin. We also liked the traditional addition of chorizo, which added meaty richness. To keep the recipe streamlined, we wilted the spinach and then set it aside before building the brothy base with canned chickpeas and aromatics. Including the chickpeas' flavorful, starchy canning liquid gave the dish more body. Finally, we added a traditional picada, which is often used in Spanish cooking as a thickener. The bread crumb–based mixture gave the stewed beans and greens just the right velvety texture and flavor boost. Our finished dish was equally at home as part of a tapas spread or served as an entrée over rice or with good crusty bread to sop up the flavorful broth. If you can't find curly-leaf spinach, you can substitute flat-leaf spinach; do not substitute baby spinach. For an accurate measurement of boiling water, bring a full kettle of water to a boil and then measure out the desired amount.

Pinch saffron threads, crumbled
2 teaspoons extra-virgin olive oil, divided
8 ounces curly-leaf spinach, stemmed
3 ounces Spanish-style chorizo sausage, chopped fine
5 garlic cloves, sliced thin
1 tablespoon smoked paprika
1 teaspoon ground cumin
¼ teaspoon pepper
2 (15-ounce) cans chickpeas
1 recipe Picada
1 tablespoon sherry vinegar

1. Combine 2 tablespoons boiling water and saffron in small bowl and let steep for 5 minutes.

2. Heat 1 teaspoon oil in Dutch oven over medium heat until shimmering. Add spinach and 2 tablespoons water, cover, and cook, stirring occasionally, until spinach is wilted but still bright green, about 1 minute. Transfer spinach to colander and gently press to release liquid. Transfer spinach to cutting board and chop coarse. Return to colander and press again.

3. Heat remaining 1 teaspoon oil in now-empty pot over medium heat until shimmering. Add chorizo and cook until lightly browned, about 5 minutes. Stir in garlic, paprika, cumin, and pepper and cook until fragrant, about 30 seconds. Stir in chickpeas and their liquid, 1 cup water, and saffron mixture and bring to simmer. Cook, stirring occasionally, until chickpeas are tender and liquid has thickened slightly, 10 to 15 minutes.

4. Off heat, stir in picada, spinach, and vinegar and let sit until heated through, about 2 minutes. Adjust sauce consistency with hot water as needed. Season with salt and pepper to taste, and serve.

PER SERVING Cal 270; **Total Fat** 14g, **Sat Fat** 3g; **Chol** 10mg; **Sodium** 660mg; **Total Carb** 26g, **Dietary Fiber** 8g, **Total Sugars** 1g; **Protein** 13g

---

TAKE IT UP A NOTCH

A picada is a traditional Spanish mixture of ground almonds, bread crumbs, and olive oil. It is used to give braised dishes body and texture.

Picada
MAKES ABOUT 1 CUP

Chopped or whole unsalted almonds can be substituted for the slivered almonds; however, they may require longer processing times.

¼ cup slivered almonds
2 slices hearty white sandwich bread, torn into quarters
2 tablespoons extra-virgin olive oil
⅛ teaspoon table salt
Pinch pepper

Adjust oven rack to middle position and heat oven to 375 degrees. Pulse almonds in food processor to fine crumbs, about 20 pulses. Add bread, oil, salt, and pepper and pulse bread to coarse crumbs, about 10 pulses. Spread mixture evenly in rimmed baking sheet and bake, stirring often, until golden brown, about 10 minutes. Let cool. (Picada can be stored in airtight container for up to 2 days.)

Stewed Chickpeas with Eggplant and Tomatoes
SERVES 6   VEGAN

WHY THIS RECIPE WORKS This easy Greek-style stew marries substantial chickpeas with silky, luxurious eggplant, while canned tomatoes offer a rustic backbone. Starting with convenient canned chickpeas helped us to avoid hours-long cooking. In fact, our combination stovetop-oven method developed an amazing depth of savory flavor and the perfect soft-creamy texture in our eggplant in less than an hour of oven time. To jump-start the cooking process, we sautéed onions, bell pepper, garlic, oregano, and bay leaves to create an aromatic base. We added our chickpeas, tomatoes, and eggplant and transferred the pot to the oven. Baking the mixture uncovered concentrated the flavors and allowed extra liquid to evaporate, eliminating the need to pretreat the eggplant. Fresh oregano added a welcome burst of herbaceous flavor. This versatile dish tasted equally good when served warm, at room temperature, or even cold as a side salad.

¼ cup extra-virgin olive oil

2 onions, chopped

1 green bell pepper, stemmed, seeded, and chopped fine

½ teaspoon table salt

¼ teaspoon pepper

3 garlic cloves, minced

1 tablespoon minced fresh oregano or 1 teaspoon dried, divided

2 bay leaves

1 pound eggplant, cut into 1-inch pieces

1 (28-ounce) can whole peeled tomatoes, drained with juice reserved, chopped

2 (15-ounce) cans chickpeas, drained with 1 cup liquid reserved

1. Adjust oven rack to lower-middle position and heat oven to 400 degrees. Heat oil in Dutch oven over medium heat until shimmering. Add onions, bell pepper, salt, and pepper and cook until softened, about 5 minutes. Stir in garlic, 1 teaspoon oregano, and bay leaves and cook until fragrant, about 30 seconds.

2. Stir in eggplant, tomatoes and reserved juice, and chickpeas and reserved liquid and bring to boil. Transfer pot to oven and cook, uncovered, until eggplant is very tender, 45 minutes to 1 hour, stirring twice during cooking.

3. Discard bay leaves. Stir in remaining 2 teaspoons oregano and season with salt and pepper to taste. Serve.

PER SERVING Cal 250; Total Fat 11g, Sat Fat 1.5g; Chol 0mg; Sodium 700mg; Total Carb 31g, Dietary Fiber 7g, Total Sugars 10g; Protein 7g

Chickpea Cakes

Chickpea Cakes
SERVES 6

WHY THIS RECIPE WORKS Fritters and croquettes are a great way to use up leftover legumes; you can add spices and aromatics to the pureed legumes, form the mixture into patties, and fry them until the exteriors are crisp and browned. But since we don't often have leftover chickpeas on hand, we decided to use canned chickpeas to make flavorful chickpea cakes that could be served as an appealing main course or side. Pureeing the chickpeas completely resulted in mushy, homogeneous cakes; instead, we pulsed them until they were coarsely ground but still had some texture. To bind the patties, two eggs and some panko bread crumbs did the trick, and for richness we added yogurt and olive oil. A combination of coriander, cayenne pepper, scallions, and cilantro ensured that these patties were ultraflavorful, and a cool yogurt sauce was the perfect accompaniment. Avoid overmixing the chickpea mixture in step 1 or the cakes will have a mealy texture.

CUCUMBER-YOGURT SAUCE

1 cucumber, peeled, halved lengthwise, and seeded

1 cup plain Greek yogurt

2 tablespoons extra-virgin olive oil

¼ cup minced fresh cilantro, parsley, or mint

1 garlic clove, minced

CHICKPEA CAKES

2 (15-ounce) cans chickpeas, rinsed

½ cup plain Greek yogurt

2 large eggs

6 tablespoons extra-virgin olive oil, divided

1 teaspoon ground coriander

⅛ teaspoon cayenne pepper

⅛ teaspoon table salt

1 cup panko bread crumbs

2 scallions, sliced thin

3 tablespoons minced fresh cilantro

1 shallot, minced

1. FOR THE SAUCE Using food processor fitted with shredding disk, process cucumber until shredded. Whisk yogurt, oil, cilantro, and garlic together in medium bowl. Stir in cucumber and season with salt and pepper to taste; refrigerate until ready to serve.

2. FOR THE CHICKPEA CAKES Pulse chickpeas in food processor until coarsely ground, about 8 pulses. Whisk yogurt, eggs, 2 tablespoons oil, coriander, cayenne, and salt together in medium bowl. Gently stir in chickpeas, panko, scallions, cilantro, and shallot until just combined. Divide mixture into 6 equal portions and gently pack into 1-inch-thick patties.

3. Heat 2 tablespoons oil in 12-inch nonstick skillet over medium heat until shimmering. Carefully lay 3 patties in skillet and cook until well browned and firm, 4 to 5 minutes per side.

4. Transfer cakes to paper towel–lined plate and tent with aluminum foil. Repeat with remaining 2 tablespoons oil and remaining 3 patties. Serve with yogurt sauce.

PER SERVING Cal 350; **Total Fat** 22g, **Sat Fat** 5g; **Chol** 65mg; **Sodium** 370mg; **Total Carb** 26g, **Dietary Fiber** 3g, **Total Sugars** 4g; **Protein** 11g

Turkish Pinto Bean Salad with Tomatoes, Eggs, and Parsley
SERVES 4 TO 6

WHY THIS RECIPE WORKS *Fasulye piyazi* is a traditional Turkish bean salad of small white beans, tomatoes, parsley, hard-cooked eggs, and more. To give our version robust flavor, we opted for pinto beans and infused them with aromatics by warming them briefly in a toasted garlic broth. We made an intense dressing with tahini and Aleppo pepper. Cherry tomatoes, onion, and parsley imparted bright, fresh flavor. A sprinkle of sesame seeds provided textural contrast and emphasized the tahini. The traditional addition of hard-cooked eggs added extra protein, giving the dish enough substance to act as an entrée as well as a complexly flavored side. If you can't find Aleppo pepper, you can substitute ¾ teaspoon of paprika and ¾ teaspoon of finely chopped red pepper flakes.

¼ cup extra-virgin olive oil, divided
3 garlic cloves, lightly crushed and peeled
2 (15-ounce) cans pinto beans, rinsed
¼ teaspoon table salt, plus salt for cooking beans
¼ cup tahini
3 tablespoons lemon juice
1 tablespoon ground dried Aleppo pepper, plus extra for serving
8 ounces cherry tomatoes, halved
¼ red onion, sliced thin

½ cup fresh parsley leaves
2 Easy-Peel Hard-Cooked Eggs
1 tablespoon toasted sesame seeds

1. Cook 1 tablespoon oil and garlic in medium saucepan over medium heat, stirring often, until garlic turns golden but not brown, about 3 minutes. Add beans, 2 cups water, and 1 teaspoon salt and bring to simmer. Remove from heat, cover, and let sit for 20 minutes.

2. Drain beans and discard garlic. Whisk remaining 3 tablespoons oil, tahini, lemon juice, Aleppo pepper, 1 tablespoon water, and ¼ teaspoon salt together in large bowl. Add beans, tomatoes, onion, and parsley and gently toss to combine. Season with salt and pepper to taste. Transfer to serving platter and arrange eggs on top. Sprinkle with sesame seeds and extra Aleppo pepper and serve.

PER SERVING Cal 360; **Total Fat** 19g, **Sat Fat** 3g; **Chol** 70mg; **Sodium** 560mg; **Total Carb** 35g, **Dietary Fiber** 9g, **Total Sugars** 3g; **Protein** 15g

---

TAKE IT UP A NOTCH

A hard-cooked egg is the perfect way to make a side dish a little heartier. Here is our foolproof method for how to cook them.

Easy-Peel Hard-Cooked Eggs
MAKES 6 EGGS

Be sure to use large eggs that have no cracks and are cold from the refrigerator. If you don't have a steamer basket, use a spoon or tongs to gently place the eggs in the water. It does not matter if the eggs are above the water or partially submerged. You can use this method for fewer than six eggs without altering the timing. You can also double this recipe as long as you use a pot and steamer basket large enough to hold the eggs in a single layer. There's no need to peel the eggs right away. They can be stored in their shells and peeled when needed.

6 large eggs

1. Bring 1 inch water to rolling boil in medium saucepan over high heat. Place eggs in steamer basket. Transfer basket to saucepan. Cover, reduce heat to medium-low, and cook eggs for 13 minutes.

2. When eggs are almost finished cooking, combine 2 cups ice cubes and 2 cups cold water in medium bowl. Using tongs or spoon, transfer eggs to ice water; let sit for 15 minutes. Peel before using. (Unpeeled eggs can be refrigerated for up to 1 week.)

Cuban-Style Black Beans and Rice

SERVES 6 TO 8 | VEGAN

WHY THIS RECIPE WORKS Beans and rice is a familiar combination the world over, but Cuban black beans and rice is unique in that the rice is cooked in the inky concentrated liquid left over from cooking the beans, which renders the grains just as flavorful. For our version, we brined dried black beans overnight, which softened their skins and helped to prevent blowouts, before simmering them with aromatics until soft. We reserved half of the ingredients for the *sofrito* (the traditional combination of sautéed garlic, bell pepper, and onion) and added them to the cooking liquid to infuse the beans with aromatic flavor. Lightly browning the remaining sofrito vegetables along with spices and tomato paste added complex flavor to this simple dish. Once the beans were soft, we combined them with the sofrito and rice to finish cooking. Baking the rice and beans eliminated the crusty bottom that can form when the dish is cooked on the stovetop. You will need a Dutch oven with a tight-fitting lid for this recipe. If you are pressed for time you can "quick-brine" your beans: In step 1, combine salt, water, and beans in a large Dutch oven and bring to a boil over high heat. Remove the pot from the heat, cover, and let stand for 1 hour. Drain and rinse the beans; they can be refrigerated for up to two days.

Cuban-Style Black Beans and Rice

2½ teaspoons table salt, divided, plus salt for brining
  1 cup dried black beans, picked over and rinsed
  2 large green bell peppers, halved, stemmed, and seeded, divided
  1 large onion, peeled and halved crosswise, divided
  1 head garlic (5 cloves minced, remaining head halved crosswise and left unpeeled), divided
  2 bay leaves
  2 tablespoons vegetable oil
  4 teaspoons ground cumin
  1 tablespoon minced fresh oregano or 1 teaspoon dried
  1 tablespoon tomato paste
1½ cups long-grain white rice, rinsed
  2 tablespoons red wine vinegar
  2 scallions, sliced thin
    Lime wedges

1. Dissolve 1½ tablespoons salt in 2 quarts cold water in large container. Add beans and soak at room temperature for at least 8 hours or up to 24 hours. Drain and rinse well.

2. In Dutch oven, combine drained beans, 4 cups water, 1 bell pepper half, 1 onion half (with root end), halved garlic head, bay leaves, and 1 teaspoon salt. Bring to simmer over medium-high heat, cover, and reduce heat to low. Cook until beans are just soft, 30 to 40 minutes.

3. Discard pepper, onion, garlic, and bay leaves. Drain beans in colander set over large bowl, reserving 2½ cups bean cooking liquid. (If you don't have enough cooking liquid, add water as needed to measure 2½ cups.) Do not wash pot.

4. Adjust oven rack to middle position and heat oven to 350 degrees. Cut remaining bell peppers and onion into 2-inch pieces and pulse in food processor until chopped into rough ¼-inch pieces, about 8 pulses, scraping down sides of bowl as needed.

5. Add oil to now-empty pot and heat over medium heat until shimmering. Add processed peppers and onion, cumin, oregano, and tomato paste and cook, stirring often, until vegetables are softened and beginning to brown, 10 to 15 minutes. Stir in minced garlic and cook until fragrant, about 1 minute. Stir in rice and cook for 30 seconds.

6. Stir in beans, reserved bean cooking liquid, vinegar, and remaining 1½ teaspoons salt. Increase heat to medium-high and bring to simmer. Cover, transfer to oven, and cook until liquid is absorbed and rice is tender, about 30 minutes. Fluff rice with fork and let rest, uncovered, for 5 minutes. Serve with scallions and lime wedges.

PER SERVING Cal 270; **Total Fat** 4g, **Sat Fat** 0.5g; **Chol** 0mg; **Sodium** 750mg; **Total Carb** 50g, **Dietary Fiber** 2g, **Total Sugars** 5g; **Protein** 9g

Red Beans and Rice with Okra and Tomatoes
SERVES 6 TO 8

WHY THIS RECIPE WORKS Staying close to home with okra's Cajun roots, we boosted the flavor profile of classic New Orleans red beans and rice by adding okra and tomatoes. To replicate this traditional dish using ingredients easily found in supermarkets, we made some simple substitutions: small red beans for Camellia-brand dried red beans and bacon for hard-to-find tasso ham. Fine-tuning the proportions of sautéed green peppers, onions, and celery gave this dish balance. To preserve some of the okra's crunchy bite, we tossed the whole pods in salt and let them sit for an hour before rinsing, cutting, and adding them to the beans for the final half hour of cooking. To save time you can "quick-brine" your beans: In step 1, combine the salt, water, and beans in a large Dutch oven and bring to a boil over high heat. Remove the pot from the heat, cover, and let stand for 1 hour. Drain and rinse the beans; they can be refrigerated for up to two days before proceeding with the recipe. While we prefer the flavor and texture of fresh okra in this recipe, you can substitute frozen cut okra, thawed and thoroughly patted dry, for fresh. If using frozen, skip step 2.

RED BEANS
- 1 teaspoon table salt, plus salt for brining
- 1 pound small red beans (2 cups), picked over and rinsed
- 1 pound okra, stemmed
- 4 slices bacon, chopped fine
- 1 onion, chopped fine
- 1 green bell pepper, stemmed, seeded, and chopped fine
- 1 celery rib, minced
- 3 garlic cloves, minced
- 1 teaspoon minced fresh thyme or ¼ teaspoon dried
- 1 teaspoon paprika
- 2 bay leaves
- ¼ teaspoon cayenne pepper
- ¼ teaspoon pepper
- 3 cups chicken broth
- 2 (14.5-ounce) cans diced tomatoes, drained
- 1 tablespoon red wine vinegar, plus extra for seasoning
- 3 scallions, sliced thin
  Hot sauce

RICE
- 1 tablespoon unsalted butter
- 2 cups long-grain white rice, rinsed
- 3 cups water
- 1 teaspoon table salt

Red Beans and Rice with Okra and Tomatoes

1. FOR THE RED BEANS Dissolve 3 tablespoons salt in 4 quarts cold water in large bowl or container. Add beans and soak at room temperature for at least 8 hours or up to 24 hours. Drain and rinse well; set aside.

2. Toss okra with 1 teaspoon salt and let sit for 1 hour, stirring halfway through. Rinse well, then cut into 1-inch pieces; set aside.

3. Cook bacon in Dutch oven over medium heat, stirring occasionally, until crispy, 5 to 7 minutes. Add onion, bell pepper, and celery and cook until vegetables are softened, 5 to 7 minutes. Stir in garlic, thyme, paprika, bay leaves, cayenne, and pepper and cook until fragrant, about 30 seconds.

4. Stir in beans, broth, and 5 cups water and bring to boil over high heat. Reduce to vigorous simmer and cook, stirring occasionally, until beans are just softened and liquid begins to thicken, 45 minutes to 1 hour.

5. Stir in okra, tomatoes, and vinegar and cook until liquid is thickened and beans are fully tender and creamy, about 30 minutes.

6. FOR THE RICE Meanwhile, melt butter in large saucepan over medium heat. Add rice and cook, stirring often, until edges begin to turn translucent, about 2 minutes. Stir in water and salt and bring to boil. Cover, reduce heat to low, and simmer until liquid is absorbed and rice is tender, about 20 minutes. Remove pot from heat, lay clean folded dish towel underneath lid, and let rice sit for 10 minutes. Fluff rice with fork.

7. Discard bay leaves from beans. Season with salt, pepper, and extra vinegar to taste. Top individual portions of rice with beans and sprinkle with scallions. Serve with hot sauce.

PER SERVING Cal 480; **Total Fat** 7g, **Sat Fat** 3g; **Chol** 15mg; **Sodium** 910mg; **Total Carb** 81g, **Dietary Fiber** 12g, **Total Sugars** 5g; **Protein** 22g

Rice and Lentils with Crispy Onions (Mujaddara)
SERVES 4 TO 6

WHY THIS RECIPE WORKS This classic Middle Eastern dish is a spectacular example of how a few humble ingredients can add up to a meal or side dish that's satisfying and complex. Tender basmati rice and lentils are seasoned with warm spices and minced garlic and topped with deeply flavorful fried onions. We microwaved the onions briefly to remove some of their liquid, then fried them in oil to a deep golden brown. We used a pilaf method to cook the rice and lentils; giving the lentils a 15-minute head start ensured that they finished cooking at the same time as the rice. Blooming the spices and toasting the rice in oil left over from frying the onions deepened their flavors and enhanced the rice's nutty flavor. Finished with a bracing garlicky yogurt sauce, this pilaf is comfort food at its best. Large green or brown lentils both work well in this recipe; do not substitute French green lentils, or *lentilles du Puy*. It is crucial to thoroughly dry the microwaved onions after rinsing. The best way to accomplish this is to use a salad spinner.

YOGURT SAUCE
- 1 cup plain whole-milk yogurt
- 2 tablespoons lemon juice
- ½ teaspoon minced garlic
- ½ teaspoon table salt

RICE AND LENTILS
- 8½ ounces (1¼ cups) green or brown lentils, picked over and rinsed
- 1 teaspoon table salt, plus salt for cooking lentils

Rice and Lentils with Crispy Onions

- 1¼ cups basmati rice
- 1 recipe Crispy Onions, plus 3 tablespoons reserved oil, divided
- 3 garlic cloves, minced
- 1 teaspoon ground coriander
- 1 teaspoon ground cumin
- ½ teaspoon ground cinnamon
- ½ teaspoon ground allspice
- ¼ teaspoon pepper
- ⅛ teaspoon cayenne pepper
- 1 teaspoon sugar
- 3 tablespoons minced fresh cilantro

1. FOR THE YOGURT SAUCE Whisk all ingredients together in bowl and refrigerate until ready to serve.

2. FOR THE RICE AND LENTILS Bring lentils, 4 cups water, and 1 teaspoon salt to boil in medium saucepan over high heat. Reduce heat to low and cook until lentils are tender, 15 to 17 minutes. Drain and set aside.

3. Meanwhile, place rice in medium bowl, cover with hot tap water by 2 inches, and let sit for 15 minutes. Using your hands, gently swish grains to release excess starch. Carefully pour off water, leaving rice in bowl. Add cold tap water to rice and pour off water. Repeat adding and pouring off cold water 4 or 5 times, until water runs almost clear. Drain rice in fine-mesh strainer.

4. Cook reserved onion oil, garlic, coriander, cumin, cinnamon, allspice, pepper, and cayenne in now-empty Dutch oven over medium heat until fragrant, about 2 minutes. Add rice and cook, stirring occasionally, until edges of rice begin to turn translucent, about 3 minutes. Stir in 2¼ cups water, sugar, and 1 teaspoon salt and bring to boil. Stir in lentils, reduce heat to low, cover, and cook until all liquid is absorbed, about 12 minutes.

5. Remove pot from heat, lay clean folded dish towel underneath lid, and let sit for 10 minutes. Fluff rice and lentils with fork and stir in cilantro and half of onions. Transfer to platter and top with remaining onions. Serve with yogurt sauce.

PER SERVING Cal 450; **Total Fat** 15g, **Sat Fat** 2g; **Chol** 5mg; **Sodium** 810mg; **Total Carb** 69g, **Dietary Fiber** 9g, **Total Sugars** 9g; **Protein** 15g

Koshari

TAKE IT UP A NOTCH

These crispy fried onions add flavorful crunch to salads and rice and grain dishes.

Crispy Onions
MAKES 1½ CUPS

It is crucial to thoroughly dry the microwaved onions after rinsing. Be sure to reserve enough oil to use in Mujaddara or Koshari. Remaining oil may be stored in an airtight container and refrigerated for up to four weeks; it tastes great in salad dressings, sautéed vegetables, eggs, and pasta sauces.

  2 pounds onions, halved and sliced crosswise into ¼-inch-thick pieces
     Table salt for salting onions
1½ cups vegetable oil

1. Toss onions and 2 teaspoons salt together in large bowl. Microwave for 5 minutes. Rinse thoroughly, transfer to paper towel–lined baking sheet, and dry well.

2. Heat onions and oil in Dutch oven over high heat, stirring frequently, until onions are golden brown, 25 to 30 minutes. Drain onions in colander set in large bowl, reserving oil. Transfer onions to paper towel–lined baking sheet to drain.

Koshari
SERVES 4 TO 6   VEGAN

WHY THIS RECIPE WORKS Considered the national dish of Egypt, *koshari* evolved as a way to use up leftovers and is now a popular street food. This hearty dish usually features lentils, rice, pasta, and chickpeas smothered in a spiced tomato sauce and topped with crispy fried onions. For a version that we could enjoy for lunch, dinner, or as a rib-sticking side, we cooked the lentils and the pasta in pots of salted boiling water, drained each of them, and set them aside while we prepared the rice and sauce. Soaking the rice in hot water before cooking eliminated some of its excess starch so it didn't clump. We preferred a tomato sauce spiked with vinegar over spicy varieties we came across in our research. Using the same spices (a blend of coriander, cumin, cinnamon, nutmeg, and cayenne) in the sauce and the rice provided a complex flavor profile and made the dish cohesive. We added the chickpeas directly to the sauce to infuse them with flavor. The finishing touch: a generous amount of ultrasavory, crunchy fried onions that brought a satisfying depth and texture to this classic Egyptian comfort food. Large green or brown lentils both work well in this recipe; do not use French green lentils, or *lentilles du Puy*. Long-grain white, jasmine, or Texmati rice can be substituted for the basmati.

1 cup elbow macaroni

1 teaspoon table salt, divided, plus table salt for cooking pasta and lentils

1 cup green or brown lentils, picked over and rinsed

1 recipe Crispy Onions, plus ¼ cup reserved oil, divided (page 457)

4 garlic cloves, minced, divided

1½ teaspoons ground coriander, divided

1½ teaspoons ground cumin, divided

¾ teaspoon ground cinnamon, divided

¼ teaspoon ground nutmeg, divided

¼ teaspoon cayenne pepper, divided

1 (28-ounce) can tomato sauce

1 (15-ounce) can chickpeas, rinsed

1 cup basmati rice

1 tablespoon red wine vinegar

3 tablespoons minced fresh parsley

1. Bring 2 quarts water to boil in Dutch oven. Add macaroni and 1½ teaspoons salt and cook, stirring often, until al dente. Drain macaroni, rinse with water, then drain again. Transfer to bowl and set aside.

2. Meanwhile, bring lentils, 4 cups water, and 1 teaspoon salt to boil in medium saucepan over high heat. Reduce heat to low and cook until lentils are just tender, 15 to 17 minutes. Drain and set aside.

3. Cook 1 tablespoon reserved onion oil, 1 teaspoon garlic, ½ teaspoon salt, ½ teaspoon coriander, ½ teaspoon cumin, ¼ teaspoon cinnamon, ⅛ teaspoon nutmeg, and ⅛ teaspoon cayenne in now-empty saucepan over medium heat until fragrant, about 1 minute. Stir in tomato sauce and chickpeas, bring to simmer, and cook until slightly thickened, about 10 minutes. Cover and keep warm.

4. While sauce cooks, place rice in medium bowl, cover with hot tap water by 2 inches, and let sit for 15 minutes. Using your hands, gently swish grains to release excess starch. Carefully pour off water, leaving rice in bowl. Repeat adding and pouring off cold water 4 or 5 times, until water runs almost clear. Drain rice in fine-mesh strainer.

5. Cook remaining 3 tablespoons reserved onion oil, remaining garlic, remaining 1 teaspoon coriander, remaining 1 teaspoon cumin, remaining ½ teaspoon cinnamon, remaining ⅛ teaspoon nutmeg, and remaining ⅛ teaspoon cayenne in now-empty pot over medium heat until fragrant, about 2 minutes. Add rice and cook, stirring occasionally, until grain edges begin to turn translucent, about 3 minutes. Stir in 2 cups water and remaining ½ teaspoon salt and bring to boil. Stir in lentils, reduce heat to low, cover, and simmer gently until all liquid is absorbed, about 12 minutes.

6. Off heat, sprinkle macaroni over rice mixture. Cover, laying clean dish towel underneath lid, and let sit for 10 minutes.

7. Return sauce to simmer over medium heat. Stir in vinegar and season with salt and pepper to taste. Fluff rice and lentils with fork and stir in parsley and half of onions. Transfer to serving platter and top with half of sauce and remaining onions. Serve, passing remaining sauce separately.

PER SERVING Cal 410; **Total Fat** 12g, **Sat Fat** 1.5g; **Chol** 0mg; **Sodium** 1250mg; **Total Carb** 64g, **Dietary Fiber** 9g; **Total Sugars** 9g; **Protein** 13g

Cauliflower Biryani
SERVES 4 TO 6

WHY THIS RECIPE WORKS The best biryani recipes place fragrant long-grain basmati center stage, enriching it with saffron and a variety of fresh herbs and pungent spices. We decided to deconstruct this dish to make it easy and fast, while staying true to its warmth and homey appeal. We paired our rice with sweet, earthy roasted cauliflower. We cut the cauliflower into florets to speed up roasting and tossed it with warm spices to give it deep flavor. While it roasted, we sautéed an onion until golden, then cooked jalapeño, garlic, and more spices until fragrant. We added the rice to this flavorful mixture and simmered it until tender. Once the rice finished cooking, we let the residual heat plump the currants and bloom the saffron while the rice rested. We stirred in lots of bright mint and cilantro and our roasted cauliflower. Biryani is traditionally served with a cooling yogurt sauce; ideally, you should make the sauce ahead to allow its flavors to meld. You can substitute long-grain white, jasmine, or Texmati rice, if necessary.

1 head cauliflower (2 pounds), cored and cut into ½-inch florets

¼ cup extra-virgin olive oil, divided

1 teaspoon table salt, divided

¼ teaspoon ground cardamom, divided

¼ teaspoon ground cumin, divided

¼ teaspoon pepper

1 onion, sliced thin

4 garlic cloves, minced

1 jalapeño chile, stemmed, seeded, and minced

⅛ teaspoon ground cinnamon

⅛ teaspoon ground ginger

1½ cups basmati rice, rinsed

2¼ cups water

¼ cup dried currants or raisins

½ teaspoon saffron threads, lightly crumbled

2 tablespoons chopped fresh cilantro

2 tablespoons chopped fresh mint

1 recipe Yogurt-Herb Sauce (page 105)

Cauliflower Biryani

1. Adjust oven rack to middle position and heat oven to 425 degrees. Toss cauliflower, 2 tablespoons oil, ½ teaspoon salt, ⅛ teaspoon cardamom, ⅛ teaspoon cumin, and ¼ teaspoon pepper together in bowl. Spread cauliflower onto rimmed baking sheet and roast until tender, 15 to 20 minutes.

2. Meanwhile, heat remaining 2 tablespoons oil in large saucepan over medium-high heat until shimmering. Add onion and cook, stirring often, until soft and dark brown around edges, 10 to 12 minutes.

3. Stir in garlic, jalapeño, cinnamon, ginger, remaining ⅛ teaspoon cardamom, and remaining ⅛ teaspoon cumin and cook until fragrant, about 1 minute. Stir in rice and cook until well coated, about 1 minute. Add water and remaining ½ teaspoon salt and bring to simmer. Reduce heat to low, cover, and simmer until all liquid is absorbed, 16 to 18 minutes.

4. Remove pot from heat and sprinkle currants and saffron over rice. Cover, laying clean folded dish towel underneath lid, and let sit for 10 minutes. Fold in cilantro, mint, and roasted cauliflower. Season with salt and pepper to taste, and serve with yogurt sauce.

PER SERVING Cal 330; **Total Fat** 12g, **Sat Fat** 2.5g; **Chol** 5mg; **Sodium** 460mg; **Total Carb** 50g, **Dietary Fiber** 4g, **Total Sugars** 10g; **Protein** 8g

Quinoa Taco Salad
SERVES 4 TO 6

WHY THIS RECIPE WORKS Taco salad hits a home run with any crowd. What's not to love about seasoned beef and the works on a bed of lettuce? We wanted a version of this salad that fulfilled all our expectations but that was lightened up enough to serve as a side or light main course. To rework taco salad into something a little less hefty, we replaced the beef with quinoa. Some tasters had doubts, but the quinoa—with its chewy texture and ability to absorb flavors—made a good stand-in for ground beef and was less filling and rich. Toasted and simmered in chicken broth with chipotles in adobo, tomato paste, anchovy paste, and cumin, it acquired a spiced meaty flavor. We substituted escarole for lettuce, cut back on cheese (opting for queso fresco) and added an extra-hefty amount of cilantro. Black beans, avocado, cherry tomatoes, and scallions completed the picture. Tasters found the salad so hearty it didn't need chips, but if you prefer, serve with your favorite tortilla or multigrain chip. We like the convenience of prewashed quinoa; rinsing removes the quinoa's bitter protective coating (called saponin). If you buy unwashed quinoa (or if you are unsure whether it's been washed), rinse it and then spread it out on a clean dish towel to dry for 15 minutes before cooking.

- ¾ cup prewashed white quinoa
- 3 tablespoons extra-virgin olive oil, divided
- 1 small onion, chopped fine
- ½ teaspoon table salt, divided
- 2 teaspoons minced canned chipotle chile in adobo sauce
- 2 teaspoons tomato paste
- 1 teaspoon anchovy paste (optional)
- ½ teaspoon ground cumin
- 1 cup chicken or vegetable broth
- 2 tablespoons lime juice
- ¼ teaspoon pepper
- 1 head escarole (1 pound), trimmed and sliced thin
- 2 scallions, sliced thin
- ½ cup chopped fresh cilantro, divided
- 1 (15-ounce) can black beans, rinsed
- 8 ounces cherry or grape tomatoes, quartered
- 1 ripe avocado, halved, pitted, and chopped
- 2 ounces queso fresco, crumbled (½ cup)

1. Toast quinoa in medium saucepan over medium-high heat, stirring frequently, until quinoa is very fragrant and makes continuous popping sound, 5 to 7 minutes; transfer to bowl.

2. Heat 1 tablespoon oil in now-empty saucepan over medium heat until shimmering. Add onion and ¼ teaspoon salt and cook until onion is softened and lightly browned, 5 to 7 minutes.

3. Stir in chipotle; tomato paste; anchovy paste, if using; and cumin and cook until fragrant, about 30 seconds. Stir in broth and toasted quinoa, increase heat to medium-high, and bring to simmer. Cover, reduce heat to low, and simmer until quinoa is tender and liquid has been absorbed, 18 to 22 minutes, stirring once halfway through cooking. Remove pan from heat and let sit, covered, for 10 minutes. Spread quinoa onto rimmed baking sheet and let cool for 20 minutes.

4. Whisk remaining 2 tablespoons oil, lime juice, remaining ¼ teaspoon salt, and pepper together in large bowl. Add escarole, scallions, and ¼ cup cilantro and toss to combine. Gently fold in beans, tomatoes, and avocado. Transfer to platter and top with quinoa, queso fresco, and remaining ¼ cup cilantro. Serve.

PER SERVING Cal 280; **Total Fat** 14g, **Sat Fat** 2.5g; **Chol** 5mg; **Sodium** 480mg; **Total Carb** 30g, **Dietary Fiber** 9g, **Total Sugars** 3g; **Protein** 9g

Hearty Pearl Couscous with Eggplant, Spinach, and Beans

SERVES 6 VEGAN

WHY THIS RECIPE WORKS Pearl, or Israeli, couscous makes for a hearty side with great visual appeal. A spice blend of zesty sumac, nutty-sweet fenugreek, and floral cardamom gave this dish a superflavorful depth. We tossed eggplant with a teaspoon of the blend before microwaving, which bloomed the spices' flavors and cooked off the eggplant's excess moisture. We seared the eggplant to develop savory browning before building an aromatic broth base in which to cook our couscous. Adding beans and baby spinach made for a more substantial dish. Do not substitute regular couscous, as it requires a different cooking method and will not work in this recipe.

    1 teaspoon ground sumac
    1 teaspoon ground fenugreek
    ½ teaspoon table salt
    ½ teaspoon pepper
    ¼ teaspoon ground cardamom
    1 pound eggplant, cut into ½-inch pieces
 1½ cups pearl couscous
    5 tablespoons extra-virgin olive oil, divided,
      plus extra for serving
    1 onion, chopped
    3 garlic cloves, minced
    1 tablespoon tomato paste
    2 cups chicken or vegetable broth
    1 (15-ounce) can great Northern beans, rinsed
    3 ounces (3 cups) baby spinach

1. Combine sumac, fenugreek, salt, pepper, and cardamom in small bowl. Line large plate with double layer of coffee filters and spray with vegetable oil spray. Toss eggplant with ½ teaspoon spice mixture and spread evenly on coffee filters. Microwave eggplant, uncovered, until dry to touch and slightly shriveled, 7 to 10 minutes, tossing halfway through microwaving.

2. Heat couscous and 2 tablespoons oil in 12-inch nonstick skillet over medium heat, stirring frequently, until about half of grains are golden brown, about 5 minutes. Transfer to bowl and wipe skillet clean with paper towels.

3. Toss eggplant with 1 teaspoon spice mixture. Heat 1 tablespoon oil in now-empty skillet over medium-high heat until shimmering. Add eggplant and cook, stirring occasionally, until well browned, 5 to 7 minutes. Transfer to separate bowl.

4. Heat remaining 2 tablespoons oil in again-empty skillet over medium heat until shimmering. Add onion and cook until softened and lightly browned, 5 to 7 minutes. Stir in garlic, tomato paste, and remaining spice mixture and cook until fragrant, about 1 minute.

5. Stir in broth, beans, and couscous and bring to simmer. Reduce heat to medium-low, cover, and simmer, stirring occasionally, until broth is absorbed and couscous is tender, 9 to 12 minutes. Off heat, stir in spinach and eggplant, cover, and let sit for 3 minutes. Season with salt and pepper to taste, and drizzle with extra oil. Serve.

PER SERVING Cal 370; **Total Fat** 12g, **Sat Fat** 1.5g; **Chol** 0mg; **Sodium** 590mg; **Total Carb** 54g, **Dietary Fiber** 5g, **Total Sugars** 6g; **Protein** 12g

Wheat Berry and Endive Salad with Blueberries and Goat Cheese

SERVES 4 TO 6

WHY THIS RECIPE WORKS The earthy, nutty, chew of wheat berries pairs well with creamy goat cheese and sweet fresh blueberries in this hearty summer salad. We cooked the wheat berries like pasta in a pot of water until they were tender but still had some nice chew (we avoided oversalting the pot, which would prevent the wheat berries from absorbing water). Endive brought an interesting bitter note. A bright champagne vinaigrette brought all the ingredients together. If using quick-cooking or presteamed wheat berries (read the package carefully to determine this), you will need to adjust the wheat berry cooking time downward in step 1.

 1½ cups wheat berries
    ½ teaspoon table salt, plus salt for cooking wheat berries
    2 tablespoons champagne vinegar
    1 tablespoon minced shallot
    1 tablespoon minced fresh chives

Italian Pasta Salad

Italian Pasta Salad
SERVES 8 TO 10 `MAKE-AHEAD`

WHY THIS RECIPE WORKS To breathe new life into typically tired, rubbery pasta salad, we started by cooking the pasta until it was a little too soft so that as it cooled and firmed up, it would have the right tender texture. Corkscrew-shaped fusilli had plenty of surface area for capturing dressing. Rather than toss raw vegetables into the mix, we took inspiration from Italian antipasto platters and used intensely flavored jarred ingredients such as sun-dried tomatoes, kalamata olives, and pepperoncini that offered a mix of textures that didn't overshadow the pasta. For heartiness, we included salami, and to balance the salt and tang, we added chunks of creamy mozzarella, fresh basil, and peppery arugula. We made a thick, punchy dressing of some of the salad ingredients—capers and pepperoncini plus some of the tangy pepperoncini brine—processed with garlic-infused olive oil, red pepper flakes, and anchovies. The pasta firms as it cools, so overcooking is key for ensuring the proper texture. We prefer a small, individually packaged, dry Italian-style salami such as Genoa or soppressata, but unsliced deli salami can be used. If the salad is not being eaten right away, don't add the arugula and basil until right before serving.

1 pound fusilli
    Table salt for cooking pasta
¼ cup extra-virgin olive oil
3 garlic cloves, minced
3 anchovy fillets, rinsed, patted dry, and minced
¼ teaspoon red pepper flakes
1 cup pepperoncini, stemmed, plus 2 tablespoons brine
2 tablespoons capers, rinsed
2 ounces (2 cups) baby arugula
1 cup chopped fresh basil
½ cup oil-packed sun-dried tomatoes, sliced thin
½ cup pitted kalamata olives, quartered
8 ounces salami, cut into ⅜-inch dice
8 ounces fresh mozzarella cheese, cut into ⅜-inch dice and patted dry

1. Bring 4 quarts water to boil in large pot. Add pasta and 1 tablespoon salt and cook, stirring often, until pasta is tender throughout, 2 to 3 minutes past al dente. Drain pasta and rinse under cold water until chilled. Drain well and transfer to large bowl.

2. Meanwhile, combine oil, garlic, anchovies, and pepper flakes in liquid measuring cup. Cover and microwave until bubbling and fragrant, 30 to 60 seconds. Set aside.

3. Slice half of pepperoncini into thin rings and set aside. Transfer remaining pepperoncini to food processor. Add capers and pulse until finely chopped, 8 to 10 pulses, scraping down sides of bowl as needed. Add pepperoncini brine and warm oil mixture and process until combined, about 20 seconds.

1 teaspoon Dijon mustard
¼ teaspoon pepper
6 tablespoons extra-virgin olive oil
2 heads Belgian endive (4 ounces each), halved, cored, and sliced crosswise ¼ inch thick
7½ ounces (1½ cups) blueberries
¾ cup pecans, toasted and chopped
4 ounces goat cheese, crumbled (1 cup)

1. Bring 4 quarts water to boil in large pot. Add wheat berries and ¼ teaspoon salt, partially cover, and cook, stirring often, until wheat berries are tender but still chewy, 50 minutes to 1 hour 10 minutes. Drain and rinse under cold running water until cool; drain well.

2. Whisk vinegar, shallot, chives, mustard, pepper, and ½ teaspoon salt together in large bowl. While whisking constantly, slowly drizzle in oil until combined. Add drained wheat berries, endive, blueberries, and pecans and toss to combine. Season with salt and pepper to taste, sprinkle with goat cheese, and serve.

PER SERVING Cal 450; **Total Fat** 28g, **Sat Fat** 5g; **Chol** 10mg; **Sodium** 350mg; **Total Carb** 43g, **Dietary Fiber** 9g, **Total Sugars** 4g; **Protein** 11g

4. Add dressing to pasta and toss to combine. Add arugula, basil, tomatoes, olives, salami, mozzarella, and reserved pepperoncini and toss well. Season with salt and pepper to taste. Serve. (Salad can be refrigerated for up to 3 days. Let come to room temperature before serving.)

PER SERVING Cal 390; Total Fat 20g, Sat Fat 7g; Chol 40mg; Sodium 790mg; Total Carb 36g, Dietary Fiber 1g, Total Sugars 2g; Protein 16g

Pimento Mac and Cheese
SERVES 8 TO 10   MAKE-AHEAD

WHY THIS RECIPE WORKS Pimento cheese takes plain macaroni and cheese and turns it into something a bit more fun and feisty to put on your plate at a cookout or for dinner. We started our recipe for a mac and cheese casserole by making a flavored béchamel, a thickened milk sauce, aiming for cohesion and silky smooth texture. Adding the cheese and cream cheese right to the sauce before adding the macaroni allowed us to bake the casserole less, therefore reducing the risk of a broken sauce. We used Frank's RedHot Original Cayenne Pepper Sauce when developing this recipe.

1 pound elbow macaroni
½ teaspoon table salt, plus salt for cooking pasta
3 tablespoons unsalted butter
2 tablespoons all-purpose flour
1 tablespoon dry mustard
¾ teaspoon pepper
2 cups whole milk
2 cups heavy cream
1 pound extra-sharp cheddar cheese, shredded (4 cups), divided
2 ounces cream cheese
2 tablespoons hot sauce
1 tablespoon Worcestershire sauce
3 (4-ounce) jars pimentoes, drained, patted dry, and minced

1. Adjust oven rack to upper-middle position and heat oven to 375 degrees. Bring 4 quarts water to boil in Dutch oven. Add macaroni and 1 tablespoon salt and cook for 5 minutes. Drain macaroni; set aside.
2. Add butter to now-empty pot and melt over medium-high heat. Stir in flour, mustard, pepper, and salt and cook until mixture is fragrant and bubbling, about 30 seconds. Slowly whisk in milk and cream and bring to boil. Reduce heat to medium-low and simmer until sauce is thick enough to coat back of spoon, about 2 minutes, whisking frequently.
3. Remove pot from heat. Add 3 cups cheddar, cream cheese, hot sauce, and Worcestershire to sauce and whisk until cheese is melted. Add pimentos and macaroni and stir until macaroni is thoroughly coated in sauce. Transfer to 13 by 9-inch baking dish and sprinkle with remaining 1 cup cheddar. (Casserole can be wrapped tightly in plastic wrap and refrigerated for up to 24 hours. When ready to serve, remove plastic and bake until heated through, 40 to 45 minutes.) Bake until edges are lightly browned and filling is bubbling, 18 to 20 minutes. Let rest for 20 minutes. Serve.

PER SERVING Cal 600; Total Fat 40g, Sat Fat 25g; Chol 125mg; Sodium 610mg; Total Carb 41g, Dietary Fiber 1g, Total Sugars 5g; Protein 21g

Stovetop Macaroni and Cheese
SERVES 4   FAST

WHY THIS RECIPE WORKS Inspired by an innovative macaroni and cheese recipe that calls for adding sodium citrate, an emulsifying salt, to cheese to keep it smooth when heated (instead of adding flour to make a béchamel), we based our sauce on American cheese, which contains a similar ingredient. Because American cheese has plenty of emulsifier but not a lot of flavor, we combined it with more-flavorful extra-sharp cheddar. A bit of mustard and cayenne pepper added piquancy. We cooked the macaroni in a smaller-than-usual amount of water (along with some milk), so we didn't have to drain it; the liquid that was left after the elbows were hydrated was just enough to form the base of the sauce. Rather than bake the mac and cheese, we sprinkled crunchy, cheesy toasted panko bread crumbs on top. Our simplified mac and cheese recipe takes only about 20 minutes from start to finish. Barilla makes our favorite elbow macaroni. Because the macaroni is cooked in a measured amount of liquid, we don't recommend using different shapes or sizes of pasta. Use a 4-ounce block of American cheese from the deli counter rather than presliced cheese.

1½ cups water
1 cup milk
8 ounces elbow macaroni
4 ounces American cheese, shredded (1 cup)
½ teaspoon Dijon mustard
Small pinch cayenne pepper
4 ounces extra-sharp cheddar cheese, shredded (1 cup)
⅓ cup panko bread crumbs

1 tablespoon extra-virgin olive oil

⅛ teaspoon table salt

⅛ teaspoon pepper

2 tablespoons grated Parmesan cheese

1. Bring water and milk to boil in medium saucepan over high heat. Stir in macaroni and reduce heat to medium-low. Cook, stirring frequently, until macaroni is soft (slightly past al dente), 6 to 8 minutes. Add American cheese, mustard, and cayenne and cook, stirring constantly, until cheese is completely melted, about 1 minute. Off heat, stir in cheddar until evenly distributed but not melted. Cover saucepan and let sit for 5 minutes.

2. Meanwhile, combine panko, oil, salt, and pepper in 8-inch nonstick skillet until panko is evenly moistened. Cook over medium heat, stirring frequently, until evenly browned, 3 to 4 minutes. Off heat, sprinkle Parmesan over panko mixture and stir to combine. Transfer panko mixture to small bowl.

3. Stir macaroni until sauce is smooth (sauce may look loose but will thicken as it cools). Season with salt and pepper to taste. Transfer to warm serving dish and sprinkle panko mixture over top. Serve immediately.

PER SERVING Cal 510; **Total Fat** 23g, **Sat Fat** 12g; **Chol** 60mg; **Sodium** 750mg; **Total Carb** 51g, **Dietary Fiber** 0g, **Total Sugars** 5g; **Protein** 24g

Baked Orzo with Eggplant and Tomatoes

Baked Orzo with Eggplant and Tomatoes
SERVES 6

WHY THIS RECIPE WORKS We wanted to put a modern spin on a classic Greek *manestra*—a simple, hearty baked dish of orzo, tomatoes, and oregano, sometimes adorned with a little cheese and a splash of olive oil. To make our interpretation of this dish into a filling side dish or simple meal, we decided to include a few additional components. Tasters particularly liked the addition of eggplant; pretreating it with salt and microwaving it rid the eggplant of excess moisture and allowed us to sauté it using a minimal amount of oil. Tomato paste, garlic, and anchovies gave the dish a rich umami core. Toasting the orzo added a nutty dimension. We found that the dish dried out in the oven unless we topped it with an unappealing amount of cheese; instead, we shingled tomato slices on top to keep the orzo moist while the casserole cooked through. As a final homage to traditional manestra, we topped the dish with feta, oregano, and olive oil.

1 pound eggplant, cut into ½-inch pieces

¾ teaspoon table salt, divided

2 cups orzo

3 tablespoons extra-virgin olive oil, divided, plus extra for serving

1 onion, chopped fine

3 garlic cloves, minced

4 teaspoons minced fresh oregano or 1 teaspoon dried, divided

2 teaspoons tomato paste

2 anchovy fillets, rinsed, patted dry, and minced

1¼ cups chicken or vegetable broth

1¼ cups water

1 ounce Parmesan cheese, grated (½ cup)

2 tablespoons capers, rinsed and minced

¼ teaspoon pepper

4 tomatoes, cored and sliced ¼ inch thick

3 ounces feta cheese, crumbled (¾ cup)

1. Adjust oven rack to upper-middle position and heat oven to 400 degrees. Line large plate with double layer of coffee filters and spray with vegetable oil spray. Toss eggplant with ½ teaspoon salt and spread evenly on coffee filters. Microwave eggplant, uncovered, until dry to touch and slightly shriveled, 7 to 10 minutes, tossing halfway through microwaving.

2. Toast orzo in 12-inch nonstick skillet over medium-high heat until lightly browned, 3 to 5 minutes; transfer to bowl. Heat 1 tablespoon oil in now-empty skillet over medium-high heat until shimmering. Add eggplant and cook, stirring occasionally, until well browned, 5 to 7 minutes; transfer to separate bowl.

3. Heat remaining 2 tablespoons oil in again-empty skillet over medium heat until shimmering. Add onion and cook until softened and lightly browned, 5 to 7 minutes. Stir in garlic, 1 tablespoon oregano, tomato paste, and anchovies and cook until fragrant, about 30 seconds. Off heat, stir in orzo, eggplant, broth, water, Parmesan, capers, and pepper. Transfer to greased 13 by 9-inch baking dish and spread into even layer.

4. Shingle tomatoes attractively over top, then sprinkle with remaining ¼ teaspoon salt. Bake until all liquid has been absorbed and orzo is tender, 30 to 35 minutes. Let cool for 5 minutes. Sprinkle feta and remaining 1 teaspoon oregano over tomatoes and drizzle with extra oil. Serve.

PER SERVING Cal 380; **Total Fat** 13g, **Sat Fat** 4g; **Chol** 15mg; **Sodium** 800mg; **Total Carb** 54g, **Dietary Fiber** 3g, **Total Sugars** 9g; **Protein** 14g

Skillet Baked Orzo

Skillet Baked Orzo
SERVES 4

WHY THIS RECIPE WORKS For a summery, satisfying dish of creamy orzo and vegetables, we settled on a stovetop-to-oven cooking method to guarantee perfectly cooked vegetables and pasta. First we sautéed our aromatics; we then briefly toasted the orzo to bring out its flavor. We added broth and wine to the skillet and simmered the orzo until it was al dente and had released its starch, creating a luscious, creamy sauce without needing any butter or cream. Stirring in the zucchini, tomatoes, and spinach right before the dish went into the oven kept the vegetables firm and bright-tasting in the finished dish. Salty bites of feta and fresh mint made the perfect finishing touches. Be sure to cook the orzo just until al dente before adding the vegetables and finishing the dish in the oven, or it will overcook and turn mushy. You will need a 12-inch ovensafe nonstick skillet for this recipe.

1 tablespoon extra-virgin olive oil
1 onion, chopped fine
4 garlic cloves, minced
2 cups orzo
1 teaspoon table salt
3½ cups vegetable broth
½ cup white wine
2 zucchini, quartered lengthwise and sliced ½ inch thick
8 ounces cherry tomatoes, halved
3 ounces (3 cups) baby spinach
1 teaspoon grated lemon zest, plus lemon wedges for serving
4 ounces feta cheese, crumbled (1 cup)
2 tablespoons chopped fresh mint

1. Adjust oven rack to middle position and heat oven to 400 degrees. Heat oil in 12-inch ovensafe nonstick skillet over medium heat until shimmering. Add onion and cook until softened and lightly browned, 5 to 7 minutes. Stir in garlic and cook until fragrant, about 30 seconds. Stir in orzo and salt and cook, stirring often, until orzo is coated with oil and lightly browned, about 4 minutes.

2. Stir in broth and wine, bring to simmer, and cook, stirring occasionally, until orzo is al dente, 10 to 12 minutes. Off heat, stir in zucchini, tomatoes, spinach, and lemon zest. Transfer skillet to oven and bake for 10 minutes.

3. Being careful of hot skillet handle, stir orzo thoroughly. Sprinkle feta over top and continue to bake until cheese is lightly browned, about 5 minutes. Sprinkle with mint and serve with lemon wedges.

PER SERVING Cal 500; **Total Fat** 11g, **Sat Fat** 5g; **Chol** 25mg; **Sodium** 1530mg; **Total Carb** 78g, **Dietary Fiber** 3g, **Total Sugars** 10g; **Protein** 18g

Orzo Salad with Radicchio, Chickpeas, and Pecorino

SERVES 4 TO 6 MAKE-AHEAD

WHY THIS RECIPE WORKS Radicchio contributes its gorgeous hue and welcome assertive chicory flavor to this flavor-packed pasta salad. Orzo performed its role here beautifully, providing enough bulk to make the salad satisfying but not so much that it became heavy and starchy. Chickpeas provided protein and a nice textural contrast. Pecorino Romano cheese has a stronger taste than Parmesan and so held up very well against the other strong flavors here. Basil added a fresh herbal note. And last but not least, the strong vinaigrette, with its high proportion of vinegar to oil and two garlic cloves, really made everything zingy.

1¼ cups orzo
½ teaspoon table salt, plus salt for cooking orzo
6 tablespoons extra-virgin olive oil, divided,
   plus extra for serving
¼ cup balsamic vinegar
2 garlic cloves, minced
½ teaspoon pepper
1 (15-ounce) can chickpeas, rinsed
½ small head radicchio (3 ounces), cored and chopped fine
2 ounces Pecorino Romano cheese, grated (1 cup)
½ cup chopped fresh basil

1. Bring 2 quarts water to boil in large saucepan. Add orzo and 1½ teaspoons salt and cook, stirring often, until al dente. Drain orzo and transfer to rimmed baking sheet. Toss with 1 tablespoon oil and let cool completely, about 15 minutes.

2. Whisk remaining 5 tablespoons oil, vinegar, garlic, pepper, and ½ teaspoon salt in large bowl until combined. Add chickpeas, radicchio, Pecorino, basil, and cooled orzo to dressing and toss to coat. Season with salt and pepper to taste.

3. Let salad sit at room temperature for 30 minutes to allow flavors to meld. Serve, drizzling with extra oil to taste. (Salad can be refrigerated for up to 2 days.)

PER SERVING Cal 350; **Total Fat** 18g, **Sat Fat** 3.5g; **Chol** 5mg; **Sodium** 560mg; **Total Carb** 38g, **Dietary Fiber** 2g, **Total Sugars** 5g; **Protein** 10g

VARIATION
Orzo Salad with Arugula and Sun-Dried Tomatoes

SERVES 4 TO 6

1¼ cups orzo
½ teaspoon table salt, plus salt for cooking orzo
¼ cup extra-virgin olive oil, divided, plus extra for serving
3 tablespoons balsamic vinegar

Orzo Salad with Radicchio, Chickpeas, and Pecorino

2 garlic cloves, minced
½ teaspoon pepper
2 ounces (2 cups) baby arugula, chopped
1 ounce Parmesan cheese, grated (½ cup)
½ cup oil-packed sun-dried tomatoes, minced
½ cup pitted kalamata olives, halved
½ cup chopped fresh basil
¼ cup pine nuts, toasted

1. Bring 2 quarts water to boil in large saucepan. Add orzo and 1½ teaspoons salt and cook, stirring often, until al dente. Drain orzo and transfer to rimmed baking sheet. Toss with 1 tablespoon oil and let cool completely, about 15 minutes.

2. Whisk remaining 3 tablespoons oil, vinegar, garlic, pepper, and ½ teaspoon salt together in large bowl. Add arugula, Parmesan, tomatoes, olives, basil, pine nuts, and orzo and gently toss to combine. Season with salt and pepper to taste. Let salad sit until flavors meld, about 30 minutes. Serve, drizzling with extra oil to taste. (Salad can be refrigerated for up to 2 days.)

HOLIDAY CLASSICS

■ FAST (30 minutes or less total time)   ■ MAKE-AHEAD   ■ VEGAN
Photos (clockwise from top left): Asparagus with Lemon-Shallot Vinaigrette; Scalloped Potatoes;
Roquefort Salad with Fennel, Dried Cherries, and Walnuts; Wild Rice Dressing

MORE HOLIDAY FAVORITES

Many holiday-appropriate side dishes can be found in other chapters. Consider some of these favorites when you're planning a Thanksgiving or other menu. The casseroles and breads can be made ahead and all of the other recipes are made on the stovetop, leaving the oven available.

VEGETABLES

SALADS

CASSEROLES

RICE AND GRAINS

BREADS

Asparagus with Lemon-Shallot Vinaigrette
SERVES 6 TO 8   VEGAN

WHY THIS RECIPE WORKS As far as vegetables go, long, verdant spears of asparagus exude elegance. For an impressive yet effortless side, we particularly like to top spears with a bright, punchy vinaigrette. Broiling cooked the asparagus quickly, concentrating its flavor and creating a lightly caramelized exterior. Working with thinner spears let us skip any tedious peeling, and as a bonus the uniform spears cooked more evenly. We placed the asparagus 4 inches from the broiler where the spears achieved a perfectly charred surface without an overcooked interior. Meanwhile, we whisked together lemon juice and olive oil, flavoring the vinaigrette with shallot, fresh thyme, and Dijon mustard for a sophisticated topping that brightened the asparagus's flavor. If you want to double this recipe, use 4 pounds of asparagus and broil in two batches. The vinaigrette can be doubled as well.

ASPARAGUS
- 2 pounds thin asparagus, trimmed
- 1 tablespoon extra-virgin olive oil
- ½ teaspoon table salt
- ¼ teaspoon pepper

LEMON-SHALLOT VINAIGRETTE
- ⅓ cup extra-virgin olive oil
- 1 shallot, minced
- 1 tablespoon minced fresh thyme
- 1 teaspoon grated lemon zest plus 1 tablespoon juice
- ¼ teaspoon Dijon mustard

1. FOR THE ASPARAGUS Adjust oven rack 4 inches from broiler element and heat broiler.

2. Toss asparagus with oil and season with salt and pepper, then lay in single layer on rimmed baking sheet. Broil, shaking sheet halfway through broiling to turn spears, until asparagus is tender and lightly browned, 8 to 10 minutes. Let asparagus cool on sheet for 5 minutes, then arrange on platter.

4. FOR THE VINAIGRETTE Meanwhile, whisk oil, shallot, thyme, lemon zest and juice, and mustard together in small bowl; season with salt and pepper to taste. Drizzle vinaigrette over asparagus and serve immediately.

PER SERVING Cal 120; **Total Fat** 11g, **Sat Fat** 1.5g; **Chol** 0mg; **Sodium** 150mg; **Total Carb** 5g, **Dietary Fiber** 2g, **Total Sugars** 2g; **Protein** 2g

Broccoli with Lemon-Oregano Dressing
SERVES 4   VEGAN

WHY THIS RECIPE WORKS Crisp-tender, brilliantly green broccoli isn't an enigma. The secret? Nuke it. Sure, you can boil broccoli, but you're often left with drab florets. Microwaving is faster and more reliable; electromagnetic waves perfectly steam it from the inside. Plus, it means one fewer pot on the stovetop. We cut the florets into 1-inch pieces and used a vegetable peeler to trim the exterior of the fibrous stems before cutting them into ½-inch pieces. A small amount of salt perked up the flavor and kept the color bright green. Since acidic dressings cause broccoli to brown, we tossed the broccoli with olive oil flavored with lemon zest and oregano to up its appeal.

1½ pounds broccoli
¾ teaspoon table salt, divided
3 tablespoons extra-virgin olive oil
2 teaspoons minced fresh oregano
1 garlic clove, minced
¾ teaspoon grated lemon zest

1. Trim broccoli florets from stalk. Cut florets into 1-inch pieces. Trim and discard lower 1 inch of stalk. Using vegetable peeler, peel away outer ⅛ inch of stalk. Cut stalk into ½-inch pieces.

2. Place broccoli in bowl and toss with ½ teaspoon salt. Microwave, covered, until broccoli is bright green and just tender, 6 to 8 minutes. Meanwhile, whisk oil, oregano, garlic, lemon zest, and remaining ¼ teaspoon salt together in bowl.

3. Drain broccoli in colander, then return to bowl. Add dressing and toss to combine. Season with salt and pepper to taste. Serve.

PER SERVING Cal 150; **Total Fat** 11g, **Sat Fat** 1.5g; **Chol** 0mg; **Sodium** 490mg; **Total Carb** 12g, **Dietary Fiber** 4g, **Total Sugars** 3g; **Protein** 5g

Maple-Glazed Brussels Sprouts

Maple-Glazed Brussels Sprouts
SERVES 6 TO 8

WHY THIS RECIPE WORKS Braising Brussels sprouts turns the crucifer sweet and tender—and the skillet stovetop method couldn't be easier for the busy holiday season. In this preparation, maple syrup and cider vinegar combine to create a sweet-sour glaze. Halving the sprouts through the stem end ensured that they cooked through evenly and stayed together in the skillet. We mimicked the caramelized edges achieved through oven roasting by sautéing the sprouts in butter before adding broth. Use pure maple syrup. You will need a 12-inch skillet with a tight-fitting lid for this recipe.

4 tablespoons unsalted butter, divided
2 pounds Brussels sprouts, trimmed and halved
½ cup chicken or vegetable broth
2 tablespoons maple syrup, divided
1 teaspoon minced fresh thyme or ¼ teaspoon dried
⅛ teaspoon cayenne pepper
4 teaspoons cider vinegar

1. Melt 2 tablespoons butter in 12-inch skillet over medium-high heat. Add Brussels sprouts and cook, stirring occasionally, until browned, 6 to 8 minutes. Stir in broth, 1 tablespoon maple syrup, thyme, and cayenne. Cover, reduce heat to medium-low, and cook until sprouts are nearly tender, 6 to 8 minutes.

2. Uncover, increase heat to medium-high, and cook until liquid has nearly evaporated, about 5 minutes. Off heat, stir in remaining 2 tablespoons butter, remaining 1 tablespoon maple syrup, and vinegar until combined. Season with salt and pepper to taste. Serve.

PER SERVING Cal 110; **Total Fat** 6g, **Sat Fat** 3.5g; **Chol** 15mg; **Sodium** 60mg; **Total Carb** 13g, **Dietary Fiber** 4g, **Total Sugars** 5g; **Protein** 4g

Braised Carrots with Apple
SERVES 6 TO 8

WHY THIS RECIPE WORKS A step beyond simple glazed carrots, this braising method infuses carrots with deep flavor and gives them an earthy-sweet sauce. Since the cooking liquid becomes your sauce when you're braising, the trick to making a great braised vegetable is to create a sauce that coats the vegetables well and flavors them through cooking but also packs a punch on its own. We found that a mixture of chicken broth and apple cider gave us a cooking medium and sauce base with depth and sweetness that complemented the carrots. Slicing the carrots ¼ inch thick ensured that they cooked through evenly and quickly. Reducing the cooking liquid slightly before the carrots were added and finishing with butter and Dijon mustard gave the sauce a silky texture and some body. A chopped apple and some fresh marjoram lent color and bright, fresh flavors to the dish.

- 3 tablespoons unsalted butter, cut into ½-inch pieces, divided
- 1 shallot, minced
- 1 cup chicken broth
- 1 cup apple cider
- 6 sprigs fresh thyme
- 2 bay leaves
- 1½ teaspoons table salt
- ½ teaspoon pepper
- 2 pounds carrots, peeled and sliced ¼ inch thick on bias
- 1 Fuji or Honeycrisp apple, cored and cut into ¼-inch pieces
- 1 tablespoon Dijon mustard
- 1 teaspoon minced fresh marjoram or parsley

1. Melt 1 tablespoon butter in Dutch oven over high heat. Add shallot and cook, stirring frequently, until softened and just beginning to brown, about 3 minutes. Add broth, cider, thyme sprigs, bay leaves, salt, and pepper; bring to simmer and cook for 5 minutes to reduce slightly. Add carrots, stir to combine, and return to simmer. Reduce heat to medium-low, cover, and cook, stirring occasionally, until tender, 10 to 14 minutes.

2. Off heat, discard thyme sprigs and bay leaves and stir in apple. Push carrots to sides of pot. Add mustard and remaining 2 tablespoons butter to center and whisk into cooking liquid. Stir to coat vegetable mixture with sauce, transfer to platter, sprinkle with marjoram, and serve.

PER SERVING Cal 110; **Total Fat** 4.5g, **Sat Fat** 2.5g; **Chol** 10mg; **Sodium** 620mg; **Total Carb** 17g, **Dietary Fiber** 3g, **Total Sugars** 11g; **Protein** 1g

Roasted Carrots with Orange Glaze and Toasted Almonds

Roasted Carrots with Orange Glaze and Toasted Almonds
SERVES 12

WHY THIS RECIPE WORKS When you want a carrot side dish to serve a crowd, baby carrots are a great way to go since you don't have to spend time peeling and cutting. This simple—and quite ingenious—recipe transforms this ubiquitous supermarket staple into something extraordinary by roasting the carrots and incorporating a simple glaze. After spreading the ready-to-use carrots across a baking sheet, we sprinkled them with brown sugar (a surefire way to boost caramelization), pieces of butter, orange marmalade for sweet-tart citrusy flavor, and a pinch of cayenne for heat. Starting the carrots under aluminum foil allowed them to cook through as the butter and marmalade melted and melded into a bubbling glaze all on their own (no separate cooking required); finishing the carrots uncovered gave the self-made glaze a chance to lightly caramelize on the vegetables. The crunch and freshness of toasted almonds and minced parsley finished this simple side. Note that some of the glaze will seep underneath the foil.

3 pounds baby carrots
⅓ cup packed brown sugar
⅓ cup orange marmalade
4 tablespoons unsalted butter, cut into small pieces
½ teaspoon table salt
    Pinch cayenne pepper
½ cup sliced almonds, toasted
2 tablespoons minced fresh parsley

1. Adjust oven rack to lowest position and heat oven to 425 degrees.

2. Line a rimmed baking sheet with aluminum foil and spray with vegetable oil spray. Spread carrots over prepared sheet and sprinkle with sugar, marmalade, butter, salt, and cayenne. Cover tightly with foil and roast, stirring occasionally, until sugar and butter have melted and sauce is bubbling, about 25 minutes.

3. Uncover carrots and continue to cook, stirring occasionally, until tender and glazed, 20 to 30 minutes. Transfer to serving bowl, stir in almonds and parsley, season with salt and pepper to taste, and serve.

PER SERVING Cal 140; **Total Fat** 6g, **Sat Fat** 2.5g; **Chol** 10mg; **Sodium** 170mg; **Total Carb** 21g, **Dietary Fiber** 3g, **Total Sugars** 16g; **Protein** 2g

Braised Celery with Vermouth-Butter Glaze
SERVES 4 TO 6

WHY THIS RECIPE WORKS Too often celery is merely a recipe building block or eaten in raw sticks with dip. But celery can star as a cooked vegetable, and its flavor becomes sweet and even more delicate when braised. Adding celery seeds to the braising liquid bolstered the aromatic celery punch, while a bit of dry vermouth contributed acidity and an herbal sweetness. Peeling the strings from the celery ribs might seem fussy, but it didn't take long and it really improved the texture. This braised celery's clean flavor is a wonderful complement to poultry or fish. You can substitute ¼ cup fresh parsley leaves for the celery leaves. You will need a 12-inch skillet with a tight-fitting lid for this recipe.

1 head celery (1½ pounds), plus
    ¼ cup minced celery leaves
1 cup water
½ cup dry vermouth
3 tablespoons unsalted butter
¼ teaspoon celery seeds
¼ teaspoon table salt
⅛ teaspoon pepper

1. Using sharp vegetable peeler, remove fibrous threads from outside of celery stalks. Halve stalks lengthwise, then slice on bias into 2-inch lengths.

2. Bring celery, water, vermouth, butter, celery seeds, salt, and pepper to simmer in 12-inch skillet over medium-high heat. Cover, reduce heat to medium-low, and cook, stirring occasionally, until celery is tender, 15 to 20 minutes. Uncover and continue to simmer, stirring occasionally, until liquid is reduced to thin glaze and begins to coat celery, 5 to 7 minutes. Transfer to platter and season with salt and pepper to taste. Sprinkle with celery leaves and serve.

PER SERVING Cal 90; **Total Fat** 6g, **Sat Fat** 3.5g; **Chol** 15mg; **Sodium** 310mg; **Total Carb** 4g, **Dietary Fiber** 2g, **Total Sugars** 3g; **Protein** 1g

Extra-Crunchy Green Bean Casserole
SERVES 6 TO 8   MAKE-AHEAD

WHY THIS RECIPE WORKS For many, the holiday table is incomplete without green bean casserole, but this old friend could use a new suit. We looked to modernize the dish with a crunchier topping and a sauce with an extra note of complexity. We jump-started the beans in the microwave, which shortened the bake time. For the sauce, we skipped canned soup, browning mushrooms to develop deep flavor and then stirring in broth, cream, and flour. Adding panko to the fried onions gave them crunch, and we didn't bake them with the beans. The onions were crunchier when not saturated with sauce, so we sprinkled them on after baking. White mushrooms can be substituted for cremini.

TOPPING
½ cup panko bread crumbs
1 tablespoon unsalted butter, melted
2½ cups canned fried onions

CASSEROLE
2 pounds green beans, trimmed and cut into
    1-inch pieces
3 tablespoons unsalted butter
1 pound cremini mushrooms, trimmed and sliced thin
1 tablespoon minced fresh thyme
2 garlic cloves, minced
1½ teaspoons table salt
½ teaspoon pepper
¼ cup all-purpose flour
1½ cups chicken broth
1½ cups heavy cream
½ cup dry white wine

1. FOR THE TOPPING Combine panko and melted butter in bowl. Microwave stirring occasionally, until panko is golden brown, about 2 minutes. Let cool completely, then stir in fried onions; set aside.

2. FOR THE CASSEROLE Adjust oven rack to middle position and heat oven to 400 degrees. Combine green beans and ½ cup water in large bowl. Cover and microwave until green beans are just tender, about 8 minutes, stirring halfway through microwaving. Drain green beans in colander; set aside.

3. Melt butter in 12-inch nonstick skillet over medium-high heat. Add mushrooms, thyme, garlic, salt, and pepper and cook until liquid is nearly evaporated, 6 to 8 minutes.

4. Stir in flour and cook for 1 minute. Slowly whisk in broth, cream, and wine and bring to boil. Cook, stirring occasionally, until sauce has thickened, 4 to 6 minutes. Transfer green beans to 13 by 9-inch baking dish. Pour sauce over green beans and toss to combine. (After cooling completely, casserole can be covered with foil and refrigerated for up to 24 hours. To serve, bake, covered until green beans are heated through and completely tender, about 40 minutes. Uncover and bake until edges begin to brown, about 10 minutes.)

5. Bake until bubbling and green beans are completely tender, about 25 minutes. Remove from oven, top with fried-onion mixture, and let cool for 10 minutes. Serve.

PER SERVING Cal 410; **Total Fat** 31g; **Sat Fat** 16g; **Chol** 65mg; **Sodium** 680mg; **Total Carb** 25g, **Dietary Fiber** 3g, **Total Sugars** 7g; **Protein** 7g

Quick Green Bean Casserole

Quick Green Bean Casserole
SERVES 8   FAST

WHY THIS RECIPE WORKS We love traditional green bean casserole (see page 471), but we wanted a streamlined technique for preparing the dish, with all the flavors of the classic—green beans, creamy mushroom sauce, delicious crispy onions—but cooked in a skillet. First, we built a sauce in the skillet with onion, garlic, chicken broth, cream, and a little flour; then we added the beans along with thyme and bay leaves, covered them, and allowed them to steam until the beans were almost done. We then stirred in browned cremini mushrooms and thickened the sauce by uncovering the skillet during the final phase of cooking. Since we were taking this dish out of the casserole, we decided to give it a refreshed topper: floured shallots that we cooked ourselves in oil until crisp. We simply sprinkled these over our easy, tasty skillet casserole.

3 large shallots, sliced thin
½ teaspoon table salt, divided
⅛ teaspoon pepper
3 tablespoons all-purpose flour, divided
5 tablespoons vegetable oil, divided
10 ounces cremini mushrooms, trimmed and sliced ¼ inch thick
2 tablespoons unsalted butter
1 onion, chopped fine
2 garlic cloves, minced
1½ pounds green beans, trimmed
3 sprigs fresh thyme
2 bay leaves
¾ cup heavy cream
¾ cup chicken broth

1. Toss shallots with ¼ teaspoon salt, pepper, and 2 tablespoons flour in small bowl. Heat 3 tablespoons oil in 12-inch nonstick skillet over medium-high heat until smoking; add shallots and cook, stirring frequently, until golden and crisp, about 5 minutes. Transfer shallots with oil to baking sheet lined with paper towels.

2. Wipe out skillet and return to medium-high heat. Add remaining 2 tablespoons oil, mushrooms, and remaining ¼ teaspoon salt; cook, stirring occasionally, until mushrooms are well browned, about 8 minutes. Transfer to plate; set aside.

3. Wipe out skillet. Melt butter in skillet over medium heat, then add onion and cook, stirring occasionally, until edges begin to brown, about 2 minutes. Stir in garlic and remaining 1 tablespoon flour; toss in green beans, thyme, and bay leaves. Add cream and broth, increase heat to medium-high, cover, and cook until beans are partly tender but still crisp at center, about 4 minutes. Add mushrooms and continue to cook, uncovered, until green beans are tender, about 4 minutes. Off heat, discard bay leaves and thyme; season with salt and pepper to taste. Transfer to serving dish, sprinkle evenly with shallots, and serve.

PER SERVING Cal 240; **Total Fat** 20g, **Sat Fat** 8g; **Chol** 35mg; **Sodium** 210mg; **Total Carb** 13g, **Dietary Fiber** 3g, **Total Sugars** 6g; **Protein** 4g

Green Beans with Bacon and Onion
SERVES 4 TO 6

WHY THIS RECIPE WORKS For a new approach to green beans that were worthy of serving at the holiday table, we sautéed green beans until tender and lightly browned and then draped them with soft, sweet caramelized onion, sprinkling crunchy bits of bacon over the top. The secret to getting all the components done at the same time was to stagger the cooking: bacon first, onion second, green beans last. We cooked the bacon, transferred it to a paper towel–lined plate to drain, and then added the onion to the skillet and cooked it in some of the rendered bacon fat for even more porky punch. Once the onion was softened and beginning to brown, we added the green beans, covered the skillet so that they would steam and cook through, and then removed the cover to cook off any residual liquid. We sprinkled the crispy bacon pieces over the green beans before serving.

  6 slices bacon, cut into ½-inch pieces
  1 onion, halved and sliced thin
  1 teaspoon packed brown sugar
  1 teaspoon table salt, divided
  ½ teaspoon pepper
  2 pounds green beans, trimmed
  ½ cup water
  2 garlic cloves, sliced thin

Green Beans with Bacon and Onion

1. Cook bacon in 12-inch nonstick skillet over medium heat until crispy, 5 to 7 minutes. Using slotted spoon, transfer bacon to paper towel–lined plate. Pour off all but 1 tablespoon fat from skillet.

2. Add onion, sugar, ½ teaspoon salt, and pepper to fat left in skillet and cook over medium heat, stirring occasionally, until onion is softened and beginning to brown, about 5 minutes.

3. Add green beans, water, garlic, and remaining ½ teaspoon salt and increase heat to medium-high. Cover and cook, stirring occasionally, until water has nearly evaporated and green beans are bright green, about 8 minutes. Uncover and continue to cook until water has completely evaporated and green beans are just spotty brown, 2 to 4 minutes. Transfer to serving platter and sprinkle with bacon. Serve.

PER SERVING Cal 170; **Total Fat** 11g, **Sat Fat** 4g; **Chol** 20mg; **Sodium** 580mg; **Total Carb** 12g, **Dietary Fiber** 4g, **Total Sugars** 6g; **Protein** 6g

Sautéed Mushrooms with Red Wine and Rosemary

Sautéed Mushrooms with Red Wine and Rosemary
SERVES 4

WHY THIS RECIPE WORKS Sautéing mushrooms the usual way means piling them in a skillet slicked with a couple of tablespoons of oil and waiting patiently for them to release their moisture, which must then evaporate before the mushrooms can brown. Instead, we accelerated the process by adding a small amount of water to the pan and steaming the mushrooms, which allowed them to release their moisture more quickly. The added benefit of steaming them is that the collapsed mushrooms don't absorb much oil; in fact, ½ teaspoon of oil was enough to prevent sticking and encourage browning. And because we used so little fat to sauté the mushrooms, we were able to sauce them with an aromatic butter-based reduction without making them overly rich. Adding broth, along with red wine and cider vinegar for punch, to the sauce and simmering the mixture ensured that the butter emulsified, creating a flavorful glaze that clung well to the mushrooms. Use one variety of mushroom or a combination. Stem and halve portobello mushrooms and cut each half crosswise into ½-inch pieces. Trim white or cremini mushrooms; quarter them if large or medium or halve them if small. Tear trimmed oyster mushrooms into 1- to 1½-inch pieces. Stem shiitake mushrooms; quarter large caps and halve small caps. Cut trimmed maitake (hen-of-the-woods) mushrooms into 1- to 1½-inch pieces.

1¼ pounds mushrooms, trimmed
¼ cup water
½ teaspoon vegetable oil
1 tablespoon unsalted butter
1 shallot, minced
1 teaspoon minced fresh rosemary
¼ teaspoon table salt
¼ teaspoon pepper
¼ cup red wine
1 tablespoon cider vinegar
½ cup chicken broth

1. Cook mushrooms and water in 12-inch nonstick skillet over high heat, stirring occasionally, until skillet is almost dry and mushrooms begin to sizzle, 4 to 8 minutes. Reduce heat to medium-high. Add oil and toss until mushrooms are evenly coated. Continue to cook, stirring occasionally, until mushrooms are well browned, 4 to 8 minutes. Reduce heat to medium.

2. Push mushrooms to sides of skillet. Add butter to center. When butter has melted, add shallot, rosemary, salt, and pepper to center and cook, stirring constantly, until aromatic, about 30 seconds. Add wine and vinegar and stir mixture into mushrooms. Cook, stirring occasionally, until liquid has evaporated, 2 to 3 minutes. Add broth and cook, stirring occasionally, until glaze is reduced by half, about 3 minutes. Season with salt and pepper to taste, and serve.

PER SERVING Cal 80; **Total Fat** 3.5g, **Sat Fat** 2g; **Chol** 10mg; **Sodium** 230mg; **Total Carb** 6g, **Dietary Fiber** 0g, **Total Sugars** 4g; **Protein** 2g

VARIATIONS

Sautéed Mushrooms with Mustard and Parsley
Omit rosemary. Substitute 1 tablespoon Dijon mustard for wine and increase vinegar to 1½ tablespoons (liquid will take only 1 to 2 minutes to evaporate). Stir in 2 tablespoons chopped fresh parsley before serving.

Sautéed Mushrooms with Soy, Scallion, and Ginger
Substitute 1 thinly sliced scallion for shallot and grated fresh ginger for rosemary. Omit salt. Substitute 2 tablespoons soy sauce for wine and sherry vinegar for cider vinegar.

Glazed Pearl Onions
SERVES 4

WHY THIS RECIPE WORKS Glazed whole pearl onions are a beautiful and fitting addition to any holiday table, since they complement just about any type of roast. For sweet, flavorful pearl onions, we found that they were best served by a dual cooking approach of browning followed by braising. Browning the onions in olive oil and butter helped to enhance their natural sweetness, while braising them in chicken broth added savoriness. Brown sugar and rosemary contributed depth. When trimming the root ends of the blanched onions, shave off the thinnest slice possible. If too much is taken off, the onion will fall apart. You can substitute frozen pearl onions for the fresh onions in this recipe; frozen pearl onions come already peeled, so skip step 1.

- 1 pound pearl onions
- 1 tablespoon unsalted butter
- 1 tablespoon extra-virgin olive oil
- ½ cup chicken broth
- 1½ tablespoons packed brown sugar
- ½ teaspoon minced fresh rosemary

1. Bring 2 quarts water to boil in large saucepan. Add onions and cook for 1 minute. Drain in colander and run under cold water until cool to touch, about 1 minute. Transfer onions to paper towel–lined plate and pat dry. Trim root and stem ends, then peel and discard onion skins.

2. Melt butter with oil in 12-inch skillet over medium heat. Add onions and cook, stirring occasionally, until onions are lightly browned, 7 to 9 minutes.

3. Add broth, sugar, and rosemary and bring to boil. Cover, reduce heat to medium-low, and simmer until onions are tender, about 12 minutes. Uncover, increase heat to medium-high, and simmer until liquid is reduced to syrupy glaze, 4 to 5 minutes. Season with salt and pepper to taste, and serve immediately.

PER SERVING Cal 140; **Total Fat** 6g, **Sat Fat** 2g; **Chol** 10mg; **Sodium** 95mg; **Total Carb** 21g, **Dietary Fiber** 0g, **Total Sugars** 9g; **Protein** 1g

Balsamic-Glazed Cipollini Onions
SERVES 6 TO 8

WHY THIS RECIPE WORKS *Cipolline in agrodolce* is a country-style Italian dish of small, flat cipollini onions braised in a sweet-and-sour vinegar-and-sugar glaze. It's the perfect foil for richer fare. But the formula, though simple, presents possibilities: balsamic or wine vinegar? White or brown sugar? Butter or olive oil? To keep the cipollinis' sweet, buttery flavor at the fore, we left the ingredient list short but impactful. We chose balsamic vinegar for its distinctive flavor and inherent sweetness, and granulated sugar over brown sugar for its clean taste. All the dish needed was a bit of extra butter swirled in for enrichment and a sprinkle of chopped fresh basil. You can use frozen cipollini onions in this recipe; they are already peeled, so skip step 1.

- 2 pounds cipollini onions
- 3 tablespoons unsalted butter, cut into 3 pieces, divided
- 2½ tablespoons sugar, divided
- ¾ teaspoon table salt
- ⅛ teaspoon red pepper flakes
- ⅓ cup balsamic vinegar
- 2 tablespoons chopped fresh basil

1. Bring 2 quarts water to boil in large saucepan. Add onions and cook for 30 seconds. Drain in colander and run under cold water until cool to touch, about 1 minute. Transfer onions to paper towel–lined plate and pat dry. Trim root and stem ends, then peel and discard onion skins.

2. Bring onions, ½ cup water, 1 tablespoon butter, 1½ teaspoons sugar, salt, and pepper flakes to boil over medium-high heat in 12-inch nonstick skillet. Cover and cook until water is nearly evaporated, about 10 minutes, stirring halfway through cooking.

3. Uncover and reduce heat to medium. Cook onions, flipping as needed, until well browned on both sides, 4 to 7 minutes.

4. Reduce heat to medium-low, and stir in vinegar, 1 tablespoon water, and remaining 2 tablespoons sugar. Simmer until liquid is reduced to syrupy glaze, 3 to 5 minutes. Off heat, stir in remaining 2 tablespoons butter. Transfer to platter, sprinkle with basil, and serve.

PER SERVING Cal 140; **Total Fat** 4g, **Sat Fat** 2.5g; **Chol** 10mg; **Sodium** 240mg; **Total Carb** 23g, **Dietary Fiber** 0g, **Total Sugars** 11g; **Protein** 1g

VARIATION
White Balsamic–Glazed Cipollini Onions with Tarragon
Substitute white balsamic vinegar for balsamic vinegar and 1 tablespoon minced fresh tarragon for basil.

Braised Parsnips with Cranberries

6 sprigs fresh thyme
2 bay leaves
1½ teaspoons table salt
½ teaspoon pepper
2 pounds parsnips, peeled and cut ¼ inch thick on bias
½ cup dried cranberries
1 tablespoon Dijon mustard
2 tablespoons minced fresh parsley

1. Melt 1 tablespoon butter in Dutch oven over high heat. Add shallot and cook, stirring frequently, until softened and just beginning to brown, about 1 minute. Add broth, cider, thyme sprigs, bay leaves, salt, and pepper; bring to simmer and cook for 5 minutes. Add parsnips, stir to combine, and return to simmer. Reduce heat to medium-low, cover, and cook, stirring occasionally, until vegetables are tender, 10 to 14 minutes.

2. Off heat, discard thyme sprigs and bay leaves and stir in cranberries. Push parsnips to sides of pot. Add mustard and remaining 2 tablespoons butter to center and whisk into cooking liquid. Stir to coat vegetable mixture with sauce, transfer to serving dish, sprinkle with parsley, and serve.

PER SERVING Cal 220; **Total Fat** 6g, **Sat Fat** 3.5g; **Chol** 15mg; **Sodium** 760mg; **Total Carb** 40g, **Dietary Fiber** 7g, **Total Sugars** 21g; **Protein** 2g

Braised Parsnips with Cranberries
SERVES 4 TO 6

WHY THIS RECIPE WORKS Parsnips have a slightly licorice-like flavor and so they can stand up to rich sauces. But if the sauce or glaze isn't correctly balanced, the finished dish can come off cloying, as parsnips are packed with their own natural sweetness. For our braising liquid, we found that a mixture of vegetable broth and apple cider gave us a base with depth, fruitiness, and a touch of acidity that complemented the parsnips perfectly and wasn't overly sweet. In addition to butter, we finished the sauce that was left after braising with emulsifying Dijon mustard, which offset the vegetable with its sharp bite. For an interesting stir-in, we chose dried cranberries; they brought a contrasting tartness and pleasing chew. Look for parsnips with bases no larger than 1 inch in diameter for this recipe.

3 tablespoons unsalted butter, 2 tablespoons cut into ½-inch pieces, divided
1 shallot, minced
1 cup chicken or vegetable broth
1 cup apple cider

Maple-Glazed Acorn Squash
SERVES 6 TO 8

WHY THIS RECIPE WORKS A sweet maple glaze beautifully highlights the earthy flavor of acorn squash. But most recipes for maple-glazed squash call for just halving the squash, pouring on some syrup, topping with a pat of butter, and roasting, which result in a stagnant pool of buttery syrup at the bottom of each half. We wanted every bite to be coated with a deeply flavored glaze. We started by cutting the squash into eighths; the increased surface area provided room for ample amounts of glaze. The problem? The smaller pieces of squash cooked so quickly that they barely browned. To remedy this, we tossed the squash wedges with vegetable oil and a small amount of granulated sugar before roasting them and then flipped them before glazing so that both sides had time to brown before being brushed. This approach boosted preglazing caramelization, producing the desired deep brown color and rich flavor beneath the maple. A final brush of syrup before serving maximized impact. We reduced the maple syrup only slightly and added butter for richness and cayenne for heat. Use pure maple syrup.

Maple-Glazed Acorn Squash

3. When bottoms of squash are deep golden, remove from oven. Flip and brush with 6 tablespoons glaze. Return to oven and roast until squash is tender and deep golden all over, about 15 minutes. Flip and brush with remaining glaze. Serve.

PER SERVING Cal 170; **Total Fat** 9g, **Sat Fat** 4g; **Chol** 15mg; **Sodium** 220mg; **Total Carb** 23g, **Dietary Fiber** 2g, **Total Sugars** 11g; **Protein** 1g

Pureed Butternut Squash
SERVES 4 TO 6   MAKE-AHEAD

WHY THIS RECIPE WORKS With its silky-smooth texture and earthy, lightly sweetened flavor, pureed butternut squash is a crowd-pleaser, but what's the best way to cook it? Most recipes for pureed squash cook the squash until tender and then puree it with some butter and/or heavy cream in a food processor. We tested a variety of squash cooking methods, including roasting, steaming, braising, and microwaving, and found that the microwave worked best. Not only was it one of the easiest cooking methods, but tasters far preferred the clean, sweet squash flavor that the microwave produced. The surprising thing about microwaving the squash was the amount of liquid released while cooking—we drained nearly ½ cup of squash liquid from the bowl before pureeing. (We tasted the liquid and found it had a slightly bitter flavor, which is why we did not opt to include it in the puree.) The squash puree needed only 2 tablespoons of half-and-half and 2 tablespoons of butter to help round out its flavor and add some richness.

2 acorn squashes (1½ pounds each),
    halved pole to pole and seeded
2 tablespoons vegetable oil
2 teaspoons sugar
¾ teaspoon table salt
½ teaspoon pepper
5 tablespoons maple syrup
4 tablespoons unsalted butter
⅛ teaspoon cayenne pepper

1. Adjust oven rack to middle position and heat oven to 475 degrees. Cut each squash half into 4 wedges. Toss squash, oil, sugar, salt, and pepper in large bowl to coat, then arrange cut side down in single layer on rimmed baking sheet. Roast until bottoms of squash are deep golden brown, about 25 minutes.

2. Meanwhile, bring maple syrup to boil in small saucepan over medium-high heat. Reduce heat to medium-low and simmer until slightly thickened, about 3 minutes. Off heat, whisk in butter and cayenne until smooth. Cover and keep warm.

2 pounds butternut squash, peeled, seeded,
    and cut into 1½-inch pieces (6 cups)
2 tablespoons half-and-half
2 tablespoons unsalted butter
1 tablespoon packed brown sugar
1 teaspoon table salt

1. Microwave squash in covered bowl until tender and easily pierced with fork, 15 to 20 minutes, stirring halfway through microwaving.

2. Drain squash in colander, then transfer to food processor. Add half-and-half, butter, sugar, and salt and process until squash is smooth, about 20 seconds, scraping down sides of bowl as needed. Transfer to serving bowl, season with salt and pepper to taste, and serve. (To make ahead, add only 2 tablespoons butter in step 2.

Cooled puree can be refrigerated for up to 4 days or frozen for up to 1 month. [If frozen, let thaw in refrigerator for 24 hours before reheating.] Microwave puree in covered bowl, stirring occasionally, until hot, 3 to 5 minutes. Stir in remaining 2 tablespoons butter and season with additional sugar, salt, and pepper to taste.)

PER SERVING Cal 120; **Total Fat** 4.5g, **Sat Fat** 2.5g; **Chol** 10mg; **Sodium** 200mg; **Total Carb** 20g, **Dietary Fiber** 3g, **Total Sugars** 6g; **Protein** 2g

VARIATIONS

Pureed Butternut Squash with Honey and Chipotle Chile
Substitute 1 tablespoon honey for sugar. Add 1½ teaspoons minced canned chipotle chile in adobo sauce to food processor with butter.

Pureed Butternut Squash with Orange
Add 2 tablespoons orange marmalade to food processor with butter.

Pureed Butternut Squash with Sage and Toasted Almonds
While squash is in microwave, cook 1 tablespoon unsalted butter with ½ teaspoon minced fresh sage in 8-inch skillet over medium-low heat until fragrant, about 2 minutes. Substitute sage butter for butter added to food processor. Sprinkle squash with ¼ cup toasted sliced almonds before serving.

Make-Ahead Mashed Potato Casserole
SERVES 8 TO 10 `MAKE-AHEAD`

WHY THIS RECIPE WORKS Mashed potato casseroles transform the humble potato into a comfort-food side dish that's more than the sum of its parts. We wanted to design our smooth, cheesy, crunchy-topped casserole so it could be made ahead and reheated for company without fuss. Keeping the potatoes creamy required mixing them with a dairy product. Whole milk and butter were obvious additions that loosened the mash to the right consistency but weren't enough to prevent dry, grainy potatoes after reheating. Sour cream added luxury that lasted and a refreshing tang. The cheddar cheese didn't incorporate well when we stirred it into the mash, so we sprinkled a cheesy layer on top. And, to complete the dish, we sprinkled a homemade bread-crumb topping over the cheese. This casserole was creamy and smooth after reheating and retained all its flavor. For a slightly spicy version, substitute pepper Jack cheese for the cheddar. For the smoothest texture, err on the side of overcooking the potatoes rather than undercooking them.

Make-Ahead Mashed Potato Casserole

TOPPING
 4 slices hearty white sandwich bread, quartered
 2 tablespoons unsalted butter, melted
 ¼ cup minced fresh parsley

CASSEROLE
 5 pounds russet potatoes, peeled and sliced ¾ inch thick
 2½ cups whole milk, warmed
 1 cup sour cream
 8 tablespoons unsalted butter, melted
 2½ teaspoons Dijon mustard
 1 garlic clove, minced
 ⅛ teaspoon cayenne pepper
 8 ounces shredded extra-sharp cheddar cheese (about 2 cups)

1. FOR THE TOPPING Adjust oven rack to middle position and heat oven to 300 degrees. Pulse bread into crumbs in food processor, about 6 pulses. Toss crumbs with melted butter and spread over rimmed baking sheet. Bake, stirring occasionally, until golden and dry, about 20 minutes. Let crumbs cool, then toss with parsley and season with salt and pepper to taste; set aside. Increase oven temperature to 350 degrees.

2. FOR THE CASSEROLE Meanwhile, place potatoes in Dutch oven and add water to cover by 1 inch. Bring to boil, then reduce to simmer and cook until potatoes are tender and paring knife inserted into potatoes meets no resistance, about 15 minutes.

3. Drain potatoes in colander. Set ricer or food mill over now-empty, but still warm, pot. Working in batches, process potatoes into pot. Stir in milk, sour cream, butter, Dijon, garlic, and cayenne until uniform. Season with salt and pepper to taste.

4. Spread potato mixture into 13 by 9-inch baking dish. Sprinkle cheddar evenly over top, then sprinkle with bread crumbs. Bake until casserole is hot throughout and crumbs are crisp, 25 to 30 minutes. Serve. (To make ahead, after sprinkling casserole with bread crumbs, cover dish tightly with plastic wrap and refrigerate for up to 2 days. To serve, remove plastic, cover with foil and bake for 20 minutes. Uncover and continue to bake until hot throughout, 20 to 30 minutes.)

PER SERVING Cal 470; **Total Fat** 25g, **Sat Fat** 15g; **Chol** 70mg; **Sodium** 280mg; **Total Carb** 48g, **Dietary Fiber** 3g, **Total Sugars** 6g; **Protein** 13g

Classic Mashed Potatoes
SERVES 4

WHY THIS RECIPE WORKS Many people would never consider consulting a recipe when making mashed potatoes, instead adding chunks of butter and glugs of cream to cooked spuds until their conscience tells them to stop. Little wonder, then, that mashed potatoes made this way are consistent only in their mediocrity. We wanted mashed potatoes that were perfectly smooth and creamy, with great potato flavor and plenty of buttery richness, every time. We began by cutting starchy russets into chunks and simmering them until tender. For smooth, velvety potatoes, we discovered that there's a bit of science involved. If the half-and-half is stirred into the potatoes before the butter, the water in the half-and-half combines with the starch in the potatoes to make them gummy and heavy. But when the butter is added first, the fat coats the starch molecules and prevents them from reacting with the water in the half-and-half, making for smoother, more velvety mashed potatoes. Melting rather than merely softening the butter enabled it to coat the starch molecules quickly and easily, so that the potatoes turned out creamy and light. For the smoothest mashed potatoes, use a potato ricer or food mill.

2 pounds russet potatoes, peeled, quartered, and cut into 1-inch pieces
8 tablespoons unsalted butter, melted
1 cup half-and-half, hot

1. Place potatoes in large saucepan and add water to cover by 1 inch. Bring to boil, then reduce to simmer and cook until potatoes are tender and paring knife inserted into potatoes meets no resistance, 20 to 25 minutes.

2. Drain potatoes in colander, tossing to remove any excess water. Wipe now-empty saucepan dry with paper towels. Return potatoes to pot and mash to uniform consistency, or process through ricer or food mill back into dry pot.

3. Using silicone spatula, fold in melted butter until just incorporated. Fold in ¾ cup half-and-half, then add remaining ¼ cup as needed to adjust consistency. Season with salt and pepper to taste, and serve.

PER SERVING Cal 430; **Total Fat** 28g, **Sat Fat** 18g; **Chol** 80mg; **Sodium** 45mg; **Total Carb** 38g, **Dietary Fiber** 3g, **Total Sugars** 4g; **Protein** 6g

VARIATIONS
Garlic Mashed Potatoes
Toasting the garlic is essential for mellowing its harsh flavor. Avoid using unusually large garlic cloves, as they will not soften adequately during toasting.

Toast about 20 unpeeled garlic cloves in 8-inch skillet over lowest possible heat until spotty dark brown and slightly softened, about 22 minutes. Remove pan from heat, cover, and let sit until garlic is completely soft, 10 to 15 minutes. Peel and mince garlic, then fold it into potatoes with butter in step 3. (If using ricer or food mill, process softened, peeled cloves whole, along with potatoes.)

Mashed Potatoes with Scallions and Horseradish
Buy refrigerated prepared horseradish, not the shelf-stable kind, which contains preservatives and additives.

Fold ¼ cup drained prepared horseradish and 3 minced scallions into potatoes with half-and-half in step 3.

Mashed Potatoes with Smoked Cheddar and Whole-Grain Mustard
Fold 2 tablespoons whole-grain mustard and 1 cup shredded smoked cheddar cheese into potatoes with half-and-half in step 3.

Whipped Potatoes

SERVES 8

WHY THIS RECIPE WORKS These whipped potatoes yield the lightest, most ethereally fluffy side of spuds you've ever tasted. We rinsed the potatoes before cooking to remove their surface starch, the main culprit behind heavy mashed potatoes. Steaming—rather than boiling—the potatoes kept them from absorbing extra liquid. A quick toss in the pot dried the potatoes further, so that they whipped up to maximum fluffiness in a stand mixer. Do not attempt to cook the potatoes in a pot smaller than 12 quarts; if you don't have a large enough pot, use two smaller pots and cook the potatoes in two simultaneous batches. If your steamer basket has short legs (under 1¾ inches), the potatoes will sit in water as they cook and get wet. To prevent this, use balls of aluminum foil as steamer basket stilts. A stand mixer fitted with a whisk attachment yields the smoothest potatoes, but you can also use a handheld mixer and a large bowl.

    4   pounds russet potatoes, peeled and cut into
        1-inch pieces
 1½   cups whole milk
    8   tablespoons unsalted butter, cut into 8 pieces
    2   teaspoons table salt
  ½   teaspoon pepper

1. Place potatoes in colander and rinse under cold running water until water runs clear, about 1 minute. Drain potatoes. Bring 1 inch water to boil in 12-quart pot over high heat. Place steamer basket in Dutch oven and fill with potatoes. Cover, reduce heat to medium, and cook until potatoes are tender, 20 to 25 minutes.

2. Heat milk, butter, salt, and pepper in small saucepan over medium-low heat, whisking until smooth, about 3 minutes; cover and keep warm.

3. Drain potatoes in colander and return potatoes to pot. Stir over low heat until potatoes are thoroughly dried, about 1 minute. Using stand mixer fitted with whisk attachment, mix potatoes on low speed until broken into small pieces, about 30 seconds. Add milk mixture in steady stream until incorporated. Increase speed to high and whip until potatoes are light and fluffy and no lumps remain, about 2 minutes. Serve.

PER SERVING Cal 280; **Total Fat** 13g, **Sat Fat** 8g; **Chol** 35mg; **Sodium** 610mg; **Total Carb** 37g, **Dietary Fiber** 3g, **Total Sugars** 3g; **Protein** 6g

---

TAKE IT UP A NOTCH

Mashed spuds are a landing pad for rich gravy, but we don't always have drippings from a roast to make gravy from scratch. This shortcut tastes great with all meals.

All-Purpose Gravy

MAKES 2 CUPS

If you would like to double the recipe, use a Dutch oven and increase the cooking times by roughly 50 percent. If you freeze the gravy, it may appear broken or curdled as it thaws, but vigorous whisking will recombine it.

    1   small carrot, peeled and chopped
    1   small celery rib, chopped
    1   small onion, chopped
    3   tablespoons unsalted butter
  ¼   cup all-purpose flour
    2   cups chicken broth
    2   cups beef broth
    1   bay leaf
  ¼   teaspoon dried thyme
    5   whole black peppercorns

1. Pulse carrot in food processor until broken into rough ¼-inch pieces, about 5 pulses. Add celery and onion; pulse until all vegetables are broken into ⅛-inch pieces, about 5 pulses.

2. Melt butter in large saucepan over medium-high heat. Add vegetables and cook, stirring often, until softened and well browned, about 7 minutes. Reduce heat to medium; add flour and cook, stirring constantly, until thoroughly browned and fragrant, about 5 minutes. Slowly whisk in chicken broth and beef broth; bring to boil, skimming off any foam that forms on surface. Add bay leaf, thyme, and peppercorns, reduce to simmer, and cook, stirring occasionally, until thickened and measures 3 cups, 20 to 25 minutes. Strain gravy through fine-mesh strainer into clean saucepan or bowl, pressing on solids to extract as much liquid as possible; discard solids. Season with salt and pepper to taste. (Gravy can be frozen for up to 1 month. To thaw, bring gravy and 1 tablespoon water slowly to simmer in saucepan over low heat. Whisk vigorously until heated through.)

Scalloped Potatoes

SERVES 8 TO 10 `MAKE-AHEAD`

WHY THIS RECIPE WORKS Most recipes for scalloped potatoes take hours of work yet still produce unevenly cooked potatoes in a curdled sauce. This faster version features layer upon layer of tender thinly sliced potatoes, creamy sauce, and nicely browned, cheesy crust. Simmering the potatoes in dairy before moving the production into a baking dish cut the cooking time significantly while also eliminating the risk of raw potatoes in the finished dish. We didn't thicken the liquid mixture with stodgy flour; the starch from the potatoes was enough. A sprinkling of cheddar cheese and a mere 20 minutes in the oven were enough to produce an appealingly browned cheesy crust. For the fastest and most even results, slice the potatoes in a food processor.

    2 tablespoons unsalted butter
    1 small onion, chopped fine
    2 cloves garlic, minced
    4 pounds russet potatoes, peeled and sliced ⅛ inch thick
    3 cups heavy cream
    1 cup whole milk
    4 sprigs fresh thyme
    2 bay leaves
    2 teaspoons table salt
    ½ teaspoon pepper
    4 ounces cheddar cheese, shredded (1 cup)

1. Heat oven to 350 degrees. Melt butter in Dutch oven over medium-high heat. Add onion and cook until softened and beginning to brown, about 4 minutes. Add garlic and cook until fragrant, about 30 seconds. Add potatoes, cream, milk, thyme sprigs, bay leaves, salt, and pepper and bring to simmer. Cover, adjusting heat as necessary to maintain light simmer, and cook until potatoes are almost tender and paring knife inserted in center of potato slice meets some resistance, about 15 minutes.

2. Discard thyme sprigs and bay leaves. Transfer potato mixture to 3-quart baking dish and sprinkle with cheese. Bake until cream has thickened and is bubbling around sides and top is golden brown, about 20 minutes. Let cool for 5 minutes before serving. (To make ahead, do not top casserole with cheddar in step 2. After transferring potato mixture to baking dish, refrigerate for up to 24 hours. To serve, cover dish tightly with greased foil and bake in 400-degree oven until hot throughout, about 1 hour. Uncover, top with cheddar, and continue to bake until cheddar is lightly browned, about 30 minutes. Let casserole cool for 15 minutes.)

PER SERVING Cal 450; **Total Fat** 33g, **Sat Fat** 21g; **Chol** 100mg; **Sodium** 580mg; **Total Carb** 33g, **Dietary Fiber** 2g, **Total Sugars** 5g; **Protein** 9g

Potato Galette

Potato Galette

SERVES 6 TO 8

WHY THIS RECIPE WORKS With its crispy exterior crust and beautifully layered presentation, a potato galette, sliced into wedges, is a sophisticated side. For even cooking and great browning, we began our galette recipe on the stovetop and then slid the pan onto the bottom rack of a hot oven. Using an ovensafe nonstick skillet averted the risk of our potato galette sticking to the pan's bottom. To keep the potatoes from sliding away from one another when we sliced our galette, we included cornstarch in the melted butter–and-herb mixture that we were using to coat the potatoes and we compressed the galette using a cake pan filled with pie weights for the first half of cooking. Slicing the potatoes ⅛ inch thick is crucial for the success of this dish; use a mandoline, a V-slicer, or a food processor fitted with a ⅛-inch-thick slicing blade. You will need a 10-inch ovensafe nonstick skillet for this recipe. A pound of dried beans or rice can be substituted for the pie weights.

2½ pounds Yukon Gold potatoes, unpeeled, sliced ⅛ inch thick
5 tablespoons unsalted butter, melted, divided
1 tablespoon cornstarch
1½ teaspoons chopped fresh rosemary
1 teaspoon table salt
½ teaspoon pepper

1. Adjust oven rack to lowest position and heat oven to 450 degrees. Place potatoes in large bowl and fill with cold water. Swirl to remove excess starch, then drain in colander. Spread potatoes on dish towels and dry thoroughly.

2. Whisk 4 tablespoons melted butter, cornstarch, rosemary, salt, and pepper together in large bowl. Add potatoes and toss until thoroughly coated. Add remaining 1 tablespoon melted butter to 10-inch ovensafe nonstick skillet and swirl to coat. Place 1 potato slice in center of skillet, then overlap slices in circle around center slice, followed by outer circle of overlapping slices. Gently place remaining sliced potatoes on top of first layer, arranging so they form even thickness.

3. Place skillet over medium-high heat and cook until potatoes are sizzling and slices around edge of galette start to turn translucent, about 5 minutes. Spray 12-inch square of aluminum foil with vegetable oil spray. Place foil, sprayed side down, on top of potatoes. Place 9-inch round cake pan on top of foil and fill with 2 cups pie weights. Firmly press down on cake pan to compress potatoes. Transfer skillet to oven and bake for 20 minutes.

4. Remove cake pan and foil from skillet. Continue to cook until paring knife inserted in center of galette meets no resistance, 20 to 25 minutes. Being careful of hot skillet handle, return skillet to medium heat on stovetop and cook, gently shaking pan (skillet handle will be hot), until galette releases from sides of skillet, 2 to 3 minutes. Carefully slide galette onto large plate, place cutting board over galette, and gently invert plate and cutting board together, then remove plate. Using serrated knife, gently cut galette into wedges; serve immediately.

PER SERVING Cal 180; **Total Fat** 7g, **Sat Fat** 4.5g; **Chol** 20mg; **Sodium** 300mg; **Total Carb** 26g, **Dietary Fiber** 0g, **Total Sugars** 0g; **Protein** 3g

Crispy Potato Latkes
SERVES 4 TO 6 (MAKES 10 LATKES) MAKE-AHEAD

WHY THIS RECIPE WORKS Lackluster latkes are no way to celebrate. To achieve latkes that were light and not greasy, with buttery, soft interiors surrounded by a shatteringly crisp outer shell, we needed to do two things: First, we removed as much water as possible from the potato shreds by wringing them out in a dish

Crispy Potato Latkes

towel. Then we briefly microwaved them. This caused the starches in the potatoes to form a gel that held on to the potatoes' moisture so it didn't leach out during cooking. With the water taken care of, the latkes crisped up quickly and absorbed minimal oil. We prefer shredding the potatoes on a coarse grater, but you can also use the large shredding disk of a food processor; cut the potatoes into 2-inch lengths first. Top with applesauce and/or sour cream.

2 pounds russet potatoes, unpeeled, shredded
½ cup grated onion
1 teaspoon table salt
2 large eggs, lightly beaten
2 teaspoons minced fresh parsley
¼ teaspoon pepper
Vegetable oil

1. Adjust oven rack to middle position, place rimmed baking sheet on rack, and heat oven to 200 degrees. Toss potatoes, onion, and salt together in bowl. Working in 2 batches, wrap potato mixture in clean dish towel and wring tightly to squeeze out as much liquid as possible into liquid measuring cup, reserving drained liquid. Let liquid sit until starch settles to bottom, 5 to 10 minutes.

2. Microwave dried potato mixture in covered bowl until just warmed through but not hot, 1 to 2 minutes, stirring mixture with fork every 30 seconds. Spread potato mixture evenly over second rimmed baking sheet and let cool for 10 minutes.

3. Pour off water from reserved potato liquid, leaving potato starch in measuring cup. Whisk in eggs until smooth. Return cooled potato mixture to bowl. Add parsley, pepper, and potato starch mixture and toss to combine.

4. Set wire rack in clean rimmed baking sheet and line with triple layer of paper towels. Add oil to 12-inch skillet until it measures about ¼ inch deep and heat over medium-high heat until shimmering but not smoking (350 degrees). Place ¼-cup mound of potato mixture in oil and press with nonstick spatula into ⅓-inch-thick disk. Repeat until 5 latkes are in pan.

5. Cook, adjusting heat so fat bubbles around latke edges, until golden brown on bottom, about 3 minutes. Turn and continue to cook until golden brown on second side, about 3 minutes longer. Drain on paper towels and transfer to baking sheet in oven. Repeat with remaining potato mixture, adding oil to maintain ¼-inch depth and returning oil to 350 degrees between batches. Season with salt and pepper to taste, and serve immediately. (To make ahead, cover cooled latkes loosely with plastic wrap and hold at room temperature for up to 4 hours, or freeze on baking sheet until firm, transfer to zipper-lock bag, and freeze for up to 1 month. Reheat latkes in 375-degree oven until crisp and hot, 3 minutes per side for room-temperature and 6 minutes per side for frozen.)

PER SERVING Cal 230; **Total Fat** 11g, **Sat Fat** 1.5g; **Chol** 60mg; **Sodium** 420mg; **Total Carb** 28g, **Dietary Fiber** 2g, **Total Sugars** 1g; **Protein** 5g

Classic Sweet Potato Casserole
SERVES 12 MAKE-AHEAD

WHY THIS RECIPE WORKS There's something nostalgic about the rich sweet potato flavor and pillowy marshmallow topping of this classic holiday table topper. Simmering the sweet potatoes in butter and cream cooked them through without drying them out or dulling their natural sweetness. Spices such as ginger, nutmeg, and cinnamon made the casserole taste like dessert, so we stuck with salt and pepper to keep things closer to the savory side. A small dose of cream cheese enriched the casserole without making it wetter and helped ensure that the dish wasn't too sweet. If you prefer a silky-smooth casserole, use a stand mixer fitted with a paddle or an immersion blender to beat the sweet potatoes in step 3. Use sharp, clean scissors sprayed with vegetable oil spray (to prevent sticking and make cleanup easier) to snip the marshmallows in half through the equator.

7½ **pounds sweet potatoes, peeled and cut into 1-inch pieces**
½ **cup heavy cream**
8 **tablespoons unsalted butter, cut into 8 pieces**
1 **tablespoon sugar**
1½ **teaspoons table salt**
¾ **teaspoon pepper**
3 **ounces cream cheese**
1 **(10-ounce) bag marshmallows, halved crosswise**

1. Combine potatoes, cream, butter, sugar, salt, and pepper in Dutch oven. Cook, covered, over medium heat, stirring occasionally, until potatoes begin to break down, about 30 minutes.

2. Reduce heat to medium-low and continue to cook, covered, until liquid has been absorbed and potatoes are completely tender, 25 to 30 minutes. Meanwhile, adjust oven rack to upper-middle position and heat oven to 450 degrees.

3. Add cream cheese to pot. Using potato masher, mash until cream cheese is fully incorporated and potatoes are smooth. Continue to cook, stirring constantly, until potatoes are thickened, about 5 minutes. Transfer potato mixture to 3-quart baking dish. (Baking dish can be covered with plastic wrap and refrigerated for up to 2 days. To serve, microwave until warm, 4 to 7 minutes before topping with marshmallows and baking as directed.)

4. Top potato mixture with single layer of marshmallows. Bake until marshmallows are browned, about 5 minutes. Serve.

PER SERVING Cal 400; **Total Fat** 13g, **Sat Fat** 8g; **Chol** 40mg; **Sodium** 470mg; **Total Carb** 64g, **Dietary Fiber** 7g, **Total Sugars** 28g; **Protein** 5g

Candied Sweet Potatoes
SERVES 6 TO 8

WHY THIS RECIPE WORKS For candied sweet potatoes that wouldn't cause a toothache, we decided to keep this rustic side simple. Peeling and cutting sweet potatoes into ¾-inch rounds promised an even, soft texture. We tossed them in oil to promote browning and roasted them on a baking sheet. While the potatoes browned in the oven, we stirred together a mellow, sweet glaze, cutting maple syrup with some water to prevent it from overshadowing the potatoes' natural roasted sweetness. A bit of cornstarch gave the glaze a clingy texture and briefly heating it thickened it nicely. To ensure easy, mess-free serving, we transferred the sweet potatoes to a baking dish, arranging the rounds with the unbrowned sides facing up. We poured the glaze over the potatoes and finished them in the oven. Whisk the syrup frequently to keep it from boiling over. A broiler-safe dish (not Pyrex) is important because of the high heat.

3 pounds sweet potatoes, peeled, ends trimmed, and sliced ¾ inch thick

2 tablespoons vegetable oil

1⅛ teaspoons table salt, divided

½ cup maple syrup

½ cup water

4 tablespoons unsalted butter

1 teaspoon cornstarch

1. Adjust oven rack to lowest position and heat oven to 450 degrees. Toss potatoes, oil, and 1 teaspoon salt together in bowl. Evenly space potatoes in single layer on rimmed baking sheet. Roast until potatoes are tender and dark brown on bottom, 18 to 22 minutes, rotating sheet halfway through baking.

2. Meanwhile, combine maple syrup, water, butter, cornstarch, and remaining ⅛ teaspoon salt in small saucepan. Bring to boil over medium-high heat and cook, whisking frequently, until thickened and reduced to 1 cup, 3 to 5 minutes.

3. Place potatoes in broiler-safe 13 by 9-inch baking dish, browned side up, shingling as necessary if you have larger potatoes. Pour syrup mixture over potatoes and bake until bubbling around sides of dish, 8 to 10 minutes. Transfer dish to wire rack and let cool for 10 minutes. Season with pepper to taste. Serve.

PER SERVING Cal 250; **Total Fat** 9g, **Sat Fat** 4g; **Chol** 15mg; **Sodium** 410mg; **Total Carb** 39g, **Dietary Fiber** 4g, **Total Sugars** 20g; **Protein** 2g

Marinated Beet Salad with Oranges and Pecorino

Marinated Beet Salad with Oranges and Pecorino

SERVES 6 MAKE-AHEAD

WHY THIS RECIPE WORKS A vibrant beet and orange salad adds freshness and color to the winter holiday table. Beets have the potential to be sweet, earthy jewels but they have baggage: Handling beets can be a messy affair, from peeling to cooking to cutting. To make easy and neat work of preparing this root vegetable, we wrapped beets in aluminum foil and roasted them until they were soft and tender and their skins were ready to slip away. The beet skins protected the insides of the beets while they were in the oven, so they emerged deeply sweet and evenly cooked. We tossed the roasted beets in a potent marinade while they were still warm so they absorbed more flavor. Orange segments, shaved Pecorino Romano cheese, and toasted walnuts arranged over the marinated beets and arugula make a complex, sweet, savory, stunning beet salad that everyone will love. Look for beets that are 2 to 3 inches in diameter.

1 pound beets, trimmed

½ cup water

¼ cup sherry vinegar

2 tablespoons extra-virgin olive oil, plus extra for drizzling

1 teaspoon fresh thyme leaves

½ teaspoon table salt

¼ teaspoon pepper

2 oranges

4 ounces (4 cups) baby arugula

2 ounces Pecorino Romano cheese, shaved

½ cup walnuts, toasted and chopped

1. Adjust oven rack to middle position and heat oven to 400 degrees. Place 16 by 12-inch piece of aluminum foil on rimmed baking sheet. Arrange beets in center of foil and lift sides of foil to form bowl. Add water to beets and crimp foil tightly to seal. Roast until beets can be pierced easily with fork, 1¼ to 1½ hours. When cool enough to handle, rub off skins with paper towels. Halve beets vertically, then cut into ½-inch-thick wedges.

2. Whisk vinegar, oil, thyme, salt, and pepper together in large bowl. Add beets and toss to combine. Cover and refrigerate for at least 30 minutes or up to 24 hours.

3. Cut away peel and pith from oranges. Holding fruit over bowl, use paring knife to slice between membranes to release segments. Arrange arugula on platter, spoon beets over top, and drizzle with remaining marinade. Arrange orange segments over salad, top with Pecorino and walnuts, and season with salt and pepper to taste. Drizzle with extra oil and serve.

PER SERVING Cal 190; **Total Fat** 14g, **Sat Fat** 3g; **Chol** 10mg; **Sodium** 380mg; **Total Carb** 12g, **Dietary Fiber** 3g, **Total Sugars** 8g; **Protein** 6g

Bitter Greens, Fennel, and Apple Salad with Warm Pancetta Dressing
SERVES 4 TO 6

WHY THIS RECIPE WORKS Softened under a hot dressing, bitter greens become a sturdy bed for flavorful ingredients. But drizzling hot vinaigrette over the greens didn't wilt them; tossing the abundant hearty greens in a preheated Dutch oven provided just the right amount of heat to wilt them without actually cooking them. After crisping some pancetta in the pot, we sautéed fennel and toasted walnuts in the rendered fat and then pulled the pot off the heat to cool slightly. We then added the greens and the vinaigrette in two stages, stirring until everything was warmed through. For mix-ins with a range of flavors and textures, in addition to the pancetta and walnuts we added sweet apple and pungent blue cheese—making this salad truly satisfying. The volume measurement of the greens may vary depending on the variety or combination used.

VINAIGRETTE
- ¼ cup red wine vinegar
- 2 tablespoons extra-virgin olive oil
- 1 tablespoon Dijon mustard
- 1 tablespoon minced shallot
- 1 teaspoon minced fresh thyme
- ¼ teaspoon table salt
- ¼ teaspoon pepper

SALAD
- 3 ounces pancetta, cut into ¼-inch pieces
- 1 small fennel bulb (8 ounces), stalks discarded, bulb halved, cored, and sliced thin
- 1 cup walnuts, chopped
- 12 ounces (10–12 cups) bitter greens, such as escarole, chicory, and/or frisée, torn into bite-size pieces
- 1 Fuji apple, cored, halved, and sliced thin
- 2 ounces blue cheese, crumbled (½ cup)

1. FOR THE VINAIGRETTE Whisk all ingredients in bowl until emulsified.

2. FOR THE SALAD Cook pancetta in Dutch oven over medium heat until browned and fat is rendered, 7 to 8 minutes. Using slotted spoon, transfer pancetta to paper towel–lined plate. Pour off all but 1 tablespoon fat from pot. Add fennel and walnuts to fat left in pot and cook over medium heat, stirring occasionally, until fennel is crisp-tender, 5 to 7 minutes. Remove pot from heat and let cool for 5 minutes.

3. Add half of vinaigrette to pot, then add half of greens and toss for 1 minute to warm and wilt. Add remaining greens, followed by remaining vinaigrette, and continue to toss until greens are evenly coated and warmed through, about 2 minutes. Season with salt and pepper to taste. Transfer greens to platter, top with apple, sprinkle with blue cheese and pancetta, and serve.

PER SERVING Cal 280; **Total Fat** 22g, **Sat Fat** 5g; **Chol** 15mg; **Sodium** 570mg; **Total Carb** 12g, **Dietary Fiber** 5g, **Total Sugars** 5g; **Protein** 9g

Shaved Mushroom and Celery Salad with Lemon-Dill Vinaigrette
SERVES 4 TO 6 **FAST**

WHY THIS RECIPE WORKS In this unique salad that combines earthy mushrooms and vegetal, crunchy celery, a lemony vinaigrette acts as both a marinade and a dressing. Thinly sliced mushrooms and shallots benefited from a mere 10-minute soak in the dressing; this was enough to soften and season them, bringing out and balancing their flavor without any cooking required. Fresh celery gave our salad a vibrant crispness. Shaved Parmesan, added just before serving, offered a layer of nutty richness and sophistication. Use a food processor or a sharp knife to slice the mushrooms and celery as thin as possible; this keeps the texture cohesive and allows the dressing to be absorbed more easily. If celery leaves are not available, increase the parsley to 1 cup. Make sure not to marinate the mushrooms for longer than 10 minutes; otherwise, the salad will be watery.

VINAIGRETTE
- 2 tablespoons lemon juice
- 1 teaspoon mayonnaise
- 1 teaspoon Dijon mustard
- ¼ teaspoon table salt
- 6 tablespoons extra-virgin olive oil
- 2 tablespoons minced fresh dill

SALAD

8 ounces cremini mushrooms, trimmed and sliced thin
1 shallot, halved and sliced thin
4 celery ribs, sliced thin, plus ½ cup celery leaves
2 ounces Parmesan cheese, shaved
½ cup fresh parsley leaves

1. FOR THE VINAIGRETTE Whisk lemon juice, mayonnaise, mustard, and salt in medium bowl until mixture is milky in appearance and no lumps of mayonnaise remain. Whisking constantly, slowly drizzle oil into vinegar mixture. Vinaigrette should be glossy and lightly thickened, with no surface pools of oil. Whisk in dill and season with salt and pepper to taste.

2. FOR THE SALAD Gently toss mushrooms and shallot with vinaigrette in large bowl and let sit for 10 minutes. Add celery ribs and leaves, Parmesan, and parsley and toss until combined. Season with salt and pepper to taste. Serve.

PER SERVING Cal 190; **Total Fat** 17g, **Sat Fat** 3.5g; **Chol** 5mg; **Sodium** 320mg; **Total Carb** 4g, **Dietary Fiber** 1g, **Total Sugars** 2g; **Protein** 5g

Brussels Sprouts Salad with Warm Bacon Vinaigrette

Brussels Sprouts Salad with Warm Bacon Vinaigrette
SERVES 6

WHY THIS RECIPE WORKS Though most often sautéed or roasted, Brussels sprouts can also make a great salad, but it's often prepared slaw-style. Shreds of sprouts are dressed and left for at least 30 minutes to soften the raw leaves. We decided to use a warm vinaigrette like we do for some hearty greens; the heat would wilt the leaves faster and a warm vinaigrette would give us fat options other than oil. And Brussels sprouts love bacon, so this was the perfect place for a bacon dressing. While we crisped a few chopped slices of bacon in a skillet, we used the microwave to lightly pickle some thinly sliced shallots in a mixture of red wine vinegar, whole-grain mustard, sugar, and salt for a punch that contrasted the rich bacon. We thought the Brussels sprouts could use a supporting vegetable, so we added some finely shredded radicchio to the skillet along with the Brussels sprouts to warm not only in the dressing but in the pan's residual heat. Sliced almonds mingled nicely with the shredded vegetables. A food processor's slicing disk can be used to slice the Brussels sprouts, but the salad will be less tender.

¼ cup red wine vinegar
1 tablespoon whole-grain mustard
1 teaspoon sugar
¼ teaspoon table salt
1 shallot, halved through root end and sliced thin crosswise
4 slices bacon, cut into ½-inch pieces
1½ pounds Brussels sprouts, trimmed, halved, and sliced thin
1½ cups finely shredded radicchio, long strands cut into bite-size lengths
2 ounces Parmesan cheese, shaved
¼ cup sliced almonds, toasted

1. Whisk vinegar, mustard, sugar, and salt together in bowl. Add shallot, cover tightly with plastic wrap, and microwave until steaming, 30 to 60 seconds. Stir briefly to submerge shallot. Cover and let cool completely, about 15 minutes.

2. Cook bacon in 12-inch skillet over medium heat, stirring frequently, until crispy and well rendered, 6 to 8 minutes. Off heat, whisk in shallot mixture. Add Brussels sprouts and radicchio and toss with tongs until dressing is evenly distributed and sprouts darken slightly, 1 to 2 minutes. Transfer to serving bowl. Add Parmesan and almonds and toss to combine. Season with salt and pepper to taste, and serve immediately.

PER SERVING Cal 170; **Total Fat** 8g, **Sat Fat** 3g; **Chol** 15mg; **Sodium** 490mg; **Total Carb** 11g, **Dietary Fiber** 4g, **Total Sugars** 3g; **Protein** 12g

VARIATION
Brussels Sprouts Salad with Warm Browned Butter Vinaigrette
Omit bacon and almonds. Substitute lemon juice for red wine vinegar, 4 ounces Manchego, shaved, for Parmesan, and 1½ ounces baby arugula for radicchio. Add ¼ cup dried cranberries to bowl with shallot before microwaving in step 1. Melt 5 tablespoons butter in 12-inch skillet over medium heat. Add ⅓ cup skinned, toasted, and chopped hazelnuts and cook until butter is dark golden brown, 3 to 5 minutes. Off heat, whisk in shallot mixture. Before serving, sprinkle with Manchego.

Citrus Salad with Arugula, Golden Raisins, and Walnuts
SERVES 4 TO 6

WHY THIS RECIPE WORKS Savory salads made with oranges and grapefruit are an impressive way to showcase the colorful citrus fruits that are plentiful during the cold months of the holiday season—but only if you can tame the grapefruit's bitterness and prevent its ample juice from drowning the other components. We started by treating the grapefruit with salt to counter its bitter notes (a technique we've used in the past with coffee and eggplant), but the salt pulled even more juice out of the fruit and onto our platter. Draining the seasoned fruit enabled us to preemptively remove the excess juice, and we used some of it in a simple mustard and shallot vinaigrette for the greens to make the salad more cohesive. Walnuts added richness that contrasted nicely with the fruit and the assertively flavored arugula, and chopped golden raisins added texture and extra sweetness. We prefer to use navel oranges, tangelos, or Cara Caras in this salad. Blood oranges can also be used, but because they are smaller you'll need four of them.

2 red grapefruits
3 oranges
1 teaspoon sugar
½ teaspoon table salt
3 tablespoons extra-virgin olive oil
1 small shallot, minced
1 teaspoon Dijon mustard
6 ounces (6 cups) baby arugula
½ cup golden raisins, divided
½ cup walnuts, chopped, divided

1. Cut away peel and pith from grapefruits and oranges. Cut each fruit in half from pole to pole, then slice crosswise ¼ inch thick. Transfer to bowl, toss with sugar and salt, and let sit for 15 minutes.

2. Drain fruit in fine-mesh strainer set over bowl, reserving 2 tablespoons juice. Arrange fruit on platter and drizzle with oil. Whisk reserved juice, shallot, and mustard together in medium bowl. Add arugula, ¼ cup raisins, and ¼ cup walnuts and gently toss to coat. Season with salt and pepper to taste. Arrange arugula mixture over fruit, leaving 1-inch border of fruit around edges. Sprinkle with remaining ¼ cup raisins and remaining ¼ cup walnuts. Serve.

PER SERVING Cal 260; **Total Fat** 15g, **Sat Fat** 1.5g; **Chol** 0mg; **Sodium** 220mg; **Total Carb** 32g, **Dietary Fiber** 7g, **Total Sugars** 24g; **Protein** 4g

Roquefort Salad with Apple, Celery, and Hazelnuts
SERVES 12   **FAST**

WHY THIS RECIPE WORKS Blue cheese is too intense, complex, and sophisticated to languish with dull salad accompaniments— tender lettuce leaves or run-of-the-mill toppings. We wanted to highlight the cheese in a robust salad that would complement its flavor profile. Strong cheese really shines when tasted with sweet, tart, bitter, and crunchy ingredients. A good shot of vinegar gave the dressing necessary tartness, and a spoonful of honey performed double duty, both tempering the acidity of the vinegar and highlighting the saltiness of the cheese. As for the greens, bitter radicchio and peppery arugula worked well mixed with milder lettuces so that their bold flavors didn't become overwhelming. Sweetness came from apple, and celery and chopped toasted hazelnuts provided textural contrast. Use sweet red apples such as Braeburn or Fuji. If you prefer a very mild and mellow blue cheese, substitute Danish blue for the Roquefort; if you prefer a sharp and piquant one, try Stilton.

6 tablespoons cider vinegar

6 tablespoons extra-virgin olive oil

2 tablespoons honey

½ teaspoon table salt

¼ teaspoon pepper

2 apples, cored and sliced very thin

4 celery ribs, sliced very thin on bias

2 heads red or green leaf lettuce (1 pound),
   torn into bite-size pieces

½ cup fresh parsley leaves, roughly torn

12 ounces Roquefort cheese, crumbled (3 cups)

1 cup hazelnuts, toasted, skinned, and chopped fine

1. Whisk vinegar, oil, honey, salt, and pepper in small bowl until combined. Toss apples, celery, and 2 tablespoons vinaigrette together in medium bowl; let sit for 5 minutes.

2. Toss lettuce, parsley, and remaining vinaigrette together in large bowl and season with salt and pepper to taste. Divide salad among individual plates; top each with portion of apple-celery mixture, Roquefort, and hazelnuts. Serve immediately.

PER SERVING Cal 270; **Total Fat** 22g, **Sat Fat** 7g; **Chol** 25mg; **Sodium** 620mg; **Total Carb** 11g, **Dietary Fiber** 2g, **Total Sugars** 7g; **Protein** 8g

VARIATION

Roquefort Salad with Fennel, Dried Cherries, and Walnuts

Omit apples and celery. Substitute red wine vinegar for cider vinegar. Reduce honey to 4 teaspoons. In step 1, whisk vinegar and honey in medium bowl. Mix in 1 cup dried sweetened cherries and microwave, covered, until cherries are plump, about 1 minute. Then whisk in oil, salt, and pepper. While still warm, add 2 thinly sliced small fennel bulbs and toss to combine; let cool completely. In step 2, substitute 2 thinly sliced small heads radicchio for parsley. Substitute 1 cup walnuts, toasted and chopped fine, for hazelnuts.

Basic Bread Stuffing
SERVES 10 TO 12 MAKE-AHEAD

WHY THIS RECIPE WORKS Hearty, rustic, and supersavory, bread stuffing is a staple of any holiday spread. This recipe streamlines it, using just cubed bread, sautéed onions and celery, and poultry seasoning, while achieving deep flavor without drippings. After toasting the bread, we browned a goodly portion of butter to unlock its nutty flavor and used some of it to impart browning to chopped onions and celery. Chicken broth promised a meaty character similar to that achieved by baking stuffing inside a turkey, so we reduced it on the stovetop for extra depth. More browned butter drizzled on before baking created a toasty crust. Use hearty white sandwich bread here; other types of bread will yield a chewy, less moist stuffing.

2 pounds hearty white sandwich bread, cut into
   ½-inch cubes (16 cups)

16 tablespoons unsalted butter, cut into 16 pieces

4 onions, chopped fine

4 celery ribs, minced

4 teaspoons poultry seasoning

1¾ teaspoons table salt

1 teaspoon pepper

6 cups chicken broth, divided

1. Adjust oven racks to upper-middle and lower-middle positions and heat oven to 325 degrees. Divide bread between 2 rimmed baking sheets and bake until golden brown, 50 to 55 minutes, stirring bread and switching and rotating sheets halfway through baking. Let cool completely on sheets, then transfer to large bowl.

2. Melt butter in 12-inch skillet over medium-low heat. Cook, stirring constantly, until butter is nutty brown, 5 to 7 minutes. Set aside 3 tablespoons browned butter in small bowl. Add onions and celery to skillet, increase heat to medium, and cook until browned, 12 to 15 minutes. Stir in poultry seasoning, salt, and pepper and cook until fragrant, about 30 seconds. Add vegetable mixture to bowl with toasted bread.

3. Increase oven temperature to 425 degrees. Add 2 cups broth to now-empty skillet and cook over high heat, scraping up any browned bits, until reduced to 1 cup, 6 to 8 minutes. Combine remaining 4 cups broth and reduced broth with vegetable-bread mixture and let sit for 10 minutes, stirring once. Transfer stuffing to 13 by 9-inch baking dish and press into even layer. Drizzle reserved browned butter evenly over top and bake on upper rack until golden brown and crisp, 35 to 45 minutes. Let cool for 15 minutes. Serve. (To make ahead, do not drizzle stuffing with reserved browned butter. Cover baking dish of stuffing with aluminum foil. Refrigerate stuffing and butter for up to 24 hours. To serve, remelt butter, drizzle stuffing with butter, cover baking dish with foil, and bake for 10 minutes. Uncover and bake until heated through and top is golden brown, 35 to 40 minutes.)

PER SERVING Cal 370; **Total Fat** 18g, **Sat Fat** 9g; **Chol** 40mg; **Sodium** 900mg; **Total Carb** 43g, **Dietary Fiber** 1g, **Total Sugars** 8g; **Protein** 6g

In addition to sitting next to slices of succulent turkey, cranberry sauce is also a great accompaniment to cheese and meat platters. This one has a clean, pure berry flavor and enough sweetness to temper the tartness of the cranberries.

Simple Cranberry Sauce

SERVES 9 (MAKES 2¼ CUPS)

The cooking time in this recipe is intended for fresh berries. If you've got frozen cranberries, do not defrost them before use; just pick through them and add about 2 minutes to the simmering time.

- 1 cup sugar
- ¾ cup water
- ¼ teaspoon table salt
- 12 ounces (3 cups) cranberries

Bring sugar, water, and salt to boil in medium saucepan over high heat, stirring occasionally to dissolve sugar. Stir in cranberries; return to boil. Reduce heat to medium and simmer until saucy, slightly thickened, and about two-thirds of berries have popped open, about 5 minutes. Transfer sauce to bowl and let cool completely before serving. (Sauce can be refrigerated for up to 1 week; let sauce stand at room temperature for 30 minutes before serving.)

VARIATIONS

Cranberry-Orange Sauce

Orange juice adds little flavor, but we found that zest and liqueur pack the orange kick we were looking for in this sauce.

Add 1 tablespoon grated orange zest to water and sugar mixture. Off heat, stir 2 tablespoons orange liqueur (such as triple sec or Grand Marnier) into cooked cranberry sauce just before serving.

Cranberry Sauce with Pears and Fresh Ginger

Peel, core, and cut 2 ripe but firm pears into ½-inch pieces; set aside. Heat 1 tablespoon grated fresh ginger and ¼ teaspoon ground cinnamon with water and sugar mixture and stir pears into liquid along with cranberries.

Classic Bread Stuffing with Sage and Thyme

Classic Bread Stuffing with Sage and Thyme MAKE-AHEAD

SERVES 8 TO 10

WHY THIS RECIPE WORKS We love the ease of our Basic Bread Stuffing (page 488), but a traditional custardy, lavish bread stuffing has its place when we have the time. As with all our stuffing recipes, we cook this one outside the turkey, since a stuffed bird takes longer to cook and often results in overcooked meat by the time the stuffing has reached a safe serving temperature. We used fresh parsley, sage, thyme, and marjoram to create an herby stuffing. Half-inch cubes of bread made the stuffing pleasantly chunky and allowed the other ingredients to be distributed evenly throughout. Tasters preferred chicken broth to other liquid ingredients, since it gave the stuffing clean, savory flavor; a couple of eggs offered richness, moisture, and structure. Covering the stuffing for only part of the baking time ensured that it was moist throughout, with a crispy, crunchy top. Instead of oven drying in step 1, you can let the bread stale overnight at room temperature. This recipe can be doubled and baked in a 15 by 10-inch baking dish for a larger crowd.

1½ pounds hearty white sandwich bread, cut into
   ½-inch cubes
6 tablespoons unsalted butter
2 celery ribs, minced
1 onion, chopped fine
¼ cup minced fresh parsley
1½ tablespoons minced fresh sage or 1 teaspoon dried
1½ tablespoons minced fresh thyme or ½ teaspoon dried
1½ teaspoons minced fresh marjoram or ½ teaspoon dried
2½ cups chicken broth
2 large eggs, lightly beaten
1 teaspoon table salt
1 teaspoon pepper

1. Adjust oven rack to middle position and heat oven to 300 degrees. Grease 13 by 9-inch baking dish. Spread bread into even layer on rimmed baking sheet and bake, stirring occasionally, until bread is dry, 45 minutes to 1 hour. Let bread cool completely on sheet, about 30 minutes.

2. Increase oven temperature to 400 degrees. Melt butter in 12-inch skillet over medium-high heat. Add celery and onion and cook until softened, about 10 minutes. Stir in parsley, sage, thyme, and marjoram and cook until fragrant, about 1 minute. Transfer to large bowl.

3. Add dried cooled bread, broth, eggs, salt, and pepper to vegetable mixture and toss to combine. Transfer mixture to prepared baking dish. (Stuffing can be covered and refrigerated for up to 24 hours; let sit at room temperature for 30 minutes before baking.)

4. Cover with aluminum foil and bake for 25 minutes. Remove foil and continue to bake until golden, about 30 minutes. Let cool for 10 minutes. Serve.

PER SERVING Cal 280; **Total Fat** 10g, **Sat Fat** 4.5g; **Chol** 55mg; **Sodium** 630mg; **Total Carb** 37g, **Dietary Fiber** 0g, **Total Sugars** 6g; **Protein** 7g

Rustic Bread Stuffing with Cranberries and Walnuts
SERVES 6 TO 8 MAKE-AHEAD

WHY THIS RECIPE WORKS Classic holiday side dishes can be on the heavy side. We wanted to introduce a lighter bread stuffing to our repertoire, something loosely textured and a bit less hefty so we had room to enjoy the table's full bounty. Eliminating eggs and cutting back on the moist broth were quick steps to achieving a rustic stuffing. We swapped the usual cubes of toasted white sandwich bread for torn chunks of airy baguette, which retain some crispness and chew through cooking, and we stirred the stuffing partway through baking to break up its texture and ensure crispness throughout. In addition to the typical stuffing aromatics we added dried cranberries for pops of sweetness and scattered earthy walnuts over the top.

3 tablespoons unsalted butter, divided
2 baguettes (10 ounces each), bottom crust and ends trimmed and discarded
3 tablespoons extra-virgin olive oil
2 cups chicken broth
3 celery ribs, cut into ½-inch pieces
1 teaspoon table salt
¼ teaspoon pepper
2 large onions, cut into ½-inch pieces
½ cup dried cranberries
3 tablespoons chopped fresh sage
3 tablespoons chopped fresh parsley
¼ cup walnuts, toasted and chopped

1. Adjust oven rack to upper-middle position and heat oven to 450 degrees. Grease 13 by 9-inch baking dish with 1 tablespoon butter and set aside. Tear baguettes into bite-size pieces (you should have about 12 cups) and spread into even layer on rimmed baking sheet. Drizzle with oil and toss with spatula until oil is well distributed. Toast in oven for 5 minutes. Stir bread, then continue to toast until edges are lightly browned and crisped, about 5 minutes longer. Transfer sheet to wire rack. Drizzle broth over bread and stir to combine.

2. Melt remaining 2 tablespoons butter in 10-inch skillet over medium heat. Add celery, salt, and pepper. Cook, stirring frequently, until celery begins to soften, 3 to 5 minutes. Add onions and cook until vegetables are soft but not browned, about 8 minutes. Add cranberries and sage and cook until fragrant, about 1 minute.

3. Add vegetable mixture to bread and toss with spatula until well combined. Transfer stuffing mixture to prepared dish and spread into even layer. (Stuffing can be wrapped in plastic wrap and refrigerated for up to 24 hours; add 5 minutes to baking time.) Bake for 20 minutes. Stir with spatula, turning crisp edges into middle, and spread into even layer. Continue to bake until top is crisp and brown, about 10 minutes. Stir in parsley, sprinkle with walnuts, and serve.

PER SERVING Cal 360; **Total Fat** 14g, **Sat Fat** 3.5g; **Chol** 10mg; **Sodium** 680mg; **Total Carb** 52g, **Dietary Fiber** 2g, **Total Sugars** 10g; **Protein** 8g

Rustic Bread Stuffing with Dates and Almonds

Substitute 3 tablespoons extra-virgin olive oil for butter (6 tablespoons oil in total). Omit pepper and sage. Substitute ½ cup chopped pitted dates for cranberries. Add 1 minced garlic clove, ½ teaspoon orange zest, ½ teaspoon paprika, ½ teaspoon ground cumin, and pinch cayenne pepper with dates. Substitute toasted sliced almonds for walnuts.

Rustic Bread Stuffing with Fennel and Pine Nuts

Substitute 3 tablespoons extra-virgin olive oil for butter (6 tablespoons in total). Substitute 1 fennel bulb, stalks discarded, bulb halved, cored, and cut into ½-inch pieces, for celery and increase pepper to ½ teaspoon. Omit cranberries. Substitute 1½ tablespoons chopped fresh rosemary, 1 minced garlic clove, and ½ teaspoon ground fennel for sage. Substitute toasted pine nuts for walnuts.

Cornbread and Sausage Stuffing

TAKE IT UP A NOTCH

Sometimes we want more than the simple sweet-tart holiday cranberry sauce. To create something with complexity, we turned to chutney. Adding vinegar, aromatics, and spices to slow-cooked cranberries and fruit yielded a jammy relish with kick and savor. And while this chutney was complex in flavor, it wasn't in process—we made the whole thing quickly in the microwave.

Cranberry Chutney

MAKES ABOUT 2 CUPS

    1 tablespoon vegetable oil
    1 shallot, minced
    2 garlic cloves, minced
    2 teaspoons grated fresh ginger
    ½ teaspoon grated orange zest plus ¼ cup juice
    ¼ teaspoon table salt
    ⅛ teaspoon red pepper flakes
    12 ounces (3 cups) fresh or thawed frozen cranberries
    6 tablespoons packed light brown sugar
    3 tablespoons apple cider vinegar

1. Combine oil, shallot, garlic, ginger, orange zest, salt, and pepper flakes in medium bowl. Microwave, uncovered, until shallot has softened, about 1 minute.

2. Stir cranberries, sugar, orange juice, and vinegar into shallot mixture. Microwave until cranberries have softened and liquid is thick and syrupy, about 8 minutes, stirring once halfway through cooking. Let cool completely and then refrigerate for at least 1 hour or up to 3 days. Serve.

Cornbread and Sausage Stuffing

SERVES 10 TO 12

WHY THIS RECIPE WORKS Store-bought or box-made cornbreads are far too sweet and crumbly to make a good sturdy cornbread stuffing—which is why so many versions don't live up to their promise of an exciting change from regular bread stuffing. We made our own cornbread so we could control our end product. Our stuffing would be plenty flavorful so we didn't have to pick up tangy buttermilk for our cornbread or make it super-rich with butter. A generous hand with the sausage and eggs and adding half-and-half to the dressing gave this dish the richness we wanted. While either fine or coarse cornmeal works well in this recipe, we recommend using stone-ground cornmeal, which has a full corn flavor. If you have time, you can skip the oven-drying in step 2 and stale the cubed cornbread overnight at room temperature.

CORNBREAD

2⅔ cups milk
½ cup vegetable oil
4 large eggs
2 cups (10 ounces) cornmeal
2 cups (10 ounces) all-purpose flour
4 teaspoons baking powder
1 teaspoon table salt

STUFFING

1½ pounds bulk pork sausage
6 tablespoons unsalted butter, divided
2 onions, chopped fine
3 celery ribs, chopped fine
4 garlic cloves, minced
1 teaspoon dried sage
1 teaspoon dried thyme
3½ cups chicken broth
1 cup half-and-half
4 large eggs
½ teaspoon table salt
⅛ teaspoon cayenne pepper

1. **FOR THE CORNBREAD** Adjust oven racks to upper-middle and lower-middle positions and heat oven to 375 degrees. Grease and flour 13 by 9-inch baking pan. Whisk milk, oil, and eggs together in bowl; set aside. Whisk cornmeal, flour, baking powder, and salt together in large bowl. Add milk mixture and whisk until smooth. Pour batter into prepared pan and bake on lower rack until golden and toothpick inserted in center comes out clean, about 30 minutes. Let bread cool in pan on wire rack, about 2 hours. (Cooled cornbread can be stored at room temperature for up to 2 days.) Reduce oven temperature to 250 degrees.

2. **FOR THE STUFFING** Cut cornbread into 1-inch squares. Divide cornbread between 2 rimmed baking sheets and bake until dry, 50 minutes to 1 hour, switching and rotating sheets halfway through baking. Let cornbread cool completely on sheets, about 30 minutes. Increase oven temperature to 375 degrees. Grease 13 by 9-inch baking dish.

3. Cook sausage in 12-inch nonstick skillet over medium-high heat, breaking it up with wooden spoon, until no longer pink, about 5 minutes. Using slotted spoon, transfer sausage to paper towel–lined plate and pour off all but 2 tablespoons fat from pan. Add 2 tablespoons butter, onions, and celery to fat in pan and cook until vegetables are softened, about 5 minutes. Add garlic, sage, and thyme and cook until fragrant, about 30 seconds. Stir in broth, remove from heat, and let cool for 5 minutes.

4. Whisk half-and-half, eggs, salt, and cayenne together in large bowl. Slowly whisk in broth mixture until incorporated. Fold in dried cornbread and sausage and let sit, tossing occasionally, until saturated, about 20 minutes.

5. Transfer cornbread mixture to prepared dish. Melt remaining 4 tablespoons butter and drizzle evenly over top. Bake on upper rack until golden brown and crisp, 30 to 40 minutes. Let cool for 15 minutes. Serve.

PER SERVING Cal 550; **Total Fat** 33g; **Sat Fat** 10g; **Chol** 195mg; **Sodium** 980mg; **Total Carb** 42g, **Dietary Fiber** 3g, **Total Sugars** 5g; **Protein** 20g

VARIATION
Cornbread and Sausage Stuffing with Red Pepper, Chipotle Chiles, and Andouille

Omit sausage and increase butter to 4 tablespoons. Melt 2 tablespoons butter in 12-inch skillet over medium-high heat. Add 2 red bell peppers, stemmed, seeded, and cut into ¼-inch pieces, along with one-third of onions and celery and cook until softened, about 5 minutes; transfer to bowl. Melt remaining 2 tablespoons butter in now-empty skillet over medium-high heat. Add remaining onions and celery and cook, stirring occasionally, until softened, about 5 minutes. Stir in ¼ cup minced chipotle chile in adobo sauce along with thyme, sage, and garlic. Add bell pepper mixture, along with softened onion mixture and 1½ pounds andouille sausage, cut into ½-inch pieces, to bowl with cornbread.

Wild Rice Dressing
SERVES 10 TO 12   `MAKE-AHEAD`

WHY THIS RECIPE WORKS Wild rice dressing is usually just another name for pilaf. While we love wild rice pilaf (see page 493), we wanted to add bread and make the dish cohesive, bringing wild rice dressing closer to the classic stuffing. While developing our recipe, we discovered that the amount of liquid that a given variety of wild rice absorbed varied drastically. To allow for this, we boiled the rice in extra liquid and then drained the excess, reserving the liquid. A combination of cream and eggs bound the dressing but was far too rich. Adding some of the rice cooking liquid lightened the dish and enhanced the nutty, earthy flavor of the rice. Large chunks of bread overpowered the small grains of rice. Chopping the bread into pea-size bits in the food processor fixed the problem. We found that toasted bread added color and crunch to our casserole and eliminated the need for staling bread. Covering the casserole with aluminum foil prevented the rice at the surface from turning toothbreakingly crunchy and a drizzle of butter before cooking ensured that this dressing, while unconventional, was rich, savory, and wholly delicious. If you have less than 1½ cups of leftover rice cooking liquid, make up the difference with additional chicken broth.

2 cups chicken broth

2 cups water

1 bay leaf

2 cups wild rice

10 slices hearty white sandwich bread, torn into pieces

8 tablespoons unsalted butter, divided

2 onions, chopped fine

3 celery ribs, minced

4 garlic cloves, minced

1½ teaspoons dried sage

1½ teaspoons dried thyme

1½ cups heavy cream

2 large eggs

¾ teaspoon table salt

½ teaspoon pepper

1. Bring broth, water, and bay leaf to boil in medium saucepan over medium-high heat. Add rice, cover, and reduce heat to low; simmer until rice is tender, 35 to 45 minutes. Strain contents of pan through fine-mesh strainer into 4-cup liquid measuring cup. Transfer rice to bowl; discard bay leaf. Reserve 1½ cups cooking liquid.

2. Adjust oven racks to upper-middle and lower-middle positions and heat oven to 325 degrees. Pulse half of bread in food processor into pea-size pieces, about 6 pulses; spread into even layer on rimmed baking sheet. Repeat with remaining bread and second rimmed baking sheet. Bake bread pieces until golden, about 20 minutes, stirring occasionally and switching and rotating sheets halfway through baking. Let bread cool completely, about 10 minutes.

3. Melt 4 tablespoons butter in 12-inch skillet over medium heat. Cook onions and celery until softened and golden, 8 to 10 minutes. Add garlic, sage, and thyme and cook until fragrant, about 30 seconds. Stir in reserved cooking liquid, remove from heat, and let cool for 5 minutes.

4. Whisk cream, eggs, salt, and pepper together in large bowl. Slowly whisk in warm broth-vegetable mixture. Stir in rice and toasted bread pieces. Transfer mixture to 13 by 9-inch baking dish. (Dressing can be refrigerated for up to 24 hours; add 20 minutes to baking time.)

5. Melt remaining 4 tablespoons butter in now-empty skillet and drizzle evenly over dressing. Cover dish with aluminum foil and bake on lower-middle rack until set, 45 to 55 minutes. Remove foil and let cool for 15 minutes. Serve.

PER SERVING Cal 380; **Total Fat** 21g, **Sat Fat** 12g; **Chol** 85mg; **Sodium** 400mg; **Total Carb** 41g, **Dietary Fiber** 2g, **Total Sugars** 5g; **Protein** 8g

Wild Rice Pilaf with Pecans and Cranberries

Wild Rice Pilaf with Pecans and Cranberries
SERVES 3 TO 4

WHY THIS RECIPE WORKS Properly cooked wild rice is chewy yet tender, and pleasingly rustic—not disappointingly crunchy or gluey. We wanted to turn out fluffy pilaf-style grains loaded with festive mix-ins. After a few trials, we found that simmering the rice in plenty of liquid and then draining it was the most reliable cooking method. A combination of water and chicken broth infused with thyme and bay leaves produced rice with nuanced savory flavor. We prepared a batch of white rice (boosted with sautéed chopped onion and carrot and studded with plumped dried cranberries) to stir in with the wild rice as a means of balancing out the latter's earthy qualities. For even more variation in this otherwise simple side, we stirred in nutty toasted pecans and minced parsley for instant freshness.

¾ cup plus 2 tablespoons chicken broth
1 bay leaf
4 sprigs fresh thyme, divided
½ cup wild rice, picked over and rinsed
¾ cup long-grain white rice
1½ tablespoons unsalted butter
½ onion, chopped fine
½ large carrot, peeled and chopped fine
1½ teaspoons table salt
6 tablespoons dried cranberries
6 tablespoons pecans, toasted and chopped
2¼ teaspoons minced fresh parsley

1. Bring broth, bay leaf, 2 thyme sprigs, and 2 tablespoons water to boil in medium saucepan over medium-high heat. Add wild rice, cover, and reduce heat to low; simmer until rice is plump and tender and has absorbed most of liquid, about 35 minutes. Drain wild rice in fine-mesh strainer. Discard bay leaf and thyme sprigs. Return wild rice to now-empty saucepan, cover, and set aside.

2. While wild rice is cooking, place white rice in fine-mesh strainer and rinse under cold running water until water runs clear. Place strainer over bowl and set aside.

3. Melt butter in medium saucepan over medium-high heat. Add onion, carrot, and salt and cook, stirring frequently, until vegetables are softened but not browned, about 4 minutes. Add white rice and stir to coat grains with butter; cook, stirring frequently, until grains begin to turn translucent, about 3 minutes.

4. Meanwhile, bring 1 cup plus 2 tablespoons water to boil in small saucepan. Add boiling water and remaining 2 thyme sprigs to white rice mixture and return to boil. Reduce heat to low, sprinkle cranberries evenly over white rice, and cover. Simmer until all liquid is absorbed, about 15 minutes. Off heat, discard thyme sprigs and fluff white rice with fork. Combine wild rice, white rice mixture, pecans, and parsley in bowl and toss with silicone spatula to combine. Season with salt and pepper to taste, and serve immediately.

PER SERVING Cal 380; **Total Fat** 12g, **Sat Fat** 3g; **Chol** 10mg; **Sodium** 1010mg; **Total Carb** 64g, **Dietary Fiber** 4g, **Total Sugars** 14g; **Protein** 8g

VARIATION
Wild Rice Pilaf with Scallions, Cilantro, and Almonds
Omit dried cranberries. Substitute ¾ cup toasted sliced almonds for pecans and 2 tablespoons minced fresh cilantro for parsley. Add 2 thinly sliced scallions and 1 teaspoon lime juice with almonds.

Make-Ahead Creamy Macaroni and Cheese
SERVES 8 TO 10 `MAKE-AHEAD`

WHY THIS RECIPE WORKS Macaroni and cheese is a nice addition to a holiday potluck and being able to make the whole dish ahead and bake before serving would be a huge help if we could do it successfully. To keep the pasta from drying out in the freezer, we increased the ratio of sauce to macaroni. The proteins in milk were causing the sauce to curdle, so we switched to heavy cream, which has more fat and therefore less protein. However, the cream produced a sauce that was too rich, so we cut it with some broth. For the cheese, we chose Colby, which melted nicely, and extra-sharp cheddar for a flavor boost. Because we made the sauce soupy to ensure creaminess after freezing, the pasta became bloated and mushy. To solve this, we undercooked the pasta and spread it on a baking sheet to cool before adding the sauce. You'll need 2 microwave-safe 8-inch square baking dishes for this recipe.

4 slices hearty white sandwich bread, torn into pieces
8 tablespoons unsalted butter, melted, plus
   6 tablespoons unsalted butter
¼ cup grated Parmesan cheese
1 garlic clove, minced
1 teaspoon table salt, plus salt for cooking pasta
1 pound elbow macaroni
6 tablespoons all-purpose flour
1 teaspoon dry mustard
⅛ teaspoon cayenne pepper
4½ cups chicken broth
1½ cups heavy cream
1 pound Colby cheese, shredded (4 cups)
8 ounces extra-sharp cheddar cheese, shredded (2 cups)
½ teaspoon pepper

1. Pulse bread, 2 tablespoons melted butter, Parmesan, and garlic in food processor until coarsely ground. Divide crumb mixture between 2 zipper-lock freezer bags and freeze.

2. Bring 4 quarts water to boil in Dutch oven over high heat. Add 1 tablespoon salt and macaroni and cook until barely softened, about 3 minutes. Drain pasta, then spread out on rimmed baking sheet and let cool.

3. Heat remaining 6 tablespoons butter, flour, mustard, and cayenne in empty pot over medium-high heat, stirring constantly, until golden and fragrant, 1 to 2 minutes. Slowly whisk in broth and cream and bring to boil. Reduce heat to medium and simmer until slightly thickened, about 15 minutes. Off heat, whisk in Colby, cheddar, 1 teaspoon salt, and pepper until smooth.

4. Stir cooled pasta into sauce, breaking up any clumps, until well combined. Divide pasta mixture between two 8-inch square baking dishes. Let cool completely, about 2 hours. Wrap dishes tightly with plastic wrap, cover with aluminum foil, and freeze for up to 2 months.

5. Adjust oven rack to middle position and heat oven to 375 degrees. Remove foil from casserole and reserve. Microwave casserole until mixture is thawed and beginning to bubble around edges, 7 to 12 minutes, stirring and replacing plastic halfway through cooking. (If preparing both dishes, microwave one at a time.) Discard plastic and cover pan with reserved foil. Bake 20 minutes, then remove foil and sprinkle with 1 bag frozen bread crumbs. (If preparing both dishes, sprinkle second bag of crumbs over second dish.) Continue to bake until crumbs are golden brown and crisp, about 20 minutes. Let cool for 10 minutes. Serve.

PER SERVING Cal 720; **Total Fat** 46g, **Sat Fat** 29g; **Chol** 135mg; **Sodium** 1070mg; **Total Carb** 49g, **Dietary Fiber** 0g, **Total Sugars** 4g; **Protein** 27g

Savory Noodle Kugel

Savory Noodle Kugel
SERVES 8 TO 10   `MAKE-AHEAD`

WHY THIS RECIPE WORKS While sweet kugels are traditionally served with Jewish holiday meals, kugel also has an excellent savory side. For our version, we caramelized onions in rendered chicken fat, or schmaltz, to build a savory base of flavor and then mixed in eggs and some parsley. We found that tossing the egg mixture with still-warm noodles helped thicken the eggs slightly so they clung to the noodles rather than sink to the bottom of the casserole. To achieve the characteristic crunchy top, we gave the baked casserole a pass under the broiler. Use a broiler-safe baking dish for this recipe. Look for rendered chicken fat (schmaltz) in the frozen food section of larger supermarkets.

- 3 tablespoons rendered chicken fat (schmaltz) or extra-virgin olive oil
- 3 onions, chopped fine
- 1½ teaspoons table salt, divided, plus salt for cooking noodles
- 6 large eggs
- 2 tablespoons minced fresh parsley
- ¾ teaspoon pepper
- 1 pound wide egg noodles

1. Adjust 1 oven rack to middle position and second rack 6 inches from broiler element. Heat oven to 350 degrees. Grease broiler-safe 13 by 9-inch baking dish. Heat rendered chicken fat in 12-inch skillet over medium-low heat. Add onions and ½ teaspoon salt and cook, stirring occasionally, until caramelized, 30 to 40 minutes. Transfer onions to large bowl and let cool for 10 minutes. (Cooled caramelized onions can be refrigerated for up to 3 days.) Whisk eggs, parsley, pepper, and remaining 1 teaspoon salt into onions; set aside.

2. Bring 4 quarts water to boil in large pot. Add noodles and 1 tablespoon salt and cook, stirring often, until al dente. Reserve 3 tablespoons cooking water, then drain noodles and let cool for 5 minutes. Whisk reserved cooking water into onion mixture. Stir still-warm noodles into onion mixture until well combined.

3. Transfer noodle mixture to prepared dish. (Kugel can be refrigerated for up to 24 hours. Increase baking time to 25 minutes.) Bake on middle oven rack until set, about 20 minutes. Remove kugel from oven and heat broiler. Once broiler is hot, broil kugel on upper rack until top noodles are browned and crisp, 1 to 3 minutes, rotating dish as needed for even browning. Serve.

PER SERVING Cal 270; **Total Fat** 9g, **Sat Fat** 2g; **Chol** 160mg; **Sodium** 460mg; **Total Carb** 35g, **Dietary Fiber** 1g, **Total Sugars** 3g; **Protein** 11g

THE BREAD BASKET

■ MAKE-AHEAD   ■ VEGAN
Photos (clockwise from top left): Rosemary Focaccia; Ultimate Flaky Buttermilk Biscuits;
Almost No-Knead Bread; Garlic and Herb Breadsticks

Easiest-Ever Biscuits

MAKES 10 BISCUITS   MAKE-AHEAD

WHY THIS RECIPE WORKS With this recipe, we combined the ease of cream biscuits (which eliminate the step of cutting cold fat into dry ingredients) with the ease of drop biscuits (which skip the rolling and cutting) to create tender, fluffy "dream" biscuits—the easiest biscuits ever. An obvious path—increasing the amount of cream in a cream biscuit recipe until the dough had a droppable consistency—produced biscuits that spread too much and were greasy. Instead of increasing the amount of cream, we found a way to increase its fluidity: We heated it to between 95 and 100 degrees, which melted the solid particles of butterfat dispersed throughout. This made a dough that was moister and scoopable but that rose up instead of spreading out in the oven, producing biscuits that were appropriately rich and tender but not greasy. These biscuits come together very quickly, so in the interest of efficiency, start heating your oven before gathering your ingredients. We like these biscuits brushed with a bit of melted butter, but you can skip that step if you're serving the biscuits with a rich accompaniment.

- 3 cups (15 ounces) all-purpose flour
- 4 teaspoons sugar
- 1 tablespoon baking powder
- ¼ teaspoon baking soda
- 1¼ teaspoons table salt
- 2 cups heavy cream
- 2 tablespoons unsalted butter, melted (optional)

1. Adjust oven rack to upper-middle position and heat oven to 450 degrees. Line rimmed baking sheet with parchment paper. Whisk flour, sugar, baking powder, baking soda, and salt together in bowl. Microwave cream until just warmed to body temperature (95 to 100 degrees), 60 to 90 seconds, stirring halfway through microwaving. Stir cream into flour mixture until soft, uniform dough forms.

2. Spray ⅓-cup dry measuring cup with vegetable oil spray. Drop level scoops of batter 2 inches apart on prepared sheet (biscuits should measure about 2½ inches wide and 1¼ inches tall). Respray measuring cup after every 3 or 4 scoops. If portions are misshapen, use your fingertips to gently reshape dough into level cylinders. Bake until tops are light golden brown, 10 to 12 minutes, rotating sheet halfway through baking. Brush hot biscuits with melted butter, if using. Serve warm. (Cooled biscuits can be stored at room temperature for up to 24 hours. Reheat biscuits in 300-degree oven for 10 minutes.)

PER SERVING Cal 340; **Total Fat** 20g; **Sat Fat** 12g; **Chol** 60mg; **Sodium** 470mg; **Total Carb** 34g, **Dietary Fiber** 0g, **Total Sugars** 3g; **Protein** 6g

Rosemary and Parmesan Drop Biscuits

Rosemary and Parmesan Drop Biscuits

MAKES 12 BISCUITS   MAKE-AHEAD

WHY THIS RECIPE WORKS Flavored with piney fresh rosemary and Parmesan cheese, these supersavory biscuits add interest to a meal of simple braised meats, or a stew or soup. We wanted a pleasantly craggy, rustic biscuit that could be easily broken apart and enjoyed piece by buttery piece. Melted butter made our biscuits rich (and simple), and using buttermilk instead of milk gave the biscuits tang and made them crisper on the exterior and fluffier on the interior. This dough required a substantial amount of leavening, but too much baking powder left a metallic aftertaste. A combination of baking powder and soda was perfect: The metallic taste was gone, and the acidic buttermilk reacted with the baking soda for even better rise. We were left with only one problem: If the buttermilk and melted butter weren't at just the right temperature when we combined them, the butter clumped in the buttermilk. Since we wanted this to be an easy recipe, we tried making a batch with lumpy buttermilk—and, surprisingly, the result was a much better biscuit, taller and less dense. The water in the lumps of butter turned to steam in the oven, which opened the crumb and created additional height, as if we'd painstakingly cut cold butter into the flour.

2 cups (10 ounces) all-purpose flour
1½ ounces Parmesan cheese, grated (¾ cup)
2 teaspoons baking powder
½ teaspoon baking soda
1 teaspoon sugar
¾ teaspoon table salt
½ teaspoon minced fresh rosemary
1 cup buttermilk, chilled
10 tablespoons unsalted butter, melted, divided

1. Adjust oven rack to middle position and heat oven to 475 degrees. Line rimmed baking sheet with parchment paper.

2. Whisk flour, Parmesan, baking powder, baking soda, sugar, salt, and rosemary together in large bowl. Stir buttermilk and 8 tablespoons melted butter together in second bowl until butter forms small clumps. Stir buttermilk mixture into flour mixture until just incorporated and dough pulls away from sides of bowl.

3. Spray ¼-cup dry measuring cup with vegetable oil spray. Drop scant ¼-cup scoops of dough 1½ inches apart onto prepared sheet (you should have 12 mounds). Bake until tops are golden brown and crisp, 12 to 14 minutes, rotating sheet halfway through baking. Brush hot biscuits with remaining 2 tablespoons melted butter, transfer to wire rack, and let cool slightly before serving. (Cooled biscuits can be stored at room temperature for up to 24 hours. Reheat biscuits in 300-degree oven for 10 minutes.)

PER SERVING Cal 190; Total Fat 10g, Sat Fat 6g; Chol 30mg; Sodium 350mg; Total Carb 19g, Dietary Fiber 0g, Total Sugars 1g; Protein 5g

VARIATION
Cheddar and Scallion Drop Biscuits
Substitute ½ cup shredded cheddar cheese for Parmesan and 2 thinly sliced scallions for rosemary.

Sweet Potato Biscuits
MAKES 16 BISCUITS MAKE-AHEAD

WHY THIS RECIPE WORKS It was only a matter of time before sweet potato–loving Southern cooks combined the fluffy texture and pleasant tang of biscuits with the earthy sweetness of this popular tuber. The key to our successful sweet potato biscuits was adding mashed potato to the biscuits without weighing down the dough. We microwaved the sweet potatoes, which decreased their moisture while concentrating flavor. To eliminate more moisture, we cut the buttermilk from our recipe. After mashing the potato flesh, we stirred in cider vinegar to mimic buttermilk's tang and

contribute to greater lift once combined with the baking powder and baking soda. To make sure these biscuits were extra tender, we used low-protein cake flour, and we opted for the molasses-y sweetness of brown sugar to complement the potatoes. Once baked, the biscuits emerged tender and subtly sweet, just as perfect smeared with butter or jam as sliced and stuffed with ham and mustard. If you can find them, Beauregard sweet potatoes are the best variety for these biscuits.

2½ pounds sweet potatoes, unpeeled, lightly pricked all over with fork
2 tablespoons cider vinegar
3¼ cups (13 ounces) cake flour
¼ cup packed (1¾ ounces) dark brown sugar
5 teaspoons baking powder
½ teaspoon baking soda
1½ teaspoons table salt
8 tablespoons unsalted butter, cut into ½-inch pieces and chilled, plus 2 tablespoons melted
4 tablespoons vegetable shortening, cut into ½-inch pieces and chilled

1. Microwave potatoes on plate until very soft and surfaces are wet, 15 to 20 minutes, flipping every 5 minutes. Immediately cut potatoes in half. When potatoes are cool enough to handle, scoop flesh into large bowl and, using potato masher, mash until smooth. (You should have 2 cups. Reserve any extra for another use.) Stir in vinegar and refrigerate until cool, about 15 minutes.

2. Adjust oven rack to middle position and heat oven to 425 degrees. Line rimmed baking sheet with parchment paper. Process flour, sugar, baking powder, baking soda, and salt in food processor until combined. Scatter chilled butter and shortening over top and pulse until mixture resembles coarse meal, about 15 pulses. Transfer flour mixture to bowl with cooled potatoes and fold with silicone spatula until incorporated.

3. Transfer dough to floured counter and knead by hand until smooth, 8 to 10 times. Pat dough into 9-inch circle about 1 inch thick. Using floured 2¼-inch round cutter, stamp out biscuits and arrange on prepared sheet. Gently pat dough scraps into 1-inch-thick circle and stamp out remaining biscuits. (You should have 16 biscuits total.) Brush tops of biscuits with melted butter and bake until golden brown, 18 to 22 minutes. Let biscuits cool on sheet for 15 minutes before serving. (Cooled biscuits can be stored at room temperature for up to 2 days. Reheat biscuits in 300-degree oven for 10 minutes.)

PER SERVING Cal 220; Total Fat 9g, Sat Fat 4.5g; Chol 15mg; Sodium 430mg; Total Carb 32g, Dietary Fiber 2g, Total Sugars 6g; Protein 3g

Ultimate Flaky Buttermilk Biscuits
MAKES 9 BISCUITS

WHY THIS RECIPE WORKS Sometimes a meal calls for a simple biscuit, and sometimes we want the ultimate—biscuits with innumerable ethereally thin layers. First, for an even distribution of butter that stayed cold through the rolling process to produce air pockets in our dough, we froze whole sticks of butter and grated them right into our dry ingredients before mixing. Then we rolled and folded the dough a total of five times. During this process the butter pieces got pressed into thin sheets between layers and layers of dough for flakes aplenty. Letting the dough rest for 30 minutes and trimming away the creased edges ensured that the biscuits would rise up nice and tall in the oven. We prefer King Arthur all-purpose flour for this recipe, but other brands will work. Use sticks of butter. In hot or humid environments, chill the flour mixture, grater, and mixing bowls before use. The dough will start out crumbly and dry in spots but will be smooth by the end of the folding process; do not add extra buttermilk. Flour the counter and the top of the dough as needed, but be careful not to incorporate large pockets of flour into the dough while folding.

- 3 cups (15 ounces) all-purpose flour
- 2 tablespoons sugar
- 4 teaspoons baking powder
- ½ teaspoon baking soda
- 1½ teaspoons table salt
- 16 tablespoons (2 sticks) unsalted butter, frozen for 30 minutes, divided
- 1¼ cups buttermilk, chilled

1. Line rimmed baking sheet with parchment paper and set aside. Whisk flour, sugar, baking powder, baking soda, and salt together in large bowl. Coat sticks of butter in flour mixture, then grate 7 tablespoons from each stick on large holes of box grater directly into flour mixture. Gently toss to combine. Set aside remaining 2 tablespoons butter.

2. Add buttermilk to flour mixture and fold with spatula until just combined (dough will look dry). Transfer dough to liberally floured counter. Dust surface of dough with flour and, using your floured hands, press dough into rough 7-inch square.

3. Roll dough into 12 by 9-inch rectangle with short side parallel to edge of counter. Starting at bottom of dough, fold into thirds like a business letter, using bench scraper or metal spatula to release dough from counter. Press top of dough firmly to seal folds. Turn dough 90 degrees clockwise. Repeat rolling into 12 by 9-inch rectangle, folding into thirds, and turning clockwise 4 more times, for total of 5 sets of folds. After last set of folds, roll dough into 8½-inch square about 1 inch thick. Transfer dough to prepared sheet, cover with plastic wrap, and refrigerate for 30 minutes. Adjust oven rack to upper-middle position and heat oven to 400 degrees.

4. Transfer dough to lightly floured cutting board. Using sharp, floured chef's knife, trim ¼ inch of dough from each side of square and discard. Cut remaining dough into 9 squares, flouring knife after each cut. Arrange biscuits at least 1 inch apart on sheet. Melt reserved butter; brush tops of biscuits with melted butter.

5. Bake until tops are golden brown, 22 to 25 minutes, rotating sheet halfway through baking. Transfer biscuits to wire rack and let cool for 15 minutes before serving.

PER SERVING Cal 370; **Total Fat** 20g, **Sat Fat** 13g; **Chol** 55mg; **Sodium** 690mg; **Total Carb** 39g, **Dietary Fiber** 0g, **Total Sugars** 4g; **Protein** 6g

TAKE IT UP A NOTCH

What's bread without butter? We love spreading a savory roll with a sweetened butter as part of a homey supper. It's easy to make your own flavored butters, and these sweet options pair well with a number of biscuits or breads.

Sweet Butters
Whip 8 tablespoons softened unsalted butter with a fork until light and fluffy. Mix in any of the ingredient combinations listed below. Wrap in plastic wrap and let rest to meld flavors, about 10 minutes, before serving, or roll the butter into a sliceable log. The butter can be refrigerated for up to 4 days or frozen, wrapped tightly in plastic wrap, for up to 2 months.

Honey Butter
- ¼ cup honey
- Pinch table salt

Molasses-Pecan Butter
- ¼ cup pecans, toasted and chopped fine
- 4 teaspoons molasses
- 2 teaspoons sugar
- ¼ teaspoon vanilla extract
- Pinch table salt

Sweet Orange Butter
- 2 teaspoons sugar
- 1 teaspoon grated orange zest
- ⅛ teaspoon vanilla extract
- Pinch table salt

Brown Soda Bread

1¾ cups (14 ounces) buttermilk
3 tablespoons sugar
3 tablespoons unsalted butter, melted, divided

1. Adjust oven rack to lower-middle position and heat oven to 400 degrees. Line baking sheet with parchment paper. Whisk all-purpose flour, whole-wheat flour, wheat germ, salt, baking powder, and baking soda together in large bowl. Whisk buttermilk, sugar, and 2 tablespoons melted butter in second bowl until sugar has dissolved.

2. Using silicone spatula, gently fold buttermilk mixture into flour mixture, scraping up dry flour from bottom of bowl, until dough starts to form and no dry flour remains.

3. Transfer dough to lightly floured counter and knead by hand until cohesive mass forms, about 30 seconds. Pat dough into 7-inch round and transfer to prepared sheet. Using sharp paring knife or single-edge razor blade, make two 5-inch-long, ¼-inch-deep slashes with swift, fluid motion along top of loaf to form cross. Bake until golden brown and skewer inserted in center comes out clean, 45 to 50 minutes, rotating sheet halfway through baking. Transfer loaf to wire rack and brush with remaining 1 tablespoon melted butter. Let cool completely, about 3 hours, before serving.

PER SERVING Cal 300; **Total Fat** 6g, **Sat Fat** 3g; **Chol** 15mg; **Sodium** 700mg; **Total Carb** 52g, **Dietary Fiber** 3g, **Total Sugars** 8g; **Protein** 10g

VARIATION
Brown Soda Bread with Currants and Caraway
Stir 1 cup dried currants and 1 tablespoon caraway seeds into flour mixture in step 1.

Brown Soda Bread
SERVES 8

WHY THIS RECIPE WORKS Robust, moist, and permeated with wheaty sweetness, brown Irish soda bread holds lots of appeal next to a stew or braised dinner. This quick bread traditionally gets its hearty, deeply flavored crumb from the addition of coarse whole-meal flour to the all-purpose flour. For a stateside version, we substituted whole-wheat flour for the hard-to-find whole-meal flour, and to highlight the bread's nutty aspects, we added toasted wheat germ. These ingredients made our bread slightly gummy, so we upped the leavener. Acidic buttermilk played double duty, yielding a moist loaf and reacting with the baking soda for a lighter crumb. The dough required only a brief knead and then we patted it into a round. Finally, brushing melted butter on the hot loaf gave this authentic soda bread a rich crust.

2 cups (10 ounces) all-purpose flour
1½ cups (8¼ ounces) whole-wheat flour
½ cup (1½ ounces) toasted wheat germ
1½ teaspoons table salt
1 teaspoon baking powder
1 teaspoon baking soda

Quick Cheese Bread
SERVES 8

WHY THIS RECIPE WORKS Quick breads aren't just sweet breakfast loaves; we employed the mixing technique to make a stellar savory cheese bread that's moist and hearty. A generous amount of baking powder lifted the heavy dough that's enriched with sour cream, melted butter, an egg, and lots of cheese. We mixed chunks (rather than shreds) of extra-sharp cheddar into the dough for pockets of rich, salty flavor. Sprinkling Parmesan on top created a bold crust. You can substitute mild Asiago, crumbled into ¼- to ½-inch pieces, for the cheddar. (Aged Asiago that is as firm as Parmesan is too piquant.) The test kitchen's preferred loaf pan measures 8½ by 4½ inches; if you use a 9 by 5-inch loaf pan, start checking for doneness 5 minutes early. Use the large holes of a box grater to shred the Parmesan. If, when you test the bread for doneness, the skewer comes out with what looks like uncooked batter clinging to it, try again. (A skewer hitting a pocket of cheese may give a false indication.) The texture of the bread improves as it cools; resist the urge to slice it when it's still warm.

3 ounces Parmesan cheese, shredded (1 cup), divided
2½ cups (12½ ounces) all-purpose flour
1 tablespoon baking powder
1 teaspoon table salt
⅛ teaspoon pepper
⅛ teaspoon cayenne pepper
4 ounces extra-sharp cheddar cheese, cut into ½-inch pieces (1 cup)
1 cup whole milk
½ cup sour cream
3 tablespoons unsalted butter, melted
1 large egg

1. Adjust oven rack to middle position and heat oven to 350 degrees. Grease 8½ by 4½-inch loaf pan, then sprinkle ½ cup Parmesan evenly in bottom of pan.

2. Whisk flour, baking powder, salt, pepper, and cayenne together in large bowl. Stir in cheddar, breaking up clumps, until cheese is coated with flour. Whisk milk, sour cream, melted butter, and egg together in second bowl.

3. Using silicone spatula, gently fold milk mixture into flour mixture until just combined (batter will be heavy and thick; do not overmix). Transfer batter to prepared pan and smooth top. Sprinkle remaining ½ cup Parmesan evenly over surface. Bake until golden brown and skewer inserted in center comes out clean, 45 to 50 minutes, rotating pan halfway through baking. Let loaf cool in pan for 15 minutes. Remove loaf from pan and let cool completely on wire rack, about 3 hours, before serving.

PER SERVING Cal 340; **Total Fat** 16g, **Sat Fat** 9g; **Chol** 65mg; **Sodium** 760mg; **Total Carb** 35g, **Dietary Fiber** 0g; **Total Sugars** 2g; **Protein** 15g

VARIATION
Quick Cheese Bread with Bacon and Onion
Cook 5 slices bacon, cut into ½-inch pieces, in 10-inch nonstick skillet over medium heat until crispy, 5 to 7 minutes. Using slotted spoon, transfer bacon to paper towel–lined plate. Pour off all but 3 tablespoons fat from skillet. Add ½ cup finely chopped onion to fat left in skillet and cook over medium heat until softened, about 3 minutes; set aside. Substitute Gruyère cheese for cheddar and omit butter. Add bacon and onion to flour mixture with cheese in step 2.

Date-Nut Bread

Date-Nut Bread
SERVES 8   MAKE-AHEAD

WHY THIS RECIPE WORKS Caramel-y dates add earthy sweetness to a nutty quick bread, but the loaf often suffers from unmitigated sweetness and hard, chewy dates. We wanted to make a quick bread rich with soft dried fruit and a moist, tender crumb. Our first step was to soak the dates in hot water with a teaspoon of baking soda; the alkaline mixture softened the dates' fibers. Rather than throw out the flavorful soaking liquid, we added it to the batter for moisture, leavening, and extra date presence throughout. Dark brown sugar (preferred over light brown here) deepened the flavor of the dates and gave our loaf an appealingly rich, dark color. Buttermilk contributed a tanginess that balanced the sweetness of the dates. For the nut component, we liked pecans and walnuts equally. Toasted, chopped, and stirred into our batter, the nuts provided needed crunch. For an accurate measurement of boiling water, bring a full kettle of water to a boil, then measure out the desired amount. The test kitchen's preferred loaf pan measures 8½ by 4½ inches; if you use a 9 by 5-inch loaf pan, start checking for doneness 5 minutes early.

10 ounces pitted dates, chopped (1⅔ cups)

1 cup boiling water

1 teaspoon baking soda

2 cups (10 ounces) all-purpose flour

1 teaspoon baking powder

½ teaspoon table salt

¾ cup packed (5¼ ounces) dark brown sugar

⅔ cup buttermilk

6 tablespoons unsalted butter, melted and cooled

1 large egg

1 cup pecans or walnuts, toasted and chopped

1. Adjust oven rack to middle position and heat oven to 350 degrees. Grease 8½ by 4½-inch loaf pan. Combine dates, boiling water, and baking soda in medium bowl, cover, and let stand until dates have softened, about 30 minutes.

2. Whisk flour, baking powder, and salt together in large bowl. Whisk sugar, buttermilk, melted butter, and egg in second bowl until smooth, then stir in date mixture until combined. Using silicone spatula, gently fold buttermilk mixture into flour mixture until just combined; do not overmix. Gently fold in pecans.

3. Transfer batter to prepared loaf pan and smooth top. Bake until golden brown and skewer inserted in center comes out clean, 55 minutes to 1 hour, rotating pan halfway through baking.

4. Let loaf cool in pan for 10 minutes. Remove loaf from pan and let cool for at least 1 hour. Serve warm or at room temperature. (Cooled loaf can be stored at room temperature for up to 3 days.)

PER SERVING Cal 470; **Total Fat** 18g, **Sat Fat** 6g; **Chol** 45mg; **Sodium** 330mg; **Total Carb** 72g, **Dietary Fiber** 4g, **Total Sugars** 42g; **Protein** 7g

Pumpkin Bread

Pumpkin Bread

SERVES 16 (MAKES 2 LOAVES) `MAKE-AHEAD`

WHY THIS RECIPE WORKS Although most recipes for pumpkin bread are pleasantly sweet and spicy, they're nothing to write home about. We wanted to make a bread that stood out, one that actually had deep pumpkin flavor. First, to rid canned pumpkin of its raw taste and bring out its rich, earthy notes, we cooked it on the stovetop just until its sugars began to caramelize. Bread made with the cooked puree was a little dry, however. To replace some of the lost moisture and offset sweetness, we added tangy buttermilk and softened cream cheese to the mix. A modest hand with spices and streusel sprinkled over the top of the loaf for textural contrast gave us pumpkin bread we'd crave. The test kitchen's preferred loaf pan measures 8½ by 4½ inches; if using a 9 by 5-inch loaf pan, start checking for doneness 5 minutes early.

TOPPING

5 tablespoons packed (2¼ ounces) light brown sugar

1 tablespoon all-purpose flour

1 tablespoon unsalted butter, softened

1 teaspoon ground cinnamon

⅛ teaspoon table salt

BREAD

2 cups (10 ounces) all-purpose flour

1½ teaspoons baking powder

½ teaspoon baking soda

1 (15-ounce) can unsweetened pumpkin puree

1 teaspoon table salt

1½ teaspoons ground cinnamon

¼ teaspoon ground nutmeg

⅛ teaspoon ground cloves

1 cup (7 ounces) granulated sugar

1 cup packed (7 ounces) light brown sugar

½ cup vegetable oil

4 ounces cream cheese, cut into 12 pieces

4 large eggs

¼ cup buttermilk

1 cup walnuts, toasted and chopped fine

1. **FOR THE TOPPING** Using your fingers, mix all ingredients in bowl until well combined and topping resembles wet sand; set aside.

2. **FOR THE BREAD** Adjust oven rack to middle position and heat oven to 350 degrees. Grease two 8½ by 4½-inch loaf pans. Whisk flour, baking powder, and baking soda together in bowl.

3. Combine pumpkin puree, salt, cinnamon, nutmeg, and cloves in large saucepan over medium heat. Cook mixture, stirring constantly, until reduced to 1½ cups, 6 to 8 minutes. Remove saucepan from heat; stir in granulated sugar, brown sugar, oil, and cream cheese until combined. Let mixture stand for 5 minutes. Whisk until no visible pieces of cream cheese remain and mixture is homogeneous.

4. Whisk eggs and buttermilk together in bowl. Add egg mixture to pumpkin mixture and whisk to combine. Using silicone spatula, fold flour mixture into pumpkin mixture until combined (some small lumps of flour are OK). Fold walnuts into batter. Divide batter evenly between prepared pans. Sprinkle topping evenly over top of loaves. Bake until skewer inserted in center of loaf comes out clean, 45 to 50 minutes. Let loaves cool in pans on wire rack for 20 minutes. Remove loaves from pans and let cool for at least 1½ hours. Serve warm or at room temperature. (Cooled loaf can be stored at room temperature for up to 3 days.)

PER SERVING Cal 280; **Total Fat** 13g; **Sat Fat** 2.5g; **Chol** 45mg; **Sodium** 230mg; **Total Carb** 37g, **Dietary Fiber** 1g, **Total Sugars** 24g; **Protein** 4g

All-Purpose Cornbread

All-Purpose Cornbread
SERVES 6 `MAKE-AHEAD`

WHY THIS RECIPE WORKS Cornbread has been around long enough to take on a distinctly different character depending on where it's made. Despite regional differences in flavor, texture, and appearance, however, most cornbread lacks convincing flavor. We wanted cornbread with a deeply browned crust, a fluffy texture, and, most importantly, rich corn flavor. While stone-ground cornmeal has great corn flavor, it didn't give us the tenderness we wanted. We went with regular degerminated cornmeal, which gave us a light, grit-free bread. To boost the corn flavor, we tried stirring in whole corn kernels, but we didn't like the chewy bites. Instead we pureed frozen corn in the food processor, which released its full flavor while breaking down the kernels, before adding it to the batter. Brown sugar added a molasses flavor that accentuated the corn flavor. Using a little baking soda with the baking powder made for a fluffy crumb; plus, the soda promoted browning. Another way to browning: Gently folding melted butter into the batter created subtle streaks of unmixed butter that rose to the surface and created a more browned, buttery top. Baking the bread at a high temperature also contributed to a nice crust. We developed this recipe with Quaker Yellow Cornmeal; a stone-ground whole-grain cornmeal will work but will yield a drier, less tender cornbread. The cornbread is best served warm.

1½ cups (7½ ounces) all-purpose flour
1 cup (5 ounces) cornmeal
2 teaspoons baking powder
¼ teaspoon baking soda
¾ teaspoon table salt
¼ cup packed (1¾ ounces) light brown sugar
¾ cup frozen corn, thawed
1 cup buttermilk
2 large eggs
8 tablespoons unsalted butter, melted and cooled

1. Adjust oven rack to middle position and heat oven to 400 degrees. Spray 8-inch square baking dish with vegetable oil spray. Whisk flour, cornmeal, baking powder, baking soda, and salt together in medium bowl; set aside.

2. Process sugar, corn, and buttermilk in food processor until combined, about 5 seconds. Add eggs and process until well combined (corn lumps will remain), about 5 seconds longer.

3. Using silicone spatula, make well in center of dry ingredients; pour wet ingredients into well. Begin folding dry ingredients into wet, giving mixture only a few turns to barely combine. Add melted butter and continue to fold until dry ingredients are just moistened. Transfer batter to prepared dish and smooth top.

4. Bake until deep golden brown and toothpick inserted in center comes out clean, 25 to 35 minutes. Let cornbread cool in dish on wire rack for 10 minutes. Remove bread from dish and let cool until just warm, about 10 minutes longer. Serve. (Cornbread can be wrapped in aluminum foil and reheated in 350-degree oven for 10 to 15 minutes.)

PER SERVING Cal 430; Total Fat 18g, Sat Fat 10g; Chol 105mg; Sodium 560mg; Total Carb 58g, Dietary Fiber 2g, Total Sugars 11g; Protein 10g

VARIATION

Spicy Jalapeño-Cheddar Cornbread
Reduce salt to ½ teaspoon. Add ½ cup shredded cheddar cheese, 1 seeded and finely chopped jalapeño, and ⅜ teaspoon cayenne pepper to flour mixture in step 1 and toss well to combine. Reduce sugar to 2 teaspoons and sprinkle ½ cup shredded cheddar over batter before baking.

Southern-Style Cornbread
SERVES 12

WHY THIS RECIPE WORKS In the South, cornbread is a satisfying skillet-baked bread that boasts hearty corn flavor; a sturdy, moist crumb; and a brown crust. And it definitely shouldn't be sweet. It's traditionally made with just cornmeal and no flour. Toasting the cornmeal in our cast-iron skillet for a few minutes intensified its flavor. After we toasted it, we created a cornmeal mush by softening the cornmeal in a mixture of sour cream and milk. We used sour cream in the mush because it added a pleasant tang and reacted with the leaveners to keep this flourless bread from being too dense. And for bread that baked up rich and tender, we whisked two eggs into the batter. Baking the cornbread in a greased, preheated cast-iron skillet gave it a seriously crunchy, golden crust. We prefer a cast-iron skillet, but any ovensafe 10-inch skillet will work. You can substitute any type of fine- or medium-ground cornmeal here; do not use coarse-ground cornmeal.

2¼ cups (11¼ ounces) stone-ground cornmeal
1½ cups sour cream
½ cup whole milk
¼ cup vegetable oil
5 tablespoons unsalted butter
2 tablespoons sugar

1 teaspoon baking powder
1 teaspoon baking soda
¾ teaspoon table salt
2 large eggs

1. Adjust oven rack to middle position and heat oven to 450 degrees. Toast cornmeal in 10-inch cast-iron skillet over medium heat, stirring frequently, until fragrant, about 3 minutes. Transfer cornmeal to large bowl, whisk in sour cream and milk, and set aside.

2. Wipe skillet clean with paper towels. Add oil to now-empty skillet, place skillet in oven, and heat until oil is shimmering, about 10 minutes. Using potholders, remove skillet from oven, carefully add butter, and gently swirl to incorporate. Being careful of hot skillet handle, pour all but 1 tablespoon oil-butter mixture into cornmeal mixture and whisk to incorporate. Whisk sugar, baking powder, baking soda, and salt into cornmeal mixture until combined, then whisk in eggs.

3. Quickly transfer batter to skillet with remaining oil-butter mixture and smooth top. Transfer skillet to oven and bake until top begins to crack and sides are golden brown, 12 to 15 minutes, rotating skillet halfway through baking. Using potholders, transfer skillet to wire rack and let cornbread cool for at least 15 minutes before serving.

PER SERVING Cal 250; Total Fat 16g, Sat Fat 6g; Chol 60mg; Sodium 310mg; Total Carb 24g, Dietary Fiber 2g, Total Sugars 3g; Protein 4g

VARIATION

Spicy Southern-Style Cornbread
Whisk 2 seeded and minced jalapeño chiles and 2 teaspoons grated lime zest into cornmeal mixture with eggs.

Cracklin' Cornbread
SERVES 12

WHY THIS RECIPE WORKS Traditionally, what makes this Southern cornbread "crackle" are crispy bits of rendered pork skin stirred into the batter. To capture this satisfying salty element, we had two options: the time-consuming task of rendering pork skin ourselves, or downgrading the bread's taste with store-bought pork rinds. Hoping to forge ahead without the cracklings, we looked to bacon. We stirred crisp bacon bits into the batter and enriched the bread with rendered fat instead of butter. Turning the loaf out of the pan minutes after it finished baking kept the bread from softening in the skillet so its crust crackled, too. We developed this recipe with Quaker Yellow Cornmeal; a stone-ground whole-grain cornmeal will make the cornbread too gritty. We prefer a cast-iron skillet, but any ovensafe 10-inch skillet will work.

6 slices bacon, chopped fine

2¼ cups (11¼ ounces) cornmeal

1 teaspoon baking powder

1 teaspoon baking soda

½ teaspoon table salt

2 cups buttermilk

¼ cup vegetable oil, divided

2 large eggs, lightly beaten

1. Adjust oven rack to middle position and heat oven to 450 degrees. Cook bacon in 10-inch cast-iron skillet over medium heat until crispy, 5 to 7 minutes. Transfer bacon to paper towel–lined plate. Pour off fat from pan, reserving ¼ cup.

2. Whisk cornmeal, baking powder, baking soda, and salt together in large bowl. Whisk in buttermilk, 3 tablespoons oil, reserved fat, eggs, and bacon.

3. Heat remaining 1 tablespoon oil in now-empty skillet over medium-high heat until just smoking. Spoon cornmeal mixture, ½ cup at a time, into skillet. Bake until top begins to crack and sides are golden brown, 12 to 16 minutes. Let bread cool in pan on wire rack for 5 minutes. Remove bread from pan. Serve.

PER SERVING Cal 220; **Total Fat** 12g, **Sat Fat** 2.5g; **Chol** 45mg; **Sodium** 380mg, **Total Carb** 23g, **Dietary Fiber** 2g, **Total Sugars** 2g; **Protein** 7g

Garlic Bread

Garlic Bread
SERVES 8

WHY THIS RECIPE WORKS Garlic bread seems like such a simple thing to make—you're dressing up a loaf of bread. Do you need a recipe? The answer is definitely yes, as this accompaniment can disappoint: There's either not enough garlic flavor or the garlic tastes acrid and harsh, or the bread is soggy or pale. For a perfectly toasted version with prominent roasty garlic flavor, we microwaved fresh garlic (grated to a paste) and butter and combined them with garlic powder to reinforce the flavor. We then combined this melted garlic butter with solid butter and a bit of cayenne and salt to make a spreadable paste that we smeared onto the bread halves. We baked the buttered bread cut side up on a baking sheet and then flipped it and compressed it with a second baking sheet. This setup pressed the buttered side onto the hot sheet so that it evenly crisped while also flattening the bread for a better balance of crust to crumb. If using a dark-colored baking sheet, the browning time after flipping will be on the shorter end of the range. A rasp-style grater makes quick work of turning the garlic into a paste. A 12 by 5-inch loaf of supermarket Italian bread, with its soft, thin crust and fine crumb that soaks up flavor, works best here. Do not use a crusty or rustic artisan-style loaf.

1 teaspoon garlic powder

1 teaspoon water

8 tablespoons unsalted butter, divided

½ teaspoon table salt

⅛ teaspoon cayenne pepper

4–5 garlic cloves, minced to paste (1 tablespoon)

1 (1-pound) loaf soft Italian bread, halved horizontally

1. Adjust oven rack to lower-middle position and heat oven to 450 degrees. Combine garlic powder and water in medium bowl. Add 4 tablespoons butter, salt, and cayenne to bowl; set aside.

2. Place remaining 4 tablespoons butter in small bowl and microwave, covered, until melted, about 30 seconds. Stir in garlic and continue to microwave, covered, until mixture is bubbling around edges, about 1 minute, stirring halfway through microwaving. Transfer melted butter mixture to bowl with garlic powder–butter mixture and whisk until homogeneous loose paste forms. (If mixture melts, set aside and let solidify before using.)

3. Spread cut sides of bread evenly with butter mixture. Transfer bread cut sides up to rimmed baking sheet. Bake until butter mixture has melted and seeped into bread, 3 to 4 minutes. Remove sheet from oven. Flip bread cut sides down, place second rimmed baking sheet on top, and gently press. Return sheet to oven, leaving second sheet on top of bread, and continue to bake until cut sides are golden brown and crisp, 4 to 12 minutes, rotating sheet halfway through baking. Transfer bread to cutting board. Using serrated knife, cut each half into 8 slices. Serve immediately.

PER SERVING Cal 260; **Total Fat** 13g, **Sat Fat** 7g; **Chol** 30mg; **Sodium** 460mg; **Total Carb** 29g, **Dietary Fiber** 0g, **Total Sugars** 2g; **Protein** 5g

Almost No-Knead Bread
SERVES 6 `MAKE-AHEAD` `VEGAN`

WHY THIS RECIPE WORKS Artisan-style bakery loaves—beautifully browned boules with a thick, crisp crust that breaks to a chewy, open interior—take professional skills to make, right? Wrong. Not only is it possible to make a rustic loaf for your table, it's easy, too, with the no-knead method. This technique replaces the kneading that develops gluten to give bread structure with a high hydration level—around 85 percent (8½ ounces of water for every 10 ounces of flour)—and an 8- to 18-hour-long (and hands-off) resting period, or autolyse. During autolyse, the flour hydrates and enzymes work to break up the proteins so that the dough requires only a brief turn to develop gluten. The dough is then baked in a Dutch oven; the humid environment gives the loaf an open crumb and a crisp crust. But the breads we tested needed more structure and flavor. To strengthen the dough, we lowered the hydration and added less than a minute of kneading to compensate. We introduced a shot of yeasty flavor from beer. We prefer to use a mild American lager, such as Budweiser, here; strongly flavored beers will make this bread taste bitter.

 3 cups (15 ounces) all-purpose flour
1½ teaspoons table salt
 ¼ teaspoon instant or rapid-rise yeast
 ¾ cup (6 ounces) water, room temperature
 ½ cup (4 ounces) mild lager, room temperature
 1 tablespoon distilled white vinegar

1. Whisk flour, salt, and yeast together in large bowl. Whisk water, beer, and vinegar together in 4-cup liquid measuring cup. Using silicone spatula, gently fold water mixture into flour mixture, scraping up dry flour from bottom of bowl, until dough starts to form and no dry flour remains. Cover bowl tightly with plastic wrap and let sit at room temperature for at least 8 hours or up to 18 hours.

2. Lay 18 by 12-inch sheet of parchment paper on counter and lightly spray with vegetable oil spray. Transfer dough to lightly floured counter and knead by hand until smooth and elastic, about 1 minute.

3. Shape dough into ball by pulling edges into middle, then transfer seam side down to center of prepared parchment.

4. Using parchment as sling, gently lower loaf into Dutch oven (let any excess parchment hang over pot edge). Cover tightly with greased plastic and let rise until loaf has doubled in size and dough springs back minimally when poked gently with your knuckle, 1½ to 2 hours.

5. Adjust oven rack to middle position. Using sharp paring knife or single-edge razor blade, make two 5-inch-long, ½-inch-deep slashes with swift, fluid motion along top of loaf to form cross. Cover pot and place in oven. Turn oven to 425 degrees and bake loaf for 30 minutes while oven heats.

6. Remove lid and continue to bake until loaf is deep golden brown and registers 205 to 210 degrees, 25 to 30 minutes. Using parchment sling, remove loaf from pot and transfer to wire rack; discard parchment. Let cool completely, about 3 hours, before serving.

PER SERVING Cal 250; **Total Fat** 0g, **Sat Fat** 0g; **Chol** 0mg; **Sodium** 580mg; **Total Carb** 52g, **Dietary Fiber** 0g, **Total Sugars** 0g; **Protein** 7g

SHAPING ALMOST NO-KNEAD BREAD

1. Transfer dough to lightly floured counter and knead by hand until smooth and elastic, about 1 minute. Shape dough into ball by pulling edges into middle.

2. Transfer dough seam side down to center of prepared parchment. Gently lower loaf into Dutch oven and let rise until loaf has doubled in size, 1½ to 2 hours.

3. Using sharp paring knife or single-edge razor blade, make two 5-inch-long, ½-inch-deep slashes with swift, fluid motion along top of loaf to form cross.

Challah

Challah

SERVES 16 ~~MAKE-AHEAD~~

WHY THIS RECIPE WORKS Beautifully braided, rich, and faintly sweet, challah is a celebratory side and impressive addition to a holiday spread. The best challah is rich with eggs, and it has a dark, shiny crust and a firm but light and tender texture. We tested many different egg combinations (challah is known as egg bread, after all); for a tender texture and a rich but not overwhelmingly eggy flavor, we found two whole eggs and an additional yolk to be optimal. We kept with tradition and made the bread dairy-free, using water and oil to hydrate and enrich the crumb instead of the milk and butter found in less authentic versions. (Happily, we found that the challah made with water had a lighter and more appealing texture.) Just ¼ cup of sugar sweetened the loaf and also contributed to its browned exterior. The recommended shape for challah in most recipes is a simple three-rope braid. Shaped this way, however, our eggy dough rose out instead of up. Some recipes call for braiding six strands for a higher loaf, but this can get complicated—unless you have skills in origami. Our solution was to make two three-strand braids, one large and one small, and place the smaller braid on top of the larger one. We brushed the loaf with egg wash before baking for a shiny crust.

3¼ cups (16¼ ounces) all-purpose flour
2¼ teaspoons instant or rapid-rise yeast
1¼ teaspoons table salt
½ cup water, room temperature
¼ cup vegetable oil
2 large eggs plus 1 large yolk, room temperature
¼ cup (1¾ ounces) sugar
1 large egg, lightly beaten with 1 tablespoon water and pinch salt
1 teaspoon poppy seeds or sesame seeds (optional)

1. Whisk flour, yeast, and salt together in bowl of stand mixer. Whisk water, oil, eggs and yolk, and sugar in 4-cup liquid measuring cup until sugar has dissolved.

2. Using dough hook on low speed, slowly add water mixture to flour mixture and mix until cohesive dough starts to form and no dry flour remains, about 2 minutes, scraping down bowl as needed. Increase speed to medium-low and knead until dough is smooth and elastic and begins to pull away from sides of bowl but sticks to bottom, about 10 minutes.

3. Transfer dough to lightly floured counter and knead by hand to form smooth, round ball, about 30 seconds. Place dough seam side down in lightly greased large bowl or container, cover tightly with greased plastic wrap, and let rise until increased in size by about half, 1½ to 2 hours.

4. Stack 2 rimmed baking sheets, line with aluminum foil, and spray with vegetable oil spray. Transfer dough to clean counter and divide into 2 pieces, one twice as large as the other (small piece will weigh about 9 ounces, larger piece about 18 ounces). Divide each piece into thirds; cover loosely with greased plastic.

5. Working with 1 piece of dough at a time (keep remaining pieces covered), stretch and roll into 16-inch rope (3 ropes will be much thicker). Arrange 3 thicker ropes side by side, perpendicular to counter edge, and pinch far ends together. Braid ropes into 10-inch loaf and pinch remaining ends together. Repeat braiding remaining ropes into second 10-inch loaf.

6. Transfer larger loaf to prepared sheet, brush top with egg mixture, and place smaller loaf on top. Tuck ends underneath. Cover loosely with greased plastic and let rise until loaf increases in size by about half and dough springs back minimally when poked gently with your knuckle, 1 to 1½ hours.

7. Adjust oven rack to middle position and heat oven to 375 degrees. Brush loaf with remaining egg mixture and sprinkle with poppy seeds, if using. Bake until deep golden brown and loaf registers 190 to 195 degrees, 20 to 25 minutes, rotating sheet halfway through baking. Transfer loaf to wire rack and let cool completely, about 3 hours, before serving.

PER SERVING Cal 160; **Total Fat** 4.5g, **Sat Fat** 0g; **Chol** 40mg; **Sodium** 200mg; **Total Carb** 24g, **Dietary Fiber** 0g, **Total Sugars** 3g; **Protein** 4g

1. Divide dough into 2 pieces, one twice as large as other.

2. Working with 1 piece of dough at a time (keep remaining pieces covered), stretch and roll into 16-inch rope (3 ropes will be much thicker).

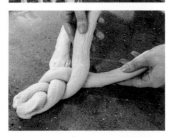

3. Arrange 3 thicker ropes side by side and pinch far ends together. Braid ropes into 10-inch loaf and pinch remaining ends together. Repeat braiding remaining ropes into second 10-inch loaf.

4. Transfer larger loaf to prepared sheet, brush top with egg mixture, and place smaller loaf on top. Tuck ends underneath.

Rosemary Focaccia
SERVES 12 (MAKES 2 LOAVES) **VEGAN**

WHY THIS RECIPE WORKS Focaccia can easily disappoint when it turns out heavy, thick, and flavorless—like bad cold pizza. We wanted to rip into a light, airy loaf, crisp-crusted and topped with just a smattering of herbs. For a bubbly crumb, we turned to a no-knead method to build our dough similar to our Almost No-Knead Bread (page 507). While we don't knead our focaccia per se, we do fold it while it rises to prevent squat loaves. Folding brings the wheat proteins into closer proximity with one another, keeping the process going at maximum clip; it aerates the dough; and it elongates and redistributes the bubbles. After turning our dough three times, we ended up with a well-risen focaccia with a tender, moist crumb. Olive oil is a key ingredient, but we found that if we added it straight to the dough, it turned the bread dense and cake-like. Instead, we baked the bread in round cake pans, where a couple of tablespoons of oil coating the exterior could be contained. Our baked focaccia boasted a crackly, crisp bottom, a deeply browned top, and an interior that was open and airy. It is important to use fresh, not dried, rosemary. Be sure to reduce the temperature immediately after putting the loaves in the oven.

SPONGE
- ½ cup (2½ ounces) all-purpose flour
- ⅓ cup water, room temperature
- ¼ teaspoon instant or rapid-rise yeast

DOUGH
- 2½ cups (12½ ounces) all-purpose flour
- 1¼ cups water, room temperature
- 1 teaspoon instant or rapid-rise yeast
- 1 tablespoon kosher salt, divided
- ¼ cup extra-virgin olive oil, divided
- 2 tablespoons chopped fresh rosemary

1. FOR THE SPONGE Stir all ingredients in large bowl with wooden spoon until well combined. Cover tightly with plastic wrap and let sit at room temperature until sponge has risen and begins to collapse, about 6 hours (sponge can sit at room temperature for up to 24 hours).

2. FOR THE DOUGH Stir flour, water, and yeast into sponge with wooden spoon until well combined. Cover bowl tightly with plastic and let dough rest for 15 minutes.

3. Stir 2 teaspoons salt into dough with wooden spoon until thoroughly incorporated, about 1 minute. Cover bowl tightly with plastic and let dough rest for 30 minutes.

4. Using greased bowl scraper (or silicone spatula), fold dough over itself by gently lifting and folding edge of dough toward middle. Turn bowl 45 degrees and fold dough again; repeat turning bowl and folding dough 6 more times (total of 8 folds). Cover tightly with plastic and let rise for 30 minutes. Repeat folding and rising. Fold dough again, then cover bowl tightly with plastic and let dough rise until nearly doubled in size, 30 minutes to 1 hour.

5. One hour before baking, adjust oven rack to upper-middle position, place baking stone on rack, and heat oven to 500 degrees. Coat two 9-inch round cake pans with 2 tablespoons oil each. Sprinkle each pan with ½ teaspoon salt. Transfer dough to lightly floured counter and dust top with flour. Divide dough in half and cover loosely with greased plastic. Working with 1 piece of dough at a time (keep remaining piece covered), shape into 5-inch round by gently tucking under edges.

6. Place dough rounds seam side up in prepared pans, coat bottoms and sides with oil, then flip rounds over. Cover loosely with greased plastic and let dough rest for 5 minutes.

7. Using your fingertips, gently press each dough round into corners of pan, taking care not to tear dough. (If dough resists stretching, let it relax for 5 to 10 minutes before trying to stretch it again.) Using fork, poke surface of dough 25 to 30 times, popping any large bubbles. Sprinkle 1 tablespoon rosemary evenly over top of each loaf, cover loosely with greased plastic, and let dough rest until slightly bubbly, about 10 minutes.

8. Place pans on baking stone and reduce oven temperature to 450 degrees. Bake until tops are golden brown, 25 to 30 minutes, rotating pans halfway through baking. Let loaves cool in pans for 5 minutes. Remove loaves from pans and transfer to wire rack. Brush tops with any oil remaining in pans and let cool for 30 minutes. Serve warm or at room temperature.

PER SERVING Cal 250; **Total Fat** 7g; **Sat Fat** 1g; **Chol** 0mg; **Sodium** 420mg; **Total Carb** 39g, **Dietary Fiber** 0g, **Total Sugars** 0g; **Protein** 6g

VARIATION

Focaccia with Caramelized Red Onion, Pancetta, and Oregano

Cook 4 ounces finely chopped pancetta in 12-inch skillet over medium heat, stirring occasionally, until well rendered, about 10 minutes. Using slotted spoon, transfer pancetta to medium bowl. Add 1 chopped red onion and 2 tablespoons water to fat left in skillet and cook over medium heat until onion is softened and lightly browned, about 12 minutes. Transfer onion to bowl with pancetta and stir in 2 teaspoons minced fresh oregano; let mixture cool completely before using. Substitute pancetta mixture for rosemary.

Fluffy Dinner Rolls
MAKES 12 ROLLS `MAKE-AHEAD`

WHY THIS RECIPE WORKS Dinner rolls are plush freshly baked, but they lose that quality as they cool. For rolls that stayed fluffy, we applied a Japanese bread-making technique called *tangzhong* that boosts dough's moisture (without making it too slack) by using a flour paste; the flour can absorb a lot more water when cooked with it to a pudding-like texture. We gradually incorporated milk, egg, flour, and yeast into the paste. We let the dough rest to encourage strong gluten bonds to form before adding tenderizing salt, sugar, and butter. Rolling portions of dough into spirals created coiled layers, which baked into light, feathery sheets in our rolls. Best of all, these rolls were just as good when reheated. The tackiness of the dough aids in flattening and stretching it in step 4; do not flour the counter.

FLOUR PASTE
- ½ cup water
- 3 tablespoons bread flour

DOUGH
- ½ cup cold milk
- 1 large egg
- 2 cups (11 ounces) bread flour
- 1½ teaspoons instant or rapid-rise yeast
- 2 tablespoons sugar
- 1 teaspoon table salt
- 4 tablespoons unsalted butter, softened, plus ½ tablespoon, melted

BAKING ROSEMARY FOCACCIA

1. Place dough rounds seam side up in prepared pans, coat bottoms and sides with oil, then flip rounds over. Cover loosely with greased plastic and let dough rest for 5 minutes.

2. Using your fingertips, gently press each dough round into corners of pan. Using fork, poke surface of dough 25 to 30 times, popping any large bubbles.

3. Sprinkle 1 tablespoon rosemary evenly over top of each loaf, cover loosely with greased plastic, and let dough rest until slightly bubbly, about 10 minutes.

4. Place pans on baking stone and reduce oven temperature to 450 degrees. Bake until tops are golden brown, 25 to 30 minutes, rotating pans halfway through baking.

Fluffy Dinner Rolls

lengthwise into 4 equal strips and cut each strip crosswise into 3 equal pieces. Working with 1 piece of dough at a time, stretch and press dough gently to form 8 by 2-inch strip. Starting at short side, roll dough to form snug cylinder. Arrange cylinders seam side down in prepared pan, placing 10 around edge of pan, pointing inward, and remaining two in center. Cover with greased plastic and let rise until doubled in size, 45 minutes to 1 hour. (Unbaked rolls can be wrapped in greased plastic, then in foil, and frozen for up to 1 month. Remove foil and plastic, let sit at room temperature for 1 hour, and bake for 40 to 45 minutes.)

5. Adjust oven rack to lowest position and heat oven to 375 degrees. Bake rolls until deep golden brown, 25 to 30 minutes. Let rolls cool in pan on wire rack for 3 minutes. Carefully invert rolls out of pan. Turn rolls right side up and brush tops and sides with melted butter. Let rolls cool on wire rack for at least 20 minutes before serving. (Cooled rolls can be stored at room temperature for up to 24 hours. Reheat rolls in 350-degree oven for 15 minutes.)

PER SERVING Cal 160; **Total Fat** 5g, **Sat Fat** 3g; **Chol** 30mg; **Sodium** 200mg; **Total Carb** 23g, **Dietary Fiber** 1g, **Total Sugars** 3g; **Protein** 5g

FORMING FLUFFY DINNER ROLLS

1. Working with 1 piece of dough at a time, stretch and press dough gently to form 8 by 2-inch strip.

2. Starting at short side, roll dough to form snug cylinder.

3. Arrange cylinders seam side down in prepared pan, placing 10 around edge of pan, pointing inward, and remaining two in center.

1. FOR THE FLOUR PASTE Whisk water and flour in small bowl until no lumps remain. Microwave, whisking every 20 seconds, until mixture thickens to stiff, smooth, pudding-like consistency that forms mound when dropped from end of whisk into bowl, 40 to 80 seconds.

2. FOR THE DOUGH Whisk flour paste and milk in bowl of stand mixer until smooth. Add egg and whisk until incorporated. Add flour and yeast. Fit stand mixer with dough hook and mix on low speed until all flour is moistened, 1 to 2 minutes. Let stand for 15 minutes.

3. Add sugar and salt and knead on medium-low speed for 5 minutes. With mixer running, add softened butter, 1 tablespoon at a time, and continue to knead for 5 minutes, scraping down dough hook and sides of bowl occasionally (dough will stick to bottom of bowl). Transfer dough to very lightly floured counter and knead briefly by hand to form ball. Place dough seam side down in lightly greased bowl and cover with greased plastic wrap. Let rise until doubled in size, about 1 hour.

4. Grease 9-inch round cake pan. Transfer dough to counter. Press down on dough to expel all air. Pat and stretch dough to form 8 by 9-inch rectangle with short side facing you. Cut dough

Rustic Dinner Rolls

MAKES 16 ROLLS `MAKE-AHEAD`

WHY THIS RECIPE WORKS Savory European-style rolls are different from their rich American cousins. The dough is lean and the crumb is open. The best part might be their crust—so crisp it shatters when you bite into it. Professionals achieve this by using steam-injected ovens to expose the developing crust to moisture. When we made the rolls, we found a dense, bland crumb beneath a leathery crust. The flavor was easy to improve: We added a bit (3 tablespoons) of whole-wheat flour for earthiness. We upped the dough's hydration; the water created steam during baking, opening up the crumb. For the crust, we came up with a process that mimicked a steam-injected oven: We misted the rolls before starting them in a cake pan at a high temperature to set the dough's shape. Next, we lowered the temperature, separated the rolls, and baked them on a baking sheet until golden all over.

Rustic Dinner Rolls

- 3 cups (16½ ounces) bread flour
- 3 tablespoons whole-wheat flour
- 1½ teaspoons instant or rapid-rise yeast
- 1½ cups plus 1 tablespoon water, room temperature
- 2 teaspoons honey
- 1½ teaspoons table salt

1. Whisk bread flour, whole-wheat flour, and yeast together in bowl of stand mixer. Whisk water and honey in 4-cup liquid measuring cup until honey has dissolved. Fit mixer with dough hook. On low speed, slowly add water mixture to flour mixture; mix until cohesive dough starts to form and no dry flour remains, about 2 minutes, scraping down bowl and hook as needed. Cover bowl tightly with plastic wrap and let dough rest for 30 minutes.

2. Add salt to dough and knead on low speed for 5 minutes. Increase speed to medium and knead until dough is smooth and slightly sticky, about 1 minute. Transfer dough to lightly greased large bowl or container, cover tightly with plastic, and let rise until doubled in size, 1 to 1½ hours.

3. Using greased bowl scraper (or your fingertips), fold dough over itself by gently lifting and folding edge of dough toward middle. Turn bowl 90 degrees and fold dough again; repeat turning bowl and folding dough 2 more times (total of 4 folds). Cover tightly with plastic and let rise for 30 minutes. Repeat folding, then cover bowl tightly with plastic and let dough rise until doubled in size, about 30 minutes.

4. Grease two 9-inch round cake pans. Press down on dough to deflate. Transfer dough to well-floured counter, sprinkle lightly with flour, and divide in half. Stretch each half into even 16-inch log and cut into 8 equal pieces (about 2 ounces each). Using your well-floured hands, gently pick up each piece and roll in your palms to coat with flour, shaking off excess. Arrange rolls in prepared pans, placing one in center and seven around edges, cut sides facing up and long side of each piece running from center to edge of pan. Cover loosely with greased plastic and let rise until nearly doubled in size and dough springs back minimally when poked gently with your knuckle, about 30 minutes. (Unrisen rolls can be refrigerated for at least 8 hours or up to 16 hours; let rolls sit at room temperature for 1½ hours before baking.)

5. Adjust oven rack to middle position and heat oven to 500 degrees. Mist rolls with water and bake until tops are brown, about 10 minutes. Remove rolls from oven and reduce oven temperature to 400 degrees. Carefully invert rolls out of pans onto baking sheet and let cool slightly. Turn rolls right side up, pull apart, and arrange evenly on sheet. Continue to bake until deep golden brown, 10 to 15 minutes, rotating sheet halfway through baking. Transfer rolls to wire rack and let cool completely, about 1 hour, before serving. (Rolls can be stored at room temperature for up to 2 days. Recrisp rolls in 450-degree oven for 6 to 8 minutes. Wrapped in aluminum foil and placed in zipper-lock bag, rolls can be frozen for up to 1 month. Unwrap rolls, thaw at room temperature, and reheat as directed.)

PER SERVING Cal 120; **Total Fat** 0g, **Sat Fat** 0g; **Chol** 0mg; **Sodium** 220mg; **Total Carb** 23g, **Dietary Fiber** 1g, **Total Sugars** 1g; **Protein** 4g

Multigrain Dinner Rolls

MAKES 18 ROLLS `MAKE-AHEAD`

WHY THIS RECIPE WORKS Often multigrain rolls either have great flavor but are as heavy as bricks, or they have a light texture but so little grain they might as well be white bread. We wanted great flavor and balanced texture. The trouble with working with whole grains is that, unlike white flour, they still contain the bran. This gives them flavor but the bran is sharp—so sharp that it cuts through the bread's gluten structure, leaving you with a dense product. So we cut some of the whole-wheat flour with all-purpose. We also added a rest that gave the flour time to hydrate and a generous kneading time that further encouraged gluten development. The result was rolls that baked up light yet chewy. For added grains, we hit upon a convenient, one-stop-shopping choice: packaged seven-grain hot cereal. To soften the cereal, we made a porridge before adding it to the dough. Topping the rolls with oats yielded a polished look. Do not substitute instant oats.

1¼ cups (6¼ ounces) seven-grain hot cereal mix
2½ cups boiling water
  3 cups (15 ounces) all-purpose flour, plus extra
    as needed
1½ cups (8¼ ounces) whole-wheat flour
  ¼ cup honey
  4 tablespoons unsalted butter, melted and cooled
2½ teaspoons instant or rapid-rise yeast
  1 tablespoon table salt
  ¾ cup raw pepitas or sunflower seeds
  ½ cup (1½ ounces) old-fashioned rolled oats or
    quick oats

1. Combine cereal mix and boiling water in bowl of stand mixer and let stand, stirring occasionally, until mixture cools to 100 degrees and resembles thick porridge, about 1 hour. Whisk all-purpose and whole-wheat flours together in large bowl.

2. Fit mixer with dough hook. Add honey, melted butter, and yeast to cooled cereal and mix on low speed until combined. Add flour mixture, ½ cup at a time, and knead until cohesive dough starts to form, 1½ to 2 minutes. Cover bowl tightly with plastic wrap and let dough rest for 20 minutes.

3. Add salt to dough and knead on medium-low speed until dough is smooth and clears sides of bowl, 8 to 9 minutes. (If dough is very sticky, add 1 to 2 tablespoons flour and mix for 1 minute.) Add seeds and knead for 15 seconds. Transfer dough to lightly floured counter and knead by hand to form smooth, round ball, about 1 minute. Transfer dough to lightly greased large bowl, cover tightly with greased plastic, and let rise until nearly doubled in size, 45 minutes to 1 hour.

4. Grease 13 by 9-inch baking dish. Transfer dough to lightly floured counter and cut into 18 equal pieces. Working with 1 piece of dough at a time (keep remaining pieces covered), form into rough ball by stretching dough around your thumbs and pinching edges together so that top is smooth. Place ball seam side down on clean counter and, using your cupped hand, drag in small circles until dough feels taut and round. Roll 1 side of each roll in oats, arrange in prepared baking dish, and cover lightly with greased plastic wrap. Let rise until nearly doubled in size, 30 to 40 minutes.

5. Adjust oven rack to middle position and heat oven to 375 degrees. Bake until rolls register 200 degrees, 30 to 35 minutes. Let rolls cool in dish for 5 minutes, then transfer to wire rack and let cool completely, about 2 hours. Serve. (Rolls can be stored at room temperature for up to 2 days. Recrisp rolls in 350-degree oven for 10 minutes. Wrapped in aluminum foil and placed in zipper-lock bag, rolls can be frozen for up to 1 month. Unwrap rolls, thaw at room temperature, and reheat as directed.)

PER SERVING Cal 230; **Total Fat** 6g, **Sat Fat** 2g; **Chol** 5mg; **Sodium** 390mg; **Total Carb** 39g, **Dietary Fiber** 2g, **Total Sugars** 4g; **Protein** 8g

Crescent Rolls

MAKES 12 ROLLS `MAKE-AHEAD`

WHY THIS RECIPE WORKS Most recipes for buttery, flaky crescent rolls require laborious repeated rolling and folding to layer softened butter into the dough. At the same time, we wouldn't think of settling for the artificial-tasting, dry, canned versions from the supermarket. After dozens of tests, we found a way to avoid either extreme: You can make rolls that are only a modicum less flaky and just as tender as labor-intensive versions by simply kneading all the ingredients together. We determined that a precise 7 tablespoons of melted butter in the dough delivered great flavor without making the dough too sticky to work with. To enhance the richness of our rolls, without weighing them down, we used half-and-half instead of milk, resulting in extra-tender rolls with big, buttery taste.

2½ cups (12½ ounces) all-purpose flour
  1 teaspoon instant or rapid-rise yeast
  1 teaspoon table salt
  ½ cup half-and-half, room temperature
  8 tablespoons unsalted butter, melted, divided
  ¼ cup (1¾ ounces) sugar
  1 large egg plus 1 large yolk, room temperature
  1 large egg lightly beaten with 1 tablespoon water
    and pinch of salt

1. Whisk flour, yeast, and salt together in bowl of stand mixer. Whisk half-and-half, 7 tablespoons melted butter, sugar, and egg and yolk in 4-cup liquid measuring cup until sugar has dissolved.

2. Fit mixer with dough hook. On low speed, slowly add half-and-half mixture to flour mixture and mix until cohesive dough starts to form and no dry flour remains, about 2 minutes, scraping down bowl as needed. Increase speed to medium-low and knead until dough is smooth and elastic and clears sides of bowl but sticks to bottom, about 8 minutes.

3. Transfer dough to lightly floured counter and knead by hand to form smooth, round ball, about 30 seconds. Place dough seam side down in lightly greased large bowl or container, cover tightly with greased plastic wrap, and let rise until doubled in size, 1 to 1½ hours.

4. Line rimmed baking sheet with parchment paper. Press down on dough to deflate, then transfer to lightly floured counter. Press and roll dough into 12-inch round. Brush top of dough with remaining melted butter and cut into 12 wedges. Starting at wide end, gently roll up each dough wedge, ending with pointed tip on bottom. Push ends toward each other to form crescent shape.

5. Arrange rolls on prepared sheet, spaced about 2 inches apart, with tip of dough underneath each roll. Cover loosely with greased plastic and let rise until nearly doubled in size and dough springs back minimally when poked gently with your knuckle, 1 to 1½ hours. (Unrisen rolls can be refrigerated for at least 8 hours or up to 16 hours; let rolls sit at room temperature for 1 hour before baking.)

6. Adjust oven rack to middle position and heat oven to 350 degrees. Gently brush rolls with beaten egg mixture and bake until golden brown, 20 to 25 minutes, rotating sheet halfway through baking. Transfer rolls to wire rack and let cool for 15 minutes. Serve warm.

PER SERVING Cal 210; **Total Fat** 9g, **Sat Fat** 6g; **Chol** 60mg; **Sodium** 220mg; **Total Carb** 26g, **Dietary Fiber** 0g, **Total Sugars** 5g; **Protein** 4g

Easy Garlic Rolls
MAKES 10 ROLLS

WHY THIS RECIPE WORKS Pizza dough isn't just for pizza, and store-bought dough is a quick way to warm, soft, chewy rolls that make just about any meal better. An egg wash alone made a perfectly golden roll, but a generous brush with garlic oil permeated the rolls, adding richness and great flavor as well as extra softness. We mixed the garlic oil together before shaping the rolls so the flavors melded, and then we brushed it on halfway through baking so the minced garlic didn't burn but turned perfectly roasty and sweet. If possible, buy bagged pizza dough that is still partially frozen; the yeast is more likely to be active, which will give the rolls a better rise. It's important to let the dough come to room temperature before beginning the recipe. Serve these rolls warm.

¼ cup extra-virgin olive oil
1 garlic clove, minced
½ teaspoon table salt
¼ teaspoon pepper
2 pounds store-bought pizza dough, room temperature
1 egg, lightly beaten

1. Adjust oven rack to middle position and heat oven to 375 degrees. Combine oil, garlic, salt, and pepper in small bowl.

2. Cut pizza dough into 10 equal pieces, roll loosely into balls, and arrange on parchment-lined baking sheet. Brush rolls with egg. Bake until golden brown, 30 to 35 minutes, brushing rolls with garlic oil halfway through baking. Transfer rolls to wire rack and let cool for 5 minutes. Serve warm.

PER SERVING Cal 290; **Total Fat** 9g, **Sat Fat** 1.5g; **Chol** 5mg; **Sodium** 530mg; **Total Carb** 44g, **Dietary Fiber** 0g, **Total Sugars** 4g; **Protein** 7g

SHAPING CRESCENT ROLLS

1. Press and roll dough into 12-inch round.

2. Brush top of dough with remaining melted butter and cut into 12 wedges.

3. Roll up each dough wedge, ending with pointed tip on bottom. Push ends toward each other to form crescent.

4. Arrange rolls on prepared sheet, spaced about 2 inches apart, with tip of dough underneath each roll.

Garlic and Herb Breadsticks

MAKES 18 BREADSTICKS

WHY THIS RECIPE WORKS Whether alongside soup or salad or a more elaborate Italian American meal, breadsticks are always welcome—and they fly off the table quickly. Using store-bought pizza dough saves time without sacrificing the pleasantly chewy texture. For flavor, we sprinkled the dough with granulated garlic, fresh thyme, dried oregano, salt, and pepper before baking. If possible, buy bagged pizza dough that is still partially frozen; the yeast is more likely to be active, which will give the breadsticks a better rise during baking. It's important to let the dough come to room temperature before beginning the recipe. Do not use Pillsbury Pizza Crust here. Wait to make the thyme mixture until just before you're ready to sprinkle it.

- 1 pound store-bought pizza dough, room temperature
- 2 teaspoons minced fresh thyme
- 2 teaspoons dried oregano
- 1 teaspoon granulated garlic
- ½ teaspoon kosher salt
- ¼ teaspoon pepper
- 3 tablespoons unsalted butter, melted, divided

1. Adjust oven rack to middle position and heat oven to 450 degrees. Line rimmed baking sheet with parchment paper.

2. Divide dough in half. Press and roll 1 piece of dough into 9 by 5-inch rectangle on lightly floured counter. Transfer dough rectangle to half of prepared sheet, with short ends parallel to long sides of sheet. Repeat with remaining dough piece and place on other half of sheet.

3. Stir thyme, oregano, granulated garlic, salt, and pepper together in bowl. Using pastry brush, brush doughs with half of melted butter. Sprinkle doughs with half of thyme mixture. Flip doughs, brush with remaining melted butter, and sprinkle with remaining thyme mixture. Using bench scraper or chef's knife, cut each dough rectangle crosswise at 1-inch intervals to create nine 5-inch breadsticks, but do not separate breadsticks. Bake until golden brown, 9 to 12 minutes. Let cool for 5 minutes. Pull breadsticks apart at seams. Serve.

PER SERVING Cal 80; **Total Fat** 2.5g, **Sat Fat** 1.5g; Chol 5mg; **Sodium** 140mg; **Total Carb** 12g, **Dietary Fiber** 0g, **Total Sugars** 1g; **Protein** 2g

Everything Breadsticks

VARIATIONS
Cinnamon Sugar Breadsticks
Substitute 2 tablespoons sugar, 1 teaspoon ground cinnamon, and ½ teaspoon ground ginger for thyme, oregano, garlic, and pepper. Reduce salt to ⅛ teaspoon.

Everything Breadsticks
Substitute 2 tablespoons sesame seeds, 1 tablespoon dried minced onion, and 2 teaspoons poppy seeds for thyme and oregano.

Onion and Rosemary Breadsticks
Substitute 1 tablespoon minced fresh rosemary and 1 tablespoon dried minced onion for thyme and oregano.

Spicy Parmesan Breadsticks
Substitute ¾ cup grated Parmesan cheese and ½ teaspoon red pepper flakes for thyme and oregano.

VEGETABLE COOKING TIMES

Sometimes you want to prepare your vegetables in the simplest (and quickest) way by steaming, boiling, or microwaving them. Just follow the times in this chart for perfectly cooked vegetables every time.

VEGETABLE	AMOUNT/ YIELD	PREPARATION	BOILING TIME (AMOUNT OF WATER AND SALT)	STEAMING TIME	MICROWAVING TIME (AMOUNT OF WATER)
Asparagus	1 bunch (1 pound)/ serves 3	tough ends trimmed	2 to 4 minutes (4 quarts water plus 1 tablespoon salt)	3 to 5 minutes	3 to 6 minutes (3 tablespoons water)
Beets	1½ pounds (6 medium)/ serves 4	greens discarded and beets scrubbed well	X	35 to 55 minutes	18 to 24 minutes (¾ cup water)
Broccoli	1 bunch (1½ pounds)/ serves 4	florets cut into 1- to 1½-inch pieces and stalks peeled and cut into ¼-inch-thick pieces	2 to 4 minutes (4 quarts water plus 1 tablespoon salt)	4 to 6 minutes	4 to 6 minutes (3 tablespoons water)
Brussels Sprouts	1 pound/ serves 4	stem ends trimmed, discolored leaves removed, and halved through stem	6 to 8 minutes (4 quarts water plus 1 tablespoon salt)	7 to 9 minutes	X
Carrots	1 pound/ serves 4	peeled and sliced ¼ inch thick on bias	3 to 4 minutes (4 quarts water plus 1 tablespoon salt)	5 to 6 minutes	4 to 7 minutes (2 tablespoons water)
Cauliflower	1 head (2 pounds)/ serves 4 to 6	cored and florets cut into 1-inch pieces	5 to 7 minutes (4 quarts water plus 1 tablespoon salt)	7 to 9 minutes	4 to 7 minutes (¼ cup water)
Green Beans	1 pound/ serves 4	stem ends trimmed	3 to 5 minutes (4 quarts water plus 1 tablespoon salt)	6 to 8 minutes	4 to 6 minutes (3 tablespoons water)
Red Potatoes	2 pounds (6 medium)/ serves 4	scrubbed and poked several times with fork	16 to 22 minutes (4 quarts water plus 1 tablespoon salt)	18 to 24 minutes	6 to 10 minutes (no water and uncovered)
Russet Potatoes	2 pounds (4 medium)/ serves 4	scrubbed and poked several times with fork	X	X	8 to 12 minutes (no water and uncovered)
Snap Peas	1 pound/ serves 4	stems trimmed and strings removed	2 to 4 minutes (4 quarts water plus 1 tablespoon salt)	4 to 6 minutes	3 to 6 minutes (3 tablespoons water)
Snow Peas	1 pound/ serves 4	stems trimmed and strings removed	2 to 3 minutes (4 quarts water plus 1 tablespoon salt)	4 to 6 minutes	3 to 6 minutes (3 tablespoons water)
Squash (Winter)	2 pounds/ serves 4	peeled, seeded, and cut into 1-inch chunks	X	12 to 14 minutes	8 to 11 minutes (¼ cup water)
Sweet Potatoes	2 pounds (3 medium) serves 4	peeled and cut into 1-inch chunks	X	12 to 14 minutes	8 to 10 minutes (¼ cup water)

X = Not recommended

GRILLING VEGETABLES

To easily grill a simple vegetable to serve with dinner, use this chart as a guide. Brush or toss the vegetables with oil and season with salt and pepper before grilling. Grill vegetables over a medium-hot fire (you can comfortably hold your hand 5 inches above the cooking grate for 3 to 4 seconds).

VEGETABLE	PREPARATION	GRILLING DIRECTIONS
Asparagus	trim tough ends	Grill, turning once, until streaked with light grill marks, 5 to 7 minutes.
Bell Pepper	core, seed, and cut into large wedges	Grill, turning often, until streaked with dark grill marks, 8 to 10 minutes.
Baby Bok Choy	halve head through stem; rinse but don't dry (water left clinging to leaves will turn to steam, helping bok choy cook evenly)	Grill, turning once, 6 to 7 minutes.
Eggplant	remove ends; cut into ¾-inch-thick rounds or strips	Grill, turning once, until flesh is darkly colored, 8 to 10 minutes.
Endive	halve lengthwise through stem end	Grill, flat side down, until streaked with dark grill marks, 5 to 7 minutes.
Fennel	slice bulb through base into ¼-inch-thick pieces	Grill, turning once, until streaked with dark grill marks and quite soft, 7 to 9 minutes.
Portobello Mushrooms	discard stems and wipe caps clean	Grill, turning once, until streaked with dark grill marks and quite soft, 7 to 9 minutes.
White or Cremini Mushrooms	trim thin slice from stems, then thread onto skewers	Grill, turning several times, until golden brown, 6 to 7 minutes.
Onions	peel, cut into ½-inch-thick slices, and skewer	Grill, turning occasionally, until lightly charred, 10 to 12 minutes.
Radicchio	cut into 4 equal wedges	Grill, turning every 1½ minutes (turn each wedge twice so that each side, including rounded one, spends some time facing fire), 4 to 5 minutes.
Scallions	trim off root end and discard any loose or wilted outer leaves (use scallions that are at least ¼ inch in diameter)	Grill, turning once, 4 to 5 minutes.
Cherry Tomatoes	remove stems, then thread onto skewers	Grill, turning often, until streaked with dark grill marks, 3 to 6 minutes.
Plum Tomatoes	halve lengthwise and seed if desired	Grill, turning once, until streaked with dark grill marks, about 6 minutes.
Zucchini or Yellow Summer Squash	remove ends; slice lengthwise into ½-inch-thick strips	Grill, turning once, until streaked with dark grill marks, 8 to 10 minutes.

COOKING RICE

Here are three simple methods for basic rice cooking: boiling, pilaf-style (which we think yields the best results), and microwaving. Boiling and simmering the rice in ample amounts of water (like pasta) on the stovetop is easy. While some may argue it doesn't produce the best rice, we think it is a great (and foolproof) method when you want rice to round out a meal or fill a burrito. The best thing about simmering rice on the stovetop is that rinsing and measuring aren't even necessary. And microwaving rice? Well, after working on it for a while in the test kitchen, we can honestly say that not only does the microwave work, it works really well. Plus you can cook the rice right in the serving bowl.

If you want to make rice for a crowd, use the boiling method and double the amount of rice (there's no need to add more water or salt). We don't recommend cooking more than 1 cup of rice in the microwave.

BOILING DIRECTIONS Bring the water to a boil in a large saucepan. Stir in the rice and 2½ teaspoons salt. Return to a boil, then reduce to a simmer and cook until the rice is tender, following the cooking times given in the chart below. Drain.

PILAF-STYLE DIRECTIONS Rinse the rice (see page 28). Heat 1 tablespoon oil in a medium saucepan (preferably nonstick) over medium-high heat until shimmering. Stir in the rice and cook until the edges of the grains begin to turn translucent, about 3 minutes. Stir in the water and ¼ teaspoon salt. Bring the mixture to a simmer, then reduce the heat to low, cover, and continue to simmer until the rice is tender and has absorbed all the water, following the cooking times given in the chart below. Off the heat, place a clean folded dish towel under the lid and let the rice sit for 10 minutes. Fluff the rice with a fork.

MICROWAVE DIRECTIONS Rinse the rice (see page 28). Combine the water, the rice, 1 tablespoon oil, and ¼ teaspoon salt in a bowl. Cover and microwave on high (full power) until the water begins to boil, 5 to 10 minutes. Reduce the microwave heat to medium (50 percent power) and continue to cook until the rice is just tender, following the cooking times given in the chart below. Remove from the microwave and fluff with a fork. Cover the bowl with plastic wrap, poke several vent holes in the plastic with the tip of a knife, and let sit until completely tender, about 5 minutes.

TYPE OF RICE	COOKING METHOD	AMOUNT OF RICE	AMOUNT OF WATER	COOKING TIME
Short- and Medium-Grain White Rice	Boiled	1 cup	4 quarts	10 to 15 minutes
	Pilaf-Style	1 cup	1¾ cups	10 to 15 minutes
	Microwave	X	X	X
Long-Grain White Rice	Boiled	1 cup	4 quarts	12 to 17 minutes
	Pilaf-Style	1 cup	1¾ cups	16 to 18 minutes
	Microwave	1 cup	2 cups	10 to 15 minutes
Short- and Medium-Grain Brown Rice	Boiled	1 cup	4 quarts	22 to 27 minutes
	Pilaf-Style	1 cup	1¾ cups	40 to 50 minutes
	Microwave	1 cup	2 cups	25 to 30 minutes
Long-Grain Brown Rice	Boiled	1 cup	4 quarts	25 to 30 minutes
	Pilaf-Style	1 cup	1¾ cups	40 to 50 minutes
	Microwave	1 cup	2 cups	25 to 30 minutes
Wild Rice	Boiled	1 cup	4 quarts	45 to 40 minutes
	Pilaf-Style	X	X	X
	Microwave	X	X	X
Basmati, Jasmine, or Texmati Rice	Boiled	1 cup	4 quarts	12 to 17 minutes
	Pilaf-Style	1 cup	1¾ cups	16 to 18 minutes
	Microwave	1 cup	2 cups	10 to 15 minutes

X = Not recommended

COOKING GRAINS

From bulgur to freekeh, the types of grains and the best methods for cooking them can vary tremendously. Some grains, such as bulgur, cook in minutes, and others, such as barley or wheat berries, take much longer. Here in the test kitchen we have homed in on three basic methods for cooking grains. We then determined which are best for each type of grain. While some grains, such as bulgur, take well to any cooking method, others will turn out best when cooked with a specific method.

BOILING DIRECTIONS Bring water to boil in large saucepan. Stir in grain and ½ teaspoon salt. Return to boil, then reduce to simmer and cook until grain is tender, following cooking times given in chart below. Drain.

PILAF-STYLE DIRECTIONS Rinse and then dry grain on towel. Heat 1 tablespoon oil in medium saucepan (preferably nonstick) over medium-high heat until shimmering. Stir in grain and toast until lightly golden and fragrant, 2 to 3 minutes. Stir in water and ¼ teaspoon salt. Bring mixture to simmer, then reduce heat to low, cover, and continue to simmer until grain is tender and has absorbed all of water, following cooking times given below. Off heat, let grain stand for 10 minutes, then fluff with fork.

MICROWAVE DIRECTIONS Rinse grain (see page 28). Combine water, grain, 1 tablespoon oil, and ¼ teaspoon salt in bowl. Cover and cook following times and temperatures given below. Remove from microwave and fluff with fork. Cover bowl with plastic wrap, poke several vent holes with tip of knife, and let sit until completely tender, about 5 minutes.

TYPE OF GRAIN	COOKING METHOD	AMOUNT OF GRAIN	AMOUNT OF WATER	AMOUNT OF SALT	COOKING TIME
Pearl Barley	Boiled	1 cup	4 quarts	1 tablespoon	20 to 40 minutes
	Pilaf-Style	1 cup	1 ⅔ cups	¼ teaspoon	20 to 40 minutes
	Microwave	X	X	X	X
Bulgur (medium- to coarse-grind)	Boiled	1 cup	4 quarts	1½ teaspoons	5 minutes
	Pilaf-Style*	1 cup	1½ cups	¼ teaspoon	16 to 18 minutes
	Microwave	1 cup	1 cup	¼ teaspoon	5 to 10 minutes
Farro	Boiled	1 cup	4 quarts	1 tablespoon	15 to 30 minutes
	Pilaf-Style	X	X	X	X
	Microwave	X	X	X	X
Freekeh	Boiled	1 cup	4 quarts	1 tablespoon	30 to 45 minutes
	Pilaf-Style	X	X	X	X
	Microwave	X	X	X	X
Wheat Berries	Boiled	1 cup	4 quarts	1½ teaspoons	60 to 70 minutes
	Pilaf-Style	X	X	X	X
	Microwave	X	X	X	X

* For pilaf, do not rinse, and skip the toasting step, adding the grain to the pot with the liquid.
X = Not recommended

CONVERSIONS AND EQUIVALENTS

Some say cooking is a science and an art. We would say that geography has a hand in it, too. Flours and sugars manufactured in the United Kingdom and elsewhere will feel and taste different from those manufactured in the United States. So we cannot promise that the loaf of bread you bake in Canada or England will taste the same as a loaf baked in the States, but we can offer guidelines for converting weights and measures. We also recommend that you rely on your instincts when making our recipes. Refer to the visual cues provided. If the dough hasn't "come together in a ball" as described, you may need to add more flour—even if the recipe doesn't tell you to. You be the judge. The recipes in this book were developed using standard

U.S. measures following U.S. government guidelines. The charts below offer equivalents for U.S. and metric measures. All conversions are approximate and have been rounded up or down to the nearest whole number.

EXAMPLE

| 1 teaspoon | = | 4.9292 milliliters, rounded up to 5 milliliters |
| 1 ounce | = | 28.3495 grams, rounded down to 28 grams |

Volume Conversions

U.S.	METRIC
1 teaspoon	5 milliliters
2 teaspoons	10 milliliters
1 tablespoon	15 milliliters
2 tablespoons	30 milliliters
¼ cup	59 milliliters
⅓ cup	79 milliliters
½ cup	118 milliliters
¾ cup	177 milliliters
1 cup	237 milliliters
1¼ cups	296 milliliters
1½ cups	355 milliliters
2 cups (1 pint)	473 milliliters
2½ cups	591 milliliters
3 cups	710 milliliters
4 cups (1 quart)	0.946 liter
1.06 quarts	1 liter
4 quarts (1 gallon)	3.8 liters

Weight Conversions

OUNCES	GRAMS
½	14
¾	21
1	28
1½	43
2	57
2½	71
3	85
3½	99
4	113
4½	128
5	142
6	170
7	198
8	227
9	255
10	283
12	340
16 (1 pound)	454

Conversions for Common Baking Ingredients

Baking is an exacting science. Because measuring by weight is far more accurate than measuring by volume, and thus more likely to produce reliable results, in our recipes we provide ounce measures in addition to cup measures for many ingredients. Refer to the chart below to convert these measures into grams.

INGREDIENT	OUNCES	GRAMS
Flour		
1 cup all-purpose flour*	5	142
1 cup cake flour	4	113
1 cup whole-wheat flour	5½	156
Sugar		
1 cup granulated (white) sugar	7	198
1 cup packed brown sugar (light or dark)	7	198
1 cup confectioners' sugar	4	113
Cocoa Powder		
1 cup cocoa powder	3	85
Butter†		
4 tablespoons (½ stick or ¼ cup)	2	57
8 tablespoons (1 stick or ½ cup)	4	113
16 tablespoons (2 sticks or 1 cup)	8	227

* U.S. all-purpose flour, the most frequently used flour in this book, does not contain leaveners, as some European flours do. These leavened flours are called self-rising or self-raising. If you are using self-rising flour, take this into consideration before adding leaveners to a recipe.

† In the United States, butter is sold both salted and unsalted. We generally recommend unsalted butter. If you are using salted butter, take this into consideration before adding salt to a recipe.

Oven Temperatures

FAHRENHEIT	CELSIUS	GAS MARK
225	105	¼
250	120	½
275	135	1
300	150	2
325	165	3
350	180	4
375	190	5
400	200	6
425	220	7
450	230	8
475	245	9

Converting Temperatures from an Instant-Read Thermometer

We include doneness temperatures in many of the recipes in this book. We recommend an instant-read thermometer for the job. Refer to the table above to convert Fahrenheit degrees to Celsius. Or, for temperatures not represented in the chart, use this simple formula:

Subtract 32 degrees from the Fahrenheit reading, then divide the result by 1.8 to find the Celsius reading.

EXAMPLE

"Roast chicken until thighs register 175 degrees."

To convert:

160°F – 32 = 128°

128° ÷ 1.8 = 71.11°C, rounded down to 71°C

Swiss Chard and Kale Gratin

INDEX

Note: Page references in *italics* indicate photographs.

E

Easier French Fries, 140, *140*

Easiest-Ever Biscuits, 498

Easy Baked Quinoa
 with Curry, Cauliflower, and Cilantro, 31
 with Lemon, Garlic, and Parsley, 30–31
 with Scallions and Feta, 31
 with Tomatoes, Parmesan, and Basil, 31

Easy Baked White Rice for a Crowd, 294

Easy Boston Beans, 36, *36*

Easy Garlic Rolls, 514

Easy Grilled Coleslaw, 371

Easy Parmesan Risotto, 29

Easy-Peel Hard-Cooked Eggs, 453

Easy White Bean Gratin, 36–37

Edamame
 Gingery Stir-Fried, 208
 Salad, 208–9, *209*
 Shiitakes, and Ginger, Quinoa Pilaf with, 321
 and Shiitakes, Pressure-Cooker Brown Rice
  with, 429, *429*
 Succotash, 334

**Egg Noodles with Browned Butter and
 Caraway, 31, *31***

Eggplant
 and Bell Peppers, Grilled, with Mint-Cumin
  Dressing, 377, *377*
 Broiled, with Basil, 15, *15*
 Broiled, with Sesame-Miso Glaze, 15
 Casserole, Slow-Cooker Turkish, 404–5
 Grilled, Tomatoes, and Basil, Pasta Salad
  with, 326
 Grilled, with Cherry Tomatoes and Cilantro
  Vinaigrette, 376–77
 Grilled Ratatouille, *392*, 392–93
 Grilled Vegetable and Halloumi Salad,
  394, *394*
 Hasselback, with Garlic-Yogurt Sauce,
  443, *443*
 Japanese
  Charred Sichuan-Style, *112*, 113
  Sesame-Basil Stir-Fried, 112

Eggplant *(cont.)*
 Stir-Fried, 112
 Sweet Chili-Garlic Stir-Fried, 113
 Marinated, with Capers and Mint,
  304, 304–5
 Pecorino, 280–81, *281*
 Salad, Crispy Thai, *438*, 438–39
 Slow-Cooker Ratatouille, 405, *405*
 Slow-Cooker Stuffed, 403–4, *404*
 Spinach, and Beans, Hearty Pearl Couscous
  with, 460
 Stuffed, 442, *442*
 Thai-Style Stir-Fried, with Garlic-Basil
  Sauce, *111*, 111–12
 and Tomatoes, Baked Orzo with,
  463, 463–64
 and Tomatoes, Stewed Chickpeas with,
  451–52
 Tunisian-Style Grilled Vegetables,
  393, 393–94
 Walkaway Ratatouille, 288, *288*
 and Zucchini Medley, Roasted, 310, *310*

Egg(s)
 Antipasti Chopped Salad, 436
 Cobb Chopped Salad, *434*, 436
 Easy-Peel Hard-Cooked, 453
 Southwestern Chopped Salad, 436
 Tomatoes, and Parsley, Turkish Pinto Bean
  Salad with, 453
 Topping, Creamy, Best Baked Potatoes
  with, 78

Egyptian Barley Salad, 318–19, *319*

Endive. *See* **Belgian Endive(s)**

Escarole
 Bitter Greens, Carrot, and Chickpea Salad,
  218–19
 Bitter Greens, Fennel, and Apple Salad with
  Warm Pancetta Dressing, 485
 Mediterranean Chopped Salad, 436–37
 and Orange Salad with Green Olive
  Vinaigrette, 249–50
 Quinoa Taco Salad, 459–60
 and Roasted Cipollini Salad, 236, *236*
 Sesame-Hoisin Braised, *114*, 114–15

Escarole *(cont.)*
 Slow-Cooker Braised Lentils with, 424
 Utica Greens, 439
 and White Beans, Sicilian, 203

Extra-Crunchy Green Bean Casserole, 471–72

F

Farro
 and Broccoli Rabe Gratin, 359, *359*
 Farrotto with Pancetta, Asparagus, and
  Peas, 186
 with Fennel and Parmesan, 295–96
 with Mushrooms and Thyme, 184–85, *185*
 Parmesan Farrotto, 185
 Salad with Asparagus, Snap Peas, and
  Tomatoes, 319, *320*
 Salad with Cucumber, Yogurt, and Mint, 320
 Slow-Cooker Creamy, with Mushrooms and
  Thyme, 416–17, *417*
 Warm, with Lemon and Herbs, 184, *184*

Fastest-Ever Baked Potatoes, 26, *26*

Fattoush, 438

Fennel
 and Arugula, Chickpea Salad with, 333
 and Asparagus Medley, Roasted, 310
 Bitter Greens, and Apple Salad with Warm
  Pancetta Dressing, 485
 Braised, with Radicchio and Parmesan, 115
 Caramelized, and Spinach, Pearl Couscous
  with, *298*, 298–99
 Confit, 281–82
 Creamy Orzo with, 35
 Dried Apricots, and Orange, Barley with, 177
 Dried Cherries, and Walnuts, Roquefort
  Salad with, 488
 and Garlic, Sautéed Cabbage with, 10
 Grapes, and Pine Nuts, Cranberry Bean
  Salad with, 208
 Grapes, Gorgonzola, and Pecans, Arugula
  Salad with, 267, *267*

V

Vegetable(s)
fried, dipping sauces for, 149
Fritters, Crispy, *138*, 159
Grilled, Tunisian-Style, *393*, 393–94
and Halloumi, Grilled, Salad, *394*, 394–95
Kebabs, Grilled, with Grilled Lemon
Dressing, 391–92
roasted, toppings for, 61
Root, and Potatoes, Slow-Cooker
Mashed, 408
Root, Gratin, 356, *356*
Root, Perfect Roasted, 60, *60*
Root, Roasted, with Lemon-Caper Sauce,
60–61
Spring, Buttery, 287, *287*
Spring, Pressure-Cooker Braised,
426, 426–27
Spring, Risotto, *294*, 294–95
see also specific vegetables
Vegetarian Refried Beans, 202
**Vermouth-Butter Glaze, Braised Celery
with, 471**
Vinaigrettes
Browned Butter–Lemon, 51
Lemon-Shallot, 368
Tomato-Basil, 368
V-slicer, working with a, 352

W

Walkaway Ratatouille, 288, *288*
Walnut(s)
and Apple, Napa Cabbage Slaw with, 311
Bitter Greens, Fennel, and Apple Salad
with Warm Pancetta Dressing, 485
Butternut Squash, and Raisins, Freekeh
Salad with, *187*, 187–88
Cape Cod Picnic Salad, 307–8

Walnut(s) *(cont.)*
and Cranberries, Rustic Bread Stuffing
with, 490
Date-Nut Bread, *502*, 502–3
-Dill Vinaigrette, Roasted Beets with, 42
Fennel, and Dried Cherries, Roquefort Salad
with, 488
Feta, and Pomegranate, Parsley-Cucumber
Salad with, *240*, 240–41
and Feta, Garlicky Swiss Chard with, *18*, 19
and Feta, Roasted Spiralized Sweet Potatoes
with, 85, *85*
Figs, Prosciutto, and Parmesan, Arugula
Salad with, *266*, 266–67
Golden Raisins, and Arugula, Citrus Salad
with, 487
and Gorgonzola, Oat Berry Pilaf with,
190–91
Hasselback Eggplant with Garlic-Yogurt
Sauce, 443, *443*
and Lemon, Roasted Brussels Sprouts
with, *38*, 44
Marinated Beet Salad with Oranges and
Pecorino, *484*, 484–85
Mediterranean Chopped Salad, 436–37
and Orange, Braised Beets with, 92
and Oranges, Slow-Cooker Beets with,
398–99
and Pomegranate, Black-Eyed Peas with,
212–13
and Pomegranate, Herbed Rice and
Pasta Pilaf with, 162
Pumpkin Bread, *503*, 503–4
and Raisins, Broccoli Salad with, 303
and Red Onion, Quick Roasted Green Beans
with, 17
Shaved Celery Salad with Pomegranate-
Honey Vinaigrette, 237
Skillet Green Beans with, 16–17
Spinach, and Parmesan, Lentil Salad with, 335
Stuffed Portobello Mushrooms with
Spinach and Gorgonzola, 444
Vinaigrette and Blue Cheese, Endive Salad
with, 271–72

Warm Farro with Lemon and Herbs, 184, *184*
**Warm Spinach Salad with Feta and
Pistachios, 226, *226***
**Warm Wheat Berries with Zucchini,
Red Pepper, and Oregano, 195, *195***
Watercress
Cape Cod Picnic Salad, 307–8
Cucumber, and Radish Salad, 271
Orange, and Avocado Salad with
Ginger-Lime Vinaigrette, 250
and Radishes, Simple Pearl Couscous
with, 33, *33*
Watermelon
-Feta Fresh Corn Salad, 238
and Purslane Salad, 252, *252*
-Tomato Salad, 252–53, *253*
Wedge Salad, *216*, 225
Wheat Berry(ies)
and Beet Salad, Slow-Cooker, with Arugula
and Apples, 419, *419*
and Endive Salad with Blueberries and
Goat Cheese, 460–61
Salad with Figs, Pine Nuts, and Goat
Cheese, 323, *323*
Salad with Orange and Carrots, 322–23
Warm, with Zucchini, Red Pepper, and
Oregano, 195, *195*
Whipped Potatoes, 480
**White Balsamic–Cipollini Onions with
Tarragon, 475**
White Bean(s)
Asparagus and Arugula Salad with
Cannellini Beans, *227*, 227–28
Boston Baked Beans, 198–99, *199*
Pressure-Cooker, 431
Quicker, 199
Broccoli Rabe with, 98
Cannellini Bean Gratin, *338*, 357
Cannellini Beans with Roasted Red Peppers
and Kale, 202
and Escarole, Sicilian, 203
Farro and Broccoli Rabe Gratin, 359, *359*
Gratin, Easy, 36–37